Law Dictionary

second edition
by

Steven H. Gifis

Associate Professor of Law
Rutgers, The State University
of New Jersey, School of Law
Newark

BARRON'S

Barron's Educational Series, Inc.

New York • London • Toronto • Sydney

All inquiries should be addressed to:
Barron's Educational Series, Inc.
250 Wireless Boulevard
Hauppauge, New York 11788

Library of Congress Catalog Card No. 84-6474

International Standard Book No. 0-8120-2085-5

Library of Congress Cataloging in Publication Data

Gifis, Steven H.
  Law dictionary.

  1. Law—United States—Dictionaries. I. Title
KF156.G53 1984   340'.03'21   84-6474
ISBN 0-8120-2085-5 (pbk.)
ISBN 0-8120-2947-X (soft)

Printed in the United States of America

7   800   9876

TO SCOTT, ROBBIE, AND LORNA

Contents

Preface to the Second Edition   vi
Preface to the First Edition   vii

Acknowledgments to the Second Edition   x
Acknowledgments to the First Edition   xi

Pronunciation Guide   xiii
Key to Effective Use of This Dictionary   xiv
Table of Abbreviations   xvi

Terms   1

Appendix   525
    The Constitution of the United States   525
    ABA Model Code of Professional Responsibility
      (with 1980 amendments)   538
    ABA Model Rules of Professional Conduct (1983)   560
    Federal Judicial Circuits   619

Preface

TO THE SECOND EDITION

It has been nearly ten years since I authored the preface to the first edition of this paperback law dictionary. In that time over 500,000 copies of the dictionary have been put in use. I have been pleased with this reception, particularly by law students, the primary audience I had in mind. During this period many users have written to me to suggest missing entries (and happily only a very few errors). This second edition is an attempt to respond to those many suggestions.

The scope of the dictionary has been broadened to include new subject areas such as corporate law, securities law, and taxation as well as numerous additional terms from the original subject areas. All the definitions have been re-examined, clarified, and refined. All citations have been brought up-to-date, especially in terms of the new Restatements of the Law and newly available hornbooks and treatises. The total number of entries and subentries has been more than doubled.

The guiding principle of this edition is faithful to that of the original mission: to make available to law students and others who are learning the language of the law a handy, portable study aid. This edition, like its predecessor, is intended to teach; readers unfamiliar with a legal term are told in clear and easily understandable language what each term means, what its significance is in a legal context, and often something about the area of law in which the term is used. Cross-references, subentries, and citations to authority are included in most terms to enable readers to fill-in gaps in their knowledge as it relates to the unfamiliar word. Concepts and phrases have been included since doctrines are often identified by name as a sort of legal shorthand. Thus, the reader will not have to wonder long about such phrases as "P.C.R. [post-conviction relief]," "piercing the corporate veil," "Regulation Z," "at-risk," "youthful offender," "pen register," or "shield laws."

The goal is not to supply all the information that might be needed to write a legal argument as it might relate to the meaning of a term. More extensive dictionaries, treatises, and legal encyclopedias remain for that task. The goal is to permit the reader to gain an immediate familiarity with the new term and after a second or third reference to master the usage sufficiently so that it becomes part of the user's vocabulary. The book should be available for *frequent immediate reference;* only by doing so while studying or reading legal materials will the reader benefit most from the effort. This dictionary is intended to be used and not merely to adorn a bookshelf.

As before I am sure errors and omissions will have penetrated our best efforts to produce a flawless and invaluable paperback law dictionary. Since 1975 several other dictionaries have added to the available choices. I believe none provides the mix of benefits offered in this new edition. I would welcome and encourage reader's comments.

STEVEN H. GIFIS

Hopewell, New Jersey

Preface

TO THE FIRST EDITION

Professions tend to insulate themselves from lay understanding by the development of specialized jargon. The legal profession has achieved this insulation so successfully that the uninitiated is overwhelmed by the incomprehensibility of his or her advocate's prose. Despite the increasing pervasiveness of law into every facet of American life, the special language of the law remains a barrier to nonlawyers. To the extent that this promotes the economic health of the profession, maintains its aura, and prevents unauthorized practice of the law, it may be regarded as a virtue. And the jargon does communicate in a unique way the tradition and stability that the society looks to its legal system to maintain.

The lawyer's language is replete with words having particular meanings. Thus, a lawyer "moves" to "evict a holdover tenant" when his or her client wants to kick the tenant out. The lawyer seeks to "partition a co-tenancy" gone sour and to "compel an accounting" to the "aggrieved party." A client's home is destroyed by earthquake and the insurance company refuses to pay. An attorney asks if the "risk" of earthquake is included in the insured's policy and, if not, whether "representations" were made to the homeowner that would support an action to "reform" the policy or that might create an "estoppel" against the company's denial of "liability." A merchant finds an umbrella in a coat rack; the attorney asks whether it has been "abandoned" or "mislaid" and explains to the merchant the "duty" which the law imposes upon a "finder" of "lost property."

Words and phrases are the tools of the lawyer's trade. Whether the lawyer is drafting a contract, negotiating a settlement, preparing a pleading, filing a tax return, attesting a will, closing a title, or arguing a motion in court, the audience is usually another lawyer. The legal communication process depends upon shared understandings of the professional language. The law school graduate taking a bar examination is counseled to "make noises like a lawyer." The successful bar applicant will not conclude that "the case should be thrown out of court;" rather, in the language of lawyers, he or she will write, "the plaintiff's action on motion should be dismissed for failure to state a cause of action upon which relief can be granted," or "for want of prosecution," or "for failure to join an indispensable party," etc.

Some of the law's reliance upon ancient or archaic terminology and Latin expression is giving way to more modern forms. But criminals still have *mens rea*, gifts are made *inter vivos*, cases still refer to legatees and *scienter*, and attorneys persist in the fiction of contracts which are written "under seal." The earlier cases upon which so much of our law is based are replete with old "forms of action" and peculiar words. They continue to confound experienced attorneys and judges, who sometimes resort to a law dictionary for an explanation. But the effect of this new jargon upon beginning law students is more than confounding. It is discouraging, frustrating, and even frightening. The first-year law student, having survived the competition for admission, now wonders with considerable anxiety whether the law can be mastered when it cannot even be comprehended. The task, it is hoped, may be eased by the massive repository of legal terms known as a law dictionary.

But the classic law dictionary weighs several pounds and contains hundreds of pages of elaborate definitions. It is a good library aid and research tool, especially helpful on rarely used legal terms. But, in my own experience as a law student, I found such dictionaries too awkward, bulky, and comprehensive to be useful study aids. It was not possible to have it with me when I was reading cases; rather, it primarily adorned the bookshelf, and was rarely consulted. When a word perplexed me, I passed it by, hoping it was unimportant or that its significance would appear in the context of the whole case. On occasion I did resort to a law dictionary, but it was always the library copy—not my own, which was safely resting at home. Few layers have an unabridged dictionary within ready reach even if they have one in their private law library. They are just not convenient.

The answer to convenience, of course, is an abridged paperback law dictionary. Those available, up to now have been written for the layperson. This dictionary, however, is intended to be a portable, useful, study aid for the law student or anyone else who, in a professional way, comes in contact with unfamiliar legal jargon and wants a comprehensible explanation which will permit a basic understanding of the word or phrase. It is hoped that first-year law students in particular will use the book constantly in their reading of cases and will find new legal terms becoming clearer in a matter of moments and becoming a permanent part of their legal vocabulary after several references.

I have been guided by this study aid focus in selecting the entries and defining those selected. First-year law students will find most of the basic terms that they will come upon in their assignments. When I am asked in class by a student what a term means, I generally try to answer the question if I am able, with a simple explanation and an example of its legal significance. I have found that these bits of legal wisdom encourage the kind of analytical questioning that is the mark of the able advocate and have therefore utilized this practice in my law dictionary to help make it stimulating as well as informative. Thus, despite its compact size this dictionary has a considerable encyclopedic dimension, an element which I consider essential for a good law dictionary.

There is always a danger that the legal significance will change, and the definition will become inaccurate or misleading. As Samuel Johnson has observed, "Definitions are hazardous." The definitions rely heavily upon cases and authority. A deliberate effort has been made to ensure that the definitions are accurate both from an historical perspective and in light of recent developments in the law. Where a treatise or hornbook has been used, the students are encouraged to go to the cited source for a fuller explanation when their interest is sufficiently aroused. In instances where the pronouns *he* and *him* appear in definitions, they have been used to conform with standard law prose. It should be understood that in every case, except where specifically stated, these references apply to both men and women. The goal of these definitions is general familiarity; no effort has been made to include all the competing definitions.

This is the first edition of this dictionary, and I welcome critical evaluations and suggestions. As for the errors which will undoubtedly be discovered, I can only repeat what Mr. Bouvier said in the preface to his law dictionary in 1839:

"To those who are aware of the difficulties of the task, the author deems it unnecessary to make any apology for the imperfections which may be found in the work. His object has been to be useful: if that has been accomplished in any degree, he will be amply rewarded for his labor."

Reader's comments should be sent to Barron's Educational Series, 113 Crossways Park Drive, Woodbury, New York 11797.

Steven H. Gifis

Hopewell, New Jersey

Acknowledgments

TO THE SECOND EDITION

The first edition of this dictionary provided the backbone for this new edition. What I said before to those who made possible the first edition I feel compelled to repeat. This edition would not have been possible without those prior efforts.

Having said that, there is a new group of extraordinarily able, industrious, and dedicated persons who joined with me in a collaborative effort to make this second edition a reality. Two third-year law students at Rutgers—The State University, School of Law, Newark, stand out for special mention. Amira Rahman served cheerfully as my General Editor. She organized the entire effort, created and supervised the now infamous "master word list," created all the cross-references and subentries and wrote from scratch many missing definitions in the wee hours of the morning to enable us to meet a deadline. Andrew Levine "spaded" the entire manuscript which means that to him the credit (or blame) must go for the accuracy of citations and the updating to new sources. He also wrote many of the new entries, again typically on very short notice.

Joseph Mahon, Esq. (class of 1980), read the entire manuscript for accuracy and contributed many of the new terms, especially in the tax area. Also assisting in the tax area was David Mills, Esq. (class of 1973). Mr. Michael Perkins, C.F.A., prepared initial drafts of most of the financial and securities terms that have been added to assist in the area of corporate law.

My wife, Susan Pollard Gifis, Esq. (class of 1973), integrated the editorial and spading suggestions into the final manuscript and read every page of galley. That she would consent to do so while fending off our three young children is something for which I am truly grateful. A special thank you to my children—to Scott, who enthusiastically and diligently operated the stamp to number the manuscript pages; to Robbie, who kept me company with his coloring books; and to Lorna, who did her best to consume several pages of manuscript she must have regarded as unworthy of submission.

The typing of the manuscript was principally the work of my secretary, Donna Villecca, and Carolyn Kappes. I am grateful for their ability to decipher handwritten manuscript, arrows, and inserts. A special thanks goes to each of them for their team spirit and skillful work.

Over the years many students contributed new entries to this manuscript. To all of them I express my sincere appreciation.

As before, the staff of Barron's rendered valuable editorial assistance. Ms. Joan Cipriano was especially helpful in assembling the various pieces of the manuscript and insuring a coherent final product.

Acknowledgments

TO THE FIRST EDITION

A work of this nature by necessity involves many persons and many sources. I am deeply indebted to a staff of second-year law students at Rutgers—The State University, School of Law, Newark, who contributed dedicated and careful labor to this dictionary: Alan Bowman, Ken Gunning, Ross London, Keith Roberts, Eric Winther, and Saul Zimmerman. Mr. London also acted as staff supervisor. Mr. Roberts served as my chief editorial assistant and to him I owe a special thanks for tireless hours of painstaking attention to detail. Research assistance on a less regular basis was also provided by Michael Dore, Joseph Finnin, Barry Moskowitz, Norman Solomon, and David Watkins. A number of first-year law students assisted in the proofreading and citation checking necessary to prepare the manuscript for publication. To all of them I extend my thanks for their contribution.

I have been especially gratified, on both a personal and professional level, by the contributions of Professors Alfred Slocum and John Payne of the Law School, whose very substantial commitment of time and scholarly resources to the energy-consuming task of critical evaluation contributed greatly to the quality of the manuscript.

Portions of the manuscript also were read by Gregory Reilly, class of 1973, and I am also indebted to him for many valuable suggestions.

I am particularly indebted to my wife, Susan Pollard Gifis, Esq., for her assistance, criticisms, and enduring affection throughout a project which often appeared interminable.

The preparation of the manuscript was the work of my secretary, Ms. Arlene Woodyard, assisted by Mrs. Sherry Zimmerman. Together they typed and retyped thousands of manuscript pages from handwritten scratches without complaint and with great skill.

This project was partially supported by research funds provided by the Law School. I take this opportunity to express my sincere appreciation.

Treatises and hornbooks often proved more helpful than case authority for many entries, and I did not hesitate to draw upon them. I am, therefore, very much indebted to the various legal publishers who have generously extended permissions to quote from their copyright publications. I commend all my sources to the student for further study.

Finally the author is very much indebted to the editorial staff of Barron's Educational Series, Inc., for expert criticisms, stylistic suggestions, and continuing patience throughout the enterprise. A special note of thanks must go to Ms. Janet Robertson who had the task of trying to produce a measure of consistency and technical accuracy to the manuscript. The author is indebted for the generous permission granted him by the following publishers to quote portions of their publications throughout this book.

We also acknowledge permission to quote from the American Law Institute *Model Penal Code* (p.o.d. 1962).

Reproduced with permission from *Survey of the Law of Real Property,* Second Edition, by Smith and Boyer, Copyright © 1971 by West Publishing Company.

Reproduced with permission from *Introduction to the Law of Real Property,* by Moynihan, Copyright © 1962 by West Publishing Company. *Constitutional Law,* by B. Schwartz, Copyright © Macmillan Publishing Co., Inc., 1972.

Rollin M. Perkins, *Criminal Law,* 2nd Ed. Copyright © 1969, The Foundation Press, Inc. Reprinted with permission of the publisher.

Civil Procedure (1965), James. Boston: Little, Brown and Company, 1965.

Various definitions draw from portions of *Restatements of the Law* published by the American Law Institute. We gratefully acknowledge permission to reprint from those various *Restatements* as indicated in appropriate entries. The copyright date for various restatements are as follows:

Agency [2d] © 1933 [1958]
Conflicts [2d] © 1934 [1971]
Contracts © 1932
Judgments © 1942
Property © 1936
Foreign Relations Law of the United States © 1962
Torts [2d] © 1934, 1938, 1939 [1965, 1966]
Trusts [2d] © 1935 [1957]
Restitution © 1937

Pronunciation Guide

The decision as to which Latin words, maxims, and expressions should be included in this dictionary, in view of the thousands which the user might encounter, was necessarily a somewhat arbitrary one; but an earnest effort has been made to translate and, where appropriate, to illuminate those terms and phrases considered likely to be crucial to a full understanding of important legal concepts. Hopefully, there are no significant omissions and we have erred only on the side of overinclusiveness.

Each of the Latin and French words and phrases—at least those which continue to be recognized as such and have not become, functionally, a part of the English language—includes a phonetic spelling designed to assist the user in the pronunciation of terms which are probably unfamiliar to her or him. The purpose in providing this pronunciation guide, however, emphatically has not been to indicate "the correct" mode of pronouncing the terms; rather, the goal has been to afford the user a guide to an acceptable pronunciation of them. In the case of Latin words, therefore, neither the classic nor the ecclesiastical pronunciation has been strictly followed; instead, the phonetic spellings provided herein reflect the often considerable extent to which pronunciation has been "Anglicized" and/or "Americanized," partly through widespread legal usage.

Of course, such a system is anything but uniform, and adoption of it is clearly hazardous from the standpoint of general acceptance as well as that of scholarship. Many, if not most, of these terms have alternative pronunciations in common usage throughout the English-speaking legal world, and there has been some deference to classical or ecclesiastical pronunciation and, we hope, to consistency. Thus, the choices made here, while in most cases meant to reflect the most commonly accepted pronunciation, inevitably have been the product of the author's personal preferences.

The phonetic symbols employed herein were drawn from what the author perceives as a commonly recognized and understood "system." The following guide should be of some assistance in interpreting them.

Vowels	
ă as in ăt	ĕ as in ĕgg
ä as in ärmy	ē as in ēvil
à as in arrive	è as in earn
ā as in āpe	ĭ as in ĭll
ähn (meant to approximate French nasal sound for which there is no English equivalent)	ī as in īce
	ŏ as in ŏx
	ô as in orgy
	ō as in ōpen

ŭ as in ŭp
û as in ûrge
ū as in dūty

Consonants
g as in gas
j as in jump or as the "g" in rouge or bourgeois

Key to Effective Use of This Dictionary

Alphabetization: The reader should note carefully that all entries have been alphabetized letter by letter rather than word by word. Thus *ab initio,* for example, is located between *abeyance* and *abortion,* rather than at the beginning of the listings. In the same manner, *actionable* appears before, not after *action ex delicto.*

Appendix: Several items thought to be of frequent use and reference have been included in the appendix. It is thought, for example, that a better understanding of many constitutional terms will be accomplished by reading the definitions in conjunction with the actual text of the Constitution. The items in the appendix include the United States Constitution, a map of the Thirteen Judicial Circuits, the ABA Model Code of Professional Responsibility, and the proposed new ABA Model Rules of Professional Conduct.

Brackets: Material in brackets [thus] represents two possibilities. One is an alternative expression for the preceding phrase. For example, "Federal Bureau of Investigation [F.B.I.]" indicates that F.B.I. is another way of expressing the entry for Federal Bureau of Investigation. Second, when the reader is referred to a different main entry for the definition of a particular word, brackets are also used to indicate that the word to be defined appears as a subentry of the main word to which the reader is referred. Thus, "COMPENSATORY DAMAGES see **damages** [ACTUAL DAMAGES]" indicates that the definition of compensatory damages appears under the subentry ACTUAL DAMAGES, which in turn is found under the heading **DAMAGES.**

Citations: All citations have been abbreviated in order to facilitate the reading of the definitions and in the interests of space economy. Case names, court, and year of decision have been generally omitted. National reporter cites have generally been given without the corresponding state reporter cite. A complete list of abbreviations used in the citations appears on the following pages. Citations to authorities other than cases are given with the last name of the author, title, page(s) or sections(s), year. No special typeface has been used to designate such authorities, and the Uniform System of Citation (bluebook form) has not been used.

Cross References: **Boldface type** has been used within the text of the definitions and at the end of them, to call attention to terms that are defined in the dictionary as separate entries and that should be understood and, if necessary, referred to specifically, in order to assure the fullest possible comprehension of the word whose definition has been sought in the first instance.

Terms emphasized in this manner include many that appear in the dictionary only in a different form or as a different part of speech. For example, although the term "alienate" may appear in boldface in the text of a definition, it will not be found as a separate entry, since it is expected that the reader can readily draw the meaning of that term from the definition given for the word "alienation;" likewise, the reader coming across the word "estop" printed in boldface should not despair upon discovering that it is not in fact an entry here, but should instead refer to the term "estoppel."

Also, the reader must not assume that the appearance of a word in regular type precludes the possibility of its having been included as a separate entry, for by no means has every such word been printed in boldface in every definition. Terms emphasized in this manner include primarily those an understanding of which was thought to be essential or very helpful in the reader's quest for adequate comprehension. Many terms which represent very basic and frequently used concepts, such as "property," "possession," and "crime," are often printed in regular type. Furthermore, boldface is used to emphasize a word only the first time that that word appears in a particular definition.

Additionally, although a strong effort was made to provide adequate cross-references, the reader should check all possible locations for a term, but should check first under the main word in the term. Thus "charitable trust" would be found under trust, and "concurrent negligence" under negligence. The reader should also keep in mind possible alternative terminology, such as "attorney," "counselor," "lawyer," or "prisoner," "convict," "inmate" when determining whether all avenues have been exhausted in a search for a term.

Gender: a serious effort was made to provide nonsexist terminology. In the event that masculine nouns and pronouns have been used, they are intended to refer to both men and women and should be so read. Many terms, however, are of feudal origin and remain masculine in standard modern language. For example, the term "and his heirs" is a basic one in property law and thus has not been altered.

Parentheses: parentheses are used to indicate additional optional words. Thus articles (of incorporation) may be read as "articles" or "articles of incorporation."

Subentries: Words printed in SMALL CAPITALS include:
   1) Those whose significance as legal concepts was not deemed sufficiently substantial to warrant their inclusion in the dictionary as separate entries, though some explanation or illumination was thought desirable, and
   2) those which, though important, are most logically and coherently defined in the context of related or broader terms.
   Words emphasized in this manner have been either separately and individually defined in the manner of "subcategories" or have been defined or illustrated, implicitly or explicitly, within the text of the definition of the main entry.

Table of Abbreviations

A [2d]	Atlantic Reporter [second series]
A.B.A. D.R.	American Bar Association, Code of Professional Responsibility, Disciplinary Rule
A.D.	Appellate Division, New York (Supreme Court)
A.L.R. [2d, 3d, 4th, Fed.]	American Law Reports [second, third, fourth, Federal series]
Am. Dec.	American Decisions
Am. Jur. [2d]	American Jurisprudence [second series]
App. Div.	Appellate Division
Barb.	Barbour's Supreme Court Reports, New York
Barn. & Ald.	Barnewall and Alderson's English King's Bench Reports
Bisph. Eq.	Bispham's Equity
Bl. Comm.	Blackstone's Commentaries [*pages refers to original pagination]
B.N.A.	Bureau of National Affairs
B.R.	Bankruptcy Reporter
Cal. [2d, 3d]	California Reports [second, third series]
Cal. App. [2d, 3d]	California Appellate Reports [second, third series]
Cal. Rptr. [2d]	California Reporter [second series]
C. C. H.	Commerce Clearing House
C. F. R.	Code of Federal Regulations
Cir. Ct.	Circuit Court
C.J.	Corpus Juris
C.J.S.	Corpus Juris Secundum
C.P.L.R.	New York Civil Practice Law and Rules
Cyc.	Cyclopedia of Law and Procedure
Dall.	Dallas' Pennsylvania and United States Reports
Del. Ch.	Delaware Chancery Reports
Edw.	Edward's New York Reports
e.g.	exemplia gratia; for example
Eng. Rep.	English Reports
eq.	equity
et seq.	et sequentes; and the following
F. [2d]	Federal Reporter [second series]
Fed. Cas.	Federal Cases
Fed. R. Civ. Proc.	Federal Rules of Civil Procedure
Fed. R. Crim. Proc.	Federal Rules of Criminal Procedure
Fed. R. Evid.	Federal Rules of Evidence
Fr.	French
F.R.D.	Federal Rules Decisions
F. Supp.	Federal Supplement
Greenl.	Greenleaf's Reports
Hale P.C.	Hale's Pleas of the Crown
Hen.	King Henry

How. Prac.	Howard's New York Practice Reports
Hun.	Hun's New York Supreme Court Reports
Ib. or Ibid.	ibidem; in the same place, volume, or case
Id.	idem; the same
i.e.	id est; that is
infra	following, ahead
I.R.C.	Internal Revenue Code
Lat.	Latin
Law Div.	Law Division
L. Ed. [2d]	United States Supreme Court Reports, Lawyer's Edition [second series]
L. Fr.	Law French
L.Q. Rev.	Law Quarterly Review
Metc.	Metcalf's Massachusetts Reports
n.b.	nota bene; note well
N.E. [2d]	North Eastern Reporter [second series]
N.J. Eq.	New Jersey Equity Reports
N.J.L.	New Jersey Law Reports
N.J.S. [A.]	New Jersey Statutes [Annotated]
N.J.Super.	New Jersey Superior Court Reports
N.Y. Bus. Corp. L.	New York Business Corporation Law
N.Y.S. [2d]	New York Supplement [second series]
N.W. [2d]	North Western Reporter [second series]
Ohio Dec.	Ohio Decisions
Ohio N.P., N.S.	Ohio Nisi Prius, New Series
P. [2d]	Pacific Reporter [second series]
Pet.	Peter's United States Supreme Court Reports
Pick.	Pickering's Massachusetts Reports
Q.B.	Queen's Bench
S. Ct.	Supreme Court Reporter
S.E. [2d]	South Eastern Reporter [second series]
Serg. & R.	Sergeant and Rawle's Pennsylvania Reports
So. [2d]	Southern Reporter [second series]
Stat.	United States Statutes at Large
Steph. Comm.	Stephen's Commentaries on English Law
supra	above, before
S.W. [2d]	South Western Reporter [second series]
U.C.C.	Uniform Commercial Code
U.S.	United States Reports
U.S.C. [A.]	United States Code [Annotated]
U.S. Const.	United States Constitution
U.S.L.W.	United States Law Week
Wall.	Wallace's United States Supreme Court Reports
Wend.	Wendell's New York Reports
Wheat.	Wheaton's United States Supreme Court Reports
W.L.R.	Weekly Law Reports [Great Britain]

A

A.B.A. see **American Bar Association.**

ABANDONMENT knowing relinquishment of one's right or claim to property without any future intent to again gain title or possession; "in law, is defined to be the relinquishment or surrender of rights or property by one person to another. It includes both the intention to abandon and the external act by which the intention is carried into effect . . . there must be the concurrence of the intention to abandon and the actual relinquishment." 164 S.W. 2d 225, 228. One who abandons his newspaper in a barbershop gives up all right and title to it; one who merely forgets to take his newspaper from the barbershop does not legally abandon it. A subsequent finder of property not legally abandoned must make reasonable effort to restore it to the true owner and must relinquish it to him upon demand. The term applies not only to tangible property but also to such things as **copyrights, easements, leases,** and **patents.**

ABATABLE NUISANCE see **nuisance.**

ABATEMENT generally, a lessening, a reduction; also a complete termination of a **cause of action;** "in the sense of common law [it] is an entire overthrow or destruction of the suit, so that it is quashed or ended. But, in the sense of a **court of equity,** an abatement signifies only a present suspension of all proceedings in the **suit.** . . . At common law a suit, when abated, is absolutely dead. But a suit in **equity,** when abated is . . . merely in a state of suspended animation, and it may be revived." 93 S.W. 164, 166. An ABATEMENT OF A LEGACY is the reduction in the amount or the extinction of a **legacy** to a **beneficiary** by the payment of debts owed by the grantor of that legacy, i.e., a **decedent.** An ABATEMENT OF TAXES is a rebate or diminution of taxes previously assessed and/or paid. See **nuisance** [ABATEMENT OF A NUISANCE]; plea [PLEA IN ABATEMENT].

ABDUCTION broadly, the criminal or tortious act of "taking and carrying away by force." This taking may be by means of **fraud,** persuasion, or open violence. Its object may be a child, ward, wife, etc., but the offense is against the family relationship and not the person taken. At **common law,** a wife could not maintain a **civil action** for abduction of her husband. In its most exclusive sense abduction is restricted to the taking of females for the purpose of marriage, concubinage, or **prostitution.** 60 A. 601, 603. In private or **civil** [as opposed to criminal] **law,** abduction is the act of taking away a man's wife by violence or by persuasion. 54 P. 847. Compare **kidnapping.**

ABET see **aid and abet.**

ABEYANCE in **property,** the condition of a **freehold** or **estate in fee** when there is no presently existing person in whom it **vests;** generally, an undetermined or incomplete state of affairs.

ABILITY TO STAND TRIAL see **capacity.**

AB INITIO *(äb ĭn-ĭ′-shē-ō)*—Lat: from the first act. 219 F. Supp. 274, 276. Most commonly used in reference to the validity of **contracts, statutes, estates, trespasses,** marriages, and **deeds** to indicate that existence, validity, etc., of such things relates back to their inception or creation; e.g., the unlawful marriage is **void** "ab initio"; the insurance policy is valid "ab initio."

ABOLISH to repeal, recall, or revoke; to cancel and eliminate entirely. Refers especially to things of a permanent nature such as institutions, customs, and usages, as in the abolition of slavery by the Thirteenth Amendment to the United States Constitution.

ABORTION the premature termination of a pregnancy. An intentionally induced abortion was at **common law** a **misdemeanor** and in American law a **felony** in most jurisdictions unless performed to save the life of the mother. See Perkins and Boyce, Criminal Law 186-197 (3d ed. 1982). The right of a woman to have an abortion during the early stages of her pregnancy without criminal sanctions applied to her or those who perform the abortion and to have it free of unreasonable governmental restraint has now been established as part of a constitutional right of personal privacy. During the first trimester the state cannot constitutionally interfere with the ABORTION DECISION which must be left to the medical judgment of the woman's physician. During the second trimester, the state may regulate the abortion procedure in ways that are reasonably related to maternal health. During the last trimester (the stage subsequent to viability) the state "in promoting its interest in the potentiality of human life may if it chooses, regulate, and even proscribe, abortion except where it is necessary, in appropriate medical judgment, for the preservation of the life or health of the mother." 410 U.S. 113, 163-64. The Supreme Court has, however, been strict in examining state statutes that limit a physician's discretion. 99 S. Ct. 675.

Subject to these constitutional guidelines, abortion may still be a criminal offense and is often grouped with other **homicide** offenses, though it usually carries a lesser maximum penalty. See, e.g., N.Y. Penal Law §§125.00, 125.05, 125.40-.60 (defining homicide as conduct which causes the death of a person or an unborn child with which a female has been pregnant for more than twenty-four weeks; defining justifiable abortion; creating two degrees of abortion with lesser felony designations; and proscribing self-abortion during the post-twenty-four-weeks period).

ABRIDGE to lessen, to shorten, to condense; a condensation of the whole, not a mere partition of the whole.

ABROGATE (ABROGATION) "to annul, destroy, revoke, or cancel; to put an end to; to do away with; to set aside," 209 N.E. 2d 172, 174; to make a law void by legislative repeal.

ABSCOND to travel covertly out of the **jurisdiction** of the courts, or to conceal oneself in order to avoid their **process.** 62 N.W. 217, 218. An absconding **debtor** is one who, with intent to avoid his **creditors,** conceals or withdraws himself from within the relevant jurisdiction for the purpose of going beyond the reach of process. An absconding debtor successfully evades the **service of process.** 32 A. 7.

ABSENTIA see **in absentia.**

ABSOLUTE LIABILITY see **strict liability.**

ABSQUE HOC *(äb'-skwā hŏc)*— Lat: but for this; apart from this; if it had not been for this. It is used as a technical word in **pleading** for purposes of **denial** of the **allegations** made. See **traverse** [SPECIAL TRAVERSE].

ABSTENTION a policy adopted by the federal courts whereby the **district court** may decline to exercise its **jurisdiction** and defer to a state court the resolution of a federal constitutional question, pending the outcome in a state court proceeding of state law **issues** that might avoid a serious constitutional question. When the court defers decision in this manner, it retains jurisdiction and may decide the federal constitutional question if the plaintiff is not satisfied with the state court outcome. Where resolution of the federal constitutional question is dependent upon, or may be materially altered by, the determination of an uncertain issue of state law, abstention may be proper in order to avoid unnecessary friction in federal-state relations, interference with important state functions, tentative decisions on questions of state law, and premature constitutional **adjudication.** 380 U.S. 578, 539.

A second variant of abstention (and a form of abstention required by some statutes) occurs when the federal court refuses to exercise jurisdiction altogether because the issues presented seem to the court more appropriate for state court resolution. In these instances the abstaining federal court actually "relinquishes" its jurisdiction to the state courts and the doctrine is more appropriately termed RELINQUISHMENT. An example of this form of abstention is the refusal of the federal courts in the interests of **comity** to enjoin state court criminal proceedings. See 401 U.S. 37.

ABSTRACT OF RECORD a complete history in short, abbreviated form of the **case** as found in the **record.** Its purpose is "to bring before the **appellate court** in abbreviated form an accurate and authentic history of all the **proceedings** in the case as they were had in the course of the **trial** below." 164 S.W. 2d 201, 207. "It would have to be complete enough to show that the questions presented for review [by the appellate court] have been properly preserved in the case." 231 S.W. 70.

ABSTRACT OF TITLE a short history of **title** to land; "a summary or epitome of the facts relied on as evidence of **title,** [which] must contain a note of all **conveyances,** transfers, or other facts relied on as evidences of the **claimant's** title, together with

all such facts appearing of record as may impair title. . . . It should contain a full summary of all **grants, conveyances, wills** and all records and judicial proceedings whereby the title is in any way affected, and all **encumbrances** and **liens** of record, and show whether they have been released or not." 107 N.E. 180, 183. See **chain of title.**

ABUSE OF DISCRETION a standard of review applied by appellate courts in reviewing the exercise of **discretion** by trial courts and administrative agencies and persons; a rationale used by reviewing courts to upset determinations made by trial courts when such determinations are wholly inconsistent with the facts and circumstances before the court and the deductions that can reasonably be made from the facts and circumstances, see 251 N.E. 2d 468, 471; any "unreasonable, unconscionable [or] arbitrary action taken without proper consideration of the facts and law pertaining to the matter submitted," 458 P. 2d 336, 338.

The "abuse of discretion" standard of review is also used in administrative settings. Thus where an agency has discretionary authority to revoke a license, the extent of that discretion is limited, and a serious or gross abuse of that discretion will provoke correction by a reviewing court. Administrative officials such as prosecutors have a very broad discretion and it is generally very difficult to upset their exercise of discretion on the grounds of arbitrary, capricious, or unfair decision-making. Davis, Administrative Law §§28.04, 28.06 (3rd ed. 1972). See **discretion.**

ABUSE OF PROCESS employment of the criminal or civil **process** for a use other than one which is intended by law; "the improper use of process after it has been issued, that is, a perversion of it." 32 A. 2d 413, 415. "Malicious use of civil process has to do with the wrongful initiation of such process, while abuse of civil process is concerned with a perversion of a process after it is issued." Id.

ABUT [ABUTTING] to adjoin; to cease at point of contact; to touch boundaries; to border on.

ACCELERATED COST RECOVERY SYSTEM see **depreciation** [ACCELERATED COST RECOVERY SYSTEM].

ACCELERATION the hastening of the time for enjoyment of an **estate** or a property right which would otherwise have been postponed to a later time. This term is applied to both the **vesting** of a **remainder** due to the premature termination of a **preceding estate** and to clauses [commonly found in **mortgage** agreements called **acceleration clauses,** stipulating that an entire debt may be regarded as due upon the default of a single **installment,** or other duty of the borrower].

ACCELERATION CLAUSE a provision in a **contract** or document establishing that upon the happening of a certain event, a party's expected interest in the subject property will become prematurely **vested.** For example, "a stipulation in a **mortgage** that, if the **mortgagor** shall fail to pay any note or **installment** of **interest,** or neglect to pay taxes or special assessments, the entire indebtedness shall become due, and payable, or that the **mortgagee** may at his option declare it to be due and payable," 9 S.W. 2d 3, 4; however, "equitable principles may be invoked to relieve a mortgagor from acceleration of the maturity of the debt and from **foreclosure** of the mortgage." 118 F. Supp. 401, 411. In law of contracts, such a clause is found often in installment contracts and can cause an entire debt to become due upon failure to pay an installment as agreed and can cause a **judgment** for the installment barring an **action** for the balance of the debt. Corbin, Contracts §950 (1952); see U.C.C. §1-208.

ACCEPTANCE act of voluntarily receiving something or of a voluntary agreement to certain terms or conditions; implies the right to reject. In **contract** law, acceptance is consent to the terms of an **offer,** which consent creates a contract. See **power of acceptance.** In com**mercial law,** acceptance of a **draft** is the **drawee's** signed engagement to honor the draft. The acceptance must be written on the draft. U.C.C. §3-410. In the law of **sales,** acceptance occurs when the buyer takes goods as his own. U.C.C. §2-606, comment 1. In **property** law, acceptance is an element essential to the completion of a **gift inter vivos;** it may be actual or implied and may also be evidenced by words and conduct; it need not be contemporaneous with delivery but may be manifested subsequently. See 36 F. Supp. 556, 564.

ACCESSION something added. Generally signifies acquisition of **title** to personalty by adding labor on it which converts it into an entirely different thing or by incorporation of property into a union with other property. 590 S.W. 2d. 607, 609. Accession is a right, derived from the **civil law,** to all of that which one's property produces, and to that which is united to it either naturally or artificially. The civil law required the thing to be changed completely, as grapes into wine, before the original owner could lose title. By com**mon law** the article in its altered form is still the property of the owner of the original material if he can prove the identity of the original material, as if leather be made into shoes. 4 Am. Dec. 368.

ACCESSORY one who aids or contributes in a secondary way or assists in or contributes to crime as a subordinate. See 216 So. 2d 829, 831. Mere silence or approval of the commission of crime does not incur accessorial liability, 81 Mo. 483, although the failure to report the commission of a felony is sometimes itself a crime. See **misprision.** An accessory does acts which **facilitate** others in the commission or attempted commission of crime or in avoiding apprehension for crime. Compare **accomplice; aid and abet; conspiracy.**

ACCESSORY AFTER THE FACT those who receive, comfort or assist a felon knowing that he has committed a **felony** or is sought in connection with the commission or attempted commission of a felony. See 234 A. 2d 284, 285. The term thus applies to one who obstructs justice by giving comfort or assistance to a criminal offender in an attempt to hinder or prevent his apprehension or punishment. 378 F. 2d 540.

ACCESSORY BEFORE THE FACT one who procures, counsels, or commands the deed perpetrated, but who is not present, actively or constructively, at such perpetration. See 282 A. 2d 154.

ACCIDENT An unforeseen, unexpected event; an occurrence by chance and not by design. In the context of an automobile insurance policy, the term includes any event that occurs unintentionally, even if due to **negligence** rather than to forces beyond anyone's control. See 62 S.W. 2d 197. An UNAVOIDABLE ACCIDENT is one that is not the product of fault of another such as one caused by an **act of God.** See 196 S.E. 915, 918.

ACCOMMODATION INDORSEMENT see **indorsement.**

ACCOMMODATION MAKER [PARTY] one who signs a **note** as acceptor, **maker,** or **indorser** without recovering value therefore, or any compensation, benefit, or **consideration** directly or indirectly by way of the transaction of which the note is a part. The accommodation maker, as **surety,** remains **liable** for the note, even though he receives no consideration. See 87 N.W. 2d 299, 302. He is, in effect, gratu-itously obligating himself to guarantee the debt of the accommodated party. The transaction must be one primarily for the benefit of the **payee.** See 264 N.W. 875, 876. If he is obliged to honor his accommodation contract he "has a right of recourse on the instrument against" the accommodated party. U.C.C. §3-415(5).

ACCOMPLICE an individual who voluntarily engages with another in the commission or attempted commission of a crime, see 165 N.E. 2d 814; one who is liable for the identical offense charged against the **defendant,** see 233 P. 2d 347; one who knowingly, voluntarily, or purposefully and with common intent with the principal offender unites in the commission or attempted commission of a crime. Mere presence combined with knowledge that crime is about to transpire, without active mental or physical contribution, does not make one an accomplice. Id. 348, 349. For example, undercover agents are not accomplices. See 478 S.W. 2d 450, 451; 473 S.W. 2d 19, 20. Essential to accomplice liability is a shared, common **mens rea** and criminal purpose between **agent** and **principal.** Compare **accessory; aid and abet; conspiracy.**

ACCORD agreement; "an agreement whereby one of the parties undertakes to give or perform, and the others to accept, in satisfaction of a **claim, liquidated** [certain] or unliquidated [in dispute] and arising either from **contract** or from **tort,** something other than or different from what he is, or considers himself, entitled to." 408 P. 2d 712, 713. "**Satisfaction** takes place when the accord is executed," 193 A. 2d 601, 602; after which there has been an "**accord and satisfaction.**" See **novation; settlement.**

ACCORD AND SATISFACTION payment of money, or other thing of value usually less than the amount owed or demanded, in exchange for **extinguishment** of the **debt.** It amounts to "something other than strict **performance** or payment. An agreement, whether actual or implied, must acknowledge that the acceptance of the smaller sum is meant to discharge the obligation to pay the larger sum.

ACCOUNT "a detailed statement of the mutual demand in the nature of debt and credit between parties, arising out of contracts or some fiduciary relation." 343 S.W. 2d 522, 524. In general business terminology, a particular client or customer. See **capital account, discretionary account; joint account; open account.**

ACCOUNT DEBTOR person who is obligated on an account. U.C.C. §9-105(1)(a).

ACCOUNT PAYABLE the amount owed by a business to its suppliers and other regular trading partners.

ACCOUNTS RECEIVABLE amounts owing on open account. 25 U.S. 178; running accounts that are usually disclosed in the **creditor's** account books, representing unsettled **claims** and transactions not reduced to writing. 327 F. Supp. 425, 427. In neither commercial nor legal contexts does an account receivable embrace an isolated transaction wholly outside of the account creditor's normal business dealings. Id. The Uniform Commercial Code has rejected "exact and detailed" descriptions in favor of those that reasonably identify what is described. All that is required under the code to describe an accounts receivable is that the financing statement be sufficiently descriptive so as reasonably to generate further inquiry. The code does not define "accounts receivable," but in the official comments to the code "accounts" is defined as "ordi-

nary commercial accounts receivable." 458 F. 2d 435, 437.

ACCOUNTING, ACTION FOR refers to an action, usually brought in **equity,** to secure a formal statement of account from one partner to others in order to obtain a judicial determination of the rights of the parties in a shared asset. If one partner feels another has been diverting funds or otherwise cheating him, he may bring an action for an accounting and ask for the appointment of a temporary **receivor.** Sometimes an equity judge will appoint a **master** to perform the accounting. 1 Am. Jur. 2d, Accounting §44.

ACCOUNTING METHOD the method by which a business (**corporation, partnership** or **sole proprietorship**) keeps its books and records for purposes of computing **income** and **deductions** and determining **taxable income.** Generally, the method of accounting affects the timing of an item of income or deduction. The two major methods of accounting are **accrual** and **cash.**

ACCRUAL METHOD an accounting method under which income is subject to tax after all events have occurred which fix the right to receive such income and deductions are allowed when the obligation to pay similarly becomes fixed, regardless of when the income is actually received or when the obligation is actually paid. Treas. Reg. §1.451-1(a) and §1.461-1(a)(2). The accrual method must be utilized by any business taxpayer which has **inventory.** Treas. Reg. §1. 446-1(c)(2)(i).

CASH METHOD an accounting method under which income is subject to tax when actually or constructively received and deductions are allowed when actually paid. Treas. Reg. §1.446-1(c)(1)(i) and §1.451-1.

INSTALLMENT METHOD OF ACCOUNTING a method of accounting which may be elected by a **taxpayer** who is either on the cash or the accrual method of accounting which allows the taxpayer to postpone the **recognition** of gain from the **sale or exchange** of assets if at least one payment is to be received after the close of the year of sale. I.R.C. §453. If this method is utilized, a pro-rata portion of the payment received each year reduces the taxpayer's **basis** and the remainder is taxed as gain from the sale or exchange of the asset.

ACCREDITED INVESTOR knowledgeable and sophisticated persons or institutions who qualify to purchase securities in transactions exempt from registration under the Securities Act of 1933. See **private offering.**

ACCRETION the adding on or adhering of something to property; a means by which a property owner gains ownership of something additional. It usually refers to "the gradual and imperceptible addition of sediment to the shore by the action of water; it is created by operation of natural causes." 198 P. 2d 769, 772. It differs from **avulsion** which "is a sudden and perceptible loss or addition to land by the action of water." 161 F. Supp. 25, 29. See **alluvion; avulsion; reliction.**

In the law of **succession,** accretion is said to take place when a co-**heir** or co-**legatee** dies before the property **vests,** or when he rejects the **inheritance** or **legacy,** or when he fails to comply with a **condition,** or when he becomes incapable of taking. The result is that the other heirs or legatees can share in his part. See 2 P. 418, 440.

In situations involving a **trust,** the term refers to any addition to the principal or income that results from an extraordinary occurrence, that is, an occurrence which is forseeable but which rarely happens.

See 213 N.W. 320, 322 and 148 F. 2d 503, 506.

ACCRUE generally, to accumulate, to happen, to come into fact or existence; as to a **cause of action,** to come into existence as an enforceable claim; as to a debt or bank account, the coming due of **interest** on **principal** sum. The point at which a cause of action is said to "accrue" also affects the length of time that a prospective plaintiff may wait to bring a suit under the **statute of limitations.**

ACCUSATION a **charge** against a person or corporation; "in its broadest sense it includes **indictment, presentment, information** and any other form in which a charge of crime or offense can be made against an individual," 151 A. 2d 127, 129; formal charge of having committed a criminal offense, made against a person in accordance with established legal **procedure** and not involving the **grand jury.**

ACCUSATORY INSTRUMENT refers to the initial **pleading** or other paper which forms the procedural basis for a criminal charge. It may take the form of an **indictment, information,** or **accusation.** If the accusatory instrument is defective, the entire proceeding will be rendered null and void.

ACCUSE to directly and formally institute legal **proceedings** against a person, charging that he has committed an offense cognizable at law; to **prosecute;** to charge with an offense judicially or by public **process.** See 73 So. 225, 228.

ACCUSED person against whom a criminal proceeding is initiated. See 73 So. 225, 228. "Accused" and "defendant" refer to one who in a legal manner is held to answer for an offense at any stage of the proceedings, or against whom a complaint in any lawful manner is made, charging an offense including all proceedings from the order of arrest to final execution. A defendant is not accused until charged with the offense or until he becomes subject to actual restraint by **arrest.** See 509 P. 2d 549, 551. The point at which a defendant is "accused" is important in determining when certain constitutional rights attach.

A.C.L.U. see **American Civil Liberties Union.**

A COELO USQUE AD CENTRUM (*ä kō-ā'-lō ūs'-kwā äd sĕn'-trūm)*— Lat: from the sky [heavens] all the way to the center of the earth; a very old **property** maxim which marked the boundaries within which an owner owned his property. This maxim no longer strictly applies because the owner of property in modern times owns subject to the rights of airplanes and oil and gas exploration. See Smith, Survey of the Law of Property 257-266 (3rd ed. 1981).

ACQUIESCENCE conduct that may imply consent; a tacit acceptance, often through silence when some objection ought to be forthcoming. 26 P. 898. Thus, if one makes a statement and another does not respond negatively, acquiescence may be inferred. An **estoppel** may be created in appropriate circumstances in this manner. See 94 N.E. 2d 479. Compare **laches** which implies a neglect to do that which we would expect another to do for his own benefit. See 5A 2d 325.

ACQUIRE to gain by any means; to obtain by any endeavor such as practice, purchase, or investment. In the law of contracts, to become the owner of property. To make something one's own. Implies some positive action as opposed to a more passive obtaining such as by an accrual. See **accrue.**

ACQUIT to set free or judicially discharge from an **accusation** of suspicion of guilt. See 65 N.Y.S. 1062, 1065. An individual is acquitted when, at the close of **trial,** either a jury or court determines that the person has been absolved of the charges which were the bases of the **action;** a **verdict** of "not guilty" acquits the defendant and prevents his retrial under the principles of **double jeopardy.**

In **contract** terminology, "to acquit" meant to release from a **debt,** duty or charge. See 26 Wend. 383, 400.

ACQUITTAL one who is acquitted receives an acquittal, which broadly means that the individual is released or discharged without any further prosecution for the same act or transaction.

A.C.R.S. see **depreciation** [ACCELERATED COST RECOVERY SYSTEM].

ACT see **overt act.** See also **wrongful act.**

ACTIO *(äk'-tē-ō)* doing, performance, action, activity; also, **proceedings, lawsuit, process, action,** permission for a suit; right or cause of action.

ACTION (AT LAW) a **judicial** proceeding whereby one party **prosecutes** another for a wrong done, or for protection of a right or prevention of a wrong; at common law, to be distinguished from an action in equity which could not be brought before the law courts but only before a court of **equity.** See **collusive action; derivative action; penal action.**

ACTIONABLE giving rise to a **cause of action;** thus, it refers to wrongful conduct which may form the basis of a civil **action,** as in ACTIONABLE NEGLIGENCE which is the **breach** or nonperformance of a **legal duty** through neglect or carelessness, resulting in damage or injury to another. See 49 A. 673.

ACTIONABLE TORT to constitute an actionable **tort** there must be a legal duty imposed by statute or otherwise owing by defendant to the one injured. 195 P. 2d 501, 511.

ACTION EX CONTRACTU see **ex contractu**.

ACTION EX DELICTO *(ĕx dĕl-ĭk'-tō)*—Lat: **cause of action** which arises out of fault, misconduct, or **malfeasance**, 100 S.W. 2d 687, 689; usually refers to an action in **tort**, arising from breach of a **legal duty** not related to a contract, rather than one based on a **contract**. "If the cause of action given expression in the **complaint** arises from a **breach of promise**, the action is EX CONTRACTU [but] if that cause of action arises from a breach of duty growing out of the contract, it is in form 'ex delicto'." 120 So. 153, 154.

ACTION FOR ACCOUNTING see **accounting, action for**.

ACTION FOR POSSESSION see **possessory action**.

ACTION IN CASE see **trespass** [TRESPASS ON THE CASE].

ACTIO NON *(äk'-tē-ō nŏn)* in **pleading,** a nonperformance, nonfeasance; a special plea by a defendant against the plaintiff. Also, a **nonsuit**.

ACTIONS IN PERSONAM see **in personam; jurisdiction**.

ACTIONS IN REM see **in rem; jurisdiction**.

ACTIONS QUASI IN REM see **jurisdiction; quasi in rem**.

ACTIVISM see **judicial activism**.

ACT OF GOD [PROVIDENCE] manifestation of the forces of nature which are unpredictable and difficult to anticipate; "the result of the direct, immediate and exclusive operation of the forces of nature, uncontrolled or uninfluenced by the power of man and without human intervention, [which] is of such character that it could not have been prevented or avoided by foresight or prudence. Examples are tempests, lightning, earthquakes, and a sudden illness or death of a person." 226 A. 2d 160, 162. In law of torts, proof that an Act of God was the sole or proximate **cause** of injury is an **affirmative defense** to an action for **negligence**. An intervening Act of God generally will not excuse an absolute contractual **duty** in the absence of statutory or contractual language to the contrary. 244 F. 2d 565. The law here is generally governed by the law of **impossibility**.

ACTUAL CASH VALUE see **market value**.

ACTUAL DAMAGES see **damages**.

ACTUAL NOTICE see **notice**.

ACTUAL POSSESSION see **possession**.

ACTUAL VALUE see **market value**.

ACTUARY one who computes various insurance and property costs; especially, one who calculates the cost of life insurance risks and insurance premiums.

ACTUS REUS *(äkt'-ŭs rā'-ŭs)*—Lat: loosely, the criminal act; but the term more properly refers to the "guilty act" or the "deed of crime." Every criminal offense has two components: one of these is objective, the other is subjective; one is physical, the other is psychical; one is the actus reus, the other is the **mens rea**. The actus reus generally differs from crime to crime. In **murder** it is **homicide;** in **burglary** it is the nocturnal breaking into the dwelling of another; in uttering a forged **instrument** it is the act of offering as good an instrument which is actually false. In like manner the mens rea differs from crime to crime. In murder it is **malice aforethought;** in burglary it is the intent to commit a **felony;** in uttering a forged instrument it is "knowledge" that the instrument is false plus an intent to defraud. Perkins and Boyce, Criminal Law 830-831 (3rd ed. 1982). The actus reus must be causally related to the mens rea for a crime to occur: "An evil intention and an unlawful action must concur in order to constitute a crime." 93 N.E. 249. Although it is frequently said that no mens rea is required for a **strict liability** offense, the actus reus alone being sufficient (see e.g., 361 U.S. 147, 150 and 342 U.S. 246, 256), it is more useful to identify a special mens rea for the civil offense that recognizes the low level of **culpability** connected with a strict or civil offense. As to the act being sufficient even in the **strict liability** setting, a "guilty act" (as opposed to a coerced act for example) would seem required. Hall, General Principles of Criminal Law 222-27 (2d ed. 1960). See **corpus delicti.**

AD DAMNUM *(äd däm'-nŭm)*— Lat: the amount of **damages** demanded. 7 A. 391, 392. In a **pleading** it fixes the amount beyond which a party may not recover on the **trial** of his **action.** 68 N.W. 2d 500, 506. In a **complaint** it is the claim for damages. 55 A. 177, 179.

ADDITUR *(ăd'-dĭ-tûr)*—Lat: it is increased. An increase by the court in the amount of **damages** awarded by the **jury.** This is a power vested in a **trial court** to assess damages and to increase an inadequate award as a condition of the denial of a **motion** by the **plaintiff** for a new trial. It cannot be done without the **defendant's** consent as this would impair his right to a jury trial on the question of damages. See 226 P. 2d 677. Increases in jury awards within the federal system are not permitted in **tort** claims. 293 U.S. 474. Compare **remittitur; set-off.**

ADEEM see **ademption.**

ADEMPTION removal or extinction of a **legacy;** a taking away; one of the ways in which a **devise** or **bequest** is adeemed is the extinction or withdrawal of the disposition by some act of the **testator** clearly indicating an intent to revoke it. In the case of a specific legacy, ademption may be effected by the testator's **inter vivos gift** of the property devised or bequeathed and/or the existence of attendant circumstances that render it impossible to effect the transfer or payment as directed by the **will.** See 167 S.W. 2d 345, 348.

ADHESION CONTRACT a contract so heavily restrictive of one party, while so non-restrictive of another, that doubts arise as to its representation as a voluntary and uncoerced agreement; implies a grave inequality of bargaining power. The concept often arises in the context of "standard-form printed contracts prepared by one party and submitted to the other on a 'take it or leave it' basis. The law has recognized there is often no true equality of bargaining power in such contracts and has accommodated that reality in construing them." 347 F. 2d 379, 383. See **unconscionable.**

AD HOC *(ăd hŏk)*—Lat: for this; for this particular purpose. An "ad hoc" committee is one commissioned for a special purpose and likewise an "ad hoc" attorney is one designated for a particular client in a special situation.

ADJECTIVE LAW the rules of legal practice and **procedure** that make **substantive law** effective. It determines the manner and means of enforcing the legal rights that are created and defined by substantive law. See 160 P. 2d. 210, 218. For instance, **service of process** is a matter of adjective law. 21 N.Y.S. 2d 791, 794.

ADJOURN to postpone; to delay briefly a court proceeding through **recess.** 2 N.J.L. 253, 254. An adjournment for a longer duration is termed a **continuance.** A session postponed indefinitely is termed an ADJOURNMENT SINE DIE. See **sine**

die. The term has a special meaning in the rule of legislatures that adjourn between legislative sessions, but recess for periods, of whatever duration, within a single session.

ADJUDICATION the determination of a controversy and a pronouncement of a **judgment** based on **evidence** presented; implies a final judgment of the court or other body deciding the matter, as opposed to a proceeding in which the merits of the cause of action were not reached, e.g., **default judgment.** Compare **disposition.**

ADJUSTED BASIS see **basis.**

ADJUSTER one who adjusts or settles an insurance claim; one who makes a determination of the amount of a claim and then makes an agreement with the insured as to a settlement.

AD LITEM *(ăd lī'-tĕm)*—Lat: for the lawsuit; for the purposes of the suit being prosecuted.

A GUARDIAN AD LITEM is a person appointed by the court to protect the interests of a minor or legally **incompetent** person in a lawsuit.

ADMINISTRATIVE AGENCY see **regulatory agency.**

ADMINISTRATIVE HEARING see **hearing.**

ADMINISTRATIVE LAW law created by administrative agencies by way of rules, regulations, orders, and decisions.

ADMINISTRATIVE LAW JUDGE the presiding officer at an administrative hearing. He does not sit as a law judge, and his power is essentially one of recommendation. In the federal system, he is empowered to administer oaths and affirmations, issue subpoenas, rule on evidence presented, take depositions, regulate the course of the hearing, and make or recommend decisions. 5 U.S.C.A. §556(c)(1) through (9). The role of Administrative Law Judges was formerly performed by hearing examiners. The Administrative Law Judge's decision can be appealed to the federal agency for which he hears cases, and then to a court of law. Mezines, et al., Administrative Law §6.01 (1977). See **Administrative Procedure Act.**

ADMINISTRATIVE PROCEDURE ACT (APA) an act designed to give uniformity to the rule-making and adjudicative proceedings of federal administrative agencies. The federal government passed the act in 1946, in response to increasing resentment of the agencies' latitude in matters affecting the rights of individuals. Following the federal lead, most of the states also passed similar statutes during the late 1940s and early 1950s.

Although the APA did not make administrative decision making into a substantially judicial process as some early reformers desired, it nonetheless brought coherence and judicial character to formerly haphazard procedures. The APA provides guidelines for rule-making hearings, adjudicative hearings, intra-agency review, judicial review, and public access to agency rules and decisions, and it creates rights of counsel at hearings, rights of public access to administrative hearings, and rights of an individual to control personal information collected by an agency. Davis, Administrative Law Text §6-11 (1972); 5 U.S.C.A. §§551 et seq., 3105, 3344, 5371, 7521.

ADMINISTRATOR (ADMINISTRATRIX) one appointed to handle the affairs of a person who has died **intestate;** one who manages the **estate** of a deceased person who left no **executor;** "an instrumentality established by law 'for performing the acts necessary for the transfer of the effects left by the deceased to those who succeed to their ownership'." 169 F. Supp. 647, 650. If decedent died with a will, an **executor** carries it out.

ADMIRALTY AND MARITIME JURISDICTION expansive jurisdiction over all actions related to events occurring at sea; "extends to all things done upon and relating to the sea, to transactions relating to commerce and navigation, to damages and injuries upon the sea, and all maritime contracts, torts, and injuries." 15 A. 49, 50. Admiralty jurisdiction is vested in the courts of the United States by the United States Constitution, Art. III, Sec. 2. See **admiralty courts**.

ADMIRALTY COURTS tribunals exercising **jurisdiction** over maritime matters, under the authority of the **United States Constitution** and the Judiciary Act. See U.S.C.A. Constitution Art. III, Sec. 2 C1.1; 28 U.S.C.A. §1333. Admiralty **jurisdiction** includes only maritime matters or subjects, and may not be extended to non-maritime matters on the ground of convenience or because a particular case involves both maritime and non-maritime matters. 360 F. Supp. 674; 14 F. 2d 949. **Federal courts,** however, do not have exclusive admiralty jurisdiction since **Congress** enacted the "saving to suitors" clause, 28 U.S.C.A. §1333(1), which reserves concurrent jurisdiction to the state courts when a suit under admiralty law may be brought to obtain other than admiralty **remedies.** State courts hearing such claims must, however, apply admiralty law as developed by the federal courts.

Admiralty law is not a complete system and in the absence of clear precedents, "admiralty courts" may look to **common law** sources or the prevailing law of the **jurisdiction.** 185 F. 2d 212; "admiralty courts" are not **courts of equity** and will not enforce an independent equitable **claim** merely because it pertains to maritime property. They may, however, grant injunctions.

ADMIRALTY LAW see **maritime law**.

ADMISSIBLE EVIDENCE evidence which may be received by a **trial court** to aid the **trier of fact** (judge or **jury**) in deciding the merits of a controversy. Each jurisdiction has established rules of evidence to determine questions of admissibility. The judge may properly receive only admissible evidence but he need not permit a party to introduce all admissible evidence. Cumulative evidence, for example, may be excluded. Moreover, under the Federal Rules of Evidence a judge may within his discretion exclude otherwise admissible evidence when the court determines that its **probative** value is outweighed by countervailing factors such as undue consumption of time, prejudice, confusion of the issues, or misleading of the jury. Federal Rules of Evidence 403. A lurid, gory photograph, for example, depicting the scene of the crime, the weapon used, or the injury to the victim may have very high probative value as to several issues in a criminal trial for atrocious assault and battery but is so highly inflammatory as to cause undue prejudice in the minds of the **jurors,** and it will be excluded if there is any other way to prove the necessary facts.

ADMISSION BY A PARTY-OPPONENT see **declaration against interest.**

ADMISSIONS in criminal law, the voluntary acknowledgment that certain facts do exist or are true; but, of themselves, admissions are insufficient to be considered a **confession** of guilt, although they are generally admissible against a defendant. Federal Rule of Evidence 801. It is a statement by the **accused** which tends to support the **charge,** but which is not sufficient to determine guilt. In civil procedure, a request for an admission is a pretrial **discovery** device by which one party asks another for a positive affirmation or denial of a material fact or **allegation** at issue. Federal Rules of Civil Procedure 36.

ADOPTION the legal process by which the parent/child relationship is created between persons not so related by blood. 31 So. 2d 819, 821. The adopted child becomes the heir and is entitled to all other privileges belonging to a natural child of the adoptive parents, including the right to inherit. 21 S.W. 82, 84. Adoption of children was unknown to the **common law,** but was a recognized practice under the **civil law** and our modern statutes of adoption are derived from the civil law. 58 N.E. 602, 604.

A.D.R. see **American Depository Receipt.**

AD TESTIFICANDUM (*äd tĕs'-tĭ-fĭ-căn'-dūm*)—Lat: for testifying. Any person sought "ad testificandum" is sought to appear as a **witness.** The term is generally used to refer to a type of **habeas corpus** writ to bring a prisoner to court to testify. See **subpoena ad testificandum.**

ADULT a person who has reached the **age of majority.**

ADULTERY voluntary sexual intercourse by a married person with someone other than his/her spouse. While most states will find the offense committed if either sexual partner is married, some states have retained the **common law** view that adultery is committed only if the woman is married. Adultery may be both a criminal offense and grounds for divorce, depending upon the jurisdiction.

   Common law distinguished adultery from **fornication** by requiring that the woman be married to commit the former and unmarried to commit the latter; in both, the marital status of the man did not matter; penetration and **consent** were necessary to commit both crimes. The element of **consent** distinguishes both crimes from **rape.**

As grounds for divorce, adultery generally applies to married persons of both sexes; however, under modern no-fault **divorce** law it is rarely used today as grounds for divorce. When adultery is the ground, the person who committed the act with the estranged spouse is called a CORRESPONDENT.

AD VALOREM (*äd và-lô'-rĕm*)— Lat: according to value; "used in taxation to designate an assessment of taxes against property at a certain rate upon its value." 74 P. 2d 47, 50. An AD VALOREM TAX is thus a tax assessed according to the value of the property. See **property tax.**

AD VALOREM TAX see **tax.**

ADVANCEMENT an irrevocable **gift** given by a parent in his or her lifetime to his or her child that is intended to represent all or part of the child's share of the estate which is to be deducted therefrom. 462 P. 2d 492, 494. For example, the mother's will provides that her son receive $20,000 upon her death. During her life, the son requires money to start up his new business. The mother gives him $10,000 without requiring repayment but informs the son that the money reduces the amount to which he will be entitled upon her death. The $10,000 constitutes an advancement.

ADVERSARY opponent or litigant in a legal controversy or litigation. See **adverse party.**

ADVERSARY PROCEEDING a **proceeding** involving a real controversy contested by two opposing **parties.** Contrast **ex parte.** See also **case or controversy; friendly suit.**

ADVERSE INTEREST against the interest of some other person, usually so as to benefit one's own interest.

ADVERSE PARTY the party on the opposite side of the **litigation.** See **adversary.**

ADVERSE POSSESSION a method of acquiring complete **title** to land as against all others, including the **record owner**, through certain acts over an uninterrupted period of time, as prescribed by statute. 13 So. 2d 649, 650; 502 P. 2d 672, 682; 226 S.W. 2d 484, 486. It is usually prescribed that such **possession** must be actual, visible, open, notorious, hostile, under claim of right, definite, continuous, exclusive, etc. 138 So. 2d 696, 699; 71 A. 2d 318, 320. The purpose of such requirements is to give **notice** that such possession is not subordinate to the claims of others. 244 P. 2d 582, 584. Possession by a **mortgagor** is not generally considered to ripen into title through adverse possession because it is not notorious or hostile. 9 N.W. 2d 421, 426. See **hostile possession; notorious possession.**

ADVERSE WITNESS see **witness.**

ADVISORY OPINION a formal opinion by a judge, court, or law officer upon a question of law submitted by a legislative body, governmental official, or other interested party, but not actually presented in a genuinely **adversary proceeding.** Such opinion therefore has no binding force as law. Compare **declaratory judgment.** See also **case or controversy.**

ADVOCACY in practice, the active espousal of a legal cause, see 268 U.S. 652; the art of persuasion.

AFFIANT the person who makes and subscribes to a statement made under oath [**affidavit**]. Compare **deponent.**

AFFIDAVIT a written, **ex parte** statement made or taken under oath before an officer of the court or a **notary public** or other person who has been duly authorized so to act.

AFFIRM the assertion of an **appellate court** that the **judgment** of the court below is correct and should stand; to approve, confirm, ratify. Compare **remand; reverse.**

Also, to attest to as in an **affirmation** of faith or fidelity.

AFFIRMATION a person's indication that one affirms the truth of one's statement. An "affirmation" serves the same purpose as an **oath,** in which a person swears the truth of the statement made. 1 U.S.C. §1. When persons object to making an oath on religious or ethical grounds, an affirmation is commonly accepted in the place of an oath. 394 F. 2d 230. A person who makes an affirmation is subject to the same penalties for **perjury** as a person who makes an oath.

AFFIRMATIVE ACTION positive steps taken in order to alleviate conditions resulting from past discrimination or from violations of a law. For example, if a discriminatory, all-white contracting firm takes a federal contract with the condition that affirmative action be taken to hire blacks, then the contracting firm must not only stop discriminating against blacks when hiring but must also take additional steps to make sure that more blacks are hired, such as apprenticeship programs or recruitment through newspaper ads. 471 F. 2d 680. Affirmative action legislation or court orders are usually remedial, not punitive. 306 U.S. 240, 257; 417 F. Supp. 377, 384. The U.S. Supreme Court upset the use of quota systems and announced **equal protection** standards for affirmative action programs in *Regents of the University of California* v. *Bakke,* 438 U.S. 265 (1978). Discrimination for its own sake, such as the presence of one social group over another, is constitutionally impermissible; but when the state pursues a legitimate state interest, such as diversity in the student body of a professional school, the state may utilize factors such as race as one of many factors to be considered. Id. Such an interest cannot be effectuated in a fashion that disregards individual rights as guaranteed by the Fourteenth Amendment. However, the use of racial quotas in furtherance of affirmative action programs is prohibited neither by the Constitution nor by federal equal rights laws.

AFFIRMATIVE DEFENSE see **defense.**

AFFIRMATIVE RELIEF that **relief** granted a **defendant** in a situation in which "the defendant might maintain an **action** entirely independent of **plaintiff**'s **claim,** and which [claim] he might proceed to establish and recover even if plaintiff abandoned his **cause of action,** or failed to establish it. In other words, [defendant's] answer must be in the nature of a [cross-claim], thereby rendering the action defendant's as well as plaintiff's." 41 N.W. 656.

AFFIX to attach to or add to permanently; to annex, as to affix a **chattel** to **realty;** e.g., to attach a chandelier to the ceiling is to affix it to the **real property.** A tree is also "affixed" to the land. See **fixtures.**

AFORETHOUGHT see **malice aforethought.**

A FORTIORI (ä fôr'-shē-ô'-rē)— Lat: from the most powerful reasoning; to draw inference that because a certain conclusion or fact is true, then a second conclusion must also be true because it is "lesser-included;" e.g., if a person is not guilty of **larceny** because he/she did not steal anything, then "a fortiori" he is not guilty of **robbery** where robbery is defined as stealing accompanied by a threat of force.

AFTER-ACQUIRED PROPERTY in **commercial law, property** acquired by a **debtor** subsequent to the execution of a **security agreement** covering property already owned by the debtor. At common law, the general rule was that mortgages on after-acquired property were illegal. Under provision of the **Uniform Commercial Code,** subject to specified conditions and restrictions, a **security interest** in after-acquired property may be created. U.C.C. §§9-108, 9-204. The term is commonly employed today in secured transactions, serving the dual purpose of subjecting additional property to the creditor's **lien** and removing doubts that may arise as to whether improvements, repairs, and additions made since execution of the agreement are included in it.

In **bankruptcy** law, the term refers to property acquired by the bankrupt after his petition for bankruptcy is filed. This property is free of all claims of the bankrupt's creditors. Exceptions to this exemption for after-acquired property include previously non-assignable real property rights that become assignable within six months after bankruptcy, and property rights vesting in the bankrupt by inheritance within six months of the bankruptcy. Collier on Bankruptcy §70.09 (1970).

AFTER-ACQUIRED TITLE a title that is not effectively conveyed at the time it is purportedly transferred, because the grantor did not have a good title to convey at that time, but which is later acquired by the unknowing grantee by operation of law because of subsequent events sufficient to perfect title in his grantor. Thus, when a person attempts to **convey title** to land which he does not in fact own, and he afterwards obtains **good title** to the same **property** or **interest** thus conveyed, such subsequent acquisition will automatically inure to the benefit of the prior grantee under this doctrine, 43 So. 2d 897, 899, provided the grantee was ignorant of non-ownership by the grantor. The same principle applies where the grantor's interest at the time of the conveyance was limited (e.g., by an outstanding **life estate** in another) in a way not known to the grantee; the grantee will enjoy the benefit of the subsequent release of the limitation on the title.

AFTER-THE-FACT see **accessory** [ACCESSORY AFTER-THE-FACT].

AGAINST THE [MANIFEST] [WEIGHT OF THE] EVIDENCE an evidentiary standard permitting the **trial court** after **verdict** to order a new trial where the verdict, though based on legally sufficient evidence, appears in the view of the trial court judge to be unsupported by the substantial credible evidence. "On such a motion it is the duty of the trial judge to set aside the verdict and grant a new trial, if he is of the opinion that the verdict is against the clear weight of the evidence, or is based upon evidence which is false, or will result in a **miscarriage of justice,** even though there may be substantial evidence which would prevent the direction of a verdict," (see **directed verdict**), 122 F. 2d 350, 352-53. It is not proper for the trial judge to substitute his judgment for that of the jury on matters of credibility or weight of the evidence, even if the judge disagrees with the jury, "unless the verdict is clearly against the undoubted general current of the evidence, so that the court can clearly see that they have acted under some mistake, or from some improper motive, bias, or feeling." 6 F. 128, 129-30. See also **judgment** (JUDGMENT N.O.V.).

AGE DISCRIMINATION the denial of privileges as well as other unfair treatment of employees on the basis of age, which is prohibited by federal law under the Age Discrimination in Employment Act of 1967. This act was amended in 1978 to protect employees up to 70 years of age.

AGENCY relation in which one person, the **agent,** acts on behalf of another with the authority of the latter, the **principal;** "a fiduciary relation which results from the manifestation of consent by one person that another shall act on the former's behalf and subject to his control, and consent by the other so to act." 122 N.W. 2d 290, 294. The acts of an agent will be binding on his principal. See also **apparent authority; regulatory agency; respondeat superior; scope of employment.** Compare **partnership.**

AGENT one who, by mutual consent, acts for the benefit of another; one authorized by a party to act in that party's behalf. Compare **servant.** See **agency.** See also **transfer agent; universal agent.**

AGE OF CONSENT age set by statute at which persons may marry without parental consent. 77 So. 2d 373. Also refers to age at which an actor may consent to sexual intercourse, 204 P. 2d 448, and below which age another commits an offense such as **statutory rape** or **sexual assault** even if the sexual conduct is engaged in voluntarily by both parties. An erroneous belief that another is at or above the age of consent is generally not a defense. See Model Penal Code §213.6.

AGE OF MAJORITY see **majority, age of.**

AGGRAVATED ASSAULT see **assault.**

AGGREGATE a total of all the parts; the whole, the complete amount; also, to combine, as to aggregate several **causes of action** in a single **suit;** similarly, to aggregate many persons whose causes of action are closely related into a **class action.** See Federal Rules of Civil Procedure 23. See **joinder.**

AGGRIEVED PARTY one who has been injured, who has suffered a loss; "a party or person is aggrieved by a **judgment, order,** or **decree** whenever it operates prejudicially and directly upon his property, pecuniary, or personal rights." 223 S.W. 2d 841, 845.

AGREEMENT a manifestation of mutual assent between two or more legally **competent** persons which ordinarily leads to a **contract.** In common usage, it is a broader term than **contract, bargain,** or **promise,** since it includes executed **sales, gifts,** and other transfers of **property,** as well as **promises** without legal obligation. While agreement is often used as a synonym for **contract,** some authorities narrow it to mean only mutual assent. The Uniform Commercial Code defines agreement as "The bargain of the parties in fact as found in their language or by implication from other circumstances. . . ." U.C.C. §1-201(3). See **postnuptial agreement; prenuptial agreement; separation agreement.**

AID AND ABET to actively, knowingly, intentionally, or purposefully facilitate or assist another individual in the commission or attempted commission of a crime. Aiding and abetting is characterized by affirmative criminal conduct and is not established as a result of omissions or negative acquiescence. 24 A. 2d 85, 87. Compare **accessory; accomplice; conspiracy.**

A.J. abbreviation for Associate Judge or Justice.

A.K.A. see **alias.**

ALEATORY uncertain; risky, involving an element of chance.

ALEATORY CONTRACT an agreement whose performance by one party depends upon the occurrence of a contingent event.

"An ALEATORY PROMISE is one the performance of which is by its own terms subject to the happening of an uncertain and fortuitous event or upon some fact the existence or past occurrence of which is also uncertain and undetermined." Corbin, Contracts 684 (One vol ed. 1952). Examples

of such contracts include life and fire insurance contracts. Such agreements are enforceable notwithstanding an uncertainty of terms at the time of the making so long as the risk undertaken is clearly apparent. A contract where performance is contingent upon the outcome of a bet, however, is a gambling contract and is generally unenforceable by statute or as matter of public policy in most jurisdictions. See generally Id. §§728-732.

ALIAS an indication that a person is known by more than one name; "means 'or', 'otherwise called' or 'otherwise known as'." 234 S.W. 2d 535, 539. "AKA" and "a/k/a" mean "also known as" and are used in **indictments** to introduce the listing of an alias.

ALIBI a provable account of an individual's whereabouts at the time of the commission of a crime which would make it impossible or impracticable to place him at the scene of the crime. An alibi negates the physical possibility that the suspected individual could have committed the crime. See 220 N.W. 328, 330. Compare **justification.**

ALIEN a person born in a foreign country, who owes his allegiance to that country; one not a citizen of the country in which he is living. A RESIDENT ALIEN is a person admitted to permanent resident status in the country by the immigration authorities but who has not been granted citizenship.

An alien is a "person" within the meaning of the due process clause of the Fourteenth Amendment. 347 U.S. 522. And alienage is treated as a "suspect" classification for purposes of **equal protection** analysis. For example, the Supreme Court has invalidated statutes that prevent aliens from entering a state's civil service and from receiving educational benefits. But where a job is "bound up with the operation of the State as a governmental entity"—policemen and public school teachers, for example—states may exclude aliens. 441 U.S. 68.

ALIENATION in the law of **real property,** the voluntary and absolute transfer of **title** and **possession** of real property from one person to another. The law recognizes the power to alienate property as one of the essential ingredients of **fee simple ownership** and therefore unreasonable restraints on alienation are generally prohibited as contrary to public policy. See 169 U.S. 353. See **restrictive covenant.** See also **restraint on alienation; rule against perpetuities.**

ALIENATION OF AFFECTIONS "a **tort** based upon willful and malicious interference with the marriage relation by a third party, without justification or excuse. . . . By definition, it includes and embraces mental anguish, loss of social position, disgrace, humiliation and embarrassment, as well as actual pecuniary loss due to destruction or disruption of the marriage relationship and the loss of financial support, if any." 415 S.W. 2d 127, 132. The interference may be in the nature of adultery (a tort then called CRIMINAL CONVERSATION) or may result from lesser acts which deprive the other spouse of affection from his or her marital partner. "More actions of this kind have been brought against parents than anyone else and the meddling mother-in-law is more frequently a defendant than the wicked lover." Prosser, Torts 876 (4th ed. 1971). Statutes in several states have abolished this **cause of action** because of the potential for abuse through **blackmail** and **extortion.** See Id. at 887. See **consortium.**

ALIENATION, ORDER OF see **marshaling [marshalling].**

ALIEN REGISTRATION see **green card.**

ALIMONY alimony or separate maintenance payments are amounts paid by one spouse to another in discharge of the paying spouse's obligation under local law to support the other spouse. For tax purposes, alimony and separate maintenance payments are payments made pursuant to a written instrument incident to divorce or separation or a decree issued by a court for support. Such payments will be **deductible** by the paying spouse and taxable **income** to the receiving spouse if they are "periodic," which means that they either must be payable over an indefinite period or if payable over a definite period, the definite period must last more than ten years. I.R.C. §71.

Generally, it has been the husband who has been ordered to support his wife but under some modern statutes the wife could be ordered to support a husband if he were in actual need. Indeed, statutes which have gender-based standards for awarding alimony have been found to be unconstitutional as a violation of **equal protection.** 440 U.S. 268.

The award of alimony is separate from **divorce** in that the court may reserve the power to modify or set aside the award of alimony. CHILD SUPPORT is a distinct obligation that may be imposed by the court upon the spouse with or without an award of alimony and is an amount of money that the court requires one spouse to pay to the other who has custody of the children born of the marriage. As with alimony, the amount of child support may be altered as changed circumstances warrant. A spouse who fails to pay alimony or child support may be held in **contempt** by the court and jailed until the past due amounts (**arrears**) are satisfied.

ALIQUOT *(ä'-lē-kwō)*—Lat: an even part of the whole; one part contained in a whole which is evenly divisible, i.e., divisible without leaving a remainder. In the case of a resulting **trust,** it is a particular fraction of the whole property involved, as distinguished from a general interest. 68 N.E. 37.

ALI TEST see **insanity** [ALI TEST].

ALIUNDE *(äl'-ē-ûn'-dā)*—Lat: from another source; from elsewhere; from outside. ALIUNDE RULE refers to the doctrine that a **verdict** may not be **impeached** by **evidence** in the possession of a juror unless the foundation for introduction of the evidence is made first by competent evidence from another source. See 141 Ohio St. 423. EVIDENCE ALIUNDE refers to evidence from an outside source.

ALLEGATION in **pleading,** an assertion of fact; the statement of the issue which the contributing party is prepared to prove.

ALLEN CHARGE an instruction given by the **court** to a **jury** which is experiencing difficulty reaching a **verdict** in a criminal case, in an attempt to encourage such jury to make a renewed effort to arrive at a decision. Such a supplementary **charge** was approved by the United States Supreme Court in *Allen* v. *United States,* where the trial court in effect told the jury "that in a large proportion of cases absolute certainty could not be expected; that although the verdict must be the verdict of each individual juror, and not a mere acquiescence in the conclusion of his fellows, yet they should examine the question submitted with candor and with a proper regard [for] and deference to the opinions of each other; that it was their duty to decide the case if they could conscientiously do so; that they should listen, with a disposition to be convinced, to each other's arguments; that, if much the larger number were for **conviction,** a dissenting juror should consider whether his doubt was a reasonable one which made no impression upon the minds of so many men, equally honest, equally intelligent with himself. If, upon the other hand, the majority was for **acquittal,** the minority ought to ask themselves whether they might not reasonably doubt the correctness of a judgment which was not concurred in by the majority." 164 U.S. 492, 501. This sort of instruction has been the target of complaints that it is coercive or constitutes a mandatory charge in terms of its likely effect on a jury. See, e.g., 309 F. 2d 852. Although use of such a charge had not yet been declared unconstitutional by any federal court, modifications of the Allen charge to ensure non-coerciveness have been insisted upon in many jurisdictions, see, e.g., 411 F. 2d 930; and its use has been banned outright by some state courts, see, e.g., 342 P. 2d. 197.

ALLOCUTION the requirement at **common law** that the trial judge address the **defendant** personally, asking him to show any legal cause why the sentence of conviction should not be pronounced upon the **verdict** of conviction. Modern **appellate procedures** have eliminated the original purposes for this formal address but it continues to be a part of the **sentencing** procedure in a majority of the states and is a mandatory part of a valid sentencing in the federal system. See Fed. R. Crim. Proc. 32(a); 365 U.S. 301 and 368 U.S. 424. The modern allocution does not ask the defendant why sentence ought not be imposed but rather for any statement that he would like to make on his own behalf in **mitigation** of punishment. It may be held to include the right of the defendant to offer evidence in mitigation beyond his own statement. 464 F. 2d 215.

ALLODIAL owned freely without obligation to one with superior right; not subject to the restriction on **alienation** which existed with feudal tenures; free of any superior rights vested in another, such as a lord. See **ownership** [ALLODIAL OWNERSHIP]. Compare **tenurial.**

ALLOWANCE see **depletion** [DE-PLETION ALLOWANCE].

ALLUVION deposits of sedimentary material (earth, sand, gravel, etc.) which have accumulated gradually and imperceptibly along the bank of a river, 47 A. 745; the term may also apply to such accumulations along the bank of the sea, 134 U.S. 178, 189; alluvion is the result of the process of **accretion,** and any alluvion is considered "an inherent and essential attribute of the original property," Id., e.i., a part of the property to which it has become attached, 192 S.W. 2d 338; whether the effect of natural or artificial causes, alluvion must accumulate so gradually that the change from moment to moment cannot be visibly perceived. 55 P. 2d. 90. See also **reliction; avulsion.**

ALTERATION see **material alteration.**

ALTER EGO (al'-tèr ē-gò)—Lat: the other self. Under the doctrine of alter ego, the law will disregard the limited personal liability one enjoys when he/she acts in a corporate capacity and will regard the act as his/her personal responsibility. To invoke the doctrine, it must be shown that the corporation was a mere conduit for the transaction of private business and that no separate identity of the individual and the corporation really existed. 106 P. 2d 974, 984.

ALTERNATIVE PLEADING at common law a pleading which alleged facts so entirely separate that it was difficult to determine upon which set of facts the person pleading intended to rely as the basis of recovery; e.g., pleading a case of personal injury alleging facts constituting negligence by the defendant, or, "in the alternative," evidence of intentional conduct by the defendant. "[W]hen a plaintiff pleads his case in the alternative, one version of which is good and the other not, his petition will, on

demurrer, be treated as pleading no more than the latter, since it will be construed most strongly against him." 93 S.E. 2d. 3, 5. See **election of remedies.** Today alternative pleading is generally permitted under modern procedure.

ALTERNATIVE WRIT OF MANDAMUS see **peremptory writ.**

AMELIORATING WASTE see **waste.**

AMEND to alter; to improve upon. Thus, one amends a bill by altering or changing an established law—the law is continued in changed form. One amends a **pleading** by making an addition to or a subtraction from an already existing pleading.

AMENDMENTS see respective entries (e.g., **First Amendment**).

AMERICAN BAR ASSOCIATION (**A.B.A**) a national organization of lawyers and law students that promotes improvements in the delivery of legal services and the administration of justice. Membership is open to any lawyer who is in good standing in any state or to any student attending an accredited law school. The AMERICAN BAR FOUNDATION is a subsidiary of the A.B.A. that sponsors and funds projects in legal research, education, and social studies.

AMERICAN CIVIL LIBERTIES UNION (**A.C.L.U.**) a nationwide organization dedicated to the enforcement and preservation of rights and civil liberties guaranteed by the federal and state constitutions. The A.C.L.U. purportedly does not take any political position, but rather strives to preserve an atmosphere in which all political positions can be heard. It was founded in 1920, by Roger Nash Baldwin, as part of a widespread nationwide movement against response to the government's persecution of conscientious objectors, pacifists and radicals, and their censorship of socialist and liberal publications during and immediately following World War I. Markman, The Noblest Cry (1965). Its activities include handling cases, opposing legislation it considers repressive, and publishing a bimonthly report and numerous informational pamphlets. The A.C.L.U.'s current membership is about 275,000. It is supported by annual contributions and has local chapters in every state.

AMERICAN DEPOSITORY RECEIPT (ADR) a receipt issued by American banks to domestic buyers as a convenient substitute for direct ownership of stock in foreign companies. ADRs are traded on **stock exchanges** and in **over-the-counter markets** like stocks of domestic companies. Stock **dividends** and similar adjustments to the underlying shares are paid in cash or ADR dividends by the bank.

AMERICAN STOCK EXCHANGE the second largest United States **stock exchange,** after the **New York Stock Exchange.** It was formerly known as the NEW YORK CURB EXCHANGE or "Curb" and is abbreviated today as either AMEX or ASE.

AMEX see **American Stock Exchange.**

AMICUS CURIAE (*à-mē'-kŭs kyŭ'-rē-ī*)—Lat: friend of the court; one who gives information to the court on some matter of law which is in doubt. See 264 F. 276, 279. The function of an amicus curiae is to call the court's attention to some matter which might otherwise escape its attention. See 64 N.Y. S. 2d 510, 512. An AMICUS CURIAE BRIEF (or AMICUS BRIEF) is submitted by one not a party to the **lawsuit** to aid the court in gaining the information it needs to make a proper decision or to urge a particular result on behalf of the public or a private interest of third parties who

will be affected by the resolution of the dispute.

AMNESTY a **pardon** that is extended to a group of persons and that excuses them for criminal offenses. A grant of amnesty is usually motivated by political reasons, and may be limited or conditioned. Amnesties often follow wars, a recent example being President Ford's forgiveness of Vietnam War draft evaders, 10 Prcs. Doc. 1149. The amnesty power is usually vested in the chief executive as part of his **clemency** power. Rubin, Law of Criminal Correction 667 (2d ed. 1973).

AMORTIZATION a gradual **extinguishment** of a **debt,** as the term is used for accounting purposes; "the provision for the gradual extinction of [a future obligation] in advance of maturity, either by an annual charge against capital account, or, more specifically, by periodic contributions to a **sinking fund** which will be adequate to discharge a debt or make a replacement when it becomes necessary." 78 F. Supp. 111, 122, n. 1. Compare **depreciation.**

AMOUNT REALIZED see **realization** [GAIN OR LOSS REALIZED].

ANCIENT DEMESNE manors that were in the actual possession of the Crown during the reign of William the Conqueror and that were recorded as such in the Domesday Book. This type of tenure was abolished in England by the Law of Property Act (1922).

ANCILLARY JURISDICTION the jurisdiction assumed by federal courts, largely as a matter of convenience to the parties, which extends beyond that conferred upon them expressly by the Constitution or by enabling statutes. Under the doctrine of ancillary jurisdiction, it is recognized "that a district court acquires jurisdiction of a case or controversy in its entirety and may as an incident to disposition of a matter properly before it, possess jurisdiction to decide other matters raised by the case of which it could not take cognizance were they independently presented. Thus when the court has jurisdiction of the principal action, it may hear also any ancillary proceeding therein, regardless of the citizenship of the parties, the amount in controversy, or any other factor that would normally determine jurisdiction." Wright, Federal Courts 99 (4th ed. 1983). The most common example of ancillary jurisdiction is represented by **compulsory counterclaims,** which the Federal Rules of Civil Procedure expressly require the defendant to bring and which accordingly have been held cognizable without regard to an independent federal jurisdictional basis. See, e.g., 286 F. 2d 631. **Permissive counterclaims** are probably not within the federal courts' ancillary jurisdiction and independent jurisdictional bases must be established. 29 F.R.D. 348. **Cross-claims, impleader** of third parties, **interpleader,** and **intervention** as of right are further examples of ancillary jurisdiction. Wright, supra. §9. **Joinder of claims** (federal and non-federal grounds) is not within ancillary jurisdiction unless the claims are so closely related as to fall within the concept of **pendent jurisdiction.**

It is generally held that where ancillary jurisdiction suffices to allow a particular claim or party to be joined in the lawsuit without an independent jurisdictional basis, it is not necessary to satisfy the **venue** requirements with respect to such a claim or party. See, e.g., 174 F. Supp. 587; but see 73 Harv. L. Rev. 1164.

AND HIS HEIRS see **heirs.**

ANIMO *(än'-ĭ-mō)*—Lat: purposefully; intentionally.

ANIMO REVERTENDI *(rĕ-vĕr-tĕn'-dē)* with the intention to return.

ANIMO REVOCANDI *(rĕ-vō-kàn'-dē)* with the intention to revoke.

ANIMO TESTANDI *(tĕs-tän'-dē)* with the intention to make a **will.**

ANIMUS see **animo.**

ANNOTATION a comment upon or collection of cases citing a particular case or statute; an annotated statute is one that has the relevant cases interpreting the statute appended to it. Thus, United States Code Annotated (U.S.C.A.) or New Jersey Statutes Annotated (N.J.S.A.) are annotated versions of the official statutes of those jurisdictions. American Law Reports is an annotated set of recent cases from the various state and federal courts. The current versions are A.L.R. 4th and A.L.R. Fed.

ANNUAL REPORT a formal financial statement issued yearly. The annual report of publicly owned corporations must comply with S.E.C. reporting requirements, which include **balance sheet, income statement** and cash flow reports audited by an independent certified public accountant. These annual reports are filed with the S.E.C. on Form 10K.

ANNUITANT one who receives the benefits of an **annuity.**

ANNUITY a fixed sum payable periodically, subject to the limitations imposed by the **grantor.** "Generally speaking, it designates a right—bequeathed, donated or purchased—to receive fixed, periodical payments, either for life or a number of years. Its determining characteristic is that the **annuitant** has an interest only in the payments themselves and not in any principal fund or source from which they may be derived." 13 A. 2d 419, 421. Compare **life estate; trust.**

ANNUL to make void; to dissolve that which once existed, as to "annul" the bonds of matrimony. A marriage which is annulled [by an "action for annulment"] is void **ab initio** as compared with a marriage which is dissolved by a decree of divorce; divorce operates only to terminate the marriage from that point forward and does not affect the former validity of the marriage.

ANSWER the principle **pleading** on the part of the **defendant** in response to **plaintiff's complaint;** it must contain a **denial** of all of the **allegations** of plaintiff's complaint which the defendant wishes to controvert; it may also contain any **affirmative defenses** which the defendant may have, which should be stated separately; it may contain a statement of any **permissive counterclaim** which the defendant has against the plaintiff and which is legally available to him in the action; **compulsory counterclaims** arising out of the same transaction must generally be pleaded in the answer or they will be barred in any subsequent separate suit. See, e.g., Fed. R. Civ. Proc. 13. See **evasive answer.**

ANTENUPTIAL AGREEMENT see **prenuptial agreement.**

ANTICIPATORY BREACH (OF CONTRACT) a breach committed before the arrival of the actual time of required performance. It occurs when one party by declaration repudiates his contractual obligation before it is due. The repudiation required is "a positive statement indicating that the promisor will not or cannot substantially perform his contractual duties." Restatement of Contracts §318(a); See U.C.C. §2-610. In the case of a **bilateral contract,** the **aggrieved party** may urge the repudiating party to perform without giving up the right to claim a present breach. Restatement of Contracts §320; U.C.C. §2-610(b). If, however, the repudiating party withdraws his repudiation before there has been a material change in position, the repudiation will be nullified. Restatements of Contracts §319; U.C.C. §2-611. A repudiation will justify a demand by the aggrieved party for an "assurance of performance" under U.C.C. §2-609. Where the anticipatory repudiation is by the party's conduct rather than by declaration it is called VOLUNTARY DISABLEMENT. Thus, in a contract for the sale of land the seller breaches through voluntary disablement if he transfers land to a third party during the executory interval before performance is due on the first contract. In some jurisdictions no distinction is drawn between the two forms of preliminary breach.

ANTI-DISCRIMINATION ACT see **Robinson-Patman Act.**

ANTI-DUMPING LAW see **dumping.**

ANTILAPSE STATUTE statutes enacted to allow the **heirs** of a **devisee** (or **legatee**) who predeceases the **testator** [the party making the devise or legacy] to be substituted as the takers of what the testator has attempted to give the deceased devisee (or legatee). Such laws abrogate the **common law** rule that such testamentary gifts "lapsed" upon the death of the specified recipient. Most American jurisdictions have adopted such laws; and in view of the fact that the common law doctrine operated most harshly on grandchildren, who became disinherited when a parent predeceased the testator/grandparent, many of these statutes apply only to relatives of the testator. See Powell, Real Property §367 (1979).

ANTITRUST LAWS Statutes aimed at promoting free competition in the market place. Any agreement or cooperative effort or intent by two or more entities that affects or restrains, or is likely to affect or restrain their competitors, is illegal under these statutes. Crotti, Trading Under EEC and US Antitrust Laws, 7 (1977).

The two major U.S. antitrust laws are the Sherman Act, 15 U.S.C. §§1-7, and the Clayton Act,

15 U.S.C. §12-27. The Sherman Act protects the right of individuals to be free to compete, which should be distinguished from preserving a freely competitive market. Section 1 of the Sherman Act makes illegal any **contract**, combination, or **conspiracy** in restraint of trade or commerce. Section 2 makes illegal **monopolies** and attempts, combinations, or **conspiracies** to monopolize.

The Clayton Act was adopted in 1914 as a reaction to the vagueness of the Sherman Act. The original Clayton Act singled out four practices for specific regulation: §2, price discrimination; §3, tying and exclusive-dealing contracts; §7, stock acquisitions; §8, interlocking directorates. Posner, Antitrust 29 (1974).

A POSTERIORI (ä pŏs'-tĕr-ē-ô'-rē)—Lat: from the most recent aspect or point of view. This concept is akin to factual knowledge which relates to those things that can only be known from experience. The term relates to the means by which a concept or proposition is known or validated. It is distinguished from **a priori** reasoning, in which a proposition is known or validated solely through logical necessity; a posteriori reasoning achieves its goal of ascertaining truth by means of actual experience or observation.

APPARENT AUTHORITY refers to a doctrine involving the accountability of a **principal** for the acts of his **agent** "which operates to make a principal liable for operative words spoken by an agent in the course of a transaction with another to whom the principal has represented that the agent has authority . . ." Seavey, Handbook of the Law of Agency §106C (1964). It refers to that situation created when a principal such as a **corporation** "manifests to a third person that an 'officer' or 'agent' may act in its behalf, and such third person in good faith believes that such 'authority' exists. In such a case, lack of actual authority, express or implied, is no **defense**. In certain cases the corporation [or other principal] may be estopped from denying the 'authority' of the 'officer' or 'agent'." Henn, Handbook of the Law of Corporations §226 (1970). The concept is also sometimes termed OSTENSIBLE AUTHORITY.

APPEAL a resort to a higher court for the purpose of obtaining a review of a lower court decision and a **reversal** of the lower court's judgment or the granting of a new **trial**. In **equity** and early **civil law**, an appeal was distinguished from a **writ of error** in that the former subjected facts as well as law to review and retrial. 214 P. 690; 9 F. 2d 256. Although the term is now used generally to denote all forms of review, in determining its more specialized meaning "it is necessary in each instance to look to (the) particular act giving an appeal, to determine powers to be exercised by (the) appellate court." 104 A. 617, 620. See **consolidated appeal**.

In the Supreme Court, an appeal is to be distinguished from a petition for **writ of certiorari** in that the former seeks review by right, while the latter seeks review through the Court's discretion. Judicial review of an administrative order may also be called an "appeal," although it constitutes the first adjudication of the legal injury complained of.

TRIAL DE NOVO historically, the appeal as it existed in **equity** allowed a trial de novo on law and facts, while proceedings **at law** allowed only a review on the **record** produced in the lower court for errors of law. Today this distinction largely has merged into one system. Equitable proceedings still, however, require a trial de novo more often than legal proceedings, unless it has been specifically prescribed by **statute**. 9 F. 2d 256, 259. For example, appeals from **probate** court **decrees** often are by trial de novo.

APPEARANCE the coming into court by a **party summoned** in an **action;** to come into court, upon being summoned, either by one's self or through one's attorney; to voluntarily submit one's self to the **jurisdiction** of the court.

COMPULSORY APPEARANCE where one has been validly served **process,** and so is compelled to appear in court.

GENERAL APPEARANCE where a party appears and participates in a **proceeding** for any reason other than for the purpose of attacking the court's jurisdiction. See 32 S.E. 2d 742, 745.

SPECIAL APPEARANCE one made for the sole purpose of attacking the **jurisdiction** of the court over the defendant's person. See 173 N.W. 468. "Whether an appearance is general or special is determined by the relief sought and if a defendant, by his appearance, insists only upon the objection that he is not in court for want of jurisdiction over his person, and confines his appearance for that purpose only, then he has made a special appearance, but if he raises any other question or asks any relief which can only be granted upon the hypothesis that the court has jurisdiction of his person, then he has made a general appearance." 209 P. 2d 843, 845

VOLUNTARY APPEARANCE where one appears in court without having had process served on him.

APPEARANCE DE BENE ESSE see **de bene esse.**

APPELLANT the party who appeals a decision; the party who brings the proceeding to a reviewing court; at common law, the PLAINTIFF IN ERROR. See also **appellee.**

APPELLATE COURT a court having jurisdiction to review the law as applied to a prior determination of the same case; "not a forum in which to make a new case. It is merely a court of review to determine whether or not the rulings and judgment of the court below upon the case as made were correct." 24 S.E. 913. A trial court first decides a law suit in most instances, with review then available in one or more appellate courts. Compare **trial** [TRIAL DE NOVO].

APPELLATE JURISDICTION see **jurisdiction.**

APPELLEE the **party** who argues, on **appeal,** against the setting aside of the **judgment;** the party prevailing in the court below; the party at whom the attack on appeal is aimed; at **common law,** the DEFENDANT IN ERROR. See also **appellant.**

APPOINTMENT OF RECEIVER the process by which one who has a proveable right or **interest** in certain **property** or a fund may obtain a **receivership** thereof in a proper case. 51 N.E. 2d 844, 847. The only **person** who can have a **receiver** is one who has some **title** or right to, **interest** in, or **lien** or **claim** on the property in question. 99 S.W. 2d 28, 30. Generally, the appointment of a receiver is discretionary, and not a matter of right. 289 U.S. 479, 504.

APPOINTMENT, POWER OF see **power of appointment.**

APPORTION to divide fairly or according to the parties' respective interests; proportionately, but not necessarily equally. See also **reapportion.**

APPRAISAL RIGHTS a statutory remedy available in many states to corporate minority **stockholders** who object to certain extraordinary actions taken by the **corporation** (such as **mergers**). This remedy allows dissenting stockholders to require the corporation to repurchase their stock at a price equivalent to its value immediately prior to the extraordinary corporate action.

This remedy is a statutory exception to the principle of corporate democracy. It allows minority stockholders the opportunity to withdraw from the corporation when the corporation takes an extraordinary action which they feel is harmful to their interests. The nature of the extraordinary corporate action which triggers this right differs in every state, but almost all include corporate consolidations and mergers. The statutory grant of appraisal rights is usually a replacement for the requirement of unanimous shareholder approval of certain corporate transactions.

APPRAISE to estimate the value; to put in writing the worth of property.

APPRECIATE to incrementally increase in value. See 300 N.W. 241, 243. Compare **depreciation.**

To be aware of the value or worth of a thing or person. See 18 N.Y.S. 2d 662, 664. In criminal law, as part of the insanity test, the word is used in some statutes to signify the defendant's subjective understanding of the wrongfulness of his conduct. See Model Penal Code §4.01(1).

APPRECIATION in general, the excess of the fair market value of property over the taxpayer's cost of or tax **basis** in such property. For example, if basis in property is $10,000 but the fair market value is $15,000, the appreciation is $5,000.

UNREALIZED APPRECIATION the amount of appreciation in property which has not yet been subject to a taxable event. See **realization.**

APPROPRIATE "to set apart for, or assign to, a particular purpose or use, in exclusion of all others." 137 P. 2d 233, 237. To wrongfully and unlawfully appropriate the property of another to one's own use constitutes theft **[larceny].** 158 S.W. 2d 796. See **misapplication of property;** compare **conversion.**

APPROPRIATION the withdrawal and designation of public funds in the Treasury by a bill or legislative grant for a specific governmental expenditure.

APPURTENANT attached to something else; in the law of **property,** it refers especially to a burden (e.g., an **easement** or **covenant**) which is attached to land and benefits or burdens the owner of such land in his use and enjoyment thereof, e.g., where A allows B the right of way over his land so that B has access to the highway, such is an EASEMENT APPURTENANT to B's land. 155 S.W. 928, 930. See **easement** [EASEMENT APPURTENANT].

A PRIORI *(ä prē-ô'-rē)*—Lat: from cause to effect, from what goes before; used in logic to denote an argument founded on analogy or abstract considerations; also refers to the process of deducing facts that must necessarily follow from a general principle or admitted truth. 185 F. 2d 679, 685.

ARBITER *(är'-bĭt-èr)*—Lat: referee, umpire; one appointed by the court to decide a controversy according to law or equity, although the decisionmaker is not a judicial officer. Unlike an arbitrator, the arbiter needs the court's confirmation of his decision for it to be final.

ARBITRAGE simultaneous purchase and sale of identical or equivalent securities, commodities, contracts, insurance, or foreign exchange in order to profit from a price discrepancy. 12 C.F.R. §220.4(d).

Any member of a national securities exchange is permitted to effect and finance bona fide arbitrage transactions in securities for any customer. 69 Am. Jur. 2d 847.

There is an exception for arbitrage transactions under the **Securities Exchange Act** provisions for recovery of profit made by directors, officers, and shareholders on short-swing speculation in corporate securities, if certain conditions are met. 208 F. 2d 600, 603-4.

KIND ARBITRAGE purchase of a security that is without restriction, other than the purchase of money, exchangeable or convertible within a reasonable time into a second security together with a simultaneous offsetting sale of the second security. 6 C.J.S. 143.

SPACE ARBITRAGE purchase in one market against sale in another market. 6 C.J.S. 143; 208 F. 2d 600, 603.

TIME ARBITRAGE most common form—the purchase of a commodity against a **present** sale of the identical commodity for future **delivery.** 6 C.J.S. 143; 352 F. 2d 156, 169.

ARBITRATION ". . . submission of controversies, by agreement of the parties thereto, to persons chosen by themselves for determination . . ." 6 C.J.S. 159. At common law, arbitration was not a favored form of settlement, and agreements to arbitratiate were generally declared invalid. Birdseye, Arbitration and Business Ethics viii (1920). Currently, arbitration is more favored and agreements to arbitrate are protected by **statute,** e.g., 9 U.S.C.A. §2 (1970). In **contracts,** arbitration is one way of allowing price terms to remain open.

In labor law, arbitration has become a major means of settling disputes. The majority of labor contracts provide for arbitration of disputes over the meaning of contract clauses, and some provide permanent arbitrators for this purpose.

Federal law has special provisions relating to arbitration in labor situations. Under the Taft-Hartley Act, **collective bargaining** is specifically authorized. 29 U.S.C.A. §171. If no agreement is thereby reached, and the dispute threatens a substantial disruption of commerce, then **mediation** is permitted. 29 U.S.C.A. §172.

COMPULSORY ARBITRATION whereby the parties are forced to agree, has been disfavored, and is generally not provided for in federal law. The states, however, have increasingly provided for compulsory arbitration in areas beyond the preemptory effect of federal law, especially in the case of policemen's and firemen's contracts.

ARBITRATION CLAUSE a clause in a **contract** providing for **arbitration** of disputes arising under the contract. Arbitration clauses are treated as separable parts of the contract so that the illegality of another part of the contract does not nullify such agreement and a **breach** or repudiation of the contract does not preclude the right to arbitrate. 6 C.J.S. 172; 271 F. 2d 402.

ARBITRATOR an impartial person chosen by the parties to solve a dispute between them, who is vested with the power to make a final determination concerning the issues in controversy. 58 U.S. 344. The decision of the arbitrator (the counterpart of a court's **order** or **judgment**) is called the AWARD. A court order enforcing an arbitrator's award is called CONFIRMATION.

In the past, agreements to submit disputes to arbitration were held void as infringing on court jurisdiction. Early in this century, courts and legislatures began to recognize and enforce such agreements. Arbitration is common in commercial disputes, labor management relations, and, recently, in uninsured motorist and **no-fault** insurance plans.

Arbitrators are bound only by

their own discretion, exercised within the scope of the authority entrusted to them by the parties, rather than rules of law, equity, procedure, or evidence.

Many states have adopted rules or statutes, based on the Uniform Arbitration Act, which govern the enforcement of arbitration awards.

ARGUENDO *(àr-gyū-ĕn'-dō)* — Lat: to put in clear light; for the sake of argument, hypothetically, e.g., "let us assume arguendo that X is true." A person arguing in this fashion is not being inconsistent if he later argues that X is not true.

ARGUMENT "a connected discourse based upon reason; a course of reasoning tending and intended to establish a position and to induce belief," 119 N.W. 289, 290; often refers especially to an ORAL ARGUMENT (see **oral**) in appellate advocacy. See also **reargument.**

ARM'S LENGTH refers to the bargaining position of two parties that are unrelated to one another and whose mutual dealings are influenced only by the independent interest of each. The term is used to describe a standard of dealing that reflects no motivation other than those normally to be expected on the part of two unconnected parties transacting in **good faith** in the ordinary course of business. For example, a good faith transaction for the **sale** of goods in the ordinary course of trade. An **agreement** made with care to avoid being overreaching, which compares favorably with the usual conduct of business within the trade generally. 363 S.W. 2d 98, 100. One-sided **contracts** involving some of the elements of **unconscionability** may not be at arm's length. Relevant elements include inequality of bargaining power, whether the contract is standardized and heavily weighed in favor of one **party** on a take-it or leave-it basis, or whether one party has taken advantage of the weaker party's ignorance, or

general business naivete. See generally, U.C.C. §2-302, §1-203. A **sale** between a parent **corporation** and its wholly owned subsidiary would not be considered a transaction at arm's length. 300 U.S. 682. See **sale.**

ARRAIGN to accuse of a wrong, see 116 N.W. 2d 68, 71; to call a person already in custody to answer the charge under which an **indictment** has been handed down. See 138 N.W. 2d 173.

ARRAIGNMENT an initial step in the criminal process wherein the defendant is formally charged with an offense, i.e., given a copy of the **complaint** or other accusatory instrument, and informed of his constitutional rights (e.g., to plead not guilty, be indicted, have a jury trial, appointed counsel if indigent, etc.). Where the appearance is shortly after the arrest it may properly be called a **presentment** since no plea is taken, at least not if it is a **felony** charge. If it is called an arraignment, it is termed an ARRAIGNMENT ON THE WARRANT [or on the complaint].

"After the **indictment** or **information** is filed, the defendant is arraigned—i.e., he is brought before the trial court, and informed of the charges against him and the pleas he might enter (usually guilty, not guilty, or **nolo contendere**)." Kamisar, LaFave, and Israel, Modern Criminal Procedure 22 (5th ed. 1980).

ARRANGEMENTS see **bankruptcy** [CHAPTER II REORGANIZATION].

ARRAY see **challenge** [CHALLENGE TO JURY ARRAY].

ARREARS that which is unpaid although due to be paid; a person "in arrears" is behind in payment.

ARREST "to deprive a person of his liberty by legal authority," 249 N.E. 2d 553, 557; in the technical criminal law sense, seizure of an alleged or suspected offender to answer for crime. See 214 N.E. 2d 114, 119. Arrest or any custodial interrogation, though not technically called "arrest" must be based on probable cause. 99 S. Ct. 2248. To be **actionable** in the event that such seizure is improper or unlawful, there must be an intent on the part of the arresting officer or agent to bring the suspect into custody. See 266 F. Supp. 718, 724. The seizure or detention must be understood by the arrested person to be an arrest. 94 Ohio App. 313. The elements are: (1) purpose or intention to effect the arrest under real or pretended authority; (2) actual or constructive seizure or detention of the person to be arrested by the person having present power to control him; (3) communication by the arresting officer of intention or purpose then and there to make the arrest; and (4) understanding by the person to be arrested that such is the intention of the arrestor. See 250 F. Supp. 278, 280. See **malicious arrest; resisting arrest.** See also **privilege from arrest.**

ARREST OF JUDGMENT the withholding of **judgment** because of some error apparent from the face of the **record;** "the method by which a court refuses to give judgment in a case, though it be regularly decided, where it appears on the face of the record, not including the **evidence,** either that intrinsically no **cause of action** exists, or that if judgment were rendered for the prevailing party it would be erroneous." 73 N.E. 2d 75, 79. See **motion** [MOTION IN ARREST OF JUDGMENT]. Compare **abstention.**

ARSON at common law, "the willful and malicious burning of the dwelling house of another." 152 A. 2d 50, 70; in some states, the burning of a house by its owner under specific circumstances, or the burning of a house by a part-owner. See 221 S.W. 2d 285, 286. Several jurisdictions divide arson into degrees.

STATUTORY ARSON refers to analogous offenses involving destruction of property other than dwellings by methods other than burning, e.g., exploding. See Perkins and Boyce, Criminal Law 287 (3rd ed. 1982). See also Model Penal Code §220.1.

ART, WORDS OF see **words of art.**

ARTICLES OF IMPEACHMENT analogous to an **indictment** in an ordinary criminal proceeding, it is the formal statement of the grounds upon which the removal of a public official is sought. A federal judge holding life tenure may be removed from office only through the **impeachment** process but he may be prosecuted for a crime while still holding office. See 493 F. 2d 1124, 1142. Under the Constitution, Articles of Impeachment are brought by the House of Representatives and a trial is conducted by the Senate. See **impeach, impeachment.**

ARTICLES OF INCORPORATION the **instrument** which creates a **corporation,** pursuant to the general corporation laws of the state.

ARTIFICE a fraud or a cunning device used to accomplish some evil; usually implies craftiness or deceitfulness.

ARTIFICIAL PERSON see **corporation.**

ASE see **American Stock Exchange.**

AS IS in the condition in which presently found; commercial term denoting agreement that buyer shall accept delivery of goods in the condition in which they are found on inspection prior to purchase, even if they are damaged or defective. Sale of goods "as is" when based on inspection of a sample requires that the goods delivered be of the same type and quality as the sample. U.C.C. §2-316. Homes and used cars are often sold "as is."

ASPORTATION the carrying away of **personal property** of another; an element of crimes involving the wrongful taking of personal property. The movement may be slight and involve any appreciable change in position of the property so long as there is a felonious **intent.** 443 F. 2d 339, 340. See **caption, larceny, robbery, trespass** [TRESPASS DE BONIS ASPORTATIS].

ASSAULT an attempt or threat, with unlawful force, to inflict bodily injury upon another, accompanied by the apparent present ability to give effect to the attempt if not prevented. 125 P. 2d 681, 690. Threat, coupled with present ability, may be an assault. 447 F. 2d 264, 273; 276 So. 2d 45, 46. As a tort, an assault may be found even where no actual intent to make one exists (as where a "joke" is intended) if the actor places the victim in reasonable fear. Because an assault need not result in a touching so as to constitute a **battery,** no physical injury need be proved to establish an assault. An assault is both a personal **tort** and a criminal offense and thus may be a basis for a civil **action** and/or a criminal **prosecution.** Some jurisdictions have by **statute** defined the criminal assault to include what at common law was the battery—the actual physical injury. In those jurisdictions an offense of "menacing" often replaces the common law assault. See e.g., N.Y. Penal Law Art. 120, Model Penal Code §211.1.

AGGRAVATED ASSAULT an assault where "serious bodily injury" is inflicted on the person assaulted, 282 P. 2d 772; a particularly fierce or reprehensible assault; an assault exhibiting peculiar depravity or atrocity—including assaults committed with dangerous or **deadly weapons;** an assault committed intentionally concomitant with further crime. See **mayhem.**

ASSEMBLY, UNLAWFUL see **unlawful assembly.**

ASSESS to determine the value of something; to fix the value of property upon which a tax rate will be imposed.

ASSESSMENT OF DEFICIENCY in general, the amount of tax which is determined to be due after a full appellate review within the **Internal Revenue Service** and a **Tax Court** adjudication (if requested) is assessed by recording the **taxpayer's** name, address, and tax liability by an assessment officer. I.R.C. §§6211–6215.

JEOPARDY ASSESSMENT an immediate assessment of the deficiency by the Internal Revenue Service without appellate review and Tax Court hearing is permitted if, in the opinion of the Internal Revenue Service, the assessment and collection of a deficiency would be jeopardized by delay. For instance, if the Internal Revenue Service has grounds to believe that a taxpayer plans to flee the country with his assets, it may make a jeopardy assessment. I.R.C. §6861. Jeopardy assessments are subject to expedited judicial review under I.R.C. §7429.

ASSETS anything owned that has monetary value; any interest in **real property** or **personal property** that can be used for payment of **debts.** 431 F. Supp. 1173, 1178. See **capital asset; hidden asset; intangible asset; marshaling** [**marshalling**] [MARSHALING ASSETS]. See also **wasting asset.**

CURRENT ASSETS for accounting purposes, property that can be easily converted into cash, such as marketable **securities, accounts receivable** (goods or services sold but not paid for), and inventories (raw materials, work in process, and finished goods intended for future sales).

FIXED ASSETS in accounting, property used for production of goods and services, such as plant and machinery, buildings, land, mineral resources. 200 So. 2d 149, 153. See **balance sheet.**

ASSET VALUE see **net asset value.**

ASSIGN to transfer one's interest in **property, contract,** or other rights to another. 19 S.E. 601. See **assignment.** Compare **delegate.**

ASSIGNED RISK in automobile **insurance,** a class of persons for whom such insurance coverage is not readily available. Generally, either these people have difficulty obtaining coverage because their behavior, e.g., prior accidents, has made them a high risk to insure, or for other reasons, such as a state-wide industry practice of not issuing new policies. Many states have **statutes** that prohibit such persons from driving unless adequate insurance has been obtained, and that compel the insurance companies doing business in the state to insure these persons. Appleman, Insurance Law & Practice §§4295, 4296 (1979), Supp. (1972). The insurance companies must then establish "assigned risk" programs so that these people can obtain insurance.

The statutes' purpose is to prevent from driving those persons who cannot bear the cost of causing an accident, and to provide adequate insurance for the state's citizens, and thus to relieve the hardships of accident victims. These laws are commonly known as FINANCIAL RESPONSIBILITY LAWS. Blashfield, Automobile Law and Practice §§272 et seq. (1966 and Supp. 1983).

ASSIGNMENT the transfer of an interest in a right or property from one party to another. Compare **subrogation.**

ASSIGNMENT FOR BENEFIT OF CREDITORS a transfer by a **debtor** of his property to an assignee in **trust** to apply that which is transferred to the debts of the assignor (debtor).

ASSIGNMENT OF A LEASE transfer of the **lessee's** entire interest in the **lease.** When there exists an express covenant in the original lease to pay rent, the assignor (original **tenant**) remains secondarily liable to the **landlord** after an assignment; i.e., the assignee is primarily liable and if he does not pay then the assignor must. Compare **sublease, subtenant.**

ASSIGNMENT OF ERROR "the **appellant's** declaration or complaint against the trial judge charging **error** in the acts of the lower court, which assignments are the basic grounds for **reversal.**" 177 So. 2d 833, 835.

ASSIGNMENT OF INCOME an attempt by a **taxpayer** to have **income** earned by him taxed to another person by directing that such income be paid to such other person, or by entering into a transaction that will result in such income being paid to such other person. For tax purposes, an assignment of income is effective if the income is taxed to such other person and ineffective if such income is taxed to the assignor. An example of an effective assignment of income would be a transfer of a share of dividend-paying stock before the dividend declaration date—in such a case the dividend would be taxed to the transferee; an example of an ineffective assignment of income would be the transfer of a share of stock after the dividend declaration date—in such a case the dividend would be taxed to the transferor. Taxpayers often attempt to assign income to another person such as a family member in order to take advantage of that person's lower tax bracket. 281 U.S. 111; 281 U.S. 376; 309 U.S. 331; 312 U.S. 579.

ASSIGNS all those who take from or under the assignor, whether by **conveyance, devise, descent** or **operation of law.** 26 N.W. 907. See **heirs** [HEIRS AND ASSIGNS].

ASSIZE ancient writ issued from a **court of assize** to the sheriff for the recovery of property, Littleton §234; actions of the special court which issues the writ. See **Court of Assize and Nisi Prius.** "A real action which proves the title of the demandant merely by showing his or his ancestor's possession," 3 Bl. Comm. *185; jury summoned to decide upon the writ of assize, 3 Bl. Comm. *185; the verdict of that jury, 3 Bl. Comm. *57, *59.

ASSOCIATE JUSTICE see **chief justice.**

ASSOCIATION a collection of persons who have joined together for a certain object. 78 So. 693, 695. See **cooperative association; freedom** [FREEDOM OF ASSOCIATION].

While a constitutional "right of association" is not expressly included in the First Amendment, its existence has been found necessary in making the Constitution's express guarantees meaningful; the "right of association" is more than the right to attend a meeting; it includes the right to express one's attitudes or philosophies by membership in a group or by affiliation with it or by other lawful means. 381 U.S. 479, 483.

ASSUMPSIT (*à-sŭmp'-sĭt*) —Lat: he promised; he undertook. Under mature English law, actions in assumpsit for expectation damages, based on **defendant's** breach of an express **contract** whose details were alleged in the **complaint,** came to be known as SPECIAL ASSUMPSIT. Actions in assumpsit to recover a **debt** came to be known as GENERAL ASSUMPSIT. In certain cases, general assumpsit was proper even though the contract was express— for example, where the **plaintiff** had not fully performed but the nonperformance was excusable, or where the plaintiff had fully performed and nothing remained but the payment of the price in money by the defendant. General assumpsit was also the appropriate action for a promise implied in either fact or in law, and was accordingly the action of choice where plaintiff was suing for **restitution**—even restitution for benefits conferred under an express contract. See Fuller & Eisenberg, Basic Contract Law 297 (4th ed. 1981). See **indebitatus assumpsit; non assumpsit.**

ASSUMPTION OF MORTGAGE see **mortgage.**

ASSUMPTION OF THE in torts, an **affirmative defense** used by the **defendant** to a **negligence** suit claiming that **plaintiff** had knowledge of a condition or situation obviously dangerous to himself and yet voluntarily exposed himself to the hazard created by defendant, thereby relieving him of legal responsibility for any resulting injury; see 70 N.E. 2d 898, 903; in **contract,** it is the express agreement by an employee to assume the risks of ordinary hazards arising out of his occupation, see 225 P. 501, 505; **contributory negligence** arises when a plaintiff fails to exercise due care, while assumption of risk arises regardless of the care used and is based fundamentally on consent. 79 Cal. Rptr. 426, 430.

Some jurisdictions have abolished the distinct defense of assumption of risk and treat it instead either as an aspect of whether the situation is one in which defendant owes plaintiff a duty of care, or as a question of plaintiff's contributory negligence in undertaking the risk. See 196 A. 2d 238; Prosser, Torts 454-57 (4th ed. 1971). Comparative negligence acts and no-fault car insurance acts also eliminate much of the need for this defense.

ASSURANCE see **covenant** [COVENANT OF FURTHER ASSURANCE].

ASSURED see **insured.**

ASYLUM a shelter for the unfortunate or afflicted, e.g., for the insane, the crippled, the poor; a POLITICAL ASYLUM is a state which accepts a citizen of another state as a shelter from prosecution by that other state.

AT BAR see **bar.**

AT EQUITY see **equity.**

AT ISSUE see **issue.**

AT LAW see **law** [AT LAW].

AT RISK see **tax shelter** [AT RISK].

ATROCIOUS outrageously wicked and vile. See 399 So. 2d 973, 977. An atrocious act is one that demonstrates depraved and insensitive brutality on the part of the perpetrator; conduct that exhibits a senselessly immoderate application of extreme violence for a criminal purpose.

ATTACHMENT a **proceeding** in law by which one's **property** is seized; "a proceeding to take a **defendant's** property into legal custody to satisfy **plaintiff's** demand. The object of the proceeding is to hold property so taken for the payment of a **judgment** in the event plaintiff's demand is established and judgment rendered therefore in his favor." 55 N.W. 2d 589, 592. Attachment of a defendant's property may also be used by the court as security for the satisfaction of such judgment as the plaintiff may recover. Restatement Judgments §34. Recent Supreme Court cases have held that attachment and other pre-judgment remedies are unconstitutional absent **due process** protections, such as a hearing in most situations. 407 U.S. 67; 419 U.S. 601. In **commercial law,** attachment means the creation of a **security interest.** It generally occurs when the debtor has agreed to the creation, received value from the secured party and obtained rights in the property security, (i.e. the **collateral**). U.C.C. §9-203. Attachment is also used when **in personam jurisdiction** is unavailable. In such cases the court acquires jurisdiction over the property seized and the proceeding essentially becomes one **in rem.** See **in rem.** Compare **garnishment; replevin.**

ATTAINDER at common law a mark of infamy caused by one's conviction for a **felony** or capital crime, which results in the elimination of all **civil rights** or liberties. See 55 N.W. 774, 781. The concept is no longer a part of American or British law. See **civil death.** Compare **bill of attainder.**

ATTAINDER, BILL OF see **bill of attainder.**

ATTAINT to pass sentence of attainder or to be under such a sentence. More generally to be stained or degraded by a conviction. In early common law practice referred to a writ used to challenge a jury verdict. 3 Bl. Comm. 402.

ATTEMPT an overt act, beyond mere preparation, moving directly toward the actual commission of a substantive offense. See 263 A. 2d 266, 271. It is an offense, separate and distinct from the object crime. See 438 S.W. 441, 446. "The overt act, sufficient to establish an 'attempt,' must extend far enough toward accomplishment of the object crime to amount to the commencement of the consummation." 500 P. 2d 1276, 1282. Various legal tests used to determine if enough has been done to cross the line between innocent preparation (mere planning of the crime) and a criminal attempt include "dangerous proximity," "indispensable element," "last act," "probable desistance," "substantial step." Acts of **solicitation** alone generally do not establish the elements of an attempt. See Model Penal Code §15.01; 252 A. 2d 321, 324.

ATTENDANT CIRCUMSTANCES loose facts surrounding an event. In criminal law the definitions of crimes often require the presence or absence of attendant circumstances. For example **statutory rape** requires that the girl be under the **age of consent,** the age of the girl being the attendant circumstance. Model Penal Code §2133.

ATTEST to affirm as true; to sign one's name as a **witness** to the **execution** of a document; to bear witness to.

ATTESTATION the act of authentication by witnessing an instrument of writing, at the request of the party making the instrument, and subscribing it as a witness. 68 P. 2d 119. Attestation entails witnessing and certification that the instrument exists. 396 A. 2d 1020, 1022.

ATTORNEY may refer to an attorney in fact or attorney at law. An ATTORNEY IN FACT is one who is an agent or representative of another given authority to act in that person's place and name. The document giving the attorney his authority is called a **power of attorney.** 155 Cal. Rptr. 843, 849.

The general reference to an attorney is usually intended to designate an ATTORNEY AT LAW. This is one of a class of persons admitted by the state's highest court or by a federal court to practice law in that jurisdiction. The attorney is regarded as an officer of the court and is always subject to the admitting court's jurisdiction as to his ethical and professional conduct. Violations of those standards of conduct may result in discipline of the attorney in the form of censure, suspension, or **disbarment.** See 296 S.E. 2d 909, 918. See also **counsel** [COUNSELLOR]; **district attorney.**

ATTORNEY-CLIENT PRIVILEGE privilege that confidential communications between an attorney and a client in the course of the professional relationship cannot be disclosed without the consent of the client. "The attorney-client privilege is the oldest of the privileges for confidential communications known to the common law. . . .Its purpose is to encourage full and frank communication be-

tween attorneys and their clients and thereby promote broader public interests in the observance of law and administration of justice. The privilege recognizes that sound legal advice or advocacy serves public ends and that such advice or advocacy depends upon the lawyer's being fully informed by the client." 449 U.S. 383, 389.

Such communications may take the form of oral or written statements or may be actions and gestures. 231 P. 2d 26. Communications made to an attorney while seeking to obtain representation, even though the attorney did not ultimately represent the client, are nonetheless privileged. 150 P. 2d 10. The privilege protects discussions of past crimes, 541 F. 2d 618, but does not extend to the client's proposed commission of future crimes. 289 U.S. 1. If third parties (generally including relatives and friends but excluding law clerks, stenographers, or interpreters) are present, the privilege may be destroyed. 564 S.W. 2d 579. The privilege extends indefinitely, and does not terminate when the attorney/client relationship ends or when either party dies. 338 P. 2d 397; 10 Pa. 519. Communications between a corporate general counsel and corporate employees have been found to be protected. 449 U.S. 383. Finally, the privilege to prohibit disclosure belongs to the client, and as such may be waived by the client. 128 U.S. 464.

ACCOUNTANT-CLIENT PRIVILEGE a statutory privilege available in about one-third of the states rendering confidential all communications to an accountant. McCormick, Evidence 159 (2d ed. 1972). Such communications are not otherwise privileged. 425 U.S. 391, 474 F. 2d 297. If the accountant is also an attorney, the **attorney-client privilege** (above) does not apply if the accountant-attorney was acting in the capacity of an accountant.

210 F. 2d 795. If, however, a client communicates to an accountant designated by the client's attorney "in confidence for the purpose of obtaining legal advice from the lawyer" it is then privileged. 296 F. 2d 918.

ATTORNEY GENERAL the chief law officer of the federal government or of each state government.

ATTORNEY, POWER OF see **power of attorney.**

ATTORNEY'S FEES in general, the charge made by the attorney for his services in representing a client; also the charge made by other professionals for services they have rendered in the course of preparing and trying a case. A CONTINGENT FEE is a charge made by an attorney dependent upon a successful outcome in the case and is often agreed to be a percentage of the party's **recovery.** Such fee arrangements are often used in **negligence** cases and other **civil** actions but it is unethical for an attorney to charge a criminal defendant a fee substantially contingent upon the result. ABA DR 2-106(C).

ATTRACTIVE NUISANCE the doctrine in tort law which holds that one who maintains a dangerous instrumentality on his **premises** which is likely to attract children is under a duty to reasonably protect those children against the dangers of that attraction. See 299 S.W. 2d 198, 199, 200. Under this doctrine the fact that the child may be a **trespasser** is merely one fact to be taken into account, with others, in determining the defendant's **duty,** and the care required of him. The basis of this liability is generally held to be nothing more than the **foreseeability** of harm to the child, and the considerations of common humanity and social policy which, in other **negligence** cases, operate to bring about a balancing of the conflicting interests, and to curtail to some reasonable extent the defendant's

privilege to act as he sees fit without taking care for the protection of others. Therefore, one has a duty to fence swimming pools, to remove doors from discarded refrigerators, to enclose partially constructed buildings, and to be sensitive to other potentially dangerous conditions which attract curious children. See Prosser, Torts §59 (4th ed. 1971).

AUCTION see **sale.**

AUDIT an inspection of the accounting records and procedures of a business, government unit, or other reporting entity by a trained accountant, for the purpose of verifying the accuracy and completeness of the records. It may be conducted by a member of the organization (internal audit) or by an outsider (independent audit).

AUDIT OF RETURN a review by an agent of the **Internal Revenue Service** of the **tax return** filed by the **taxpayer** and the books and records supporting the information contained on the tax return.

AUTHORITY the permission or power delegated to another. This may be express or implied. See **de facto** [DE FACTO AUTHORITY]. If express it is usually embraced in a document called a **power of attorney.** 328 F. 2d 662, 664. IMPLIED AUTHORITY stems from a relationship such as that of **principal** and **agent.** If the agent does not have EXPRESS AUTHORITY by some writing, he nonetheless will have **apparent authority.** Restatement (second) Agency §8. If the authority is given to the agent for a **consideration** it is said to be an AUTHORITY COUPLED WITH AN INTEREST. Where not to infer an authority would result in an injustice, the law will imply an authority so as not to mislead another. In this circumstance the law speaks of an AUTHORITY BY ESTOPPEL. 405 N.E. 2d 462, 465. Where the principal intended his agent to have the right to act on his behalf, the authority is called an ACTUAL AUTHORITY. 391 A. 2d 196, 197.

The term may also refer to the jurisdiction of a court such as within the court's authority. It is also used to denote judicial or legislative precedent.

AUTHORIZED ISSUE the total number of shares of capital stock which a corporation may issue under its charter. Henn, Corporations 282 (1970). If the corporation wishes to issue more shares than the authorized issue, it must amend its charter through a resolution approved by shareholders. The OUTSTANDING ISSUE is the total shares actually issued to shareholders less **treasury stock** and must be less than the authorized issue.

AUTOMOBILE, DEATH BY see **homicide; manslaughter** [DEATH BY AUTOMOBILE].

AUTOMOBILE GUEST STATUTE see **guest statue.**

AUTOPSY the dissection of a body to determine the cause of death. It may involve inspection and exposure of important organs of a dead body in order to determine the nature of a disease or abnormality. The medical examiner of a county will often conduct an autopsy to determine the cause of death. A coroner's **inquest** will be called if a criminal act is suspected.

AVERMENT a positive statement or **allegation** of facts in a pleading as opposed to an **argumentative** one or one based on inference. See **negative averment; notice** [AVERMENT OF NOTICE].

AVOID to **annul**, cancel, make **void,** or to destroy the efficacy of anything. 211 A. 2d 38, 41.

AVOIDANCE see **confession and avoidance.**

AVOIDANCE OF TAX the method by which a taxpayer reduces his tax liability without committing **fraud** —e.g., by investing in a **tax shelter**. Compare **evasion of tax.**

AVULSION an abrupt change in the course or channel of a stream which forms the boundary between two parcels of land, resulting in the loss of part of the land of one **riparian** landowner and a consequent increase in the land of the other. 341 S.W. 2d 18, 21. The sudden and perceptible nature of this change distinguishes avulsion from **accretion.** This distinction is important, for when the change is abrupt, the boundary between the two properties remains unaltered. 143 U.S. 359.

AWOL see **desertion** [ABSENT WITHOUT LEAVE].

B

BAD CHECK a check which is dishonored on presentation because of **non-sufficient funds** [NSF] or a closed bank account. Issuing a bad check is a form of **larceny** [theft] and is generally punished as a **misdemeanor** although in some jurisdictions it is a more serious offense if the amount of the check is substantial. An affirmative defense is usually provided if the maker of the check, upon notice of dishonor, promptly satisfies the **payee.** See Model Penal Code §224.5. See also **check kiting.**

BAD DEBT a debt that becomes uncollectable because the debtor is insolvent. A non-business bad debt is **deductible** from **gross income** as a **short-term capital loss** whereas a BUSINESS BAD DEBT is allowable as a **deduction** against **ordinary income.** I.R.C. §166.

BAD DEBT RESERVE rather than take deductions for specific debts that become worthless during the **taxable year,** a businessman may deduct in each year a reasonable percentage of his receivables which percentage then becomes an addition to the reserve for bad debts. For example, if a taxpayer determines that on the average 3 percent of his **accounts** receivable becomes worthless during the taxable year, the taxpayer may deduct 3 percent and add it to his reserve for bad debts. I.R.C. §166(c).

NON-BUSINESS BAD DEBT is a debt that is neither (1) created or acquired in connection with the **taxpayer's** trade or business; nor (2) incurred in a transaction entered into for profit.

BAD FAITH "**breach** of faith, willful failure to respond to plain, well-understood statutory or contractual obligations." 124 F. 2d 875, 883. "GOOD FAITH means being faithful to one's duty or obligation; bad faith means being recreant thereto." 235 N.W. 413, 414. It is thus the absence of **good faith.**

BADGES OF FRAUD facts or circumstances surrounding a transaction which indicate that it may be fraudulent, especially that it may be in **fraud** of **creditors.** These "badges" include fictitious consideration, false statements as to consideration, transactions different from the usual method of doing business, transfer of all of a debtor's property, insolvency, confidential relationship of the parties, and transfers in anticipation of suit or execution. 92 S.W. 2d 733, 736.

BAD TITLE one which is legally insufficient to **convey** property to the purchaser, 36 N.Y.S. 668; a title which is not a **marketable title** is not necessarily a bad title, 4 App. D.C. 283, but a title which is bad is not marketable and is one that a purchaser may not be compelled to accept.

BAIL a monetary or other form of security given to insure the **appearance** of the **defendant** at every stage of the **proceedings.** See 120 P. 2d 980. Those posting bail are in the position of **surety** and the money is the **security** for the accused's appearance. It is thus used as a means "to procure release of a **prisoner** by securing his future attendance." 42 F. 2d 26, 28; object is to relieve the **accused** of imprisonment, and the state of the burden of keeping him pending **trial** or **hearing,** and at the same time to secure the appearance of the accused at the trial or hearing. 190 F. 2d 16, 19. Compare **release on recognizance.** See **excessive bail; jump bail.**

BAIL BOND the document executed in order to secure the release of an individual in **custody** of the law. The surety forfeits his security in the event the defendant fails to appear as required for court dates, subject to the right of the surety to petition to set aside all or part of the forfeiture. The **surety's** obligation is satisfied by the **appearance** of the accused in court on the day or days required.

BAILEE "one to whom the property involved in the **bailment** is delivered," 55 A. 346, 348; "species of agent to whom something movable is committed in **trust** . . . for another." 75 So. 711, 713; generally, party who holds the goods of another for a specific purpose pursuant to an agreement between the parties. See U.C.C. §7-102(a). However, an involuntary bailee is one whom possession is "thrust upon" without his consent. See **bailment.**

BAILIFF a court attendant; "a person to whom some authority, care, **guardianship** or **jurisdiction** is delivered, committed or entrusted," 92 S.E. 2d 89, 95; "a servant who has the administration and charge of lands, goods and chattels to get the best benefit for the owner . . . and also a person appointed by private persons to collect their rents and manage their estate," 202 Ill. App. 387, 391; "signifies a keeper or protector," 20 So. 818, 819, especially one appointed as such by the court, as in the case of a court-appointed guardian of a feeble-minded person, 189 A. 753, 755.

BAILMENT "delivery of **personal property in trust**," 277 S.W. 2d 695, 698; "delivery of a thing in trust for some special object or purpose and upon a **contract,** express or implied, to conform with the object or purpose of the trust," 75 S.W. 2d 761, 764; also, that relationship which arises where one delivers property to another to keep for hire, and control and **possession** of the property passes to the keeper or **bailee.** 108 A. 2d 168, 170. "An express agreement between the parties is not always necessary. The element of lawful **possession,** however created, and the duty to account for the article as the property of another is sufficient," 351 P. 2d 840, 842; e.g., the finder of **mislaid property** becomes a bailee thereof.

ACTUAL BAILMENT one established by an actual or constructive delivery of the property to the bailee or his **agents.**

BAILMENT FOR HIRE one that arises from contract in which the bailor agrees to compensate the bailee as, for example, in the case of delivering one's car to a garage attendant. 326 N.Y.S. 2d 776, 785. If the bailment is intended to result in some additional benefit for the bailor, such as a repair of his vehicle during the bailment, it may be referred to as a BAILMENT FOR MUTUAL BENEFIT.

BAILMENT FOR MUTUAL BENEFIT one in which the parties contemplate some compensation for benefits flowing from the bailment resulting from an express or implied undertaking to that ef-

fect. 88 Cal. Rptr. 39, 43. Compare BAILMENT FOR HIRE.

CONSTRUCTIVE BAILMENT one which arises when the person having possession holds it under such circumstances that the law imposes an obligation to deliver to another, even where such person did not come into possession voluntarily, and where therefore no bailment was voluntarily established. See 140 N.Y.S. 955, 956.

GRATUITOUS BAILMENT "results when care and custody of **bailor's** property is accepted by **bailee** without charge and without any expectation of benefit or **consideration.** In a gratuitous bailment, the bailee is liable to bailor for the loss of bailed property only if the loss is proximately caused by bailee's **gross negligence.**" 197 P. 2d 1008, 1014. It "consists of gratuitous loaning of **personal property** to be used by bailee and returned **in specie.**" 120 A. 2d 552.

INVOLUNTARY BAILMENT "arises by the accidental leaving of **personal property** in the **possession** of any person without **negligence** on the part of its owner." 152 P. 816, 817. Such a bailment arises whenever the goods of one person have by an unavoidable casualty or accident been lodged upon another's land or person. If the person upon whose land the personal property is located should refuse to deliver the goods to their owner upon demand or to permit him to remove them, he might be liable for **conversion** of said property. 67 S.E. 722, 724. Compare **lost property; mislaid property.**

BAILOR "person who delivers **personal property** to another to be held in **bailment**—the one who places the thing in trust." 27 S.E. 487, 488. The bailor need not be the owner of the property involved.

BAIT AND SWITCH a method of consumer deception practiced by retailers which "involves advertising in such an attractive way as to bring the customer in, followed by disparagement of the advertised product so as to cause the customer to switch to a more expensive product." 50 A.L.R. 3d 1008. It "consists of an attractive but insincere offer to sell a product or service which the seller in truth does not intend or desire to sell." 493 P. 2d 660, 665. This device is also frequently termed DISPARAGEMENT. Id. at 666. Statutes in many states prohibit this sort of advertising. See Model Penal Code §224.7(5).

BALANCE SHEET a financial statement that gives an accounting picture of property owned by a company and of claims against the property on a specific date. Generally, a summation of **assets** is listed on one side and **liabilities** is listed on the other side. Both sides are always in balance.

BALLOON NOTE a promissory note repayable in periodic installments of a specified amount, usually representing interest, with a much larger final payment, usually of the entire principal amount, often called the BALLOON PAYMENT.

BANC bench. See **en banc.**

BANK generally, a corporation formed for the purposes of maintaining savings accounts and checking accounts, issuing loans and credit, and dealing in negotiable securities issued by governmental entities and corporations. Michie, Banks and Banking, Ch. 1, §2 (1973). By law, banks are usually permitted to engage in activities and offer numerous services incidental to and beyond those listed above, e.g., buying and selling gold and silver, or disbursing the payroll of depositors. N.J.S. §§17:9A-24 through 26. See **member bank; nonmember bank.** See also **thrift institutions.**

Banks earn money by investing their customers' deposits. In order to protect the customers against loss, banks are strictly regulated, and fall into the following three categories according to their limitations:

COMMERCIAL BANK by far, the most common and most unrestricted type of bank. It is allowed the most latitude in the services it offers and the investments it makes. Its major limitation is that it must keep on reserve a larger percentage of its deposits than the other two types of banks. This reserve is used to cover the bank's daily needs, to guard against a money shortage at the bank and a resulting panic, and to shield the customers against the bank's failure and the consequent loss of deposits. Commercial banks are often public corporations owned through stock. White, Banking Law 33-37 (1976).

SAVINGS BANK prevalent only on the East coast and in the Midwest, this is the least common type of bank. Traditionally, it developed to encourage frugality among the poorer sections of the population, and offered limited services. Its major service was the "time" savings account, or deposit, from which money, once deposited, could be withdrawn only after a set period elapsed or 30 days' notice was given. Its services, however, have been expanded in some instances. By law a savings bank's investments are usually limited to certain corporate and government bonds and securities. Its advantages are that it can pay higher interest rates than commercial banks, has certain tax benefits, and can keep a smaller percentage of its deposits on reserve. Usually, the bank is owned by its depositors as creditors whose dividends are paid in the form of interest on their accounts.

SAVINGS AND LOAN ASSOCIATION similar to savings banks in history and operation, except that the savings and loan associations' primary purpose has been not only to encourage thrift but also to provide loans for purchasing and building homes. Also known as building and loan association. These institutions are authorized to offer a variant of a checking account called a NEGOTIABLE ORDER OF WITHDRAWAL ("NOW") which operates to allow depositors to write checks against their interest-bearing savings account.

BANKRUPTCY popularly defined as **insolvency;** technically, however, it is a legal process under federal law intended to not only insure fairness and equality among creditors but also to help the **debtor** by enabling him to start anew with **property** he is allowed to retain as exempt from his **liabilities,** unhampered by pressure and discouragement of preexisting **debts.** 402 U.S. 637. See generally Collier, Collier Bankruptcy Manual Ch. 1 (2d ed. 1959). Mere financial embarrassment does not constitute bankruptcy; person is not bankrupt within the meaning of federal bankruptcy law until he has been adjudicated bankrupt. A **corporation** is not bankrupt until it, by law, performs an "act of bankruptcy," or when **proceedings** in bankruptcy have been instituted by or against it.

Bankruptcy, as it was first developed by the British, was a quasicriminal proceeding instituted only by a creditor against an insolvent debtor, who was considered an offender. Under American law, the Constitution gave Congress the power to legislate on the subject of bankruptcies (U.S. Constitution Art. 1, Sec. 8 Cl. 4). However, the **remedies** of the first U.S. Bankruptcy Act in 1898 were initially available only to creditors. The concept of bankruptcy was subsequently broadened to allow the debtor to

initiate the proceedings. The term now refers to not only proceedings for the voluntary or involuntary adjudication of a debtor, but also for the relief of the debtor by reorganization and readjustments. 299 U.S. 445. See **discharge in bankruptcy.**

The BANKRUPTCY ACT generally refers to the law in effect prior to October 1, 1979. The BANKRUPTCY CODE refers to the Bankruptcy Act of 1978 which took effect October 1, 1979 and governs all requests for relief filed on or after that date. 11 U.S. C. §101 et seq.

BANKRUPTCY COURT is the forum in which most bankruptcy proceedings are conducted. Some aspects of the organization of these courts, which are nominally appendages of the federal district courts, were declared unconstitutional. 102 S. Ct. 2858. This required Congress to modify the structure of these courts. 28 U.S.C. §151.

BANKRUPTCY TRUSTEE refers to the person who takes legal title to the property of the debtor and holds it "in trust" for equitable distribution among the creditors. 11 U.S.C. §321 et seq. In most districts, the trustee is appointed by the bankruptcy judge or selected by the creditors and approved by the judge. In a limited number of "pilot districts," a UNITED STATES TRUSTEE, appointed by the Attorney General, serves as or supervises the trustee. 11 U.S.C. §1501 et seq. The 1978 Bankruptcy Act envisions an experimental period before determining whether United States Trustees should serve in all districts.

CHAPTER 11 REORGANIZATION (formerly ARRANGEMENTS) in addition to voluntary and involuntary petitions whereby a debtor is adjudged as a bankrupt, petitions for relief under Chapter 11 permit the debtor to undertake a reorganization to pay his debts. While the purpose of the Chapter 7 case is to **liquidate** the debtor, the purpose of a Chapter 11 reorganization case is to restructure finances so that the debtor can continue to operate. The general policy underlying both the Chapter 9 and Chapter 11 reorganizations is to give the debtor a breathing spell from debt collection efforts to allow him to work out a repayment plan with creditors. The goal is a plan that specifics how much creditors will be paid, in what form they will be paid and other details. 11 U.S.C.A. §1123. See **debt; insolvency.**

DEBTOR REHABILITATION refers to those provisions of the Code that enable the rehabilitation and reorganization of the debtor. Creditors are paid out of future earnings of the debtor rather than the liquidation of the debtor's property. This includes business reorganizations, (see CHAPTER II REORGANIZATION) above and the "WAGE EARNER'S PLAN" (below).

INVOLUNTARY PROCEEDINGS an **equitable** proceeding for the purpose of impounding all the debtor's non-exempt property, to distribute it equally among creditors, and to release the debtor from liability. Only a creditor entitled to benefit under the Bankruptcy Act may file a petition to have the debtor adjudged bankrupt. Additional qualified creditors have an absolute right to join in the original petition at any time before **judgment** is entered. Under the Bankruptcy Code of 1978, involuntary proceedings are available only under Chapter 7 and Chapter 11, but cannot be commenced against a farmer or against certain corporations. 11 U.S.C.A. §303.

In STRAIGHT BANKRUPTCY (Chapter 7 of the Code) most assets of the **debtor** are **liquidated** as quickly as possible to pay off his creditors to the extent possible and to free the debtor to start anew. The debtor receives a **discharge** from most debts incurred prior to the time he filed for relief.

VOLUNTARY PROCEEDING a proceeding whereby any debtor entitled to benefits of the Bankruptcy Act may file a **petition** to be adjudged a voluntary bankrupt. A voluntary bankruptcy is the surrender of the debtor's property to his creditors in order to **discharge** him from his debts. 161 S.W. 2d 866. The amendment to the Bankruptcy Act in 1910 permitted corporations as well as persons to take advantage of proceedings for voluntary bankruptcy. 88 F. 2d 212.

WAGE EARNER'S PLAN relief, available to individual filing petition pursuant to Chapter 13 of the Bankruptcy Act, under which the debtor retains possession of his property, but under the supervision of a court-appointed trustee and according to a court-approved schedule pays creditors over a period of time. 11 U.S.C.A. §1322.

BANKRUPTCY PETITION see **petition in bankruptcy.**

BAR in procedure, barrier to the relitigating of an **issue.** "Where **causes of action** are the same, final **judgment on the merits** in the first action is a complete bar to the second action." 179 S.W. 2d 441, 444. Issues which have been decided by a court become bars in further **litigation** as between the **parties** to the decision. A bar operates to deny a party the right or privilege of rechallenging issues in subsequent litigation. The prevailing party in a lawsuit can use his favorable decision to bar retrial of the cause of action. See **plea** [PLEA IN BAR].

A particular position in the courtroom is also termed a "bar;" hence, the defendant standing before the judge is sometimes called the "prisoner AT BAR." The complete body of attorneys is called "the bar" because they are the persons privileged to enter beyond the bar that separates the general courtroom audience from the bench of the judge. The CASE AT BAR refers to the particular action before the court. See **collateral estoppel; double jeopardy; estoppel; merger; res judicata.**

BARGAIN a mutual voluntary **agreement** between two parties for the **exchange** or **purchase** of some specified goods. "An agreement of two or more persons to exchange promises or to exchange a promise for a performance or to exchange performances." Restatement, Contracts (Second), §3. The term also "implies negotiation over the terms of an agreement." 118 P. 77, 78.

BARGAIN AND SALE a **contract,** or **deed** in the form of a contract, which conveys **property** and raises a **use** in the buyer thereof; by operation of the **Statute of Uses,** such contract or deed is also effective to transfer **title** to the buyer. See 137 S.E. 744, 745. Absent the inclusion of a "**convenant** against the grantor's acts" this deed lacks any guarantee from the seller as to the validity of the title. Compare **warranty deed; quitclaim deed.**

BARGAINING UNIT the labor union or other group that represents employees in **collective bargaining.** 148 N.W. 2d. 902, 904.

BARRATRY at common law the crime of stirring up suits and quarrels. An **indictment** was required to charge the offender with being a common barrato and proof required at least three instances of offending. Generally, the **statutory** crime of barratry is narrower, being restricted to the practice of instigating groundless judicial proceedings. Soliciting personal injury cases, or "ambulance chasing," although unethical, is not a violation of the barratry statute but may constitute **champerty.**

BARRISTER in England one of two classes of legal practitioners, whose function is "the advocacy of causes in open court" and related duties. 29 A. 559. His function is somewhat similar to that of the American trial lawyer, but the barrister, unlike the American trial lawyer, does not prepare the case from the start. His **soliciter** assembles the materials necessary for presentation to the court and settles cases out of court.

BARTER the exchange of goods or services without using money. See **exchange.**

BASIS an amount that usually represents the **taxpayer**'s cost in acquiring an asset. I.R.C. §1011 et seq. It is used for a variety of tax purposes, including computation of **gain or loss** on the **sale or exchange** of the asset and **depreciation** with respect to the asset. Tax basis is subject to adjustment due to depreciation and other transactions in which a taxpayer engages.

ADJUSTED BASIS during the time that a taxpayer holds an asset, certain events require that the taxpayer adjust (either up or down) his original basis to reflect the event. I.R.C. §1016. The original basis adjusted by such events constitutes the adjusted basis. For example, depreciation deductions taken or allowable in a taxable year with respect to an asset reduce the taxpayer's basis in the asset. On the other hand, if the taxpayer made a **capital expenditure** with respect to the asset, the amount of the expenditure would increase the taxpayer's basis.

CARRYOVER BASIS a taxpayer's basis which is determined by reference to the basis of the property when held by the person who transferred it to the taxpayer. For example, if a taxpayer does not purchase property but receives it as a **gift,** his basis in the property is the transferor's basis in the property. I.R.C. §1015.

RECOVERY OF BASIS the process by which a taxpayer recoups his basis through **distributions** or payments with respect to the property. For example, the amount realized on sale of property is allocated in part to gain, and in part to basis recovery.

STEP-UP BASIS the process by which a taxpayer's basis is increased to a certain level (usually fair market value) as of a certain date. For instance, inherited property receives a basis equal to its fair market value on the decedent's date of death. I.R.C. §1014.

SUBSTITUTED BASIS in certain cases, a taxpayer's basis is determined by reference to property that he has transferred in order to receive other property. The basis of the transferred property is substituted as the basis of the property received. For instance, in a like-kind exchange, the taxpayer does not recognize gain or loss, but substitutes the basis of the property transferred as the basis of the property received in order to preserve the gain or loss for recognition at a later date. I.R.C. §1031.

BASTARD "an illegitimate child," 281 So. 2d 587, 588; "children who are not born either in lawful wedlock or within a competent time after its termination," 93 P. 2d 825; also, a child of a married woman conceived with one who is not the husband of the mother. See 17 N.W. 2d 546. "A child born out of lawful matrimony or born to a married woman under conditions where the presumption of legitimacy is not conclusive and has been rebutted." 30 N.E. 2d 587, 589.

BASTARDY PROCEEDING see **paternity suit [bastardy proceeding]**.

BATTERY "the unlawful application of force to the person of another," Perkins and Boyce, Criminal Law 152 (3d ed. 1982); the least touching of another's person **willfully,** or in anger, 3 Bl. Comm.

*120; the actual touching involved in an "**assault** and battery." In **tort** law the legal protection from battery extends to any part of one's body or to "anything so closely attached thereto that it is customarily regarded as a part thereof." Restatement (Second), Torts §18. "Thus, contact with the plaintiff's clothing, or with a cane, . . . the car which he is riding [sic] or driving" will be sufficient to create civil tort liability. Prosser, Torts 34 (4th ed. 1971). If the contact is offensive, even though harmless, it entitles the plaintiff to an award of **nominal damages.** In the criminal law, every punishable application of force to the person of another is a criminal battery (a **misdemeanor** at common law). Conviction of battery may be based upon **criminal negligence** but not ordinary civil negligence. See Perkins and Boyce, supra at 156-158.

BEARER PAPER commercial paper which is negotiable upon delivery by any party in possession of it, or which does not purport to designate a specific party by whom it is negotiable. U.C.C. 3-202 (1), 3-111. Such commercial paper is said to be PAYABLE TO BEARER.

BEFORE-THE-FACT see **accessory** [ACCESSORY BEFORE-THE-FACT].

BELIEF see **information and belief.** See also **reasonable belief.**

BENCH the court; the judges composing the court collectively. The place where the trial judge sits (as "approach the bench"). Compare **bar.**

BENCH TRIAL see **trial.**

BENCH WARRANT an order from the court empowering the proper legal authorities to seize a person; most commonly used to compel one's attendance before the court to **answer a charge** of contempt or for failure of a **witness** to attend in response to a **subpoena** which has been duly served. See 321 P. 2d 15, 17.

BENEFICIAL INTEREST the interest of the beneficiary as opposed to the interest of the trustee who holds legal **title;** the **equitable** interest in property held in **trust** which the **beneficiary** may enforce against the **trustee** according to the terms of the trust; any person who under the terms of a trust instrument has the right to income or principle of the trust fund has a beneficial interest in the trust." 27 N.Y.S. 2d 648, 652. It "is such a right to its enjoyment as exists where the legal title is in one person, and the right to such beneficial use or interest is in another, and where such right is recognized by law, and can be enforced by the courts." 200 U.S. 118, 128.

In a trust the beneficial equitable interest must be distinct from the legal interest or a **merger** will occur and the effort by the creator of the trust **[settlor]** to create separate legal and equitable interests in particular property will be ineffective. "Where a single individual has the whole legal interest and the whole beneficial interest, there is no trust. Where the sole trustee has also the whole beneficial interest, he simply holds the property free of trust. He cannot maintain a bill in equity against himself to compel himself to carry out the terms of the trust; and since there is no one else who has any interest in the property, there is no one who can prevent him from dealing with the property as he likes. Where the intended trustee and the intended beneficiary are the same, no trust is created. Where at the outset a trust existed, but a single individual subsequently holds the whole legal interest and the whole beneficial interest, the trust terminates." Scott, Abridgement of the Law of Trusts §99 (1960). A valid trust can be created even though a trustee holds a part of the beneficial interest and even where a group of beneficiaries holds the whole beneficial interest and the identical persons hold the whole legal title, although some courts have found ineffective any attempts to create trusts in such circumstances. See Id. at §§99.1-99.5.

BENEFICIAL USE with respect to property, the right to its full and profitable enjoyment as exists where legal **title** is in one person while right to such use or interest is in another. 131 P. 2d 189, 191. A person who has beneficial use does not hold legal title of property. Legal title is held in **trust** by another. See **beneficial interest; mortgage; trusts; use.**

BENEFICIARY "one receiving [or designated to receive] benefit or advantage, or one who is in receipt of benefits, profits, or advantage." 244 F. 902, 908; "person for whose benefit property is held in **trust,**" Restatement (Second), Trusts, §3(4); "person to whom another is in a **fiduciary** relation, whether the relation is one of **agency,** trust, **guardianship, partnership,** or otherwise." Restatement, Restitution §190; "one for whose benefit a trust is created," 180 S.W. 2d 268, 271; "the person named in an **insurance** policy as the one to receive proceeds or benefits accruing thereunder," 155 P. 2d 772, 774. The person named in a will to receive certain property is a beneficiary under the **will.** See **contingent beneficiary: favored beneficiary.** See also **third party beneficiary.**

INCIDENTAL BENEFICIARY a person who may incidentally benefit from the creation of a trust. Such a person has no actual interest in the trust and cannot enforce any right to incidental benefit. "The beneficiaries of a trust include only those persons upon whom the **settlor** intended to confer a **beneficial interest** under the trust, or persons who have succeeded to their interests." Scott, Abridgement of the Law of Trusts §126 (1960).

BENEFIT advantage, useful aid, financial help. 262 F. Supp. 535,

536. The receiving as the exchange for a promise of some performance or forbearance which the promisor was not previously entitled to receive. 255 N.E. 2d 793, 795. In **tax** law, any event that results in an economic value to a taxpayer. Not all benefits, however, are included in the gross income of a **taxpayer** since many benefits are not realized in the **taxable year** or are not subject to tax under the **Internal Revenue Code** or judicially or administratively developed principles.

FRINGE BENEFITS benefits other than direct salary or compensation (such as parking, health insurance, tuition reimbursement) received by an employee from an employer. So long as the fringe benefits are not construed as an alternative form of compensation, they are generally not subject to tax.

BEQUEATH the appropriate term for making a **gift** of personalty by means of a **will.** 134 N.W. 498, 500. Strictly, it signifies a gift of **personal property**, which distinguishes it from a **devise,** which is a gift of **real property.** A **disposition** is the generic name encompassing both a bequest of personalty and a devise of realty. However, when a testator's intention is obvious, "bequeath" is considered synonymous with "devise."

BEQUEST a **gift** of **personal property** contained in a **will,** see 133 P. 2d 626, 634; "a **disposition** of personal property by will," 9 P 2d 1065, 1067. "A **devise** ordinarily passes **real estate** and a 'bequest' personal property." 103 N.Y.S. 36, 44. It is regarded as synonymous with **legacy.**

CONDITIONAL BEQUEST a bequest, "the taking effect or continuing of which depends upon the happening or nonoccurrence of a particular event." See 42 N.E. 465, 467.

EXECUTORY BEQUEST a bequest of personalty or money which does not take effect until the happening of a possible or certain future event, upon which it is thus said to be contingent. See 36 S.E. 404, 408.

RESIDUARY BEQUEST bequest consisting of that which is left in an **estate** after the payment of **debts** and general legacies and other specific gifts. See 155 P. 353, 355.

SPECIFIC BEQUEST a bequest of "particular items or a part of a testator's estate which is capable of identification from all others of the same kind and which may be satisfied only by delivery of the particular thing (given by the will), not merely a corresponding amount in value or like property." 477 S.W. 2d 771, 773.

BEST EVIDENCE RULE a rule of evidence law requiring that to prove the content of a writing, recording, or photograph, the original writing, recording, or photograph is required. See Fed. R. Ev. 1002. "Where the terms are material, the original writing must be produced unless it is shown to be unavailable for some reason other than the serious fault of the proponent." McCormick, Evidence §229 (2d ed. 1972).

BESTIALITY sexual intercourse with an animal; constitutes a **crime against nature.** 122 P. 2d 415, 416. See also **sodomy.**

BEYOND A REASONABLE DOUBT see **reasonable doubt.**

B.F.O.Q. See **bona fide occupational qualification [B.F.O.Q.].**

B.F.P. see **bona fide purchaser.**

BID an offer by an intending purchaser to buy goods or services at a stated price, or an offer by an intended seller to sell his goods or services for a stated price. In the building construction trade, general **contractors** usually solicit bids based on building specifications from several subcontractors in order to complete the project. Governmental agencies are often required by law to construct highways and buildings, and to buy goods and services, only in accordance with a procedure wherein competitive bids are solicited by advertisement from the public, with the lowest competent bid winning the contract.

BID SHOPPING "the practice of a **general contractor** who, before the award of the prime contract, discloses to interested **subcontractors** the current low subbids on certain subcontracts in an effort to obtain lower subbids." 482 P. 2d 226, 228.

BIGAMY the criminal offense of "the having of two or more wives or husbands at the same time." 194 P. 877. "The state of a man who has two wives, or of a woman who has two husbands, living at the same time." 189 S.E. 321, 323. A bigamous marriage is **void**. See Model Penal Code, §230.1.

BILATERAL CONTRACT see **contract.**

BILATERAL MISTAKE see **mistake.**

BILL a proposition or statement reduced to writing. In commercial law, an "account for goods sold, services rendered and work done," 11 Cal. Rptr., 893, 897; in the law of negotiable instruments, bills are "all forms of paper money," 127 S.W. 961, 962; a single **bond** without condition, 36 U.S. 257, 328; an order drawn by one person on another to pay a certain sum of money absolutely and in all events. 61 N.Y. 251, 255.

In legislation, a draft of a proposed statute submitted to the legislature for enactment. 226 F. 135, 137.

In **equity pleadings,** the name by which the complainant sets out his cause of action.

BILL FOR A NEW TRIAL one submitted to a **court of equity** stating equitable grounds for enjoining the execution of a judgment rendered in a **court of law** and proposing a new suit in **equity.**

BILL OF ATTAINDER see **bill of attainder.**

BILL OF CERTIORARI see **certiorari.**

BILL OF DISCOVERY see **discovery.**

BILL OF EXCEPTIONS a writing submitted to a trial court stating for the **record** objections to rulings made and instructions given by the trial judge. See **exceptions.**

BILL OF EXCHANGE an order written from one party to another directing him to pay a certain sum to a third party.

BILL OF INTERPLEADER see **interpleader.**

BILL OF LADING see **bill of lading.**

BILL OF PARTICULARS see **bill of particulars.**

BILL OF REVIEW see **bill of review.**

BILL OF RIGHTS the first eight amendments to the United States Constitution creating individual rights. Because they were adopted at the same time, Amendments 9 and 10 are referred to by many as part of the Bill of Rights. See **Bill of Rights.**

BILL OF SALE a written agreement under which **title** to personal **chattels** is transferred. See 172 S.E. 672.

CROSS BILL brought in a court of equity by defendant against plaintiff or against another defendant in the suit concerning a matter related to the original bill; similar to **cross-claim** and **counter-claim** at law.

TREASURY BILL see **treasury bill.**

BILL OF ATTAINDER a legislative act, in any form, that applies "either to named individuals or to easily ascertainable members of a group in such a way as to inflict punishment on them without a judicial trial," 381 U.S. 437, 448; such enactments are prohibited in the United States Constitution, Art. 1, §9, Cl. 3. At the time of the adoption of the federal constitution it "was a legislative judgment of conviction, an exercise of judicial power by parliament without a hearing, and in disregard of the first principles of natural justice." 35 N.E. 951. It should be noted, however, that a "legislature, like a court, must of necessity, possess the power to act immediately and instantly to quell disorder in the chamber," and therefore a legislature may punish and impose a jail sentence for **contempt** of the legislature as long as its procedures conform with **due process** requirements, i.e., the **accused** must have some opportunity to appear and to respond to the charges against him. 404 U.S. 496, 503, 504. An example of a bill of attainder was Section 304 of the Urgent Deficiency Appropriation Act of 1943 which forbade the paying of salaries to certain named government employees because Congress objected to their political views. See 328 U.S. 303.

BILL OF EXCHANGE see **draft.** See also **bill** (BILL OF EXCHANGE); **exchange.**

BILL OF LADING in commercial law, the receipt a **carrier** gives to a shipper for goods given to the carrier for transportation. U.C.C. §1-206(6). The bill evidences the contract between the shipper and the carrier, and can also serve as a document of **title** creating in the person possessing the bill ownership of the goods shipped. 430 N.E. 2d 1185, 1189. See generally U.C.C. Art. 7.

ORDER BILL OF LADING a negotiable bill of lading that can be negotiated like any other negotiable instrument, so that the shipper can sell it to anyone, not just the intended recipient of the goods. 109 S. 205, 207. It not only states that the carrier is to deliver the goods to a specified person at a specified place, but also requires the carrier to release the goods only when the bill of lading is given to him. An "order" bill operates as a document of title and must be presented before possession of the goods will be delivered. Under this arrangement, the shipper can withhold the bill of lading, and thus the goods themselves, from the intended recipient of the goods until he pays for them.

STRAIGHT BILL OF LADING a nonnegotiable bill of lading. It merely states that the carrier is to deliver the goods to a specified person at a specified place.

BILL OF PARTICULARS the criminal law **procedural** equivalent of a **civil action** request for a "more definite statement." 1 F.R.D. 229, 231. Its function "is to inform the defense of the specific occurrences intended to be investigated on the trial and to limit the course of the **evidence** to the particular scope of the inquiry." 155 S.E. 2d 802, 810. It is "in the nature of an amplification of the **pleading** to which it relates, and it is to be construed as part of it for certain purposes." 216 P. 2d 151, 155. "In legal effect, [it] is a more specific statement of details of offenses charged and is designed to advise the court, and more particularly, the **defendant,** of what facts he will be required to meet." 10 F.R.D. 191, 192.

A bill of particulars may also be used in civil actions in some states. See, e.g., N.Y.C.P.L.R. §§3041 et seq.

Generally the defendant can only demand a bill of particulars as to those matters upon which the state or plaintiff has the **burden of proof.**

BILL OF REVIEW form of **equita-**

ble **proceedings** brought to secure an explanation, alteration, or **reversal** of a final **decree** by the court which rendered it. 192 N.E. 229, 234. Most commonly, only errors of law appearing on the face of the **record,** new evidence not susceptible to use at the trial and coming to light after the decree is issued, and **new matter** arising after entry of the decree, could have been the basis for a successful bill of review. 84 N.E. 2d 318, 322. It is also appropriate where there is evidence of **fraud** impeaching the original transaction. 114 N.E. 592, 593.

BILL OF RIGHTS the first ten amendments to the United States Constitution; that part of any constitution which articulates fundamental rights of citizenship. It is a declaration of rights that are substantially immune from governmental interference, and thus constitutes a reservation of limited individual sovereignty.

Among such rights guaranteed in the federal Constitution are the rights to speak, assemble, and practice religion free from federal governmental regulation, the right to be free from unreasonable **searches and seizures,** and the right to a jury trial when tried for a criminal offense. Originally restrictive only on federal power, the Bill of Rights has now been largely "incorporated" into the **due process** clause of the Fourteenth Amendment, and thus made applicable to actions by the states as well. The various theories used to justify this incorporation, and the extent to which the incorporation has been effected is a subject of study and some controversy within modern constitutional law. It is clear, however, that as a limitation on political power, the Bill of Rights offers no protection against the interference with such rights by private individuals.

While given the highest constitutional protection, these rights may not be absolute. Courts will of necessity balance and limit them when they clash with one another. Thus, the First Amendment guarantee of free speech and publication has in some cases been found to conflict with the Sixth Amendment guarantee of a fair trial, with the result of a judicial balancing of the two values. The rights may also be balanced against other social values which are considered of equal importance, such as national security. Thus, it has been said that freedom of speech does not extend to the right to yell "fire" in a crowded theater. And, the free exercise of religion will be constrained where its practice seriously endangers the lives of others, or violates other fundamental social values, such as laws forbidding **bigamy.**

BIND something which obligates or constrains the bound individual. "To **guaranty,** to promise, to secure, to warrant, and to defend." 1 Ark. 325, 333. A bind places one under legal duties and obligations. One can "bind" himself as in a **contract** or one can be "bound" by a **judgment.**

BINDER a "contract for temporary insurance," 120 A. 2d 501, 502; "merely a written memorandum of the most important items of a preliminary contract," 155 S.E. 2d 246, 251; "insurer's bare acknowledgment of its contract to protect insured against casualty of a specified kind until a formal policy can be issued or until insurer gives notice of its election to terminate," 142 S.E. 2d 659; "a cover note." 185 P. 2d 832, 836.

BINDER RECEIPT evidence of an application for insurance previously accepted; "a contract of insurance in praesenti, temporary in nature, intended to take the place of an ordinary policy until it can be issued." 104 S.E. 2d 633, 637.

BINDING "as used in statute, commonly means obligatory," 172 N.E. 2d 703, 705. See **binder.**

BINDING AGREEMENT a conclusive agreement, see 148 S.W. 290, 291.

BINDING INSTRUCTION an instruction "which directs jury how to determine a case only if the conditions stated in that one instruction are shown to exist." 207 S.W. 2d 304, 307.

BIND OVER to order that a defendant be placed in custody pending the outcome of a proceeding (usually criminal) against him. He may be released on bail or other conditions of release thereafter. See 124 N.W. 492, 493. When **probable cause** is found to exist at a **preliminary hearing,** the court will direct that the defendant be "bound over" for action by the **grand jury** [or for trial on a prosecutor's information].

BLACK LETTER LAW see **hornbook law.**

BLACKMAIL extortion, 68 N.E. 2d 464, 465; "the exaction of money either for the performance of a duty, the prevention of an injury, or the exercise of an influence," 24 P. 979, 980; "malicious threatening to do injury to person of another or to accuse one of crime or offense, to compel him to do an act against his will," 258 N.W. 62; "extortion of things of value from a person by menaces of personal injury, or by threatening to accuse him of crime or any immoral conduct, which, if true, tends to degrade or disgrace him." 82 N.E. 1039. Often labeled as "criminal coercion" in criminal statutes. See Model Penal Code §212.5.

BLACKMAIL SUITS see **strike suits.**

BLANK INDORSEMENT see **indorsement.**

BLASPHEMY at **common law,** the **misdemeanor** of reviling or ridiculing the established religion (Christianity) and the existence of God, see 168 Eng. Rep. 1140, 1149. Blasphemy statutes exist in the United States in many jurisdictions, but are rarely, if ever, enforced, and hence have not been the subject of major constitutional attack even though there appears to be a basis for such attack. Perkins and Boyce, Criminal Law 475 (3rd ed. 1982). See **establishment clause.**

BLOOD, CORRUPTION OF THE see **corruption of blood.**

BLUE CHIP STOCK the common stock of a company known nationally for the quality and wide acceptance of its products or services, and for its ability to generate consistent profits and pay increased dividends. The term probably evolved from its use in gambling casinos, where blue chips are valued at $100, since common stocks of leading companies were offered at $100 per share around the turn of the last century.

BLUE LAWS see **Sunday closing laws.**

BLUE RIBBON JURY see **jury** [BLUE RIBBON JURY].

BLUE SKY LAWS popular name given to state statutes regulating the sales of **corporate securities** through investment companies, imposed to prevent the sale of securities of **fraudulent** enterprises. See 242 U.S. 539.

BOARD OF DIRECTORS a group elected by shareholders to set company policy and appoint the chief executives and operating officers. See **de facto** [DE FACTO BOARD OF DIRECTORS].

BOARD ROOM a stockbroker's office where registered representatives (securities salespersons registered with the S.E.C.) work and where the public is allowed to visit and obtain stock price quotations throughout the market day. Offices are equipped with electronic machines that provide information on trading in **listed stocks,** and **over-the-counter markets** and also provide business news.

BOILERPLATE any standard or formal language in a legal document; language found almost universally in documents of a given type, often in small print. See 163 N.W. 2d 140, 141.

In contract law, a person often binds himself to boilerplate language that he has not even read merely by signing the contract. Such contracts can sometimes be voided because of mistake of fact.

For this reason, contract boilerplate has been much criticized in the field of consumer protection. Courts have increasingly used the principle of **unconscionability** to invalidate industrywide standardized contracts that give the seller too many benefits and/or an excessive price. Standardized contract clauses can also be avoided by crossing them out, writing over them, or adding language to invalidate them.

BOILER ROOM [OR SHOP] a place devoted to high-pressure promotion by telephone of stocks, bonds, diamonds, commodities, contracts, etc., which are of very questionable value. Extensive fraud is usually involved, but successful prosecution may be difficult since operations often disband before detection and since little tangible evidence is obtainable.

BONA *(bō'-nà)*—Lat: good, virtuous; also, goods and chattels, property.

BONA FIDE *(bō'-nà fĭde)*—Lat: in good faith; without fraud or deceit, 80 Cal. Rptr. 89, 97; 458 P. 2d 33, 41; genuine, 20 A. 2d 414, 416.

BONA FIDE OCCUPATIONAL QUALIFICATION [B.F.O.Q.] statutory provision that permits discriminatory practices in employment if a person's "religion, sex, or national origin is a bona fide occupational qualification reasonably necessary to the normal operation of that particular business or enterprise." 42 U.S.C. §2000e-2(e). It is also permissible for an educational institution with a particular religious orientation to hire only employees of that religion. Id. Courts have placed the burden of proof of establishing a "B.F.O.Q." on the defendant. 502 F. 2d 34, and the exception provided by the "B.F.O.Q." has been narrowly interpreted. 380 F. Supp. 197. In this manner it is more difficult to justify a "B.F.O.Q." than to defend against a constitutionally based claim of sex discrimination under the Equal Protection Clause of the 14th Amendment. The "B.F.O.Q." exception would only be permitted if, in the example of a woman working at a job requiring the frequent lifting of substantial amounts of weights, the defendant proved by a preponderance of the evidence that all or substantially all females would be unable to perform safely and efficiently the duties involved in the job. 540 F. 2d 718. Sex has been found to be a "B.F.O.Q." in terms of community standards of morality where, for example, a man works as an attendant in a men's washroom and a woman works as a fitter in a lingerie establishment. 482 F. Supp. 681.

BONA FIDE PURCHASER (BFP) "one who pays a valuable **consideration,** has no notice of outstanding rights of others and who acts in **good faith**" concerning the purchase, 303 S.W. 2d 110, 117; "one who acquires the apparent legal **title** to **property** in good faith for a valuable consideration and without notice of a claim or interest of a third person under the common source of title," 294 S.W. 2d 308, 311; innocent purchaser for value. 498 S.W. 2d 73, 75. The Uniform Commercial Code defines "bona fide purchaser" as a "purchaser for value in good faith and without notice of any adverse claim who takes delivery of a security in bearer form or of one in registered form issued to him or indorsed to him or in blank." U.C.C. §8-302.

BONA FIDE PURCHASE "one made in **good faith** for valuable consideration and without notice of an inconsistent third-party claim." 69 S.W. 2d 603, 609. See **holder in due course.**

BOND "written **instrument** with **sureties,** guaranteeing faithful **performance** of acts or duties contemplated," 71 N.E. 2d 742, 749; evidence of a debt; a binding agreement, a **covenant** between two or more persons, [or] an instrument under **seal** by which the **maker** binds himself, and usually also his **heirs, executors** and **administrators** or, if a **corporation,** their **successors,** to do or not to do a specified act." 166 N.Y.S. 2d 679, 680. See **bail bond.**

A bond may thus be the "obligation of a state, its subdivision, or a private corporation, represented by certificate for principal, and by detachable coupons for current interest; includes all interest-bearing obligations of persons, firms, and corporations," 95 S.W. 2d 39, 40; "certificate of indebtedness," 52 S.W. 2d 650; "security." 74 F. Supp. 133, 134. See **municipal bond.** See also **state or municipal bonds.**

The rights of the holder are specified in the bond **indenture,** which contains the legal terms and conditions under which the bond was issued. Bond debt is secured or guaranteed primarily by the ability of the issuer (borrower) to pay the interest when due and to repay the principal at maturity.

Bonds are available in two forms. REGISTERED BONDS are recorded on the books of the issuer by the trustee, and interest is paid by mail to the **holder** of record. **Bearer bonds** are **negotiable instruments** that must be safeguarded by the owner to prevent loss. Interest is paid by **coupon** redemptions. See **security** [BOND]; **treasury bond.**

BOND DISCOUNT occurs where bonds are sold on the market for cash at a price less than the face amount of the bonds. 469 F. 2d 340, 345. Since bonds may **mature** [become due] many years hence, they are "discounted" to reflect present value, i.e., $20 due in five years may be worth only $10 today. The exact discount will depend upon the interest rate, inflation, and economic market conditions.

BONDED DEBT that "part of the entire indebtedness of a **corporation** or state which is represented by **bonds** it has issued; . . . A debt contracted under the obligation of a bond." 40 S.E. 523, 527.

BOND FOR DEED [TITLE] "an instrument given by the owner of **real estate** to **convey** the same upon being paid money," 137 So. 2d 387; "an agreement to make **title** in the future, and so long as it remains **executory** [not yet performed] the title is **vested** in the original owner." 41 N.E. 177.

BOND FOR GENERAL PURPOSES "bonds which are a charge against the taxpayers generally as distinguishable from those for improvements the cost of which is charged to the property specially benefited." 251 P. 413.

BOND ISSUE the offering of bonds for sale to investors; "commonly intended to distribute **indebtedness** among many investors over a period of years." 137 So. 665. The distribution of a bond or bonds. 138 S.W. 381, 383.

BOND PREMIUM amount that purchaser pays in buying a bond that exceeds face or call value of the bond. Generally reflects the difference between the nominal interest rate born by such bonds and the actual or effective rate of return determined by the current market. 332 N.E. 2d 886, 888.

BOND YIELD see **yield.**

PERFORMANCE BOND a contractor's bond, guaranteeing that the contractor will perform the contract and providing that, in the event of a default, the surety may complete the contract or pay damages up to the bond limit. 440 P. 2d 600, 605.

SERIAL BOND bond issue consisting of a number of bonds with different maturity dates. Bonds are issued at the same time as distinguished from series bonds which are issued at different times.

SERIES BONDS groups of bonds normally issued at different times but under same indenture.

SURETY BOND a bond issued by one party, the surety, guaranteeing that he will perform certain acts promised by another or pay a stipulated sum, up to the bond limit, in lieu of performance, should the principal fail to perform. In a criminal case, the surety bond assures the appearance of the **defendant** or the repayment of bail forfeited upon the defendant's failure to appear in court.

BONDSMAN a **surety;** one who is bound or gives surety for another, 59 N.E. 557, 558; a person who obtains surety bonds for others for a fee; also, the individual who arranges for the defendant in a criminal case to be released from jail by posting a **bail bond.**

BONUS STOCK common stock offered as an additional incentive to underwriters or buyers of a **bond** or **preferred stock issue.**

BOOK VALUE in reference to corporations, the worth of the assets minus the cost of the liabilities. However, since the ways of computing assets and liabilities vary so greatly, there is no standard method for ascertaining book value. 51 A.L.R. 2d 606.

BORDELLO see **prostitution.**

BOROUGH ENGLISH see **primogeniture.**

BOYCOTT to refrain from com-
mercial dealing with by concerted effort; "[r]efusal to work for, purchase from or handle the products of an employer," 292 N.E. 2d 647, 655; "within the meaning of the 'Sherman Act,' [it] includes even the peaceful persuasion of a person to refrain from doing business with another." 344 F. Supp. 118, 141. Although boycotting is not necessarily illegal, 284 N.W. 126, 130, a conspiracy to injure business through intimidation or coercion may violate **antitrust laws** such as the Sherman Act.

SECONDARY BOYCOTT economic pressure by a union upon an employer with whom the union has no dispute. By engaging in such activity the union hopes to compel the person to cease doing business with the employer with which the union has its dispute. Secondary boycotts are a violation of the **Taft-Hartley Act.** 29 U.S.C. §141 et seq.

BRAIN DEATH the irreversible cessation of brain function; statutory or case law definitions of death are being expanded in many jurisdictions to include this. Among the factors considered are the failure to respond to external stimuli, the absence of breathing or spontaneous movement, the absence of reflex movement, and a flat electroencephalograph reading following a 24-hour observation period. 366 N.E. 2d 744.

BREACH [OF CONTRACT] a party's failure to perform some contracted-for or agreed-upon act, or his failure to comply with a duty imposed by law which is owed to another or to society. 682 F. 2d 883, 885.

ANTICIPATORY BREACH see **anticipatory breach.**

BREACH OF DUTY a failure to perform a duty owed to another or to society; a failure to exercise that care which a **reasonable man** would exercise under similar circumstances. 56 A. 498, 500.

BREACH OF PROMISE failure to do what one promises, where he has promised it in order to induce action in another. The phrase is often used as a shorthand for "breach of the promise of marriage."

BREACH OF THE COVENANT OF WARRANTY a failure of the seller's guarantee of **good title** which occurs when the buyer [**covenantee**] is evicted by a person claiming under a **paramount** title; since it is a future covenant it is not breached until that eviction occurs; see Cribbit, Principles of the Law of Property 274-276 (1975).

BREACH OF THE PEACE an offense embracing a great variety of conduct destroying or menacing public order and tranquility. It includes not only violent acts but acts and words likely to produce violence in others. 310 U.S. 296, 308. In its broadest sense the term refers to any criminal offense (or at least any **indictable offense,** 207 U.S. 425). Today the term is generally used to describe conduct which unreasonably threatens the public peace and which lacks a specific criminal label; by statute such conduct is often called "disorderly conduct" as the specific criminal offense. See, e.g., New York Penal Law §240.20. The term has been defined by state courts as "disturbances of the public peace violative of order and decency or decorum," 147 N.W. 2d 886, 892; "any violation of any law enacted to preserve peace and good order." 236 P. 57, 59. It "signifies disorderly, dangerous conduct disruptive of public peace." 261 A. 2d 731, 739. See also **fighting words; slander.**

BREACH OF TRUST "violation by a **trustee** of a **duty** which **equity** lays upon him, whether willful and **fraudulent,** or done through **negligence,** or arising through mere oversight and forgetfulness." 150 P. 2d 604, 648. See Restatement (second), Torts §201.

BREACH OF TRUST WITH FRAUDULENT INTENT "a **larceny** after **trust,** which includes all of the elements of larceny except the unlawful taking in the beginning." 31 S.E. 2d 906, 907.

BREACH OF WARRANTY "infraction of an express or implied agreement as to the title, quality, content or condition of a thing sold or **bailed.**" 151 N.W. 2d 477, 482. A **warranty** is a **guarantee** and is breached when the thing so guaranteed is deficient according to the terms of the warranty. See U.C.C. §2-312 et seq.

CONSTRUCTIVE BREACH this occurs when the party bound to perform does some act that disables him from performing under the contract or announces in advance of his time for performing that he has no intention to do so. This creates an **anticipatory breach.** 19 F. 2d 388, 389.

MATERIAL BREACH in contract law a breach that is substantial and operates to excuse further performance by the **aggrieved** party. A material breach destroys the value of the contract and gives rise to an action for breach of contract.

PARTIAL BREACH a **breach** that gives rise to a claim for **damages** but that is so slight that it does not substantially impair the value of the **contract** to the injured party and thus does not give the injured party cause to abandon the whole contract. 11 Williston on Contracts 8-9 (3rd ed. 1940). For instance, if a person contracts to buy a white yacht, and is delivered a yellow yacht, he might have to purchase the yacht and seek damages for the cost of painting the yacht white.

BREAKING A CLOSE the **common law trespass** of unlawful entering upon the land of another. 187 S.E. 349, 350.

BREAKING AND ENTERING two of the elements necessary to constitute a **burglary.** The "breaking and entering" necessary to constitute a **burglary** may be any act of physical force, however slight, by which obstruction to entrance is removed. 381 P. 2d 178, 182. For example, the pushing open of a door that is ajar followed by entrance into a building will be sufficient to constitute the "breaking and entering" elements of burglary.

BREAKING BULK refers to a doctrine whereby a **bailee** could be charged with **larceny** by trespass if he opened a chest, parcel, or case containing goods entrusted to his care and converted same to his own use; the trespass necessary for larceny was complete even if the goods were not in a container but were themselves delivered in bulk provided that the bailee separated only a portion of the goods entrusted to him. If he converted all of the goods, there was, however, no breaking bulk and hence no trespass and no larceny. Perkins & Boyce, Criminal Law 320-321 (3rd ed. 1982).

BREATHALYZER a chemical test of a person's breath to determine whether he or she is intoxicated, usually when he or she is suspected of drunken driving. The test is normally administered by a police officer trained in the use of the equipment, and the equipment must be calibrated on a regular basis. A person operating a motor vehicle is usually presumed to have consented to taking the test, e.g., N.J.S.A. §39:4-50.2, and refusal to take the test may result in the automatic loss of one's driver's license. The results of the test are admissible as evidence in court. See 378 A. 2d 95.

BRIBERY "voluntary giving of something of value to influence performance of official duty." 237 F. Supp. 638, 641. The "essential elements are offer of gift, purpose to corruptly influence, and official status of offeree." 103 S.E. 2d 666, 670. "At common law the voluntary giving or receiving of anything of value in unlawful payment of an official act done or to be done." 119 P. 901, 907. See Model Penal Code §240.1. COMMERCIAL BRIBERY is a statutory expansion of the crime to include the breach of duty by an employee in accepting secret compensation from another in exchange for the exercise of some discretion conferred upon the employee by his employer. See, e.g., Model Penal Code §224.8; New York Penal Law Art. 180.

BRIEF a written argument concentrating upon legal points and authorities, which is used by the lawyer to convey to the court (trial or appellate) the essential facts of his client's case, a statement of the questions of law involved, the law that he would have applied, and the application that he desires made of it by the court; it is submitted in connection with an application, motion, trial, or appeal. See 107 P. 630, 631. Compare **memorandum.**

BROKER "one who for commission or fee, brings parties together and assists in negotiating contracts between them." 170 P. 2d 727. "Persons whose business it is to bring buyer and seller together." 110 S.W. 206, 208. Compare **jobber.**

BRUTUM FULMEN *(brū'-tŭm fŭl'-měn)*—Lat: inert thunder. It refers to an empty threat or charge, or a void **judgment** which is in legal effect no judgment at all. See 179 S.W. 2d 346, 348. Brutum fulmen are any potentially powerful and effective orders, documents, **decrees,** or judgments that are powerless due to some imperfection causing them to be unenforceable. The following statement is exemplary: "Any decree by this court directed against the legislature would be unenforceable and no basis for a charge of contempt, if ignored. It would be a classic example of what the law describes as brutum fulmen." 153 A. 2d 888, 892.

BUGGERY see **sodomy.**

BUGGING see **wiretap.**

BUILDING PERMIT see **certificate of occupancy.**

BULK SALE ACTS "a class of statutes designed to prevent the defrauding of **creditors** by the secret sale in bulk of substantially all of the merchant's stock of goods." 125 S.E. 870. These laws generally require that notice be given to creditors before any sale of debtor's goods in bulk and out of the ordinary course of business. See generally U.C.C. Art. 6. See **bulk transfer.**

BULK TRANSFER a type of commercial **fraud** wherein a merchant (or the owner of a business) transfers the business or a major part thereof for **consideration** and then fails to pay his **creditors** with the proceeds. Any transfer in bulk of a major part of the materials, supplies, merchandise or other inventory, not in the ordinary course of the retailer's business, is subject to the provisions of Article 6 of the Uniform Commercial Code. The purpose of the article is to prevent the above-described transfer after which the merchant pockets the proceeds and disappears thus leaving his creditors unpaid. The article also contributes toward the prevention of the type of frauds wherein the merchant, owing debts, sells out his stock in trade to a friend for less than it is worth, pays his creditors less than what he owes them and hopes to come back into the business through the "back door." See White and Summers, Uniform Commercial Code, §19-3 (2d ed. 1980).

BUNCHING a term referring to the concentration of **gross income** in one or more **taxable years;** this results in adverse tax consequences because of the progressive **tax rate** structure that results in a higher effective rate of tax in the years that have the larger amount of income. These adverse effects are minimized to a certain degree by the availability of **income averaging,** I.R.C. §1301, and by the preferential tax treatment afforded to **capital gains,** I.R.C. §1201.

BURDEN generally, anything that is grievous, wearisome, or oppressive. 297 S.W. 2d 39, 44.

In property law, burden refers to any restriction on the use of land, including zoning ordinances, 548 P. 2d 538, 540, or restrictive covenants or other restrictions running with the land such as easements in favor of other property. A **servient estate** is property that is "burdened" with an obligation (servitude) that benefits other property. 125 N.E. 834.

See **burden of proof** for discussion of burden in procedure.

BURDEN OF PROOF the duty of a party to substantiate an **allegation** or **issue** either to avoid the **dismissal** of that issue early in the trial or in order to convince the "trier of facts" as to the truth of that claim and hence to prevail in a civil or criminal **suit.** Thus defined, the burden of proof embodies at least two distinct concepts:

The burden of proof may refer to the RISK OF NONPERSUASION, 9 Wigmore, Evidence §2485 (3rd ed. 1940), [also called simply PERSUASION BURDEN]. This means essentially that the party carrying it will lose if the trier of fact in deliberating the final outcome of the case, remains in doubt or is not convinced to the degree required. "If at the close of the evidence the [trier of fact] finds itself in doubt as to the facts, the decision must go against the party who has the burden of persuasion on the particular issue in question." 251 F. Supp. 474, 476. In civil cases this burden is met by proving a case by a **preponderence** of the evidence, while in criminal cases the state's persuasion burden is met only by proof beyond a **reasonable doubt.** 397 U.S. 358. In some **equity** matters the burden of persuasion is met by **clear and convincing** evidence (e.g., to **reform** a **contract** the party seeking reformation must present clear and convincing evidence that the writing does not accurately reflect the agreement of the parties).

The burden of proof may also refer to the DUTY OF PRODUCING EVIDENCE [also called BURDEN OF EVIDENCE or simply PRODUCTION BURDEN]. This is the duty that the **plaintiff** has at the beginning of the trial to produce evidence sufficient to avoid a preemptory finding at the close of his case [such as a **nonsuit, directed verdict; dismissal**], 54 Cal. Rptr. 528, 530; the duty of producing evidence is the "burden of making a **prima facie** [sufficient on its face] showing as to each fact necessary to establish a prima facie case." 126 S.W. 2d 915, 918. This burden is met if the court determines that there are enough facts on an issue sufficient to support a decision by the trier of fact favorable to the party who has the production burden [in a jury trial, sufficient to "permit the case to go to jury"]; if the burden is not met, that party loses on that issue. This burden, once allocated, often is shifted in the course of the trial to the opposing side. See generally, James & Hazard, Civil Procedure §7.5 (2d ed. 1979).

A third distinct burden which may be included within the phrase "burden of proof" is the PLEADING BURDEN. This burden refers to the obligation to plead each element of a **cause of action** or **affirmative defense** on pain of suffering a dismissal.

See also **moral certainty; presumption; res ipsa loquitur.**

BURGLARY at common law, an actual breaking of a dwelling, in the nighttime, with intent to commit a **felony.** See 90 P. 2d 520, 521. The common law offense has been expanded by statutes so that today burglary "connotes the entering of a building [not necessarily a dwelling] in the night season with intent to commit a felony or with intent to steal property of value." 116 N.E. 2d 311, 312. Modern statutes have expanded the crime to include any unlawful entry into or remaining in any building, with intent to commit any crime. See, e.g., Model Penal Code §221.1, N.Y. Penal Law Art. 140.

BUSINESS, COURSE OF see **ordinary course of business.**

BUSINESS CYCLE the periodic expansion and contraction of economic activity.

BUSINESS GUEST see **invitee.**

BUSINESS INVITEE see **invitee.**

BUSINESS RECORDS EXCEPTION see **hearsay rule.**

BUSINESS TRUST see **Massachusetts trust.**

BUT FOR in **tort** and in criminal law, a test of whether an individual's action caused a particular event. 409 P. 2d 340, 341. The test is applied by asking whether the event would have occurred "but for," or in the absence of, the individual's act. Since every event has several causes, the test can describe any and all of them, and therefore is widely regarded as being of little or no benefit in assigning civil or criminal liability in many types of situations. For example, the test fails to distinguish those causes that should give rise to legal liability from those causes that are an accepted part of everyday life. Thus, if A, driving a car, hits B, crossing the street, the accident has two causes: A's driving and B's crossing. Whether the accident was A's or B's fault would be impossible to determine without factual investigations beyond the "but for" test. Inquiries of this sort are conducted under more complex legal doctrines such as **proximate cause.** 25 How. L. Rev. 103, 109 (1911).

The "but for" test also fails to define cause conclusively when independent, concurrent causes are present. Thus, if both A and B toss matches into a hayloft, and either one's acts would have produced the resultant fire, applying the "but for" test will define neither actor as the cause when in fact both were. 2 Harper & James, The Law of Torts §20.2 (1956).

BUYER IN ORDINARY COURSE OF BUSINESS a person who, in **good faith** and without knowledge that the sale to him is in violation of the ownership rights or **security interest** of a third party in the **goods** buys goods in the usual manner from a person in the business of selling goods of that kind. A buyer in the **ordinary course of business** takes free of a **security interest** created by his seller even though the buyer knows of its existence. U.C.C. §1-201(9). See **holder in due course.**

BY-LAWS or BYLAWS rules adopted for the regulation of a group's own actions, by the group itself; a subordinate law adopted by a **corporation,** association, or other body for its self-government or to regulate the rights and duties of its officers and members. 19 A. 2d 588, 592. In the absence of law to the contrary, under the **common law,** the power to make by-laws resides in the constituent body of members or **stockholders.** 249 A. 2d 623, 624. When used by corporations, the term by-law deals with matters of corporate structure and machinery as distinguished from a regulation imposed by a board of directors to deal with problems relating to management of **property** of the corporation.

BY OPERATION OF LAW see **operation of law.**

BY THE ENTIRETY see **tenancy** [TENANCY BY THE ENTIRETY].

C.A.B. see **Civil Aeronautics Board.**

CADAVER the body of a deceased person.

CALENDAR CALL a hearing in court in a pending cause to ascertain the status of the matter and to establish a date for trial.

CALL in property law, an identifiable natural object serving to mark the boundary of the land conveyed and designated as a landmark in an **instrument** of **conveyance,** 98 F. 913, 922.

In the **securities** trade, the term refers to a call option which is a **contract** giving the buyer the right to purchase **stock** at a specified price, called the "strike" price, until a specified date called the expiration date. The chief advantage of such listed option contracts is that they are **fungible** as a result of centered clearing, certificateless trading, uniform strike prices, and expiration dates. Trading in over-the-counter option contracts, which are not fungible and which as a result have a very poor secondary market, has declined to a very low level. See also **option.**

CALLABLE BOND a bond which the issuer may retire at any time before its maturity. Usually the issuer must pay a premium (an amount more than the face value of the bond) to call the bond.

CALL OPTION see **stock option.**

CALUMNY slander, defamation; false prosecution or accusation; a word once used in **civil law** "which signified an unjust prosecution or defense of a suit, and the phrase is still said to be used in the courts of Scotland and the **ecclesiastical** and **admiralty** courts of England." 30 Ohio St. 115, 117.

CAMERA see **in camera.**

CANNABIS see **controlled substances** [CANNABIS].

CANON a rule of **ecclesiastical law,** primarily concerning the clergy, but also at times, embracing lay members of a congregation. A rule of **construction;** one of an aggregate of rules indicating the proper way to construe statutes, ordinances, etc. See 161 N.Y.S. 484, 487.

A professional canon is a rule or standard of conduct adopted by a professional group to guide or discipline the professional conduct of its members. The Canons of Professional Ethics were originally 32 in number and were adopted by the American Bar Association in 1908. Today a new Code of Professional Responsibility containing seven broad canons and a large number of "ethical considerations" and "disciplinary rules" have replaced the original Canons. A familiar Canon, Number Seven, provides that "A Lawyer Should Represent a Client Zealously Within the Bounds of the Law." The new Code has been adopted by most of the states' highest courts.

CAPACITY "mental ability to make a rational decision, which includes the ability to perceive and appreciate all relevant facts. Capacity is not necessarily synonymous with sanity." 563 S.W. 2d. 197, 209. No one can be guilty of a **crime** who lacks the legal capacity to commit it. 22 C.J.S. 193. To render a **contract** binding, the parties involved must have the capacity to contract. 17 C.J.S. 630. **Testamentary** capacity with respect to personalty is governed by the law of

the **testator's domicile,** and, with respect to **realty,** by the law of the place where the realty is situated. 94 C.J.S. 684. The **objection** of lack of capacity to sue refers to a general legal **disability** to maintain the **action.**

CAPACITY TO SUE see **legal capacity to sue.**

CAPIAS *(kā'-pē-as)*—Lat: that you take. The term refers to a species of **writ** executed by seizure of either the **property** or the person of the **defendant** for the purpose of requiring him to answer a particular charge in court. It embraces several types of judicial writs of **process,** by which actions **at law** were commenced. 3 Bl. Comm. *282; 178 A. 843, 844.

CAPIAS AD AUDIENDUM JUDICIUM *(ăd äw-dē-ĕn'-dŭm jū-dĭ'-shē-ŭm)* —Lat: you take to hear judgment. A writ to bring the defendant who has appeared and has been found **guilty** of a **misdemeanor** to receive judgment. 4 Bl. Comm. *375.

CAPIAS AD RESPONDENDUM *(ăd rĕs'-pŏn-dĕn'-dŭm)*—Lat: you take to respond. Commonly abbreviated CA. RESP., a writ directing the **arrest** and production of a defendant before **judgment.** It not only notifies a defendant to defend **suit,** like a **summons,** but also authorizes his **arrest** as security for the plaintiff's claim. 4 A. 2d 883, 885.

CAPIAS AD SATISFACIENDUM *(ăd să'-tĭs-fā'-shē-ĕn'-dŭm)*—Lat: you take to satisfy. Commonly abbreviated CA. SA., a writ for the arrest of a judgment **debtor** until the debt claim is satisfied. 3 Bl. Comm. *414; 274 A. 2d 283, 286. See also **service of process.** See, generally, 26 Rutgers L. Rev. 853 (1973).

CAPITA see **per capita.**

CAPITAL broadly, all the money and other property of a corporation or other enterprise used in transacting its business, 61 N.W. 851, 852; each investment. A corporation's legal **liability** is ordinarily limited by its capital. See also **risk capital.**

CAPITAL ACCOUNTS that part of a business's accounting records where capital assets and expenditures, and the liabilities incurred to acquire such assets and make such expenditures, are taken into account. The capital account usually consists of CAPITAL ASSETS [below] and capital liabilities, such as long term debt, and stock and other **equity** ownership.

CAPITAL ASSET property with a relatively long life, or fixed assets in a trade or business. For tax purposes, property, the **sale or exchange** of which gives rise to **capital gain or loss** rather than **ordinary income** or a **deduction.** Capital assets include most property other than inventory, stock in trade, depreciable business property, and business real property. I.R.C. §1221.

CAPITAL EXPENDITURES the cost of an acquisition of or repair to property which property or improvement has a **useful life** extending substantially beyond the taxable year. Such costs are not deductible for income tax purposes. I.R.C. §263. However, they may be subject to **depreciation** or **depletion.** Compare **expenses.**

CAPITAL GAINS OR LOSSES gains or losses **realized** from the **sale or exchange** of CAPITAL ASSETS [above], calculated as the difference between the **amount realized** on the sale or exchange and the taxpayer's **basis** in the assets. I.R.C. §1222. LONG-TERM CAPITAL GAINS OR LOSSES are capital gains or losses from the sale or exchange of capital assets held for the required **holding period**

(generally, one year for **taxable years** beginning after 1977). Individual taxpayers may deduct 60 percent of the excess of their net long term capital gains over their net short term capital losses for income tax purposes, resulting in a 20 percent maximum federal income tax rate on such gains. I.R.C. §1202. Corporate taxpayers are subject to a 28 percent alternative tax on the excess of their net long-term capital gains over their net short-term capital losses. I.R.C. §1201. SHORT-TERM CAPITAL GAINS OR LOSSES are gains or losses from the sale or exchange of capital assets held for a period shorter than the required **holding period.**

CAPITAL INTENSIVE an industry or economic sector that requires a large amount of machinery, equipment, etc., relative to the quantity of labor or land required. The energy industries— oil production and refining, coal mining, and electric power generation—require large amounts of capital equipment per unit of output. Historically, coal mining was a labor intensive industry requiring a large labor force to dig the product using hand tools. This is no longer the case, however, as modern strip-mining machinery can dig more coal per hour than fifty miners using hand tools could dig in a shift.

CAPITAL INVESTMENT money paid out for acquisition of a capital asset, or something for permanent use or value in a business or home, see 205 F. 2d 538, 542; also, monies paid out for an interest in a business as in the purchase of **stock.**

CAPITAL MARKET the organized buying and selling of long-term fixed-income securities such as **bonds** or **mortgages,** proceeds from the sale of which are used to finance CAPITAL EXPENDITURES [above]. In contrast to the capital market, the money market is used to raise short-term funds and the EQUITY MARKET (see **equity**) is used to obtain permanent capital through the sale of stock.

CAPITAL STOCK the amount of money or property contributed by **shareholders** to be used as the financial foundation from which the business of **incorporation** is to be carried on. See 74 Cal. Rptr. 920, 925. The **charter** of the corporation limits the total capital stock, which is divided into **shares,** to be offered to the public.

§1231 PROPERTY depreciable business property, business real property, and certain other types of property are §1231 property. These assets produce long term capital gain and ordinary loss. I.R.C. §1231.

CAPITAL GAINS OR LOSSES see **capital** [CAPITAL GAINS OR LOSSES].

CAPITAL INVESTMENT see **capital** [CAPITAL INVESTMENT].

CAPITALIZATION 1. for accounting purposes, the allocation of an item of expense to the capital account because of the relatively long life of the asset acquired by the expense. 2. "[A] method of computation which gives value to land in relation to the income it produces." 363 N.E. 2d 1018, 1021. 3. The total of long-term **capital,** such as long-term loans and notes, bonds, mortgages, and stock, used by a business to purchase assets.

CAPITALIZED VALUE the current worth of money expected to be earned or received in the future, calculated by discounting the amount to be received by an appropriate rate that takes into account the time value of money.

CAPITAL MARKET see **capital** [CAPITAL MARKET].

CAPITAL OFFENSE a criminal offense punishable by death. **Bail** is generally unavailable to **defendants charged** with a capital offense. Where the death penalty is no longer in force, offenses heretofore "capital" have been held to be bailable by most courts.

CAPITAL PUNISHMENT the penalty of death. The death penalty does not *per se* violate the U.S. Constitution's injunction against cruel and unusual punishment, at least when the offense involves homicide. 428 U.S. 153. States are prohibited by U.S. Supreme Court interpretations of this constitutional provision from enacting mandatory death penalty **statutes** for certain offenses. A death penalty statute may not preclude consideration of relevant mitigating factors; thus, the **sentencing** authority in a capital case must not be denied the consideration of any aspect of a **defendant**'s character or **record** and any of the circumstances of the offense that the defendant offers as a basis for a sentence less than death. 431 U.S. 633.

CAPITAL STOCK see **capital** [CAPITAL STOCK].

CAPITE see **in capite.**

CAPTION the heading of a legal document containing the names of the **parties,** the court, index or docket number of case, etc.

The term also refers to the seizing, asportation, or carrying away of an object, which is one element of common law **larceny.**

CARE attention, charge, or management implying responsibility for safety; also **custody,** temporary charge. 245 P. 2d 577, 581. In the law of **negligence,** the care owed by a **defendant** to those who may be injured by his or her actions is measured by the risks that those actions create. Occasionally, statutes fix the duty of care owed and an unexplained violation of that statutory standard renders the defendant negligent as a matter of law. 281 F. 2d. 626, 629. Generally, degrees of care set a relative standard by which conduct is tested to determine whether it constitutes negligence. See **due care; duty** [DUTY OF CARE]. See also **utmost care.**

GREAT CARE degree of care usually exercised in similar circumstances by the most competent, prudent, and careful class of persons engaged in similar conduct. Care greater than that usually bestowed by persons of ordinary prudence in similar circumstances. 28 S.W. 520, 522. For example, the great care expected of an airplane pilot is the care that would be exercised by the most competent, conscientious, prudent, and careful airplane pilot in similar circumstances.

ORDINARY CARE reasonable diligence and exercise of good judgment 140 So. 2d. 445. Care a reasonably careful person would use under similar circumstances. 255 N.E. 2d. 47, 49.

REASONABLE CARE degree of care which under the circumstances would usually be exercised by or might be reasonably expected from an ordinary, prudent person. 268 So. 2d. 290, 292. Often viewed as the only true measure of care. Reasonable care is synonymous with ordinary and due care. 134, So. 428, 429.

SLIGHT CARE such as persons of ordinary prudence usually exercise about their own affairs of slight importance. 116 P. 51, 54. Includes such care as careless or inattentive persons usually exercise. 114 S.E. 2d 289, 292.

CA. RESP. see **capias** [CAPIAS AD RESPONDENDUM].

CARNAL KNOWLEDGE sexual intercourse; the slightest penetration of the female sexual organ by the male sexual organ. 52 S.W. 2. At common law and under statute,

rape can be committed only where the unlawful carnal knowledge of a female is had without her consent. 89 A. 968. Carnal knowledge with a female under the **age of consent** constitutes STATUTORY RAPE.

CARRIER [COMMON CARRIER] one who is in the business of transporting goods or persons for hire, as a public utility. A private carrier, in contrast, is not in the business of transporting as public employment, but hires out to deliver goods in particular cases.

CARRYBACK a process by which the **deductions** or **credits** of one **taxable year** which cannot be used to reduce tax liability in that year are applied against tax liability in an earlier year or years. Carrybacks are available, for example, with respect to operating losses of businesses and investment tax **credits.** I.R.C. §§172(b) and 46(b). Compare **carryover.**

CARRYOVER a process by which the **deductions** and **credits** of one **taxable year** which cannot be used to reduce tax liability for that year are applied against tax liability in subsequent years. For example, carryovers are available with respect to net operating losses, charitable contributions, and investment tax credits. I.R.C. §§172(b), 170(d), and 46(b). Compare **carryback.** See also **basis** [CARRYOVER BASIS].

CARTEL a group of independent industrial **corporations,** usually on an international scale, which agree to restrict trade to their mutual benefit. Although prevalent outside the United States, such groups are generally found to violate federal **antitrust laws.** See **monopoly; oligopoly.**

CARVE OUT the process by which a **taxpayer** separates the present **income** stream of property from the property itself. For example, if an owner of mineral property sells for a certain number of years a portion of the future mineral production from such property, the sale of such future production is a "carved out" interest in the mineral property.

CA. SA. see **capias** [CAPIAS AD SATISFACIENDUM].

CASE an **action**, cause, **suit**, or controversy, **at law** or in **equity**, see 220 S.W. 2d 45, 51; also, abbreviation for **trespass** [ON THE CASE]. See also **test case**.

ACTION IN CASE see **trespass** [TRESPASS ON THE CASE].

PRIMA FACIE CASE see **prima facie case**.

CASE, ON THE see **trespass** [TRESPASS ON THE CASE].

CASE AT BAR see **bar; sub judice**.

CASE LAW see **common law**.

CASE OF FIRST IMPRESSION see **first impression**.

CASE OR CONTROVERSY see **controversy** [CASE OR CONTROVERSY].

CASH EQUIVALENT DOCTRINE see **income** [CASH EQUIVALENT DOCTRINE].

CASHIER'S CHECK see **check** [CASHIER'S CHECK].

CASH SALE if a contract for the sale of **goods** does not specify the manner of payment, the law requires that the purchase price be paid in cash. White & Summers, Uniform Commercial Code §3-6 (1980); U.C.C. §§2-310(a); 2-507(1); 2-507, Comment 2.

Under the "cash sale doctrine" a seller who sells to a middleman under "cash sale" terms has priority over other secured creditors to that middleman's assets if he or she goes bankrupt. 1 B.R. 255, 260.

CASH SURRENDER VALUE the amount the insurance company will pay on a given life insurance policy if the policy is canceled prior to the death of the insured.

CASH VALUE see **market value**.

CASUALTY LOSS a loss of property due to fire, storm, shipwreck, or other casualty, which is allowable as a **deduction** in computing **taxable income**. I.R.C. §165(c)(3). For a loss to qualify as a casualty loss it must be due to an event that is sudden, unexpected, or unusual. Thus, while damage to property due to a storm would normally qualify as a casualty loss, gradual erosion by wind, water, etc. would not.

CAUSA *(käw'-zà)*—Lat: lawsuit, case; grounds, cause, motive, purpose, reason; good reason; pretext, pretense; inducement, occasion.

CAUSA MORTIS *(käw'-zà mōr'-tĭs)*—Lat: in anticipation of approaching death. A gift causa mortis will be void if the donor survives the contemplated death.

CAUSA PROXIMA *(käw'-zà prŏk'-sĭ-mà)*—Lat: **proximate cause**, most closely related cause. It is used to indicate legal cause. That which is sufficiently related to the result as to justify imposing liability on the actor who produces the cause, or likewise, to relieve from liability the actor who produces a less closely related cause.

CAUSA SINE QUA NON *(käw'-zà sē'-nà kwä nŏn)*—Lat: a cause without which it would not have occurred; used most often in connection with the "but for" test of causation. See **cause**.

CAUSE that which effects a result. 169 F. 2d 203, 206. In law "cause" is not a constant and agreed-upon term. The following is a list of some of the attempts to conceptualize "that which effects a result":

DIRECT CAUSE the active, efficient cause that sets in motion a train of events that brings about a result without the intervention of any other independent source, see 6 N.E. 2d 879, 881; often used interchangeably with "proximate cause," 199 F. Supp. 951, 954. See also **probable cause.**

IMMEDIATE CAUSE the nearest cause in point of time and space; it is not necessarily the direct or proximate cause.

INTERVENING CAUSE [SUPERVEN-ING] "one which comes into active operation in producing the result after the negligence of the defendant. 'Intervening' is used in a time sense; it refers to later events. If the defendant sets a fire with a strong wind blowing at the time, which carries the fire to the plaintiff's property, the wind does not intervene, since it was already in operation; but if the fire is set first, and the wind springs up later, it is then an intervening cause." Prosser, Torts 271 (4th ed. 1971).

PROXIMATE CAUSE that which in natural and continuous sequence unbroken by any new independent cause produces an event, and without which the injury would not have occurred, see 323 P. 2d 108, 114. In criminal and tort law, one's **liability** is generally limited to results "proximately caused" by his conduct or omission.

REMOTE CAUSE that which does not necessarily produce an event without which injury would not occur. Thus, a cause which is not considered to be "proximate" will be regarded as "remote."

SUPERSEDING CAUSE an intervening cause which is so substantially responsible for the ultimate injury that it acts to cut off the liability of preceding actors regardless of whether their prior negligence was or was not a substantial factor in bringing about the injury complained of. Courts sometimes use "superseding" interchangeably with "interven-ing" in which case it does not have this meaning. Properly, the term "superseding" is limited to an intervening cause which "by its intervention prevents the actor from being liable for harm to another which his antecedent negligence is a substantial factor in bringing about." Restatement (second), Torts §440.

SUPERVENING CAUSE see INTER-VENING CAUSE, above.

CAUSE OF ACTION a claim in law and fact sufficient to demand judicial attention; the composite of facts necessary to give rise to the enforcement of a right. 254 A. 2d 824, 825. A RIGHT OF ACTION is the legal right to sue; a cause of action is the facts which give rise to a right of action. If the **complaint** fails to state a proper cause of action, it will be **dismissed.** See also **splitting a cause of action.**

CAUTIONARY INSTRUCTION that part of a judge's charge to a **jury** telling them not to allow any extraneous or outside matter to influence their **verdict.** Instruction by judge cautioning jury against regarding instructions as the opinion of the court on the facts. Instruction that the jury should not consider certain rulings of the court as an intimation of opinion. Instruction that after the **trial** the jury should advise no one as to what happened in the jury room. Instruction cautioning jury to consider **evidence** in a certain way.

"The giving of cautionary instructions is within the discretion of the court and is not improper if it does not prejudice either party, but there is authority holding that such instructions should not be given if unnecessary." 88 C.J.S. 809.

CAVEAT *(kä'-vē-ät)*—Lat: let him beware. In general, a warning or emphasis for caution; "an intimation given to some judge or officer notifying him that he ought to beware how he acts in some particular affair, and suspend the **pro-**

ceedings until the merits of the caveat are determined," 38 N.J. Eq. 485, 488; also, "an **in rem** proceeding attacking the validity of an **instrument** purporting to be a **will**," 118 S.E. 2d 17, 18; also, "a remedy given to prevent a **patent** from issuing in certain cases where the directions of the law have been violated." 5 U.S. 45, 101.

CAVEAT EMPTOR *(kä'-vē-ät ĕmp'-tôr)*—Lat: let the buyer beware. Expresses the rule of law that the purchaser buys at his own risk. 26 S.W. 148, 149. This harsh principle has been modified substantially by statutes and court decisions that have given consumers certain rights respecting the purchase of goods, e.g., **warranties** of fitness and merchantibility (except where the goods are bought expressly as is) and in landlord tenant law, e.g., the implied covenant of **habitability**. The maxim is still applicable to **sheriff's sales** and forced **sales**.

C.D. see **certificate of deposit [C.D.].**

CEASE AND DESIST ORDER an order of a court or other body having judicial authority prohibiting the person or entity to which it is directed from undertaking or continuing a particular activity or course of conduct. Such an order may be issued upon a showing, to a degree of certainty or probability, that the conduct is unlawful or likely to be found unlawful. 651 P. 2d. 802, 805. Distinguished from **mandatory injunction** in that a mandatory injunction commands the performance of some positive act, 187 F. Supp. 36, whereas a cease and desist order commands the prohibition of an act. See **injunction**.

CELL PARDE see **sentence** [CELL PAROLE].

CENSURE the official reprimand by a legislative or other formal body of one of its own members. Synonymous with **obloquy**. 11 P. 713, 716. A censure is more severe than a simple reprimand. Being under censure makes one the object of disgrace.

In **ecclesiastical law**, a spiritual punishment consisting in withdrawing from a baptized person, whether belonging to the clergy or the laity, a privilege which the church gives him, or in wholly expelling him from the christian community. 14 C.J.S. 100.

The House of Representatives has voted to censure or reprimand a member only twenty-six times in its history, and only eight times in the last fifty years. The most recent cases of censure involved two representatives in 1983 for sexual relations with congressional pages.

CENTER OF GRAVITY see **conflict of laws**.

CERT. see **certiorari**.

CERTIFICATE OF DEPOSIT [C.D.] "an acknowledgment by a bank of receipt of money with an engagement to repay it." U.C.C. §3-104(2)(c). The writing may or may not be a **negotiable instrument** depending on whether it meets the requirements for negotiability. See id. at §3-104(3).

CERTIFICATE OF INCORPORATION see **articles of incorporation**.

CERTIFICATE OF OCCUPANCY a document by a local government agency signifying that a building or dwelling conforms to local building code regulations. Generally, entry or transfer of title requires a valid certificate of occupancy.

The certificate of occupancy is complementary to a building permit. The BUILDING PERMIT in effect states that what the applicant proposes to do will be in conformity with the pertinent ordinance provisions; the certificate of occupancy certifies that what has actually been done meets municipal requirements and that the use stated in the certificate is a lawful use in the district in which the structure or land is located at the time of its issuance. Rathkopf, The Law of Zoning and Planning 55-20 (4th ed. 1975).

Occupancy of a building without a certificate of occupancy is illegal. 255 N.Y.S. 996.

CERTIFICATION see **certiorari.**

CERTIFIED CHECK see **check.**

CERTIORARI *(sèr-shē-ô-rä'-rē)*— Lat: to be informed of a means of gaining **appellate** review; a **common law writ,** issued from a superior court to one of inferior jurisdiction, commanding the latter to certify and return to the former the record in the particular case. 6 Cyc. 737. The writ is issued in order that the court issuing the writ may inspect the proceedings and determine whether there have been any irregularities. In the United States Supreme Court the writ is discretionary with the Court and will be issued to any court in the land to review a **federal question** if at least 4 of the 9 justices vote to hear the case. A similar writ used by some state courts is called CERTIFICATION.

CESTUI QUE *(sĕs'-tĭ kā,* or *sĕs'-twē kā;* plural: CESTUIS QUE) Old French: the one who; the person who.

CESTUI QUE TRUST (plural: TRUSTENT, *trŭst'-tĕnt)*—O.F.: the one who trusts; the beneficiary of a **trust.** 96 N.W. 860, 861.

CESTUI QUE USE (plural: USENT, *yū'-zĕnt)*—O.F.: the one who uses. The person for whose use the property is held by another. **Cestui que use** enjoys the beneficial rights to the profits and income of the estate, while the legal title and obligations remain in the **trustee.**

CESTUI QUE VIE *(vē)*—O.F.: the one who lives; the person by whose life the duration of an estate is measured.

C.F.I. see **C.I.F.**

CHAIN OF TITLE the successive **conveyances** of a certain property, "commencing with the patent from the government [or other original source], each being a perfect conveyance of the **title** down to and including the conveyance to the present holder." 46 S.W. 2d 329, 332.

The recorded chain of title consists only of the documents affecting title, recorded in a manner that makes the fact of their existence readily available to a **bona fide purchaser.** See Cribbet, Property 290 (2d ed. 1975). Of the two systems in general use for recording such documents, the TRACT INDEX is the one best-equipped to insure accessibility of title-affecting documents, since it records in the same place all **instruments** relating to a particular piece of property. Id. The GRANTOR-GRANTEE INDEXING systems, on the other hand, index all such instruments under the names of the various grantors or grantees of the property. See **abstract of record; clear title, title search; Recording Acts; warranty deed.**

CHALLENGE in general, to call one out to answer for something, 68 A. 210, 214; a request to fight a duel. In a legal sense an objection or exception calling into question the capability of a person for a particular function, the existence of a right, or the sufficiency or validity of an **instrument.** 14 C.J.S. 350.

An objection by a party or the party's lawyer to the inclusion of a particular prospective juror as a member of the jury that is to hear that party's cause or trial, with the result that the prospective juror is disqualified from the case. See **voir dire.**

CHALLENGE FOR CAUSE a request to a judge that a prospective juror not be allowed to serve on the jury for some specific cause or reason, e.g., he is not qualified under the provisions of a statute. 118 S.W. 612.

CHALLENGE TO JURY ARRAY a formal objection to the entire panel of grand jurors. 621 F. 2d. 951. The basis of such a challenge is that something has been done or omitted to the prejudice of the substantial rights of the challenging party. 337 F. Supp. 140.

GENERAL CHALLENGE a type of challenge for cause based on grounds from which, if shown to exist, the disqualification of the juror follows as a legal conclusion. 98 U.S. 145. Known as **challenge for principal cause** at common law.

PEREMPTORY CHALLENGE challenges which may be made without any specific reason or cause. 380 U.S. 202. The right to a peremptory challenge is not intended to enable a party to select particular jurors but to exclude from the jury persons whom he is unable successfully to challenge for cause. 403 F. 2d. 528. The number of peremptory challenges allowed is usually prescribed by statute or court rule. E.g., Fed. R. Crim. P. 24. If a specific reason exists why a particular juror may not fairly decide a matter, the juror may be challenged for cause. This conserves the peremptory challenges. These challenges are also available to the government.

CHAMPERTY at common law, an agreement between an attorney and his client that the attorney would sue and pay the costs of the client's suit in return for a portion of the damages awarded. The strict common law rule against champerty has been greatly relaxed in modern times, and survives only in a few jurisdictions and only in modified form. See **criminal maintenance;** compare **barratry.**

CHANCELLOR in early English law, the name of the King's minister who would dispense justice in the King's name by extraordinary equitable relief where the remedy at law was inadequate to do substantial justice. Later, the name given to the chief judge of the court of chancery. In American law it is the name used in some states to signify any judge sitting in a court of **chancery.**

CHANCERY that jurisprudence which is exercised in a **court of equity,** originally by the **chancellor;** synonymous with **equity** or equitable jurisdiction.

CHAPTER 11 see **bankruptcy** [CHAPTER 11 REORGANIZATION].

CHARACTER WITNESS see **witness.**

CHARGE in criminal law, the underlying substantive offense contained in an **accusation** or indictment. In trial practice, an address delivered by the **court** to the **jury** at the close of the **case,** instructing the jury as to what principles of law they are to apply in reaching a decision, 168 N.E. 2d 285, 287-8; the charge may also, in some jurisdictions, comprehend any instructions given for the jury's guidance at any time during the trial, 15 S.E. 758; the charge to the jury need not originate with the court, but may be, and often is, requested by the **parties.** 168 N.E. 2d 285, 287. In its broader signification, the term means simply to entrust, by way of responsibility, with duty, etc. Compare **complaint.**

CHARITABLE CONTRIBUTION a contribution for the use of a state, the United States, or a **corporation** organized and operated exclusively for religious, charitable, scientific, literary, educational, or like purposes. For individuals, most charitable contributions are deductible up to a limit of one-half the individual's adjusted gross **income.** To qualify, contributions must be made to qualified charitable organizations; additionally, if the contribution is to a private foundation, a lower percentage limitation on the deductions is applicable. Deductions above the ceiling may be carried over into later taxable years. (See **carryover.**) **Corporations** are limited to charitable deductions amounting to 5 percent of their taxable income (calculated with special adjustments) and also may carryover unused deductions to later taxable years. I.R.C. §170.

POLITICAL CONTRIBUTION donations to political candidates, parties, and newsletter funds. Fifty percent of the amount contributed is allowed as a tax credit, limited to fifty dollars per tax year. I.R.C. §41.

CHARITABLE DEDUCTION see **charitable contribution.**

CHARITY a gift or an activity which benefits an indefinite number of persons by the promotion of religion, education, or relief from disease, by assisting people to establish themselves in life, or by erecting or maintaining public works. 221 A. 2d 280, 287. The essence of charity is that it is for the public at large, rather than for specific individuals. For income tax purposes, a nonprofit institution organized and operated exclusively for charitable, religious, scientific, literary, educational or like purposes, whose income is exempt from federal income tax. I.R.C. §501(c)(3). Contributions to such organizations are allowable, with limitations, as a deduction in computing one's taxable **income.** I.R.C. §170. The word charity is given a narrower meaning in tax exemption cases. 146 S.E. 2d 903, 905.

PRIVATE FOUNDATIONS all charities which do not receive a major portion of their support from the public. I.R.C. §509. Unlike a public charity, a private foundation is subject to additional restrictions with respect to the activities in which the organization may engage, and with respect to its financial dealings, including accumulation of income. I.R.C. §4940 et seq. These restrictions are designed to prevent abuses arising from a single individual or a small group of individuals controlling the assets of a private foundation.

PUBLIC CHARITY for income tax purposes, any charity which, under certain specified tests, is deemed to receive the major portion of its support from the public rather than from a small group of individuals. Income tax deductions for contributions to public charities are allowed in larger amounts than deductions for contributions to private foundations. I.R.C. §170(b).

CHARTER a document issued by the government [sovereign] establishing a corporate entity. See **certificate of incorporation.**

In earlier law, the term referred to a grant from the sovereign guaranteeing to the person or persons therein named certain rights, privileges, and powers. Thus, the earlier American colonies were recognized by charters granted by the King of England.

The Magna Charta or the GREAT CHARTER, granted by King John to the barons of England in 1215, established the basis for English constitutional government. See **Magna Carta** [MAGNA CHARTA].

CHATTEL any tangible, movable thing; personal, as opposed to real, property, 170 S.E. 660, 662; goods. See **personal property** [PERSONALTY].

PERSONAL CHATTEL movable things; personalty which has no connection to real property. The Uniform Commercial Code uses the term **goods** to refer to "all things . . . which are movable" and specifically includes the unborn young of animals and growing crops. UCC §2-105.

REAL CHATTEL an interest in real estate less than a freehold or fee; leasehold estates. See **fixture.**

CHATTEL MORTGAGE a conveyance of some present legal or **equitable** right in **personal property**, as security for the payment of money, or for the performance of some other act. 271 N.Y.S. 2d 312. Most commonly used in buying high-priced consumer goods on credit, such as automobiles and large appliances. Like a real **mortgage,** a chattel mortgage can be viewed either as a transfer of **title** from borrower to lender or as a **lien** on the goods, and it terminates when the debt, plus interest, has been paid in full.

Since the adoption in many jurisdictions of the **Uniform Commercial Code,** the law relating to transactions intended to create a security interest in personal property is now generally controlled by Article 9 of the U.C.C.

CHATTEL PAPER "a writing or writings which evidence both a monetary obligation and a **security interest** in or a **lease** of specific goods." U.C.C. §9-105(1)(b). Chattel paper and other non-negotiable instruments creating a security interest are subject to special rules as to priority over other security interests in the same collateral. See id. at §9-308.

CHECK a "**draft** drawn upon a bank and payable on **demand,** signed by the **maker** or **drawer,** containing an unconditional promise to pay a **sum certain** in money to the order of the **payee,**" 503 P 2d 1063, 1066. See U.C.C. 3-104(2)(b).

BAD CHECK see **bad check.**

CASHIER'S CHECK one "issued by the authorized officer of a bank directed to another person, evidencing the fact that the **payee** is authorized to demand and receive upon presentation from the bank the amount of money represented by the check." 277 S.W. 625, 627. The cashier's check is drawn upon the bank's own account and not that of a private person and as such has a higher guarantee that it will be honored and is accepted for many transactions where a personal check would not be.

CERTIFIED CHECK check containing a "certification that the drawer of the check has sufficient funds to cover payment of the check." 286 N.E. 2d 80, 82. It indicates that the bank will retain a sufficient amount of the drawer's funds to cover the payment of the check on demand; it makes the bank liable to a **bona fide** holder of the check for value. See U.C.C. §3-411; 85 P. 81, 82.

MEMORANDUM CHECK it "is in the ordinary form of a bank check, with the word 'memorandum' written across its face, and is not intended for immediate presentation, but simply as evidence of an indebtedness by the **drawer** to the **holder.**" 84 U.S. 496, 502.

NSF [NON-SUFFICIENT FUNDS] CHECK see **NSF [non-sufficient funds] check.**

RAISED CHECK see **raised check.**

CHECK KITING an illegal scheme whereby a false line of credit is established by the exchanging of worthless checks between two banks. For instance, a "check kiter" might have empty checking accounts at two different banks, A and B. The kiter writes a check for $50,000 on the Bank A account and deposits it in the Bank B account. If the kiter has good credit at Bank B, he will be able to draw funds against the deposited check before it clears, i.e., is forwarded to Bank A for payment and paid by Bank A. Since the clearing process usually takes a few days, the kiter can use the $50,000 for a few days, and then deposit it in the Bank A account before the $50,000 check drawn on that account clears. See **bad check.**

CHIEF JUSTICE the presiding member of certain courts which have more than one judge; especially, the presiding member of the Supreme Court of the United States, who is a member of the United States Supreme Court. Presiding judges of inferior federal courts are called CHIEF JUDGES. Some, but not all, states call the presiding judge of their highest court the chief justice. All other judges, who sit on the same court but do not preside, are called ASSOCIATE JUSTICES.

The Chief Justice of the United States is the principal administrative officer of the federal judiciary. The statutory duties and powers of this office are extensive, ranging from summoning the annual judicial conference and reporting thereon to Congress to making temporary reassignments of circuit court judges and establishing the regulations of the library of the Supreme Court. The internal rules by which the Court organizes itself provide special influence for the Chief Justice who, for example, will usually assign the justice who will write the Court's majority opinion.

CHILD AND DEPENDENT CARE CREDIT a **tax credit** allowed for 20 percent of the child care and household services expenses incurred to allow a taxpayer to be employed where a taxpayer maintains a household which includes one or more dependents under fifteen years of age or certain other individuals who are mentally or physically incapacitated. I.R.C. §44A.

CHILD CUSTODY see **custody of children.**

CHILD SUPPORT see **alimony** [CHILD SUPPORT].

CHILL [CHILLING EFFECTS] the relinquishment of legitimate First Amendment rights by individuals fearful of the possible or threatened application of laws or sanctions and subsequent prosecutions, whether or not successful, indirectly resulting from the exercise of those legitimate rights.

In recognition of the chilling effect of statutes that may be constitutionally **overbroad,** a facial attack on such statutes is permitted by any person properly before the court even if he lacks personal **standing** to assert the facial invalidity of the statute because his own conduct falls squarely within some valid application of the statute. See 380 U.S. 479; 415 U.S. 452.

CHOATE *(kō'-āt)* completed or perfected; a right in regard to which no additional events need occur for it to be operative. Compare **inchoate.**

CHOSE *(shōz)*—Fr: thing; A thing, either presently possessed [chose in possession] or claimed [chose in action].

CHOSE IN ACTION a **claim** or **debt** upon which a recovery may be made in a **lawsuit.** It is not a present possession, but merely a right to sue; it becomes a "possessory thing" only upon successful completion of a lawsuit.

CHOSE IN POSSESSION as opposed to **chose in action,** a thing actually possessed or possessable. 372 P. 2d 470, 476.

CHURNING excessive trading in a stock investment account in order to generate commissions for a broker with relatively little concern for the welfare of his customer. 310 N.Y.S. 2d 266, 268. The practice is unethical and recovery of damages by the customer is possible.

C.I.F. cost, insurance, and freight, see 264 F. 2d 405, 408; also written c.f.i. See 182 N.Y.S. 30, 33. In a **contract** of sale it means that the cost of the goods, insurance thereon, and freight to the destination is included in the contract price, and "[u]nless there is something in a c.i.f. contract to indicate to the contrary, the seller completes his contract when he delivers the merchandise called for to the shipper, pays the freight thereon to point of destination, and forwards to the buyer **bill of lading,** invoice, insurance policy and receipt showing payment of freight." 135 N.E. 329, 330.

CIRCUIT judicial divisions of a state or the United States; originally so called because judges traveled from place to place within the circuit, holding court in various locations. There are now thirteen federal judicial circuits wherein the United States Courts of Appeal are allocated the appellate jurisdiction of the United States. 28 U.S.C. §41.

CIRCUIT COURT one of several courts in a given jurisdiction; a part of a system of courts extending over one or more counties or districts; formerly applied to United States Courts of Appeal. See **federal courts.** Compare **district court.**

There are thirteen Circuit Courts of Appeal in the federal court system. 28 U.S.C. §41.

CIRCUMSTANTIAL EVIDENCE indirect evidence; secondary facts by which a principal fact may be rationally inferred.

CITATION a reference to a source of legal authority, e.g., a citation to a statute or case. It is analogous to a **summons** at law, in that it commands the appearance of a party in a proceeding; "a writ issued out of a court of competent **jurisdiction,** commanding the person named therein to appear on the day named, and do something therein mentioned, or show cause why he should not." 56 P. 725, 726. Compare **subpoena.**

CITIZEN as a member of a nation or political community, one who owes allegiance to, and may claim protection from its government. 153 N.E. 13, 17. Under the Constitution, all persons born or naturalized in the United States, and subject to the jurisdiction thereof, are citizens of the United States and of the State wherein they reside. United States Constitution, Fourteenth Amendment.

Citizenship is the status of being a citizen. In the United States there is usually a double citizenship, that is, citizenship in the nation and citizenship in the state in which one resides.

Generally in the United States one may acquire citizenship by birth in the United States or by naturalization therein. 59 S.Ct. 884. A child of alien parents born in the United States is a citizen of the United States. 75 F. Supp. 268. A foreign-born child of citizens of the United States, subject to certain qualifications and limitations, is a citizen of the United States. 42 F. Supp. 13. A child born in the United States of a diplomatic representative such as an ambassador or minister, takes the nationality of such representative. 47 F. Supp. 952. The adoption of an alien child by a citizen of the United States does not render the child a citizen thereof. 14 C.J.S. 1137. The term citizen may include or apply to Indians. 279 P. 2d 349, 352.

For purposes of **diversity jurisdiction:** a municipality may be considered a citizen, 532 F. 2d 491, 495; a corporation is deemed a citizen of the state in which it maintains its principal place of business, 386 F. Supp. 430, 433; counties are citizens, 366 F. Supp. 1299, 1301; the United States is not a citizen, 441 F. Supp. 715 and states are not citizens, 688 F. 2d 1147, 1150.

CITIZEN, NATURALIZED see **naturalized citizen.**

CIVIL that branch of law that pertains to suits outside of criminal practice, pertaining to the rights and duties of persons in **contract, tort,** etc.; also refers to **civil law** as opposed to **common law.**

CIVIL ACTION action maintained to protect a private, **civil** right, or to compel a civil remedy, as distinguished from a criminal **prosecution.**

CIVIL AERONAUTICS BOARD an independent federal agency established by Congress in 1938 to foster and regulate commercial aviation, and to provide public air safety and navigation facilities. Meteorological services, the establishment of airways, the publication of aviation charts, registration of aircraft, the investigation of aviation accidents, and the development and maintenance of navigation facilities were originally entrusted to this Board. 52 Stat. 973-1030. In 1958, Congress transferred all these functions except the economic regulation of air carriers, the registration of aircraft and licensing of pilots, and accident investigation, to the newly established Federal Aviation Agency. P.L. 85-726, 72 Stat. 731-811. When the F.A.A. was expanded into the Federal Aviation Administration, under the new Department of Transportation, some CAB functions were transferred to the Secretary of Transportation, which in turn delegated certain safety-related responsibilities to the National Transportation Safety Board. 49 U.S.C. §1655(d) and §1657(g). In the Airline Deregulation Act of 1978 Congress provided that the Board be phased out of existence by January 1, 1985, with its rate and route regulatory functions greatly reduced and transferred to the Department of Justice, the Department of Transportation and the U.S. Postal Service. 92 Stat. 1744-47, 49 U.S.C. §1601.

CIVIL CONTEMPT see **contempt of court.**

CIVIL DAMAGE ACTS see **dram shop act.**

CIVIL DEATH at common law, civil death was the status given to a person who, though alive, had been convicted of a **felony** and sentenced to life imprisonment. It referred to the fact that the convict had lost all his **civil rights** and was thus thought to be dead as regards his participation in society. He could not, for example, sue or inherit since in contemplation of law he did not exist. In fact, a **next friend** was often designated to represent the interests of a civilly dead person. Perkins & Boyce, Criminal Law 27 n. 35 (3d. ed. 1982). Some states still apply civil death to persons serving life sentences. However, there is no general agreement as to the scope of the civil rights lost. Most states deny specific rights to convicted felons such as the right to vote or to hold public office. See 23 Vand. L. Rev. 929.

CIVIL DISOBEDIENCE the refusal to obey a law for the purpose of demonstrating its unfairness or social undesirability; generally does not apply to violent efforts to oppose laws. 361 F. Supp. 427, 430.

CIVIL DISORDER any public disturbance involving acts of violence by a group of three or more persons causing immediate danger, damage, or injury to the property or person of another individual. 18 U.S.C. §232.

CIVIL LAW Roman law embodied in the Justinian Code (Codex Justinianeus) and presently prevailing in most Western European States. It is also the foundation of the law of Louisiana. The term may also be used to distinguish that part of the law concerned with noncriminal matters, or may refer to the body of laws prescribed by the supreme authority of the state, as opposed to **natural law.** See 244 P. 323, 325.

CIVIL LIABILITY amenability to **civil action,** as opposed to criminal action, 50 A. 2d 39, 43; liability to actions seeking private remedies or the enforcement of personal rights, based on contract, tort, etc.

CIVIL LIBERTIES see **civil rights.**

CIVIL PENALTIES generally, fines or money **damages** imposed by a regulatory scheme. See, e.g., 15 U.S.C.A. §45(1). Civil penalties, however, have been distinguished from civil **remedies** in that civil penalties are imposed as a punishment for certain activity and have the character of a **criminal** sanction, while civil remedies seek to redress wrongs or compensate for injuries suffered.

CIVIL PROCEDURE see **procedure** [CIVIL PROCEDURE].

CIVIL RIGHTS rights given, defined, and circumscribed by **positive laws** enacted by civilized communities. 252 N.E. 2d 463, 474. Civil rights differ, in theory at least, from CIVIL LIBERTIES in that civil rights are positive in nature, and civil liberties are negative in nature; that is, civil liberties are immunities from governmental interference or limitations on governmental action (such as those embodied in the First Amendment) which have the effect of reserving rights to individuals.

CIVITAS *(sĭ'-vĭ-täs)*—Lat: in the Roman Law, any body of people living under the same laws; citizenship, state, commonwealth, community.

CIVIL RIGHTS ACT OF 1964 federal act passed to amend statutes passed after the Civil War to provide stronger protection for rights guaranteed by the Constitution. The Act affected voting rights, 42 U.S.C. §§1971 et seq., the Civil Rights commission, 42 U.S.C. §§1975 et seq., and discrimination in public accommodations, 42 U.S.C. §§2000a et seq. The Act was passed during the Johnson presidency as part of his program to upgrade the status of minorities.

C.J. abbreviation for **Chief Justice** or Chief Judge.

CLAIM the assertion of a right to money or **property;** the aggregate of operative facts giving rise to a right enforceable in the courts, 309 F. Supp. 1178, 1181. A claim must show the existence of a right, an injury, and a **prayer** for **damages.** See 149 F. Supp. 615, 618. One who makes a claim is the CLAIMANT. See **counterclaim; crossclaim.**

CLAIMANT the **party** who asserts a right to money or property. See **claim.**

CLAIM FOR REFUND the procedure by which a **taxpayer** informs the **Internal Revenue Service** in writing of his view that he is entitled to a refund of all or part of the **taxes** paid by him in earlier years. A claim is subject to **statutes of limitation,** and the filing of a timely claim is a necessary prerequisite to any allowance of a refund by the Service or of any suit by the taxpayer against the Service for the disallowance of the claimed refund.

CLAIM OF RIGHT in property law, "that claimant is in **possession** as owner with intent to claim the land as his own and not in recognition of or subordination to the record title owner." 624 P. 2d 747, 748. In tax law, a doctrine which requires a **taxpayer** to include in his **gross income** all amounts which are received by him under any claim by him that he is entitled to the amounts, whether or not the taxpayer is in fact legally entitled to keep the amounts and whether or not he is required to repay the amounts in a subsequent year. 345 U.S. 278. for instance, when a taxpayer receives salary in one year, and he is sued for repayment of the salary in a later year, he must still include the salary in income in the year he received it. When a repayment occurs, a **deduction** is allowed for the year of repayment. I.R.C. §1341.

CLASS ACTION a **lawsuit** brought by a representative member(s) of a large group of persons on behalf of all the members of the group. See Fed. R. Civ. Pr. 23. The trial court must specifically certify a lawsuit as a class action. To receive that certification the class must be ascertainable, the members must share a common interest in the issues of law and fact raised by the plaintiff(s), and the action must satisfy a variety of other special requirements applicable to class actions. If so certified, all members of the class must receive **notice** of the pendency of the action and an opportunity to exclude themselves from the class if they so desire. Members not so excluding themselves are bound by the **judgment.** Subclasses may be formed to reach an identifiable and manageable class size for purposes of litigation. See 417 U.S. 156.

CLASS GIFT "a gift of an aggregate sum to a body of persons uncertain in number at the time of the gift, to be ascertained at a future time, who are all to take in equal, or other definite proportions, the share of each being dependent for its amount upon the ultimate number. . . ." 331 A. 2d. 408, 410.

CLASSIFIED STOCK common stock divided into two or more classes. A typical approach is for a company to issue Class A **stock** to raise the bulk of **equity** capital while vesting voting rights in Class B stock, which is retained by management and/or founders. The practice is usually confined to promotional ventures, and very few publicly held companies have classified stock as part of their **capitalization.**

CLAUSE see respective entries, e.g. **escalator clause.**

CLAYTON ACT a federal statute amending the **Sherman Antitrust Act.** 15 U.S.C. §§12-27. The Act prohibits certain types of price and other discriminations, now covered by the **Robinson-Patman Act;** tying, exclusive dealing, and total requirements agreements 15 U.S.C. §§13, 13a; mergers or acquisitions tending substantially to lessen competition in any line of commerce, 15 U.S.C. §§18a, and interlocking directorates, 15 U.S.C. §19. See Henn & Alexander, Law of Corporations §312 (3d ed. 1983). See **antitrust laws.**

CLEAN HANDS [DOCTRINE] the concept in **equity** that **claimants** who seek **equitable relief** must not themselves have indulged in any impropriety in relation to the transaction upon which relief is sought; freedom from participation in unfair conduct. A party with "unclean hands" cannot ask a court of conscience [the equity court] to come to his aid. See also **unclean hands.**

CLEAR see **free and clear.**

CLEAR AND CONVINCING as a standard of proof, it is that quantum of evidence beyond a mere **preponderance,** but below that of "beyond a **reasonable doubt,**" 464 F. 2d 471, 474; and such that it will produce in the mind of the **trier of fact** a firm belief as to the facts sought to be established. 220 N.E. 2d 547, 574. It "indicates a degree of proof required in [some] civil cases [e.g., **reformation** of a contract] . . . less than the degree required in criminal cases but more than required in the ordinary civil action." 110 N.E. 493. In the ordinary civil cases the degree of proof is characterized as a preponderance; in the exceptional civil case (e.g., a contract to pay for services between persons in a family relation), it should be clear and convincing. See 110 N.E. 493.

CLEAR AND PRESENT DANGER in constitutional law, a standard used to determine if one's First Amendment right to speak may be curtailed or punished. "[T]he character of every act depends upon the circumstances in which it is done. . . . The most stringent protection of free speech would not protect a man in falsely shouting fire in a theatre and causing a panic. It does not even protect a man from an injunction against uttering words that may have all the effect of force [fighting words]. The question in every case is whether the words used, are used in such circumstances and are of such a nature as to create a clear and present danger that they will bring about the substantive evils that [the government] has a right to prevent." 249 U.S. 47, 52.

CLEARINGHOUSE an association, usually formed voluntarily by banks, to exchange checks, drafts, or other forms of indebtedness held by one member and owed to another. 399 N.E. 2d 930, 932. The object of such an association is to effect at one time and place the daily settlement of balances between the banks of a city or region with a minimum of inconvenience and labor.

In a stock or commodities exchange, the term signifies an organization to facilitate the settlement of debits and credits of its members with each other. In essence, it operates on the same principles of centrality and convenience as does the clearinghouse association for banks. For example, if broker A is obligated to deliver 5000 shares of XYZ stock and is entitled to receive 4500 such shares from B, C, and D brokers, he would deliver at the end of the day to the clearinghouse only 500 shares.

CLEAR TITLE title free from any encumbrance, obstruction, burden or limitation that presents a doubtful or even a reasonable question of law or fact. See 29 N.E. 2d 41, 43. See **good title; marketable title.** See also **title** [CLEAR TITLE OF RECORD].

CLEMENCY the act of forgiving a person the criminal liability of his acts. 192 S.W. 2d 280, 282. The term is generic and embraces **pardon, amnesty,** and **commutation.** The power of clemency is usually vested in the chief executive. For instance, the President is vested with the federal pardoning power

by the United States Constitution, Art. II, Sec. 2(1). See generally, Rubin, The Law of Criminal Correction 651 et seq (2d ed. 1973). See **executive clemency.**

CLERGYMEN'S PRIVILEGE see **priest-penitent privilege.**

CLERICAL ERROR immediately correctable mistake resulting from the copying or transmission of legal documents. As opposed to a **judicial error,** a clerical error is not made in the exercise of judgment or discretion, but is made by a mechanical or other inadvertence. A clerical error is known by the character of the error, and is not dependent on who makes the error, be it clerk or judge.

CLERK an assistant or a subordinate. A **court clerk** is an officer whose duty is to keep records, issue process, enter judgment and the like. A **law clerk** is an assistant to a lawyer or a judge. The primary job of a law clerk is to aid in the research and writing of briefs or opinions and the handling of cases.

CLOSE an ancient term referring to an enclosure, whether surrounded by a visible or an invisible boundary; land rightfully owned by a party, the **trespass** upon which is **actionable** at law. See 4 Ill. 258, 259. See **breaking a close.**

CLOSE CORPORATION see **corporation** [CLOSE CORPORATION].

CLOSED END FUNDS see **investment company** [TRUST].

CLOSED-END MANAGEMENT COMPANY a management **investment company** that issues a fixed number of **shares.** The shares are redeemable through secondary market transactions rather than directly from the investment management company as in an open-end management investment company [**mutual fund**]. The shares of a closed-end management company are generally listed for trading on a **stock exchange.**

CLOSED-END MORTGAGE see **mortgage** [CLOSED-END MORTGAGE].

CLOSED SHOP an enterprise subject to a collective bargaining agreement between a labor union and the owners/managers of the enterprise that requires all workers to be union members as a condition of their employment. 611 F. 2d 684, 692. "The closed shop—which might provide, 'The employer hereby agrees to employ only members in good standing of the Union'— gives greatest power to the union, because it permits the union to determine the eligibility of job applicants (as well as retention of a job already had) by controlling admission to union membership and by expelling from membership persons who fail to comply with internal rules and regulations." Gorman, Labor Law, 640-642 (1979).

Even though the closed shop was disallowed by the Taft-Hartley Act of 1947 and was further declared illegal under numerous state laws, it still exists in effect for musicians, longshoremen, and crafts workers in the building trades, among others. Compare **open shop; union shop.**

CLOSING as pertaining to the sale of real estate, the consummation of a transaction involving the sale of real estate or of an interest in real estate, usually by payment of the purchase price (or some agreed portion), delivery of the **deed** or other **instrument of title,** and finalizing of collateral matters. Additional documents exchanged at closing may include the **mortgage,** mortgage note, survey of the property, **leases, insurance** policies, **assignments,** and receipts for taxes, special assessments, and utilities. 136 A. 140, 143.

CLOSING AGREEMENT a written agreement between a **taxpayer** and the **Internal Revenue Service** which conclusively settles the tax liability of the taxpayer for a **taxable year** ending prior to the date of the agreement or settles one or more issues affecting the taxpayer's tax liability. Such an agreement is a determination conclusive on both the taxpayer and the Internal Revenue Service unless fraud or misrepresentation as to a material fact is demonstrated. I.R.C. §7122.

CLOSING LAWS see **Sunday closing laws.**

CLOSING STATEMENT see **statement** [CLOSING STATEMENT].

CLOTURE in legislative assemblies that permit unlimited debate (**FILIBUSTER**), a procedure or rule by which debate is ended so that a vote may be taken on the matter. In the United States Senate, a two-thirds majority vote of the body is required to invoke cloture and terminate debate.

CLOUD ON TITLE any matter appearing in the record of a **title** to real estate that on its face appears to reflect the existence of an outstanding claim or **encumbrance** that, if valid, would defeat or impair title, but that might be proven invalid by evidence outside the title record. 429 S.W. 2d 531, 534. Clouds on title may be removed by a court of **equity** by means of an action to **quiet title.** A valid cloud on title reflects a real obstacle to the free **enjoyment** of one's land. One test is if the person claiming under the alleged cloud should bring an action against the true owner, would the owner be required to offer evidence to defeat the action. If so, the cloud exists. 51 So. 348, 350.

CO-CONSPIRATOR EXCEPTION see **hearsay rule.**

CODE a systematic compilation of laws. The criminal code refers to the penal laws of the jurisdiction, the motor vehicle code to the laws relating to automobiles, etc. Today most jurisdictions have codified a substantial part of their laws. See **penal law** [CODE].

All jurisdictions record each new law in a volume of session laws or Statutes at Large; e.g., Public Law No. 91-112 (i.e., the 112th law passed by the 91st Congress of the United States, etc.). If the laws are not codified they will appear only in these volumes.

CO-DEFENDANT a **defendant** who has been joined together with one or more other defendants in a single **action**. See **joinder.**

CODE OF MILITARY JUSTICE see **military law** [CODE OF MILITARY JUSTICE].

CODE OF PROFESSIONAL RESPONSIBILITY "an inspirational guide to the members of the (legal) profession and . . . a basis for disciplinary action when the conduct of a lawyer falls below the required minimum standards stated in the Disciplinary Rules" Preliminary Statement to the Code.

On August 14, 1964, the House of Delegates of the American Bar Association created a Special Committee on Evaluation of Ethical Standards to examine the then current Canons of Professional Ethics and to make recommendations for changes. That committee produced the Model Code of Professional Responsibility which was adopted by the House of Delegates in 1969 and became effective January 1, 1970. The new Model Code revised the previous Canons in four principal particulars: (1) there were important areas involving the conduct of lawyers not effectively covered in the Canons; (2) editorial revision of some of the Canons; (3) most of the Canons did not lend themselves to sanctions for violation; and (4) changed and changing conditions in our legal system and urbanized society required new statements of professional principles. Preface to the Code.

The Code has been replaced with the **Model Rules of Professional Conduct** which was adopted by the A.B.A. on August 2, 1983. The various states will consider whether to adopt, reject or amend the new rules.

CODE PLEADING "the term applied to the system of **pleading** developed in this country through practice codes enacted in the majority of the states, beginning with the New York Code of 1848, as a consolidation and improvement of the **common law** and **equity** systems of pleading previously in vogue. Since the union of law and equity procedures is basic in present-day procedural reform, it has now become appropriate to regard modern English and American pleading as advanced systems of code pleading." Clark, Code Pleading 1-26 (2d ed. 1947).

CODICIL a supplement to a **will;** "an instrument of a **testamentary** nature, the purpose of which is to change or alter an already executed will by adding to and enlarging, subtracting from and restricting, or qualifying, modifying, or revoking the provisions of a prior existing will." 176 P. 2d 281, 288. Compare **testamentary disposition.**

COERCION any form of compulsion or constraint which compels or induces a person to act otherwise than freely; it may be physical force but is more often used to describe any pressure which is brought to bear on another's free will. In testamentary law, if undue influence is exerted upon the **testator,** the coercion will vitiate the effect of the instrument. In criminal law, improper conduct which coerces the defendant interfering with his ability to decide whether or not to incriminate himself will void the **confession.** 385 U.S. 493. See also **criminal coercion; duress.**

COGENT appealing forcibly to the mind or reason; compelling; convincing. The word is frequently used to describe the quality of a particular legal argument. It is derived from the Latin "cogo," "cogere," which means "to bind, drive or compress into a mass." See Oxford Latin Dictionary, Fascicle 11, p. 347. "A forcible argument tells strongly, but may not convince; cogent reasoning is more apt to be conclusive or to compel assent." 22 N.W. 2d 218, 219.

COGNIZABLE within the **jurisdiction** of the court. An interest is cognizable in a court of law when that court has power to **adjudicate** the interest in controversy. See 113 F. 2d 703, 707. See **jurisdiction.**

COGNOVIT JUDGMENT see **confession of judgment.**

COGNOVIT NOTE a **promissory note** in which the debtor authorizes an attorney to enter a confession of judgment against him in the event of non-payment. 289 F. Supp. 930, 935.

COHABITATION literally, the act of living together; often statutorily expanded to include living together publicly, as husband and wife. Cohabitation among unmarried persons of the opposite sex is often proscribed by local laws. Such cohabitation will produce an **inference** of criminal **fornication.**

CO-HEIR one who inherits the same property together with another. The co-heirs will be deemed **joint-tenants** or tenants in common according to the language employed in the **conveyance** and the controlling law of the jurisdiction, the latter being the preferred designation in most jurisdictions. Moynihan, Introduction to the Law of Real Property, 216-17 (1962). The term "co-heir" grew out of the concept of **coparceners.**

COIF headdress formerly worn by English sergeants at law. "Order of the Coif" is an honorary legal fraternity in the United States.

COINSURANCE a scheme of **insurance** wherein the **insurer** provides **indemnity** for only a certain percentage of the insured's loss. The scheme reflects "a relative division of the risk between the insurer and the **insured,** dependent upon the relative amount of the policy and the actual value of the property insured thereby." 160 N.Y.S. 566, 569. A typical coinsurance clause, commonly called the New York Standard Coinsurance Clause, is as follows: "This company shall not be liable for a greater proportion of any loss or damage to the property described herein than the sum hereby insured bears to the percentage specified on the first page of the policy of the actual cash value of said property at the time such loss shall happen, nor for more than the portion which this policy bears to the total insurance thereon." See Keeton, Insurance Law §3.7(b) (1971).

COLLATERAL secondary; not of the essence of the principal thing; on the side, divergent or auxiliary. See 57 S.W. 2d 222, 223. In commercial transactions, "collateral means the property subject to a **security interest,** and includes accounts, contract rights, and **chattel paper** which have been sold." U.C.C. §9-105(c). To obtain credit it is sometimes necessary to offer some collateral, i.e., to place within the legal control of the lender some property which may be sold in the event of a default and applied to the amount owing.

In contracts, a COLLATERAL PROMISE is one ancillary to an integrated contractual relationship; its enforcement is not precluded by the **parol evidence rule.** The term may also refer to a promise ancillary to a principal transaction; its **breach** does not entitle the other party to rescind [see **rescission**]. Such promises are generally used to guarantee payment of a debt by the third-party promisor.

IMPAIRMENT OF COLLATERAL lessening of the effect of the collateral; an act whose effect is to reduce the value of the collateral as security for the obligation it is intended to assure.

COLLATERAL ATTACK a challenge to the integrity of a prior **judgment**, brought in a special **proceeding** intended for that express purpose. A **direct attack**, on the other hand, is an attempt to impeach a judgment within the same **action** in which the judgment was rendered, through an appeal, request for a new trial, etc. Lack of proper jurisdiction and constitutional infirmities in the original judgment are often grounds for collateral attack. See 145 P. 2d 402, 405. **Habeas corpus** is a "collateral attack" remedy.

COLLATERAL ESTOPPEL the doctrine recognizing that the determination of facts **litigated** between two **parties** in a **proceeding** is binding on those parties in all future proceedings against each other; also known as issue preclusion. "In a subsequent **action** between the parties on a different **claim,** the judgment is conclusive as to the **issues** raised in the subsequent action, if these issues were actually litigated and determined in the prior action." Restatement, Judgments §45. The constitutional prohibition against **double jeopardy** includes within it the right of the **defendant** (but not the state) to **plead** "collateral estoppel" and thereby preclude proof of some essential element of the state's case found in the defendant's favor at an earlier trial. 397 U.S. 436. Thus, if D is charged with robbing six persons at a poker game and his defense in the first trial involving the alleged robbery of only one of the victims is that he wasn't there **[alibi],** and if he is **acquitted** at that trial, the state will be **estopped** to relitigate the alibi

question with respect to the other related robberies. See id. See **estoppel.** See also **bar; merger; res judicata.**

COLLATERAL FRAUD see **fraud** [EXTRINSIC [COLLATERAL] FRAUD].

COLLATION "the bringing into the **estate** of an **intestate** [person who dies without a **will**] an estimate of the value of advancements made by the intestate to his or her children, in order that the whole may be divided in accordance with the **Statute of Descents.**" 267 N.W. 743, 744.

COLLECTIVE BARGAINING in labor law, the negotiation of employment matters between employers and employees through the use of a bargaining agent designated by an uncoerced majority of the employees within the bargaining unit. Jenkins, Labor Law §9.114 (1969). It is an **unfair labor practice** for employers to interfere with their employees' right to bargain collectively. 29 U.S.C. §158(a)(5).

Employers have an obligation to bargain with their employees in good faith, that is to meet with the representative at reasonable hours and negotiate about working conditions, hours and wages. Jenkins, Labor Law §9.1 et seq. (1969). See **arbitration, bargaining unit.**

COLLOQUIUM allegation in a **declaration** or **complaint** of **libel** under **common law pleadings,** which purport to connect the libelous words with the **plaintiff** by setting forth extrinsic facts showing that they applied to him and were so intended by defendant. See 69 N.E. 288, 289.

COLLUSION the making of an agreement with another for the purposes of perpetrating a **fraud,** or engaging in illegal activity, or in legal activity while having an illegal end in mind. In divorce law, the term refers to an agreement by husband and wife to suppress facts or fabricate **evidence** material to the existence of lawful grounds for divorce. 5 N.W. 2d 133, 137.

COLLUSIVE ACTION an impermissible **action** maintained by non-**adversary parties** to determine a hypothetical point of law, or to produce a desired legal precedent. Such suits will not be entertained in federal courts because the Constitution requires an actual case or **controversy.** 319 U.S. 302. State courts also prohibit collusive actions. 140 P. 2d 666, 669, 670. Compare **advisory opinions, declaratory judgment.**

COLOR semblance; disguise. Color is often used to designate the hiding of a set of facts behind a sham, taking advantage of the confidence but technically proper, legal theory or legal right.

COLORABLE that which presents an appearance which does not correspond with the reality, or an appearance intended to conceal or to deceive. See 172 P. 23, 24.

COLOR OF LAW "mere semblance of legal right." 202 N.W. 144, 148. An action done under color of law is one done with the apparent authority of law but actually in contravention of law. A federal **cause of action** may be maintained against a state officer who under "color of law" deprives a person of his **civil rights.** 42 U.S.C. §1983.

COLOR OF TITLE lending the appearance of **title,** when in reality there is no title at all; an **instrument** which appears to pass title, and which one relies on as passing title, but which fails to do so; an instrument which, on its face, professes to pass title, but which fails to do so either because title is lacking in the person conveying or because the **conveyance** itself is defective. Thus, one possessing a forged or false **deed** has mere color of title. Color of title is sometimes an element of **adverse possession.**

COMITAS see **comity.**

COMITY a rule of courtesy by which one court defers to the concomitant **jurisdiction** of another. "Judicial comity is not a rule of law, but one of practical convenience and expediency based on the theory that a court which first asserts jurisdiction will not be interfered with in the continuance of its assertion by another court . . . unless it is desirable that one give way to the other." 177 U.S. 485, 488. Comity will ordinarily prevent a federal court from interfering with a pending state criminal prosecution. 401 U.S. 37. The doctrine of comity, rather than **full faith and credit,** is applicable when a state is asked to honor a judgment (e.g., a **divorce** decree) of a foreign country.

COMMENT refers to the statements made by a judge or counsel concerning the defendant, such statements not being based on fact, but rather on alleged facts. A judge may comment "on the weight of the evidence and indicate his own opinion concerning the credibility of witnesses and the relative strength of competing permissible inferences, provided always that he makes it clear to the jury that it is their province to decide such questions of weight and credibility." James & Hazard, Civil Procedure §7.14 (2d ed. 1977). However, a prosecutor may not "comment" on the refusal of a defendant in a criminal proceeding to testify, and the court may not instruct a jury that such silence is evidence of guilt. See 380 U.S. 609. Compare **fair comment**

COMMERCIAL BANK see **bank** [COMMERCIAL BANK].

COMMERCIAL BRIBERY see **bribery.**

COMMERCIAL FRUSTRATION see **frustration [of purpose].**

COMMERCIAL PAPER a **negotiable instrument,** i.e., a writing **indorsed** by the **maker** or **drawee,** containing an unconditional promise or order to pay a certain sum on demand or at a specified time, made payable to order or to bearer. U.C.C. §3-104(1). The term comprehends **bills** of exchange, **checks, notes, and certificates of deposit.** U.C.C. §3-104(2). Article 3 of the U.C.C. generally governs the use of commercial paper.

COMMERCIAL UNIT a unit considered by trade or usage to be a whole which cannot be divided without materially impairing its value, character, or use. For example, a machine or a suite of furniture would be considered a "commercial unit." Since acceptance of any part of a commercial unit constitutes acceptance of the whole, the term becomes significant when a buyer attempts to reject part of a contract for non-conformance. If the item rejected is determined to be part of a commercial unit, the rejection will not be allowed. U.C.C. §2-105(b).

COMMINGLING OF FUNDS the act of a **fiduciary** or **trustee,** including a lawyer, in mixing his or her own funds with those belonging to a client or customer; generally prohibited unless the fiduciary maintains an exact accounting of the client's funds and how they have been used.

An attorney commingles funds when a client's money is intermingled with that of his attorney and its separate identity lost so that it may be used for the attorney's personal or business expenses or subjected to claims of the attorney's creditors. 483 P. 2d. 1106, 1110.

COMMISSION in **contracts,** a form of payment for services performed. The ordinary understanding of the word is compensation based on a percentage of an amount collected, received, or agreed to be paid for results accomplished, as distinguished from "salary" which is a fixed and periodic amount payable without regard to actual results achieved. 356 F. Supp. 235, 239.

COMMITTEE a person or persons to whom the consideration or determination of certain business is referred or confided. 87 A. 361. A "committee is a subordinate body charged with investigating, considering and reporting to a parent body upon a particular subject, leaving the parent body to act." 69 Cal Rptr. 480, 486. In legislative practice, a body which investigates some matter or area of interest and reports its findings and recommendations to the legislative body.

The "committee" of an incompetent is one who stands in the place of and who acts in the stead of the alleged incompetent, and who is charged with full responsibility for his acts in managing the incompetent's affairs.

COMMISSION, MILITARY see **military law** [MILITARY COMMISSION].

COMMODITY [COMMODITIES] any tangible **good;** commercially, commodities refer to products that are the subject of **sale** or barter. See also **futures.**

COMMON AREA in landlord-tenant law portions of premises used in common by all tenants. A large number of cases have imposed **liability** on the **landlord** on the basis of "retained control" with injuries sustained when the landlord has failed to maintain in reasonably safe condition common areas. 406 So. 2d 521. Implicit in these decisions is the notion that since no individual **tenant** controls the common area, control remains with the landlord. 372 S.W. 2d 844, 849. Common areas to which the landlord's obligation has been extended include stairways, porches, hallway and entrance areas, elevators, yards, and basements. See Schoshinski, American Law of Landlord and Tenant, §4.4 (1980).

COMMON CARRIER see **carrier** [COMMON CARRIER].

COMMON LAW the system of jurisprudence, which originated in England and was later applied in the United States, which is based on judicial **precedent** rather than statutory laws, which are legislative enactments; it is to be contrasted with **civil law** (the descendant of Roman Law prevalent in other western countries). Originally based on the unwritten laws of England, the common law is "generally derived from principles rather than rules; it does not consist of absolute, fixed, and inflexible rules, but rather of broad and comprehensive principles based on justice, reason, and common sense. It is of judicial origin and promulgation. Its principles have been determined by the social needs of the community and have changed with changes in such needs. These principles are susceptible of adaptation to new conditions, interests, relations, and usages as the progress of society may require." 37 N.W. 2d 543, 547.

COMMON LAW COPYRIGHT see **copyright.**

COMMON LAW MARRIAGE one based not upon ceremony and compliance with legal formalities, but upon the agreement of two persons, legally competent to marry, to cohabit with the intention of being husband and wife, followed by a substantial period of living together as husband and wife.

The term was adopted by American law from England. Such marriages were recognized as valid by the **ecclesiastical** courts of England prior to 1753. In America such marriages were recognized in some of the colonies and in a number of states after independence from England. 2 Hagg. Cons. 54; 96 U.S. 76. At present the recognition of common law marriage seems to be on the decline, with a majority of the states having decided, either by statute or case law, that common law marriages will not be recognized, e.g., N.J.S.A. 37:1-10.

Where such marriages are recognized, the standards courts generally apply in order to find a common law marriage are consent and mutual assumption of the marital relationship, 269 F. 2d 249, together with "a long continued and consistent marital cohabitation . . . ," Clark, Law of Domestic Relations 50, n. 43.

COMMON NUISANCE see **nuisance.**

COMMON PROPERTY see **community property; property.**

COMMONS land set aside for public use, e.g., public parks; also, the untitled class of Great Britain, represented in Parliament by the House of Commons.

COMMON STOCK see **securities.**

COMMUNITY PROPERTY all property that a husband or wife acquires by their joint efforts during their marriage. 144 S.W. 2d 529, 531; all property owned at the time of marriage, or that was acquired by gift, devise, bequest, or descent, and the rents and profits therefrom is considered **separate property.** All other acquisitions arising from the earnings of either husband or wife during marriage constitute community property. The community property system of **concurrent** ownership is applicable only to the ownership of property by husband and wife. The basic theory underlying this system is that a husband and wife both contribute to the property acquired after their marriage and should, therefore, share equally in the ownership of any interest resulting from their joint efforts. Currently, there are eight states that have adopted the Civil Law doctrine of community property. Some states that do not espouse the community property doctrine have adopted **equitable distribution** statutes to achieve a similar distribution of the marital estate upon the dissolution of the marriage. Community property is similar to but should be distinguished from, **tenancy by the entirety** and **joint tenancy**. See American Law of Property §7.1 et seq. (1952).

COMMUTATION substitution, change; the substitution of a lesser penalty or punishment for a greater one, such as from death to life imprisonment, or from a longer term to a shorter one. The chief executive officer [President, governor] has the constitutional power of **executive clemency** which includes the broad power in his discretion to commute a sentence. Compare with **pardon** and **reprieve**.

COMPANY broadly, any group of people voluntarily united for performing jointly any activity, business, or commercial enterprise. See 23 Tex. 295, 303.

In reference to trades, "company" applies to the combination of individuals' capital, skill and labor for the purpose of business carried on for such individuals' common benefits. 6 So. 362, 364.

The term also applies to a wide range of activities, and under statutory construction has been held to include private **corporations,** joint stock companies (see below), all **partnerships,** etc. See 222 S.W. 736, 739. "Company" has also been considered synonymous with "firm."

HOLDING COMPANY see **holding company.**

JOINT STOCK COMPANY a company or association, usually unincorporated, which has the capital of its members pooled in a common fund; the capital **stock** is divided into **shares** and distributed to represent ownership **interest** in the company, see Henn, Law of Corporations §50 (1961); a form of partnership, but one which is distinguished from a "partnership"

in the ordinary sense of that term in that the membership of a joint stock company is changeable, its shares are transferable, its members can be many and not necessarily known to each other, and its members cannot act or speak for the company. See 154 S.E. 357, 361. There is an important distinction between joint stock companies at common law, and those under statutory authority in certain states; in certain jurisdictions, "joint stock companies" are regulated more like corporations than partnerships, and thus have extensive power unknown at common law. See 279 F. 2d 785. See also **trust company.**

COMPARATIVE NEGLIGENCE see **negligence.**

COMPELLING INTEREST see **equal protection of the laws.**

COMPENSATION "remuneration for work done; indemnification for injury sustained," 245 P. 2d 352, 355; recompense, remuneration, equivalence; pay for injury done or service performed; "that which constitutes, or is regarded as, an equivalent or recompense; that which compensates for loss or privation; amends." 112 A. 2d 716, 719. As used in constitutional law the word means "a compensation which is just and fair both to the owner of the property being taken and to the public represented by the **condemning** authority." 131 A. 2d 180, 182. See also, **just compensation.**

COMPETENT capable of doing a certain thing; capacity to understand, and act reasonably. **Competent evidence** is evidence generally admissible due to its relevance and materiality to the issues being **litigated;** a competent court is one having proper **jurisdiction** over the person or property at issue. An individual is competent to make a

will if he understands the extent of his **property,** the identity of the natural objects of his bounty, and the consequences of the act of making a will. 26 N.Y.S. 2d 96. An individual declared incompetent to attend to his daily affairs may nevertheless be competent to make a will. See 63 N.Y.S. 2d 572. A criminal defendant is competent to stand trial if he "has sufficient present ability to consult with his lawyer with a reasonable degree of rational understanding and . . . has a rational as well as a factual understanding of the **proceedings** against him." 362 U.S. 402. Compare **insanity.** See **compos mentis.**

COMPLAINANT the party who initiates the **complaint** in an **action** or **proceeding.** "[F]or all practical purposes it is synonymous with **petitioner** and **plaintiff.** The nature of the proceeding and the court in which it is instituted determines which term is the more appropriate under the circumstances." 62 S.E. 2d 80, 81.

COMPLAINT in a civil action, the first **pleading** of the **plaintiff** setting out the facts on which the claim for relief is based. Fed. R. Civ. Proc. 3. Under modern court rules, the purpose of the complaint is to give notice to the adversary of the nature and basis of the claim asserted.

In criminal law, the complaint is the preliminary **charge** or accusation made by one against another to the appropriate court or officer, usually a magistrate. Fed. R. Crim. Proc. 3 However, court proceedings, such as a trial, cannot be instituted until an **indictment** or **information** has been handed down against the defendant. Fed. R. Crim. Proc. 4.

COMPOS MENTIS *(kŏm'-pōs měn'-tĭs)* mentally competent. See **non-compos mentis.**

COMPOUNDING A FELONY the offense of refusing to **prosecute** a **felon,** by one who was injured by the felony, in exchange for which the party injured receives a bribe or reparation for his **forbearance;** "[t]he offense consists of perverting public justice in some way by making a bargain to allow the criminal to escape conviction or showing some favor to him for that purpose." 106 N.E. 215, 217. Compare **accessory.** See Model Penal Code §242.J.

COMPOUND INTEREST see **interest.**

COMPROMISE VERDICT see **verdict.**

COMPULSORY ARBITRATION see **arbitration.**

COMPULSORY APPEARANCE see **appearance.**

COMPULSORY COUNTERCLAIM see **counterclaim.**

COMPULSORY JOINDER see **joinder.**

COMPULSORY PROCESS the right of a **defendant** to have the resources of the court (i.e, the **subpoena** power) utilized on his behalf to compel the **appearance** of **witnesses** before such court. See Fed. R. Civ. Proc. 45; 44 A. 2d 520. See **process.** In civil actions, the right to compulsory process is often secured through state constitutional or statutory provisions. 97 C.J.S. Witnesses §3. State constitutions and statutes may also provide this right to legislative or administrative bodies conducting **hearings** or investigations. 133 N.E. 2d 104; 118 F. 2d 8. In any criminal proceeding, this right is guaranteed the defendant by the 6th Amendment to the United States Constitution. See 388 U.S. 14. Defendant must exercise this right, i.e., request the attendance of witnesses, reasonably and diligently, especially where their attendance is sought to be secured at government expense. See 224 F. 2d 801; the constitutional right extends, however, as reasonably necessary throughout the trial. 257 P. 385. It may be asserted only with respect to competent, **material witnesses** subject to the court's process whose expected testimony will be admissible. 97 C.J.S. Witnesses §9.

COMPURAGATOR in early English law, one of a group of neighbors called by a person accused of a crime to swear that the accused was testifying truthfully. 3 Bl. Comm. * 341. See **wager of law.**

CONCEALMENT an act making more difficult the discovery of that which one is legally obligated to reveal or not withhold, such as the failure of a **bankrupt** to schedule all his **assets,** or the failure of an applicant for an insurance policy to disclose information relevant to the insurer's decision to insure the risk. "A concealment in the law of insurance implies an intention to withhold or secrete information so that the one entitled to be informed will remain in ignorance." 236 N.E. 2d 63, 70.

CONCERTED ACTION [CONCERT OF ACTION] "action which has been planned, arranged, adjusted, agreed upon, and settled between parties acting together, in pursuance of some design or in accordance with some scheme." 416 F. 2d 857, 860. Thus, in the criminal law, concerted action is found only where there has been a **conspiracy** to commit an illegal act, i.e., all must share the criminal intent of the actual perpetrator. 6 S.E. 2d 647, 649. But there cannot be a conspiracy or concerted action when the crime, by its nature, requires participation of at least two people. 184 A. 2d 814, 820.

The term also applies to joint **tort-feasors** where there is tort liability for conspiracy. See Prosser, Torts §46 (4th ed. 1971).

CONCLUSION OF FACT conclusion reached solely through use of facts and natural reasoning, without resort to rules of law; inferences from evidentiary facts. 22 P. 2d 819, 822. See **finding** [FINDING OF FACT].

CONCLUSION OF LAW conclusion reached through application of rules of law. "Where the ultimate conclusion can be arrived at only by applying a rule of law, the result so reached embodies a conclusion of law, and is not a finding of fact." 229 N.W. 194, 197. See **finding** [FINDING OF LAW].

CONCLUSIVE EVIDENCE evidence which is incontrovertible, that is to say, "either not open or not able to be questioned, as where it is said that a thing is conclusively proved, it means that such result follows from the facts shown as the only one possible." 21 So. 2d 878, 880.

The term contemplates degree of proof, and its meaning in a particular statute depends largely on its context and the intention of the legislature. 82 N.Y.S. 2d 577.

CONCLUSIVE PRESUMPTION see **presumption.**

CONCUR to agree. A concurring opinion states agreement with the conclusion of the **majority,** but may state different reasons why such conclusion is reached. An opinion "concurring in the result only" is one which implies no agreement with the reasoning of the prevailing opinion, but which fails to state reasons of its own. Compare **dissent.**

CONCURRENT to run together, in conjunction with; to exist together. "The words, 'concurrent' [or] 'consecutive' . . . are generally used to indicate the intention of the Court. . . . When used in ordinary legal parlance and especially as adapted to **judgments** in criminal cases, the opposite of concurrent is consecutive and accumulative. If the sentences are not concurrent they are consecutive, and accumulative, and they are to be served in their numerical order." 122 F. 2d 85, 87. In many jurisdictions the presumption is that multiple sentences imposed at the same time upon the same defendant by a court are concurrent unless the court otherwise directs. See 100 F. 2d 280. See **sentence** [CONCURRENT SENTENCE].

CONCURRENT CONDITION see **condition.**

CONCURRENT COVENANTS see **covenant.**

CONCURRENT JURISDICTION see **jurisdiction.**

CONCURRENT NEGLIGENCE see **negligence.**

CONCURRING OPINION see **opinion.**

CONDEMN to declare as legally useless or unfit for habitation as when an unsafe building is condemned and demolished; as to land, a taking of private property for public use such as building a highway which raises a duty of **just compensation** under the laws governing **eminent domain.** 626 S.W. 2d 561, 563. The term is also used in criminal law to refer to the imposition of a penalty or pronouncement of judgment, especially the pronouncement of a sentence of death upon conviction of a **capital offense.**

CONDITION "the equivalent of 'requisite' or 'requirement.' In legal signification, the term 'condition' denotes something attached to and made a part of a grant or privelege." 67 N.E. 2d 439, 442. A condition is a possible future event, the occurrence of which will trigger the **performance** of a legal obligation.
   In the law of contracts, conditions may be precedent, subsequent, or concurrent. A CONDITION PRECEDENT is a fact [act or event] which must exist or occur before a duty of immediate performance of a promise arises. Corbin, Contracts §628 (1960). A CONDITION SUBSEQUENT is a fact which will extinguish a duty to make compensation

for **breach of contract** after the breach has occurred. Id. A CONCURRENT CONDITION is a condition precedent which exists only when parties to a contract are found to render performance at the same time. Id. at §629. Real property interests can be affected by like conditions. Conditions can also be express or implied. See **determinable fee; estate; fee simple conditional.**

CONDITIONAL dependent upon the happening or non-happening of the **condition;** implies a type of **incumbrance.**

CONDITIONAL DISCHARGE see **sentence** [SUSPENDED SENTENCE].

CONDITIONAL BEQUEST see **bequest.**

CONDITIONAL CONTRACT see **contract.**

CONDITIONAL DISCHARGE see **sentence** [CONDITIONAL DISCHARGE].

CONDITIONAL FEE [ESTATE] a **fee simple** [complete ownership of **real property**] which is limited in that it must eventually pass from the **donee** to certain **heirs** or the **issue** [children] of the donee [**heirs of the body**]. 194 S.E. 817. Should the designated heir fail to be in existence at the time of the death of the donee, the property **reverts** [goes back] to the donor of his **estate.** However, the entire estate rests with the donee until his death, the donor having the mere **possibility of reverter.** Such a reverter may be released to the donee, thereby converting his estate from a fee simple conditional to a fee simple absolute. 275 P. 45, 52. See also **determinable fee; defeasible fee; life estate.**

CONDITION PRECEDENT see **condition.**

CONDITION SUBSEQUENT see **condition.**

CONDOMINIUM "a system of separate ownership of individual units in multiunit projects. . . . In addition to the interest acquired in a particular unit, each unit owner is also a **tenant in common** in the underlying **fee** and in the spaces and building parts used in common by all the unit owners," such as elevators. Rohan & Reskin, 1 Condominium Law and Practice §1.01(1). A condominium is distinguished from a COOPERATIVE, which consists of "a **corporate** or business **trust** entity holding **title** to the **premises** and granting rights of occupancy to particular apartments by means of proprietary **leases** or similar arrangements." Id. at §1.01(2).

CONFERENCE, PRE-TRIAL see **pre-trial conference.**

CONFESSION an admission of guilt or other incriminating statement made by the **accused;** not admissible against the **defendant** at his **trial** unless the state demonstrates that it was voluntarily made and, if applicable, consistent with the **Miranda** doctrine. The voluntariness of the confession must be established at least by a **preponderance of the evidence,** 404 U.S. 477, 489; and in some jurisdictions must be **beyond a reasonable doubt.** Id. at n. 1. See **involuntary** [INVOLUNTARY CONFESSION]; **oral** [ORAL CONFESSION].

CONFESSION AND AVOIDANCE **pleading** by which a **party** admits the **allegations** against him, either expressly or by implication, but which presents **new matter** which **avoids** the effect of the failure to deny those allegations. Thus, a litigant "confesses," rather than denies, the allegation, but his presentation of new matter acts to "avoid" a **judgment** against him. See Stephen, Pleading 230, 233 (Williston ed. 1895).

CONFESSION OF JUDGMENT entry of a judgment upon a written **admission** or **confession** of the **debt-** or without the formality, time or expense of an ordinary legal **proceeding,** 105 N.W. 698, 701; also called COGNOVIT JUDGMENT. It is accomplished through an advance, voluntary submission to the **jurisdiction** of the court as when a buyer of goods on **credit** agrees in his purchase **contract** that if he fails to pay the amounts due timely that he will consent to the entry of a judgment against him for the amount outstanding (and often reasonable **attorney's fees** not exceeding a fixed percentage [commonly 20 percent]). A judgment entered upon an attorney's **affidavit** that his client owes the **plaintiff** the sum **pleaded** in the lawsuit and consents to the entry of a judgment for that amount. These procedures are now regulated and often prohibited by statute because of their coercive effect on debtors and because of the potential for abuses. The confession of judgment procedures may also offend **due process.** See 407 U.S. 67, 94.

CONFIDENCE GAME "[a]ny scheme whereby a swindler wins the confidence of his victim and then cheats him out of his money by taking advantage of the confidence reposed in him." 95 N.E. 2d 80, 83. The elements of the crime of the confidence game are "(1) an intentional false representation to the victim as to some present fact . . . (2) knowing it to be false . . . (3) with the intent that the victim rely on the representation . . . (4) the representation being made to obtain the victim's confidence . . . and thereafter his money and property." 304 A. 2d 260, 275.

CONFIDENTIAL COMMUNICATION see **privileged communications.**

CONFIRMATION see **arbitrator** [CONFIRMATION].

CONFISCATE to take private property without **just compensation;** to transfer property from a private use to a public use. 561 S.W. 2d 645, 650; to appropriate private property as a result of a criminal conviction or because the possession was itself a crime. See also **condemn.**

CONFLICT OF INTEREST[S] "a situation in which regard for one duty leads to disregard of another," 463 F. 2d 600, 602, or might be reasonably be expected to do so. For instance, an attorney representing several persons accused of the same crime might be required to cast guilt upon one in order to exonerate the others. With reference to disqualification of a public officer to perform his sworn duty, the concept "refers to a clash between the public interest and the private pecuniary interest of the individual concerned." 514 F. 2d 38, 41.

Conflicts of interest may be actual or potential. An actual conflict, such as where an attorney has a personal financial interest adverse to his client, precludes the attorney from representing the client under the **Code of Professional Responsibility.** A potential conflict arises where conflicting interests may develop but do not exist such as when an attorney is asked to represent both the buyer and seller of real estate. Some jurisdictions permit such potential conflicts of interest to exist with full disclosure to the clients while others do not permit such potential conflicts. In all cases, once an actual conflict of interest exists, the attorney must withdraw and new counsel must be engaged to represent each party.

CONFLICT OF LAWS [CHOICE OF LAW] that body of law by which the court in which the **action** is maintained determines or chooses which law to apply where a diversity exists between the applicable law of that court's state [the forum state] and the applicable law of another jurisdiction interested in the controversy. The considerations comprising that decison formerly rested on simple and traditional rules such as LEX LOCI CONTRACTUS or place of making a con-

tract, and LEX LOCI DELICTI or place of the wrong in tort. More modern doctrine focuses on an interest analysis which very often arrives at the same choice but includes, along with the traditional considerations of place of contracting and place of the wrong, the public policy of the forum and in general which jurisdiction maintains the most significant relationship or contacts with the subject matter of the controversy. The "interest analysis" is referred to as CENTER OF GRAVITY or CONTACTS APPROACH. As a general rule the forum state will apply its own law on questions of **procedure** regardless of a "conflict."

A federal court must follow the choice of laws principles of the forum state. See 313 U.S. 487. Where a controversy has been reduced to a judgment in the courts of one of the states, the choice of laws principles employed cannot be challenged in another state unless the full **faith and credit** doctrine would permit a challenge. See also **comity; forum non conveniens.**

CONFORMED COPY an exact copy of a document, often certified to be so by a **clerk** of a **court,** with hand-written notations duplicating those on the original document. Thus, an order may have the date, precise terms, and signature of the judge written by hand on another copy of a proposed order which had not been signed. This then becomes a conformed copy of the order which was completed and signed by the court.

CONFORMING USE see **nonconforming use.**

CONFRONTATION CLAUSE under the Sixth Amendment of the Constitution, the accused in a criminal prosecution is entitled "to be confronted with the witnesses against him." This right entitles the accused to be present at the trial, and to hear and cross-examine all witnesses against him. Evidence which is not subject to confrontation, such as the confession of a codefendant who is not subject to cross-examination, may not be used against the accused. 380 U.S. 400; 272 U.S. 542.

CONFUSION OF GOODS "results when **personal property** belonging to two or more owners becomes intermixed to the point when the property of any of them no longer can be identified except as part of a mass of like goods." 264 P. 2d 283.

CONGLOMERATE a group of **corporations** engaged in unrelated businesses which are controlled by a single corporate entity. "The term conglomerate . . . describes a company that controls a group of other companies engaged in unrelated businesses. . . ." 339 N.Y.S. 2d 347, 348.

A **merger** of corporations into a single conglomerate, standing alone, does not violate the antimonopoly sections of the federal **antitrust** laws, the reason for this is that there were no economic relationships between the acquiring and acquired corporations and hence there is no lessening of competition in any relevant market. See 386 U.S. 568, 577; and 258 F. Supp. 36, 56. See **merger** [CONGLOMERATE MERGER].

CONGRESS a formal body of delegates; in American law, the national legislative body consisting of the Senate and House of Representatives. The lawmaking power of the United States vests in this body. United States Constitution, Art. I, Sec. 1; 377 U.S. 533. The Constitution of the United States provides for the eligibility, election and qualification of members of Congress. Art. I, Sec. 2 and 3 et seq. It allows each house to determine the rules of its proceedings, provided those rules are constitutional and do not violate fundamental rights, and it enumerates the powers of Congress in detail. Art. I, Sec 4 et seq. The two houses of Congress possess not only those powers granted to them specifically by the constitution, but also implied auxiliary powers as are necessary to effect the express powers. 72 F. 2d 560. See generally, Schwartz, Constitutional Law, Ch. 3, p. 73 (1979).

CONGRESSIONAL REFERENCE CASES see **Court of Claims.**

CONJECTURE a tenuous inference based upon facts within a person's knowledge. A witness may only testify as to facts within his knowledge and may not present conjecture to the jury. McCormick, Evidence 21, 22 (1972). A jury cannot render a verdict on the basis of conjecture, but must find its verdict based upon the evidence admitted in the trial of the matter.

CONJUGAL RIGHTS the rights of married persons which include "the enjoyment of association, sympathy, confidence, domestic happiness, the comforts of dwelling together in the same habitation, eating meals at the same table, and profiting by the joint property rights, as well as the intimacies of domestic relations." 286 P. 747. In the prison setting, a CONJUGAL VISITATION permits sexual intercourse between the inmate and his spouse. See Hopper, Sex in Prison (1969). See also **consortium; visitation rights.**

CONJUNCTIVE DENIAL see **denial.**

CONSANGUINITY the familial relationship of persons united by one or more common ancestors. **Lineal consanguinity** refers to persons who are descended in a direct line from a common ancestor. **Collateral consanguinity** refers to persons who are descended from a common ancestor but not in a direct line. Degrees of collateral consanguinity are determined by counting generations up to the common ancestor, and then down to the related party. 54 A.L.R. 2d 1012. Degrees of consanguinity sometimes control **inheritance**. See **descent and distribution**.

CONSCIENCE OF THE COURT refers to the power of the **court of equity** to resolve a controversy by applying common standards of decency and fairness. The term does not refer to the private opinion of a particular judge but to uniformly held judgment of the community. The proper application of the doctrine rests upon general principles of equitable law and to established precedent. Conduct which shocks the conscience of the court will lead to the invalidation in part or in whole of an **unconscionable contract,** U.C.C. §2-302, or to the **suppression** of evidence as violative of **due process of law.**

CONSCIENTIOUS OBJECTOR any person who, by reason of religious training and belief, is conscientiously opposed to participation in war in any form. Such a person is not only exempt from participation in combat, and, under the 1967 Selective Service Act, can be required to serve the nation in a noncombatant military or civilian capacity, such as working in a hospital. 50 U.S.C. App. §456. Participation in an organized religion is a factor contributing toward, but not essential to, conscientious objector status. The objection to war must nonetheless be founded on religious beliefs, and cannot be based upon essentially political, sociological, or economic considerations. The exemption is extended through statute by the sovereign's grace and is not a **constitutional right.** 401 U.S. 437.

CONSCIOUS PARALLELISM knowledge that a particular course of conduct has been followed by a competitor combined with an independent decision by another party to follow the same course of conduct; it is distinguished from **conspiracy,** which requires an agreement, either tacit or express, between the parties engaged in the parallel conduct. See 346 U.S. 537, 540-41.

Conscious parallelism alone is not a violation of the **anti-trust statutes.** See 75 Harv. L. Rev. 655 (1962). Evidence of such consciously parallel conduct, however, is highly probative on the issue of whether an actual conspiracy did exist. See 306 U.S. 208.

CONSENT DECREE see **consent judgment** [CONSENT DECREE]; **decree.**

CONSENT, INFORMED see **informed consent.**

CONSENT JUDGMENT "the **contract** of the parties entered upon the **record** with the approval and sanction of a court of competent **jurisdiction,** [which] contract cannot be nullified or set aside without the consent of the parties thereto, except for **fraud** or **mistake** . . ." 78 S.E. 2d 323, 326. Consent **judgments** have the same force and effect as any other judgment. 47 Am. Jur. 2d, Judgments §1088 (1969). Because the agreement of the parties waives exception to irregularities in the proceedings occurring prior to the time of agreement, **appeal** from a consent judgment is limited to attack for mistake, fraud, or lack of jurisdiction. 89 P. 2d 624, 629; 69 A.L.R. 2d 755. Since a consent judgment is contractual in nature, it should be construed as a written contract. 47 Am. Jur. 2d Judgments §108.5.

CONSENT DECREE the **equitable** counterpart of consent judgment. However, as a decree, it is only as binding as any other equitable remedy. For instance, in antitrust cases, the court has the power to modify a consent decree according to changing circumstances. 286 U.S. 106.

CONSENT ORDER generally, any court **order** to which the opposing party agrees; in **antitrust** law, an agreement between the Federal Trade Commission and a party being investigated whereby the party consents to cease activities that could be the subject of an antitrust action and the FTC refrains from initiating suit. 16 C.F.R. §§2.31-2.35 (1977).

CONSENT ORDER see **consent judgment** [CONSENT ORDER].

CONSENT SEARCH a search made by an authorized person after the subject of the search has voluntarily consented. The constitutional immunity from unreasonable searches and seizures may be waived by consent to a search or seizure. 343 U.S. 747. Once an individual has consented to a search he cannot later **challenge** the **search.** In order to constitute a lawful waiver the consent must be given intelligently and voluntarily. 412 U.S. 218.

CONSEQUENTIAL DAMAGES see **damages.**

CONSERVATOR court-appointed custodian of property belonging to person determined to be unable to properly manage his property. Uniform Probate Code §5-401(2). The term is sometimes used interchangeably with **guardian** or **committee.** In some jurisdictions the conservator can be a public or private agency rather than a person.

CONSIDERATION the inducement to a contract, something of value given in return for a performance or a promise of performance by another, for the purpose of forming a **contract;** one element of a contract that is generally required to make a promise binding and to make the agreement of the parties enforceable as a contract. To find consideration there must be a performance or a return promise which has been bargained for by the parties. Restatement (second), Contracts §71(1) (1981). Consideration represents the element of bargaining to indicate that each party agrees to surrender something in

return for what it is to receive. It is consideration which distinguishes a contract from a mere **gift.**

Courts have used the word "consideration" with many different meanings. "It is often used merely to express the legal conclusion that a promise is enforceable. Historically, its primary meaning may have been that the conditions were met under which an action of **assumpsit** [an early form of contract action] would lie. It was also used as the equivalent of the **quid pro quo** required in an action of **debt.** A **seal,** it has been said, 'imports a consideration,' although the law was clear that no element of bargain was necessary to enforcement of a promise under seal. On the other hand, consideration has sometimes been used to refer to almost any reason asserted for enforcing a promise, even though the reason was insufficient [as in] promises 'in consideration of love and affection,' 'illegal consideration,' 'past consideration,' and consideration furnished by reliance on a gratuitous promise" where in fact there has been no consideration at all. Id. at Comment A.

The phrase SUFFICIENT CONSIDERATION is used by some courts to express the legal conclusion that one requirement for an enforceable bargain has been met. This is redundant and misleading, however, since any performance or return promise which has been bargained for and received is legally sufficient to satisfy the consideration element of a contract. Other unnecessary qualifications to the word consideration include LEGAL CONSIDERATION and VALUABLE CONSIDERATION. The law will not in general inquire into the adequacy of "consideration" and hence these terms do not add anything of substance to the phrase consideration. So long as the bargained for promise is not **illusory** or the performance a sham pretext, a sufficient exchange will have taken place to justify the enforcement of the agreement so far as consideration is at issue.

The performance may be any lawful act done for the benefit of the other contracting party or a third person and may include an act of forebearance. A MORAL [EQUITABLE] CONSIDERATION will not generally qualify as consideration so as to render the promise enforceable unless the promise is "made in recognition of a benefit previously received by the promisor from the promisee" in which instances it is "binding to the extent necessary to prevent injustice." Id. at §86(1).

FAILURE OF CONSIDERATION refers to the circumstance in which consideration was bargained for but has either become worthless, has ceased to exist, or has not been performed as promised. Failure of consideration may be partial or total. The term is often used interchangeably with WANT OF CONSIDERATION.

CONSIDERED DICTUM see **dictum.**

CONSIGNMENT a **bailment** for care or **sale.** The term does not ordinarily imply a sale but an **agency.** It most commonly refers to a transaction wherein goods are delivered to a dealer for sale by him/her rather than sold to him/her. The dealer must either sell the goods for the person making delivery and remit to him/her the price or, if he does not sell the goods, return the goods to the person making delivery. 156 S.E. 2d 137, 140.

A **conditional** sale is distinguished in that the buyer in such sale undertakes an absolute obligation to pay for the property.

CONSIGNEE a person to whom goods are shipped for sale under a consignment contract; one to whom a **carrier** may lawfully make delivery in accordance with his contract of carriage; the person named in a **bill of lading** to whom or to whose order the bill promises delivery. U.C.C. §7-102(b).

CONSIGNOR one who sends or makes a consignment; a shipper of goods; the person calling on a common carrier for transportation service. The person who actually consigns the goods is not necessarily the person in whose name a **bill of lading** is made. The existence of a consignee is implied and the term does not apply to a transaction where the purchaser of goods carries them with him from the point of sale to the point of destination. U.C.C. §7-102(c).

CONSOLIDATED APPEAL if two or more persons are entitled to **appeal** from a **judgment** or order of a district court and their interests are such as to make **joinder** practicable, they may file a joint notice of appeal, or may join in appeal after filing separate notices of appeal, and they may thereafter proceed on appeal as a single appellant. Appeals may be consolidated by order of the court of appeals upon its own motion or upon motion of a party, or by stipulation of the parties of the several appeals. Fed. R. App. P. 3(b).

CONSOLIDATION see **merger.**

CONSORTIUM "the conjugal fellowship of husband and wife, and the right of each to the company, cooperation and aid of the other in every conjugal relation." 134 Mass. 123. Where a person willfully interferes with this relation, he deprives one spouse of the consortium of the other, and is liable in damages. 119 S.E. 222. Willful interference with consortium may give rise to an action for **alienation of affection;** more generally, loss of consortium often figures in the award of damages in a **tort** action for injury or **wrongful death** of a spouse.

CONSPIRACY "a combination of two or more persons to commit a criminal or unlawful act, or to commit a lawful act by criminal or unlawful means; or a combination of two or more persons by **concerted action** to accomplish an unlawful purpose, or some purpose not in itself unlawful by unlawful means. It is essential that there be two or more conspirators; one cannot conspire with himself." 314 P. 2d 625, 631. Some jurisdictions, however, permit prosecution of one person for a conspiracy when, for example, the other party(ies) cannot be located or is otherwise unavailable for prosecution. A conspiracy to injure another is an actionable **tort;** it may also be a criminal offense if the object of the conspiracy is within the reach of the definition of criminal conspiracy in the particular jurisdiction. See, generally, Model Penal Code §5.03. Compare **accessory; accomplice; aid and abet.**

CONSPIRATOR one involved in a **conspiracy;** one who acts with another, or others, in furtherance of an unlawful transaction. "It is not necessary that all of the conspirators either meet together or agree simultaneously. . . . It is not necessary that each member of a conspiracy know the exact part which every other participant is playing; nor is it necessary in order to be bound by the acts of his associates that each member of a conspiracy shall know all the other participants therein; nor is it requisite that simultaneous action be had for those who come on later, and cooperate in the common effort to obtain the unlawful results, to become parties thereto and assume responsibility for all that has been done before." 47 F. Supp. 395, 400-01. According to the Model Penal Code, a conspirator is one who, with another person or persons with the purpose of promoting or facilitating the commission of a crime "a) agrees with such other person or persons that they or one or more of them will engage in conduct which constitutes such crime or an **attempt** or **solicitation** to commit such crime; or b) agrees to **aid** such other person or persons in the planning or commission of such crime or an attempt or solicitation to commit such crime." Model Penal Code 5.03(1).

CONSTITUTION the organic **law** framing a governmental system; the original and fundamental principles of law by which a system of government is created and according to which a country is governed. A constitution represents a mandate to the various branches of government directly from the people acting in their sovereign capacity. It is distinguished from a law which is a rule of conduct prescribed by legislative agents of the people and subject to the limitations of the constitution. 229 A. 2d 388, 394.

In American law, the word **Constitution** specifically refers to a written instrument which is the basic source from which government derives its power, but under which governmental powers are both conferred and circumscribed. It is the emphasis on restrictions of power that distinguishes the American concept. Schwartz, Constitutional Law, Ch. 1, p. 1 (1979). The Constitution gives a permanence and stability to government and is not designed to protect majorities, who can protect themselves, but to preserve and protect the rights of minorities against the arbitrary actions of those in power. 208 U.S. 412, 420. The Constitution is the basic law to which all others must conform. 140 F. Supp. 925. It is the supreme law of the land and it cannot be **abrogated** even in part by **statute.** Like the federal Constitution, a state constitution is the supreme law within the state. 140 F. Supp. 925.

CONSTITUTIONAL RIGHT individual liberties granted by state or the federal constitutions and protected from governmental interference. 389 U.S. 258. Such rights are usually those asserted by the minority, since the governmental instruments of the majority, the legislative and the executive branches, are usually sought to be checked by the supremacy of constitutional provisions as interpreted by the judiciary.

Most of the federal constitutional rights are found in the Bill of Rights, which was created originally as a limitation on action by the federal government, but many of whose rights are now applicable to the states by reason of the **Fourteenth Amendment.** 391 U.S. 145. See **bill of attainder; due process; equal protection; establishment clause; ex post facto; freedom of contract; free exercise clause; guarantee clause; obligation of contract; search and seizure; self-incrimination, privilege against; void for vagueness.** See also **unconstitutional.**

CONSTRUCTION the giving of an interpretation to something, which thing is less than totally clear, e.g., to determine the construction of a statute or **constitution** is to determine the meaning of an ambiguous part of it; to give a coherent meaning to; the act of CONSTRUING.

STRICT [LITERAL] CONSTRUCTION an interpretation of a **statute** or a provision according to its letter, leaving nothing for inference; a literal construction of a statute which accepts the precise language in its exact and technical sense, giving no effect to practical or equitable considerations. A **penal** statute is generally accorded a strict construction so that only conduct plainly within the reach of the statute is proscribed as criminal.

LIBERAL [EQUITABLE] CONSTRUCTION a liberal construction expands the meaning of a statute or provision to give broad effect to its purposes so as to encompass circumstances clearly within the spirit if not the letter of the statute. Statutes which are intended to be remedial in purpose are generally accorded a liberal construction so as to meet the evils which the statute was intended to remedy.

CONSTRUCTIVE not actual, but accepted in law as a substitute for whatever is otherwise required. Thus, anything which the law finds to exist "constructively" will be treated by the law as though it were actually so. If an object is not in one's actual possession but he intentionally and knowingly has dominion and control over it, the law will treat it as though it were in his actual possession by finding a "constructive possession." The same is true in many other contexts.

[For the meaning of "constructive" as applied to various legal concepts, refer to specific entries.]

CONSTRUCTIVE BAILMENT see **bailment.**

CONSTRUCTIVE CONTEMPT see **contempt of court.**

CONSTRUCTIVE DELIVERY see **delivery.**

CONSTRUCTIVE EVICTION see **eviction.**

CONSTRUCTIVE FRAUD see **fraud.**

CONSTRUCTIVE POSSESSION see **possession.**

CONSTRUCTIVE SERVICE see **service.**

CONSTRUE to interpret a statute, case, regulation, treaty or other legal authority; **construction** requires the determination of the meaning of the language of the authority in light of the background of the authority, such as the legislative history of a statute or the particular facts of and cases leading to a particular case. 27 S.E. 133, 140.

CONSUMER in economics, an individual who buys goods and services for personal use rather than for manufacture. It has been said that the consumer is the last person to whom property passes in the course of ownership and that this is the test of a retail transaction. 55 So. 2d 812, 823.

CONSUMER GOODS goods which are "used or bought for use primarily for personal, family, or household purposes." U.C.C. §9-109. "Consumer goods" is one of four categories of goods distinguished by the Uniform Commercial Code; the classifications are important for such purposes as determining the rights of persons who buy goods subject to a security interest, rights after a default, and rights among those with conflicting security interests in the same collateral. Thus, consumer goods are to be distinguished from EQUIPMENT, which are goods used or bought for use primarily in business; from FARM PRODUCTS, which are goods in the possession of one engaged in a farming operation "if they are crops or livestock or supplies used or produced in farming operations or if they are products of crops or livestock in their unmanufactured states" and from INVENTORY, which are goods held for sale. U.C.C. §9-109. The classification of goods is determined by its primary use.

CONSUMER PROTECTION refers to laws designed to aid retail consumers of goods and services that have been improperly manufactured, delivered, performed, handled, or described. Such laws provide the retail consumer with additional protections and remedies not generally provided to merchants and others who engage in business transactions, on the premise that consumers do not enjoy an "**arm's-length**" bargaining position with respect to the businessmen with whom they deal and therefore should not be strictly limited by the legal rules that govern **recovery** for **damages** among businessmen.

CONTACTS APPROACH see **conflict of laws.**

CONTEMPLATION OF DEATH see **causa** (CAUSA MORTIS).

CONTEMPT OF COURT an act or omission tending to obstruct or interfere with the orderly administration of justice, or to impair the dignity of the court or respect for its authority. There are two kinds, direct and constructive. 249 S. 2d 127, 128. DIRECT CONTEMPT openly and in the presence of the court, resists the power of the court, 102 A. 400, 406; and consequential, or CONSTRUCTIVE CONTEMPT results from matters outside the court, such as failure to comply with orders. 114 P. 257, 258.

Another classification differentiates between civil and criminal contempt. CIVIL CONTEMPT consists of failure to do something which is ordered by the court for the benefit of another party to the proceedings (sometimes called RELIEF TO LITIGANTS), while CRIMINAL CONTEMPTS are acts in disrespect of the courts or its processes which obstruct the administration of justice. 199 S.W. 2d 613, 614.

The penalty for civil contempt is usually payment of a fine, or imprisonment for an indefinite period of time until the party in contempt agrees to perform his legal obligation, unless the imprisonment clearly fails to act as coercion and acts merely to punish; 65 N.J. 257. The penalty for criminal contempt is a fine or imprisonment for a specific period of time, intended as punishment which must be tried by a jury if postconviction contempt proceedings impose sentences exceeding an aggregate of six months. 94 S.Ct. 2687.

CONTIGUOUS near or in close proximity to. 78 N.W. 2d 86, 91.

CONTINGENT BENEFICIARY one who will receive the benefit or proceeds of an estate, trust, life insurance policy or the like but only if some particular event or circumstance, whose happening or outcome is not presently known or assured, does in fact occur.

CONTINGENT ESTATE an **interest** in land which commences at some future point depending upon either the occurrence of a specific but uncertain event or upon the determination or existence of the person(s) to whom the estate is limited, see 260 S.W. 357, 359; e.g., if property is granted "to **A** for life and then to the heirs of **B**," there is a contingent estate (a "contingent **remainder**") in the heirs of **B**, which will **vest** [become certain] at the death of **A** unless **B** is without heirs. If **B** is without heirs, the estate **reverts** [goes back] to the original **grantor**. Because a contingent estate was regarded as a mere possibility or expectancy it was not **alienable inter vivos** [transferable during one's lifetime] at common law. Contingent remainders were made alienable in England in 1845 and are freely alienable today in the majority of American jurisdictions. Moynihan, Introduction to the Law of Real Property 135-137 (1962). Compare **conditional fee; determinable fee** [FEE SIMPLE DETERMINABLE]. See also **condition; future interest.**

CONTINGENT FEE see **attorney's fee.**

CONTINGENT LIABILITY a liability which will not accrue unless facts or circumstances which are not certain to occur do in fact occur at some future time. 347 N.Y.S. 2d 898. For instance, in a contract to sell a business, the seller will incur a contingent liability if he agrees to refund some or all of the purchase price in the event that the purchaser is sued for the seller's negligent acts in operating the business.

CONTINUANCE the adjournment or postponement to a subsequent date of an **action** pending in a court. 257 A. 2d 705, 709. See **recess.**

CONTRA (*kôn'-trà*)—Lat: against; in opposition to; in answer to, in reply to; contrary to; in violation of; the reverse of; in defiance of. Thus, "the Court's most recent decision is contra an established line of **precedent.**"

CONTRABAND any property the possession or transportation of which is illegal. For instance, narcotic drugs, firearms, counterfeit money, or cigarettes which an individual intends to illegally distribute or use are contraband. 49 U.S.C. §781.

CONTRA BONOS MORES (*kôn'-trà bō'-nōs mô'-rāz*)—Lat: against good morals; "conduct of such character as to offend the average conscience, as involving injustice according to commonly accepted standards." 231 F. 950, 969.

CONTRACT a promise, or set of promises, for **breach** of which the law gives a **remedy**, or the performance of which the law in some way recognizes as a **duty.** 1 Williston, Contracts §1. The essentials of a valid contract are "parties **competent** to contract, a proper subjectmatter, **consideration, mutuality** of agreement, and mutuality of obligation," 286 N.W. 844, 846; "a transaction involving two or more individuals whereby each becomes obligated to the other, with reciprocal rights to demand performance of what is promised by each respectively." 282 P. 2d 1084, 1088. "The total legal obligation which results from the parties' agreement as affected by law." U.C.C. §1-201 (11). Types of contracts include:

ALEATORY CONTRACT see aleatory contract.

BILATERAL CONTRACT one in which there are mutual promises between two parties to the contract, each party being both a **promisor** and a **promisee.** Corbin, Contracts §21.

CONDITIONAL CONTRACT a contract, the performance of which depends on an operative fact (a fact or event that affects legal relations; it is a cause of some change in those legal relations). Corbin On Contracts, One Volume Edition, §627 (1952). A contract, the performance of which depends on an event, not certain to occur, which must occur, unless its non-occurrence is excused before performance under the contract becomes due. See Restatement (Second), Contracts § 224.

CONTRACT OF ADHESION see **adhesion contract.**

CONTRACT OF HAZARD see **sale in gross.**

CONTRACT UNDER SEAL see SPECIAL CONTRACT (below). See also **sealed instrument; specialty.**

COST-PLUS CONTRACT "one where the total cost to the contractor represents the whole payment to be made to him, plus a stated percentage of profit," 59 N.W. 2d 368, 370; frequently used in government contracts and in situations where the production or construction costs are not presently determinable. See, e.g., 139 F. 2d 661, 667; 144 F. 2d 207, 208.

FREEDOM OF CONTRACT see **freedom of contract.**

FORMAL CONTRACT see **sealed instrument.**

IMPLIED CONTRACT see QUASI [IMPLIED] CONTRACT (below).

INSTALLMENT CONTRACT see **installment contract.**

OPTION CONTRACT see **option.**

ORAL CONTRACT one which is not in writing or which is not signed by the parties; "within the **statute of frauds** [it] is a real existing contract which lacks only the formal requirement of a memorandum [signed by the party to be charged] to render it enforceable in **litigation.**" 84 N.E. 2d 466, 467.

OUTPUT CONTRACT where one promises to deliver his entire output to another and the other promises to accept the entire output supplied. See U.C.C. §2-306.

QUASI [IMPLIED] CONTRACT a contract created by the law for reasons of justice, without any expression of assent and sometimes even against a clear expression of dissent. For example, B finds or steals A's money and refuses restitution; he is under a quasi-contractual duty to make such restitution. The chief reason why such contracts were classified as quasi or "implied in law" was that they were classified as such both in Roman Law and in English Common Law. See Corbin on Contracts, One Volume Edition, §19 (1952).

REQUIREMENTS CONTRACT where one party agrees to purchase all his requirements of a particular product from another. See 276 F. 2d 1; U.C.C. §2-306.

SEVERABLE CONTRACT see **severable contract.**

SPECIAL CONTRACT a CONTRACT UNDER SEAL; a **specialty.** See **sealed instrument.**

UNILATERAL CONTRACT one in which no promisor receives a promise as consideration for his promise, Corbin, Contracts §21; one-sided agreement whereby one makes a promise to do, or refrain from doing something in return for a performance not a promise.

See also **adhesion contract; breach [of contract]; privity [PRIVITY OF CONTRACT]; retail installment contract; tender; usurious contract; yellow dog contract.**

CONTRACT OF ADHESION see **adhesion contract.**

CONTRACTOR one who is a party to a contract; also one who contracts to do the work for another. An INDEPENDENT CONTRACTOR is "one who makes an agreement with another to do a piece of work, retaining in himself control of the means, method and manner of producing the result to be accomplished, neither party having the right to terminate the contract at will." 45 N.E. 2d 342, 345. A GENERAL CONTRACTOR in a building contract context is one who contracts directly with the owner of the property upon which the construction occurs, as distinguished from a **subcontractor** who would only deal with one of the general contractors. It is not necessary that the individual perform the entire construction involved. See 66 Va. 509, 511. See also **subcontractor.**

CONTRACTUAL BREACH see **breach of contract.**

CONTRACT UNDER SEAL see **sealed instrument.**

CONTRA PACEM (*kôn'-trà pä'-kĕm*)—Lat: against the peace. This phrase was used in the Latin forms of **indictments,** and also in **actions** for **trespass** as a signification that the offense alleged was committed against the public peace. Modern **pleading** uses the phrase "against the peace of the commonwealth," "of the people," etc.

CONTRIBUTION the legal right enjoyed by one required to compensate a victim for his injury to demand reimbursement from another person jointly responsible for that injury. Equal sharing of a common burden. In the law of *torts,* a right of contribution exists, if at all, generally by statutes although some courts have upheld the right of contribution that persons who are equals in the duty of bearing a common burden may be compelled by their associates to bear their share

of that burden." 34 F. Supp. 77, 80. The duty generally involves an equal sharing of the loss but in some jurisdictions it may be apportioned among the **joint tortfeasors** according to their degrees of relative fault. See, e.g., 114 N.W. 2d 105. Compare **indemnity.** See **charitable contribution.**

CONTRIBUTORY NEGLIGENCE see **negligence.**

CONTROLLED SUBSTANCES drugs whose general availability is restricted; any one of a number of drugs or other substances which are strictly regulated or outlawed because of their potential for abuse or addiction. Such drugs include those classified as narcotics, stimulants, depressants, hallucinogens, and cannabis.

In illegal trade, controlled substances are known as "drugs" or "dope." Commonly known controlled substances can be classified as follows:

NARCOTICS can be broken into two groups—opiates, including opium, heroin, morphine and codeine, which are derived from the opium poppy, and nonopiate synthetic narcotics such as demerol and methadone. Their major medicinal use is as a painkiller and a tranquilizer. Outside of medicine, the recreational use of the drugs produces euphoria although the exact pleasurable effect has not been identified. All narcotics are physically addicting, with the likelihood of addiction depending upon the drug, the frequency and duration of its usage, and its dosage. Symptoms of withdrawal from the addiction include weakness, depression, nausea, vomiting, irritability, insomnia, and anorexia. During the 19th century, opiates were common as a pain-reliever and as an ingredient in patent medicines. The U.S. first outlawed the sale of opiates except for medicinal purposes through the Harrison

Act in 1914 because of trade difficulties with China and Britain.

STIMULANTS this group includes cocaine, a drug extracted from the leaves of the South American coca plant, amphetamines, synthetic drugs first developed during the late 1800s, and other amphetamine-like synthetic drugs. These drugs stimulate the central nervous system and are used medicinally to combat depression and narcolepsy. Excessive doses produce hyperactivity, paranoia, and other psychotic symptoms. Prolonged use and large doses are followed by fatigue and depression. Cocaine can be psychologically addicting, with withdrawal resulting in depression. Cocaine was first outlawed with narcotics in 1914; sale of amphetamines was first regulated in 1954.

DEPRESSANTS this class includes barbiturates and tranquilizers such as librium and valium. These drugs are used to produce sedation, to induce sleep, to combat anxiety and to treat epilepsy. Excessive doses cause a drunken-like state, and have side effects similar to alcohol, including a hangover.

HALLUCINOGENS this class includes LSD (lysergic acid diethylamide), mescaline, and peyote. These drugs are often described as psychoactive, that is, affecting the mind. While hallucination is common, other effects of the drug depend upon the conditions surrounding the taker while using the drug. LSD is sometimes used in psychotherapy, but its ultimate effectiveness has not yet been established. These drugs are non-addictive. Peyote has been used in American Indian rituals since before America was discovered. LSD was discovered in 1938, and has been regulated since the early 1950s. It became very popular during the 1960s counter culture, at which time numerous repressive laws were passed.

CANNABIS this class includes marijuana, hashish, and hashish oil. Normally smoked, this drug is essentially an intoxicant, and has no psychoactive effect or hallucinogenic effect. While it currently has no general medicinal use in this country, it was recently recognized as a treatment for glaucoma. Cannabis is non-addictive. Between 1850 and 1937, marijuana was used medicinally as a treatment for a wide range of conditions, from insanity to gout. During Prohibition, recreational use of marijuana became widespread as a response to the lack of alcohol. After Prohibition ended, the Bureau of Narcotics campaigned against marijuana and by 1937, forty-six of the states had outlawed the substance.

CONTROVERSY a dispute; occurs when there are adversaries on a particular **issue;** an **allegation** on one side and a **denial** on the other. In constitutional law, in order to constitute a CASE OR CONTROVERSY sufficient to permit a constitutional **adjudication** within the limits of Article III of the United States Constitution, a controversy "must be definite and concrete, touching the legal relations of parties having adverse legal interests. . . . It must be a real and substantial controversy admitting of **specific relief** through a decree of a conclusive character, as distinguished from an option advising what the law would be upon a hypothetical state of facts." 300 U.S. 227, 240-41. Compare **advisory opinion.** See also **justiciable; separable controversy.**

CONTUMACY willful disobedience to the **summons** or orders of a court; signifies overt defiance of authority. 133 N.E. 2d 796, 800. Contumacious conduct may result in a finding of **contempt of court.**

CONVERSATION, CRIMINAL see **alienation of affections.**

CONVERSION the **tortious** deprivation of another's property without his authorization or **justification.** "To constitute a 'conversion' there must be a wrongful taking, or a wrongful detention, or an illegal assumption of ownership, or an illegal [use or misuse]. . . . A 'conversion' in the sense of the law of **trover** consists either in **appropriation** of a thing to the party's own use and beneficial enjoyment, or in destruction, or in exercising dominion over it, in exclusion or defiance of plantiff's right, or in withholding **possession** from plaintiff under **claim of title** inconsistent with his own." 339 F. Supp. 506, 511. See also **involuntary** [INVOLUNTARY CONVERSION].

CONVERTIBLE SECURITIES bonds and **preferred stock** that can be exchanged for **common stock** or other lesser security usually of the same **corporation.** Terms of the exchange specify the exchange ratio and expiration of the right to exchange.

CONVEY in the law of **real property,** to transfer property from one to another; in its widest sense, it means the "transfer of property or the **title** to property from one person to another by means of a written **instrument** and other formalities." 47 S.E. 784, 787. Compare **alienation.** See also **grant.**

CONVEYANCE see **convey.**

CONVICT one who has been determined by the court to be guilty of the crime charged; also, so to determine such guilt. "As ordinarily used, [the term] carries with it the idea that the person of whom it is spoken is **guilty** of a crime of such infamous character as to be punishable by imprisonment . . . and therefore is to be taken **prima facie** as importing guilt of such crime and imprisonment in consequence." 32 A. 19. One is convicted upon a valid plea of guilty or a verdict of guilty and judgment of conviction entered thereupon.

CONVICTION that legal act by judge or jury which declares the guilt of a **party** and upon which **sentence** or **judgment** is founded. 205 N.E. 2d 391, 393. The **confession** of an **accused** in open court or a verdict which ascertains and publishes the fact of guilt are both sufficient to constitute a conviction. 414 P. 2d 54, 56. See **guilty.** See also **judgment** [JUDGMENT OF CONVICTION].

COOPERATIVE see **condominium.**

COOPERATIVE ASSOCIATION a "union of individuals, commonly laborers, farmers, or small capitalists, formed for the prosecution in common of some productive enterprise, the profits being shared in accordance with the capital or labor contributed by each." 164 N.W. 804, 805.

CO-ORDINATE JURISDICTION see **jurisdiction** [CONCURRENT JURISDICTION].

COPARCENARY at common law, the estate of two or more females inherited from a common ancestor in default of male heirs. The rights of coparceners were in the nature of a **joint tenancy** in that they could sue and be sued jointly in regards to the property, but were in the nature of a **tenancy** in common in that no right of survivorship existed. Moynihan, Introduction to the Law of Real Property 235-236 (1962).

COPARCENERS at common law, two or more females who, in default of male heirs, inherited land from a common ancestor. Estates in coparcenary are not recognized in the United States. Moynihan, Introduction to the Law of Real Property 235-236 (1962).

COPY, CONFORMED see **conformed copy.**

COPYHOLD a medieval form of land tenure in England. A copyhold was a parcel of land granted to a peasant by a lord in return for agricultural services. The transaction was recorded on the rolls of the manor by the steward, who gave the tenant an authenticated copy of the recordation. Transfer of lands held by copyhold was achieved by surrender and admittance; that is, the copyholder surrendered his land to the baronial court and the steward admitted the person designated by the previous holder to the land by recording the transfer on the rolls and issuing a copy to the new tenant. Tenure was at the will of the lord, but in time the custom of the manor arising over many years gave the tenant a degree of security against arbitrary action by the lord. 57 Tenn. (10 Heisk) 621. Thus copyhold, though not originally entitling the holder to the absolute ownership characteristic of a freehold estate, came to represent a form of permanent tenure with rights of descent and alienability, while money rents or symbolic consideration were substituted for agricultural services. Copyhold was abolished in England in 1926. Moynihan, Introduction to the Law of Real Property 17 (1962).

Also used to refer generally to any form of land tenure other than a **freehold.**

COPYRIGHT the protection of the works of artists and authors giving them the exclusive right to publish their works or determine who may so publish.

Following the enactment of the Copyright Act of 1976, almost all copyright law in the United States is governed by federal statute. (Title 17, U.S.C.) This abrogated a system in which state COMMON LAW COPYRIGHT protected works prior to "publication" and the federal statute protected works following "publication." A small class of art work which are not fixed in a tangible medium (e.g. a perfor-

mance) may still be protected by common law copyright.

Under current federal law, copyright protection for most works is for the life of the "author" plus 50 years.

Copyrights under the 1976 Act "subsist" in "original works of authorship fixed in any tangible medium of expression." 17 U.S.C. §102. The level of "originality" required is not susceptible to a precise definition and is the subject of a considerable body of case law. Similarly, the degree of unauthorized use which constitutes INFRINGEMENT is difficult to delineate. For example, as to written work, the copyright is said to extend "only to the arrangement of words. A copyright does not give monopoly in any incident in a play. Other authors have a right to exploit the facts, experiences, and field of thought and general ideas, provided they do not substantially copy a concrete form, in which the circumstances and ideas have been developed, arranged, and put into shape." 133 F. 2d 889, 891.

CORAM NOBIS, WRIT OF see **writ of coram nobis.**

CORONER a public official who investigates the causes and circumstances of deaths that occur within his jurisdiction and makes a finding in a CORONER'S INQUEST. See also **post mortem.**

CORPORAL PUNISHMENT punishment inflicted upon the body, such as whipping. 69 F. 2d 905. The term may or may not include imprisonment. Id. Thus it often serves simply to distinguish physical punishment from non-physical punishment, such as a fine. See 43 P. 1026. Whipping has been found to violate contemporary standards of civilized conduct, and thus to be prohibited by the 8th Amendment's ban on "cruel and unusual punishment," whether administered pursuant to a **sentence** or in the course of prison discipline. 404 F. 2d 571.

The use of reasonable corporal punishment, however, has been upheld in the schools. 430 U.S. 651.

CORPORATE OPPORTUNITY the opportunity that a person having a close relationship to a **corporation** has to take advantage of the special knowledge he thereby acquires for personal gain. The term refers to the legal doctrine that directors or others invested with a **fiduciary** duty toward a corporation may not appropriate for their own benefit and advantage a business opportunity properly belonging to the corporation. 219 F. 2d 173, 176. Such a business opportunity has been held to arise when a director attempts to acquire property interests adverse to the interest of the corporation, or property in which the corporation has an interest or expectancy as, for example, the purchase of property under lease to the corporation; drawing away its existing customers; purchasing property the firm needs or has resolved to acquire; taking advantage of an offer made to the corporation, knowledge of which came to him as a director. 380 F. 2d 897, 901. Persons found guilty of this practice are deemed to hold the property or profits thus obtained in **constructive trust** for the benefit of the corporation, 222 N.W. 2d 71, and injunctive relief as well as money damages may be available. 380 F. 2d 897. See also **conflict of interests**.

CORPORATE POWER see **power, corporate**.

CORPORATION an association of **shareholders** (or even a single shareholder) created under law and regarded as an ARTIFICIAL PERSON by courts, "having a legal entity entirely separate and distinct from the individuals who compose it, with the capacity of continuous existence or **succession,** and having the capacity as such legal entity, of taking, holding and conveying **property,** suing and being sued, and exercising such other powers as may be conferred on it by law, just as a **natural person** may." 200 N.W. 76, 87. See 17 U.S. 518, 657. See also **subsidiary** [SUBSIDIARY CORPORATION].

A corporation's **liability** is normally limited to its **assets** and the **stockholders** are thus protected against personal liability in connection with the affairs of the corporation. [But see **piercing the corporate veil**.] The corporation is taxed at special corporate tax rates and the stockholders must pay an additional tax upon **dividends** or other profits obtained from the corporation. Corporations are subject to regulation by the state of incorporation and by the jurisdictions in which they carry on their business. State laws in some jurisdictions give the corporate board of directors and officers more freedom from stockholder consent and scrutiny than other states and thereby induce many corporations to form within their jurisdictions. Delaware is the leading example. Special statutes have been enacted in many jurisdictions to permit single individuals or closely-knit groups of individuals to form corporations to limit their personal liability but to carry on business without all of the formality of annual meetings, action by boards of directors, etc. These corporations are called CLOSE CORPORATIONS. They generally have only a single or a very small number of stockholders. See, Henn & Alexander, Law of Corporations 705 (3rd ed. 1983).

ACQUIRED CORPORATION a corporation which has been the target of a successful acquisition attempt.

ACQUIRING CORPORATION the corporation seeking to acquire the target corporation.

AFFILIATED CORPORATION generally applied to any member of an affiliated group of corporations related through common ownership.

BROTHER-SISTER CORPORATION two or more corporations having a common parent corporation.

CONTROLLED CORPORATION a corporation which is deemed to be controlled by another entity or individual who satisfies certain control requirements relating to stock ownership. Control is usually established by voting rights; for some purposes, however, it can be defined by the relative fair market value of a shareholder's stock.

DE FACTO CORPORATION one existing **de facto,** i.e., without actual authority of law. Three elements of de facto corporations are: the existence of a statute under which the corporation might have been validly incorporated; a **colorable** attempt to comply with such statute; and some use or exercise of corporate privileges. Henn & Alexander, Law of Corporations 330 (3rd ed. 1983).

MEMBER CORPORATION see **member corporation.**

MUNICIPAL CORPORATION see **municipal corporation.**

NOT-FOR-PROFIT CORPORATION one organized for some charitable, civil, social or other purpose that does not entail the generating of profit or the distribution of its income to members, principals, shareholders, officers or others affiliated with it. Such corporations are accorded special treatment under the law for some purposes, including federal income taxation.

NON STOCK CORPORATION see **non stock corporation.**

PRIVATE CORPORATIONS the common corporation, created by and for private individuals for non-governmental purposes.

PROFESSIONAL CORPORATION see **professional corporation.**

PUBLIC CORPORATION [POLITICAL CORPORATION] those created by the state to fulfill certain purposes and which possess governmental powers and functions, such as lesser governmental bodies (towns, cities), school districts, water districts. The United States Post Office is now a public corporation (called United States Postal Service). 39 U.S.C. §201.

QUASI CORPORATION a body which exercises certain functions of a corporate character, but which has not been established as a corporation by any statute, general or special. 103 U.S. 707, 708, See **quasi.**

SUB-CHAPTER S CORPORATION see S CORPORATION below.

S CORPORATION a small corporation which elects to be taxed as a partnership for federal income taxation purposes. Prior to 1982 these entities were called SUBCHAPTER S CORPORATIONS. The number of shareholders is limited; individual shareholders enjoy the benefits under state law of limited corporate liability but avoid corporate federal taxation.

TARGET CORPORATION a corporation which is the subject of an acquisition attempt.

CORPOREAL HEREDITAMENT see **hereditaments.**

CORPUS *(kôr'-pŭs)*—Lat: body. The principal mass of a physical substance. It is the principal or **res** of an **estate, devise** or **bequest** from which income is derived. 101, P. 2d 533, 536-537; 136 F. 2d 390, 391. In the law of trusts, any valid **trust** must have a valid subject matter or corpus; the corpus can consist of "any transferable interest, **vested** or contingent, legal or equitable, real or personal, tangible or intangible, as long as the subject matter is "certain." 102 N.E. 293, 295. Bogert, Handbook of the Law on Trusts (5th ed. 1973). Intangible things such as a **copyright** or the good will of a business or a trade secret, if transferable by **gift, inter-vivos** or by **will,** can constitute the corpus of a trust. See Restatement (Second), Trusts, §§74, §82 (1959).

In the law of **real property,** the term refers to all tangible objects; thus, the roadway, embankment and equipment constitute the corpus of railroad property. 99 U.S. 513. Royalties from oil and gas in a well also constitute the corpus of the land. 168 S.W. 2d 531, 534. The term generally is found in **civil law** denoting a positive fact as distinguished from a possibility. See **corpus delicti.** It also refers to an aggregate of a substance such as the law. See **corpus juris.**

CORPUS DELICTI *(kôr'-pŭs dĕ-lĭk'-tī)*—Lat: body of the crime. It is the objective proof that a crime has been committed. It is sometimes thought of mistakenly as the body of the victim of a **homicide,** but correctly understood, a corpus delicti in a **murder prosecution** is a "**prima facie** showing that the alleged victim met death by a criminal agency." 323 P. 2d 117, 123. The body of the victim is often helpful in this regard, and in the absence of the victim's body, it is frequently very difficult to establish either that the victim is dead or that he died by a criminal agency. In such instances the corpus delicti must be established to a **moral certainty.** See 1 Q.B. 388.

Corpus delicti applies to every crime. In order for the state to introduce a **confession** or convict the **accused** it must prove a corpus delicti, the elements of which are "first, the occurrence of the specific kind of injury or loss (as, in homicide, a person deceased); [and] secondly, somebody's criminality (in contrast, e.g., to mere accident) as the source of the loss. These two together [involve] the commission of a crime by somebody." 7 Wigmore, Evidence §2072 (Chadbourn rev. 1981). Only a prima facie showing of the corpus delicti is nec-

essary to admit a confession. 323 P. 2d 117, 123. **Proof beyond a reasonable doubt** is necessary if the corpus delicti is used to refer to all of the elements of the crime charged. 247 P. 2d 665.

CORPUS JURIS *(kôr'-pŭs jûr'-ĭs)*—Lat: body of law. Refers to a series of texts which contained much of the **civil,** as well as **canon** [**ecclesiastical**] law.

CORRECTIONAL INSTITUTION a general term used to describe a **jail,** prison, reformatory, or other government-maintained detention facility.

CORRESPONDENT see **adultery.**

CORROBORATING EVIDENCE evidence complementary to evidence already given and tending to strengthen or confirm it; additional evidence of a different character on the same point. 501 S.W. 2d 283, 289.

In relation to **rape,** corroboration of the testimony of the prosecutrix was necessary to support a conviction under the express provisions of some statutes, 65 N.W. 2d 448, although this requirement is now disfavored and rare.

CORRUPTION OF THE BLOOD incapacity to **inherit** or pass **property,** usually because of **attainder,** such as for treason; "the doctrine of corruption of blood was of feudal origin . . . the blood of the attainted person was deemed to be corrupt, so that neither could he transmit his **estate** to his **heirs,** nor could they take by **descent** from the ancestor." 18 N.E. 148, 150. This doctrine has been constitutionally abolished in the United States. See United States Constitution, Art. III, Sec. 3.

CO-SIGN a signature in addition to the **principal** signature of another in order to verify the authenticity of the principal signature. 163 A. 787, 789. The term does not have a definite legal significance as to whether the signature is one of a **principal** or a **surety.** 121 Cal. Rptr. 453, 455. However, an **indorsement** which clearly shows that it is not in the chain of **title** is **notice** that it is there only as an **accommodation.** U.C.C. §3-415(4).

COST, INSURANCE AND FREIGHT see **c.i.f.**

COST OF COMPLETION in a **breach of contract** situation, a measure of damages representing the total amount of additional expense, over and above the **contract** price, that the injured party would have to incur in order to obtain a substituted **performance** that would place him in the same position he would have been in if the contract had not been breached. See 212 N.Y.S. 222, 226; and 187 N.Y.S. 807, 813; often used as a measure of damages for breaches of construction contracts. Compare **diminution in value; expectation damages; specific performance.**

COST OF LIVING CLAUSE in a long-term contract, a clause which adjusts the price paid for the goods or services received in an amount equal to the change in the cost of living. For instance, in a lease of commercial property, the contract often provides that the rent will be increased once a year in an amount equal to the rise in the consumer price index for the area, published by the Bureau of Labor Statistics.

COST-PLUS CONTRACT see **contract.**

COSTS pecuniary reimbursement to the successful **party** for the expenses of **litigation;** an allowance which is incidental to judgment and is authorized by law to be awarded to the prevailing party and which compensates a party for the expense of asserting his rights in court. 43 F. Supp. 209; 245 P. 2d 67, 70; 30 A.L.R. 2d 1141. Costs may be allowed to a **plaintiff** if the **default** of the **defendant** made it necessary to sue him, and to a defendant if the plaintiff sued him

without cause. 142 N.Y. 580. Generally, **costs** and expenses of litigation are recoverable by right but only if authorized by **statute.** If there is no applicable statute, Rule 54d of the Federal Rules of Civil Procedure provides that costs are allowed to the prevailing party unless the trial court otherwise directs. State court rules usually have similar provisions. See generally 176 F. 2d 1; 374 P. 2d 289, 296.

At **common law,** a party could not recover costs. 102 N.W. 2d 376. Courts originally awarded reimbursement of costs to punish the defeated party rather than to compensate the successful party. Under some statutes the law of costs is still penal in nature. 135 N.Y.S. 2d 72.

COSTS TO ABIDE THE EVENT court order requiring the losing party to pay for legal expenses of the prevailing party "up to and including the decision of the [highest court of the jurisdiction]." 200 N.Y.S. 796, 797, and sometimes on retrial.

COTENANCY possession of a unit of property by two or more persons; does not refer to an **estate,** but rather a relationship between persons as to their **holding** of property; encompasses both **tenancy** in common and **joint tenancy** [and thus, **tenancy** by the entirety as well].

COUNSEL [COUNSELLOR] an **attorney;** lawyer.

COUNT a distinct statement of **plaintiff's cause of action.** See 126 F. Supp. 395, 397. In **indictments,** a count, like a **charge,** is an **allegation** of a distinct offense. See 167 S.W. 2d 192, 193. A complaint or indictment may contain one or more counts.

COUNTERCLAIM a counter-demand made by **defendant** in his favor against the **plaintiff.** It is not a mere **answer** or **denial** of plaintiff's allegations, but rather asserts an independent **cause of action,** 275 N.E. 2d 688, 690, the purpose of which is to oppose or deduct from plaintiff's claim, 16 F.R.D. 225, 228.

In federal practice and in many states, counterclaims may be either: COMPULSORY—"those arising out of the transaction or occurrence that is the subject matter of the opposing party's claim," Green, Civil Procedure 125 (2d ed. 1979); or PERMISSIVE—any other, i.e., those not arising out of the present claim. See **set-off.** Compare **cross-claim.**

COUNTERFEIT "[f]orged; false, fabricated without right; made in imitation of something else with a view to defraud by passing the false copy for genuine or original," 197 F. Supp. 264, 265; e.g., counterfeit coins, paper money, bonds, deeds, stocks, etc.

COUPLED WITH AN INTEREST see **authority** [AUTHORITY COUPLED WITH AN INTEREST].

COUPONS certificates, usually attached to an instrument evidencing a loan, which may be detached (clipped) and presented separately for payment of a specific sum of money representing interest on the main instrument. 106 U.S. 589. See **bond** [BEARER BONDS].

COURSE OF BUSINESS see **ordinary course of business.**

COURSE OF DEALING see **trade usage** [COURSE OF DEALING].

COURT the branch of government which is responsible for the resolution of disputes arising under the laws of the government. A court system is usually divided into various parts which specialize in hearing different types of cases. Trial courts are responsible for receiving evidence and determining the application of the law to facts which it finds. Trial courts are usually divided into CIVIL COURTS, which hear disputes arising under the common law and civil statutes, CRIMINAL COURTS which hear prosecutions under the criminal laws, MATRIMONIAL COURTS which hear divorce proceedings, and SURROGATE'S COURTS which hear proceedings regarding the estates of deceased and incompetent persons. Appellate courts review the decisions of trial courts to determine whether the trial court made an error of law in deciding the case. Appellate courts are frequently divided into intermediate appellate courts to which a party may always appeal, and a supreme appellate court, which has discretion over which cases it chooses to hear. James & Hazard, Civil Procedure §1.11 (2d ed. 1977). See **de facto** [DEFACTO COURT]; **district court; federal courts; inferior court; international court of justice; juvenile courts; kangaroo court; moot court; open court.** See also **probate** [PROBATE COURT]; **small claims court; supreme court; tax court; term of court; territorial court; trial court.**

COURT EN BANC see **en banc.**

COURT-MARTIAL (plural "courts-martial") the basic trial court of the military courts system. Depending upon the circumstances, a court-martial may consist of from one to six or more members, 10 U.S.C. §816, and may be convened by the President, secretaries of military departments, or by senior commanding officers, 10 U.S.C. §§822, 823. A court-martial may impose sentences of confinement and/or discharge. 10 U.S.C. §§858, 858a.

In order for a crime to be subject to court-martial rather than civilian criminal proceedings, it is not enough that the accused has military "status;" the crime itself must be "service-connected;" such as being committed on a military post, 401 U.S. 355, 369, or while wearing a service uniform, 395 U.S. 258, 283. Thus, a soldier on an evening pass is not subject to discipline by a court-martial for attempted rape or burglary while away from his base, but must be prosecuted under civilian authority. Id. See **military law** [COURT-MARTIAL].

The Uniform Code for Military Justice, Chapter 47 establishes three kinds of court-martial in each of the armed forces:

GENERAL COURT-MARTIAL presided over by a law officer and not less than five members, has jurisdiction over all members of the armed services of which it is a part, and is authorized to try defendants for all military offenses, and to prescribe any permitted sanctions. It deals generally with capital offenses, 10 U.S.C. §818.

SPECIAL COURT-MARTIAL presided over by three members, may try all non-capital offenses, but is limited in its authority to prescribe sanctions as dismissal, hard labor, and extended confinement, and may not authorize execution, 10 U.S.C. §819.

SUMMARY COURT-MARTIAL presided over by a single commissioned officer, and is limited in respect to the military personnel over whom it has jurisdiction and the sanctions it may prescribe. The accused may refuse trial by a summary court-martial, but the charges may then be referred to a higher level court-martial, 10 U.S.C. §820.

COURT OF APPEALS see **appellate court.**

COURT OF ASSIZE AND NISI PRIUS an English law court "composed of two or more commissioners, who [were] twice in every year sent by the king's special commission all around the kingdom to try by jury cases under their jurisdiction." See 3 Bl. Comm. *58, *59.

COURT OF CLAIMS a court of the United States created in 1855 to hear and determine claims against the United States. The purpose of the tribunal was to relieve Congress of the burden of disposing of such claims through **the enactment** of private bills. At first the court's decisions were merely recommendations for congressional action but in 1866 its decisions were declared by Congress to be final. The TUCKER ACT of 1887 expanded the jurisdiction of the court. 24 Stat. 505. The Supreme Court determined that the court was an Article III court and that its judges enjoyed life tenure. 370 U.S. 530. In 1982 Congress replaced this court with a new UNITED STATES CLAIMS COURT "established under Article I"; the judges of the new court hold office for fifteen year terms and decide CONGRESSIONAL-REFERENCE CASES. 28 U.S.C. §1492. These congressional-reference cases are cases in which Congress asks the court to make findings of fact or recommendations that Congress will then use in deciding whether to afford a party legislative relief.

COURT OF CUSTOMS AND PATENT APPEALS see **federal courts.**

COURT OF EQUITY "a court having jurisdiction in cases where a plain, adequate and complete remedy cannot be had at **law.**" 3 N.Y. 498, 499. Courts of equity were common law courts but had their own principles (e.g., **clean hands doctrine**) and their own unique remedies (e.g., **injunction, specific performance**). Actions were brought either equitably "in **chancery**" or legally "at law." Courts which are guided primarily by equitable doctrine are said to be courts of equity. Thus, a **bankruptcy** court is a court of equity. "A court of equity is a court of conscience, and whatever, therefore, is unconscionable is odious in its sight." 47 A. 693, 695. Courts of equity, which arose independently of courts of law in England, have merged with the latter in most jurisdictions of the United States. See **equity.**

COURT OF EXCHEQUER (*ĕks'-chĕk-ėr*) an ancient English court of **record.** It was established by William the Conqueror to recover the King's **debts** and **duties;** it was inferior to both the court of the **Kings bench** and the court of common pleas, but served as both a **court of law** and **equity.** It took its name from the chequered cloth which covered its table and was marked and scored when the King's accounts were prepared. It consisted of two divisions, one that handled the royal revenue and the court, which was subdivided into courts of **equity** and **common law.** 3 Bl. Comm. *44-45.

THE COURT OF EXCHEQUER CHAMBER a court of **appeal** established to determine causes upon **writs** of error from the **common law** side of the **court of exchequer.** Id. at 46.

COURT OF INQUIRY see **military law** [MILITARY COURT OF INQUIRY].

COURT OF KING'S [QUEEN'S] BENCH see King's [Queen's] Bench.

COURT OF LAW a **tribunal** which has **jurisdiction** over cases **at law.** The term applies to courts which administer justice according to federal or state law or **common law,** as distinguished from courts which follow the rules and principles of **equity** and are called **chancery** courts. Law courts and **equity** courts, however, are generally no longer distinguished, and a **court of law** is any **tribunal** administering the law.

COURT OF MILITARY APPEAL see **military law** [COURT OF MILITARY APPEAL].

COURT OF MILITARY REVIEW see **military law** [COURT OF MILITARY REVIEW].

COURT OF STAR CHAMBER see **star chamber.**

COVENANT an agreement or promise to do or not to do a particular thing; to enter into a formal agreement; to **bind** oneself in **contract;** to make a stipulation; a promise incidental to a **deed** or contract, which is either express or implied; "an agreement, convention or promise of two or more parties, by deed in writing signed, and delivered, by whichever of the parties pledges himself to the order that something is either done or shall be done or stipulates for the truth of certain facts." 279 P. 2d 276, 278.

CONCURRENT COVENANTS those which require the performance by one party of his obligation when the other party is ready and offers his performance.

COVENANT NOT TO COMPETE see **covenant not to compete.**

DEPENDENT COVENANTS those in which the obligation to perform one covenant arises only upon the prior **performance** of another and therefore, until the prior **condition** of performance has been met, the other party is not liable to an **action** on his covenant.

INDEPENDENT [MUTUAL] COVENANTS those which must be performed by one party without reference to the obligations of the other party. See 125 F. 536, 541.

In deeds, the usual covenants for **title** include:

COVENANT AGAINST THE ACTS OF THE GRANTOR often inserted into a **bargain and sale** deed and assures that the grantor has not done, nor caused to be done, any act by means of which the premises or any part thereof may be impeached or encumbered in any way. See 8 N.J.L. 90.

COVENANT AGAINST ENCUMBRANCES a guarantee given to the **grantee** of an estate that such estate is without **encumbrances.**

COVENANT OF FURTHER ASSURANCE obligates the covenantor to perform whatever acts are reasonably demanded by the covenantee for the purpose of perfecting or "assuring" the title which is conveyed. See Burby, Real Property §125 (3rd ed. 1965). This type of covenant is no longer in general use.

COVENANT OF HABITABILITY see **warranty of habitability.**

COVENANT OF QUIET ENJOYMENT see **quiet enjoyment.**

COVENANT OF WARRANTY AND QUIET ENJOYMENT obligates the **covenantor** to protect the estate against the existence of lawful claims of ownership. A cause of action arises only when there is an actual or constructive **eviction.**

COVENANTS OF SEISIN AND RIGHT TO CONVEY covenant that the **grantor** has an **estate,** or the right to **convey** an estate, of the quality and quantity which he purports to convey.

"Covenants such as **warranty,** quiet enjoyment, and further assurance are continuous in nature and may be enforced by a remote party. Other covenants, such as **seisin,** right to convey, and against encumbrances, are not continuous in nature and do not **'run with the land.' "** Burby, Real Property 126 (3rd ed. 1965). See **warranty** [WARRANTY OF HABITABILITY, WARRANTY OF MERCHANTABILITY].

RESTRICTIVE COVENANT see **restrictive covenant.**

COVENANTEE one who receives the **covenant,** or for whom it is made.

COVENANT NOT TO COMPETE a contractual term or condition by which a party promises to refrain from conducting business or professional activities of a nature similar to those of another party. These covenants are encountered principally in contracts of employment, partnership, or sale of a business. 62 A.L.R. 3d 1014. In a contract for the sale of a business, a covenant not to compete is generally enforceable provided it is reasonable and limited as to time and territory. In partnership contracts, covenants not to compete are generally upheld for the duration of the partnership. In employment contracts, covenants not to compete are generally enforceable during the period of employment. But covenants imposing restrictions after termination of employment may be held invalid unless reasonable in scope and duration or supported by adequate consideration. Reasonableness is assessed by the court considering factors such as the adequacy of **consideration,** the danger an employer seeks to avert, the economic hardship the covenant would impose on the employee, the public interest, the adequacy of time and territorial limits, and the scope of the covenant's restrictions. 390 A. 2d 1161. The protection of **trade secrets,** customer lists, business methods specific to a particular employer, and unique qualifications of an employee have been held to constitute legitimate interests for protection by covenants not to compete. 274 A. 2d 577.

COVENANTOR one who makes a **covenant.**

COVER in commercial law, to find a source of supply of similar goods through purchases on the open market after a seller of goods has breached a contract of sale by failing to deliver the goods as agreed. Under U.C.C. §2-712, after a seller breaches and the buyer "covers," the buyer can recover the difference between the cost of the substitute goods and the original contract price, 200 F. Supp. 59, 66, provided the buyer has acted in good faith and without reasonable delay in effecting such "cover." The U.C.C. formula thus seeks to put the buyer in the economic position that performance by the seller would have placed him in. This result is a significant departure from prior law whereby, if an aggrieved buyer made a cover purchase, there was no assurance that the court, applying general contract principles, would measure the market at or near the time he made his covering purchase. White & Summers, Uniform Commercial Code, 216-222 (2d ed. 1980).

Under the Code, the buyer is not required to cover as a means of minimizing damages; failure to effect cover does not bar him from any other remedy except compensatory (actual) **damages** which could have been avoided by reasonable cover. U.C.C. §2-712(3).

In **insurance** law, the term means to hold protected as against a particular risk. An oral contract to "cover" is ordinarily construed to mean that the insured is at the present time protected against loss, and not merely that a notation has been made that at some future date a policy will issue. See 295 N.W. 837, 841.

COVERTURE at common law, a married woman's legal condition; "a term used to describe the condition or state of a married woman whereby the civil existence of the wife was for many purposes merged with that of her husband." 327 S.W. 808, 811. "In England, and in all of the United States except the **community property** jurisdictions, statutes have been enacted which give a wife almost unlimited control over her **real** and **personal property.** Known as "Married Woman's Property Acts," these statutes generally provide that her property shall be wholly free from the husband's claims or control. Accordingly, they have the practical effect of abolishing the husband's estate by the marital right." 1 American Law of Property §5.56 (1952).

CREDIT that which is extended to a buyer or borrower on the seller or lender's belief that that which is given will be repaid. The term can be applied to unlimited types of transactions. Under the Uniform Commercial Code, any credit transaction creating a **security** interest in property is called a "secured transaction." U.C.C., Art. 9. In accounting, a credit is money owing and due to one, and is considered an **asset.** The word is also used with respect to one's reputation or business standing in a given community. For example, a person with a healthy, profitable business who has always repaid debts in the past, will be considered a good "credit risk" by a prospective lender. The use of credit in consumer transactions is strictly controlled by federal and state law. See **U.C.C.C. [Uniform Commercial Credit Code].** See also **full faith and credit; revolving credit; tax credit.**

CREDITOR one to whom money is owed by the **debtor;** one to whom an obligation exists. "In its strict legal sense, [a creditor] is one who voluntarily trusts or gives credit to another for money or other property, but in its more general and extensive sense it is one who has a right by law to demand and recover of another a sum of money on any account whatever." 38 S.W. 13, 14. See **judgment creditor.**

CREDITOR BENEFICIARY see **third party beneficiary** [CREDITOR BENEFICIARY].

CREDITOR'S BILL [OR SUIT] a **proceeding** in **equity** in which a **judgment creditor** [a creditor who has secured **judgment** against a **debtor** and whose **claim** has not been satisfied] attempts to gain a discovery, accounting, and deliverance of **property** owed to him by the **judgment debtor,** which property cannot be reached by execution [seizure and forced sale] at law. See 42 A. 2d 872, 875.

CRIME any act which the sovereign has deemed contrary to the public good; a wrong which the government has determined is injurious to the public and, hence, prosecutable in a **criminal proceeding**. Crimes include **felonies** and **misdemeanors**. A "common law crime" was one declared to be an offense by the developed case law method of the common law courts. Today, nearly all criminal offenses are statutory, as most jurisdictions either do not recognize common law crimes at all, or at least refuse to develop "new" offenses not punishable under the early common law. See 427 P. 2d 928; 1 Wheat. 415. See also **vice crime**; **white-collar crime**.

CRIMEN FALSI (krī'-měn făl'-sē) –Lat; literally, a crime of deceit. At **common law** a crimen falsi was a crime containing the elements of falsehood and fraud. See 141 N.E. 2d 202, 206. A person who had committed such a crime, which was described as one which "injuriously affects the administration of justice by the introduction of falsehood and fraud," was generally disqualified from appearing as a **witness** in any judicial **proceeding**. See 1 F. 784, 787 and 207 F. 527, 531. Examples of crimen falsi include **forgery**; **perjury**; **subornation of perjury**; suppression of testimony by, or **conspiracy** to procure the absence of, a **witness**; and the fraudulent making or alteration of a writing. See 5 A. 2d 804, 805.

CRIME OF PASSION a crime committed under the influence of sudden or extreme passion. For instance, a man's attack on another person with an axe after that person insulted the attacker's wife might be considered a crime committed in the heat of passion. 3 So. 551. More frequently, killing an adulterer or adulteress upon the sudden discovery of adultery is characterized as a crime committed in the heat of passion. Heat of passion is a defense to the mens rea, or intent element of murder, the rationale being that a person whose passions are sudden-

ly provoked is ... itation. Id. Th ... a murder charg... charge and ... dant's possible ... Proc & Crim. ... (1979) to determ... act was impelled by ... or by malice, all ... must be taken into ac... ing the length of time ... provocation and killing ... of the killing, and the p... tions of the parties. 22... 600. See **manslaughter**.

CRIME, ORGANIZED s... nized crime; racketeering

CRIMES AGAINST NAT... ual deviations which were ... ered crimes at common la... have been carried over by sta... include sodomy and bestiality.

CRIMINAL, one who has be... convicted of a violation of the crim... inal laws; also, an adjective which denotes "an act done with mali... cious **intent**, from an evil nature, or with a wrongful disposition to harm or injure other persons or property." 96 P. 2d 588, 591. After the criminal has satisfied whatever sanction has been imposed upon him, he is called today an EX OFFENDER. An HABITUAL OFFENDER (or HABITUAL CRIMINAL) is a person convicted on numerous occasions of crime, and who for that reason is subject to an extended term of imprisonment under the habitual offender laws of many jurisdictions. See **recidivist**; **sentence** [EXTENDED TERM]. See also **quasi** [QUASI-CRIMINAL].

CRIMINAL CODE see **penal law** [CODE].

CRIMINAL COERCION the common law offense of **extortion** has been broadened by modern statutes to encompass any person who, acting with purpose to restrict unlawfully another's freedom of action to his detriment, threatens to commit any criminal offense, accuse any-the buyer in the economic position that performance by the seller would have placed him in. This result is a significant departure from prior law whereby, if an aggrieved buyer made a cover purchase, there was no assurance that the court, applying general contract principles, would measure the market at or near the time he made his covering purchase. White & Summers, Uniform Commercial Code, 216-222 (2d ed. 1980).

Under the Code, the buyer is not required to cover as a means of minimizing damages; failure to effect cover does not bar him from any other remedy except compensatory (actual) **damages** which could have been avoided by reasonable cover. U.C.C. §2-712(3).

In **insurance** law, the term means to hold protected as against a particular risk. An oral contract to "cover" is ordinarily construed to mean that the insured is at the present time protected against loss, and not merely that a notation has been made that at some future date a policy will issue. Sec 295 N.W. 837, 841.

COVERTURE at common law, a married woman's legal condition; "a term used to describe the condition or state of a married woman whereby the civil existence of the wife was for many purposes merged with that of her husband." 327 S.W. 808, 811. "In England, and in all of the United States except the **community property** jurisdictions, statutes have been enacted which give a wife almost unlimited control over her **real** and **personal property.** Known as "Married Woman's Property Acts," these statutes generally provide that her property shall be wholly free from the husband's claims or control. Accordingly, they have the practical effect of abolishing the husband's estate by the marital right." 1 American Law of Property §5.56 (1952).

CREDIT that which is extended to a buyer or borrower on the seller or lender's belief that that which is given will be repaid. The term can be applied to unlimited types of transactions. Under the Uniform Commercial Code, any credit transaction creating a **security** interest in property is called a "secured transaction." U.C.C., Art. 9. In accounting, a credit is money owing and due to one, and is considered an **asset.** The word is also used with respect to one's reputation or business standing in a given community. For example, a person with a healthy, profitable business who has always repaid debts in the past, will be considered a good "credit risk" by a prospective lender. The use of credit in consumer transactions is strictly controlled by federal and state law. See **U.C.C.C. [Uniform Commercial Credit Code].** See also **full faith and credit; revolving credit; tax credit.**

CREDITOR one to whom money is owed by the **debtor;** one to whom an obligation exists. "In its strict legal sense, [a creditor] is one who voluntarily trusts or gives credit to another for money or other property, but in its more general and extensive sense it is one who has a right by law to demand and recover of another a sum of money on any account whatever." 38 S.W. 13, 14. See **judgment creditor.**

CREDITOR BENEFICIARY see **third party beneficiary** [CREDITOR BENEFICIARY].

CREDITOR'S BILL [OR SUIT] a **proceeding** in **equity** in which a **judgment creditor** [a creditor who has secured **judgment** against a **debtor** and whose **claim** has not been satisfied] attempts to gain a discovery, accounting, and deliverance of **property** owed to him by the **judgment debtor,** which property cannot be reached by execution [seizure and forced sale] at law. See 42 A. 2d 872, 875.

CRIME any act which the sovereign has deemed contrary to the public good; a wrong which the government has determined is injurious to the public and, hence, prosecutable in a **criminal proceeding.** Crimes include **felonies** and **misdemeanors.** A "common law crime" was one declared to be an offense by the developed case law method of the **common law** courts. Today, nearly all criminal offenses are statutory, as most jurisdictions either do not recognize common law crimes at all, or at least refuse to develop "new" offenses not punishable under the early common law. See 427 P. 2d 928; 1 Wheat. 415. See also **vice crime; white-collar crime.**

CRIMEN FALSI *(krĭ'-mĕn fäl'-sē)*—Lat: literally, a **crime** of **deceit.** At **common law** a crimen falsi was a crime containing the elements of falsehood and **fraud.** See 141 N.E. 2d 202, 206. A person who had committed such a crime, which was described as one which "injuriously affects the administration of justice by the introduction of falsehood and fraud," was generally disqualified from appearing as a **witness** in any judicial **proceeding.** See 1 F. 784, 787 and 207 F. 327, 331. Examples of crimen falsi include **forgery; perjury; subornation of perjury;** suppression of testimony by, or **conspiracy** to procure the absence of, a **witness;** and the fraudulent making or alteration of a writing. See 5 A. 2d 804, 805.

CRIME OF PASSION a crime committed under the influence of sudden or extreme passion. For instance, a man's attack on another person with an axe after that person insulted the attacker's wife might be considered a crime committed in the heat of passion. 3 So. 551. More frequently, killing an adulterer or adulteress upon the sudden discovery of adultery is characterized as a crime committed in the heat of passion. Heat of passion is a defense to the mens rea, or intent element of murder, the rationale being that a person whose passions are sudden-

ly provoked is incapable of premeditation. Id. The defense will reduce a murder charge to a manslaughter charge and hence reduce a defendant's possible punishment. LaFave & Scott, Criminal Law 572 (1972). In determining whether the act was impelled by heat of passion or by malice, all circumstances must be taken into account, including the length of time between the provocation and killing, the manner of the killing, and the previous relations of the parties. 220 N.E. 2d 600. See **manslaughter.**

CRIME, ORGANIZED see **organized crime; racketeering.**

CRIMES AGAINST NATURE sexual deviations which were considered crimes at common law and have been carried over by statute; include **sodomy** and **bestiality.**

CRIMINAL one who has been convicted of a violation of the criminal laws; also, an adjective which denotes "an act done with malicious **intent,** from an evil nature, or with a wrongful disposition to harm or injure other persons or property." 96 P. 2d 588, 591. After the criminal has satisfied whatever sanction has been imposed upon him, he is called today an EX-OFFENDER. An HABITUAL OFFENDER (or HABITUAL CRIMINAL) is a person convicted on numerous occasions of crime and who for that reason is subject to an extended term of imprisonment under the habitual offender laws of many jurisdictions. See **recidivist; sentence** [EXTENDED TERM]. See also **quasi** [QUASI-CRIMINAL].

CRIMINAL CODE see **penal law** [CODE].

CRIMINAL COERCION the common law offense of **extortion** has been broadened by modern statutes to encompass any person who, acting with purpose to restrict unlawfully another's freedom of action to his detriment, threatens to commit any criminal offense, accuse anyone of a criminal offense, expose any secret tending to subject any person to hatred, contempt or ridicule, impair his credit or business repute, or threatens to take or withhold action as an official, or cause an official to take or withhold action. Model Penal Code §212.5 Common law extortion was limited to the corrupt collection of an unlawful fee by an officer acting under **color** of office with no proof of threat, force, or **duress** required. 621 F. 2d 123, 124. If property is obtained as the result of criminal coercion, the conduct then constitutes **theft** by extortion since that form of theft encompasses today any conduct which is now proscribed by the criminal coercion statute. See **coercion.**

CRIMINAL CONTEMPTS see **contempt of court.**

CRIMINAL CONVERSATION see **alienation of affections.**

CRIMINAL MAINTENANCE unauthorized interference in a lawsuit by helping one party, with money or otherwise, to prosecute or defend a **cause of action** so as to obstruct justice, promote unnecessary litigation or unsettle community peace. Unlike **champerty,** criminal maintenance does not necessarily involve personal profit. See **barratry.**

CRIMINAL   NEGLIGENCE see **negligence.**

CRIMINAL POSSESSION see **possession.**

CRIMINAL PROCEDURE see **procedure** [CRIMINAL PROCEDURE].

CROSS-CLAIM claim **litigated** by co-**defendants** or co-**plaintiffs** against each other, and not against a party on the opposite side of the litigation. See 424 F. 2d 52, 55. Compare **counterclaim.**

CROSS-EXAMINATION the questioning of a witness, by a party or lawyer other than the one who called the witness, concerning matters about which the witness has testified during **direct examination.** The purpose is to discredit or clarify testimony already given so as to neutralize damaging testimony or present facts in a light more favorable to the party against whom the direct testimony was offered.

All the evidence presented in **litigated** cases must be so presented as to give the parties to whom it is adverse the opportunity for cross-examination, 213 A. 2d 491, and a person may not be deprived of property or liberty without an opportunity to cross-examine adverse witnesses. 380 U.S. 400. As a general rule, and sometimes by virtue of statute, a wide latitude is, or should be, permitted in the cross-examination of an adverse witness. Although such examination must conform with well recognized rules of evidence, more latitude is allowed than on direct examination. 98 C.J.S. 130; Fed. R. Evid. 611.

DIRECT EXAMINATION the initial questioning of a witness by the party who called the witness. The purpose is to present testimony containing the factual argument the party is making. Leading questions should not be used on the direct examination of a witness except as may be necessary to develop his testimony. Fed. R. Evid. 611.

REDIRECT EXAMINATION the questioning of a witness by a party who called the witness after that witness has been subject to cross-examination. The purpose of redirect examination is to rebut or clarify any damaging testimony elicited on cross-examination. In general, the redirect examination of a witness may extend to matters brought out on cross-examination, and ordinarily it should be limited to the scope of the cross-examination, although the court may permit it to go beyond the scope thereof. 98 C.J.S. 221.

CRUEL AND UNUSUAL PUNISH-MENT such punishment as is found to be offensive to the ordinary person; Amendment VIII to the United States Constitution provides: "Excessive bail shall not be required, nor excessive fines imposed, nor cruel and unusual punishment inflicted." "The term cannot be defined with specificity. It is flexible and tends to broaden as society tends to pay more regard to human decency and dignity and becomes . . . more humane. Generally speaking, a punishment that amounts to torture, or that is grossly excessive in proportion to the offense for which it is imposed, or that is inherently unfair, or that is shocking or disgusting to people of reasonable sensitivity is a 'cruel and unusual punishment.' And a punishment that is not inherently cruel and unusual may become so by reason of the manner in which it is inflicted," 309 F. Supp. 362, 380; ". . . [t]he beatings, physical abuse, torture, running of gauntlets, and similar cruelty—was wholly beyond any force needed to maintain order [in a prison]" and thus constituted cruel and unusual punishment. 453 F. 2d 12, 22. "Although lawful incarceration . . . deprives the prisoners of many rights enjoyed by others . . . they are still entitled to protection against cruel and unusual punishment by the **Eighth Amendment.**" Id. at 22-23. Imposition of the death penalty is not per se cruel and unusual punishment. 428 U.S. 153. A mandatory sentence of death for a crime without consideration of particularized mitigating factors, however, has been held unconstitutional as a violation of the Eighth Amendment. 431 U.S. 633. The rendering of a death penalty by juries exercising broad **discretion** has also been held unconstitutional. 428 U.S. 153; 408 U.S. 238.

CUCKOLD a man whose wife is unfaithful; the husband of an adulteress. It is explained that the word alludes to the habit of the female cuckold, which lays her eggs in the nests of other birds to be hatched by them. To make a cuckold of a man is to seduce his wife. 166 S.W. 770.

CULPA (*kŭl'-pă*)—Lat: a term from the civil law meaning fault, neglect, or negligence. Compare DOLUS, also from the civil law meaning fraud, guile, or deceit.

CULPABLE deserving of moral blame; implies fault rather than guilt; "criminal, reckless, gross . . . it means disregard of the consequence which may ensue from the act, and indifference to the rights of others," 183 N.E. 273, 275; as well as intentional wrong-doing.

CULPABLE MENTAL STATE generally, the state of mind which is necessary in order to commit a crime. At common law both an intent to commit a crime, called the **mens rea,** and the acts which constitute the crime were required to establish guilt. 4 Bl. Comm.*21. During the 19th century, American law developed the doctrine that punishment for crimes resulting in death depends upon the intent of the actor. Generally, willful, deliberate, and premeditated killing was classified as first degree murder, while a killing with malice, or mere intent to kill, would be classified as second degree murder. The distinction is statutory and varies widely among jurisdictions. Most modern criminal codes define the culpable mental states in specific terms such as acting intentionally, purposefully, knowingly, recklessly, or negligently. Model Penal Code §2.02. See **mens rea.**

CUMULATIVE DIVIDEND see **dividend.**

CUMULATIVE VOTING a system of shareholder voting for a board of **directors** designed to give minority shareholders representation on the board. Under a straight voting system each share of voting stock carries one vote for each position to be filled on the board. Under cumulative voting all the votes can be cast for a single position. For example, the owner of a single share of stock voting in an election for five directors would be able to cast one vote for each position under a straight voting system, but would be able to cast all five votes for a single position, or distribute them in any manner desired, under a cumulative voting system. Henn & Alexander, Handbook of the Law of Corporations 495-496 (3d ed. 1983).

CURATIVE correcting a legal error or defect. A judge will give a curative **instruction** to the jury to negate the effect of an erroneous instruction or of tainted evidence. 23 A. 2d 288. A curative statute is enacted to remedy a defect in previously enacted legislation.

CURIA REGIS *(kyū'-rē-à rā'-gĭs)*—Lat: the King's Court.

CURRENT ASSETS see **asset; balance sheet.**

CURRENT LIABILITIES debts incurred by the reporting entity as part of normal operations and expected to be repaid during the following twelve months. Examples are **accounts payable,** short-term loans and that portion of long-term loans due in one year. 135 F. 2d 679, 684. See **balance sheet.**

In accounting, the term refers to the credit side of the **balance sheet** where the sum of liabilities and **net worth** exactly offset **assets** on the debit side of the balance sheet. Current liabilities as opposed to long-term or fixed liabilities are to be paid within one year or less (such as salaries, taxes due, etc.).

CURTESY the husband's right, at common law, upon the death of his wife, to a **life estate** in all the **estates** of **inheritance** in land which his wife possessed during their marriage; "a life estate to which the husband was entitled in all lands of which his wife was **seised** in **fee simple** or in **fee tail** at any time during the marriage, provided that there was **issue** born alive capable of inheriting the estate. On the birth of such qualified issue the husband's **tenancy** by the marital right was enlarged to an estate for his own life. . . . Although . . . the husband's estate for his life was called 'curtesy initiate' prior to his wife's death and 'curtesy consummate' after her death, he had a present life estate in both situations and there was no substantial difference between the two types of curtesy." Moynihan, Introduction to the Law of Real Property 54 (1962). Curtesy is no longer as important or as useful a concept in the law of estates as it once was. Compare **dower.**

CURTILAGE at common law the land around the dwelling house; "a piece of ground within the common enclosure belonging to a dwelling-house, and enjoyed with it, for its more convenient occupation." Land found to constitute curtilage is protected under the constitutional prohibition against searches and seizures. 313 A. 2d 730, 732. 29 N.J.L. 468, 474.

CUSTODY as applied to property, not **ownership,** but "a keeping, guarding, care, watch, inspection, preservation, or security of a thing, [which] carries with it the idea of the thing being within the immediate personal care and control of the person to whose 'custody' it is subjected." 74 P. 962, 968. As applied to persons, it is such restraint and physical control over persons as to insure their presence at any **hearing,** or the actual imprisonment resulting from a criminal **conviction.** See 193 N.W. 789, 790. Custody of children is legal **guardianship,** often an **issue** between parents in a **divorce** action. Compare **possession.** See also **protective custody.**

CUSTODY OF CHILDREN the care and control of minor children awarded by the court to one parent in a divorce proceeding. Where parents both make application for JOINT CUSTODY, and circumstances render the arrangement feasible, some courts have awarded custody to both parents so that responsibility for the children is shared. Under a joint custody order, each parent assumes custody of the children for a fixed period, such as for six months or for the school year or for the summer vacation.

Litigation over the custody of children arises in many contexts, although **divorce** and judicial separation account for most of it. Custody must be so awarded as to promote the child's best interest. 150 F. 2d 152. The power to protect children and act for their welfare was acknowledged to be part of **equity** jurisdiction in England at least as far back as the seventeenth century, although the origin of the jurisdiction remains in dispute. Since each custody case differs in its facts from all others, and since the particular facts of each case are crucial in its decision, custody cases have less importance as **precedents** than do decisions in other branches of law. See Clark, Domestic Relations 572 et seq. (1968).

CUSTOM DUTIES taxes imposed on the importation of foreign goods into the United States. Customs duties and other restrictions are imposed in order to regulate trade between the United States and other countries. 19 U.S.C. §1351.

CUSTOMS COURT see **federal courts.**

CY-PRES *(sē'-prĕ)*—Fr: so near, as near; in the law of trusts and wills the principle that **"equity** will, when a charity is illegal or later becomes impossible or impracticable of fulfillment, substitute another charitable object which is believed to approach the original purpose as closely as possible." 93 So. 2d 483, 486. "The courts will exercise this power, however, only

when the purpose for which the fund was established cannot be carried out, and diversion of the income to some other purpose can be found to fall within the general intent of the donor expressed in the instrument establishing the trust." 133 A. 2d 792, 794.

D.A. abbreviation for **District Attorney.**

DAILY see **per diem.**

DAMAGE see **injury; irreparable injury** [DAMAGE, HARM].

DAMAGES monetary compensation which the law awards to one who has been injured by the action of another; recompense for a legal wrong such as a **breach of contract** or a **tortious** act. There are various measures used for calculating damages, including **diminution in value** and **cost of completion.** Compare **specific performance.**

ACTUAL [COMPENSATORY; GENERAL] DAMAGES those damages directly referrable to the breach or tortious act; losses which can readily be proven to have been sustained, and for which the injured party should be compensated as a matter of right.

COMPENSATORY DAMAGES see ACTUAL DAMAGES above.

CONSEQUENTIAL [SPECIAL] DAMAGES those damages which are caused by an injury but which are not a necessary result of the injury. 279 P. 279, 281. Special damages should be distinguished from ACTUAL [GENERAL] DAMAGES, which are directly caused by the injury. 176 F. 512, 515. Because special damages do not necessarily flow from the injury, they must be specially pleaded and proven. 167 A. 310, 312. The distinction between special and general damages is not absolute but, rather, is relative and depends upon the circumstances of each case. For instance, in an action for failure to provide widgets as agreed in a contract, the general damages would be the price paid under the contract. Any claim for damages to business reputation for reliability would be special damages. In an action for the tort of interference with a business relationship, however, damage to the business reputation would be the general damage. Under the U.C.C., in order for a buyer to recover consequential damages resulting from a seller's breach, the damages must not have been avoidable by **cover.** U.C.C. §2-715(2)(a).

DOUBLE [TREBEL] DAMAGES twice [or three times] the amount of damages that a court or jury would normally find a party entitled to, which is recoverable by an injured party for certain kinds of injuries pursuant to a statute authorizing the double [or treble] recovery. See 6 Fed. Cas. 892, 893. They are intended, in certain instances, as a kind of punishment for improper behavior. See EXEMPLARY [PUNITIVE] DAMAGES below.

EXEMPLARY [PUNITIVE] DAMAGES compensation in excess of actual damages; a form of punishment to the wrongdoer and excess enhancement to the injured; nominal or actual damages must exist before exemplary damages will be found and then they will be awarded only in instances of **malicious** and **willful** misconduct.

EXPECTATION DAMAGES a measure of the money damages available to **plaintiff** in an action for **breach of contract** based on the value of the benefit he would have re-

ceived from the contract if the **defendant** had not breached, but had completed **performance** as agreed. The amount is generally the monetary value of full performance of the contract to the plaintiff minus costs plaintiff avoided by not performing his own part of the contract. When the buyer breaches, the expectation damages will ordinarily be the contract price, less costs saved; when the seller breaches, the buyer's expectation damages will be measured by the fair **market value** of the promised performance at the time and place of promised **tender** (delivery) or performance.

GENERAL DAMAGES see ACTUAL DAMAGES above.

INCIDENTAL DAMAGES includes losses reasonably incident to, or conduct giving rise to, a claim for actual damages. A buyer's incidental damages would include "expenses reasonably incurred in inspection, receipt, transportation, and care and custody of goods rightfully rejected . . .," U.C.C. §2-715; while the seller's incidental damages would include "any commercially reasonable charges, expenses or commissions incurred in stopping delivery, in the transportation, care and custody of goods after the buyer's breach, in connection with return or resale of the goods. . . ." U.C.C. §2-710.

LIQUIDATED DAMAGES an amount stipulated in the **contract** which the **parties** agree to as a reasonable estimation of the **damages** owing to one in the event of a **breach** by the other. 151 F. 534. In order for such a provision to be enforceable as a measure of damages, the liquidated damages provision must constitute a reasonable forecast of the damages likely to actually result from the breach. 134 A. 252. Where these conditions are met, the amount thus provided for establishes a maximum limitation on the defaulting party's **liability.** 25 F. Supp. 478. If the provision does not meet these conditions, or if it otherwise appears that inclusion of the provision was motivated by a desire to deter a breach rather than by a **good faith** effort to estimate probable damages, the provision will be considered a "penalty" and will be unenforceable; recovery will then be limited to actual damages, if any. 72 A. 2d 233. See U.C.C. 2-718.

NOMINAL DAMAGES a trivial sum awarded, frequently $1.00, as recognition that a legal injury was sustained, though slight; in actuality the amount is usually so small as to not really constitute damages. Nominal damages will be awarded for a technical violation of a contract or for an intentional tort to vindicate the plaintiff's claim where no recoverable loss can be established.

PUNITIVE DAMAGES see EXEMPLARY [PUNITIVE] DAMAGES above.

SPECIAL DAMAGES see CONSEQUENTIAL [SPECIAL] DAMAGES above.

TREBLE DAMAGES see DOUBLE [TREBLE] DAMAGES above.

DAMNUM ABSQUE INJURIA *(dăm'-nūm äb'-skwā ĭn-jû'-rē-à)*— Lat: harm without **injury.** The gist of this maxim is that there is harm or damage without a legally recognized injury, which means that the law provides no **cause of action** to recover for one's loss. See 330 P. 2d 459, 462. These situations arise where a lawful act causes injury, where there is damage without any violation of a legal right, where there is damage for which the law provides no remedy, and where damage is caused by nature (such as damage from running water). Thus, "loss to a party . . . not caused by any breach of legal or equitable duty is damnum absque

injuria." See 29 A. 2d 823. Where the loss cannot be attributed to the defendant in terms of legal **fault** there can be no **recovery** against him. For example, if the operation of a hospital causes **depreciation** of neighborhood property values and discomfort and inconvenience to the residents, it is "damnum absque injuria." See 46 N.E. 2d 823, 824.

DANGEROUS WEAPON [INSTRUMENTALITY] almost any instrumentality which is used, or attempted to be used, which has the potentiality to cause serious bodily injury or endanger a life; not synonymous with **deadly weapon.** "A dangerous weapon may possibly not be deadly; but a deadly weapon, one which is capable of causing death, must be dangerous." 33 A. 978, 979.

DAY IN COURT a time when a person who is a party to a lawsuit "has been duly cited to appear [before the court] and has been afforded an opportunity to be heard [by the court]." 45 A. 1035, 1036. See **appearance.**

DEAD HAND see **Mortmain.**

DEADLY FORCE see **force** [DEADLY FORCE].

DEADLY WEAPON any instrumentality that is capable of producing death or serious bodily injury; an instrument may be intrinsically deadly, e.g., knife, pistol, rifle, or deadly because of the way it is used or the force with which it is used, e.g., a wrench, hammer, stick. See Model Penal Code §210.0.

DEALER one who produces or buys or otherwise acquires something in order to sell it. 100 A. 2d 98, 101. A person is a "dealer" in a commodity if he has so structured his business that he can, upon reasonable **notice, deliver** that commodity once a sale has been made. 138 F. Supp. 454, 461. A "dealer" must habitually engage in the buying and selling of a commodity. For example, a merchant who sometimes takes lumber in payment of a **debt,** or in exchange for **goods** kept by him for sale, is not a dealer in lumber. 35 S.E. 605, 606. Compare **merchant.**

DEATH the point at which life ceases; permanent and irreversible termination of vital signs. Several states have adopted statutes defining death to include brain criteria. See, e.g., Iowa Criminal Code §702.8. See **brain death; civil death.**

When one has left his home and has not been heard from for a period ranging in state statutes from two to seven years, a statutory presumption of death for purposes of **inheritance,** or a defense in cases such as **bigamy,** is provided.

DEATH BY AUTOMOBILE see **homicide; manslaughter** [DEATH BY AUTOMOBILE].

DEATH PENALTY the ultimate punishment imposed for **murder** or other **capital offenses.** The U. S. Supreme Court has determined that the death penalty is not considered unconstitutional as cruel and unusual punishment in every instance. 428 U.S. 153. State death penalty statutes deemed to be constitutional now provide for a separate hearing after the establishment of guilt to determine the sentence. At the second hearing evidence is heard in extenuation, mitigation or aggravation, and punishment is determined in accordance with strict guidelines. Statutes providing for mandatory sentences of death are unconstitutional. 431 U.S. 633. See also **cruel and unusual punishment.**

DEBAUCHERY over-indulgences in sensual pleasures; sexual immorality; as used in the Mann Act [prohibiting travel across state lines for immoral purposes], it is "a broad term and includes all sexual immoralities, whether for hire or not for hire, or for **cohabitation.**" 274 F. 2d 15, 18.

DE BENE ESSE *(dā bā'-nā ĕs'-sĕ)*—Lat: conditionally; provisionally.

APPEARANCE DE BENE ESSE a conditional **appearance.**

DEPOSITIONS DE BENE ESSE conditional **depositions** which are non-usable if the **witness** is available at the trial.

EVIDENCE DE BENE ESSE refers to the doctrine of conditional relevancy, and stands for the situation where the admission of **evidence** is conditioned upon a subsequent showing of facts necessary to demonstrate valid admissibility. See 100 A. 2d 246, 252.

DEBENTURE a written acknowledgment of a **debt** with a promise to pay, see 16 N.E. 2d 352; unsecured **bonds;** financial obligation of **corporations** often bought and sold as **investments.** Compare **certificate of deposit; note.**

Holders of debentures representing corporate indebtedness, as creditors of the corporation, are entitled to payment before stockholders [the owners of the corporation] upon dissolution of the corporation. See Henn & Alexander, Corporations §156 (3d ed. 1983).

DEBIT a sum charged as due or owing. In bookkeeping, a term used to denote an entry on the left, or **asset** side of a ledger or account indicating the creation of or addition to an asset or an expense, or the reduction or elimination of a **liability.** Also, the balance of an account where it is shown that something remains due to the person keeping the account. 25A C.J.S. 1042. Compare **credit.**

DEBT money, goods, or services owing from one person to another. See 238 P. 316, 323. An absolute promise to pay a certain sum on a certain date, see 281 S.W. 968, 972;

or any obligation of one person to pay or compensate another. See **bankruptcy; bad debt; bond** [BOND-ED DEBT]; **creditor; floating debt; insolvency.** See also **satisfaction (of a debt).**

DEBT CAPITAL see **security** [DEBT CAPITAL].

DEBTOR one who has the obligation of paying a **debt;** one who owes a debt; "one who owes another anything, or is under any obligation, arising from express agreement, implication of law, or from the principles of natural justice, to render and pay a sum of money." 38 S.W. 13, 14. See U.C.C. §9-105 (1)(d). See **judgment debtor.**

DECEASED one who has ceased to live; in property, the alternative term DECEDENT is generally used. In criminal law, "the deceased" refers to the victim of a **homicide.**

DECEDENT see **deceased.**

DECEIT the **tort** of **fraudulent** representation. "The elements of actionable deceit are: a false representation of a material fact made with knowledge of its falsity, or recklessly, or without reasonable grounds for believing its truth, and with intent to induce **reliance** thereon, on which **plaintiff** justifiably relies to his **injury.**" 300 P. 2d 14, 16.

DECISION ON THE MERITS see **judgment on the merits.**

DECLARATION at common law, the formal document setting forth plantiff's **cause of action,** which includes those facts necessary to sustain a proper cause at action and to advise defendant of the grounds upon which he is being sued. See 103 A. 228. A declaration may contain one or more **counts.** See 82 S.W. 115, 117-118.

DECLARATION AGAINST IN-TEREST a statement which at the time of its making was so contrary to the declarant's pecuniary, proprietary, or penal interest that a reasonable person would not have made the statement unless he believed it to be true. Further, the declarant must be unavailable at the time of trial and must have personal knowledge. Because of its special trustworthiness, a declaration against interest is an exception to the **hearsay** rule. Fed. R. Evid. 804(b)(3). 34 A.L.R. Fed. 412.

ADMISSIONS BY A PARTY-OPPONENT distinguishable from declarations against interest in that admissions of a party-opponent are **per se** admissible and thus do not have to satisfy the above requirements for a declaration against interest and they do not have to, although they may, be against interest when made. Further, the party making the admission need not be unavailable and need not have personal knowledge. McCormick, Evidence §276 (2d ed. 1972).

DECLARATION OF ESTIMATED TAX see **return** [DECLARATION OF ESTIMATED TAX].

DECLARATION OF TRUST see **trust** [DECLARATION OF TRUST].

DECLARATORY JUDGMENT [RELIEF] a **judgment** of the court the purpose of which is "to establish the rights of the parties or express the opinion of the court on a question of law without ordering anything to be done. The distinctive characteristic of a declaratory judgment is that it stands by itself, and no executory process follows as a matter of course. A declaratory judgment is distinguished from a direct action in that the former does not seek execution or performance from the defendant or the opposing litigants." 258 So. 2d 555, 558-59. If it becomes necessary, a more coercive remedy such as an **injunction** may be sought by the **aggrieved party.** Compare **advisory opinion.** See also **controversy; justiciability.**

DECLARATORY STATUTES

those which merely declare the existing law without proposing any additions or changes, for the purpose of resolving conflicts or doubts which have arisen concerning the meaning of a previous statute or portion of the **common law.** 34 N.W. 2d 640, 642.

DECREE "the judicial decision of a **litigated** cause by a **court of equity.** It is also applied to the determination of a cause in courts of **admiralty** and **probate.** It is accurate to use the word **judgment** as applied to **courts of law,** and 'decree' to courts of equity, although the former term is now used in a larger sense to include both." 146 A. 372, 375.

Historically, "[a] judgment at law was either simply for the **plaintiff** or for the **defendant.** There could be no qualifications or modifications of the judgment. But such a judgment does not always touch the true justice of the cause or put the parties in the position they ought to occupy. While the plaintiff may be entitled, in a given case, to general **relief,** there may be some duty connected with the subject of litigation which he owes to the defendant, the performace of which, equally with the fulfillment of his duty by the defendant, ought, in a perfect system of remedial law, to be exacted. This result was attained by the decree of a court of equity which could be so molded, or the execution of which could be so controlled and suspended, that the relative duties and rights of the parties could be secured and enforced." Bishop. Eq. §7 (10th ed. 1925).

CONSENT DECREE an agreement of the parties made under the sanction of, and approved by, the court not as the result of a judicial determination, but merely as their agreement to be bound by certain stipulated facts. A consent decree is not appealable in the sense that no errors will be considered which were in law waived by the consent given. 104 U.S. 767, 768.

DECREE NISI in English Law, a provisional decree of divorce, which becomes absolute only upon the passage of a specified interval of time, usually six months, during which time parties have the opportunity of showing cause why the decree should not become absolute. 2 Steph. Com. 281.

FINAL DECREES those which ultimately dispose of every matter of contention between the parties and constitute a bar to another **bill of equity** filed between the same parties for the same subject matter. 2 Del. Ch. 27.

INTERLOCUTORY DECREES those made upon some point arising during the progress of the suit which do not determine finally the **merits** of the questions involved.

DECREE NISI see **decree** [DECREE NISI]; **nisi** [DECREE NISI].

DECRIMINALIZATION the adoption or repeal of legislation, the effect of which is that acts or omissions formerly considered criminal are no longer so characterized, and penal sanctions for such acts or omissions are removed.

DEDICATION a **conveyance** of land by a private owner in the nature of a gift or grant and an acceptance of that land by or on behalf of the public. 143 P. 941, 943. Streets in a development are usually acquired by the town through a dedication to the public of the property comprising the streets. See **public easement.**

DEDUCTIONS amounts allowed to taxpayers under the **Internal Revenue Code** as offsets against **gross income** or **adjusted gross income.** See **income.**

ITEMIZED DEDUCTIONS deductions allowed under the various provisions of the Code for specific costs or expenses incurred by the taxpayer during the taxable year. These deductions are allowed in computing taxable income to the extent they exceed the ZERO BRACKET AMOUNT (below). I.R.C. §63(f).

MARITAL DEDUCTION an amount allowed as a deduction for federal estate and gift tax purposes for certain interests in property transferred to a spouse. The deduction is currently unlimited in amount. I.R.C. §2056.

PERSONAL EXPENSES DEDUCTIONS personal expenses as opposed to expenses for income producing or business expenses. In general, personal expenses are not allowed as deductions, except for certain expenses such as taxes, interest payments, etc., as specifically enumerated in the Internal Revenue Code. I.R.C. §262.

STANDARD DEDUCTION provision allowing a taxpayer to deduct, in lieu of itemized deductions, a percentage of gross income up to certain specific amounts; repealed and replaced by the ZERO BRACKET AMOUNT (below).

ZERO BRACKET AMOUNT the minimum amount of deductions allowed to a taxpayer. I.R.C. §63(d). This amount is reflected in the tax tables and therefore a taxpayer who has income less than or equal to the zero bracket amount is not subject to income taxes.

DEED an instrument in writing which conveys an interest in land from the grantor to the grantee; instrument used to effect a transfer of realty, 201 S.E. 2d 889, 893; main function is to pass a title to land. 409 So. 2d 114, 120. Deeds are generally classified as bargain and sale, general warranty deeds, or quit-claim deeds. See estoppel [ESTOPPEL BY DEED]. See also registry (of deeds).

DEED OF TRUST a transfer of legal title to property from the trustor [settlor] to the trustee, for the purpose of placing the legal title with the trustee as security for the performance of certain obligations, monetary or otherwise, 399 A. 2d 68, 71. See mortgage.

DEED POLL a deed made by and obligatory to one party alone. See 120 U.S. 464.

DEEP ROCK DOCTRINE a doctrine that makes available a remedy for improper conduct in connection with a loan to a corporation by a controlling shareholder. 306 U.S. 307. Whereas loans made by any shareholder to a corporation are generally entitled to equal priority with loans made by outside creditors, the doctrine allows, when there are insolvency proceedings involving the corporation, subordination of the shareholder loans to the claims of other creditors where it would be "manifestly unfair" to permit a controlling shareholder to participate equally with these other creditors.
   The "unfairness" occurs most commonly where the corporation is undercapitalized and frequently involves a parent corporation as the controlling shareholder of an insolvent subsidiary. 360 F. 2d 741, 752.

DE FACTO *(dā fäk'-tō)*—Lat: in fact; by virtue of the deed or accomplishment; in reality; actually. Compare de jure. Used to qualify many legal terms:

DE FACTO AUTHORITY authority exercised in fact. See 139 P. 1057, 1059.

DE FACTO BOARD OF DIRECTORS the board which in fact is in charge of the affairs of a company and is recognized as such and is performing the legitimate functions and duties of a board. See 71 N.W. 2d 652, 658.

DE FACTO CORPORATIONS those

which have inadvertently failed to comply with the provisions of the laws relating to the creation of a **corporation** but have made a good faith effort to do so and have in **good faith** exercised the **franchise** of a corporation. See 261 S.W. 2d 127, 131.

DE FACTO COURT one established and exercising judicial functions under the authority of an apparently valid statute. If the statute is subsequently declared invalid, the court exists in fact though not in law [**de jure**].

DE FACTO INCUMBENT one who was elected in an election which is later declared void. See 370 S.W. 2d 829, 839.

DE FACTO JUDGE one acting under color of right, and who exercises the judicial functions he assumed while the appointment is contested. See 77 P. 2d 114, 115.

DE FACTO JURY a jury selected in pursuance of a void law. See 97 P. 96, 98.

DE FACTO OFFICER one whose title is not good in law, but who in fact possesses an office and discharges his duties. See 197 A. 667, 669.

DE FACTO SEGREGATION segregation which results without purposeful action by government officials; real or actual segregation which results from social, psychological, or economic conditions. See 269 F. Supp. 401, 445.

DE FACTO TRUSTEE one who assumes an office or position under **color** of right or title and who exercises the duties of the office. See 403 F. 2d 16, 20, 21.

DEFALCATION failure of one entrusted with money to pay over when it is due to another. The term is like misappropriation and **embezzlement,** but is wider in scope because it does not imply any crim-

inal **fraud.** See 123 N.Y.S. 403, 410. See also **misapplication.**

DEFAMATION the publication of anything injurious to the good name or reputation of another, or which tends to bring him into disrepute. A defamation designed to be read is a **libel;** an oral defamation is a **slander.** 207 N.E. 2d 482, 484. There is no legal cause of action called defamation; "libel and slander may be founded on defamation, but the right of action itself is libel or slander. . . ." 221 So. 2d 772, 775.

DEFAULT a failure to discharge a duty, to one's own disadvantage; anything wrongful—some omission to do that which ought to have been done by one of the parties. 90 N.Y.S. 589, 590.

The term is most often used to describe the occurrence of an event which cuts short the rights or **remedies** of one of the parties to an agreement or a legal dispute. It is often used in the context of **mortgages** to describe the failure of the mortgagor to pay mortgage **installments** when due, and in the context of judicial **proceedings** to describe the failure of one of the parties to take the **procedural** steps necessary to prevent the entry of a **judgment** against him. See **default judgment.**

DEFAULT JUDGMENT a **judgment** entered against a **defendant** due to his failure to respond to the **plaintiff's action** or to appear at the **trial;** "one taken against a defendant who, having been summoned in an action, fails to enter an appearance," 80 N.W. 2d 548, 553; judgment which is given without the defendant being heard in his own defense. 303 A. 2d 139, 140.

DEFEASANCE an **instrument** which, in effect, negates the effectiveness of a **deed** or of a **will;** a **collateral** deed which defeats the force of another deed upon the performance of certain conditions. See 82 N.E. 1064.

DEFEASIBLE subject to revocation upon the occurrence or nonoccurrence of certain conditions, 280 P. 2d 81, 85; capable of being avoided or annulled or liable to such avoidance or annulment. See **condition** [CONDITION PRECEDENT, CONDITION SUBSEQUENT].

DEFEASIBLE FEE see **determinable fee.**

DEFECT see **latent defect; patent defect.**

DEFECTIVE something that is wanting as to an essential; incomplete, deficient, faulty, 331 S.W. 2d 140, 143; also, not reasonably safe for a use which can be reasonably anticipated or for which reason it was purchased. 148 A. 2d 261, 265. See **warranty** [WARRANTY OF FITNESS, WARRANTY OF MERCHANTIBILITY]. See also **products liability; strict liability.**

DEFECTIVE PLEADING any **pleading** [complaint, answer, cross-claim, etc.] which fails to conform in form or substance to minimum standards of accuracy or sufficiency. Under strict common law pleading rules, a defective pleading was often fatal to the **lawsuit.** Under modern relaxed standards, such occurrences are rare and are curable by amendment. See Fed. R. Civ. Proc. 15.

DEFECTIVE TITLE one which is unmarketable. With reference to **title** in land, it means that land **conveyed** by a person claiming to have **good title** is actually subject to the partial or complete **ownership** of the title by someone else. As to **negotiable instruments,** the term denotes title obtained through illegal means or means that amount to **fraud.** See U.C.C. §33-201; 23 N.E. 2d 431. A defective title is unmarketable.''

DEFENDANT in **civil proceedings,** the **party** responding to the **complaint;** ''one who is sued and called upon to make satisfaction for a wrong complained of by another, [the **plaintiff**].'' 203 S.W. 2d 548, 552. In criminal proceedings, also called the **accused.**

CO-DEFENDANT see **co-defendant.**

DEFENDANT IN ERROR the prevailing party in the lower court who is the adverse party in the **appellate proceeding** wherein review has been sought on a **writ of error.** The person who brings the **action** at the appellate level is called the PLAINTIFF IN ERROR. See also **appellee.**

DEFENSE a denial, answer, or plea opposing the truth or validity of the plaintiff's case. This may be accomplished by cross-examination or by **demurrer.** It is more often done by introduction of testimony or other evidence designed to refute all or part of the allegations of the plaintiff's case. See also **self-defense.**

AFFIRMATIVE DEFENSE one which serves as a basis for proving some new fact; in such a defense, defendant does not simply **deny** a **charge,** but offers new **evidence** to avoid **judgment** against him; defendant must raise the defense in his answer and he has the **burden of proof** on defense.

EQUITABLE DEFENSE a defense which is recognized by **courts of equity** acting solely upon inherent rules and principles of **equity.** 78 A. 2d 572, 576. Examples of such defenses include **fraud, duress,** illegality. With the merger of **courts of law** and **courts of equity,** such defenses can now be asserted in courts of law as well. James & Hazard, Civil Procedure §8.2 n. 5 (2d ed. 1977). The term also refers to equitable doctrines such as **unclean hands** which may operate to **bar** a plaintiff from pursuing an equity action and thus constitute equitable defenses to such an action.

DEFERMENT postponing or putting off to a future time. May apply to the vesting or enjoyment of an estate, or to the calling of a person to serve in the armed forces. 50 U.S.C. App. §456 To defer does not mean to abolish, 17 S.E. 2d 22, 23, or omit, 90 F. 2d 549, 551.

DEFERRED COMPENSATION see **retirement plans** [DEFERRED COMPENSATION].

DEFERRED PAYMENTS payments extended over a period of time or put off to a future date. **Installment** payments are usually a series of equal deferred payments made over a course of time.

DEFICIENCY the excess of a **taxpayer's** correct tax liability for the **taxable year** over the amount of **taxes** previously paid for such year. I.R.C. §6211. The **Internal Revenue Service** is authorized to assess such deficiencies during an **audit** of the taxpayer's return, and such deficiency may be used to assess penalties for the underpayment of tax, such as for negligence or fraud in filing the return.

DEFICIT want or insufficiency in an account or number. 19 Fla. 127, 135. While the term is broad enough to cover shortages due to **defaults** and misappropriations, it neither necessarily nor ordinarily implies misapplication, and may result from insufficiencies occasioned by mistake or by shrinkage in values. 53 N.W. 2d 230, 232.

DEFINITE FAILURE OF ISSUE see **failure of issue.**

DEFRAUD to deprive a person of **property** or **interest, estate** or right by **fraud, deceit** or **artifice;** to misrepresent some fact knowing it to be false and intending that another person be deceived as a consequence. 438 P. 2d 250, 252.

DEGREE a measure. Also, the certificate of achievement that a school, college, or university gives to a student who completes a specified course of study or curriculum.

DEGREE OF CONSANGUINITY [KINSHIP] see **consanguinity.**

DEGREE OF CRIME the measure of the seriousness of a criminal act which determines the range of criminal sanctions that may be imposed for the crime. For instance, under the Model Penal Code, assault can be classified into any of four degrees depending upon the victim or the manner of commission. A simple assault could be a petty misdemeanor carrying a sentence of not more than 30 days, or a misdemeanor carrying a sentence of not more than one year; an aggravated assault could be a crime of the third degree exposing the defendant to five years, or a crime of the second degree carrying a maximum sentence of ten years. Model Penal Code §§211.1 et seq. 6.06, and 6.08.

DEGREE OF NEGLIGENCE the measure of **negligence** necessary for liability to result. Parties under an obligation to exercise great **care,** such as common **carriers,** may be liable for **slight negligence,** whereas parties only required to exercise slight **care,** such as the driver of an automobile in a state which has a **guest statute,** will be liable to a passenger only for **gross negligence.** Prosser, Torts §34 (4th ed. 1971).

DEGREE OF PROOF the measure of probability necessary in order for a **court** or other fact-finder to render a decision or a **verdict** with regard to the evidence **presented** to it. See **preponderance of the evidence; clear and convincing,** and **reasonable doubt.**

DE JURE (dā jū'-rā)—Lat: by right; by justice; lawful; legitimate. Generally used in contrast to **de facto** in that de jure connotes "as a matter of law" while de facto connotes "as a matter of conduct or practice not founded upon law." For example, "de jure segregation" refers to segregation directly intended and approved by law or otherwise issuing from an official racial classification. See 269 F. Supp. 401, 443.

DELEGABLE DUTY a **duty** that an obligor is able to transfer to another; the term does not imply a giving up of authority but, rather, the conferring of authority to another to do things that otherwise must be done by the obligor. When delegation occurs, it does not free the obligor from his duty to see to it that performance is properly complied with. Only by **novation** may the original obligor totally discharge his responsibilities and liabilities.

Where performance by the delegate would vary materially from the performance of the obligor, the duty is NON-DELEGABLE. U.C.C. §2-210(1). Thus, under a contract to paint a portrait or where a contract is premised on the unique abilities of the obligor, the duties are nondelegable. 31 Cal. 240. Construction contracts, however, are generally held to be delegable because it is contemplated by the parties that the work will be performed by persons other than the obligor. 91 N.Y. 153. See Corbin, Contracts §865 (one vol. ed. 1952).

DELEGATE to appoint, authorize or commission. The **transfer** of authority by one person to another, which may infer a general power to act for another's benefit or which may assign a **debt** to another. A **trustee** may delegate the exercise of **trust** power to an agent if a reasonably prudent owner of this **property** would similarly employ assistance. If the transactions are so important that the **trustee** must personally manage them, then the **trust** power may not be delegable. In fact, the **trustee,** as a **fiduciary,** is under a duty to perform his fiduciary duties personally. Restatement (Second), Trusts §171 (1959). A delegate is a person commissioned to act instead of another. 450 S.W. 2d 281, 288. See **delegable duty.** See also **assign.**

DELEGATED POWER authority conferred by one person on another to act for his benefit. It is not synonymous with "surrender" of power, which implies abandonment or a yielding of power in favor of another. 2 So. 2d 11, 15, 16. Compare **novation.**

DELIBERATE to consider all of the evidence and arguments presented in regard to a particular matter. For instance, after the evidence has been presented, the parties to a lawsuit have made their closing arguments, and the judge has given the jury its instructions, the jury will retire to deliberate and render its verdict. 565 S.W. 2d 893, 895.

DELIBERATE SPEED forthwith, immediately, 172 S.E. 2d 579, 583. In certain instances, such as the desegregation of public facilities, the term implies that desegregation should occur as quickly as the maintenance of law and order and the welfare of all citizens will allow. 347 U.S. 483.

DELIBERATION any method used to weigh and examine the reasons for and against a **verdict** including careful and mature consideration. While verdicts should be the consensus of the individual judgments of each **juror,** the purpose of the deliberation process is to allow for opinions to be changed by conference in the **jury** room. The **law presumes** that jurors shall harmonize their opinions by a discussion of the **evidence.** 164 U. S. 492. However, the length of time taken by the jury in reaching its verdict has no effect upon the validity of its verdict. 91 A.L.R. 2d 1235. Jurors are **presumed** to limit their "deliberation" to the evidence or lack of **evidence** presented at **trial** and not to any outside knowledge.

DELICT a **tort,** a wrong or injury, any statutory violation, 89 N.E. 2d 111, 116; sometimes used in the sense of a default on a monetary obligation, 78 P. 936, 940.

DELICTUM Latin for tort. 2 Bl. Comm. *117. An ACTION EX DELICTO is an action in tort as opposed to one EX CONTRACTU, in contract. This distinction was significant when the early forms of code pleading were very strict. If, for example, one alleged a cause of action ex delicto for fraud but the proof established a breach of warranty, an action ex contractu, the case would be dismissed for **variance.** Pomeroy, Code Remedies §452 (4th ed. 1904).

DELINQUENT in a monetary context, something which has been made payable and is overdue and unpaid; implies a previous opportunity to make payment. With reference to persons, implies carelessness, recklessness. See also **juvenile delinquent.**

DELISTING removal of an issue from authorized trading on an organized exchange such as the New York Stock Exchange. Organized exchanges have minimum listing requirements which must be met before listed trading is allowed. If the issuer fails to maintain the minimum requirements, trading in its listed securities can be suspended or eliminated entirely by the governing body of the exchange.

DELIVERY a voluntary transfer of **title** or **possession** from one **party** to another; a legally recognized handing over of one's possessory rights to another. Where actual delivery would be cumbersome or impossible, the courts will find a CONSTRUCTIVE DELIVERY sufficient, provided the intention is clearly to transfer title. Thus, one may deliver the contents of a safety deposit box by handing over to another the key thereto together with any necessary authorization. Such an action is also called a SYMBOLIC DELIVERY. In some instances, courts unequivocally require actual delivery. See **gift; livery of seisin.** Compare **bailment; conveyance;** grant. See also **tender of delivery.**

DELUSION a false belief which is produced by a mental disorder and which people of the same age, class, and education would find incredible. A delusion can be the basis for the **insanity defense** to a **crime.** Perkins & Boyce, Criminal Law 964 (3d ed. 1982).

DEMAND see **on demand.**

DEMAND NOTE an **instrument** which by its express terms is payable immediately on an agreed-upon date of **maturation** without requiring any further demand; the **maker** of the **note** acknowledges his **liability** as of the due date; also includes those instruments payable at sight, or upon presentation, or those in which no time for payment is stated. See 448 S.W. 2d 495, 497.

DEMESNE *(de-mēń)*—Fr: domain; own; held in one's own right and not of a superior; not allotted to tenants. In the language of pleading, own; proper, or original. 26A C.J.S. 174. See **ancient demesne.**

DE MINIMIS *(dā mǐ'-nǐ-mǐs)*— Lat: insignificant; minute, frivolous. Something or some act which is "de minimis" in interest is one which does not rise to a level of sufficient importance to be dealt with judicially. "Trifles, or matters of a few dollars or less." 121 F. 2d 829, 832. A crime which is "de minimis" may be dismissed under the Model Penal Code and similar statutes. Model Penal Code §2.12.

DE MINIMIS NON CURAT LEX *(nǒn kyū'-rät lěx)*—Lat: the law does not care for small things; the law does not bother with trifles.

DEMISE term used to describe a **conveyance** of an estate in **real property.** Most commonly used as a synonym for "let" in a **lease.** "The word 'demise' used as a noun, means a lease for a term of years; a conveyance **in fee,** or for life, or for years, most commonly the latter.

As a verb, it means to lease for a term of years. In its primitive meaning, it was always used in reference to a lease, and while it has been held that, where the context clearly justified such construction, it meant a conveyance or transfer; this is not its usual signification." 142 P. 131, 133.

DEMONSTRATIVE EVIDENCE evidence consisting of an object or thing, such as a weapon used in a crime, a stolen item, or a photograph or x-ray, that may aid the jury in understanding the crime before it but which has no effect on the question of guilt; evidence other than a person's oral testimony but which may help to explain that testimony. See McCormick, Evidence 524 et seq. (2d ed. 1972).

DEMUR to present a **demurrer.** More broadly, to take an exception to a point of law or an allegation of facts on the basis that even if it is so it does not advance the interests of the party making the statement.

DEMURRER *(dē-mûr'er)*—Fr: to stop, stay or rest; in **pleading,** a formal objection attacking the legal sufficiency of the opponent's pleadings. It is an assertion, made without disputing the facts, that the pleading does not state a **cause of action,** and the demurring party is entitled to **judgment.** In demurring, the answering party requests a **dismissal** of the action based only on the law. 290 A. 2d 85, 87

Since the **common law** placed heavy emphasis on both the substance and the form of pleadings, a party would demur in order to prevail on the basis of the opponent's defective pleading, and thus avoid **trial.** The danger was that by so challenging the pleadings' legal sufficiency, the party had to admit the truth of the facts. At **common law** a demurrer was either **sustained** or **overruled,** which in either event ended the case with judgment for the prevailing **party.** James & Haz-

ard, Civil Procedure, §4.2 (2d ed. 1977).

There were two kinds of demurrers at common law: GENERAL DEMURRER, which went to the **merits** of the case and SPECIAL DEMURRER, which challenged defects in form. 120 A. 2d 228, 231.

In diminishing the importance of the pleading procedure, the Federal Rules of Civil Procedure deemphasized the demurrer. Rule 12 (b)(6) allows a party to move for dismissal because of the opponent's failure to state a **claim** upon which relief can be granted, and 12(c) allows either party, after the pleadings, to move for judgment on the pleadings. Since **affidavits** and other evidentiary material outside the pleadings are often relevant, this **motion** is usually treated as one for **summary judgment** and the parties proceed according to Rule 56.

Since pleadings are no longer required to be as precise as at common law, it is now more diffcult to challenge their legal sufficiency. The well settled rule of federal practice is that a motion to dismiss for failure to state a claim should not be granted unless it appears to a certainty that the complaining party would not be able to recover under any state of facts which could be proved in support of his claim. 414 F. 2d 320, 321. Compare **summary judgment.**

DENIAL a contradiction or **traverse;** in practice, a controverting of affirmative **allegations** in a **pleading** by an adversary. A defendant in his **answer** must admit, deny, or state he has insufficient information upon which to admit or deny the allegations. The latter amounts to a denial. See Fed. R. Civ. Proc. 8(b). Any allegations in a complaint not denied (or given an insufficient information response) are taken as true. See Fed. R. Civ. Proc. 8(d). See also **confession and avoidance.**

CONJUNCTIVE DENIAL a denial which denies all of the allegations as wholly untrue.

DISJUNCTIVE DENIAL a denial which denies the allegations as untrue in the alternative.

GENERAL DENIAL a denial of all of the plaintiff's allegations.

SPECIFIC DENIAL a denial of one or several, but not all, of the plaintiff's allegations.

DE NOVO (dā nō'-vō)—Lat: new, young, fresh; renewed, revived. A second time. See 47 N.W. 2d 126, 128. See also **appeal** [APPEAL DE NOVO]; **trial** [TRIAL DE NOVO]; **venire** [VENIRE DE NOVO].

DE NOVO HEARING a new hearing. "In a 'de novo hearing,' the judgment of the trial court is suspended and [the reviewing court] determine[s] the case as though it originated in [the reviewing court] and give[s] no attention to the findings and **judgment** of the **trial court** except as they may be helpful . . . in the reasoning." 46 N.E. 2d 429, 430.

DEODAND scc **forfeiture.**

DEPENDENCY a territory or possession not within the boundaries of the country which has jurisdiction to govern it. Dependencies of the United States include Puerto Rico, the Virgin Islands, Guam and various other islands located in the Pacific Ocean. See 48 U.S.C.§731 et seq.

DEPENDENT "one who looks to another for support in whole or in part, 135 F. Supp. 327, 330; unable to exist or sustain oneself without support, 202 N.E. 2d 317, 318; any person with respect to whom **a taxpayer** can claim a dependency **exemption;** defined by the **Internal Revenue Code** to mean any individual supported by the taxpayer and who bears a specific relationship to the taxpayer (e.g., son or daughter, brother or sister, father or mother, etc.) or who makes his principal abode in the taxpayer's household. Support means that the taxpayer provided at least one-half of the dependent's support requirements during the **taxable year.** However, a dependency exemption is not allowed where the dependent has $1,000 or more of gross income and is not a child of the taxpayer, under 19, and a student; the exemption is also denied where a married dependent files a joint return with his spouse. I.R.C. §152.

DEPENDENT CARE see **child and dependent care credit.**

DEPENDENT COVENANTS see **covenant.**

DEPENDENT RELATIVE REVOCATION the doctrine which provides that when a **will** revokes an earlier will executed by the same person, the earlier will is only revoked if the latter will is effective; otherwise the earlier will remains in full effect and force. 550 F. 2d 9, 12.

DEPLETION the exhaustion of a natural resource, the amount of the original deposit being hidden from view and thus necessarily unknown. 103 S.E. 2d 823, 825. In taxation, DEPLETION ALLOWANCE is a **deduction** allowable to an owner of oil, gas, mineral, or timber property (DEPLETABLE PROPERTY). I.R.C. §611 et seq. It allows an owner to recover the capital cost of the natural resource property as he exhausts the natural resources. This should be contrasted with **depreciation** deduction provisions which deal with the wear and tear and deterioration of tangible physical **property** incident to its use which results in the shortening of its useful life. 513 S.W. 2d 319, 322.

COST DEPLETION cost depletion requires a determination of the number of units which will be produced by the property. I.R.C. §611. Then, the portion of the basis allocable to the reserves of depletable property is divided by the number of units to be produced. This amount is then deductible as each unit is sold during the **taxable year**. The basis of the property is reduced by the depletion taken and once basis allocable to the depletable reserves reaches zero no further depletion is allowed.

PERCENTAGE DEPLETION a special method for computing depletion which is allowable with respect to all depletable property except timber. I.R.C. §613. Percentage depletion allows as a deduction from **gross income** a percentage of the gross income received with respect to such property. Although percentage depletion reduces the owner's **basis** in the property, percentage depletion continues to be allowed even if the **basis** is reduced to zero.

DEPONENT a **witness**; one who testifies as to information or facts known to him, under oath in a **deposition**. Compare **affiant**.

DEPORTATION the transfer of an **alien** excluded or expelled from one country, to a foreign country. 162 F. Supp. 890, 892. In effect, it is simply the refusal by a government to harbor persons whose presence is deemed to be inconsistent with the public welfare. 149 U.S. 698.
Deportation is not a **prosecution** for, or conviction of, a **crime**, nor is it a punishment, although the facts underlying its implementation may constitute a crime. It is a sovereign's right to remove an alien who, by his conduct in violation of **statute,** makes himself subject to removal. 32 F. Supp. 508, 517. In the United States, an alien being deported is entitled to fundamental fairness in the procedural processes of deportation, particularly including notice, the opportunity to be heard, and a fair hearing.
Deportation is to be distinguished from EXCLUSION, which is the denial of entry to a country, 6 F. 2d 336, TRANSPORTATION, which is punishment of one convicted of an offense against the **laws** of a country, 149

U.S. 698, **extradition**, which is the surrender to another country (or state), of one **accused** of an offense against its **laws,** 149 U.S. 698, and EXPULSION, which is the permanent deprivation of the privileges of a society, 102 So. 637, 639.

DEPOSE to give **evidence** or **testimony**, or to bear **witness**. 47 Me. 248, 252. Used in a deposition reciting that the **witness** is under **oath.** 200 N.W. 225, 226. The term also is used to refer to the taking of a deposition of another, particularly by a lawyer pursuant to rules governing **discovery** prior to the **trial** of a case. See **deposition**.

DEPOSITION a method of pre-trial **discovery** which consists of "a statement of a **witness** under oath, taken in question and answer form as it would be in court, with opportunity given to the **adversary** to be present and cross-examine, with all this reported and transcribed stenographically." James & Hazard, Civil Procedure §6.3 (2d ed. 1977). Such statements are the most common form of discovery, and may be taken of any witness (whether or not a **party** to the **action**). When taken in the form described it is called an ORAL DEPOSITION. Depositions may also be taken upon written **interrogatories** where the questions are propounded to the witness by the officer who is taking the deposition [called in that case DEPOSITIONS ON WRITTEN INTERROGATORIES]. Compare **affidavit, interrogatory.**

DEPOSITIONS DE BENE ESSE see **de bene esse.**

DEPRECIATION a **deduction** allowed to a **taxpayer** representing a reasonable allowance for the exhaustion, wear, and tear of property used in a trade or business, or property held for the production of income. I.R.C. §167. The amount of deduction may be calculated under one of several methods depending on the type of property involved. The amount allowed as a deduction depends upon several factors, including the taxpayer's **basis,** the useful life of the property, and its salvage value.

ACCELERATED COST RECOVERY SYSTEM [ACRS] a method of depreciation allowable for tangible depreciable property placed in service after 1980. ACRS places property into one of four categories (3 year, 5 year, 10 year, and 15 year property) and allows the taxpayer to take accelerated depreciation deductions for the property. ACRS is designed to simplify depreciation by eliminating issues concerning useful life, salvage value, and method of depreciation. I.R.C. §168.

ACCELERATED DEPRECIATION any one of a number of allowed methods of calculating depreciation which permit greater amounts of deductions in earlier years than are permitted under the straight line method.

SALVAGE VALUE the estimated value of the property when the taxpayer completes his use of the property. In determining the amount of depreciation allowable, salvage value must be subtracted from **basis.**

STRAIGHT LINE a method which calculates the depreciation deduction available by subtracting the asset's salvage value from its total value and dividing the difference by the asset's useful life.

USEFUL LIFE the reasonable estimate of the term of an asset's usefulness to the taxpayer in his business.

DEPRECIATION RESERVE [AC-CUMULATED DEPRECIATION] the total **depreciation** charged against all productive **assets** as stated on the **balance sheet.** The charge is made to allow realistic reduction in the value of productive assets

and to allow tax-free recovery of the original investment in assets.

DEPRESSANTS see **controlled substances.**

DERELICTION "a recession of the waters of the sea, a navigable river, or other stream, by which land that was before covered with water is left dry." 260 S.W. 2d 257, 259. "In such case, if the alteration takes place suddenly and sensibly, the ownership remains according to former bounds; but if it is made gradually and imperceptibly, the derelict or dry land belongs to the **riparian** owner from whose shore or bank the water has so receded." Id. The term may also refer to the land itself which is thus left uncovered. 188 S.W. 2d 550. In order for **contiguous** landowners to gain ownership of the newly uncovered land, the withdrawal of the water must appear permanent, and not merely seasonal. 156 N.W. 591. Compare **accretion; avulsion.**

DERIVATIVE ACTION an action based upon a primary right of a **corporation,** but asserted on its behalf by the **stockholder** because of the corporation's failure, deliberate or otherwise, to act upon the primary right, see 138 N.Y.S. 2d 163, 166; shareholder's action on behalf of corporation.

Such suits are the only civil remedy a stockholder has for breach of a fiduciary duty on the part of those entrusted with the management and direction of their corporation. Many states have enacted statutes requiring small stockholders to provide security for the costs which may be incurred by the corporation in defending these suits in order to prevent abuse of this remedy. See N.Y. Bus. Corp. L. §627. Recovery in a derivative action generally inures to the benefit of the corporation because the action asserts a corporate rather than an individual right. In some instances, however, individual shareholders may recover a pro rata share. See Henn &

Alexander, Corporations §373 (3rd ed. 1983). See **strike suits.**

Also used to describe a **cause of action** that is founded upon an injury to another, as when a husband sues for loss of **consortium** or services of his wife on account of an injury to her by the defendant, or when a father sues for loss of services of children. See 36 N.Y.S. 2d 465, 467.

DERIVATIVE TORT an action in **tort** based on the **criminal** conduct of **defendant** which resulted in **injury** to **plaintiff,** and for which injury plaintiff seeks **compensation.** The action is distinct from any criminal prosecution which may result from the same conduct by defendant.

The term also applies to liability imposed on a **principal** for the wrongs committed by his **agent.** See **vicarious liability.**

DEROGATION partial taking away of the effectiveness of a law; to partially repeal or abolish a law. A rule (or canon) of statutory **construction** is that "statutes derogating from the **common law** are to be strictly construed." Cardozo, The Paradoxes of the Legal Science 9, 10 (1928).

DESCENT AND DISTRIBUTION transmission of the **real** or **personal property** of someone who dies without a valid **will,** i.e., dies **intestate.** State laws which determine the **inheritance** of an intestate's property are frequently called "statutes of descent and distribution." Descent applies to the transmission to an **heir** of real property on the death of an owner intestate or by inheritance according to the rules of law; personalty is distributed to the next of kin by an **administrator** or **executor** who pays the **debts** and allots the remaining property to the entitled persons. Atkinson, Wills, Ch. 1,4 (2d ed. 1953). On the death intestate of a **beneficiary** of a **trust,** devolution of his trust interest is governed by the same rules of descent and distribution as govern his legal interests. Restatement, (Second), Trusts §142 (1959).

Descent in its broadest sense signifies an inheritance of real or personal property cast upon anyone capable of receiving it whether or not that person is a **common law heir.** 306 S.W. 2d 573, 576. It has been interpreted, however, to apply only to inheritance by operation of law rather than provision by **will.** 129 F. Supp 609, 614. It is synonymous with **"succession"** as used in most **statutes,** 242 P. 2d 655, 656, and is distinguished from **"purchase"** whereby land is acquired by act or **agreement** of the **parties.** 171 S.W. 2d 691, 695.

Distribution generally is the division by the court of the residue of a personal **estate** of an intestate after payment of all debts. It can, however, refer to division according to terms of a will. 274 N.Y.S. 208, 210. The duty of distribution falls on an administrator or **trustee** of the estate and the distributee is the person entitled to the estate under a statute of distribution. 67 F. 2d 662, 92 A.L.R. 862. The distributee may be an heir, but is generally not a devisee, **legatee,** or **creditor.** 12 F. 2d 572.

While the law of the place where the **property** is situated generally governs the descent irrespective of the deceased owner's **domicile,** the law of the domicile state governs the succession to and distribution of personalty and movable property. 41 F. 2d 464, 465; 34 F. 2d 690, 691. See also **doctrine of worthier title; intestate; per capita; per stirpes.**

DESERTION act of abandonment of a relation or service in which one owes duties; the withdrawal, unexcused, from the obligations of some condition or status. 76 S.E. 2d. 533, 535. The **common law** does not punish this violation of duty if no harm results but if the neglect is with the requisite **mens rea** and causes bodily harm, it is a common-law crime which, if death ensues, may be

manslaughter or even **murder.** 72 Ga. 164. A negative act; a crime by omission. In matrimonial law, an unjustified cessation from cohabitation, with intent not to resume it and without the other spouse's consent, is desertion and is a ground for divorce. 75 A. 2d. 397, 399. Desertion may or may not be accompanied by NONSUPPORT, which is the wilful failure to provide support (food, clothing, and shelter) and maintenance to the spouse and minor children when able and when legally obliged to do so.

In military law, ABSENT WITHOUT LEAVE [AWOL] signifies an intention by a member of the armed forces not to return to service, and punishable under the Code of Military Justice. 10 U.S.C. §885.

DESIST see **cease and desist order.**

DESTINATION CONTRACT see **tender** [TENDER OF DELIVERY].

DESTRUCTIBILITY OF CONTINGENT REMAINDERS a **common law** rule "that a **freehold contingent remainder** which does not **vest** at or before the termination of the preceding freehold estate is destroyed. Such termination of the preceding estate might result from the natural expiration of that estate, or from forfeiture, or from **merger.**" Moynihan, Introduction to the Law of Real Property 129 (1962).

DESUETUDE a term applied to obsolete laws and practices that have grown out of use. A long desuetude of any law amounts to its repeal. 266 F. Supp. 318, 325. Usually, discontinued practices, customs or laws will be rendered obsolete when their objects have vanished or their reasons have ceased to be applicable. Thus, an ordinance regulating the speed of horse-drawn carriages for the purpose of controlling the generation of dust in the streets, particularly in a city whose streets are now paved, will be regarded as having been impliedly repealed under the principle of desuetude. See generally 49 Iowa L. Rev. 392.

DETAINER keeping a person from goods or land to which he has a legal right; "a **writ** or **instrument,** issued or made by a competent officer, authorizing the keeper of a prison to keep in his **custody** a person therein named." 131 S.E. 2d 382, 388.

FORCIBLE DETAINER see **forcible detainer; forcible entry** [FORCIBLE ENTRY AND DETAINER].

UNLAWFUL DETAINER refusal to deliver on demand, as in a **lease** situation where the **tenant** remains after his lease has ended or has been terminated; actual repudiation of owner's rights must exist. Compare **tenancy** [AT SUFFERANCE]; **trespass.**

DETENTION restraining a person for some official purpose, by establishing control over the person, 418 N.E. 2d 1359, 1364. PRE-TRIAL DETENTION refers to holding a defendant (called a PRE-TRIAL DETAINEE) prior to his trial on criminal charges either because he cannot post the established **bail** or because he has been denied pre-trial release under a PRE-TRIAL DETENTION STATUTE. Those statutes have been adopted by some jurisdictions and usually require a hearing where evidence is examined, and a preliminary decision reached, that the defendant meets certain limited conditions for the denial of bail. Those statutes raise constitutional questions under state and federal constitutional guarantees of pre-trial liberty and the **presumption of innocence.**

Pre-trial detainees are entitled to enjoy a higher standard of confinement conditions than persons who have been committed to prison after conviction of a crime. See also **preventive detention.**

INVESTIGATIVE DETENTION refers to the holding of a suspect without formal arrest during the investigation of his possible participation in a crime. Such investigative detention is unconstitutional if **probable cause** does not exist to charge him with the crime. 442 U.S. 200.

DETERMINABLE FEE [FEE SIMPLE DETERMINABLE] an **interest** in **property** which may last forever, except upon the happening or non-happening of a specified event, at which point it will automatically terminate, e.g., "A, owner of Blackacre in **fee simple absolute,** conveys it 'to B and his heirs so long as Brookline remains a town [and no longer] and if Brookline becomes a city then the said premises shall **revert** to A and his heirs.' B has a fee simple determinable. . . . If the town becomes a city [or ceases to exist as a town] B's estate expires automatically and A becomes the owner in fee simple." Moynihan, Introduction to the Law of Real Property 95-96 (1962).

DETERMINATION a decision by a court or other adjudicative body. See **holding; judgment; verdict.**

DETINUE at **common law,** an **action** for the wrongful detention of **personal property;** an action for the recovery of the item itself and for **damages** based on its unlawful detention. In rare cases, the value of the item will be awarded if the item cannot be located, but the action must originally lie for the return of the item and not for its monetary value. 59 N.E. 265, 267. See **detainer, unlawful; replevin; trover.** Compare **conversion.**

DEVISE traditionally a gift of real property made by will. As defined by Restatement, Property §12 (1), "A testamentary act by which a now-deceased person manifested his intent to create one or more interests in land or in a thing other than land, irrespective of whether

such act is effective to create such interest." "Simplicity of statement requires that a single word be available to describe a testamentary act intended to dispose of interests in land, interests in things other than land or both these types of interests. The employment of two words, such as 'devise' and 'bequeath,' is awkward. . . ." Id., Comment (a). Compare **bequest; legacy.**

DEVOLVE "when by **operation of law,** and without any voluntary act of the previous owner, [an **estate**] passes from one person to another; it does not devolve from one person to another as the result of some positive act or agreement between them. . . ; [the word] implies a result without the intervention of any voluntary actor." 29 P. 495.

DICTA plural form of **dictum.**

DICTUM (pl. dicta) a statement, remark, or observation in a judicial **opinion** not necessary for the decision of the case. Dictum differs from the **holding** in that it is not binding on the courts in subsequent cases. See 14 Ohio N.P., N.S. 97. Holdings are guides to future conduct, whereas dicta [plural] are not. CONSIDERED DICTUM is a phrase used to refer to a discussion of a point of law that, though it is dictum, is nevertheless so well developed that it is later adopted or incorporated into an opinion of a court as though it were authority.

DIE WITHOUT ISSUE see **failure of issue.**

DILATORY PLEA at **common law,** a **plea** not going to the **merits,** but constituting rather a **defense** which simply delays or defeats the present **action,** leaving the **cause of action** unsettled, 32 S.W. 2d 674, 675; such as a challenge to **jurisdiction** or other plea in abatement on the grounds of disability of the **plaintiff** or the **defendant,** etc. If a defendant can defeat the plaintiff's cause of action in whole or in part, upon establishing the facts, or can obtain any substantial relief against the plaintiff, the plea is not dilatory, but rather **on the merits.** 68 S.E. 1086. This kind of plea has largely disappeared under modern practice, James & Hazard, Civil Procedure §4.2 (2d ed. 1977). Instead these defenses are now raised by **motion** or in an **answer.** See **plea** [PLEA IN ABATEMENT].

DILIGENCE attention to the matter at hand. DUE DILIGENCE or REASONABLE DILIGENCE is that diligence which is required by the circumstances, the rendering of which prevents liability for **negligence.** This measure is a relative one, and is determined by considering the facts of each particular case. 18 So. 2d 282, 284. See **care.**

DILUTING THE SHARES see **watered stock.**

DIMINISHED CAPACITY in criminal law, the inability to have the mens rea required for the commission of a crime. 79 Cal. Rptr. 155, 161. The states which allow the defense treat it variously. Some limit it to crimes requiring a **specific intent;** others recognize it in crimes involving different **degrees.** About half the states do not recognize it as a separate defense, but limit questions concerning the mental state to the defense of insanity. 30 Vand. L. Rev. 213-15 (1977). A successful defense of diminished capacity will usually result in conviction of a lesser offense, not in acquittal. LaFave & Scott, Criminal Law 326 (1972). Compare **insanity.**

DIMINISHED RESPONSIBILITY see **diminished capacity.**

DIMINUTION OF VALUE a measure of **damages** for **breach of contract** which reflects a decrease, occasioned by the breach, in the value of property with which the **contract** was concerned. In a building contract it "is the difference between the value of the building as constructed and its value had it

been constructed conformably to the contract." 143 N.E. 2d 802, 803. "There are two general rules with variations where there are damages to **realty** and, in some cases, personalty attached to realty. There is the before and after value of realty rule, sometimes referred to as the diminution rule. There is also the restoration or replacement rule which will generally be applied by the court if the injury is temporary and replacement is possible, or if it involves an amount less than that derived from application of the diminution rule." 388 F. 2d 165, 168. Compare **cost of completion; damages** [EXPECTATION DAMAGES]; **specific performance.**

DIRECT ATTACK as applied to a judicial **proceeding,** an attempt by **appellants** to **avoid** or correct a **judgment** in some manner provided by law, 191 S.E. 779, 782; an attempt to amend, correct, reform, **vacate** or enjoin **execution** of a judgment in a proceeding instituted for that purpose, 441 S.W. 2d 653, 655; generally an attack is "direct" where it constitutes a resort to the primary appellate review procedure. Compare **collateral attack.**

DIRECT CAUSE see **cause.**

DIRECT CONTEMPT see **contempt of court.**

DIRECTED VERDICT a verdict entered in a jury trial by the court, without consideration by the jury, because the facts elicited during the trial, together with the applicable law, made it clear that the directed verdict was the only one which could have been reasonably returned, 123 F. 2d 438, 440. In **civil proceedings** either party may receive a directed verdict in its favor if the opposing party fails to present a **prima facie case,** or fails to present a necessary **defense.** In criminal proceedings, while there may be a directed verdict of acquittal (sometimes called a "judgment of acquittal''), there may be no directed verdict of conviction as such a procedure would violate the defendant's constitutional right to a jury determination of his guilt or innocence. 67 S.E. 265. A directed verdict may be issued on the **motion** of a party or on the court's own initiative [**sua sponte**].

DIRECT ESTOPPEL see **estoppel**.

DIRECT EXAMINATION see **cross-examination** [DIRECT EXAMINATION].

DIRECTOR one who sits on a board of directors of a **company** or **corporation,** and who has the legal responsibility of exercising control over the officers and affairs of the company or corporation.

A director has a **fiduciary duty** to the corporation and to its **stockholders** to manage the affairs of the corporation in a manner which is consistent with their interests. Any **breach** of his fiduciary duty may subject him to personal liability to both the shareholders and the corporation.

DIRECT ORDER OF ALIENATION see **marshaling [marshalling]** [DIRECT ORDER OF ALIENATION].

DISABILITY state of not being fully capable of performing all functions, whether mental or physical. 258 N.W. 558, 567. Any want of legal capacity such as **infancy, insanity,** or past criminal conviction which renders a person legally **incompetent.** 108 N.E. 275, 276. In property, one person's inability to alter a given legal relation with another person. Restatement, Property, §4a. The term is defined by statute for worker's compensation and social security purposes, and may include partial, permanent, temporary, or total disability, 288 P. 2d 31, 34. See also **Durham Rule; non compos mentis; minority; total disability.**

DISBAR to deprive an attorney of the right to practice law by rescinding his license to so practice, as a result of illegal or unethical conduct by the attorney.

DISCHARGE general word covering methods by which a legal **duty** is extinguished, 375 S.W. 2d 85, 92; to release, annul or dismiss the obligations of **contract** or **debt.** See 41 N.E. 2d 979, 981. See also **satisfaction.**

"When it is said that a contract is discharged, it is always meant that one or more of the legal relations of the parties have been terminated. The meaning that is most commonly intended is that the legal duty of one of the parties has been terminated. A party who is asserted to be under a legal duty by virtue of his contract may reply that the duty has been discharged by some factor that has occurred since the making of the contract." Corbin, Contracts §1228 (one- vol. ed. 1952). The factors bringing about discharge of contractual obligation include full **performance, rescission, release,** informal written **renunciation,** contract not to sue.

Discharge also refers to the termination of one's employment by his employer.

In criminal law, to release from custody, acquit. See **sentence** [SUSPENDED SENTENCE (CONDITIONAL DISCHARGE; UNCONDITIONAL DISCHARGE)]. Compare **reprieve.**

DISCHARGE A DEBT settlement of a debt is discharged and the **debtor** is released when the **creditor** has received something from the debtor which satisfies him. It may be money or its equivalent. It may consist of **offsetting** mutual demands, or wiping out mutual, disputed **claims** by mutual concessions, in which event no money is required to pass from one to the other. See 79 Mich. 484.

DISCHARGE IN BANKRUPTCY the release of the debtor from most of his debts; a bar to all future proceedings for enforcement of the discharged debt. 243 A 2d 722,

725. Some debts, such as those unscheduled by the debtor in his request for **bankruptcy** relief, those arising from certain types of fraudulent conduct, **alimony** support and maintenance, liability for willful and malicious conduct, and certain student loans, are not dischargeable. At the conclusion of bankruptcy proceedings, a debtor is usually granted discharge. See 11 U.S.C. §§523, 524, 727.

DISCLAIMER a voluntary denial or repudiation of a person's **claim** or right to a thing, though previously that person insisted on such a claim or right; complete renunciation of right to **possess** and claim of **title.** See 67 P. 662, 663. Denial of a right of another, e.g., where an **insurer** disclaims an allegation of **liability** against its **insured** and thereby refuses to defend the insured in a **lawsuit.** In such instances the insured can sue the insurance company to challenge the DIS-CLAIMER OF LIABILITY.

QUALIFIED DISCLAIMER a disclaimer which meets certain requirements and which results in the taxpayer not being considered as having an interest, for federal unified estate and gift tax purposes, in the disclaimed property. I.R.C. §2518.

DISCONTINUANCE in practice, the cessation of the **proceedings** in an **action** where the **plantiff** voluntarily puts an end to it, with or without judicial approval; judicial approval may be required, depending upon each jurisdiction's rules of practice. See also **dismissal; nonsuit.**

DISCOUNT a deduction from a specified sum. Often used in connection with transactions in negotiable **commercial paper** in which the buyer purchases an instrument due at a future date at a price below its face amount with the intention of ultimately collecting the full val-ue of the instrument. Sellers offer instruments at a discount because of an immediate need for cash or out of a fear of never being able to collect on them. "To discount" in finance is to purchase or pay an amount in cash less a certain per cent, as on a promissory note which is to be collected by discounter or purchaser at maturity. 117 So. 124, 126.

Discount is the difference between the price and the amount of the debt, the evidence of which is transferred. 14 Ill. App. 566, 570.

DISCOUNT BOND see **bond** [BOND DISCOUNT].

DISCOUNTED CASH FLOW a measure of the present value of a future income stream generated by a **capital** investment. The discount rate chosen usually equals or exceeds the return on a risk-free investment. "A discounted cash flow analysis is an investor-oriented method that determines a . . . required return on equity." See 376 A. 2d 687, 696. See **present value.**

DISCOVERY modern pre-trial procedure by which one **party** gains information held by another party; the disclosure by a party of facts, deeds, documents, and other such things. The scope of material available for discovery is quite broad under the Federal Rules of Civil Procedure. See Fed. R. Civ. Proc. 26. The discovery provisions of the federal rules reflect an accommodation between full and open discovery, and safeguard against unwarranted intrusions into the opponent's files. This new approach in discovery has been adopted in whole or substantial part by most states. James & Hazard, Civil Procedure §6.2 (2d ed. 1977). Similar discovery is now available to defendants and the prosecution in criminal cases. See Fed. R. Crim. Proc. 16. In criminal cases, any state discovery procedure must be reciprocal to be constitutional. 412 U.S. 470. See **depositions; interrogatories; work product.**

DISCRETION the reasonable exercise of a power or right to act in an official capacity; involves the idea of choice, of an exercise of the will, so that **abuse of discretion** involves more than a difference in judicial opinion between the **trial** and **appellate** courts, and in order to constitute an "abuse" of discretion, the **judgment** must demonstrate a perversity of will, a defiance of good judgment, or bias. 94 N.W. 2d 810, 811.

ABUSE OF DISCRETION see **abuse of discretion.**

JUDICIAL DISCRETION the reasonable use of judicial power, i.e., freedom to decide within the bounds of law and fact. See 5 F. 2d 188.

LEGAL DISCRETION the use of one of several equally satisfactory provisions of law. 32 N.E. 2d 431, 432.

PROSECUTORIAL DISCRETION the wide range of alternatives available to a prosecutor in criminal cases, including the decision to prosecute, the particular charges to be brought, plus bargaining, mode of trial conduct, and recommendations for sentencing, parole, etc. See La Fave, Arrest 72 (1967).

DISCRETIONARY ACCOUNT in the **securities** trade, one in which the customer gives the **broker** or a third party complete or partial discretion to buy and sell securities. Such discretion typically extends to selection, price, timing, and amount purchased. 288 F. Supp. 836, 839.

A public officer has discretion whenever the effective limits on his power leave him free to make a choice among possible courses of action or inaction. Davis, Administrative Law §4.02 (3rd ed. 1972).

DISCRIMINATION the unequal treatment of parties who are similarly situated. Federal law prohibits discrimination on the basis of race, sex, nationality, religion, and age in matters of employment, housing, education, voting rights, and access to public facilities. Furthermore, states or any governmental bodies may not engage in any actions which result in discrimination on grounds of race, sex, nationality, religion, or age. See, e.g., 42 U.S.C. §1983, 18 U.S.C. §245; **age discrimination; civil rights.** See also **price discrimination; reverse discrimination.**

DISHONOR to refuse to make payment on a **negotiable instrument** when such an instrument is duly presented for payment. A negotiable instrument may be either rightfully or wrongly dishonored. See U.C.C. §§3-507, 4-402. When a bank, for example, refuses to pay a check which has been presented to it for payment, it may do so because there are not adequate funds in the **drawer's** account to "cover" the check, or it may do so for other reasons. When such an instrument is dishonored, for whatever reason, the holder may pursue his **remedies** against either the principal party [drawer or **maker**] or any subsequent **indorser.** U.C.C. §3507(2). See **notice of dishonor.**

DISINHERIT (DISINHERITANCE) the act by the **donor** which dissolves the right of a person to **inherit** that **property** to which he previously had such right; the act of terminating another's right to inherit.

DISINTERMEDIATION movement of savings from banks and savings and loan associations into money market instruments, such as **treasury bills** and **notes** in order to obtain higher interest rates.

DISJUNCTIVE ALLEGATIONS [DENIAL] "those which **charge** that the **defendant** did one thing *or* another. The rule is that, whenever the word 'or' would leave the **averment** uncertain as to which of two or more things is meant, it is inadmissible." 419 P. 2d 569, 574. An **allegation** that charges the commission of a **crime** by one act 'or' another is defective if it is not sufficiently clear to enable the defendant to be properly informed of what he is charged with so that he can prepare a **defense**. See 419 P. 2d 569, 574. The same standard is applied to **pleadings** in **civil** cases, where both disjunctive allegations and DISJUNCTIVE DENIALS generally constitute **defective pleadings** and are therefore inadmissible. See 41 A. 2d 270, 271. Compare **alternative pleading; denial** [LITERAL DENIAL, CONJUNCTIVE DENIAL]. See also **negative pregnant.**

DISMISS in a legal context, to remove a **case** out of the court; to terminate a case without a complete **trial**. See **demurrer; motion** [MOTION TO DISMISS]. Compare **summary judgment.**

DISMISSAL equivalent of a cancellation, 91 N.E. 748, 749; dismissal of a **motion** is a denial of the motion, 57 P. 684, 685; a dismissal of an **appeal** places the parties in the same condition as if no appeal had been taken or allowed, and thus acts as a confirmation of the judgment below. See **judgment** [JUDGMENT OF DISMISSAL]. Compare **summary judgment.**

DISMISSAL WITH PREJUDICE usually considered an **adjudication** upon the **merits** and will operate as a **bar** to future action. 135 P. 2d 71, 74. See **res judicata.**

DISMISSAL WITHOUT PREJUDICE usually an indication that the dismissal affects no right or **remedy** of the parties, i.e., is not **on the merits** and does not bar a subsequent **suit** on the same **cause of action.** See **collateral estoppel; res judicata.**

DISORDERLY CONDUCT a generic term embracing certain minor offenses generally below the grade of **misdemeanor** which are yet quasi-criminal in character. The term has been so variously defined in different jurisdictions that no general, precise definition is available, although it may be said to broadly signify conduct which tends to **breach the peace,** disturb those who hear or see it, or endanger the morals, safety, or health of the community. 173 N.W. 887, 888. Specific offenses often proscribed by disorderly conduct statutes include drunkenness, brawling, **loitering,** or the use of offensive language in a public place, and refusing to move on when lawfully ordered by the police. But acts as diverse as fortune telling, wearing signs which misstate facts while **picketing,** and the unauthorized changing of a door's lock by a roomer have been considered disorderly conduct. The offense is broader than, and often includes within its meaning, the related offenses of breach of the peace and vagrancy.

Since the term lacks precise meaning, disorderly conduct statutes will be held **void for vagueness** unless the proscribed conduct is further and sufficiently specified. 274 F. Supp 658. As a limitation on speech and the right of assembly, within circumstances defined by the statutes, offenses defined as disorderly conduct may be scrutinized for conflict with First Amendment values.

DISPARAGEMENT see **bait and switch.**

DISPOSITION the giving up of, or the relinquishment of, anything, 13 F. 2d 756, 758; often used in reference to a testamentary **proceeding,** e.g., "the disposition of the estate;" **satisfaction** of a debt. Courts are also said to "dispose of" **cases,** i.e., finally determine the rights of the parties or otherwise terminate the proceedings. In criminal law, the **sentence** the **defendant** receives is the disposition; i.e., the post-adjudicative phase of the criminal proceeding is called the disposition or the dispositionary stage [process]. See also **bequeath; testamentary disposition.**

DISPOSSESS to oust, eject or exclude another from the possession of lands or premises, whether by legal process (as where a landlord lawfully evicts a tenant) or wrongfully. Compare **disseisin.**

DISPUTABLE PRESUMPTION see **presumption** [REBUTTABLE PRESUMPTION].

DISQUALIFICATION the inability to perform some act due to the existence of factors rendering the performance improper or inappropriate. See 117 F. 448, 451. For instance, a judge may be disqualified from hearing a particular case because of having previously represented one of the parties involved.

DISSEISIN the act of wrongfully depriving a person of the **seisin** of land, see 49 A. 1043, 1044; to take **possession** of land under claim or **color of title,** see 5 Conn. 255, 257; the dispossession of the **freeholder,** and the substitution of the disseisor as **tenant,** see 3 Watts 69, 71; an **estate** gained by wrong and injury. See 5 Conn. 371, 374. Mere entry on another's land is not disseisin unless accompanied by expulsion or refusal to allow one claiming paramount title to enter, see 163 S.W. 984, 988; but it is any act the necessary effect of which is to divest the estate of the former owner. See 74 Ala. 122, 130. There are two self-explanatory categories of disseisin: (1) at the election of the owner of the land; (2) in spite of the true owner. See 3 Me. (3 Greenl.) 174, 175.

DISSENT to differ in opinion; to disagree; to be of contrary sentiment. See 201 F. 2d 607, 609. The most common usage is in a situation where a judge's **opinion** of the **case** differs from that of the majority of the court and the "dissenting judge" will note his or her dissent

and may write a contrary opinion explicating the deficiencies of the majority opinion and his or her reasons for arriving at a contrary conclusion. See **opinion** [DISSENTING OPINION]. Compare **concur.**

DISSENTING OPINION see **opinion.** [DISSENTING OPINION].

DISSOLUTION in the law of **corporations,** the end of the legal existence of a corporation. It is a termination in any manner, whether by expiration of **charter, decree** of court, act of legislature or other means. 276 N.Y.S. 72. The process is governed by statute in most jurisdictions.

VOLUNTARY DISSOLUTION occurs where the proposal to dissolve is initiated by the corporation's board of directors and usually requires approval by a majority of voting **shares.**

INVOLUNTARY DISSOLUTION occurs upon the granting of a petition presented to the court by a specified percentage of **shareholders,** on grounds which have been defined by statute. Cox, Corporations. §§13.3111-3120 (1973).
    After the filing of a certificate of dissolution with the secretary of state the corporation is technically dissolved but the powers of the corporation and its directors continue to wind up the affairs of the corporation. Cox §13.3112. The right to dissolve a corporation without its consent belongs exclusively to the state. 19 Am. Jur. 2d 954.

DE FACTO DISSOLUTION occurs when a corporation suspends all its operations due to **insolvency** or other reasons, and goes into **liquidation** without availing itself of the statutory procedure provided for that purpose. A dissolution by any other means is a dissolution by law. 19 C.J.S. 1412.
    In matrimonial law, the act of terminating a marriage. A di-

vorce decree will dissolve the marriage. Compare **annulment.**

In a parliamentary system of government, refers to the ending of a sitting parliament by the Crown or by proclamation.

DISTINGUISH to demonstrate that an apparently similar case is so sufficiently different from the case at hand that it is of limited value as a **precedent.**

DISTRAINT see **distress.**

DISTRESS the act or process of DISTRAINT whereby a person (the DISTRAINOR), without prior court approval, seizes the **personal property** of another located upon the distrainor's land in satisfaction of a claim, as a pledge for performance of a duty, or in reparation of an injury. Where goods are seized in satisfaction of a claim, the distrainor can hold the goods until the claim is paid and, failing payment, may sell them in satisfaction. Originally, distress was a landlord's remedy [see **lien** (LANDLORD'S LIEN), 324 A. 2d 102, 104,] and was distinguishable from **attachment,** which is a court ordered seizure of goods or property. The persons whose goods are distrained upon has recourse against the wrongful distrainor in **replevin.**

Distraint has been superseded in most states of the United States by statutory provisions for debt collection, the enforcement of security interests, and landlord-tenant relations.

See also **impounding; garnishment; replevin.**

DISTRIBUTION a distribution is a payment in cash or in property by an entity to the owner of such entity. For example, when a **corporation** pays a dividend to its shareholder, such payment of a dividend constitutes a corporate distribution. See also **secondary distribution.**

CORPORATE DISTRIBUTION a distribution by a corporation to its shareholders. If the corporation has current or accumulated **earnings and profits,** such distribution constitutes a **dividend** to the shareholders. To the extent the distribution exceeds earnings and profits, distribution constitutes a return of **basis** to the shareholder and to the extent that it exceeds basis, such distribution constitutes the equivalent of a receipt of property or cash as a result of a **sale or exchange** of the stock. I.R.C. §301. A corporate distribution is not **deductible** by the corporation.

PARTNERSHIP DISTRIBUTION a distribution by a **partnership** to its partners. A **partnership,** as a nontaxpaying entity, has all of its income taxed to its partners. To the extent a distribution exceeds the partnership's current income, it reduces the **basis** of the partner's interest in the partnership and such distribution is not taxable unless it exceeds the partner's basis. I.R.C. §§705, 731. If the distribution does exceed his basis and is in cash, the partner is taxed as if the distribution were an **amount realized** from the **sale or exchange** of the partner's interest in the partnership; if the distribution is of property, it is not taxed to the partner, and the partner receives a **carryover basis** in the property. I.R.C. §732.

TRUST DISTRIBUTION a distribution by a **trust** to the beneficiaries of the trust. If a trust has current or accumulated income of a character which may be distributable to the beneficiaries [generally, **ordinary income**] such a distribution is taxed to the beneficiary as ordinary income and deductible by the trust. I.R.C. §§643(a), 651, 652, 661 and 662. If such trust does not have distributable income, then it is considered to be a distribution of corpus to the beneficiaries of the trust and not income to such beneficiaries.

DISTRICT ATTORNEY an officer of the governmental body under which he or she is operating, such as a state, county, or municipality, with the duty to prosecute all those accused of crimes. A district attorney will frequently have assistants who are similarly empowered. In the federal government, district attorneys are called UNITED STATES ATTORNEYS. See 28 U.S.C. §§541 et seq.

DISTRICT COURT with respect to the judicial system of the United States, constitutional courts each having territorial **jurisdiction** over a district which may include a whole state or only a part of it. Thus the designation "S.D.N.Y." refers to District Court for the Southern District of New York. They have **original jurisdiction,** exclusive of courts of the individual states, of all offenses against laws of the United States, 255 F. 2d 9, 13, and are courts of general **jurisdiction** for **suits** between **litigants** of different states [see **diversity of citizenship**]. Also refers to inferior courts in several states having limited jurisdictions to try certain minor cases. See also **federal question jurisdiction.**

DISTURBANCE OF THE PEACE "to agitate, to arouse from a state of repose, to molest, to interrupt, to hinder and to disquiet." 156 So. 2d 448, 449. "Any act which molests inhabitants in enjoyment of peace and quiet or which excites disquietude or fear among normal persons." 138 So. 851. See **breach of the peace.**

DIVERS many, several, sundry; a grouping of unspecified persons, things, acts, etc.

DIVERSIONARY PROGRAMS see **pre-trial intervention [P.T.I.]** [DIVERSIONARY PROGRAMS].

DIVERSITY JURISDICTION see **diversity of citizenship.**

DIVERSITY OF CITIZENSHIP that basis of federal **jurisdiction** first promulgated in the First Judiciary Act which grants to federal courts **original jurisdiction** over cases and **controversies** between citizens of different states or between a citizen of a state and an alien, subject to a **jurisdictional amount** of $10,000. See Wright, Federal Courts §§23-37 (4th ed. 1983); 28 U.S.C.A. §1332. The constitutional grant of diversity jurisdiction extends "to Controversies . . . between Citizens of different states . . . and between a State, or the Citizens thereof, and foreign States, Citizens or Subjects." United States Constitution Art. III Sec. 2. See **removal.**

DIVESTITURE a remedy, by virtue of which the court orders the offending party to rid itself of property or assets before the party would normally have done so. Divestiture, like **restitution,** has the purpose of depriving a defendant of the gains of his wrongful conduct, 91 F. Supp. 333, and is commonly used to enforce **antitrust** laws. A court will not invoke this extreme remedy unless it finds divestiture to be both necessary and practicable in preventing a **monopoly** or restraint of trade.

DIVIDEND profits appropriated for division among **stockholders.** See 378 S.W. 2d 161, 167, 169; a distribution of profits or earnings to shareholders. See 224 N.Y.S. 2d 985, 988. The amount any stockholder receives depends upon whether the stockholder owns common or preferred **stock.**

CUMULATIVE DIVIDEND a dividend which provides that, if at any time it is not paid in full, the difference shall be added to the following payment.

DIVIDEND ADDITION as used in a life-insurance policy, it means **insurance** purchased with dividends in addition to the face [value] of the policy. See 19 N.E. 2d 854, 857.

EX-DIVIDEND see **ex-dividend.**

EXTRAORDINARY   DIVIDENDS
" 'ordinary dividends' are usual
or customary dividends [such] as
6 percent, or sum per share, paid
at regular periods, while 'extraordinary dividends' may assume unusual form and amount,
paid at irregular intervals from
accumulated surplus or earnings,
and require investigation into
their source and apportionment
according to equitable principles
rather than application of common law rule that a dividend
belongs to the party entitled to it
at the date of its declaration."
193 A. 33, 37.

LIQUIDATION DIVIDEND act or operation in **winding up** affairs of
firm or **corporation,** a settling
with its **debtors** and **creditors,**
and an appropriation and distribution to its stockholders proportionately of the amount of profit
and loss. See 68 F. 2d 763, 765.

PREFERRED DIVIDEND fund paid to
one class of stockkholders in priority to that to be paid to another
class. 55 Utah 129.

SCRIP DIVIDEND a dividend not
payable in cash, but in certificates of indebtedness which give
the holder certain rights against
the corporation. See 142 N.Y.S.
847, 849.

STOCK DIVIDEND a dividend paid
not in cash, but in **stock** so that
each stockholder obtains a greater absolute number of shares but
the same relative number of
shares.

DIVISIBLE CONTRACT see **severable contract.**

DIVORCE dissolution of bonds of
marriage. 61 Cal. Rptr. 178, 180. It
is not a punishment for a wrong
done by one spouse to the other,
but is the result of the determination by the state of **domicile** that the
continuation of the marital relationship between the parties concerned

will be contrary to the policy of the
law. 75 A. 2d 889, 892.

While a divorce puts an end to
the marital relation, it does not
relate back to the act of marriage
and render it null and **void.** It is
based upon the theory of an invalid
marriage for some cause arising
after the marriage ceremony. This
is to be contrasted with an **annulment** proceeding which relates back
and erases the marriage and all its
implications from the outset on the
theory that for some reasons existing at the time of marriage no valid
marriage existed. 104 A.L.R.
1290.

NO-FAULT DIVORCE a divorce
which is granted without the necessity of finding a spouse to have
been guilty of some marital misconduct. The most common "no-
fault" ground is voluntary separation for a period of time. Prior
to the enactment of no-fault
divorce statutes, the traditional
concept of divorce required
proof of marital misconduct as a
prerequisite. There had to be a
specified fault, a wholly innocent
plaintiff spouse and a wholly **guilty** or aggressor **defendant**
spouse.

The Uniform Marriage and Divorce Act §§302(2), 305 (1971)
supports a pure no-fault concept.
It allows for divorce unilaterally
upon the application by either
spouse without proof of marital
misconduct and without a mandatory waiting period either before or after the divorce is
decreed.

SEPARATION [DIVORCE A MENSA ET
THORO] (ā měn'-să ĕt thō-ŕō)—
Lat: from table and bed. A partial
divorce decree, usually entered
in the course of divorce proceedings, which directs the parties to
live separately—indeed, forbids
cohabitation—but does not dissolve the marriage.

See **community property; equitable distribution.**

DOCKET a list of cases on a court's calendar. In **procedure,** a formal record, included in a **brief,** of the proceedings in the court below.

DOCTOR-PATIENT PRIVILEGE see **physician-patient privilege.**

DOCTRINE OF WORTHIER TITLE see **worthier title, doctrine of.**

DOCUMENT any writing, recording, computer tape, blueprint, x-ray, photograph, or other physical object upon which information is set forth by means of letters, numbers or other symbols. 324 N.Y.S. 2d 483, 486.

DOCUMENTARY EVIDENCE a **document** having legal effect which is offered as **evidence.** For instance, a **contract** or a **deed.** Prior to being admitted as evidence, the authenticity of the document must be established by testimony as to how the writing was produced or the circumstances under which it has been kept. McCormick, Evidence §218 et seq. (2d ed. 1972).

DOCUMENT OF TITLE a **bill of lading,** dock warrant, warehouse receipt, or order for the delivery of **goods,** or any other document which in the regular course of business or financing is treated as adequate evidence that the person in possession of it is entitled to receive, hold, and dispose of the document and the goods it covers. U.C.C. §1-201(15).

DOCUMENT, ORIGINAL see **best evidence rule.**

DOLUS see **culpa.**

DOMAIN "ownership of **land;** immediate or absolute ownership; paramount or ultimate ownership, an estate or patrimony which one has in his own right; land of which one is absolute owner," 30 Cal. 645, 648; territory. See **public domain.**

DOMESDAY BOOK a record made in the time of William the Conqueror (1081-1086) consisting of accurate and detailed surveys of the lands in England and the means by which the alleged owners obtained title. See 2 Bl. Comm. *49.

DOMICILE the place where an individual has his permanent home or principal establishment, to where, whenever he is absent, he has the intention of returning, 168 So. 2d 873, 877; "the one technical preeminent headquarters, which as a result either of fact or of fiction, every person is compelled to have in order that by aid of it certain rights and duties which have been attached to it by the law may be determined." 51 N.E. 531, 532. "Every person has at all times one domicile, and no person has more than one domicile at a time." 1 Restatement, second, Conflict of Laws §11 (1971). Residence is not equal to domicile since a person can have many transient residences where he may temporarily be found but only one legal domicile which is the residence to which he always intends to return and to remain indefinitely.

A business or corporation may have a domicile which refers to the place where the establishment is maintained or where the governing power of the corporation is exercised. For purposes of taxation, it is often a principal place of business. 123 S.W. 353, 359.

DOMICILIARY an individual who is domiciled in a particular state or country is a domicilary of that state or country. See **domicile.**

DOMINANT ESTATE [TENEMENT] an estate whose owners are entitled to the **beneficial use** of another's property; **property** retained by an original grantor when a particular tract is subdivided and a portion is conveyed, and to which certain rights or benefits are legally owed by the conveyed or **servient estate.** 116 S.W. 668. These rights and benefits may be in the nature of an **easement,** so that the owner of the retained land [dominant estate] is said to have a right of easement in the servient estate.

DOMINION having both **title** to and possession of **property;** having control of both ownership and use. 522 F. 2d 1299, 1307.

DONATED SURPLUS see **unearned surplus** [DONATED SURPLUS].

DONATIO (*dō-nä'-shē-ō*)—Lat: a **gift.** A donation.

DONATION see **contribution.**

DONATIVE INTENT see **gift.**

DONEE the recipient of a **gift** or **trust;** one who takes without first giving **consideration.** See 76 N.C. 82, 83. One who is given a power, see 70 S.W. 742, 743, e.g., one who exercises a **power of appointment.** 274 S.W. 2d 431, 439. Compare **bailee; trustee.**

DONEE BENEFICIARY see **third party beneficiary** [DONEE BENEFICIARY].

DONOR one who gives or makes a **gift;** creator of a **trust,** 195 N.E. 557, 564; the party conferring a power, e.g., the grantor of a **power of appointment.** 274 S.W. 2d 431, 439. See also **settlor** [DONOR; TRUSTOR].

DOUBLE DAMAGES see **damages** [DOUBLE [TREBLE] DAMAGES].

DOUBLE JEOPARDY provision in the Fifth Amendment to the Constitution of the United States which provides that "No person . . . shall . . . be subject for the same offense to be twice put in jeopardy of life or limb." This provision has been fundamental to the common law and finds expression in state constitutions. See 18 Wall. 163, 168. It has now been held applicable to the states through the due process clause of the Fourteenth Amendment. See 395 U.S. 784. The clause operates only in criminal settings and prevents a second prosecution, regardless of the outcome of the first trial (acquittal, conviction, or mistrial) unless there has been an appeal from a conviction, see 163 U.S. 662, or a **mistrial** granted upon manifest necessity. See 410 U.S. 458; 400 U.S. 470.

The bar against double jeopardy applies only after "jeopardy has attached," i.e., after the jury has been sworn or after a judge in a non-jury trial receives the first piece of evidence at the trial. A dismissal prior to jeopardy attaching does not preclude a second or renewed prosecution under the double jeopardy clause.

Double jeopardy bars double punishment as well as double prosecution. While a higher penalty upon a retrial following a successful appeal does not itself violate the double jeopardy guarantee, there must generally appear independent justification for the increased penalty in order to insure that the higher penalty is not vindictive. See 395 U.S. 711. See also **collateral estoppel.**

DOUBT see **reasonable doubt.**

DOWAGER generally, a widow supported by the property of her deceased husband. In real property, a widow who has a life estate in the real property of her husband by her right of **dower.** Moynihan, Introduction to the Law of Real Property 55 (1962).

DOWER a **life estate** to which a wife is entitled upon the death of her husband. 290 S.W. 244, 250. At **common law,** the widow was entitled to one-third of all the property in which her husband was **seized** in **fee** at any time during the marriage [coverture]. See 278 Ill. App. 564; 261 N.Y.S. 400; 131 S.E. 585, 586. Her dower is a **freehold** estate, and cannot derive from an **estate for years.** 42 So. 290, 298. Compare **homestead rights.** See **curtesy; inchoate dower.**

Dower rights have been abrogated in many jurisdictions or limited to interests which the husband holds at his death. American Law of Property §§5.31-5.32. Where they still exist, a wife can join in a **conveyance** and thereby give up her dower rights. Id. at §18.95.

DOWRY money and personalty which the wife brings to the husband to support the expenses of marriage; a donation to the maintenance and support of the marriage. See 22 Mo. 206, 254.

DRAFT an order in writing directing a person other than the **maker** to pay a specified sum of money to a named person; automobiles are often purchased by used car dealers through "dealer's drafts," i.e., by a document setting forth a bank's promise to pay on the dealer's behalf for the automobile once it has been properly **indorsed** by the dealer. Drafts may or may not be **negotiable instruments** depending upon whether the elements of negotiability are satisfied. See U.C.C. §3-104(3). Draft is synonymous with BILL OF EXCHANGE although "draft" is the preferred term. See id. at §3-104(2)(a).

SIGHT DRAFT a draft payable on demand. 276 P. 262; U.C.C. §3-108. A bill of exchange for immediate collection. 405 P. 2d 488, 490.

TIME DRAFT a draft which is not payable until a specified future time. For instance, a post-dated check is a time draft. U.C.C. §3-109.

In a military context, the term connotes the compulsory conscription of citizens into the military service.

More generally, it refers to the preliminary form of a legal document (e.g., the draft of a contract—often called "rough draft"). It also refers to the process of preparing or DRAWING a legal document (e.g., drafting a will) or piece of proposed legislation.

DRAM SHOP ACT a legislative enactment imposing **strict liability** upon the seller of intoxicating beverages when the sale results in harm to a third party's person, **property,** or means of support. Under **common law,** no **cause of action** existed against the person dispensing intoxicating beverages for the resulting damages that might be inflicted by the intoxicated person. The common law theorized that the **proximate cause** of the injury was not the furnishing of liquor but rather the act of the purchaser in drinking the liquor. 143 P. 2d 952. In many jurisdictions, the legislature has enacted CIVIL DAMAGE ACTS or "dram shop acts" creating a statutory remedy against the seller of intoxicating beverages, provided that the resulting intoxication causes the injury. Under such acts, the **plaintiff** has a cause of action against the vendor when, by reason of the intoxication of another, he sustains personal injury, property damage, or loss of support. Under this theory, some jurisdictions have held that a wife may recover "for injuries to means of support" when her husband dies as a result of intoxication, either his own or another's. 158 N.E. 2d 7. Since the statute involves strict liability, the plaintiff need not show negligence on the part of the seller. The law is unsettled though, as to the seller's rights of **indemnity** from the intoxicated person who proximately caused the injury. 45 Am. Jur. 2d 612.

DRAW see **draft.**

DRAWEE one to whom a **bill of exchange** or a **check** directs a request to pay a certain sum of money specified therein. In the typical checking account situation, the bank is the drawee, the person writing the check is the **maker** or **drawer,** and the person to whom the check is written is the **payee.**

DRAWER person who draws a **check** or **bill of exchange.**

DRIVING WHILE INTOXICATED [D.W.I.] the offense of operating a motor vehicle while under the influence of alcohol or drugs. State law controls both the definition of "operating," such as whether it includes the actual driving of the car or merely sitting in the car, and the level of intoxication needed in order to be found in violation of the law. Some statutes refer to DRIVING UNDER THE INFLUENCE [D.U.I.] or DRIVING WHILE IMPAIRED and it is possible to do so without being intoxicated. 73 N.W. 2d. 135.

DROIT *(drwäh)*—Fr: a right; law; the whole body of the law.

DRUG ABUSE the repeated or uncontrolled use of **controlled substances.** While possession or use of controlled substances may be a crime, addiction to drugs is a disease which cannot be made a crime under the **due process** clause of the Constitution. 370 U.S. 660. Drug abuse or addiction is a ground for **divorce** in some states.

DRUG LAW see **generic** [GENERIC DRUG LAW].

DRUGS see **controlled substances; driving while intoxicated.**

DUAL CITIZENSHIP "where two different sovereigns within their respective territorial confines claim citizenship of the same person and he of them." 76 F. Supp. 664, 666. A person having dual citizenship can lose his United States citizenship after attaining the age of twenty-two unless he resides in the United States or takes an oath of allegiance to the United States. 8 U.S.C. §1482.

DUCES TECUM see **subpoena** (SUBPOENA DUCES TECUM).

DUE CARE a concept used in **tort** law to indicate the standard of care or the **legal duty** one owes to others. **Negligence,** in the context of due care, is the failure to use that degree of care which a person of ordinary prudence and reason [the **reasonable man**] would exercise under the same circumstances. See 198 S.E. 2d 526, 529. Also, the "[F]ailure to exercise due care is the failure to perform some specific duty required by law." 153 S.E. 2d 356, 359. It "means care which is reasonably commensurate with a known danger and the seriousness of the consequences which are liable to follow its omisssion. . . . Due care may be either ordinary care or a high degree of care, according to the circumstances of the particular case." 438 P. 2d 477, 482.

DUE COURSE see **payment in due course.**

DUE DATE time fixed for payment of debt, tax, etc.

DUE PROCESS OF LAW a phrase which was first expressly introduced into American jurisprudence in the Fifth Amendment to the Constitution which provides that "nor [shall any person] be deprived of life, liberty, or property, without due process of law;" This provision is applicable only to the actions of the federal government. 7 Pet. 243 (1833). The phrase was made applicable to the states with the adoption of the Fourteenth Amendment, Section 1, which states that "Nor shall any State deprive any person of life, liberty or property, without due process of law"; The phrase does not have a fixed meaning but expands with jurisprudential attitudes of fundamental fairness. 302 U.S. 319. The legal substance of the phrase is divided into the areas of substantive due process, and procedural due process. The constitutional safe-guard of SUBSTANTIVE DUE PROCESS requires that all legislation be in furtherance of a legitimate governmental objective. Since the late 1930s, the Supreme Court has generally limited judicial review on the basis of "substantive due process" to determine whether the law is rationally related to a legitimate goal. Only where legislation restricts what the Court characterizes as "fundamental rights" will the Court allow stricter scrutiny. Such rights include first amendment, voting, and sexual privacy rights (410 U.S. 113). STRICT SCRUTINY involves determining whether the law is necessary to further a compelling governmental interest.

The original content of the phrase was a PROCEDURAL DUE PROCESS protection, i.e., in guaranteeing procedural fairness where the government would deprive one of his property or liberty. This requires that notice and the right to a fair hearing be accorded prior to a deprivation. 237 U.S. 309. The enumeration of those procedures required by due process varies according to the factual context. The extent to which procedural due process must be afforded a person is influenced by the extent to which he may be "condemned to suffer grievous loss . . . and depends upon whether the [person's] interest in avoiding that loss outweighs the governmental interest in summary adjudication. Accordingly . . . 'considerations of what procedures due process may require under any given set of circumstances must begin with a determination of the precise nature of the government function involved as well as the private interest that has been affected by governmental action'." 397 U.S. 254, 262-263. In recent years, the bulk of problems in determining the scope of procedural due process has involved the characterization of **property.** The due process clause of the Fourteenth Amendment has been used as the vehicle for the application of most of the substantive and procedural rights in the Bill of Rights to state action.

Due process of law does not have a fixed meaning. As the constitution itself it adjusts with changing jurisprudential values. Said Justice Frankfurter: "The requirement of 'due process' is not a fair weather or timid assurance. It must be respected in periods of calm and in times of trouble; it protects aliens as well as citizens. But 'due process,' unlike some legal rules, is not a technical conception with a fixed content unrelated to time, place and circumstances. Expressing as it does in its ultimate analysis respect enforced by law for that feeling of just treatment which has been evolved through centuries of Anglo-American constitutional history and civilization, 'due process' cannot be imprisoned within the treacherous limits of any formula. Representing a profound attitude of fairness between man and man, and more particularly between the individual and government, 'due process' is compounded of history, reason, the past course of decisions, and stout confidence in the strength of the democratic faith which we profess. Due process is not a mechanical instrument. It is not a yardstick. It is a delicate process of adjustment inescapably involving the exercise of judgment by those whom the Constitution entrusted with the unfolding of the process." 341 U.S. 123, 162-163.

DUMMY a strawman, a sham.

DUMMY CORPORATION a **corporation** which has no business purpose other than to provide protection from liability or the disclosure of the principal behind its activities.

DUMMY DIRECTOR a **director** who serves in name only and has no real control over the corporation's activities. See 92 P. 2d 316, 319.

DUMMY SHAREHOLDER a **shareholder** who owns **stock** in name only and has no financial interest in the corporation.

DUMPING the sale of manufactured goods for a price lower than its fair value; "sale of commodities in foreign market at a price which is lower than the price or value of comparable commodities in the country of their origins," 494 F.

Supp. 1161, 1169. Under the ANTI-DUMPING LAW, the United States may impose special **custom duties** on foreign manufacturers which attempt to import goods into this country for less than their fair value if an industry in the United States is or may be materially injured. 19 U.S.C. §1671 et seq. Also, discharge of waste material into the environment.

DUMPOR'S CASE see **Rule in Dumpor's Case.**

DUPLICITOUS refers to a **pleading** which joins in the same **count** two or more distinct grounds of **action** to enforce a single right; to allege more than one distinct claim in the same **indictment** is 'duplicitous.'

DUPLICITY in practice, the technical invalidity resulting from uniting two or more **causes of action** in one **count** of a **pleading,** or multiple defenses in one plea, or multiple **crimes** in one count of an **indictment**, or two or more incongruous subjects in one legislative act, which may be contrary to proper **procedural** or constitutional requirements, see, e.g., 47 F. Supp. 524, 529, 530 (pleadings); 173 N.E. 2d 474, 475 (indictments); 273 P. 928, 930 (legislation). Fed. R. Civ. Proc. 8(e) permits duplicity in the federal courts. See also **joinder; misjoinder.**

DURESS action by a person which compels another to do what he would not otherwise do. It is a recognized **defense** to any act, such as a **crime**, contractual **breach** or **tort**, which must be voluntary in order to create **liability** in the actor. Restatement, Second, Contracts, provides that the manifestation of assent required for a valid contract is defeated if the assent is compelled by duress, §174; that a contract is voidable by a victim if his assent is induced by an improper threat leaving the victim no reasonable alternative, §175(a); and that a contract is voidable if assent is induced by one who is not a party to the transaction, unless that party transacts in good faith, gives value, or relies on the assent, and has no knowledge of the duress. §175(b). Duress negates the free assent necessary to create a binding **contract**, and may be accomplished by force or threat of force to a person or his property. Neither the threats alone nor the fear alone is sufficient to prove duress, and the test of fear is the actual state of mind of the victim, without resort to an objective standard of reasonableness. See 50 N.E. 555. To qualify as duress, threats must be unlawful. See Dobbs, Remedies 10.2 (1973). Thus, the "threat" to pursue a legal remedy (such as a lawsuit) will not qualify as duress, as long as the "threat" is made in good faith. See 274 F. Supp. 1003, 1005.

In tort law, duress is most often used to invalidate the consent which will otherwise exclude the defendant's liability. Prosser, Torts 106 (4th ed. 1971).

In criminal law, duress is an **affirmative defense** which will excuse the action under some circumstances, if a person of reasonable firmness could not have resisted the fear induced by another. 180 N.W. 418, 422. At common law, duress was not recognized as a defense to felonious **homicides**, 12 So. 301, 303, but this limitation does not exist in the Model Penal Code. M.P.C. §2.09. See **coercion; self help.**

DURHAM RULE a test of criminal responsibility, adopted by the District of Columbia Court of Appeals in 1954, which states that "an accused is not criminally responsible if his unlawful act was the product of mental disease or defect." 214 F. 2d 862, 874-75. The Durham Rule was the first major modification of the **common law M'Naghten Rule** but is no longer in force in the District of Columbia, having been negated by the American Law Institute's Model Penal Code test,

§4.01(1), now used by a number of jurisdictions. 471 F. 2d 969, 971. See **insanity defense.**

DUTY obligatory conduct owed by a person to another person. In **tort** law, duty is a legally sanctioned obligation the **breach** of which results in the **liability** of the actor. See 247 F. Supp. 188, 191. Thus, under the law of **negligence,** if an individual owes to others a DUTY OF CARE, he must conduct himself so as to avoid negligent injury to them. See **breach** [BREACH OF DUTY]; **due care.**

In tax law, a duty is a levy [tax] on **imports** and **exports.** See 119 F. Supp. 352, 354.

See **delegable duty.**

DUTY, LEGAL see **legal duty.**

DUTY OF PRODUCING EVIDENCE see **burden of proof.**

DUTY TO MITIGATE DAMAGES see **mitigation of damages.**

DWELLING HOUSE one's residence or abode; a structure or apartment used as a home for a family unit. As used in a **restrictive covenant** the term PRIVATE DWELLING may be limited to single-family occupation even though two-family use does not change the outward character of the house. 198 N.Y.S. 311, 312. In the law of real property, it "includes everything pertinent and accessory to the main building and may consist of a cluster of buildings." 121 Ga. App. 240.

In criminal law, a house in which the occupier and his family usually reside, temporary absence being insufficient to destroy the status of the structure as a dwelling. 4 Bl. Comm. *225. For the purpose of the crime of **burglary** the dwelling house includes mobile homes, 46 A. 2d 35, 36; apartment units, 26 N.Y. 200; even a hotel room if one is living therein and thus is not a mere transient. Compare 99 N.E. 357, 359 with 86 N.Y. 360. See generally, Perkins and Boyce, Criminal Law 255-59 (3rd ed. 1982).

D.W.I. see **driving while intoxicated.**

DYING DECLARATIONS see **hearsay rule.**

E

EARNEST at **civil law,** something of value given by one party to another to bind a **contract,** usually a sales agreement. Derived from Roman law and the Napoleonic Code, the earnest serves both as part payment or performance and as a method of predetermining liquidated damages for breach of contract. On breach by buyer, seller retains the earnest, while in seller's breach, buyer is entitled to twice the value of the earnest. Justinian, Institutes, III, 23; Code Napoleon, Art. 1590 (1804); La. Rev. Stat. Art. 2463 (1978).

At common law, earnest is often used to denote a down payment but, unlike a down payment, earnest is by definition forfeited on breach of contract. 255 N.W. 2d 827, 829. The earnest was originally used as a device to render a contract enforceable despite the **Statute of Frauds** requirement of a writing. 255 N.W. 134. Unlike **escrow,** in which a neutral third party holds the goods or money pending distribution to a proper party, an earnest is transferred directly to the other contracting party.

An earnest differs from an **option** to purchase in that the earnest serves to bind the actual contract of sale, while money given for an option results in the buyer acquiring only a right to purchase, without the obligation to do so. 65 S. 2d 185.

EARNINGS AND PROFITS generally, a tax term referring to the income of a **corporation** which, if distributed to its shareholders, would constitute a **dividend** to the distributee shareholder. I.R.C. §316 "reflects a corporation's capacity to pass along tax consequences to its **shareholders** through distributions to them." 508 F. 2d 1076, 1082.

ACCUMULATED EARNINGS AND PROFITS the amount of earnings and profits from prior years earned by a corporation but which has not been distributed as dividends to its shareholders.

CURRENT EARNINGS AND PROFITS the earnings and profits of a corporation which are earned during the current taxable year. For dividend purposes, distributions to shareholders are deemed to be made first out of current earnings and profits.

EARNINGS REPORT see **income statement.**

EASEMENT a right, created by an express or implied agreement, of one owner of land to make lawful and **beneficial use** of the land of another. 46 Cal. Rptr. 25, 33; 62 Cal Rptr. 113; 172, S.W. 2d 885, 887. Such use must not be inconsistent with any other uses already being made of the land. See 45 N.W. 2d 895. An easement is an **inchoate** privilege connected with the land, and is therefore not an **estate** or **fee.** 91 P. 2d 428. See also **public easement.**

AFFIRMATIVE EASEMENT an easement that allows its owner to do affirmative acts on the subservient property, such as to use the subservient property as a right of way. Boyer, Law of Property, 562 (1981).

EASEMENT APPURTENANT a "pure" easement, or "easement proper," i.e., one that requires a **dominant estate** to which the ben-

efit of the easement attaches, or "appertains." In contrast to an **easement in gross,** an "easement appurtenant" "passes with the dominant estate to all subsequent **grantees** and is **inheritable.**" 206 N.Y.S. 42, 44. See 258 N.Y.S. 695.

EASEMENT BY PRESCRIPTION see PRESCRIPTIVE EASEMENT below.

EASEMENT IN GROSS a personal privilege to make use of another's land. It is not **appurtenant** to a **dominant estate** and is therefore not **assignable** or **inheritable,** but "dies" with the person who acquired it. See 156 A. 121, 122; 210 P. 2d 593, 596.

EASEMENT OF NECESSITY an **easement** necessary for the continued use of the land when a larger tract of land has been subdivided. The existence of such an easement is determined by assessing the facts surrounding the original **conveyance** severing the **dominant estate** from the **servient estate.** If without the easement either the **grantee** or **grantor** cannot make use of his property, then the existence of an "easement of necessity" is implied by **operation of law.** See 146 N.E. 2d 171, 175, 137 A. 2d 92, 98, 99, 139 A. 2d 318, 322.

EQUITABLE EASEMENT an **equitable servitude,** and therefore only enforceable in **equity.** To be enforceable at **law,** there must be **privity** between the **grantor** and **grantee.** As an equitable servitude, however, privity is not necessary to enforce the easement so long as the subsequent grantee has either actual or constructive **notice** of the easement. 344 P. 2d 221. Violation of this easement is remedied by an **injunction** rather than money **damages.**

IMPLIED EASEMENT An easement that is not expressly created but rather is implied at the time real property is transferred from the prior continuous and apparent use of the subservient property and the necessity of the easement to the enjoyment of the dominant property. Boyer, Law of Property 563 (3rd ed. 1981).

NEGATIVE EASEMENT an easement which restricts an owner of land from doing certain acts on or in connection with the owner's land. "A negative easement is one the effect of which is not to authorize the doing of an act by the person entitled to the easement, but merely to preclude the owner of the land subject to the easement from doing that which, if no easement existed, he would be entitled to do." 66 P. 2d 792, 794. Restrictive covenants are sometimes viewed to have the same legal consequences as negative easements, 107 A. 205; 274 N.Y.S. 549, 554, although technically a covenant is merely a personal undertaking while an easement is a claim on lands. 21 C.J.S. 885.

PRESCRIPTIVE EASEMENT [EASEMENT BY PRESCRIPTION] an easement acquired through the uninterrupted use of another's land for the same statutory period of time necessary to satisfy adverse possession requirements. At common law, prescriptive easements were based on the fictitious "lost grant doctrine" which conclusively presumed [see presumption] that there had been a grant of the right which had been lost. This fiction has generally been discarded and prescriptive easements now operate by analogy to adverse possession, under the application of the Statute of Limitations. 16 F. 2d 395, 169 N.E. 428. The use must be adverse to the rights of the owner, open and notorious, continuous and uninterrupted, and with knowledge and acquiescence of the owner. 201 N.W. 880. There can be no prescriptive rights acquired where the use is with the permission of the record owner or his agent. The easement only permits a certain use, and has no effect on the underlying title.

PUBLIC EASEMENT any easement enjoyed by the public in general, e.g., the right of passage of the public over the surface of streets, alleys, highways, etc. It is also called a DEDICATION, meaning that the use of the land has been devoted for such purposes by the owner of the fee. A "public easement" carries with it the right to construct and properly maintain the passageway, and includes necessary light and air. See 42 A. 583, 584, 134 A. 77, 79.

RECIPROCAL NEGATIVE EASEMENTS an implied covenant which can be raised in equity against the retained lands of the grantor or his successors in interest, when a common grantor has failed to insert the restrictions placed on prior purchases in his later conveyances. "If the owner of two or more lots, so situated as to bar the relation to a general scheme of development, sells one with an easement of benefit to the land retained, the servitude becomes mutual, and, during the period of restraint, the owner of the lot or lots retained can do nothing forbidden to the owner of the lot sold. For want of a better descriptive term, this is styled a reciprocal negative easement." 319 S.W. 2d 855. The essential elements necessary for a court to find the existence of reciprocal negative easements are: a common grantor, a general scheme of development evincing an original intent that all lands within the development be similarly and mutually restricted, and restrictive covenants running with the land in accordance with the scheme contained in deeds granted to parcels previously granted by the common grantor. 96 N.W. 2d 743, 747. Reciprocal negative easements are not personal to the original owner but are operative upon the use of the land by any subsequent owner having actual or constructive **notice** of their existence.

EAVESDROPPING the monitoring of communications by a third party without the knowledge of the communicating parties. See **invasion of privacy, wiretapping.**

ECCLESIASTICAL LAW English **law** pertaining to matters concerning the church. This law was administered by ecclesiastical courts and is considered a branch of English **common law;** it was intended to vindicate the dignity and peace of the church by reforming the ecclesiastical state and persons, and "all manner of errors, heresies, schisms, abuses, offenses, **contempts** and enormities." 3 Bl. Comm. *67. Today, in **equity** and **divorce** cases, courts still rely on the principles and doctrines established by ecclesiastical law in so far as these principles are consistent with relevant constitutional and statutory law. 44 S.E. 861, 862. American law specifically adopted the practice of granting **alimony,** as incident to **divorce,** from English ecclesiastical law. Clark, Law of Domestic Relations §14.1 (1968).

Historically, the ecclesiastical courts had undisturbed jurisdiction over rights of marriage, actions for divorce, restitution of **conjugal rights** and testamentary and intestacy cases. 3 Bl. Comm. *87-98. There is, however, a conflict of opinion as to whether ecclesiastical law has been adopted as part of the common law of this country. Some courts hold that this code of laws cannot be considered part of the common law since it is based on a union of church and state which has no place in our legal system. 108 A. 2d 882. Other courts consider some of this law part of the common law, especially if these laws afford a good rule of **construction** for a particular American law. See generally, Clark, Law of Domestic Rela-

tions §13.1 (1968); 10 S.E. 2d 893, 896-897. See **canon, corpus juris.**

ECU see **eurodollar.**

E.E.O.C. see **equal opportunity.**

EFFECTS, PERSONAL see **personal effects.**

EGRESS see **ingress and egress.**

EIGHTH AMENDMENT one of the Bill of Rights passed in 1791 prohibiting **cruel and unusual punishment** and excessive **bails** and fines. The ban against cruel and unusual punishment has been applied against a state's imposition of a penalty for the status of being addicted to the use of narcotics." 370 U.S. 660, but the Supreme Court has given the state courts great deference in determining what constitutes cruel and unusual punishment in terms of sentencing for various crimes, 454 U.S. 370. However, the amendment does limit the kinds of punishment that can be imposed, proscribes punishment grossly disproportionate to the severity of the crime, and imposes substantive limits on what can be made criminal and punished as such. 430 U.S. 651.

EJECTMENT a legal action brought by one claiming a right to possess **real property** against another who possesses the premises adversely or who is a holdover **tenant** who remains beyond that termination of a **lease** but who is not merely a **trespasser.** See 469 F. 2d 211, 214. At **common law,** the action was originally commenced by a copyholder or **lessee** against an intruder. Later it became a possessory action brought by a fictitious lessee to **try the title** of the possessor or **real party in interest.** See 51 A. 509, 510. Under modern statutory law the action is generally between real parties in interest, and the holder of legal title is entitled to recover possession from one holding under an invalid title. See 244 N.W. 160. See also **adverse posses-**

sion; **tenancy** [TENANCY AT SUFFER-ANCE]; **trespass.**

EJUSDEM GENERIS *(ĕ-yūs'-dĕm jĕn'-ĕr-ĭs)*—Lat: of the same kind. a rule of statutory **construction**, generally accepted by both state and federal courts, that where general words follow enumerations of particular classes or persons or things, the general words shall be construed as applicable only to persons or things of the same general nature or kind as those enumerated. 49 F. Supp. 846. Thus, in a statute forbidding the concealment on one's person of "pistols, revolvers, derringers, or other dangerous weapons," the term "dangerous weapons" may be contrued to comprehend only dangerous weapons of the kind enumerated, i.e., firearms, or perhaps more narrowly still, handguns.

ELECTION the selection of a public official by the citizens of a country, state, or other political body. The choice between two or more legal rights, whether they arise under a statute, by contract, or otherwise.

ELECTION OF REMEDIES a choice of possible **remedies** permitted by law for an **injury** suffered; a rule of **procedure** which requires that the party make a choice between two or more alternative and inconsistent remedies allowed by law on the same facts. See 112 F. Supp. 365, 367; 85 A. 2d 493, 496; 231 P. 2d 39, 47. Once the choice is made, the alternatives not chosen are waived. See 194 P. 721, 722. Thus, while the plantiff may seek the alternative remedies of **specific performance** or **damages** for a **breach of contract,** he may not ask for alternative inconsistent remedies such as **recission** and damages, since the recission elects to treat the **contract** as **void** and the request for damages seeks to enforce a valid contract. See **alternative pleading.**

ELECTION UNDER A WILL the principle that to take under a will is to adopt and require conformity to all its provisions. See 191 S.E. 14, 16. More specifically, it consists of a legatee's choice to accept a benefit given under a will and relinquishment of a claim to property which the will disposes of to another, or to retain the claim and reject the benefit. See 136 N.E. 695, 696, 284 P. 411, 414. See also **widow's election.**

ELECTION, WIDOW'S see **widow's election.**

ELECTIVE FRANCHISE see **franchise.**

ELECTIVE SHARE see **widow's election.**

ELEGIT see **fieri facias** [ELEGIT].

ELEMENT generally, an ingredient or factor; the constituent parts of a criminal offense which the prosecution must prove **beyond a reasonable doubt** to sustain a conviction. The elements of a crime consist of the acts and mental state, if any, which the statute defines as constituting the criminal offense. Elements constituting prerequisites to criminal liability may also include **attendant circumstances** and, sometimes, specified results. See LaFave & Scott, Criminal Law 45 (1972).

ELEMENTS the forces of nature: fire, air, earth, and water. Reference to "caused by the elements" is used synonomously with "caused by an **Act of God.**"

ELEVENTH AMENDMENT an amendment to the U.S. Constitution effectively prohibiting the federal courts from hearing cases against a state by citizens either of that state or from another state unless that state consents to be sued. The amendment is rooted in **sovereign immunity doctrine** and was intended to overrule *Chisholm v. Georgia,* 2 U.S. (2 Dall.) 419(1793). 134 U.S. 1. The amendment has been interpreted to premit suits against state officials in federal court for **injunctive** and **declaratory** relief based on federal law. 209. U.S. 123 See also **immunity** [OFFICIAL IMMUNITY].

EMANCIPATION the freeing of someone from the control of another; a parent's express or implied relinquishing of rights in, or authority and control over, a **minor** child. While emancipation frees the child of parental control, and gives him the right to his own earnings and the right to purchase property free from his parent's claims, the child surrenders his right to maintenance and support from the parents. See 269 N.Y.S. 667; 118 S.W. 956, 958. It is sometimes said that the acts of a child alone are not enough to establish emancipation; that some act or omission by the parent is necessary, see 117 N.E. 2d 42, 43; but it may be sufficient for a child merely to enter into a relation, such as marriage, which is inconsistent with his subjection to control by the parent. 37 Vt. 528, 529; 63 A. 2d 586, 587-8.

EMBEZZLEMENT the **fradulent** appropriation to one's own use of property lawfully in his **possession.** It is a type of **larceny** which did not exist at **common law** because it does not involve a **trespassory** or wrongful taking; thus it is a crime created by statute. See generally Model Penal Code §223. Embezzlement is often associated with bank employees, public officials, or officers of organizations, who may in the course of their lawful activities come into possession of property, such as money, actually owned by others. Compare **misapplication; theft.**

EMBLEMENT the right of a **tenant** of agricultural land to remove crops he has planted, even if the tenancy has expired before harvest. An irrevocable license to go upon the land to care for and harvest the crop. 112 N.W. 570. It is applicable only as to crops planted during the continuance of the **lease.** 75 N.W. 323.

The doctrine of emblements is applicable only if the tenancy is terminated through no fault on the part of the tenant. 198 A. 687. The doctrine is applied as a means by which to encourage agricultural activities and out of fairness to tenants. Burby, Real Property 18 (1965).

Vegetable **chattels** such as corn produced annually as the result of one's labor are deemed **personal property** in the event of the death of the farmer before harvest.

EMBRACERY the **common law misdemeanor** of attempting to bribe or corruptly influence a juror. 4 Comm. *140. It is immaterial that the influence might be in the direction of a just or proper **verdict** since the **crime** is the impermissible interference with the jury function. The crime is complete when the **attempt** is made; hence, "there can be no such crime as an attempt to commit embracery." 130 S.E. 249, 251. It has been held that embracery may also be committed by corruptly attempting to influence members of the **grand jury** as well as the petit [trial] **jury.** 115 S.E. 2d 576, 579.

The crime need not involve bribery as such but where it does it is often assumed today under modern statutes broadly defining the bribery offenses. Modern statutes have also treated the remaining aspects of embracery under the general offense of **obstructing justice** and the offense of embracery itself is tending to disappear as a distinct offense. Perkins & Boyce, Criminal Law 550-551 (3rd ed. 1982). See N.J.S.A. 2C:29-8.

EMINENT DOMAIN the right of the state or **sovereign** to take private property for **public use;** since "eminent domain" is an inherent attribute of sovereignty, 15 A. 2d 647, the individual property owner's consent to the taking is immaterial. 29 N.E. 1062. The Fifth

Amendment to the United States Constitution requires that **just compensation** be made whenever private property is taken for public use by the Congress. See **condemn.**

EMOLUMENT profit derived from office, employment, or labor, including salary, wages, fees, rank, and other compensation. "Emoluments" are not generally considered to include travel or other business expenses, vacation or compensatory time, or other items not thought of as strictly profit. See 508 P. 2d 1151, 1156; 360 S.W. 2d 307, 311; 122 A. 2d 800, 801.

EMPLOYMENT RETIREMENT INCOME SECURITY ACT OF 1974 see **ERISA.** [Employment Retirement Income Security Act of 1974].

EMPLOYEE SHARE OWNERSHIP PLAN (ESOP) a plan designed to provide a retirement benefit and a stake in the corporation for the employee. Henn & Alexander, Corporations 674 (3d ed. 1983). Such plans are also used by employees to purchase plants that are being closed.

EMPLOYEE STOCK OPTION see **stock option.**

EMPLOYER'S LIABILITY ACTS statutes specifying the extent to which employers shall be **liable** to make **compensation** for injuries sustained by their employees in the course of employment. 53 Am. Jur. 2d, Master and Servant §§341, 353. Unlike **worker's compensation** laws, which have replaced these acts in many states, the employer is made liable only for injuries resulting from his **breach** of a **duty** owed the employee—i.e., his negligence—and is not **strictly liable.** 52 So. 878. Like worker's compensation, however, many of these acts do abolish the use by the employer of the common law defenses of **contributory negligence, assumption of the risk,** and the **fellow servant rule.**

See 53 Am. Jur. 2d 354. See also **federal Employer's Liability Acts.**

ENABLING CLAUSE a provision in most new laws or statutes that gives appropriate officials the power to implement and enforce the law.

ENACTING CLAUSE generally, the preamble of a **statute,** or that part which identifies the statute as a legislative act and authorizes it as law. See 61 N.E. 1116, 1117; 139 F. Supp. 922. Thus, "Be it enacted by the Senate and House of Representatives of the United States in Congress assembled," etc., is the enacting clause used in Congressional legislation.

EN BANC [IN BANC] *(ähn bähnk)*—Fr: by the full court. Many **appellate courts** sit in parts or divisions of three or more judges from among a larger number on the full court. These parts will generally decide a particular case but sometimes either on the court's **motion** or at the request of one of the **litigants** the court will consider the matter by the full court rather than by only a part thereof; a matter may also be reconsidered by the whole court after a part thereof has rendered its decision. This is called a REHEARING EN BANC, (occasionally spelled "en bank"). Courts which generally hear matters by the full court may use an "en banc" notation at the head of the opinion.

ENCLOSURE see **inclosure.**

ENCROACH to gain unlawfully upon the lands, property, or authority of another; to intrude slowly or gradually upon the rights or property of another. 82 N.Y.S. 961, 964. An ENCROACHMENT is any infringement on the property or authority of another. Id.

ENCUMBRANCE a burden on **title** or a charge on **property.** It is a third **party's** lawful **interest** in real or **personal property** that diminishes the value of that property, 299 A. 2d 552, 554; 243 F.2d 863, 867, and impairs the **transfer** of **marketable title.** 86 A. 2d 827, 828. An encumbrance is sometimes construed broadly to include not only **liens** such as **mortgages** and **taxes,** but also **attachments, leases, inchoate dower** rights, water rights, **easements,** and other restrictions on **use.** 533 P. 2d 9, 12.

There are two general forms of encumbrance: 1) those affecting title, such as liens, which may be removable and 2) those affecting the physical condition of the property such as a road or a right of way, which is usually permanent in character. 196 F. Supp 134, 136. A **warranty deed** usually contains a **covenant** of good right to convey, against encumbrances and for quiet **possession,** and property can not be sold with such a **deed** if there are encumbrances existing against the land. See **warranty.** 57 A.L.R. 1376-1377. Donahue, Property §2B (1974). See, generally, Restatement of Property §129(h) (1936).

Although encumbrance usually refers to **real property,** it can refer to a **chattel mortgage** or lien on personal property. Consequently, if a **bona fide purchaser** of personal property is deprived of that property because of an unknown prior encumbrance, he may recover from his **vendor** for breach of implied **warranty** of title. See U.C.C. §2-312. See **ground rent.**

ENDORSEMENT see **indorsement.**

ENDOWMENT a permanent fund of **property** or money bestowed upon an institution or a person, the income from which is used to serve the specific purpose for which the "endowment" was intended. See 45 F. 2d 345, 346, 187 A. 632, 636. For example, an endowment may be bestowed on a college or hospital for the support of the institution.

ENFEOFF to create a **feoffment** [early common law means of conveying **freehold** estates]. "Enfeoff" has been used as a word granting **title** in some modern **deeds.** See 31 N.J.L. 143, 151.

EN GROS *(ähn grō)*—Fr: in gross (large) amount; total; by wholesale.

ENJOIN to command or instruct with authority; to abate, suspend, or restrain. See 138 F. 2d 320, 326; 32 Hun. 126, 129. For example, one may be "enjoined" or commanded by a court with **equitable** powers, either to do a specific act or to refrain from doing a certain act. See **injunction.**

ENJOYMENT substantial present economic benefit. It refers to beneficial **use, interest,** and purpose to which **real** or **personal property** may be put and implies rights, profits, and income therefrom, rather than a technical **vesting** of **title.** Enjoyment of certain transferred property may determine if it is taxable. 408 U.S. 125. In common usage, it is synonomous with "use" and "occupancy," and usually implies **possession.** A **vested remainder** without present **possession,** however, has a certainty of enjoyment. A **remainderman** has a **vested interest** as long as that interest can become a present **estate** when the preceding **freehold** determines, and as long as it is not subject to a **condition precedent,** even though there is no certainty that he will ever enjoy possession. Moynihan, Introduction to the Law of Real Property 116 (1962). Even if the remainderman dies before the **interest** becomes present, the enjoyment is still considered certain to go to his **heirs.** It does not mean personal enjoyment, it only means control. Restatement of Property §157 comment f (1936); 92 S.W. 2d 723, 726. If the remainder is not certain but **contingent** on a prior event, enjoyment is postponed until actual possession. Restatement of Property, Supra. §157, comment j.

ADVERSE ENJOYMENT see **adverse possession.**

COVENANT OF QUIET ENJOYMENT see **quiet enjoyment.**

ENJOYMENT, QUIET see **quiet enjoyment.**

ENLARGEMENT a rule of civil procedure permitting a court to extend the expiration period for any act required or allowed to be done at or within a specified time. See F. R. Civ. P. 6(b). Once cause is shown, the court may act in its discretion with or without motion or notice if the period has not expired; if the period has expired, the court can only act upon motion where the failure to act was the result of excusable neglect. Certain of the time periods found in specific rules may not be enlarged by this general rule, but can only be enlarged by conditions within those rules themselves. Id.

ENRICHMENT see **unjust enrichment.**

ENTAIL to create a **fee tail;** to create a fee tail from a **fee simple.**

ENTIRETY see **tenancy** [TENANCY BY THE ENTIRETY].

ENTRAPMENT in criminal law, an **affirmative defense** created either by statute or by court decision which excuses a **defendant** from criminal liability for **crimes** induced by certain governmental persuasion or trickery. The prevailing "subjective" view of entrapment requires that the particular defendant demonstrate that but for the objectionable police conduct, he would not have committed the crime. This means that the predisposition of the defendant to commit the offense must be balanced against the police conduct to determine whether the police can be said to have caused the crime. The "objective" test favored by only a minority of United States Supreme Court justices in 1932 and again in 1973 (but recommended by the

Model Penal Code §2.13(2)(b)) looks solely to the police conduct to determine if an ordinary, law-abiding citizen would have been persuaded to commit the crime. "Under the objective test the prosecution is not permitted to introduce evidence of the defendant's character, past criminal convictions, rumored criminal activities, or reaction to the Government's offer since such evidence relates only to the defendant's predisposition to commit the crime. Because the subjective test focuses on such evidence, it is open to substantial abuse." 87 Harv. L. Rev. 243, 244 n. 5; 287 U.S. 435. Merely presenting the opportunity is not entrapment under either test. Entrapment as such is not a **due process** guarantee applicable to the states, but "outrageous" governmental conduct may violate due process of law and condemn a **prosecution** which is the fruit thereof. 411 U.S. 423, 431-32.

ENTRY, FORCIBLE see **forcible entry.**

ENTRY, UNLAWFUL see **unlawful entry.**

ENURE see **inure.**

EN VENTRE SA MERE in gestation; in the womb of one's mother. 100 N.W. 2d 445, 447. In the law of property, a person who is en ventre sa mere has the same rights as, and is entitled to the same protections as, a person who has been born. Powell, Real Property §796(3).

ENVIRONMENTAL PROTECTION AGENCY [EPA] a federal agency created to allow for the coordinated and effective governmental action to protect the environment through the **abatement** and control of pollution on a systematic basis. 5 U.S.C. App, Reorganization Plan No. 3 of 1970. The EPA is responsible for various research, monitoring, standard-setting, and enforcement activities controlling air pollution, water pollution, hazardous waste disposal, and other threats to the environment.

EO INSTANTI immediately; instantly.

EPA see **environmental protection agency.**

EQUAL OPPORTUNITY employment practices which do not discriminate on the basis of race, color, religion, sex, or national origin. Such discrimination is outlawed by Title VII of the Civil Rights Act of 1964. 42 U.S.C. §2000e.

Title VII created the EQUAL EMPLOYMENT OPPORTUNITY COMMISSION [EEOC] to implement an equal opportunity policy by working with local agencies, paying the expenses of witnesses before the Commission, affording persons subject to Title VII technical assistance to further compliance, helping to conciliate employers and labor organizations with employees or members refusing to cooperate, making technical studies, and intervening in civil actions on the part of an aggrieved party. The Commission is composed of five members, appointed by the President and approved by the Senate. They serve for five-year terms. No more than three of the five may belong to the same political party. 42 U.S.C. §2000e-4.

EQUAL EMPLOYMENT OPPORTUNITY COMMISSION [EEOC] see **equal opportunity.**

EQUAL PROTECTION OF THE LAWS constitutional guarantee embodied in the Fourteenth Amendment to the U.S. Constitution, which states in relevant part that "No State shall . . . deny to any person within its jurisdiction the equal protection of the laws." This has not been interpreted to imply that all persons in the state must be equally affected by each statute that the legislature enacts. "The equal protection clause of the Fourteenth Amendment does not take from the State the power to classify in the adoption of police laws, but admits of the exercise of a wide scope of discretion in that regard, and avoids what is done only when it is without any reasonable basis and therefore is purely arbitrary." 220 U.S. 61, 78. Thus, in the general case, courts presume the validity of a state statute if there is any rational basis for it. See **rational basis test.** However, in certain special instances, the court will subject the law to "strict scrutiny." This test requires that the law be held to violate the equal protection clause unless the state can show a COMPELLING INTEREST which can only be furthered by enactment of the statute in question. 394 U.S. 618, 634. One situation that will trigger the "strict scrutiny" test occurs where the statute singles out for special treatment a class of persons that the court finds to be a SUSPECT CLASSIFICATION. The criteria for suspectness are that the class must be "saddled with such disabilites, or subjected to such a history of purposeful unequal treatment, or relegated to such a position of political powerlessness as to command extraordinary protection from the majoritarian process." 411 U.S. 1, 28. Classifications based upon the following have been held to be suspect: alienage, 403 U.S. 365, 372; nationality, 332 U.S. 633, 644-646; race, 379 U.S. 184, 191-192.

Classifications based on gender have not been labeled "suspect" but have been subjected to scrutiny less strict than strict scrutiny and more strict than the rational relationship analysis. Gender-based distinctions must "serve important governmental objectives and must be substantially related to achievement of those objectives." 429 U.S. 190, 197. In some instances the courts have required the statute to pass the stricter test where the law infringed upon the exercise of a "fundamental right," such as those embodied in the First Amendment. 394 U.S. 618, 634 (right to travel). Although wealth classifications have not been held to be inherently suspect the courts have struck down legislation which denied indigents free trial transcripts and hence in effect access to appellate review of their criminal convictions. "There can be no equal justice where the kind of trial a man gets depends on the amount of money he has." 351 U.S. 12, 19. Under the equal protection guarantee indigents have also won the right to appointed counsel, first in felony cases, 372 U.S. 335; and today in any instance where they are exposed to any period of imprisonment. 407 U.S. 25.

The equal protection clause applies only to states; however, any denial of equal protection by the Federal government is treated as a violation of the due process clause of the Fifth Amendment. 347 U.S. 497. 55 N.C.L. Rev. 540 (1977). Section 5 of the Fourteenth Amendment empowers Congress to enforce the Amendment. Congress therefore may on its own initiative take steps to outlaw discrimination. 42 U.S.C. §§1981 2000h. See **affirmative action.**

EQUAL RIGHTS AMENDMENT [E.R.A.] a proposed amendment hoping to eliminate sex as a basis for any decisions made by a state of the United States. This amendment was never ratified by a sufficient number of states to qualify as a constitutional amendment, but the basic premise underlying the proposal has become an accepted standard in many statutes and court decisions.

EQUAL TIME see **fairness doctrine.**

EQUITABLE according to natural right or natural justice; marked by due **consideration** for what is fair, unbiased, or impartial. 62 F. Supp. 968, 970.

In Anglo-American jurisprudence, the term is often used to distinguish remedies, defenses, doctrines, and the like that are recognized by **courts of equity,** as distinguished from those that are "legal" because they are recognized by **courts of law.**

EQUITABLE DISTRIBUTION a fair and just meting out of **property,** etc., between interested **parties.** For example, a **constitutional** provision requiring an "equitable distribution" of income of a school fund requires distribution thereof to the several districts in proportion to school children enumerated and living in each district. 259 N.W. 168. In matrimonial law, the term refers to statutorily authorized division of **property,** both real and personal, which was acquired during the marriage. See, e.g., N.J.S.A. 2A:34-23. The court does not necessarily divide the property equally, but attempts to make a fair and just allocation taking into account such factors as length of marriage, ages of the participants, earning capacities, etc. The concept of equitable distribution represents a profound change in matrimonial law by recognizing the essential role played by a non-working spouse (usually the wife) as homemaker and helpmate in the acquisition of family assets. Marriage is therefore viewed as a joint undertaking, similar to a partnership, entitling both partners to a fair share of the assets. 320 A. 2d 496, 501. In contrast, the traditional purpose underlying **alimony** was to prevent a wife and children from becoming public charges. Keezer, Marriage and Divorce §560 (3d ed., 1946). Absent statutory authority, the courts have no power to transfer property from one spouse to another. 24 Am. Jur. 2d 1054.

EQUITABLE DEFENSE see **defense.**

EQUITABLE ESTATE see **estate.**

EQUITABLE ESTOPPEL see **estoppel** [EQUITABLE ESTOPPEL].

EQUITABLE RECOUPMENT a doctrine applicable in limited circumstances to a taxpayer who erroneously paid a tax and is later properly assessed a tax arising from the same taxable event. The doctrine allows the taxpayer to offset the tax properly assessed by the tax erroneously paid, even if the statute of limitations would otherwise prevent the taxpayer from recovering the earlier overpayment through a **claim for refund.** 295 U.S. 247.

EQUITABLE RELIEF see **relief.**

EQUITABLE SEISIN see **seisin.**

EQUITABLE SERVITUDE building restrictions and restrictions relating to land-use that are enforceable in **equity** by and between **landlords. Covenants** pertaining to land-use may be enforceable in equity either when the equitable enforcement is supplementary to the legal remedies at law for **breach** of contract or the invasion of a property right or when the restriction is cognizable only in equity. Burby, Real Property 100 (1965). For a covenant to be valid at **law,** as to remote **grantees** of the affected property, there must exist **privity of estate** between **covenator** and **covenantee,** but such a relationship is not necessary to create an enforceable equitable servitude so long as the subsequent grantee has either actual or constructive **notice** of the covenant. Id. at 98, 108.

Usually equitable servitudes are created as the result of covenants relating to the use of land and embodied in a **deed** that **conveys** a possessory **estate.** The conveyance of a possessory estate in land is not essential to the creation of equitable servitudes; landowners in a specified area may join together in the execution of a document placing restrictions on their land which are enforceable among themselves. Restatement, Property §539, Comment i.

EQUITABLE TITLE see **title.**

EQUITY most generally, "justice." Historically, "equity" developed as a separate body of law in England in reaction to the inability of the **common law** courts, in their strict adherence to rigid **writs** and **forms of action,** to entertain or provide a **remedy** for every injury. The King therefore established the high court of **chancery,** the purpose of which was to administer justice according to principles of fairness in cases where the common law would give no or inadequate redress. Equity law to a large extent was formulated in maxims, such as "equity suffers not a right without a remedy," or "equity follows the law," meaning that equity will derive a means to achieve a lawful result when legal procedure is inadequate. Equity and **law** are no longer bifurcated but are now merged in most jurisdictions, though equity jurisprudence and equitable doctrines are still independently viable. See 29 N.Y.S. 342, 343, 6 N.Y.S. 2d 720, 721, 293 F. 633, 637.

An action brought in a **court of equity** is said to be AT EQUITY.

"Equity" also refers to the value of **property** minus **liens** or other **incumbrances.** See 67 Cal. Rptr. 104, 107. For example, one's "equity" in a home he has **mortgaged** is the value of the property beyond the amount of the mortgage to be paid. See **equity of redemption shareholder** [SHAREHOLDER EQUITY].

EQUITY CAPITAL see **security** [EQUITY CAPITAL].

EQUITY OF REDEMPTION right of **mortgagor** to redeem his property after defaulting in the payment of the **mortgage debt,** by the subsequent payment of all costs and interest, in addition to the mortgage debt to the **mortgagee.** See 95 F. 2d 487, 489. It is a right available to mortgagors and is **extinguished** by actual **foreclosure.** The concept is more applicable in **title jurisdictions** than in **lien jurisdictions,** because in the former, redemption actually brings title to the mortgaged property back to the mortgagor. 230 P. 724. Equity of redemption has been held to be an interest in **real property** and, as such, subject to the ordinary rules of **conveyancing.** 272 P. 1063, 1064.

ERA see **equal rights amendment [ERA].**

ERGO *(ĕr'-gō)*—Lat: therefore; consequently; hence; because.

ERISA [EMPLOYEE RETIRE- MENT INCOME SECURITY ACT OF 1974] a Congressional attempt to attack a multitude of problems that were affecting employee benefit plans, especially the lack of employee information and adequate safeguards concerning their operation. 29 U.S.C. §1001. Through various statutes and regulations, the act creates minimum standards to assure the equitable character and financial soundness of these plans.

ERRONEOUS involving a mistake; signifies a deviation from the requirements of the law. 15 F. 2d 285. It does not connote a lack of legal authority, and is thus distinguished from "illegal." See 23 P. 508. "It means having the power to act, but [committing] error in its exercise." 15 F. 2d 285, 286.

ERRONEOUS JUDGMENT "one rendered according to course and practice of court, but contrary to law, upon mistaken view of law, or upon erroneous application of legal principles." 157 S.E. 434. An erroneous judgment is not **void,** and is not subject to **collateral attack,** but remains in effect until **reversed** or modified on **appeal.** 81 S.E. 2d 409.

ERROR an act involving a departure from truth or accuracy; a mistake. 252 P. 2d 550, 555. After the jury has rendered its verdict, an erroneous ruling on a legal issue [an ERROR OF LAW] occurring during the trial is subject to review by an appellate court. However, a claim that the trier of fact improperly found a fact [an ERROR OF FACT] may be reversed by the trial court on the ground that the verdict was against the weight of the evidence, or by an appellate court on the more limited ground that the jury could not have reasonably found the facts it did. James & Hazard, Civil Procedure, §7.20; §13.8 (2d ed. 1977). See **assignment of error; clerical error, harmless error; plain error, reversible error.** See also **motion** [MOTION IN ERROR]; **writ of error.**

ESCALATOR CLAUSE that part of a **lease** or **contract** which provides for an increase in the contract price upon the determination of certain acts or other factors beyond the parties' control, such as an increase in the cost of labor or of a necessary commodity, or the fixing of maximum prices by a governmental agency. See 176 F. 2d 675, 212 S.E. 2d 293. For example, an escalator clause in a lease may permit an increase in rent whenever the rent control laws are relaxed so that the landlord can charge more; a wife's **alimony** may have an escalator clause to increase her alimony as the cost of living increases or as her husband's income increases.

ESCAPE CLAUSE provision in a **contract,** insurance policy, or other agreement or document allowing parties to avoid **liability** or performance. For example, a contract to purchase a home may include a provision allowing the buyer to break the contract without any penalty or loss of deposit within three days of signing the contract. Certain transactions, such as door-to-door purchase contracts or other consumer credit transactions, may by statute be rescinded within three business days following the consummation of the transaction. 15 U.S.C. §1635.

ESCHEAT the reversion of **prop-**

erty to the state or **sovereign,** as the ultimate proprietor of **realty,** by reason of the lack of anyone to **inherit** it, or by reason of a breach of **condition,** etc. See 252 N.W. 826, 104 N.W. 2d 338, 340. Compare **forfeiture.**

ESCROW a written **instrument,** such as a **deed,** temporarily deposited with a neutral third party (called the ESCROW AGENT), by the agreement of two parties who have entered into a valid **contract.** The escrow agent will hold the document until the conditions of the contract are met, at which time he will deliver it to the **grantee** or **obligee.** The depositor has no control over the instrument after it is in "escrow." At **common law,** "escrow" applied to the deposits only of instruments for the **conveyance** of land, but it now applies to all instruments so deposited. Money so deposited is also loosely referred to as "escrow." See generally 74 N.E. 2d 619, 622.

ESOP see **Employment Share Ownership plan [ESOP].**

ESQUIRE term originally used to designate a rank of English landed gentry, and afterward used to designate English barristers, sergeants and judges. See 1 Bl. Comm.*406. Used now as an appendage to the name of a person admitted to practice law in the United States.

ESSENCE see **time of the essence.**

ESTABLISHMENT CLAUSE that provision in the First Amendment of the Federal Constitution and made applicable to the states by the Fourteenth Amendment prohibiting the enactment of laws respecting "the establishment of religion." The Supreme Court has stated that the establishment clause "means at least this: Neither a state nor the Federal government can set up a church. Neither can pass laws which aid one religion, aid all religions, or prefer one religion over another. Neither can force a person to go to or to remain away from a church against his will or force him to profess a belief or disbelief in any religion. . . . No tax in any amount, large or small, can be levied to support any religious activities or institutions, whatever they may be called, or whatever form they may adopt to teach or practice religion. . . . In the words of Jefferson, the clause against establishment of religion was intended to erect a 'wall of separation between Church and State'." 330 U.S. 1, 15.

Since the **free exercise clause** prohibits the government from opposing religious activity, it is not always clear whether government programs that may benefit religious groups violate the establishment clause. Under the test currently used, government action does not violate the establishment clause if the action (1) has a secular purpose, (2) has primarily a secular effect, and (3) does not involve excessive entanglement with religion. School text book programs and school busing programs that incidentally aid parochial schools have been upheld. 392 U.S. 236, 330 U.S. 1. Traditional local tax exemptions for church-owned property have been upheld. 397 U.S. 664. But most direct state aid to primary and secondary schools has been held to violate the establishment clause. 403 U.S. 602 (salary assistance), 413 U.S. 756 (tuition assistance), 413 U.S. 472 (payments to cover costs of state mandated services). Non-denominational prayers to be said aloud by public school students violate this clause. 370 U.S. 421. Many financial assistance programs to aid students attending religiously affiliated colleges and state assistance in construction have been upheld. 426 U.S. 736, 413 U.S. 734.

ESTATE interest, right, or **ownership** in land; technically, the degree, quantity, nature, and extent of a person's interest or ownership of land. In its broad sense, "estate" applies to all that a person owns, whether **real** or **personal property.** See 205 P. 2d 1127, 1130. 175 S.E. 2d 351, 353. See also **privity** [PRIVITY OF ESTATE].

CONTINGENT ESTATE see **contingent estate.**

DOMINANT ESTATE see **dominant estate [tenement].**

EQUITABLE ESTATE an estate or interest which can only be enforced in **equity;** especially applies to every **trust,** express or implied, which is not converted to a legal estate by the **statute of uses.** "In law, the legal estate is the whole estate, and the holder of the legal title is the sole owner. But this title may be held for the beneficial interest of another, which interest has come to be called an 'equitable estate.' It is not, however, strictly speaking, an interest in the land itself, but a right which can be enforced in equity." 35 A. 213.

ESTATE IN FEE SIMPLE see **fee simple.**

ESTATE IN FEE TAIL see **fee tail.**

FUTURE ESTATE [ESTATE IN FUTURO] an estate in land which is not **possessory** but which will or may become so at some time in the future. "Future estates" are either **vested** or **contingent,** and include **remainders** and **reversions.** See 112 N.Y.S. 310, 311. See also **future interest.**

LEGAL ESTATE originally, an interest in land that was enforced by courts of **common law,** as opposed to an equitable estate, enforced by **courts of equity.** Prior to the fifteenth century, the law conceived of only one type of ownership in the same property, which was the "legal estate." The development of **uses** and **trusts,** however, led to the present dual system of ownership whereby a **title** to property does

not necessarily imply the right to **beneficial use** and enjoyment. For example, in a trust relationship the **trustee** possesses legal title to the trust **property;** however, the **beneficiary** of the trust has the equitable estate and is entitled to the exclusive benefit of the trust. Similarly, one who purchases property under an installment land contract has an "equitable estate" and is entitled to possession. However, the seller holds the "legal estate" or "title" to the property, until the property is paid in full. See Restatement of Property §6. See **Statute of Uses; lien jurisdiction.**

NET ESTATE see **net estate.**

PRECEDING ESTATE see **preceding estate.**

RESIDUARY ESTATE see **residuary estate.**

SERVIENT ESTATE see **servient estate.**

VESTED ESTATE one either presently in **possession** or one owned by a presently existing person to whom the property interest will automatically accrue upon the termination of a **preceding estate.** See 68 N.E. 1057. Such an estate thus represents a present interest and as such is neither subject to any contingency nor otherwise capable of being defeated. Compare **contingent estate.** See **vested.**

ESTATE AT SUFFERANCE see **tenancy** [TENANCY AT SUFFERANCE].

ESTATE AT WILL see **tenancy** [TENANCY AT WILL].

ESTATE BY THE ENTIRETY see **tenancy** [TENANCY BY THE ENTIRETY].

ESTATE FOR LIFE see **life estate.**

ESTATE FOR YEARS see **tenancy** [TENANCY FOR YEARS].

ESTATE FROM YEAR TO YEAR [PERIOD TO PERIOD] see **tenancy** [PERIODIC TENANCY].

ESTATE IN COMMON see **tenancy** [TENANCY IN COMMON].

ESTATE IN COPARCENARY see **coparcenary.**

ESTATE OF INHERITANCE a **freehold estate** that may descend to **heirs.** It is a type of freehold estate that the **tenant** can both enjoy during his life and pass on after his death according to an established order of **descent.** 50 S.W. 690, 692. Estates of inheritance include estates in **fee simple absolute,** fee simple conditional, fee simple determinable and estates in **fee tail.** An estate for life or **per autre vie** are not estates of inheritance, since they exist for a lifetime only and cannot be inherited. 542 P. 2d 928, 930; 2 Bl. Comm. *120; Restatement of Property §18 (1936). At **common law** an inheritable estate in fee simple was only created if the grantor used words of inheritance, e.g., "to B and his heirs." Id. at §27. This requirement has been abolished in most **jurisdictions** by **statute.** Moynihan, Introduction to the Law of Real Property Ch. 2 §3 (1962). To entitle a widow to **dower,** the husband's estate must be an estate of inheritance. 50 S.W. 690. Such an estate can be created by a **vested remainder** following a **life estate.** 9 A. 2d 311, 327. See **estate** and **ground rent.**

ESTATE PER AUTRE VIE [PUR AUTRE VIE] see **per [pur] autre vie.**

ESTATE TAX see **tax,** [ESTATE TAX].

ESTOPPEL a bar; preclusion, also known as issue preclusion "a bar which precludes a person from denying the truth of a fact which has, in contemplation of law, become settled by the facts and proceedings of judicial or legislative officers, or by the act of the party himself, either by conventional writing, or by representations, express or implied. An estoppel arises where man has done some act which the policy of the law will not permit him to gainsay or deny." 51 S.E. 514, 521. It is an **equitable** doctrine, and as such, is used when good conscience requires it. Thus, some injury to a party invoking the doctrine of estoppel is generally required, and the elements of the claim, then, consist of ignorance on the part of the person invoking estoppel, representation by party estopped which misleads, and an innocent and detrimental change of position in reliance on the representation. See 159 A. 2d 345, 351. Estoppel is distinguished from **waiver** in that a waiver generally refers to a voluntary surrender or relinquishment of some known right, benefit, or advantage; estoppel creates an inhibition or inability to assert it. 106 F. 2d 687, 691. Compare **res judicata.**

AUTHORITY BY ESTOPPEL see **authority by estoppel.**

COLLATERAL ESTOPPEL see **collateral estoppel.**

DIRECT ESTOPPEL the prohibition of the relitigation of an issue by two parties who have previously litigated the issue and had it decided by a court. See **res judicata; collateral estoppel.**

ESTOPPEL BY DEED a bar which precludes a party from denying the truth of his deed. It may be invoked only in a suit on the deed or concerning a right arising out of it. See 170 S.W. 2d 240, 243.

ESTOPPEL BY JUDGMENT see **judgment.**

ESTOPPEL BY LACHES. see **laches.**

ESTOPPEL IN PAIS [EQUITABLE ESTOPPEL] strictly, an estoppel which arises out of a person's statement of fact, or out of his silence, acts, or omissions, rather than from a deed or record or written contract. 35 P. 512.

EQUITABLE ESTOPPEL see ESTOPPEL IN PAIS [EQUITABLE ESTOPPEL] above.

MUTUALITY OF ESTOPPEL the doctrine which prohibits one party from raising an issue or a matter as to which the other party is estopped.

PROMISSORY ESTOPPEL see **promissory estoppel.**

ESTOVERS the right of the **tenant** to use during the period of his **lease** whatever timber there may be on the leased **premises** to the extent necessary to promote good husbandry . . . "The right includes, when necessary for that purpose, timber for fencing, bridges, corn cribs; cotton houses, fire wood, repairs and other necessary purposes." 13 So. 2d 652, 653. The term also referred to an allowance out of an estate or other thing for a person's support.

ET AL. (*ĕt äl*)—Lat: the abbreviated form of "et alii," which means "and others."

ETHICAL see **unethical.**

ET NON (*ĕt nŏn*)—Lat: and not. This phrase is used primarily in introducing the negative averments of a special **traverse** in **pleading** and thus is called the "inducement to the traverse." Synonymous in use with **absque hoc** which means "without this." 18 N.J.L. 339, 352.

ET SEQ. (*ĕt sĕk*)—Lat: the abbreviated form of "et sequentes" or "et sequentia," which means "and the following." It is most commonly used in denominating page reference and statutory section numbers.

ET UX. (*ĕt ŭx*)—Lat: the abbreviated form of "et uxor" which means "and wife" for the purpose of **wills** and other **instruments** which purport to **grant** or **convey.**

EURODOLLAR a U.S. dollar held as a deposit in a European commercial bank. Eurodollars were created after World War II by United States foreign defense and aid expenditures. Since the dollar was backed by gold, it became a popular reserve currency in Europe and among all the trading partners of the United States.

EUTHANASIA the act or practice of painlessly terminating the life of a person or animal. As applied to animals, it is sometimes referred to as "humane disposal." N.J.S.A. §45:16-14. As applied to persons, it is accepted in some cultures but in the United States is treated as criminal, subjecting those responsible to prosecution under the homicide statutes. An exception has been developed in some jurisdictions, however, in which the termination of an incurably ill patient is no longer treated as criminal if done by a guardian or immediate family member after consultation with an ethics committee of a hospital, and if accomplished by the negative means of withdrawing life-support systems or extraordinary medical care rather than by some affirmative act. 355 A. 2d 647. See also **brain death.**

EVASION OF TAX, see **tax evasion.**

EVASIVE ANSWER an **answer** which which fails to admit or deny the allegations set forth in the **complaint.**

EVICTION originally, the physical expulsion of someone from land by the assertion of paramount title or through legal proceedings. See 173 S.E. 812. In reference to modern landlord-tenant law, "eviction" is sometimes used to refer to what is actually a "constructive eviction."

ACTUAL EVICTION an actual expulsion of the tenant out of all or some part of the leased premises, and involving a physical ouster or dispossession from the very thing granted. Actual eviction relieves the tenant of any further duty to pay rent. 43 N.E. 2d 147, 155.

CONSTRUCTIVE EVICTION refers to circumstances existing under the control of the **landlord** which compel the **tenant** to leave the **premises** though he is not asked to do so by the landlord. The tenant may be deemed constructively evicted if the premises are rendered unfit for occupancy in whole or in substantial part, or if the use and enjoyment has been substantially impaired. No physical expulsion or legal **process** is necessary, see 95 N.Y.S. 2d 883, 886; and the tenant is not responsible for further rent, 263 N.Y.S. 695; but the tenant must actually vacate the premises. Compare **ejectment; ouster; warranty** [WARRANTY OF HABITABILITY].

PARTIAL ACTUAL EVICTION occurs where the tenant is wrongfully excluded from a portion of the premises, or when part of the leased premises has been rendered unusable through the fault of the landlord. If the lease rental is not apportioned by room, nor the premises partitioned in the lease agreement, the tenant is not responsible for any part of the lease rental while actually evicted from a part of the leased premises, and he need not vacate the habitable part of the premises. 48 N.E. 781; 117 N.E. 579.

RETALIATORY EVICTION eviction of a **tenant** based on the tenant's complaints against the landlord. Such evictions against residential tenants are illegal in many states. See e.g., N.J.S.A. 2A: 42-10.10. When a landlord seeks to evict a tenant within a specified period of time after the tenant has filed a complaint against the landlord, a **presumption** may arise that the eviction is in reprisal or retalia-

tion for the tenant's complaints.

EVIDENCE all the means by which any alleged matter of fact, the truth of which is submitted to investigation at judicial **trial,** is established or disproved. See 16 A. 2d 80, 89. Evidence includes the **testimony** of **witnesses,** introduction of records, documents, exhibits, objects or any other **probative** matter offered for the purpose of inducing belief in the **party's** contention by the **fact-finder.** An **allegation** is not itself evidence but rather is something to be proved or disproved through the introduction of **competent** admissable evidence. See **best evidence rule; circumstantial evidence; conclusive evidence; corroborating evidence; demonstrative evidence; documentary evidence; illegally obtained evidence; incompetent evidence; indirect evidence; indispensable evidence; newly discovered evidence; preponderance of the evidence; real evidence; presumptive evidence; insufficient evidence; hearsay; mere evidence rule; parol evidence rule; rebuttal evidence; suppression of evidence; traditionary evidence.** See also **weight of the evidence.**

EVIDENCE ALIUNDE see **aliunde.**

EVIDENCE DE BENE ESSE see **de bene esse.**

EX AEQUO ET BONO (ex é-quō et bō-nō)—Lat: from equity and conscience.

EXAMINATION see **cross-examination; cross-examination** [DIRECT EXAMINATION].

EXCEPTIONS something that otherwise ought to be included in the category from which it is eliminated. 157 F. 2d 661, 665. "Exceptions" arise in numerous contexts. STATUTORY EXCEPTIONS are intended to restrain the **enacting clause** or to exclude something which would otherwise be within it, or to modify it in some manner. 102 P. 2d 251, 256.

An "exception" to a court's ruling is an objection to such ruling or the calling of an error to the attention of the court in some manner. 168 N.E. 2d 285, 287.

"Exception" is also generally used as a term meaning to withhold from a conveyance of land an **estate** or **interest** which has previously been severed and which is usually not owned by the grantor. 506 P. 2d 1236, 1238.

EXCESSIVE BAIL an amount of **bail** which is set at a higher figure than is reasonably calculated to fulfill the purpose of assuring that the accused will stand trial and submit to sentence if found guilty. 342 U.S. 1. Excessive bail is prohibited by the Eighth Amendment to the United States Constitution and by the constitutions of the various states. The prohibition against excessive bails has been held to forbid a person from being capriciously held, by demanding bail in such amount that there is in fact a denial of bail where a right to bail exists. 342 U.S. 524. The prohibition against excessive bail has been held not to confer a right to bail on anyone but to provide only that if bail is permitted it may not be set at an excessive amount. 416 A. 2d 137. See also **detention.**

EXCHANGE to give goods or **services** and to get goods or services of equal value in return. 276 A. 2d 708, 711. Generally, a transaction is a **sale** where the **consideration** is paid in money and is an "exchange" if the **consideration** is paid in specific **property** susceptible of valuation. 202 N.Y.S. 2d 470, 476. Exchange is synonymous with **barter,** and should be distinguished from **sale,** which involves a transfer of goods or services in return for money. 2 S.W. 112, 113. It has also been stated that the criterion in determining whether a transaction is a **sale** or "exchange" is whether there is a determination of value of things "exchanged," and if no price is set for either, it is an "exchange." 142

F. 2d 363, 366. See **sale or exchange.**

EXCHANGE, LIKE-KIND see **sale or exchange.**

EXCHEQUER see **court of exchequer.**

EXCISE broadly, "any kind of tax which is not directly on property or the rents or incomes of real estate." 4 A. 2d 861, 862. "An inland impost upon articles of manufacture or sale and also upon licenses to pursue certain trades, or to deal in certain commodities." 184 U.S. 608. It is imposed directly and without assessment and is measured by amount of business done and other means. 161 So. 735, 738. See **tax** [EXCISE TAX].

EXCLUSION an amount which otherwise would constitute **gross income** but which, under some specific provision of the **Internal Revenue Code,** is excluded from gross income. For example, some items specifically excluded from gross income include certain life insurance and employee death benefits, I.R.C. §101, **gifts** and inheritances, I.R.C. §102, interest on governmental obligations, I.R.C. §103, certain compensatory payments for injury or sickness and accident and health plan payments, certain **scholarships and fellowships,** I.R.C. §117, some meals and lodging furnished by an employer, I.R.C. §119, and gain realized on the sale of a residence by certain taxpayers over 55 years of age, I.R.C. §121. Compare **Deductions.**

EXCLUSIONARY RULE a constitutional rule of law based upon Court interpretation of the constitutional prohibition against unreasonable **searches and seizures,** which provides that otherwise admissible evidence may not be used in a criminal trial if it was the product of illegal police conduct. The rule does not apply in civil proceedings although statutes sometimes specifically provide for exclusion of such evidence. See **fruit of the poisonous tree.**

EXCLUSIVE USE see **use.**

EX CONTRACTU *(ĕks kŏn-trak'-tū)*—Lat: arising out of contract. See **action ex delicto.**

EXCULPATORY refers to **evidence** and/or statements which tend to clear, justify, or excuse a **defendant** from alleged fault or **guilt.** See 501 S.W. 2d 101, 103. Contrast **incriminate.**

EXCULPATORY   CLAUSE a clause in a legal document which excuses a party from liability for its acts other than those caused by willful neglect or gross negligence. 420 F. 2d 787, 789.

EXCUSABLE NEGLECT the failure to perform a required act, usually procedural in nature, because of unusual circumstances. 477 P. 2d 903, 906. The party failing to perform the act is usually given the opportunity by the court to cure his neglect. See, for example, Fed. R. Civil Proc. 6(b).

EX-DATE see **ex dividend** [EX DIVIDEND DATE].

EX DELICTO *(ĕks dĕ-lĭk'-tō)*— Lat: arising out of wrongs. See **action ex delicto.**

EX-DIVIDEND without a right to a declared **dividend.** When a stock trades ex-dividend the buyer does not receive the declared dividend because the date on which he will officially own the stock will occur after the record date of ownership for purposes of receiving same. A stock will trade ex-dividend during the settlement period, usually five business days, between the execution of an order to buy or sell the security by a broker and the date of settlement when the certificate and funds change hands. The PAYMENT DATE refers to when the dividend is actually paid and is usually sometime after the ex-dividend date

(sometimes called simply EX-DATE) and the record date.

EXECUTE "to complete, as a legal **instrument;** to perform what is required to give validity to, as by signing and perhaps **sealing** and **delivering;** as to execute a **deed, will,** etc." 171 N.E. 2d 553, 563. For example, a **contract** is "executed" when all acts necessary to complete it and to give it validity as an instrument are carried out, including signing and delivery. See 3 S.W. 2d 185. It is synonymous with "make."

The term also refers to the killing of a person by the authority of the State, as a criminal sanction pursuant to his **conviction** for a **capital offense.**

EXECUTED fully accomplished or performed; leaving nothing unfulfilled; signed; opposite of **executory.** See **execution of instrument.**

EXECUTED INTEREST see **interest.**

EXECUTION the process of carrying into effect a court's **judgment, decree,** or **order.** 302 P. 2d 11, 13. It is "the end of the law. It gives the successful **party** the fruits of his judgment." 34 U.S. 8, 27. For instance, when a claim has been reduced to judgment, the **judgment creditor** can enforce, or execute, the judgment by having the sheriff seize and sell the judgment debtor's property, and by then using the proceeds to pay the judgment. See also **writ of execution.**

In criminal law, execution refers to a convicted defendant serving his sentence. 306 So. 2d 701, 702. Execution also refers specifically to carrying out a death sentence. 199 P. 376, 379. Death sentences have been carried out in this country by shooting, 99 U.S. 130; hanging, 91 A. 417; electrocution, 329 U.S. 459; and the use of lethal gas, 30 A.L.R. 1443. Recently, a new method of "execution," lethal injection, has come into use. See **capital punish-**

ment. See also **stay** [STAY OF EXECUTION].

EXECUTION OF INSTRUMENT to sign a legal instrument such as a **deed** or **contract** so that it is legally binding and enforceable. 367 So. 2d 1381, 1383.

EXECUTION SALE see **sheriff's sale** [JUDICIAL SALE].

EXECUTIVE AGREEMENT see **treaty.**

EXECUTIVE CLEMENCY the power constitutionally reposed in the President, as Chief Executive Officer, and by most State Constitutions in the governor, to **pardon** or **commute** (i.e., reduce) the **sentence** of one convicted by a court within his **jurisdiction.**

EXECUTIVE ORDER an order that is issued by the executive head of a government, such as the President of the United States or a governor of a state, and which has the force of law. An executive order of the President must find support in the Constitution, either in a clause granting the President specific power, or by a delegation of power by Congress to the President. 343 U.S. 579. Antieau, Modern Constitutional Law, §13:24 (1969).

EXECUTIVE PARDON see **pardon.**

EXECUTIVE PRIVILEGE the **privilege** of the executive branch of government to refuse to disclose confidential communications, the disclosure of which could impair its ability to function. 422 N.Y. S. 2d 867, 868; 362 So. 2d 228, 232. The executive privilege is intended to insure the effective functioning of the executive branch 40 F.R.D. 318, 325, and is generally limited to matters of state and national security secrets. 389 F. Supp 107, 148; 5 U.S.C. §552 (b) (1). An executive privilege accrues to the President of the United States under the doctrine of **separation of powers,** 418 U.S. 683, 711; however, that privi-

lege may be overcome in the interests of the "fundamental demands of due process of law in the fair administration of criminal justice." 418 U.S. 713. See **privilege.**

EXECUTIVE PROCLAMATION see **proclamation** [PRESIDENTIAL PROCLAMATION].

EXECUTOR [EXECUTRESS OR EXECUTRIX] "a person who either expressly or by implication is appointed by a **testator** [one who dies leaving a **will**] to carry out the testator's directions concerning the dispositions he makes under his will." 285 N.E. 2d 548, 550. Compare **administrator.**

EXECUTORY not fully accomplished or completed, but contingent upon the occurrence of some event or the performance of some act in the future; not **vested;** opposite of **executed.** An executory **contract** is one in which some performance remains to be accomplished. See **interest** [EXECUTORY INTEREST].

EXECUTORY BEQUEST see **bequest.**

EXECUTORY INTEREST see **interest.**

EXECUTORY WAIVER see **waiver.**

EXEMPLAR nontestimonial identification evidence such as fingerprints, blood samples, handwriting samples, **voice exemplars,** and the like. See **search and seizure.**

EXEMPLARY DAMAGES see **damages.**

EXEMPT see **tax exempt.**

EXEMPTION a **deduction** allowed to a **taxpayer** because of his status (e.g., having certain **dependents,** being over 65, being blind, etc.) rather than because of specific economic costs or expenses incurred during the **taxable year.** I.R.C. §151. Personal exemptions are allowed for the taxpayer, and for his spouse if a **joint return** is not filed and the spouse has no **income** and is not the dependent of another taxpayer. Additional exemptions are allowed for each dependent as well as if the taxpayer is over sixty-five (and for the spouse, if over sixty-five and if the taxpayer can claim a normal exemption with respect to her) or blind (and for the spouse if also blind, under the same limitation as above). See **dependency exemption.**

EX GRATIA *(ĕx grä'-shē-à)*—Lat: out of grace; out of favor. That which is done as a favor rather than as a required task or as a duty to another's right.

EXHAUSTION OF REMEDIES a judicial policy or statutory requirement that certain administrative or non-federal judicial remedies be pursued by a litigant before a state or federal court will consider the controversy. 228 N.W. 2d 640, 642.

EXHAUSTION OF ADMINISTRATIVE REMEDIES the doctrine of all courts, adopted either as judicial policy or by statutory directive, that the courts will not interfere with or review an administrative decision or process until the available administrative channels of review have been attempted. 299 N.W. 2d 259, 264. This requirement stems from the usual requirement that courts review only "final" administrative actions. The doctrine avoids piecemeal interruption of administrative processes, conserves scarce judicial resources, and insures that the expertise of administrative agencies will be fully employed. In some extreme cases, where irreparable harm to public or private interests may be caused by honoring the doctrine, it will be held inapplicable.

EXHAUSTION OF STATE REMEDIES the practice of federal courts of not intervening in matters where state administrative remedies are available to the litigant seeking federal relief. 430 F. Supp. 920, 930. This is a policy of **comity** and may be excused when it would be unjust or inappropriate to await state administrative consideration. 261 U.S. 290. The doctrine applies only to state administrative remedies and not state judicial remedies except in cases involving state prisoners seeking federal habeas corpus relief. In those instances, the federal habeas corpus statute requires that state prisoners first exhaust state judicial remedies, provided they are then currently available. 28 U.S.C. §2254; 372 U.S. 391. Even in the context of habeas corpus petitions by state prisoners, the doctrine of exhaustion is not absolute. If the prisoner can demonstrate that resort to state remedies would be "ineffective" he need not exhaust; also, he need not present the state with more than one opportunity based on the same issue provided he has pursued all available appeals in that previous state application. 344 U.S. 443.

The Supreme Court has held that exhaustion of state remedies is not required when federal courts are asked to remedy a violation of one's civil rights pursuant to the Civil Rights Act. 42 U.S.C. §1983; 102 S. Ct. 2557.

EXHIBIT an item of **real evidence** which has been presented to the court. 5 Am. Jur. 2d Trials §553 et seq.

EXIGENCY an emergency situation which excuses some particular procedure or right from being followed or enforced. Thus, an exigency may justify speeding to the hospital with a critically ill person, breaking into someone's home to secure shelter from life-threatening harm, or dispensing with the **warrant** requirement to effect a **search and seizure** under the **Fourth**

Amendment. 292 S.W. 2d 650, 657. See **exigent circumstances.**

EXIGENT CIRCUMSTANCES emergency situations or conditions which the law recognizes as excusing compliance with some procedural requirement or recognition of another's property or other interests. Most commonly used to refer to the variety of contexts in which a valid **search and seizure** may be conducted without a **warrant.** If the police action must be taken on a "now or never" basis to preserve evidence, it may be reasonable to permit a seizure without obtaining prior judicial approval. 413 U.S. 496. Exigent circumstances may be found when substantial risk of harm to others or the police would exist if police were to delay a search until a warrant could be obtained. 627 F. 2d 906, 909. The mobility of a motor vehicle has been held in itself to create an exigent circumstance. In every instance where a search or arrest warrant has been dispensed with on grounds of **exigency, probable cause** must be present to justify the intrusion. 453 U.S. 454.

EXIGIBLE demandable; capable of being required.

EXILE to drive or force out, eject, or cut off from membership in or the privileges of. 46 A. 2d 137, 143. The punishment of forced expulsion by a political authority on the ground of expediency, 149 U.S. 698, inflicted upon **criminals** by compelling them to leave a city, place, or country, for a period of time or for life. 198 U.S. 253.

EX-OFFENDER see **criminal.**

EX OFFICIO (*ĕx ō-fē'-shē-ō*)— Lat: from the office, by virtue of his office, see 44 S.E. 2d 88, 95; officially. See 90 So. 423, 424.

EX OFFICIO MEMBER one who is the member of a board, committee or other body by virtue of his title to a certain office, and who does not require warrant or fur-

ther appointment. See 31 N.W. 2d 5, 9.

EX OFFICIO SERVICES services which are imposed by law on a public officer by virtue of his office. See 251 N.W. 395. See **oath ex officio.**

EX PARTE (*ĕx pär'-tā*)—Lat: in behalf of, on the application of, one party, by or for one party. An ex parte judicial **proceeding** is one brought for the benefit of one party only, without notice to or challenge by an **adverse party.** It refers to an application made by one party to a proceeding in the absence of the other. Thus, an ex parte **injunction** is one having been granted without the adverse party having had **notice** of its application. An uncontested application where notice was given is not ex parte.

EXPECTANCY contingency as to **possession** or enjoyment. In the law of **property, estates** may be either in possession or in expectancy; if an expectancy is created by the parties it is a **remainder;** if by **operation of law** it is a **reversion.** In either situation, there is no vested right to the property so long as it remains an expectancy. 2 Bl. Comm.*163. See also **future interest; vested.**

EXPECTATION DAMAGES see **damages.**

EXPENSES costs that are currently deductible as opposed to **capital expenditures** which may not be currently deducted but which either must be **depreciated** or amortized over the useful life of the property, or which may not be deducted at all.

LOBBYING EXPENSE those incurred in promoting or evaluating legislation; a lobbying expense may be deductible by a **taxpayer** if paid or incurred either (a) in direct connection with an appearance before Congressional committees, Congress, state legislatures, etc., with respect to legislation which is directly of business interest to the taxpayer, or (b) with respect to direct communication between the taxpayer and a trade or business organization, of which he is a member, concerning legislation which directly interests both the taxpayer and the organization. Other lobbying expenses, however, such as expenses incurred in attempts to influence the general public or segments of the general public, are not deductible. I.R.C. §162(e).

MEDICAL EXPENSE a **deduction** allowed to a taxpayer for amounts actually expended during the **taxable year** for diagnoses, cure, mitigation, treatment or prevention of any disease or affecting any structure or function of the body and associated transportation costs. However, such deduction is only allowed to the extent it exceeds five percent of adjusted gross income. Moreover, expenses for medicine and drugs are allowed as a deduction only if they must be obtained by prescription. I.R.C. §213.

MOVING EXPENSE deduction allowed to a taxpayer for the reasonable expenses of moving his residence from one location to another if such move meets certain specified technical requirements regarding distance moved and length of stay. I.R.C. §217.

ORGANIZATION EXPENSE deduction allowed to a newly formed **corporation** may deduct the costs of organizing the corporation over a period of not less than five years if such costs are paid or incurred before the end of the first **taxable year** in which the corporation commences business. I.R.C. §248. Similarly, a **partnership** may deduct the amounts paid or incurred in organizing the partnership or in promoting the sale of an interest in the partner-

ship, over a period of not less than five years. I.R.C. §709.

PERSONAL EXPENSE in general, a personal living or family expense is not allowable as a deduction from gross **income**. I.R.C. §262. Certain expenses, however, such as interest, certain **taxes, bad debts,** medical expenses, and **charitable contributions** are deductible if the taxpayer itemizes his deductions.

TRADE OR BUSINESS EXPENSE deduction allowed to a taxpayer for all "ordinary and necessary" expenses incurred with respect to the taxpayer's trade or business. I.R.C. §162.

EXPERT TESTIMONY [EVIDENCE] see **expert witness.**

EXPERT WITNESS a **witness** having "special knowledge of the subject about which he is to **testify,**" 26 A. 2d 770, 773; that knowledge must generally be such as is not normally possessed by the average person. 22 A. 2d 28. The expert witness is thus "able to afford the tribunal having the matter under consideration a special assistance." 139 P. 2d 239, 242. This expertise may derive from either study and education, or from experience and observation. 43 P. 2d 716. An expert witness must be qualified by the court to testify as such. To qualify, he need not have formal training, but the court must be satisfied that the testimony presented is of a kind which in fact requires special knowledge, skill or experience. 83 F. Supp. 722. Such testimony, given by an expert witness, constitutes EXPERT EVIDENCE or EXPERT TESTIMONY. 168 Ill. App. 419. Hypothetical questions [asking the witness to assume certain stated facts] may be asked of an expert witness as a way of educating the **trier of fact** in the area of the expert's knowledge or experience. See generally McCormick, Evidence, 29-41 (2d ed. 1972).

EXPORT to transport out of one country and into another; also, the article transported. The Constitution gives the federal government the power to regulate exports as part of its power to regulate trade with foreign nations, United States Constitution, Art. 1, Sec. 8, Cl. 3, and it also gives the federal government the power to tax exports as part of its taxing power. United States Constitution, Art. 1, Sec. 8, Cl. 1. It also forbids the States from taxing exports to another country. United States Constitution, Art. 1, Sec. 9, Cl. 5. This constitutional prohibition does not apply to goods exported from one state to another. 114 U.S. 622, 626-27. The constitutional protections against state taxes, however, are not applicable until the article begins its physical entry into the stream of exportation. Hence, a state may tax an item where it is made, but may not tax it when it is exported—an act which would discriminate against a foreign market.

EXPORTATION the act of transporting goods from one country to another; the severance of goods from the mass of things belonging to the U.S. with the intention of adding them to the mass of things belonging to some foreign country. Another country as the intended destination of the goods is essential to **exportation.** See **import.**

EX POST FACTO (*ĕx pōst fäk'-tō*)—Lat: after the fact; "every law that makes an action done before the passing of the law and which was innocent when done to be criminal and punishable as [a crime]; every law that aggravates a **crime** or makes it greater than when it was committed; every law that changes and inflicts a greater punishment; and every law that alters the legal rules of **evidence,** and requires less, or different, testimony than the law required at the time of the commission of the offense, in order to convict the offender." 171

S.W. 2d 880. Such a law violates Art. 1, Secs. 9 (Cl. 3) & 10 of the Constitution of the United States which provide that neither Congress nor any state shall pass an ex post facto law; these provisions have been held applicable only to criminal statutes. 3 U.S. (3 Dall.) 386. Compare **bill of attainder.**

EXPRESS to make known explicitly and in declared terms. To set forth an actual **agreement** in words, written or spoken, which unambiguously signifies intent. As distinguished from "**implied**" the term is not left to implication or inference from conduct or circumstances. 195 N.E. 2d 877, 882. When parties show their **agreement** in words they create an express **contract** as contrasted to a contract implied by circumstances alone, or a quasi-contract, which is implied in law in order to obtain justice. 451 F. 2d 690, 695. Compare **implied.**

EXPRESSIO UNIUS EST EXCLUSIO ALTERIUS (*ĕx-prĕ'-shē-ō ū-nē'-ūs ĕst ĕx-klū'-shē-ō äl-tĕr'-ē-ūs*)—Lat: The expression of one thing is the exclusion of another. In construing statutes, contracts, wills, and the like under this maxim, the mention of one thing within the statute or other document implies the exclusion of another thing not so mentioned. See 95 P. 2d 1007, 1012. "The maxim . . . though not a rule of law, is an aid to construction, and is applicable where, in the natural association of ideas, that which is expressed is so set over by way of contrast to that which is omitted that the contrast enforces the affirmative inference that that which is omitted must be intended to have opposite and contrary treatment." See 34 So. 2d 132. Thus a statute granting certain rights to "police, fire, and sanitation employees" would be interpreted to exclude other public employees not enumerated from the legislation. This is based on presumed legislative intent and where for some reason this intent cannot be reasonably inferred the court is free to draw a different conclusion. See 16 N.E. 2d 459.

EXPROPRIATION the right of the **sovereign** to take private property which, under the United States Constitution, must be for public purpose and only on the payment of **just compensation.** The right had its origin in the inherent power of the sovereign over its citizens. The right is grounded in public policy which deems the good of the community to take priority over individual interest. An individual who owns property under the protection of the laws of the community tacitly agrees to subject that property to the needs of the community. Although the power of expropriation is a sovereign right, it can be delegated. It has been extended by statute to municipalities and even private corporations serving a public purpose, such as public utilities. 200 So. 2d 428, 433 (1967). See **eminent domain.**

EXPULSION see **deportation** [EX-PULSION].

EXPUNGEMENT OF RECORDS a procedure whereby a court orders the annulment and destruction of records of an arrest or other court proceedings. Some jurisdictions provide that an individual arrested and not convicted may apply to a court for an order of expungement and that if such an order is granted the individual may regard the arrest and all subsequent proceedings had as having not occurred in contemplation of law. See, e.g., N.J.S.A. 2C: 52-6. Court-ordered expungements may also be available as a remedy for unlawful arrests. See LaFave, Search and Seizure §1.9. Many states permit an expungement remedy as a means of removing civil disabilities following a period of good behavior after a conviction. See, e.g., N.J.S.A. 2C: 52-2. Even an expunged record may be used for sentence enhancement and as a basis for denial of a federal fire-

arms permit. 103 S.Ct. 986. Compare **sealing of records.** See also **executive clemency, pardon.**

EX REL. *(ĕx rĕl)*—Lat: the abbreviated form of "ex relatione" which means "upon relation or report." Legal **proceedings** which are initiated "ex rel." are brought in the name of the state but on the information and at the instigation of a private individual with a private interest in the outcome. The **real party in interest** is called the "relator." The action is captioned "State of X [or United States] ex rel. Y v. Z."

EX-RIGHTS refers to stock sold without **rights** to purchase stock subsequently offered by the same **corporation.** Rights normally have value, since the new issue is usually priced at a **discount** from the prevailing market price.

EXTENDED TERM see **sentence** [EXTENDED TERM].

EXTENDI FACIAS see **fieri facias** [EXTENDI FACIAS].

EXTENSION an increase in the date of expiration or due date for a term or obligation. In a **lease** an extension represents a continuation of the existing lease on the same terms, whereas a renewal may involve new terms in a different lease. In **procedure,** extensions of time are governed by rules of the court. See, for example, Fed. R. Civil Proc. 6(b); Fed. R. Crim. Proc. 45; Fed. R. App. Proc. 26. For favorable action it is usually important that an application by a party for an extension of time be made in advance of the due date. When this is not possible, the court may entertain such a motion **nunc pro tunc.**

EXTENUATING CIRCUMSTAN-CES unusual factors related to and tending to contribute to the consummation of an illegal act, but over which the actor had little or no control. These factors therefore reduce the responsibility of the actor and serve to mitigate his punishment or his payment of **damages.** See **mitigating circumstances.** Compare **justification.**

EXTINGUISHMENT a discharge of an obligation or contract by **operation of law** or by express agreement. Compare **merger.**

EXTORTION at common law, the corrupt collection by a public official under **color** of office of an excessive or unauthorized fee. It was punishable as a **misdemeanor.** Under modern statutes the offense is broadened to include the illegal taking of money by anyone who employs threats, or other illegal use of fear or coercion in order to obtain the money, and whose conduct falls short of the threat to personal safety required for **robbery.** Model Penal Code §223.4. See 148 A. 2d 848, 850; 2 Mass. 522, 523; 160 F. 2d 754, 756. Extortion is used interchangeably with **blackmail** and is commonly punished as a felony. See generally Perkins & Boyce Criminal Law 442-452 (3d ed. 1982). Compare **bribery.**

EXTRADITION the surrender by one sovereign to another of an **accused** or convicted person. 668 F. 2d 805, 810. A state's chief executive has the right to demand from the **asylum** state the return of a person who has been accused of a crime based on **probable cause.** Extradition prevents the escape of fugitives who try to seek sanctuary in another state. It enables the state in which the offense occurred to bring the offender swiftly to trial.

The Supreme Court has interpreted extradition to be a summary and mandatory executive proceeding derived from the Extradition Clause, (United States Constitution Art. IV, Sec. 2). 197 U.S. 324, 332. It does not contemplate that the asylum state will conduct a preliminary inquiry before the defendant's trial in the demanding state. The purpose of extradition is to foster national unity by requiring **comity** and **full faith and credit** between the states. 439 U.S. 282.

On receiving a requisition for extradition, the asylum state is bound by the requirements of the Constitution, its implementing statute, 18 U.S.C. §3182, and, where adopted, the Uniform Criminal Extradition Act which establishes extradition guidelines. The Uniform Criminal Extradition Act requires, **inter alia,** that the demanding state "must substantially charge" the fugitive with the commission of a crime. The Supreme Court, however, has emphasized the duty of the asylum state to surrender the person, based upon the presumption that the demanding state has probable cause. The asylum state may make no independent assessment of that probable cause in order not to frustrate the "summary and mandatory executive proceeding" that the Constitution contemplates once a demand for extradition has been properly issued by the governor of the demanding state. 439 U.S. 282.

EXTRAJUDICIAL that which is done outside of a court's **jurisdiction;** not founded upon or dependent upon the authority of a court. Suspects may be compelled to perform extrajudicial acts not in the presence of a judge or jury, such as appearing in police line-ups or trying on certain garments, without violating their privilege against self-incrimination. 388 U.S. 218.

An EXTRAJUDICIAL REMEDY is one engaged in by a person without the formal sanction of a court order. Thus, if a secured party retakes possession of collateral through self-help, he would be employing an extrajudicial remedy. U.C.C. §9-503. Courts generally will not grant an injunction in disputes among members of clubs or associations where there exists other extrajudicial means of redress before a quasi-judicial body within the organization or association itself. 303 U.S. 41.

EXTRAORDINARY DIVIDENDS see **dividend.**

EXTRAORDINARY REMEDY see **remedy.**

EXTREMIS see **in extremis.**

EXTRINSIC FRAUD see **fraud.**

EX TURPI CAUSA NON ORITUR ACTIO *(ĕx tûr'-pē käw'-zà nŏn ôr'-ē-tûr äk'-shē-ō)*—Lat: no disgraceful, [foul, immoral, obscene] matter can be the basis of an **action.** 24 S.E. 2d 895, 897.

EYEWITNESS a person who can testify as to what he has experienced by his presence at an event. 86 N.W. 2d 142, 144. An "eyewitness" does not have to be one who has obtained knowledge of the act by the sense of sight alone. For example, an "eyewitness" may be one who has obtained knowledge of the act via voice recognition and identification. 166 S.W. 2d 30.

F

F.A.A. see **Federal Aviation Administration [FAA].**

FACE VALUE the stated value expressed in the language of the **instrument.** 16 S.E. 906, 907. Face value differs from **market value,** which refers to the value of the instrument when it matures or becomes due. For example, a **bond** is issued with a face value of **par** and pays a certain interest rate. That bond's market value will be greater if the prevailing interest rates for like periods are lower; its market value will be lower if the prevailing interest rates for like periods are higher, assuming in

each instance comparable credit risks are involved.

FACIAL INVALIDITY see **void for vagueness.**

FACILITATION in criminal law, a statutory offense rendering one guilty when, believing it probable that he is aiding a person who intends to commit a **crime,** he engages in conduct which assists that person in obtaining the means or opportunity to commit the crime and in fact his conduct does aid the person to so commit it. See N. Y. Penal Law §115. For example, if a store owner sells a gun to someone who is enraged and uttering threats about killing a third party, the store owner may be guilty of criminal facilitation. At **common law,** knowing facilitation may give rise to **liability** for **aiding and abetting** if the requisite **mens rea** can be established for the **accessorial** liability, but there was no distinct offense of criminal facilitation as such at common law. Compare **accomplice; conspiracy.**

FACINUS QUOS INQUINAT AEQUAT *(fä'-sĭ-nŭs kwōs ĭn'-kwĭ-nät ī'-kwät)*—Lat: villany and guilt make all those whom it contaminates equal in character.

FACT an event that has occurred or circumstances that exist, events whose actual occurrence or existence is to be determined by the evidence. 179 S.E. 2d 138, 141. In deciding a case, a **court** will find facts on the basis of the **evidence** presented to it, and then apply the **law** to those facts. In a **jury trial,** the judge will instruct the jury how to apply the law to the facts, and the jury will then find the facts and render a **verdict.** Facts may be so well known that a court will take **judicial notice** of it, that is, take the fact into consideration without the presentation of evidence on the fact. McCormick, Evidence §§328 et seq. (2d ed. 1972). Otherwise, facts must be established by **compe-**

tent evidence, such as the testimony of **witnesses** or the presentation of **real evidence** to the court. McCormick, Evidence §5 (2d ed. 1972). See **conclusion of fact; error** [ERROR OF FACT]; **mistake** [MISTAKE OF FACT]. See also **ultimate facts.**

FACTA SUNT POTENTIORI VERBIS *(fäk'-tà sŭnt pō-tĕn'-tē-ô'-rē vĕr'-bēs)*—Lat: the facts, deeds, or accomplishments are more powerful than words.

FACT-FINDER in a judicial or administrative **proceeding,** the person or group of persons that has the responsibility of determining the facts relevant to decide a controversy. It is the role of a **jury** in a jury trial; in a non-jury trial the judge sits both as a fact-finder and as the trier of law; in administrative proceedings it may be a hearing officer or a hearing body. The term TRIER OF FACT generally denotes the same function.

FACTO *(fäk'-tō)*—Lat: in fact; by a deed, accomplishment or exploit. See also **de facto; ipso facto.**

FACTOR a person who receives and sells goods for a commission (which is called FACTORAGE); he is entrusted with the **possession** of the goods he sells and generally sells them in his own name. 209 N.W. 660, 661. In this respect, a factor differs from a **broker** in that a broker just brings parties together but never takes possession of the goods. For example, a used car dealer is a "factor" when a car is placed in the dealer's possession so that the dealer can sell it. See 285 P. 2d 632, 634. Consignee. A financier who lends money and takes in return an **assignment** of accounts receivable or some other security. 294 F. 2d 126, 129. The **garnishee** in states where "factorizing" is the name for **garnishment.** 33 A. 147, 157. See **factor's acts.** Compare **jobber.**

FACTOR'S ACTS the name of cer-

tain English statutes, which have also been enacted in a number of states, whose "general effect is to make a **factor's [agent's] possession** of property or documents of **title** such evidence of ownership as to enable him to do all acts which the true owner might, thus making the owner responsible for the factor's acts and protecting **bona fide purchasers** in any transaction fairly effected with the apparent owner [factor]." 32 Am. Jur. 2d Factors §53. The purpose of such statutes is to protect the purchaser where the agent has exceeded his authority. See 30 N.E. 2d 876. 880. The policy is now incorporated in U.C.C. §2-403.

FACT, QUESTION OF see **question of fact.**

FACTS, PROBATIVE see **probative** [PROBATIVE FACTS].

FACTUAL IMPOSSIBILITY see **impossibility.**

FACTUM *(fäk'-tūm)*—Lat: literally, a deed, act, exploit or accomplishment. When used with respect to a change in a person's domicile, the "factum" is the person's physical presence in the new domicile. See 169 Va. 548. In the civil law the word "factum" is used to distinguish a matter of **fact** from a matter of **law.** See **fraud** [FRAUD IN THE FACTUM].

FACTUM PROBANDUM *(fäk'-tūm prō-bän'-dūm)*—Lat. in the law of **evidence,** the **fact** to be proved.

FAILURE OF CONSIDERATION see **consideration.**

FAILURE OF ISSUE words used in a **will** or **deed** to refer to a **condition** which operates in the event either no children be born or no children survive the decedent. Often the words "die without issue" are employed. The words may fix a condition whereby an estate, instead of being alienable and therefore capable of being conveyed to a third person, will, in the event of "failure of issue," pass automatically to an alternative designated in the original instrument. Unless the instrument indicated to the contrary, the common law read the condition as operating ad infinitum. This construction is termed INDEFINITE FAILURE OF ISSUE. Thus, if children of the first taker themselves fail to leave children, the estate will still go to the alternative. The first taker is regarded as possessing a **fee tail,** and his descendants continue as **tenants in tail.** 9 Watts 447, 450; 20 A. 560. A majority of American jurisdictions by statute have reversed this presumption and construe "die without issue" as a DEFINITE FAILURE OF ISSUE; i.e., the condition is satisfied fully if the first taker has issue surviving at the time of his death. 5 Amer. Law of Property §21.50 (1952). Alternative expressions include "if he dies before he has any issue;" "for want of issue;" "without leaving issue."

FAILURE TO PROSECUTE see **default judgment; dismissal; non prosequitur.**

FAIR COMMENT a defense by one involved in a **libel** suit that the statements made, even if untrue, were not made with malice nor intended to create ill will or malice but rather were intended to state the facts as the writer honestly understood them to be. **"Defendant** is not entitled to publish defamatory misstatements of fact without reasonable grounds for a belief of truth, with conscious indifference to truth, or without ascertaining reasonably available facts. Only honest and unintentional mistake of facts are protected." 139 F. Supp. 35, 38.

FAIR COMPETITION see **unfair competition.**

FAIR HEARING a statutorily authorized extra-judicial hearing which is granted primarily in situa-tions where the normal judicial processes would be inadequate to secure **due process,** either because a judicial remedy does not exist, or because one would suffer grievous harm or substantial prejudice to his rights before a judicial remedy became available. Thus, fair hearings have been authorized as forums for the administrative determination of a citizen's rights in the event of termination of welfare benefits (42 U.S.C.A. §602(a)(4)), before deportation of an alien (8 U.S.C.A. §1252(b)), where the granting or revocation of a broadcasting license is at issue (47 U.S.C.A. §409(b)), etc; and it has been determined judicially that due process requires in some situations the opportunity for a fair hearing. See, e.g., 294 F. 2d 150. The fair hearing must be conducted in a manner consistent with the requirements of due process, including the opportunity to present evidence in his favor, as well as to be apprised of the evidence against him in the matter so that he will be fully aware of the basis for the judgment. See 212 F. 275.

FAIR LABOR PRACTICE see **unfair labor practice.**

FAIR MARKET VALUE see **market value.**

FAIRNESS DOCTRINE a requirement that broadcasting stations present contrasting viewpoints on controversial issues of public importance. This doctrine imposes two affirmative responsibilities on the broadcaster: (1) to present adequate coverage of controversial public issues, and (2) to ensure that this programming presents differing viewpoints so that the public is fully and fairly informed. 412 U.S. 94, 111. The rule evolved from the First Amendment and has been given statutory approval. 47 U.S.C. §315 (a).

Methods of programming, format, and choice of spokesmen on differing views are left to the broadcaster's discretion, subject only to the standard of reasonableness and **good faith.** The fairness doctrine does not require a broadcaster to give differing views equal time, which is the rule for political broadcasting. Its purpose is only to ensure that the public hears both sides of controversial issues. When a controversial editorial is broadcast, it is the station's duty to offer broadcast time to responsible spokesmen with opposing views. The broadcaster must provide free time for the presentation of opposing views if a paid sponsor is unavailable and it must initiate programming on public issues if no one else seeks to do so. 412 U.S. at 111. This requirement does not include a duty to accept editorial advertisements. Id at 122. While this doctrine has been upheld by the Supreme Court, constitutional questions remain concerning the "**chilling effect**" the doctrine may have on a broadcaster's First Amendment rights of free speech. 395 U.S. 367.

The PERSONAL ATTACK RULE, another aspect of the fairness doctrine, imposes stricter requirements on the broadcaster. If during the presentation of views on a controversial public issue an attack is made on the honesty, character, integrity, or like personal qualities of a person, the broadcaster must notify that person within seven days. That person has an absolute right personally to be heard in his or her **defense.**

FAIR TRADE LAWS state statutes that permit a manufacturer to establish minimum resale prices which cannot be varied by the wholesaler or distributor.

Almost all vertical minimum pricing agreements are **per se** violations of the **conspiracy** sections of the Federal **Anti-Trust** Acts. Under the provisions of the McGuire Act, 15 U.S.C. §45 (1952) such agreements did not violate the antitrust laws when they were entered into under the provisions of state Fair Trade Statutes. However, in 1975 the fair trade exception was repealed, so that such state statutes are no longer viable. Austin, Antitrust §4.11 (1976).

FAIR USE in federal **copyright** law 17 U.S.C. §§101 et seq., refers to specific use of copyrighted materials without payment of royalties or which otherwise does not constitute an infringement of copyright, permitted use by copying and acknowledgment; refers to a "privilege in others than the owner of the copyright to use the copyrighted material in a reasonable manner without his consent, notwithholding the monopoly granted to the owner by the copyright." 366 F. 2d 303, 306. Whether a use is considered a fair use depends upon the purpose and character of the use, the nature of the copyrighted work, the amount and substantiality of the portion used, and the effect of the use upon the market value of the copyright. Important factors include whether the copied material was creative or research-oriented; the status of the user (reviewer, scholar, compiler, parodist); extent of use (both qualitatively and quantitatively); the absence of an intent to plagiarize as evidenced by proper acknowledgment; the original contribution of the user. See Kaplan and Brown, Copyright 309-351 (1960).

The doctrine was originally judge-made in an effort to balance the economic incentives to creators of copyrighted works and the dissemination of those works to the public. 422 U.S. 151, 156. It was codified in the Copyright Act of 1976 and in its statutory form restated the language of the case law. 17 U.S.C. §107. It has been held that the fair use codification by Congress was not intended to depart from court-created principles and use factors developed in case law to determine fair use defense.

207 U.S.P.Q. 977; 542 F. Supp. 1156.

FALSE ARREST unlawful **arrest;** unlawful restraint of another's personal liberty or freedom of locomotion. 193 N.E. 2d 485, 489. It may be a criminal offense and/or the basis of a **civil action** for **damages.** See **false imprisonment.**

FALSE IMPRISONMENT as a **tort,** the unjustified detention of a person. The restraint must be total so that it amounts to an imprisonment; mere obstruction, stopping, locking one out of his room, etc., is not enough. 219 F. 2d 622. The total restraint may, however, be of any appreciable duration. 70 So. 734. No physical force need be used so long as the victim reasonably believes that he is being restrained against his will. 195 S.W. 2d 312 (woman remained in a store when her purse was wrongfully taken from her). The tort must be intentional, Restatement Torts §35; but no actual **damages** need be proved. 109 A. 2d 128.

Where the restraint is imposed by virtue of purported legal authority and an arrest occurs, it will be a **false arrest** resulting in a false imprisonment; the defendant need not be a police officer but must merely assert improper legal authority to detain. 116 P. 234 (railroad conductor).

As a **common law misdemeanor** it is the unlawful confinement of a person. This need not consist of wrongfully locking him in a jail, but comprehends "any unlawful exercise or show of force by which a person is compelled to remain where he does not wish to remain or to go where he does not wish to go." 172 N.E. 2d 380, 381-82. In many states, an unlawful knowing restraint which interferes substantially with a person's liberty gives rise to criminal liability. See Model Penal Code §217.3.

FALSE OATH see **false swearing.**

FALSE PRETENSE the statutory offense of obtaining property by false pretense. Essential elements include an intent to defraud, an implied or express false representation, and obtaining property as a result of that misrepresentation. 183 N.W. 2d 813, 815. The crime also requires at least the intent that **title** to the property pass, even if there is not an actual passing of title. 152 N.W. 2d 714, 716, and in that respect differs from **larceny** by trick, in which the false pretense persuades the owner of property to permit another to take possession but not title. Thus, if one borrows another's vehicle under a false credit card, it becomes larceny by trick but if one buys the vehicle by making false statements on a credit application, it is false pretense. See Perkins & Boyce, Criminal Law 366 (3rd ed. 1982).

Modern statutes have expanded the false pretense to include false promises, i.e., statements as to future fact provided that the falsity of the statement in fact is not alone a sufficient basis to prove that the defendant knew the statement was false when made. See Model Penal Code §223.3. Compare **embezzlement.**

FALSE RETURN a **return** (statement) to a **writ** made by a ministerial officer in which there is a false statement that is injurious to a party having an interest in such writ. 266 S.W. 723, 726. For example, if a sheriff is supposed to serve a **summons** and claims on his return that he did serve it, when he actually did not serve the summons, this would constitute a false return.

In tax situations, an incorrect return in which there appears either an intent to mislead or deceive on the part of the taxpayer, or at least **negligence** that is sufficiently gross to warrant holding the taxpayer liable for his error. See 52 N.E. 635, 638.

FALSE SWEARING a **common law misdemeanor** which would amount to **perjury** except that it is not committed in a judicial **proceeding;** the giving of a false oath in connection with some proceeding or matter in which an oath is required by law. "A FALSE OATH is a willful and corrupt sworn statement made without sincere belief in its truthfulness." Perkins and Boyce, Criminal Law 511 (3rd ed. 1982). Thus, the giving of a false oath in an **affidavit** used to obtain a marriage license will not support a charge of perjury because it is extrajudicial but it will support a charge of false swearing which is a separate offense. 3 S.W. 662. Many jurisdictions now have statutes proscribing false swearing. Model Penal Code §241.2. Other statutes group perjury, false swearing, and "making false written statements" together as different degrees of the same crime, often called loosely "perjury." See, e.g., N.Y. Penal Law Art. 210.

FALSE VERDICT see **verdict** [FALSE VERDICT].

FALSI CRIMEN see **crimen falsi.**

FAMILY [WIDOW'S] ALLOWANCE an amount awarded to a widow for support during the administration of her deceased husband's estate, regardless of whether the widow has any right in the corpus or income of the estate. 48 F. 2d 135.

FAMILY, CRIMINAL see **organized crime.**

FAMILY PURPOSE DOCTRINE doctrine establishing **tort liability** of the owner of a "family car" when that car is operated negligently by another member of the family. The rule thus imputes a relationship of **principal** and **agent** where one maintains an automobile for pleasure or other use of members of his family. See 180 S.W. 2d 102, 104; 79 P. 2d 965. It is synonymous with "FAMILY AUTOMOBILE DOCTRINE" and "FAMILY GROUP."

The doctrine has been rejected or limited in many states which follow the theory that automobiles are merely one type of **chattel,** similar to guns or golf clubs, to which liability does not attach to a head of a household who, without negligence, entrusts such chattel to a family member. Prosser, Torts 485 (4th ed. 1971).

FAMOSUS LIBELLUS *(fä-mō'-sŭs lē'-bĕl-ŭs)*—Lat: literally, a **slanderous** or **libelous** letter, handbill, advertisement, petition, written **accusation** or **indictment.** Its legal usage is that of a libelous writing.

F.A.S. see **free alongside.**

FATAL VARIANCE see **variance.**

FAULT generally, error or mistake; all conduct falling below a certain standard. 349 So. 2d 1345, 1348. In describing conduct, it is the responsibility for or cause of wrongdoing or failure. 156 P. 2d 441, 445.

In describing **goods,** a fault is a defect in either the quantity or quality of the goods. See **negligence.**

FAVORED BENEFICIARY "[o]ne who, in the circumstances of the particular case, has been favored over others having equal claim to the **testator**'s bounty." 1 So. 2d 890, 892. "Confidential relations, accompanied with activity of a favored beneficiary in the preparation and execution of a will, raises a presumption of **undue influence.**" 112 So. 313, 316.

F.B.I. see **Federal Bureau of Investigation [F.B.I.].**

F.C.I. see **jail** [FEDERAL CORRECTIONAL INSTITUTION [F.C.I.].

F.D.A. see **Food and Drug Administration [F.D.A.].**

FEALTY in feudal times, "the oath sworn by the **tenant** to be faithful to his lord." Moynihan, Introduction to the Law of Real Property 18 (1962). It was one of the **incidents** of free **tenures.** See also **homage.**

FEATHERBEDDING in labor law, the **unfair labor practice** of creating or spreading employment by unnecessarily maintaining or increasing the number of employees or the time used to complete a particular job. 547 F. Supp. 1336, 1341. Minimum crew regulations on the railroad is a typical example. Unions attempt to justify such practices on grounds of health and safety although job security is their primary motivation. See **labor organization [union]**.

FEDERAL AVIATION ADMINISTRATION [F.A.A.] an agency of the U.S. Department of Transportation, charged with regulating air commerce, promoting aviation safety and overseeing the operation of airports, including air traffic control.

FEDERAL BUREAU OF INVESTIGATION [F.B.I] an agency of the U.S. Department of Justice, charged by law with investigating violations of all laws of the U.S. government, except those expressly assigned to other agencies.

FEDERAL COMMON LAW the body of decisional law developed by the federal courts, not resting on state court decisions. Before the decision in *Erie Railroad* v. *Tompkins,* 304 U.S. 64, it referred primarily to the decisional law that federal courts developed in **diversity of citizenship** cases. After *Erie,* federal courts sitting in diversity cases have been bound to follow the general (substantive) **common law** of the state from which, respectively, each case arose. See **preemption**.

FEDERAL CORRECTIONAL FACILITY see **jail** [FEDERAL CORRECTIONAL INSTITUTION].

FEDERAL COURTS the courts of the United States, as distinguished from the courts of the individual states. These courts derive their legitimacy from the Constitution, Art. III, Sec. I. Clause 1: "The judicial Power of the United States, shall be vested in one supreme court, and in such inferior courts as the Congress may from time to time ordain and establish." Presently, the principal federal courts are the **district courts** (gencral courts of **original jurisdiction;** federal **trial courts**), the courts of appeal (formerly circuit courts of appeals; principally **appellate** review courts), and the **Supreme Court** (only court created directly by the Constitution; court of last resort in federal system; having final appellate review of lower federal courts, and of state court decisions involving questions of federal law). All of these courts are limited in their power to hear cases by the grant of **jurisdiction** in the Constitution (Art. III, Sec. 2). The principal instances of federal jurisdiction are those cases "arising under [the] Constitution, [and] the laws of the United States," those "to which the United States shall be a Party" and those either between two states, a state and the citizen of another state or between the citizen of two different states [**diversity of citizenship**].

There are a few other specialized courts within the federal system: COURT OF CLAIMS (hears suits involving such claims against the United States government as are allowed by federal law); COURT OF CUSTOMS AND PATENT APPEALS established to review Customs Court decisions; CUSTOMS COURT (review decision of the several collectors of customs). See Wright, Federal Courts §§1-5 (4th ed. 1983). See also **bankruptcy**.

With the exception of the Supreme Court, federal courts have no jurisdiction except as conferred by statute. Therefore, any person asserting a claim in federal court must demonstrate a statutory jurisdictional basis.

FEDERAL EMPLOYER'S LIABILITY ACT the federal law imposing liability on railroads for injuries sustained by their employees in the course of employment. 45 U.S.C. §51. It is based upon the federal government's power over **interstate commerce.** Compare **Jones Act.**

FEDERAL INSURANCE CONTRIBUTION ACT see **F.I.C.A.**

FEDERALISM a system of government wherein power is divided by a constitution between a central government and local governments, the local governments maintaining control over local affairs and the central government being accorded sufficient authority to deal with national needs and affairs. Since the United States is a federal "republic," considerations of federalism play a major role in the interpretation of the Constitution. See **pre-emption.**

FEDERAL MAGISTRATE see **magistrate** [UNITED STATES [FEDERAL] MAGISTRATE].

FEDERAL MAGISTRATE'S ACT OF 1968 see **magistrate** [FEDERAL MAGISTRATE'S ACT OF 1968].

FEDERAL QUESTION JURISDICTION one kind of **original jurisdiction** given to federal courts by virtue of Article III of the Constitution and enabling legislation, it allows federal courts to hear **cases** wherein the meaning or application of something in the Constitution, laws, or treaties of the United States is being disputed. For example, if the meaning of a federal law or the application of a provision of the federal Constitution were raised in a case, then the case would present a federal question, and if federal law granted federal courts jurisdiction to hear that specific federal question, then there would be federal question jurisdiction. Federal district courts are granted jurisdiction under 28 U.S.C. §1331 to hear federal question cases, although there are also many statutes which grant jurisdiction in particular federal question cases. Previously, a

jurisdictional amount of $10,000 was required, but such an amount requirement was abolished in 1980. Wright, Law of Federal Courts §17 et seq. (4th ed. 1983). See also **diversity of citizenship.**

FEDERAL RESERVE SYSTEM established under the Federal Reserve Act of 1913 to hold the cash reserves of member banks and to provide for other service functions such as furnishing currency for circulation, facilitating the clearance and collection of checks, and issuing and redeeming government obligations such as savings bonds. The duties and functions of the agency were expanded in 1933 and 1935 to place a greater emphasis on governmental control of the money supply, the credit structure, and the economy in general. Twelve Federal Reserve Banks are located throughout the country and act as the operating arms of the Federal Reserve system. All national banks are member banks; state banks may join at their option.

FEDERAL TORT CLAIMS ACT [F.T.C.A.] see **Tort Claims Act.**

FEDERAL TRADE COMMISSION [F.T.C.] a federal administrative agency established in 1914 to protect consumers against unfair methods of competition and deceptive business practices, including sales frauds and violation of the **antitrust** laws. The agency's Bureau of Competition is responsible for the enforcement of the **antitrust** laws. The Bureau of Consumer Protection protects consumers against sales, frauds, and any other unfair or deceptive business practices. The Bureau of Economics performs economic analysis both for informational purposes and for use in litigation by the trial staff. It accomplishes this goal chiefly through its authority to order the offender to "cease and desist" from a prohibited practice. If its order is disobeyed, the F.T.C. must go to federal court to seek enforcement.

FEDERAL TRADE COMMISSION IMPROVEMENT ACT see **Magnuson-Moss Warranty Act.**

FEE in **real property,** an **estate** of complete **ownership** which can be sold by the owner or **devised** to his **heirs.** 106 F. 2d 217, 224; 7 A. 2d 696, 698-99. "Fee" derives from "feudal," or "feodor," meaning "land," importing that such land is held by some superior to whom certain **services** are due. "Fee," "fee simple," and "fee simple absolute," are often used as equivalents. The word "fee" indicates that it is an estate of **inheritance;** the word "simple" signifies that there are no restrictions on the inheritable characteristics of the estate. See **fee simple.** But a fee may be qualified, such as a **conditional** or **determinable fee** which could continue forever but would be discontinued upon the happening of a certain event.

IN FEE Outright ownership of real property; the ownership of all aspects of title, including the ability to transfer the totality of such title.

FEE SIMPLE a **freehold estate** of virtually infinite duration and of absolute **inheritance** free of any condition, limitations, or restriction to particular **heirs.** 78 P. 2d 905, 907, 908. Also called FEE SIMPLE ABSOLUTE. At **common law,** it was mandatory that the words "to B and his heirs" be used to create a fee simple; a transfer "to B in fee simple" gave B only a **life estate** under the common law. Today, the presumption is in favor of fee simple estates unless an intention to create a more limited estate clearly appears. Compare **fee tail.** See also **words of limitation.**

FEE SIMPLE CONDITIONAL see **conditional fee [estate].**

FEE SIMPLE DEFEASIBLE see **determinable fee.**

FEE SIMPLE DETERMINABLE see **determinable fee.**

FEE TAIL a **conveyance** created by a **deed** or **will** to a person "and the heirs of his body." A fee tail establishes a fixed line of inheritable **succession** and cuts off the regular succession of **heirs** at law. 243 P. 2d 1030. It is a limited estate in that **inheritance** is through lineal descent only, which, if exclusively through males, is called FEE TAIL MALE, while exclusively through females is called FEE TAIL FEMALE. If the family line runs out **(failure of issue)** the fee **reverts** to the **grantor** or his successors in interest. See **words of limitation.**

FELA see **Federal Employer's Liability Act; Employer's Liability Acts.**

FELLOW SERVANT a co-worker, defined for the purpose of the FELLOW SERVANT RULE which absolves an employer of **liability** for **injury** to a worker resulting from the **negligence** of a co-worker. Fellow servants, who were said to **assume the risk** of each other's negligence, are employees engaged in the same common pursuits under the same general control, serving the same master, engaged in the same general business and deriving authority and compensation from a common source. See 16 F. 2d 517, 519. **Employer's Liability Acts** and **Worker's Compensation** statutes have abrogated the fellow servant doctrine.

FELLOWSHIPS see **scholarships and fellowships.**

FELONY generic term employed to distinguish certain high crimes from minor offenses known as **misdemeanors;** crimes declared to be such by statute or as "true crimes" by the **common law.** Statutes often define felony in terms of an offense punishable (or punished in fact) by death or imprisonment generally, (180 So. 717; 126 P. 2d 406, 408), or by death or imprisonment for more than one year (18 U.S.C. §1). The original common law felonies were felonious **homicide, mayhem, arson, rape, robbery, burglary, larceny,** prison breach [escape], and rescue of a felon. Perkins & Boyce, Criminal Law 14-15 (3rd ed. 1982).

Conviction for felony meant at common law that the felon "forfeited life and member and all that he had." 2 Pollock & Maitland, History of English Law 462 (2d ed. 1899). Originally all felonies were punishable by death except for mayhem which was punished by mutilation (as were the other felonies very early [pre-13th century]); "the fiction of benefit of clergy [under which clergymen were exempt from trial or punishment for crime in the secular courts] was extended ultimately to the point where the death penalty was not applied to one convicted of felony unless by statute that offense had been declared to be without benefit of clergy. Hence, . . . it is better to define felony . . . in terms of an offense punishable by forfeiture." Perkins & Boyce, supra at 14. See also **misprision of felony.**

FELONY, MISPRISION OF see **misprision of felony.**

FELONY MURDER an unlawful **homicide** that occurs in the commission or **attempted** commission of a **felony,** which is considered first degree **murder** by operation of this doctrine. In many modern statutes, only homicides that occur in the course of certain specified felonies are "felony murders." See N.J.S.A. 2C:11-3 (3). The evil mind or **malice** that is necessary to find someone **guilty** of murder is implied or imputed from the actor's intent to commit a felony. See 383 F. 2d 421, 426. For example, if someone burned down a warehouse and thereby committed **arson,** which resulted in the death of a person in the building, the arsonist is guilty of first degree murder ("felony murder") even if he did not know of the presence of the person and he had taken special precautions to try to avoid any loss of life. The harshness of this doctrine has led to a limitation of its use except against the person who actually committed the underlying felony. See Model Penal Code §§210.1 et seq.

FENCE a structure erected in order to enclose **real property.** A fence may be used to determine a boundary for purposes of **trespass.**

In criminal law, an individual who receives stolen property and resells it for profit. A "fence" commits the crime of **receiving stolen property.** Model Penal Code §223.6.

FEOFFMENT the name given at common law to the means of conveying title to freehold estates, which required the **livery of seisin** or other corporeal **hereditaments.** At the site of the land and in the presence of neighboring **tenants,** the **vendor** would point out the boundaries to the purchase and hand over to the vendee the appropriate symbol of seisin. 3 N.H. 234, 260. The method was used until the use of the written deed came to be prescribed by statute. See **enfeoff.**

FERAE NATURAE (*fĕr'-ī nä-tûr'-ī*)—Lat: wild beasts of nature. "Ferae naturae" are wild animals, that is to say, animals of natural disposition and character in that their nature, unlike that of domestic animals, is untamed.

FERTILE OCTOGENARIAN a legal fiction which means that, for the purposes of the **Rule Against Perpetuities,** a woman in her eighties can conceive and give birth. "For the purpose of the rule against perpetuities every living person is conclusively presumed capable of having children as long as he lives." Smith, and Boyer, Survey to the Law of Real Property 119 (2d ed. 1971). Thus, even though it may be biologically impossible for one to reproduce, for the purposes of the rule this is not so. The impact of this fiction under the rule against perpetuities has been modified by statute in many jurisdictions today.

FEUDALISM a system of government and a means of holding property in England and Western Europe that grew out of the chaos of the dark ages. Through a ceremony, called **homage,** in which mutual duties of support and protection were promised, the "vassal" in effect gave his land to the "lord" and the lord then had a duty to protect it and the vassal. Though the vassal thenceforth owned no land, he held the land of the lord as a **tenant** and retained a **use** in that land. The land which the vassal held was called his feud, fief, or feudum. The relationship between the lord and his vassals could become more indirect by the process of **subinfeudation,** so that theoretically there could be placed between the lord and his vassal any number of persons at different levels, each serving as a link in the chain of relations between the lord at the top and the least of the vassals. Eventually, the king became the ultimate lord over all, and all land in England was held of him. Only in England was feudalism the sole method of holding land, although it was the general method elsewhere in Western Europe. See Cribbet, Principles of the Law of Property 27-29 (2d ed. 1975).

The fedual land holding system influenced all of the early common law concerning real property, and despite the fact that the feudal system never existed in the United States, it has played a vital role in shaping modern land law. Id. at 37.

FIAT JUSTITIA (*fē'-ät jūs-tǐ'-shē-à*)—Lat: let justice be done.

F.I.C.A. [FEDERAL INSURANCE CONTRIBUTION ACT] this Act imposes a tax on employees and employers that is used to fund the Social Security system. I.R.C. §3101 et seq.

FICTION, LEGAL see **legal fiction.**

FIDUCIARY a person having a **legal duty,** created by his undertaking, to act primarily for the benefit of another in matters connected with his undertaking, 34 N.E. 2d 68, 70; in the nature of a position of trust or holding confidence. For example, a **trustee** has fiduciary obligations to the beneficiary of the **trust** and acts as a fiduciary in his management of the trust property. An attorney has a fiduciary relationship with a client, etc.

FIERI FACIAS (*fēě'-rē fä'-shē-ăs*)—Lat: that you cause to be made; a common law writ to enforce the collection of a claim that has gone to judgment and has become final. 22 So. 384, 385. By this early English writ, a creditor with judgment was, in effect, ordering the sheriff to enforce against the debtor by seizure and sale of the debtor's personal property to the extent necessary to satisfy the judgment. 185 F. Supp. 867, 870. At common law, the real property of the debtor could not be sold at execution. See 259 N.W. 871, 873. Today, the law of execution is for the most part statutory, and most state laws provide for a single writ for the enforcement of judgments out of the real and personal property of the debtor. Other common law writs made virtually obsolete by modern statutory provisions include:

ELEGIT (*ē-lē'-jǐt*)—Lat: that he has chosen; a writ resulting in the appraisal and transfer of a debtor's goods to his creditor, and, if necessary to satisfy the judgment, the transfer of an interest in the rents and profits from all (originally only a **moiety**) of his real property. 5 Sandford's Reports 197, 200.

EXTENDI FACIAS (*ěx těn'dī fä'-shē-ăs*)—Lat: you cause to be extended; also known as "extent," a writ calling for the setting off of lands of a debtor for purposes of appraisal as to its sufficiency to satisfy the writ of the creditor. See 33 C.J.S. Executions §403.

LEVARI FACIAS *(lĕ-vä'-rī fā'-shē-ăs)*—Lat: a writ authorizing enforcement of a judgment out of both the debtor's goods and the profits and rents of his land. 6 Watts & S. (Pa.) 483, 484.

FIFO see **first-in, first-out.**

FIFTEENTH AMENDEMENT the amendment to the United States Constitution, ratified in 1870, which guarantees each citizen the right to vote, regardless of race, color, or previous condition of servitude.

FIFTH AMENDMENT the amendment to the U.S. Constitution, part of the Bill of Rights, that establishes certain protections for citizens from actions of the government by providing (1) that a person shall not be required to answer for a capital or other **infamous crime** unless an **indictment** or **presentment** is first issued by a grand **jury,** (2) that no person will be placed in **double jeopardy,** (3) that no person may be required to testify against himself, (4) that neither life, liberty nor property may be taken without **due process of law,** and (5) that private property may not be taken for public use, without payment of just compensation.

FIGHTING WORDS "those which by their very utterance inflict injury or tend to incite an immediate **breach** of the peace." 315 U.S. 568, 572. The utterance of fighting words is not protected by the First Amendment guarantee of free speech. Id. Later cases support the view that it is not merely the words themselves, but the context in which they are uttered that qualify them as "fighting words," and there is often a further requirement that the words be spoken with intent to have the effect of inciting

the hearer to an immediate breach of the peace. 266 A. 2d 579, 584.

In tort law one who uses fighting words towards another, and who thereby creates reasonable apprehension in that person, may be guilty of an **assault** despite the doctrine that words alone do not constitute an assault. See generally Prosser, Torts 40 (4th ed. 1971). See also **defamation; slander.**

FIGURE see **public figure.**

FILIBUSTER see **cloture** [FILIBUSTER].

FILING see **return** [FILING].

FINAL DECISION decision that settles the rights of **parties** respecting the subject-matter of the **suit** unless it is **reversed** or set aside. 291 N.W. 118, 121. It ends the **litigation** on the **merits** and leaves nothing for the court to do but execute the **judgment.** 183 F. 2d 29, 31. 403 F. 2d 674, 678. The expression is equivalent to **final decree** or **final judgment.** 150 F. 32, 34. Compare **interlocutory.**

FINAL DECREE see **decree.**

FINAL HEARING see **hearing.**

FINAL JUDGMENT the decision of a trial court which prevents the relitigation of a matter. The finality of a judgment may be overturned on appeal, and the matter is then returned to the trial court for redetermination. James and Hazard, Civil Procedure §11.4 (2d ed. 1977).

FINAL ORDER see **order.**

FINANCE CHARGES any charge for an extension of credit. Under the federal **Truth in Lending Act,** finance charges specifically include interest; service or carrying charges; loan fees or finders' fees; fees for credit investigations; and charges protecting the creditor against the default. Finance charges are also subject to state prohibitions against **usury.**

FINANCIAL INTERMEDIARY an institution or organization such as a bank that brings together lenders (in the form of depositors) and borrowers. Other examples include savings and loan associations, credit unions, **real estate investment trusts** (REITs), and various kinds of finance companies.

FINANCIAL RESPONSIBILITY LAWS see **assigned risk.**

FINANCIAL STATEMENT see **balance sheet; income statement.**

FINDER OF FACT see **fact-finder.**

FINDER'S FEE a fee or commission paid to an individual or organization for "finding" what that party needs or desires; it is not dependent on whether the party ultimately consummates a transaction. 566 P. 2d 449, 453. In **merger** activities, the finder either locates a buyer when the client company wants to sell out or locates a seller when the client company is looking for acquisitions. In real estate activities, finder's fees are paid for locating property, for obtaining mortgage loans, and for referring buyers, sellers, and mortgage loans.

FINDING decisions of a court on **issues** of fact or law. The purpose of it is to answer questions raised by the **pleadings** or charges. It is designed to facilitate review by disclosing the grounds on which the **judgment** rests. See 2 Cal. Rptr. 719, 721.

FINDING OF FACT factual determinations made by the trier of fact (court or jury) or an administrative body based upon the evidence which has been presented to it. If the case is presented to a jury, the jury makes the finding of facts. Otherwise, the judge or administrative officer will make the findings of fact. When the jury returns a general **verdict** ("we find for the plaintiff" or "not guilty") the factual basis of the jury's verdict will not be known and may not easily be ascertained unless there was only one issue of fact in the case. When the jury returns a special verdict, it answers specific factual questions which have been presented to it.

Under Fed. R. Civ. Proc. 52(d), an appellate court can only set aside a finding of fact made by a trial judge if it determines that the finding is **clearly erroneous,** i.e., that reasonable men could not possibly make such a finding. 265 F. 2d 463.

FINDING OF LAW a determination of the court as to the application of a rule of law to particular facts. Also referred to as a CONCLUSION OF LAW.

FINE a sum of money imposed upon a defendant as a penalty for an act of wrongdoing. The fine is payable to the public treasury as opposed to **restitution** which is payable to the **victim** of the wrongdoing. Modern statutes favor restitution over fines and sometimes provide that courts may not impose a fine if its satisfaction would interfere with the making of restitution. See Model Penal Code §7.02(3)(b). Since an individual may no longer be imprisoned for debt, the courts must make a determination as to a defendant's ability to make prompt or installment payment of a fine before imposing same. 450 U.S. 261. The familiar "$30 or 30 days" sentence has been held to violate **equal protection.** 401 U.S. 395; 399 U.S. 235, 243.

FIRM OFFER an **offer** which is irrevocable for a period of time. At common law the mere fact that an offer stated that it would remain open for a definite period of time did not make it so since the promise not to revoke was generally not supported by **consideration** and was hence unenforceable. 109 A. 2d 793; Corbin, Contracts §38 (1952). The Uniform Commercial Code introduced a statutory basis to enforce firm offers in the sale of **goods**. The offer must be in writing, state that it is to remain open for a reasonable period of time (not more than three months), and if part of a form supplied by the offeree must be separately signed by the offeror. U.C.C. §2-205. Even if the specific requirements of the U.C.C. are not met, an offer reasonably expected to induce another to act will be binding as an **option** contract to the extent necessary to avoid injustice. Restatement (Second), Contracts §89(b)(2).

The courts have also recognized valid firm offers that create option contracts as to real estate transactions. To be enforceable, the firm offer must be in writing, for an option for a reasonable period of time on fair terms, and must state a separate purported consideration for the option itself. The failure to actually pay the separate consideration to support the option is immaterial. Restatement (Second), Contracts §87(1)(a).

FIRST AMENDMENT the first of the ten amendments added to the federal Constitution in 1791 by the Bill of Rights. While originally intended to limit the power of the federal government, the various rights of political and religious freedom articulated in this amendment have been held applicable to the states through the due process clause of the **Fourteenth Amendment.** Thus, the freedoms of speech, press, assembly, petition, free exercise of religion, and nonestablishment of religion, were, one by one, incorporated into the due process clause of the Fourteenth Amendment, beginning in 1927 through 1947. Tribe, Constitutional Law 567-568 (1978). Although freedom of **association** is not specifically mentioned in the text of the First Amendment, it has been recognized as at least a derivative safeguard of an individual's rights of speech and assembly when exer-

cised in a group. 357 U.S. 449.

The First Amendment has been the basis for a constitutional theory categorizing a number of its rights as PREFERRED RIGHTS subject to special constitutional protection. 319 U.S. 105, 115. Some of the more recent areas of litigation arising under the First Amendment include the use of prayer in the public schools, censorship of the press in military and national security affairs, the right of professionals to advertise, and the right of communities to regulate obscene materials. See **freedom.**

FIRST-DEGREE see **murder** [FIRST-DEGREE MURDER]; **principal** [PRINCIPAL IN THE FIRST DEGREE].

FIRST-DEGREE MURDER see **murder** [FIRST-DEGREE MURDER].

FIRST DEVISEE the first person who is to receive an **estate devised** by **will.** "Next devisee" refers to those who will receive the **remainder** in **tail.** 5 N.J.L. 689, 709-10. See **fee tail.**

FIRST IMPRESSION first discussion or consideration; refers to the first time a question of law is considered for determination by a court. A case is one of "first impression" when it presents a **question of law** that was never before considered by any court, and thus is not influenced by the doctrine of **stare decisis.**

FIRST-IN, FIRST-OUT [FIFO] see **inventory.**

FISC the treasury of a political entity.

FISCAL of or pertaining to the public finance and financial transactions. See 14 So. 2d 19, 26. Belonging to the public treasury (called the FISC).

FISCAL POLICY the use of public finance and financial transactions to achieve desired economic goals. Taxing and spending power are used along with monetary policy to arrest and reverse declines in business activity. By cutting taxes, more money is left in the hands of consumers and businessmen which increases their spendable income. The government can act more directly on the economy by increasing purchases from the private sector and by pursuing public works projects. Taken together, tax cuts, increased government spending and "easy money" provide powerful and effective stimulation to the economy.

FISCAL YEAR any twelve-month period used by government or business as its fiscal accounting period. 291 A. 2d 336, 337. Such accounting period, may, for example, run from July 1 of one year through June 30 of the next year. See **taxable year** [FISCAL YEAR].

FIT see **unfit.**

FITNESS see **warranty** [WARRANTY OF FITNESS].

FIXED ASSETS see **assets** [FIXED ASSETS], **balance sheet.**

FIXED CAPITAL the amount of capital permanently invested in a business.

FIXED INCOME income that does not change. For instance, bonds paying interest at a specified rate that does not change are fixed-income securities.

FIXED INVESTMENT TRUST see **nondiscretionary trust.**

FIXED SALARY a salary that is set at a dollar amount, and does not increase or decrease as a result of certain events occurring or not occurring, such as a level of business being done by the employer.

FIXING, PRICE see **price fixing.**

FIXTURE something which was once a chattel but has become physically attached to **real property** such that its removal would damage the property; it is thus considered a part of the realty. 35 Am. Jur. 2d Fixtures §§1-2. A lighting fixture will not be a fixture in the legal sense if it can easily be removed; area carpets are not fixtures but wall to wall carpeting may be. A built-in bookcase or a furnace will almost always be considered a fixture.

TRADE FIXTURE an article that a tenant has annexed to the leased premises to aid him in a business conducted thereon. Leases often expressly permit (or require) removal at the end of the term with a payment for any damage sustained, or make other provision for restoring the premises to their original condition.

FLIGHT any leaving or self-concealment to avoid **arrest** or **prosecution** after arrest; 184 A. 2d 321, 324; the act of leaving the scene of the crime, done by one who feels **guilt**, in order to avoid arrest. See also **abscond**; **fugitive from justice.**

FLOAT refers to checks that are in transit between banks and that have not yet been paid; checks in the process of collection, which, when entered in a depositor's account, remain conditional credits until the checks are paid to the bank in money; also refers to the practice of writing a check with insufficient funds and then covering the check before it returns to the bank for payment. 15 B.R. 937, 941.

FLOATING DEBT any short-term obligation of a business, such as bank loans due in one year and **commercial paper.** Government floating debt consists of **treasury bills** and short-term **treasury notes.** Long-term debt is referred to as FUNDED DEBT.

F.O.B. see **Free on Board.**

F.O.I.A see **Freedom of Information Act.**

FOOD AND DRUG ADMINISTRATION [F.D.A] an administrative

agency regulating the safety and quality of foodstuffs, pharmaceuticals, cosmetics, and medical devices. Its activities presently include (1) establishing mandatory standards of identity, quantity and quality of food; (2) safety regulation of additives to food, drugs, and cosmetics; (3) ensuring that drugs, foods, cosmetics, and devices are fairly packaged and labeled and not adulterated or mishandled. The F.D.A. is a part of the Department of Health and Human Services and is, thus, not an independent regulatory commission. The federal Food, Drug, and Cosmetic Act covers products that are prepared for interstate commerce, and applies until the ultimate sale to the consumer. The remedies available to the F.D.A. are seizure of adulterated goods, criminal prosecution, and injunction. See 21 U.S.C. §§301 et seq.

FORBEAR to refrain from doing an act. See **forbearance.**

FORBEARANCE act of declining, usually for a period of time, to enforce a legal right. For purposes of the law of **usury,** the term is often used to refer to a contractual obligation of a creditor to refrain for a specific period from enforcing or claiming a debt that has already become payable, 210 N.W. 2d 550, 561; such forbearance is in substance a loan for which a creditor may impose a charge. In contract law, forbearance of a valid claim, if bargained for, constitutes **consideration.** Corbin, Contracts §132 (one volume ed. 1952).

FORCE physical acts or the threat of physical acts intentionally used to do an act or to commit a crime.

DEADLY FORCE in criminal law, force which is intended or is likely to cause death or great bodily harm. The doctrine of **self-defense** justifies the use of deadly force only to repel deadly force. See **self-defense.**

UNLAWFUL FORCE In the law of torts, the use of force without the consent of the person against whom it is directed, for which the user may be liable. See **battery.** Prosser, Torts §9 p. 36 (4th ed. 1971).

FORCED HEIRS persons who cannot be disinherited, such as a person's spouse or children. In the United States, a spouse may elect to take a share of a decedent's **estate,** usually one-third, instead of taking what the decedent has given the spouse under a last **will** and testament. Civil law countries such as France and Switzerland have forced heirship laws under which members of a person's family, including children, are entitled to **inherit** a certain portion of the estate, regardless of the person's wishes as expressed in a last will and testament.

FORCED SALE see **sale.**

FORCIBLE DETAINER 1. **detainer** by the use of **force** or the show of force. See **forcible entry.** 2. a summary action based on a statutory right to obtain possession of premises by one entitled to actual possession. 444 P. 2d 521.

FORCIBLE ENTRY entry on **real property** in the **possession** of another, against his will and without authority of law, by actual force, or with such an array of force and apparent intent to employ it for the purpose of overcoming resistance that occupant, in yielding and permitting possession to be taken from him, must be regarded as acting from a well-founded fear that resistance would be perilous or unavailing. 193 S.W. 2d 643, 644. In many states a mere **trespass** without any force will be considered "forcible" and a simple refusal to surrender possession after a lawful demand will constitute a "forcible **detainer.**" See 198 P. 646.

FORCIBLE ENTRY AND DETAINER after a forcible entry and detainer the aggrieved party is entitled to bring "a **summary** statutory **proceeding** for restoring to the **possession** of land one who is wrongfully kept out or has been wrongfully deprived of the possession, in the particular cases mentioned in the statute. It is a possessory action only and it usually arises where one's possession has been forcibly invaded between **landlord** and **lessee, vendor** and **vendee,** or the purchaser at a **judicial sale** and a party to the judicial proceeding. The question of **title** cannot be tried, but only the right to possession." 100 N.E. 520, 521. Its purpose is "to protect the actual possession of **real estate** against unlawful and forcible invasion, to remove occasion for actual violence in defending such possession, and to punish **breaches** of the peace committed in the entry upon the detainer of **real property.**" 17 N.Y.S. 522, 523. Compare **try title.**

.**FORECLOSURE** generally, the cutting off or termination of a right to **property;** specifically, an **equitable** action to compel payment of a **mortgage** or other **debt** secured by a **lien.** As to **real property,** it is precipitated by non-payment of the debt, and leads to the selling of the property to which the mortgage or lien is attached in order to satisfy that debt. As a consequence, the mortgagor's **equity of redemption** is irrevocably destroyed subject to any statutory redemption rights which may survive for a limited time in some jurisdictions. A **security interest** in **personal property** can also be foreclosed by a **judicial sale** of the **collateral.** See U.C.C. §9-501.

FOREMAN [FOREPERSON] OF JURY the presiding member of the jury and the person who speaks on the jury's behalf when communicating with the court or in rendering the jury's verdict. Normally the individual selected first or seated in the number one position in the jury box is designated the foreperson.

FORENSIC belonging to the courts of justice. The word indicates the application of a particular subject to the law. For example, FORENSIC MEDICINE is a branch of science that employs medical technology to assist in solving legal problems.

FORESEEABILITY a concept used in various areas of the law to limit **liability** of a party for the consequences of his acts to consequences that are within the scope of a FORESEEABLE RISK, i.e., risks whose consequences a person of ordinary prudence would reasonably expect might occur.

In a contract setting, a party's liability for consequential or special **damages** is limited, under the *Hadley* v. *Baxendale* rule, to damages arising from the foreseeable consequences of his breach. See Calamari and Perillo, Contracts, §14.5 (2d ed. 1977). Compare U.C.C. §2-715(2)(a).

In tort law, in most cases, a party's actions may be deemed **negligent** only where the injurious consequences of those actions were "foreseeable." See 73 S.W. 2d 626, 628.

FORFEITURE the permanent loss of **property** for failure to comply with the **law;** the **divestiture** of the **title** to **property** to the sovereign power without compensation, as a result of a **default** or an offense. 294 F. Supp. 176, 178; aff'd 394 U.S. 456. A right of a **vested interest** can be forfeited in one of two ways: (1) **common law** or judicial forfeiture where the defendant suffers in an action **in personam,** and (2) a legislative or statutory **in rem** forfeiture against the property itself. 235 A. 2d 247, aff'd 246 A. 2d 476. If the holder of a **life estate** commits **waste** according to judicial determination, he forfeits his **estate.** Restatement of Property §199(d) (1936). Under early law, as a punishment for a crime, the **property** of the convicted individual was extinguished when forfeited to the lord or king. 40 A.L.R. 1275; Moynihan, Introduction to the Law of Real Property 21 (1962).

While the terms forfeiture and penalty are often used interchangeably, the generic term "penalty" includes a forfeiture; forfeiture in its strict sense relates to a loss of real or personal property, while a penalty most often relates to money. 91 S.W. 419. It differs from **escheat** in feudal law because the whole **fee escheated,** whereas any part of an interest can be forfeited.

The federal **Racketeer Influenced and Corrupt Organizations Act [RICO]** (18 U.S.C. §1961) provides that whoever violates the act shall, in addition to a **fine** or **imprisonment,** forfeit directly (as part of a criminal prosecution rather than a separate **in rem** proceeding) any interest in any enterprise which he has participated in in violation of the Act. 18 U.S.C. §1963. For example, forfeiture of ownership of a motel can be warranted where the defendant operated the motel as a place of prostitution and corrupted local officials to maintain his business. 667 F. 2d 1182.

FORGERY fraudulent making or altering of a writing with the intent to prejudice the rights of another, 167 N.E. 101, 104; making of a false **instrument** or the passing of an instrument known to be false, 72 P. 2d 656, 660; the false making or material altering, with intent to defraud, of any writing which, if genuine, might apparently be of legal efficacy or the foundation of a legal liability. 97 P. 2d 779, 785. See generally Model Penal Code §224.

The fabrication or **counterfeiting** of **evidence;** the artful and fraudulent manipulation of physical objects, or the deceitful arrangement of genuine facts or things, in such a manner as to create an erroneous impression or a false inference in the minds of those who may observe them. 466 F. 2d 748, 752. See Model Penal Code §241.7.

FORM model of a document containing the phrases and **words of art** that are needed to make the document technically correct for **procedural** purposes as opposed to the elements necessary to meet substantive requirements. Forms are used by lawyers in drafting legal documents.

FORMAL CONTRACT see **sealed instrument.**

FORMA PAUPERIS see **in forma pauperis.**

FORMS OF ACTION technical categories of personal actions developed at **common law,** containing the entire course of legal proceedings particular to those actions. The forms of actions are no longer required, but they continue to affect modern civil procedure and **tort law.**

Forms of action consisted of proceedings for recovery of debts, and recovery of money damages resulting from **breach of contract,** or injury to one's person, property or relations. The forms can be classified as (a) actions in form **ex contractu,** including **assumpsit, covenant,** debt and account; and (b) actions in form **ex delicto** (i.e., those not based on contracts) including **trespass, trover, case, detinue** and **replevin.** See Shipman, Handbook of Common-Law Pleading, Chap. 2 (3rd ed. 1923).

"In the early English law, remedies for wrongs were dependent upon the issuance of **writs** to bring the defendant into court. . . . The number of such writs available was very limited and their forms were strictly prescribed; and unless the plaintiff's cause of action could be fitted into the form of some recognized writ he was without a remedy. The result was a highly formal and artificial system of procedure." Prosser, Torts 28 (4th ed. 1971).

FORNICATION generally, sexual intercourse of two unmarried persons of different sexes, which is punished as a **misdemeanor** by statute in some states. 10 A. 727, 731. In some states, it refers to illicit sexual intercourse between a man, whether married or single, and an unmarried woman. See 425 S.W. 2d 183, 188. 175 N.E. 661, 662. In some states, illicit intercourse can be fornication for the party who is not married, and **adultery** for the party who is married. See 23 N.E. 747, 748. It is not a **common law** crime and is not part of modern penal codes. See Model Penal Code §213. Some courts have held that such statutes are unconstitutional as violations of the right to privacy. See, e.g., 381 A. 2d 333, 340. Compare **cohabitation.**

FORUM a court; a place where disputes are heard and decided according to law and justice; a tribunal; a place of **jurisdiction;** place where **remedies** afforded by the law are pursued. See 292 N.W. 584, 586.

A FORUM STATE is one which, through one party's residence, **domicile,** presence, transaction of business, ownership of real estate, commission of a tortious act, or other reasonable relationship, establishes a sufficient **minimum contact** for the court to exercise jurisdiction. Courts may constitutionally deny jurisdiction in cases that do not meet one of the above criteria. James and Hazard, Civil Procedure §§12.14 and 12.29 (2d ed. 1977).

FORUM NON CONVENIENS (fôr'-ūm nōn kôn-vē'-nē-ĕns)—Lat: an inconvenient court. Under this discretionary doctrine, a court which has jurisdiction of a case, may decline to exercise it where there is no substantive reason for the case to be brought there, or where presentation of the case in that court will create a hardship on the **defendants** or on relevant **witnesses** because of its distance from them. The court will not **dismiss** the case under the doctrine unless the **plaintiff** has another **forum** open to him. If the forum is changed due to hardship rather than jurisdiction, the applicable law will usually be that of the state where the case is originally brought. Green, Civil Procedures 67 (2d ed. 1979).

FOUNDATION In **evidence** law, preliminary evidence necessary to establish the admissibility of other evidence. A lawyer will lay a foundation to establish the relevancy of evidence that does not otherwise appear relevant to the matter at hand. McCormick, Evidence, §53 (2d ed. 1972).

Also, an organization whose assets are dedicated to charitable purposes. See **charity.**

FOUNDER one who provides the first **gift** to establish a charitable institution, such as a college. One who organizes or begins an entity.

FOUNDER'S SHARES **shares** in a **corporation** or **company** issued to the organizers and often carrying special privileges.

FOUR CORNERS the doctrine that requires that the meaning of a document be derived from its entire contents as they relate to one another, and not from its individual parts. 361 S.W. 2d 419, 423.

FOURTEENTH AMENDMENT one of the so-called Civil War Amendments to the Constitution ratified in 1868 shortly after the civil war ended which guarantees that all persons born in any state of the United States is a citizen of that state and of the United States and is guaranteed the **privileges and immunities** due to citizens of the United States and to **due process** and **equal protection** of the laws.

The Fourteenth Amendment was originally passed to provide federal protection for the rights of individuals freed from slavery by the **Thirteenth Amendment.** Until 1954, these rights were protected by the doctrine of **separate but equal** under which a system of segregation of blacks from whites arose. In the landmark case of *Brown v. Board of Education*, 347 U.S. 483 (1954), the United States Supreme Court declared that separate but equal violated the constitutional guarantee of equal protection and that integration of public school systems is required. Within the following years, the Supreme Court expanded the concepts of equal protection and due process to any societal function involving state action in order to prevent discrimination against individuals on the grounds of race, sex, religion, or age. In the Civil Rights Act of 1964, Congress passed laws to affirmatively protect the constitutional rights of citizens and to guarantee equal access to public accommodations and facilities and employment opportunities. 42 U.S.C. §§1981 et seq. See **rational basis test.**

The due process clause of the Fourteenth Amendment has been the vehicle for applying nearly all of the specific guarantees in the first ten amendments to **state action** by selectively incorporating these rights into this amendment. Tribe, Constitutional Law §11-2 (1978).

FOURTH AMENDMENT constitutional **amendment** guaranteeing the right of persons to be secure in their homes and property from unreasonable **searches and seizures** and consisting of the following elements: (1) the issuance of a **warrant** upon **oath** or affirmation; (2) upon **probable cause,** as determined by a neutral and detached **magistrate;** and (3) particularly describing the place to be searched and the items or persons to be seized.

The Fourth Amendment is most frequently encountered in cases involving the use of illegally seized evidence, or **fruits of the poisonous tree,** and is applied through the **exclusionary rule.** It was initially incorporated in the **Bill of Rights** to counter the abuses from searches conducted without warrants, with general warrants, or with **writs of assistance** and designed to safeguard the public's legitimate or reasonable expectation of privacy. LaFave, 1 Search and Seizure, §1.1(a) (1978). Such expectations of privacy extend to a person's home (in such areas as use of contraceptives, obscene materials, or marijuana in a private residence), and to lesser extents, to a person's place of business, automobile, or even body. Courts have upheld invasions of a person's body in the areas of compulsory vaccinations, blood tests, rectal and vaginal searches, and surgical removal of a bullet. See Tribe, Constitutional Law §15-9 (1978). See **search warrant.**

FOUR UNITIES see **unities.**

FRANCHISE special privilege which is "conferred by the government upon individuals and which do[es] not belong to the citizens of the country generally, of common right." 93 P. 2d 872, 879. For example, a municipality may grant a "franchise" to a local bus company that will give them the sole authority to operate buses in the municipality for a certain number of years.

ELECTIVE FRANCHISE (sometimes called simply "the franchise") refers to the right of citizens to vote in public elections.

"Franchise" also refers to the right given to a private person or **corporation** to market another's product within a certain area. Thus, gas stations that sell brandname gasoline often operate the station through a franchise granted by the oil company.

FRATRICIDE the murder of one's brother.

FRAUD intentional deception resulting in **injury** to another. Elements of fraud are: a false and material misrepresentation made by one who either knows it is falsity or is ignorant of its truth; the maker's intent that the representation be relied on by the person and in a manner reasonably contemplated; the person's ignorance of the falsity of the representation; the person's rightful or justified reliance; and proximate injury to the person. See 310 F. 2d 262, 267.

It usually consists of a misrepresentation, concealment of nondisclosure of a material fact, or at least misleading conduct, devices, or contrivance. 234 F. Supp. 201, 203. It embraces all the **multifarious** means which human ingenuity can devise to get an advantage over another. It includes all surprise, trick, cunning, dissembling and unfair ways by which another is cheated. At **law,** fraud must be proved, in **equity** it suffices to show facts and circumstances from which it may be presumed. 425 P. 2d 974, 978. See generally Model Penal Code §224. See also **deceit.**

BADGES OF FRAUD see **badges of fraud.**

CONSTRUCTIVE [LEGAL] FRAUD comprises all acts, omissions, and concealments involving **breach** of **equitable** or **legal duty,** trust or confidence and resulting in damage to another, 38 Cal. Rptr. 148, 157; i.e., no **scienter** is required. Thus, the party who makes the misrepresentation need not know that it is false. See 437 S.W. 2d 20, 27.

EXTRINSIC [COLLATERAL] FRAUD fraud that prevents a party from knowing about his rights or **defenses** or from having a fair opportunity of presenting them at a trial, or from fully **litigating** at the trial all the rights or defenses that he was entitled to assert. 468 S.W. 2d 160, 163. It is a ground for equitable **relief** from a **judgment.** See 247 P. 2d 801, 803.

FRAUD IN FACT [POSITIVE FRAUD] actual fraud. Deceit. Concealing something or making a false representation with an evil intent

[scienter] when it causes injury to another. It is used in contrast to CONSTRUCTIVE FRAUD (above) which does not require evil intent. See 144 A. 2d 836, 838.

FRAUD IN LAW fraud that is presumed from circumstances, where the one who commits it need not have any evil intent to commit a fraud; it is a CONSTRUCTIVE FRAUD (above). See 225 N.E. 2d 813, 814 and 109 N.W. 136, 138. For example, if a **debtor's transfer** of **assets** impairs the rights of his **creditors,** then the transfer might be a fraud in law and the **conveyance** could be set aside although the debtor had no intention of prejudicing the creditors' rights.

FRAUD IN THE FACTUM generally arises from a lack of identity or disparity between the **instrument** executed and the one intended to be executed, or from circumstances which go to the question as to whether the instrument ever had any legal existence; as for example, when a blind or illiterate person executes a deed when it has been read falsely to him after he asked to have it read. 5 S.E. 2d 138, 141. Fraud in the factum provides a stronger basis for setting aside an instrument than FRAUD IN THE INDUCEMENT (below).

FRAUD IN THE INDUCEMENT fraud which is intended to and which does cause one to execute an **instrument,** or make an agreement, or render a **judgment.** The misrepresentation involved does not mislead one as to the paper he signs but rather misleads as to the true facts of a situation, and the false impression it causes is a basis of a decision to sign or render a judgment. See 255 N.Y.S. 2d 608, 610. It renders an agreement **voidable.** See 174 N.E. 2d 304, 308.

INTRINSIC FRAUD fraudulent representation that is presented and considered in rendering a **judgment**. 208 S.W. 2d 111, 112. Generally, "intrinsic fraud" is not a sufficient ground for granting **equitable relief** from a judgment. For example, **perjury** is only intrinsic fraud because it does not prevent a completely **adversary proceeding**. It only influences the judgment, so it will not be a ground for equitable relief from a judgment resulting from it. 299 N.W. 108, 109.

FRAUDULENT CONVEYANCE any conveyance made, or presumed to have been made, with the intention to delay or defraud **creditors**, where such intention is known to the party to whom the conveyance is made. It is generally characterized by a lack of fair and valuable **consideration** and is usually made by a debtor to place his **property** beyond the reach of creditors. See **preference** [VOIDABLE PREFERENCE].

FREE ALONGSIDE [F.A.S.] a commercial **delivery** term which signifies that the seller must at his own risk and expense deliver the **goods** to the side of the transporting medium in the usual manner and obtain and **tender** a receipt for the goods in exchange for which the carrier must issue a **bill of lading**. U.C.C. §2-319(2). Compare **Free on Board [F.O.B.]**.

FREE AND CLEAR unincumbered. In property law, a **title** is "free and clear" if it is not incumbered by any **liens;** one conveys land "free and clear" if he transfers a **good** or **marketable title** (i.e. unincumbered by any interest in the land held by another). 53 A. 477, 480.

FREEDOM the state of being free; the absence of restrictions.

FREEDOM OF ASSOCIATION the right to peaceably assemble as guaranteed by the **First Amendment.**

FREEDOM OF EXPRESSION general term referring to the freedom of press, religion, and speech.

FREEDOM OF PRESS the right to publish and circulate one's views, as guaranteed by the First Amendment. 167 A.L.R. 1447. Closely related to FREEDOM OF SPEECH (below). See **open court.**

FREEDOM OF RELIGION see **establishment clause.**

FREEDOM OF SPEECH the right to express one's thoughts without governmental restrictions on the contents thereof, as guaranteed by the First Amendment. 333 U.S. 507.

FREEDOM OF CONTRACT the liberty or ability to enter into agreements with others. "Freedom of contract" is "a basic and fundamental right reserved to the people" by the Fifth and Fourteenth Amendments to the Constitution which prohibit "the deprivation of liberty without due process of law." 32 F. Supp. 964, 987. "Freedom of contract" is subject to legislative regulation in the interests of public health, safety, morals or welfare." 57 A. 2d 421, 423. See also **obligation of a contract.**

FREEDOM OF INFORMATION ACT [F.O.I.A.] a federal law (5 U.S.C. §552) requiring that, with specified exceptions, documents and materials generated or held by federal agencies be made available to the public and establishing guidelines for their disclosure. The primary purpose of the Act is to establish a general policy of full agency disclosure unless information is clearly exempted. 543 F. Supp. 38. See 38 A.L.R. Fed. 701 and 29 A.L.R. Fed. 606.

FREE EXERCISE CLAUSE provision in **First Amendment** to the United States Constitution providing that "Congress shall make no law . . . prohibiting the free exercise" of religion. It is applicable to both the federal and state governments through the due process clause of the Fourteenth Amendment. See 293 U.S. 245. The clause is distinguished from its counterpart, the **"establishment clause,"** in that the free exercise clause guarantees against governmental compulsion in religious matters while the establishment clause insures that the government will maintain neutrality towards religion.

In the exercise of one's religion one cannot insist on conduct which threatens important interests of the society in an unreasonable manner. The courts must, therefore, balance the importance of a religious exercise claim against the state interest involved in a rule or practice which prevents or hinders the exercise. Thus, although the state can prescribe educational standards, it may not require public education (vs. private or sectarian education) of a religious group. A state may not require a person to take an oath requiring a belief in God in order to qualify for public employment. 367 U.S. 488. Nor may a state bar ministers from public office. 435 U.S. 618. See 268 U.S. 510.

On the same reasoning, mandatory education beyond the eighth grade in violation of Amish history of informal education, has been held violative of the right to free exercise. See 406 U.S. 205. But the balance has been struck in favor of laws prohibiting polygamy and bigamy against the challenge that they offend the tenets of the Mormon church, see 136 U.S. 1; and compulsory vaccination or x-ray laws have been sustained against objections by Christian Scientists or others claiming an invasion of their religious principles. See 197 U.S. 11. The clause has not been so broadly interpreted as to allow the practice of all religions or the practice of all aspects of a particular religion in **prisons** due to difficulties in supervision in such an institutional setting. 479 F. Supp. 1311.

FREEHOLD an estate in **fee** or a **life estate.**

FREEHOLD ESTATE **estate** or **interest** in **real property** for life or of uncertain duration, lasting at least as long as the life of the present holder. 144 P. 457, 460. It is an "estate of inheritance or for life in either a corporeal or incorporeal **hereditament** existing in or arising from **real property** of free **tenure.**" 33 P. 144, 147. Estates created under the common law could only be conveyed by engaging in the **livery of seisin;** upon assuming title by such livery, the **tenant** [or owner] became **seised** to the land and established ownership. Although a charter of enfeoffment may have recorded the ceremonious livery of seisin, under the common law, initially, no writing was required to transfer a freehold estate.

At **common law,** "freehold" referred to those interests in land which could be associated with one who was considered a free man. "In medieval times the only estates fully recognized by the law and given protection in the King's courts were the freehold estates: the **fee simple,** the **fee tail** and the **life estate.**" Moynihan, Introduction to the Law of Real Property 28 (1962). In the later common law, non-freehold estates (**copyholds**) such as estates for a term of years were given protection through the development of the action for ejectment through which the **tenant for years** could recover **possession** of his property. Id. at 64.

FREE ON BOARD [F.O.B.] a commercial term that signifies a contractual agreement between a buyer and a seller to have the subject of a sale delivered to a designated place, usually either the "place of shipment" or the "place of destination," without expense to the buyer. Thus a shipment "f.o.b. shipping point" requires the seller to bear the expense and the risk of putting the subject of the sale into the possession of the carrier, but the **duty** to pay the transportation charges from the f.o.b. point is on the buyer. 334 P. 2d 808, 814. Where the shipment is "f.o.b. destination point," the seller is required to bear the transportation charges and the risk of transport until the buyer point of destination. U.C.C. §2-319. The term is not merely a pricing agreement as to who shall bear the cost of transportation but is also a "delivery term" designating where **title** and **risk of loss** shall pass. An f.o.b. contract that does not designate any point of delivery is commonly held to be an f.o.b. shipping point agreement. When in addition to designating a delivery point, the agreement specifies a vessel, car or other vehicle, the seller must also load the goods aboard said vessel, car, or other vehicle at his own expense. U.C.C. §2-319(1)(c). Compare **Free Alongside [F.A.S.]**.

FREIGHT FORWARDER a shipper who accepts small shipments, consolidates them into larger shipments, and takes responsibility for their safe arrival at their point of destination. 475 F. 2d 1086, 1090.

FRESH PURSUIT in criminal law, "the **common law** right of a police officer to cross jurisdictional lines in order to arrest a felon." 112 N.W. 2d 693, 697. Also refers to the power of a police officer to make an arrest without a **warrant** when he is in immediate pursuit of a criminal. 11 So. 632.

FRIENDLY SUIT an action brought by agreement between the **parties** in order to obtain a **judgment** which will have a binding effect in circumstances where a mere agreement or settlement will not. For example, the friendly suit is employed to settle a claim concerning an infant, since the infant cannot effectively **release** the claim by **contract**, the entry of a judgment will bind him. The friendly suit is

usually brought without formal **process** but the court will demand some kind of proof (often **affidavits** are sufficient) that the settlement is a just and fair one. Suits that are **"collusive,"** that is, those wherein the parties purport to have a controversy but do not, or where they agree to certain facts in order to obtain a particular legal result (as in divorce cases), will be **dismissed.** Compare **adversary proceeding; controversy; declaratory judgment.**

FRIEND, NEXT see **next friends.**

FRIEND OF THE COURT see **amicus curiae.**

FRINGE BENEFIT see **benefit** [FRINGE BENEFIT].

FRISK quick, superficial search. It is "a contact or patting of the outer clothing "to detect, by the sense of touch, if a concealed weapon is being carried." 235 A. 2d 235, 239. See **stop and frisk.**

FRIVOLOUS clearly lacking in substance; clearly insufficient as a matter of law, 185 N.E. 2d 583, 593; presenting no debatable question. 227 F. Supp. 735, 740. For example, a **claim** is "frivolous" if it clearly appears either that it is insufficient because it is not supported by the facts or that it is one for which the law recognizes no remedy. An appeal is frivolous if it presents no **justiciable** question or merit. "If a court of appeals shall determine that an appeal is frivolous, it may award . . . damages. . . ." Fed. App. R. 38.

FRONT-END LOAD PLAN a contractual agreement to buy **mutual fund** shares through periodic payments, usually monthly, in which the sales commission and other expenses, called "load," are taken out of the initial payments.

FRUCTUS INDUSTRIALES (*frŭk'tŭs in-dŭs-trĭ-ā'lēz*)—Lat: the produce of a land resulting from manual labor, such as crops. 182 A. 2d 60, 61.

FRUCTUS NATURALES *(fruk'tus na-tu-rā'lez)*—Lat: the produce of land which grows naturally, such as timber. 182 A. 2d 60, 61.

FRUIT OF THE POISONOUS TREE DOCTRINE under this rule evidence which is the direct result or immediate product of illegal conduct on the part of an official is inadmissible in a criminal trial against the victim of the conduct (or other person with **standing**) under the **due process** clause of the Fourteenth Amendment. See 371 U.S. 471. An exception has been made in that such evidence may be used to impeach the **testimony** of a defendant who takes the stand in his own defense. See 401 U.S. 222. This rule does not apply to evidence resulting from illegal conduct by private persons unless there has been some complicity on the part of the state. See 256 U.S. 465. Several state courts do exclude evidence obtained through unreasonable private-party searches. 485 P. 2d 47. Also, if evidence is acquired in a way sufficiently distinct from the original illegal activity, it may be used if the taint has dissipated. Thus, where the defendant has been illegally arrested, then released, then sometime thereafter returns to confess, his confession has been held admissible. See 371 U.S. 971.

The doctrine draws its name from the idea that once the tree is poisoned (the primary evidence is illegally obtained) then the fruit of the tree (any secondary evidence) is likewise poisoned or tainted and may also not be used. "Evidence obtained by independent means, not search-connected to the poisonous tree, and otherwise admissible, may, however, still be used, although the burden of showing nontaint is upon the proponent [the government]." Forkosch, Constitutional Law 479 (1969).

FRUITS OF CRIME the results of a criminal act.

FRUSTRATION [OF PURPOSE] occurs in contract law when an implied **condition** of an agreement does not occur or ceases to exist without fault of either party, and the absence of the implied condition "frustrates" one party's intentions in making the agreement. It may be a basis for terminating or **rescinding** an agreement if there has been no previous **breach** of the agreement and if there has been no specific **warranty** that the condition would continue to exist or would occur. 127 P. 2d 1027, 1028. The concept is also termed COMMERCIAL FRUSTRATION. See also U.C.C. §2-615. Compare **impossibility**.

F.T.C. see **Federal Trade Commission [F.T.C.]**.

FUGITIVE FROM JUSTICE "one who commits a **crime** within a state, and then withdraws himself from that state without waiting to abide the consequences of the crime he there committed," 270 S.W. 2d 39, 42; also one who conceals himself within the state in order to avoid its **process**; is applicable even to those who leave the state for another purpose. 255 U.S. 52. The fugitive status will toll the **statute of limitations. See flight; long-arm statute.**

FULL FAITH AND CREDIT federal constitutional requirement that the "public Acts, Records, and judicial Proceedings" of one state be respected by each of the sister states. Art. 4, §1. Thus it has been said that "if a **judgment** is conclusive in the state where it was pronounced, it is equally conclusive everywhere in the courts of the United States." 72 U.S. 290, 302. Not even a claim of fraud will be a sufficient basis to challenge the judgment of a sister state—at least not beyond that permitted by the original **forum** itself. Id.; 356 U.S. 604. The sister state's judgment may be challenged in the second state, however, if proper **jurisdiction** was lacking in the sister state which rendered the judgment. 325 U.S. 226. But the "judgment is entitled to full faith and credit—even as to questions of jurisdiction—when the second court's inquiry discloses that those questions have been fully and fairly **litigated** and finally decided in the court which rendered the original judgment." 375 U.S. 106, 111.

Full faith and credit does not apply to foreign judgments where principles of **comity** operate instead.

FUND an amount of money that may be available either for general uses or purposes or that may be dedicated to a specific use or purpose; to pay such an amount.

FUND IN COURT an amount deposited in court because parties are contesting title to it or so that money will be available to pay a liability that is contingent.

GENERAL FUND a fund that is not dedicated to a specific purpose but that may be used to pay any debt or liability.

HEDGE FUND see **hedge fund.**

INDEX FUND see **index fund.**

MUTUAL FUND see **mutual fund.**

SINKING FUND in finance, a bond issue under the terms of which the issuer is obligated to repurchase a portion of the bonds each year until all of the bonds have been repurchased, rather than to redeem all of the bonds at the end of the term of the issue.

TRUST FUND see **trust fund.**

FUNDED DEBT see **floating debt.**

FUNGIBLE a term applied to **goods** that are interchangeable or capable of substitution by nature or agreement. U.C.C. §1-201(17). Oil, grain and coal are examples of naturally fungible goods. When storing fungible goods, warehousemen are exempt from the legal requirement of keeping stored goods from one depositor separate from the goods of another. 63 A. 2d 262, 265; U.C.C. §7-207. **Securities** of the same issue are considered fungible; hence a person obligated to deliver securities may deliver any security of the specified issue. U.C.C. §8-107(1).

FUTURE ESTATE see **estate.**

FUTURE INTEREST an **interest** in presently existing **real** or **personal property,** or in a **gift** or **trust,** which may commence in **use, possession,** and/or enjoyment at a time in the future. 213 F. 2d 520, 521, 145 So. 2d 455, 462. A **legatee** to receive an annual income upon reaching the age of twenty-one has a "future interest" which, when that age is reached will ripen into a "present interest." Future interests may constitute either a **vested** or a **contingent estate.** 138 F. 2d 254, 257. Compare **remainder.**

FUTURES agreements whereby one person agrees to sell a commodity at a certain time in the future for a certain price. The buyer agrees to pay that price, knowing that the person will have nothing to deliver at the time. Instead, the buyer understands that at the delivery date, he will pay the seller the difference between the market value of that commodity and the price agreed upon if the commodity's value declines; if its value advances, the seller is to pay to the buyer the difference between the agreed-upon price and the market price. See 58 S.E. 401, 410; 14 R.I. 131, 138. Essentially, if the price of the commodity rises, the buyer makes a profit, and if the price declines, the buyer suffers a loss.

Formerly, such speculative agreements were generally unenforceable in courts of law as being against public policy because they were a form of gambling. See 26 N.E. 568, 569. Today, futures are traded on commodity futures exchanges. In order to make the transactions legal, the parties must intend to deliver or receive delivery of the commodity, each party being obligated to make delivery or accept delivery of the commodity unless the contract has been **liquidated** by offset on the exchange. If a trader insists on literal satisfaction of his contract rights, it must be fulfilled by conveyance of the physical commodity." 73 Yale L. J. 174 (1963). "Thus, the fundamental principle underlying all commodity exchanges is that a person who buys or sells a futures contract and does not offset it by a contra-transaction on the exchange must receive the commodity or be called upon to deliver it. The fact that most persons who trade on a commodity exchange expect to offset their contracts before the date of delivery or receipt is not a denial of this principle." 311 F. 2d 52, 56.

G

GAG ORDER a court-imposed order to restrict information or comment about a case. The ostensible purpose of such an order is to protect the interests of all parties and preserve the right to a fair trial by curbing publicity likely to prejudice a jury. A gag order cannot be directly imposed on members of the press because this constitutes an impermissible prior restraint and violates the First Amendment. 427 U.S. 539. Also an order to restrain an unruly defendant who is disrupting his criminal trial. 397 U.S. 337.

GAIN see **recognition** [NONRECOGNITION OF GAIN; RECOGNITION OF GAIN].

GAINFUL EMPLOYMENT [OCCUPATION] generally, any employment that is suited to the ability and potentiality of the one em-

ployed. For purposes of disability covered by insurance, it may mean "the ordinary employment of the particular person insured, or such other employment, if any, approximating the same livelihood, as the insured might fairly be expected to follow, in view of his station, circumstances, and physical and mental capabilities." 30 S.E. 2d 879, 883.

GAIN OR LOSS REALIZED see **realization** [GAIN OR LOSS REALIZED].

GAINS OR LOSSES see **capital** [CAPITAL GAINS OR LOSSES].

GAMBLING "a play for value against an uncertain event in the hope of gaining something for value," 283 N.Y.S. 2d 760, 761, whose elements include the "payment of a price for a chance to gain a prize." 310 P. 2d 834, 837. Gambling is illegal in most jurisdictions, although many states permit state-run lotteries. See **aleatory** [ALEATORY CONTRACT].

GAME LAWS laws whose "general aim is to protect from unauthorized pursuit and killing certain birds and animals." 174 S.E. 253. These laws may include outright prohibitions, or may restrict the hunting seasons, classes of animals, or type of weapons used.

GAOL the British and early-American spelling of "jail."

GARAGEMAN'S LIEN see **lien.**

GARNISH to bring a **garnishment** proceeding or to **attach** wages or other property pursuant to such a proceeding.

GARNISHEE a person who receives notice to retain **custody** of **assets** in his control that are owed to or belong to another person until he receives further notice from the court; the garnishee merely holds the assets until legal **proceedings** determine who is entitled to the property. The term thus signifies one on whom process of **garnishment** is served. In a statutory garnishment proceeding the garnishee may be directed to pay over to the **creditor** a portion of the **debtor's** property (often employee's wages). 298 S.W. 2d 785, 787.

GARNISHMENT process in which money or **goods** in the hands of a third person which are due a **defendant,** are attached by the **plaintiff;** e.g., **property** controlled by a third person which is owed to or belongs to a **debtor** is used to repay a debt of the debtor.

It is a statutory remedy that consists of notifying a third party to retain something he has belonging to the defendant (debtor), to make disclosure to the court concerning it, and to dispose of it as the court shall direct. 267 So. 2d 18, 20. Garnishment of wages must be preceded by notice of the action and an opportunity to be heard to comply with due process of law. 395 U.S. 337. Compare **attachment.**

G.A.T.T. General Agreement on Tariffs and Trade. See **tariff.**

GAVELKIND at common law, a form of feudal land ownership that required land to descend to all sons equally. Moynihan, Introduction to the Law of Real Property 15 n. 7 (1962). By the end of the first quarter of the 20th century all land ownership, or **tenure,** was reduced to a single form of common **socage** and peculiar customary tenures such as gavelkind were abolished.

By distributing land to all sons equally, gavelkind **tenure** differed from the English doctrine of **primogeniture** which allowed only the oldest son to inherit. In the United States, **statutes** of **descent and distribution** in each state govern **intestate succession.** These **statutes** generally provide that all children share equally. See **primogeniture** and **descent and distribution.**

GENERAL APPEARANCE see **appearance.**

GENERAL CONTRACTOR see **contractor.**

GENERAL COURTS-MARTIAL see **court-martial; military law** [COURT-MARTIAL].

GENERAL INTENT see **intent.**

GENERAL PARTNERS see **partnership** [GENERAL PARTNERS].

GENERAL POWER see **power of appointment** [GENERAL POWER].

GENERAL WARRANT see **search warrant.**

GENERAL WARRANTY DEED see **warranty deed** [GENERAL WARRANTY DEED].

GENERATION SKIPPING TRANSFER a transfer that passes over one generation in favor of a younger generation. For example, a transfer by a grandfather to a grandchild would constitute a generation skipping transfer since it skips the grandchild's parent. A GENERATION SKIPPING TRUST is a **trust** created in order to make a generation skipping transfer. Certain generation skipping transfers made by a generation skipping trust or its equivalent may avoid the **estate** or the **gift tax,** but are nonetheless subject to the generation skipping transfer tax. I.R.C. §§2601 et seq.

GENERIC general, relating to a group or class of related things; something not specific, not referring to a particular thing. "The term 'generic' has reference to a class of related things. . . . While the term 'specific' is limited to a particular, definite, or precise thing." 2 F. 2d 113, 114.

GENERIC DRUG LAW refers to modern statutes enacted by many states that permit or require pharmacists in certain circumstances to substitute a drug product with the same active ingredients and of the same generic type for the drug prescribed by the physician. See, e.g., Calif. Bus. & P. Code §4047.6.

GERRYMANDER to create a civil division of an unusual shape within a particular locale for improper purpose, as for example, to redistrict a state with unnatural boundaries, isolating members of a particular political party, so that a maximum number of the elected representatives will be of that political party.

If the process creates legislative districts of unequal population, the constitutional rule of "one man-one vote" required by equal protection of the laws is violated. 377 U.S. 533, 581.

GIFT a voluntary transfer of property made without **consideration,** that is, for which no value is received in return. 551 S.W. 2d 823. The essential components of a valid completed gift of personal property are: **competency** of the **donor** to understand the nature of his act; voluntary intent on the part of the donor to make a gift (called DONATIVE INTENT); **delivery** either actual or **symbolic; acceptance,** actual or imputed; complete divestment of all control by the donor; and a lack of **consideration** for the gift. A transfer that constitutes a gift may be of significance in several tax contexts. For example, receipt of a gift is excluded from the **gross income** of the recipient but the transferor may be subject to the **unified estate and gift tax.** I.R.C. §§ 102, 2501 et. seq.

CLASS GIFT see **class gift.**

SPLIT GIFT if one spouse makes a gift, the other spouse may "split" the gift with the first spouse for federal gift tax purposes, so that the gift will be deemed to be made one-half by each spouse. I.R.C. §2513. Splitting gifts allows spouses to take maximum advantage of exclusions, credits, and progressive tax rates for gift tax purposes.

GIFT CAUSA MORTIS see **causa** [CAUSA MORTIS].

GIFT INTER VIVOS see **inter vivos.**

GIFT IN CONTEMPLATION OF DEATH former provisions of federal tax law provided that transfers made within three years of donor's death were deemed to have been made in contemplation of death and thus includible in his gross estate "unless shown to the contrary." The three-year rule has been continued but without reference to contemplation of death and with certain other exclusions. See I.R.C. §2035.

GIFT OVER an estate created upon the expiration of a **preceding estate,** e.g., a gift over to C is established when in default of the exercise of a **power of appointment** by the donee B, the donor A has provided that C take in default, rather than that the property which is the subject matter of the power **revert** to A's estate.

GIFT TAX a tax which is imposed on transfers of property by gift during the transferor's lifetime. While the federal government imposes a gift tax I.R.C. §2501 et seq., most states do not. The federal gift tax is imposed at the same rates as the federal estate tax. I.R.C. §2502(a).

G.N.P. see **Gross National Product [G.N.P.].**

GOING CONCERN VALUE the value attributed to a business entity as an on-going enterprise vs. its simple **book value.** The going concern value reflects the ability of the company's assets to generate a return on investment and incorporates **good will** which may not be included as an aspect of the book value. The going concern value for a profitable enterprise will often be higher than its liquidation value; if the enterprise is not profitable, liquidation may produce a higher value than the continued operation of the business.

GOOD CAUSE substantial or legally sufficient reason for doing something. 319 P. 2d 983, 986. For example, if a statute provides for granting a new **trial** upon a showing of "good cause," such "good cause" might include the existence of fraud, lack of **notice** to **parties,** or new **evidence.** In virtually every situation where it is used, good cause must be considered within the context of a particular case and not by any standardized formula.

GOOD FAITH a total absence of any intention to seek an unfair advantage or to defraud another party; an honest and sincere intention to fulfill one's obligations. In the case of a merchant, good faith refers to honesty in fact and the observance of reasonable commercial standards of fair dealing in the trade. U.C.C. §2-103(1)(b). More generally, the term means "honesty in fact in the conduct or transaction concerned." U.C.C. §1-201(19). In property law, a "good faith" purchaser of land pays the value of the land and has no knowledge or notice of any facts that would cause an ordinary, prudent person to make inquiry concerning the validity of the conveyance. See 220 N.W. 795, 797. See also **bona fide; bona fide purchaser; notice-inquiry.**

GOODS every species of **property** that is not **real estate, choses** in action, or investment **securities** or the like. 380 A. 2d 843, 846. Under the Uniform Commercial Code, "goods refers to all things, (including specially manufactured goods) existing and movable other than the money in which the price is to be paid, investment securities, and things in action. Unborn young of animals and growing crops may be included. U.C.C. §2-105(1)(2). See **chattel.** See also **confusion of goods; consumer goods.**

GOOD TENANTABLE REPAIR as used in a lease, describes the obligation of a tenant to maintain the condition of property which has been rented. Eg. 111 Mass. 531.

GOOD TITLE a **title** free from present **litigation,** obvious defects and grave doubts concerning its validity or merchantability, 227 P. 476, 477; a title valid in fact which is marketable and which can be sold to a reasonable purchaser or **mortgaged** to a person of reasonable prudence as security for a loan of money. In a **contract** to **convey** "good title," the term also means there are no **incumbrances** on the land. 244 P. 424, 425. The term is often said to be synonymous with **marketable title** (174 S.W. 2d 830, 831) and **clear title** (96 S.W. 2d 808). See **recording acts; warranty deed.**

GOOD UNTIL CANCELLED see **order** [GOOD UNTIL CANCELLED].

GOOD WILL an intangible but recognized business asset which is the result of such features of an ongoing enterprise as the production or sale of reputable brand name products, a good relationship with customers and suppliers, and the standing of the business in its community. Good will can become a **balance sheet asset** when a going business is acquired through a purchase transaction in which the price paid exceeds the net asset value (**assets** and **liabilities**). Under current accounting practice, the term good will has been replaced by the terminology "excess of cost of investment in consolidated subsidiaries over net asset value," and the total must be **amortized** over a period not to exceed 40 years.

GOVERNMENT the exercise of authority in the administration of the affairs of a state, community, or society. 110 P. 304, 309; an instrument to preserve an ordered society, 183 So. 759, 764; the authoritative direction and restraint exercised over the actions of men, 41 N.Y.S. 858.

In the United States, the federal and state governments operate under a written constitution from which their sovereignty and authority emanate.

GOVERNMENTAL FUNCTIONS activity done or furnished for general public good, 654 P. 2d 855, 856; "limited to legal duties imposed by state upon its creatures which it may not omit with impunity, but must perform at its peril." 279 P. 2d 472.

When a jurisdiction engages in a governmental function, such as operating a police department, 255 S.E. 2d 48, 49, conducting safety inspections, 304 N.W. 2d 841, 843, suing to enforce public policy as manifested by city ordinances, 309 N.E. 2d 763, 764, or generally is not acting in a proprietary manner it is immune from tort liability for its actions unless a lawsuit is specifically permitted by statute. 253 N.W. 2d 355, 356; Prosser, Torts. 979 (4th ed. 1971). See **sovereign immunity.**

GOVERNMENTAL IMMUNITY doctrine of implied limitation on the power of the federal government to tax a state or any of its instrumentalities, and of the power of any state to tax the federal government or any of its instrumentalities. The doctrine stems from *McCulloch* v. *Maryland,* 4 Wheat 316, and results from the dual governmental nature of our political system. The principle applies only to the taxing relationships between the federal and state governments. 21 A. 2d 228, 229. For instance, a state would not be permitted to tax a federal defense installation because of "governmental immunity." The term may also be used as synonymous with **sovereign immunity.**

GOVERNMENT, MILITARY see **military law** [MILITARY GOVERN-MENT].

GRACE PERIOD in general, any period specified in a **contract** during which payment is permitted, without penalty, beyond the due date of the debt. In the insurance context, it is a span of time after an insurance policy premium was due to be paid, during which the insurance nevertheless remains in force. 404 So. 2d 684, 686. See also **binder.**

GRADED OFFENSE one where an offender is subject to different penalties for various degrees of the offense, according to the terms of a statute. Modern criminal codes rely upon degrees of an offense to distribute sanction ranges according to the danger of harm caused or risked by the actor. See **degree of crime.**

GRAFT the fraudulent obtaining of public money by the corruption of public officials, 199 F. 2d 44, 48; "a dishonest transaction in relation to public or official acts;" also commonly used to "designate an advantage which one person by reason of his peculiar position or superior influence or trust acquires from another." 104 P. 181, 183. See **bribery.**

GRANDFATHER CLAUSE provisions allowing persons, engaged in a certain business before the passage of an act regulating that business, to receive a license or prerogative without meeting all the criteria that new entrants into the field would have to fulfill. For example, The Interstate Commerce Act included a provision requiring the Interstate Commerce Commission to grant a permit upon application authorizing any carrier to operate over all routes on which it or its predecessor in interest were in **bona fide** operation on July 1, 1935. See 355 U.S. 554, 555.

GRAND JURY a body of people (generally 23 in number) drawn, selected, and summoned according to law to serve as a constituent part of a court of criminal **jurisdiction.** The purpose of the body is to investigate and inform on crimes committed within its jurisdiction and to accuse persons of (indict them for) crimes when it has discovered sufficient evidence to warrant holding a person for a trial. See **indictment; jury.**

GRAND LARCENY see **larceny.**

GRANT to give, confer, consent, allow, surrender or transfer something to another with or without compensation; a gift or bestowal of land made by one having control or authority over it, 191 F. Supp. 495, 537; any transfer of **real property.** 299 S.W. 2d 591, 594. Also, generally, to yield or concede, as to grant a request. Compare **convey.**

LAND GRANT a governmental grant to another level of government, a corporation, or an individual, without compensation. Many of the first colleges in the United States were established as land-grant colleges, with the land being donated to the schools by the federal or state governments.

GRANTOR-GRANTEE INDEX see **chain of title.**

GRATIS free; given or performed without reward or **consideration.** 29 S.E. 2d 161.

GRATUITOUS   BAILMENT see **bailment.**

GRATUITOUS PROMISE one by which a person promises to do, or refrain from doing, something without requiring any **consideration** in return. See Calamari & Perillo, Contracts, §4-4 (2d ed. 1977). Such a promise is generally not legally enforceable as a **contract.** Id. See **mutuality.** Compare **illusory promise.**

GRATUITY see **gift.**

GRAVAMEN the material part, substance, or essence of a com-plaint, charge, grievance, cause of action, etc. See 153 P. 2d 990, 991. For example, the gravamen of a complaint alleging that someone struck plaintiff and then went to Los Angeles would be the fact that he struck plaintiff.

GREAT   CHARTER see **Magna Carta [Magna Charta].**

GREAT WRIT see **habeas corpus.**

GREEN CARD a common name for the alien registration card carried by permanent resident aliens in the United States. Permanent resident status is a first step towards becoming a **naturalized citizen.** 689 F. 2d 21, 23.

GRIEVANCE one's allegation that something imposes an illegal obligation or burden, or denies some equitable or legal right, or causes injustice. See 137 P. 400, 402. An employee may be entitled by a collective bargaining agreement to seek relief through a particuler series of steps called a GRIEVANCE PROCEDURE.

GROSS conduct which is willful and flagrant, 264 N.E. 2d 792, 794; out of all measure, beyond allowance, not to be excused, 354 P. 2d 56, 66, as in **gross negligence.**

Consideration, profit or income before charges and deductions, 241 N.E. 2d 209, as in gross **income.** Compare **net income.** See **easement** [EASEMENT IN GROSS].

GROSS ESTATE see **net estate.**

GROSS INCOME see **income.**

GROSS NATIONAL PRODUCT [G.N.P.] the total money measure of a nation's annual production of goods and services. G.N.P. is defined both in terms of factor consumption (goods and services purchased by private citizens and government, gross private investment, and the net foreign trade-investment balance) and in terms of factor earnings (wages, taxes, rents, interest and profits, and **depreciation**). G.N.P. is a gross production measure since no allowance is made for capital consumption; i.e., depreciation is part of G.N.P. Since economists consider G.N.P. to be one of the most important concepts in economic science, the United States and other national governments expend considerable effort in collecting, analyzing, and publishing G.N.P. statistics. Results are reported in both current dollars, including inflation, and constant dollars.

GROSS NEGLIGENCE see **negligence.**

GROUND RENT an **estate of inheritance** in the **rent** of lands, i.e., an inheritable **interest** in and right to the rent collected through the **leasing** of certain lands, 48 A. 636, 637; it is a **freehold** estate, 69 N.E. 658, and as such is subject to **incumberance** by **mortgage** or **judgment (lien, attachment,** etc.). The ground rent is an incorporeal **hereditament** and is therefore an interest distinct from that held by the owner of the property, whose estate is in the land itself and is therefore corporeal. 163 A. 2d 297, 298; 48 A. 636, 637. The term most frequently signifies the long-term rent paid on land upon which office buildings, hotels, and other structures are built, where the owner of the land retains title.

GROWTH STOCK the **stock** of a company which has achieved above-average earnings growth in the past and has good prospects for continued increases in the future. Growth companies generally have other characteristics in common, including above-average profit margins and return on **shareholder's equity,** above average expenditures for product development and research, and patented and/or proprietary products. Markets served by growth companies are typically large and expanding and the company is usually a dominant force in the markets it serves. Earnings reinvestment in the business is high resulting in low **dividends.** Initially, capital appreciation potential is the primary attraction of growth stocks for investors. If above-average growth continues for a long enough period, dividend payouts compared to original cost of purchased stock can become substantial.

GUARANTEE one who receives a **guaranty,** see 168 S.E. 838, 839; also used, as in "guaranty," to mean a promise to answer for the **debt,** default or miscarriage of another; a **warranty** or promise to undertake an original obligation, see 292 S.W. 1079, 1083; something given as security for the performance of an act or the continued quality of a thing, see 109 N.E. 2d 795, 799; to assure the performance of an act or the continued quality of a thing.

GUARANTEE CLAUSE Art. IV, Sec. 4 of the United States Constitution, which states that "the United States shall **guarantee** to every state in this Union a Republican Form of Government." That section of the Constitution has been held to provide that the United States "shall protect each of them [the states] against invasion; and on the application of the legislature or of the executive (when the legislature cannot be convened) against domestic violence." 48 U.S. 1, 42. The Court has declined to use the clause to identify a state's lawful government, 7 How. 1, or to enforce a representative form of government, *Baker* v. *Carr,* 369 U.S. 186; but has instead used the **equal protection clause** of the Constitution to achieve legislative apportionment of a representative character and thus invalidate some forms of **gerrymandering.** Id.; 377 U.S. 533.

GUARANTEED SECURITY a **bond** or **stock** that is guaranteed as to principal or interest or both by someone other than the issuer. A current example is tax-free INDUSTRIAL DEVELOPMENT [REVENUE] BONDS issued by local government authorities to build facilities for industrial corporations. The corporation leases the property and guarantees payments which will return the interest and retire the principal on the bonds. This method of financing results in substantial interest savings by the corporation since tax-free interest rates are substantially less than taxable interest rates.

GUARANTOR one who makes the **guaranty** for the benefit of the guarantee. See **guaranty.**

GUARANTY an agreement or promise to answer for the debt, default or miscarriage of another; a promise or contract to answer for the debt, default or miscarriage of another. 204 So. 2d 547, 549. One giving a guaranty agrees to perform the act promised to be done or properly done by another person if that person does not fulfill his obligation. 392 S.W. 2d 761, 766. Compare **surety.**

GUARDIAN one who legally has care and management of the person or estate, or both, of an incompetent who cannot act for himself, 63 A. 2d 883, 885; an officer or agent of the court who is appointed to protect the interests of minors or incompetent persons and to provide for their care, welfare, education, maintenance and support, 429 S.W. 2d 612. The term when used without words of limitation describes one who is responsible for the care and custody of both the property and person of the **ward,** though the guardianship may by its terms embrace only one or the other. 23 N.W. 746. In guardianship matters, the court is said to be the superior guardian and can regulate the conduct of the guardian toward his ward. 125 P. 2d 318. Some essential features of the relationship of guardian and ward include the fact that a fiduciary relationship exists between them, 79 N.E. 2d 17, that the ward has a duty to live where the guardian tells him to live, and that the guardian does not hold legal title to the ward's property but may prevent the ward from entering into a **contract** respecting his property. 196 P. 2d 456. See **committee, next friend, ward.**

GUARDIAN AD LITEM a guardian who is appointed by the court to represent a **ward** in legal proceeding. 411 N.E. 2d 390, 396. Compare **next friend.** See **ad litem** [GUARDIAN AD LITEM].

GUEST a transient who rents a room at an inn or hotel. See 218 N.W. 510, 511. Someone to whom hospitality is extended; one entertained without being charged. See 185 P. 2d 784, 786.

An AUTOMOBILE GUEST is one who rides in an automobile for his own benefit without giving the driver any compensation for the ride. See 219 A. 2d 374, 376. See **guest statute.**

For purposes of **tort** law, a SOCIAL GUEST is considered a "bare **licensee**" with respect to his entry upon the host's premises, so that, unlike an **invitee,** no duty of affirmative care or inspection is owed to him; he is thus entitled to no more than a warning as to dangers or defective conditions actually known to the occupier. Prosser, Torts §60 at 378-9 (4th ed. 1971). Some states have decided, however, that considering the social guest as an invitee is more in harmony with contemporary social realities. See, e.g., 98 So. 2d 730; 167 N.W. 2d 477.

GUEST STATUTE law which provides that a special standard of care is owed by an automobile owner or driver toward his gratuitous passenger. These statutes differ from state to state in their particulars, but all require more than just ordinary **negligence** on the part of an owner or driver in order for a "guest" to recover damages in a **civil suit.** Some statutes require intentional misconduct, some require "heedlessness and reckless disregard" of others' rights, some require "gross **negligence**," and some require "intoxication or willful misconduct." Prosser, Torts §60 at 382-385 (4th ed. 1971).

GUILD see **National Lawyers Guild.**

GUILTY the condition of having been found by a **jury** to have committed the **crime charged,** or some **lesser-included** crime. The term may, though rarely does, refer to the commission of a **civil** wrong or **tort.**

In criminal cases, a judicial finding of guilt—i.e., a **verdict** of "guilty"—requires that the **evidence** indicate beyond a **reasonable doubt,** or to a **moral certainty,** that the **defendant** committed the crime. 397 U.S. 358. In civil cases involving an alleged tort, "guilt" indicates that the evidence shows by a **preponderance** that the defendant committed the wrongful act. Thus, the "standards of proof" of guilt are different in the two areas. Compare **conviction.** See also **not guilty.**

GUN CONTROL LAW a law restricting or regulating the sale, purchase or possession of firearms, or establishing a system of licensing, registration or identification of firearms or their owners or users. See **Second Amendment.**

H

HABEAS CORPUS (*hā'-bē-ŭs kôr'-pŭs*)—Lat.: you have the body. The **writ** of habeas corpus, known as the GREAT WRIT, has varied use in criminal and civil contexts. It is a procedure for obtaining a judicial determination of the legality of an individual's custody. Technically, it is used in the criminal law context to bring the petitioner before the court to inquire into the legality of his confinement. 488 F. 2d 218, 221.

The writ of federal habeas corpus is used to test the constitutionality of a state criminal conviction. It pierces through the formalities of a state conviction to determine whether the conviction is consonant with **due process of law.** 261 U.S. 86. Issues not raised in the state proceeding generally cannot be raised in a federal habeas petition under the doctrine of **exhaustion.** 456 U.S. 107. The writ's usage has been limited by recent Supreme Court opinions. See, e.g. 455 U.S. 509. The writ is used in the civil context to challenge the validity of child custody, deportations, and civil commitment to mental institutions. See **post conviction proceedings.**

HABENDUM that clause of the deed which names the **grantee** and limits and defines the **estate** to be granted. Its function is to qualify the general language that appears in the granting clause, 213 N.W. 59, 60, 20 So. 877, 878; begins with the words "to have and to hold. . . ."

HABITABILITY the condition of residential or other premises being reasonably fit for occupation, 33 A. 445, and which does not impair the health, safety, or well-being of the occupants. 425 N.E. 2d 781, 785. If this condition is not met, due to a failure to provide heat, for example, the occupant may be eligible for a rent **abatement** or may under some circumstances vacate the premises. See **eviction** [CONSTRUCTIVE EVICTION]; **warranty** [WARRANTY OF HABITABILITY].

HABITUAL OFFENDER see **criminal; sentence** [EXTENDED TERM].

HAEC VERBA see **in haec verba.**

HALFWAY HOUSE a residence established to assist persons who have left highly structured institutions to adjust to and reenter society and live within its accepted norms. Mental patients and prisoners may be released to facilities of this kind located within the community and usually with no security other than supervised regimen of sign-in, sign-out, and curfew rules. Release to halfway houses is sometimes a first step in a **parole** program. Modern statutes permit courts to sentence defendants directly to such facilities, known as RESIDENTIAL COMMUNITY TREATMENT CENTERS as a condition of **probation.** See, e.g., 18 U.S.C. §§3651, 4082.

A **work-release program** may utilize a halfway house instead of a more secure institution for nighttime confinement and weekend supervision. The halfway house provides a "supervised and restricted environment in which to ascertain the convict's ability to form a productive life in society [while simultaneously fulfilling] the functions of a penal institution in its concern for security and rehabilitation." 400 F. Supp. 1046, 1048.

Although states are not required to utilize such modern correctional concepts as halfway houses, if they choose to do so, the procedures for assigning inmates to such facilities must meet standards of procedural due process and equal protection of the laws. 617 F. 2d 996.

HALLUCINATION a state of mind whereby a person senses something that in reality does not exist; a perception of an object having no reality. 90 S.E. 2d 593, 596. Any of the senses may be involved, although sight or hearing are most commonly affected. The state of hallucination most often results from mental illness or from ingesting drugs designed to create these perceptions. See **controlled substance** [HALLUCINOGENS].

HALLUCINOGENS see **controlled substances** [HALLUCINOGENS].

HANGED, DRAWN, AND QUARTERED a common law punishment for convictions of high treason or other atrocious crimes where the defendant was "drawn to the place of execution, disemboweled alive, and then beheaded and quartered." 28 N.E. 533. See **cruel and unusual punishment.**

HARASSMENT in criminal matters generally, a **prosecution** brought without reasonable expectation of obtaining a valid conviction. 437 F. Supp. 201, 221. Any exercise of authority in such manner as to be unnecessarily oppressive; connotes purposeful actions and conduct motivated by a malicious or discriminatory purpose.

SEXUAL HARASSMENT "an employee policy or acquiescence in a practice of compelling female employees to submit to the sexual advances of their male superiors." 552 F. 2d 1032. This policy constitutes an artificial barrier to promotion in employment and therefore violates Title VII of the Civil Rights Act of 1964 (42 U.S.C. §2000 et seq.). 568 F. 2d 1044. Recently, lawsuits brought as discrimination on the basis of gender have applied to both men and women and apply in instances of verbal or physical harassment.

HARD CASES cases that produce decisions deviating from the true principles of law in order to meet the exigencies presented by the extreme hardship of one **party.**

It is sometimes said that "hard cases make bad law" because logic is often shortcut in a hard case, and later attempts to justify the new law thus created often compound the original inadequacy of reasoning.

HARDSHIP, UNNECESSARY see **unnecessary hardship.**

HARM see **injury; irreparable injury [damage, harm].**

HARMLESS ERROR error which is not sufficiently prejudicial to an **appellant** or does not affect his substantial rights so as to warrant the reviewing court overturning or otherwise modifying the lower court decision. See 178 P. 2d 341.

In the criminal law context, some violations of defendant's constitutional rights may be considered harmless error and thus permit a **conviction** to withstand constitutional challenge. Whether a particular error is harmless or not is a matter of federal and not state law as to federal constitutional questions. The prosecution has the burden of proving "beyond a reasonable doubt that the error . . . did not contribute to the verdict obtained." 386 U.S. 18, 24. Other properly received evidence may be considered in determining whether the valid proof was so overwhelming as to preclude the possibility that the constitutional violation contributed to the verdict. 395 U.S. 250. See also **error; plain error.**

HEAD NOTE summary of an issue covered in a reported case; summaries of all the points discussed and issues decided in a case, which are placed at the beginning of a case report.

HEAD OF HOUSEHOLD an unmarried **taxpayer** who maintains as his home a household which is the principal place of residence of a specifically designated person who constitutes a **dependent.** A person who qualifies as a head of household is subject to a **tax rate** that is less than the tax rate applied to a person who is not a head of household. I.R.C. §§1(b) and 2(b).

HEARING a **proceeding** wherein **evidence** is taken for the purpose of determining an issue of fact and reaching a decision on the basis of that evidence, 426 P. 2d 942, 951; describes "whatever takes place before magistrates clothed with judicial functions and sitting without jury at any stage of the proceeding subsequent to its inception." 15 N.E. 2d 1014, 1015. Thus a hearing, such as an ADMINISTRATIVE HEARING, may take place outside the judicial process, before officials who have been granted judicial authority expressly for the purpose of conducting such hearings.

FINAL HEARING "is sometimes used to describe that stage of proceedings relating to the determination of a **suit** upon its **merits**, as dis-

tinguished from those of preliminary questions." 15 N.E. 2d 1014, 1015. See **preliminary hearing; fair hearing.** See also **due process of law.**

HEARING DE NOVO see **de novo** [DE NOVO HEARING].

HEARSAY RULE a rule that declares not **admissible** as **evidence** any statement other than that by a **witness** while testifying at the **hearing** and offered into evidence to prove the truth of the matter stated. Uniform Rule of Evidence 63. The reason for the hearsay rule is that the credibility of the witness is the key ingredient in weighing the truth of his statement; so when that statement is made out of court, without benefit of cross-examination and without the witness's demeanor being subject to assessment by the trier of fact (judge or jury), there is generally no adequate basis for determining whether the out-of-court statement is true. 6 Wigmore, Evidence §1766 (chadbourne rev. 1976). The statement may be oral or written and includes non-verbal conduct intended as a substitute for words. If, for example, a witness's statement as to what he heard another person say is elicited to prove the truth of what that other person said, it is hearsay; if however, it is elicited to merely show that the words were spoken, it is not hearsay. The witness's answer will be admissible only to show that the other person spoke certain words and not to show the truth of what the other person said.

There are many exceptions to the hearsay rule of exclusion based on a combination of trustworthiness and necessity. Thus, official written statements, such as police reports, where the declarant's statements are based on firsthand knowledge and where the officer is under an official duty to make the report (and hence has no motive to falsify) are admissible under the BUSINESS RECORDS EXCEPTION. See, e.g., Uniform Rule 63(13). Another common exception is made for DYING DECLARATIONS, see, e.g., Uniform Rule 63(5). Under this rule a statement made by a person with knowledge or hopeless expectation of his impending death is admissible through another who overheard that statement where the declarant is unavailable because he died. Originally it was strongly believed that a dying person would tell the truth; thus W's testimony as to what the dying declarant said became admissible both on the grounds of trustworthiness and necessity. Today, with more skepticism about the effect of religiosity on truth-telling, necessity remains as a major factor in determining admissibility. The question of W's credibility is subject to demeanor examination and cross-examination for bias, memory, etc. Some jurisdictions permit any admission by a party to be offered by his adversary in a civil proceeding through any competent witness as another broad exception to the hearsay rule. See Uniform Rule 63(7).

Hearsay exceptions may jeopardize the constitutional guarantee of confrontation and thus criminal exceptions may be more narrow (e.g., compare the "declaration against interest exception" with the "admissions exception." Id. R.R. 63(10) and 63(7)). The confrontation clause has been held not identical with the general common law hearsay rule, see 399 U.S. 149; and state exceptions have been upheld where they have sufficient trustworthiness to satisfy the confrontation clause interests. See 400 U.S. 74 (permitting an unusually broad CO-CONSPIRATOR EXCEPTION which permits statements made by one conspirator to be admissible against the other conspirators even though the statement was made after the conspirators were in custody— contrary to the generally accepted rule that the exception does not extend to the post-custody stage, see 336 U.S. 440). See also 380 U.S. 400; 390 U.S. 719; 392 U.S. 293. See **evidence.**

HEDGE FUND an investment partnership or **mutual fund** that uses **selling short** to **hedge** long positions in **stocks.** If stock selection is correct, the stocks sold short decline more in a falling market than the stock owned, and the stocks owned appreciate more in a rising market than the stocks sold short. The goal is to generate trading and investment profits no matter what the direction of the general market. Hedge funds may borrow money to increase their **leverage.**

HEDGING a concept that involves offsetting a risk position. In the **commodities** trade, it might involve a processor position or a speculative position. For example, a potato chip manufacturer can hedge or protect his profit margin on a large order of chips to be delivered in the future by buying potatoes in the **futures** market; a potato farmer may sell the futures contract to the process to protect some or all of his investment in raising his crop. A speculator in potato contracts might hedge a long position in old crop futures by selling new crop futures in anticipation of a bumper crop and, therefore, lower prices. **Arbitrage** is a type of hedge involving the buying of securities in one market and selling in another market when the price difference between markets offers a profitable trade. Hedged trades are used in the stock **option** market where the various positions are referred to as **spreads,** straddles, etc. In securities trading and investment, **selling short** is used to hedge stock ownership positions against a decline in the general market. See **hedge fund.**

HEIR APPARENT one who has the rights to heirship (or **inheritance**) provided that he live longer than his ancestor; "before the death of the ancestor, persons who would become heirs on his death are only heirs apparent; and no inheritance which can descend to their children passes to heirs apparent who die before the ancestor." 42 S.E. 2d 215, 216. An **antilapse statute** may operate to save a **gift** to an heir apparent who predeceases the **testator.**

HEIRS strictly, those whom statutory law would appoint to inherit an **estate** should the ancestor die without a **will** [**intestate**]. 29 Cal. Rptr. 601, 605, 606, 332 P. 2d 773, 775. Synonyms: "heirs at law," "rightful heir," "legal heirs." The term is often applied indiscriminately to those who inherit by will or **deed** as well as by **operation of law.** Compare **devise; grant; inheritance.** See **co-heir; intestate succession; pretermitted heir.**

AND HIS HEIRS at **common law** these words had to be included in order to convey a **fee simple.** See 112 S.W. 53, 55. The formal requirement has been abolished or modified by statute in most of the states, and now one may **convey** or devise **real property** without using these technical words. See 300 N.Y.S. 1279. These words are **"words of limitation** [describing the nature of the **estate** granted, a fee simple] not **words of purchase** [describing the persons to whom it is given]. . . . This construction prevails unless it plainly appears from the context of the will [or other instrument] that such was not the **testator's** [or grantor's] intention." 157 A. 328.

HEIRS AND ASSIGNS words describing that a **fee simple** estate is being **conveyed;** 335 A. 2d 157, 161; words of limitation, not of substitution, 536 S.W. 2d 109, 115, or of purchase, 285 N.Y.S. 309. When used in a **will,** the words are descriptive and do not set up an independent class of **legatees.** 46 S.E. 2d 305.

COLLATERAL HEIRS an heir who is

not of the direct line of the deceased, but comes from a collateral line, as a brother, sister, an aunt or uncle, nephew, niece, or a cousin of the deceased. 196 N.E. 2d 16, 19.

LINEAL HEIR one who inherits in a line either ascending or descending from a common source as distinguished from a collateral heir. 196 N.E. 2d 16, 19.

HEIRS OF THE BODY issue of the body, offspring engendered by the person named as parent. These words are used in instruments of conveyance, such as **deeds** and **wills,** to create a **conditional fee** or a **fee tail.** 2 So. 2d 160, 162.

HEREDITAMENTS anything which can be inherited, including real, personal or mixed **property.** 160 N.W. 716, 719. There are two kinds of hereditaments: CORPOREAL and INCORPOREAL. The former generally refers to tangible things. 69 Cal. Rptr. 612, 625. The latter refers to rights growing out of or connected to any property including such items as an **easement** or **rent.** 286 S.W. 2d 380, 383. For example, the right to use water flowing across one's own land is not an easement and is therefore a "corporeal hereditament." The right to have the water flow to the land across the land of another, however, is an incorporeal hereditament. 46 Mass. 236, 238.

HEREDITARY SUCCESSION the passing of **title** according to the laws of **descent;** the title to an **estate** acquired by a person by **operation of law** upon the death of an ancestor without a valid **will** affecting the property inherited. 163 P. 118, 120. Synonymous with **inheritance, descent.** Compare **devise.**

HIDDEN ASSET a property value understated on the **balance sheet** of a company due to accounting convention and/or deliberate action of management. Recent high rates of inflation have served to increase asset values that are carried at historic cost less **depreciation, depletion,** and **amortization.** The result is understated asset values in terms of current dollars. A more traditional example is the practice by many oil exploration companies of expensing oil field discovery and development costs even though a very valuable asset is created by successful efforts.

HIDDEN DEFECT defect not recognizable upon a reasonable inspection of a good or product, or which is not readily apparent, 411 N.E. 2d 648, for which a seller is generally liable and which would give rise to a right to revoke a prior **acceptance.** U.C.C. §2-608(1)(b). See **latent defect.** Compare **patent defect.** See also **as is.**

HIDDEN INFLATION a price increase implemented by offering a smaller quantity or poorer quality for the old price. For example, a candy bar manufacturer might reduce the weight of a two-ounce bar to one and three-quarter ounces and offer the new bar at the old price. The result is 14.3 percent inflation in the candy's cost.

HIDDEN TAX an indirect tax paid unwittingly by the consumer, such as taxes levied on goods at some point in their production or transport prior to retail sale.

HIT-AND-RUN STATUTES statutes requiring that a motorist involved in an accident stop and identify himself and give certain information about himself to the other motorist and to the police. These laws have been upheld as not violative of the privilege against **self-incrimination** on the ground that they call for neutral acts, not intended to be probative of guilt, and pose only an insignificant hazard of self-incrimination. 402 U.S. 424.

HOARDING the excess accumulation of commodities, goods, or currency in anticipation of scarcity and/or higher prices. Hoarding is a common practice during periods of high inflation, during wartimes, and during periods of economic or political instability.

HOBBY LOSSES a loss incurred by a **taxpayer** in an activity not engaged in for profit. In general, hobby losses are **deductible** only to the extent of income generated by the hobby. I.R.C. §183.

HOLDER "a person who is in possession of a document of **title** or an **instrument** or an investment security **drawn,** issued or **indorsed** to him or to his order or to **bearer** or in blank." U.C.C. 1-201 (20) See **holder in due course.**

HOLDER IN DUE COURSE in commercial law, "nothing more than a highly refined species of **bona fide purchaser** who takes free of most defenses of prior parties to the [**negotiable**] **instrument** and free of conflicting title claims to the instrument itself." White and Summer, Uniform Commercial Code 456. A holder in due course generally takes free of "personal defenses" which the **maker** or any other prior party may have against the original **payee** or any subsequent **holder** but not free of "real defenses" such as **fraud** in the factum, **incapacity, duress,** illegality, etc. U.C.C. §3-305 (2). Thus, S sells B a car and takes B's check as payment. If S negotiates the check to a holder in due course, B may not assert some fault with the car as a defense against such a holder collecting on the check (a personal defense good only between S and B) but may defend if he was forced to sign the check against his will (duress—a real defense). The protections afforded to holders in due course have been limited in some jurisdictions in transactions involving consumer goods. See, e.g., N.J.S.A. 17:16C-38.1.

To qualify for this special status one must be a holder, who takes the negotiable instrument, for value, in

good faith, without notice that it is overdue or has been dishonored or of any defense against or claim to it on the part of any person. U.C.C. §3-302(1).

HOLD HARMLESS see **save harmless.**

HOLDING in commercial and property law, **property** in which one has legal **title** and of which one is in **possession,** 246 S.W. 2d 990; the term may be used to refer specifically to ownership of stocks, or **shares,** of **corporations.** 36 S.E. 2d 5, 8.

In procedure, any ruling of the court, including rulings upon the admissibility of evidence or other questions presented during trial, may be termed a "holding." See 218 P. 2d 888, 893. Compare **dictum.**

HOLDING CELL see **jail** [HOLDING CELL].

HOLDING COMPANY a corporation organized to hold the stock of other corporations; any company, incorporated or unincorporated, which is in a position to control or materially influence the management of one or more other companies by virtue, in part at least, of its ownership of **securities** in the other company or companies. 20 P. 2d 460, 468. See **personal holding company.**

HOLDING PERIOD the period of time which property must be held before its disposition will give rise to long-term **capital** gain or loss (for **tax years** beginning after 1977 this period is one year). I.R.C. §§1222 and 1223. In certain situations, **taxpayers** calculating their holding period must "tack" onto the period during which they actually held the property the period during which the property was held by a previous holder.

HOLDOVER TENANCY see **tenancy** [TENANCY AT SUFFERANCE].

HOLDUP SUIT a lawsuit that has no legal basis and is instituted solely to prevent or block something from occurring. A party harmed by such a suit may have an action for **malicious prosecution.** See also **strike suit.**

HOLOGRAPHIC WILL "a **will** that 'is entirely written, dated and signed by the hand of the **testator** himself.'" It is sometimes written "OLOGRAPHIC." In some states, under statute, such a will need not be witnessed and is valid under a statute of **descent and distribution** to pass **property.** 34 P. 614, 615.

HOMAGE during the **feudal** period, the ceremony "wherein the vassal knelt before the lord, acknowledged himself to be his man, and swore **fealty** [an oath of loyalty to the lord]. It was frequently accompanied by a grant of land from the lord to the vassal, the land to be held of the lord by the vassal as **tenant.**" Moynihan, Introduction to the Law of Real Property 4 (1962). As a consequence, any attempt by the vassal [or **tenant**] to convey more than the estate which had been granted him (e.g., an attempt by the vassal to convey a **fee simple** when his grant from the lord consisted only of a **life estate**), was not only **tortious** conduct with regard to the lord, but was also treasonous. See **fealty.**

HOME PORT DOCTRINE in maritime law, refers to the rule that a vessel which is an instrumentality of foreign commerce and engaged therein is subject to property tax only at its "home port" regardless of where it happens to be actually located on tax assessment day, 366 F. Supp. 1133; "home port" referring either to the place of a vessel's place of registration or the domicile of the owners. Id. Vessels engaged in interstate commerce may be taxed by jurisdictions other than its home port, but only on an apportioned basis.

The doctrine does not bar the

placing of **liens** on vessels in ports other than the vessel's home port for supplies or repairs to the vessel. 17 U.S. 438.

HOME RULE means of apportioning power between state and local governments by the granting of "power to the electorate of a local governmental unit to frame and adopt a charter of government." 48 Minn. L. Rev. 643, 645. The effect of this grant is to enable local government to legislate without first obtaining permission from state legislatures. Id. at 650. See also **preemption.**

HOMESTEAD any house, outbuildings, and surrounding land that is owned and used as a **dwelling** by the head of the family. 590 S.W. 2d 635, 637. Under modern HOMESTEAD EXEMPTION LAWS, enacted in most states, any property designated as a homestead is exempt from **execution** and **sale** by **creditors.** 106 N.W. 684, 685. This homestead exemption applies in some states to property taxes as well.

The exemption from claims of creditors may be extended by a **probate** court upon the death of the head of the family to ensure the surviving spouse and minor children uninterrupted **possession** and enjoyment of the family home. A home so protected is referred to as a PROBATE HOMESTEAD. See **life estate.**

HOMICIDE any killing of a human being by another human being; most commonly used to refer to an unlawful homicide such as **murder** or **manslaughter.** "The destruction of the life of one human being by the act, agency, procurement or **culpable** omission of another. The destruction of life must be complete by such act or agency; but although the injury which caused death might not, under other circumstances, have proved fatal, yet if such injury be the cause of death, without it appearing that there has been any gross neglect or improper

treatment by some person other than the defendant . . . it would be homicide." 108 S.W. 699, 701.

JUSTIFIABLE HOMICIDE "the killing of a human being by commandment of the law, in the execution of public justice, in **self-defense,** in [lawful] defense of habitation, property or person." etc. 45 S.E. 2d 798, 799.

HONORABLE DISCHARGE a formal final judgment passed by the government upon the entire military record of the soldier, and it is an authoritative declaration that he has left the service in a status of honor. 115 F. Supp. 509. A person's classification after retirement from the armed services directly affects his ability to take advantage of benefits provided to members of the services.

HONORARY generally refers to a position held without profit, fee, or reward, and in consideration of the honor conferred by holding a position of responsibility and trust 81 N.Y. 255; a position recognizing honor or commitment. An HONORARY DEGREE is one conferred without formal qualification in recognition by an educational institution of an individual's non-academic accomplishments.

HORNBOOK a book intended to aid one with the fundamentals of the subject being studied; a primer for the student studying in an area of knowledge.

HORNBOOK LAW those principles of law which are known generally to all and are free from doubt and ambiguity. They are therefore such as would probably be enunciated in a **hornbook.** Such basic and accepted legal principles were formerly called BLACK LETTER LAW.

HORS *(ôr)*—Fr: outside of, besides, other than (sometimes: dehors *(dĕ-ôr')*).

HOSTILE POSSESSION actual occupation or **possession** of **real**

estate without the permission of anyone claiming **paramount title**, coupled with a **claim,** express or implied, of **ownership.** Hostile possession is to be contrasted with **holding** in recognition of or in subordination to the true owner, as in the case of possession under a **lease.** 138 P. 2d 846, 851, 852, 350 S.W. 2d 729, 732. Hostile does not imply ill will or actual enmity but merely that the occupant claims ownership against all others, including the **record owner.** 468 P. 2d 702, 706. The term is usually used in connection with and as a condition for **adverse possession.** See also **notorious possession.**

HOSTILE WITNESS see **witness.**

HOUSE all-inclusive and may include any and every kind of structure, depending upon the context in which it is used and the purpose sought to be effected. 169 A. 2d 65, 68. Whether a structure is defined as a "house" or "home" may have constitutional implications. For **Fourth Amendment** purposes, "houses" include curtilage. 375 F. Supp. 949, 958. See **domicile; dwelling house; residence.** See also **halfway house; prostitution** [IIOUSE OF PROSTITUTION].

HUNG JURY one whose members [jurors] cannot reconcile their differences of opinions and therefore cannot reach a **verdict** by whatever degree of agreement is required (generally unanimity, but sometimes by a substantial majority, e.g., 10-2).

HUSBAND-WIFE PRIVILEGE see **marital communications privilege [husband-wife privilege];** compare **spousal disqualification.**

HYPNOSIS a state of heightened concentration with diminished awareness of peripheral events, increasing the suggestibility of the subject while hypnotized. 432 A. 2d 86, 90. In those jurisdictions permitting the use of hypnotically refreshed testimony, the results of

hypnosis, as with the results of any scientific test, are admissible only when they have "sufficient scientific basis to produce uniform and reasonably reliable results and will contribute materially to the ascertainment of the truth." Id. at 91.

HYPOTHECATE to pledge something as security without turning over possession of it. 522 S.W. 2d 552, 554. Hypothecation creates a right in the creditor to have the thing pledged sold in order that the claim may be satisfied out of the sale proceeds. 57 N.E. 455, 457. A **mortgage** on real property is a form of hypothecation contract. Intangibles and securities are most often the subject of hypothecation contracts. In the case of buying stock on **margin** the owner signs a hypothecation agreement with the broker who handles the transaction; the broker is then free to pledge the customer's securities as **collateral** for a bank loan or to lend the customer's securities in connection with short sales transactions.

HYPOTHETICAL QUESTION a question which assumes facts [that] the evidence tends to show and calls for an opinion based on the hypothesis. 112 N.E. 2d 537, 538. In trials, hypothetical questions can only be posed to an expert witness who is qualified to give an opinion on the matter in issue. See Fed. R. Evid. 703, 705.

IBID. (*ĭb'-ĭd*)—Lat: in the same place, at the same time, in the same manner; abbreviated form of the word "ibidem." It is used to mean "in the same book" or "on the same page." It functions to avoid repetition of source data contained in the reference immediately preceding.

ID. *(ĭd)*—Lat: the same, the very same, exactly this, likewise; abbreviated form of the word "idem." This term is used in citations to avoid repetition of the author's name and title when a reference to an item immediately follows another to the same item.

I.D.B. **[Industrial Development Bond]** see **guaranteed security.**

IGNORANCE lack of knowledge. Ignorance of the law does not justify an act, since every person is presumed to know the law. However, **mistake** of fact may provide a legal excuse. Perkins and Boyce, Criminal Law, 1028 (2d ed. 1982). See **ignorantia legis non excusat.**

IGNORANTIA LEGIS NON EX-CUSAT *(ĭg-nō-rän'-shē-à lā'-gĭs nŏn ĕx-kū'-zät)*—Lat: ignorance of the law is no excuse; i.e., the fact that defendant did not think his act was against the law does not prevent the law from punishing the prohibited act. See **mistake** (MISTAKE OF FACT and MISTAKE OF LAW).

ILLEGAL against the law. Behavior that can result in either criminal sanctions, such as prison sentences or fines, or civil sanctions, such as liability or injunctions, is illegal.

ILLEGALLY OBTAINED EVIDENCE evidence obtained by the police through circumstances in which the police or a police agent violated a person's right against unreasonable search and seizure as guaranteed by the **Fourth Amendment** or analogous state constitutional provisions. See **fruit of the poisonous tree; exclusionary rule; search and seizure.**

ILLEGITIMATE illegal or improper; as applied to children, it means those born out of wedlock, i.e., **bastards.**

ILLUSORY PROMISE a promise so indefinite that it cannot be enforced or which, by virtue of provisions or conditions contained in the promise itself, is one whose fulfillment is optional or entirely discretionary on the part of the promisor. 287 P. 2d 735. Since such a promise does not constitute a legally binding obligation, it is not sufficient as **consideration** for a reciprocal promise and thus cannot create a valid **contract.** See 17 Am. Jur. 2d Contracts §§11-13, 1-5. See **mutuality.**

IMMATERIAL not **material; irrelevant;** evidence that "is offered to prove a proposition which is not a matter in **issue** or probative of a matter in issue." McCormick, Evidence §185 (2d ed. 1972).

IMMEDIATE CAUSE see **cause.**

IMMIGRATION the movement of persons into a foreign country for the purpose of permanently residing in that country. See 128 F. 375, 380.

IMMORAL CONDUCT that "conduct which is willful, flagrant, or shameless, and which shows a moral indifference to the opinions of the good and respectable members of the community." 20 P. 2d 896, 897. It is sometimes the basis for suspension or revocation of authority to practice certain professions such as law and teaching. See id., 421 P. 2d 586, 589.

IMMUNITIES, PRIVILEGES AND see **privileges and immunities.**

IMMUNITY a right of exemption from a duty or penalty; a favor or benefit granted to one and contrary to the general rule; immunity from prosecution, such as that granted a **witness** to compel answers to questions he might otherwise refuse to answer on Fifth Amendment grounds. See **self-incrimination** (TRANSACTIONAL IMMUNITY; USE IMMUNITY); Federal Tort Claims Act.

OFFICIAL IMMUNITY the personal immunity accorded to a public official from liability to anyone injured by any of his actions that are the consequence of the exercise of his official authority or duty. See 18 Ark. L. Rev. 82 (1964). This immunity is complete for judges, so long as they act within the jurisdiction of their respective courts; administrative officers, however, are generally immune only for **discretionary** as opposed to **ministerial acts** that are done honestly and in **good faith.** Prosser, Torts §132 (4th ed. 1971). See also **waiver** [WAIVER OF IMMUNITY].

SOVEREIGN IMMUNITY see **sovereign immunity.**

TRANSACTIONAL IMMUNITY see **self-incrimination** (TRANSACTIONAL IMMUNITY).

USE IMMUNITY see **self-incrimination** (USE IMMUNITY).

IMPACT RULE the requirement of a physical contact with an individual person in order for damages for emotional distress to be imposed. Prosser, Torts 51–52 (4th ed. 1971).

IMPAIR THE OBLIGATION OF A CONTRACT see **obligation of a contract.**

IMPANEL see **panel** (IMPANEL).

IMPANELING the process by which jurors are selected and sworn in to their task, 119 N.E. 916; the listing of those selected to serve on a particular jury.

IMPEACH to charge a public official with a wrongdoing while in office. "The object of prosecutions of impeachment in England and the United States 'is to reach high and potent offenders, such as might be presumed to escape punishment in the ordinary tribunals, either from their own extraordinary influence, or from the imperfect organization and powers of those tribunals. These prosecutions are, therefore, conducted by the representatives of the nation, in their public capacity, in the face of the nation, and upon a

responsibility which is at once felt and reverenced by the whole community.' " 188 P. 2d 592, 595, citing Story, Const., Sec. 688. Impeachment proceedings against officers of the United States are governed by the Constitution. See **Articles of Impeachment.**

With reference to the testimony of a **witness,** to impeach "means to call into question the **veracity** of the witness by means of evidence offered for that purpose, or by showing that the witness is unworthy of belief." 190 P. 2d 193, 195. Court rules applicable to the introduction of **evidence** used to impeach a witness are less strict than the rules pertaining to evidence used to convict a **defendant.**

IMPERTINENT MATTER an inappropriate matter; facts that are irrelevant to the controversy. Under the Federal Rules of Civil Procedure, impertinent matter consists of any allegation which is not responsive nor relevant to issues involved in the action and which could not be put in issue or be given in evidence between the parties. See 56 F.R.D. 116, 120.

IMPLEADER the procedure by which a third party is brought into a suit between a **plaintiff** and **defendant,** where that third party may be liable, so as to settle all **claims** in a single **action.** See 143 N.Y.S. 2d 327, 330. It is a **procedural** device available to any defendant where a third party is or may be liable to him for any damages that the defendant owes the plaintiff. The defendant is considered a "third-party plaintiff" vis-a-vis the third party thus joined. Fed. Rule Civil Proc. 14. The device is also available to a plaintiff against whom a **counterclaim** has been made. Id. Compare **interpleader; joinder.** See also **cross-claim.**

IMPLICATION intention, meaning; that which is inferred; though not expressly stated, a state of mind or facts which is deduced.

NECESSARY IMPLICATION "one which results from so strong a probability of intention that an intention contrary to that imputed to the testator cannot be supposed." 220 N.W. 25, 27.

IMPLIED not explicitly written or stated; referring, e.g., to a condition, consent, power, warranty, a state of mind, or a fact which is determined by deduction or inference from known facts and circumstances. Compare **express.**

IMPLIED CONSENT consent "manifested by signs, actions or facts, or by inaction or silence, which raises a presumption that consent has been given," 487 S.W. 2d 624, 629; or consent that arises from a course of conduct or relationship between the parties, in which there is mutual acquiescence or a lack of objection under circumstances signifying assent. 195 S.E. 2d 711, 713. In criminal law, generally used as a defense against rape, whereby the defendant claims that he acted under a reasonable and honest belief based on the fact that the woman consented to his advance.

IMPLIED CONTRACT see **contract** [QUASI [IMPLIED] CONTRACT].

IMPLIED EASEMENT see **easement** (IMPLIED EASEMENT).

IMPLIED NOTICE see **notice** (IMPLIED NOTICE).

IMPORT the transportation of goods into one country and out of another; also, the article imported. The term under the **customs** laws requires that the goods be brought voluntarily into this country, into the proper port of entry, and with an **intent** to unload them. If customs officials determine that an article has been imported into the United States, it is assessed a **duty** under customs laws, unless clear **evidence** is proved to the contrary. 375 F. Supp. 1360, 1361-1363. To be imported within the scope of the tariff laws, the goods must be from a country subject to our tariff laws and the goods must pass through the custody and control of the customs officials, and into the custody and control of the importer. See generally 146 F. 484, 486–487. See **export.**

IMPORTATION the act of transporting goods into a country from a foreign country. 262 U.S. 100. As used in tariff statutes the term means merchandise to which the status of an **import** has attached. 266 F. Supp. 175 (1967). Compare **exportation.**

IMPOSSIBILITY a **defense** to nonperformance of a **contract.** It arises when **performance** is impossible due to the destruction of the subject matter of the **contract** (as, for example, by fire) or the death of a person necessary for the performance of it; performance is then excused and the contract **duty** terminated. In civil law, impossibility is an excuse for nonperformance of a contract where the promised performance has become **illegal.** At common law, impossibility did not reach the cases where performance simply became very expensive or difficult. Thus, a builder was held not excused for his failure to perform even though the building collapsed in two attempts to build it due to unforeseen difficulties, 20 Minn. 494; and it has no application at all if the promise has been expressly made unconditional even as against unforeseen difficulties. But "the essence of the modern defense of 'impossibility' is that the promised performance was at the making of the contract, or thereafter became, impracticable owing to some extreme, or unreasonable difficulty, expense, injury or loss involved, rather than that it is scientifically or actually impossible." Williston on Contracts §1931 (3d ed. 1978). The Uniform Commercial Code recognizes this broader "commercial impracticability" modification of the common law impossibility doctrine. Under the Code provision, if a contingency arises, the non-occurrence of which was an essential basis of the contract between the parties, then the seller is excused from performing and is required to follow certain procedures in allocating his available capacity to perform on like contracts. U.C.C. §§2-615, 2-616.

In the criminal law the term applies to situations in which an actor does an act which would otherwise be criminal except that the facts or circumstances render the crime impossible to commit. Thus, it is impossible to **murder** another if he is already dead. If the actor thought he was alive, however, in some jurisdictions he will be held for an **attempted** murder.

FACTUAL IMPOSSIBILITY prevents liability for the object crime of murder but in those jurisdictions it will not operate to prevent liability for an attempt to commit that crime. See New York Penal Law §110.10.

LEGAL IMPOSSIBILITY the term in the criminal law context has sometimes been used to describe the failure to consummate a crime because of some legal bar. Thus, it has been said that one cannot legally receive stolen property that was never stolen in the first instance. 78 N.E. 169. Holdings of this kind have been much criticized and the recognized rule is that attempt liability will be attached for this conduct as well. If legal impossibility is limited to instances in which the actor lacks capacity to commit the crime in question, then legal impossibility is a complete defense. Perkins, Criminal Law 570-72 (2d ed. 1969). See **frustration of purpose.** Compare **mistake.**

IMPOST a tax; a charge or levy in the nature of a tax.

IMPOUND to place merchandise, funds or records in the **custody** of an officer of the law.

IMPOUNDING [IMPOUNDMENT] at **common law,** impounding originally related to the restraining of stray cattle. It then became the second step in a **distress** action, whereby the **distrainor,** having seized the chattels, was required to bring the goods to a public pound for safekeeping pending the outcome of the action. 30 A. 2d 516, 519–520. It has now been extended to apply to any goods, including automobiles, funds, account books, and records, taken into custody of a law or court officer. See 242 F. Supp. 191, 202.

IMPRESSION, CASE [MATTER] OF FIRST see **first impression, case of.**

IMPRIMATUR the license granted by the government permitting the publication of a particular book.

IMPRISONMENT the confinement of an individual to a particular place, usually in order to punish him for a crime; any deprivation of liberty or detention of a person contrary to his will. 402 S.W. 2d 424, 425. Status of imprisonment may affect certain constitutional rights—for example, a right of bail guaranteed to imprisoned persons may not include juveniles held pending delinquency proceedings. 416 A. 2d 137, 139. Synonymous with **incarceration.** See **false imprisonment.**

IMPROVEMENT any development of land or buildings through the expenditure of money or labor that is designed to do more than merely replace, repair, or restore to the original condition. 27 S.E. 2d 164, 172, 19 P. 2d 644, 49 S.E. 2d 779, 783. "Improvements" are generally thought of as permanent and fixed, and supposedly increase the value of the property. 203 N.Y.S. 2d 35, 38, 122 N.W. 2d 189, 190. See **ameliorating waste.**

IMPUTE to assign vicariously to a person or other entity the legal responsibility for the act of another, because of the relationship between the person so made liable and the actor, rather than because of actual participation in or knowledge of the act. See **vicarious liability.**

IMPUTED LIABILITY see **vicarious liability.**

IN ABSENTIA *(ĭn ăb-sĕn'-shē-à)*— Lat: in absence.

INALIENABLE RIGHTS fundamental rights, including the right to practice religion, freedom of speech, due process, and equal protection of the laws, that cannot be transferred to another nor surrendered except by the person possessing them. See **Bill of Rights.**

IN ARTICULO MORTIS *(in är-tik'-ū-lō môr'-tis)*—Lat: in the moment of death.

IN BANC see **en banc.**

IN CAMERA *(ĭn kă'-mĕ-rà)*—Lat: in chambers; generally, refers to proceedings held in a judge's chambers or where the public is not present. "The meaning of the word 'chambers' varies with the context in which it is used. It may mean a room adjacent to a courtroom in which a judge performs the duties of his office when his court is not in session. The word 'chambers' is also commonly used in a different sense. When a judge performs a judicial act while the court is not in session in the matter acted upon, it is said that he acted 'in chambers' whether the act was performed in the 'judge's chambers,' the library, at his home, or elsewhere." 66 Cal. Rptr. 825, 829.

Confidential or otherwise sensitive documents are often examined "in camera" to determine whether the information therein should be revealed to the jury and thereby made a matter of public record.

INCAPACITY to lack the ability;

the quality or state of being incapable; the lack of legal, physical, or intellectual power; inability, 161 N.E. 2d 189, 194. In a legal sense, it means the inability to stand trial; in a physical sense, it means the inability to procure employment due to some injury or the inability to perform usual tasks of one's job. 435 S.W. 2d 248, 249. See **incompetency; minority; non compos mentis.** Compare **insanity.**

IN CAPITE *(ĭn kă'-pēt)*—Lat: in chief; with reference to feudal tenures, an estate in land held by direct grant of the king.

INCARCERATION confinement in a jail, prison, or penitentiary. Synonymous with **imprisonment.**

INCENDIARY arsonist; one who maliciously and willfully sets property on fire; also, an object or thing capable of starting and sustaining a fire; e.g., an "incendiary device."

INCEST a criminal offense which involves sexual intercourse between members of a family, or those among whom marriage would be illegal because of blood relations. 75 P. 166. See Model Penal Code §230.2.

IN CHIEF principal, primary. At trial, the initial presentation of a party's evidence constitutes that party's case in chief, to which rebuttal is allowed.

INCHOATE that which is not yet completed or finished; 349 S.W. 2d 453, 462. Inchoate offenses are those offenses such as **attempt, solicitation,** or **conspiracy** to commit a crime, all of which involve conduct designed to culminate in the commission of a substantive offense but has either failed or has not yet achieved its culmination because there is something that the actor or another still must do. See 389 A. 2d 601, 603.

INCHOATE DOWER [INCHOATE RIGHT OF DOWER] the **interest** which a wife has in her husband's lands prior to his death and contingent upon his predeceasing her. The right of **dower** of a widow is considered "inchoate" until that death, at which time it becomes a **vested** right to a **life estate.** 1 S.E. 2d 853, 855, 258 P. 295, 297. An "inchoate dower" cannot be **alienated,** 32 N.E. 681, 683; and it cannot be reached by **creditors.** It can be released by the wife if she joins with her husband in a deed.

INCIDENTAL BENEFICIARY see **beneficiary.**

INCIDENTAL DAMAGES see **damages** (INCIDENTAL DAMAGES).

INCIDENT OF OWNERSHIP an aspect of the legal title to property, for federal estate tax purposes, if a decedent possessed any "incidents of ownership" over life insurance at the time of his death, the value of these insurance policies would be includable in the decedent's gross estate. I.R.C. §2042.

INCLOSURE any land enclosed by something other than an imaginary boundary line, i.e., some wall, hedge, fence, ditch or other actual obstruction. See 39 Vt. 326, 332, 113 N.W. 384, 388. The word "town" derives from the Anglo-Saxon word "tun," meaning "inclosure." See 23 P. 405, 406, 6 N.W. 607, 608. Compare **close.**

INCOME an economic **benefit,** 348 U.S. 426; money or value received.

ADJUSTED GROSS INCOME the **gross income** of the taxpayer reduced by certain specified **deductions** that generally represent the taxpayer's business deductions. I.R.C. §62.

CASH EQUIVALENT DOCTRINE if a taxpayer receives either services or property as the result of a transaction that would ordinarily result in the receipt of income, then the taxpayer is considered to have received a cash equivalent which is subject to income

tax. Treas. Reg. §1.61-2(d). Whether **promissory notes** constitute property which is a cash equivalent is the subject of controversy. 524 F. 2d 788.

CONSTRUCTIVE RECEIPT OF INCOME a doctrine under which a taxpayer is required to include in gross income those amounts which, though not actually received, are deemed received during the tax year. Treas. Reg. §1.451-2(a). Thus there is constructive receipt when income is made available to a taxpayer without substantial restriction or condition on the taxpayer's right to exercise control over the income. It is under this theory that interest credited on a savings account is required to be included in income even though the taxpayer does not withdraw it since he had the right to withdraw it. The doctrine is to be distinguished from the CASH EQUIVALENT DOCTRINE discussed above.

FIXED INCOME see **fixed income.**

GROSS INCOME the total of the taxpayer's income from whatever source derived except those items specifically excluded from income by the Internal Revenue Code and other items not subject to tax, such as the return of capital or **fringe benefits.** Gross income includes such items as salary, **alimony,** gains from dealing in property, uncashed checks, or unclaimed wages, I.R.C. §61.

IMPUTED INCOME imputed income is an economic benefit a taxpayer obtains for himself through the performance of his own services or through the use of his own property. In general, imputed income is not subject to **income taxes.** For example, if a taxpayer is a plumber and repairs his own toilet, such repair service is not subject to tax.

INCOME AVERAGING a method of

calculating tax liability that averages income over a five-year period. It is designed to minimize the adverse consequences of **bunching** of **income** which results from fluctuations in income from year to year. The method permits such a taxpayer to compute his tax as if the higher amount of income had been earned equally over that year and the previous four years. I.R.C. §§1301 et seq.

INCOME IN RESPECT OF A DECEDENT income earned by a taxpayer before his death but received by the taxpayer's **heirs** or personal representatives. Such income is not taxed to the deceased taxpayer but to his heirs or personal representatives. I.R.C. §691.

INCOME SPLITTING the division of income between two or more taxpayers in order to reduce the overall tax liability imposed on the income by taking advantage of the taxpayer's low initial tax brackets. Compare **assignment of income**. See **joint return**.

NET INCOME in accounting, the income in excess of costs.

ORDINARY INCOME ordinary income is income that is fully subject to the ordinary income tax rates as opposed to being subject to the benefit of special deductions for **capital gains and losses**.

TAXABLE INCOME taxable income is gross income reduced by deductions allowable in obtaining adjusted gross income and further reduced by those deductions allowable in calculating itemized deductions. I.R.C. §63.

INCOME STATEMENT a financial statement that gives operating results for a specific period; also referred to as EARNINGS REPORT, OPERATING STATEMENT, and PROFIT-AND-LOSS STATEMENT. Statements normally cover 12 months of operations with interim statements at quarterly periods in current fiscal or calendar years. Operations divide into two categories of transactions—sales or revenue generation and expenses incurred in the production of sales or revenues. A typical manufacturing business sells products to its customers which, net of returns and discounts, results in "net sales" income. Net **income** or profit is "net sales" less all expenses. Net income is obtained after taxes are deducted at the prevailing rate. Net income (or "loss" should expenses exceed sales) is available to invest in the business, pay dividends, etc., as decided by owners of the enterprise. The principal expense item is usually cost-of-goods sold which includes purchase of raw materials, direct labor and factory overhead such as power, rent, etc. Next comes selling, general, and administrative expenses, which include salaries of salespersons, staff personnel, managers and offices, cost of administrative buildings and support services, and advertising expenses. **Depreciation,** which is a factory cost, is stated separately since it is not an actual cash outlay and since additional comment on the method used in calculating depreciation is required. As discussed under **balance sheet,** depreciation can be either straight line or accelerated. Both methods result in approximately the same total depreciation, but accelerated methods move most of the charge into early years which reduces reported profits and taxes on production from new machinery and equipment. Interest on debt is deducted next, resulting in pretax profit.

INCOME TAX see **tax; return, income tax.**

INCOMPETENCY inability; "a relative term which may be employed as meaning disqualification, inability or **incapacity.** The term can refer to lack of legal qualifications or fitness to discharge the required duty. It may be employed to show want of physical or intellectual or moral fitness." 116 So. 2d 566, 567.

When a person is adjudicated an "incompetent," a **guardian** is appointed by the court in which the incompetency hearing was held, who will manage the incompetent's affairs until and unless the incompetent recovers his competency to the satisfaction of the court, at which time the guardian is discharged. An adjudicated incompetent lacks capacity to contract and his contracts are void. An incompetent who has not been so adjudged enters into contracts which are **voidable**. See **competency; minority; non compos mentis.**

INCOMPETENT EVIDENCE evidence that is not **admissible**. See **admissible evidence.**

INCONSISTENT contradictory to one another. In pleading, inconsistent facts or legal theories may be pled in the alternative. Fed. R. Civ. 8(e) (2). James & Hazard, Civil Procedure 2.12 (2d ed. 1977).

INCONSISTENT STATEMENT see **prior inconsistent statement.**

INCONTESTABILITY CLAUSE see **non-contestability (incontestability) clause.**

INCONVENIENT FORUM see **forum non conveniens.**

INCORPORATE to combine together or unite so as to form one whole; to form a **corporation,** to organize and be granted status as a corporation by following procedures prescribed by law. See **articles of incorporation.**

When used in a document in reference to another writing, it means that the writing referred to is "incorporated" into or adopted and made part of the document. See 256 S.W. 2d 421, 422, 423.

INCORPORATION, SELECTIVE see **selective incorporation.**

INCORPOREAL intangible; having no physical reality. See **corporeal.**

INCORPOREAL HEREDITAMENT see **hereditament.**

INCORPOREAL PROPERTY intangible property, evidencing something of value but having no inherent value independent thereof, such as a stock certificate. See **intangible property.**

INCORPOREAL HEREDITAMENT see **hereditament.**

INCORRIGIBLE uncorrectable; a person, usually a juvenile, whose behavior cannot be made to conform to the standards dictated by law. See **criminal** (HABITUAL OFFENDER); **recidivist.**

INCREMENT an amount of increase or gain in number, amount or value; as to salaries, increments "are the periodic, consecutive additions or increases which do not become a part of the salary . . . until they accrue under the rule making such provision. . . ." 29 A. 2d 890, 891.

INCRIMINATE to hold another, or oneself, responsible for criminal misconduct; to involve someone, or oneself, in an accusation of a crime. See also **self-incrimination.**

INCROACH to use unlawfully or otherwise impair possession or title to another's property. See **encroach; trespass.**

INCULPATORY that which tends to **incriminate** or bring about a criminal conviction. Compare **exculpatory.**

INCUMBENT person in present possession of an office or position. See **de facto** [DE FACTO INCUMBENT].

INCUMBRANCE every right to, interest in, or legal **liability** upon **real property** which does not prohibit passing **title** to the land but which diminishes its value. See 113

F. 2d 748, 751. Incumbrances include **easements, licenses, leases,** timber privileges, **homestead** privileges, **mortgages,** judgment **liens,** etc.

INDEBITATUS ASSUMPSIT *(in-de-bi-tā'-tus as-sump'-sit)*—Lat: to be indebted, to have undertaken a debt. At common law, a form of action founded in contract in which the plaintiff alleges that the defendant has undertaken a debt and has failed to satisfy it.

INDEBTEDNESS, INVOLUNTARY see **bankruptcy** [INVOLUNTARY PROCEEDING].

INDECENT vulgar, offensive, obscene.

INDEFEASIBLE cannot be defeated, or altered. An "indefeasible" estate is absolute and cannot be changed by any **condition.** 80 N.Y.S. 2d 380, 381. An "indefeasible" estate **in fee simple** implies a perfect **title.** 131 U.S. 75.

INDEFINITE FAILURE OF ISSUE see **failure of issue.**

IN DELICTO *(ĭn dĕ-lĭk'-tō)*—Lat: in fault, though not in equal fault. See **in pari delicto.**

INDEMNIFY to secure against loss or damage which may occur in the future, or to provide compensation for or to repair loss or damage already suffered; to insure; to save harmless. See 235 App. Div. 382.

INDEMNITY refers to "the obligation [or duty] resting on one person to make good any loss or **damage** another has incurred or may incur by acting at his request or for his benefit," 92 S.E. 2d 54, 55; or, alternatively, the right which the person suffering the loss or damage is entitled to claim. 18 A. 2d 807; an assurance or **contract** by one party to compensate for the damage caused by another. A party seeking indemnity from another acknowledges that a duty is (or was) in fact owed by him; at the same time he

asserts that for some specified reason(s), that duty should be (or should have been) performed by the other. "Indemnity" therefore comprehends a right to insist that the duty be performed by the other, or that one be compensated by the other if the duty has already been performed. "Indemnity refers to a total shifting of the economic loss to the party chiefly or primarily responsible for that loss," 124 N.Y.S. 2d 634, 636, rather than to the party contractually responsible.

INDENTURE a **deed** between two parties conveying **real estate** by which both parties assume obligations. 94 N.Y. 86, 89. "Indenture" implies a **sealed instrument.** See 3 Ark. 565, 568. Historically, "indenture" referred to a crease or wavy cut that was made in duplicates of the deed so their authenticity could be verified later. 10 Serg. & R. 416, 417.

In a business context, an indenture is a lengthy written agreement which sets forth the terms under which **bonds** or **debentures** may be issued. Terms include the amount of the issue, the interest rate, the maturity, the property pledged as collateral (if any), and the so-called "protective covenants." An independent trustee, usually a bank or trust company, is named to oversee the issuance of the bonds, to collect and pay interest and principal, and to protect the bondholder's rights as specified in the indenture.

INDEPENDENT CONTRACTOR see **contractor.**

INDETERMINATE SENTENCE see **sentence.**

INDEX FUND a portfolio of stocks selected to match a stock market **index number,** usually the Standard & Poor's Industrial Index or the Standard & Poor's Composite Index. The guiding principle is creation of a proxy for the selected index since the index itself contains an unmanageably large number of stocks.

INDICIA *(ĭn-dĭ'-shē-à)*—Lat: indications; signs or circumstances which tend to support a belief in a proposition as being probable, but which do not prove to a certainty the truth of the proposition. It is often said to be synonymous with **circumstantial evidence.** 53 S.E. 2d 122, 125. Where one exercises dominion and control over **personal property** as if it were his own, such behavior is an indicium of ownership, see id.; a carbon copy of a bill of sale has also been held to be an indicia of title. 277 S.W. 2d 413, 416.

"Indicia" is important in many contexts. Thus, where the owner of property is responsible for giving another indicia of ownership, that other person may effectively transfer the owner's interest to a **bona fide purchaser.** See 34 N.Y.S. 2d 1008, 1009. Indicia of reliability are necessary to use information supplied by an informer as a basis to support a **search warrant.** 393 U.S. 410 (1969).

INDICIUM *(ĭn-dĭ'shē-ŭm)*—Lat: singular of **indicia.**

INDICTABLE OFFENSES crimes that can be **prosecuted** by the **grand jury** that indict the accused. At **common law,** these crimes were known as **felonies** and were placed in that category on the basis of the punishment associated with them—either death, **forfeiture** of all one's property, or mutilation. They included **murder, treason, robbery, assault, rape, arson, burglary,** and **larceny.** These crimes could also be prosecuted by individuals bringing lawsuits against the **defendants.** Under the Constitution the federal government must prosecute all **"infamous crimes,"** such as felonies, by indictment. Today states have the choice of prosecuting either by indictment or by **information.** That choice is regulated by **statute** or by state constitutional provisions. The

method of **prosecution** often depends upon whether the crime is classified as a **felony** or a **misdemeanor.** If a crime is an indictable offense, it gives rise to certain constitutional protections for the accused, such as the right to **Miranda Warnings** before being subject to custodial interrogation. 258 A. 2d 675, 679. Crimes are now usually classified according to punishment (i.e., first degree, second degree, disorderly persons offense, etc.), and do not always fall within the historical definition given above.

INDICTMENT a formal written accusation, drawn up and submitted to a **grand jury** by the public **prosecuting attorney,** charging one or more persons with a crime. The indictment is presented under oath by the prosecuting attorney to the grand jury so that it may determine whether the accusation, if proved, would be sufficient to bring about a conviction of the accused, in which case the indictment is indorsed by the foreman as a TRUE BILL. See 137 A. 370, 372. Once an indictment is filed, the matter passes to the court and a prosecutor must proceed to trial unless the court approves a **dismissal.** Indictments also serve to inform an accused of the offense with which he is charged, and must do so with sufficient clarity to enable him to prepare his defense adequately. See 143 f. 2d 953, 955. Compare **accusation; charge; complaint; information; presentment.**

INDIGENT generally, a person who is poor, financially destitute; in a legal context, a person found by a court to be unable to hire a lawyer or otherwise meet the expense of defending a criminal matter, at which point defense counsel is appointed by the court. Such status also affects his responsibility to pay a criminal fine, 497 P. 2d 523, 525; to pay certain fees, such as court costs, 452 F. Supp. 939, 942; or to be eligible for medical or hospital assistance. 425 P. 2d 316, 318. See **in forma pauperis.**

INDIGNITY in divorce law, an "affront to the personality of another, a lack of reverence for the personality of one's spouse." 176 A. 2d 919, 920. "Indignity" is a ground for divorce in some states; "the offense is not predicated upon a single act but consists of a persistent or continuous course of conduct which has the ultimate effect of rendering cohabitation intolerable." 363 P. 2d 86, 87, 88. Generally, indignities "consist of vulgarity, unmerited reproach, habitual contumely, studied neglect, intentional incivility, manifest disdain, abusive language, malignant ridicule, and any other plain manifestation of settled hate and estrangement." 180 A. 2d 82, 83. See **mental cruelty.**

INDIRECT ATTACK see **collateral attack.**

INDIRECT EVIDENCE a **circumstantial evidence;** evidence that supports a factual theory but that does not make it explicit.

INDISPENSABLE EVIDENCE evidence that is necessary to prove a submitted **fact.**

INDISPENSABLE PARTY a party whose interest in a lawsuit is such that a final **decree** cannot be issued without either affecting that interest or leaving the controversy in such a condition that its final determination may be wholly inconsistent with **equity** and good conscience. 254 U.S. 80. Therefore, an **action** may not proceed without an indispensable party, 316 P. 2d 296, 299; an indispensable party must be **joined** because his nonjoinder would result in prejudice to his rights and the rights of other parties to the **action.** See 50 F.R.D. 311, 314.

INDIVIDUAL RETIREMENT ACCOUNT [I.R.A.] a **retirement** account for individuals not eligible to participate in a qualified **pension** or profit-sharing plan for an entire **taxable year.** Such individuals may pay into the account a specified sum (in general, no more than $2,000). Such amounts are deductible to the employee and the income earned thereon is not recognized if the account provides that the employee may not make withdrawals, except if he dies or becomes disabled, prior to age 59½ and that withdrawal must commence no later than age 70½. I.R.C. §408.

INDORSEE one to whom a negotiable **instrument** is assigned by indorsement. For instance, the payee or holder of a check may write "pay to X" and sign the check on the back. X is the indorsee. In the absence of fraud or illegality, an indorsee has all of the right, title, and interest in a negotiable instrument which the indorser had prior to assignment. U.C.C. §3-201.

INDORSEMENT signature placed upon the back of an **instrument,** with or without other words, whose effect is to transfer the instrument and create "a new and substantive **contract** by which the indorser becomes a party to the instrument and liable, on certain conditions, for its payment." 370 S.W. 2d 811, 813, n. 4. Conditions giving rise to the indorser's liability generally comprehend the failure of the party primarily liable under the instrument to make payment in accordance with the terms thereof. 71 S.E. 148, 149. Indorsements are made primarily for the purpose of continuing the negotiability or enhancing the commercial value of the instrument. See 36 So. 668, 669. To constitute an indorsement, the writing must be effective to transfer the entire instrument to which it is affixed; otherwise it operates as only a partial **assignment,** U.C.C. §3-202(3), which is merely a partial transfer of title. 182 N.W. 409, 413.

ACCOMMODATION INDORSEMENT one made in the absence of any **consideration** solely for the benefit of the holder. 34 A. 201. **Credit** is thereby extended to the holder by the indorser, 12 A. 566, generally for the purpose of enabling such holder to obtain credit or money from another on the basis of the indorsement. 97 N.W. 694. See U.C.C. §3-415.

BLANK INDORSEMENT one which specifies no particular party to whom the indorsed instrument is exclusively payable, and which therefore authorizes negotiation by the **bearer** upon **delivery** alone. U.C.C. §3-204(2).

RESTRICTIVE INDORSEMENT one which is conditional, or which places restrictions on transferability through the use of certain words, including "for collection," "for deposit," "pay any bank." Id. at 3-205.

SPECIAL INDORSEMENT one which specifies the party to whom or to whose **order** the instrument shall be payable; the instrument is then negotiable only by such person unless he makes a further indorsement. Id. at 3-204(1).

INDORSER one who indorses negotiable paper. For instance, the payee or holder of a check may indorse the check by signing it on the back. An indorser is liable to pay the negotiable **instrument** in case it is dishonored. U.C.C. §3-414.

INDUSTRIAL DEVELOPMENT BOND [I.D.B.] see **guaranteed security.**

INDUSTRIAL RESERVE BANK [I.R.B.] see **guaranteed security.**

INELIGIBILITY disqualification; legal inability to perform some task or assume some office. 47 N.E. 223, 224. See **disqualify.**

IN ESCROW held in an **escrow** account, held by one who is not a party to a transaction for future delivery to a party upon the occurrence or nonoccurrence of a specific event or events.

IN ESSE (ĭn ĕs'ē)—Lat: in existence. Compare **in posse.**

IN EXTREMIS (ĭn ĕx-trĕ'-mĭs)—Lat: in extremity; at an end; especially, in anticipation of death. But "the term 'in extremis' is not exclusively applicable to an actor's anticipation of imminent death. It characterizes any situation in which the actor is 'in extremity' or in 'extreme circumstances.'" 67 Cal. Rptr. 297, 302. The fact that one has executed a document under such circumstances may affect its interpretation as his or her will. Id. Compare **causa** (CAUSA MORTIS).

INFAMOUS CRIME a crime which works infamy in the person who commits it. 189 S.E. 441. At **common law,** any infamous crime was one that rendered the person convicted thereof incompetent as a **witness.** 4 N.Y. Cr. R. 545, 546. This was based on the theory of untrustworthiness whereby a testimonial disqualification was imposed to prevent the introduction of **evidence** thought not entitled to credence. In this sense, infamous crimes comprehended **treason,** felonies and any crime involving the element of deceit **[crimen falsi]** 23 F. 136, 137 and examined the nature of the crime rather than the nature of the punishment inflicted. The modern view of infamous crimes, which under Art. V of the Constitution must be prosecuted by **indictment,** is any crime that is punishable by death or imprisonment in a state **penal institution,** with or without hard labor for more than one year. See 604 F. 2d 569, 572. Under this view, it is determined by the nature of the punishment, which a court is authorized to impose, and not by the character of the crime. The common law procedure of excluding witnesses because of prior infamous convictions is no longer followed, although such convictions may affect the **credibility** of the witness. See 182 A. 2d 15, 16.

INFANCY the period prior to reaching the age of legal **majority**; minority. In some states it is terminated upon marriage regardless of age.

An infant's contracts are generally **voidable**, except that by statute infants within certain age groups can validly contract for necessities and for business ventures on reasonable terms. Educational loans constitute a frequent exception to the ordinary contract defense of infancy. See 23 Vt. 378.

An infant will be liable for his own **torts** although special rules relating to the capacity of very young actors to form necessary states of mind may apply and insulate them to some extent. See Prosser, Torts §134 (4th ed. 1971).

"At common law, children under the age of seven are conclusively presumed to be without criminal capacity, those who have reached the age of fourteen are treated as fully responsible, while as to those between the ages of seven and fourteen there is a rebuttable **presumption** of criminal incapacity. About one-third of the states have made some change by statute in the age of criminal responsibility for minors. In addition, all jurisdictions have adopted **juvenile court** legislation providing that some or all criminal conduct by those persons under a certain age (usually eighteen) must or may be adjudicated in the juvenile court rather than in a criminal proceeding." LaFave & Scott, Criminal Law 351 (2d ed. 1982). See **emancipation**. See also **incompetence**.

IN FEE [IN FEE SIMPLE] describes absolute ownership of an **estate** in land. It is not used to describe a quality of a title to an **easement,** or other appurtenance or incorporeal interest. 139 So. 2d 135, 138. See **fee simple**.

INFERENCE a deduction from the facts given, which is usually less than certain but which may be sufficient to support a finding of fact; "a process of reasoning by which a fact or proposition sought to be established . . . is deducted as a logical consequence from other facts, or a state of facts, already proved or admitted. . . . It has also been defined as 'a deduction of an ultimate fact from other proved facts, which proved facts, by virtue of the common experience of man, will support but not compel such deductions.' " 186 A. 2d 632, 633. Compare **presumption**.

INFERENCE, NECESSARY see **necessary inference**.

INFERIOR COURT a court whose decision is subject to review by another court, which is referred to as a SUPERIOR COURT.

INFEUDATION the act of granting a **freehold estate;** same as **feoffment** or enfeoffment.

INFIRM sickly; a weak person. In particular circumstances the testimony of an "infirm" person may be obtained in a manner that differs from regular procedure to prevent its loss through the death of the witness. See **de bene esse.**

INFLUENCE, UNDUE see **undue influence.**

INFORMAL PROCEEDINGS in probate law, the admission of a will to probate without the requirements necessary in an adversarial proceeding, such as notice to interested parties. Uniform Probate Code §1-201 (19).

IN FORMA PAUPERIS (*ĭn fôr'-mà päw'-pĕr-ĭs*)—Lat: in the manner of a pauper. With regard to **pleadings,** opportunity to sue "in forma pauperis" grants a party the right to proceed without assuming the burden of **costs** or formal niceties of pleading, such as page size and numbers of copies required. A criminal **defendant** granted permission to proceed in forma pauperis may be entitled to the assistance of court-appointed **counsel.** See **indigent.**

INFORMATION a written accusation of crime signed by the **prosecutor,** charging a person with the commission of a crime; an alternative to **indictment** as a means of starting a criminal prosecution. The purpose of an information is to inform the **defendant** of the charges against him and to inform the court of the factual basis of the charges.

Although the U.S. Constitution's Fifth Amendment requires that the federal government prosecute all **infamous crime** only upon presentment of an indictment by the grand jury, the states are free to prosecute any crime by means of an information.

INFORMATION AND BELIEF refers to a degree of certainty which falls short of actual knowledge, but which comprehends reasonable, **good faith** efforts to determine truth or falsity. See Fed. R. Civ. Proc. 36. The term is used with reference to documents requiring verification, such as requests for **search warrants,** 122 P. 2d 815, 817, responses to **interrogatories, complaints, pleadings,** etc.; statements made "on information and belief" may or may not achieve the degree of certainty required for these various types of statements, depending on the jurisdiction, the circumstances, etc.

INFORMED CONSENT consent accompanied by full notice as to that which is being consented to; constitutionally required in certain areas where one may consent to what otherwise would be an unconstitutional violation of a right. See, e.g., **Miranda Rule.**

The phrase is also used in **tort** law with respect to the requirement that a patient be apprised of the nature and risks of a medical procedure before the physician can validly claim exemption from liability

for **battery** or from responsibility for medical complications, etc. 104 N.W. 12; 159 So. 2d 888.

INFORMER one who, on a confidential basis, gives information about some wrongdoing to the police or other governmental authorities.

INFORMER'S PRIVILEGE the privilege of the government to not reveal the identity of an informer. The identity of an informant need not be disclosed to the defendant at a suppression hearing so long as the person relying upon the informer's information has testified and has been cross-examined as to what the informant told him and as to why the information was believed to be trustworthy. 386 U.S. 300. The privilege may not survive a demand for disclosure at the trial level, however, if necessary to insure a fair trial. 353 U.S. 53. And in no event can the informer's true identity be withheld from the accused once the prosecution decides to use the informer as a government witness in a criminal trial. 390 U.S. 129.

INFRA *(in'-frà)*—Lat: below, beneath; when seen in text, refers to a discussion or a citation appearing subsequently in the text; opposite of **supra** (above or before).

INFRINGEMENT OF COPYRIGHT see **copyright** (INFRINGEMENT); **plagiarism.**

INFRINGEMENT OF PATENT see **patent infringement.**

IN FUTURO *(in fyū-tyū'-rō)*—Lat: in the future; at a later date. Contrast **in praesenti.**

IN GENERE *(in jĕ'-nĕ-rā)*—Lat: in kind; in the same class or species. Articles or things in the same genus are "in genere"; expresses any class relationship. Laws on the same subject are likewise said to be "in genere." However, an in genere relationship between two statutes does not mean they are identical. Thus, laws in one area, though broadly designed to regulate one general field may be aimed at different portions of that field, and still be in genere. The term imports singleness in general purpose but permits diversity of individual purposes.

INGRESS AND EGRESS the entering upon and departure from the lands in question, and the means of entering and leaving; the right of **lessee** to enter and leave leasehold. See **easement.**

IN GROSS at large. See **easement** (EASEMENT IN GROSS).

IN HAEC VERBA (*in hēc ver'ba*)— Lat: in these words.

INHERENT DEFECT a defect that exists in an item regardless of the use made of that item. Although an inherent defect may not be readily detectable, a manufacturer is nonetheless strictly liable for any injury caused by it. Prosser, Law of Torts 656, 657. (4th ed. 1971). Synonymous with **latent defect.**

INHERENT POWERS those powers an authority such as a court or a government must have in order to achieve the purposes for which it was created. See 437 N.E. 2d 164, 168.

INHERENT CONSTITUTIONAL POWERS the federal government possesses "all those inherent and implied powers which, at the time of adopting the Constitution, were generally considered to belong to every government as such, and as being essential to the exercise of its functions." 12 Wall. 457, 556. These powers include the ability to conduct foreign affairs, 299 U.S. 304, 315-16; to exclude and deport aliens, 142 U.S. 651, 659; to protect persons in federal custody or employment, 135 U.S. 1; to protect federal elections, 110 U.S. 651; to protect federally created or fed-

erally guaranteed rights, 112 U.S. 76. Antieau, Modern Constitutional Law §§11:5 to 11:12 (1969).

INHERENT RIGHT a right that exists by reason of an individual's status as an individual and is not derived from any other source.

INHERIT technically, to take as an **heir at law** solely by **descent,** rather than by **devise.** More commonly used to signify taking either by devise, i.e., by **will,** or by descent, i.e., from one's ancestor as a matter of law. See 113 U.S. 340.

INHERITANCE real or personal **property** which is inherited by **heirs** according to the laws of **descent and distribution.** 216 P. 446, 449. 154 S.E. 2d 37, 39. **Real property vests** in the inheritor immediately on the death of the ancestor, subject to the rights of creditors. 70 P. 2d 1059, 1060. A nontechnical meaning of "inheritance" refers to the estate passed by **will.** 277 S.W. 197, 198.

IN HOC (*in hŏk*)—Lat: in this; respecting this.

IN INVITUM (*in in-vē'-tŭm*)—Lat: against the will of the other party.

INJUNCTION a judicial **remedy** awarded for the purpose of requiring a party to refrain from doing or continuing to do a particular act or activity. 104 A. 2d 884. Injunctions were first used by the **courts of equity** to restrain parties from conduct contrary to **equity** and good conscience. 344 S.W. 2d 257. Today, with the widespread merger of law and equity, injunctions are used as well in general **courts of law** whereas law courts were formerly constrained to use the writ of **mandamus.**

The injunction is a preventative measure which guards against future injuries rather than affording a remedy for past injuries.

Types of injunctions include:

FINAL INJUNCTIONS see PERMA-
NENT [FINAL] INJUNCTIONS below.

INTERLOCUTORY INJUNCTIONS see
TEMPORARY [INTERLOCUTORY]
INJUNCTIONS below.

MANDATORY INJUNCTIONS require
positive action, rather than restraint.

PERMANENT [FINAL] INJUNCTIONS
issued upon completion of a trial
wherein it has been actively
sought by a party.

TEMPORARY [INTERLOCUTORY] IN-
JUNCTIONS usually used to prevent threatened injury, maintain
the **status quo,** or preserve the
subject matter of the litigation
during trial.

INJURIA ABSQUE DAMNO *(ĭn-
jû'-rē-à äb'-skwā däm'-nō)*—Lat:
wrong without damage; insult without damage. "Injuria" means a **tortious** act in legal terminology. See 7
Ill. App. 438, 446. Where a **cause of
action** requires that damages be
pleaded as an element, this maxim
expresses the rule that a wrong
which causes no damage recognized as such by the law cannot
give rise to a cause of action. While
this maxim applies to a **negligence**
suit, it is not applicable in any cause
of action in which **nominal damages**
can be recovered, such as in the
case of intentional torts (assault
and battery) and actions for **breach
of contract.** See **damages** (NOMINAL
DAMAGES).

**INJURIA NON EXCUSAT INJU-
RIAM** *(ĭn-jû'-rē-à nŏn ĕx-kū'-sät
ĭn-jû'-rē-äm)*—Lat: one wrong
does not justify another.

INJURY any wrong or damage
done to another, either in his person, rights, reputation, or property.
24 So. 2d 623, 626. Unlike the ordinary meaning of injury (that which
damages the body), a LEGAL INJU-
RY is any damage resulting from a
violation of a legal right, and which
the law will recognize as deserving

of redress. See 33 A. 1, 2. See **damnum absque injuria; irreparable injury.** Compare **damages.**

IN KIND of the same kind; to
return something of the same or
similar type or quality to that which
was received, though not necessarily the identical article. See **in genere.**

IN LIMINE *(ĭn lĭ'-mĭ-nē)*—Lat: at
the beginning or the threshold. See
motion in limine.

IN LOCO PARENTIS *(ĭn lō'-kō pä-
rĕn'-tĭs)*—Lat: in the place of a parent; "according to its generally
accepted common law meaning, refers to a person who has put himself
in the situation of a lawful parent by
assuming the obligations incident to
the parental relation without going
through the formalities necessary
to legal adoption. It embodies the
two ideas of assuming the parental
status and discharging the parental
duties." 159 F. 2d 683, 686. The
term is commonly used with reference to the relationship between a
minor and a residential institution
such as a boarding school.

INMATE one who is committed to
an institution, such as a prisoner at
a prison.

IN MORTMAIN see **mortmain.**

INNOCENT PURCHASER see
bona fide purchaser.

INNS OF COURT four private societies in England that prepare students for the practice of law and
that alone may admit them to the
bar; that is, confer the rank of **barrister.** The four inns of court are
Inner Temple, Middle Temple, Lin-
coln's Inn, Gray's Inn.

INNUENDO that part of a **pleading**
in an **action** for **libel** which explains
words spoken or written and an-
nexes to them their meaning as construed by the plaintiff. 41 A. 781,
782. The plaintiff in a libel action
cannot enlarge or change original
language by innuendo, since the

purpose of innuendo is to explain the application of words used, and words which are not libelous in themselves cannot be made so by innuendo. See 81 N.Y.S. 2d 920, 921.

IN OMNIBUS *(ĭn ŏm'-nĭ-būs)*— Lat: in all things; in all the world; in all nature; in all respects.

IN PAIS *(ĭn pĕ'-ĭs)*—Fr: in the country, neighborhood; applies to a transaction handled outside the court or without a legal **proceeding.**

IN PARI DELICTO *(ĭn pä'-rē dĕ-lĭk'-tō)*—Lat: in equal fault. The term is used with reference to an exception to the general rule that illegal transactions or contracts are not legally enforceable; thus, where the parties to an illegal agreement are not "in pari delicto," the agreement may nevertheless be enforceable at **equity** by the innocent or less guilty party. 23 A. 2d 607. Such a situation may arise where one party's consent to the arrangement is made under **duress,** see id., or is obtained **fradulently,** see 113 P. 2d 190; or where one party is but an instrument in the hands of another, see 39 P. 270; or where the law violated by the agreement was one designed especially for the protection of one class of persons from oppression by another, see 70 N.E. 258. The term may also be used with reference to liability in tort, where the party most negligent may be required to bear the entire burden of the loss or injury. 178 F. 2d 628. See **clean hands.**

IN PARI MATERIA *(ĭn pä'-rē mä-tĕr'-ē-à)*—Lat: on like subject matter. **Statutes** or document provisions that are "in pari materia" are those that relate to the same person or subject. In the **construction** or interpretation of a particular statute or instrument, the various portions of the statute or instrument, and all other acts or instruments relating to the same subject or having the

same general purpose, are to be read together, as constituting one law or agreement, such that equal dignity and importance will be given to each. 43 Okl. 652.

IN PERPETUITY to exist forever; perpetually.

IN PERSONAM *(ĭn pĕr-sō'-näm)* —Lat: into or against the person. In **pleading,** the term refers to an **action** against a person or persons, founded on personal **liability,** and requiring **jurisdiction** by the court over the person sought to be held liable, i.e., the **defendant;** actions whereby "the plaintiff either seeks to subject defendant's general **assets** to execution in order to satisfy a money **judgment,** or to obtain a judgment directing defendant to do an act or refrain from doing an act under sanction of the court's contempt power." 237 So. 2d 592, 594. An action **in rem** is distinguished from an action **in personam;** "in an action 'in rem' a valid judgment may be obtained without personal **service of process** so far as it affects the **res** involved, but in an action to recover a judgment 'in personam,' process must usually be personally served or there must be compliance with the substituted service specifically provided by some statute. A judgment in rem is conclusive upon all who may have or claim any interest in the subject matter of the litigation." 267 S.W. 2d 18, 22. Compare **in rem.**

IN POSSE *(ĭn pŏs'-ē)*—Lat: in the future, that which is not yet but which may exist. Compare **in esse.**

IN PRAESENTI *(ĭn prā-sĕn'-tē)*— Lat: in the present; often signifies an act or interest which is presently effective as distinguished from one operative or effective **in futuro.**

IN QUANTUM MERUIT see **quantum meruit.**

INQUEST a judicial inquiry; an inquiry made by a **coroner** to determine the cause of death of one who has been killed, has died suddenly, has died under suspicious circumstances, or has died in prison. Generally, it is "a trial of an issue of fact where the plaintiff alone introduces testimony [and which] does not necessitate a jury." 6 How. Prac. 118, 119.

INQUIRY NOTICE see **notice** (IMPLIED NOTICE).

IN RE (ĭn rā)—Lat: in the matter of; usually used to signify a legal proceeding where there is no opponent, but rather some judicial disposition of a thing, or **res,** such as the **estate** of a decedent. See **ex parte.**

IN REM (ĭn rĕm)—Lat: signifies actions that are against the **res,** or thing, rather than against the person. A proceeding "in rem" is one taken against property, and has for its object the disposition of the property, without reference to the title of individual **claimants.** 71 A. 2d 911, 914. The outcome of the proceeding is binding on all who claim title to the property. Compare **in personam; quasi** (QUASI IN REM).

ACTIONS IN REM those which seek not to impose personal liability but rather to affect the interests of persons in a specific thing (or **res**). A few such actions purport to affect the interests of all persons ("all the world") in the same thing; most of them seek to affect the interests of only certain particular persons in the thing. Typical modern examples are actions for **partition** of, or for **foreclosure** of a lien upon, or to **quiet title** to, real estate. The concept of in rem actions has been extended to those which seek to affect status.

ACTIONS QUASI IN REM actions based on a claim for money damages begun by **attachment** or **garnishment** or other seizure of property where the court has no **jurisdiction** over the person of

the defendant but has jurisdiction over a thing belonging to the defendant or over a person who is indebted or under a duty to the defendant.

INSANE DELUSION see **delusion.**

INSANITY not mentally responsible, to some degree (the degree depending on the legal transaction in relation to which it is employed). 232 F. Supp. 255, 257. The term may be used to signify lack of criminal responsibility, need for commitment to a mental institution, inability to transact business, inability to stand trial (i.e., unable to assist in one's own defense). See 214 A. 2d 393, 405. "In criminal law, 'insanity,' by whatever test it may be ascertained, may be said to be that degree or quantity of mental disorder which relieves one of the criminal responsibility for his actions." 316 P. 2d 917, 919. Compare **incompetence.** See also **non compos mentis; diminished capacity.**

There are three main tests governing insanity defenses:

The M'NAGHTEN RULE was the common law test of criminal responsibility. 8 Eng. Rep. 718. A person was not responsible for criminal acts if as a result of a mental disease or defect he did not understand what he did or that it was wrong, or if he was under a delusion (but not otherwise insane) which, if true, would have provided a good **defense.** The person is unable to distinguish right from wrong. See **M'Naghten Rule**

The first major modification of the M'Naghten Rule was the DURHAM RULE which states that "an accused is not criminally responsible if his unlawful act was the product of mental disease or defect." 214 F. 2d 862, 874–75. See **Durham Rule.**

Most federal courts and many state courts and legislatures have adopted the American Law Institute's Model Penal Code §4.01(1) (1962) test which combines many of the elements of the M'Naghten and Durham tests. The ALI TEST states that "A person is not responsible for criminal conduct if at the time of such conduct as a result of mental disease or defect he lacks substantial capacity either to appreciate the criminality [or alternatively, wrongfulness] of his conduct or to conform his conduct to the requirements of law." The ALI TEST further provides that the "terms 'mental disease or defect' do not include an abnormality manifested only by repeated criminal or otherwise antisocial conduct." Id. at §4.01(2). This language is designed to exclude the sociopathic or psychopathic criminal.

Since a person found to be insane at the time of the commission of the criminal act could not have the necessary mental state to commit a crime, the finding of insanity is a complete acquittal to the charge. Moreover, since such a finding is based on the defendant's state at the time of the crime, the finding does not necessarily relate to the defendant's mental state at the time of trial and therefore does not logically lead to the conclusion that the defendant is sufficiently **incompetent** to be involuntarily committed in a mental institution.

Further, insanity provides a ground for rescinding a **contract** or **will** when it is shown that the contracting party did not understand the nature of his act or the extent of his property.

The insanity defense must be distinguished from the concept of "capacity to stand trial," which is based on the defendant's ability to assist in his defense and his understanding of the charges against him. See Beran and Toomey, eds., Mentally Ill Offenders and the Criminal Justice System 11 (1979). While the insanity defense affects a person's culpability, lack of capacity to stand trial does not bar a subsequent trial for the charges against him when and if the condition ceases.

INSANITY, PLEA OF see **plea.**

IN SE *(ĭn sā)*—Lat: in and of itself, e.g., **malum in se** refers to that which is evil in and of itself.

INSIDER Section 16(a) of the Securities and Exchange Act, 15 U.S.C. § 78p(a) (1964), defines an insider as every officer and director of a **corporation** and any person who owns more than 10% of the **stock** of that corporation.

Under federal law, such insiders are forced to return to the corporation the "SHORT SWING" PROFITS which they made on the sale or exchange of corporate stock. Such profits are defined under the federal statute as those made by the insider through sale or other disposition of the corporate stock within six months after purchase.

Both federal securities acts and state **blue sky laws** regulate the stock transactions of individuals who have access to inside information concerning a corporation. The laws were enacted so that the general investing public would not hesitate in purchasing securities for fear that they have been artificially inflated or deflated by **insider trading.** Under the Bankruptcy Act of 1978, special rules for preferences apply to insiders, who are defined as individuals or business entities closely related to the debtor. See 11 U.S.C. 101(25), 547. See insider trading.

INSIDER TRADING buying or selling corporate stock by a corporate officer or other **insider** who profits by his access to information not available to the public. Such trading is illegal under state and federal law based on a policy that all persons trading in stock should have equal access to information and that insiders should not profit personally from something that belongs to the corporation. For these reasons, the courts have used the Securities Exchange Act of 1934 to require insiders either to disclose all material inside information or to abstain from trading. The prohibition against trading on inside information is enforced regardless of whether the trading is done by the insider or by an unscrupulous investor who has been tipped off by the insider.

INSOLVENCY a financial condition in which one is unable to meet his obligations as they mature in the ordinary course of business or in which one's liabilities exceed his assets at any given time. 317 P. 2d 182. In the absence of statutory definition, the former description of insolvency is the more widely recognized, Id.; however, statutory definition is common today. See, e.g., 11 U.S.C.A. §101(26) (Bankruptcy Act); U.C.C. §1-201(23). See also **bankruptcy.**

INSOLVENCY PROCEEDINGS see **bankruptcy.**

IN SPECIE *(ĭn spē'-shē)*—Lat: in kind; in like form; e.g., to repay a loan "in specie" would be to return the same kind of goods to the lender as were borrowed.

INSPECTION OF DOCUMENTS right of parties in a **civil action** to view and copy documents essential to the adverse party's **cause of action,** which are in his or the court's possession. Fed. R. Civ. P. 34. This is done as part of the **discovery** process before trial; but apart from the production for pretrial inspection, a party may require the production of documents at the time of trial for the purpose of introducing them into **evidence.** James & Hazard, Civil Procedure §6.5 (2d ed. 1977). See **subpoena duces tecum.**

INSTALLMENT the partial satisfaction of a debt or other obligation.

INSTALLMENT CONTRACT a contract in which the obligation of one or more of the parties—such as an obligation to pay money, deliver goods, or render services—is divided into a series of successive performances.

The contact is one and entire in its origin and simply looks to a series of performances for the fulfillment of its terms. The fact that performance is not rendered all at once does not mean there is more than one contract between the parties, and it is not necessarily a divisible contract. The Uniform Commerical Code takes a broad approach to the term, including any contract that requires or authorizes the delivery of goods in separate lots to be separately accepted; even though the contract contains a clause, each delivery is a separate contract or its equivalent. U.C.C. §2-612. See also **retail installment contract.**

INSTALLMENT METHOD see **accounting method** (INSTALLMENT METHOD OF ACCOUNTING).

INSTALLMENT SALE a contract by which goods are purchased now but paid for over a period of time by a number of installments. Consumers have extensive protection against abusive installment sales of consumer goods under the Truth-in-Lending Act, 15 U.S.C. §§1601 et seq., which governs advertising, the computation of interest on unpaid installments, and other aspects of such sales.

INSTANT MATTER see **sub judice.**

IN STATU QUO *(ĭn stă'-tū kwō)*—Lat: in the existing situation or condition. IN STATU QUO ANTE in a contract means "being placed in the same position in which a party was at the time of the inception of the contract which is sought to be **rescinded.**" 28 P. 764, 767.

INSTITUTION see **correctional institution; penal institution.**

INSTRUCTION directions given by the judge to the **jury** prior to their deliberation, informing them of the law applicable to the facts of the **case** before them, which is to guide them in reaching a correct verdict according to law and the **evidence.** See 155 S.W. 2d 550. An instruction to the jury is a **"charge"** to the jury, 47 S.W. 2d 443, 447; "and denotes more in the nature of a 'command' than request." 29 A. 2d 705. See **Allen charge.**

INSTRUMENT in commercial law, a written document that records an act or agreement and that is regarded as the formal expression thereof, and that therefore provides the evidence of that act or agreement. 54 P. 2d 553.

In the law of evidence, the term "has a still wider meaning, and includes not merely documents, but witnesses, and things animate and inanimate, which may be presented for inspection" by the tribunal. 39 P. 783, 785. See **negotiable instrument.** See also **written instrument.**

INSUFFICIENT EVIDENCE decision by a trial judge that the evidence offered by a plaintiff or prosecutor to prove his case has failed to provide even the minimum degree of evidence necessary to submit the case to the jury, if it is a jury trial, or for the judge to hear the defendant's case, if it is a judge trial. This decision results in a directed verdict in favor of a defendant. If an appellate court decides that the evidence was insufficient, it will reverse the decision and dismiss the suit or charges against the defendant.

INSURABLE INTEREST that relationship with a person or thing that will support the issuance of an insurance policy. "A person is usually regarded as having an insurable interest in the subject matter insured when he will derive pecuniary benefit or advantage from its preservation, or will suffer pecuniary loss or damage from its destruction. . . ." 255 S.W. 2d 990, 991. Ownership or other possessory interest is not necessary, 54 So. 2d 764; so long as there is a reasonable expectation of pecuniary advantage. 15 P. 2d 483.

An insurable interest in the life of another requires that the person holding the insurance be "so connected with [the other] as to make the continuance of [his] life a matter of some real interest" to the insuring party. 94 U.S. 457, 460. The connection may be pecuniary in nature (such as when a **creditor** insures the life of his **debtor**), or it may consist of familial or other such ties of affection. Id.

INSURANCE the benefit arising from an agreement by the insurer to provide the insured, for a **consideration,** money or some other benefit in the event of the destruction or loss of, or injury to, a specified person or thing in which the other has an interest. 30 A. 2d 44. Thus, payment under the agreement by the insurer is based entirely on contingencies, 155 F. Supp. 612; which may include loss or injury not only of a specified subject, but also from a specified peril. See 172 P. 2d 4. "[T]here must be a risk of loss to which one party may be subjected by contingent or future events and an assumption of it by legally binding arrangement by another." 107 F. 2d 239, 245.

ENDOWMENT INSURANCE life insurance for a specified amount which is payable to the insured at the expiration of a certain period, or to a designated **beneficiary** immediately upon the death of the insured. 129 U.S. 252.

NO FAULT INSURANCE a system of automobile insurance where a party injured in an automobile accident recovers damages up to a specific amount against his own insurance company regardless of who was at fault in the accident. Damages in excess of the specified amount are recovered by a lawsuit against the party who caused the accident. "No fault insurance" is designed to reduce the amount of litigation resulting from minor automobile accidents and to make the system of compensating victims of such accidents more efficient. Prosser, Torts 566–567 (4th ed. 1971).

TERM INSURANCE insurance for the period for which a premium has been paid. 291 N.W. 72, 77. "Term insurance" is most often associated with life insurance policies. In that connection it is a **contract** in which the insured is required to pay from one assessment period to another the actual cost of insurance during that period, without paying an additional sum to make up a deficit in future years, where the cost of carrying the risk on the insured's life becomes greater. 122 F. 853, 856. Term insurance has no cash surrender value nor loan value and may be terminated at any time by a refusal to pay the premium. 552 P. 2d 471, 473. Automobile liability insurance, 212 So. 2d 471, 479, and health and accident insurance, 223 S.W. 2d 759, 761, also have the status of term insurance.

WHOLE LIFE INSURANCE insurance upon the life of the insured for a fixed amount at a definite premium which is paid each year in the same amount during the entire lifetime of the insured. 271 P. 2d 674, 676. Essentially, it continues for the whole of the insured's life and provides for the payment of the amount insured at the insured's death. 512 P. 2d 1245, 1250. The term is synonymous with "ordinary" life insurance or "straight" life insurance.

INSURED the person whose interests are protected by an **insurance** policy. The term refers to the person who **contracts** for a policy of insurance that indemnifies him against loss of **property,** life or health, or in the event of accident.

In a strict sense, the insured party is the owner or purchaser of the policy even though the benefit of the insurance may **accrue** to someone else. 158 N.W. 2d 99, 104. In a life insurance policy, ownership may be considered divided between the insured and the **beneficiary;** the insured owns the loan and cash surrender value of the policy, and the beneficiary owns the benefit of the proceeds at the death of the insured, subject to the insured's right of **revocation.** In a fire insurance policy, the term insured usually refers to the owner of the property insured, to whom the property was insured, and by whom the premiums were paid; and does not include a person appointed to receive a portion of the proceeds.

In its broad sense, the insured in a policy is not limited to the insured named in the policy, but applies to anyone who is insured under the policy. 251 N.E. 2d 349, 352. There is no requirement that a person must be described by name in order to be insured under a policy, as long as an insured can be ascertained by the description contained in the policy. See **insurable interest, insurance.**

INSURRECTION a violent uprising of part or all of the people against the government or other authority.

INTANGIBLE ASSET an asset that has no physical being, apart from a writing which evidences its existence. For instance, the debt of another which is evidenced by a **promissory note** is an intangible asset. The intangible assets of a business include **going concern value** and **good will.**

INTANGIBLE PROPERTY property that does not have value in itself, but that simply represents value, such as **stock certificates, bonds, promissory notes, franchises** (contracts giving right to manufacture certain items). 60 F. 2d 827, 828.

INTEGRATION the process by which the parties to an agreement adopt a writing or writings as the full and final expression of their agreement, see 3 A. 2d 180; also, the writing or writings so adopted. Restatement, Contracts, 2d §209. Thus, where the parties to a contract have agreed to it as an integration, **parol evidence** is not admissible to supplement or vary its terms. 436 P. 2d 561. See **merger.** Also refers to the process by which peoples of different races are brought together and treated equally, without discrimination on the basis of race or color.

INTENDMENT OF LAW the true meaning of or purpose behind a law.

INTENT a state of mind wherein the person knows and desires the consequences of his act which, for purposes of criminal **liability,** must exist at the time the offense is commited. 473 P. 2d 169, 170. The existence of this state of mind is often impossible to prove directly; consequently, it must be determined from reasonable deductions, such as the likelihood that the act in question would result in the consequent injury. See 262 S.W. 2d 748, 751. Two general classes of "intent" exist in the criminal law: GENERAL INTENT, which must exist in all crimes, and SPECIFIC INTENT, which is essential to certain crimes and which, as an essential element of the crime, must be proved beyond a reasonable doubt. See 261 P. 2d 614. **Assault** is a general intent offense requiring only the general **mens rea** common to any offense; "assault with intent to **rape**" is a specific intent offense requiring in addition to the general mens rea for an assault a special mens rea consisting of intent to rape the victim. In tort law, intent refers to an actor's desire to cause the consequences of his act or signifies that he believes that the consequences are substantially certain to result from it. Restatement 2d, Torts §8A. See animo; **mens rea; scienter.**

TRANSFERRED INTENT see **transferred intent.**

INTER ALIA (*ĭn'-tèr ä'-lē-à*)— Lat: among other things, as in, "the statute provides inter alia . . . ."

INTERCEPTION see **wiretap.**

INTEREST in commercial law, **consideration** or **compensation** paid for the use of money loaned or forebearance in demanding it when due. Interest is a means of compensation, 133 F. 2d 442, 444, 445, and expresses a formula consisting of the amount charged (a percentage), the amount loaned, and the time involved. 36 A. 2d 33, 36.

COMPOUND INTEREST interest paid not only upon the principal sum, but also upon the interest previously paid on that sum. Thus, interest already paid or accrued becomes part of the principal, for purposes of subsequent interest calculations.

INTEREST RATE the amount of interest paid, usually expressed as a percentage of the amount of the underlying debt.

In practice, the term connotes concern for the advantage or disadvantage of parties to the cause of action, 42 So. 2d 445, 446; or bias, 165 So. 2d 294, 297. Its existence is a factor affecting the credibility of witnesses. A third party must have an interest or concern in a lawsuit in order to **intervene;** such interest or concern is also a ground for disqualifying a **judge** or **juror.**

In real property, the broadest term applicable to claims in or on **real estate,** including any right **title,** or **estate** in or **lien** on real property, 268 N.W. 665, 667; the legal concern of a person in the property, or in the right to some of the benefits or uses from which the property is inseparable. 107 So. 103, 104. See also **security interest; terminable interest; undivided interest (right); unities** (UNITY OF INTEREST).

EXECUTED INTEREST an interest presently enjoyed and possessed by a party.

EXECUTORY INTEREST interest which may become actual at some future date or upon the happening of some contingency.

SHIFTING INTEREST a future interest arising in derogation of or out of a preceding interest, other than from the **grantor.**

SPRINGING INTEREST a future interest arising from an estate which the grantor possesses.

VESTED INTEREST one in which there is a fixed right to present or future enjoyment. See 95 A. 510.

INTERIM FINANCING debt that is incurred on a short-term basis until permanent financing can be arranged.

INTERIM ORDER a temporary order, made until another or final **order** takes its place or a specific event occurs. 39 N.W. 2d 809. See also **interlocutory.**

INTERLOCKING DIRECTOR-ATE two or more **boards of directors** of corporations that have one or more common members. Common control of the corporations may result from interlocking directorates, and can be used to restrict competition. Consequently, interlocking directorates are subject to prohibition and regulation under the Clayton Antitrust Act. 15 U.S.C. §19.

INTERLOCUTORY provisional; temporary; not final, 507 P. 2d 530, 532. "An **order** or **judgment** is interlocutory if it does not determine the **issues** (at trial) but directs some further **proceeding** preliminary to a final **decree.** Such an order or judgment is subject to change by the court during the pendency of the action to meet the exigencies of the case." 120 S.E. 2d 82, 91. For that reason it is often not appeal-

able until the entire matter has been disposed of by a final judgment.

INTERLOCUTORY DECREE see **decree** (INTERLOCUTORY DECREES)

INTERLOCUTORY ORDER order determining an intermediate issue, made in the course of a pending litigation which does not dispose of the case, but abides further court action resolving the entire controversy. See 205 S.W. 2d 612, 614. Such orders are not generally appealable until after the entire matter has been disposed of by final order or judgment. 28 U.S.C. §§1291-1293.

INTERMEDDLER see **officious intermeddler.**

INTERNAL REVENUE CODE the massive statute that sets forth the federal tax law. It is located in Title 26, United States Code. Its various subtitles include provisions relating to the **income tax, gift tax, estate tax, generation skipping tax,** and other less important and less well-known taxes; as with all federal statutes it is enacted and amended by Congress, and is implemented by the executive branch through the **Internal Revenue Service** by the Commissioner of Internal Revenue who is appointed by the President.

INTERNAL REVENUE SERVICE the federal agency primarily concerned with the administration of the federal tax laws; the Commissioner of Internal Revenue is in charge of this agency and is charged with responsibility for the **assessment** and collection of federal taxes; the Service is divided into its central office (known as the National Office) and various field offices in major cities; the field offices are divided into regional and district offices. The most important division at the regional office level is the Appellate Division which is responsible for handling administrative appeals by taxpayers concerning their tax liabilities.

EXAMINATION DIVISION responsible for examination of **returns, deficiency assessments** and for initial conferences and settlement activities respecting tax liability.

CRIMINAL INVESTIGATION DIVISION responsible for investigations into cases involving potential tax fraud.

COLLECTION DIVISION responsible for actual collection of taxes.

INTERNATIONAL AGREEMENTS agreements between nations such as **treaties,** conventions, and protocols.

INTERNATIONAL COURT OF JUSTICE the principal judicial tribunal of the United Nations, consisting of 15 members elected by the General Assembly and the Security Council for a definite, limited term. The only **appeal** from a **judgment** of this Court is to the U.N. Security Council. The seat of the Court is at the Hague, though it may meet elsewhere at its discretion.

INTERNATIONAL LAW the law governing relations between nations; rules and principles that govern questions of right between nations. See 45 Am. Jur. 2d International Law §1. These rules emanate from nations' own free will, as expressed in conventions, or by generally accepted usages. See generally Restatement 2d, Foreign Relations Law of the United States, §§1–5. The Charter of the United Nations provides for the General Assembly to initiate studies and make recommendations toward encouraging the progressive development of international law and its codification. Charter of the United Nations c.IV art. 13. In its broadest sense it is both public and private law. The public law regulates the political relations between nations. The private law refers to the comity of nations giving effect to each other's national laws relating to the rights of individuals in each country. See generally 246 U.S. 304. International law may be founded on either abstract reasoning, custom and usage, conclusions of publicists based on established practice, or judicial precedents. See generally 311 F. 2d 547. Various conferences and commissions have also codified international law. See Restatement 2d, Foreign Relations Law of the United States, §§1–5. International law is part of the law of the United States so that even though a court may be without **jurisdiction** to enforce international law, such law is legally paramount when international rights and duties are involved. 313 U.S. 69, 246 P. 2d 585. See **International Court of Justice.**

INTER PARES *(ĭn'-tèr pär'-ās)*— Lat: among peers; among those of equal rank.

INTER PARTES *(ĭn'-tèr pär'-tās)*—Lat: between the parties.

INTERPLEADER an **equitable action** in which a **debtor,** not knowing to whom among his **creditors** a certain debt is owed, and having no claim or stake in the fund or other thing in dispute other than its proper disposition, will petition a court to require that the creditors litigate the claim among themselves. The person interpleading is called the STAKEHOLDER. "Interpleader" is used to avoid double or multiple liability on the part of the debtor. See Fed. R. Civ. Proc. 22; Green, Basic Civil Procedure 90 (1979). Interpleader is a procedure used often by insurance carriers, which will deposit the proceeds of a policy in court where several persons with conflicting rights have made claims. Compare **cross-claim; impleader; joinder.**

INTERROGATION informal term used to describe the process by which **suspects** are rigorously questioned by police; must be preceded by **"Miranda warnings."** See **self-incrimination.**

INTERROGATORIES in civil actions, a pretrial **discovery** tool in which written questions are propounded by one party and served on the adversary, who must answer by written replies made under oath. 149 A. 761. "Interrogatories" can only be served on **parties** to the action, and while not as flexible as **depositions,** which include opportunity of cross-examination, they are regarded as a good and inexpensive means of establishing important facts held by the adversary. Fed. R. Civ. Proc. 33.

IN TERROREM *(ĭn tĕ-rô'-rĕm)*— Lat: in fear. A CONDITION SUBSEQUENT (see condition) placed in a will or contract that has the purpose of intimidating the **beneficiary** and thereby perhaps securing his compliance. Such clauses may be unenforceable if the condition they attempt to impose is impossible, illegal or against public policy. In many states, for example, an in terrorem clause stating that if a person contests a will that person cannot take anything under that will is unenforceable.

INTER SE [INTER SESE] *(ĭn'-tèr sā; ĭn'-tèr sĕ'-sā)*—Lat: among or between themselves; commonly applied to **trust** instruments to signify that only the rights of **shareholders** and **trustees** are involved. 13 Am. Jur. 2d Business Trusts §41.

INTERSTATE COMMERCE intercourse and traffic between citizens or inhabitants of different states; includes not only the transportation of persons and property and the navigation of public waters for that purpose, but also the purchase, sale, and exchange of commodities. U.S.C.A. Const. Art. I, Sec. 8, Cl. 3. 57 F. Supp. 57, 62.

INTERVAL OWNERSHIP see **time-sharing.**

INTERVENING CAUSE [FORCE] see **cause** (INTERVENING [SUPERVENING] CAUSE).

INTERVENTION a **proceeding** permitting a person to enter into a law suit already in progress. The term in **civil** law proceedings refers to admission of a person not an original **party** to the **suit,** so that person can protect some right or **interest** that is allegedly affected by the **proceedings.** The intervening party may wish to join the **plaintiff** or the **defendant** or demand something adverse to both of them. A person generally can become an intervenor only upon a showing that he has an **interest** in the subject matter of the original **litigation.** The purpose of intervention is to prevent delay and unnecessary duplication of lawsuits; it may be denied, however, if it interferes excessively with the rights of original parties to conduct the suit on their own terms. Fed. R. Civ. Proc. 24.

INTERVENOR the person who voluntarily interposes in a pending proceeding.

INTER VIVOS *(ĭn'-tèr vē'-vōs)*— Lat: between the living; transactions made "inter vivos" are those made while the parties are living, and not upon death (such as in the case of **inheritance**) or upon contemplation of death **[causa mortis].** A **deed,** therefore, is an **instrument** that **conveys** inter vivos a present **interest** in land, or which conveys the **corpus** of a **trust** to the **trustees** [a **deed of trust**]. Gifts are transferred inter vivos, by **will,** or causa mortis. See also **trust** [INTER VIVOS TRUST].

INTESTATE [INTESTACY] to die without leaving a valid **will.** INTESTATE PROPERTY (i.e., property not **devised**) is that which a **testator** has failed to dispose of [devise] by will. 33 A. 2d 322, 326. There can be partial intestacy if a will does not provide for distribution of all of the decedent's property or if a clause in the will is invalid. An INTESTATE ESTATE may result if the person to whom the decedent left a life estate dies and the decedent did not provide for a **remainderman.** 47 N.E. 2d 454, 456.

INTESTATE SUCCESSION the disposition of property according to the laws of **descent** and distribution upon the death of a person who has left no **will** or who has not accounted for a portion of his **estate.** 116 N.E. 2d 439, 441. See **intestate; heirs.**

IN TOTO (ĭn tō'-tō)—Lat: in entirety; in total; e.g., to repay a debt **in toto.**

INTOXICATION state of drunkenness or inebriation or some similar condition caused by use of drugs other than alcohol. In the criminal law, voluntary intoxication is no **defense** against crimes of "general **intent,**" but may operate to refute the existence of **mens rea** necessary for crimes of "specific intent." Intoxication may also be a mitigating factor reducing punishment meted out for certain crimes. Involuntary intoxication will render an actor's conduct involuntary and thereby allow him to avoid criminal **liability.** See Model Penal Code §2.08. Compare **incompetence.**

INTRINSIC FRAUD see **fraud.**

INURE to take effect, to operate; to serve to the use, benefit or advantage of someone; in property, to **vest.** 154 S.W. 2d 961, 964.

IN VACUO (ĭn văk'ū-ō)—Lat: in space.

INVALID ON ITS FACE see **void for vagueness.**

INVASION OF PRIVACY the wrongful intrusion into a person's private activities by other individuals or by the government. Tort law protects one's private affairs with which the public has no concern against unwarranted exploitation or publicity that causes mental suffering or humiliation to the average person. The right to be left alone is not always superior to the rights of the public and it may or may not

exist or may exist to a lesser degree with regard to the life of a public figure, such as a politician or other person in whom the public has a rightful **interest.** The right to personal privacy is encompassed as an aspect of liberty protected against government interference by the Constitution's **due process** clause. Some of the personal decisions protected from unwarranted government interference include decisions relating to marriage, procreation, contraception, family relationships, child rearing, and education. 431 U.S. 678. See **privacy, right of; wiretapping.**

INVENTION see **patent** [PATENT OF INVENTION].

INVENTORY the category on a **balance sheet** reflecting the cost of **goods** purchased by a business for future sale. Inventories are generally required in every business in which the sale of merchandise is a material **income** producing factor. Treas. Reg. §1.471-1. To determine the gross profit from the business operation involving the sale of merchandise, the **taxpayer** reduces from gross receipts the cost of goods sold. To determine costs of goods sold, the taxpayer adds the inventory on hand at the beginning of the year to the cost of goods purchased during the year and subtracts the inventory on hand at the close of the year. In general, there are two methods available for determining the **basis** of inventory on hand at the end of the year—LIFO and FIFO.

FIRST-IN, FIRST-OUT [FIFO] a method of inventory accounting in which the goods sold during the year are assigned the cost of the goods purchased earliest and the goods on hand at the end of the year are given the value of the goods most recently purchased. The underlying assumption of FIFO is that a business sells its inventory in the order in which it was purchased, i.e., the items purchased first are sold first. During a period of rapid inflation, FIFO will cause large profits to result, since the least expensive goods, i.e., those purchased earliest, are considered sold. To avoid the distortion of income that may result from FIFO, business may change to the LAST-IN, FIRST-OUT method of inventory accounting discussed below.

LAST-IN, FIRST-OUT [LIFO] a method of inventory accounting under which the goods sold during the year are assigned the cost of the goods most recently purchased, and the goods on hand at the end of the year are given the value of the goods purchased earliest. I.R.C. §472. The underlying assumption of LIFO is that a business sells its most recently purchased goods first. During a period of inflation, LIFO tends to understate profits since the most expensive goods, i.e., those most recently purchased, are considered to be sold.

LOWER COST OR VALUE a method of valuing inventory in which the goods on hand are valued at the lower of the price paid to purchase them or their fair market value at the time of valuation.

IN VENTRE SA MERE *(in věn'-tre sa mār)*—Leg. Fr: in the mother's womb; an unborn child.

INVERSE ORDER OF ALIENATION see **marshaling (marshalling)** (INVERSE ORDER OF ALIENATION).

INVEST to place **capital** in such a way that it is hoped will secure income or profit for the investor. See 12 F. Supp. 245, 247.

INVESTIGATORY POWERS the powers given to governmental agencies and other entities to investigate violations of laws and to gather information regarding laws that are proposed to be enacted.

INVESTITURE at **common law,** a ceremony demonstrating the transfer of **possession** of land. An open and notorious **livery of seisin** or corporeal possession in the presence of other vassals was essential to transfer land in the system of feudal **tenure.** During the early English period, when the art of writing was not widely known, this ceremony demonstrated who had title in case title was disputed at a later time. Investitures were probably first used in conquered countries to demonstrate the legitimate possession of lands by the lord. See **seisin.**

INVESTMENT BANKER a **broker** of **stocks** who acts as an **underwriter** of **securities.** The investment banker can act as **principal** by buying the entire issue from the selling **corporation** or from selling **shareholders,** or as **agent** by selling the offering on a "best-efforts" basis. In either event, the investment banker sells the issue to other dealers who together with the lead banker have formed an underwriting **syndicate.** Members of the syndicate in turn sell the **shares** to the investing public and to institutional investors such as pension funds (see **retirement plan**) or **mutual funds.** Investment banking is not banking as generally defined, and investment banking activities are illegal for commercial banks.

INVESTMENT COMPANY ACT OF 1940 see **Securities Acts** [INVESTMENT COMPANY ACT OF 1940].

INVESTMENT COMPANY [TRUST] a company or trust formed to pool the money resources of many individual investors in a large fund offering potential for investment diversification and professional management. Such a corporation typically invests in real estate or stocks and bonds, distributing the profit therefrom to its shareholders in the form of **dividends.** These companies are regulated by the Investment Company Act of 1940. 15 U.S.C. §77000. See **Securities Acts.**

In terms of organization, public investment companies are of two types: closed-end or open-end. CLOSED-END FUNDS establish their capitalization upon their inception and do not redeem shares. A number of closed-end funds are traded on the New York Stock Exchange. OPEN-END FUNDS, which are more commonly known as **mutual funds,** do not have a fixed capitalization; rather they continuously offer to sell or buy shares. See Henn and Alexander, Corporations §301 (3d ed. 1983).

INVESTMENT STOCK see **restricted securities.**

INVESTMENT TAX CREDIT see **tax credit** [INVESTMENT TAX CREDIT].

INVESTORS ADVISORS ACT OF 1940 see Securities Acts [INVESTORS ADVISORS ACT OF 1940].

INVITEE one who comes upon the land of another by the other's invitation, 23 A. 2d 917, 918; whether express or implied. 189 P. 2d 442, 444. In **tort** law, the occupier is not an insurer of the safety of invitees, but he owes a duty to them to exercise reasonable care for their protection from latent defects in the premises that might cause them injury. Prosser, Torts 392 (4th ed. 1971). Compare **licensee; trespass.**

BUSINESS INVITEE [GUEST] one who is invited to enter onto another's land or premises for the purpose of doing business. The person who invites the business invitee onto the property has a high duty of care with regard to the business invitee and must take reasonable care to protect the invitee against injury. Prosser, Torts 61 (4th ed. 1971).

INVOLUNTARY unwilling; forced; opposed; in criminal law, can act as a defense to a charge of committing a crime. See **duress.**

INVOLUNTARY CONFESSION a confession to a crime obtained in violation of the defendant's right against **self-incrimination** under the **Fifth Amendment.** Such confessions can never be used at trial, and their use results in reversal of any subsequent conviction.

INVOLUNTARY CONVERSION the conversion of property into money or similar property as a result of its destruction in whole or in part by theft, seizure, requisition, condemnation or threat thereof. For income tax purposes, gain is not recognized on property that is involuntarily converted, if the taxpayer acquires property similar in service or use within two years of the loss. I.R.C. §1033.

INVOLUNTARY BAILMENT see **bailment.**

INVOLUNTARY MANSLAUGHTER see **manslaughter** [INVOLUNTARY MANSLAUGHTER].

INVOLUNTARY NONSUIT see **nonsuit** [INVOLUNTARY NONSUIT].

IPSE DIXIT (*ĭp'-sā dĭx'-ĭt*)—Lat: he himself said it; an assertion by one whose sole authority for it is the fact that he himself has said it.

IPSO FACTO (*ĭp'-sō fäk'-tō*)— Lat: by the fact itself; in and of itself, 270 N.Y.S. 737; e.g., "the sale of his property should 'ipso facto' end any interest he may have in it."

IPSO JURE (*ĭp'-sō jû'-rā*)—Lat: by the law itself; merely by the law.

I.R.A. see **Individual Retirement Account.**

I.R.B. [Industrial Reserve Bond] see **guaranteed security.**

I.R.C. see **Internal Revenue Code.**

IRRELEVANT immaterial; not relevant; generally used in the context of a rule of evidence, whereby one party objects to the introduction at trial of evidence that is not connected to the issue being decided. See generally, McCormick, Evidence Ch. 16 (2d ed. 1972).

IRREPARABLE INJURY [DAMAGE, HARM] a type of **injury** for which no remedy **at law** suffices, and which requires a **court of equity** to intervene, often by issuing an **injunction** to prevent the conduct or conditions that are causing or that threaten the injury. In fact, a showing of imminent irreparable injury is ordinarily a prerequisite to a request for an injunction. It is any injury of such a nature that the injured party cannot be adequately compensated therefore in **damages**. 317 S.W. 2d 260, 263. An irreparable injury may not be necessarily very large or beyond the possibility of repair; it can also be an injury that is constantly recurring. See 130 N.E. 2d 758, 763; 297 N.E. 2d 557, 561. See **injury**.

I.R.S. see **Internal Revenue Service.**

ISSUE in general, to put into circulation; to send out, as to a buyer. See 73 F. 2d 799, 803. In the law of **real property**, "issue" are descendants. All persons who are descendants from a common ancestor may be regarded as issue, but in some contexts the term has a more restricted meaning and may refer to **heirs** only as a term of limitation (see **words of limitation**). See 24 A. 297. See also **failure of issue; fee tail; tender** [TENDER OF ISSUE].

In practice, an issue is a single, certain point of fact or law disputed between **parties** to the **litigation**, generally composed of an affirmative assertion by one side and a denial by the other. See 249 F. 285, 287.

In corporation law, a STOCK ISSUE is the process by which a corporation authorizes, executes, and delivers shares of stock for sale to the public. The term is also used to describe the shares thus offered by the corporation for sale at a particular time.

MATERIAL ISSUE see **material issue.**

ISSUED see **when issued.**

ISSUE PRECLUSION the rendering of a decision that precludes the issue decided from being relitigated. James & Hazard, Civil Procedure §§11.1 et seq. (2d ed. 1977). See **res judicata, collateral estoppel.**

J

J. abbreviation for a **judge** or justice. Other abbreviations include A.J., Associate Judge/Justice; C.J., Chief Judge/Justice; J.A.G., Judge Advocate General; JJ., Judges/Justices; J.P., Justice of the Peace; L.J., Law Judge; P.J., Presiding Judge; etc.

J.A.G. abbreviation for Judge Advocate General; a designation used in **military justice**.

JAIL place used for the detention of persons in the lawful custody of the government, such as a person accused of a crime who is held for **trial**, or a person convicted of a crime who is serving his **sentence**. If the inmate is confined in a local police station, it is generally referred to as a LOCK-UP; if he is temporarily confined in a courthouse during a trial, it is generally called a HOLDING CELL; if he is confined in a county facility for a period of 18 months or less, it is often called a WORKHOUSE. Most long-term confinement is now held in a CORRECTIONAL FACILITY such as the Federal Correctional Institution at [particular place]. These are referred to as F.C.I. at [place]. Older usage called such long-term confinement facilities PRISONS or PENITENTIARIES. See **penal institution**.

JAILHOUSE LAWYER Inmate who, through self-study of law, assists fellow inmates in the preparation of their appeals but does not possess formal training and is not licensed to practice law. Reliance upon jailhouse lawyers is often the only means by which indigent prisoners can be assured of access to the courts. Thus, the use of such assistance has been declared to be constitutionally protected. 393 U.S. 483.

J.D. Juris Doctor. Degree awarded today upon completion of formal legal studies by most American law schools. The degree was formerly designated LL.B.

JENCKS ACT a statute entitling a criminal **defendant** in a federal prosecution to **discover** any **witness** statement against him which is relevant to the witness's testimony and which is in the possession of the United States government. 18 U.S.C §3500. It was enacted after the U.S. Supreme Court held that defendants were entitled to such material. 353 U.S. 657. Since the Act restricts the defendant's access to such material until after the witness has testified in court against him, pretrial discovery of such material is not permitted. Fed. R. Crim. P. 16(2). Testimony of a **grand jury** witness is specifically included in the definition of "statement" by virtue of a later-enacted amendment to the Act. 18 U.S.C. §3500(e) (3).

JEOPARDY the danger of conviction and punishment in which a person is placed when he is put on trial for a criminal offense. See **double jeopardy**.

JEOPARDY ASSESSMENT see **assessment of deficiency** [JEOPARDY ASSESSMENT].

JJ. abbreviation for judges or justices.

JOBBER a "middleman" in the **sale** of **goods**, 119 N.Y.S. 325; typically, one who buys goods from a "wholesaler" and then sells them to a "retailer." See 66 F. Supp. 555. A jobber is distinguished from a **broker** or **agent**, who sells goods on another's behalf; a jobber actually purchases the goods himself, and then resells them. Compare **wholesaler**.

JOBS CREDIT see **tax credit** [JOBS CREDIT].

JOHN/JANE DOE fictional names used to identify persons in a hypothetical situation in order to explain an issue; name used when a person refuses to identify himself or when a person cannot be identified. See 3 Bl. Comm. *295.

JOINDER uniting of several **causes of action** or **parties** in a single **suit**. In federal practice, a party "may join, either as independent or as alternative **claims**, as many claims, legal, **equitable**, or **maritime**, as he has against the opposing party." Fed. R. Civ. Proc. 18(a). See also id. at Rules 19-23. See **class action; cross-claim; counterclaim; impleader; interpleader; misjoinder; real party in interest**.

COMPULSORY JOINDER the mandatory joining of certain parties which are required for the just adjudication of a **controversy;** the mandatory joining of a party to a lawsuit if his presence as a party will not deprive the court of jurisdiction and if complete relief to the existing parties may not be given in the absence of the party to be joined, or if the failure to join such party will impede the party's ability to protect his interest or subject existing parties to multiple or inconsistent liabilities. Fed. R. Civ. Proc. 19(a). If an indispensable party may not be joined, the court may dismiss the lawsuit so that it can be brought in another court. Fed. R. Civ. Proc. 19(b). In criminal law, some jurisdictions require that the **prosecutor** join in a single prosecution all offenses within the jurisdiction of the court and known to the prosecutor which arise from the same conduct or criminal episode. Model Penal Code §1.07(2); 333 A. 2d 257. Federal principles of **double jeopardy** do not require such joinder although the failure to join may bar relitigation by the state of a fact issue necessarily determined in the defendant's favor in a prior proceeding. 397 U.S. 496.

JOINDER OF ACTIONS OR CLAIMS the joinder of two or more claims or actions in a single law suit. See PERMISSIVE JOINDER below.

JOINDER OF ISSUE the act by which an **issue** is formally fashioned and structured for the purpose of its consideration and determination by a court. Under the code system of pleading, an issue is joined when one side asserts a set of facts and the other side denies it. 71 C.J.S. §513. In criminal law joinder of issue occurs when the defendant pleads "not guilty" in response to an indictment filed against him. 21 Am. Jur. 2d §458.

JOINDER OF PARTIES the naming of a person or entity as a party to a lawsuit. See COMPULSORY JOINDER above and PERMISSIVE JOINDER below.

MISJOINDER the improper joinder of a party or a claim. In **civil** cases, the remedy is to remove the improper party or claim from the suit. Fed. R. Civ. Proc. 21. In **criminal** cases, the remedy is separate trial of the misjoined offenses or defendents. Fed. R. Crim. Proc. 14. This remedy is also available to criminal defendants if the joinder prejudices any of the defendants. *Id.*

PERMISSIVE JOINDER the joining of parties in a single lawsuit for claims arising under the same transaction or occurrences, or involving a question of law or fact common to claims against such parties. Fed. R. Civ. Proc. 20(a). Such joinder is allowed but is not required. The court may order separate trials and grant such other relief as is necessary to prevent a party from being prejudiced by permissive joinder. Fed. R. Civ. Proc. 20(b).

Also, the joining in a single lawsuit of as many alternative and separate claims as a party may have against an opposing party, Fed. R. Civ. Proc. 18(a). The permissive joinder of claims is encouraged as furthering **judicial economy** since it avoids the multiplicity of suits that would otherwise result. However, the failure to raise claims could result in a party being barred from pursuing them at a later date due to the doctrines of **res judicata, direct estoppel** and **collateral estoppel**. The failure to join a compulsory counterclaim will similarly bar a separate, later suit by the claimant. Fed. R. Civ. Proc. 13(a).

JOINT united; combined; not solitary in interest or action. In criminal law, a slang expression for a marijuana cigarette. See **controlled substances.**

JOINT ACCOUNT a bank account in the name of two or more persons, each of whom has the power to withdraw funds.

JOINT AND SEVERAL refers to the sharing of rights and **liabilities** among a group of people collectively and also individually. Thus, if **defendants** in a negligence suit are "jointly and severally" liable, the injured party may sue some or all of the defendants together, or each one separately, and may collect equal or unequal amounts from each in satisfaction of his damages. See 108 F. Supp. 386, 387. However, while the injured party may have a choice as to whom he will collect damages from, he may not collect in total for more than the amount of his damages found by the court. See **contribution; indemnity.** Compare **severally.**

JOINT CUSTODY see **custody of children.**

JOINT ENTERPRISE enterprise or undertaking founded on consensual agreement of parties. Its essential elements are agreement, common purpose, community of interest, and equal right of control. 466 P. 2d 413, 418. Those who engage in a joint enterprise that is unlawful or causes injury may be liable as **joint tortfeasors,** accessories, or conspirators.

JOINT LIABILITY shared **liability** which entitles any one party who is sued to insist that others be sued jointly with him. See 38 F. Supp. 404, 407. See **joinder.**

JOINT LIVES a period which lasts until the death of the last to survive of two or more specified persons.

JOINT OWNERSHIP see **joint tenancy [ownership].**

JOINT STOCK COMPANY see **company** [JOINT STOCK COMPANY].

JOINT TENANCY [OWNERSHIP] an interest in property consisting of a single **estate** in land or other property owned by two or more persons, created by the same grantor or grantors under one **instrument** and, at one time, with all such persons having an equal right to share in the use and enjoyment of the property during their respective lives and being entitled to the full ownership of such property upon the death of each other such person. 309 P. 2d 1022, 1025. The property can be conveyed by a **deed** joined in by all the co-tenants or by a forced judicial **partition.** See **survivorship; unities.**

JOINT TORT-FEASORS two or more persons who owe to another person the same **duty** and whose **negligence** results in injury to such other person, thus rendering the tort-feasors both **jointly and severally** [individually] liable for the injury, 194 N.W. 2d 564, 565; 277 F. Supp. 457, 461; the parties must either act in **concert** or must by independent acts unite in causing a single injury. See also **contribution.**

JOINTURE an **estate** in **property** secured to a prospective wife as a marriage settlement, to be enjoyed by her after her husband's decease. See 74 N.W. 1077, 1078. The estate existed under the **common law** as a means of protecting the wife's future, upon the death of her husband, in lieu of **dower.** See also **curtesy.**

JOINT VENTURE a business undertaking by two or more parties in which profits, losses, and control are shared. See 447 P. 2d 609. Usually connotes an enterprise of a more limited scope and duration than a **partnership,** although the terms are often considered synonymous and both indicate similar types of **joint liability** for debts and torts. See 27 N.Y.S. 785. Compare **corporation.**

JONES ACT the federal statute that gives a seaman who suffers a personal injury in the course of his employment, or the personal representative of a seaman who dies as the result of a personal injury suffered in the course of his employment, the right to sue for **damages** at law. 46 U.S.C. §688. See also **Federal Employer's Liability Act.**

JOURNALIST'S [NEWSPERSON'S] PRIVILEGE some states have enacted **shield laws** granting media persons the privilege of declining to reveal confidential sources of information. No constitutional basis for such a privilege has been found in the **First Amend-**

ment's guarantee of freedom of the press. 408 U.S. 665. Such a privilege, however, must yield to a defendant's need for discovery and for a fair trial as constitutionally guaranteed under the **Sixth Amendment,** 394 A. 2d 330, 581 P. 2d 812, and similarly must yield in any circumstance where the interests of justice so require, 444 F. Supp. 1195. However, disclosure can only be required if **relevant** to issues at trial. 424 F. Supp. 229.

JOYRIDING the illegal taking of an automobile for the purpose of using it for a short period of time. Joyriding is a specific offense, usually lesser in degree than **larceny,** and is in many states punishable by fines and/or imprisonment. In other states, it is one of many acts that may constitute the more serious crime of **larceny.** Perkins & Boyce, Criminal Law 333–334 (3d ed. 1982).

J.P. abbreviation for Justice of the Peace.

JUDGE one who conducts or presides over a court of justice. 295 P. 2d 174, 178. The function of judges is to determine controversies between parties; they are not advisors or investigators. 160 N.E. 655, 658.

JUDGE-MADE LAW law made in the **common-law** tradition; law that exists by judicial **precedent** rather than by statute; judicial **construction** of statutes so different from their original legislative intent that the resulting application of them can be attributed to the **judiciary,** rather than to the legislature. See **stare decisis.**

JUDGMENT the determination of a court of competent **jurisdiction** upon matters submitted to it, 30 N.E. 2d 994, 995; a final determination of the rights of the **parties** to a lawsuit. 28 N.W. 2d 567, 568. See also **recall a judgment; warrant** [WARRANT TO SATISFY JUDGMENT].

COGNOVIT JUDGMENT see **confession of judgment.**

CONFESSION OF JUDGMENT see **confession of judgment.**

DEFAULT JUDGMENT a judgment entered on behalf of a plaintiff when the defendent **defaults,** or fails to appear in the proceeding. See **default judgment.**

ESTOPPEL BY JUDGMENT **estoppel** brought about by the judgment of a court, the essence of which is that a similar question of fact presently in dispute has been previously determined by a court of competent jurisdiction between the same parties or their **privies.** 117 F. 2d 672, 678.

FINAL JUDGMENT a judgment conclusively determining the rights of the parties and disposing of the entire controversy before the court, or of some separable portion thereof, so that, immediately after the judgment or an **appeal** therefrom is rendered, the only judicial business that remains is enforcement of that judgment. James & Hazard, Civil Procedure 527 (2d ed. 1977). The term also refers to the **sentence** imposed in a criminal case. See **final decision; final judgment.**

JUDGMENT BY DEFAULT see **default judgment.**

JUDGMENT IN PERSONAM see PERSONAL JUDGMENT below.

JUDGMENT IN REM one which is pronounced upon the status of some particular subject matter, property, or thing, as opposed to one pronounced upon persons. See 259 P. 2d 953, 954. See **in rem.**

JUDGMENT NOT WITHSTANDING THE VERDICT see **N.O.V** [Non Obstante Veridicto].

JUDGMENT N.O.V. see **N.O.V.** [Non Obstante Veridicto].

JUDGMENT OF CONVICTION the **sentence** in a criminal case formally entered in the clerk's records.

JUDGMENT OF DISMISSAL an order that finally disposes of a matter without a trial of the issues involved on their merits. See **dismissal.**

JUDGMENT ON THE MERITS judgment rendered through analysis and adjudication of the factual issues presented, rather than by the existence of a technical or **procedural** defect that requires one party to prevail. A "judgment on the merits" is binding and issues so adjudged become subject to the force of **res judicata** and **collateral estoppel.** Judgments not rendered on the merits are frequently considered **dismissed without prejudice** so that the factual issues may eventually be decided upon.

JUDGMENT ON THE PLEADINGS see SUMMARY JUDGMENT below.

PERSONAL JUDGMENT a judgment rendered against an individual or an entity such as a corporation for the payment of money damages. To be distinguished from a JUDGMENT IN REM above. See **in personam.**

SUMMARY JUDGMENT a preverdict judgment rendered by the court on the basis of the pleadings because no material issue of fact exists and one party or the other is entitled to judgment as a matter of law. Either party may move for summary judgment at any time after all pleadings have been filed. James & Hazard, Civil Procedure, 149–50 (2d ed. 1977). See **summary judgment.**

JUDGMENT CREDITOR a **creditor** who has obtained a **judgment** against a **debtor** [called a **judgment debtor**] through which he can obtain the sum now due him. The debtor must have **notice** of the creditor's **action** before the judgment

may be enforced. See 345 U.S. 361. Judgment creditor status creates against other creditors certain **priority liens** with regard to the right to have the debt satisfied out of the debtor's **property** and **assets.** See U.C.C. §9-301(3). In addition, it extends the life of the claim under the **statute of limitations,** permitting suit upon the judgment debt for a much longer period of time than would be possible if a judgment had not been rendered. See **levy; writ of execution.** Compare **judgment debtor.**

JUDGMENT DEBTOR a person owing a **debt,** and against whom legal **judgment** for that debt has been entered. The effect of becoming a judgment debtor is that property in the debtor's possession may be subject to **creditors'** claims. The creditor can enforce his judgment by filing a judgment **lien** against the debtor's **real property** or by having the debtor's personal property seized by the sheriff and sold. The judgment lien is merely a charge upon the property or a security for the judgment debt, and does not affect the title or occupancy of the judgment debtor. A **judgment creditor** also has the power to subject to **sale** any further **interest** in real property which the judgment debtor has the power to **transfer.** Restatement of Property §166(b) (1936).

PROPERTY OF JUDGMENT DEBTOR property of which the debtor has possession. It includes not only property that the judgment debtor owns but also his future wages. As used in the Bankruptcy Act, the term includes property in the debtor's actual or **constructive** possession and is not limited to property to which the debtor has **title.** See **creditor's bill; garnishment; sheriff's sale; writ of execution.** Compare **judgment creditor.**

JUDGMENT PROOF a person who lacks the financial resources necessary to satisfy a judgment for **damages** or whose wages or property is protected from judicial **attachment** by law.

JUDICATURE that department of government established to interpret and administer the law, 11 N.W. 424, 426; the judiciary and all those connected with the practice of law.

JUDICIAL ACTIVISM the theory of judicial behavior that advocates basing decisions not on the judicial **precedent** but on achieving what the court perceives to be for the public welfare, or what the court determines to be fair and just on the facts before it. Compare **judicial restraint.**

JUDICIAL ADMISSION see **stipulation.**

JUDICIAL DISCRETION see **discretion.**

JUDICIAL ECONOMY the most efficient use of judicial resources; often used as the rationale underlying doctrines in civil procedure such as **permissive joinder** or **res judicata,** and sometimes offered as the justification for a **judge's** decision in a particular **case.**

JUDICIAL IMMUNITY the immunity of a judge from civil liability for any acts performed in the judge's official capacity. The immunity is absolute provided only that the judge is acting within his or her jurisdiction. The scope of the judge's jurisdiction must be construed broadly to protect the court's independence; therefore, the judge will not be deprived of immunity because the action taken was in error, was done maliciously, or was in excess of the judge's authority; rather, the judge will be subject to liability only when the action taken was in clear absence of all jurisdiction. 435 U.S. 349. Where the relief sought is **injunctive** or **declaratory** and not money damages, immunity is not provided

under the Civil Rights Act of 1964, 42 U.S.C. §1983 and state courts may be sued for such relief. 446 U.S. 719. See generally Prosser, Torts §132 (4th ed. 1971).

JUDICIAL NOTICE a rule of judicial convenience whereby the court takes note of certain facts that are capable of being known to a veritable certainty by consulting sources of indisputable accuracy, thereby relieving one party of the burden of producing **evidence** to prove these facts. 187 N.W. 2d 845, 847. A court can use this doctrine to admit as "proved" such facts that are common knowledge to a judicial professional or to an average, well-informed citizen. See 322 S.W. 2d 916, 924. Thus, the court could take judicial notice that regular mail is not delivered on New Year's Day or that a given day was a certain day of the week (by resort to a calendar). See McCormick, Evidence §328 (2d ed. 1972).

JUDICIAL RESTRAINT the theory of judicial behavior that advocates basing decisions on grounds that have been previously defined by judicial **precedent** rather than on the basis of achieving some public good, which is viewed as the proper role of the **legislature.** Compare **judicial activism.**

JUDICIAL REVIEW the review by a court of law of some act, or failure to act, by a government official or entity, or by some other legally appointed person or organized body; the review of the decision of a **trial** court by an **appellate** court.

In a constitutional law context, judicial review expresses the concept first articulated in *Marbury v. Madison,* 5 U.S. (1 Cranch) 137 (1803) that it is "the province and the duty of the judicial department to say what the law is." Id. at 177–178. Under this doctrine the U.S. Supreme Court and the highest courts of every state have assumed the power and responsibility to decide the constitutionality of the acts of the legislative and executive branches of their respective jurisdictions.

JUDICIAL SALE see **sheriff's sale.** **[judicial sale].**

JUMP BAIL with reference to a **defendant** in a criminal trial, a colloquial expression meaning to leave the **jurisdiction** or to avoid **appearance** in a criminal trial after **bail** has been posted, thus causing a forfeiture of bail; to **abscond** after the posting of bail. See also **flight.**

JURAL of or pertaining to law or justice.

JURAT *(jûr'-ät)*—Lat: the clause appearing at the end of an **affidavit** reciting the date, location, and person before whom the statement was sworn; a certificate designating the competency of the administrating officer.

JURE UXORIS *(jū'rĕ ŭ-xō'rĭs)*— Lat: right of the wife.

JURIS *(jū'rĭs)*—Lat: of law.

JURISDICTION the power to hear and determine a case. 147 P. 2d 759, 761. This power may be established and described with reference to particular subjects or to parties who fall into a particular category. In addition to the power to adjudicate, a valid exercise of jurisdiction requires fair **notice** and an opportunity for the affected parties to be heard. Without jurisdiction, a court's judgment is void. A court must have both SUBJECT MATTER JURISDICTION and PERSONAL JURISDICTION (see below). See also **territorial jurisdiction; title jurisdiction.**

SUBJECT MATTER JURISDICTION refers to the competency of the court to hear and determine a particular category of cases. Federal district courts have "limited" jurisdiction in that they have only such jurisdiction as is explicitly conferred by federal statutes. 28 U.S.C. §1251 et seq. See

LIMITED [SPECIAL] JURISDICTION below. Many state trial courts have "general" jurisdiction to hear almost all matters. The parties to a lawsuit may not waive a requirement of subject matter jurisdiction.

PERSONAL [IN PERSONAM] JURISDICTION refers to the court's power over the parties involved in a particular law suit. The court can obtain in personam jurisdiction over the defendant as a result of the defendant's physical presence within the state. A court can also obtain in personam jurisdiction where a defendant's activity can be characterized as meeting the "minimum contacts" test: "[I]n order to subject a defendant to a judgment in personam, if he be not present within the territory of the **forum,** he [must] have certain minimum contacts with it such that the maintenance of the suit does not offend 'traditional notions of fair play and substantial justice.' " 326 U.S. 310, 316. See **minimum (minimal) contacts (forum).**

In the ACTION IN PERSONAM the plaintiff seeks either to subject defendant's general **assets** to **execution** in order to satisfy a money **judgment,** or to obtain a judgment directing defendant to do an act or refrain from doing an act, under sanction of the court's **contempt** power. James & Hazard Civil Procedure 628–29 (2d ed. 1977). The court obtains in rem jurisdiction by the presence of a tangible or intangible asset within a state or territory. An ACTION IN REM seeks not to impose personal liability but rather to affect the interests of persons in a specific thing (or **res**). A few such actions purport to affect the interests of all persons ("all the world") in the thing; most of them seek to affect the interests of only certain particular persons in the thing. Typical modern examples are actions for **partition** of, or **foreclosure** of a lien upon, or to **quiet title** to, real estate. The concept of in rem actions has been extended to those that seek to affect status (e.g., divorce actions), the status being given a situs (e.g., where one of [the] spouses is domiciled). Id.

An ACTION QUASI IN REM is based on a claim for money damages begun by **attachment** or **garnishment** or other seizure of property where the court has no jurisdiction over the person of the defendant but has jurisdiction over a thing belonging to the defendant or over a person who is indebted or under a duty to the defendant. Id. (citing Restatement of Judgments Second. §75).

The constitutionality of some forms of quasi in rem jurisdiction such as where the property is not the source of the underlying controversy between the plaintiff and defendant has been questioned. 433 U.S. 186.

A state court can exercise jurisdiction in personam over persons within its territory and jurisdiction in rem with respect to things within its territory. In both instances **due process** requirements of notice and opportunity to be heard must be satisfied. The usual manner of obtaining jurisdiction over a person within the court's territorial jurisdiction is by personal service of process within such territorial jurisdiction. See also **long-arm statutes.**

The word "jurisdiction" is also used to refer to particular legal systems, as in "the law varies in different jurisdictions," and in the sense of territory (coupled with authority to reach conduct within the territory) as in "within the jurisdiction of X state."

ANCILLARY JURISDICTION the concept that a federal court acquires jurisdiction of the entire case or controversy, even though some of the matters contained therein would not independently be subject to the jurisdiction of the federal court. Wright, Federal Courts, 28 (4th ed. 1983).

APPELLATE JURISDICTION the power vested in a superior **tribunal** to correct legal errors of an inferior tribunal and to revise their judgments accordingly. See 106 S.W. 326, 331.

CONCURRENT JURISDICTION equal jurisdiction; that jurisdiction exercised by different courts at the same time, over the same subject matter and within the same territory, and wherein litigants may, in the first instance, resort to either court indifferently. 242 Ill. App. 139.

DIVERSITY JURISDICTION that jurisdiction in federal courts brought about by the fact that opposing parties come from different states. See **diversity of citizenship.**

FEDERAL QUESTION JURISDICTION the jurisdiction of the federal courts arising under Article III of the U.S. Constitution allowing the courts jurisdiction over all cases arising under the Constitution, Laws, and Treaties of the United States. Wright, Federal Courts 90 (4th ed. 1983).

IN PERSONAM JURISDICTION see PERSONAL (IN PERSONAM) JURISDICTION above.

IN REM JURISDICTION see ACTION IN REM above.

JURISDICTION OF THE PERSON see PERSONAL (IN PERSONAM) JURISDICTION above.

JURISDICTION OF THE SUBJECT MATTER see SUBJECT MATTER JURISDICTION above.

LIMITED [SPECIAL] JURISDICTION jurisdiction of a court that is limited to specified types of cases as set forth by statute. See **limited jurisdiction.**

ORIGINAL JURISDICTION the jurisdiction of a court to hear a matter in the first instance; for example, the U.S. Supreme Court has original jurisdiction to hear cases affecting ambassadors, other public ministers and counsels, and those in which a state shall be a party. U.S. Constitution Art. III, Sec. 2, Cl. 2.

PENDENT JURISDICTION the concept that a federal court may hear claims based on both federal and state law arising from the same facts, if the court's jurisdiction in the first instance is FEDERAL QUESTION JURISDICTION, see above. James & Hazard, Civil Procedure 613 (2d ed. 1977).

SPECIAL JURISDICTION see LIMITED (SPECIAL) JURISDICTION above

JURISDICTIONAL AMOUNT a requirement that a certain amount be in **controversy** in order for a particular court at the trial or appellate level to have jurisdiction to hear a case. In the federal system ever since the First Judiciary Act of 1789 there has been a jurisdictional amount, exclusive of interest and costs, which must be sued for in order to create **diversity jurisdiction.** Until 1980 **federal question jurisdiction** also required an amount in controversy. The present jurisdictional amount required for diversity actions in the federal district courts is $10,000. 28 U.S.C. §1332.

The method of determining the jurisdictional amount may vary according to the nature of the case. It may be the amount of **damages** claimed, money demanded, or the value of **property** in cases of disputed ownership, or the value of a claimed right such as a right to have injury prevented as in a case seeking an **injunction.** See 236 S.W. 111,

112. The court determines jurisdiction according to the amount in controversy when the suit is begun, and this jurisdiction is not affected if the amount in controversy changes during the course of the **trial.** 99 S.W. 92. Similarly, if an amount in controversy is required for **appellate** jurisdiction, the trial court **record** must show that the jurisdictional amount has been met. 427 S.W. 2d 807. Whether **claims** can be aggregated to satisfy the required jurisdictional amount often is not clear. See generally Wright, Federal Courts §§32–37 (4th ed. 1983).

JURIS DOCTOR see **J.D.**

JURIS IGNORANTIA EST CUM NOSTRUM IGNORAMUS *(jù'-rĭs ĭg-nō-rän'-shē-ā ĕst kŭm nōs'-trŭm ĭg-nō-rä'-mŭs)*—Lat: it is ignorance of the law when we are unfamiliar with our own rights.

JURISPRUDENCE the science of law; the study of the structure of legal systems, i.e., of the form, as distinguished from the content, of systems of law; also, a collective term denoting the course of judicial decision or case law, as opposed to legislation; sometimes used simply as a synonym for "law." See Pound, 1 Jurisprudence 7–9 (1959).

JURIST a legal scholar; one versed in law, particularly the **civil law** or the law of nations; also sometimes used to refer to a judge.

JUROR person sworn as member of a **jury;** a person selected for jury duty, but not yet chosen for a particular case. 144 N.E. 338, 340.

JURY a group of people summoned and sworn to decide on the facts in issue at a trial; a jury is composed of the peers or a cross-section of the community. See 328 U.S. 217; 407 U.S. 493.

BLUE RIBBON JURY a jury that was chosen from prominent members of the community, such as well-educated persons or persons in positions of high responsibility, thought to be particularly well-qualified to serve as jurors. These juries were used for certain highly publicized cases where ordinary juries were thought to be too influenced to judge impartially. Such special juries raised serious constitutional questions of the right to trial by a jury of one's peers selected from a "fair cross-section of the community," 419 U.S. 522, and are thus no longer used.

GRAND JURY a body of persons summoned and sworn to determine whether the facts and accusations presented by the prosecutor warrant an indictment and eventual trial of the accused. Called "grand" because of the relatively large amount of jurors impaneled (traditionally twenty-three) as compared with a **petit jury**. See also **grand jury**.

JURY OF THE VICINAGE literally, a jury from the neighborhood where a crime was committed. 82 S.W. 643, 644. The phrase embodies the same notion as "jury of one's peers."

PETIT [PETTY] JURY ordinary trial jury, as opposed to a **grand jury**. Its function is to determine issues of fact in civil and criminal cases and to reach a verdict in conjunction with those findings. Petit juries have been composed traditionally of 12 members, whose verdict was required to be unanimous. This remains the case in most jurisdictions today, but six person juries, 399 U.S. 78 (1970); and less than unanimous verdicts have been held constitutionally permissible in state (but not federal) criminal proceedings. 406 U.S. 404 (1972).

POLLING THE JURY the practice of a **judge** asking each individual **juror** his or her decision on the

verdict which has been rendered. The polling of the jury usually takes place at the request of a criminal defendant who has been convicted or a party to a civil suit who has lost, and occurs after the foreman of the jury has announced the verdict of the jury.

JURY TRIAL the **trial** of an issue of **fact** before a **jury**. The parties to a suit present their **evidence** to the jury. The **judge** then instructs the jury as to how the law applies to their **findings of fact,** and the jury then **deliberates** and renders its **verdict** in the matter. In **civil** cases, the jury consists of at least six jurors, and may consist of up to 12. James & Hazard, Civil Procedure 389–91 (2d ed. 1977). The **Sixth Amendment** of the Constitution guarantees an accused the right to a jury trial in all **criminal** prosecutions. This right does not apply to trials for **petty** offenses, those for which the punishment may not exceed 6 months' imprisonment. 399 U.S. 66. In all federal criminal trials the jury consists of 12 members, in which case proof **beyond a reasonable doubt** must be established by the unanimous vote of all 12 jurors. States are free to convict upon a nonunanimous vote of as low as nine to three. 406 U.S. 356. Criminal juries of as few as six members are constitutionally permissible, however the vote of such a six-member jury must be unanimous for conviction. 441 U.S. 130.

The Sixth Amendment also guarantees an accused the right to be tried by an impartial jury. The jury must be chosen from a fair cross section of the community, 419 U.S. 522, and may not discriminate against any class of potential jurors, 396 U.S. 320. In the event of excessive pretrial publicity that may prejudice any potential jury in an area, the court may have to take specific measures designed to insure that the jury is nonetheless impartial. The court may delay the trial for a period of time, grant a change of venue, or conduct a voir dire of the potential jurors concerning the publicity. 366 U.S. 717.

JURY VOIR DIRE see **voir dire.**

JUS ACCRESCENDI (*jūs à-krĕ-sĕń dī*)—Lat: right of survivorship. See **joint tenancy [ownership].**

JUST COMPENSATION with regard to a government's taking of property under its power of **eminent domain,** just compensation is "full indemnity or remuneration for the loss or damage sustained by the owner of the property taken or injured," 319 S.W. 2d 930, 934; it consists of a "settlement with a citizen which leaves him no poorer and no richer than he was before the property was taken." 40 F. Supp. 811, 819. The measure generally used is the fair **market value** of the property at the time of taking, 418 P. 2d 1020; which means the value which the land could have if put to the most profitable use for which it is adapted. 33 F. Supp. 519. "Just compensation" need not take account of anticipated or possible future profitability, 155 F. 2d 905; or of sentimental or other nonobjective values, but is to be based on the property's value to a willing seller and a willing buyer. 150 F. Supp. 347.

JUS TERTII (*yūs tĕr'-shē*)—Lat: the right of a third; the legal right of a third party. The term is often employed in **title** actions over **real property,** wherein it is said that because a possessor's title is good against all the world except those with a better title, one seeking to **oust** a possessor must do so on the strength of his own title, and may not rely on a jus tertii, or the better title held by a third party.

JUSTICE synonymous with **judge.** However, a judge of an appellate court is commonly given the formal title of "Justice." For instance, a member of the U.S. Supreme Court is called a Justice. 28 U.S.C. §451.

In New York, a "justice" is a trial judge of the trial court (which is called the Supreme Court) while a member of the state's highest court (the Court of Appeals) is called a judge.

JUSTICE OF THE PEACE a judicial officer of inferior rank, who presides in a court of statutorily limited **civil jurisdiction** and who is also a protector of the peace with limited jurisdiction in minor criminal **proceedings, prosecutions,** and commitments of offenders as fixed by **statute.** 94 S.W. 2d 632. This office has been abolished in most states, with similar powers transferred to municipal or district courts.

JUSTICIABLE capable of being tried in a court of law or equity. "Justiciability" is a question of feasibility, i.e., whether it is feasible for a court to carry out and enforce its decision, as opposed to a question of **jurisdiction,** which involves a court's power or authority to hear a case. A court can have jurisdiction, but at the same time have a "non-justiciable" **issue** before it.

JUSTICIABLE CONTROVERSY a real and substantial controversy that is appropriate for judicial determination, as distinguished from a hypothetical, contingent, or abstract dispute, 155 S.E. 2d 618, 621; a dispute that involves legal relations of parties who have real adverse interests, and upon whom judgment may effectively operate through a decree of conclusive character. 249 So. 2d 908, 918. See **controversy; political question.**

JUSTIFIABLE HOMICIDE see **homicide.**

JUSTIFICATION just cause or excuse; just, lawful excuse for an act; reasonable excuse. 342 F. Supp. 1048, 1062; showing of a sufficient reason in court why defendant did what he is called upon to answer for, so as to excuse **liability.**

The defense of justification [also called NECESSITY] in criminal and tort law excuses the defendant from liability for an otherwise criminal or tortious act when he has unavoidably been forced to make a "choice of evils;" e.g., intentionally setting fire to "real property of another for the purpose of preventing a raging forest fire from spreading into a densely populated community." New York Penal Law §35.05, Commentary (McKinney ed. 1967). See Model Penal Code §3.01 et seq. In tort law a PUBLIC NECESSITY will provide a complete justification while a PRIVATE NECESSITY will provide a more limited **privilege.** Prosser, Torts §24 (4th ed. 1971). See also **duress; mistake.**

JUVENILE COURTS tribunals first established in the United States in the late 1800s and designed to treat youthful offenders separately from adult persons accused. Fashioned after the Chancery Court of Crime of England, the framework was intended to place the state, through the presiding judge, in the position of **parens patriae** and to remove the adversary nature of normal proceedings, replacing it with a paternal concern for the child's wellbeing. Because of this changed atmosphere, the minimal procedural due process requirements guaranteed to adult offenders through the **Bill of Rights** were not afforded to the young persons coming before such courts. Offenders were referred to as "delinquents" rather than "criminals," although the allowable period of incarceration in detention homes to which they were liable was often longer than that to which an adult would be subject. The landmark decision of the Supreme Court in the case of *In Re Gault,* 387 U.S. 1 (1967), found that the **due process** clause of the Fourteenth Amendment requires that persons before such courts facing possible incarceration be assured of timely notice of charges, right to counsel, the privilege

against **self-incrimination,** and the opportunity to cross-examine witnesses. See 18 Crime and Delin. 68-78 (1972). The due process rights of juveniles are not, however, identical to adults.

JUVENILE DELINQUENT term used to describe minors who have committed an offense ordinarily punishable by criminal processes, but who are under the statutory age for criminal responsibility. When a juvenile commits an offense it is considered an act of JUVENILE DELINQUENCY. See **juvenile court.** See also **youthful offenders.**

KANGAROO COURT a court that has no legal authority and that disregards all the rights normally afforded to persons; its conclusions are not legally binding. This is a slang term referring to a court that is biased against a party and thus renders an unfair **verdict** or **judgment.**

KEOGH PLAN see **retirement plan.**

KEY NUMBERS a numbering system used by the West Publishing Company in their publications to break down legal research into manageable topic areas with subcategories. It is a quick and useful method of finding **cases** pertaining to a given subject.

KICKBACK the practice of a **seller** of **goods** or services paying the purchasing agent of those goods or services a portion of the purchase price in order to induce the agent to enter into the transaction. In the context of public officials purchasing goods or services for a government entity, kickbacks are plainly illegal, since they cause the official to act in his own, and not the public's, interest. In most commercial contexts, they are illegal and prohibited by criminal **commercial bribery** statutes. Perkins & Boyce, Criminal Law 531 (2d ed. 1982). The principal of the purchasing agent may also have a cause of action against the agent to recover the amount of the bribery. For tax purposes, amounts paid as kickbacks or bribes generally are not deductable. I.R.C. §162(c).

KIDNAPPING unlawful taking and carrying away of a person against that person's will. 178 S.E. 2d 407, 411. Kidnapping is **false imprisonment** with the added element of removal of the victim to another place. See 174 N.E. 162, 163.

The **common law** offense required that the victim be sent out of the country. This was expanded by statute to include any significant removal. Under the Model Penal Code, kidnapping includes any unlawful removal from one's home, place of business, or a substantial distance from where one was found; or the unlawful confinement of a person for a substantial time period in an isolated place for the purpose of obtaining an award, facilitating a felony, physically harming or terrorizing the victim or any other person, or interfering with any government function. Model Penal Code §212.1.

Kidnapping was a **misdemeanor** at common law, 4 Bl. Comm. *219; but it is a serious **felony** in the United States. Simple kidnapping is often distinguished from the more aggravated forms involving ransom demands or child-stealing. Compare **abduction**. See also **false arrest**.

KIN [KINSHIP] see **consanguinity**.

KIND see **in kind**.

KING'S [QUEEN'S] BENCH Court of King's Bench or Court of Queen's Bench (depending on who is the reigning monarch); the high-est English **common law** court, both civil and criminal, so called because the king or queen formerly presided; now known as the King's Bench or Queens Bench Division of the High Court of Justice, embracing the jurisdiction of the former **Courts of Exchequer** and Courts of Common Pleas.

KITING see **check kiting**.

KNOWINGLY see **mens rea**.

LABOR-MANAGEMENT RELATIONS ACT see **Taft-Hartley Act**.

LABOR ORGANIZATION [UNION] any association of workers whose main purpose is to bargain on behalf of workers with employers about the terms and conditions of employment; "any organization of any kind, or any agency or employee representation committee or plan in which employees participate and which exists for the purpose, in whole or in part, of dealing with employers concerning grievances, labor disputes, wages, rates of pay, hours of employment, or conditions of work." 29 U.S.C. §152(5).

In England, unions were originally indictable as criminal **conspiracies**. When statutes were enacted freeing them from this criminal **liability** they were still condemned by the courts as being organizations in restraint of trade, and therefore not deserving legal enforcement of their rights, an attitude that persisted for some time in the United States. 28 Am. Dec. 501. Today, labor unions are recognized in full by the law and are subject to regulation by the federal government under the **National Labor Relations Act**. See 29 U.S.C. §§151-168. See also **closed shop; union shop.** Compare **cooperative association.**

LABOR PRACTICE see **unfair labor practice.**

LACHES a doctrine providing a party with an **equitable defense** where long-neglected rights are sought to be enforced against the party. Laches signifies an undue **lapse** of time in enforcing a right of **action,** and **negligence** in failing to act more promptly. 100 A. 110, 113. It recognizes that because of the delay, the defendant's ability to defend may be unfairly impaired because witnesses or evidence needed to defend against the stale claim may have become unavailable or lost. The doctrine also recognizes that if the delay has led the adverse party to change his or her position as to the property or right in question, it is inequitable to allow the negligent delaying party to be preferred in their legal right. 118 S.W. 324, 326. The consequent preclusion of the negligent party's action constitutes a species of equitable estoppel known as ESTOPPEL BY LACHES. See **estoppel** [ESTOPPEL IN PAIS].

LADING, BILL OF see **bill of lading.**

LAME DUCK an elected official who has not been reelected but who continues to serve until his present term of office expires.

LAND broadly, any ground, soil, or earth. More specifically, the term refers to **real estate** or **real property,** 42 P. 2d 292; or to any tract which may be **conveyed by deed.** 125 F. 2d 430, 434. "Land" may comprehend an **estate** or **interest** in real property. 161 S.E. 2d 163, 166. It often refers not only to the soil and earth itself, but also to things of a permanent nature found there or affixed thereto. 166 S.E. 570, 580. See **grant** [LAND GRANT]; **run with the land; tide land.**

LANDLORD one who leases **real property.** See **lease.**

LANDRUM-GRIFFIN ACT officially known as the Labor-Management Reporting and Disclosure Act, 29 U.S.C. §§401 et seq., the Act created broad reporting and disclosure provisions "to eliminate or prevent improper practices on the part of labor organizations, employers, labor relation consultants, their officers and representatives . . . " 29 U.S.C. §401(c).

LAND TRUST also called an ILLINOIS LAND TRUST. This device vests **title** to **real property** "in the name of a **trustee** under a recorded deed of trust while a second unrecorded agreement between the trustee and the **beneficiaries** declares the trustee to be vested with full **legal** and **equitable** title subject to certain specified rights of the beneficiaries which are declared to be personal property of the beneficiaries." 351 So. 2d 1094, 1095.

LAPSE the expiration of a right. The term generally refers to a right or **privilege** that can no longer be exercised due to the failure of a particular contingency. A **legacy** may lapse when the **beneficiary** dies before the death of the **testator,** or the **beneficiary** is in some way incapable of taking under the **will.** 337 A. 2d 205, 207; 82 F. 2d 806. The doctrine of lapse applies to all forms of **devises** and **gifts** in **real** or **personal property** to persons or charitable institutions; but it will not be extended beyond cases to which it strictly applies. 76 A. 2d 327. See **antilapse statute.**

In **contracts** cases, the unaccepted **offer** can lapse or expire at the end of the time limit set for its **acceptance.** If no time limit is fixed, the **offer** generally lapses in a reasonable time. 263 F. 2d 919; 147 F. 2d 3. See also, Calamari & Perillo, Contracts 74–77 (2d ed. 1977).

LARCENY the taking of another's **property** unlawfully, with the intention of depriving the owner of its use; "the **felonious** taking and carrying away from any place the **personal property** of another, without his consent, by a person not entitled to the **possession** thereof, with the intent to deprive the owner of the property and to convert it to the use of the taker or some person other than the owner." 53 So. 2d 533, 536. In some modern penal statutes, "larceny" includes common-law larceny by **trespassory** taking, common-law larceny by trick, **embezzlement,** and obtaining property by false pretenses; it may also include acquiring lost property by any means, and issuing a bad **check.** The Model Penal Code and the statutes of many states modeled after the Model Penal Code now call all forms of larceny "THEFT." See Model Penal Code §223.

Larceny was classified by early statutes as either GRAND LARCENY or PETIT LARCENY (now often spelled "petty"). If the value of the property taken did not exceed 12 pence it was termed petit larceny and the death penalty was not exacted. Statute of Westminster I, c. 15 (1275). Today the distinction based on value is retained in the present criminal codes with the frequent addition of automobile theft and larceny by extortion added to the dollar value as aggravating factors leading to grand larceny classification and a higher sanction range. The dollar amount varies by statute from $50 to $250. Some states have more than one degree of grand larceny, again according to the value of property taken or the method used or both. Compare **burglary; robbery.**

LAST ANTECEDENT DOCTRINE in statutory **construction,** under the last antecedent doctrine, relative or modifying phrases are to be applied only to words immediately preceding them, and are not to be construed as extending to more remote phrases, 195 P. 2d 82, 84, unless such is clearly required by the con-

text of the statute or the reading of it as a whole. 272 N.W. 50, 52.

LAST CLEAR CHANCE the doctrine in some jurisdictions that a defendant may be liable for the injuries he caused, even though the plaintiff was guilty of **contributory negligence,** if the defendant could have avoided injury to the plaintiff by exercising ordinary care; "the essential elements of the docrine are: that the plaintiff by his own **negligence** placed himself in a position of danger; that the plaintiff could not extricate himself from the danger; that the defendant, seeing the plaintiff in a position of danger, or by the exercise of **due care** should have seen the plaintiff in such position, by exercising due care on his part had a clear chance to avoid injuring the plaintiff; that the defendant failed to exercise such due care; and that as a result of such failure on the defendant's part plaintiff was injured." 470 P. 2d 748, 753.

LAST-IN, FIRST-OUT [LIFO] see **first-in, first-out [FIFO]; inventory.**

LAST WILL AND TESTAMENT see **will.**

LATENT AMBIGUITY language of legal effect that can be interpreted to have more than one meaning. **Extrinsic evidence,** when allowable, is often necessary to determine the correct interpretation of a latent ambiguity. U.C.C. §2-202. In **contract** law, a latent ambiguity that one party interprets differently from the other party can prevent the **meeting of the minds** necessary to the formation of a valid contract. Simpson, Contracts §42 (2d ed. 1965).

LATENT DEFECT a defect not discoverable even by the exercise of ordinary and reasonable care. 202 A. 2d 560, 563. A **landlord** may not be liable for injuries to **tenants** resulting from latent defects in the leased premises, since the landlord's duty with respect thereto extends only to making a reasonably careful inspection, which would not uncover such defects. See 261 N.W. 354. The same may be true of a host's liability to an **invitee** injured on the host's premises. A defect known to the landlord but latent to the tenant creates a duty in the landlord to warn the tenant as to that known latent defect. Prosser, Law of Torts 393, 401 (4th ed. 1971). See **warranty** (WARRANTY OF HABITABILITY).

Consumers who are injured due to a fault of the product that they had no ability to protect themselves against may recover against the manufacturer under a theory of **products liability.** Prosser, Law of Torts 658 et seq. (4th ed. 1971). See **products liability.** Compare **inherent defect; patent defect.**

LATERAL SUPPORT an owner of **real property** has the right to have his land, in its natural condition, supported and held in place from the sides by his neighbor's land. Boyer, Property 267 (3d ed. 1981).

LAW the legislative pronouncement of the rules which should guide one's actions in society; "the aggregate of those rules and principles of conduct promulgated by the legislative authority [court decisions], or established by local custom. Our laws are . . . derived from a combination of the divine or moral laws, the laws of nature, and human experience, as [each] . . . has been evolved by human intellect influenced by the virtues of the ages. Human laws must therefore of necessity continually change as human experience shall prove the necessity of new laws to meet new evils, or evils which have taken upon themselves new forms, or as the public conscience shall change, thus viewing matters from a different moral viewpoint." 123 N.W. 504, 508. See also **case law; common law; session laws; statute; substantive law; uniform laws; wager of law.**

AT LAW that which pertains to or is governed by the rules of law, as opposed to the rules of **equity.** Also may be used to mean by **operation of law.**

LAW, CHOICE OF see **conflict of laws [choice of law].**

LAW, QUESTION OF see **question of law.**

LAWFUL any act performed within the bounds of law or authorized by law and that does not give rise to any legal liability; "activity which is not illegal and is not contrary to public policy." 516 F. Supp. 399, 404.

LAW MERCHANT a body of commercial law governing merchants in England, with similar rules existing in other European states. These laws were first enforced by special English mercantile courts, and later enforced in **common law courts of law** and **equity.** It is particularly noted for contributions to the law of **negotiable instruments;** the modern doctrine of **holder in due course** had its genesis in the law merchant.

The law merchant was the common law's recognition of usages and procedures that had developed over a long period of time among merchants in England and other European countries. As part of the common law of England, it was incorporated into American law and has been largely supplanted by common law evolution and statutory enactment.

LAW OF ADMIRALTY see **maritime law.**

LAW OF THE CASE doctrine whereby a determination of law once made will be treated as correct throughout all subsequent stages of the proceeding except when the issue is raised in a higher court. Thus, a trial court will decline to reconsider its own earlier ruling in subsequent trial proceedings. James & Hazard, Civil Procedure 535–536 (2d ed. 1977). This is true even where the appellate court on an **interlocutory appeal** considers the case a second time in the interlocutory stage before final judgment. 132 P. 2d 471, 474. Some courts have permitted exceptional reexamination. 492 P. 2d 686, 691. "The doctrine of 'the law of the case' permits, wisely, of a change of decision, where, among other things, intervening between a first and second appeal, there has been a material change in the situation either as to the facts or in the applicable law." 143 F. 2d 484, 486. The "law of the case" should be distinguished from **res judicata** in that the law of the case doctrine applies within one action regarding issues of law previously determined while the rules of res judicata bar relitigation of the same issues in successive actions. Restatement of Judgments Second §78. See also **collateral estoppel.**

LAW OF THE LAND phrase first used in the **Magna Carta** to refer to the then established law of the Kingdom as distinguished from Roman or **civil law.** 56 Cal. 229, 238. Refers today to fundamental principles of justice commensurate with **due process** of law, i.e., those rights that the legislature cannot abolish or significantly limit, because they are so fundamental to our system of liberty and justice; also refers to the law as developed by the courts or in statutes in pursuance of those principles or rights. The United States Constitution (Art. VI, §2) establishes itself, and laws made under its authority, and treaties of the United States, as the "supreme law of the land."

LAWSUIT see **suit.**

LAY WITNESS any **witness** not **testifying** as an **expert witness** and who is thereby generally precluded from testifying in the form of an **opinion.** However, a "lay witness" is able to testify in the form of an opinion or inference if the testimo-

ny is "(a) rationally based on the perceptions of the witness and (b) helpful to a clear understanding of his testimony or the determination of a fact in issue." Fed. R. Evid. 701. The witness may be a LAY EXPERT WITNESS, "meaning a person whose expertise or special competence derives from experience in a field of endeavor rather than from studies or diplomas." 186 N.W. 2d 258, 262.

LEADING CASE a case continually cited for a proposition of law which controls in that particular area. For example, *Katz v. United States,* 389 U.S. 347 (1967), is a leading case in the area of **search and seizure,** and *Marbury v. Madison,* 5 U.S. (1 Cranch) 137 (1803), is a leading case in constitutional law.

LEADING QUESTION a question posed by a trial lawyer which is ordinarily improper on direct examination because it suggests to the **witness** the answer he is to deliver, or in effect prompts the answer that is to be given irrespective of actual memory. See 223 So. 2d 843, 847, 274 A. 2d 742, 745. Leading questions may be asked on cross-examination and when a witness is hostile to the party examining him. McCormick, Evidence §6 (2d ed. 1972).

LEASE an agreement whereby one party (called the **landlord** or **lessor**) relinquishes his right to immediate possession of property while retaining ultimate legal ownership (**title).** "Ordinarily when a lease is made we find an agreement by the owner-**lessor** to turn over specifically-described premises to the exclusive possession of the **lessee** for a definite period of time and for a **consideration** commonly called **rent.** Although no absolute requirement exists for the use of particular words, the instrument is usually studded with such terms as 'lease,' 'let,' **'demise,'** 'grant,' and the like." 197 A. 2d 176, 182.

The difference between a lease and a **license** (or permit, privilege, limited custodial use) is that a lease gives exclusive possession of the premises against all the world, including the owner, while a license confers a privilege to occupy under the owner. A license, or similar status is generally revocable at the pleasure of the owner (except if there has been detrimental reliance upon the granting of the license, see 83 P. 808) and gives occupancy only so far as necessary to engage in the agreed acts or the performance of agreed services; a lease gives the right of exclusive possession for all purposes not prohibited by its terms. See 197 A. 2d 176, 182. The difference may be vital inasmuch as the lease must ordinarily be in writing under the **statute of frauds** (at least if for a long term) while a mere license may be valid although only orally agreed to. See 18 N.E. 2d 362.

A lease creates an estate in real property (called a **copyhold estate**) and although contractual in form it is governed more by property doctrine than by contract doctrine. However, the contractual nature of the lease is gaining increasing recognition by the courts. Burby, Real Property 112-113 (3rd ed. 1965). If a tenant vacates his leasehold interest before his term expires he does not, for example, affect his estate and rent is still due periodically unless the lease specifically provides (as most do) that vacating the premises before the end of the term accelerates the entire term rental. Id. Older property doctrines held that the various covenants, such as to pay rent and to make essential repairs, were not dependent and hence a landlord's breach did not permit a rent set-off for repairs made by a tenant. Some jurisdictions now permit a rent set-off for certain essential repairs that the landlord has failed to make. 265 A. 2d 526, 535. See also **release** [LEASE AND RELEASE]; **sublease.**

PROPRIETARY LEASE a lease that the resident/stockholder in a cooperative apartment maintains with the cooperative as owner of the building. See **condominium.**

SUBLEASE [UNDER-LEASE] "a transition whereby a **tenant** [one who has **leased premises** from the owner, or **landlord**] grants an **interest** in the leased premises less than his own, or reserves to himself a **reversionary** interest in the term." 390 S.W. 2d 703, 707. See **assignment,** which connotes the **conveyance** of the whole term of a lease.

LEASEHOLD the **estate** in **real property** of a **lessee,** created by a **lease.** See 299 P. 838, 841. It generally refers to an estate whose duration is fixed, such as an estate for years, see 10 S.E. 2d 901; but may also be used to describe a "**tenancy at will,**" 151 A. 81, 83, a month-to-month tenancy, periodic tenancy, etc.

LEAVE OF COURT "permission obtained from a court to take some action which, without such permission, would not be allowable." 556 S.W. 2d 726, 728. This permission in some instances may come before or after the expiration of the period in which the action was to be taken. Fed. R. Civ. Proc. 6(b). For instance, a **trustee** may need "leave of court" in order to spend trust **corpus** for the support of the trust **beneficiary;** an attorney will need "leave of court" in order to file papers after the time allowed for filing the papers has elapsed. Id.

LEGACY gift or **bequest** by **will** of **personal property,** 264, So. 2d 496, 505. The term is frequently confused with **devise,** which refers to a disposition of **real property,** but the technical distinction between "legacy" and "devise" will not defeat a **testator's** intention, so that either term may be used to dispose of real or personal property. It is regarded as synonymous with **bequest.** Compare **devise.**

ALTERNATE LEGACY disposition whereby testator leaves one of two or more gifts to a person without specifically stating which gift should pass.

CONTINGENT LEGACY a legacy which will only pass upon the happening of some event, such as "if she reaches the age of twenty-five."

DEMONSTRATIVE LEGACY "a gift of stated value that identifies a particular asset as the primary source of payment but permits **executor** to draw on general assets of estate once the primary source has been exhausted," 439 A. 2d 516, 520. Therefore, a "demonstrative legacy" is in nature both a GENERAL LEGACY (see below), since it bequeaths a specified amount, and a SPECIFIC LEGACY (see below) in that it designates the fund from which the payment is made, 408 N.Y.S. 2d 295, 296.

GENERAL LEGACY "one designated primarily by quantity or amount and may be paid out of general assets without regard to any particular fund or thing," 120 S.E. 2d 241, 247. For example, a bequest of 270 shares of stock that testator did not describe as specified shares by numbers or otherwise was a general legacy. 388 N.Y.S. 2d 853, 855.

LEGATEE recipient of personal property by virtue of a will—i.e., the recipient of a "legacy."

RESIDUARY LEGACY "a GENERAL LEGACY (see above) wherein fall all the assets of the estate after all other legacies have been satisfied and all charges, debts, and costs [of the estate and its administration] have been paid," 106 So. 2d 215, 217.

SPECIFIC LEGACY "a bequest of some definite or specific part of a testator's estate which is capable of being designated, identified and distinguished from other like things composing the estate," 380 N.E. 2d 601, 602; that which can be distinguished from other articles of the same general nature in the estate, 301 N.E. 2d 263, 265.

LEGAL AGE see **age of majority.**

LEGAL AID a nationwide system of **non-profit** offices established throughout the country to deliver legal services to financially needy **litigants,** that is, those unable to afford to retain private **counsel.** See also **Legal Services Corporation.**

LEGAL CAPACITY TO SUE requirement that a person bringing suit have a "sound mind, **lawful** age, and [be] under no restraint or legal disability," 125 P. 2d 1010, 1016, such disability referring to "infancy, lunacy, or want of title in plaintiff in the capacity in which he sues." 198 N.W. 554. The term "has no reference to failure of the petition to show a right of action in the plaintiff." 186 S.W. 1004, 1006.

LEGAL CONSIDERATION see **consideration.**

LEGAL DETRIMENT giving up something a person was privileged to retain, or "doing or refraining from doing something which he was privileged not to do, or not to refrain from doing," Williston, Contracts §102A (3d ed. 1957), where a person "changes his legal position, or assumes duties or liabilities not therefore imposed on him." 163 S.W. 2d 948, 953. That change of position constitutes the **consideration** necessary to form a **contract** and therefore imposes duties on the person benefitting from the detriment. 255 N.E. 2d 793, 795.

LEGAL DISCRETION see **discretion.**

LEGAL DUTY that which the law requires be done or forborne by a determinate person. 278 N.E. 2d

504, 510. **Breach** of a legal duty owed another is an element of **negligence** and is the essence of most actions in **tort**. Legal duties not otherwise imposed may be created by a **contract** or by one's entering into some other such relationship (landlord-tenant, host-invitee, spousal duty to support each other and the children, etc.). See **duty.**

LEGAL ESTATE see **estate.**

LEGAL FICTION an assumption that certain facts exist, whether or not they really do exist, so that a principle of law may be applied in order to achieve justice on the facts as they do exist. Application of this doctrine frequently avoids undue delay in disposing of uncontroverted matters, permitting the court to focus attention instead on matters that are in dispute. E.g., the **domicile** of the owner is presumed to be the situs of **personal property** for taxing purposes regardless of where it is actually located. The term "legal fiction" commonly occurs in cases where adherence to the fiction is perceived as working an injustice. E.g., when the personal property has never been in the state where the owner is domiciled and it would clearly be unfair to tax the property, the court will dispense with the situs presumption as a mere legal fiction.

LEGAL HEIRS see **heirs.**

LEGAL IMPOSSIBILITY see **impossibility.**

LEGAL SEPARATION see **divorce,** (SEPARATION [DIVORCE A MENSA ET THORO]); **separation agreement.**

LEGAL SERVICES CORPORATION a **corporation** established by Congress in 1974 to provide "financial support for legal assistance in noncriminal proceedings or matters to persons financially unable to afford legal assistance." 42 U.S.C. §2996 b(a). The Corporation is empowered to make **grants** to qualified

programs and to **contract** with outside organizations. See also **Legal Aid.**

LEGAL TENDER money that is lawfully acceptable for payment of a **debt** or obligation where the medium of payment is not specified by statute or agreement. See U.C.C. §2-511 (2). All legal tender is **money,** but all money is not legal tender. Congress has the power to determine what constitutes legal tender. 116 S.E. 465, 468. Under 31 U.S.C. §392 all coins and currencies of the United States (including Federal Reserve Notes and circulating notes of Federal Reserve Banks and national banking associations) are legal tender.

LEGATEE one who takes a **legacy.**

RESIDUARY LEGATEE "a person to whom is **bequeathed** what is left of an estate after payment of debts, expenses of administration and other legacies," 252 N.Y.S. 2d 948, 952; "one who is designated by the **testator** in his **will** to receive the residue, being the personal estate of testator not effectually disposed of by his will and which remains after payment of debts and satisfaction of particular legacies," 196 So. 2d 225, 227.

LEGISLATION "the act of giving or enacting **laws;** the power to make laws," 22 N.E. 644, 646; "act of legislating; preparation and enactment of laws; the making of laws by express decree," 182 So. 676, 678; "the exercise of **sovereign** power," 24 Ark. 161, 166.

LEGISLATION, SPECIAL see **special legislation.**

LEND parting with a thing of value for either a fixed or indefinite period. Such item or something equivalent to it must be returned at the time originally established or when **lawfully** demanded. 78 N.Y. 159; when used in a will, it means "give" or "devise" "unless it is manifest that the testator intended otherwise," 193 S.E. 275, 276.

LESSEE one who holds an **estate** by virtue of a **lease**, 253 P. 553, 554; the **tenant** of a **landlord**. See **lease**.

LESSER-INCLUDED OFFENSE "one which is necessarily established by proof of the greater offense and which is properly submitted to the jury, should the **prosecution's** proof fail to establish **guilt** of the greater offense charged, without necessity of multiple **indictment**," 407 F. 2d 1199, 1228; also defined as that offense committed "when it is impossible to commit a particular crime without concomitantly committing, by the same conduct, another offense of lesser grade or degree," which latter offense is, in respect to the former, the "lesser-included offense." See New York Criminal Procedure Law §1.20 (37). For example, **larceny** is necessarily lesser-included in the crime of **robbery**, just as **assault** is ordinarily a lesser-included element of **murder**. See **double jeopardy; graded offense.**

Criminal cases are often disposed of by a **plea bargain** in which the prosecutor accepts a **plea** of guilty to a lesser-included offense and the more serious charge is dismissed.

LESSOR one who grants a **lease** to another, 252 P. 2d 624, 626, thereby transferring an exclusive right of **possession** of certain land, subject only to rights expressly retained by the lessor in the lease agreement. 18 N.W. 2d 88, See **landlord.**

LET to **lease**; to grant the use of **realty** for a compensation; to hire out for compensation. 118 S.W. 881, 883. The term does not always connote the act of "leasing," but may simply involve the granting of a **license**. See 119 N.Y.S. 222, 223.

LETTER OF CREDIT in commercial law, a promise by a **bank** or other issuer that it will honor on behalf of one of its customer's demands for payment, upon compliance with specified conditions. U.C.C. §5-103 (1) (a). A letter of credit is intended to facilitate long-distance commercial transactions by allowing a **buyer** of **goods** to establish a credit line against which a **seller** can draw. A seller in France might negotiate with a United States buyer for the buyer to send a letter of credit which can be drawn against when the goods arrive in the United States. Letters of credit guard against risks of insolvency and uncertainty in delivery and settlement due to market fluctuations over time. White & Summers, Uniform Commercial Code Ch. 18 (1980).

LETTER OF INTENT "customarily employed to reduce to writing a preliminary understanding of the parties," 330 F. Supp. 22, 25. This letter is not a **contract,** and it does not constitute a binding agreement. McCarthy, Acquisitions and Mergers 130 (1963). Rather, it is "an expression of tentative intentions of the parties," 308 F. Supp. 195, 198, and creates no liability as between the parties. It is, in essence, "an agreement to agree," id. If a formal writing is contemplated by the parties, a binding contract may arise between them before the writing is executed as long as there has been a **meeting of the minds** concerning the essential elements of the writing, 330 F. Supp. at 25.

LETTER RULING "a written statement . . . issued to a taxpayer by the office of Assistant Commissioner [of Tax] and in which interpretations of tax laws are made and applied to a specific set of facts," 362 F. Supp. 1298, 1301.

LETTERS ROGATORY see **rogatory letters.**

LETTER STOCK see **restricted securities.**

LEVARI FACIAS see fieri facias [LEVARI FACIAS].

LEVERAGE the use of debt to finance **capital investment,** for the purpose of increasing the investor's **rate of return** on the investor's **equity.** Thus, property is purchased or investments are made with small down payments, the balance being supplied by borrowed money. As long as the return (income and appreciation) on the total investment exceeds the interest paid on the debt, the investor benefits.

LEVY to raise or collect; to seize; to assess, as to levy a tax; also a seizure or levying, as of land or other property or rights, through lawful **process** or by force. When one levies, or places a levy upon some property, right, or a **chose in action,** it is seized and may be sold to satisfy a **judgment.** See **writ of execution.**

LEXIS a computerized legal research system that enables the user to type in various search terms and receive information and cases that fit the designated query. Another popular system is called WESTLAW. Both are private sector innovations in legal research and more are likely to be developed as microcomputer technology becomes more common in offices of every size.

LEX LOCI CONTRACTUS *(lĕx lō'-kī kŏn-trăk'-tŭs)*—Lat: place of making a **contract.** See **conflict of laws.**

LEX LOCI DELICTI *(lĕx lō'-kī dĕ-lĭk'-tē)*—Lat: the place of the wrong. See **conflict of laws.**

LIABILITY an obligation to do or refrain from doing something; a duty which eventually must be performed; an obligation to pay money; signifies money owed, as opposed to an **asset;** also used to refer to one's responsibility for his conduct, such as contractual liability, tort liability, criminal liability, etc. See also **products liability; strict liability; transferee liability; vicarious liability.**

ABSOLUTE LIABILITY see **strict liability.**

CURRENT LIABILITIES in accounting, debts due within one year, including such items as salary payable to employees, purchase costs payable to suppliers, taxes, and portion of long-term debt due in one year.

JOINT AND SEVERAL LIABILITY "when **tortious** conduct is the cause of a single and indivisible harm, each contributing **tort-feasor** is liable to the same extent and in the same manner as if they had performed the wrongful act themselves," 655 P. 2d 116, 118. See also **joint and several.**

JOINT LIABILITY created where two or more persons, who may or may not have a legal relationship to each other, 452, A. 2d 75, 77, owe another a joint duty and by common neglect of that duty the other person is injured. 137 So. 479, 482. See also **joint liability.**

LIABILITY WITHOUT FAULT see **strict liability.**

LONG-TERM LIABILITIES in accounting, debts due after one year, including term bank loans, mortgages payable, bonds outstanding, and liabilities under long-term lease and rental agreements.

PRIMARY LIABILITY liability imposed upon the party directly responsible for the loss or injury.

SECONDARY LIABILITY that which arises only when the party directly liable fails to perform or otherwise **defaults** in performance. Frequently refers to the liability of a guarantor.

STRICT LIABILITY see **strict liability.**

VICARIOUS LIABILITY see **vicarious liability.**

LIABILITY WITHOUT FAULT see **strict liability.**

LIABLE to be responsible for; to be obligated in law. See **liability.**

LIBEL a **tort** consisting of a false and malicious publication printed for the purpose of defaming one who is living; (spoken defamation is called **slander**). In tort law, only a living person may be defamed; statutes in several states have made defamation of the dead a crime but no civil liability has been implied. Prosser, Torts 744-45 (4th ed. 1971). "Libel" includes "any unprivileged, false and **malicious** publication which by printing, writing, signs or pictures tends to expose a person to public scorn, hatred, contempt or ridicule . . . and also embraced therein is any such publication that relates to a person's office, trade, business or employment, if the publication imputes to him some incapacity or lack of due qualifications to fill the position, or some positive past misconduct which will injuriously affect him in it." 252 A. 2d 755, 772. The truth of the published statement creates a valid **defense** to an **action** for libel.

The First Amendment protects the press against certain libel actions unless actual malice is shown. Public officials and public figures must prove that the published information is false and that the defendant published it with reckless disregard of the truth. 376 U.S. 254 (public officials); 388 U.S. 130 (public figures). In contrast, the common law presumed that published information was false and forced the publisher to prove its truthfulness. The constitutional limitation does not apply to **defamation** by a newspaper of private persons, where only some degree of fault on the part of the newspaper is required. 418 U.S. 323, 347. See also **seditious libel.** Compare **slander.**

LIBERTY freedom; the ability to enjoy all the rights granted by the United States and a particular state's constitution, as well as other rights such as the right to earn a living, the right to acquire knowledge, the right to marry, etc.; refers to the fullest scope of freedoms one has but at the same time limits those freedoms so as not to interfere with another person's exercise of them. See **Bill of Rights.**

LIBERTY, CIVIL see **civil rights.**

LICENSE a right granted which gives one permission to do something which he could not legally do absent such permission; "leave to do a thing which the LICENSOR [the party granting the license] could prevent. . . . [G]enerally speaking, [it] means a grant of permission to do a particular thing, to exercise a certain privilege, or to carry on a particular business or to pursue a certain occupation." 160 P. 2d 37, 39. Licenses may be granted by private persons or by governmental authority, such as in the case of a license permitting another to infringe upon a patent, driver's license, liquor license, etc. See **franchise; monopoly.**

In the law of property, a license is a personal privilege or permission with respect to some use of land, and is revocable at the will of the landowner. 230 S.W. 2d 770, 775. The privilege attaches only to the party holding it and not to the land itself since, unlike an **easement,** a license does not represent an **estate** or **interest** in the land. 41 A. 2d 66, 68. For the same reason, a license is distinguished from a **lease,** which is an estate that includes an exclusive right of possession. 5 F. Supp. 435, 437.

Because a license represents only a personal right, it is generally not **assignable.** 34 N.Y.S. 693.

LICENSEE one to whom a **license** has been granted; in property, one whose presence on the premises is not invited but tolerated. Thus, a licensee is "a person who is neither a customer, nor a servant, nor a **trespasser,** and does not stand in any contractual relation with the owner of the **premises,** and who is permitted expressly or impliedly to go thereon merely for his own interest, convenience, or gratification." 118 S.E. 697, 698. In **tort** law, one's status as a licensee may affect the **duty** of care owed to him. Typically, "the law places those who come upon the premises of another in three classes: **invitees** are those who are expressly or impliedly invited, as a customer to a store; licensees are persons whose presence is not invited, but tolerated; **trespassers** are persons who are neither suffered nor invited to enter. The duty of the owner toward an invitee is to exercise reasonable care to keep the premises in a safe condition, but licensees take the premises as they find them, the only duty of the occupier being to give notice of traps or concealed dangers [of which the occupier himself has knowledge]. Toward trespassers the occupier need only refrain from willful or wanton injury as modified by the 'attractive nuisance' line of cases." 282 N.W. 389, 392. Some jurisdictions have abandoned the tort law distinction between invitees and licensees. See Prosser, Law of Torts §62 (4th ed. 1971).

LICENSE TAX the fee or tax charged by a government to issue the license required for engaging in some regulated activity such as the sale of liquor or the practice of a profession.

LICENSOR one who grants a **license.**

LIE DETECTOR TEST see **polygraph.**

LIEN a charge, hold, claim, or incumbrance upon the **property** of another as security for some **debt** or charge, 227 A. 2d 423, 426; not a **title** to property but rather a charge

upon it; the term connotes the right which the law gives to have a **debt** satisfied out of the property, 429 S.W. 2d 381, 382, by the sale of the property if necessary. 170 S.W. 86, 89.

ARTISAN'S LIEN a statutory lien permitting an artisan to retain possession of a piece of work until payment for the labor performed on it is received.

EQUITABLE LIEN a right in **equity,** but not **at law** to have specific property applied in satisfaction of a debt. 404 F. 2d 856, 861. Whenever parties enter into an agreement indicating an intention to post some particular property, real or personal, as security for an obligation, an equitable lien is created on such property. 353 N.E. 2d 30, 33. An equitable lien may also be created by implication, and is based on the doctrine of **unjust enrichment.** 407 F. Supp. 164, 183. When real property is involved, it is not an **estate** or a right to recover the property and it is not a right which may be the basis of a possessory action. 338 N.E. 2d 140, 143.

FACTOR'S LIEN a lien that a **factor** has on goods **consigned** to him while in his possession for any money advanced by him and for his **commissions.** At **common law,** it was purely a possessory lien and was lost by surrender of **possession,** but today, under the Uniform Commercial Code, a written security agreement will cause the lien to survive the loss of possession. U.C.C. §9-312.

FEDERAL TAX LIEN a lien of the United States on "all property and rights to property" of a taxpayer who fails to pay a tax for which he is liable to the federal government, 26 U.S.C. §6321. It reaches not only all property owned by the taxpayer when the lien arises but also property acquired subsequently, and such a lien attaches to property that would otherwise be exempt by state law, from the reach of creditors.

The statutory scheme does not confer priority upon the lien; such priority is determined on the basis of whichever is first in time.

FLOATING LIEN in commercial law, one that covers not only inventory and accounts of a debtor in existence at the time of original loan but also his **after-acquired property** of inventory or accounts. The floating lien allows a buyer's complete operations to be financed with periodic advances and repayments secured by changing collateral or raw materials, work in progress, finished goods, proceeds, etc. This financing may be accomplished in a single security agreement with only one filing required. U.C.C. §9-108, White & Summers, Uniform Commercial Code §24-5 (1980).

GARAGEMAN'S LIEN see MECHANIC'S LIEN below.

JUDGMENT LIEN a lien on a **judgment debtor's** property in favor of a **judgment creditor.** When judgment has been entered in a civil case, and the party liable for the judgment fails to pay it, the judgment creditor may file a lien against the property of the party liable, to give notice that the property is subject to sale in satisfaction of the judgment. The judgment creditor may enforce the lien by having the sheriff seize the property and sell it at a **sheriff's sale.**

LANDLORD'S LIEN at common law, the **landlord's** right to **levy [distress]** upon the goods of a tenant in satisfaction of unpaid rents or property damage; now generally a statutory lien giving the lessor the status of a preferred creditor with regard to the lessee's property.

MECHANIC'S LIEN one "created ... for the purpose of securing priority of payment of the price or value of work performed and materials furnished in erecting or repairing a building or other structure, and as such attaches to the land as well as buildings and improvements erected thereon." 142 U.S. 128, 130. Statutes giving priority to the satisfaction of the debt represented by a mechanic's lien are found in most jurisdictions and extend to automobiles and other **goods** as well as to structures; as applied to automobiles, sometimes called GARAGEMAN'S LIEN. 20 F. Supp. 465, 466.

PRIOR LIEN "as between two liens, or in a class of liens, the one superior to the others," 81 F. 439.

STATE TAX LIEN a security interest in the property of a taxpayer established by statute, of which the tax collector may avail himself upon default of payment of taxes. Unlike liens on personal property, which may be made a charge upon other personal property of the owner, such lien on real property does not extend to property other than that being assessed unless expressly authorized by statute. Most jursidications give these liens priority over **mortgages** and other liens existing against the property.

TAX LIEN "a statutory lien which exists in favor of a state or municipality," 125 N.E. 2d 298, 299; "merely a security established by statute of which a tax collector may avail himself in default of taxes," 33 So. 2d 852, 854, and is analogous to a "judgment lien," 135 F. 2d 527, 528. See **judgment lien.**

WAREHOUSEMAN'S LIEN right of a warehouseman to maintain possession of goods until all storage charges have been paid. See U.C.C. §§7-209, 7-210.

LIEN JURISDICTION jurisdiction in which **title** to **mortgaged premises** remains with the **mortgagor** pending payment of the mortgage price. See **mortgage; title jurisdiction.**

LIEN THEORY OF MORTGAGE see **mortgage** [LIEN THEORY].

LIFE ESTATE an **estate** whose duration is limited to or measured by the life of the person holding it or that of some other person [**pur autre vie**], 282 P. 2d 141, 143. It is a **freehold interest** in land, whereas a right of **homestead** includes only right of occupancy and use of the surface of the land. 291 S.W. 757, 759.

LIFE EXPECTANCY the period of time a person is predicted to live, based on their present age and sex. This figure is most frequently used by **actuaries** to determine **insurance premiums.**

LIFE INTEREST an interest in property measured by the life of either the person using the property or by another's life. See **life estate.**

LIFE TENANT tenant whose legal right to remain in possession of certain lands is measured either by his life or the life of another. See **life estate.**

LIFO last-in, first-out. See **first-in, first-out; inventory.**

LIKE-KIND EXCHANGE see **sale or exchange.**

LIMINE see **in limine.**

LIMITATION a restriction or restraint; the act of limiting. A state constitution constitutes a "limitation" on the power which the state may exercise, not a "grant" of power. 190 P. 2d 665, 669. "Limitation" also declares the nature and extent of the **estate** granted, and the uses for which the grant is made. 35 A. 1072, 1075. For example, in an estate granted "to A and his heirs," the phrase **"and his heirs"** constitutes **words of limitation** and indicates that A has a **fee simple,** and can use the land as he pleases. Also, "a limitation determines an estate upon the happening of the event itself without the necessity of doing any act to regain the estate, such as re-entry," 132 S.W. 2d 553, 563. See **statute of limitations.**

LIMITATION, WORDS OF see **words of limitation.**

LIMITATIONS PERIOD see **statute of limitations.**

LIMITATIONS, STATUTE OF see **statute of limitations.**

LIMITED JURISDICTION refers to courts that are only authorized to hear and decide certain or special types of cases. Examples include **small claims courts** and the **court of claims.** Also known as SPECIAL JURISDICTION. See **jurisdiction.**

LIMITED LIABILITY the limitation placed on the amount an investor of a corporation can lose resulting from a lawsuit against the corporation or other loss suffered by the corporation; the **liability** for losses that is limited to the amount an investor or shareholder invests in the corporation, unless that amount is determined by a court to have been fraudently insufficient. The corporation itself also enjoys limited liability inasmuch as the corporation's obligations are always limited to its **assets** unless, with regard to particular transactions, personal responsibility is assumed by an officer or shareholder of the corporation.

LIMITED PARTNERSHIP see **partnership.**

LINEAL refers to descent by a direct line of **succession** in ancestry. See 87 A. 2d 485, 486.

LINEUP a police procedure in which a person suspected of a crime is placed in a line with several other persons of similar dress, height, and ethnic group and a witness to the crime attempts to identify the suspect as the person who committed the crime. The procedure must not be "unduly suggestive," (such as placing the suspect who is 5 feet 2 inches tall in a lineup with persons 6 feet tall) or the identification will not be admissible in a criminal trial. 338 U.S. 293; 409 U.S. 188.

LIQUIDATE to settle; to determine the amount due, and to whom due, and having done so, to extinguish the indebtedness. See 29 N.C. 143, 61 N.E., 2d 801. Although the term more properly signifies the adjustment or **settlement** of **debts,** "to liquidate" is often used simply to mean "to pay." 68 N.W. 628. Also, to sell; to reduce the value of an object or an asset to its cash value.

LIQUIDATE A BUSINESS "to assemble and mobilize the **assets,** settle with the **creditors** and **debtors,** and apportion the remaining assets, if any, among the stockholders (see **shareholder**) or owners." 281 N.W. 172, 175.

LIQUIDATE A CLAIM "to determine by agreement or **litigation** the precise amount" of the claim. 298 F. 125.

LIQUIDATED AMOUNT [OBLIGATION] amount that may be readily ascertained by a mere computation based on the terms of the obligation or instrument. See **liquidate; sum certain.** Compare **unliquidated.**

LIQUIDATED DAMAGES an amount stipulated in the **contract** which the **parties** agree is a reasonable estimation of the **damages** owing to one in the event of a **breach** by the other. 151 F. 534. In order for such a provision to be enforceable as a measure of damages, the liquidated damages provision must constitute a reasonable forecast of the damages likely to actually result from the breach. 134 A. 252. Where these conditions are met, the amount thus provided for establishes a maximum limitation on the defaulting party's **liability.** 25 F. Supp. 478. If the provision does not meet these conditions, or if it otherwise appears that inclusion of the provision was motivated by a desire to deter a breach rather than by a **good faith** effort to estimate probable damages, the provision will be considered a "penalty" and will be unenforceable; recovery will then be limited to actual damages, if any. 72 A. 2d 233. See U.C.C. §2-718.

LIQUIDATED SUM CERTAIN see **sum certain** [LIQUIDATED SUM CERTAIN].

LIQUIDATION DIVIDEND see **dividend.**

LIS PENDENS *(lēs pěn'-děns)*— Lat: a suspended **lawsuit;** a pending lawsuit. In a legal sense the term is equivalent to the maxim that pending the suit nothing should be changed. The doctrine of lis pendens is that one who acquired any **interest** in **property** during the pendency of **litigation** respecting such property from a party to the litigation, takes subject to the **decree** or **judgment** in such litigation and is bound by it. 288 N.W. 832.

NOTICE OF LIS PENDENS may be required in some jurisdictions to be placed in the public records to warn persons (such as prospective purchasers or others having an interest in the property under suit) that the **title** to the property is in litigation and that they will be bound by the possibly adverse judgment. See 33 P. 153. See also **pendente lite.**

LISTED STOCK stock of a company traded on an organized **stock exchange.** In addition to satisfying the registration requirements imposed by the **Securities and Exchange Commission,** a company must comply with the rules imposed by the exchange on which its stock is traded. The **New York**

LISTING 275 LOBBYISTS

Stock Exchange has the most stringent standards among the various exchanges. Some of the requirements are: national interest in the company; a minimum of one million publicly held shares and not less than 2,000 round-lot shareholders; the minimum total value of publicly held shares is sixteen million dollars, and net income should exceed two and one-half million pretax dollars for the latest 12 months and must exceed two million in the two most recent fiscal years. Unlisted stock trades **over-the-counter** [OTC] either through the **National Association of Securities Dealers Automated Quotation** system, called NASDAQ, or through a broker-dealer network of market-makers who are listed in daily PINK SHEETS.

LISTING in **real estate,** "an agency relationship between the seller and broker with the purpose of effecting a juncture between buyers and sellers of **real property** with an ultimate pecuniary reward to the broker for his part in bringing the parties together," 365 N.E. 2d 1274, 1277. See also **listed stock.**

LITE PENDENTE see **pendente lite.**

LITIGANTS the parties involved in a **lawsuit;** those involved in **litigation;** refers to all parties whether **plaintiffs** or **defendants.** The term is usually limited to those actively involved in the suit.

LITIGATION a controversy in a court; a judicial contest through which legal rights are sought to be determined and enforced. The term refers to **civil actions.** 34 F. Supp. 274, 280. See also **action; case; suit; vexatious litigation.**

LITIGIOUS most commonly used to refer to one's fondness for or propensity to become engaged in **litigation.** Thus, a citizen who repeatedly sues his neighbor over various issues would be called "litigious." Also, the subject of a law-suit or action. Compare **malicious prosecution.** See also **vexatious litigation.**

LIVERY OF SEISIN an ancient ceremony signifying an **alienation** of land by **feoffment.** "It consisted of a formal delivery of **possession** of the **premises,** symbolized by the manual **delivery** of a clod or piece of turf from the land, all of which was done in the presence of **witnesses.**" 140 P. 242, 244. See **seisin.**

LIVING TRUST see **trust.**

L.J. abbreviation for Law **Judge.**

LL.B. see **J.D.**

LOAN "delivery of a sum of money to another under **contract** to return at some future time an equivalent amount with or without an additional sum agreed upon for its use; and if such is the intent of parties, such transaction shall be deemed a loan regardless of its form" 428 P. 2d 190, 194. The characterization of a transaction as a loan or some other type of borrowing has significance in ascertaining whether **usury** laws apply to the amount of **interest** being charged.

LOAN SHARKING the practice of loaning money at **usurious** rates of **interest.** Many states have laws that render usurious interest and in some instances even the underlying debt uncollectable. The use or the threat to use violence in order to collect the interest or the debt constitutes the crime of **extortion.** 18 U.S.C. §§891 et seq. See **extortion; usury.**

LOBBYISTS persons engaged in the business of persuading legislators to pass laws that are favorable, and to defeat those that are unfavorable, to their interests or the interests of their clients. The activities of lobbyists are regulated by statute in most jurisdictions; at the federal level such activities are subject to the provisions of the Lobbying Regulation Acts, 2 U.S.C. §§261 et seq.

LOCKDOWN a temporary confinement of inmates in a correctional facility to their cells on a 24-hour basis with no outside contact and little if any ordinary privileges or recreation. Such a restriction on normal activity of prisoners is done as a security measure following an escape or riot or during the course of some other prison emergency. Prison officials have been accorded considerable latitude by the courts in the use of such lockdowns both in terms of duration and quality. Any measures taken by prison officials that are "unnecessarily cruel" or completely unjustified may violate an inmate's right to be free from cruel and unusual punishment. 452 U.S. 337; 441 U.S. 520.

LOCKUP see **jail.**

LOCO PARENTIS see **in loco parentis.**

LOCUS *(lō'-kŭs)*—Lat: the place.

LOCUS CONTRACTUS *(kŏn-trăk'-tūs)*—Lat: the place where the **contract** was made.

LOCUS DELICTI *(dĕ-lĭk'-tē)* the place where the wrong occurred. Where the "defendant's conduct occurs in one state and the **injury** is done in another; . . . the locus delicti is taken by courts in this country to be the state where the last event necessary to make the actor **liable** occurs." 242 S.W. 2d 285, 288.

LOCUS IN QUO *(ĭn kwō)* the place in which or where; refers to the locale where an offense was committed or a **cause of action** arose.

LOCUS POENITENTIAE *(pō-ĕ-nĭ-tĕn'-shē-ī)* a place for repentance; the opportunity for one to change his mind as to certain things, such as the revoking of a gift **inter vivos;** or **withdrawing** or **renunciating** before the consummation of a crime.

LOCUS SIGILLI *(lō'kŭs sĭ-jĭl'-lī)*— Lat: the place of the **seal;** usually abbreviated "L.S." It is commonly seen within brackets on copies of documents to indicate the position of the seal in the original. 71 S.E. 142, 143. It may also be used to call the attention of the signer to the place for making his seal [signature].

At **common law,** a **contract** under seal was a formal contract. Seals were gradually replaced by the phrase "locus sigilli" or the abbreviation "L.S." Under modern law anything indicating a seal serves the purpose, since it is the intent of the signers rather than the seal that determines the validity of the contract. In many states the distinction between sealed and unsealed instruments has been abolished altogether by statute. The **Uniform Commercial Code** provides that the use of the seal is inoperative in a contract involving a sale of **goods.** U.C.C. §2-203. See generally Corbin on Contracts §241 (1963).

LOG ROLLING schemes used by legislators to force the passage of desired **bills** without actually convincing their colleagues concerning the merits of their proposals. One type of log rolling is the inclusion of several sub-bills under one bill, each sub-bill of which probably would not have been approved if voted on singly. See 36 P. 2d 549, 552. Another practice is for two (or more) legislators to agree to vote on each other's bills, even if neither has any interest in the other's bill.

LOITER to linger idly by; to move slowly about; to be dilatory, particularly in a public place, around a school, or near a transportation facility. Criminal prohibitions against "loitering" include proscription of such behavior as remaining or wandering around a public place for purposes of begging, gambling, soliciting another to engage in sexual intercourse, or for the purpose of selling or using drugs; being masked or disguised in an unusual manner; or simply not being able to give a satisfactory explanation of one's behavior. See New York Penal Law §§240.35-240.36. Loitering statutes are often quite vague and may operate to permit **arrest** for mere suspicion. In either instance the law will be unconstitutional. See 405 U.S. 156; 347 N.Y.S. 2d 33. See **probable cause; void for vagueness.**

LONG ARM STATUTES statutes that allow local **courts** to obtain **jurisdiction** over nonresident **defendants** when the **cause of action** is generated locally and affects local **plaintiffs.** The Supreme Court, in *International Shoe Co. v. State of Washington,* 236 U.S. 310, 316, authorized such expanded jurisdiction where "the contacts of the nonresident defendant with the forum are such that exercise of jurisdiction does not offend our traditional notions of fair play and substantial justice." Green, Basic Civil Procedure 37 (2d ed. 1979). Such statutes are commonly employed to allow a local court to exercise jurisdiction over nonresident motorists who cause automobile accidents within the state. See also **service** (CONSTRUCTIVE SERVICE).

LONG POSITION in finance, the ownership of a **stock** or **security,** subjecting the owner to risk of loss in case the security declines in value. Compare **selling short.**

LONG-TERM CAPITAL GAIN see **capital** [CAPITAL GAINS OR LOSSES].

LONG-TERM LIABILITY see **liability** [LONG-TERM LIABILITIES].

LOOKOUT "person . . . specifically charged with duty of observing lights, sounds, echoes or any obstruction to navigation." 304 F. Supp. 49, 54. Such a person must devote his undivided attention to the task 466 F. Supp. 403, 409, with "that watchfulness which a prudent and reasonable person must maintain for his own safety and the safety of others." 388 S.W. 2d 8, 11.

The doctrine of PROPER LOOKOUT requires that one operating a motor vehicle use such care, prudence, and watchfulness as a person of ordinary care and prudence would use under similar circumstances to avoid liability for negligent operation of the vehicle. In popular usage, it refers to a person stationed outside the area where a crime is being committed, to watch for police or persons who may alert police or be witnesses to the crime.

LORD at **common law,** one who granted a feudal **estate** in land to a tenant. For instance, the King would be the Lord of the Dukes and other nobles to whom the Crown had granted property; the dukes and other nobles were the lords of the persons to whom they in turn granted property. The lord was responsible for protecting and maintaining order among his tenants, for which purpose he maintained a court. In return, the tenant was responsible for providing services to the lord. Moynihan, Real Property 8-10 (1962). Under the English Parliamentary system of government, the House of Lords arose to provide representation for nobles. Traditionally, membership in the House of Lords was hereditary. In recent times, the Crown has appointed individuals as lords for life only, with the individual's title ceasing at his death. See Winchester, Their Noble Lordships 11-22 (1982).

LORD CAMPBELL ACT the English statute that first provided that the surviving family of a person who suffered a **wrongful death** may sue the **tort-feasor** for **damages.** 9 & 10 Vict. c. 93 (1846). It is to be distinguished from the WRONGFUL DEATH STATUTE, which provides that the personal representative of a person who has suffered a wrongful death may sue for damages, thus contravening the **common law** rule that an action for personal injuries did not survive the plaintiff's death. Most states have enacted some form of a Lord Campbell Act or wrongful death statute. Prosser, Law of Torts §127 (4th ed. 1971).

LOSS the act of losing or the thing lost, 158 So. 2d 924, 927; synonymous with **"damage,"** 121 Cal. Rptr. 794, 798; as used in an insurance policy, "a state of fact of being lost or destroyed, ruin or destruction," 182 N.E. 2d 448, 450; and where a policy requires notice of a loss, refers to the date that a fraud was discovered, 224 F. Supp. 666, 670. See also **casualty loss; lost property; risk of loss; total loss.**

LOST PROPERTY property with which the owner has involuntarily parted through neglect, carelessness or inadvertence, 284 S.W. 2d 333, 335; **mislaid property,** on the other hand, is property which the owner intentionally has placed where he could again resort to it, but then forgot where he placed it. Id. at 336. A person may commit an act of theft by acquiring lost property without making a reasonable effort to return the property to its rightful owner. Model Penal Code §223.5. Compare **abandonment.**

LOT, ODD see **odd lot.**

LOTTERY a gambling scheme in which **consideration** is taken in return for the offering of a prize that will be given on the basis of chance and not merit. 212 F. 662. The use of **interstate commerce,** the U.S. mail, or radio or television to distribute or advertise a lottery constitutes a federal crime. 18 U.S.C. §§1301 et seq. However, these laws do not apply to any lottery conducted by a state, 18 U.S.C. §1307, nor to a SWEEPSTAKES (for which no consideration is required) conducted by a business entity.

LOWER OF COST OR MARKET a method of valuating **inventory,** using the lower of either the price of the item as of the time it was pur-

chased or the present **market value** of the item.

L.S. See **locus sigilli.**

LUMP-SUM PAYMENT a single amount of money; a sum paid all at once rather than in part or in installments. For instance, under an insurance policy the proceeds may be paid immediately, as a lump-sum payment, or at the option of the payee over time as an annuity or in installment payments.

LUMP-SUM ALIMONY PAYMENT the discharge of one's obligation to pay **alimony** by the payment of a single lump sum. For income tax purposes, the payment of lump-sum alimony may or may not shift the income tax burden on the alimony to the payee, depending on the circumstances. I.R.C. §71.

LUMP-SUM DISTRIBUTION lump-sum payment to an employee from a **pension** or profit-sharing plan upon termination of employment either by retirement or death.

LYING IN WAIT hiding or concealing oneself for the purpose of committing a crime when the opportunity arises. Regarding **murder,** "lying in wait" implies **premeditation** or **malice aforethought** necessary for first-degree murder. Perkins & Boyce, Criminal Law 130 (3rd ed. 1982).

M

MACHINATION "that which is devised; a device; a hostile or treacherous scheme; an artful design or plot." 125 N.E. 2d 225, 230.

MAFIA see **organized crime.**

MAGISTRATE a public **civil** officer, invested with some part of the legislative, executive, or judicial power. In a narrower sense, the term only includes inferior judicial officers, such as justices of the peace. 16 S.W. 903, 905.

UNITED STATES [FEDERAL] MAGISTRATE appointed by U.S. District Court judges, magistrates are governed by 28 U.S.C. §§631-636 [FEDERAL MAGISTRATE'S ACT OF 1968]. Their powers include the ability to hear and determine any pre-trial motion pending before a district court except for several specified motions, to conduct hearings, including evidentiary hearings, and to submit proposed findings of facts and recommendations for disposition. 28 U.S.C. §636(b)(1)(A). See 447 U.S. 667.

MAGNA CARTA [MAGNA CHARTA] the "great charter" to which King John gave his assent in 1215, and which is considered the fundamental guarantee of rights and privileges under English law.

MAGNUSON-MOSS WARRANTY ACT federal statute requiring warranties for consumer products to be written in plain and easily understood language and providing the Federal Trade Commission with better means of protecting consumers. See 15 U.S.C. §2301 et seq.

MAIL BOX RULE a common law doctrine providing that an **acceptance** made in response to an offer is valid and forms a binding **contract** at the time of its dispatch, as when it is placed in the mail box, if that method of accepting is a reasonable response to the offer. It originated in the case of *Adams* v. *Lindsell,* 1 Barn. & Ald. 681 (King's Bench 1818). The Mail Box Rule controls the situation in which an **offeror,** after making his **offer,** dispatched to the **offeree** a **revocation,** but, before receiving the revocation, the offeree sent by mail an

acceptance of the offer. It became necessary, therefore, to determine the point at which each of these communications has legal effect, either upon dispatch or upon receipt. According to the Mail Box Rule, the acceptance is effective upon dispatch. The rule generally prevails today provided that the means chosen for communication of the acceptance are reasonable. The Mail Box Rule does not apply to the revocation, which is effective only upon receipt. Restatement, 2d, Contracts §63; U.C.C. §§1-201(38), 2-206(1)(a).

MAIM at common law, "to deprive a person of such a part of his body as to render him less able in fighting or defending himself than he would otherwise have been." 132 N.E. 2d 761, 763. See **mayhem.**

MAIN PURPOSE RULE see **statute of frauds.**

MAINTAIN to continue, to support, to sustain, 192 N.Y.S. 2d 342, 344; to hold or keep in any particular state or condition, 243 F. 2d 927, 931; in terms of "maintaining" a **nuisance,** includes both knowledge of the nuisance and preserving and continuing its existence by some positive act or by acquiescence. 256 N.Y.S. 2d 467, 469. Compare **maintenance.**

MAINTENANCE in matrimonial law, food, clothing, and shelter, as well as reasonable living and household expenses of person claiming alimony, 319 So. 2d 479, 481; in a law suit, an officious intermeddling by a party who has no interest in the suit, 178 N.E. 2d 713. It was considered an offense against justice since it kept alive strife and contention, and changed the remedial process of the law into a weapon of oppression. 4 Bl. Comm. 134. Like **champerty,** its strictness has been greatly relaxed in modern times and it only survives in a few jurisdictions in modified form. 14

Am. Jur. 2d 843 (1964). While maintenance refers to the upkeep or preservation of property, 97 S.E. 2d 672, 682, **"maintain"** is more frequently used in this context. See **criminal maintenance.**

MAJORITY, AGE OF the age when a person is considered legally capable of being responsible for all his or her actions, such as entering into contracts, and becomes legally entitled to the rights held by citizens generally, such as voting. In most states, the age of majority was traditionally 21 but is now generally 18, due at least in part to the enactment in 1972 of the 26th Amendment to the United States Constitution, allowing those 18 years of age to vote in federal elections. Many states, however, have set a higher legal age for the consumption and purchase of alcoholic beverages, ranging from 19 to 21.

MAJORITY OPINION see **opinion.**

MAKER in commercial law, one who **executes** a **note** and thus promises that he or she will pay the note at the time it is due. The maker's obligation is primary and unconditional while the obligation of an **endorser** is only secondary since it is conditioned on **dishonor** by the maker. U.C.C. §3-413(1).

MALA IN SE see **malum in se.**

MALA PROHIBITA see **malum prohibitum.**

MALFEASANCE the doing of a wrongful or unlawful act; "a wrongful act which the actor has no legal right to do . . . as any wrongful conduct which affects, interrupts or interferes with the performance of official duty; . . . as an act for which there is no authority or warrant of law; . . . as an act which a person ought not to do at all. . . ." 97 S.E. 2d 33, 42. Compare **misfeasance; nonfeasance.**

MALICE the state of mind that accompanies the intentional doing of a wrongful act without **justification** or excuse. 99 A. 2d 849, 854. It refers to an "intent to cause the very harm that results or some harm of the same general nature, or an act done in **wanton** or **wilful** disregard of the plain and strong likelihood that some such harm will result. It requires also on the negative side the absence of any circumstance of justification, excuse or recognized mitigation." 118 N.W. 2d 422, 425. It denotes "a reckless disregard of human life which proceeds from a heart and mind devoid of a just sense of social duty and fatally bent on mischief." 234 A. 2d 442, 443. Blackstone first said that malice may be either express or implied in law. EXPRESS [ACTUAL] MALICE is that type of **malice aforethought** that includes an **intent** to kill. IMPLIED [CONSTRUCTIVE, PRESUMED] MALICE is a state of mind sufficient for murder but lacking specific intent. It is inferred from the conduct of the actor and the injury which results. Perkins & Boyce, Criminal Law 75-76 (3rd ed. 1982). See 43 Yale L.J. 537 (1934).

With respect to **slander** and **libel,** it is the mental state that accompanies the making of a false statement when the maker knows it to be false or when the maker recklessly disregards the truth or falsity of it. See 362 F. 2d 188, 195.

In cases of **malicious prosecution,** it embodies an intent to institute a **prosecution** for a purpose other than "bringing an offender to justice." 164 So. 2d 745, 750. It includes any prosecution "undertaken from improper wrongful motives or [in] reckless disregard of the rights of the plaintiff." 461 P. 2d 557, 559.

MALICE AFORETHOUGHT the distinguishing state of mind which may render an unlawful homicide **murder** at common law; it is characterized by a "man-endangering" mental disposition for which there is no justification or excuse and as to which no mitigating circumstances exist. See Perkins & Boyce, Criminal Law 75 (3rd ed. 1982).

" 'Malice aforethought' is the characteristic mark of all murder, as distinguished from the lesser crime of **manslaughter** which lacks it. It does not mean simply hatred or particular ill-will, but extends to and embraces generally the state of mind with which one commits a wrongful act. It may be discoverable in a specific deliberate intent to kill. It is not synonymous with **premeditation,** however, but may also be inferred from circumstances that show a wanton and depraved spirit, a mind bent on evil mischief without regard to its consequences." 362 F. 2d 770, 774.

Malice aforethought is not "malice in its ordinary understanding alone, a particular ill-will, a spite or a grudge. Malice is a legal term, implying much more. It comprehends not only a particular ill-will but every case where there is a wickedness of disposition, hardness of heart, cruelty, recklessness of consequences, a mind regardless of social duty, although a particular person may not be intended to be injured. Murder, therefore, at common law embraces cases where no intent to kill existed, but where the state or frame of mind termed malice, in its legal sense, prevailed." 58 Pa. 9, 15.

Modern homicide statutes do not employ malice aforethought but instead rely upon an intent to cause death and the absence of extenuating circumstances. See Model Penal Code §§210.2 and 210.3.

MALICIOUS ARREST the arresting of a person on a criminal **charge** without **probable cause,** or with knowledge that that person did not commit the offense charged. See **malicious prosecution.** Compare **false arrest.**

MALICIOUS PROSECUTION an action for recovery of damages that have resulted to person, **property** or reputation from previous unsuccessful **civil** or criminal **proceedings** which were prosecuted without **probable cause** and with **malice.** 52 N.W. 2d 86, 90. See also **false arrest.**

MALPRACTICE a professional's improper or immoral conduct in the performance of duties, done either intentionally or through carelessness or ignorance. 134 S.E. 527; 234 N.Y.S. 52, 53. The term is commonly applied to a physician, surgeon, dentist, lawyer, or public officer to denote the negligent or unskillful performance of duties resulting from such person's professional relationship with patients or clients. 72 F. Supp. 394, 399; 236 N.Y.S. 641.

MALUM IN SE *(mǎ'-lǔm ǐn sā)*— Lat: evil in itself; "naturally evil, as adjudged by the sense of a civilized community." 259 P. 893, 898. It refers to an **"act** or **case** involving illegality from the very nature of the transaction, upon principles of natural, moral and public law." 373 S.W. 2d 90, 93. For example, murder is "malum in se" because even without a specific criminal prohibition the community would think it to be an evil and wrongful act. Compare **malum prohibitum.**

MALUM PROHIBITUM *(mǎ'-lǔm prō-hǐ'-bǐ-tǔm)*—Lat: wrong because it is prohibited; made unlawful by statute for the public welfare, but not inherently evil and not involving moral turpitude. See 223 N.E. 2d 755, 757. Refers to acts prohibited solely because of the existence of statutes. See 262 F. 2d 245, 248. It is contradistinguished from **malum in se.** For example, driving at excessive speeds is malum prohibitum because statutes prohibit it as a result of a determination that it is dangerous to the community, though it may not be inherently dangerous; whereas, reckless driving would be regarded as malum in se.

MANAGEMENT COMPANY see **closed-end management company.**

MANDAMUS *(măn-dā'-mŭs)*— Lat: we command. An extraordinary **writ** issued from a court to an official compelling performance of a ministerial act that the law recognizes as an absolute duty, as distinct from other types of acts that may be a matter of the official's discretion. It is extraordinary in the sense that it is used only when all other judicial remedies have failed or are inadequate. 9 F. Supp. 422, 423. It is an emergency writ. 74 P. 695, 501. See **ministerial act.**

MANDATE a judicial command; especially, an official mode of communicating the **judgment** of the **appellate court** to the lower court, 151 P. 228, 230; also, a **bailment** in which the bailee performs services gratuitously. 190 P. 12, 16.

MANDATORY INJUNCTION see **injunction.**

MANDATORY SENTENCING see **sentence** [MANDATORY SENTENCE].

MANDATUM in civil law, "a delivery of goods to have some service performed about them by the **bailee** without recompense." 84 S.E. 33, 35.

MANIFEST WEIGHT see **against the [manifest] [weight of the] evidence.**

MANIPULATION under Section 10 (b) of the Securities Exchange Act of 1934, 15 U.S.C. §78, refers to practices that are intended to mislead investors by artificially affecting market activity. 430 U.S. 462, 476. Such practices include WASH SALES or MATCHED ORDERS, i.e., buy and sell orders of substantially the same size at the same time to create a false impression of active trading, 405 S.W. 2d 457, or RIGGED ORDERS. See also **wash sale.**

MANN ACT a federal statute prohibiting the transportation of a woman or girl in interstate or foreign commerce for the purpose of prostitution, debauchery or any other immoral purpose; also known as the WHITE SLAVE TRAFFIC ACT. 18 U.S.C. §§2421-2424. See 363 F. 2d 348.

MANSLAUGHTER an unlawful killing of another person without **malice aforethought.** The crime of manslaughter was developed as an alternative to murder and its attendant death penalty for homicides that were not as extreme and that were explainable. Most jurisdictions distinguish between voluntary and involuntary manslaughter. In general VOLUNTARY MANSLAUGHTER is an intentional killing committed under circumstances that mitigate the homicide, although they do not justify it. The classic example of voluntary manslaughter is where the accused kills in the heat of passion as a result of the deceased's provocation. See, e.g., 59 N.J. 515. Heat of passion, such as rage, fright, terror, or wild desperation is a necessary element of this crime. 80 A. 571; 325 P. 2d 97. Such heat of passion must have been provoked by the deceased. To mitigate the intentional homicide sufficiently to reduce it to manslaughter, this provocation must cause a reasonable man to lose his normal self-control. Voluntary manslaughter is also committed when the killing, although unintentional, resulted from unreasonable and grossly reckless conduct. See Model Penal Code §210.3.

INVOLUNTARY MANSLAUGHTER consists of "criminally-negligent homicide" and "unlawful-act manslaughter." A typical example of criminally negligent homicide is where a death results from the negligent operation of an automobile. See Anno., 99 A.L.R. 756; 160 A.L.R. 515. In some jurisdictions, the crime is specifically labelled "DEATH BY AUTOMOBILE." Model Penal Code §210.4. The standard form of the offense exists where the defendant has killed someone as the consequence of his gross negligence or recklessness. The conduct of the defendant under the circumstances must have involved an unreasonable and high degree of risk of death or serious bodily injury. See 59 N.J. 515. The cases differ, however, as to whether the defendant must be conscious that his conduct produces an unreasonable and high degree of risk. See 55 N.E. 2d 902.

Unlawful-act manslaughter occurs when someone dies as the result of the defendant's doing of an unlawful act, usually a **misdemeanor.** The unlawful act referred to can be any act prohibited by law. See 75 S.E. 523. Unlawful acts which are **malum in se,** and which cause a death, constitute involuntary manslaughter. Unlawful acts that are **malum prohibitum** and have death as a foreseeable consequence of committing the act also constitute involuntary manslaughter. La Fave & Scott Criminal Law (1972). Thus, misdemeanor-manslaughter is analogous to **felony-murder.** Many states have been leaning towards the abolition of the unlawful-act doctrine. See, e.g., N.Y. Penal Law §125.15.

MARGIN the payment, as a percentage of purchase cost, that a buyer of regulated **securities** must make when buying on **credit** from a **stockbroker.** In order to open a margin account with a stock brokerage firm the customer must have good credit standing and must make a minimum deposit of $2,000 in cash or securities. The initial margin requirement is set by the Federal Reserve Board under **Regulation T,** and has ranged from 40 percent to 100 percent since its enactment in 1934. Once the initial "Reg. T" margin call is met the account must be maintained at a minimum **equity** level set by the **New York Stock Exchange** at 25 percent and higher (30 percent or more) by the **member firm** carrying

the account. If the account falls below the carrying firm's minimum equity requirement due to a drop in the price of shares held on credit, the firm will make a margin maintenance call or "house call." Should the customer not meet the call for more money, the firm has a right to sell as much of the customer's securities as is required to raise the customer's equity to house requirements.

Brokerage firms, under Regulation T, are allowed to extend credit only on "regulated securities," that is, securities listed on a **stock exchange** or included on the Federal Reserve Board's list of **over-the-counter** stocks. Other securities are unregulated and cannot be purchased on credit from a stockbroker, but they can be used as **collateral** to obtain a loan from a bank. Bank lending on stocks and bonds is controlled by **Regulation U** which usually specifies the same terms for regulated securities purchase as Regulation T. However, banks can lend more on regulated securities than brokers provided the loan is for a nonregulated purpose, such as to purchase a home, car, etc. Banks indirectly fund most securities loans since brokers obtain most of their margin credit monies from banks under call loans using customers' securities as collateral.

MARIHUANA [MARIJUANA] see **controlled substance** [CANNABIS].

MARITAL AGREEMENT see **prenuptial agreement; separation agreement.**

MARITAL COMMUNICATIONS PRIVILEGE [HUSBAND-WIFE PRIVILEGE] principle that either spouse is precluded from disclosing a confidential communication (oral, written, or expressive action) made by one to the other. 291 U.S. 7. The privilege is only valid during a legal marriage and communications made before the marriage, 347 U.S. 1, or after the marriage terminates, 80 F. 2d 665, are not protected.

However, those communications made during the marriage continue to be protected even after divorce or death. 549 F. 2d 1150. Its purpose is to preserve the marital status and to encourage free and open communication and confidence between spouses. See 445 U.S. 40, 51. Numerous courts have held that the privilege does not apply to persons living together without being married, 555 F. 2d 737, 364 N.E. 2d 756, nor to those in a bigamous marriage. 475 F. 2d 1136. The privilege does not apply if third persons are present, 347 U.S. 1, whether or not such presence was known to the spouses, 260 P. 2d 331, unless the third party lacks the capacity to be a witness, 169 N.E. 833. A presumption does exist that the communication was confidential. 347 U.S. 1. Where a spouse or child is the victim of a crime by the other spouse, the privilege does not apply as to that crime. 137 F. 2d 1006. The privilege belongs to the spouse against whom testimony is offered, 176 N.E. 2d 81, and while it may be waived, many courts feel both spouses, not merely the spouse making the communication, must consent for a valid waiver. 137 F. 2d 1006. See McCormick, Evidence §78 et seq. (2d ed. 1972). Compare **spousal disqualification.**

MARITAL DEDUCTION an **estate** or **gift tax deduction** permitting an individual or the individual's estate to deduct the value of certain property which has passed to his or her spouse for purposes of determining the amount of the taxable gift or estate. Outright transfers, life estates, and certain interests in property that will terminate will qualify for the marital deduction. I.R.C. §§2056, 2523.

MARITIME JURISDICTION see **admiralty and maritime jurisdiction.**

MARITIME LAW the traditional body of rules and practices particularly relating to commerce and nav-

igation, to business transacted at sea or relating to navigation, ships, seamen, harbors, and general maritime affairs, 318 U.S. 36; it "is entirely distinct from the municipal law of the land. It is, and always has been, a body of law separate and distinctive from every other **jurisprudence.** The Constitution of the United States transferred this jurisprudence from the sovereignty of the states to that of the nation. The maritime law proper finds its expression now only in the national will." 73 F. 350, 351. See **admiralty and maritime jurisdiction.**

MARKETABLE TITLE one that a reasonably well-informed purchaser would, in exercise of ordinary business prudence, be willing to accept. See 172 S.W. 472, 473. "A **title,** to be marketable, need not be perfect, (i.e., free from every possible technical criticism), but it must be reasonably safe. . . ." 136 P. 849. It should be free from reasonable doubt so that it will not expose the party who holds it to the hazards of litigation. 510 P. 2d 1223, 1230. See also **good title.**

MARKET MAKERS see **over-the-counter market** [MARKET MAKERS].

MARKET PRICE "established by public sales or sales in the way of ordinary business," 171 N.E. 2d 207, 213; "figure fixed by sales in ordinary business transactions, established when other property of the same kind and in the same or comparable location has been bought or sold in so many instances that such value may reasonably be inferred," 120 A. 2d 77, 80. This price is based on a theoretical transaction between a free seller and buyer dealing at arm's length. 367 F. 2d 104, 110. This term is synonymous with ACTUAL VALUATION, ACTUAL VALUE, MARKET VALUE, and FAIR VALUE. In determining a buyer's damages for non-delivery or repudiation of goods, "market price is determined as of the place for tender or, in cases of rejection after arrival or revocation of acceptance, as of the place of arrival." U.C.C. §2-713(2).

MARKET VALUE the price that goods or **property** would bring in a market of willing buyers and willing sellers, in the ordinary course of trade. See 27 F. Supp. 65. It cannot be determined on the basis of a price that would be acceptable to a buyer or seller operating under pressures or constraints. See 63 F. 2d 241.

For **condemnation** purposes, to determine **just compensation,** market value is not to be based necessarily on the use to which the land is presently put, but on the best and most profitable use to which it is reasonably adaptable. 470 P. 2d 967.

Market value is generally established on the basis of sales of similar goods or property in the same locality, but where there have been no such prior sales, there is no single measure of value, and other evidence of value must be considered. 108 F. 2d 95. Market value is generally regarded as synonymous with ACTUAL VALUE, CASH VALUE, and FAIR MARKET VALUE. 288 F. 2d 232; 216 A. 2d 439. See **book value.**

MARRIAGE a voluntary union for life (or until divorce) of a man and a woman; the union is solemnized in accordance with local law by a wedding ceremony and the filing of a certificate of marriage. A license is required before a marriage can be performed. Such license can only be obtained after medical testing of the couple and, in the case where either the man or woman is a **minor,** by consent of a parent. "The freedom to marry has long been recognized as one of the vital personal rights essential to the orderly pursuit of happiness." 388 U.S. 1, 12. The common law recognized a marital status from a period of **cohabitation** as husband and wife but such **common-law marriages** are no

longer recognized as valid in most jurisdictions. Compare **bigamy.**

MARRIED WOMEN'S ACTS see **tenancy** [TENANCY BY THE ENTIRETY].

MARSHAL "an officer of the peace, appointed by authority of a city or borough, who holds himself in readiness to answer such calls as fall within the general duties of a constable or sheriff." 9 S. 7, 10. An officer in each federal district who performs the same duties as the sheriffs do for the states. Federal marshals also execute **writs** and **orders** issued by the federal courts.

MARSHALING [MARSHALLING] "an equitable principle employed to adjust the rights of various parties by ranking their priorities and determining the order in which the mortgaged property will be sold to satisfy the mortgage debt or debts. Two common techniques are the "two funds" doctrine, and the "inverse order of alienation" rule.

The "TWO FUNDS" DOCTRINE applies when a senior mortgagee has a first mortgage on two or more parcels and a junior mortgagee has a security interest on only one. The doctrine applies to require the senior creditor to proceed first against the parcel that is subject only to his lien. In this way, the junior lienor will receive the maximum possible protection and will not be arbitrarily deprived of his security by the prior mortgagee proceeding first against the property subject also to the junior's claim. The doctrine is not applied automatically; it is incumbent on the one asserting the right to request the equity court to apply it.

The "INVERSE ORDER OF ALIENATION" rule applies when a mortgaged tract of land is "sold off" or conveyed in parcels and the various grantees pay full value to the mortgagor without getting a release from the mortgagee. Thereafter, if the mortgagor defaults and the mortgagee forcloses, the "inverse order" rule will require the mortgagee to proceed first against the lands still owned by the mortgagor, and then proceed against the other parcels in the inverse order in which they were sold until the mortgage is fully satisfied. The rationale is that the buyer of the first parcel sold acquired the most equity, and likewise down the line until the land still held by the mortgagor has the least. As between the mortgagor and the grantees, the mortgagor should pay the debt, and his land should be sold first for that purpose.

The opposite of the "inverse order" rule should apply when one or more grantees of a portion of the mortgaged property assumes the mortgage debt. In this situation, as between the grantee and the mortgagor, the equity resides with the grantor-mortgagor, and the grantee should pay and his land be sold to satisfy the debt. Thus, the "DIRECT ORDER OF ALIENATION" rule would apply in this situation, and the mortgagor's remaining land would be last sold to satisfy the debt." Boyer, Survey of the Law of Property 511-512 (3d ed. 1981).

Probate courts marshall assets to meet the stated wishes of a **testator** (testatrix) in a **will** when appointed property (i.e., property disposed of in the will by the exercise of a **power of appointment**) would because of technical impediments pass into an inappropriate **residuary clause** rather than within the intended disposals. Marshaling of assets in probate courts to achieve this objective is also called SELECTIVE ALLOCATION.

MARSHALING ASSETS a rule of ranking assets that seeks to achieve an equitable distribution of assets among as many claims as possible according to the equities of the different parties. "Broadly defined, the rule of marshaling assets is one which courts of equity sometimes invoke to compel a **creditor,** who has the right to make his **debt** out of either of two funds, to resort to that one of them which will not interfere with or defeat the rights of another creditor who has recourse to only one of these funds. It is not a **vested** right or **lien** founded on **contract,** but rests upon equitable principles called into action by the benevolence of the Court." 192 N.Y. 266, 282, 283. See also 81 N.Y.S. 2d 404.

MARSHALING LIENS "doctrine whereby one claiming a **lien** against two or more classes of property, one of which is also subject to a junior lien [a lien inferior to another] will be required to exact satisfaction from the property not subject to the junior lien. Thus, the junior lien is preserved where other assets exist sufficient to satisfy the senior lien." 171 F. Supp. 655, 660.

MARSHALING REMEDIES "where one creditor has security on two funds of his debtor, and another creditor has security for his debt on only one of those funds, the latter has a right in equity to compel the former to resort to the other fund, if [such an action] is necessary for the satisfaction of both creditors, provided it will not prejudice the rights or interests of the party entitled to the double fund, nor do injustice to the common debtor, nor operate inequitably on the interests of other persons," 27 A. 2d 166, 174.

MARTIAL LAW law of military necessity, where the military exercises great control over civilians and civilian affairs, usually because of the existence of war. "When instituted, [it] is complete and represents the arbitrary will of the commander, controlled only by consideration of strategy, tactics and policy and subject only to the orders of the President. Under martial law the commander can seize men and hold them in confinement without trial. He can try them before a military commission for a violation of the laws of war or his own regulations. Finally, he can legislate and bind citizens and others by rules established by him and governing their conduct in the future." 48 F. Supp. 40, 49. Under a constitutional government, martial law may be imposed only in time of war or when civil authority has become ineffective. See **court-martial.** Compare **military law.**

MASSACHUSETTS TRUST a business trust that confers limited liability on the holders of trust certificates; also called a common-law trust. A Massachusetts trust is a form of business organization in which investors form a voluntary association and transfer contributed cash or other property to trustees who have legal authority to manage the business. Ownership interest is represented by certificates of beneficial interest, also called trust certificates and, less properly, shares. The business trust is a very common form of organization among **real estate investment trusts** (REITs).

MASTER [MASTER IN CHANCERY; SPECIAL MASTER] a judicial officer appointed by **courts of equity** to hear **testimony** and make reports which, when approved by the presiding judge, become the **decision** of the court.

The term also refers to the employer in an employment relationship. See **master and servant.**

MASTER AND SERVANT an employer-employee relationship; the relation that develops from an **express** or **implied** employment **contract** between a master, or employer, and a **servant,** or employee. Restatement Agency 2d §2 (1958). The servant is expected to perform services, usually for a salary, and is under the master's control. While "servant" sometimes refers specifically to hired help in domestic matters, in its broadest sense, the term refers to a person of any rank or position who is subject to the control of another. Such a relationship is distinguished from that of an **independent contractor** who is not under the employer's direct control, but serves the employer only as to the results of his work and not as to the method by which the work is done. Essentially, the power to control is the test in determining whether a master and servant relationship exists. 166 So. 2d 106; Restatement Agency 2d §220. The engagement of a lawyer does not create a master and servant relationship. Under the master and servant relationship, the master will be liable for the actions of his servant committed while the servant was acting within the **scope of his employment.** See **agent; respondant superior; servant.**

MASTER PLAN a long-term, general outline of a project or governmental function, 239 N.Y.S. 2d 185, 189. For instance, in **zoning** law, a planning board or zoning commission will adopt a master plan for an area or a development project, which will regulate the height, density, and other characteristics of structures that may be erected. 209 A. 2d 179, 181.

MATCHED ORDERS see **Manipulation** [MATCHED ORDERS].

MATERIAL important, necessary; relating to a given matter; "[g]enerally speaking, any evidence is relevant and material which tends to prove or disprove any ultimate **issue** made by the **pleadings,** or to make the proposition at issue more or less probable, or which can throw any light on the transaction involved." 155 S.W. 2d 624, 625.

In contract law, a material **breach** is a breach that excuses further performance by the **aggrieved** party and gives rise to an action for **breach of contract.** See **breach** [MATERIAL BREACH].

MATERIAL ALTERATION any alteration of a document that changes its legal effect, 384 A. 2d 906, 909, i.e., that changes the rights, interests, and obligations of the parties to the instrument, 217 A. 2d 400, 406.

MATERIAL BREACH see **breach** [MATERIAL BREACH].

MATERIAL ISSUE an issue that is of legal consequence or other importance.

MATERIAL WITNESS see **witness.**

MATERNAL of the mother; belonging to or coming from the mother.

MATRICIDE the crime of killing one's mother.

MATRIMONIAL ACTION a lawsuit for the purpose of establishing or altering the marital status of the parties through an **annulment** or a **divorce.** 275 N.Y.S. 2d 68, 69; 443 N.Y.S. 2d 181, 182. See **custody; equitable** [EQUITABLE DISTRIBUTION].

MATTER the substantial facts upon which a claim or defense is based, 101 So. 2d 408, 410; the subject of litigation, upon which issue is brought before the court and joined. 368 F. 2d 648, 654.

MATTER OF FACT see **question of fact.**

MATTER OF LAW see **question of law.**

MATURITY the date at which legal rights in an obligation ripen; in the context of **commercial paper** [**negotiable instruments**], it is the "time when the paper becomes due and demandable, that is, the time when an action can be maintained thereon to enforce payment." 221 F. 2d 402, 405.

MAXIMS statements espousing general principles of law; not usually used to justify a court decision based on law, but frequently used to determine the equities of a situation. For example: "Equity treats as done what ought to be done." (The court will order the party to do what he or she should in good conscience already have done); "First in time is first in right." (If the claim of two parties is equal, the first in time is the party who will normally prevail.)

MAYHEM the common law **felony** of maliciously **maiming** or dismembering or in any other way depriving another of the use of any part of his body so as to render him less able to fight in the king's army.

Some states have retained mayhem as a separate offense, although usually the specific intent to maim or disfigure rather than the general intent to act with malice, must be established. Many states simply treat the crime of mayhem as an **aggravated assault.**

McNABB-MALLORY RULE renders incriminating statements inadmissible in federal court if they are obtained from a suspect while he is being held in violation of the speedy **arraignment** provisions of federal law, i.e., if there is an unreasonable delay in arraignment. This doctrine is a matter of judicial policy based on federal law and is not constitutionally mandated. See Fed. R. Crim. Proc. 5(a); 318 U.S. 332, 341, 345; and 354 U.S. 449, 453, 456. The Omnibus Crime Control and Safe Streets Act of 1968 states that a voluntary confession is admissible if it is made within six hours following arrest or detention; if the delay in arraignment is longer than six hours, a voluntary confession is admissible if the delay was reasonable in view of the means of transportation and the distance to be travelled to the nearest magistrate. See 18 U.S.C. §3501(c). Compare **Miranda Rule [warnings].**

MECHANIC'S LIEN see **lien.**

MEDIATE DATA facts from which **ultimate facts** may be inferred for purposes of **collateral estoppel.** See 246 F. Supp. 19, 21.

MEDIATELY indirectly; deduced from proven facts.

MEDIATION a method of settling disputes outside of a court setting; the imposition of a neutral third party (see **party**) to act as a link between the parties; similar to **arbitration** and conciliation. Compare **negotiation.**

MEDICAL EXAMINER see **coroner.**

MEETING OF THE MINDS in reference to the parties to a **contract,** a mutual manifestation of assent to the same terms. It is one of the traditional rules of contract law that the legally enforceable agreement between contracting parties is exclusively that which has been expressed by the terms of the contract they create, for therein lies the requisite "meeting of the minds." A hidden or private intent on the part of either party will not change the effect of the agreement as expressed. 200 F. 287. Where, however, there has been a **mutual mistake,** id., or where the circumstances indicate that one party knew or should have known of the other's undisclosed intent, that intent might no longer be considered "hidden" and might affect interpretation of the contract. 84 S.E. 2d 516.

MEMBER BANK a member of the **Federal Reserve System.**

MEMBER CORPORATION a **securities brokerage** firm, organized as a corporation, with at least one member of the **New York Stock Exchange** who is a director and a holder of voting **stock** in the corporation. See **member firm.**

MEMBER FIRM a **securities** brokerage firm organized as a **partnership** and having at least one general partner who is a member of the **New**

York Stock Exchange. See **member corporation.**

MEMORANDUM (pl. memoranda) an informal record; "a brief note, in writing, of some transaction or an outline of some intended instrument; an instrument drawn up in brief and compendious form." 43 P. 896, 899.

MEMORANDUM OF LAW an argument by an **advocate** in support of his position. It is much like a **brief** but in less formal style without argument headings, tables of cases, etc.

OFFICE MEMORANDUM an informal discussion of the merits of a matter pending in a lawyer's office; usually written by a law clerk or junior associate for the benefit of a senior associate or partner. It is protected from **discovery** by the **work-product** doctrine.

MEMORANDUM CHECK see **check.**

MENACING see **assault.**

MENS REA a guilty mind; the mental state accompanying a forbidden act. For an act to constitute a criminal offense, the act usually must be illegal and accompanied by a requisite mental state. Criminal offenses are usually defined with reference to one of four recognized criminal states of mind that accompanies the actor's conduct: (1) intentionally; (2) knowingly; (3) recklessly; and (4) grossly [criminally] negligent. See Model Penal Code §2.02. The mens rea may be GENERAL, i.e., a general intent to do the prohibited act, or SPECIFIC, which means that a special mental element is required for a particular offense such as "**assault** with intent to rape" or **larceny** which requires a specific intent to appropriate another's property. In a criminal prosecution, the state must prove beyond a reasonable doubt that the required mental state coexisted with the doing of the proscribed act. Defenses of insanity, intoxication and mistake may either nullify or mitigate the existence of a SPECIFIC MENS REA. Crimes that are **malum prohibitum** often do not require any specific mens rea. See, e.g., 343 U.S. 790. These are usually crimes of **strict liability.**

MENTAL ANGUISH compensable **injury** embracing all forms of mental pain, as opposed to mere physical pain, including deep grief, distress, anxiety and fright. See 114 So. 529. Compare **pain and suffering.**

MENTAL CRUELTY a ground for **divorce,** consisting of a course of behavior by one spouse toward the other which imperils the mental and physical health of the other to the extent that continuing the marriage relationship is rendered unbearable. 102 So. 2d 837, 838.

Although probably intended to reach only the most extreme cases when divorce was morally objectionable to most persons, the term has been given an expansive and liberal construction by courts willing to permit divorces practically upon request, even where specific no-fault divorce reform legislation has not yet been enacted. See Clark, Law of Domestic Relations §12.4 (1968).

MERCANTILE LAW the branch of law (often called commercial law) that deals with the rules and institutions of commercial transactions. It is derived from the **law merchant.** The **Uniform Commercial Code** generally governs commercial transactions.

MERCHANT under the **Uniform Commercial Code,** "a person who deals in goods of the kind or otherwise by his occupation holds himself out as having knowledge or skill peculiar to the practice or goods involved in the transaction or to whom such knowledge or skill may be attributed by his employment of an agent or broker or other intermediary who by his occupation holds himself out as having such knowledge or skill." U.C.C. §2-104(1). A one-time **seller** who was not engaged in the business of selling goods in question, or holding himself out as a person who deals in such goods, was not a "merchant" for purposes of implied **warranty.** 473 F. Supp. 35, 38.

Merchants include car dealers, 397 N.Y.S. 2d 677, 681; producers of remanufactured engines, 551 F. Supp. 771, 777; manufacturers of mobile homes, 548 P. 2d 279, 286; and with respect to the leasing of an apartment, a landlord is also considered a merchant, 338 N.Y.S. 2d 67, 69.

A warranty of merchantability will only be implied if the seller is a merchant with respect to goods of the kind in the contract of sale. U.C.C. §2-314(1).

Under the Uniform Commercial Code, risk of loss passes to the **buyer** on his receipt of goods only if the seller is a merchant; otherwise, the risk passes to the buyer on tender of delivery. U.C.C. §2-509(3). See **warranty** [WARRANTY OF MERCHANTABILITY].

MERCHANTABLE salable and fit for the market; "the quality of being reasonably fit for the general purpose for which an article is manufactured and sold," 242 N.W. 895, 896; having at least an average or ordinary quality, in light of the quality of the same or similar products produced previously or elsewhere. See U.C.C. §2-314.

MERCHANTABLE TITLE see **marketable title.**

WARRANTY OF MERCHANTABILITY see **warranty.**

MERE EVIDENCE RULE a former rule of criminal procedure prohibiting the **seizure** of objects of evidential value whether pursuant to a **warrant,** 255 U.S. 298, or incident to arrest. 285 U.S. 452. The rule is no longer in effect and thus there is no distinction between "mere evidence" and instrumentalities, fruits of crime and contraband, in terms of seizure under the reasonableness standards of the Fourth Amendment. 387 U.S. 294. Even private personal papers may be seized as long as the **privilege against self-incrimination** is not violated by compelling a person to make a record or to authenticate the papers by their production. 427 U.S. 463.

MERGER the combination of two or more acts, rights, or entities into a single act, right, or entity. In criminal law, the process by which, when a single criminal act constitutes two offenses, the **lesser-included offense** "merges" or becomes a part of the more serious or higher offense. See 90 S.W. 440, 444.

In the law of **corporations,** a merger is effected when one (or more) corporation(s) become(s) a part of or merge(s) with another corporation; the former corporation(s) cease(s) to exist but the latter corporation continues to exist. In a merger, the company that continues to exist retains its name and identity and acquires the assets, liabilities, franchises, and powers of the corporation(s) that cease(s) to exist. By contrast, in CONSOLIDATION, two or more corporations unite to form a new corporation and the original corporations cease to exist. Thus, in the merger of A and B corporation, one will survive; but in consolidation of A and B, a new corporation, C, will be formed. In both merger and consolidation, the surviving or consolidated corporation acquires the assets of the former corporations, assumes their liabilities, and issues its shares or pays fair consideration for the shares of the former corporation. See Henn & Alexander, Law of Corporations §346 (3rd ed. 1983); 272 N.E. 2d 105, 108.

In civil procedure, "merger" is used to describe the effect of a **judgment** in plaintiff's favor. "Such a judgment extinguishes the entire **claim** or **cause of action** which was the subject of the former action and merges it in the judgment. . . . Plaintiff may no longer sue on the original cause of action or any item thereof even if that item was omitted from the original action." James & Hazard, Civil Procedure 533 (2d ed. 1977). Thus, a judgment in plaintiff's favor merges and puts an end to all issues he raised or could have raised in the cause of action litigated.

A marital separation agreement may either merge into the judgment of divorce or "survive" (i.e., not merge) that judgment according to the intention of the parties and the law of the jurisdiction. The same is true of representations made and agreements entered into prior to the delivery of the executed deed in a real property conveyance. So, if the seller and buyer agreed in the contract of sale that the seller was to provide **warranties (covenants)** of title, of **quiet enjoyment,** against encumbrances, and of further assurances, but the deed delivered at closing of title was not a full warranty but instead a **quit claim** deed, the buyer could not then, after he accepted the deed, sue on the warranties, as they merged into and were extinguished by the deed. An agreement to landscape the property which by the terms of the contract was to survive the delivery of the deed will not merge into that executed deed.

In **property** law, the term applies to the process by which, since the **Statute of Uses,** equitable ownership becomes legal ownership as well, and a conveyance of the former is effective to convey the latter.

It also signifies the absorption of an **estate** of inferior degree into an estate of a higher degree when the two estates vest in the same person at the same time and without any intermediate estate separating them. 1 S.E. 2d 853, 857. Thus, when a **tenant for years** purchases or inherits the **reversion** in **fee simple,** the term for years is **merged** in the inheritance. 57 S.W. 721, 723. Similarly, an **easement** is extinguished when the ownership of the easement and the ownership of the land burdened or affected by it is united in the same person, so that the nonpossessory interest is merged into the possessory interest. A well-known application of the doctrine of merger is found in the **Rule of Shelley's Case,** whereby a remainder in the heirs of the life tenant is converted to a remainder in the life tenant himself, so that the life estate and the remainder are lodged in the same person to form a fee simple title.

CONGLOMERATE MERGER a merger wherein the merged corporations are neither competitors nor potential or actual customers or suppliers of each other, 258 F. Supp. 36, 56; where there are no economic relationships between the acquiring and the acquired firm, 467 F. 2d 67, 75.

GEOGRAPHIC MARKET EXTENSION MERGER a merger between firms that produce the same or similar product line but who sell in separate geographic markets and are not direct rivals. 301 F. Supp. 1161, 1190.

HORIZONTAL MERGER acquisition of one company by another company producing the same or similar product and selling it in the same geographic market. 306 F. Supp. 766, 774.

MERGER OF PROPERTY INTERESTS merger of a smaller and larger estate whenever successive **vested estates** are owned by the same person. There cannot be a merger if a vested estate intervenes between the two **estates,** and a **contingent remainder,** which would otherwise be destroyed by a merger of a life estate and the next vested estate, will not be

destroyed if those two estates are created simultaneously with the contingent remainder since that would defeat the intention of the transferor. Moynihan, Real Property 131-32 (1962).

PRODUCT EXTENSION MERGER a merger between firms that are not direct rivals but that produce products that are functionally related either in marketing or in production to the other. 301 F. Supp. 1161, 1190.

PURE CONGLOMERATE MERGER a residual category of mergers in which all mergers are placed that do not fit anywhere else and in which there seems to be no functional or meaningful relationship between the firms involved. 301 F. Supp. 1161, 1190.

SHORT FORM MERGER a statutory method of merging corporations without the approval of the shareholders of either corporation, usually requiring that the corporation desiring the merger own at least 90 percent of the outstanding shares of each class of the other corporation. Henn & Alexander, Corporations 984 (3d ed. 1983).

VERTICAL MERGER acquisition of one company which buys the products sold by the acquiring company or which sells the product bought by the acquiring company. 324 F. Supp. 19, 39.

MERGER CLAUSE see **Parol Evidence Rule [Merger Clause].**

MERITS the substance of a **litigant's** claim or refutation of a claim; the various elements that enter into or qualify plaintiff's right to the relief sought, see 271 U.S. 228, or defendant's right to prevail in his defense; the totality of the elements of a party's claim that tend to establish or refute the validity or credibility of his cause; the grounds of an action or defense. 112 F. 2d 886, 887. See also **judg-**

ment [JUDGMENT ON THE MER-
ITS].

MESNE intermediate: between two
extremes.

MESNE LORD in English law, a lord
who held lands under authority
of the King and who then gave
others inferior in class to himself
the right to use those lands, and
thus became a lord to those
grantees. See **feoffment, servitudes.**

MESNE PROFITS those profits that
are obtained from the land by one
who has no legal right to the land
and holds it in derogation of the
rights of the true owner.

METES AND BOUNDS a method
of describing the territorial limits of
property by means of measuring
distances and angles from designated landmarks and in relation to
adjoining properties. See 177 S.W.
2d 231, 234.

MILITARY JURISDICTION refers to the constitutional set-up of
three types of military jurisdiction:
military law, which provides for
governing the armed forces in both
peace and war; **military government,** which is exercised in times of
foreign war outside the United
States or in times of rebellion and
civil war within states occupied by
rebels, supersedes local law, and is
exercised by a military commander
under the authority of the President; and **martial law,** which can
only be declared by Congress, or
by the President for a temporary
period, to be used in time of invasion or insurrection within the
United States where ordinary law
no longer adequately secures public
safety and private rights. 71 U.S. (4
Wall.) 2, 141. See **court-martial.**

MILITARY LAW a statutory code
of rules and articles provided by
Congress for the government and
discipline of troops. 44 Ill. 142. It
only applies to those in military service, 200 N.W. 278, 280, but is

enforced in both peace and war, 46
N.J.L. 328, 331. See **military jurisdiction.** Compare **martial law.**

CODE OF MILITARY JUSTICE see
[UNIFORM] CODE OF MILITARY
JUSTICE below.

COURT OF MILITARY APPEAL the
final appellate court which may
review court-martial convictions
of any armed service. It is not an
Article III constitutional court
but is established by Congress
under its power to raise and regulate the land and naval forces of
the United States. U.S. Constitution, Art. I, Section 8; 10 U.S.C.
§867. Its decisions are subject to
review by the President of the
United States. 10 U.S.C. §871.

COURT OF MILITARY REVIEW an
intermediate appellate court established by each branch of the
armed forces for purposes of
reviewing **court-marital** cases. 10
U.S.C. §866.

COURT-MARTIAL see **court-martial.**

MILITARY COMMISSION in time of
war, a court appointed by a field
commander to try alien enemy
combatants for offenses against
the laws of war. 327 U.S. 1, 9.

MILITARY COURT OF INQUIRY a
board of three or more commissioned officers which is convened by any person authorized
to convene a general court-martial for the purpose of making an
investigation and advising
whether further proceedings
shall be had. 10 U.S.C. §935.

MILITARY GOVERNMENT **military
jurisdiction** established under the
Constitution, 48 F. Supp. 40, 46,
superseding local law and exercised by the military commander
under the direction of the President with the express or implied
sanction of Congress. 71 U.S. (4
Wall.) 2. It is exercised either
outside the boundaries of the
United States or in time of rebel-

lion and civil war within states or districts occupied by rebels. 51 F. Supp. 227, 230. When a military government exists, any offense against the "law of war" is tried before a military court. See **martial law.**

[UNIFORM] CODE OF MILITARY JUSTICE the statute that sets forth the procedures by which the armed forces may enforce discipline within its ranks. 10 U.S.C. §§801 et seq. The military justice code establishes a system of courts to try members of the armed forces for service-related crimes. Service-related crimes are those committed on military posts, 401 U.S. 355, 369, or while wearing a service uniform, 395 U.S. 258, 283, but may extend to "nonmilitary" offenses in appropriate circumstances. Id. The military courts function as a part of the executive branch of government, not the judicial branch, and are specifically exempted from the requirement of a grand jury. U.S. Constitution, Amendment V. The proceedings of the military courts are not generally subject to review by the federal courts; however, the federal courts may hear habeas corpus applications from military prisoners who allege the denial of basic constitutional rights. 28 U.S.C. §2241.

MINIMUM [MINIMAL] CONTACTS that degree of contact with a **forum** state sufficient to maintain a **suit** there and not offend traditional notions of fair play and substantial justice which are part of the constitutional guarantee of **due process of law.** 326 U.S. 310, 316. Such contacts include transacting business within the forum, 681 F. 2d 1003, 1007, advertising within the forum, or accepting insurance payments from persons within the forum. James & Hazard, Civil Procedure 632 (2d ed. 1977). The requirement is not met if, for example, a person buys an item outside

the forum and is then injured in the normal use of that item within the forum.

MINIMUM WAGE minimum hourly wages established by Congress, 29 U.S.C. §206, under the Fair Labor Standards Act, 29 U.S.C. §201, to maintain the health, efficiency, and general well-being of workers, 29 U.S.C. §202. That Act has been held inapplicable to state and local governments, 426 U.S. 833.

MINISTER a person ordained in conformity to the customs of any organized religion. To be exempt from military training and service, but not from registration, under the Universal Military Training and Service Act, §6(g), 50 App. U.S.C. §456(g), a person must be ordained in accordance with the formalities required by their religious denomination and preach and teach its religious tenets as their regular and customary vocation, not merely irregularly or incidentally. 387 F. 2d 909, 911.

MINISTERIAL ACT those acts performed by a subordinate official according to explicit directions, usually embodied in a statute rather than directed by judicial order; "the term 'ministerial' . . . is generic rather than specific, and ministerial acts may be divided into two classes: (1) those that are ministerial solely and involve no judgment or discretion; and (2) those that are quasi judicial. . . . A purely ministerial act . . . is one which a person performs on a given state of facts in a prescribed manner, in obedience to the mandate of legal authority, without regard to or the exercise of his own judgment upon the propriety of the act being done." 139 N.W. 83, 88. A public servant or official may be compelled to perform ministerial acts through a **mandamus** proceeding, while **discretionary** acts may be outside the scope of such a proceeding, at least unless a clear **abuse of discretion**

can be demonstrated. See id; 102 P. 2d 970, 973; and 157 N.E. 792, 794.

MINORITY "In the context of the constitutional guarantee of **equal protection,** 'minority' does not have a merely numerical denotation; rather it refers to an identifiable and specially disadvantaged group." 343 F. Supp. 704, 730. Also refers to one who is not of legal age. See **incompetency; majority, age of.**

MINUTES records of the proceedings of a court or any other duly constituted body, such as a legislature or the board of directors of a corporation. While the minutes kept by a judge are neither a memorial of the **judgment** nor records required by **law** to be kept, they do constitute legal **evidence** of the **judgment,** and as such they may serve as the foundation for the correction of **errors.** 140 S.W. 629, 630. Where the clerk puts the minutes of **record,** they constitute sufficient journal entries of **record.** 62 F. 2d 981, 982. Compare **transcript.**

MIRANDA RULE [WARNINGS] the requirement that a person receive certain warnings relating to his privilege against **self-incrimination** (right to remain silent) and his right to the presence and advice of an attorney before any custodial **interrogation** by law enforcement authorities takes place. The actual rule was enunciated in *Miranda* v. *Arizona:* "[t]he prosecution may not use statements, whether exculpatory or inculpatory, stemming from custodial interrogation of the defendant unless it demonstrates the use of **procedural** safeguards effective to secure the privilege against self-incrimination. By custodial interrogation, we mean questioning initiated by law enforcement officers after a person has been taken into custody or otherwise deprived of his freedom of action in any significant way. As for the procedural safeguards to be employed, unless other fully effective means are devised to inform accused persons of their right of silence and to assure a continuous opportunity to exercise it, the following measures are required. Prior to any questioning, the person must be warned that he has a right to remain silent, that any statement he does make may be used as **evidence** against him, and that he has a right to the presence of an attorney, either retained or appointed. The defendant may waive effectuation of these rights, provided the waiver is made voluntarily, knowingly, and intelligently. If, however, he indicates in any manner and at any stage of the process that he wishes to consult with an attorney before speaking there can be no questioning. Likewise, if the individual is alone and indicates in any manner that he does not wish to be interrogated, the police may not question him. The mere fact that he may have answered some questions or volunteered some statements on his own does not deprive him of the right to refrain from answering any further inquiries until he has consulted with an attorney and thereafter consents to be questioned." 384 U.S. 436, 444-45. An explicit statement of waiver of rights is not always necessary to support a finding of waiver; waiver can be inferred from the circumstances of the interrogation. 441 U.S. 369.

Unless being used to cross-examine the defendant, 401 U.S. 222, statements and evidence obtained in violation of this rule are not admissible in the defendant's criminal **trial** and are grounds for federal constitutional challenge to any **conviction** obtained thereby.

MISADVENTURE an accident. A homicide by misadventure results from a lawful act unaccompanied by criminal carelessness or recklessness. 179 So. 591, 600. It differs from involuntary manslaughter in that the homicide by misadventure must be the result of a lawful act. 10 So. 667, 669.

MISAPPLICATION [MISAPPROPRIATION] OF PROPERTY the use of funds or property for a purpose other than that for which they are intended or legally required to be used; implies a conscious misappropriation or illegality. See 66 A. 420, 424. "Misapplication" and "misappropriation" particularly apply to the acts of a **fiduciary** [one in a position of trust], including public servants as well as private **trustees**. The terms can include the misapplication of funds intended for another purpose, e.g., the misapplication of public money, or the **conversion** of another's funds for one's own benefit. See 147 F. 349, 357. Thus **embezzlement** is included as a type of misapplication or misappropriation. See 64 P. 692, 693. Compare **larceny**.

MISCARRIAGE OF JUSTICE damage to the rights of one **party** to an **action** that results from errors made by the court during trial and that is sufficiently substantial to require **reversal**. Where the **appellate court** is seriously doubtful that without committed errors the result in the case would have been the same, the errors may require a reversal on the grounds of a miscarriage of justice. 71 P. 2d 220, 253-254. See **plain error**.

MISCEGENATION a mixing of the races; usually referred to marriage between a caucasian (white) and a member of any of the other races. Such marriages can no longer be validly proscribed nor deemed criminal. 379 U.S. 184; 388 U.S. 1.

MISCONDUCT IN OFFICE corrupt misbehavior by an officer in the exercise of the duties of the office or while acting under color of the office, 185 A. 2d. 45, 47; includes any act or omission in breach of a duty of public concern by one who has accepted public office, 318 A. 2d 783, 786. See **bribery**.

MISDELIVERY includes both **delivery** to the wrong party and delivery of **goods** damaged by the **carrier**, 71 N.E. 685, 689; failure to deliver goods within terms of **bill of lading**, 174 N.E. 801, 803; a total failure to deliver the goods, or leaving them at the wrong place, which is also deemed a **conversion**, 71 N.E. 685, 689. In a **bailment** for hire, the bailee is held strictly accountable for a misdelivery and is liable for conversion when such misdelivery occurs. Boyer, Survey of the Law of Property 693 (3rd ed. 1981). For purposes of commercial **contracts**, a delivery pursuant to a forged delivery order is a misdelivery rather than a **theft**. 339 F. 2d 295, 298.

MISDEMEANOR a class of criminal offenses consisting of those offenses less serious than **felonies** and which are sanctioned by less severe penalties. It is generally distinguished from a felony by the duration or place of imprisonment and the severity of the possible or actual punishment. See 121 N.W. 2d 457, 459; 402 P. 2d 998, 1000. At common law, "misdemeanors" applied to all indictable offenses below felonies.

The distinction between felony and misdemeanor may have important consequences depending upon the locality of the crime. For example, **burglary**, under the common law, could only be committed by entering a dwelling house at night with the intent to commit a felony. In criminal procedure, an alleged felon may have to be tried by a state rather than municipal court, and may have to be **indicted** by a **grand jury**, while a misdemeanant may receive less in the way of procedural safeguards. The convicted felon may also be disqualified from holding office, serving on a jury, or engaging in particular licensed occupations, while one convicted of a misdemeanor may not be similarly handicapped. LaFave & Scott, Criminal Law 27-28 (1972).

Some modern criminal statutes no longer retain the misdemeanor/felony distinction. Instead, crimes and offenses are classified according to degrees. Model Penal Code §1.04. See **degree of crime.**

MISFEASANCE the doing of a proper act in a wrongful or injurious manner; the improper performance of an act which might have been lawfully done. See **malfeasance; misconduct; nonfeasance.**

MISJOINDER the joining together of distinct counts in a single **indictment** or **complaint,** which counts ought not to be tried together. See Fed. R. Civ. Proc. 42(b) and Fed. R. Crim. Proc. 8. "The charging in separate counts, of separate and distinct offenses arising out of wholly different transactions having no connection or relation with each other." 13 F. 2d 11, 12. Also, the improper consolidation of separate indictments, or actions. The term may also be used with reference to the improper joining of parties in a single action. See Fed. R. Civ. Proc. 19 21 and Fed. R. Crim. Proc. 8. See **joinder** [COMPULSORY JOINDER, PERMISSIVE JOINDER].

MISLAID PROPERTY property that owner has intentionally placed where he can resort to it, but which place is then forgotten. See 284 S.W. 2d 333, 335. The finder of mislaid property acquires no **interest** or right to **possession,** and thus the proprietor of the place in which the mislaid object is found is the only one entitled to retain possession pending the search for the true owner. Compare **lost property.**

MISNOMER a mistake in the word or combination of words constituting a person's name and distinguishing him from other individuals. See 1 A. 2d 178, 181. The MISNOMER RULE, which affords relief from the **statute of limitations,** "ap-plies to situations in which the **plaintiff** has actually sued and **served** . . . the party he intends to sue, but merely mistakenly used the wrong name of the **defendant.**" 284 F. Supp. 635, 641.

MISPRISION OF FELONY at common law, the **misdemeanor** of observing a **felony** and failing to prevent it, or of knowing about a felony and failing to disclose the fact of its occurrence, or concealing the felony without any previous agreement with or subsequent assistance to the **felon.** "Misprision of felony" should be distinguished from the crime of being an accessory before- or after-the-fact, which requires some agreement with the party committing the felony. See 217 A. 2d 432, 433. The offense of misprision of felony has not been accorded general recognition in the United States. Perkins & Boyce Criminal Law 576 (3rd ed. 1982). Today, in order to be guilty of the federal crime of "misprision of felony," in addition to knowing about a felony and failing to disclose information about it, one must take an affirmative step to conceal the felony. See 38 F. 2d 515, 517, 18 U.S.C. §4. Compare **accomplice; conspiracy.**

MISREPRESENTATION see **false pretense.**

MISTAKE "an act or omission arising from ignorance or misconception," 31 Ohio Dec. 130, which may, depending upon its character or the circumstances surrounding it, justify **rescission** of a **contract,** or exoneration of a defendant from tort or criminal **liability.**

Commercial law distinguishes two types of mistake:

MUTUAL [BILATERAL] MISTAKE signifies error on the part of both parties regarding the same matter, i.e., "where both parties understood that the real agreement was what one party alleges it to be, but had unintentionally prepared and executed one which did not express the true agreement." 237 P. 879, 880. In the event of such a mistake, the contract may be subject to **rescission** (i.e., it may be **voidable,** 423 S.W. 2d 427), or **reformation,** 160 S.E. 2d 833, by either of the parties. See Restatement, Contracts 2d, §§152, 155.

UNILATERAL MISTAKE a mistake on the part of only one of the parties. It can never justify reformation or alteration of the contract, although such a mistake may be the basis for rescission if the parties can be restored to their original positions (**status quo ante**) and one party is seeking an unconscionable advantage over the other. 140 A. 749.

A further distinction is drawn between a MISTAKE OF LAW and a MISTAKE OF FACT. With respect to a contract, the latter is the sort that may justify rescission, subject to the mistake's **materiality** to the transaction. See 24 S.E. 677. However, a mistake of law—which consists of one's ignorance of the legal consequences of his conduct, though he is fully cognizant of the facts and substance of that conduct—is not generally regarded as sufficient to justify rescission or reformation of a contract, unless the mistake is a mutual one concerning private legal rights of one of the parties, which rights the contract was expected to secure. 47 N.E. 2d 284.

The criminal law has traditionally recognized the same dichotomy, allowing a mistake of fact in some cases to constitute a valid defense to a criminal prosecution, but relying on the maxim, "ignorance of the law is no excuse," with regard to mistakes of law. LaFave & Scott, Criminal Law 347 (1972). [See **ignorantia legis non excusat.**] The more modern and far less confusing rule is that either type of mistake supplies a valid defense if it necessarily negates the **culpable** mental state (intent, knowledge, etc.) required by the criminal statute for one to be guilty of the crime in question. Model Penal Code §2.04(1)(a). Nevertheless, he could be guilty if what he erroneously thought he was doing also constitutes a crime. Id. §2.04(2). See **impossibility** [LEGAL IMPOSSIBILITY].

MISTRIAL a **trial** terminated and declared void prior to the return of a **verdict.** A mistrial most commonly arises due to a deadlock in a jury's deliberations (**hung jury**), but may also be due to some extraordinary circumstance, such as death or illness of a necessary juror or of an attorney. It may also be due to a fundamental error prejudicial to the defendant that cannot be cured by appropriate instructions to the jury, such as the inclusion of highly improper remarks in the prosecutor's summation. It does not result in a **judgment** for any party, but merely indicates a failure of **trial.** See 157 S.W. 2d 879, 881. Mistrials in a criminal prosecution may prevent retrial under the doctrine of **double jeopardy,** unless due to manifest necessity or required by the interests of justice. 400 U.S. 470; 410 U.S. 458.

MITIGATING CIRCUMSTANCES circumstances that do not exonerate a person from the act with which he is charged but which reduce the penalty connected to the offense, or the **damages** arising from the offense; for example, **murder** may be reduced to **manslaughter** where there were present mitigating circumstances, i.e., that the killing was committed in a sudden heat of passion caused by legally adequate provocation. See 407 P. 2d 917, 920. Mitigating circumstances may also influence the choice of sanction by the court so that a defendant pleading mitigating circumstances might receive a more lenient **sentence.** See **comparative negligence.** Compare **defense.**

MITIGATION OF DAMAGES a requirement that one injured by reason of another's **tort** or **breach** of an agreement exercise reasonable diligence and ordinary care to avoid aggravating the injury or increasing the **damages.** 236 So. 2d 57. The term also refers to a defendant's request to the court for a reduction in damages owed to the plaintiff, a request that the defendant justifies by reason of some evidence that shows the plaintiff not entitled to the full amount that might otherwise be awarded to him. 360 F. 2d 643.

DUTY TO MITIGATE DAMAGES not actually a duty in the sense that its breach will give rise to a **cause of action** against the person who violates it. Rather it expresses the general rule that one who was wronged must act reasonably to avoid or limit losses or be precluded from recovering damages that could reasonably have been avoided. In this sense the rule has been termed a "RULE OF AVOIDABLE CONSEQUENCES" rather than a duty to mitigate damages. McCormick, Damages, §§33, 160 (1935). Thus, if a wrongfully discharged employee failed to look for alternative work and work was readily available of the same kind that was the subject of the breached contract, the employer would be allowed to deduct what the earnings could have been from the damages claimed. In **commercial law,** a buyer has a duty to either follow a seller's instructions as to the goods which the buyer rightfully rejected or to make reasonable efforts to sell them if they are perishable or threaten to decline in value. See U.C.C. §2-603.

MIXED NUISANCE see **nuisance** [MIXED NUISANCE].

M'NAGHTEN RULE See **insanity** [M'NAGHTEN RULE].

M.O. see **modus operandi.**

MOB see **organized crime.**

MODEL RULES OF PROFESSIONAL CONDUCT most recent pronouncement of rules governing professional conduct of lawyers recommended by the Amercian Bar Association in 1983 to replace the Code of Professional Responsibility. Generally consists of rules of reason prescribing terms for resolving ethical problems that arise from "conflict between a lawyer's responsibility to clients, to the legal system and to the lawyer's own interest in remaining an upright person while earning a satisfactory living." Preamble to the Rules. The adoption of the Rules recognizes that the legal profession is largely self-governing, a status that can be maintained only as long as the profession can assure that its regulations are conceived in the public interest and not in furtherance of parochial or self-interested concerns of the bar. The Rules, however, simply provide a framework for the ethical practice of law. They do not exhaust the moral and ethical considerations that should guide a lawyer. Id. Moreover, the Rules are not designed to be a basis for civil liability. Each state body that regulates lawyer conduct within its jurisdiction is free to adopt all or part of the Rules, or to reject them. Presently, state courts follow the **Code of Professional Responsibility** which was a successor version of the original Canons of Ethics.

The Rules address eight separate areas: (1) the client-lawyer relationship, (2) the lawyer as a counselor, (3) the lawyer as an advocate, (4) transactions with persons other than lawyers, (5) law firms and associations, (6) public service, (7) information about legal service, and (8) maintaining the integrity of the profession.

One of the more controversial rules, Rule 1.6, concerns Confidentiality of Information, which essentially requires the lawyer to not reveal any information the client tells to the lawyer, even if that information concerns the commission of a crime or fraud upon others, except if the crime is likely to result in imminent death or substantial bodily harm, or establishes a claim or defense on behalf of the lawyer in a controversy between the lawyer and client.

MODUS OPERANDI *(mō'-dŭs ŏp'-ér-än'-dē)*—Lat: the manner of operation; the means of accomplishing an act; "characteristic method employed by defendant in performance of repeated criminal acts," 249 C.A. 2d 81; e.g., the modus operandi of the murderer was suffocation by a pillow; abbreviated M.O.

MOIETY denotes the half part, in contrast to **entirety** which denotes the whole. 9 N.Y.S. 275. To hold a moiety is to hold one-half of the thing held.

MOLLITER MANUS IMPOSUIT *(mō'-lĭ-tér mä'-nŭs ĭm-pō'-zū-ĭt)*— Lat: the gentle laying of hands upon; in a **tort** action, refers to assertion by one of the **parties** that he used only such force as was necessary to protect himself or his **property** from injury by the other party. See also **self-defense.**

M-1 [M-2, M-3] see **money supply [M-1, M-2, M-3].**

MONEY coined metal, usually gold or silver, upon which a government has impressed its stamp to designate its value. While money was once limited to "coin of the realm," in common usage the term refers to any currency, tokens, bank notes or the like accepted as a medium of exchange. Under the **Uniform Commercial Code,** money is defined as "a medium of exchange authorized or adopted by a domestic or foreign government as a part of its currency." U.C.C. §1-201(24). Compare **legal tender.**

MONEY DEMAND any demand or **action** arising out of **contract,** tort,

or statute, express or implied, where the relief demanded is a recovery of money, 8 Ind. 339, 341, and may be enforced by **attachment** when the amount due is fixed or can be ascertained. 24 So. 847, 848.

MONEY HAD AND RECEIVED in early common law pleading, one of the categories in the action for general **assumpsit.** The plaintiff declared that the defendant "had and received certain money . . .." The other two related declarations in the same category were "for money lent" and "for money paid."

MONEY JUDGMENT a judgment ordering the payment of a sum of money, 275 S.E. 2d 673, 675. Such judgments may be executed under a writ of **execution,** 306 So. 2d 869, 874.

MONEY ORDER a credit instrument, either **negotiable** or nonnegotiable, calling for payment of money to a named **payee,** and involving the payee, **drawee,** and remitter. 261 N.W. 2d 586, 589.

MONEY SUPPLY [M-1, M-2, M-3] the various measures of money used by the Federal Reserve System. M-1 is currency plus demand deposits or checking account balances; M-2 is M-1 plus net time deposits other than large **certificates of deposit;** M-3 is M-2 plus deposits at nonbank thrift institutions such as savings and loan associations. Various other components and combinations are also used.

MONOGAMY see **polygamy.**

MONOPOLY a description of a market condition where all or nearly all of an article of trade or commerce within a community or district is brought within the single control of one person or company, thereby excluding competition or free traffic in that article. 18 N.W. 2d 905, 908.

Monopolization is prohibited by Section 2 of the **Sherman Act.** Conviction can lead to criminal penalties and **divestiture.** The offense of monopoly has two elements: "1) the **possession** of monopoly power in the relevant market, and 2) the willful acquisition or maintenance of that power as distinguished from growth or development as a consequence of a superior product, business acumen, or historical accident." 384 U.S. 563, 570-71.

The term also comprehends a privilege or **license** granted to a group or company which gives it the sole authority to deal in produce, or provide a product or service in a specified area. For example, utilities are usually lawful monopolies within their assigned areas.

There can be "natural" monopolies, where one company exercises monopoly power through no effort on its part and over which the company has no power. Such natural monopolies are not unlawful. See **antitrust laws.**

MOOT CASE a case seeking to determine an "abstract question which does not rest upon existing facts or rights, or which seeks a **judgment** in [an alleged] controversy when in reality there is none; [a case] which seeks a decision in advance about a right before it has actually been asserted or contested, or a judgment upon some matter which when rendered for any cause cannot have any practical effect upon the existing controversy." 32 N.W. 2d 190, 192. See also **advisory opinion.** Compare **declaratory judgment.**

MOOT COURT a fictitious court established to argue a **moot case;** usually found in law schools as an instrument of learning oral advocacy skills.

MORAL CERTAINTY to be reasonably certain or certain beyond a **reasonable doubt** but short of being absolutely certain; "a reasonable certitude or conviction based on convincing reasons and excluding all reasonable doubts that a con-

trary or opposite conclusion can exist based on any reasons." 104 N.W. 2d 379, 382. A juror is said to be morally certain of the truth of a fact sought to be proved when he would act in reliance upon its truth in matters of the greatest importance to himself.

The term is sometimes used to express the criminal law standard of proof [proof "beyond a reasonable doubt"] but may also be used to indicate an even higher standard, as in regard to an allegation that an unlawful **homicide** has been committed when the victim's body is missing. [1955] 1 Q.B. 388. Compare **preponderance.**

MORAL CONSIDERATION see **consideration.**

MORAL TURPITUDE baseness, vileness, or dishonesty of a high degree. See 44 So. 2d 802. Conviction of a crime of "moral turpitude" may lead to disqualification from governmental office, loss of one's license to practice law, or deportation of immigrants. See, e.g., 8 U.S.C. §1251(a)(4) [deportation]. The term lacks precision but has been held not unconstitutionally vague. 450 F. 2d 1022, 1024. A crime of "moral turpitude" is one demonstrating depravity in the private and social duties which a man owes to another and society at large, contrary to what is accepted and customary. See 99 S.W. 2d 1079. This category of offenses is sufficiently broad to include such relatively commonplace crimes as bribery, 187 F. Supp. 753, and larceny, 112 F. Supp. 324.

MORTGAGE at **common law,** a **conveyance** of a **conditional fee** of a **debtor** to his **creditor,** intended as a security for the repayment of a loan, usually the purchase price (or a part thereof) of the **property** so conveyed. The transfer was to be **void** upon repayment of the loan, i.e., the property reverted to the debtor upon the discharge of the mortgage by the timely payment of the sum loaned. Since the mortgage actually conveyed the legal **title,** the creditor had all of the incidents of legal ownership including the right to **possession** itself. But the **courts of equity** recognized the security nature of the transaction and protected the debtor's right of possession. See Osborne, Mortgages 8-22 (2d ed. 1970).

In American jurisdictions three theories of mortgages are recognized: title theory, **lien** theory, and hybrid theory. The TITLE THEORY is the modern version of the common law mortgage under which the creditor has the legal right to possession (though in fact the debtor remains in possession of his property). Under the HYBRID THEORY the creditor's right to possession arises only upon default by the debtor. Under the LIEN THEORY, the **mortgagee** [creditor] takes only a lien on the property, and is not entitled to possession until he has pursued his remedy in **foreclosure** and the mortgaged **premises** have been sold; i.e., the right to possession arises only when the **equity of redemption** had been foreclosed. See id. at 23-26. In the mortgage relationship, the debtor is called the **mortgagor** and the creditor is called the mortgagee. In most home purchase transactions the buyer is the mortgagor who gives a mortgage in the home he is purchasing either to the bank or to the seller (and sometimes to both parties if there are first and second mortgages upon the same property). The bank (or the seller) is the mortgagee. See also **wraparound mortgage.** Compare **deed of trust.**

ASSUMPTION OF MORTGAGE acceptance of the obligations of a mortgagor towards a mortgagee, generally as a part of the purchase price of a parcel of real estate. By assuming the mortgage rather than taking "subject to the mortgage," the purchaser becomes personally liable on the debt. 245 So. 2d 221, 223.

CHATTEL MORTGAGE conveyance of an interest in **personal property,** generally made as security for the payment of money, such as the purchase price of the property, or for the performance of some other act. The mortgagor retains possession. It is thus distinguished from a **pledge,** which establishes a **bailment** and which therefore establishes the pledgee as **bailee** and grants him possession of the personalty. The term "chattel mortgage" is now rarely used. Chattel mortgages are now dealt with as **security** interests under article 9 of the **Uniform Commercial Code.**

CLOSED-END MORTGAGE a mortgage that does not permit additional borrowing without the consent of the first mortgagee.

EQUITABLE MORTGAGES "usually defined as security transactions that fail to satisfy the requirements of legal mortgages but nevertheless are treated as mortgages in equity. Stated thus broadly they include cases in which the **interest** in the property in the hands of the creditor is the full legal ownership and the aid of equity is necessary to cut it down to a security interest and to establish the rights of the debtor as a mortgagor." Id. at 32. Also included are cases where the transaction is technically insufficient to create a mortgage at law, but where equity intervenes to protect the mortgagee.

PURCHASE MONEY see **security interest.**

SUBJECT TO MORTGAGE a condition or term of sale describing the purchase of land that is encumbered by a mortgage that survives the sale. The purchaser's obligation to the mortgage is limited to the value of the property subject to the mortgage, unless the purchaser becomes personally liable on the debt by "assuming the mortgage." See ASSUMP-

TION OF MORTGAGE above. 514 P. 2d 1003, 1005.

MORTGAGE MARKET origination of mortgage loans in the primary mortgage market and resale of mortgages in the secondary mortgage market, especially mortgage certificates that are **bond**-like securities backed by blocks of mortgage loans. Primary origination is conducted by mutual savings banks, savings and loan associations, mortgage bankers, commercial banks, and insurance companies. The same institutions are active in the secondary market with mortgage certificate issues directed to the general public and traditional investment groups such as pension funds. Mortgage loans represent first liens on real estate property which, unlike bonds, require periodic payment (usually monthly) of both principal and interest over the term of the mortgage. The federal government has assumed a major economic role in the mortgage loan market because real estate development is a major sector of the U.S. economy. The Federal Housing Authority and the Veterans Administration promote primary mortgage originations by guaranteeing home mortgages. The government National Mortgage Association (Ginnie Mae) and the Federal National Mortgage Association (Fannie Mae) promote the secondary mortgage market in government-insured loans. The Federal Home Loan Bank Board regulates savings banks, which are the primary originators of home mortgages, and promotes the secondary market in government-insured mortgages, privately insured mortgages and conventional uninsured mortgages.

MORTGAGEE the party lending the money to a **mortgagor,** who takes a security interest in property owned by the mortgagor.

MORTGAGOR the party borrowing money from a bank or other lending agency, who secures the loan with property the party owns in whole or in part.

MORTIS CAUSA see **causa** [CAUSA MORTIS].

MORTMAIN literally, "dead hand"; applies to **real property** that, from the nature of the purposes to which it is devoted, or the character of the ownership to which it is subjected, is for every practical purpose in a dead or unserviceable hand. 9 Barb. 324, 333 (N.Y.). At common law it was used to refer to land where the alienability was restricted because it was owned by an ecclesiastical or temporal corporation. In England, the MORTMAIN ACTS restricted the transfer of property to corporations in response to the use of corporations by the church and other ecclesiastical bodies to control land. The concept has been used with reference to any sort of corporation that may hold property in perpetuity, and thus with a "DEAD HAND." 259 P. 2d 49, 51.

MOST FAVORED NATION CLAUSE in international law, a clause in a **treaty** by which each signatory country grants to the other the broadest rights and privileges which it accords to any other nation in treaties it has made or will make. 417 P. 2d 581, 583.

MOTION an application to the court requesting an **order** or rule in favor of the applicant. See 347 S.W. 2d 211, 216. Motions are generally made in reference to a pending **action** and may be addressed to a matter within the discretion of the judge, or may concern a point of law as in the case of a MOTION TO DISMISS which tests the adequacy of the **pleadings.** Motions may be made orally, or, more formally, in writing, by a NOTICE OF MOTION. They may be determined without notice to the adverse parties [**ex parte**] or argued by adverse parties.

MOTION FOR JUDGMENT a motion

admitting an agreed-upon statement of facts that leaves the dominant issue in the case as one of a **matter of law,** thereby relegating the issue for a determination by the **court** rather than by a **jury.** See **judgment** [JUDGMENT NOTWITHSTANDING THE VERDICT]; **summary judgment.**

MOTION IN ARREST OF JUDGMENT application made by defendant to withhold judgment after verdict. The motion, like a **demurrer,** must point out some fatal defect arising as a matter of law from the record. See 112 F. 972, 983.

MOTION IN ERROR same as **writ of error,** except no notice to opponent is required, since both parties are before the court when a motion in error is made. 21 Conn. 283, 284.

MOTION IN LIMINE a motion used to exclude reference to anticipated **evidence** claimed to be objectionable until the **admissibility** of the questionable evidence can be determined either before or during the trial by presenting to the **court,** out of the presence of the **jury, offers** and **objections** to the evidence. 220 N.W. 2d 919, 922. The motion seeks to avoid injection into **trial** of irrelevant, inadmissible, or prejudicial evidence at any point, including the **voir dire** examinations, opening statements, and direct and cross examinations, and therefore prevents **mistrials** based on evidentiary irregularities.

MOTION TO SET ASIDE JUDGMENT exactly like motion in arrest of judgment, except that while a motion to arrest must be made during term of court which renders judgment, a motion to set aside judgment can be made at any time within the applicable **statute of limitations.** Both motions must be based on a legal defect appearing on the face of the **record.** See 121 S.E. 648, 649.

MOTOR VEHICLE CODE see **code.**

MOVANT the moving party; applicant for an **order** by way of **motion** before a court.

MOVE to make a **motion;** in practice, to make application to a court or other tribunal for a ruling, **order,** or particular **relief.**

MULCT a **fine** or penalty imposed for an offense, 93 N.W. 372, 378; a **forfeiture,** 137 P. 841, 844.

MULTIFARIOUS SUIT suit wherein "distinct and independent matters are improperly **joined** . . ., and thereby confounded—as for example, where several perfectly distinct and unconnected matters against one **defendant** are united in one bill," 69 N.E. 912, 913; also refers to **misjoinder** of **causes of action** and misjoinder of **parties** in a suit. See 65 S.E. 656, 658. Modern practice favors **joinder** of distinct claims in the interest of judicial economy, thereby eliminating most problems of multifarious suits. See **counterclaim.**

MULTIPARTITE consisting of two or more parts or parties, as where several nations join in a treaty.

MULTIPLICITY OF ACTIONS [SUITS] the existence of several separate **actions** at law brought against the same defendant to **litigate** the same right. In exercise of its equity powers, the court can enjoin the proceedings at law and hear all of the claims at a single proceeding. A mere multitude of suits is not sufficient to invoke this remedy. Rather, the court must find that the remedy at law is not sufficient and that the proceedings will be vexatious for the defendant and wasteful for the courts. 51 N.E. 2d 436, 438-440. **Class action** suits are permitted as an attempt to alleviate this problem. See Fed. R. Civ. Proc. 23. See also **litigious; malicious prosecution.**

MUNICIPAL BOND a **bond** issued by a state or local government body such as a county, city, or town. Interest paid on municipal bonds is exempt from federal income tax and from state and local income taxes within the state of issue. This tax exempt feature keeps interest rates paid on municipal bonds lower but it results in an effectively higher yield, especially for bond holders in higher tax brackets.

MUNICIPAL CORPORATIONS usually **incorporated** cities, towns, and villages having subordinate and local powers of legislation. 117 S.E. 2d 872, 874. At times the term is used in a broader sense to include every **corporation** formed for governmental purposes, so as to embrace counties, townships, school districts, and other governmental subdivisions of a state. Id. They are created by and derive their powers from the state's legislature. 92 U.S. 307. See **governmental functions; sovereign immunity.**

MUNICIPAL COURT city court that administers the law within the city. These courts generally have exclusive **jurisdiction** over violations of city **ordinances**, and may also have jurisdiction over criminal cases arising within the city and over certain minor civil cases. See 82 N.E. 521, 523. They are thus inferior courts of limited jurisdiction.

MUNICIPAL ORDINANCE a law of local application, whose violation is an offense against the city enacting it, 52 S.E. 751, 755. See **ordinance.**

MURDER a common law offense of unlawful homicide; unlawful killings of another human being with **malice aforethought.** This requires a premeditated intent to kill plus an element of hatred. See LaFave & Scott, Criminal Law §67 (1972). The development of the law of the crime led to several other categories of murder such as intentional killings in the heat of an unreasonable passion; **felony-murder,** where the defendant unintentionally kills another person in the commission of a **felony;** and where the defendant kills another while intending to do him only serious bodily harm.

Today, legislatures have distinguished between the different degrees of homicide in order to limit the possible infliction of the death penalty to the most egregious form, "first degree" murder. The modern classification of murder includes first degree murder and second degree murder.

FIRST DEGREE MURDER has been often defined as an unlawful killing that is willful, deliberate, and premeditated, see e.g., N.J.S.A. 2A:113-2; willfulness being the requirement of intent, deliberation requiring a conscious consideration of the decision to kill, and premeditation requiring that the intent to kill be fashioned prior to the killing. Each one of the requisite elements can be formed within a time of a moment's duration. First degree murder also includes the category of felony-murder.

SECOND DEGREE MURDER is the unlawful killing of another with malice aforethought but without deliberation and premeditation. Such malice may be in the form of express malice as the actual intention to kill, or of implied malice where there is no intent, but where death is caused by an act that discloses such a reckless state of mind as to be equivalent to an actual intent to kill, such as where the accused shoots into a crowd. See 222 S.W. 244. Compare **manslaughter.**

MUTE see **standing mute.**

MUTINY to rise against lawful or constituted authority, particularly in the naval or military service, 249 F. 919, 925; at sea, an attempt to usurp command of a vessel from its master, 54 F. 533, 534; includes resisting a federal warden or subordinate officers in the free and lawful exercise of their legal authority.

MUTUAL FUND popular name for the shares of open-end management **investment companies** or **trusts** that invest, reinvest, hold, and trade **securities** of other issuers, who do not have a fixed capitalization, who sell their own new shares to investors and buy back or redeem their old shares at net asset values, and who are not listed on securities exchanges. Henn & Alexander, Corporations 838-39 (3rd ed. 1983). Compare **closed-end management company.**

MUTUAL FUND SHARE a security reflecting an undivided ownership in a **mutual fund** company which is not traded by the shareholders but is redeemable upon its request, 286 F. Supp. 914, 917.

MUTUALITY OF ESTOPPEL see **estoppel** [MUTUALITY OF ESTOPPEL].

MUTUALITY OF OBLIGATION the requirement that each party to a **bilateral contract** be bound to perform in some way, otherwise the agreement will lack **consideration** and not be a valid contract. "[A] promise whose performance depends upon the mere will of the promisor imposes no obligation upon him and is insufficient consideration to support the promise of the other party to the supposed contract." 159 F. 2d 642, 643. See **illusory promise.** Compare **mutuality of remedy.**

MUTUALITY OF REMEDY the availability of both parties to a transaction of a remedy available to either. The term is used with reference to the requirement that the remedy of **specific performance** be granted in favor of one party only when it could have been available to the other party. In certain instances, mutuality of remedy will not apply for specific performance. For example, although a buyer could sue a seller for sale of a par-

ticular condominium pursuant to a contract (if the condominium has been built), a seller may not be able to force the buyer to purchase that condominium, especially if the seller can be adequately compensated by money damages. 320 A. 2d 194. The doctrine of mutuality of remedy is founded on the idea that one party should not obtain from **equity** that which the other party could not obtain. 8 P. 2d 930. Accordingly, whenever a contract is incapable of being specifically enforced against one party because of the personal nature of the contract, that party cannot specifically enforce it against the other. 476 S.W. 2d 724. However, the general requirement of mutuality does not compel each party to have precisely the same remedies available against each other, since the means of enforcement may differ without necessarily affecting their reciprocal obligation. 139 So. 2d 166. See **mutuality of obligation.**

MUTUAL MISTAKE see **mistake.**

NAKED POWER see **power of appointment** [NAKED POWER].

NAMED INSURED the party who contracts for insurance and who is named in the policy. 401 N.Y.S. 2d 374, 377. It sometimes happens that one who is a named insured has a claim in tort against another who is an additional insured under the policy. For example, the owner of an insured automobile may lend it to another whose operation of the vehicle injures the owner (the named insured). 197 N.E. 516.

NARCOTICS see **controlled substances** [NARCOTICS].

N.A.S.D see **National Association of Securities Dealers** [N.A.S.D.].

NASDAQ the national automated quotation service for **over-the-counter securities.** Operation is supervised by the **National Association of Securities Dealers [N.A.S.D.]** and input is provided by hundreds of **over-the-counter market** makers. NASDAQ is an acronym for National Association of Securities Dealers Automated Quotations.

NATIONAL ASSOCIATION OF SECURITIES DEALERS [N.A.S.D.] a body empowered by the **Securities and Exchange Commission** to regulate **over-the-counter market** brokers and dealers. It is charged to adopt, administer and enforce rules of fair practice and rules to prevent fraudulent and manipulative acts and practices, and in general to promote just and equitable principles of trade for the protection of investors. It publishes quotations for national and regional over-the-counter transactions and supervises operation of NASDAQ, the national automated quotation service for over-the-counter stocks.

NATIONAL LABOR RELATIONS ACT comprehensive federal law that regulates the relations of employees and employers and establishes the **National Labor Relations Board.** 29 U.S.C. §§151 et seq. See **labor organization [union].**

NATIONAL LABOR RELATIONS BOARD [N.L.R.B.] an independent agency created by Congress that oversees relationships between unions and employees. 29 U.S.C. §153. The Board has the power to adjudicate claims before it and to enforce its judgments in the federal courts. See **labor organization [union].**

NATIONAL LAWYERS GUILD an association of lawyers, law students, legal workers, and **jailhouse lawyers** dedicated to the need for basic change in the political and economic system of the country. It actively seeks to eliminate racism and to maintain and protect civil rights and civil liberties. It was founded in 1937 as a progressive alternative to the **American Bar Association.**

NATURALIZED CITIZEN one who, having been born in another country or otherwise reared as a foreigner, has been granted U.S. citizenship and the rights and privileges of that status. The process by which such a person attains citizenship is called NATURALIZATION. 8 U.S.C. §§1421 et seq. The person seeking naturalization must satisfy the burden of establishing good moral character and must be a resident of the United States for five years. 8 U.S.C. §1427.

NATURAL LAW law "which so necessarily agrees with the nature and state of man, that without observing its maxims, the peace and happiness of society can never be preserved . . . [K]nowledge of [natural laws] may be attained merely by the light of reason, from the facts of their essential agreeableness with the constitution of human nature." 11 Ark. 519, 527. Natural law exists regardless of whether it is enacted as **positive law,** although there may be instances where natural law cannot be judicially enforced. See also **positivism.**

NATURAL LAW THEORY in jurisprudence, the view that the nature and value of any legal order is best understood by studying how the **positive law** of that legal order agrees or contrasts with **natural law.** See d'Entreves, Natural Law (1951).

NATURAL PERSON a human being, as opposed to artificial or fictitious "persons" such as **corporations.** See 209 F. 749, 754; 104 N.Y.S. 510, 511. The phrase "natural person" does not include corporate entities, but the phrase "person" without qualification may or may not include artificial persons, depending on the context. Thus, the phrase "no person" in the Fourteenth Amendment's **equal protection** clause has been held to include natural and artificial persons, see 118 U.S. 394, 396, but the same phrase "no person" in the Fifth Amendment's "privilege against **self-incrimination**" clause has been held to include only natural persons and not corporations since the privilege is personal and may not be asserted by an artificial person. See 201 U.S. 43. Business premises are protected from unreasonable searches and seizures and corporations do enjoy Fourth Amendment rights. 429 U.S. 338, 353.

NAVIGABLE WATERS within meaning of congressional acts, when waters form (in their ordinary condition by themselves or by uniting with other waters) a continued highway over which commerce is or may be carried on with other states or foreign countries in customary modes in which such commerce is conducted by water. 278 F. Supp. 254, 256. See **admiralty and maritime jurisdiction.**

N.B. nota bene.

NECESSARY AND PROPER CLAUSE constitutional provision, U.S. Constitution, Art. I, Sec. 8, Cl. 18, empowering Congress to make all laws which shall be "necessary and proper" for carrying into execution the enumerated powers of Congress. The phrase is not limited to such measures as are absolutely necessary, but includes all appropriate means that are conducive to the end to be accomplished, and which in the judgment of Congress, will most advantageously effect it. 110 U.S. 421, 440. The clause is not a grant of power but a declaration that Congress possesses all the means necessary to carry out its specifically granted powers. 361 U.S. 234.

NECESSARY IMPLICATION see **implication.**

NECESSARY INFERENCE inference or deduced fact that "is inescapable, or unavoidable from the standpoint of reason; an inference is not inescapable or unavoidable if another and a different inference may be reasonably drawn from the facts as stated." 9 So. 2d 644, 646. Compare **presumption.**

NECESSARY PARTY see **party.**

NECESSITY, DEFENSE OF see **justification.**

NEGATIVE AVERMENT an averment in some of the **pleadings** in which a negative is asserted. 16 F. 2d 816, 819. Generally a party need not prove a negative averment, but the point in issue is to be proved by the party who asserts the affirmative. 68 P. 487.

NEGATIVE EASEMENT see **easement** [NEGATIVE EASEMENT].

NEGATIVE PREGNANT refers to a **denial** which implies an affirmation of a substantial fact and hence is beneficial to opponent. Thus, when only a qualification or modification is denied while the fact itself remains undenied, the denial is "pregnant" with the affirmation. See 115 S.W. 2d 330.

"Negatives pregnant come in two varieties. One is the literal denial. If the complaint alleges that the defendant was driving his car at 75 miles an hour and the defendant denies that he was driving his car at 75 miles an hour, this would be an admission that he may have been driving it at any other speed, i. e., 74 or 76 miles per hour. The other type of negative pregnant is the conjunctive denial. If the complaint alleges that the defendant was careless and negligent and reckless and the defendant denies that he was careless and negligent and reckless this would constitute an admission that he was guilty of any combination less than all three. To avoid this the defendant should have denied the facts in the disjunctive, i.e., denied that he was careless *or* negligent *or* reckless." Green, Basic Civil Procedure 122 (2d ed. 1979).

NEGLECT the omission of proper attention; avoidance or disregard of duty from heedlessness, indifference, or willfulness; failure to do, use, or heed anything; **negligence,** as neglect of business, of health, or of economy. 10 A. 2d 203, 205. See also **excusable neglect.**

NEGLIGENCE failure to exercise that degree of care which a person of ordinary prudence (a **reasonable man [person]**) would exercise under the same circumstances. The term refers to conduct which falls below the standard established by law for the protection of others against unreasonable risk of harm. It does not comprehend conduct recklessly disregardful of the interests of others. Restatement, Second, Torts §282; nor does it include intentional infliction of injury on another. Unless the actor is a child, the standard of conduct to which he must conform to avoid being negligent is that of a reasonable man under like circumstances. See id. §283. Negligent conduct may involve either a) an act that the actor as a reasonable man should recognize as involving an unreasonable risk of causing an invasion of an interest of another, or b) a failure to do an act necessary for the protection or assistance of another and which the actor is under a duty to perform. See id. §284.

In the law of torts, the degrees of negligence, in general, are: SLIGHT NEGLIGENCE, which is failure to use great care; ORDINARY NEGLIGENCE, which is failure to use ordinary care; and GROSS NEGLIGENCE, which is failure to use even slight care. Prosser, Torts §34 (4th ed. 1971).

COMPARATIVE NEGLIGENCE the allocation of responsibility for damages incurred between the **plaintiff** and **defendant,** based on the relative negligence of the two; the reduction of the damages to be recovered by the negligent plaintiff in proportion to his fault. See id. §407.

CONCURRENT NEGLIGENCE the wrongful acts or **omissions** of two or more persons acting independently but causing the same injury. The independent actions do not have to occur at the same time, but must produce the same result. The actors are all responsible for paying the damages, and can usually be sued together in one lawsuit or individually in separate lawsuits.

CONTRIBUTORY NEGLIGENCE conduct on the part of the plaintiff that falls below the standard to which he should conform for his own protection, and which is a legally contributing cause in addition to the negligence of the defendant in bringing about the plaintiff's harm. At common law, any amount of contributory negligence would bar recovery by the plaintiff. Id. §483. As an **affirmative defense,** the defendant has the **burden of proof** on this issue. Most states have overcome the harshness of the contributory negligence rule by adopting a COMPARATIVE NEGLIGENCE (see above) rule. Prosser, Torts 416 (4th ed. 1971). Compare **assumption of risk.**

CRIMINAL [CULPABLE] NEGLIGENCE such negligence as is necessary to incur criminal liability; in most jurisdictions, culpable [criminal] negligence is something more than the slight negligence necessary to support a civil action for damages. 133 N.Y.S. 2d 423, 427. Thus, culpable negligence, "under criminal law, is recklessness or carelessness resulting in injury or death, as imports a thoughtless disregard of consequences or a heedless indifference to the safety and rights of others." 85 S. E. 2d 327, 332; see also Perkins & Boyce,

Criminal Law 841 (3d ed. 1982).

CULPABLE NEGLIGENCE see CRIMI-NAL [CULPABLE] NEGLIGENCE above.

NEGLIGENCE PER SE negligence as a matter of law, 3 Cal. Rptr. 274, 275; an act or omission that is recognized as negligent either because it is contrary to the requirements of the law or because it is so opposed to the dictates of common prudence that one could say without hesitation or doubt that no careful person would have committed the act or omission. See 278 S.W. 2d 466, 470; 31 F. 755, 756. "The distinction between negligence and 'negligence per se' is the means and method of ascertainment. The first must be found by the jury from the facts, the conditions, and circumstances disclosed by the evidence; the latter is a violation of a specific requirement of law or ordinance; the only fact for determination by the jury being the omission or commission of the specific act inhibited or required." 196 N.E. 274, 278.

In a considerable minority of jurisdictions the violation of a statutory duty of care creates only evidence of negligence which the jury may accept or reject. See Prosser, Torts §36 (4th ed. 1971). Even in the majority of jurisdictions the per se negligence doctrine operates only to create a mandatory finding of negligence leaving open as a defense lack of **proximate causation,** contributory negligence, and assumption of risk. See id.

RECKLESS NEGLIGENCE see WAN-TON NEGLIGENCE below.

WANTON NEGLIGENCE an intentional act of an unreasonable character in disregard of a risk known, or so obvious that it must have been known, and so great as to make it highly probable that harm would follow. The act is usually accompanied by a conscious indifference to the consequences amounting almost to willingness that they shall follow. 34 A. 2d 523.

The term "wanton" is used synonymously with WILLFUL and RECKLESS. The result is that wanton, WILLFUL, or RECKLESS conduct tends to take on the aspect of highly unreasonable conduct, or an extreme departure from ordinary care in a situation where a high degree of danger is apparent. Prosser, Torts, 184-186 (4th ed. 1971).

WILLFUL NEGLIGENCE see WAN-TON NEGLIGENCE above.

NEGOTIABLE INSTRUMENT a writing which is signed by the **maker** or **drawer,** contains an unconditional promise or order to pay a sum certain in money, is payable on demand or at a definite time, and is payable to **order** or to **bearer.** A **draft, check, certificate of deposit,** and **note** may or may not be a negotiable instrument depending upon whether the above elements of negotiability are satisfied. See U.C.C. §3-104. A **transferee** of a negotiable instrument may have rights superior to the assignee of other obligations if the transferee qualifies as a **holder in due course.** See also **holder.**

NEGOTIABLE ORDER OF WITH-DRAWAL [N.O.W.] see **bank** [NE-GOTIABLE ORDER OF WITHDRAWAL [N.O.W.]].

NEGOTIATION a method of dispute resolution where either the parties themselves or the representatives of each party attempt to settle conflicts without resort to the courts; an impartial third party is not involved. Compare **arbitration; mediation.**

NEMO EST SUPRA LEGIS (nā'-mō ĕst sū'-prà lāg'-ĭs)—Lat: nobody is above the law.

NET ASSET VALUE an accounting term similar in meaning to **book value** and net worth. The term is most often used in reference to the value of **mutual fund** shares and similar investment companies. Investment companies compute their net asset value at the end of each market day by taking the total market value of securities, cash, etc., owned, less any **liabilities.** See **balance sheet.**

NET ESTATE the portion of an **estate** subject to federal and state estate taxes; the estate remaining after all debts of decedent, funeral and administrative expenses, and/or other deductions prescribed by law, have been deducted from the GROSS ESTATE [total valuation of the estate's assets at decedent's death]. See 136 N.Y.S. 2d 923, 925. The term thus refers generally to that estate left to be distributed after all deductions have been made. See 225 N.Y.S. 190.

NET INCOME the **gross [total] income** less deductions and exemptions allowed by law, 221 S.W. 2d 51; "gross income less the legitimate expenses of realizing same." 240 F. 2d 324.

NET OPERATING LOSS the excess of expenses over income. For tax purposes, a net operating loss is the excess of allowable **deductions** over **gross income** with certain adjustments. A taxpayer is allowed a deduction for the net operating loss in a year in which deductions do not exceed gross income. A taxpayer may carryback the net operating loss to three prior tax years, or carryover the net operating loss to 15 subsequent tax years. For individual taxpayers, the net operating loss is limited to business losses. I.R.C. §172.

NET WORTH the excess of **assets** over **liabilities.** For tax purposes, the net worth method is one of several used by the **Internal Revenue Service** to reconstruct a **taxpayer's** income when it is determined that the taxpayer has either failed to file a **return** or the tax liability shown is not correct. Under this method the taxpayer's net worth for the start of the period and at the end of the period in question is determined, with the difference, less any nontaxable amounts received, deemed to be the taxpayer's income for the period. This approach is often used in cases involving suspected **evasion** by the taxpayer, but it is also used in normal civil or civil fraud contexts.

NEUTRALITY LAWS laws governing a country's abstention from participating in a conflict or aiding a participant of such conflict, and the duty of participants to refrain from violating the territory, seizing the possession, or hampering the peaceful commerce of the neutral countries. 166 U.S. 1. For example, the Neutrality Act of 1939, 22 U.S.C. §§441 et seq., was passed by Congress for the purpose of preserving the neutrality of the United States and averting the risks that brought the United States into World War I. 37 F. Supp. 268. The codified law of traditional neutrality is to be found in The Hague Conventions Nos. V and XIII of 1907.

NEWLY DISCOVERED EVIDENCE evidence in existence at the time of trial of which a party was unaware. 344 So. 2d 160, 163. Newly discovered evidence may be grounds for a new trial, but an aggrieved party is not entitled to similar relief for evidence that has come into existence after the trial is over since such a procedure could result in perpetual trials. Id. Newly discovered evidence which will entitle a party to new trial on such grounds must be material and such as will probably produce a different result on retrial, and it must appear that with reasonable diligence, such evidence could not have been discovered and produced at trial. 315 P. 2d 5, 11. See Fed. R. Crim. Proc. 33; Fed. R. Civ. Proc. 60(b).

NEW MATTER matters raised by defendant that go beyond mere denials of plaintiff's allegations. It involves new issues, with new facts to be proved, and purports to show that the alleged **cause of action** never did exist and that material allegations are not true. See 3 P. 2d 768, 769. More generally, the term refers to any factual matter not previously alleged by a party, which can then be added by an **amended** or **supplemental pleading.**

NEWSPAPERMAN'S PRIVILEGE see **journalist's [newsperson's] privilege.**

NEWSPERSON'S SHIELD see **shield laws.**

NEW YORK CURB EXCHANGE see **American Stock Exchange.**

NEW YORK STOCK EXCHANGE [N.Y.S.E.] the oldest organized stock exchange in the United States, which has been active since its organization in establishing listing requirements for companies whose stocks are traded on the Exchange and in encouraging accurate and timely disclosure of listed company **income statement** and **balance sheet** results. See **American Stock Exchange.**

NEXT FRIEND a person who, although not an appointed **guardian,** acts in the behalf of a party who is unable to look after his or her own interests or manage his or her own lawsuit, 50 A. 644; one who represents an infant or other party, who by reason of some disability, is not **sui juris.** 54 S.E. 870, 871. A next friend is not considered a party to the suit, but is regarded as an agent or officer of the court to protect the rights of the disabled person. 95 A. 790. Any persons, whether related or not, may serve as next friends provided that their interests are not adverse to the disabled person and that they are not themselves incompetent. 79 S.E. 2d 479, 55 So. 418.

NEXT-IN, FIRST-OUT [N.I.F.O.] a method of inventory valuation. See **inventory** [NEXT-IN, FIRST-OUT [N.I.F.O.]].

NEXT OF KIN the term is used generally with two meanings: (1) nearest blood relations according to law of **consanguinity** and (2) those entitled to take under statutory distribution of **intestates' estates.** In the latter case, the term is not necessarily confined to relatives by blood, but may include a relationship existing by reason of marriage, and may well embrace persons, who in the natural sense of the word, bear no relation of kinship at all. 309 P. 2d 1070, 1073.

NIHIL *(ni'-hĭl)*—Lat: nothing, not, not at all, in no respect. NIL is an often-used form to express the noun. Describes a sheriff's **return** after an unsuccessful attempt to **serve** a **summons** or otherwise gain **jurisdiction** over an individual.

NIL see **nihil.**

NINTH AMENDMENT one of the **Bill of Rights** stating that the rights enumerated in the Constitution shall not be construed to deny or disparage other rights retained by the people. These rights are "those so basic and fundamental and so deeply rooted in our society to be truly 'essential rights,' and which nevertheless, cannot find direct support elsewhere in the Constitution." 576 F. 2d 165. The Amendment was included in an abundance of caution and together with the reserved powers amendment **(Tenth Amendment)** was intended to emphasize the limited powers conferred upon the new central government. The Ninth Amendment has been cited by the United States Supreme Court very few times but was relied upon by some members of the Court to identify a right of marital privacy to bar a state from prohibiting the use of contraceptives by married persons. 381 U.S. 479, 486-494; id. at 490 n.6.

NISI (*nē'-sē*)—Lat: unless; "It is used in law after **'decree,' 'order,' 'rule'** to indicate [that the adjudication referred to] shall take permanent effect at a specified time unless cause is shown why it should not or unless it is changed by further proceedings." 215 A. 2d 779, 783. A "DECREE NISI" usually refers to a conditional divorce, becoming absolute upon the expiration of a stipulated period unless cause to the contrary is shown within the time period. 92 A. 791.

NISI PRIUS (*nē'-sē prē'-ŭs*)—Lat: unless the first. In American law, sometimes used to describe any court where a case is first heard by a **judge** and **jury,** distinguishing such courts from the **appellate courts.** Literally translated it means "unless the first," i.e., unless it is the original or first **forum** it is not a "nisi prius" court. See **original jurisdiction.**

N.L.R.A. National Labor Relations Act. 29 U.S.C. §§151 et seq. See **labor organization [union].** See also **National Labor Relations Board.**

N.L.R.B. see **National Labor Relations Board.**

NO FAULT a system of insurance whereby all persons who are injured in an automobile accident may be compensated for any injuries resulting therefrom, without regard to who was at fault. Under traditional insurance principles, the right to be compensated for injuries resulting from an automobile accident was predicated on a clear showing of **negligence** on the part of the actor. This **tort** system has been accused of being slow, expensive, and, most importantly, impractical because of the difficulty in ascertaining who was at fault. See **insurance** [NO FAULT INSURANCE].

NO-FAULT DIVORCE see **divorce** [NO-FAULT DIVORCE].

NOLENS VOLENS (*nō'-lenz vō'-lenz*)—Lat: whether willing or unwilling.

NOLLE PROSEQUI *nōl'-ē prōs'-ē-kwī*)—LAT: unwilling to prosecute, 91 So. 2d 857, 859; the prosecution's abandonment of a charging document, **count,** or part of a count; "a discontinued prosecution by the authorized attorney for the state," 443 A. 2d 86, 89; the formal entry of a declaration that a case will not be further prosecuted, 419 N.E. 2d 47, 51. If applicable **statutes of limitation** have not run, the defendant can be re-indicted and prosecuted again, 418 S.W. 2d 629, 632. A "nolle prosequi" cannot be pleaded as **former jeopardy** or **res judicata,** 213 S.E. 2d 91, 93. Sometimes abbreviated as NOL. PROS. See **dismissal.**

NOLO CONTENDERE (*nō'-lō kôntĕn'-dĕ-rā*)—Lat: I do not wish to contend, fight or maintain (a **defense**); "not strictly a **plea** at all, but a statement that the **defendant** will not contend [a] **charge** made by the government." 119 F. Supp. 288. Like a **demurrer** to an **indictment,** it admits all facts stated in the indictment for the purposes of a particular **case,** but it cannot be used as an **admission** elsewhere, as it is an implied **confession** only of the offense charged. See 139 P. 2d 682. Thus, corporations often plead "nolo contendere" in order to avoid any collateral civil effects from their plea in criminal **antitrust** cases. The plea of nolo contendere is equivalent to a plea of guilt for the purposes of the criminal matter and is accepted only in the discretion of the trial court, which must be satisfied that it is voluntarily and intelligently entered and that there is a factual basis to support it. See, e.g., Fed. R. Crim. Proc. 11(b).

NOL PROS see **nolle prosequi.**

NOMINAL DAMAGES see **damages.**

NOMINAL PARTY see **party.**

NON-ASSESSABLE STOCK stock purchased from the issuer at full par value or more per share. Fully paid stock cannot be assessed to pay debts of the issuer in the event of bankruptcy liquidation and is, therefore, non-assessable. Almost all domestic stock issues are non-assessable and instances of assessments against shareholders are extremely rare. See Henn & Alexander, Corporations 428 (3d ed. 1983).

NON ASSUMPSIT a form of **pleading** in which the **defendant** claims that he did not undertake or promise any obligation in the manner or form set forth in the **plaintiff's complaint**. See **assumpsit**.

NON-COMPETITION CLAUSE see **covenant** [COVENANT NOT TO COMPETE].

NON COMPOS MENTIS *(nŏn kŏm'-pōs mĕn'-tĭs)*—Lat: not having control over the mind or intellect. Not of sound mind; insane. See 108 A. 2d 820, 822. In certain circumstances its effect is lessened to mean only "not legally **competent**." See 1 S.E. 2d 768, 770. Compare **incompetent; non sui juris.**

NONCONFORMING USE a **use** of land "which lawfully existed prior to the enactment of a **zoning** ordinance and which may be maintained after the effective date of the ordinance" although it no longer complies with the use restrictions applicable to the area. 508 P. 2d 190, 192. Continuation of the existing use comprehends preservation of both the functional use of the land and the physical structures thereon, and neither of these aspects of "use" may be extended or enlarged once the zoning restriction has taken effect. 102 A. 2d 84. Only actual uses are protected by this doctrine, and not merely uses for which the land might be suitable. 86 A. 2d 74. The protection may extend to a use not yet in existence, but whose development has reached a certain stage. 508 P. 2d 190. Compare **variance**. See **grandfather clause.**

NON-CONTESTABILITY [IN-CONTESTABILITY] CLAUSE a provision in an insurance policy that precludes the insurer from disputing the validity of the policy on the basis of **fraud** or **mistake** after a specified period. If the insurer wishes to contest the policy on any grounds that would justify **rescission** of it, it must do so within the prescribed period, either by suing to cancel the policy or by asserting fraud or misrepresentation as a defense in an action instituted by the policyholder or beneficiary. 237 P. 2d 510, 512. The purpose of the clause is to require the insurer to investigate the accuracy of the information provided by the policyholder with reasonable promptness. It prevents the insurer from lulling the policyholder into a sense of security during the time when facts could best be ascertained, only to litigate them belatedly. Couch on Insurance 2d §72.1 (1968).

NON-CUSTODIAL SENTENCE see **sentence.**

NONDISCRETIONARY TRUST [FIXED INVESTMENT TRUST] an **investment trust** that may buy only those **securities** on a list set forth when the trust is organized. The percentage of total assets that may be invested in a specific security or type of securities is usually predetermined. See **unit investment trust.**

NONFEASANCE in the law of agency, "the total omission or failure of an **agent** to enter upon the performance of some distinct duty or undertaking which he has agreed with his **principal** to do." 191 N.E. 2d 588, 591. Also, it is the "substantial failure [of an officer] to perform a duty, or, in other words, the neglect or refusal, without sufficient excuse, to do that which it [is an] officer's legal duty to do." 115 N.W. 2d 411, 413. It differs from **misfeasance,** which is the improper doing of an act that one might lawfully do, and from **malfeasance,** which is the doing of an act that is wholly wrongful and unlawful. See 323 P. 2d 301, 309. See **misconduct.**

NONMEMBER BANK a bank that is not a member of the **Federal Reserve System** and is regulated only by the banking laws in the state in which it is chartered. The main advantages of being a nonmember bank are the right to keep required reserves in interest-bearing **securities** and the generally less stringent regulations of most states.

NON-NEGOTIABLE INSTRUMENTS see **negotiable instruments.**

NON OBSTANTE VEREDICTO *(non ob-stan'-te ve-re-dik'tō)*— Lat: notwithstanding the verdict. See **N.O.V.** [NON OBSTANTE VEREDICTO].

NON-PERFORMANCE the failure to fulfill an obligation. The non-performance must be material and substantial to justify suspension of another's return performance. See **performance.** See also **consideration** [FAILURE OF CONSIDERATION].

NON-PROFIT [NOT-FOR-PROFIT] CORPORATION an incorporated organization chartered for other than profit-making activities. Most such organizations are engaged in charitable, educational, or other civic or humanitarian activities although they are not restricted to such activities. See **charity.**

NON PROSEQUITUR *(non prō-sek'-wi-tèr)*—Lat: he has not proceeded. An entry by the defendant that the plaintiff has not continued his action. Under modern rules, such failure on the part of the plaintiff would result in either a **dismissal** of the action or in a **default judgment** for the defendant. Fed. R. Civ. Proc. 41, 55. Abbreviated ''NON PROS.''

NONQUALIFIED PENSION OR PROFIT SHARING PLAN See **retirement plans** [NONQUALIFIED PENSION OR PROFIT SHARING PLAN].

NON-REBUTTABLE PRESUMPTION see **presumption.** [NON-REBUTTABLE PRESUMPTION].

NONRECOGNITION OF GAIN see **recognition** [NONRECOGNITION OF GAIN].

NONRECOURSE without personal liability. An obligation that is nonrecourse does not provide a **basis** for federal taxation purposes for individuals or partnerships except in certain limited cases such as when real estate is involved. If a promisor has limited his exposure in the event of a **default** to a particular pledged asset such as his equity in a building or entity, his obligation will be regarded as nonrecourse. Individuals often structure transactions in corporate form to achieve similar limited personal liability.

NON SEQUITUR *(nŏn sĕ'-kwĭ-tûr)*—Lat: it does not follow; it does not come after (in time). ''Non seq.'' is an often-used abbreviated form. When an action or decree is non sequitur it is unrelated to the preceding events. A non sequitur is something that has no logical or temporal purpose for its place in the progression of events; it is logically, temporally and spatially incoherent.

NONSTOCK CORPORATION a **corporation,** owned by its members under the membership charter or agreement, which confers all rights and liabilities, rather than through the issue of **shares.** Examples include mutual companies such as mutual savings banks and mutual insurance companies, fraternal lodges, private clubs.

NON-SUFFICIENT FUNDS CHECK see **nsf [non-sufficient funds] check.**

NON SUI JURIS (*nŏn sū'-ē jû'-rĭs*)—Lat: not by his own authority or legal right. This maxim refers to those who are not legally **competent** to manage their own affairs as regards **contracts** and other causes; this **incompetency** restricts their granting **power of attorney** or otherwise exercising self-judgment. Compare **non compos mentis.**

NONSUIT a **judgment** rendered against a **plaintiff** who "fails to proceed to trial [known as a VOLUNTARY NONSUIT] or is unable to prove his case [known as an INVOLUNTARY NONSUIT]." 12 S.E. 2d 553, 554. See Fed. R. Civ. Proc 41(a) and (b). Since the adjudication is made when the **complainant** has simply failed to provide evidence sufficient to make out a case, it does not decide the **merits** of his **cause of action,** 78 P. 2d 1010, and thus does not preclude his bringing it again. 42 S.E. 2d 648. The term is sometimes broadly applied to various terminations of an action which do not amount to a **judgment on the merits.** 78 P. 2d 1010. Compare **acquit;** see **dismissal.**

NON-SUPPORT the failure to provide **support** that one can provide and that one is legally obliged to provide to a spouse, child, or other dependent. Although non-support of wife and child were apparently not crimes at common law, statutes in all states contain provisions making such acts crimes with respect to children and in nearly all states with respect to spouses. See Model Penal Code §230.5. Most jurisdictions treat the offense as a **misdemeanor.** See **desertion; support.**

NON VULT (*nŏn vŭlt*)—Lat: abbreviation of non vult contendere ("He will not contest"). Refers to a plea by one charged with a crime that does not expressly admit guilt, but acknowledges that the defendant will not contest the charge and therefore agrees to be treated as though he had been found guilty. See also **nolo contendere.**

NO-PAR [NONPAR] STOCK stock issued with no stated value on the stock certificate. At one time new issues of stock were made as par value, but this practice was abandoned when states began to tax corporations based on par values. At present, par value is arbitrarily set as a low value with no-par stock preferred when allowed by state law. In accounting for stock issues, the par value is carried as a separate item with the balance of stock issue proceeds carried as capital surplus.

NORMAL COURSE OF BUSINESS see **ordinary course of business.**

NOSCITUR A SOCIIS (*nō'-si-ter ā sō'-she-is*)—Lat: it is known by its associates. Under this rule of statutory construction, the meaning of a word in a statute is ascertained in light of the meaning of the words with which it is associated. 250 N.W. 2d 412, 413. When two or more words in a statute are grouped together, and ordinarily have a similar meaning but are not equally comprehensive, the general word will be limited and qualified by the specific word. 218 S.E. 2d 735, 740. Compare **ejusdem generis.**

NO STRIKE CLAUSE a clause in a labor agreement that prohibits employees from striking for any reason during the life of the contract. Such a clause regulates relations between the employer and the employees. 356 U.S. 342, 350. It is not an "unfair labor practice" under the **National Labor Relations Act** for an employer to bargain in good faith for such a clause.

NOTA BENE (*nō'-tà bā'-nā*)—Lat: note well; written as the original note N.B. to indicate an important portion of the text to be studied.

NOTARY PUBLIC a public officer under civil and commercial law, authorized to administer oaths, to attest to and certify certain types of documents, to take **depositions,** and to perform certain acts in commercial matters, such as **protesting commercial paper.** See 164 A. 253, 254. The seal of a "notary public" authenticates a document. Id. Documents so certified are valid as such in other jurisdictions. In some jurisdictions an attorney admitted to practice within the jurisdiction can act as a notary public. In many jurisdictions private persons can apply for and receive authority to act as notaries to witness documents. Thus, secretaries in law offices, bank officers, insurance and real estate agents, small town grocery clerks, drug store clerks, etc. are often licensed notaries. See **rogatory letters.**

NOTE a writing acknowledging a **debt** and promising payment. 155 S.E. 2d 701, 703. For the **instrument** to be **negotiable** it must be signed by the **maker** and contain an unconditional promise to pay a **sum certain** in money on **demand** or at a definite time to **order** or to **bearer.** U.C.C. §3-104(1). A note is not payment but only a promise to pay. 131 P. 2d 894, 896. The term note is synonomous with the term PROMISSORY NOTE. The term may be qualified by its unique characteristics. For example, a note that is backed by a pledge of **collateral** such as real or personal property is called a SECURED NOTE; when no such collateral is behind the promise it is called an UNSECURED NOTE. If the note is payable at any time it is called a DEMAND NOTE. If the note is payable over a specified period of time in more than one payment, it is called an INSTALLMENT NOTE. If the note evidences a loan for which real estate has been encumbered it is called a MORTGAGE NOTE. If the note is negotiable it is called a NEGOTIABLE NOTE. These various terms can also be combined so that a note that is payable at any time, secured by collateral may be called a "negotiable secured promissory demand note," and so forth. See also **treasury note.**

NOT-FOR-PROFIT CORPORATION see **corporation** [NOT-FOR-PROFIT CORPORATION]; **non-profit [not-for-profit] corporation.**

NOT GUILTY a **plea** by the **accused** in a **criminal** action that denies every essential **element** of the offense charged. 287 F. 2d 435, 440-441. A **plea** of not guilty on **arraignment** obliges the government to prove the defendant's guilt beyond a reasonable doubt and preserves the right to defend. 128 F. 2d 265, 273. A jury **verdict** of not guilty does not mean the **jury** found the accused innocent, but simply that the state failed to prove its case beyond a reasonable doubt. 87 P. 2d 251, 256.

NOT GUILTY BY REASON OF INSANITY a special form of verdict or finding usually followed by **commitment** of the defendant to a mental institution. The **insanity defense** differs from other defenses in that if successful, it is not an **acquittal** and does not result in the outright release of the accused unless the defense is temporary insanity and the court finds that the defendant poses no present danger to himself or to others. LaFave & Scott, Criminal Law 268 (1972).

NOTICE "information concerning a fact, actually communicated to a person by an authorized person, or actually derived by him from a proper source." 215 F. 2d 415, 417. Notice to a **defendant** of a **lawsuit** which has been instituted against him or of an **action** in which he may have an interest to defend is accomplished by **service of process** on him. See also **recording acts** [NOTICE].

ACTUAL NOTICE direct positive knowledge of fact in question or information sufficient to put a prudent person on inquiry as to such fact. 122 P. 2d 140, 142. "Actual notice" embraces those things of which one has express information and which reasonably diligent inquiry would have disclosed. 237 S.W. 2d 286.

AVERMENT OF NOTICE a statement included in the **pleadings** that a **party** to an action has received proper notice thereof.

CONSTRUCTIVE NOTICE that notice which is presumed by law to have been acquired. 226 P. 697. It is often accomplished by the posting of notices or by the mailing of notification to the defendant if he cannot be personally **served** with **process**. Green, Basic Civil Procedure 44 (1972).

IMPLIED NOTICE notice that may be inferred from facts that a person had means of knowing, which was his duty to use and which he did not use. Persons have no right to avoid information and then say that they had no notice. 402 So. 2d. 1197, 1200. "Implied notice" is distinguished from CONSTRUCTIVE NOTICE, above, in that the latter rests upon strictly legal presumptions whereas the former is a form of ACTUAL NOTICE, above, arising from inferences of fact. 334 A. 2d. 542, 544.

INQUIRY NOTICE with respect to one who claims to have been a **bona fide purchaser** without notice, "information from whatever source derived, which would excite apprehension in an ordinary mind and prompt a person of average prudence to make inquiry." 311 P. 2d 676, 678.

JUDICIAL NOTICE see **judicial notice.**

NOTICE BY PUBLICATION method of bringing a lawsuit to the attention of parties which may have an interest therein by publishing notification of it in a newspaper of general circulation. This type of notice is permissible only where specifically allowed by statute, and is generally limited to actions involving land, estates, or status.

Green, Civil Procedure 55 (1979).

PERSONAL NOTICE communication of notice orally or in writing, according to the circumstances, directly to the person affected or to be charged. 215 F. 2d 415, 418.

NOTICE OF DISHONOR notice, given in any reasonable manner, that an **instrument** has been dishonored. Notice of dishonor may be given to any person who may be liable on the instrument by or on behalf of the holder or any party who has himself received notice, or any other party who can be compelled to pay the instrument. In addition an agent or bank in whose hands the instrument is dishonored may give notice to a principal or customer or to another agent or bank from which the instrument was received. U.C.C. §3-508(1). Delay in giving notice of dishonor completely discharges an **indorser.** U.C.C. §3-502(2).

NOTICE OF LIS PENDENS see **lis pendens.**

NOTICE OF MOTION see **motion.**

NOTORIOUS POSSESSION possession of **real property** that is open, undisguised, and conspicuous to the point where such possession is generally known or recognized. See 108 S.W. 2d 489, 493. The term is used as one of the elements in defining and/or determining the existence of **adverse possession,** which involves a claim of right to property not by **title** but by possession for a statutory period of time; such possession is required to be "actual," "continuous," "notorious," and "hostile," in order that the title owner without actual **notice** of such possession may be legally presumed to have notice. 14 So. 805, 806. See also **hostile possession.**

N.O.V. [NON OBSTANTE VERDICTO] —Lat: nonwithstanding

the verdict. A JUDGMENT N.O.V. is one that reverses the determination of the jury, and is granted when a judge determines that the jury **verdict** had no reasonable support in fact or was contrary to law. See 170 S.W. 2d 303, 306. The motion for a judgment n.o.v. provides a second chance for the trial court to render what is, in effect, a **directed verdict** for the moving party. See, e.g., Fed. R. Civ. Proc. 50(b).

NOVATION the substitution of a **party** for one of the original parties to a contract with the consent of the remaining party. The result is that the old contract is extinguished, and a new contract, with the same content but with at least one different party, is created. See 248 N.Y.S. 89. It often involves a transaction whereby the original debtor is discharged from liability to his creditor by the substitution of a second debtor. If an **assignment** or a **lease** is consented to by the **landlord**, it will amount to a novation and the original lessee will be discharged from further liability under the lease agreement.

NOW ACCOUNT [NEGOTIABLE ORDER OF WITHDRAWAL ACCOUNT] an interest-bearing savings account against which depositors are permitted to write checks. See **bank** [NEGOTIABLE ORDER OF WITHDRAWAL [N.O.W.]].

NSF [NON-SUFFICIENT FUNDS] CHECK a check that the **drawer** does not have sufficient funds to cover when it is presented for payment, and which for that reason is dishonored by the **drawee.** In such a case, the presenter will have no power to make the drawee pay the check. White & Summers, Uniform Commercial Code §16-4 (1980). If, however, the drawee does honor the check, it is possible that he may bear the risk of loss in the event funds to cover it are never secured from the drawer. Id. See **bad check.**

NUDUM PACTUM *(nū'-dŭm päk'-tŭm)*—Lat: a bare **contract** or agreement that amounts to merely a naked **promise.** See 22 S.E. 2d 186. "A contract, naked of any obligation or duty on one side, a 'nudum pactum' is not enforceable." 151 P. 270. Contracts must generally be supported by a **consideration** on each side. A naked contract is one that is bare of a valid consideration on one side and hence unenforceable. See **mutuality of obligation.**

NUGATORY void; of no effect; invalid. For example, **judicial proceedings** in a court that lacks **jurisdiction** are sometimes considered "nugatory." See 121 S.E. 828, 829. Compare **voidable.**

NUISANCE in tort law, it is a broad concept characterizing "the defendant's interference with the plaintiff's interests." Prosser, Law of Torts 571 (4th ed. 1971); "anything which annoys or disturbs the free use of one's property, or which renders its ordinary use or physical occupation uncomfortable. . . . [I]t extends to everything that endangers life or health, gives offense to the senses, violates the laws of decency, or obstructs the reasonable and comfortable use of property." 391 S.W. 2d 5, 9. It thus refers to "a wrong arising from an unreasonable or unlawful use of property to the discomfort, annoyance, inconvenience or damage of another, and usually comprehends continuous or recurrent acts." 483 S.W. 2d 633, 637.

ABATABLE NUISANCE a nuisance that can be suppressed, or extinguished, or rendered harmless, and whose continued existence is not authorized under the law. 113 S.W. 996, 1000.

ABATEMENT OF A NUISANCE the removal, termination or destruction of a nuisance.

ATTRACTIVE NUISANCE see **attractive nuisance.**

COMMON NUISANCE see PUBLIC [COMMON] NUISANCE below.

MIXED NUISANCE a nuisance which is both a public nuisance [see below] and a private nuisance [see below] at the same time; it interferes with a right of the general public and also interferes with a particular person's use and enjoyment of his land. See 132 A. 2d 445, 448.

PRIVATE NUISANCE "an actionable interference with a person's interest in the private use and enjoyment of his land." 212 N.W. 2d 505, 508.

PUBLIC [COMMON] NUISANCE "an unreasonable interference with a right common to the general public. . . . It is behavior which unreasonably interferes with the health, safety, peace, comfort or convenience of the general community." 299 A. 2d 155, 158. A public nuisance offends the public at large or a segment of the public, a private nuisance offends only a particular person or persons. See 303 A. 2d 544, 567.

NUISANCE PER SE an act, occupation, or structure that is a nuisance at all times and under any circumstances, regardless of its location or surroundings; acts that are denounced as illegal by law, when perpetration of them invades rights of others. 281 S.W. 2d 721, 723. From an evidentiary point of view once a nuisance per se is established by proof, it becomes a nuisance as a **matter of law.** 268 N.W. 2d 525, 528.

NULL AND VOID see **nullity.**

NULLITY "in law, a void act or an act having no legal force or validity—invalid—null." 64 F. Supp. 865, 870. It is "the highest degree of an irregularity, . . . and is such a defect as renders the proceeding in which it occurs totally null and void, of no avail or effect whatever

and incapable of being made so; . . . a proceeding that is essentially defective, or that is expressly declared to be a nullity by statute." 4 N.W. 220, 222.

NUL TIEL RECORD see trial [TRIAL BY THE RECORD].

NUNC PRO TUNC (nŭnk prō tŭnk)—Lat: now for then; permits action to be taken after the point when it should have been performed, giving the action retroactive effect.

NUNC PRO TUNC ORDER an **order** used by the courts to correct the **record.** It supplements a prior **judgment** or order in any matter over which the court originally had **jurisdiction.** If the time for taking an appeal has expired, the party may seek leave to file a notice of appeal "out-of-time." If it is permitted, the notice would be filed nunc pro tunc and thus render the appeal timely.

NUNCUPATIVE WILL oral declarations of a person made with dispositive intent during a last illness, where a written **will** would not be possible. Such oral wills are rarely upheld because of the opportunity for fraud and because of the detailed requirements for their validity. Such requirements are that the testator, during sickness, indicate that the disposition is to be a will; that it be reduced to writing by a witness within a short time; that more than one witness prove the will, and that the witnesses are disinterested and competent. See 189 A. 315. The requirements are strictly adhered to, except for persons in actual military service. Nuncupative wills are generally restricted to **personalty** under the **statute of frauds** and thus cannot operate to transfer **real property.** See 46 Va. L. Rev. 613 (1960); Atkinson on Wills 368 (1953).

N.Y.S.E. see **New York Stock Exchange [N.Y.S.E.].**

O

OATH swearing to the truth of a statement; if one makes a statement under oath and knows it to be false, one may be subjected to a prosecution for perjury or other legal proceedings. Writings, (e.g., **affidavits**) as well as oral testimony may be made "under oath." Compare **affirmation.**

OATH EX OFFICIO at **common law,** an oath administered by an **ecclesiastical court** whereby a clergyman accused of a crime would have to swear to his innocence. [An accused was also obliged to put forward proof of his innocence, after which the ecclesiastical judge, not a jury, decided innocence or guilt.] 3 Bl. Comm. *101.

The phrase has also referred to a process whereby the court, upon an accusation, could order the accused into court to swear an oath. 3 Bl. Comm. *447. After the courts abused their right by turning their proceedings into inquisitions, the English Parliament abolished the oath.

OBITER DICTA *(ō'-bĭ-tèr dĭk'-tà)*—Lat: passing or incidental statements; statements made or decisions reached in a court opinion which were not necessary to the disposition of the case. It is the plural of "obiter dictum." See **dictum.**

OBJECTION a procedure whereby a party asserts that a particular witness, line of questioning, piece of **evidence** or other matter is improper and should not be continued, and asks the court to rule on its impropriety or illegality. A timely objection on the record, stating the grounds thereof, must be made to evidence rulings admitting or excluding evidence if the ruling is to be challenged later on appeal.

This is necessary to preserve the point on appeal. See Fed. R. Evid. 103 (a)(1). As to other rulings or orders entered by a trial court, the failure to object will not prejudice a party's right to challenge on appeal the action taken if he had no opportunity to object. Fed R. Civ. Proc. 46, Fed R. Crim. Proc. 51. See also **challenge; motion** [MOTION IN LIMINE].

OBLIGATION, MUTUALITY OF see **mutuality of obligation.**

OBLIGATION OF A CONTRACT "the civil obligation, the binding efficacy, the coercive power, the legal duty of performing the contract." 25 U.S. 212. Refers to the legal requirement binding the contracting parties to the performance of their undertaking and not the duties arising out of the contract itself. 71 P. 301. Except where **specific performance** is available as a remedy, one cannot be compelled to actually perform a contract obligation; rather, he merely subjects himself to liability in **damages** if he fails to honor the obligation of a contract.

IMPAIR THE OBLIGATION OF A CONTRACT "to weaken [the contract], or lessen its value, or make it worse in any respect or in any degree. . . . Any law which changes the intention and legal effect of the original parties, giving to one a greater and to the other a less interest or benefit in the contract, impairs its obligation." 115 A. 484, 486. "The extent of the change is immaterial. Any deviation from its terms by hastening or postponing the time of performance which it prescribes, or imposing conditions not included in the contract, or dispensing with the performance of those that are included . . . impairs the obligation of a contract." Id. Impairment is also said to exist where the right to enforce a contract is eliminated or substantially lessened. See 185

A. 401. State statutes which do so are prohibited by Art. I, Section 10 of the United States Constitution.

OBLIGEE one who is entitled to receive a sum of money or to have an act or deed performed as promised or agreed to by the **obligor.**

OBLIGOR one who has promised or is otherwise obligated to perform an act or deed, such as the payment of a sum of money under a promissory **note** or other **contract.** Compare **obligee.**

OBLOQUY blame, censure, reproach, 11 P. 713; to expose one to obloquy is to subject one to blame or disgrace and may constitute **defamation.** 258 P. 242.

OBSCENE MATERIAL material which, taken as a whole, appeals to the **prurient** interest and lacks serious literary, artistic, political or scientific value. Matter so classified is not protected by the "free speech" guarantee of the First Amendment. 354 U.S. 476. Guidelines for determining obscenity have changed through the years, but as of 1974, material is "obscene" when a) the subject as a whole appeals to the prurient interest of the average person, using contemporary community standards, b) the work depicts or describes in a patently offensive way sexual conduct proscribed by state statute, and c) the work as a whole lacks serious literary, artistic, political or scientific value; note that the former test of "utterly without redeeming social value" is rejected. See 413 U.S. 15. Evidence of **pandering** may be used to establish obscenity. 383 U.S. 463, 474.

The issue of how "local" the community must be by whose standards obscenity is to be determined is largely a statutory matter. It has been held that "contemporary community standards" is a sufficient jury instruction without specifying the geographical extent of the

community. 418 U.S. 153. See **pornography.**

OBSCENITY see **obscene material.**

OBSOLESCENCE the process by which property becomes useless, not because of physical deterioration but because of scientific or technological advances. In determining **useful life** for purposes of calculating **depreciation,** obsolescence is taken into account. Treas. Reg. §1-167(a)-9.

OBSTRUCTION OF JUSTICE the "impeding or obstructing [of] those who seek justice in a court, or those who have duties or powers of administering justice therein." 214 S.W. 788. It was an offense at common law. Id. at 789. It includes acts such as attempting to influence, intimidate or impede any **juror, witness** or officer in any court regarding the discharge of his duty, as well as the actual impeding or obstructing of the due administration of justice. See 16 A. 2d 642, 644. When the statue addressing this subject reaches beyond interference with the judicial process and proscribes as well interference with police officers and other such administrative officials, it is sometimes called "obstruction of governmental administration." See generally Model Penal Code §242. See **embracery; misprision of felony.**

OBVIOUS RISK a risk that is readily apparent, 45 S.E. 706. At common law, a master was not liable to servants for any obvious risks of the employment, 63 P. 645, rather, the servant was held to have assumed the risk of the employment. Prosser, Torts §80 (4th ed. 1971).

OCCUPANCY the act of occupying or taking possession, 153 P. 2d 420, 422; to hold or use, 203 P. 2d 540. See **certificate of occupancy.**

OCCUPANT one who "takes possession; one who has the actual use or possession, or is in possession of, a thing. One who holds possession and exercises dominion (or control) over it," 77 N.Y.S. 2d 732, 734; one who has actual possession, such as a tenant, in contrast to a landlord, who retains legal **ownership**. See 67 N.W. 2d 481, 487.

OCCUPATIONAL DISEASE [INJURY] "a disease which is the natural incident or result of a particular employment, usually developing gradually from the effects of long-continued work at the employment." 176 S.W. 2d 471, 476. It results from the conditions of a particular employment that involve a risk of contracting the disease greater than the risk that exists in employment and living conditions in general. See 418 P. 2d 769, 777. See also **employers' liability acts; worker's compensation.**

OCCUPATIONAL HAZARD a risk that is peculiar to a particular type of employment or workplace, and which arises as a natural incident of such employment or of employment in such a place.

OCCUPATIONAL SAFETY AND HEALTH ACT [OSHA] a law passed by Congress in 1970 for the purpose of preventing employees from being injured or contracting illnesses in the course of their employment. 29 U.S.C. §651. Under OSHA, the Secretary of Labor is empowered to promulgate national safety and health standards, 29 U.S.C. §655, and to enforce such standards by seeking the imposition of civil and criminal injunctions and penalties. 29 U.S.C. §§659, 662, and 666. Broad congressional authority granted to OSHA to make warrantless inspections of business premises has been held to be unconstitutional. 436 U.S. 307. Thus, an OSHA inspection may be made only in accordance with the administrative inspections permitted in other con-

texts. Id. at 320-321; 387 U.S. 523, 538. See **search and seizure**.

OCCUPYING THE FIELD see **pre-emption**.

OCCURRENCE TEST see **transaction or occurrence test.**

ODD LOT in the securities trade, a quantity of **stock** that is less than 100 shares or a number of **bonds** less than 100 bonds. In buying or selling an odd lot, a premium or discount to the round lot price is charged; this charge is referred to as the ODD LOT DIFFERENTIAL.

ODIOUS base, vile, scandalous, detestable, disgraceful. 39 N.E. 498, 499.

ODIUM hatred, dislike. 29 N.E. 417.

OF COUNSEL refers to an attorney who aids in the preparation of a case, but who is not the principal attorney of record for the case. He or she usually assists the attorney who has been hired for the case. See also **on the brief**.

OFFENSE any violation of law for which a penalty is prescribed, including both **felonies** and **misdemeanors**. See **degree of crime**.

OFFER a "manifestation of willingness to enter into a bargain, so made as to justify another person in understanding that his assent to that bargain is invited and will conclude it," Restatement, Contracts (2d) §24; "a promise, a commitment to do or refrain from doing some specified thing in the future. The offer creates a power of **acceptance** permitting the offeree by accepting the offer to transform the offeror's promise into a contractual obligation." Calamari & Perillo, Contracts 28 (2d ed. 1977).

A communication addressed to numerous persons will not generally be an offer but will rather be considered an invitation for offers (which may then become **contracts** through acceptance). This is the case in most mail-order settings and in newspaper advertisements. If, however, there is a "principle of selection" among the offerees (such as "first-come, first-served," "first ten persons," etc.) then the "ad" may amount to an offer that generates a power of acceptance and which by acceptance may lead to a contract. See, e.g., 86 N.W. 2d 689.

To constitute an offer there must be "language of promise" (i.e., "I may" or "I want" is not as likely to be construed as an offer as a communication using the language "I will . . .") and a sufficiently definite statement of terms so that an acceptance may be made without suggesting new terms. The Uniform Commercial Code permits an offer, if intended to operate as such, to be missing many terms (such as price, time of delivery) provided that there is a reasonable basis for framing a remedy in the event of a **breach** of contract. See U.C.C. §§2-305, 2-308, 2-309, and 2-204.

In the **securities** trade, the term is used to indicate the price and volume available from open market sellers of **stocks** and **bonds.** The term is also used to refer to an **underwriting** in which a **broker** offers a large quantity of a specific **issue** at a fixed price called an OFFERING. See also **private offering [placement]; tender offer.**

OFFER OF PROOF to offer **evidence** for acceptance at **trial.** Such an offer of evidence is governed by the appropriate **jurisdiction's** rules of evidence. For example, if a **party** offers evidence through the **testimony** of a **witness,** certain of the questions asked by counsel may be objected to. Should the court inquire as to the propriety of the questioning, counsel would then ordinarily offer to the court, or "proffer," the relevance of the question. In such an instance the offer of proof would not ordinarily be made within the hearing of the **jury** if one is present. If the court

sustains the objection, the **appellate court** will assume that the proffer could have been established for the purposes of reviewing the trial court's ruling. McCormick, Evidence §51 (2d ed. 1972).

OFFICER a person invested with the authority of a particular position or office. An officer may be either public or private in that the office he occupies may or may not be invested with a public trust. The term is often used to designate corporate personnel who are appointed by the directors and are charged with the duty of managing the day-to-day affairs of the **corporation.** The term embraces the idea of **tenure,** duration, **emoluments** and duties, the latter being continuing and permanent and not occasional or temporary, 99 U.S. 508; and, in light of those characteristics, it is distinguished from "employee."

OFFICIAL IMMUNITY see **immunity.**

OFFICIOUS   INTERMEDDLER one who performs an act that confers a benefit upon another, although he had neither a contractual duty to do the act nor a legally recognized interest in seeing to it that the act was done, and who nevertheless seeks payment or **restitution** for the benefit conferred. See 153 F. 2d 798, 799.

OFFSET see **set-off.**

OF THE ESSENCE see **time of the essence.** Compare **on or about.**

OLIGOPOLY an industry in which a few large sellers of substantially identical products dominate the market, see 118 F. Supp. 41, 47; e.g., the automobile industry is an oligopoly. An oligopolistic industry is more concentrated than a competitive one but is less concentrated than a **monopoly.**

OLOGRAPHIC see **holographic will.**

OMISSION a "neglect or failure to

do something; that which . . . is left undone,'' 175 So. 358, 364; the ''neglect to perform what the law requires,'' 109 N.E. 2d 385, 387; may be intentional or unintentional. An act of omission will not give rise to liability unless there is a **duty** to act. Thus a parent owes a duty of protection to his child and if he fails to do what is required to protect the child, he may face criminal liability; a nurse who neglects a patient may face tort and/or criminal liability. Thus, an omission, though it consists of a failure to act, may constitute the **actus reus** which is a component of criminal liability.

OMNIBUS see **in omnibus.**

OMNIBUS CLAUSE a clause in an automobile liability insurance policy that serves the purpose of giving ''additional assureds, other than the person named in the liability policy as assured, with certain specified limitations, the benefit of the policy. . . . It extends protection to one 'permitted' to use the car, although the 'assured' may not be liable for the accident under the doctrine **respondeat superior.** The object of such clause is to cover the liability of the operator of the car as unnamed assured, and to protect any person so injured by giving him a **cause of action** against the insurer for injuries deemed by law to have been caused by the operation of the car.'' 30 So. 2d 123, 125. Statutes have been passed in some jurisdictions requiring the inclusion of omnibus clauses for the protection of automobile accident victims. See 84 N.W. 2d 84.

Also applies to a clause in a **will** or distribution decree passing all property not specifically mentioned or known of at the time.

ON ALL FOURS an expression used to describe a case that is on point and therefore useful as **precedent.** It is derived from the Latin maxim: nullum simile est idem nisi quatuor pedibus currit, meaning:

nothing similar is identical unless it runs on all four feet.

ON DEMAND when requested; when asked for. For example, a note payable ''on demand'' is payable when the sum is requested. Such a note is called a demand **note** if no due date is stated on it. U.C.C. §3-108.

ONE MAN, ONE VOTE see **reapportionment** [ONE PERSON, ONE VOTE PRINCIPLE].

ON ITS FACE see **void for vagueness** [FACIAL INVALIDITY].

ON OR ABOUT language used in legal documents to qualify a time or a place as approximate. Unless the parties expressly provide, any reference to time of performance is presumed to be approximate so that the failure to perform as specified is not a **breach.** Where the parties intend otherwise, they generally provide in the legal document that **''time is of the essence''** or words to that effect.

ON THE BRIEF designation on a **brief** indicating the names of persons who contributed to the written product. Such persons may or may not be listed as the attorneys of record. Many reported cases list the attorneys of record and all persons ''on the brief.'' See **of counsel.**

ON THE MERITS refers to a decision or **judgment** based upon the essential facts of the case rather than upon a technical rule of practice, such as a failure of proper **service** or other **jurisdictional** defect. See 2 Wyo. 465, 472. A decision on the merits is rendered by the **trier of fact** after a full presentation of the evidence and determines finally the rights of the party, barring **appeal** or subsequent relitigation. 133 P. 2d 15, 17. A **summary judgment** may also be on the merits; however, a default judgment may not. See **dismissal** [DISMISSAL WITH PREJUDICE]; **trial** [TRIAL ON THE MERITS]; **res judicata.**

ON THE PLEADINGS See **judgment** [SUMMARY JUDGMENT].

OPEN visible, free from concealment, 289 F. 493, 495; exposed to public view, 79 Ill. App. 308; unobstructed, such as land without trees or fences, 229 S.W. 2d 80, 85. See **notorious possession; plain view.**

An account or matter that is not final and not closed.

An attorney OPENS a trial by addressing the trier of fact and briefly summarizing the facts and theory of the case which he or she intends to develop during the trial. This is known as an OPENING STATEMENT.

OPEN ACCOUNT account that has not yet been settled or paid, 323 U.S. 111; a series of transactions that give rise to credits and debits, but that results in a single liability. 437 P. 2d 705, 706.

OPEN AND NOTORIOUS See **notorious possession**.

OPEN COURT "a court [that] is formally opened and engaged in the transaction of judicial affairs, to which all persons who conduct themselves in an orderly manner, are admitted." 43 Ill. App. 573, 574. Most legal proceedings take place in open court except where confidentiality is a recognized interest (e.g., matrimonial, adoption, or juvenile delinquency proceedings).

There is a potential conflict between a criminal defendant's right to a fair trial and the public's right to a public trial and more particularly to the freedom of the press to report thereon. Criminal trials are presumptively open and may be closed to the public and the press only in rare cases and for good cause. 448 U.S. 555, 573; 104 S. Ct. 819, 824. When a portion of a criminal trial is to be closed, the state bears a heavy burden of demonstrating that the denial of public access is necessitated by a compelling governmental interest and that

that interest is being narrowly served. 457 U.S. 596, 606-607.

Electronic coverage of judicial proceedings is now permitted in many states. In the absence of a showing of actual prejudice, it is not unconstitutional for a state to broadcast a criminal trial over the defendant's objection. 449 U.S. 560.

OPEN END FUNDS See **investment company [trust].**

OPENING STATEMENT see **statement** [OPENING STATEMENT].

OPEN POSSESSION see **notorious possession.**

OPEN PUBLIC MEETINGS LAWS see **sunshine laws.**

OPEN SHOP an enterprise that employs workers without regard to whether they are members of a **labor union.** Section 14(b) of the **National Labor Relations Act,** 29 U.S.C. §164(b), permits each state to adopt an open shop policy. A minority of many states have adopted such statutes, which range from strongly prohibiting to merely discouraging mandatory union membership as a condition of employment (the **closed shop**). Frequently these statutes simply prohibit an employer from collecting dues on behalf of a union. This has the practical effect of creating an open shop, since the union then has no means of enforcing compulsory membership or the payment of dues.

OPERATING LOSS see **net operating loss.**

OPERATION OF LAW by or through law; refers to the determination of rights and obligations through the automatic effects of the law and not by any private agreement or direct act of the party affected. Thus, when one dies without leaving a valid will [**intestate**], his **heirs** take according to the statute of descent and distribution, that is, by operation of law. So too, in certain instances the law will impose a constructive **trust** upon a transaction "by operation of law" to protect certain classes of persons.

OPINION the reason given for a court's judgment, finding, or conclusion, as opposed to the **decision,** which is the judgment itself. See 107 P. 2d 1104, 1106, 1107. An opinion of a court implies its adoption by a majority of the judges. See 123 S.W. 2d 83, 85. Opinions are usually written by a single judge and if there were more than one judge deciding the matter, as in an appeal to a three-member appellate tribunal, other judges will join in the opinion.

CONCURRING OPINION one that is basically in accord with the majority opinion, but written to express a somewhat different view of the issues, to illuminate a particular judge's reasoning, to expound a principle which he holds in high esteem, etc. An opinion that concurs "in the result only" is one that entirely rejects the reasoning and conclusions concerning the law and/or the facts on the basis of which the majority reached its decision, and which expresses a different view, but has coincidentally led the judge or justice writing it to recommend the same disposition of the case (affirmance, dismissal, remand, etc.) as was agreed upon by the majority (or plurality).

DISSENTING OPINION one that disagrees with the disposition made of the case by the court, the facts or law on the basis of which the court arrived at its decision, and/ or the principles of law announced by the court in deciding the case. Opinions may also be written which express a dissent "in part."

EXPERT OPINION see **expert witness.**

LAY OPINION see **lay witness.**

MAJORITY OPINION one that is joined by a majority of the court. Generally known as "the opinion."

PER CURIAM OPINION an opinion "by the court," which expresses its decision in the case but whose author is not identified.

PLURALITY OPINION one agreed to by less than a majority of the court but the result of which is agreed to by the majority. A plurality opinion carries less weight under **stare decisis** than does a MAJORITY OPINION (above).

"Opinion" also refers to the conclusions reached by a witness which are drawn from his observations of the facts; such an "opinion" is merely evidence from which the **trier of fact** will make an ultimate finding. See 129 N.W. 2d 393, 396; 13 So. 2d 669, 672. See **expert witness.**

OPTION see **option contract; stock option.**

OPTIONAL WRIT see **peremptory writ.**

OPTION CONTRACT a binding promise in which the owner of property agrees that another shall have the privilege of buying the property at a fixed price within a stated period of time. 121 P. 358, 136 A. 379. It is the offeror's acceptance of **consideration** in exchange for his promise to keep the offer open for a designated period of time, thus rendering the offer irrevocable. See **firm offer.**

An option must be supported by consideration, often the payment of a small sum of money which may be, though need not be, applied as a down payment if the option is exercised. It exists only when the option holder himself has the right to determine whether he shall require the performance called for by the option. If the agreement states that the option may be exercised only with the consent of the other party, it is not an option even though so-called by the agreement. 307 S.W. 2d 758. Some types of option contracts are formed without consideration: "An offer is binding as an option contract if it is in writing and signed by the offeror, recites a purported consideration for the making of the offer and proposes an exchange on fair terms within a reasonable time . . . ," Restatement of Contracts, 2d §87(1); "An offer which the offeror should reasonably expect to induce action or forbearance of a substantial character on the part of the offeree before acceptance and which does induce such action or forbearance is binding as an option contract to the extent necessary to avoid injustice." Id. §87(2). Under the Uniform Commercial Code a seller can offer a buyer an option contract without consideration by making an irrevocable offer and complying with other statutory requirements. U.C.C. §2-205 [**firm offer**]. See also **stock option.**

ORAL spoken

ORAL ARGUMENT legal arguments given in court proceedings by attorneys in order to persuade the court to decide a legal issue in favor of their client.

ORAL CONFESSION an acknowledgment by a criminal defendant that he did the act of which he is accused and that he is guilty of a crime as a result of it. See **self-incrimination, privilege against.**

ORAL CONTRACT see **contract** [ORAL CONTRACT].

ORAL TRUST a **trust** created by the agreement of the **grantor** and the **settlor,** but for which no document is executed setting forth the terms of the trust. Trusts of land are subject to the **Statute of Frauds.** Most states will recognize an oral trust of **personal property;** however, a few states also subject trusts of personal

property to the Statute of Frauds. 1 Scott on Trusts §§40, 52 (3rd ed. 1967).

ORAL WILL see **nuncupative will.**

ORDER a direction of the court on some matter incidental to the main proceeding which adjudicates a preliminary point or directs some step in the proceeding. See 420 S.W. 2d 530, 533. A FINAL ORDER is an appealable order. "If an order closes the matter and precludes future hearing and investigation it is final; but an order which does not completely dispose of the subject matter and settle the rights of the **parties** is not final." 146 N.W. 2d 450, 452. See **interlocutory order protective order; restraining order.**

In the securities trade, an order is an instruction to buy or sell a specified security under specified conditions. The most common type of order is a MARKET ORDER which is specified as to volume with price determined by the market level at the time of sale. Instructions can include a limit as to price to be paid or received (LIMIT ORDER) and a limit as to the time the bid or offer is available. If the order is for the day only it is a DAY ORDER; if it is good until cancelled, it is a standing order called a GTC.

ORDERED LIBERTY a concept in constitutional law that the **due process** requirements applicable to the states through the Fourteenth Amendment to the United States Constitution do not incorporate all the provisions of the first 10 amendments (the so-called **Bill of Rights**), but only those measures essential for the preservation of a scheme of "ordered liberty." All that is meant is that due process contains within itself certain minimum standards which are 'of the very essence of a scheme of ordered liberty.' " 332 U.S. 46, 65 n. 28 quoting 302 U.S. 319, 325.

The restrictive view of due process expressed by this doctrine has been largely replaced today by a broader view of incorporating nearly all of the Bill of Rights as a national standard of fundamental fairness. If a right embodied in the Bill of Rights is "fundamental to the American scheme of justice," it will today be regarded as applicable to the states through the due process clause of the Fourteenth Amendment. See 391 U.S. 145. For instance, the right to trial by jury, recognized almost universally in American law, has been held applicable to the states in all but petty cases, which have been defined as those involving possible sanctions involving less than six months imprisonment. New York City alone in the nation defined petty in terms of one year which was held to be an impermissible deviation from the national norm. See 399 U.S. 66.

ORDER PAPER a negotiable instrument which is payable to order, i.e., payable to a specified person or his **assignee.** An instrument will be negotiable only if it is payable to the order of a specified person or to the bearer. U.C.C. §§3-104 (1) (d), 3-110. See **bearer paper; indorsement.**

ORDER TO SHOW CAUSE see **show cause order.**

ORDINANCE a local law that applies to persons and things subject to the local jurisdiction. See 90 F. 2d 175, 177. It is used to mean an act of a city council or local governmental entity that has the same force and effect as a **statute** when it is duly enacted; it differs from a law in that laws are enacted by a state or federal legislature and ordinances are passed by a municipal legislative body. See 7 S.E. 2d 896, 898. Ordinances are enacted to regulate zoning, highway speed, parking, refuse disposal, and other matters typically and traditionally of local concern. Some criminal violations (such as loitering) are based on ordinances rather than state penal law, though the more serious offenses are covered by state laws. See **home rule; pre-emption.**

ORDINARY COURSE OF BUSINESS according to the common practices and customs of commercial transactions. The term refers to a usual and necessary activity that is normal and incidental to the business. Occasional isolated or casual transactions are not frequent or continuous enough to constitute the ordinary course of business. See generally 46 A.L.R. 2d 648. **Sales** in the ordinary course of business refers to **property** usually available for **sale** to customers of the trade. Id. In banking, the term generally means receiving deposits, paying withdrawals, making loans, and discounting **commercial paper.** 77 F. 2d 14, 17. Treasury regulations exempt from **gift tax** any **transfers** made in the ordinary course of business. 176 F. 2d 233, 236.

Entries in accounting books may be admissible into **evidence** if made in the regular course of business by a person other than the **party** himself. Even if the person who made the entry is dead or otherwise unavailable as a **witness,** such entries are usually admissible. The rationale for this exception to the **hearsay rule** is the probability of the trustworthiness of routine records in the day-to-day operation of a business. Fed. R. Evid. 803(6). See generally 237 F. 2d 79, 89; 60 A.L.R. 2d 1119, 1123.

ORDINARY INCOME for tax purposes, income subject to being taxed at the highest rates, as opposed to **capital gains,** which may be taxed at lower rates. Generally, only **capital losses** may be deducted against capital gains, and only ordinary income may be offset by the other **deductions.**

ORDINARY NEGLIGENCE see **negligence.**

ORGANIC LAW the fundamental law of a country, state, or society; the law upon which its legal system is based, whether that law is written, such as a constitution, or unwritten.

ORGANIZED CRIME a syndicate of professional criminals who rely on unlawful activities as a way of life. 383 F. Supp. 346, 350. Often called the FAMILY, the MAFIA, or the MOB. See **racketeering.**

ORIGINAL DOCUMENT RULE see **best evidence rule.**

ORIGINAL ISSUE the initial sale or issue of a **security.**

ORIGINAL JURISDICTION authority to consider and decide cases in the first instance as distinguished from APPELLATE JURISDICTION, which is the authority to review a decision or **judgment** of an inferior tribunal and to **affirm, reverse,** or modify the decision. 513 P. 2d 960, 964. When an **appellate court** tries a case **de novo** on **appeal,** however, it is said to exercise its original jurisdiction rather than its appellate jurisdiction. Consequently, the test of whether a court exercises original jurisdiction is not the manner in which the case reaches the court but the nature of the court's authority. See generally 16 N.W. 2d 275.

The **Supreme Court** has original jurisdiction in all cases affecting ambassadors, other public ministers and consuls, and those in which a state is a party. U.S. Constitution, Art. III, Section 2. The constitutional grant of original jurisdiction to the Supreme Court has been regarded as self-executing; Congress can neither restrict nor enlarge this grant of original jurisdiction to the Supreme Court. 5 U.S. (1 Cranch) 137. The federal district courts exercise that original jurisdiction which the Congress by statute expressly provides such as **federal question jurisdiction** (28 U.S.C. §1331) and **diversity of citizenship** jurisdiction (28 U.S.C. §1332). See **jurisdiction.**

ORIGINAL PACKAGE DOCTRINE the constitutional prohibition of state and local taxation of **goods** while they are still in their original packages. 199 S.E. 2d 665, 667. The U.S. Constitution, Art. I, Section 10, Cl. 2, prohibits states from imposing import or export **duties.** In an early case, the Supreme Court held that an item in its original package retained its character as an import and was thus free of tax by a state while "in the original form or package in which it was imported." 25 U.S. 419.

OSHA see **Occupational Safety and Health Act [OSHA].**

OSTENSIBLE AUTHORITY see **apparent authority.**

OTC see **Over-the-Counter Market [OTC].**

OUSTER the wrongful dispossession of a person, or exclusion of him from property. Usually applied to the acts of a co-tenant which exclude other co-tenants from their legal right to share **possession.** See 91 Cal. Rptr. 170. The ouster of co-tenants with proper notice will commence the running of the **statute of limitations** for purposes of **adverse possession.** See 226 S.W. 2d 484, 486.

OUT-OF-COURT SETTLEMENT in civil cases, the resolution of a dispute between parties prior to the rendering of a final judgment by the trial court. Compare **plea bargaining.**

OUTPUT CONTRACT see **contract [OUTPUT CONTRACT].**

OUTSTANDING ISSUE see **authorized issue [OUTSTANDING ISSUE].**

OVERBREADTH a term used to describe a statute which may legitimately proscribe certain conduct, but which also forbids or inhibits conduct that is constitutionally protected, e.g., by the First Amendment's safeguards of freedom of speech and press. See 305 F. Supp. 842, 851. An overbroad statute may be challenged by another who, though engaged in so-called core conduct which clearly falls within the permitted scope of the statute, will still be permitted to argue the rights of those "chilled" by the existence of the overbroad statute. See **chilling effect; void for vagueness.**

OVERREACHING in commercial law, taking an unfair advantage over another through fraudulent practices or abuse of superior bargaining power, see 112 So. 2d 838, 841; synonymous with **fraud.** See 285 N.Y.S. 648, 670. **Contracts** that are the product of overreaching in an unequal bargaining context may be unenforceable today under modern concepts of fraud or the **unconscionability** doctrine. See U.C.C. §2-302.

OVERRULE to overturn or make void the **holding** of a prior **case;** occurs when a court in a different and subsequent case makes a decision on a point of law exactly opposite to the decision made in a prior case. A decision can only be overruled by the same court or a higher court within the same **jurisdiction.** Once overruled, a decision no longer has **precedential** value. The term should be distinguished from **reverse,** which applies to a higher court's overturning of a lower court's decision in the same case.

Sometimes without expressly overruling a prior precedent, the court will dispose of a matter in such a way that it has in fact overruled the prior authority **sub silentio.** Also, in some cases, rather than overrule a prior case, the court may announce in its decision that the former authortiy is "disapproved," which has the same effect. If a court does not desire to expressly overrule or disapprove one of its prior decisions it may limit the prior case to its facts or otherwise distinguish or limit the prior case.

Overrule also applies to a court's denial of any **motion** or point raised to the court, such as in "overruling

a motion for a new trial" or "objection overruled."

OVERT ACT open act; "in criminal law, . . . an outward act done in pursuance of [a] crime and in manifestation of an intent or design, looking toward the accomplishemnt of [a] crime." 275 F. 2d 813, 817. An "overt act" is required to find criminal liability for **attempt, conspiracy,** or **treason.** In the case of a conspiracy, the existence of an "overt act" is necessary to establish criminal liability, but the act itself need not be illegal. See 175 P. 2d 724, 732.

OVER-THE-COUNTER MARKET [OTC] a securitites market created by dealers who primarily handle trading in securities that are not **listed stocks** on an organized exchange. OTC trading differs from exchange trading in two significant ways: (1) transactions are carried out through telephone contact and negotiation with a number of dealers, called MARKET MAKERS, as compared to the single specialist, single location auction market mechanism used for listed securities trading, and (2) the market maker acts as principal in the transaction which involves the dealer as buyer and seller from his own inventory. The bulk of **bond** trading is carried out in the OTC market. See **National Association of Securities Dealers [NASD].**

OWNER the person who has legal **title** to property, 381 S.W. 2d 821, 826; the person in whom ownership, dominion, or title of property is vested. 65 N.W. 2d 856. See also **record owner.**

OWNERSHIP "one's exclusive right of possessing, enjoying, and disposing of a thing." 72 S. 891. The term has been given a wide range of meanings, but is often said to comprehend both the concept of **possession** and, further, that of **title** and thus to be broader than either. See 139 N.W. 101. See **fee simple.**

ALLODIAL OWNERSHIP free ownership, not subject to the restrictions or obligations associated with **feudal** tenures. See 28 Wis. 367.

TENURIAL OWNERSHIP the holding of land subject to specific **services** or obligations owed to another.

OYER hearing. At common law, the reading to a defendant upon his demand the writ upon which the action is brought. See generally 3 Bl. Comm. *299.

OYER AND TERMINER in English law, special tribunals empowered to hear and determine cases within their criminal **jurisdiction,** commissioned by the King when the delay involved in ordinary prosecution could not be tolerated, as in the case of sudden insurrection. Some states use the term to refer to their higher courts of criminal jurisdiction.

OYEZ hear ye. An exclamation used to get attention for an official proclamation or proceeding. 4 Bl. Comm. *340. In many courtrooms, the **bailiff** normally cries "oyez" to signal the beginning of the court proceeding.

P.A. Professional Association. See **professional corporation.**

PACKAGE, ORIGINAL see **original package doctrine.**

PACTUM *(päk'-tūm)*—Lat: pact, **contract,** agreement. An agreement unenforceable because it lacks **consideration** is said to be **nudum pactum,** meaning a naked or bare agreement.

PAID-IN-SURPLUS in corporate finance, the amount paid for stock in excess of its **par value.**

PAIN AND SUFFERING a species of **damages** that one may recover for physical or mental "pain and suffering" that result from a wrong done or suffered. The loss of ability or capacity to work because of physical pain or emotional or mental suffering is a type of pain and suffering and a proper element of damages. See 48 S.E. 2d 137. Recovery for the pain and suffering of a deceased person is sometimes permitted by such person's personal representative, though some states by statute forbid such a recovery. See 217 F. 2d 344, 348, and 37 A. 571, 572. See **survival statute.**

PAINTING THE TAPE expression for a person or group making transactions without a true change of ownership to give the impression that a stock is trading actively. See **manipulation** [RIGGED ORDERS; WASH SALE].

PAIS *(pā, pās)*—Fr: the countryside.

PALIMONY an award of support similar to **alimony** but made to a partner in a dissolved nonmarital relationship. Where the partners had an **express contract,** founded on consideration other than sexual services, some courts have held the contract enforceable; where no such formal agreement exists, the court may determine whether the conduct of the parties warrants a finding of **implied** contract or other understanding to support an award. See 134 Cal. Rptr. 815; 403 A. 2d 902.

PANDER to pimp, to cater to the lust of another; a PANDERER is thus a pimp, procurer, male bawd, one who caters to the lust of others. See 209 S.W. 2d 99, 100. PANDERING is the crime of inducing any female to become a prostitute. See 158 S.W. 1120, 1125. With reference to **obscenity,** pandering is the promotion of obscene literature or movies by appeals to prurient interests and such conduct is not protected by the **First Amendment.** See 383 U.S. 463. See also **aid and abet; solicitation.**

PANDERER see **pander; prostitution.**

PANEL the list of persons who have been summoned for **jury** duty and from whom a jury may be chosen. 56 S.W. 2d 592. To IMPANEL a jury means to summon and select a jury. Id.

Panel also refers to the group of appellate judges who will hear an appeal. Typically, intermediate appellate courts consist of several judges who sit in panels of three.

PAPER see **bearer paper; chattel paper; commercial paper; order paper.**

PAPER PROFIT unrealized gain; profit that exists and is reflected in financial statements but that has not been reduced to cash and realized for tax purposes. See **realization.**

PAR equal to the established value. When used in connection with **negotiable instruments** and **stocks** and **bonds,** it denotes the face amount of the instrument or security, and not the actual value such instrument or security would receive on the open market.

AT PAR negotiable instruments or securities that sell at their nominal value. They are "above" or "below par" when they sell for more or less than their nominal value. 17 S.E. 49, 53. The usual par is 100.

PAR VALUE the stated value [**face value** or nominal value] of a stock, bond, or negotiable instrument. On the corporation's **balance sheet,** the par value of the stock issued is allocated to stated capital. Many states once required that a corporation have assets equal to the par value of its stock in order to guard against the issue of **watered** stock. Most

states have now either abolished or diminished the importance of par value with regard to stock. Henn & Alexander, Laws of Corporations, §§123, 159, and 319 (1983). Thus, par value has little significance now for common stock, and the current practice is to issue **no-par stock,** or stock with an arbitrary low value. In the case of **preferred stock,** par value takes on added importance since it specifies the dollar value upon which dividends are paid, and preferred stocks ("preferreds") are usually offered for sale or exchange at par value. The par value on bonds specifies both the maturity payment and interest base.

PARALEGAL a person other than a licensed attorney who is employed, usually by a law office, to perform a variety of tasks associated with a law practice, any of which may be performed properly and conveniently by one not trained or authorized to practice law.

PARALLELISM see **conscious parallelism.**

PARAMOUNT TITLE a **title** that will prevail over another title asserted against it. 231 S.W. 49. It signifies an immediate right of **possession,** and is generally referred to as the basis for **eviction** of a **tenant** by one with a right of possession superior to that of the tenant, i.e., his eviction by one with a "paramount title." 1 Nev. 433.

PARAMOUR a lover; one who stands in the place of a husband or wife, but ordinarily without the legal rights attached to the marital relationship. See 292 S.W. 2d 74.

PARCENER at common law, one who jointly holds an **estate** by virtue of **descent** (i.e., **inheritance**). 27 Mo. App. 218. The **holding** of a parcener is generally known as an "estate in coparcenary," see 56 S.W. 2d 783, and usually refers to the estate held by each inheritor before the inheritance has been divided (i.e., **partitioned**). See 147 N.E. 602. The term is no longer widely used, since it is now said to be indistinguishable from a **tenancy in common**. See 194 N.E. 2d 921.

PARDON "an exercise of the sovereign prerogative of mercy, relieving the person on whom it is bestowed from further punishment and from legal disabilities because of the crime named." Rubin, The Law of Criminal Correction 555 (2d ed. 1973). Its effect is that of "relaxing the punishment and blotting out the existence of guilt, so that in the eyes of the law the offender is as innocent as if he had never committed the offense." 17 F. 2d 534, 535. But the majority of cases hold that a pardon does not obliterate the conviction or restore the defendant's good character. Most civil rights lost due to the conviction are, however, restored. See Id. at 690. "An UNCONDITIONAL PARDON goes no further than to restore the accused to his civil rights and remit the penalty imposed for the particular offense of which he was convicted in so far it remains unpaid." 127 P. 2d 257, 259. The pardoning power is usually vested in the chief executive with few restrictions on its use. The only frequent exceptions in state constitutions are treason and a judgment on impeachment. See Rubin, supra at 679.

CONDITIONAL PARDON any pardon imposing some condition, precedent or subsequent, that is not illegal, immoral, or impossible of performance. See 65 So. 2d 721, 722.
See **amnesty; commutation; executive clemency; parole.**

PARENS PATRIAE (*pa'-renz pa'-tri-ē*)—Lat: parent of his country; refers traditionally to the role of the state as sovereign and guardian of persons under legal disability. 440 F. 2d 1079, 1089. The term is a concept of **standing** often used by courts of **equity** when acting on behalf of the state to protect and control the **property** and **custody** of minors and incompetent persons.

The court, as an arm of the state, acts in the capacity of parens patriae when it awards **custody** of a minor to one parent in a **divorce, separation,** or **habeas corpus** proceeding. By exercising this authority the state emphasizes that a child is not the absolute property of a parent, but is a "trust" reposed in a parent by the state. 26 A. 2d 799, 809. States have used the doctrine to recover damages to quasi sovereign interests such as the "health and welfare" of its people and pollution-free air and waters; states have had less success in their attempts to use the doctrine in **antitrust** claims. 440 F. 2d 1079, 1089.

Historically, parens patriae has embodied the duty of the sovereign to protect both the public interest and those with disabilities. It has been called into play when such persons could be a danger to themselves and to the public if not held under protective custody of the sovereign. While the term originated in England and referred to the power of the king, in America it refers to the people or the state. 41 N.W. 2d 60, 70.

PARENTAL LIABILITY responsibility of parents for tortious acts committed by their minor children. While at common law, parents did not have such liabilities, the fact that juvenile misbehavior resulted in uncompensated victims led many states to enact statutes imposing liability on parents for the tort of their minor child. These statutes vary widely, but usually limit the parents' liability to a small dollar amount. Prosser, Torts 871 (4th ed. 1971).

PARENT CORPORATION see **subsidiary.**

PARI DELICTO see **in pari delicto.**

PARI MATERIA see **in pari materia.**

PARITY equality. 31 S.W. 2d 427, 431.

PARLIAMENT a legislative body. The term was first used to describe the legislative body of England, Scotland, and Ireland and still is used to describe that of the United Kingdom. Many countries and localities that are former British colonies call their legislative bodies "Parliament."

PARLIAMENTARY LAW general body of rules governing the orderly procedure of any legislative or other deliberative body. 67 N.E. 189. The most commonly followed rules are "Robert's Rules of Order."

PAROLE in criminal law, a conditional release from imprisonment that entitles the person receiving it to serve the remainder of the term outside the prison if all the terms and conditions connected with the person's release are satisfactorily complied with. Typical conditions of parole include periodic meetings with parole officers, foregoing the possession of weapons, and not associating with known criminals. See 76 A. 2d 150, 153. Compare **pardon; probation.**

PAROL EVIDENCE testimony of a witness; oral rather than written **evidence.** See **parol evidence rule** [merger clause].

PAROL   EVIDENCE   RULE [MERGER CLAUSE] the doctrine that renders any evidence of a prior or contemporaneous understanding of the parties inadmissible if offered to contradict or modify the terms of a written agreement. It is best understood as a rule of substantive law concerning the legal effect of the expression of an agreement in a final, fully integrated contract; it declares that when the terms of a contract have been embodied in a writing [called the **integration** of the agreement] to which both parties have assented as the final expression of their agreement, parol [oral] evidence of contemporaneous or prior oral agreements is not admissible for the purpose of varying or contradicting the written contract. Agreements relating to different subject matter and all subsequent agreements (whether oral or written), regardless of their effect on the writing, are not subject to the rule. A subsequent written or oral agreement discharges and supercedes prior agreements, whether oral or written. Even a clause in a written agreement forbidding oral modification may be orally rescinded and the prior agreement orally modified unless prohibited by a statute, such as U.C.C. §2-209(2) which requires written modifications or a rescission of contracts for goods governed by the statute. Prior agreements and understandings, oral or written, are not affected by a subsequent written contract if they are not inconsistent in meaning and operation even though they deal in some way with the same subject matter unless there is a MERGER CLAUSE stating that the written agreement is intended as exclusive (or a finding by the court to that effect, see U.C.C. §2-202(b)).

All relevant evidence is admissible to determine whether the agreement is final and exclusive, including parol evidence. Moreover, the parol evidence rule does not exclude evidence offered to prove **fraud, duress, mistake,** misrepresentation, illegality, special communications necessary to establish liability for consequential **damages, conditions precedent,** or evidence offered for the purpose of **rescission** or **reformation.** Parol evidence may be offered to show that the written contract does not accurately reflect the intention of the parties. See generally 3 Corbin, Contracts §§573-596 (1960); Restatement, Contracts 2d §§213-218.

PARTIAL   ACTUAL   EVICTION

see **eviction** [PARTIAL ACTUAL EVICTION].

PARTIAL BREACH see **breach** [PARTIAL BREACH].

PARTIALLY DISCLOSED PRINCIPAL see **principal.**

PARTICULARS, BILL OF see **bill of particulars.**

PARTITION a judicial separation of the respective interests in land of joint owners or **tenants in common** thereof, "so that each may take **possession** of, enjoy, and control his separate **estate** at his own pleasure." 23 N.E. 2d 57, 59. Partition is thus the dissolution of the **unity** of possession existing between common owners, 30 A. 2d 574, with the result that the parties hold their estates in **severalty.** 77 S.W. 2d 1086. Partition is available whenever desired by any co-tenant in a tenancy in common. A **joint tenancy** can be destroyed by either the **sale** or the **mortgaging** of a joint owner's interest in the estate and the resultant tenancy in common is then subject to partition, thus defeating the **survivorship** rights of other joint tenants in the subject of the sold or mortgaged property. A joint tenancy is not subject to partition until and unless the joint tenancy is destroyed; but partition is a matter of right and such right is not affected by the difficulty of the partition or any inconveniences which may result to the other tenants. 48 A. 384. When partition is not feasible, a court may order a sale, in which case the proceeds from the sale are distributed in the same proportion as interest held in the realty.

PARTNERSHIP "a contract of two or more competent persons to place their money, effects, labor and skill, or some or all of them, in lawful commerce or business, and to divide the profit and bear the loss in certain proportions; . . . [an] association of two or more persons to carry on as co-owners a business for profit." 187 S.W. 2d 941, 944.

See also Uniform Partnership Act §6(1). Partners are individually liable for the debts of the partnership and assets individually owned will be subject to execution to satisfy any such debt when partnership assets are insufficient. Crane & Bromberg, Law of Partnership Chap. 6 p. 342 (1968). An essential element of partnerships is the agreement to share profits and to make good any losses. See 12 N.Y.S. 2d 464. A partnership is not subject to income taxes; rather its partners are directly taxed individually on the income, taking into account their share of partnership gains and losses. I.R.C. §761(a). Compare **corporation; joint venture.** See also **distribution** [PARTNERSHIP DISTRIBUTION].

ARTICLES OF PARTNERSHIP the written agreement, setting forth each partner's rights in and obligations to the partnership.

LIMITED PARTNERSHIP generally, "an entity in which one or more persons, with unlimited liability (called GENERAL PARTNERS) manage the partnership, while one or more other persons only contribute capital; these latter partners (called LIMITED PARTNERS) have no right to participate in the management and operation of the business and assume no liability beyond the capital contributed." 243 A. 2d 130, 133.

PART PERFORMANCE see **statute of frauds.**

PARTY in a judicial proceeding, a **litigant (plaintiff** or **defendant);** a person directly interested in the subject matter of a case; one who could assert a **claim,** make a **defense,** control proceedings, examine **witnesses,** or **appeal** from the **judgment.** See 55 A. 2d 705, 708. The term also refers to a person or entity that enters into a contract, lease, deed, etc.; sometimes called "the party of the first part," "the party of the second part," etc.

AGGRIEVED PARTY see **aggrieved party.**

INDISPENSABLE PARTY one whose interest in the subject matter of a **controversy** is of such a nature that his interests will be affected thereby or without whose **joinder** in the action complete relief cannot be granted, so that the suit cannot in equity and good conscience proceed without him. See Fed. R. Civ. Proc. 19(b). See also **indispensable party.**

NECESSARY PARTY one whose interests will be affected by the suit or without whom complete relief cannot be granted, but who will not be joined if doing so would deprive the court of **jurisdiction** in the case. See Fed. R. Civ. Proc. 19(a).

NOMINAL PARTY party appearing on the **record** not because he has any real interest in the case, but because technical rules of **pleading** require his presence in the record. See 134 S.W. 2d 850, 852. See **real party in interest.**

PARTY WALL see **party wall.**

POLITICAL PARTY a group of persons uniting to pursue common political goals, specifically including the election of their members to public office.

PREVAILING PARTY see **prevailing party.**

PROPER PARTY one who has an interest in the subject matter of the litigation, but, as compared with a necessary party, without whom substantial relief may nonetheless be accorded. Such decree, however, will not settle all questions at issue in the controversy with respect to such party.

REAL PARTY IN INTEREST see **real party in interest.**

SECONDARY PARTY see **secondary party.**

THIRD PARTY someone other than the parties directly involved in the action or transaction; an outsider with no legal interest in the matter.

PARTY TO BE CHARGED see **statute of frauds.**

PARTY WALL a dividing wall between adjoining landowners. 94 N.E. 2d 55. It exists for the common benefit of both properties which it separates, and of which any use may be made by either party, so long as such use is not detrimental to the other. 34 N.Y.S. 2d 445. The two landowners own the wall as **tenants in common,** 106 N.W. 357, where the wall stands upon ground which is itself held in common, 94 N.E. 2d 55, or where it stands partly upon each of the two adjoining properties. 131 A. 290. A party wall may be constructed wholly upon property belonging to one of the parties, 220 N.Y.S. 2d 752, or it may be owned entirely by only one of them, in which case it is said to be subject to an **easement** or right in the other to have it maintained. 43 N.Y.S. 1016. A party wall is often one that provides support for one or more separately owned structures. 79 A. 2d 382; 222 S.W. 2d 197.

PAR VALUE see **par** [PAR VALUE].

PASSIVE USE see **use.**

PATENT evident; obvious; manifest.

PATENT OF INVENTION (often called simply "a patent") a grant of a right to exclude others from the making, using or selling of an invention during a specified time; it constitutes a legitimate **monopoly.** See 304 F. Supp. 357, 367.

PATENT OF LAND an instrument by which the government conveys a **fee simple** interest in land to another. See 70 U.S. 478; 144 P. 499, 503.

PATENT PENDING (often abbreviated PAT. PEND.) a notice to others that the product on which it is ascribed has been the subject of an application for patent protection and that if a patent does issue those with notice will be subject to the applicant's prior rights.

PATENT APPEALS see **federal courts** [COURT OF CUSTOMS AND PATENT APPEALS].

PATENT DEFECT a defect that could be recognized upon reasonably careful inspection or through the use of ordinary diligence and care. See 83 S.E. 2d 26, 29; U.C.C. §2-605(1). Compare **latent defect.**

PATENT INFRINGEMENT "the act of trespassing upon the incorporeal rights secured by a **patent**. . . . Any person who, without legal permission, [makes, uses, or sells] to another to be used, the thing which is the subject matter of any existing patent, is guilty of an infringement, for which **damages** may be recovered at law . . . or which may be remedied by a **bill in equity** for an **injunction.**" 273 F. 698, 704.
"The test of infringement is whether the accused device does substantially the same work in substantially the same way and accomplishes the same result. One appropriating the principle and mode of operation of a patent, and obtaining its results by the same or equivalent means, may not avoid infringement by making a device different in form, even though it be more or less efficient than the patented device." 79 F. 2d 685, 692.
Copyrights and **trademarks** can also be the subject of infringement action.

PATERNITY SUIT [BASTARDY PROCEEDING] a suit initiated to determine the paternity [father] of a child born out of wedlock and to provide for the support of that child once paternity is proved. 234 P. 412.

PAT. PEND. see **patent** [PATENT PENDING].

PATRICIDE the killing of one's own father.

PATRONAGE giving either protection or support. 74 N.Y.S. 2d 156, 161. POLITICAL PATRONAGE is the use of political office to protect one's friends and supporters through the influence of the office, and to support them by hiring them for government jobs. The **Civil Service Commissions** were established to create professional bodies of government employees who would be free of political patronage. 5 U.S.C. §1101.

PAUPER indigent; one who is unable to provide his own support and is otherwise without financial resources. Under the **Equal Protection Clause** to the United States Constitution, indigents and paupers may be excused from paying certain court costs and other legal fees, so that they may have equal access to the courts. 428 F. Supp. 728. See **in forma pauperis; indigent.**

PAWN to give **personalty** to another as security for a loan; "property deposited with another as security for the payment of a **debt.**" 42 S.E. 474, 475.

PAYABLES see **account** [ACCOUNT PAYABLE]; **balance sheet; liabilities.**

PAYABLE TO BEARER see **bearer paper.**

PAYABLE TO ORDER see **order paper.**

PAYEE any **person** to whom a **debt** should be paid, 156 S.W. 301, 303; one to whose order a **negotiable instrument,** such as a **bill of exchange, note** or **check,** is made payable.

PAYER [PAYOR] one who pays a **debt** or is obligated to pay a debt under a promissory **note** or other **instrument.**

PAYMENT satisfaction of a claim. 144 P. 2d 466, 468. Delivery of money in fulfillment of an obligation. 54 P. 130, 132.

PAYMENT DATE see **ex dividend** [PAYMENT DATE].

PAYMENT IN DUE COURSE payment of a **negotiable instrument** at or after its date of **maturity,** made to its **holder** in **good faith** and without **notice** of any defect in **title.** 10 Williston on Contracts 483 (1967). Under the Uniform Negotiable Instruments Law, payment in due course would discharge the **payor's** liability on the note. The Uniform Commercial Code eliminates the "in due course" requirement and discharges the payor upon payment to the holder even though the payor has knowledge of a third party's claim to the instrument. The third party consequently must proceed against the holder, not the payor, for satisfaction of the claim. U.C.C. §3-603 (Comment 3).

PAYMENT INTO COURT the payment by a party of a sum of money or other subject matter of a lawsuit into court for the duration of the lawsuit. The court disposes of the money or other property as the parties agree in their settlement of the lawsuit, or in accordance with the court's judgment. Fed. R. Civ. Proc. 67.

PAYOR see **PAYER [PAYOR].**

P.C. see **professional corporation.**

PCR ACTIONS see **post-conviction relief proceedings [PCR actions].**

P.D. public defender.

PEACEABLE POSSESSION possession that is continuous and not interrupted by adverse **suits** or other hostile action intended to **oust** the possessor from the land. 472 S.W. 2d 825. The term often refers to parties in **adverse possession** of land, and thus has nothing to do with actual **ownership.** 167 P. 2d 390. "Peaceable possession" does

not preclude the existence of adverse claims, so long as no actual attempt to dispossess is made. 57 So. 706. Actions to **quiet title** generally require a showing of peaceable possession by the one bringing the action. See 47 So. 202.

PEACEFUL ENJOYMENT see **quiet enjoyment.**

PECULATION "the fraudulent **misappropriation** by one to his own use of money or goods intrusted to his care." 164 S.E. 375, 378. See also **embezzlement; larceny.**

PECUNIARY relating to money and monetary affairs, 136 N.E. 2d 550, 554; consisting of money or that which can be valued in money. Many **wrongful death statutes** limit recovery to PECUNIARY LOSS, i.e., a loss of money or of something which can be translated into an economic loss. The loss of affections that a parent suffers by the negligent death of a child is not such a loss, whereas the loss of actual or anticipated financial support by the deceased child is pecuniary loss.

PENAL ACTION a civil suit brought for the recovery of a statutory penalty imposed as a punishment for an offense against the public. 92 S.W. 191, 212.

PENAL INSTITUTION any place of confinement for convicted criminals. See 230 N.E. 2d 536, 541. Penal institutions include local and county **jails** and workhouses, reformatories, penitentiaries, prison camps and farms, as well as the modern CORRECTIONAL INSTITUTION (new nomenclature used to describe many penal institutions previously called "prisons"). See **jail.**

PENAL LAW [CODE] a law enacted to preserve the public order by defining an offense against the public and imposing a penalty for its violation. See 191 N.Y.S. 2d 54, 57. Statutes that grant a private [civil] **action** against a wrongdoer are not considered penal, but remedial, in nature. See 218 S.W. 2d 75, 78; 59 S.W. 952, 953.

PENALTIES see **civil penalties.**

PENALTY CLAUSE a **contract** clause that provides for the payment of an amount as forfeiture in the event a party defaults. Penalty clauses are generally not enforced by the courts when the amount of the penalty is unrelated to the damages incurred. However, the courts will sometimes enforce a penalty on the grounds that the parties were free to agree to it. 5 Corbin on Contracts, §1057 (1964). Courts will enforce a **liquidated damage clause** when the amount of actual damages is difficult to ascertain and the liquidated damages are a reasonable attempt to approximate the actual damages. U.C.C. §2-718(1); White & Summers, Uniform Commercial Code 160 (1980).

PENDENTE LITE [LITE PENDENTE] *(pĕn-dĕn'-tā lē'-tā)*—Lat: suspended by the **lawsuit; pending** the lawsuit. Matters that are pendente lite are contingent upon the determination of a pending lawsuit. Thus, funds may be deposited with the clerk of the court pendente lite, so that those funds can be used to make payment to the opposing party in the event that the depositing party loses the lawsuit. See also **lis pendens.**

PENDENT JURISDICTION federal court doctrine whereby a plaintiff may rely upon both federal and non-federal grounds for the **relief** which is sought in a **complaint;** i.e., the plaintiff joins a federal claim with a state law claim based on "a common nucleus of operative fact," i.e., closely related or identical conduct of the defendant. Whether the federal court will hear and determine the state law claim if it dismisses the federal claim (and thus be without an independent jurisdictional basis for proceeding with the adjudication of his suit) is discretionary with the district court, although current practice would seem to favor retaining jurisdiction and deciding the state law claim. See 383 U.S. 715. Compare **ancillary jurisdiction.** See **abstention.**

PENITENTIARY see **jail** [PENITENTIARIES].

PEN REGISTER see **wiretap** [PEN REGISTER].

PENSION FUND see **retirement plan** [PENSION FUND [PLAN]].

PENSION PLAN see **retirement plan** [PENSION FUND [PLAN]].

PEONAGE see **Thirteenth Amendment** [PEONAGE].

PER ANNUM *(pĕr ăn'-nŭm)*—Lat: through the course of a year; annually. Anything (e.g., interest, wages, rent) which is calculated "per annum" is calculated on the basis of a year in time; sometimes a per annum rate will be fixed at 1/360th instead of 1/365th per day.

PER [PUR] AUTRE VIE *(pĕr(pûr) ô'-tr vĕ)*—Fr: for or during the life of another. An **estate** per autre vie is a **life estate** measured by the life of a third person rather than the life of the **grantee.**

PER CAPITA *(pĕr kăp'-ĭ-tä)*—Lat: through the head, top, summit; through the leader or capital (of country); "defined by the heads or polls; according to the number of individuals, share and share alike." 32 S.E. 2d 291. Anything which is figured per capita is calculated by the number of heads (people) involved and is divided equally among each individual. The term is used frequently in the law of **descent and distribution** and in that context means "to take in one's own right," as opposed to taking by **representation** (i.e., **per stirpes**).

PERCENTAGE DEPLETION see **depletion** [PERCENTAGE DEPLETION].

PER CURIAM *(pĕr kū'-rē-äm)*— Lat: by the court. See **opinion** [PER CURIAM OPINION].

PER DIEM *(pĕr dē'-ĕm)*—Lat: through the course of a day. As used in relation to compensation, wages, or salary, it describes pay for a day's services. See 160 S.E. 596, 599. Government and private business travel allowances are often allocated on a "per diem" basis.

PEREMPTORY "absolute, conclusive, final, positive, not admitting of question or appeal," 178 S.W. 2d 274, 279; e.g., a peremptory trial date may be established by the court on its own **motion** or at the request of a **party** to insure a timely disposition of the case. In the selection of a **jury** each side has a right to a fixed number of **peremptory challenges** to the seating of potential jurors. See **challenge** [PEREMPTORY CHALLENGE]; **peremptory writ**.

PEREMPTORY CHALLENGE see **challenge** [PEREMPTORY CHALLENGE].

PEREMPTORY PLEA see **plea** [PEREMPTORY PLEA].

PEREMPTORY WRIT a species of original **writ** commencing certain lawsuits at common law and directing the sheriff to have the **defendant** appear in court, provided that the **plaintiff** has given the sheriff security for the prosecution of the claim. The writ initially included the words "si te fecerit securum," which means "if he shall give you security." The writ was used when no specific damages were requested, but rather when general damages, arising from **trespass** or **trespass on the case,** were requested. In modern practice, a **summons** has replaced the peremptory writ. The alternative species of original writ was the OPTIONAL WRIT which the plaintiff used to demand something certain of the defendant, such as the restoration of the possession of land, the payment of a certain liqui-

dated debt, or the rendering of an accounting. 3 Bl. Comm. * 274. See **prerogative writ**.

The term also refers to a form of **mandamus** which requires that the act commanded be done absolutely. 199 A. 619, 620. In comparison, an ALTERNATIVE WRIT OF MANDAMUS [OPTIONAL WRIT] permits the public official the choice of either doing the act commanded or showing legal cause why it need not be done. 55 C.J.S. 608. Before a peremptory writ of mandamus can issue, the official must be given notice of the legal action and an opportunity to defend. Id. Compare **prerogative writ**.

PERFECTED completed, executed, enforceable, merchantable; refers especially to the status ascribed to **security interests** after certain events have occurred or certain prescribed steps have been taken, such as filing evidence of the interest and taking possession of the collateral. A perfected security interest has **priority** over an unperfected interest. The date of perfection is also the time from which courts judge priority contests with other perfected creditors. See U.C.C. §§9-301 et seq.

In practice, after all steps necessary to entitle a litigant to proceed in an **appellate** court have been accomplished, the appeal is said to be "perfected."

PERFORMANCE the fulfillment of an obligation; a promise kept, 42 S.E. 2d 910; refers especially to completion of one's obligation under a **contract**. See **specific performance; substantial performance.** See also **non performance**.

PERFORMANCE BOND a bond used in building contracts to guarantee that a contractor will perform the contract. 440 P. 2d 600, 605. In the event the contractor defaults or otherwise breaches the contract, the owner of the building project may use the proceeds of the bond to complete the project. 423 N.E. 2d

390, 393. Depending upon its terms, the proceeds of a performance bond may also be used to pay subcontractors who furnish labor and materials. 187 A. 2d 799, 802.

PERIL risk, such as the risk that is insured in an insurance policy.

PER INFORTUNIUM *(per in-for-tu'-ni-um)*—Lat: by accident.

PERIODIC TENANCY see tenancy [PERIODIC TENANCY].

PERJURY criminal offense of making false statements under **oath** or **affirmation;** at **common law,** only a willful and corrupt sworn statement made without sincere belief in its truth, and made in a judicial **proceeding** regarding a material matter, was perjury. Today, statutes have broadened the offense so that in some jurisdictions any **false swearing** in a legal instrument or legal setting is perjury, even if it is not material and even though it is not presented in a judicial proceeding. See Perkins & Boyce, Criminal Law 511 (3d ed. 1982); Model Penal Code §241.1. See also **subornation of perjury.**

PERMANENT FIXTURE see **fixture.**

PERMANENT INJUNCTION see **injunction** [PERMANENT [FINAL] INJUNCTION].

PERMISSION OF COURT see **leave of court.**

PERMISSIVE COUNTERCLAIM see **counterclaim; joinder.**

PERMISSIVE JOINDER see **joinder.**

PERMISSIVE USE see **use.**

PERMISSIVE WASTE see **waste.**

PER MY ET PER TOUT *(pĕr mē ā pĕr tū)*—Law Fr: by half and by whole. In joint **tenancy,** each tenant's share is the whole, for purposes of **tenure** and **survivorship** [tout], and each share is an **aliquot** portion for purposes of **alienation**

[my]. Cribbett, Principles of the Law of Property 96 (2d ed. 1975). Compare **per tout et non per my.**

PERPETUITIES, RULE AGAINST see **rule against perpetuities.**

PERPETUITY see **in perpetuity.**

PER QUOD *(pĕr kwōd)*—Lat: through which; by which; whereby; requiring extrinsic circumstances (context); acquiring meaning only by reference to external facts. "False imputations may be **actionable per se,** that is, in themselves, or per quod, that is, on allegation and proof of **special damage.**" 161 F. 2d 335. In a **libel** and **slander** action, words not injurious on their face or in their usual and natural usage, but which become so as a consequence of extrinsic facts and which require an innuendo, are actionable per quod. See 121 So. 459.

PER SE *(pĕr sā)*—Lat: through itself, by means of itself; not requiring extraneous evidence or support to establish its existence; e.g., NEGLIGENCE PER SE refers to acts that are inherently negligent, i.e., which implicitly involve a **breach** of duty, obviating the need to expressly allege the existence of the duty.

In defamation, statements that damage a person's reputation, without reference to the circumstances that give the language their injurious meaning, are LIBELOUS or SLANDEROUS PER SE. Language imputing any of the following characteristics to a person is slanderous per se: having a loathsome disease; having committed a crime; unchastity in a woman; and incompetence in one's profession. 408 So. 2d 1126, 1133.

In antitrust law, some types of business conduct are considered per se restraints of trade. Since proof of such conduct proves a violation of the **Sherman Antitrust Act,** there is no need to prove any injury to competition, which is otherwise a necessary **element** in an antitrust claim. One example of a per se violation is **price fixing**. 339 U.S. 485.

PERSON "in law, an individual or incorporated group having certain legal rights and responsibilities." 124 N.E. 2d 39, 41. This has been held to include foreign and domestic **corporations**. See 134 U.S. 594. Precise definition and delineation of the term has been necessary for purposes of ascertaining those to whom the Fourteenth Amendment to the U.S. Constitution affords its protection, since that Amendment expressly applies to "persons." Compare **natural person**.

PERSON AGGRIEVED see **aggrieved party**.

PERSONAL ATTACK RULE see **fairness doctrine** [PERSONAL ATTACK RULE].

PERSONAL CHATTEL see **chattel** [PERSONAL CHATTEL].

PERSONAL EFFECTS a vague phrase used to describe tangible property having an intimate relation to the decedent, such as clothing and jewelry. 110 N.Y.S. 2d 584, 585.

PERSONAL HOLDING COMPANY a **corporation** having a limited number of **shareholders** and a high percentage of passive **income**, such as **interest, dividends, rents, royalties**, and **capital gains**. A special income tax was imposed on personal holding companies in 1937 in order to prevent taxpayers from avoiding taxes by placing their **assets** in corporations. Previously, taxpayers would avoid income taxes by placing their assets in one or more corporations, thereby splitting their income among several taxpayers and taking advantage of the lower marginal tax brackets. The PERSONAL HOLDING COMPANY TAX is imposed on the undistributed income of such corporations at the flat rate of 50 percent. The purpose of the tax is to force the share-holders to distribute the corporation's income to themselves as dividends so they may be taxed on it at their regular rate of income tax. I.R.C. §§541 et seq.

PERSONAL JUDGMENT judgment imposed on defendant requiring sums to be advanced from whatever assets he has within the **jurisdiction** of the issuing court, as opposed to a judgment directed against particular property (called an **in rem** judgment) or a judgment against a **corporate** entity. See **jurisdiction** [IN PERSONAM JURISDICTION].

PERSONAL JURISDICTION see **jurisdiction**.

PERSONAL PROPERTY [PERSONALTY] things movable, as distinguished from **real property** or things attached to the **realty**. 3 Ill. App. 275, 279. However, things attached to the realty may be considered personalty if by their nature they are severable without injury to the realty. 25 S.E. 2d 315. See **fixture**. The term "personalty" embraces both tangible property other than realty and intangible property. 84 N.E. 2d 99.

PERSONAL RECOGNIZANCE see **release on own recognizance** [ROR].

PERSONAL REPRESENTATIVE a person who manages the affairs of another, either under a **power of attorney** or due to the incapacity of the principal either through death, incompetency, or infancy; for example, the **executor** appointed under the will of a decedent or the **committee** of an incompetent.

PERSONAL SERVICE see **service**.

PERSONALTY see **personal property** [personalty].

PERSONAM see **in personam**.

PER STIRPES (*pĕr stŭr'-pāz*)— Lat: "through or by roots or stocks, by representation." 282 S.W. 2d 478. The essential characteristic of a distribution of an **intestate's estate** per stirpes is that each distributee takes in a representative capacity and stands in the place of a deceased ancestor. See 82 N.E. 2d 866. "A distribution per stirpes is a division with reference to the intermediate course of descent from the ancestor. It is literally a distribution according to 'stock.' It gives the beneficiaries each a share in the property to be distributed, not necessarily equal, but [in proportion] to which the person through whom he claims from the ancestor would have been entitled. [As such, the person is said to take] 'by right of REPRESENTATION.' " 63 N.W. 2d 352. It is distinguished from a distribution **per capita,** which is "an equal division of the property to be divided among the beneficiaries, each receiving the same share as each of the others, without reference to the intermediate course of descent from the ancestor." Id.

PERSUASION BURDEN see **burden of proof.**

PER TOUT ET NON PER MY *(pĕr tū ā nŏhn pĕr mē)*—Law Fr: by the whole and not by half; describes the type of **seisin** that exists in a **joint tenancy** or **tenancy by the entirety.** Thus, the joint tenants or husband and wife who own property by the entirety own an **undivided interest** in the whole of the property but not an individual interest in half the property. In a tenancy by the entirety one spouse cannot seize or end the tenancy by his acts alone. See Cribbet, Principles of the Law of Property 96 (2d ed. 1975). See **partition; tenancy** [TENANCY IN COMMON]. Compare **per my et per tout.**

PETITION "a formal written request or **prayer** for a certain thing to be done." 104 S.W. 1009, 1010. As related to **equity** procedure, the petition is the functional equivalent of a **complaint** at law. It "connotes

an application in writing addressed to a court or judge, stating facts and circumstances relied upon as a cause for judicial action, and containing a **prayer** [formal request] for relief." 110 S.E. 2d 909, 911.

PETITIONER one who presents a petition to a court or other body either in order to institute an **equity** proceeding or to take an **appeal** from a **judgment.** The adverse party is called the **respondent.**

PETITION IN BANKRUPTCY the petition by which an insolvent debtor declares bankruptcy and invokes the protection of the bankruptcy court from creditors. 11 U.S.C. §301. Under Art. I, Sec. 8, Cl. 1 of the United States Constitution, Congress is given power to establish uniform laws of bankruptcy. It has used this power to preempt all state laws and state court actions by granting an automatic stay of any proceedings against the bankrupt debtor upon the filing of a bankruptcy petition. 11 U.S.C. §362. Creditors must seek their remedies against the debtor in the bankruptcy court.

PETIT [PETTY] JURY see **jury.**

PETIT [PETTY] LARCENY see **larceny.**

PETTY JURY see **jury.**

PETTY LARCENY see **larceny.**

PHYSICAL WASTE see **waste.**

PHYSICIAN-PATIENT PRIVILEGE privilege protecting communications (including oral statements by the patient and visual observations by the physician) between a physician and a patient in the course of their professional relationship from disclosure unless consent is given by the patient. 328 N.E. 2d 825. This privilege is statutory and did not exist under common law. 444 F. 2d 691. Its purpose is to allow persons to secure medical service without the fear of betrayal, 273 N.W. 478, or humiliation, 2 N.E. 2d 638. Treatment need not be rendered, 138 N.E. 2d 799. However, such privilege does not extend if a physician examines a patient for a purpose other than treatment, such as by court order (e.g., compelling an examination for purposes of determining sanity or obtaining a blood sample to determine intoxication). 501 S.W. 2d 619. The privilege does not preclude a physician from giving expert opinion testimony in response to a **hypothetical question** involving the physical or mental condition of the patient where such testimony is not dependent upon information protected by the privilege. 295 N.W. 2d 29. In general, the privilege does not apply to a nurse, unless acting as the doctor's assistant, 254 A. 2d 812, nor to medical students, 57 P. 2d 235, dentists, druggists, or chiropractors, and does not extend after the death of the patient. 121 F. 2d 104. Public records, such as certificates of death, do not sustain a privilege. 5 N.W. 2d 463. Similarly, the fact of treatment, 209 F. 2d 122, and the number and dates of visits, 23 F.R.D. 255, are not privileged. See McCormick, Evidence §§98 et seq. (2d ed. 1972).

PSYCHOTHERAPIST-PATIENT PRIVI-LEGE many states recognize a privilege similar to the **physician-patient privilege** (above) for disclosures to psychiatrists or those general practitioners or psychologists treating mental disease or emotional conditions such as drug or alcohol dependence. Such a privilege arises from the special therapeutic need to assure the patient that disclosures will not be made. McCormick, Evidence 213 n. 9 (2d ed. 1972); Unif. R. Evid. 503.

PICKETING the practice, often used in labor disputes, of patrolling, usually with placards, to publicize a dispute or to secure support for a cause. It is a constitutionally protected exercise of free expression when done peaceably, see 63 N.Y.S. 2d 860, 862, but may be prohibited when violent or dangerous to public safety, see 100 P. 2d 339, 343, or when done to propagandize falsely. See 139 P. 2d 963, 971.

PIERCING THE CORPORATE VEIL the process of imposing liability for corporate activity, in disregard of the corporate entity, on a person or entity other than the offending corporation itself.

Generally, the corporate form isolates both individuals and **parent corporations** (see **subsidiary** [SUB-SIDIARY CORPORATION]) from liability for corporate misdeeds. However, the courts will ignore the corporate entity and strip the organizers and managers of the corporation of the limited liability that they usually enjoy when, for example, the incorporation itself was accomplished to perpetrate a **fraud.** In doing so, the court is said to "pierce the corporate veil." 93 Cal. Rptr. 338, 341; Henn & Alexander, Laws of Corporations §146 (3d ed. 1983).

PIMP see **pander; prostitution.**

PINK SHEETS see **listed stock** [PINK SHEETS].

PIRACY at common law, the commission of acts of robbery and depredation on the high seas which if committed on land would constitute felonies. 244 N.Y.S. 720, 722. Piracy is also used to refer to the commercial reproduction and distribution of property protected by copyright, patent, trademark, or trade secret law.

P.J. presiding **judge.**

PLAGIARISM appropriation of the literary composition of another and passing off as one's own the product of the mind and language of another. The offense of plagiarism is known in the law as INFRINGE-MENT OF COPYRIGHT and comes into being only when the work allegedly copied is protected by **copyright.** Some states have made it unlawful to sell term papers, theses, etc., from which students plagiarize for academic credit. See, e.g., N.Y. Education Law §213-b.

PLAIN ERROR rule requiring an appellate court to reverse a conviction and award a new trial when an obvious error in the trial proceedings, 635 P. 2d 1161,1164, which was not objected to during the trial and went uncorrected by the trial court, affected the defendant's fundamental right to a fair trial. 597 F. 2d 1170, 1199. See Fed. R. Crim. P. 52(b).

For example, where unduly damaging **evidence** is introduced to which no **objection** is made and the trial judge fails to give an **instruction** to the **jury** limiting its consideration of that evidence, despite an obvious need for limiting instructions, the error so prejudices the defendant's rights that an appellate court will conclude there was plain error and direct that defendant be retried. Compare **harmless error; miscarriage of justice.**

PLAINTIFF the one who initially brings the **suit;** "he who, in a personal **action,** seeks a remedy in a court of justice for an injury to, or a withholding of, his rights." 147 F. 44, 46. See also **complainant; defendant; petitioner.**

PLAINTIFF IN ERROR **appellant;** one who appeals from a judgment against him in a lower court, whether he was plaintiff or defendant in that court. See **appellant;** compare **defendant** [DEFENDANT IN ERROR].

THIRD-PARTY PLAINTIFF refers to a **defendant** who files a **complaint** against a third party not named as a defendant by the plaintiff, and so not otherwise a party to the **proceeding.** Fed. R. Civ. P. 14(a).

PLAIN VIEW an exception to the general requirement of a valid search warrant to legitimize a search or seizure. "A search implies a prying into hidden places for that which is concealed, and it is not a search to observe that which is open to view." 193 N.E. 202, 203. Thus, it is not a search for an officer to observe or hear something by one of his natural senses, 474 F. 2d 1071, nor when common means of enhancing the senses such as a flashlight, 422 F. 2d 185, or binoculars, 319 N.E. 2d 332, are used. But the use of such devices may be so intrusive as to constitute a search in the case of a high-powered telescope, 415 F. Supp. 2152 or x-ray machine, 495 F. 2d 799. See LaFave, Search and Seizure §2.2 (1978). In all cases there must be a legal justification to be in the position in which seizable property is observed. "The plain view doctrine may not be used to extend a general exploratory search from one object to another until something incriminating at last emerges." 403 U.S. 443, 466. See **search or seizure.**

PLAN see **master plan.**

PLAT in property law, a map that shows the location of real estate in a town or county in relation to adjoining lots and landmarks such as roads.

PLEA in **equity,** a special answer indicating why a **suit** should be dismissed, delayed, or barred. Story, Equity Pleading §649. At law, broadly, any one of the common law **pleadings.** Technically, the defendant's answer by a factual matter, as distinguished from a **demurrer,** which is an answer by a matter of law. In criminal procedure, a defendant's plea entered at arraignment of either "guilty" or "not guilty," or in some jurisdictions, **nolo contendere** or **non vult** ("no contest"). A criminal defendant's plea may include an explanation for his or her acts, such as insanity at the time of committing the act or that the act was committed to prevent a greater harm. The COMMON LAW PLEAS which have been abolished or made obsolete by the Federal Rules of Civil Procedure included:

AFFIRMATIVE PLEA "one that sets up a single fact not appearing in the bill, or sets up a number of circumstances all tending to establish a single fact, which, if existing, destroys the complainant's case." 42 A. 1055, 1056.

DILATORY PLEA plea asserted to defeat an action by contesting grounds other than the merits of a plaintiff's case, such as improper **jurisdiction,** wrong defendant, or other procedural defects. See PLEA IN ABATEMENT (below). Compare PEREMPTORY PLEA (below). See also **dilatory plea.**

DOUBLE PLEA "one which consists of several distinct and independent matters alleged to the same point and requiring different answers." 36 A. 588.

INSANITY PLEA one by which the defendant claims innocence because of a mental disorder or inability to reason that prevented him from having a culpable mental state, i.e., from having the sense of purposefulness (intent, willfulness, recklessness) that is a necessary element of the crime charged. See **insanity.**

PEREMPTORY PLEA a type of PLEA IN BAR (below) which answers the merits of the plaintiff's complaint, as compared to a DILATORY PLEA (above) which defends on grounds other than the merits.

PLEA IN ABATEMENT a DILATORY PLEA (above) objecting to the place, mode, or time of asserting the plaintiff's claim, but not addressing any of the underlying merits. These errors can be corrected, as opposed to claims made in a PLEA IN BAR (below), at which time the claim can be renewed. 162 N.E. 2d 313, 315. Compare PEREMPTORY PLEA (above).

PLEA IN BAR a plea that "sets forth matters which per se destroy the plaintiff's right of action and bar its prosecution absolutely, such as a bar due to a statute of limitations or a constitutional guarantee against self-incrimination." 234 F. 2d 97, 99. This plea denies a plaintiff's right to maintain the action and which, if established, will destroy the action. 104 S.E. 2d 861, 862.

PLEA BARGAINING the process whereby the accused and the prosecutor negotiate a mutually satisfactory disposition of the case. "The disposition of criminal **charges** by agreement between the prosecutor and the accused, sometimes loosely called 'plea bargaining,' is an essential component of the administration of justice. Properly administered, it is to be encouraged. . . . Disposition of charges after plea discussions is not only an essential part of the process but a highly desirable part for many reasons. It leads to prompt and largely final disposition of most criminal cases; it avoids much of the corrosive impact of enforced idleness during pretrial confinement for those who are denied release pending trial; it protects the public from those accused persons who are prone to continue criminal conduct even while on pretrial release; and, by shortening the time between charge and disposition, it enhances whatever may be the rehabilitative prospects of the guilty when they are ultimately imprisoned." 404 U.S. 257, 260-261.

Plea negotiations can center around the defendant's pleading guilty to a lesser offense, or to only one or some of the counts in a multi-count **indictment.** In return, the defendant seeks to obtain concessions as to the type and length of the **sentence** or a reduction of counts. The recognition of plea bargaining has led to the promulgation of standards for the conduct of the negotiations. See, e.g., ABA Minimum Standards for Criminal Justice—Standards Relating to Pleas of Guilty (1968). All plea bargains must be placed upon **record** in **open court** at the time that the guilty plea is entered. Furthermore, a judge has discretion whether to accept or reject the plea and its attendant bargain. See, e.g., N.J. Court Rule 3:9-2. However, once the guilty plea is accepted, the state must adhere to the terms of the bargain. See 404 U.S. 257.

PLEAD to make any **pleading;** to answer **plaintiff's common law declaration;** in criminal law, to answer to the **charge,** either admitting or denying guilt.

PLEADING BURDEN see **burden of proof.**

PLEADINGS statements, in logical and legal form, of the facts that constitute plaintiff's **cause of action** and defendant's ground of **defense.** They are either **allegations** by the parties affirming or denying certain matters of fact, or other statements by them in support or derogation of certain principles of law, which are intended to have the effect of disclosing to the court or jury the real matter in dispute. 77 S.W. 2d 464, 469. At common law, pleadings were a rigorous process of successive statements the aim of which was to progressively narrow the issue. The common law pleadings were the plaintiff's declaration, the defendant's plea, the plaintiff's replication, the defendant's rejoinder, the plaintiff's surrejoinder, the defendant's rebutter, the plaintiff's surrebutter. Modern code procedure often includes only a **complaint,** an **answer,** and where necessary, a **reply** to the answer. See, e.g., Fed R. Civ. Proc. 7(a). Pleadings may be on the **merits,** and thus **peremptory,** or else they may be based on some other ground which

prevents the case from going to the jury, in which case they are referred to as **dilatory pleas.** Modern procedure permits liberal amendments to pleadings and thus defects in pleadings will directly affect a party's case only in rare instances. See **burden of proof.**

AFFIRMATIVE PLEADINGS any defensive pleadings that affirmatively allege the existence of facts, rather than merely deny the existence of the facts alleged by the plaintiff. For instance, if a plaintiff alleges the non-payment of a promissory **note,** the defendant may deny that the note exists, or he may affirmatively plead that the note has been paid. James & Hazard, Civil Procedure §4.7 (2d ed. 1977).

AMENDED PLEADINGS pleadings submitted to the court later in time than the original pleadings and which correct the original pleadings or arguments therein, such as by the addition of a cause of action or a defense. James & Hazard, Civil Procedure §5.2 (2d ed. 1977).

CODE PLEADINGS pleadings pursuant to the procedural codes adopted after 1848 in order to simplify the pleading process. New York was the leading state in developing and adopting the first code of legal procedure. The codes attempted to simplify pleading by requiring that a civil plaintiff set forth in the complaint only the facts upon which the cause of action was based, whereupon the court would determine the law applicable to such facts. Such pleading was an improvement over the common law practice of requiring the plaintiff to set forth as a separate count each cause of action under which the plaintiff might recover on the same facts. However, code pleading developed distinctions between pleading facts, law, and evidence which resulted in the dismissal of lawsuits without any justice being done between the parties. Accordingly, when the Federal Rules of Civil Procedure were adopted, they abandoned the requirement that only facts be pleaded, and instead added the requirement that the complaint contain a short statement showing that the pleader is entitled to relief. Fed. R. Civ. Proc. 8(a)(2); James & Hazard, Civil Procedure §§2.1 to 2.11 (2d ed. 1977).

DEFECTIVE PLEADING see **defective pleading.**

PLEADINGS IN THE ALTERNATIVE see **alternative pleading.**

RESPONSIVE PLEADINGS answers that either admit or deny the allegations contained in the complaint, and thus respond to them, rather than raise grounds upon which the complaint should be dismissed, such as the expiration of the **Statute of Limitations.**

SUPPLEMENTAL PLEADINGS pleadings that assert a claim or a defense based upon events occurring after the filing of the original pleading which they supplement. James & Hazard, Civil Procedure §5.8 (2d ed. 1977).

PLEADING THE FIFTH AMENDMENT see **self-incrimination, privilege against.**

PLEDGE a deposit of **personal property** as security for a **debt;** delivery of goods by a **debtor** to a **creditor** until the debt is repaid; generally defined as a **lien** or a **contract** that calls for the transfer of personal property only as **security.** The pledgor can pledge intangible as well as tangible **personalty** as long as it is capable of delivery, and it can confer ownership rights upon the person to whom delivery is made. Certain intangible personal property, however, such as accounts receivable and contract rights, may not be the subject of a

pledge or possessory **security interest.** Generally, the personal property subject matter of a pledge is referred to as "**collateral** security" or collateral. See **bailment; collateral; lien.**

PLEDGEE person who takes property to hold as security for a **debt** in accordance with a contract.

PLEDGOR person who delivers the property.

PLENARY "literally, . . . full, entire, complete, absolute, perfect or unqualified; but with reference to judicial proceedings, it denotes a [complete, formally pleaded suit wherein] a **petition** or **complaint** is filed by one or more persons against one or more other persons who file an **answer** or a response." 315 S.W. 2d 521, 525. A PLENARY ACTION is one in which a full trial or PLENARY HEARING is had on the merits of a complaint following full **discovery,** as distinguished from a summary proceeding.

PLURALITY OPINION see **opinion.**

POCKET VETO a means by which the President of the United States may effectively veto an act of Congress without exercising the presidential veto right. Under the U.S. Constitution, Art. I, Sec. 7, Cl. 2, the President must veto legislation within 10 days after it has been passed by both the Senate and the House of Representatives, or else the legislation will become law. However, if Congress adjourns before the end of the 10-day period, the legislation will only become law if the President has signed it. Accordingly, the President may effectively veto legislation that was passed within the last 10 days of the congressional session merely by not signing it into law. 279 U.S. 655.

POINT RESERVED at **trial,** the holding of a legal issue in abeyance for argument, so that the testimony or other matters at hand may proceed.

POISONOUS TREE see **fruit of the poisonous tree.**

POLICE COURT usually, an inferior municipal court with limited jurisdiction in criminal cases. See 91 P. 147, 148. Minor cases can be disposed of by such courts but otherwise they generally have the power only to arraign the accused and set **bail.**

POLICE POWER inherent power of state governments, often delegated in part to local governments, to impose upon private rights those restrictions that are reasonably related to promotion and maintenance of the health, safety, morals, and general welfare of the public. See 57 N.W. 331. "Police power must be confined to such restrictions and burdens as are thus necessary to promote the public welfare, or, in other words to prevent the infliction of public injury." See 71 N.W. 400. "In the exercise of its police powers a state is not confined to matters relating strictly to the public health, morals, and peace, but, there may be interference whenever the public interest demands it; and in this particular, a large discretion is necessarily vested in the legislature, to determine not only what the interests of the public require, but what measures are necessarily for the protection of such interests." 9 N.W. 2d 914, 919. Restrictions upon the use of one's property, such as **zoning** laws, or upon the conduct of one's business, such as environmental regulations, are imposed by state and local governments pursuant to the police power. Such power is conferred upon the states by the **Tenth Amendment** but is subject to and limited by due process considerations.

POLITICAL ASYLUM see **asylum.**

POLITICAL CONTRIBUTION see **charitable contribution.**

POLITICAL CORPORATION see **corporation; public corporation.**

POLITICAL PARTY see **party.**

POLITICAL QUESTION a question that a court determines to be not properly subject to judicial determination (i.e., which is not **justiciable**) because resolution of it is committed exclusively to the jurisdiction of another branch of government (legislature or executive), because adequate standards for judicial review are lacking, or because there is no way to insure enforcement of the court's judgment. Jurisdiction is not lacking, since the court has the power to decide political questions but chooses not to. Cases challenging the composition of state legislative bodies had been held political and nonjusticiable, 328 U.S. 549, until the Court determined that no other remedy existed and an **equal protection** of the laws violation was found, resulting in the formulation of the "one-man-one-vote" remedy. See 369 U.S. 186.

POLLING THE JURY see **jury** [POLLING THE JURY].

POLL TAX a capitation tax; a tax "of a fixed amount upon all the persons, or upon all the persons of a certain class, resident within a specified territory, without regard to their property or the occupation in which they may be engaged." 88 So. 4, 5.

State laws requiring the payment of a poll tax to register or vote in federal elections are now barred by the Twenty-Fourth Amendment; as to state elections, required payment of a poll tax as a prerequisite to registration or voting has been held to discriminate against poor persons and thus violate the Fourteenth Amendment's guarantee of **equal protection of the laws.** 383 U.S. 663.

POLYGAMY in criminal law, the offense of having more than one spouse at one time. See Model Penal Code §230.1. Community insistence upon MONOGAMY [having only one spouse at one time] has been so important that notwithstanding the **First Amendment's** guarantee of **free exercise** of religion, a polygamy conviction of a member of the Mormon faith was upheld despite the doctrine of the Mormon church that had imposed a duty upon its male members to practice polygamy. 98 U.S. 145.

POLYGRAPH a lie detector test. 139 A.L.R. 1171. It is an electromechanical instrument that simultaneously measures and records certain physiological changes in the human body which it is believed are involuntarily caused by the subject's conscious attempts to deceive the questioner. 348 F. Supp. 1377, 1380. Once the machine has recorded the subject's responses to the questions propounded by the operator, the operator interprets the results and determines whether the subject is lying. The courts almost uniformly reject the results of a "polygraph," when offered in **evidence** for the purpose of establishing guilt or innocence, due to its unreliability. 225 A. 2d 805, 809. Some **jurisdictions** will not allow evidence of a polygraph to be introduced for any purpose, even if all **parties** have stipulated to its admission, 541 P. 2d 871. Others, however, will allow the results of a polygraph to be admitted upon stipulation, 297 A. 2d 849, or even without stipulation and over objections, so long as certain requirements are met concerning the qualification of the operator, the reliability of the testing procedure, and the validity of the particular test made. 539 P. 2d 204.

POOL a group or combination of individuals or entities organized for the purpose of eliminating competition between the members and combining their resources in order to accomplish a benefit for each member. A pool sufficiently large or powerful so as to restrict competition throughout a particular trade or industry is illegal under Section 2 of the **Sherman Antitrust Act** of 1890. 15 U.S.C. §2. Sullivan, Antitrust §42 (1977).

PORNOGRAPHY books, magazines, films, pictures, and other such material depicting sexual acts that appeal to one's **prurient interests.** See **obscene material.**

PORTFOLIO a group of **securities** held by an individual or institutional investor, which may contain a variety of common and preferred **stocks,** corporate and municipal **bonds, certificates of deposit,** and **treasury bills**—that is, appropriate selections from the **equity, capital** and **money markets.**

POSITIVE FRAUD see **fraud** [FRAUD IN FACT].

POSITIVE LAW existing law created by legally valid procedures; ". . . law set by political superiors to political inferiors." Austin, The Province of Jurisprudence Determined 9 (1954 ed.).

POSITIVISM in **jurisprudence,** the view that any legal system is best studied by concentrating on the **positive law** of that system; formed in reaction to **natural law theory.** See Hart, The Concept of Law (1961), for a full discussion.

POSSE see **in posse.**

POSSE COMITATUS *(pŏ'-sä kŏm'-ĭ-tä'-tūs)*—Lat: to be able to be an attendant. "In a proper case the sheriff may summon to his assistance any person to assist him in making an **arrest** for a **felony.** A posse comitatus, i.e., those called to attend the sheriff, may be summoned verbally. The mode is immaterial, so long as the object is to require assistance. A person so summoned is neither an officer nor a mere private person but occupies the legal position of a posse comitatus and, while acting under the sheriff's orders, is just as much clothed with the protection of the law as the sheriff himself. It is not essential for a posse comitatus to be and remain in the actual physical presence of the sheriff; it is sufficient if the two are actually endeavoring to make the arrest and acting in concert with a view to effect their common design." 449 S.W. 2d 656, 661.

POSSESSION dominion and control over **property;** "the having, holding, or detention of property in one's power or command." 50 N.Y. 518. When distinguished from mere **custody,** it is said to involve custody plus the assertion of a right to exercise dominion and control. See 488 P. 2d 316. See also **unities** [UNITY OF POSSESSION].

ACTUAL POSSESSION immediate and direct physical control over property. 426 F. 2d 992. With regard to **real property,** it involves actual occupation of the property, see 92 S.E. 550, or direct appropriation of the benefits it yields. See 175 P. 247.

ADVERSE POSSESSION see **adverse possession.**

CHOSE IN POSSESSION see **chose** [CHOSE IN POSSESSION].

CONSTRUCTIVE POSSESSION the condition of having the conscious power and intention to exercise dominion and control over property but without direct control of or actual presence upon it.

CRIMINAL POSSESSION possession for which criminal sanctions are provided, because the thing (or property) either may not lawfully be possessed, may not be possessed by a particular category of persons, or may not be possessed under certain circumstances.

HOSTILE POSSESSION see **hostile possession.**

NOTORIOUS POSSESSION see **notorious possession.**

PEACEABLE POSSESSION see **peaceable possession.**

POSSESSORY ACTION a lawsuit brought for the purpose of obtaining or maintaining possession of real property and not for a determination of rightful title. In a common instance, a landlord will bring a possessory action to evict **holdover tenants,** praying that the court will issue a writ of possession against the holdover tenants.

POSSESSORY INTEREST a right to exert control over certain land to the exclusion of others, coupled with an intent to exercise that right. Restatement, Property §7. It is this "privilege of exclusive occupation" which distinguishes possessory from non-possessory interests. Restatement, Property, Div. V, Part I, Introductory Note. One holding a non-possessory interest is subject to specific restrictions with respect to the use he may make of the land, but the holder of a possessory interest is limited only by the rights of others (including co-owners, neighbors, **remaindermen,** etc.). Id. Examples of non-possessory interests include **easements, remainders,** the rights retained by the **grantor** of a **life estate,** etc. Restatement, Property §7 Comment. See also Restatement (second), Property, Landlord and Tenant §1.2 Comment a.

POSSIBILITY OF A REVERTER the possibility of the return of an **estate** to the **grantor,** if a specific event should occur or a particular act be performed in the future. It is thus a **reversionary** interest subject to a **condition** precedent. 108 N.W. 2d 548. The possibility does not itself constitute an estate, present or future. 2 So. 2d 344. It describes the interest remaining in the **grantor** who conveys a **conditional** or **determinable fee.** 106 S.E. 2d 913. Distinguished from a **right of reen-**

try for condition broken, in which case the grantor must assert his right by judicial process before the preceding estate is terminated. Also distinguished from the occurrence of the condition in a determinable fee situation in which the estate is terminated automatically without any further act of the grantor. This construction works a forfeiture with less protection to the grantee and thus is disfavored in law.

POST-CONVICTION RELIEF PROCEEDINGS [PCR ACTIONS] a statutory or court rule procedure whereby a criminal defendant may challenge collaterally a **judgment** of **conviction** which has otherwise become final in the normal **appellate** review process. See **collateral attack.** The availability of a PCR avenue of relief generally operates to preclude state or federal **habeas corpus.** The federal PCR statute is 28 U.S.C. §2255, enacted by Congress in 1948. The remedy has been interpreted as providing "a remedy exactly commensurate with that which had been available by habeas corpus." 368 U.S. 424, 427. A federal petitioner complaining of a federal judgment of conviction must bring a 2255 action rather than a writ of habeas corpus unless the 2255 remedy would be "inadequate or ineffective to test the legality of his detention." 28 U.S.C. §2255. The rules governing a 2255 motion are very much like those governing federal habeas, with the exception that the motion is brought not in the district of confinement, but in the sentencing court. See 373 U.S. 1.

Many states have adopted similar PCR statutes (or court rules) that encompass all constitutional challenges to the judgment of conviction, 381 U.S. 336, 338, but some statutes limit the scope of the remedy and the timeliness with which a motion for relief must be made (e.g., not more than five years after the conviction). A **writ of coram nobis** is available in some states as a form of PCR relief and in others an out-of-time motion for a new trial to correct a miscarriage of justice services this function. See generally, ABA Minimum Standards for Criminal Justice, Post-Conviction Remedies (App. Draft 1968).

POST FACTO see **ex post facto.**

POST HOC ERGO PROPTER HOC (*pōst hōk er'-gō prop'-ter hōk*)—Lat: after this, therefore because of this; a maxim setting forth the false logic that because one event occurs after another event, it was caused by the prior event.

POSTING to affix physically in order to display. In civil procedure, posting of certain required information is a substitute form of **service of process.** In order to satisfy **due process,** it must be sufficiently conspicuous to insure public **notice.** Posting in a public place is sometimes required by **statutes** governing service of process by publication, and a public place has been defined as a place where the public has a right to go and be. A notice posted on private property, however, may still be considered a posted public notice if it is likely to be seen by affected or interested persons.

In commercial law, posting is the procedure that a bank follows in deciding to finally pay a **negotiable instrument** and in recording its payment. It includes verifying any signature, ascertaining that sufficient funds are available, marking the item paid, charging the customer's account and correcting or reversing an entry or erroneous action with regard to the item. Posting also refers to the exhibition of notices on real property, warning potential trespassers that trespass for fishing or hunting is not permitted by the property owner.

POST MORTEM (*pōst môr' -tĕm*) —Lat: after death. The term generally refers to the examination of the body of a deceased to determine the cause of death; it may comprehend only such examination as that undertaken by a **coroner** and may consequently not extend to a true medical determination of the cause of death which would involve **autopsy** and dissection. See 31 N.Y.S. 865, 866.

POST-NUPTIAL AGREEMENT an agreement entered into by a husband and wife to determine the rights of each in the other's property in the event of death or divorce. 494 P. 2d 208, 212. Generally, each spouse must disclose his or her assets to the other and must have independent counsel for a post-nuptial agreement to be valid. Even then, most jurisdictions will not permit a post-nuptial agreement unless it is made to accommodate the rights of the parties in an already failing marriage. See **separation agreement.** Compare **prenuptial agreement.**

POT slang for marijuana. See **controlled substance** [CANNABIS].

POUROVER a provision in a will, or a whole will, declaring that money or other valuables are to be distributed to a previously established trust; in rare instances, a provision in a trust placing the trust assets in a will. See also **trust** [POUROVER TRUST].

POWER, CONSTITUTIONAL in a constitutional form of government, enumerated and implied power vested in a particular branch or designated authority, for example, the spending power and the taxing power under the United States Constitution. In addition, the COMMERCE POWER describes the whole range of authority granted the Congress to regulate **interstate commerce.** See **inherent powers** [INHERENT CONSTITUTIONAL POWERS]; **necessary and proper clause; privileges and immunities.**

POWER, CORPORATE a corporation's capacity or right to do certain acts or engage in certain activities, such as to sue or be sued, to enter into contracts, to borrow money, and to do such other things as are necessary to obtain its purposes. Fletcher, Cyclopedia Corporations §2475 (1979).

POWER COUPLED WITH AN INTEREST a power over property that is accompanied by or connected with an interest in the property subject to the power. 340 S.W. 2d 93, 95. Under the law of agency, when an agent has a power over property and also has a beneficial interest in that property, the principal may not revoke the agent's power until the interest has expired or unless the principal and agent have agreed otherwise. 3 Am. Jur. 2d 460 (1962).

POWER OF ACCEPTANCE the ability of an **offeree** to create a **binding contract** by consenting to the terms of an **offer.** A "power of acceptance" resides only with the persons in whom the **offeror** intends it to reside, and an offer can be accepted only by persons invited by the offeror to furnish the **consideration.** When the power of acceptance resides with many persons, the **acceptance** of the offer by one person may or may not terminate the power of acceptance of the remaining persons, depending upon the terms of the offer. The offeror controls the offer and the power of acceptance rests upon his or her manifested intent. Restatement 2d of Contracts §§52, 53. The power of acceptance is always terminated by rejection or counter-offer by the offeree, **revocation** by the offeror prior to acceptance, lapse of time, or death or incapacity of the offeror or offeree. Id. at §§35, 36.

POWER OF APPOINTMENT a power or authority given by a **donor** to a **donee** to appoint the **beneficiaries** of the donor's property, or any interest therein, which is vested in a person other than the donee of the power. 136 Cal. Rptr. 807, 809. The power may be created by **deed** or will, id., and it may be reserved by the donor for him or herself. The instrument creating the power delineates the extent to which the donee may choose the beneficiaries of the donor's property. Under a GENERAL POWER, the power may be exercised in favor of any person, including the donee. Under a SPECIAL POWER, the power may be exercised only in favor of a limited group, not including the donee or his or her estate. Present day powers of appointments are more flexible in determining beneficiaries than if a disposition irrevocably named all takers, a flexibility that allows for unforeseen future events. For example, a father's will may give his daughter the power of appointment over the principal of a trust, with the result that the daughter can allocate the principal as needed when she exercises the power. Under a more inflexible procedure whereby the father names all the beneficiaries and the amount to which they are entitled, adjustments could not be made for differing needs. If the father wants to insure that only the daughter's children are the beneficiaries, he can so provide by giving a "special power of appointment" to the daughter. The instrument creating the power usually will include a provision disposing of the property if the power is not effectively exercised. Title to the property or interest passes directly from the donor of the power to the beneficiary; the donee is merely the conduit through which title passes, 92 S.E. 2d 503. Moreover, since a power of appointment does not constitute an estate or interest, it is termed a NAKED POWER. If in the same instrument creating the power of appointment the donee is granted a present or future interest in the property over which the power is to be exercised, the donee is said to have a power coupled with an interest. 227 P. 2d 670.

I.R.C. §2041 defines a general power of appointment for tax purposes (subject to exceptions) as "a power which is exercisable in favor of the decedent, his estate, his creditors, or the creditors of his estate. . . ." If that definition is met, the value of the underlying property is includable in the value of the decedent's taxable gross estate. Therefore, special powers of appointment are generally better from a tax viewpoint.

POWER OF ATTORNEY "an instrument in writing by which one person, as principal, appoints another as his agent and confers upon him the authority to perform certain specified acts or kinds of acts on behalf of the principal. The primary purpose of a power of attorney is not to define the authority of the agent as between himself and his principal, but to evidence the authority of the agent to third parties with whom the agent deals." 248 A. 2d 446, 448. Powers of attorney may be either general, as in the authorization to sell property, or specific, as in the authorization to sell to a particular person.

POWER OF DISPOSITION see **power of appointment.**

POWER OF POLICE see **police power.**

PRACTICE refers to the rules governing all aspects of a court proceeding.

PRAECIPE *(prē'-si-pe)*—Lat: order; command. A writ commanding the defendant to do the thing required or to show reason why it has not been done. The clerk of the court is ordered by a praecipe to issue an **execution** for a **judgment creditor.** 257 U.S. 10.

PRAESENTI see **in praesenti.**

PRAYER [FOR RELIEF] request contained in **complaint** or **petition** that asks for relief to which plaintiff thinks him or herself entitled, see 256 P. 195, 196; that part of the **pleading** in which relief is requested.

In addition to whatever specific kinds of **relief** or **remedy** (e.g., money **damages, injunction**) the party may request, it is common to add a general prayer to enable the court to grant whatever relief it feels is appropriate, i.e., "and such other and further relief as to the court may seem just and proper."

PREAMBLE an introductory clause in a constitution, statute, or other legal **instrument** which states the intent of that instrument; "a prefatory statement or explanation or a finding of facts by the power making it, purporting to state the purpose, reason, or occasion for making the law to which it is prefixed." 177 P. 742, 744. Compare **purview.**

PRECATORY advisory; words of "entreaty, request, desire, wish or recommendation, employed in **wills,** as distinguished from direct and imperative terms." 264 N.W. 2d 746, 749. See **trusts** [PRECATORY TRUSTS].

PRECEDENT a previously decided case which is recognized as authority for the disposition of future cases. At **common law,** precedents were regarded as the major source of law. A precedent may involve a novel question of common law or it may involve an interpretation of a **statute.** In either event, to the extent that future cases rely upon it or distinguish it from themselves without disapproving of it, the case will serve as a precedent for future cases under the doctrine of **stare decisis.**

PRECEDENT CONDITION see **condition.**

PRECEDING ESTATE a prior estate upon which a **future interest** is limited. Thus, a **remainder** is said to **vest** upon the termination of a preceding estate, such as a **life estate.**

PRECLUSION OF ISSUE see **estoppel; issue preclusion.**

PRE-EMPTION a judicial doctrine asserting the supremacy of federal legislation over state legislation of the same subject matter; it "rests upon the **supremacy clause** of the federal constitution, and deprives a state of jurisdiction over matters embraced by a congressional act regardless of whether the state law coincides with, is complementary to, or opposes the federal congressional expression." 398 P. 2d 245, 246. When Congress legislates in an area of federal concern, it may specifically pre-empt all state legislation (thus, OCCUPYING THE FIELD), or may bar only inconsistent legislation; where Congress does not directly indicate its intention in this regard, the court will determine that intention based on the nature and legislative history of the enactment. See 312 U.S. 52; 350 U.S. 497. State legislatures may also "pre-empt" local governments in the same manner.

At common law, the term expressed the king's right to buy provisions and other necessaries for the use of his household in preference to others. In international law, it expresses the right of a nation to detain goods of a stranger in transit so as to afford its subjects a preference of purchase.

PRE-EMPTIVE RIGHTS the right specified in the **charter** of a corporation, granting to existing shareholders the first opportunity to buy a new issue of **stock.** Corporations implement such a charter provision by distributing, in advance of a new issue, subscription rights or **warrants** to existing shareholders in proportion to their current holdings. Shareholders have the choice of exercising the rights by purchasing shares of the new issue or of selling the rights in the open market. Rights usually have market value slightly below the prevailing market due to pricing of the new issue.

The purpose of pre-emptive rights is to protect the shareholder against the dilution of the shareholder's ownership interest in the corporation. Most states allow the existence of pre-emptive rights to be determined by the **articles of incorporation.** Pre-emptive rights are commonly used in **close corporations** and rarely used in widely held public corporations. Henn & Alexander, Laws of Corporations §127 (3d ed. 1983). At one time, pre-emptive rights were a popular proviso in corporate charters. The provision has been largely eliminated due to the size, diversity, and professional management of most public companies.

PREFERENCE the paying or securing by an **insolvent debtor,** to one or more of his **creditors,** the whole or a part of their claims, to the exclusion or detriment of other creditors. See 157 P. 392, 394. Under the **Bankruptcy Act** of 1978, a transfer of the debtor's property to a creditor is a "preference" if it occurs within 90 days preceding the filing of petition for bankruptcy and the transfer enables the creditor to obtain more than the creditor would receive in bankruptcy. Under certain circumstances, a transfer to an **insider** within a year preceding the filing of the petition is a preference. The **trustee** in bankruptcy may avoid a preferential transfer and recover the property, 11 U.S.C. §547.

VOIDABLE PREFERENCE a transfer of property by a bankrupt person to a creditor within four months of filing the petition in bankruptcy. Since such transfers deprive the bankrupt's other creditors from sharing in the property, the transfer is set aside and the property is brought back into the bankrupt's estate. The technical requirements of a voidable preference are: a transfer of the debtor's property to or for the benefit of the creditor; while the debtor was insolvent; within four months of filing the bankruptcy petition; on account of an exist-

ing debt; when the creditor has cause to know of the debtor's insolvency; and which allows the creditor to obtain a greater portion of the debtor's estate than the other creditors in the same class. 11 U.S.C. §547(b); Hensen, Secured Transactions §7-7 (1979).

PREFERENCE ITEMS see **tax preference items.**

PREFERRED DIVIDEND see **dividend.**

PREFERRED RIGHTS see **First Amendment.**

PREFERRED STOCK see **security** [PREFERRED STOCK].

PREGNANT, NEGATIVE see **negative pregnant.**

PREJUDICE a bias, a leaning toward one party in a lawsuit, a prejudging of a case; "an opinion or judgment formed beforehand or without due examination." 232 P. 2d 949. A fixed anticipatory judgment as contradistinguished from those opinions that may yield to evidence. 82 S.E. 777, 780. For a criminal defendant to obtain a severance from other co-defendants under Fed. R. Crim. P. 14, the prejudice required to be shown is that the movant will be unable to secure a fair trial unless severance is granted. 573 F. 2d 455, 480. In the context of **laches,** prejudice means a disadvantage in asserting and establishing a claimed right or defense, or other damage caused by a detrimental reliance on the plaintiff's conduct, 632 F. 2d 1279, 1283, barring plaintiff from prevailing. Under rules of evidence, **evidence** that is probative may still be excluded if it will cause unfair prejudice to the opposing party. See Fed. R. Evid. 403. As a ground for disqualification of a judge, prejudice is a "condition which sways the judgment and renders the judge unable to exercise his functions impartially in a particular case. It refers to the mental attitude or disposition of the judge toward a party to the litigation and not to any views he may entertain regarding the subject matter involved." 330 N.Y.S. 2d 248, 254. See **dismissal** [DISMISSAL WITHOUT PREJUDICE; DISMISSAL WITH PREJUDICE].

PREJUDICIAL ERROR see **reversible error.**

PRELIMINARY HEARING in criminal law, a hearing conducted for the purpose of determining whether or not **probable cause** for the arrest of a person existed, held prior to the issuing of an **indictment;** "the sole purpose of a preliminary hearing . . . is to determine whether there is sufficient evidence to warrant the defendant's (continued) detention (and whether submission of such evidence to the grand jury is justified) . . . (T)he filing of the indictment conclusively establishes probable cause for such detention, thereby eliminating the necessity for a preliminary hearing." 42 F.R.D. 421, 423. In a jurisdiction .that does not use indictments but relies instead upon a prosecutor's **information,** there must be a prompt judicial determination of probable cause to justify any extended restraint on liberty. This is true whenever the arrest was without a **warrant** and where no similar probable cause determination has been made by the **grand jury** through the issuance of an indictment. 420 U.S. 103. The judicial determination required may be **ex parte** although more typically the preliminary hearing format is utilized with limited defense participation. Id. Compare **arraignment.** See also **fair hearing.**

PRELIMINARY INJUNCTION see **injunction, temporary restraining order.**

PREMEDITATION forethought; the giving of consideration to a matter beforehand "for some length of time, however short." 56 S.E. 2d 678, 681. As one of the **elements** of first-degree murder, the term is often equated with **intent** and "deliberateness," though it is said that premeditation should require more substantial contemplation and should be confined to instances of "real and substantial reflection." Perkins & Boyce, Criminal Law 132 (3rd ed. 1982). See also **mens rea.**

PREMISE in logic, the propositions upon which a conclusion is based.

PREMISES land and its **appurtenances,** see 98 So. 444; land or a portion thereof and the buildings and structures thereon. See 131 S.E. 11. The term is an elastic one whose meaning depends on the context in which it is used. See 97 So. 2d 828. It is generally said to include a tract of land in the context of conveyancing, or to signify the right, title, or interest conveyed. See 71 N.E. 22. For purposes of insurance on a building, or in defining the crime of **burglary,** the scope of the term may be restricted so as to embrace only a building. See 287 S.W. 2d 714. The range of the term may be very unclear with respect to **search warrants.** See 1 R.I. 464. With respect to the **Workers' Compensation Acts,** "premises" may include any place where the employee may go in the course of his employment. See 270 So. 2d 104.

In drafting legal documents, such as contracts, the word is often used to refer to the introductory language of the documents that sets forth the reason why the document is being executed.

PREMIUM the sum paid to an insurer as **consideration** for a policy of **insurance.** 275 So. 2d 680, 682. A premium may also be money paid by a buyer for an **option** to buy or sell corporate **stock.** 200 F. Supp. 193, 195. The term has also been used to denote a reward for an act done. 136 P. 2d 617, 619. See **bond** [BOND PREMIUM].

PRENUPTIAL AGREEMENT an agreement entered into by two people who intend to marry each other which sets forth the rights of each person in the property of the other in the event of divorce or death. Generally, the entering into marriage constitutes sufficient consideration to make a prenuptial agreement enforceable. Such an agreement is also termed an ANTENUPTIAL AGREEMENT.

PREPONDERANCE OF THE EVIDENCE general standard of **proof** in civil cases. "Evidence preponderates where it is more convincing to the trier [of fact] than the opposing evidence." McCormick, Evidence 793 (2d ed. 1972). It thus refers to proof which leads the **trier of fact** to find that the existence of the fact in issue is more probable than not. Compare **reasonable doubt; clear and convincing.**

PREROGATIVE WRIT writs formerly issued by the king. Today, a class of writs issued by courts in furtherance of their discretionary powers. They are not granted as a matter of right. See 12 P. 879, 884. The prerogative writs are the writ of **procedendo,** the writ of **mandamus,** the writ of **prohibition,** the writ of **quo warranto,** the writ of **habeas corpus,** and the writ of **certiorari.** Compare **peremptory writ.**

PRESCRIPTION a means of acquiring an **easement** in or on the land of another by continued regular use over a statutory period. See 81 A. 2d 137. Requisite elements are similar to those of **adverse possession,** except that acquisition by prescription does not require **hostile possession** or use and therefore, an easement can be acquired through permissive use (i.e., without an assertion of right). Adverse possession may eventually give one absolute title, but prescription only provides one with an easement.

PRESCRIPTIVE EASEMENT see **easement.**

PRESENT DANGER see **clear and present danger.**

PRE-SENTENCE REPORT material prepared by a probation department to assist the trial court in **sentencing** a criminal defendant after he has been convicted. 533 F. 2d 1110, 1111. Pre-sentence reports usually include prior convictions, prior arrests, employment history, education history, and family and social background.

PRESENTMENT in criminal law, "a written accusation of crime made and returned by the **grand jury** upon its own initiative in the exercise of its lawful inquisitorial powers." 487 S.W. 2d 672, 675. In formal terms a "presentment" is the result of the grand jury's "investigation on its own without the consent or participation of a prosecutor." 370 F. Supp. 1219, 1222. "A presentment is in the form of a bill of **indictment** and . . . is [usually] signed individually by all the grand jurors who return it, whereas only the Grand Jury Foreman signs an indictment." 487 S.W. 2d 672, 675.

In commercial law, presentment is the production of a **negotiable instrument** such as a **promissory note** to the party on whom it is drawn for his acceptance, or to the person bound to pay for payment. Where the instrument has been **executed** and the parties bound thereby, presentment means presentment for payment, as distinguished from presentment for acceptance which must be made before the instrument is due. 141 S.E. 394, 395. See U.C.C. §3-504.

PRESIDENTIAL PROCLAMATION see **proclamation** [PRESIDENTIAL PROCLAMATION].

PRESUMPTION a rule of law which requires the assumption of a fact from another fact or set of facts. The term "presumption" indicates that certain weight is accorded by law to a given evidentiary fact, which weight is heavy enough to require the production of further evidence to overcome the assumption thereby established. It thus constitutes a rule of evidence which has the effect of shifting either the **burden of proof** or the burden of producing evidence. Compare **inference.**

CONCLUSIVE [NON-REBUTTABLE] PRESUMPTION one which no evidence, however strong, no argument, or consideration, will be permitted to overcome. See 2 S.E. 2d 343, 348. Since a presumption always properly refers to a rebuttal assumption of a fact, when the term presumption is used in this conclusive sense, it is not a true presumption but is merely a statement by the court of a rule of law. See McCormick, Evidence 804 (2d ed. 1972).

NON-REBUTTABLE PRESUMPTION see CONCLUSIVE [NON-REBUTTABLE] PRESUMPTION above.

REBUTTABLE PRESUMPTION an ordinary presumption which must, as a matter of law, be made once certain facts have been proved, and which is thus said to establish a **prima facie** conclusion; it may be rebutted or overcome through the introduction of contrary evidence, but if it is not, it becomes conclusive. See 145 A. 2d 289, 293; 114 P. 975, 976. After rebutting evidence is introduced, under prevailing doctrine the competing facts are weighed on their own merits, without further reference to the presumption. See McCormick, Evidence 821 (2d ed. 1972).

PRESUMPTION OF INNOCENCE
in criminal law, the principle that a person is innocent of a crime until he is proven guilty. Its primary manifestation is the constitutional requirement that the prosecution establish the defendant's guilt by proof beyond a **reasonable doubt.** 397 U.S. 358. The presumption of innocence thus refers to a burden of proof, and not a determination by the justice system that the accused is innocent. To the contrary, the accused would not be on trial unless the justice system had made some determination that the accused may have committed a crime. Thus the grand jury's indictment was based on a finding of **probable cause.** While not mentioned in the Constitution, the presumption of innocence has been recognized as part of our jurisprudence from time immemorial. 156 U.S. 432, 454. Recently it has been used as the basis for a defendant's right to appear in court in his everyday clothes rather than prison clothes. 425 U.S. 501.

PRESUMPTIVE EVIDENCE evidence that is indirect or **circumstantial; prima facie** evidence or evidence that is not conclusive and that may be contradicted; evidence that must be received and treated as true and sufficient until and unless rebutted by other evidence, i.e., evidence that a statute deems to be presumptive of another fact unless rebutted. See 166 S.W. 2d 828. See **presumption.**

PRETERMITTED HEIR an **heir** who was born after a **decedent executed** his **will,** but before he died. Because the heir was not alive when the testator executed his will, the pretermitted heir is not mentioned in and may not take under the will. However, most states have statutes that allow a child of the decedent who was born after the will was executed but before the time of death to take a share of the decedent's estate equal to the share the child would have received if the decedent had died **intestate.** A child who may so take a share of the decedent's estate is called a pretermitted heir. 2 Page on Wills §21.105 (1960).

PRE-TRIAL CONFERENCE in civil procedure, a conference held after the pleadings have been filed and before the trial begins, for the purpose of bringing the parties together to outline **discovery** proceedings and define the issues to be tried. Courts often use the pre-trial conference as an opportunity to encourage settlement. James & Hazard, Civil Procedure §6.16 (2d ed. 1977).

In criminal procedure, a "pretrial conference" is also used to review evidentiary issues prior to trial, but because of the privilege against **self-incrimination** and the **presumption of innocence,** it is not as comprehensive or useful to the parties as in civil cases. Fed. R. Crim. Proc. 17.1.

PRE-TRIAL DETAINEE see **detention** [PRE-TRIAL DETAINEE].

PRE-TRIAL DETENTION see **detention** [PRE-TRIAL DETENTION].

PRE-TRIAL DISCOVERY see **discovery.**

PRE-TRIAL INTERVENTION [PTI] a remedial program by which first-time or petty criminal offenders are not subjected to the regular judicial process, but rather are immediately placed under probationary supervision for a period usually no longer than one year. The program allows persons accused of crime to avoid the stigma of conviction and a permanent criminal record by correcting their criminal behavior during the period of probation. Preconviction probationary programs divert persons from the ordinary criminal process without an admission of guilt or a conviction, and, for this reason, are called DIVERSIONARY PROGRAMS. Compare **parole; probation.**

PREVAILING PARTY the party in a lawsuit who has successfully obtained a judgment in his or her own favor. 42 U.S.C. §1988 allows for the awarding of attorney's fees to the prevailing party, other than the United States, in proceedings in vindication of civil rights. Courts have broadened the interpretation

of "prevailing party" in such a context to include preliminary relief or relief obtained as the result of a consent decree, 604 F. 2d 352, or settlement, 676 F. 2d 92, and the party need only prevail on the merits of some of the claims, 664 F. 2d 639. The plaintiff's lawsuit must be found to be causally linked to the achievement of relief of pain, and the defendant must not have acted gratuitously in response to a frivolous or legally insignificant claim. 683 F. 2d 1068.

PREVARICATION deceitful, dishonest, or unfaithful conduct.

PREVENTIVE DETENTION pretrial confinement imposed upon a criminal defendant under the terms of a statute authorizing the denial of **bail** to certain defendants charged with particular offenses. A hearing is required at which the court must determine that the defendant is likely to be found guilty of an enumerated serious offense and that he poses an immediate danger to the public if released on bail. The constitutionality of preventive detention has been upheld by one court but has yet to receive review by the United States Supreme Court. 322 A. 2d 579. Only a small number of jurisdictions have such statutes. In many instances, however, the same result is accomplished **de facto** by a magistrate setting bail beyond a defendant's reach. See **detention.**

PRICE DISCRIMINATION the practice of charging different persons different prices for the same goods or services. When price discrimination is engaged in for the purpose of lessening competition, for instance, through tying the lower prices to the purchase of other goods or services, it constitutes a violation of the **Sherman Antitrust Act.** 15 U.S.C. §2. Unlawful price discrimination is also specifically covered by the **Clayton Act,** 15 U.S.C. §13, and by the **Robinson-Patman Act,** 15 U.S.C. §§13-13b, 21a.

PRICE FIXING under the federal **antitrust laws,** "a combination or **conspiracy** formed for the purpose and with the effect of raising, depressing, fixing, pegging, or stabilizing the price of a commodity in interstate commerce. The test is not what the actual effect is on prices, but whether such agreements interfere with the freedom of traders and thereby restrain their ability to sell in accordance with their own judgment." 235 F. Supp. 705, 720.

HORIZONTAL PRICE FIXING price fixing engaged in by those in competition with each other at the same level, such as retailers. 133 N.Y.S. 2d 908, 924.

VERTICAL PRICE FIXING price fixing engaged in by members of different levels of production, such as manufacturer and retailer.

PRIEST-PENITENT PRIVILEGE communications made by a person to a priest, rabbi, or minister in the course of confession, or similar course of discipline by other religious bodies, that are privileged from disclosure. The communications to clergy members must be made while clergy members are acting in the professional capacity of a spiritual adviser and with the purpose of dispensing religious counsel, advice, solace, or absolution. 419 N.Y.S. 2d 426. Some states have broadened their privilege to include all forms of individual or group counseling for marital and other personal problems. See, e.g., N.J. R. Evid. 29. The definition of "clergy" is the subject of controversy, 49 A.L.R. 3d 1205, but has not been found to include nuns. 279 A. 2d 889.

PRIMAE IMPRESSIONIS *(prī'-mē im-pre-she-ō'-nis)*—Lat: first impression.

PRIMA FACIE *(prī'-mä fā'-shē-à; prē'-mà fā'-shē-à)*—Lat: at first view, on its face; not requiring fur-

ther support to establish existence, validity, credibility, etc.

PRIMA FACIE CASE a case sufficient on its face, being supported by at least the requisite minimum of **evidence,** and being free from palpable defects. State of facts that entitles a party to have the case go to the jury. See 105 N.E. 2d 454, 458. One that will usually prevail in the absence of contradictory evidence; "one in which the evidence is sufficient to support but not to compel a certain conclusion and does no more than furnish evidence to be considered and weighed but not necessarily to be accepted by the trier of the facts." 185 N.E. 2d 115, 124. Sufficient to avoid a **directed verdict** or a **motion to dismiss.** See **presumption; prima facie.**

PRIMARY DISTRIBUTION see **underwriting.**

PRIMARY LIABILITY see **liability** [PRIMARY LIABILITY].

PRIMARY OFFERING see **underwriting.**

PRIMOGENITURE *(prē-mō-jĕn'-ĭ-tûr)*—Lat: first born. Ancient common law of **descent** in which the eldest son takes all property of his deceased father. The opposite of primogeniture, BOROUGH ENGLISH, existed under local custom in at least one jurisdiction even while primogeniture prevailed elsewhere in England. Under Borough English, the youngest son inherited on the death of the father. Under the local custom of GAVELKIND, all sons took equally. In the event all **issue** of the **decedent** were daughters, they took equal shares in **coparceny.** See generally, 2 Pollack & Maitland, History of English Law 261-266 (2d ed. 1903).

PRINCIPAL most important; manifest ranking. In the criminal law, one who commits an offense or an accomplice who is present actually or constructively during the commission of the offense. "A principal is any person concerned in the commission of a criminal offense, regardless of whether he profits from such involvement." 111 P. 1096. A PRINCIPAL IN THE FIRST DEGREE is "one who with the requisite mental state, engages in the act or omission concurring with the mental state which causes the criminal result." LaFave & Scott, Criminal Law 496 (1972). A PRINCIPAL IN THE SECOND DEGREE is one who is actually or constructively present at the commission of a criminal offense and who aids, counsels, commands, or encourages the principal in the first degree in the commission of that offense. See id. at 497. The Model Penal Code has not retained the distinction between a principal in the first degree and the second degree.

In commercial law, the principal is the amount which is received, in the case of a loan, or the amount from which flows the interest. See 154 A. 315, 316.

In the law of agency, a principal is "one who has permitted or directed another to act for his benefit and subject to his direction or control." Seavey, Law of Agency §3 (1964). Master is a species of principal. Id. "In a transaction conducted by an **agent,** the principal is DISCLOSED if the other party has notice of his identity; he is PARTIALLY DISCLOSED if the other party has notice of his existence but not his identity; he is UNDISCLOSED if the other party has no notice that the agent is acting for a principal." Id. at §4.

PRIOR INCONSISTENT STATEMENT in evidence, a **witness's** out-of-court statement that contradicts his or her testimony in court; a prior inconsistent statement may constitute **hearsay,** since the evidence of the prior inconsistent statement may be based only on the witness's out-of-court statement rather than the evidence about which he or she testified. Regardless of its character as hearsay, a prior inconsistent statement is nonetheless admissible in evidence for purposes of **impeaching** the witness. McCormick, Evidence §34 (1972). **Extrinsic** evidence of a prior inconsistent statement is not admissible unless the witness is first given the opportunity to explain or deny the same, and the opposite party is given an opportunity for interrogation thereon, or the interests of justice otherwise require. Fed. R. Evid. 613(b). Compare **admission by a party-opponent; declaration against interest.**

PRIORITY preference; the condition of coming before, or of coming first; e.g., in a **bankruptcy** proceeding, the right to be paid before other **creditors** out of the assets of the bankrupt party. The term is also used to signify such a right in connection with a **prior lien,** prior **mortgage,** etc.

PRIOR LIEN a first or superior **lien,** though not necessarily one antecedent to others. 231 F. 205, 210.

PRIOR RESTRAINT any prohibition on the publication or communication of information prior to such publication or communication. Under the **First Amendment** guarantees of the right to free speech and press, prior restraints are subject to strict scrutiny and bear a heavy presumption against constitutional validity. 372 U.S. 58, 70. While prior restraints are theoretically permissible when a publication presents a **clear and present danger** or constitutes **obscenity,** they are in fact rarely upheld. 403 U.S. 713; 427 U.S. 539, 558; Tribe, Constitutional Law §12-31 (1978).

PRISON see **jail, penal institution.**

PRISONER generally, anyone who is held against his or her will. Specifically, one who has been committed to a prison, **jail,** or **penal institution** for the purpose of detention until he or she may be tried for a crime of which he or she is accused, or for the purpose of punishment after conviction of such crime. See **detention; sentence.** Compare **inmate.**

PRIVACY, INVASION OF see **invasion of privacy.**

PRIVACY, RIGHT OF a general right to be left alone, 389 U.S. 347; a right to "live life free from unwarranted publicity," 127 So. 2d 715, 717. A "generic term encompassing various rights recognized . . . to be 'inherent in the concept of ordered liberty,' . . . including protection from governmental interference . . . to intimate personal relationships or activities, freedoms of the individual to make fundamental choices involving himself, his family, and his relationships with others." 540 S.W. 2d 668, 679. The right is not absolute and so does not apply to private conduct harmful to individual participants or to society. 553 F. Supp. 1121.

Although the federal Constitution does not explicitly provide for this right, "zones of privacy have been created by specific Constitutional guarantees and impose limits upon governmental power." 424 U.S. 693, 712. These "zones" have been implied from the general thrust of the **Bill of Rights,** 381 U.S. 479, and specifically the **First,** Third, **Fourth, Fifth,** and **Ninth Amendments,** to cover a broad spectrum of areas, including the right to have an abortion, 410 U.S. 113, to counsel married persons concerning birth control, 381 U.S. 479, to view **obscene** materials in the home, 413 U.S. 49, and to keep certain types of information private, 440 U.S. 301, 318. The right may not exist where there is some other compelling state interest, such as curbing the use of illegal drugs, 429 U.S. 589. See Warren & Brandeis, The Right to Privacy, 4 Harv. L. Rev. 193 (1890).

Invasions of one's privacy constitute a tort for which remedies are available. The four different types of torts are: (1) appropriation, or the use of a person's name, picture, or likeness as a symbol of his or her identity without compensation; (2) an intrusion upon a person's physical solitude or seclusion; (3) the public disclosure of private facts; and (4) placing a person in a false light in the public eye by associating this person with beliefs or activities with which this person has no connection. Prosser, Torts §117 (4th ed 1971).

PRIVATE CORPORATION see **corporation.**

PRIVATE DWELLING see **dwelling house.**

PRIVATE FOUNDATIONS see **charity** [PRIVATE FOUNDATIONS].

PRIVATE NECESSITY see **justification.**

PRIVATE NUISANCE see **nuisance.**

PRIVATE OFFERING [PLACEMENT] generally, any sale of securities in a corporation not subject to registration requirements under the Securities Act of 1933. Transactions by an issuer not involving any public offering are exempt. 15 U.S.C. §77d(2). These include placements with large institutional investors such as insurance companies and pension funds, securities issued to key employees of a company, and securities issued to acquire the stock of a closely held corporation. The Securities and Exchange Commission has general authority to issue regulations concerning exempt transactions and is specifically authorized to issue regulations exempting offerings if the aggregate amount of the securities to be sold does not exceed $5,000,000. 15 U.S.C. §§77c(6) and 77s. The SEC issued REGULATION D in 1982, under which offerings of various amounts of securities are exempt from registration if they meet specific requirements, the most important of which is that the purchasers of the securities be ACCREDITED

INVESTORS, that is, an institutional investor such as a bank, an insurance company, a pension fund, or a charitable foundation with assets of at least $5 million; a director or officer of the issuer; an individual with a minimum net worth of $1 million or a minimum annual income of $200,000; or an individual who purchases at least $150,000 of the securities offered, provided that the purchase does not exceed 20 percent of his net worth. Rule 501. If the securities issued total less than $5 million, then up to 35 of the purchasers do not have to be accredited investors. Rule 505.

PRIVATE PLACEMENT see **private offering [placement]**.

PRIVATE RULING see **revenue ruling** [PRIVATE RULING].

PRIVILEGE an advantage not enjoyed by all; "a particular or peculiar benefit enjoyed by a person, company, or class beyond the common advantages of other citizens; an exceptional or extraordinary exemption; or an immunity held beyond the course of the law. And, again, it is defined to be an exemption from some burden or attendance, with which certain persons are indulged, from a supposition of the law that their public duties or services, or the offices in which they are engaged, are such as require all their time and care, and that therefore, without this indulgence, those duties could not be performed to that advantage which the public good demands." 55 S.E. 820, 823. See **executive privilege; informer's privilege; rape crisis counselor privilege.**

PRIVILEGE AGAINST SELF-INCRIMINATION see **self-incrimination, privilege against.**

PRIVILEGED COMMUNICATIONS communications which occur in a context of legal or other recognized professional confidentiality. The fact that certain communication is termed privileged allows the speakers to resist legal pressure to disclose its contents. See McCormick, Evidence §72 (2d ed. 1972). When communications are termed privileged, a **breach** of the concurrent confidentiality can result in a **civil suit** in **tort.** There are several forms of privileged communications, including: (1) communications in the sanctity of the marital relationship; (2) communications between a physician and patient; (3) communications between psychological counselors and their clients; (4) priest-and-penitent communications; (5) communications between an attorney and client; and (6) in some jurisdictions, communications between journalists and their sources. See N.J. R. Evid. 26-29. Notably absent, however, are a teacher-student privilege, 279 A. 2d 889, and a parent-child privilege, 326 F. Supp. 400, 406. The evidentiary privileges recognized in a federal court will depend upon federal common law or state rules of privilege since there are no specific evidentiary privileges embodied in the federal rules of evidence. Fed. R. Evid. 501. See generally McCormick, supra, §§78-113. The usual effect of the legal determination of privileged communication is that the participants cannot be forced under legal compulsion to state the substance of the communication. Furthermore, one of the participants can enjoin the other from disclosing. See **attorney-client privilege; journalist's privilege; marital communications privileges; physician-patient privilege** (including psychotherapist-patient privilege); **priest-penitent privilege.** See also **informer's privilege; rape crisis counselor privilege; self-incrimination, privilege against.**

PRIVILEGE FROM ARREST the right of certain persons, granted by either a constitution, statute, or public policy, against being arrested while engaging in certain activities. For instance, the U.S. Constitution, Art. I, Sec. 6, Cl. 1, grants

Senators and Representatives the privilege from arrest during their attendance at the session of their respective houses, and in going to or returning from the same.

PRIVILEGES AND IMMUNITIES the phrase used in the **Fourteenth Amendment** to the Constitution to describe the rights that citizens of the United States have by virtue of their citizenship. These rights derive from the establishment and existence of the federal government and thus were assumed to exist prior to the enactment of the Fourteenth Amendment. That provision makes it clear that the federal government may protect such rights from state as well as individual denials. Privileges and immunities include the right to travel, 73 U.S. (6 Wall.) 35; the right to vote in federal elections, 313 U.S. 299; the right to assemble to petition federal officers and to discuss national legislation, 92 U.S. 542; and any other personal right arising out of federal statutes, 83 U.S. (16 Wall.) 36; 112 U.S. 76. Such rights are to be distinguished from those that exist regardless of the federal government, such as the right to assembly or of jury trial. 92 U.S. 542; 92 U.S. 90; 176 U.S. 581. See generally, Antieau, Modern Constitutional Law §§9:8, 9:9 (1969).

PRIVITY a relationship between parties out of which there arises some mutuality of interest. 443 P. 2d 39, 43.

In the law of judgments, the doctrine of **res judicata** is said to apply not only to one who was a party to the **litigation,** but also to those "in privity" with him, since their mutual or subsequently acquired interests can be considered so related to the interest of the actual party litigant that it is proper to hold them bound by the judgment as well. 200 N.W. 2d 45, 47. Privity in this context is said to exist, and to invoke res judicata, especially where a party has, subsequent to the rendition of the judgment, acquired an inter-

est in the subject matter affected by the judgment, 289 N.E. 2d 788, 793, or where one not a named party to an action controls it, or where one has his interest protected by a party to an action (e.g., in **class actions**). Green, Basic Civil Procedure 241 (2d ed. 1979).

HORIZONTAL PRIVITY the privity of estate that exists between the covenantor and covenantee. Horizontal privity is satisfied anytime an estate is conveyed from one party to another, provided that the covenant is made at the time of the conveyance (and is contemporaneous with the transfer).

PRIVITY OF CONTRACT "the relationship that exists between two or more contracting parties. It is essential to the maintenance of an **action** on any contract that there should subsist a privity between the plaintiff and defendant in respect to the matter sued on." 47 A. 929, 935. This requirement has been abrogated in the area of **products liability.** See U.C.C. §2-318; Prosser, Torts §§96, 100 (4th ed. 1971).

PRIVITY OF ESTATE denotes mutual or successive relation to the same right in property. "A privy in estate is one who derives from another **title** to property, by contract (grant, **will,** or other voluntary transfer of possession), or law (**descent,** judgment, etc.)." 60 S.E. 404, 405.

VERTICAL PRIVITY the privity of estate that exists between the covenantor and his successor in interest who acquires the property subject to the covenant. In most states, both vertical and horizontal privity must be present before a covenant can **run with the land at law,** although some states relax the horizontal privity requirement and only demand vertical privity.

PRIVY persons connected with

one another, or having mutual interests in the same action or thing, by some relation other than that of actual **contract** between them. 274 N.Y.S. 875. See **privity.**

PROBABLE CAUSE a requisite element of a valid **search and seizure** or **arrest,** consisting of the existence of facts and circumstances within one's knowledge and of which one has reasonably trustworthy information, sufficient in themselves to warrant a person of reasonable caution to believe that a crime has been committed [in the context of an arrest] or that property subject to seizure is at a designated location [in the context of a **search and seizure**]. See 267 U.S. 132. The issue of whether probable cause to search exists must be determined on the basis of the independent judgment of a "detached magistrate"; it must be based on **affidavits,** in support of a request for a search warrant; or if the police officer conducts a warrantless search, the issue of probable cause may be later determined by a judge at a hearing if a **motion** is filed to suppress the **evidence** as illegally obtained.

Probable cause can be established in many ways. It may be established on the basis of the cumulative knowledge of the investigating officers. See 380 U.S. 102, 111. However, probable cause cannot be based on facts which are completely innocent in themselves. See 393 U.S. 410. Furthermore, the fact that the suspect has been previously involved in similar crimes is not of important value. See 393 U.S. 410. Probable cause must be based on particular facts in the affidavit and not by mere conclusions. See 378 U.S. 108. Particularly difficult problems in determining probable cause arise when an informer's tip standing alone does not create probable cause. It must be corroborated by the informer's reliability or by the cumulative effect of other information and observations made by the police. See 393 U.S. 410. A **"totality of circumstances"** test is applied. An affidavit must provide the magistrate with a "substantial basis" for determining the existence of probable cause for the issuance of a search warrant. 103 S. Ct. 2317. Probable cause is required at the time of the arrest or search, see 287 U.S. 206, and may not be created by the fruits of the search or arrest.

PROBATE the act of proving that an **instrument** purporting to be a **will** was signed and otherwise executed in accordance with legal requirements, and of determining its validity thereby, see 301 S.W. 2d 310; also, the combined result of all the procedural acts necessary to establish the validity of a will. See 22 N.E. 2d 679. In some jurisdictions a PROBATE COURT is a special court having jurisdiction of proceedings incident to the settlement of a decedent's **estate.** See 169 N.E. 2d 591. Some states give probate courts jurisdiction over the estates of juveniles and those persons determined unable to take proper care of their property or themselves. In such situations the court may appoint a **committee, conservator,** or **guardian.** See **surrogate.** See also **homestead** [PROBATE HOMESTEAD].

PROBATION a procedure whereby a **defendant** found guilty of a crime is released by the court without imprisonment, subject to conditions imposed by the court, under the supervision of a probation officer. A VIOLATION OF PROBATION can lead to REVOCATION OF PROBATION and the imposition of a custodial [prison] sentence. One of the conditions permitted in some jurisdictions as a condition of probation is a short period of incarceration. This is called a SPLIT SENTENCE since part of it is served in a jail and the balance on probation [see **sentence**]. Under the federal statute no more than six months imprisonment may be imposed as a condition of probation. 18 U.S.C. §3651.

Probation is part of the sentencing process and the defendant is entitled to be represented by counsel under the **Sixth Amendment.** 389 U.S. 128. Compare **parole** which, unlike probation, is not part of the sentencing process, but is the supervised release from confinement of a prisoner who is permitted to serve part of a custodial sentence in the community and who is subject to REVOCATION OF PAROLE by the parole board should he violate the terms and conditions of his release. The revocation of parole or probation is not part of the sentencing process, but the defendant is nevertheless entitled to procedural **due process** safeguards, including a **hearing** with **notice** and an opportunity to be heard. The defendant is not entitled to appointed counsel [at state expense] unless the issues are complex or fundamental fairness otherwise requires that he have the aid of counsel to be dealt with justly. 408 U.S. 471; 411 U.S. 778.

PROBATIVE tending to prove a particular proposition or to persuade one as to the truth of an allegation.

PROBATIVE FACTS matters of evidence required to prove ultimate facts; "facts from which the ultimate and decisive facts may be inferred . . . are probative." 21 S.E. 2d 873.

PROBATIVE VALUE the relative weight of particular evidence. For example, if a trial involves the question of whether the defendant was driving at an excessive rate of speed through a school zone, evidence tending to prove that he was going 50 miles an hour less than a block from the school zone would be of very high probative value; evidence that he was going 50 miles an hour two blocks away (without

an intervening stop sign) would have less but still high probative value; evidence that he was going 50 miles an hour six blocks away in a residential zone would have even less but still some probative value; evidence that he was speeding several miles away or that he ran a traffic signal the previous day would have very little probative value. Whatever value the traffic violation the previous day may have would be outweighed by its prejudicial impact upon the jury and it would likely be excluded. See **admissible evidence.**

PRO BONO PUBLICO *(prō bō'-nō pūb'-lē-kō)*—Lat: for the public good or welfare. When attorneys take on cases without compensation to advance a social cause, they are said to be representing the party "pro bono publico" or "pro bono."

PROCEDENDO *(prō-sā-děn'-dō)* —Lat: duty to have proceeded. Refers to a **writ** issued by a superior court when a cause has been improperly removed to it, as by **certiorari,** commanding the inferior court from which it was removed to assume **jurisdiction** and proceed to judgment on the cause. It is more frequently called a **remand.**

PROCEDURAL DUE PROCESS see **due process of law.**

PROCEDURE legal method; the machinery for carrying on the **suit,** including pleading, process, evidence and practice. The term thus refers to the mechanics of the legal process—i.e., the body of rules and practice by which justice is meted out by the legal system—rather than the substance and content of the law itself. See **substantive law.**

CIVIL PROCEDURE the body of rules of **practice** to be adhered to in adjudicating a controversy before a court of civil, as opposed to criminal, **jurisdiction.** The term refers to matters of form rather than to the principles of **substantive law** that must be applied to determine the rights of the parties.

Procedural rules govern the decisional forms whereby substantive rights may be maintained or redressed when they have been violated, or when their violation has been threatened. Generally, procedural rules concern the incidents of **adjudication** or one of its institutional equivalents such as **arbitration** or the **administrative** process.

The law of procedure is both a means of augmenting other inducements to individuals for conducting their relations in conformity with the substantive law's prescriptions, and a model of dispute resolution technique. James and Hazard, Civil Procedure, Introduction (2d ed. 1977).

CRIMINAL PROCEDURE the process by which the government imposes **sanctions** for **crimes,** from the investigation of the crime, through the **arrest** and **trial** of the person accused of committing the crime, to the **punishment** of the convicted criminal. The primary sources of criminal procedure are: **statutes** governing police activities, court procedures and sentencing matters; and **court rules** such as the Federal Rules of Criminal Procedure. Constitutional limitations on criminal procedure to protect the rights of defendants are found in state and federal guarantees such as the ban on unreasonable **searches and seizures,** and the privilege against **self-incrimination.**

PROCEEDING the succession of events constituting the process by which judicial action is invoked and utilized, 80 A. 2d 100, 102; the form in which actions are to be brought and defended, the manner of intervening in suits and of conducting them, the mode of deciding them, opposing them, and of executing judgments. 37 F. 470, 488. It is thus broader in meaning than the term **action.** 136 F. 2d 790, 791.

COLLATERAL PROCEEDING any proceeding not instituted for the express purpose of annulling, correcting, or modifying a **judgment.** 68 P. 757, 764. Instead, a collateral proceeding will attempt to change or affect the result of the judgment while allowing the judgment to remain intact. See **collateral estoppel.**

INFORMAL PROCEEDING see **informal proceedings.**

SUMMARY PROCEEDING see **summary proceeding.**

PROCESS "a formal writing [**writ**] issued by authority of law," 38 F. Supp. 142, 143; any "means used by the court to acquire or to exercise its **jurisdiction** over a person or over specified property," 282 N.E. 2d 452, 456; usually refers to the method used to compel the attendance of a **defendant** in court in a civil suit. 283 N.E. 2d 456, 458. See **abuse of process; compulsory process; due process of law; service of process.**

PROCLAMATION a public announcement giving notice of an act done or to be done by the government. 62 Md. 244, 247. A PRESIDENTIAL PROCLAMATION is the President's official, public announcement of an **executive order** or act. 156 U.S. 548.

PROCTOR one who manages another's affairs, acting as that person's **agent;** an attorney who is admitted to practice in a **probate, admiralty,** or **ecclesiastical court.** Compare **administrator.**

PRODUCT see **work product.**

PRODUCTION BURDEN see **burden of proof.**

PRODUCTS LIABILITY doctrine in the law of torts that holds a manufacturer, or other party involved in selling a product, **strictly liable** when an article, placed into the market with knowledge that it is to be used without inspection for defects, proves to have a defect that causes a personal injury. 377 P. 2d 897, 900. Consumers who are injured because of a fault with a product that the consumers had no ability to protect themselves against may recover against the manufacturer under a theory of products liability. Prosser, Law of Torts §96 et seq. (4th ed. 1971). See 111 N.E. 1050. Thus, one who sells any product in a defective condition unreasonably dangerous to the user or consumer or to property may be liable for physical harm caused thereby even though there is no contractual or other relationship (i.e. no **privity of contract**) between the seller and user, and even though the seller has not been negligent. Restatement 2d of Torts §402A.

One area of products liability, the manufacture of pharmaceutical drugs, has always presented questions of latent defects. Courts have tended to hold manufacturers to a high standard of care in preparing, testing, and labeling drugs, but absent evidence of any lower standard of care, they have refused to hold the manufacturer liable for the unforeseeable harm, on the theory that the utility and social value of the drug normally outweighs the known and unknown risks. Prosser, Law of Torts 661 (4th ed. 1971). See **warranty.**

PROFESSIONAL ASSOCIATION see **professional corporation [association].**

PROFESSIONAL CONDUCT see **code of professional responsibility; model rules of professional conduct.**

PROFESSIONAL CORPORATION [ASSOCIATION] a corporation formed for the purpose of engaging in one of the learned professions, such as law, medicine, or architec-

ture. Traditionally, corporations were prohibited from engaging in such professions because they lacked the human, personal qualifications necessary to pursue them. However, within recent years most states have enacted a professional corporation or association act that allows professional persons to practice in the corporate form provided that all shareholders are members of the profession. A professional corporation has at least two advantages. First, it allows a professional to join together with one or more other professionals without assuming personal liability for the acts or omissions of the others. Second, it allows the professional to enjoy certain tax advantages not available to him or her as an individual taxpayer. Fletcher, 1A Cyclopedia Corporations §§97, 112.1 (1983).

PROFESSIONAL RESPONSIBILITY see **code of professional responsibility; model rules of professional conduct.**

PROFFER to offer; a term sometimes used to describe an **offer of proof.** McCormick, Evidence §51 (n. 7) (2d ed. 1972).

PROFIT gain; the excess of an amount received over the amount paid for goods and services. 42 A. 2d 419, 422. See **capital gains or losses; earnings and profits; paper profit; realization.** See also **profit à prendre.**

PROFIT-AND-LOSS STATEMENT see **income statement.**

PROFIT À PRENDRE (*prō-fē ah prŏn-dre*)—Fr: the right to take. In **real property** law, the right to take soil, gravel, minerals, and the like from another's land. 283 S.W. 754, 759.

PRO FORMA (*prō fôr'-mà*)—Lat: for the sake of form; as a matter of form. In an appealable **decree** or **judgment,** the term usually means "that the decision was rendered, not upon intellectual conviction that the decree was right, but merely to facilitate further proceedings." 267 F. 564, 568.

In accounting, the term is used in reference to the presentation of financial statements that represent proposed events in the form in which they will appear if or when the event actually occurs. Examples include presentation of consolidated statements in connection with a proposed corporate **merger** and presentation of **balance sheet** data showing the effect of a proposed financing.

PROGRESSIVE TAX see **tax** [PROGRESSIVE TAX].

PRO HAC VICE (prō häk vē'- chā)—Lat: for this turn; for this one particular occasion; the allowance of that which under ordinary circumstances is not permitted. Usually the term is used to describe the permission granted an out-of-state lawyer to appear in a particular case with the same standing as a local attorney admitted to practice in the jurisdiction. 184 F. 2d 119, 123. Ordinarily, a local attorney admitted to the bar of the state will be "attorney of record" and officially responsible for the case. Admission of out-of-state attorneys is within the discretion of each court and the refusal to permit an attorney who is not licensed to practice in the particular jurisdiction does not violate either the client's right to counsel of his or her choice nor the attorney's right to practice his or her profession. 439 U.S. 438.

PROHIBITION see **writ of prohibition.**

PROLIXITY any unnecessary language or facts in **pleadings** or in **evidence.**

PROMISE a declaration of one's intention to do or to refrain from doing something. 119 S.E. 235, 236. It can bind the person making the declaration to the thing declared.

See **contract; covenant; promissory estoppel.**

BREACH OF PROMISE see **breach of promise.**

COLLATERAL PROMISE see **collateral promise.**

GRATUITOUS PROMISE see **gratuitous promise.**

ILLUSORY PROMISE see **illusory promise.**

PROMISSORY ESTOPPEL an **equitable** doctrine declaring that "a promise which the promisor should reasonably expect [will] induce action or forebearance on the part of the promisee or a third person and which does induce such action or forbearance is binding if injustice can be avoided only by enforcement of the promise. . . ." See Restatement 2d, Contracts §90. The promisor, having induced **reliance** on his promise by the other party, is said to be **estopped** from denying the existence of a contract, though in fact one has not been made. Thus, promissory estoppel departs from traditional contract law in that no bargain is involved. For instance, the doctrine of promissory estoppel is invoked when a pension is promised to an employee and at the fruition period, the promise is not honored.

Promissory estoppel is a recognized alternative to the requirement of **consideration** in appropriate cases. However, some jurisdictions do not accept it and demand that the traditional requirements of **consideration** be met. See also **estoppel; waiver** [EXECUTORY WAIVER].

PROMISSORY NOTE a note; a kind of **negotiable instrument** wherein the **maker** agrees (promises) to pay a sum certain at a definite time.

PROMOTER in corporate law, generally anyone who undertakes to form a corporation and to procure for it the rights, instrumentalities, and capital by which it is to carry out the purpose set forth in its charter. 379 N.E. 2d 1298. Under Securities and Exchange Commission Rule 405(g), a promoter is "any person who, acting alone or in conjunction with one or more persons, directly or indirectly takes initiative in founding or organizing the business or enterprise of an issuer [of securities]," or any person who receives 10 percent or more of any class of securities of an issuer on the proceeds therefrom in consideration for services or property. See generally, Fletcher, Cyclopedia Corporation §189 (1983).

PROOF [PROOFS] the **evidence** that tends to establish the existence of a fact in issue; the persuasion of the trier of fact by the production of evidence of the truth of a fact alleged. See also **burden of proof; degree of proof; inference; judgment proof; moral certainty; offer of proof; preponderance of evidence; presumption; reasonable doubt.**

PROOF BEYOND A REASONABLE DOUBT see **reasonable doubt.**

PROOF TO A MORAL CERTAINTY see **moral certainty.**

PROPER see **necessary and proper clause.**

PROPER LOOKOUT see **lookout** [PROPER LOOKOUT].

PROPER PARTY see **party.**

PROPERTY "every species of valuable right or interest that is subject to **ownership,** has an exchangeable value, or adds to one's wealth or **estate.**" 107 A. 2d 274, 276. "Property" describes one's exclusive right to possess, use, and dispose of a thing, 202 P. 2d 771, as well as the object, benefit, or prerogative which constitutes the subject matter of that right. 331 U.S. 1.

COMMON PROPERTY that which belongs to the citizenry as a whole, 7 P. 2d 868; property owned by tenants in common, 108 P. 2d 377, or in some jurisdictions where designated by statute, that owned by husband and wife. 3 Cal. 83. Compare **community property.**

INCORPOREAL PROPERTY see **incorporeal** [INCORPOREAL PROPERTY].

INTANGIBLE PROPERTY see **intangible property.**

PERSONAL PROPERTY see **personal property [personalty].**

PUBLIC PROPERTY see **public property.**

TANGIBLE PROPERTY see **tangible property.**

PROPERTY SETTLEMENT in matrimonial law, the division of property owned or acquired by spouses during their marriage. Since a property settlement merely allocates the property between the parties and does not satisfy the obligation of either spouse to support the other, it is not subject to judicial modification if the circumstances of either spouse later change. 438 A. 2d 295, 297; 403 P. 2d 19, 21. See **post-nuptial agreement; prenuptial agreement; separation agreement.**

PROPERTY TAX see **tax** [PROPERTY TAX].

PROPORTIONAL REPRESENTATION a system of election designed to insure that different groups will have their interests represented, something that may not necessarily occur in a majority rule scheme.

PROPRIETARY owned by a particular person. In **trade secrets** law, proprietary property is information or knowledge in which the person developing it has ownership rights. Such rights are usually protected by contract and have not been the subject of a **patent** application. In the law of municipal corporations, a proprietary function is one that a government may undertake for the benefit of its citizens. Government activities fall into two general categories: those fundamental to its nature as a government, such as passing of legislation or providing police services, and those proprietary or done for the benefit of particular citizens, such as providing a swimming pool. A government may not be held liable for the former, but it may be liable for negligence with regard to the latter. See **governmental function; sovereign immunity.**

PROPRIETARY LEASE see **lease** [PROPRIETARY LEASE].

PROPRIETOR owner; the person who holds **title** to property. See **proprietary.** See also **sole proprietorship.**

PRO RATA *(prō rā'-tà)*—Lat: according to the rate, i.e., in proportion; "according to a measure which fixes proportions. It has no meaning unless referable to some rule or standard." 39 A. 134, 135. Thus, a lease terminated by agreement before the expiration of the full term may call for the payment of rent on a pro rata basis for the expired term of the lease; an adjudicated bankrupt, after establishing **insolvency,** is relieved of liability to all listed creditors after engaging in a pro rata distribution of his assets among those creditors.

PRO SE *(prō sā)*—Lat: for himself; in one's own behalf; e.g., one appears "pro se" in a legal **action** when one represents oneself without the aid of counsel.

PROSECUTION the act of pursuing a lawsuit or criminal trial; also, the party initiating a criminal suit, i.e., the state. Where the civil **litigant,** or the state in a criminal trial, fails to move the case towards final resolution or trial as required by the court schedule, the matter may be dismissed for WANT OF PROSECUTION or for FAILURE TO PROSE-CUTE. See **malicious prosecution.**

PROSECUTOR a person who prepares and conducts the prosecution of persons accused of crime. It is usually a public official but in some instances involving minor offenses, it may be the complainant or a private attorney designated by the court to act on the complainant's behalf. In certain cases, the legislature may appoint a SPECIAL PROSE-CUTOR to conduct a limited investigation and prosecution. The state prosecutors are usually called district attorneys or county prosecutors. The federal prosecutor is known as the United States Attorney for a certain federal district.

The basic role of the public prosecutor is to seek justice and not convictions. His office is charged with the duty to see that the laws of his jurisdiction are faithfully executed and enforced. In the enforcement of the laws, the prosecutor has broad discretion in deciding whom and when to prosecute. See generally, ABA Minimum Standards Relating to the Prosecution Function and the Defense Function §§1.1-3.9 (Approved Draft 1971).

The term also refers to the person who initiates the action by "prosecuting" the case.

PROSECUTRIX term used to refer to the complaining witness in a rape case; less frequently, it refers to a female prosecutor.

PROSECUTORIAL DISCRETION see **discretion.**

PROSPECTIVE future, in the future. A law or decision that is to be applied "prospectively" is to be applied only after the date it was enacted or decided. Constitutional decisions in the area of criminal procedure are often applied prospectively only to minimize the disruptive effect on law enforcement and the administration of justice. If the new decision does not affect the integrity of the fact finding process and represents a clear break from prior **precedent,** it will be applied prospectively only. 394 U.S. 244; 422 U.S. 531; 102 S. Ct. 2579. Compare **retroactive.**

PROSPECTUS a document that discloses financial information about a corporation to potential purchasers of **securities** in that corporation and explains the plans and objectives of the business's undertakings. The Securities Act of 1933, 15 U.S.C. §77a, requires that whenever a corporation makes a public offering of its securities, it file a prospectus wih the **Securities and Exchange Commission,** and provide a copy of the prospectus to each buyer of the securities. Information required to be disclosed in the prospectus includes financial history, current financial statements, and summary of earnings of the corporation and its subsidiaries. Rappaport, SEC Accounting Practice and Procedure 1-3, 9-5 (3d ed. 1972). A prospectus must be written in a clear, unambiguous manner since any injurious misrepresentation constitutes **fraud** and the complaining party may sue for **damage** or **rescission.** 18 C.J.S. 864.

PROSTITUTION sexual activity for hire. See, e.g., N.J.S.A. §2c:34-1. A person who sells his or her body for sexual intercourse is a PROSTITUTE; a person who arranges such a sale with the customer is a PIMP or a PANDERER. 30 N.E. 920, 921. **Solicitation** sometimes refers specifically to the crime of encouraging or asking someone to engage in prostitution. A place where people regularly engage in prostitution is known variously as a HOUSE OF PROSTITUTION, a HOUSE OF ILL FAME, a BORDELLO, and a BROTHEL.

At common law, prostitution per se was not a crime, but keeping a bawdy house and wandering the streets as a prostitute were punishable as public nuisances. 4 Bl. Comm. ★167. Laws prohibiting prostitution per se were enacted by the federal government and most of the states during the late 1800s and early 1900s because of prevailing social mores and fear of venereal disease. 64 Cal. L. Rev. 1235, 1238-39. While proscribing prostitution is regarded as a valid exercise of the state's **police power,** some antisolicitation statutes have been declared unconstitutional because of **overbreadth,** vagueness, denial of **due process,** and infringement upon the privilege against **self-incrimination.** 77 A.L.R. 3rd 519. See **pander; solicitation.**

PRO TANTO (*prō tän'-tō*)—Lat: to such extent; for so much; as far as it goes; "to the extent, but only to the extent." 104 N.W. 2d 462, 466. See **in tanto.**

PROTECT [**PROTECTION**] to preserve in safety; to keep intact; to take care of and to keep safe. 72 N.Y.S. 2d 669, 672. "Protection" is any measure which attempts to preserve that which already exists. For instance, trade protection attempts to preserve domestic industry through the imposition of tariffs and custom duties on imported goods. See **tariff** [PROTECTIVE TARIFF]; see also **consumer protection.**

PROTECTIVE CUSTODY the confinement of an individual by the state in order to protect the individual from being harmed either by himself/herself or some other person. For instance, a prisoner who is the subject of attack by other prisoners will be segregated from those prisoners and placed in protective custody.

PROTECTIVE ORDER any order issued for the purpose of protecting a party from some abuse of the legal system. Under Fed. R. Civ. P. 26(c), the court may make any order that justice requires to protect a party or person from annoyance, embarrassment, oppression or undue burden or expense. The rule specifically mentions various discovery matters, including the time, place, and subject matter of discovery, and the protection of trade secrets. Under Fed. R. Crim. P. 16(d)(1), the court is specifically authorized to limit discovery in criminal cases as may be appropriate.

PRO TEMPORE [PRO TEM] *(prō těm'-pō-rā)*—Lat: for the time being.

PROTEST a formal statement that either objects to some act that has been, is being, or is about to be performed, or that demands the performance of some act not being done. For instance, a party to a contract may protest the nonperformance of the other party under the contract in order to create a record that the contract is being breached. In commercial law, a protest is a certificate of dishonor made under the hand and seal of a United States Consul or Vice Consul or a notary public or other person authorized to certify dishonor under the law of the place where the dishonor occurs. U.C.C. §3-509. In the case of an international promissory note, a protest must be obtained in order to hold a drawer or indorser liable for nonpayment of the note. White & Summers, Uniform Commercial Code 509 (2d ed. 1980). See **under protest.**

PROVISIONAL REMEDY see **remedy.**

PROVISO a condition or stipulation. Its general function is to "except something from the basic provision, to qualify or restrain its general scope, or to prevent misinterpretation." 108 F. 2d 936, 940.

PROXIMATE CAUSE see **cause.**

PROXY an individual who is the recipient of a grant of authority to act or speak for another. "A proxy is one permitted to vote in place of a **stockholder** of a **corporation,** and is presumably voicing the judgment and the will of his principal." 59 A. 778, 783. Sometimes used to identi-

fy the instrument used to grant this authority.

The ultimate control of any corporation rests in the hands of the stockholders. These stockholders exercise this power by means of voting their shares at duly constituted stockholders' meetings. Because many stockholders are unable to attend such meetings they delegate their authority to vote these shares through the issuance of proxies to individuals whom they feel will represent their interests. Such proxies are revocable until they are voted, unless there is a specific contractual agreement to the contrary. Compare **voting trust.**

Association by-laws sometimes permit voting by proxy on stated issues. The absent voting member actually casts a written vote and delivers it to the chairperson in advance of the meeting. If the absent voting member can ultimately attend or if the issues at the meeting differ from that voted upon by the written proxy, the proxy becomes ineffective. This is distinguished from the instances in which one authorizes another, the proxy, to vote on his or her behalf (with or without confidential instructions).

PRUDENT MAN RULE a flexible legal investment standard that allows a **fiduciary** to purchase **securities** that a prudent man of discretion and intelligence would choose to earn a reasonable income and to preserve the **principal.** In some states, fiduciaries who act as **trustees** for pension funds, estates, and similar funds representing a public trust or interest are restricted to buying from a so-called legal list rather than the less restrictive "prudent man" requirement.

REASONABLY PRUDENT PERSON see **reasonable man [person].**

PRURIENT INTEREST shameful and morbid interest in nudity, sex, or excretion, 230 N.E. 2d 241, 250. It is one criteria in determining whether or not something is obscene. See obscenity.

PSYCHOTHERAPIST - PATIENT PRIVILEGE see **physician-patient privilege** [PSYCHOTHERAPIST-PATIENT PRIVILEGE].

PTI see **pretrial intervention.**

PUBLICATION, SERVICE BY see **service** [SERVICE BY PUBLICATION].

PUBLIC CHARITY see **charity** [PUBLIC CHARITY].

PUBLIC CORPORATION see **corporation.**

PUBLIC DEFENDER an attorney hired by the government to defend persons who are accused of crimes and unable or unwilling to hire any other attorney. Under the **Sixth** and **Fourteenth Amendments,** every defendant in a criminal proceeding is entitled to the assistance of counsel in conducting his or her defense, e.g., 407 U.S. 25, 37, and if a defendant is too poor to hire counsel and qualifies as an **indigent,** then the government is obligated to provide counsel at no expense to the defendant. 372 U.S. 335, 344.

PUBLIC DOMAIN "comprehends all lands and waters in the possession or ownership of the United States, and including all lands owned by the several states, as distinguished from lands possessed by private individuals or corporations." 143 F. 740, 748.
"Information, the source of which is available to anyone, . . . and not subject to **copyright"** is considered to be in the "public domain." 46 F. Supp. 468, 471.

PUBLIC EASEMENT see **dedication; easement** [PUBLIC EASEMENT].

PUBLIC FIGURE in **libel** law, a person of "general fame and notoriety in the community, and pervasive involvement in the affairs of society." 418 U.S. 323, 352. Under the **First Amendment,** a public figure is required to show actual **malice** before recovering damages for libel.

PUBLIC NECESSITY see **justification.**

PUBLIC NUISANCE see **nuisance.**

PUBLIC OFFERING see **offer** [OFFERING].

PUBLIC PROPERTY that which is dedicated to the use of the public, see 84 P. 685, and/or that over which the state has dominion and control. See 173 S.W. 2d 631. Thus the term may be used either to describe the use to which the property is put, or to describe the character of its ownership. 25 Ohio St. 229. See also **public domain.**

PUBLIC SALE see **sale.**

PUBLIC SECURITIES see **securities.**

PUBLIC TRIAL see **open court.**

PUBLIC TRUST a charitable trust (see **trust**); also, the public's confidence reposed in their elected officials and expectation that these elected officials will faithfully perform the duties of public office.

PUBLIC TRUST DOCTRINE a doctrine under which the state is said to own lands lying under navigable waters and to hold such lands in trust for the benefit of the people of the state. According to this doctrine, these submerged lands may not be sold or otherwise alienated by the state except in a manner that promotes the public interest.

PUBLIC USE the public's right to use or to benefit from the use of **property** condemned by the government, which under the U.S. and state constitutions is a prerequisite to the government's exercise of its power of **eminent domain.** Some **jurisdictions** define the term broadly to mean benefit or advantage, while other **jurisdictions** define it to mean only actual use by the public. 147 S.E. 2d 131. In its broader sense, "public use" could constitute anything that contributes to the general welfare and prosperity of the whole community. Most courts agree that exercising the power of eminent domain is permissible only where a public use exists and not where a mere public interest is found. 130 S.E. 764.

PUBLIC UTILITY a company which, because of the nature of its business, has characteristics of a natural **monopoly.** For instance, an electric company will have a natural monopoly over the sale of electricity to that area, since having a single supplier of electricity for any given area is the most efficient method of producing and distributing electricity. Because no free market or competition exists for the services or goods sold by public utilities, they are subject to government regulation of the price they may charge and the means in which they may distribute their goods. 1 Priest, Principals of Public Utility Regulation Chs. 1-2 (1969).

PUBLIC UTILITY HOLDING COMPANY ACT OF 1935 see **securities acts** [PUBLIC UTILITY HOLDING COMPANY ACT OF 1935].

PUBLISH to make known to the general public; to inform one or more persons of a fact or matter that they would not otherwise have reason to know of. In the law of torts, a statement does not constitute defamation unless it is published, i.e., unless it is made known to some third party other than the party making the statement or the party defamed. Prosser, Torts §113 (1971). In the law of wills, a will is not valid unless the testator publishes it, i.e., informs the witnesses that he is signing the document as his will. In civil practice, the court may allow the service of process by publication if the parties may not otherwise be given notice of the

lawsuit. Service by publication is normally done by publishing the appropriate notice in local newspapers. See, e.g., N.J. Ct. R. 4:4-5(c).

PUFFING a statement of opinion or belief not meant as a representation of fact, 150 F. 2d 106, 109; a seller's commendatory expressions or extravagant statements, made to enhance the wares and induce others to enter into a bargain, 130 A. 509, 511. Such "dealer's talk" or salesmanship talk cannot be made the basis of a charge of **fraud** or **express warranty,** as the buyer has no right to rely on them. 12 P. 2d 75, 273 N.W. 895. The courts will usually examine the form and manner of the representation, together with any of the relevant surrounding circumstances, before concluding whether or not the buyer had a right to rely on the statement. 245 N.W. 70. The characterization of the representation as "puffing" results from a conclusion that such reliance was not justified, in view of the nature of the statements and the surrounding circumstances. Thus a statement by a seller that "this is a wonderful car" is mere puffing whereas the statement "this car has been driven less than 10,000 miles" is an express warranty. U.C.C. §2-313.

PUNISHMENT sanctions imposed on a person because that person has been found to have committed some act. Historically, punishment for various acts has included fines, prison sentences, loss of rights or privileges, banishment or deportation, physical dismemberment, and execution. Some forms of punishment, such as banishment and dismemberment, have fallen into disuse. The Constitution specifically forbids **cruel and unusual punishment.** United States Constitution Amendment VIII. This prohibition has been held to apply to torture or other treatment "beyond the limits of civilized standards." 356 U.S. 86. However, courts have generally had difficulty in defining the exactness of the constitutional limitation. See generally, Antieau, Modern Constitutional Law §5:125 (1969). See also **capital punishment; corporal punishment.**

PUNITIVE DAMAGES see **damages** (EXEMPLARY [PUNITIVE] DAMAGES).

PUR AUTRE VIE see **per autre vie.**

PURCHASE the acquisition of property by furnishing valuable **consideration.**

PURCHASE, WORDS OF see **words of purchase.**

PURCHASE-MONEY SECURITY INTEREST see **security interest.**

PURCHASER one who acquires property by giving valuable consideration for it. See **bona fide purchaser.**

PURCHASER IN DUE COURSE see **holder in due course.**

PURLOIN to steal; to commit **larceny.**

PURPOSELY deliberately or intentionally, 383 P. 2d 726, 728. As used in criminal statutes to define murder, "purposely" means intentionally, and as an act of the will, not accidentally. 249 N.E. 2d 78, 80. In the Model Penal Code it is one of the four defined mental states. Model Penal Code §2.02(1). "A person acts purposely with respect to a material element of an offense when . . . it is his conscious object to engage in conduct . . . or cause a result." Model Penal Code §2.02(2) (a).

PURSUIT OF HAPPINESS one of the "unalienable rights" of people enumerated in the Declaration of Independence, along with "life" and "liberty." "The right to pursue any lawful business or vocation, in any manner not inconsistent with the equal rights of others, which may increase their prosperity or

develop their faculties, so as to give them their highest enjoyment." 111 U.S. 746, 757. Because the right is not set forth in the Constitution, it is not enforceable by the courts. However, the right to the pursuit of happiness is often raised in arguments against government regulations, because its mention in the Declaration of Independence gives it a degree of forcefulness.

PURVIEW the enacting part or body of a statute as distinguished from other parts of it, such as the preamble. 173 N.E. 229, 231. Conduct is said to be "within the purview" of a statute when it properly comes within its scope, purpose, operation, or effect.

PUTATIVE alleged; supposed; commonly used in family law, e.g., a "putative" marriage is one which is actually void but which has been contracted in good faith by the two parties, or by one of the parties. See 136 S.W. 1145, 1148. The "putative father" in a **paternity suit** is the person alleged to have fathered the child whose parentage is at issue in the suit.

PUT OPTION see **stock option** [PUT OPTION].

PYRAMIDING the use of paper profits from an investment to finance purchases of additional investments. Pyramiding makes the buying of securities on **margin** more speculative. During the 1920s, stocks could be purchased for as little as 10 percent of their total value which, in the rising market prior to 1929, allowed speculators to pyramid small amounts of capital into very large holdings of common stocks. The speculative excesses of that period contributed to the subsequent crash in stock prices during the early 1930s. In 1934, as part of congressional legislation designed to reform the securities industry, the Federal Reserve Board was empowered to control the use of credit in stock purchase transactions. Since 1934 the required initial payment, called margin, has ranged from a low of 40 percent to a high of 100 percent. Although credit use in stock speculation remains popular, the 1920s style of pyramid investment is largely confined to real estate speculation where extensive use of credit is encouraged. Compare **margin.**

Q

QUAERE *(kwē'-rē)*—Lat: a **query.**

QUALIFIED DISCLAIMER see **disclaimer** [QUALIFIED DISCLAIMER].

QUALIFIED PENSION OR PROFIT-SHARING PLAN see **retirement plans** [QUALIFIED PENSION OR PROFIT-SHARING PLAN].

QUANTUM MERUIT *(kwän'-tŭm mĕ'-rū-ĭt)*—Lat: as much as he deserved. Historically, it was a common count in the action of **assumpsit,** allowing recovery "for services performed for another on the basis of a **contract** implied in law or an implied **promise** to pay the performer for what the services were reasonably worth." 121 N.W. 2d 744, 746. To recover under quantum meruit today, the **plaintiff** must have performed valuable services for or furnished materials to the person sought to be charged and that person must have accepted such services or goods under circumstances which gave notice that the plaintiff expected to be paid. See 459 S.W. 2d 691, 694. Quantum meruit establishes **liability** for a contract implied in law, which "arises not from the consent of the parties but from the law of natural justice and equity, and is based on the doctrine of **unjust**

enrichment." For instance, when a physician renders emergency services to an unconscious accident victim, the consent of the injured party is implied in law, so that the physician may bring an action in quantum meruit to recover the reasonable value of his services. 432 P. 2d 386, 390. See **quasi** [QUASI CONTRACT]. Compare **officious intermeddler.**

QUANTUM VALEBANT *(kwän'-tūm văl ē'bănt)*—Lat: as much as they were worth. A common law action of **assumpsit** for goods sold and delivered, founded on an implied assumpsit or promise by the defendant to pay the plaintiff as much as the goods are reasonably worth. 108 S.E. 2d 299, 303.

QUARE CLAUSUM FREGIT *(kwä'-rā klŏw'-sŭm frā'-gĭt)*—Lat: wherefore he broke the close. An early form of **trespass** designed to obtain **damages** for an unlawful entry upon another's **land.** The **form of action** was called TRESPASS QUARE CLAUSUM FREGIT, or TRESPASS QU. CL. FR. in its abbreviated form. **Breaking a close** was the **common law** expression for an unlawful entry upon land. Even without an actual fence the **action** would **plead** that the "defendant with force and arms broke and entered the close of the **plaintiff,**" 182 S.E. 156, 157, since in the eyes of the common law, every unauthorized entry upon the soil of another was a trespass.

QUASH to annul, overthrow, or vacate by judicial decision. 162 S.E. 1, 2. Oppressive and unreasonable **subpoenas** can be "quashed," as can **injunctions, orders,** etc.

QUASI *(kwā' -sī; kwä' -sē)*—Lat: as it were, so to speak; about, nearly, almost, like.

QUASI CONTRACTS those which, "unlike true **contracts,** are not based on the apparent intention of the **parties** to undertake the **performances** in question, nor are they promises. They are obligations created by law for reasons of justice." Restatement of Contracts 2d §4b. The doctrine of quasi contracts is based upon the principle that a party who has received a benefit which was desired, under circumstances rendering it inequitable for the party to retain the benefit without making compensation, must do so. 298 P. 184. See **quantum meruit; unjust enrichment.**

QUASI CORPORATION see **corporation.**

QUASI CRIMINAL refers to a **proceeding** which, though not actually a criminal **prosecution,** is sufficiently similar in terms of the sanction to be imposed (civil fine, loss of employment, loss of license, suspension from school, etc.) or the stigma to be attached that some of the special **procedural** safeguards of a criminal proceeding are warranted. For instance, a **parole** revocation is not a criminal proceeding, but it is quasi criminal in the sense that the parole board must accord substantial procedural **due process** to the parolee facing revocation. 408 U.S. 471.

QUASI IN REM "actions based on a claim for money **damages** begun by **attachment,** or **garnishment** or other **seizure** of property where the court has no **jurisdiction** over the person of the defendant but has jurisdiction over a thing belonging to the defendant or over a person who is indebted or under a duty to the defendant." James & Hazard, Civil Procedure 629 (2d ed. 1977). The constitutionality of some quasi in rem actions is questionable. 433 U.S. 186. See **jurisdiction.**

QUEEN'S BENCH see **King's [Queen's] Bench.**

QUERY question; indicates that the proposition or rule that it introduces is unsettled or open to some question. Thus, a law professor might say, "Query: whether a **pardon** can reach pre-**indictment** offenses of a public official?"

QUESTION, LEADING see **leading question.**

QUESTION, POLITICAL see **political question.**

QUESTION OF FACT disputed factual contention which is traditionally left for the jury to decide. In a **battery** case, a question of fact would be whether A touched B. The legal significance of the touching of B by A is left for the judge to decide since it amounts to a **question of law.** If no jury is present, the judge serves as the **trier of fact** and decides both questions of fact and of law.

The distinction between fact and law is often nebulous. However, the way an issue is characterized in this regard can trigger many different legal consequences. There are different standards of review for findings of fact and findings of law. The doctrine of **res judicata, collateral estoppel,** and **stare decisis** often center on this problem.

QUESTION OF LAW disputed legal contentions which are traditionally left for the judge to decide. The occurrence or non-occurrence of an event is a **question of fact;** their legal significance is a question of law.

The resolution of a question of law is paid less deference in an **appeal** than is a determination of fact. It must be noted that often the line between fact and law is impossible to objectively determine. In those situations, there may be a compound conclusion of law and fact.

QUIA EMPTORES, STATUTE OF (*quī'ă ĕmp-tō'rēz*)—Lat: an act passed by Parliament in 1290 which abolished the restraint upon alienation or transfer of land that had been imposed under the feudal system. The process of **subinfeudation** [creation of new manors by the subject of a lord] was terminated, and after that date only the king was able to infeudate. The statute's practical effect on land transactions and ownership was that after the land was sold, the seller had no further connection with it. See Cheshire, The Modern Law of Real Property 15 (11th ed. 1972). Thus subinfeudation was replaced by strict **alienation.**

QUICK alive, living.

QUICKENING the point at which a fetus first moves within the womb. 12 N.W. 2d 670, 671. The term VITALIZED [alive] applies to the fetus both before and after quickening. 181 P. 609.

QUID PRO QUO *(kwĭd prō kwō)*—Lat: what for what; something for something; in some legal contexts, synonymous with **consideration,** see 209 S.W. 2d 851; sometimes referred to simply as the QUID and always indicating that which the party receives or is promised in return for something he promises, gives, or does, e.g., a defendant's willingness to testify for the state may be the quid pro quo for the government's willingness to accept a **plea** of guilty to a lesser offense.

QUIET ENJOYMENT the right to unimpaired use and enjoyment of **property leased** or **conveyed.** As to leased premises a guarantee of quiet enjoyment is usually expressed by a COVENANT OF QUIET ENJOYMENT in a written lease, but such a covenant may be implied today from the landlord-tenant relationship when it is not so expressed. This covenant is violated if the tenant's enjoyment of the premises is substantially disturbed either by wrongful acts or omissions of the landlord or by persons claiming a superior or **paramount title** against the landlord. The covenant does not extend to interference with **possession** by a stranger, i.e., a person not claiming under the lessor or under a title paramount to the les-

sor's. 128 P. 222. The covenant may be and often is included in the **deed** conveying title to property, but in this context it does not arise by implication. If it is present in a deed, the **grantor** is obligated to protect the estate of his **grantee** against lawful claims of ownership by others. Burby, Real Property 315, (3rd ed. 1965). See **constructive eviction; covenant.**

QUIET TITLE an **equitable action** to determine all adverse claims to the property in question; a **suit** in **equity** brought to obtain a final determination as to the **title** of a specific piece of **property;** such a suit is usually the result of various individuals asserting contradictory rights to the same parcel of land. In such a situation, the court, in order to prevent a **multiplicity of suits,** will bring all interested parties together to determine the right and ultimately issue an injunction. 164 N.W. 338, 341. A "quiet title" action is distinguished from an action to REMOVE CLOUD ON TITLE. The latter is brought to determine and resolve problems of **instruments** conveying a particular piece of land, rather than to resolve the actual claims to that land.

QUI TAM *(quī tam)*—Lat: who as well. A "qui tam" action is a lawsuit under a statute, which gives to the plaintiff bringing the action a part of the penalty recovered and the balance to the state. The plaintiff describes himself as suing for the state as well as for himself. 21 N.W. 2d 287, 289.

QUITCLAIM DEED a **deed** which conveys only that right, **title,** or **interest** which the **grantor** has, or may have, and which does not require that the grantor thereby pass a **good title.** A quitclaim deed may be purchased for a small sum as protection against the possibility that the grantor has a substantial interest unknown to him. The grantor of a quitclaim deed does not represent that he or she has any interest whatever in the property for which the deed was given—merely that whatever interest is had may be **conveyed** to the grantee. Compare **warranty deed.**

QUORUM the number of members of any body who must necessarily be present in order for the body to transact business. "A quorum is such a number of officers or members of any body as is sufficient to transact business." 179 P. 2d 870, 873. Usually, but not necessarily, it requires a majority.

A quorum is required to render legitimate any actions voted on or taken by any limited membership body. While a quorum is usually a majority of either the total membership or the members present, this general principle can be altered by the body to require or permit that more or less than a majority of the body is necessary to transact business.

QUOTATION in commercial usage, a statement of the price of an item or of the market price of a security or commodity; it also refers to the price stated in response to an inquiry, see 2 Cal. Rptr. 310, 314. More generally, the word for word repetition of a statement from some authority, case, or law. See also **citation.**

QUOTIENT VERDICT see **verdict** [QUOTIENT VERDICT].

QUO WARRANTO *(kwō wär'-ràntō)*—Lat: by what right or authority; an ancient **common law writ,** issued out of **chancery** on behalf of the king against one who claimed or usurped any office, **franchise** or liberty, to inquire by what authority he asserted such a right thereto in order that its assertion might be determined. 38 N.E. 2d 2, 5. "Formerly a criminal method of **prosecution,** it has long since lost its criminal character, and is now a **civil proceeding,** expressly recognized by statute, and usually employed for **trying the title** to a corporate franchise or to a corporate or public

office." 234 S.W. 344, 347. Only the state may bring an action quo warranto.

"Quo warranto" proceedings may be brought against **corporations** where the company has abused or failed for a long time to exercise its franchise; in the case of an official it may be brought to cause him to forfeit an office for misconduct. If in these cases a quo warranto proceeding determines that a company no longer properly holds a franchise or that an officer no longer properly holds office, it will oust the wrongdoer from enjoying the franchise or office. The purpose of the writ is not to prevent an improper exercise of power lawfully possessed; its purpose is to prevent an official, corporation, or persons acting as such from usurping a power which they do not have. See 148 S.W. 2d 527, 530.

R

RACE a term commonly used in antidiscrimination statutes that refers to ancestry, as opposed to national origin. See 402 F. Supp 363, 367. For its use in a property law context, see **recording acts.**

RACKETEER INFLUENCED AND CORRUPT ORGANIZATIONS ACT [RICO] see **racketeering.**

RACKETEERING originally, an organized **conspiracy** to commit **extortion.** Today, punishable offenses created by Congress to "seek the eradication of **organized crime** by establishing new penal prohibitions and by providing enhanced sanctions and new remedies to deal with the unlawful activities of those engaged in organized crime." Pub. L. 91-452, §1, 84 Stat. 922 (1970). The federal statute is entitled "RACKETEER INFLUENCED AND

CORRUPT ORGANIZATIONS ACT [RICO]" under Title IX of the Organized Crime Control Act of 1970 (18 U.S.C. §§1961-68) and many states have adopted similar statutes, e.g., N.J.S.A. 2C:41-1.1 et seq.

There are four punishable racketeering offenses under the federal statute: (1) directly or indirectly investing income derived from a pattern of racketeering activity or through collection of an unlawful debt in any enterprise affecting trade or commerce; (2) acquiring or maintaining any interest in an enterprise through a pattern of racketeering activity or collection of an unlawful debt; (3) conducting or participating in the affairs of the enterprise through a pattern of racketeering activity or collection of an unlawful debt; or (4) conspiring to violate the racketeering provisions. 18 U.S.C. §1962. See also, N.J.S.A. 2C:41-2a to 2C:14-2d. "Pattern of racketeering activity" requires engaging in at least two incidents of racketeering conduct (specified offenses ranging from murder, kidnapping, criminal usury, and theft to forgery, alteration of motor vehicle identification numbers, and possession or use of firearms or explosives) within 10 years of each other, and where at least one of the incidents occurs after the effective date of the act. Some states also require that there be a showing that the incidents of racketeering are interrelated in some way. The term "enterprise" in the federal act includes any individual, partnership, corporation, or any union or group of individuals associated in fact though not a legal entity, and some states have expanded the meaning to include sole proprietorships, business or charitable trusts, governmental entities, and illicit as well as licit entities. A criminal **forfeiture** provision is included in the act that allows for forfeiture of "any interest in money or property acquired in violation of the act." 18 U.S.C. §1963. Some state racketeering statutes have civil forfeiture provisions as well. N.J.S.A. 2C: 41-3. Finally, the provisions of the acts are directed to be liberally construed to best effect the overall purpose. The acts are felt to be a powerful tool in assisting prosecutors in apprehending and convicting those persons involved in organized crime and are preferred to viable alternatives under traditional conspiracy or professional criminal or **habitual offender** statutes. See 571 F. 2d 880.

RADAR an electrical device used for determining the speed, direction, or range of an object. The term stands for Radio Detection and Ranging. Radar was developed during World War II and since the late 1940s, has been used by police to monitor the speed of motor vehicles. Radar is generally admissible in court as probative **evidence** that a person was driving in excess of the speed limit. However, the accuracy of a particular radar reading may be attacked on the grounds of the inadequacy of the training of the police officer operating the unit; whether the unit has been recently tested for accuracy or is properly calibrated, and whether it was operated properly on a given occasion. Furthermore, the type of radar device used may affect whether the evidence produced by it is admissible. Baily & Rothblatt, Handling Misdemeanor Cases §§730-739 (1976).

RAISED CHECK a **check** whose face amount has been increased from the amount for which the check was originally issued. That change constitutes a **material alteration** under U.C.C. §3-407(1)(c), and "discharges any party whose contract is thereby changed unless that party asserts or is precluded from asserting the defense." U.C.C. §3-407(2)(a). A **holder in due course** of the raised check may enforce it for its original amount. U.C.C. §3-407(3).

RANSOM the money or other consideration paid for the release of a

kidnapped person; to redeem from captivity by the payment of money or other consideration. Holding a person for ransom is an element of kidnapping. 18 U.S.C. §1201; Model Penal Code §212.1(a).

RAPE unlawful sexual intercourse with a female person without her consent. 18 U.S.C. §2031. At common law, it was a felony. An essential element of rape was penetration, however slight. In the absence of penetration, only the crime of attempted rape could be established. Perkins & Boyce, Criminal Law 201 (3rd ed. 1982). In many states, a valid conviction for rape required that certain material elements such as force, penetration, or identity be corroborated by evidence other than the victim's testimony. The modern trend is, however, to abandon all such requirements. Also, the former requirement of **utmost resistance** has also been abandoned. Id. at 210-212; N.J.S.A. 2C:14-5(a). See **shield laws.**

At common law, a man could not commit rape by having sex with his wife, even if he did so by force and against her will. Id. at 202. But it has been held that this exemption was unavailable where the parties were separated. 426 A. 2d 38. Also, only a male actor could be charged with the rape of a female person. The Model Penal Code incorporated both the male only defendant and the marital exemption in its recommended final draft, Model Penal Code §213.11, but several states have adopted "SEXUAL ASSAULT" statutes to replace the common law rape definition with gender-neutral provisions and to eliminate any marital exemption. See, e.g., N.J.S.A. 2C:14-2. See also **carnal knowledge.**

SEXUAL CONTACT the unlawful intentional touching of intimate parts for the purpose of degrading or humiliating the victim or sexually gratifying the actor. It is treated as **lesser-included** to the crime of rape or sexual assault in jurisdictions which have adopted the new offense.

STATUTORY RAPE the crime of having sexual intercourse with a female under an age set by statute, regardless of whether or not she consents to the act. The common law set the age of consent at 10 years and the statutes of the various states ranged from 11 to 18 years. The trend in modern statutes is to reduce the age of consent to 12 or 14 and require that the male actor be some years older than the female victim. See Perkins & Boyce, Criminal Law 198-199 (3rd ed. 1982). A mistake of fact as to the age of the female is generally not recognized as a defense to the crime of statutory rape except by a few jurisdictions. Id. at 917.

RAPE CRISIS COUNSELOR PRIVILEGE privilege against disclosure of records and notes afforded by some states to professionals who give victims of sexual assault counseling and emotional support. The privilege is usually available in both civil and criminal proceedings. The privilege is relatively novel and is presently recognized in only a small number of jurisdictions. See, e.g., N.J.S.A. 2A:84A-22.11. Where it has been adopted, its availability represents a judgment that the confidentiality of a rape victim and a rape crisis counselor is sufficiently important to justify limiting the right of the criminal defendant to confront the witnesses against him under the Sixth Amendment. See 428 A. 2d 126; Women's Rights Law Reporter vol. 8:1 (1984).

RAPE SHIELD LAWS see **shield laws.**

RATABLE taxable, 44 P. 516, 519; proportional, capable of estimation. In **bankruptcy,** a RATABLE DISTRIBUTION is a **pro rata** share of the bankrupt's **assets,** 173 U.S. 131,

161. Ratable does not mean "equal," but rather "pro rata" according to some measure fixing proportions. 171 S.W. 2d 386, 387.

RATE a stated or fixed price for some commodity or service measured by a specific unit or standard, 185 A. 2d 917, or which may be stated as a percentage of a fixed figure, such as a percentage of profits, 377 U.S. 235, 243; an amount of charge or payment with reference to some basis of calculation. 307 F. Supp. 1396, 1399.

RATE OF RETURN a return on investment, frequently used to describe the rate that a **utility**, such as an electric company or telephone company, is entitled to earn on its investment, and is determined by combining the capital structure of the utility with the proper cost of capital. 448 A. 2d 272, 286. It is expressed as a percentage of the utility's rate base. 611 S.W. 2d 908, 909.

RATE OF TAX see **tax rate.**

RATIFICATION to sanction or affirm. In the law of agency, a voluntary election to adopt an act purportedly done on one's behalf and to treat the act as originally authorized by that person, 500 P. 2d 1401; a confirmation of the acts of another regardless of whether the act was originally done with or without authority, 526 S.W. 2d 839, 846. By ratifying an act, a person is responsible for the consequences of the act. Ratification is also the process by which society approves a fundamental change in the law. Congress, by a two-thirds vote, may either propose an amendment or call a convention for proposing amendments to the Constitution. Any proposed amendments must be ratified, or approved, by either the legislature or a convention in three-fourths of the states before becoming effective. U.S. Constitution, Art. V. Antieau, Modern Constitutional Law §§12:173-12:179 (1969).

RATIO DECIDENDI *(rä'-shē-ō dā-sē-dĕn'-dē)*—Lat: the principle which the case establishes; the reason for the decision.

RATIO LEGIS *(rä'-shē-ō lāg'-ĭs)*—Lat: the underlying principle; reasoning; grounds; scheme; theory, doctrine, or science of the law. Thus, the ratio legis of a loitering statute is to allow law enforcement officers more latitude in attempting to prevent crime rather than relying solely on apprehension and sentencing as a deterrence.

RATIONAL BASIS TEST a method of constitutional analysis under the **equal protection clause** used to determine whether a challenged law bears a reasonable relationship to the attainment of some legitimate governmental objective. 431 U.S. 471, 489; the principle that the constitutionality of a statute will be upheld, if any rational basis can be conceived to support it. The standard is "relatively relaxed. . . [to reflect] the Court's awareness that the drawing of lines that create distinctions is peculiarly a legislative task and an unavoidable one." 427 U.S. 307, 314. The test is used when a general constitutional objection is raised to a law's reasonableness, and not when the violation of specific constitutional rights is alleged. If the violation of a fundamental right, such as the right to vote or the right to an abortion, or the creation of a **suspect classification** such as color, religion, national origin, or indigence, is alleged, then the law is subject to **strict scrutiny,** and may only be upheld if the government shows a compelling interest in sustaining the statute. Schwartz, Constitutional Law §§9.2-9.5 (1979).

RAVISH generally, synonymous with **rape.** Literally, to "ravish" is to seize or take by force. Traditionally, a valid **indictment** for rape required the use of the term "ravished," which implied the element of force or violence; it would thus constitute an "essential word in all indictments for rape, [importing] not only force and violence on the part of the man but resistance on the part of the woman." 6 Minn. 279, 285. Also, it "includes the meaning of the phrase 'carnally known by force and against her will.'" Id.

RE see **in re.**

REAL CHATTEL see **chattel** [REAL CHATTEL].

REAL ESTATE land, and such property permanently affixed to it, such as a building; any possible **interest** in land, except for a mere **chattel** interest one may have; "every estate, interest, and right, legal and equitable, in lands, tenements, and hereditaments." 4 S.W. 56, 59. See **fixture; real property.**

REAL ESTATE INVESTMENT TRUST [REIT] a corporation that is given special income tax treatment in order to allow individuals to invest in real estate through centralized management without being subject to corporate income taxes. REITs fall into two basic categories: companies that invest directly in real estate so as to have equity ownership of it; and companies that lend funds and take mortgages on real estate. The income of a REIT is not taxed to the corporation but rather is taxed directly to the shareholders. In order to qualify as a REIT, a corporation must: (1) be organized in the United States; (2) have at least 100 shareholders; (3) have a high percentage of its assets invested in real estate and its income derived from real estate; and (4) meet other technical requirements. I.R.C. §§856-859. Bittker, Federal Taxation of Income, Estates and Gifts §95.7.2 (1982).

REAL EVIDENCE an object relevant to facts in issue at a trial, 329 N.E. 2d 880, 885, and produced for inspection at trial rather than described by a witness. 259 S.E. 2d 510, 533. Real evidence may include any object produced for inspection at a trial, from the murder weapon to a tape recording of a telephone conversation or a photograph of where an event occurred to the exhibition of a physical injury. Real evidence is one type of **demonstrative evidence.** See generally, McCormick Evidence §§212-217 (2d ed. 1975).

REALIZATION the occurrence of an event or transaction deemed to be a sufficiently substantial change in the **taxpayer's** economic situation to warrant the imposition of an **income tax.** 348 U.S. 426. If the tax is imposed, the event gives rise to **recognition.** Thus, if a taxpayer buys an asset for $10 and sells it for $20, the sale constitutes a realization of the amount received. If the amount received in excess of the taxpayer's cost basis is subject to tax, it is considered **recognized.**

GAIN OR LOSS REALIZED the difference between the amount realized on a **sale or exchange** of an asset and the taxpayer's **basis** in such asset.

REAL PARTY IN INTEREST the person who will be entitled to the benefits of a court action if successful; one who is actually and substantially interested in the subject matter, as opposed to one who has only a nominal, formal, or technical interest in or connection with it. See 167 P. 619, 620. For example, if an insurance company pays its insured for damage done the insured's automobile under a collision insurance provision of the insured's policy and if the insurance company attempts to collect its loss from the responsible party, the suit may be brought in the name of the insured, but the "real party in interest" will be the insurance company. Some states, however, would require that the action be brought in the name of the real party in interest, e.g., the insurance company. See, e.g., Md. R. Civ. P. 203. See **nominal party.**

REAL PROPERTY land, including the surface, whatever is attached to the surface such as buildings or trees, whatever is beneath the surface, such as minerals, and the area above the surface, i.e., the sky. Burby, Real Property §§8-11 (3rd ed. 1965). See **fixture.**

Originally, the distinction between real property and **personal property** did not depend upon the nature of the property, but rather depended upon the **action** by which rights in the property were vindicated. This distinction later evolved into the definition of real property and personal property, which consists of **chattels,** or movable **goods.**

An interest in a **leasehold** is sometimes treated as real property because it concerns land or buildings, and is sometimes treated as **personalty** because of its contractual nature. See Brown, The Law of Personal Property 10-11 (3rd ed. 1975).

REALTY an interest in land; another word for **real property** or **real estate.**

REAPPORTIONMENT the changing of the boundaries of a legislative district or number of legislative representatives to which a district is entitled in order to reflect the population of the district. The object of reapportionment is to give effect to the ONE PERSON, ONE VOTE PRINCIPLE. Under Article I, Section 2 of the Constitution, the U.S. House of Representatives is to be chosen "by the people of the several States." Under this provision, reapportionment of congressional districts is required in order to make "as nearly as practicable, one [person's] vote in a congressional election . . . worth as much as another's." 376 U.S. 1. Under the **equal protection clause** of the Constitution, the seats in a state legislature must also be apportioned on a population basis. 369 U.S. 186. Compare **gerrymander.**

REARGUMENT the oral presentation of additional arguments to a court after it has already heard argument, for the purpose of demonstrating that "there is some decision or principle of law which would have a controlling effect and which has been overlooked, or that there has been a misapprehension of facts." 18 N.Y.S. 2d 107, 110. Reargument usually occurs prior to the court rendering a decision in a matter and may be distinguished from a **rehearing** which also presents some new or overlooked principle of law or fact but which usually occurs after the court has rendered its decision.

REASONABLE see **unreasonable.**

REASONABLE BELIEF in criminal law, similar to the **probable cause** standard in that it is a subjective standard used to validate a **warrantless search and seizure** or **arrest** and that considers whether an officer acted on personal knowledge of facts and circumstances which are reasonably trustworthy, and that would justify a person of average caution to believe that a crime has been or is being committed; in insurance law, a subjective standard used to determine the extent to which an automobile insurance policy covers a driver, based on the reasonableness of the driver's belief that owner's permission had been granted to use the vehicle, whether or not such permission was directly granted.

REASONABLE CARE "that degree of **care** which under the circumstances would ordinarily or usually be exercised by or might be reasonably expected from an ordinary prudent person." 268 So. 2d 290, 292. The exercise or absence of reasonable care, which is a jury question, is often dispositive of tort cases or of cases involving injury to others. See **reasonable man [person]**.

REASONABLE DILIGENCE see **diligence.**

REASONABLE DOUBT refers to the degree of certainty required for a juror to legally find a criminal **defendant** guilty. These words are used in **instructions** to the jury in a criminal trial to indicate that innocence is to be presumed unless guilt is so clearly proved that the jury can see that no "reasonable doubt" remains as to the guilt of the person charged. The term "reasonable doubt" does not signify a mere skeptical condition of the mind. Nor does it require that the proof be so clear as to eliminate any possibility of error since under such a rule no criminal prosecution would prevail. It means simply that the proof must be so conclusive and complete that all reasonable doubts of the fact are removed from the mind of the ordinary person, see 25 F. 556, 558, or "would cause prudent men to hesitate before acting in matters of importance to themselves." 367 F. Supp. 91, 101. See also **moral certainty; preponderance.**

REASONABLE MAN [PERSON] a hypothetical person who exercises "those qualities of attention, knowledge, intelligence and judgment which society requires of its members for the protection of their own interest and the interests of others." Restatement Torts 2d, §283(b); a test used to determine whether or not one person was **negligent** towards another. Negligence will exist upon a failure to do "something which a reasonable man, guided by those considerations which ordinarily regulate the conduct of human affairs, would do, or [the doing of] something which a reasonable and prudent person would not do." 43 S.W. 508, 509. The phrase does not apply to a person's ability to reason, but rather the prudence with which he acts under the circumstances. See id. Similar phrases include: "reasonably prudent person," "ordinarily prudent man," etc.

REASONABLE TIME a subjective standard based on the facts and circumstances within a particular case, with applicability in a variety of contexts. Within commercial law, the term applies to the amount of time in which to accept an **offer,** 471 P. 2d 647, 648, to inspect goods prior to payment or acceptance, U.C.C. §2-513(1), 148 N.W. 2d 385, 389; to await performance by a party who repudiates a contract, U.C.C. §2-610(a); or the time in which a seller may substitute conforming goods for goods rejected by a buyer as non-conforming, U.C.C. §2-508(2). If not governed by statute, the term may also refer to the time allowed to set aside a **default judgment,** 400 P. 2d 345, 347, to inform an insurance company of an accident, 223 F. Supp. 953, 956, to file certain claims, 430 S.W. 2d 340, 341, and to make various motions. Compare **time of the essence.**

REBUTTABLE PRESUMPTION see **presumption.**

REBUTTAL generally, the time either party is given to refute or oppose a claim or claims made by the opposing party that would not otherwise belong in that party's case in chief. See 254 N.W. 2d 628, 634; also refers to the time given to the party who presented the first closing argument to rebut any claims made by the opposing party in the closing argument, which followed. This rebuttal can only attack those claims made in the opposing party's argument and cannot raise any new issues.

REBUTTAL EVIDENCE "any evidence that repels, counteracts or disproves evidence given by a witness," 158 P. 2d 799, 803; "that which explains away, contradicts, or otherwise refutes the adverse party's evidence 'by any process which consists merely in diminishing or negating the force' of it." 202 N.W. 896, 898. Rebuttal evidence is offered to contradict other evidence or to rebut a **presumption** of fact.

REBUTTER a form of **common law** pleading which was a defendant's answer of fact to the plaintiff's **surrejoinder**. See **pleadings**.

RECALL a method of removing a public official from office by submitting to popular vote the issue of whether the official should continue in office, 101 N.W. 2d 312. In insurance law, the invalidation of an insurance policy before it becomes effective, 243 N.W. 904, 906. Under the federal Consumer Safety Act, a recall is the process by which a manufacturer is required to replace or repair potentially defective products in order to bring them into conformity with consumer product safety rules. 15 U.S.C. §2064(d).

RECALL A JUDGMENT reversing or **vacating** a decision based on a **matter of fact**, as opposed to a **matter of law**.

RECAPITALIZATION a recasting of the **capital** structure of a **corporation**. A typical **capitalization** will contain debt (usually **bonds, debentures** or other loans), **equity, preferred stock** and **common stock**. Voluntary recapitalization could involve exchanging an existing bond issue or exchanging a preferred stock issue for bonds. Recapitalizations are common when public companies emerge from **bankruptcy**. See **refinancing**.

RECAPTURE a term generally applied to situations in which an event or transaction requires a **taxpayer** to repay earlier tax savings by payment of additional tax in the current **taxable year**. Upon a **sale or exchange** of property which constitutes a **capital asset**, for example,

the **gain realized** on such sale or exchange constitutes **capital gain**. However, under certain circumstances, if the taxpayer has taken excess **depreciation (accelerated depreciation** over **straight line depreciation)** with respect to real property or any depreciation with respect to personal property, the gain realized on sale or exchange of such property is taxed, to the extent of such depreciation, as **ordinary income** and not as **capital gains**. This taxation of the proceeds of the sale or exchange of the capital asset as ordinary income is recapture. I.R.C. §§1245 and 1250. For example, if a taxpayer purchased an item of personal property for $1,000 and depreciated the property so that his **adjusted basis** was $500 and then sold such property for $750, the $250 of gain realized could be taxed as ordinary income notwithstanding the fact that the sale of such property under general circumstances would constitute the **sale** or exchange of a capital asset. Similarly, if a taxpayer takes an **investment tax credit** with respect to certain property and then sells the property in a subsequent tax year, the sale may trigger a recapture of all or part of the credit taken earlier, and the taxpayer's income taxes will be increased accordingly. I.R.C. §47.

RECEIVABLES see **account** [account receivable]; **balance sheet**.

RECEIVER a person appointed by the court to receive and preserve the property or fund that is the subject of the **litigation,** see 115 S.W. 2d 1212, 1216; a "person appointed by a court or judicial officer to take charge of property during the pendency of a **civil action,** suit, or proceeding, or upon a judgment, decree, or order therein, and to manage and dispose of it as the court or officer may direct." 76 P. 774, 775. The court takes possession of the property in controversy through its **agent,** the receiver, during the litigation or after the decree or judgment, for the benefit of the people entitled to the property, when the court does not deem it proper that either party should have control of it during that time. 76 P. 774, 775. Although the "receiver" is the custodian of the assets involved in the litigation, title to the assets remains in those owners who are parties to the litigation while the receiver manages the property for the benefit of the parties. See 275 N.E. 2d 724, 728.

A receiver is frequently appointed in **insolvency** proceedings to manage the property of the insolvent for the benefit of his creditors. See **appointment of receiver.**

In criminal law, one who obtains possession of property which he knows or believes to have been stolen is a "receiver" (colloquially called a "fence") of stolen property and commits an offense thereby.

RECEIVERSHIP an equitable remedy used by a court to place property under the control of a **receiver** so that it may be preserved for the benefit of affected parties. A failing company may be placed in receivership in an action brought by its creditors. The business is often continued but is subject to the receiver's control. A receivership is ancillary to or in aid of the main **relief** sought in an action; it is sometimes used to carry out an **order** or **decree** but is generally used for the purpose of preserving property during **litigation** involving rights in the property. See 60 F. Supp. 716, 719; 175 N.E. 2d 655, 659. The term is also used to refer to the status of property affected by this remedy. For example, property is said to be "in receivership." Compare **bankruptcy.**

RECEIVING STOLEN PROPERTY a crime at common law, and under most modern statutes, requiring as its elements, that property be stolen by someone other than the person charged with receiving it; that the person receiving it has actually received the property or

aided in concealing it; that the person has knowledge that the property has been stolen; and, in some jurisdictions, that the person received it with wrongful intent. 96 N.E. 2d 446, 448. The receiver is popularly known as a "fence," and his or her blameworthiness is sometimes considered greater than the thief's since the fence has induced the thief to commit the crime. Perkins & Boyce, Criminal Law 394-395 (3rd ed. 1982). The crime may be a **felony** or **misdemeanor,** or its degree may vary, depending on the value of the property received. See **fence.**

RECESS a temporary adjournment of a trial or hearing which may be either very short, for lunch, overnight, or for a few days. If it amounts to a substantial delay in the proceedings it is called a **continuance.** It also refers to "the intermission between sittings of the same [legislative] body at its regular or adjourned session, and not . . . the interval between the final adjournment of one body and the convening of another at the next regular session. . . . A temporary dismissal, and not an adjournment **sine die.**" 74 S.W. 298.

RECIDIVIST a second offender; a "habitual criminal"; often subject to extended terms of imprisonment under **habitual offender** statutes.

RECIPROCAL NEGATIVE EASEMENT see **easement** [RECIPROCAL NEGATIVE EASEMENT].

RECIPROCITY generally, a relationship between persons, states, or countries whereby favors or privileges granted by one are returned by the other. Thus, if state A certifies engineers already certified by state B to work in state A, "reciprocity" exists when state B similarly certifies engineers previously certified by state A. Reciprocity does not involve a **vested right** that would exist without it. See 103 S.E. 2d 205, 208. See also **comity.**

RECKLESS careless, heedless, inattentive to duty. The word "reckless" has a wide range of meaning that may vary in color and content according to the circumstances and the time in which it is used. Some cases hold that the term implies more than carelessness, and in fact reaches the equivalent of "willfulness." In this sense, the term may be used as meaning "foolishly heedless of danger; headlong; impetuously or rashly adventurous; indifferent to consequences; mindless; not caring or noting; . . . rash; . . . or very negligent." 26 P. 2d 573.

In the criminal area the modern trend is to define "recklessly" with regard to a material element of an offense as conscious disregard of a "substantial and unjustifiable risk that the material element exists or will result from his conduct. The risk must be of such a nature and degree that, considering the nature and purpose of his conduct and the circumstances known to him, its disregard involves a gross deviation from the standard of conduct that a reasonable person would observe in the actor's situation." Model Penal Code §2.02. Recklessness in this sense imports wanton indifference to the consequences of one's acts. Compare **negligence**.

RECKLESS DISREGARD refers to "an act or conduct destitute of heed or concern for consequences; especially, foolishly heedless of danger; headlong, rash; wanton disregard or indifference to consequences. This implies a consciousness of danger and a willingness to assume the risk." 305 P. 2d 752, 757. The phrase is often associated with **guest statutes** and refers to the actions of a driver. "Reckless disregard" is more severe than ordinary **negligence,** but does not necessarily require a criminal intent to cause harm, either in general or to a particular victim. See 404 P. 2d 677, 678. In the context of libel and publishing, "reckless disregard," if proven, shows serious doubt as to truth of publication or an informant or the informant's accuracy. 294 F. Supp. 1087, 1088.

RECKLESS NEGLIGENCE see **negligence** [WANTON NEGLIGENCE].

RECOGNITION subjecting to tax, under the federal income tax system; the inclusion of gain in income so that it may be subject to federal income taxes. I.R.C. §1001 (c). Compare **realization.**

NON-RECOGNITION OF GAIN gain or loss from the sale or exchange of an asset is not recognized when such gain or loss is not subject to tax. For example, if a taxpayer sells his or her principal residence and within a period ending two years after the date of the sale of such principal residence the taxpayer reinvests the proceeds from the sale, the gain realized (the excess of the selling price over the basis of the property) is not recognized. I.R.C. §1034(a).

RECOGNITION OF GAIN gain or loss realized from the **sale or exchange** of property is recognized when such gain or loss is subject to tax. In general, whenever an asset is disposed of, the gain realized is taxed unless specifically exempted from recognition. I.R.C. §1001(c).

RECOGNIZANCE an obligation of record, entered into before a court or other officer duly authorized for that purpose, with a condition to do some act required by law, upon failure of which the recognizor is obligated to pay a specific sum to the court or a party. 46 N.W. 988, 989. For instance, in criminal law, a recognizance is an undertaking entered into before a court of record by the defendant and his sureties by which they bind themselves to pay a sum of money to the court unless the defendant appears for trial. 3

S.W. 346. See **bond, release on own recognizance [ROR]**.

RECOGNIZANCE, ONE'S OWN see **release on own recognizance [ROR]**.

RECORD to preserve in a writing or printing, or by film, tape, etc. It often refers to "a precise history of a suit from its commencement to its termination, including the conclusions of law thereon drawn by the proper officer for the purpose of perpetuating the exact state of facts." 159 N.E. 591, 592. The RECORD ON APPEAL consists of those items introduced in **evidence** in the lower court, as well as a compilation of **pleadings, motions, briefs,** and other papers filed in the proceeding in the inferior court. Thus, if an argument by an **appellant** is based on facts other than those presented in the court below, the appellant will be going "outside the record" (**hors** the record) which the appellant ordinarily cannot do.

In real property law, to enter in writing in a book or other repository maintained as a public record any interest affecting real property, such as a mortgage upon or sale of land, located within the jurisdiction of the governmental entity maintaining the public record. See **recording acts**.

RECORD DATE the date on which a **shareholder** must be registered on the books of a **corporation** in order to receive **dividends** and other distributions or to vote on company business. See **ex-dividend**.

RECORDING ACTS in real property law, statutes that afford a means of giving **constructive** notice of **ownership** respecting **estates** or **interests** in land by providing for recording the existence of that estate or interest. These statutes generally provide for recording **deeds, mortgages, executory contracts** of **sale,** and **leases** of specified duration. When one's interest or ownership in land is recorded, the recording prevents a subsequent purchaser or mortgagee of the land from qualifying as a **bona fide purchaser** for value without notice, because the instrument recorded would provide at least **constructive** notice of another's prior ownership or interest in the land. Usually recording acts apply to derivative titles and not to original titles, so that anyone who obtains an original title by **adverse possession** will continue to hold title even if the record holder of title conveys his interest to one who is a **bona fide purchaser** for value and without notice. See Burby, Real Property § 130 (3rd ed. 1965).

The different types of recording acts are "pure race," "race-notice" (with or without a period of grace) and "notice" (with or without a period of grace). Under the RACE type of recording act, the person who records first takes in preference to other persons who receive an interest from the same source, even if the first recorder had notice of a prior unrecorded conveyance. A RACE-NOTICE type of act operates in the same way as the race statute, but only if the first recorder had no notice of the prior unrecorded conveyance.

NOTICE type recording acts favor a bona fide purchaser over a prior purchaser so long as the second purchaser had no knowledge of the prior conveyance at the time the purchase was made. This can only happen where the first purchaser has failed to record his or her deed at the time the second purchase is made, since the act of recording puts all subsequent purchasers on constructive notice of the recorded conveyance, depriving them of the right to assert that they are bona fide purchasers.

Where there is a **grace period** provided by a recording act, a prior conveyee is protected as against a subsequent conveyee even if he or she doesn't record first, as long as he or she records within the period of grace defined by the recording act. See Cribbet, Principles of Law of Property 285 (2d ed. 1975); Boyer, Survey of the Law of Property 478 (3d ed. 1981). See also **chain of title.**

While not technically recording acts, other statutes provide for maintenance of public records which give constructive notice of a person's interest in the property of another. For example, Article 9 of the Uniform Commercial Code provides for the filing of **security interests** in personal property.

RECORD OWNER the owner of **real estate** or other property, such as **stocks, bonds,** etc., at the time in question as revealed by public records. 284 N.Y.S. 777, 785. The term is frequently found in tax statutes, and therefore has importance in terms of which party is liable for a certain tax. It also may permit a party to have notice of certain events, such as land **foreclosure.**

RECOUPMENT the right of the **defendant** to have **plaintiff's** award of **damages** against defendant reduced; a right of deduction against the plaintiff's claim which arises either because of a prior payment thereon, or because of the plaintiff's breach of the contract on which the plaintiff's claim is based. It has been defined as "a keeping back of something which is due because there is an equitable reason for withholding it. . . ." The word is nearly if not completely synonymous with "discount" or "deduction" or "reduction." 143 F. 929, 936. It is distinguished from **set-off** in that the latter refers to a reduction of a plaintiff's claim based on a separate transaction, while a recoupment looks to a reduction based on the same transaction. See also **counter claim.**

RECOURSE the act of satisfying a claim, i.e., "recourse in the courts." If persons fail to obtain a desired result in court, they might claim that they will seek "recourse in the legislature." In financing, the

ability to pursue a judgment for a default on a **note** not only against the property underlying the note, but against the party or parties signing the note. In **nonrecourse financing,** only the property used as **collateral** for the underlying loan may be reached to satisfy a **default judgment.** See also **without recourse.**

RECOVERY "the establishment of a right by the judgment of a court." 18 F. 2d 752, 753. Thus a person who is successful in a suit to obtain a judgment "recovers" that which the court deems the person lost, though recovery does not necessarily imply a return to whole or normal. See 347 F. Supp. 955, 962; 429 P. 2d 379, 381. It also refers to the amount of the judgment as well as the amount actually collected pursuant to it. See 167 N.Y.S. 217, 219.

RECOVERY OF BASIS see **basis** [RECOVERY OF BASIS].

RECUSATION the process of disqualification of a judge, jury, or administrative hearing officer by reason of prejudice, bias, or interest in the subject matter. Judges may be recused by the objections of either party or they may voluntarily disqualify themselves if they fear they may not act in an impartial manner. 103 So. 835. Under most state statutes, judges may also be disqualified because they are closely related to a party litigant, 190 S.E. 654. The appearance of impropriety must be avoided at all costs.

REDEEMABLE BOND a **bond** that is callable for payment by the issuer.

REDEMPTION "to purchase back; to regain **possession** by payment of a stipulated price; repurchase," 139 N.W. 802, 803; the "process of cancelling and annulling a **defeasible title,** such as is created by a mortgage or tax sale, by paying the debt or fulfilling other obligations," 253 P. 2d 957, 960.

In corporate finance, the repurchase of outstanding corporate debt or equity.

For income tax purposes, a redemption is any purchase by a corporation of its own stock. The proceeds of a redemption that meet certain requirements will qualify as a **sale** or **exchange** of the stock redeemed, taxable to the shareholder as a **capital gain,** whereas the proceeds of a redemption that fail to qualify will constitute a **dividend,** taxable as ordinary income. I.R.C. §302.

RIGHT OF REDEMPTION statutory right in some jurisdictions to redeem property that has been forfeited because the **mortgagor** defaulted on the mortgage payments; it can be exercised only after the **foreclosure** and sale of the property; it is a personal privilege and not an **interest** or **estate** in land, and can be exercised only by persons permitted by statute and on specified conditions. This right arises only after the **equity of redemption** period ends. See 133 F. 2d 287, 289; 156 P. 1085, 1086. It is frequently found with reference to tax foreclosure statutes. See **equity of redemption.** See **sale** [SALE WITH RIGHT OF REDEMPTION].

RED HERRING an issue, whether legal or factual, raised in a case or law school exam which may be important generally but which has no relevant importance to the question at hand. Also, a preliminary **prospectus,** concerning a future stock issue, distributed during the WAITING PERIOD—the period from the filing date to the effective date of a registration statement. Henn & Alexander, Laws of Corporations 805 (3d ed. 1983).

RE-DIRECT EXAMINATION see **cross-examination** [RE-DIRECT EXAMINATION].

REDLINING an unlawful credit discrimination based on the characteristics of the neighborhood surrounding a would-be borrower's dwelling. 604 F. 2d 1256, 1259; 12 U.S.C. §§2801 et seq.

REDRESS relief or **remedy.** It may be damages or equitable relief. See **recovery; restitution.**

REDUCTIO AD ABSURDUM *rā-dŭk'-tē-ō äd äb-sûr' -dŭm)*—Lat: to reduce to the absurd, e.g., to disprove a legal argument by showing that it ultimately leads to an absurd position.

RE-ENTRY, RIGHT OF the resumption of **possession** pursuant to a right reserved when former possession was parted with. It was a remedy originally given by the feudal law for nonpayment of rent, and now also refers to a right reserved in the conveyance of a **fee** which is subject to a **condition** subsequent. See **conditional fee.** Under the common law the grantor was permitted to exercise the right through **self-help.** Contemporary decisions usually deny a right to use self-help even though the right is formally reserved in the instrument of conveyance. A suit to **quiet title** is preferred. In the landlord-tenant relationship the right can be exercised only when it "is expressly reserved in the lease, for without such reservation the remedy of the **lessor** under the lease . . . is confined to an action on the convenant. The method of exercising the right is by an action of **ejectment** to recover possession of the demised premises." 62 N.E. 425, 427.

REFEREE a quasijudicial officer appointed by a court for a specific purpose to whom the court refers the power and duty to take **testimony,** determine issues of fact and report the findings to the court upon which the court can enter judgment. See 46 N.W. 193, 76 Cal. Rep. 803, 806. "Referee" derives from "refer," i.e., the matters before the referee have been "referred" by the court. See **bankruptcy** (BANKRUPTCY COURT); **master.**

REFERENDUM referring of legislative acts to the voters for final approval or rejection. 281 S.W. 918, 920. A referendum limits the legislature's power by reserving for the electorate the final approval of a law. 38 P. 2d 802, 803. Most states utilize the referendum for one or more types of legislation; the federal system does not use it at all. State constitutions: usually provide that state constitutional amendments must be referred for approval by the electorate; sometimes provide that certain types of legislation, such as state borrowing for public works or the relocating of the state capitol, must be referred; and sometimes provide that upon the filing of a petition by a certain percentage of the people, any specified law must be referred. The legislature can also voluntarily refer a law. Abernathy, Constitutional Limits on the Legislature 88-91 (1959). State legislatures will often by law require a local referendum when a town or city wishes to create a long-term debt to fund a public work such as a new school building. Compare **initiative.**

REFINANCING to repay existing debt with funds raised by creating new debt; usually implies selling a new **bond** issue to provide funds for **redemption** of a maturing issue. See **recapitalization.**

REFORM to correct, modify, or rectify; synonymous with "amend." 517 S.W. 2d 379, 382.

REFORMATION an equitable remedy consisting of a "rewriting" of a contract or other document in cases where the written terms of the contract do not express what was actually agreed upon. Reformation is generally only decreed upon a **clear and convincing** showing of mutual **mistake,** for "[i]f only one party was mistaken, reformation will not be decreed unless the mistake on one side was caused by the other party's **fraud.**" Simpson, Contracts 200 (1965). **Parole evi-**dence is admissible for its **probative value** in establishing that a mistake has been made. 100 F. 2d 294.

Because reformation deals with written contracts incorrectly stating a prior agreement, it is not an action for the removal of provisions to which a party had never agreed. See Corbin, Contracts 395 (one vol. ed. 1952). Compare **rescission.**

REFUND see **claim for refund; tax** [TAX REFUND]

REFUNDING the process of selling a new **issue** of **securities** to obtain funds needed to retire existing securities. Debt refunding is done to extend maturity and/or to reduce debt service cost. See **refinancing.**

REFUSAL the rejection of something to which a person is entitled, such as the rejection of **goods** under a **contract,** e.g., U.C.C. §2-601.

The denial of an obligation to perform a legal duty such as the refusal to complete a contract. 163 A. 2d 803, 806.

A refusal may be an affirmative act, or it may be the mere failure or neglect to perform an act that one is obligated to do without a demand therefore, such as the payment of money. 248 N.W. 261, 265; 72 Mass. 224, 225.

REGIONAL STOCK EXCHANGE a domestic exchange located outside New York City such as the Boston or Philadelphia Stock Exchange. See **stock exchange.**

REGISTER to record formally and exactly; to enroll; to enter precisely in a list or the like. 452 P. 2d 930, 933. For instance, every citizen must register with the local government to be able to vote. Corporations must register securities with the **Securities and Exchange Commission** before they may be sold to the public. See also **draft.**

REGISTERED [COUPON] BOND see **bond** [REGISTERED BOND].

REGISTERED REPRESENTA-TIVE a commission salesperson qualified to take orders for **securities** from the general public. A securities sales trainee must be trained in the securities trade for at least six months and must pass tests prepared by the **National Association of Securities Dealers** and the **New York Stock Exchange;** when all the training and testing is successfully completed, the trainee is "registered" with the Securities and Exchange Commission, the NASD, the American and New York Stock Exchanges, and regional exchanges, and is registered in the various states in which the salesperson intends to do business.

REGISTRAR a record keeper, such as the official at a university who is responsible for maintaining academic records. In corporate law, an agent appointed by a corporation to record the names of stock and bondholders.

REGISTRATION the act of making a list, catalogue, schedule, or register which has the purpose and effect of giving notice and preventing fraud and deception; within the meaning of election laws, a method of proof for ascertaining and identifying electors who are eligible to vote.

In securities law, registration is the process by which a company submits financial data to the **Securities and Exchange Commission** so that it may have its securities bought and sold on public markets. The Securities Act of 1933 sets forth the basic requirements for registration. 15 U.S.C. §§77a et seq.

REGISTRATION STATEMENT a document required by the Securities Act of 1934 that must be submitted to and approved by the **Securities and Exchange Commission** [SEC] prior to a **public offering** of new **securities** by a company through the mails or in interstate commerce. The registration statement must describe the securities offered and must disclose, in detail, information on the nature of the business including accounting statements, the identity of the management and key stockholders, and the purpose of the offering, including the use to be made of the proceeds.

The SEC does not pass on the merits of the offering as an investment, but it does require adequate and accurate disclosure so that potential investors can be adequately informed on the offering. Less detail is required for offerings of $500,000 or less. No statement is required for intrastate offerings when the mails are not used or for offerings made by exempt entities, such as federal, state, and local governmental bodies, or companies supervised by another federal agency, such as railroads under Interstate Commerce Commission jurisdiction.

When a company applies for **listing** on an **exchange,** a registration statement must be submitted to both the SEC and the listing exchange. Information on company operations, outstanding securities, and management must be included.

REGISTRY (OF DEEDS) a book or other record used to give notice to all third parties of the true ownership of property and to put them on notice of any change of ownership that was effected by a **conveyance** of that property. See 54 A. 397, 398. See **recording acts.**

REGULAR COURSE OF BUSINESS see **ordinary course of business.**

REGULATION A the "small-issues" exemptions governing the sale of **securities** that are exempt from registration filing requirements. 15 U.S.C. §77c(b). See Henn & Alexander, Laws of Corporations 801 (3rd ed. 1983).

REGULATION D see private **offering [placement]** [REGULATION D].

REGULATIONS rules or other directives issued by administrative agencies that must have specific authorization to issue directives and upon such authorization must usually follow prescribed conditions, such as prior notification of the proposed action in a public record and an invitation for public comment. See **Administrative Procedure Act.**

REGULATION T a regulation of the **Securities and Exchange Commission** that governs the maximum amount of credit that **securities** brokers and dealers may extend to customers for the initial purchase of regulated securities. The Federal Reserve Board sets the limits under Regulation T which have required customers to supply between 40 percent and 100 percent of the purchase price of regulated stock and bonds since 1934 when the regulation was authorized by Congress. Regulated securities include all listed stocks and bonds as well as a small portion of **over-the-counter** securities. See **margin; regulation U.**

REGULATION U a regulation of the **Securities and Exchange Commission** that governs the maximum amount of credit banks may extend for the purchase of regulated **securities.** Unlike **stock** and **bond** brokers and dealers, banks can extend credit on unregulated securities with no stated limits. Both banks and brokers can extend credit against securities as collateral for any purpose; however, under Regulation U banks can usually lend more than brokers can under **Regulation T** for such "unregulated" purposes.

REGULATION Z the body of regulations included in the federal **Truth-in-Lending Act,** 15 U.S.C. §§1601 et seq., which governs the Federal Reserve Board's supervision of compliance by all banks in the federal reserve system with regard to the credit disclosure requirements established under the Act. The regulation is set forth in 12 C.F.R. §§226.1 et seq.

REGULATORY AGENCY a government body responsible for control and supervision of a particular activity or area of public interest. For example, the Federal Communications Commission [FCC], in addition to its other duties, administers the laws regulating access to communication facilities such as television and radio airwaves. Regulatory agencies are also called ADMINISTRATIVE AGENCIES.

REGULATORY OFFENSE those crimes not inherently evil but which are wrong only because prohibited by legislation i.e., one which is **malum prohibitum.** See 51 S.E. 945, 946. "Generally a crime involving 'moral turpitude' is **malum in se,** but otherwise it is **malum prohibitum.**" LeFave & Scott, Criminal Law 29 (1972). Some examples of regulatory offenses are: "driving over the speed limit, . . . sale of intoxicating liquors, public intoxication, hunting without permission, carrying a concealed weapon, shooting in a public place, keeping slot machines, and passing through a toll gate without paying the toll." Id. at 30. Regulatory offenses are also called STATUTORY OFFENSES and often impose **strict liability** upon defendants for their violation.

REHEARING a retrial or reconsideration of the issues by the same court or body; "a new hearing and a new consideration of the case by the court [or other body] in which the suit was originally heard, and upon the **pleadings** and **depositions** already in the case." 14 A. 490, 494. A **litigant** must usually show "good cause" to obtain a rehearing. Compare **reargument.**

REHEARING EN BANC see **en banc.**

REINSTATE restore to a former state, authority, station, or status from which one has been removed; as applied to insurance, to restore all benefits accruing under a policy, 89 P. 2d 36, 37. As applied to employment practices, if the former position no longer exists or is occupied by another with senior service, an obligation to reinstate may be satisfied by placing the person on a preferential employment list rather than by restoring the person to active employment. 393 N.Y.S. 2d 446, 447.

REIT see **real estate investment trust [REIT].**

REJOINDER at common law, a **pleading** made by the defendant in response to the plaintiff's **replication.**

RELATION BACK the principle that an act done at a later time is deemed by law to have occurred at a prior time. In practice, an amended **complaint** will relate back to the time of the filing of the initial complaint for the purpose of the statute of limitations. See Fed. R. Civ. Proc. 15(c). To take advantage of this principle, in pleading, the claim or defense sought to be added must have been based on or related to, or have arisen from, the original transaction or claim.

RELATOR the **real party in interest** in whose behalf certain suits are brought by the state or the Attorney General when the right to sue resides solely in that official, 329 P. 2d 118, 133; the real party in interest in an **ex rel.** suit; also, "a person in whose behalf certain **writs** are issued, such as **informations** in the nature of **quo warranto,**" 175 S.W. 940, 942. Thus, a habeas corpus action is styled "United States ex rel. [defendant] vs. [warden]."

RELEASE the act or writing by which, or a written document whereby, some **claim,** right, or interest is given up to the person against whom the claim, right, or interest could have been enforced. See 149 N.E. 137, 138; 20 S.W. 1081, 1085. For example, a person may sign a "release" that ends the person's right to sue someone for an injury caused by that person.

In the law of property, the holder of a fee simple may convey to another a term of years and then subsequently "release" his **reversionary** interest [LEASE AND RELEASE] to the possessor of the term of years; conversely, should the possessor of the term of years quit the premises before the end of the term, the possessor may be said to have "surrendered" the remainder of the term to the grantor.

RELEASE ON OWN RECOGNIZANCE [ROR] a condition under which an individual is released in lieu of **bail,** i.e., upon his or her promise to appear and answer a criminal charge. See, e.g., 18 U.S.C. §3146. Bail is intended to assure the defendant's appearance when required by the trial court. The ROR procedure permits his or her release on non-monetary conditions, generally involving only his or her promise to appear but sometimes involving special conditions (e.g., remaining in the custody of another, abiding by travel restrictions, etc.).

In determining whether to permit ROR, the court must "take into account the nature and circumstances of the offense charged, the weight of the evidence against the accused, the accused's family ties, employment, financial resources, character and mental condition, the length of residence in the community, record of convictions, and record of appearance at court proceedings or of flight to avoid prosecution or failure to appear at court proceedings." Id. at §3146(1)(b).

RELEVANCY [RELEVANT] a test concerning the **admissibility** of **evidence** under Fed. R. Evid. §§401 et seq. which looks to the logical relationship between proposed evidence and the fact to be established by that evidence. The standard is established where a fact offered tends to prove or disprove a fact in controversy, however slight the relationship. 239 S.E. 2d 811, 820. Relevancy must be distinguished from **materiality**; the former concerns admissibility while the latter looks to weight and credibility. 215 N.E. 2d 919, 924.

RELEVANT MARKET a term used by the courts in determining whether a violation of an **antitrust statute** has occurred. Identification of the relevant market "takes into account not only the product (the line of commerce) but also its geographic area of distribution (the section of the country). . . . A geographic market must include commercial realities and at the same time be economically significant." 345 F. Supp. 117, 120-121. "[C]ommodities reasonably interchangeable by consumers for the same purposes make up that 'part of the trade or commerce' monopolization of which may be illegal." 351 U.S. 395.

RELIANCE dependence, confidence, trust, repose of mind upon what is deemed sufficient support or authority.

DETRIMENTAL RELIANCE involves reliance by one party on the acts, representations, or promises of another that cause the first party to allow or to effect a change for the worse in his or her position, and is an important element in many legal contexts. If such a detrimental change of position is established, and if the reliance appears to have been justified under the circumstances, it may preclude revocation of an offer of waiver, and may support a promise as a **contract** even without **consideration** (see **promissory estoppel**). Such reliance is also a necessary ingredient in an action to recover upon a claim of **fraud.**

RELICTION the gradual and imperceptible withdrawal of water from land which it covers "by the lowering of its surface level from any cause." 91 N.W. 2d 57, 58. If the retreat of the waters is permanent—i.e., not merely seasonal—the owner of the contiguous property acquires ownership of the dry land thus created. See 152 N.W. 796. See **dereliction;** see also **accretion, avulsion.**

RELIEF the **redress** or assistance awarded to a **complainant** by a court, especially a court of equity, including such remedies as **specific performance, injunction, rescission** of a contract, etc.; but the term generally does not comprehend an award of money **damages.** Thus the term **affirmative relief** is often used to indicate that the gist of relief is protection from future harm rather than compensation for past injury.

In feudal property law, "a relief was a sum payable to the lord by the **heir** of a deceased **tenant** for the privilege of succeeding to his ancestor's lands." Moynihan, Introduction to the Law of Real Property 18 (1962). Thus, it operated as a kind of inheritance tax. Because inheritance was a privilege to be paid for, the lord possessed unlimited discretion in fixing the price payable by the tenant for the privilege. Abuses of this prerogative led to the charging of exorbitant reliefs, which effectively disinherited the tenant's descendant, and therefore inspired many ingenious efforts to avoid them. Inheritance later became a matter of right, but the payment of relief to the lord continued.

In a more general sense, relief refers to the assistance society gives to those in need, usually administered by a branch of the government. Relief in this sense is often called public assistance or more simply "welfare." See **declar-**

atory judgment [relief]. See also prayer for relief.

RELIEF TO LITIGANTS see contempt of court.

RELINQUISHMENT see abandonment; abstention.

REM see in rem.

REMAINDER that part of an **estate** in property which is left upon the termination of the immediately preceding estate (often a life estate or an estate for a term of years) and which does not amount to a **reversion** to the original grantor or the grantor's heirs. The legal conditions for a remainder are that "there must be a precedent particular estate, whose regular termination the remainder must await; the remainder must be created by the same conveyance, and at the same time, as [the precedent] estate; the remainder must **vest** in right during the continuance of the [preceding] estate . . . [and that] no remainder can be [created in connection with] a **fee simple.**" 57 S.W. 584, 599. Thus, "if A, being the owner of land [in fee simple] gives it by deed or will to B for life, and after the death of B, to C in fee, the estate given to C is called a 'remainder,' because it is the remnant or remainder of the estate or title which is left after taking out the lesser estate [life estate] given to B." 101 N.W. 195, 197.

CONTINGENT [EXECUTORY] REMAINDER "any remainder which is created in favor of an ascertained person but is subject to a **condition** precedent; is created in favor of an unborn person; or is created in favor of an existing but unascertained person. It was not, according to the older common law definition, an estate, but merely the possibility of an estate. . . . A contingent remainder becomes a **vested** remainder if any condition precedent is fulfilled and if the **remainderman** is ascertained before the termina-

tion of the preceding estate. Thus, A conveys to B for life, then to C and his heirs if C marries. At the time of the conveyance C is unmarried. The state of the title at that time is: life estate in B, contingent remainder in fee simple in C, reversion in fee simple in A. C marries while B is yet living. C's remainder becomes vested immediately on his marriage and all of the characteristics of a vested remainder attach thereto. The vesting of C's remainder operates to divest the **reversion** in A." Moynihan, Real Property 123 (1962).

EXECUTED REMAINDER a remainder interest which is **vested** as of the present time, though the enjoyment of it may be withheld until a future date.

EXECUTORY REMAINDER see CONTINGENT [EXECUTORY] REMAINDER above.

VESTED REMAINDER "a remainder [in favor of] a person in existence and ascertained who is given the right to immediate possession whenever and however the preceding estate or estates come to an end. It is an estate the owner of which is entitled to immediate possession subject only to the existence of a prior right to possession in another person which created the remainder," Moynihan, Real property, 116 (1962), e.g., A, owner in fee simple of Blackacre, conveys Blackacre to B for life, then to C and his heirs. C has a vested remainder of which he can take possession upon the death of B.

REMAINDERMAN one who has an interest in land **in futuro;** one who has an interest in an estate which becomes possessory at some point in the future after the termination, by whatever reason, of a present possessory interest. "Remainderman" usually refers to one who holds an interest in a **remain-**

der whether **vested** or **contingent.** It may also refer to one who holds an interest in an executory limitation.

REMAND to send back, as for further deliberation; to send back a matter to the tribunal [or body] from which it was appealed or moved. 155 N.W. 2d 507, 511. When a judgment is **reversed,** the **appellate court** usually remands the matter for a new trial to be carried out consistent with the principles announced in its opinion. Often, the court will simply direct that "the matter be remanded [to the lower court] for further proceedings not inconsistent with this opinion."

REMEDY "the means employed to enforce or redress an injury." 272 F. 538, 539. The most common remedy at law consists of money **damages.**

EXTRAJUDICIAL REMEDY see **extrajudicial** [EXTRAJUDICIAL REMEDY].

EXTRAORDINARY REMEDY a **remedy** not usually available in an **action at law** or in **equity,** and ordinarily not employed unless the evidence clearly indicates that such a remedy is necessary to preserve the rights of the party. See 39 N.E. 2d 162, 166. Examples include an appointment of a **receiver,** a decree of **specific performance,** the issuing of a writ of **mandamus,** or **writ of prohibition.**

PROVISIONAL REMEDY a proceeding incidental to and in connection with a regular **action,** invoked while the primary action is pending in order to assure that the claimant's rights will be preserved or that he or she will not suffer irreparable injury. Its connection to the primary action is termed **collateral.** Examples include **attachment,** temporary **restraining orders,** preliminary **injunctions, appointment of receivers, arrest** and **bail,** etc.

REMEDY, MUTUALITY OF see **mutuality of remedy.**

REMITTER the act by which a person, who has a good title to land, and enters upon the land with less than his or her original title, is restored to his or her original good title, see 3 Bl. Comm.* 19; the doctrine whereby the law will relate back from a defective title to an earlier valid title.

REMITTITUR *(rē-mĭt'-tĭ-tûr)*— Lat: "in its broadest sense, the **procedural** process by which the **verdict** of a jury is diminished by subtraction. . . . The term is used to describe generally any reduction made by the court without the consent of the jury." 116 S.E. 2d 867, 871. "The theory of **additur** is a corollary to that of remittitur, the former to increase an inadequate verdict, the latter to decrease an excessive verdict. It is a universal rule . . . that a remittitur may not be granted by a court in lieu of a new trial unless consented to by the party 'unfavorably affected thereby.'" 258 F. 2d 17, 30.

REMOTE CAUSE see **cause** [REMOTE CAUSE].

REMOVAL a change in place or position; a petition made by a defendant to transfer a case from one court, where the plaintiff originally brought the action, to another. Generally used to refer to the transfer of a state action to a federal district court; the petition must be filed within 20 days of the plaintiff's pleadings and must allege jurisdiction in the federal court. 28 U.S.C. §§1441 et seq.

REMOVE CLOUD ON TITLE see **quiet title** [REMOVE CLOUD ON TITLE].

RENDER to officially announce a decision, either orally in open court or by memorandum filed with the clerk, 614 S.W. 2d 203, 205.

RENOUNCE an affirmative declaration of abandonment, 162 A. 560,

563; giving up of a title or claim, 77 S.E. 2d 415, 418. See **renunciation.**

RENT compensation for the use or possession of property for a period of time; a profit in money, goods, or labor issuing out of land and tenements, constituting a periodic return for the privilege of use, 262 N.Y.S. 217; the compensation, a return of value given at stated times for the possession of lands and tenements corporeal. 282 N.Y.S. 282. See **ground rent.**

RENUNCIATION in criminal law, the voluntary and complete abandonment of criminal purpose prior to the commission of a crime, or an act otherwise preventing its commission; in some jurisdictions it is an **affirmative defense** to inchoate offenses such as **attempts, conspiracy, solicitation,** or offenses dependent upon the conduct of another (i.e., accessorial crimes). "Renunciation" is "not voluntary if it is motivated, in whole or in part, by circumstances, not present or apparent at the inception of the actor's course of conduct, which increase the probability of detection or apprehension or which make more difficult the accomplishment of the criminal purpose. Renunciation is not complete if it is motivated by a decision to postpone the criminal conduct until a more advantageous time or to transfer the criminal effort to another but similar objective or victim." Model Penal Code §5.03(6).

In property law, the voluntary forebearance of claiming title to property. Individuals often renounce property to achieve estate and gift tax savings. The period within which a renunciation or a disclaimer may be made while achieving the desired tax consequences is limited by statute. I.R.C. §2518. See also **disclaimer.** Compare **withdrawal.**

RENVOI (*rähn'-vwä*)—Fr: "rule in some jurisdictions that in a **suit** by a nonresident upon a cause arising locally, his capacity to sue will be determined by looking to the law of his **domicile** rather than to the local law," 174 A. 508, 511; the problem of renvoi is nothing more than the question whether the whole law including its **conflict of laws** of a foreign state is looked to for solution when a reference is made to the law of another state. If the reference is to the whole law, as is often the case, an application of the renvoi concept is involved. . . . Take, for example, the case of a citizen of the United States permanently residing in France who dies leaving movables in New York. Assuming the New York conflict of laws rule to be that the law of the **decedent's domicile** will govern this matter, the New York **forum** would look to the "law" of France. If the forum should look to the law applicable to a French person dying in France leaving movables there, the court would be rejecting the use of renvoi. If, however, the forum looks to the whole law, i.e., including the French conflicts rule, this is using the renvoi. See 181 N.Y.S. 336, 342.

REORGANIZATION in corporate income tax law, a group of transactions including mergers, consolidations, recapitalizations, acquisitions of the stock or assets of another corporation, and changes in form or place of organization. The common element in each of these transactions is that if various technical requirements are met, the corporations or shareholders involved may not recognize any gain for income tax purposes, and the transaction will occur tax free. I.R.C. §368. Bittker, Federal Taxation of Income, Estates and Gifts §94.2 (1982).

REPAIR see **tenantable repair.**

REPEAL abolish, rescind, annul by legislative act; "the abrogation or annulling of a previously existing law by the enactment of a subsequent statute, which either declares that the former law shall be revoked and abrogated, or which contains provisions so contrary to or irreconcilable with those of the earlier law that only one of the two can stand in force; the latter is the 'implied' repeal . . . the former, the 'express' repeal." 139 S.W. 443, 445. Compare **amend.**

REPLEVIN an **action** for the recovery of property taken, rather than for the value of that property; a possessory **remedy;** "a legal form of action ordinarily employed only to recover possession or the value of specific personal property unlawfully withheld from the plaintiff plus **damages** for its detention. . . . It is primarily a possessory action in which the issues ordinarily are limited to the plaintiff's title or right to possession of the goods." 182 A. 2d 219, 221. Compare **trespass; trover.** See U.C.C. §2-716(3).

REPLEVY to deliver to the owner; to redeliver goods which have been kept from the rightful owner. See 30 So. 788, 789. See **replevin.**

REPLICATION the plaintiff's answer or reply to the defendant's **plea** or **answer.** See 6 So. 374, 375. See **pleadings.**

REPLY a defensive **pleading** by a plaintiff, the sole purpose of which is to interpose a **defense** to **new matter** pleaded in the **answer.** 255 S.W. 935, 937. In modern practice a reply is an extraordinary pleading and is not permitted except to respond to a **counterclaim** or by leave of court to an answer or third-party answer. See, e.g., Fed. R. Civ. Proc. 7(a).

REPOSSESSION seizure or **foreclosure;** the method by which a secured **creditor** satisfies a **debtor's** obligation after the debtor has defaulted. 441 S.W. 2d 15, 27. The creditor may take possession either of the property in which he or she has a security interest, or of the collateral securing the property. U.C.C. §9-503. To repossess prop-

erty, the creditor must usually file a **complaint,** an **affidavit** and post a **bond,** whereupon the sheriff will seize the **property.** While repossession of the collateral from the debtor is relatively simple, repossession of the collateral from third parties is more difficult. Before the creditor can resell the repossessed collateral, he or she must take the reasonable steps necessary to inform the debtor and other interested parties so each can protect his or her own interests. U.C.C. §9-504. Compare **foreclosure; seizure.**

REPRESENT [REPRESENTATION] to stand in another's place, to speak with authority on behalf of another, 90 S.E. 2d 22, 25; to appear on one's behalf. As an element of actionable fraud, representation includes "deeds, acts or artifices calculated to mislead another, as well as words or positive assertions." 446 S.W. 2d 188, 193. In insurance law, a representation is an oral or written statement preceding the insurance policy and, though not part of it, is used to enable the **underwriter** to form a judgment as to whether he or she will accept the risk. 584 S.W. 2d 529, 532. Only a false misrepresentation that materially affects the risk will permit the insurer to rescind the policy. 172 A. 2d 206, 210. In commercial law, a representation is anything short of a **warranty** and is sufficient to create a distinct impression of fact conducive to action. 382 F. Supp. 1365, 1368.

In constitutional law, the **Sixth Amendment's** right of assistance of counsel in a criminal case includes the right to adequate and effective representation. This standard includes the right to an attorney who knows the relevant law, does not have any conflicts in the case at hand, adheres to all legal procedural requirements so as not to forfeit any rights, and vigorously pursues a client's case at trial through direct and cross-examinations, the filing of motions, and the raising of objections. Representation so lacking in competence creates a duty on a trial judge to correct such to prevent a mockery of justice. 229 So. 2d 582, 583.

In property law, "representation" permits children or more remote lineal descendents of a predeceased relative of the **intestate** to stand in their predeceased ancestor's shoes for purposes of inheritance. Representation is equivalent to **per stirpes** (meaning by the stock or roots). Compare **per capita.** See **proportional representation.**

REPRESENTATIVE agent; one who acts for another in a special capacity, 249 P. 2d 24, 27. One's status as a representative entitles the person to a number of rights, including the right to discovery of trial preparation materials, 53 F.R.D. 594, 595, and the right to bargain collectively on behalf of employees, 318 F. 2d 472, 476. See **personal representative; registered representative.**

REPRIEVE in criminal law, "the withdrawing of a **sentence** for an interval of time whereby the execution is suspended. . . . It is merely the postponement of the sentence for a time. It does not and cannot defeat the ultimate execution of the judgment of the court, but merely delays it." 131 S.W. 2d 583, 585. Reprieves are most commonly granted by the governor or president to postpone the execution of a death sentence. If the death sentence is to be modified, the action will be a **commutation** or **pardon.** See also **executive clemency.**

REPUBLICATION an affirmative act of **reviving** a **will** after it has been destroyed or otherwise replaced by a subsequent will, and is frequently accomplished by use of a **codicil.** In those jurisdictions permitting republication, the mere revocation of the subsequent will shall not revive the earlier will without some type of affirmative act.

REPUDIATION the renunciation of a duty, 87 N.E. 1062, 1063; a denial of responsibility or obligation. A repudiation of a contract is an act or declaration by a contracting party indicating unequivocally that he or she will not perform, or further perform, his or her contract. A repudiation is said to be in the nature of an **anticipatory breach** but does not operate as such unless the promisee elects to treat the repudiation as a **breach** and brings suit for **damages.** 36 P. 2d 821, 825.

REPUTATION EVIDENCE see **witness** [CHARACTER WITNESS].

REQUIREMENTS CONTRACT see **contract** [REQUIREMENTS CONTRACT].

RES *(rēz)*—Lat: the thing; the subject matter of **actions** that are primarily **in rem,** i.e., actions that establish rights in relation to an object, as opposed to a person, or **in personam.** See 42 N.Y.S. 626, 628. For example, in an action that resolves a conflict over **title** to **real property,** the land in question is the res. Tangible **personal property** can also be a "res," as in the corpus of a trust. In a **quasi in rem proceeding,** land or **chattels** that are seized and **attached** at the beginning of the action, in order that they may later be used to satisfy a personal **claim,** are the res of such suits. The term refers as well to the status of individuals. Thus, in a divorce suit, the marital status is the res. The purpose of a res is to establish a court's **jurisdiction,** i.e., if the property lies within the state where the action is brought, or an individual in a divorce action is a **domiciliary** of the state, then jurisdiction is established.

RES AJUDICATA see **res judicata.**

RESCIND to abrogate a **contract,** release the parties from further obligations to each other and restore the parties to the **status quo**

ante, or the positions they would have occupied if the contract had never been made. See 163 N.W. 2d 35, 38. For instance, in "rescinding" a sales contract, any monies paid or goods received would usually be returned to their original holders, although the parties could agree otherwise.

RESCISSION the cancellation of a **contract** and the return of the parties to the positions they would have occupied if the contract had not been made. Rescission may be brought about by the mutual consent of the parties, by the conduct of the parties, or by a **decree** to that effect by a **court of equity.** For instance, there is a "rescission" of a contract if both parties expressly or by their actions implicitly agree not to go through with the contract before their positions have been altered by the performance of their duties under contract. Grounds for rescission, in addition to mutual agreement, include the original invalidity of the contract, **fraud, failure of consideration, material breach,** or **default.** 112 N.W. 2d 654.

In a broad sense, rescission is the act of canceling, **vacating,** or **annulling.** In a strict sense, rescission means a mutual intent to restore the **parties** to the status quo ante, or the position each was in prior to their entering into the contract, 314 N.Y.S. 2d 77, 80; 80 Cal. App. 3d 610.

The general rule is that in the absence of breach or default by the other party, no party has the unilateral right to rescind a valid contract. Parties can, however, rescind or annul a contract of **sale** by their mutual consent, which consent may even be inferred from conduct which indicates they consider the contract at an end, 94 U.S. 29, 49; 124 U.S. 385, 390. A fully executed contract cannot be rescinded. A party who substantially violates the contract himself cannot seek rescission. See **revocation, repudiation.**

RESCRIPT a statement of the decision of the highest appellate tribunal; a direction from that tribunal to a lower court to enter a **decree** in accordance with that direction, in effect remanding the case to the lower court for the entry of a decree. 31 N.E. 2d 564, 568.

RESCUE the act of aiding a person in imminent and serious peril, which, as a matter of law, cannot give rise to a charge of contributory negligence against the rescuer in risking his or her own life or serious injury in attempting to effect the rescue, provided the attempt is not made recklessly or rashly. 372 P. 2d 55, 59.

RESCUE DOCTRINE tort rule holding a **tortfeasor** liable to his or her victim's rescuer, should the latter injure himself or herself during a reasonable rescue attempt; "one who had, through his **negligence,** endangered the safety of [himself or] another, may be held liable for injuries sustained by a third person [who attempts] to save such other from injury." 393 S.W. 2d 48, 57. The doctrine derives from the fact that "the original wrong which imperils life is not only a wrong insofar as the imperiled victim is concerned, but is a wrong also to his rescuer." 146 A. 2d 705, 712. One who attempts such a rescue cannot be charged with **contributory negligence,** provided his or her rescue attempt was not rash or reckless. See 188 P. 2d 121, 123, 124.

RESERVATION a clause in any **instrument** of **conveyance,** such as a **deed,** which creates a lesser **estate,** or some right, interest, or **profit** in the estate granted, to be retained by the **grantor.** See 214 P. 2d 212, 214, 85 A. 2d 775, 778. Compare **reversion.**

Also refers to a tract of land, usually substantial, set aside for specific purposes such as military grounds, parks, Indian lands.

In practice, the term refers to the

act of a court or other body in delaying decision on a point of law. The court may "reserve decision" and proceed with the matter or may adjourn the proceedings pending its decision. When the court "takes the matter under advisement" it in effect reserves decision, often so that it may render a written decision.

A performance "under reservation" will preserve the rights of the performing party in a disputed contract context. See **under protest.**

RESERVE funds kept available to meet future contingencies. Examples include funds banks must keep on hand to meet depositors' withdrawals, insurance company liabilities, and pension payments. The funds that must be presently retained are usually a percentage of the institution's full liability for the particular need. See **depreciation reserve.**

RESERVE CLAUSE generally found in sports contracts, giving a team that first signs a player a continuing and exclusive right to that player's services, even beyond the length of the contract, and *to the point* of obligating other teams to respect and enforce those rights. 346 U.S. 356. Such clauses have less effect than they once did, and players in most sports are free to move to other teams after their contract expires.

RESERVED POINT see **point reserved.**

RESERVED POWERS see **Tenth Amendment.**

RES GESTAE *(rēz jes'tē)*—Lat: things done. Rule that covers spoken words that are so closely connected to an occurrence that the words are considered part of the occurrence, 257 N.E. 2d 816, 818; spontaneous exclamations or statements, made by either the participants, victims, or spectators to a crime or other litigation immediately before, during, or after the event,

432 S.W. 2d 349, 352; "the circumstances, facts and declarations which grow out of the main fact, are contemporaneous with it, and serve to illustrate its character," 266 P. 2d 992, 1003. In **evidence,** such written or oral statements are admissible as "excited utterances," declarations as to present bodily conditions, declarations of present mental states and emotions, and declarations of present sense impressions, 383 A. 2d 858, 860, and as such do not violate the **hearsay rule.** Fed. R. Evid. 803.

RESIDENCE broadly, any place of abode that is more than temporary. See 88 Cal. Rptr. 628, 630. The term is often used as being synonymous with **domicile,** since a person's residence is usually also his or her domicile and since the two terms have been held equivalent in judicial construction of some statutes. However, in a strict sense, "residence" applies to the mere fact of a person dwelling in a particular abode, while "domicile" is a person's legal home, or the place that the law presumes is his or her permanent residence, regardless of temporary absence. See 67 A. 2d 273, 275. Traditionally, one may have more than one residence, but only a single domicile. See **retreat, duty to; search and seizure; self-defense.**

RESIDENT ALIEN see **alien.**

RESIDENTIAL COMMUNITY TREATMENT CENTERS see **halfway houses.**

RESIDUARY BEQUEST see **bequest; residuary legacy.**

RESIDUARY CLAUSE clause in a **will** conveying to one or more beneficiaries, referred to as the residuary beneficiaries or legatees, everything in a **testator's estate** not **devised** to a specific **legatee;** "includes in its gift any property or interest in the will which, for any reason, eventually falls into the general residue. It will include **legacies** that were originally **void,** either because the disposition was illegal, or because for any other reason it was impossible that it should take effect; and it includes such legacies as may lapse by events subsequent to the making of the will. (But see **antilapse statutes.**) It operates to transfer to the **residuary legatee** such portion of his or her property as the **testator** has not perfectly disposed of." 20 N.E. 602, 604.

RESIDUARY ESTATE that part of a **testator's** estate which remains after all of the **estate** has been distributed through the satisfaction of all claims and specific legacies with the exception of the dispositions authorized by the **residuary clause;** "that portion of the estate that remains after the payment of debts and other classes of legacies; it is conditional upon something remaining after the paramount claims on the testator's estate are satisfied." 43 N.E. 2d 769, 775.

RESIDUARY LEGACY "a general **legacy** into which fall all the assets of the estate after the satisfaction of other legacies and the payment of all debts of the estate and all costs of administration." 44 S.E. 2d 659, 664.

RESIDUUM the substance or part remaining after some other part has been taken away.

RESIDUUM RULE in administrative law, the principle that a decision rendered by an administrative agency and based in part on incompetent **evidence** will be upheld on judicial review if it is supported by a residuum of competent evidence. The federal courts have rejected the residuum rule. 402 U.S. 389.

RES IPSA LOQUITUR *(rēz ip'sa lo'qui-ter)*—Lat: the thing speaks for itself. A rule of **evidence** whereby **negligence** of the alleged wrongdoer may be inferred from the mere fact that the accident happened, provided: (1) the occurrence is the kind of thing that does not ordinarily happen without negligence; (2) the occurrence must have been caused by an agency or instrumentality within the exclusive control of the defendant; (3) the occurrence was not due to contribution or voluntary action by the plaintiff. Prosser, Torts 214 (4th ed. 1971). The rule may not apply when direct evidence of negligence exists. See 270 So. 2d 900, 904. "The gist of it, and the key to it, is the inference, or process of reasoning by which the conclusion is reached. This must be based upon the evidence given, together with a sufficient background of human experience to justify the conclusion. It is not enough that plaintiff's counsel can suggest a possibility of negligence. The evidence must sustain the **burden of proof** by making it appear more likely than not." Prosser, Torts 212 (4th ed. 1971). The procedural effect of successfully invoking the doctrine is to shift the **burden** of going forward with the evidence, which normally attaches to the plaintiff, to the defendant, who is thereby charged with introducing evidence to refute the presumption of negligence which has been created.

RESISTANCE see **utmost resistance.**

RESISTING ARREST common law offense involving physical efforts to oppose a lawful arrest: "In every case where one person has a right to arrest or restrain another, the other can have no rights to resist, since the two rights cannot coexist. . . . No right of **self-defense** can arise out of such a circumstance." 173 P. 1076, 1080-1081. Most often, the person attempting to make the arrest is a police officer in whose presence an offense has occurred, and the resistance is classified as an **assault** and **battery** upon the officer. See, e.g. 274 S.W. 17. Some modern statutes specifically

label the crime "resisting arrest."
See N.J.S.A. 2C:29-2.

RES JUDICATA *(rēz jū-di-kā'ta)*—Lat: the thing has been decided; a matter has been adjudged. Doctrine by which "a final judgment by a court of competent **jurisdiction** is conclusive upon the **parties** in any subsequent **litigation** involving the same cause of action. . . . The policy underlying the doctrine of res judicata is one of repose, the same policy which is reflected in the **statute of limitations** with stale claims." Green Civil Procedure 227-228 (2d ed. 1979). Compare **collateral estoppel**. See also **bar; merger.**

RESPITE a delay, postponement, or **forebearance** of a **sentence,** not comprehending a permanent suspension of execution of the judgment, see 237 P. 525, 527; a **reprieve;** also, a delay in repayment, granted to a debtor by his creditor. See **grace period.**

RESPONDEAT SUPERIOR *(rā'-spôn-dā'-ät sū-pĕr'-ē-ôr)*—Lat: let the superior reply. This doctrine is invoked when there is a master-**servant** relationship between two parties. The "respondeat superior" doctrine stands for the proposition that when an employer, dubbed "master," is acting through the facility of an employee or **agent,** dubbed "servant," and tort **liability** is incurred during the course of this agency due to some fault of the agent, then the employer or master must accept the responsibility. Implicit in this is the **common law** notion that a duty rests upon every person to conduct his or her affairs so as not to injure another, whether or not in managing the affairs he or she employs agents or servants. See 143 P. 2d 554, 556. This doctrine is **civil** in its application. See 9 N.W. 2d 518, 521. See **scope of employment.** Compare **vicarious liability.**

RESPONDENT in **equity,** the party

who answers a **bill** or other **pleading.** "Anyone who answers or responds may properly be called a 'respondent'." 158 N.W. 2d 809, 812. The term also refers to the party against whom an **appeal** is brought.

RESPONSIBILITY the obligation to answer for an act and to repair any injury caused by that act, 426 P. 2d 828, 835; the state of being answerable for an obligation, 316 S.W. 2d 662, 671; as used in statutes such as those governing awards of local public contracts to "RESPONSIBLE BIDDERS," the term refers to "the characteristic the absence of which would cause fair-minded and reasonable men to believe it was not in the best interests of the municipality to award the contract to the lowest bidder," 432 A. 2d 564, 566, and may involve experience, financial ability and adequate facilities. 149 A. 2d 228, 234.

RESPONSIBILITY, DIMINISHED see **diminished capacity.**

RESPONSIVE PLEADING [ALLEGATION] see **pleadings** [RESPONSIVE PLEADING].

RESTATEMENT an attempt by the American Law Institute ". . . to present an orderly statement of the general **common law** of the United States, including in that term not only the law developed solely by judicial decision, but also the law that has grown from the application by the courts of statutes. . . ." Restatement, Torts viii, ix (1st ed). Restatements are compiled according to subject matter; those compiled include contracts, torts, property, trusts, agency, conflict of laws, judgments, restitution, security, and foreign relations.

The policy of the A.L.I. in the restatements 2nd has turned away from a mere head count of the jurisdictions in determining what the general state of the law is and has taken into account other factors, such as the modern trend of the law according to influential jurisdictions and well-thought out opinions. See Wechsler, The Course of the Restatements 55 A.B.A.J. 147 (1969).

RESTITUTION act of making good, or of giving the equivalent for, any loss, damage, or injury; **indemnification.** 3 A. 2d 521, 525. As a remedy, restitution is available to prevent **unjust enrichment,** to correct an erroneous payment, and to permit an **aggrieved party** to recover deposits advanced on a contract. Under the Uniform Commercial Code, an aggrieved party is entitled to restitution and **damages** for a breach to the extent the latter can be proved. See U.C.C. §2-711. At common law, the plaintiff would have to elect between restitution and damages. See 22 Pick. 457 (Mass. 1839). As a contract remedy, restitution is limited to the value of a performance rendered by the injured party, see Restatement, Contracts 2d, §373, and ordinarily requires that both parties to a transaction be returned to the **status quo** ante. See 22 Pick. 457.

In criminal law, restitution is sometimes ordered as a condition of a **probationary sentence.** See, e.g., N.Y. Penal Law §65.10(2)(f).

RESTRAINING ORDER an order granted without notice or hearing, demanding the preservation or the **status quo** until a hearing can be had to determine the propriety of any **injunctive relief,** temporary or permanent. A restraining order is always temporary in nature inasmuch as it is granted pending a hearing and thus is often called a T.R.O. [TEMPORARY RESTRAINING ORDER]. The restraining order is issued upon application of a plaintiff who requests the court to forbid an action or threatened action of defendant; the form of the restraining order will generally be an order to show cause why the injunctive relief the plaintiff seeks ought not be granted. After a hearing a preliminary or permanent injunction may issue.

Although sometimes used interchangeably, a restraining order is distinguished from an injunction in that the restraining order issues without a hearing whereas the injunction will follow a hearing.

RESTRAINT, JUDICIAL see **judicial restraint.**

RESTRAINT, PRIOR see **prior restraint.**

RESTRAINT OF TRADE at common law and as used in the **Sherman Antitrust Act,** illegal "restraints" interfering with free competition in business and commercial transactions, which tend to restrict production, affect prices, or otherwise control the market to the detriment of purchasers or consumers of goods and services. Ordinarily reasonable restraints of trade are made unreasonable if they are intended to accomplish the equivalent of an illegal restraint. 255 F. 2d 214, 230.

RESTRAINT ON ALIENATION restriction on the ability to **convey real property** interests; any attempt to restrict alienation was in derogation of the **common law** public policy favoring free alienability; interests thus created were void or voidable as an unlawful restraint on alienation.

Although fees on condition subsequent and fee simple determinables are, in general, permissible **estates,** a condition which states, "but if any attempt is made to alienate the land, the **grantor** and his **heirs** reserve the right to re-enter and declare the estate forfeit," would be against the policy. As a consequence, a rule exists which requires that there be a person capable of transferring absolute interest in possession within a certain period of time. See 201 P. 2d 69, 73. See **alienation; rule against perpetuities.** In **estates** created by short-term **leases,** however, such restraints are permissible. The determination of validity is based upon the nature and quality (duraton) of the restraint, the type of estate in question, and the penalty imposed for violation of the restraint.

RESTRICTED SECURITIES securities acquired from an issuer in a non-public transfer, that is, on terms and at a price not offered to the general public through an **underwriter.** Since the securities were not part of a public offering and thus not subject to the safeguards of the Securities Act of 1933, such as the registration of the securities and the issuing of a prospectus, their sale to the public is restricted. Under S.E.C. Rule 144, restricted stock must be held at least two years prior to its sale on an established securities market, and may only be sold in small amounts. Restricted stock is often referred to as LETTER STOCK since the certificate must bear a legend reciting the restrictions to which it is subject. It is also known as INVESTMENT STOCK.

RESTRICTIVE COVENANT a promise included in an agreement restricting the use of **real property** or the kind of buildings that may be erected thereupon; the promise is usually expressed by the creation of an express **covenant,** reservation, or exception in a **deed.** In order for a grantor to enforce the covenant against remote grantees [i.e., subsequent owners who take title from the first grantee], the covenant must **"run with the land."** Some restrictive covenants, such as those that discriminate racially by, e.g., limiting the use of the property or its transfer to white persons, may be unenforceable since a court will be unable to enforce them and remain consistent with the **equal protection clause** of the Fourteenth Amendment. See 334 U.S. 1; 346 U.S. 249. It does not matter that a racially restrictive covenant is expressed as a condi-

tion a.id thus purports to automatically cause a **reversion** to the grantor. See 316 P. 2d 252; but see 388 S.E. 2d 114. See also 382 U.S. 296.

RESTRICTIVE INDORSEMENT see **indorsement** [RESTRICTIVE INDORSEMENT].

RESULTING TRUST see **trust** [RESULTING TRUST].

RESULTING USE see **use** [RESULTING USE].

RETAIL INSTALLMENT CONTRACT generally, a **contract** consisting of a promissory **note** and a **chattel mortgage,** 143 N.E. 2d 824, 825; a contract whereby the seller retains **title** to, or a security or property interest in, **goods** purchased by a buyer who is obligated to make periodic payments for the goods. In some states, the term also includes certain types of **leases.** 353 N.Y.S. 2d 217, 219. See **installment contract.**

RETAINER compensation paid in advance to a professional, such as an attorney, for services to be performed in a specific case. A "retainer" includes fees "not only for the rendition of professional services when requested, but also for the attorney taking the case, making himself available to handle it, and refusing employment by [the client's] adversary." 201 S.E. 2d 794, 796. A retainer may represent the whole sum to be charged (plus expenses) but more often is in the nature of a deposit with the attorney, rendering from time to time or at the conclusion of the matter a statement of amounts owed by the client for services rendered.

RETALIATORY EVICTION see **eviction** [RETALIATORY EVICTION].

RETIRE in reference to **bills of exchange,** "to recover, redeem, regain by the payment of a sum of money; . . . to withdraw from circulation or from the market; to take up and pay." 110 F. 2d 878, 879.

For example, the federal government retires a Series E bond when the holder turns it in for cash upon **maturity.**

The term also refers to the voluntary withdrawal from office, a public station, business, or other employment. See 131 A. 2d 512, 515.

A **jury** is "retired" at that point when the judge has submitted the case for its consideration and **verdict.** See 192 S.W. 922, 923.

RETIREMENT PLANS the general term referring to any plan provided by an employer or a self-employed individual for employees' or a self-employed individual's retirement. Most retirement plans give rise to tax advantages by allowing the employer a present **deduction** while the employee will be permitted to avoid **recognizing** the **income** until he or she has actually or **constructively** received it.

DEFERRED COMPENSATION a plan whose terms permit an employee to defer payment of a portion of his or her salary in return for the employer's promises to pay the employee the salary at some time in the future. Generally, if such plan is not funded by irrevocably setting the fund aside for the employee or guaranteed by insurance, the employee will not recognize income from the plan until the employee is actually paid, and the employer does not obtain a deduction until the employee recognizes the income. See QUALIFIED and NON-QUALIFIED Plans below.

INDIVIDUAL RETIREMENT ACCOUNT [IRA] a retirement plan permitting any individual who receives compensation to pay a specified amount into the plan, called an individual retirement account. Amounts so deposited are deductible to the employee and the income earned thereon is not taxable until the individual withdraws it. Except in the case of death or disability, if an individual withdraws the funds prior to age 59½, a 10 percent penalty is imposed in addition to the income tax. Withdrawals must commence no later than age 70½. I.R.C. §219.

KEOGH PLAN a qualified pension or profit-sharing plan set up by a self-employed individual. Also known as an "HR-10 plan." I.R.C. §401(c).

NON-QUALIFIED PENSION OR PROFIT-SHARING PLAN a plan created by an employer for an employee but which does not qualify for a present deduction to the employer and deferral of income recognition to the employee. Generally, in such cases the employer will not be permitted to take a deduction for the amount set aside until the employee recognizes such amount as income.

PENSION FUND [PLAN] any plan, fund, or program that provides retirement income to employees or results in a deferral of income by employees for periods extending to the termination of covered employment or beyond. 29 U.S.C. §1002(2). This definition is intended to reach a wide variety of retirement benefit structures, including profit-sharing plans that meet these requirements, with the only limitation being the express language of the plan providing for retirement benefits or deferral of income. 526 F. Supp. 510, 515.

QUALIFIED PENSION OR PROFIT-SHARING PLAN a plan set up by an employer for an employee or a group of employees which allows the employer to pay into a trust a certain sum or percentage of compensation for the employees. The employer obtains a present deduction for the contributions but the employee does not recognize the income until it is actually paid to him or her. I.R.C. §401 et seq.

ROLLOVER procedure permitting an employee to convert from one qualified plan to another without the recognition of income on such conversion. I.R.C. §402(a)(5).

RETIREMENT SECURITY ACT see **ERISA.**

RETRACTION the withdrawing of a plea, declaration, **accusation,** promise, etc. As to a **defamation,** "it has been held that a retraction . . . can be effected only if it is a full and unequivocal one that does not contain lurking insinuations or hesitant withdrawals. It must, in short, be an honest endeavor to repair all the wrong done by the defamatory imputation." 123 A. 2d 473, 477.

RETRAXIT a voluntary renunciation by a **plaintiff** in open court of his or her suit and cause of action and which bars a second action between the same parties on the same grounds, 91 S.E. 2d 415, 419; it is **dismissal with prejudice,** equivalent to a **verdict** and **judgment on the merits** of the case. 260 P. 2d 194, 197; 107 Cal. Rptr. 270, 273.

RETREAT, DUTY TO a duty found in some jurisdictions obligating a person to retreat from a dangerous situation rather than employ **self-defense** and injure another. However, one is not usually required to retreat when attacked in one's own home. In tort law, the failure to exercise one's duty to retreat may create liability in the party who could have retreated. Prosser, Law of Torts 111 (4th ed. 1971). In criminal law, the failure to retreat except from one's home or from a robber will foreclose the defense of self-defense in a minority of states. Perkins & Boyce, Criminal Law 1130 (3d ed. 1982).

RETRIAL a new trial in which an issue or issues already litigated, and as to which a verdict or decision by the court has been rendered, are reexamined by the same court for some sufficient reason, such as a recognition that the initial trial was improper or unfair as a result of procedural errors. Compare **mistrial.**

RETROACTIVE refers to a rule of law, whether legislative or judicial, relating to things already decided in the past. "Retroactive" includes both RETROSPECTIVE and **ex post facto,** the former technically applying only to civil laws, the latter to criminal or penal laws. A retrospective law relates back to a previous transaction and gives it some different legal effect from that which it had under the law when it occurred; it is constitutionally objectionable, if it impairs **vested** rights acquired under existing laws, or creates a new obligation or attaches a new disability with respect to past transactions. Similarly, in respect to ex post facto laws, "retroactivity" refers to the imposition of criminal liability on behavior that took place prior to the enactment of the criminal statute. State constitutions may prohibit their legislatures from enacting retrospective laws; ex post facto laws are prohibited by the Constitution of the United States. It should be noted, however, that judicially created law (**common law**) is often "retroactive" in its effect since the court decides on the basis of a fact pattern wherein the responsible actors could not possibly have predicted the court's eventual interpretation of the law at the time the act occurred, but are nevertheless held accountable to the decision.

In constitutional law, decisions announcing new or different rights for criminal defendants may be given full retroactive effect so as to permit a **collateral attack** on previously finalized judgments. Because of the tremendous impact on the administration of justice, the U.S. Supreme Court has held some decisions not retroactive where the integrity of the fact-finding process was not challenged by the new rules and where there has been reliance by law enforcement authorities upon the former practice. Compare 393 U.S. 5 (holding fully retroactive a right to counsel) with 384 U.S. 719 (limiting the new **Miranda** rights to be applicable only to trials not yet begun when that decision was handed down) and 394 U.S. 244 (holding new search and seizure rules applicable only to searches not yet conducted). Where no such reliance has been justified, the doctrine is fully retroactive, at least as to cases still on direct review. 457 U.S. 537.

RETROSPECTIVE see retroactive.

RETURN a report from an official, such as a sheriff, stating what he has done in respect to a command from the court, or why he has failed to do what was requested. See B1. Comm.*287. A **false return** is a false or incorrect statement by the official acting to the detriment of an interested party. See 70 S.W. 192. See also **rate of return.**

For income tax purposes, a document by which a **taxpayer** or a taxpayer's representative provides information to the **Internal Revenue Service** relevant to the determination of the taxpayer's tax liability for a specified period. I.R.C. §§6011 et seq.

AMENDED RETURN a return by which a taxpayer or a taxpayer's representative corrects information contained in an earlier return. Thus, an amended return may require an additional payment of tax (possibly with interest and/or penalties) or be accompanied by a **claim for refund.**

DECLARATION OF ESTIMATED TAX a return required of any taxpayer whose tax withheld from his or her income does not satisfy his or her tax liability for the year. The declaration is accompanied by payments of estimated tax. I.R.C. §6015.

FALSE RETURN see **false return.**

FILING the process by which the taxpayer transmits the return to the Service. The **Internal Revenue Code** sets forth the due dates for the filing of the various returns and rules exist for determining whether or not the returns are timely filed. E.g., I.R.C. §6012.

INFORMATION RETURN any of a number of returns that only communicate information to the Service relevant to tax liability but which do not compute the actual liability of any taxpayer or accompany the actual payment of tax; thus, since a **partnership** is not subject to tax, it merely files an information return with information relevant to the tax liabilities of the various partners. I.R.C. §6031 et seq.

JOINT RETURN a return filed by a husband and wife, setting forth tax information concerning each of them, and computing a joint tax liability. I.R.C. §6013.

REVALUATION SURPLUS see **unearned surplus** [REVALUATION SURPLUS].

REVENUE income from whatever source derived; that which returns or comes back from an investment.

REVENUE BILLS bills that levy taxes. Federal revenue bills are required to originate in the House of Representatives. U.S. Constitution, Art. I, Sec. 7, Cl. 1. Many states have similar constitutional provisions requiring that such bills originate in a particular house of a legislature, 315 A. 2d 860, 865, or that the bills shall not be passed in the last five days of the legislative session, 115 So. 2d 484, 485; 294 P. 2d 809, 811.

REVENUE RULING a published decision by the **Internal Revenue Service** in the Internal Revenue Bulletin applying the federal tax laws to a particular set of facts. Revenue rulings (as opposed to private rulings) may be relied upon by **taxpayers** in determining the **tax** impact upon them of a similar set of facts. I.R.C. §7805.

PRIVATE RULING a determination by the Internal Revenue Service issued to a taxpayer who has asked for a determination as to the tax impact upon such taxpayer of a particular transaction. The determination is binding with respect to the taxpayer only and may not be relied upon by other taxpayers. These private rulings are published with the identifying characteristics of the taxpayer and the transaction deleted.

REVENUE PROCEDURE a published determination by the Internal Revenue Service concerning the administrative practices in the Internal Revenue Service. For example, the method and requirements for obtaining a private ruling are often published in revenue procedure.

REVERSAL as used in opinions, judgments, and mandates, the setting aside, annulling, vacating, or changing to the contrary the decision of a lower court or other body. Compare **overrule; remand.** See also **affirm.**

REVERSE DISCRIMINATION a term referring to the practice of excluding a classification or race of people who have not been historically discriminated against, usually whites, from positions that are made available exclusively to persons or groups that have traditionally been the subject of discrimination, or who otherwise benefit from **affirmative action** programs. The term has been applied to the practice of reserving positions for minorities in school admissions programs, corporate promotions, and rehiring of blacks with less job seniority than whites. The contention that affirmative action violates the **equal protection clause** of the **Fourteenth Amendment** and Title VI of the **Civil Rights Act,** 42 U.S.C. §§2000d et seq., has been the cause of differing opinions by members of the Supreme Court. 438 U.S. 265.

REVERSIBLE ERROR error substantially affecting **appellant's** legal rights and obligations which, if uncorrected, would result in a miscarriage of justice and which justifies reversing a judgment in the court below even if the error was not objected to in the lower court; synonymous with prejudicial error. See 314 P. 2d 973, 976. Compare **harmless error; plain error.**

REVERSION an **interest** created by operation of law by a **conveyance** of property but not transferred by that conveyance which thus remains in the **grantor;** "a **future estate** created by operation of law to take effect in possession in favor of a **lessor** or a **grantor** or his **heirs,** or their heirs of a **testator,** after the natural termination of a prior particular estate leased, granted or **devised.**" 30 A. 2d 57. Reversion may also refer to a present estate, constituting that part of an estate that the grantor retains upon the conveyance of the rest of the estate. Compare **remainder.**

REVERTER see **reversion.** See also **possibility of a reverter.**

REVEST returning to the possession of the **donor** or the former **proprietor,** 24 N.E. 734, 739.

REVIEW judicial reexamination of the proceedings of a court or other body; a reconsideration by the same court or body of its former decision; often used to express what an **appellate court** does when it examines the **record** of a lower court or agency determination on appeal. See **bill of review, judicial review.**

REVISED STATUTES statutes that have been changed, altered, reorganized, or simply reenacted. Their enactment is generally regarded as repealing and replacing the former laws. Abbreviated REV. STAT., REV. ST., or R.S. See 171 S.W. 2d 41 at 45.

REVIVAL in the law of **wills,** the act reinstituting a former will (which had been **revoked** by a latter will) once the latter will is canceled or destroyed. A few jurisdictions recognize the former will automatically upon the latter will's cancellation; most require some affirmative act, such as **republication,** before the former will is effective.

REVOCABLE able to be terminated at the **maker's** discretion. See **revocation.**

REVOCATION the recall of a power or authority conferred, or the cancellation of an **instrument** previously made, 300 N.Y.D. 351, 361; often used to signify the cancellation of an **offer** by the offeror, which, if effective, terminates the offeree's power of **acceptance.**

REVOCATION OF PAROLE [PROBATION] see **probation** [REVOCATION OF PAROLE; REVOCATION OF PROBATION].

REVOCATION OF WILL an affirmative act, such as writing "annulled" or "void" across the face of the **will,** 17 So. 2d 405, 409, or other marks on the words of the instrument and not just on the margin, 27 N.E. 2d 19, 21; or by tearing off the signatures at the end of the will, 102 N.E. 2d 818, all of which operate to render the instrument invalid for purposes of **probate.** Some courts require that the markings must affect the entire will or there is no revocation, 28 N.Y.S. 2d 390, 393, while others allow particular names to be eliminated, 184 N.W. 2d 718, although attempts to write in a new name will not be effective unless independently signed and witnessed.

REVOKE to recall a power or authority previously conferred, vacate an **instrument** previously made, or annul, repeal, **rescind** or cancel privileges. 67 N.E. 2d 570, 572. For example, in many states, motorists who receive more than a specified number of points for motor vehicle moving violations may have their licenses revoked.

REVOLVING CREDIT renewable **credit line** over a prescribed period of time. The term relates generally to an arrangement whereby a banker or merchant extends a certain amount of credit that can be repaid periodically. 297 F. 971, 979. Most states have **statutes** expressly regulating revolving charge accounts and some states authorize higher service charge rates on these accounts. The courts of other states have ruled that the service charge is interest on a loan and have subjected the credit transactions to **usury** laws.

REV. STAT. scc **revised statutes.**

RICO see **Racketeer Influenced and Corrupt Organizations Act [RICO].**

RIDER an amendment or addition attached to a document usually found as an attachment to an insurance policy identifying changes or increases in coverage. In the legislative process, a provision in a bill that is not germane to the main purpose of the law.

RIGGED ORDERS see **manipulation** [RIGGED ORDERS].

RIGHT see **claim of right; rights.**

RIGHT, WRIT OF see **writ of right.**

RIGHTFUL HEIRS see **heirs.**

RIGHT OF ACTION see **cause of action.**

RIGHT OF ELECTION in probate law, the statutory right of a surviving spouse to elect to take either what the deceased spouse gave under the **will,** or a share of the deceased spouse's estate as set forth by statute. Page, Wills §47.1 et seq. (3d ed. 1962). Compare **dower.**

RIGHT OF FIRST PUBLICATION see **copyright.**

RIGHT OF PRIVACY see **privacy, right of.**

RIGHT OF REDEMPTION see **redemption.**

RIGHT OF RE-ENTRY see **re-entry, right of.**

RIGHT OF WAY an **easement** for passage or access upon or across the lands of another, 149 P. 2d 61, 64. The right of a vehicle or pedestrian to proceed on the road, while others yield. Right of way statutes give preference to one of two vehicles (or between a vehicle and a pedestrian) when they are attempting to pass over the same part of the road at the same time. 21 N.W. 2d 522, 526.

RIGHT OR WRONG TEST see **insanity** [M'NAGHTEN RULE].

RIGHTS individual liberties either expressly provided for in the state or federal constitutions, such as the right to assembly or free speech, or which have been found to exist as those constitutions have been interpreted, such as the right to an abortion; that which a person is entitled to have, or to do, or to receive from others, within the limits prescribed by law; an enforceable legal right or the capacity to enforce that right; a claim or title to or an interest in anything that is enforceable by law, 263 P. 2d 769, 773. See also **civil rights; constitutional rights; inalienable rights; inherent right; pre-emptive rights; subscription rights; vested** [VESTED RIGHTS]; **visitation rights; voting right; voting rights act.**

In **securities** trading, a negotiable privilege to buy a new **issue** of stock at a subscription price lower than the market price of outstanding stock. As a result of the subscrip-

tion discount, rights have value and are often traded actively until they expire. Stock purchase rights are issued to existing shareholders in proportion to their holdings. In cases where the corporate charter includes **pre-emptive rights,** a RIGHTS OFFERING or similar mechanism is required. In other cases, rights offerings are used to aid in the distribution of a new issue by giving existing shareholders a convenient method to subscribe to the issue. Compare **stock option; warrant.**

RIGHT TO CONVEY see **covenant** [COVENANT OF SEISIN AND RIGHT TO CONVEY].

RIGHT TO REMAIN SILENT see **Miranda Rule [warnings].**

RIGHT TO WORK LAWS see **open shop.**

RIGOR MORTIS *(rǐ'-gôr môr'-tǐs)*—Lat: medical terminology depicting the stiffness, numbness, or hardness, of the muscles, which occurs after death.

RIPARIAN RIGHTS rights that accrue to owners of land on the banks of waterways, such as the use of such water, ownership of soil under the water, etc.; "rights not originating in grants, but [arising] by **operation of law,** and [which] are called 'natural rights,' because they arise by reason of the ownership of lands upon or along streams of water, which are furnished by nature, and the lands to which these natural rights are attached are called in law 'riparian lands.' Riparian lands, in the language of the cases and treatises, include by nature the lands over as [well as] those along which the stream flows, and riparian rights are incident to lands on the bank, as well as those forming the bed of the stream." 70 A. 472, 479.

RIPE FOR JUDGMENT the point in a case when everything seems to have been done that ought to be done before entry of a final adjudication upon the rights of the parties. 150 N.E. 2d 545, 548. See also **ripeness doctrine.**

RIPENESS DOCTRINE doctrine in constitutional law under which the Supreme Court, in accordance with its policy of self-restraint, will not decide cases "in advance of the necessity of deciding them." 331 U.S. 549. Compare **justiciable; moot.**

RISK hazard, danger, peril, exposure to loss, injury, disadvantage, or destruction. 203 S.E. 2d 739, 740. In **tort** law, the risk that should be reasonably perceived and avoided defines the common law duty concerning the probability or foreseeability of injury to another. 95 N.W. 2d 657, 664; 162 N.E. 99, 100. See **assigned risk; obvious risk.**

RISK, FORSEEABLE see **forseeability** [FORSEEABLE RISK].

RISK ASSUMPTION see **assumption of the risk.**

RISK CAPITAL money invested in a business venture for which **stock** is issued; in **security** law, a security transaction whereby an investor subjects money to the risks of an enterprise over which he or she exercises no managerial control. 371 F. Supp 395, 397. If a transaction is so characterized, it is subject to the various securities laws. Id.

RISK OF LOSS the financial risk of and responsibility for damage or destruction when property is being transferred between a buyer and a seller. The **Uniform Commercial Code** uses a contractual approach in allocating the risk of loss and assumes that the risk is upon the seller until some event occurs that shifts the risk to the buyer. Where the goods are identified and the contract authorizes the seller to ship the goods by carrier, the event necessary to shift the risk of loss is dependent upon whether the contract is a "shipment" or "destination" contract. See U.C.C. §2-509. Where the contract does not require the transfer of the goods by carrier, risk of loss passes to the buyer upon the taking of physical possession, unless an agreement to the contrary is made. U.C.C. §2-509(3), (4).

The phrase is also an insurance term denoting the hazards and perils that an insured is protected against, i.e., the contingencies or unknown events that are contemplated by the insured and that are covered by the insurance policy. 45 C.J.S. §753.

RISK OF NONPERSUASION see **burden of proof.**

ROBBERY forcible stealing; a common law offense defined as "the **felonious** taking of property from the person of another by violence or by putting him in fear. A felonious taking in his presence is a taking from the person when it is done by violence and against his will. . . . The violence or putting in fear must be at the time of the act or immediately preceding it." 152 F. 2d 808, 809. Under the Model Penal Code, a person commits robbery, "if, in the course of committing a theft, he: (a) inflicts serious bodily injury upon another; or (b) threatens another with or purposely puts him in fear of immediate serious bodily injury; or (c) commits or threatens to commit any felony of the first or second degree. An act shall be deemed in the course of committing a theft if it occurs in an attempt to commit theft or in flight after the attempt or commission." Model Penal Code §222.1

ARMED ROBBERY robbery aggravated by the fact that it is committed by a defendant armed with a dangerous weapon, whether or not the weapon is used in the course of committing the crime. Under the Model Penal Code, armed robbery is not a separate crime from robbery but raises the degree of the offense. Compare **burglary.**

ROBERTS RULES OF ORDER see **parliamentary law.**

ROBINSON-PATMAN ACT section 2(a) of the **Clayton Act,** the Robinson-Patman Act, also known as the ROBINSON-PATMAN ANTI-DISCRIMINATION ACT, prohibits price discrimination between purchasers of commodities of like grade and quality, where the effect of the discrimination may be to substantially lessen competition or tend to create a **monopoly** in any line of commerce. 15 U.S.C. §13(a). The illegal discrimination may include payment or acceptance of commissions, brokerage fees, or other compensation, §13(c), payment for services or facilities for processing or sale, §13(d), furnishing services or facilities for processing or handling, §13(e), knowingly inducing or receiving discriminatory price, §13(f), or the discriminatory use of rebates, discounts, advertising service charges, or underselling in particular localities. 15 U.S.C. §13(a). See **antitrust laws.**

ROGATORY LETTERS "a formal communication from a court in which an **action** is pending, to a foreign court, requesting that the **testimony** of a **witness** residing in such foreign jurisdiction be taken under the direction of the court addressed and transmitted to the court making the request." 215 N.W. 21, 22. See Fed. R. Civ. Proc. 28(b). The term is applicable to interstate as well as to international affairs. See 269 N.W. 498, 499.

ROLLOVER see **retirement plans** [ROLLOVER].

ROR see **release on own recognizance [ROR].**

ROUND LOT SHAREHOLDERS **shareholders** holding blocks of 100 shares per block. The term also refers to bondholders holding **bonds** with a $1,000 **par value.**

ROYALTY a share of the product or of the proceeds therefrom reserved by an owner for permitting another to exploit and use his or her **property**; the rental that is paid to the original owner of property based on a percentage of profit or production. 148 F. 2d 671, 673. The term is employed with respect to mining leases, conveyances, literary works, inventions, and other intellectual productions. Compare **commission.**

R.S. see **revised statutes.**

RUBRIC the title of a statute; a statute regarded as authoritative.

RULE prescribed guide for action or conduct, regulation or principle, 370 P. 2d 307, 309; includes commands to lower courts or court officials to do **ministerial acts.** 102 S.W. 6, 9. If a standard or directive by a governmental agency is characterized as a "rule," it must be promulgated in accordance with the procedures set down in the **Administrative Procedure Act.** A rule of a **court,** such as a federal rule of civil or criminal procedure, is adopted by the court itself and is subject to legislative action. Wright, Law of Federal Courts §62 (3d ed. 1976).

RULE AGAINST PERPETUITIES the rule that "no [contingent] **interest** is good unless it must **vest,** if at all, not later than twenty-one years after some life in being at the creation of the interest." Gray, Rule Against Perpetuities, 191 (4th ed., 1942).

The weight of authority is that the rule against perpetuities is directed against the remoteness of vesting of **estates** or interests in property. The minority view is that a perpetuity involves the suspension of the power of **alienation** beyond the time permitted by law. See Burby, Real Property 412 (3rd ed. 1965). "Its ultimate purpose is to prevent the clogging of title beyond reasonable limits in time by contingent interests and to keep land freely alienable in the market places." Boyer, Survey of the Law of Real Property 158 (3rd ed. 1981).

RULE IN SHELLEY'S CASE "When in the same **conveyance** an **estate** for life is given to the ancestor with **remainder** to the ancestor's **heirs,** then the ancestor takes both the life estate and the remainder in **fee simple** and the heirs take nothing"; e.g., 'A,' fee owner, conveys "to 'B' for life, then to the heirs of 'B.' 'B' takes both the life estate and the remainder in fee simple." Boyer, Survey of the Law of Real Property, 146 (3rd ed. 1981). The rule, created in 1324, has been abolished in England and in a majority of American jurisdictions. Id. at 106.

RULE IN WILD'S CASE in property law, a rule of construction by which a devise to "B and his children," where B has no children at the time the gift **vests** in B, was read to mean a gift to B in **fee tail,** the words "and his children" thus being construed as **words of limitation** and not **words of purchase.** The popularity of the fee tail has declined and most American jurisdictions have repudiated the Rule in Wild's Case so that in such conveyances the language quoted is construed to be a gift of a **life estate** to B, with a **remainder** to his children. See Moynihan, Introduction to the Law of Real Property 46-47 (1962).

RULE NISI procedure by which one party through an **ex parte** application or an order to **show cause** calls upon another to show cause why the rule set forth in the proposed order should not be made final by the court. If no cause is shown the court will enter an order rendering "absolute" [i.e., final] the rule, thereby requiring whatever was sought to be accomplished by the rule.

RULE OF AVOIDABLE CONSEQUENCES see **mitigation of damages.**

RULE OF LAW see **question of law.**

RULE OF REASON in **antitrust law,** the principle first enunciated by the Supreme Court in 1911 that the law is to be applied only to "unreasonable" restraints of trade, 221 U.S. 1. Since then, the rule of reason has evolved into a complex set of factors that may be considered in resolving an antitrust case. Givens, Antitrust: An Economic Approach, App. D (1983). The rule of reason has been rejected for certain types of business conduct such as **price fixing** agreements, which have been found to be illegal **per se,** that is, likely to harm competition and so lacking in potential benefit that they are illegal in and of themselves. 273 U.S. 392. See **Sherman Antitrust Act.**

RULES OF PROFESSIONAL CONDUCT see **code of professional responsibility; model rules of professional conduct.**

RUN WITH THE LAND a phrase used with respect to **covenants** in the law of real property to mean that the burdens, benefits, or both of the covenant pass to the persons who succeed to the interests of the original contracting parties, the idea being that the covenant "runs" because it is attached to the estate in the land as it is conveyed from one to another in the **chain of title.** Boyer, Survey of the Law of Property 516 (3rd ed. 1981). Covenants so characterized, therefore, bind the owners of the property to which they attach (with which they "run"), no matter who those owners are; such covenants therefore represent a more-or-less permanent limitation upon the estate held by the owner of the "burdened" property, and an enhancement of the estate held by the owner of the "benefited" property.

In order for a covenant to run with the land at law, the necessary formalities for creation of such a covenant must be met: the covenant must "touch and concern the land" [meaning that it must increase the use or value of the land benefited, or it must decrease the use or value of the land burdened]; the parties must intend that the covenant will run with the land; and there must be **privity** of estate. See id.; Cribbet, Principles of the Law of Property 353 (2d ed. 1975). In some jurisdictions such a covenant can only be created at the time a conveyance of land takes place.

S

SALABLE merchantable; an item fit for sale in usual course of trade, at usual selling prices. 178 P. 430. The item salable shall be of ordinary marketable quality, bring the average price, be lawful merchandise, be good and sufficient of its kind, and be free from any remarkable defects. 92 A. 180.

SALARY, FIXED see **fixed salary.**

SALE a **contract** or agreement by which **property** is transferred from the seller [vendor] to the buyer [vendee] for a fixed price in money, paid or agreed to be paid by the buyer. 172 F. 940, 942. "A 'sale' contemplates a free **offer** and **acceptance,** a seller and purchaser dealing at **arm's length,** and the fixing and payment of a purchase price." 46 N.E. 2d 184, 191. The **Uniform Commercial Code** Article 2 generally governs the sale of **goods.** Compare **bailment; exchange; gift.**

ABSOLUTE SALE a sale wherein the property passes to the buyer upon completion of the agreement between the parties. See 32 A. 227, 228.

AUCTION SALE a public sale to the highest bidder; the sale of real property or goods by public outcry and competitive **bidding.** With the fall of the auctioneer's hammer, or some other customary manner of ending bidding, the sale by auction is complete. If the buyer **bids** while the hammer is falling, the auctioneer may in his or her discretion reopen the bidding. U.C.C. §2-328(2).

The auction sale is "WITH RESERVE," meaning the auctioneer reserves the right to withdraw the goods from the auction block anytime before completion of sale, unless the goods are explicitly put up "WITHOUT RESERVE." The Uniform Commercial Code retains the **common law** rule for sales "without reserve" in that once the auctioneer calls for a bid, the article for sale cannot be withdrawn unless there is no bid within a reasonable time. In sales both with and without reserve, the bidder may retract the bid before completion of the sale. This retraction, however, does not revive any previous bid. U.C.C. §2-328(3); Calamari & Perillo, Contracts 36-37 (2d ed. 1977).

BARGAIN AND SALE see **bargain and sale.**

BILL OF SALE see **bill** [BILL OF SALE].

CASH SALE see **cash sale.**

CONDITIONAL SALE "a sale in which the vendee receives the **possession** and right of use of the goods sold, but transfer of the **title** to the vendee is made dependent upon the performance of some condition, usually the full payment of the purchase price." 434 P. 2d 655, 657. The "conditional sale" becomes absolute on the occurrence of the condition. See 131 N.E. 816, 817. It also refers to a "purchase accompanied by an agreement to resell upon particular terms." Id.

EXECUTED SALE in contrast to an EXECUTORY SALE (see below), it exists when "nothing remains to be done by either party to effect a complete transfer of the title to the subject matter of the sale." 167 S.W. 2d 407, 411.

EXECUTION SALE see **sheriff's sale.**

EXECUTORY SALE in contrast to an EXECUTED SALE, it is an agreement to sell wherein "something remains to be done by either party before delivery and passing of title," 167 S.W. 2d 407, 411; an agreement to sell where something more remains to be done before all the terms of the agreement are performed.

FORCED SALE "a sale which the vendor must make immediately, without the time or opportunity to find a buyer who will pay a price representing a sum approaching the reasonable worth of the [property] sold." 131 N.E. 2d 397, 403. The phrase is used synonymously with JUDICIAL SALE, whereby the court forces the sale of property as a result of a prior judicial **decree.** Many states have adopted constitutional provisions protecting **homesteads** from forced sales. 54 A. 2d 357, 359; 10 F. 601. However, a sale of a homestead consented to by the owner, or a sale in probate proceedings, to procure funds to pay for a testator's indebtedness have been held not to constitute forced sales. 35 P. 2d 154, 29 P. 2d 966. See **sheriff's sale.**

INSTALLMENT SALE see **installment sale.**

JUDICIAL SALE see FORCED SALE above; **sheriff's sale.**

PUBLIC SALE a sale upon notice to the public and in which members of the public may bid. See 99 N.W. 2d 885, 888. See also U.C.C. §2-706.

SALE BY SAMPLE a sale of goods in existence in bulk, but not present for examination, where it is mutually understood that the goods not exhibited conform to the sample; such a sale carries with it an implied **warranty** that the bulk of the goods purchased conforms to the sample. See 83 S.W. 78, 81; 120 S.E. 427, 429; U.C.C. §2-313(1)(c).

SALE IN GROSS as applied to a sale of land, a sale by the tract or as a whole, without regard to any warranty as to quantity [acres]; sometimes referred to as a CONTRACT OF HAZARD. See 77 Va. 610, 616; 169 A. 203, 205.

SALE ON APPROVAL a transaction in which goods delivered primarily for use may be returned if the buyer is unsatisfied with them even though they may conform to the contract. U.C.C. §2-326(1)(a); 175 S.W. 2d 218. If the goods are delivered primarily for resale, rather than for use, the transaction is termed a SALE OR RETURN or a **consignment.** U.C.C. §2-326(1)(b). Goods so consigned may be returned if unsold in a reasonable amount of time at the buyer's risk and expense. Id. at §2-327(2)(b).

SALE OR EXCHANGE see **sale or exchange.**

SALE WITH RIGHT OF REDEMPTION sale where seller reserves the right to take back title to property he or she has sold upon repayment of the purchase price; it is distinct from transactions where a purchaser grants an option to his or her seller to repurchase. See 263 So. 2d 96, 105.

SHERIFF'S SALE see **sheriff's sale.** See also FORCED SALE above.

TAX SALE a sale of land for the nonpayment of taxes. See 25 So. 105, 108. See **foreclosure.**

SALE AND LEASEBACK a procedure whereby an owner of property sells it to another party who immediately leases the property back to the original owner. This method is frequently employed for tax purposes or for situations where the original owner needs cash rather than property.

SALE IN INSTALLMENTS see **installment sale.**

SALE OR EXCHANGE a phrase used in tax law to describe a disposition of property in a value for value exchange as opposed to a disposition by gift, contribution, or the like; the **realization** of **gain or loss** for **income tax** purposes on the disposition of property is based on the sale or exchange of that property, e.g., I.R.C. §§1001, 1222.

SALES TAX see **tax** [SALES TAX].

SALVAGE generally, the value of property following its destruction or loss; in maritime law, a service rendered to a vessel which removes it from some distress, 332 F. Supp. 44, 47; to be entitled to a salvage award, the distressed vessel must be in impending peril of the sea from which it is rescued from the voluntary efforts of others, 90 U.S. (23 Wall) 1; 342 F. Supp. 976, 982; in insurance law, the value of the property following a loss, which can be deducted from the amount recovered by the insured, 109 F. 2d 172, 174; in tax law, "the amount, determined at the time of acquisition, which is estimated will be realizable upon sale or other disposition of an asset when it is no longer useful in the taxpayer's business and is to be retired from service." 181 F. Supp. 887, 889. That amount is then calculated into a taxpayer's permissible **depreciation** of the asset. See I.R.C. §167(f).

The **accelerated cost recovery system** does not provide for salvage value.

EQUITABLE SALVAGE an equitable right of the last person to preserve a property's value to have priority over others in either that property or its value upon real-ization, since without that person's actions the property would be worthless.

SALVAGE VALUE see **depreciation** [SALVAGE VALUE].

SAMPLE that which is taken out of a large quantity as a fair representation of the whole; a part shown as evidence of the quality of the whole. 189 P. 2d 258, 259. See, e.g., 402 F. 2d 1009, 1012. "Any sample or model which is made part of the basis of the bargain creates an express warranty that the whole of the goods shall conform to the sample or model." U.C.C. §2-313(1)(c).

SANCTION a punishment for violation of accepted norms of social conduct, which may be of two kinds: those which redress **civil** injuries, i.e., civil sanctions; and those which punish crimes, i.e., penal sanctions. See 81 S.W. 526, 528. Also, to approve; "convey[s] the idea of sacredness, or of authority." 43 N.E. 80, 81.

SANE [SANITY] the state of sound mental condition; all persons are presumed sane until the opposite is demonstrated. All jurisdictions require the defendant in a criminal case to produce some evidence to challenge this presumption. In some jurisdictions, the burden of persuasion is borne by the state; in others, the defendant carries the ultimate burden of proof. The allocation of this burden is apparently within the individual state's rules of procedure and placing the burden on the defendant does not violate the presumption of innocence. 429 U.S. 877. See LaFave, Modern Criminal Law 345 (1978). Compare **insanity.**

SANITY HEARING a proceeding authorized by statute for investigating the sanity of a person accused of a felony. Such a hearing is not a **trial** placing the accused in jeopardy, but is a "collateral inquiry" in the nature of an inquest to determine the competency of a person to stand trial. See Fed. R. Crim. Proc. 12.2.

SATISFACTION [OF A DEBT] a discharge and subsequent release of obligation by the payment thereof. 105 P. 2d 342, 345. See **accord; accord and satisfaction; ademption.**

SAVE HARMLESS protect from loss or liability; **indemnify;** guaranty. 50 N.W. 496.

In contract law, the phrase is used to signify a commitment by one party to make good or repay another party to an agreement in the event of a specified loss. The agreement commits the **obligor** to reimburse the **obligee** if the obligee suffers the stated loss, and not to bear the loss in the first instance. Thus, where a lease states, "the lessee [tenant] shall save harmless the lessor [landlord] against claims for injuries to persons on the premises," the lessee is required to reimburse the lessor in the event such a claim is successfully prosecuted by an injured third party and damages are recovered against the lessor. 12 A. 797, 801.

SAVING CLAUSE a clause in a statute restricting the scope of the repeal of prior statutes; language inserted in a statute to maintain the force of the law repealed as to existing rights, 198 So. 2d 94, 97; a **grandfather clause** as to rights abrogated by the repeal of a legislative act.

SAVINGS AND LOAN ASSOCIATION see **bank** [SAVINGS AND LOAN ASSOCIATION].

SAVINGS BANK see **bank** [SAVINGS BANK].

SCHOLARSHIPS AND FELLOWSHIPS tuition or subsistence aid given to an individual for participation in an educational program. In general, a fellowship or scholarship grant at an educational institution is not subject to income taxes. However, it must not constitute compensation for services primarily for the benefit of the grantor of the fellowship or scholarship unless the employment is required in order for the taxpayer to obtain a degree. If the individual receiving the grant is not a candidate for a degree, the grantor must be a tax-exempt educational organization or a governmental unit. The amount **excludable** in any one year is $300 multiplied by the number of months for which the recipient received amounts under the scholarship or fellowship grant during the **taxable year.** I.R.C. §117.

SCIENTER *(sē'-ĕn-têr)*—Lat: knowledge; previous knowledge of an operative state of facts; frequently signifies "guilty knowledge." As used in **pleadings,** scienter signifies that "the alleged **crime** or **tort** was done designedly, understandingly, knowingly or with guilty knowledge," 211 N.W. 346; "a term usually employed in legal **issues** involving **fraud,** means knowledge on the part of a person making representations, at the time they were made, that they are false . . . the false statements must have been made intentionally to deceive or with what is recognized as the legal equivalent to a deliberately fraudulent intent to deceive." 444 S.W. 2d 498, 505. See also **culpable; mens rea.**

SCINTILLA [SCINTILLA OF EVIDENCE] evidence which is speculative and conjectural and is something less than substantial evidence, 491 P. 2d 1342, 1344; if at least a scintilla of evidence is presented, some courts have held that the party against whom the evidence is offered should not be granted a **summary judgment.** 374 So. 2d 872, 873.

SCOPE OF AUTHORITY in the law of agency, those acts proper for the accomplishment of the goal of the agency, including "not only actual authorization conferred upon agent by his principal, but also that which has apparently or impliedly been delegated to the agent." 290 N.Y.S. 204, 208. As applied to doctrine of **respondeat superior,** masters are liable civilly for damages occasioned by the torts of their servants and agents committed while acting within the scope of their authority. "The proper inquiry is whether the act was done in the course of the agency and by virture of the authority as agent." 62 N.W. 899, 903. See also **apparent authority.**

SCOPE OF EMPLOYMENT the range of activities encompassed by one's employment; refers to those acts done while performing one's job duties; "[t]he phrase . . . [was] adopted by the courts for the purpose of determining a master's **liability** for the acts of his **servants,** [and] has 'no fixed or technical meaning,' . . . 'the ultimate question is whether it is just that the loss resulting from the servant's acts should be considered one of the normal risks of the business in which the servant is employed which that business should bear.' " 145 So. 743, 745. The phrase is "a convenient means of defining those **tortious** acts of the servant not ordered by the master for which the policy of law imposes liability upon the master." 181 A. 2d 565, 569. The master (usually, the employer) is **vicariously liable** only for those torts of the servant (employee) which are committed within the scope of his or her employment. See **respondeat superior.** See also **Employers' Liability Acts; Worker's Compensation Acts.**

S CORPORATION see **corporation** [S CORPORATION].

SCRIP DIVIDEND see **dividend.**

SCRIVENER a term, infrequently used in the United States, signifying a writer or scribe, particularly one who draws legal documents. Also, one who acts as the **agent** for another, investing and managing

that other's property, whether money or otherwise, for a fee.

SCRUTINY see **strict scrutiny.**

SCUTAGE in feudal law, a tax imposed on landholders to help pay for the King's army.

SEAL at common law, an impression on wax, wafer, or other substance placed on a document and having legal effect. See 30 S.W. 132, 133. "The purpose of a 'seal' is to attest in a formal manner to the execution of an **instrument.**" 42 So. 959, 960. "Among the forms of 'seal' that are in use in most of the states are wax, a gummed wafer, an impression in the paper itself, the word 'seal,' the letters 'L.S.' (signifying LOCUS SIGILLI for "place of the seal"), [and] a pen scrawl." Corbin Contracts 3241 (one-volume ed. 1952).

A **seal** of a corporation is sometimes called a COMMON SEAL. See 65 A. 526, 527. See **locus** [LOCUS SIGILLI]; **sealed instrument.**

SEALED INSTRUMENT one that is signed and has the **seal** of the signer attached. "To render a **contract** a sealed instrument, it must be so recited in the body of the instrument and a seal or scroll must be placed after the signature." 16 S.E. 2d 502, 504. A sealed contract was a FORMAL CONTRACT (as opposed to a contract without a seal which was called a SIMPLE CONTRACT) and is often called a CONTRACT UNDER SEAL; such a contract did not require **consideration** at **common law,** Corbin Contracts §252 (1952); a deed under seal likewise required no consideration. Today any symbol, even the word "seal" or the letters "L.S." printed on a form, will, if so intended, constitute the necessary seal. Statutes have eliminated most of the special effects of sealed instruments at common law in most of the states, though a number of states continue the common law significance of sealed instruments. Even in many states which have purported to abrogate these effects, longer periods for enforcing debts founded upon sealed instruments exist under their **statutes of limitations.** See id. §254.

Under the Uniform Commercial Code, the use of a seal is intended to have no effect upon the transaction; the use of a seal "does not constitute the writing of a sealed instrument and the law with respect to sealed instruments does not apply." U.C.C. §2-203.

SEALING OF RECORDS the sealing of criminal records, required in some states with respect to **youthful offenders,** so that such records may be examined only by court order. See **expungement.**

SEARCH AND SEIZURE a police practice whereby a person or place is searched and evidence useful in the investigation and prosecution of crime is seized. The extent of a search and seizure is constitutionally limited by the Fourth and Fourteenth Amendments to the United States Constitution and by provisions in the several state constitutions, statutes, and rules of court. One limitation requires that the search and seizure be reasonable, which usually requires the existence of **probable cause** to believe that the item searched for was involved in criminal activity and will be located at the place to be searched. In most circumstances a **search warrant** is required prior to the search and seizure. However, there are several exigent circumstances where such warrants are not required: (1) searches that are incident to an arrest, see 267 U.S. 132, 399 U.S. 30, [which must be limited to the person and the immediately surrounding area, see 395 U.S. 752 (1969)]; (2) frisks conducted as part of an investigative stop [limited to the outer frisk for a weapon, see 392 U.S. 1]; (3) seizures of items in **plain view,** see 390 U.S. 234; (4) seizures of abandoned property, see 265 U.S. 57; (5) circumstances where it would

be impossible or unwise to secure a warrant, see 387 U.S. 294; (6) searches where there is proper consent, see 255 U.S. 313; 412 U.S. 218; and (7) searches at international borders. See 413 U.S. 266.

If there is an unreasonable or otherwise unconstitutional search, the evidence seized will be excluded at any criminal proceeding where the defendant has **standing** to object to its introduction. See 439 U.S. 128. Furthermore, all fruits of the illegal search are excluded. See 251 U.S. 385. Victims of an illegal search may also bring a civil **tort** suit against the officers for the violation of their civil right of privacy. See 403 U.S. 388. See **exclusionary rule; illegally obtained evidence.** Compare **unreasonable search and seizure.**

SEARCH, CONSENT FOR see **consent search.**

SEARCH OF TITLE see **title search.**

SEARCH WARRANT an order issued by a judge directing certain law enforcement officers to conduct a search of specified premises for specified things or persons, and to bring them before the court. It has long been a requirement of fundamental law that searches be conducted after the obtaining of a search warrant. The requirement was embedded in American law by the Fourth Amendment to the Constitution, which is now applicable to the states through the Fourteenth Amendment, see 338 U.S. 25, and requires that all searches be reasonable and that search warrants issue only upon **probable cause** supported by sworn allegations and that the warrant "particularly describe the place to be searched, and the persons or things to be seized." The paramount evil to which the Fourth Amendment is addressed was the use of GENERAL WARRANTS to be used by the government to conduct unreasonable searches. See 116 U.S. 612. Thus, general searches of the described premises and the seizure of things not described in the warrant, except in certain instances where the unmentioned thing is in **"plain view,"** have been proscribed by Supreme Court construction of the Fourth Amendment. See 403 U.S. 443.

The "reasonableness" requirement of the Fourth Amendment does not mean that a warrant is required for all searches since there are exceptional circumstances under which a warrant is not required, although probable cause may be required. **Warrants** are constitutionally preferred and may be dispensed with only in certain exigent circumstances. 380 U.S. 102. A major exception to the warrant requirement is that a search of the person and the area within his control is permitted without warrant, incident to a valid **arrest** [i.e., one made upon probable cause]. See 414 U.S. 218.

In those cases where warrants are required, only a neutral and impartial judge or magistrate can issue it 407 U.S. 345 and only upon a showing of probable cause that the described item is located in the designated place and that it was involved in the planning or commission of a crime. See 333 U.S. 10, 403 U.S. 443, 103 S. Ct. 2317.

SEASONABLE timely, in due season or time, 277 S.W. 372, 373; the time in which action is appropriate and can be effective, 2 F. Supp. 999, 1000. The word "seasonably" has been used synonymously with "reasonably" to mean in a timely manner. 277 S.W. 372, 373. See **time of the essence.**

SEASONAL relating to a specific time of the year. 204 N.W. 391, 393. Seasonal employment is the kind of occupation that can be performed only during certain periods of the year, and does not include such occupations that may be carried on throughout the entire year. 284

N.W. 756, 760. Compare **seasonable.**

S.E.C. see **Securities and Exchange Commission [S.E.C.].**

SECOND AMENDMENT the provision in the U.S. Constitution that gives each state the right to maintain a "well regulated Militia" and "the people to keep and bear Arms." The debates that led to the adoption of the Second Amendment indicate that its purpose was to prevent federal interference with state militia and the creation of a national army that would destroy local autonomy. The Second Amendment thus does not apply to private conduct, 92 U.S. 542, 553, to **state action,** 116 U.S. 252, 265, or to federal gun control laws that do not interfere with state militia, 307 U.S. 174. See generally, Tribe, American Constitutional Law, 226, n.6 (1978).

SECONDARY BOYCOTT see **boycott** [SECONDARY BOYCOTT].

SECONDARY DISTRIBUTION an organized **offering** of **stock** already issued and outstanding. Typical sources of large blocks of stock for redistribution are corporate founders, **insiders,** and major investors. If the block involves **letter stock** and if the volume is large compared to average trading volume, then a **registration statement** must be filed with the **Securities and Exchange Commission.** In cases requiring a full registration, the **corporation** involved usually offers a comparable quantity of new shares for its own account. In cases involving **listed** securities and where no registration statement is required to be delivered with the shares, the secondary distribution can be handled as a **stock exchange** distribution. In either case, the distribution is usually handled by a **syndicate,** which is organized by the lead **investment bank,** and trades are initiated in the open market to stabilize the price of the publicly traded shares while the offering is underway.

SECONDARY LIABILITY see **liability** [SECONDARY LIABILITY].

SECONDARY PARTY a person obligated to pay a **debt** if the person incurring the debt fails to pay it. The person from whom a **creditor** is first obliged to attempt to collect a debt is "primarily **liable**"; the parties from whom the creditor may then collect the debt are "secondarily liable." All the **assets** of the person secondarily liable may be used to satisfy the personal liability of the primary obligor. 276 F. 2d 714, 717.

SECOND-DEGREE see **murder** [SECOND-DEGREE MURDER]; **principal** [PRINCIPAL IN THE SECOND-DEGREE].

SECOND MORTGAGE a **mortgage** without intervening liens between it and the first mortgage, 97 Pa. 342, 347; one which does not contemplate a mortgage on a buyer's interest in a land contract, 425 P. 2d 891, 894.

SECRETS OF TRADE see **trade secrets**.

SECTION 1231 PROPERTY see **capital** [§1231 PROPERTY].

SECUNDUM *(sĕ-kūn'-dŭm)*—Lat: immediately after, beside, next to. In law publishing, the second series of a treatise may be called secundum as in Corpus Juris Secundum (C.J.S.).

SECURED CREDITOR a **creditor** who holds **security** that will cover the amount the **debtor** owes him or her. Among these securities may be mortgages, deeds, bills of sale, liens upon goods, etc., 289 N.Y.S. 771, 785. The definition in the Bankruptcy Act, 11 U.S.C. §§101 et seq., is narrower in that it applies only to those creditors who hold security belonging to the bankrupt. 539 F. 2d 487, 491. See White & Summers, Uniform Commercial

Code §§24-1 et seq. (2d ed. 1980). See **credit, security interest**.

SECURED TRANSACTIONS see **credit, security interest**.

SECURITIES stock   certificates, bonds, or other **evidence** of a secured indebtedness or of a right created in the holder to participate in profits or **assets** distribution of a profit-making enterprise; more generally, written assurances for the return or payment of money, 91 P. 2d 892, 895; 15 U.S.C. §78c(10); **instruments** giving to their legal holders the right to money or other property. As such, securities have value and are used in regular channels of commerce. The basic purpose of the sale of securities is to raise capital for businesses and government. Historically, securities have been an area of major investment and speculation by **banks** and individuals. Unbridled trading by unscrupulous speculators which led to inflated securities markets and contributed to the great financial crash of the late 1920s resulted in the passage of the Securities Act, 15 U.S.C. §77a et seq., and the Securities Exchange Act, 15 U.S.C. §78a et seq., in 1933 (See **Securities Acts**), both of which strictly regulate the buying and selling of securities. Parrish, Securities Regulation and the New Deal 108 (1970). Securities are also regulated by state laws known as **Blue Sky laws**.

The most common types of securities are:

BLUE CHIP STOCK see **blue chip stock**.

BOND essentially, a loan agreement representing a debt. In return for the **capital** given to a corporation or a government entity, the bondholder gets a promise of repayment of **principal** and **interest** over time, instead of ownership rights. Since the holder of a bond is a **creditor** instead of an owner, his claims against the assets of a corporation are satisfied first in case of a failure of the business venture. Most bonds are secured by some kind of **collateral,** so that in case of **default,** the debt might still be satisfied. Consequently, bonds are generally a lower risk investment. See Henn & Alexander, Law of Corporations, §§154-56 (3d ed. 1983). Unsecured bonds are called **debentures,** 16 N.E. 2d 352. Bonds raise money commonly known as DEBT CAPITAL. See **bond.**

BONUS STOCK see **bonus stock.**

CAPITAL STOCK see **capital** [CAPITAL STOCK].

CLASSIFIED STOCK see **classified stock.**

COMMON STOCK see STOCK below.

CONVERTIBLE SECURITY see **convertible securities.**

DEBT CAPITAL see BOND above.

DIVIDEND see **dividend.**

EQUITY CAPITAL see STOCK below.

GROWTH STOCK see **growth stock.**

GUARANTEED SECURITY see **guaranteed security.**

INVESTMENT STOCK see **restricted securities.**

JOINT STOCK COMPANY see **company** [JOINT STOCK COMPANY].

LETTER STOCK see **restricted securities.**

LISTED STOCK see **listed stock.**

NON-ASSESSABLE STOCK see **non-assessable stock.**

NONSTOCK CORPORATION see **nonstock corporation.**

NO-PAR [NONPAR] STOCK see **no-par [nonpar] stock.**

PREFERRED STOCK see STOCK below.

PUBLIC SECURITIES those certificates and other **negotiable instruments** evidencing the debt of a governmental body.

RESTRICTED SECURITIES see **restricted securities.**

STOCK an equity or ownership interest in a **corporation,** 375 F. 2d 730, 731, usually created by a contribution to the **capital** of the corporation. Its unit of measurement is the **share,** and the owner of one or more shares of stock in a company is entitled to participate in the company's management and profits, and in distribution of assets upon **dissolution** of the company. Ownership of stock may be evidenced by a written **instrument** known as a **stock certificate.** 308 So. 2d 352, 354. Distribution of profits to stockholders occurs through the payment of **dividends.** However, for tax purposes, not all corporations pay dividends to their stockholders, but rather reinvest profits in the business, thereby increasing the value of the stock to the investor. See Cavitch, Business Organizations with Tax Planning, §68.01 (1978 ed.).

There are two general types of stock. COMMON STOCK is the ordinary stock of a corporation. It is distinguished not by its own features but by the advantages given other types of securities. Generally, common stock is last in priority when profits or assets are distributed. 18 C.J.S. Corporations §216 (1939). PREFERRED STOCK is a class of stock entailing certain rights beyond those attached to common stock; "corporate stock having preference rights. It represents a contribution to the capital of the corporation and is in no sense a loan of money. . . . By general definition preferred stock is stock entitled to a preference over other kinds of stock in the payment of **dividends.** The dividends come out of earnings [income] and not out of **capital.** Unless there are net earnings there is no right to dividends.'' 41 N.W. 2d 571, 575. Other rights which may be attendant to preferred stock are limitless; however, whatever rights are given must be clearly noted. It is part of the capital **stock** of a **corporation** which enjoys **priority** over the remaining stock, or **common stock,** in the distribution of profits and, in the event of dissolution of the corporation, in the distribution of assets as well. The issuance of stock raises money commonly known as EQUITY CAPITAL.

STOCK ISSUE see **issue** [STOCK ISSUE].

TREASURY STOCK see **treasury stock.**

UNLISTED STOCK see **unlisted security.**

WATERED STOCK see **watered stock.**

WHEN ISSUED SECURITIES see **when issued securities.**

SECURITIES ACT OF 1933 see **Securities Acts** [SECURITIES ACT OF 1933].

SECURITIES ACTS popular name given to the two major federal statutes regulating the issuing of and market trading in **corporate securities.**

The SECURITIES ACT OF 1933, 15 U.S.C. §§77a et seq., deals primarily with the initial distribution of securities by the issuer, and its objective is to provide full disclosure of facts material to the securities for sale so that investors are able to make informed investment decisions. Cox, Corporations 234 (1975).

The SECURITIES EXCHANGE ACT OF 1934, 15 U.S.C. §§78a et seq., is designed to regulate post-distribution trading in securities and provides for the registration and regulation of securities exchanges, including disclosure of information about the issue for the purpose of prohibiting fraud and manipulation in connection with the sale or purchase of securities. See 69 Am. Jur. 2d Securities Regulation-Federal §183. Federal securities laws specifically preserve the jurisdiction of state commissions to regulate securities transactions as long as there is no conflict with federal law. See **blue sky laws; prospectus.** The other acts constituting the remainder of the federal securities statutes are as follows:

The INVESTMENT COMPANY ACT OF 1940 act that regulates publicly owned companies engaged primarily in the business of investing and trading in securities. 15 U.S.C. §§80a-1-80a-52.

The INVESTORS ADVISERS ACT OF 1940 act that establishes a scheme of registration and regulation of investment advisers comparable to that contained in the Securities Exchange Act of 1934 (above) with respect to broker-dealers but not as comprehensive. A limited private cause of action for **rescission** but not **damages** has been found to be implied in the Act. See 444 U.S. 11; 15 U.S.C. §§80b-1 et seq.

The PUBLIC UTILITY HOLDING COMPANY ACT OF 1935 act that regulates the financing and operation of electric and gas public utility holding company systems. 15 U.S.C. §§79 et seq.

The SECURITIES INVESTOR PROTECTION ACT OF 1970 act that established the **Securities Investor Protection Corporation [S.I.P.C.]** and gave it the power to supervise the liquidation of financially troubled securities firms and the payment of the claims of their customers. 15 U.S.C. §§78aaa et seq.

The TRUST INDENTURE ACT OF 1939 act that regulates public issuers of large debt securities, i.e., over $5,000,000. 15 U.S.C. §§77aaa-77bbb.

SECURITIES AND EXCHANGE COMMISSION [S.E.C.] an agency empowered to regulate and supervise the selling of securities; a commission expressly authorized by the Securities Exchange Act of 1934 to make rules and regulations to effectuate the provisions of the Act. 15 F. Supp. 144. The SEC, although it exercises some quasi judicial functions, does not constitute a court, but is an administrative agency exercising regulatory powers. See **Securities Acts.**

SECURITIES EXCHANGE ACT OF 1934 see **Securities Acts** [SECURITIES EXCHANGE ACT OF 1934].

SECURITIES INVESTOR PROTECTION ACT OF 1970 see **Securities Acts** [SECURITIES INVESTOR PROTECTION ACT OF 1970].

SECURITIES INVESTOR PROTECTION CORPORATION [S.I.P.C.] a **non-profit corporation,** supported by its membership of **securities brokers** and dealers, designed to protect customers of securities brokers and dealers and to promote confidence in the securities markets. It was created by Congress as a result of the enactment of the Securities Investors Protection Act of 1970. 15 U.S.C. §§78aaa et seq. See **Securities Acts.**

SECURITY protection, safety, 213 N.E. 2d 191, 195; the instrument of protection or safety, 155 S.E. 2d 32, 34; a person who becomes the **surety** for another, 192 F. Supp. 93, 94. Generally, "instruments for the payment of money, or evidencing title or equity, with or without some collateral obligation, and which are commonly dealt in for the purpose of financing and investment." 289 N.Y.S. 2d 301, 304. Also, an investment in some private or public business enterprise. 330 N.E. 2d 794, 800. Components of a security are: (1) an investment of money, (2) in a common enterprise, (3) with an expectation of profits solely from the efforts of others. 392 A. 2d 419, 420. See U.C.C. §8-102(1)(a); Uniform Probate Code §1-201(37); **Securities Exchange Act of 1934** §3, 15 U.S.C. §78c; I.R.C. §6323(h); **Bankruptcy Act** 11 U.S.C. §101(35). See generally **Securities; Securities Acts.**

SECURITY DEPOSIT the pledge of property, money, or some additional personal obligation of the debtor or tenant to secure an obligation. Most commonly refers to money that a **tenant** deposits with a **landlord** to insure the landlord that the tenant will abide by the lease agreements; "represents a fund from which the landlord may obtain payment for damages caused by the tenant during his occupancy." 172 So. 2d 26, 28. Leases sometimes provide that the landlord may retain the security deposit as **liquidated damages** in the event that the lease is terminated at the tenant's request prior to the expiration of the full term of the lease. In some jurisdictions, statutes require that no more than a certain sum (often 1 or 1½ times the monthly rental) be required as security and that it be held separately from the landlord's other funds in an interest paying account. See, e.g., N.J.S. §46:8-19. Compare **surety.**

SECURITY INTEREST an **interest** in **real** or **personal property** which secures the payment of an obligation. Under the Uniform Commercial Code security interests are limited to personal property and **fixtures.** See U.C.C. §1-201 (37).

At common law, security interests are either consensual or arise by **operation of law.** Security interests that arise by operation of law include judgment **liens** and statutory liens. The Uniform Commercial Code does not govern most interests that arise by operation of law.

The clearest examples of security interests are the **mortgage,** the **pledge** and the **conditional sale.** The mortgage involves the situation wherein the mortgagor gives the mortgagee a security interest in a specific asset, which is usually real property. The pledge deals with the situation wherein the creditor takes possession of the property. The conditional sale involves the situation wherein the seller gives credit and takes a security interest. The Uniform Commercial Code ignores differences of form and treats all secured interests in personal property simply as "security interests." See U.C.C. §9-102. Compare **security deposit.**

PURCHASE-MONEY SECURITY INTEREST one "taken or retained by the seller of the **collateral** to secure all or part of its price; or is one taken by a person who, by making advances or incurring an obligation, gives value in order to enable the debtor to acquire rights in or the use of collateral if such value is in fact so used." U.C.C. §9-107.

SEDITION illegal action tending to cause the disruption and overthrow of the government. The United States had enacted an Alien and Sedition Act as early as 1798. Sedition acts were also enacted during World War I, prohibiting types of communication advocating the overthrow of the government. In 1919, the Supreme Court held that seditious communications could be punished consistent with the First Amendment, if they presented a **clear and present danger** of bringing about an evil (violence) which the government had a right to prevent. See 249 U.S. 47.

The state governments also have the power to prevent harmful sedition. See 254 U.S. 325. However, the states cannot punish sedition against the United States where

Congress has already **preempted** legislation in this area by "occupying the field" with legislation of its own. See 350 U.S. 497. See **treason.**

SEDITIOUS LIBEL in English law a misdemeanor involving the publishing of any words or document, with a seditious intention. "A seditious intention means an intention to bring into contempt or excite disaffection against the government or to promote feelings of ill will between the classes. If the seditious statement is published, the publisher is guilty of a seditious libel." Black, Constitutional Law 543 (2d ed. 1897). The law of seditious libel is now severely circumscribed in **the United States** by the **First Amendment** to the Constitution. See **freedom** [FREEDOM OF PRESS]; [FREEDOM OF SPEECH].

SEDUCTION "[i]nducing a chaste, unmarried woman, by means of temptation, deception, acts, flattery, or a promise of marriage, to engage in sexual intercourse." 151 So. 2d 752, 757. A woman may also entice a man to commit sexual intercourse. 138 So. 2. Force is not an **element** of "seduction." At common law, seduction merely created a **civil** liability and in some states the woman could recover **damages** for her seduction. In states where seduction is now a criminal offense, the chastity or reputation of chastity of the victim prior to seduction may be essential for conviction. See 18 U.S.C. §2198; Model Penal Code §213.3. Other states have barred actions for seduction. See N.Y. Civ. Rights L. §80a. Perkins & Boyce, Criminal Law 462 (3d ed. 1982). See **fornication.** Compare **rape.**

SEGREGATION to set apart; the separation of some persons or things from others. 170 S.E. 189, 191. For instance, a contract may require a party to keep certain funds segregated so that they will be available for payment 160 A. 711, 712.

In constitutional law, segregation is the maintenance of separate facilities and institutions for people of different races. The racial segregation that prevailed in this country until the 1950s was based on the theory that **separate but equal** facilities met the constitutional requirements of the equal protection clause. 163 U.S. 537. In the landmark case of *Brown v. Board of Education,* 347 U.S. 483 (1954), segregation resulting from **state action** was held to be violative of the **equal protection clause.** After a period of 15 years, the **deliberate speed** with which all vestiges of public school segregation was to end was rejected in favor of a standard of immediate implementation. See 396 U.S. 19. Schwartz, Constitutional Law §§9.15-9.16 (2d ed. 1979). See **de facto** [DE FACTO SEGREGATION].

SEIGNEUR **[SEIGNIOR]** *(sē'-nyôr)*—generally, Fr: master, lord; more specifically, the lord of a **fee** or of a manor. 79 C.J.S. 1023.

SEISED the condition of legally **owning** and **possessing realty.** Thus, one seised of **real property** legally owns and possesses it. The phrase imports legal **title** as opposed to **beneficial ownership.** See 110 A. 770, 773. See **seisin.**

SEISIN in early English property law, the term that properly described the **interest** in land of one who held a **freehold estate.** The term "**ownership**" was not used, since the sovereign was considered, technically, the owner of all lands in England; a landholder was instead said to be "seised of" his estate. The concept embraced more than mere **possession,** involving as well some legal right to hold; an **ouster** effected a **disseisin** of the original holder, requiring the original holder to resort to self-help or the legal process to regain his land. A voluntary transfer of the holder's interest was accomplished by **livery of seisin.** See Cribbet, Principles of the Law of Property 14 (1975).

Today, "seisin" is generally considered synonymous with OWNERSHIP. See 83 U.S. 352, 361. See **livery of seisin.**

SEISIN, COVENANT OF see **covenant** [COVENANT OF SEISIN AND RIGHT TO CONVEY].

SEIZURE the act of forcibly dispossessing an owner of property, under actual or apparent authority of law; also, the taking of property into the **custody** of the court in **satisfaction** of a **judgment,** or in consequence of a violation of public law. See 94 N.W. 18. See **attachment; garnishment; in rem; levy; search and seizure.**

SELECTIVE ALLOCATION see **marshaling [marshalling]** [SELECTIVE ALLOCATION].

SELECTIVE INCORPORATION the process by which certain of the guarantees expressed in the **Bill of Rights** become applicable to the states through the **Fourteenth Amendment.** Under the TOTAL INCORPORATION APPROACH, an approach never adopted by a majority of the Supreme Court, all the Bill of Rights and the attendant case law interpreting them, are applied to the states. Under the selective incorporation approach, each guarantee in the Bill of Rights and its related case law is applied to the states, 391 U.S. 145.

SELECTIVE SERVICE SYSTEM the system established under the Selective Service Act by which persons are selected to serve in the armed forces in order to ensure the security of this country. 50 U.S.C. App. §451. Every male citizen or resident of the United states who is between the ages of 18 and 26 years is required to register for potential selection to serve in the armed forces. 50 U.S.C. App. §453. The requirement that only men and not women register does not violate the

Fifth Amendment. Since women are not eligible for combat duty and the purpose of the registration system is to ensure the availability of combat troops, the statute has been found to bear a reasonable relationship to a legitimate legislative purpose. 453 U.S. 57. While males are required to register, none has been drafted into the armed forces since the end of the Vietnam War. See also **military law.**

SELF-DEALING transactions in which a **fiduciary** uses or obtains the property held in his or her fiduciary capacity for his or her own benefit; for instance, a **trustee** using trust property for his or her own benefit. Self-dealing is a violation of the fiduciary's duty of loyalty. In such cases the beneficiary of the trust usually has the option to affirm or disaffirm the transactions. See Scott, Law of Trusts §170 (3d ed. 1967). Many states have enacted statutes prohibiting self-dealing; see, e.g., N.Y.E.P.T.L. §11-2.2(a)(2). Federal statutes also address self-dealing in specific situations. For example, the Employee Retirement Income Security Act [ERISA] prohibits self-dealing by the trustee of an employee **pension plan.** 29 U.S.C. §§1104(a)(1)(A) and 1106. A director, officer, or employee of a corporation also owes the corporation a duty of loyalty, which may be breached by self-dealing. Henn & Alexander, Laws of Corporations §237 (3d ed. 1983).

SELF-DEFENSE the right to protect one's person, or members of one's family, and, to a lesser extent, one's property, from harm by an aggressor. It is a valid **defense** to a criminal **charge** or to tort liability. The essential elements of self-defense are, "[f]irst, that the defendant must be free from fault, must not say or do anything for the purpose of provoking a difficulty, nor be unmindful of the consequences in this respect of any wrongful word or act; second, there must be

no convenient mode of escape by retreat or by declining the combat; and, lastly, there must be a present impending peril . . . either real or apparent, [so] as to create the **bona fide** [or reasonable] belief of an existing necessity." 23 So. 2d 19, 20. Whether or not retreat is required depends upon the jurisdiction and the circumstances and **deadly force** may be used only when necessary to meet imminent danger of death or serious bodily injury.

There are two classes of self-defense, perfect and imperfect. "A perfect right of self-defense can only obtain and avail where the party **pleading** it acted from necessity, and was wholly free from wrong or blame in occasioning or producing the necessity which required his action. If, however, he was in the wrong—if he was himself violating or in the act of violating the law—and on account of his own wrong was placed in a situation wherein it became necessary for him to defend himself against an attack made upon himself, which was superinduced or created by his own wrong, then the law justly limits his right of self-defense, and regulates it according to the magnitude of his own wrong. Such a state [is] . . . the imperfect right of self-defense." 162 U.S. 466, 472. See also **justification.**

SELF-HELP the protection of one's person or property through personal means without resort to legal process; "the right or fact of redressing or preventing wrongs, by one's own action, without recourse to legal proceedings." 201 S.W. 2d 24, 25. For example, under Section 9-503 of the Uniform Commercial Code, a secured party may, upon **default,** take **possession** of the **collateral** without judicial process as long as there will be no **breach of the peace.** Conversely, some types of self-help, such as a retaliatory assault not justified by **self-defense,** are patently illegal.

A prisoner who attempts to break

out of jail is guilty of escape even though he or she may be able to show an unlawful imprisonment, since the doctrine of self-help is not available to a prisoner in a penal or correctional institution. 252 F. 2d 398. Intolerable prison conditions may, however, create a defense of **duress** if the prisoner attempts to surrender to authorities promptly after escape. See 362 N.E. 2d 319; 444 U.S. 394.

SELF-INCRIMINATION, PRIVILEGE AGAINST the constitutional right of a person to refuse to answer questions or otherwise give **testimony** against himself or herself which will subject him or her to an incrimination. This right under the **Fifth Amendment** (often called simply PLEADING THE FIFTH AMENDMENT) is now applicable to the states through the **due process** clause of the **Fourteenth Amendment,** 378 U.S. 1, and is applicable in any situation, civil or criminal, where the state attempts to compel incriminating testimony. See 369 U.S. 556. The right may be waived where the defendant testifies, 356 U.S. 148, and the privilege does not preclude the use of voluntary **confessions,** 377 U.S. 201; 384 U.S. 436, provided that the requirements of the **Miranda rule** have been complied with.

The requisite compulsion will include any threat calculated to interfere with the unfettered free will of the suspect. Thus, the privilege has been held to bar the use in a criminal trial of the testimony of a police officer obtained after threat of job dismissal if he or she did not testify. This was so even though the police officer could have been validly dismissed for refusing to testify, 392 U.S. 273, but the testimony could not validly be compelled by using such a threat to induce him or her to testify. 385 U.S. 493.

In general, only criminal sanctions are within the privilege and testimony can be compelled despite the personal, social, or economic costs to the witness. For example, a mother having no statutory evidentiary privilege could be compelled to testify against her child and would not be able to plead the privilege against self-incrimination unless she too feared a personal criminal sanction. If she persisted in her refusal to testify, she could be found in **contempt.** The Court has, however, held that a lawyer facing a disbarment proceeding may plead the privilege, 385 U.S. 511, and a juvenile facing **juvenile delinquency** charges enjoys the full protection of the privilege. 387 U.S. 1.

The **hit-and-run statutes** requiring that a motorist involved in an accident stop and identify himself or herself and give certain information to the other motorist and to the police have been upheld on the ground that such forced disclosures are not incriminating in that they are all neutral acts, not intended to be probative of guilt and posing only an insignificant hazard of self-incrimination. Requiring a person to buy a gambling tax stamp, however, does identify such a person as participating in an activity illegal nearly everywhere and as such violates the privilege. 390 U.S. 39.

The privilege can be displaced by a grant of TESTIMONIAL [USE] IMMUNITY which guarantees that neither the compelled testimony nor any fruits will be used against the witness. Given such immunity, the witness can no longer fear incrimination and thus cannot plead the privilege against self-incrimination, 406 U.S. 441; 406 U.S. 472. Some states give such witnesses a broader form of TRANSACTIONAL IMMUNITY which protects them not merely from use of their testimony but from any prosecution brought about relating to transactions about which relevant testimony was elicited. See, e.g., N.Y. Crim. Proc. Law §50.10. Transactional immunity was previously the federal standard, 18 U.S.C. §2514, but was replaced in 1970 by testimonial immunity, 18 U.S.C. §6002. Immunity from federal prosecution may only be given by a federal prosecutor, not a judge. As such, a witness may invoke a broad self-incrimination privilege in a civil suit, in which the federal prosecutor is not involved. See 103 S. Ct. 608. Once granted immunity, a witness who refuses to testify can be punished for **contempt.** The privilege against self-incrimination, like all constitutional rights, may be **waived. Miranda warnings** are generally necessary before such a waiver will be found to qualify a **confession** as admissible evidence for a criminal trial.

The rule does not extend to nontestimonial compulsion. Thus, blood tests may be compelled from the accused because they are "noncommunicative," i.e., the evidence is considered physical or real and not testimonial so as to invoke the protection of the privilege. On the same reasoning, the Court has permitted compelled **line-ups,** 388 U.S. 218, and handwriting exemplars. 388 U.S. 263.

SELLER in commercial law "a person who sells or contracts to sell goods," U.C.C. §2-103(1)(d); in securities law, entities whose conduct is a substantial factor in causing a purchaser to buy a **security.** 545 F. Supp. 1314, 1354. Compare **merchant.**

SELLING SHORT refers to the selling of **securities, commodities,** or foreign exchange that is not actually owned by the **seller.** In making a short sale, the seller hopes to "cover," that is, buy back the item sold at a lower price and thus earn a profit. Selling short is most commonly associated with stock transactions in which positions are established by borrowing shorted securities from the broker who handled the transaction. At a later time, the short is covered and purchased stock is used to return the borrowed securities. Short sales of securities are regulated by the **Securities and Exchange Commission** and **margin** requirements are set by the **Federal Reserve Board.** Selling short is not a popular activity among securities investors and total volume seldom exceeds a few days' trading volume in the typical case. Dealers and exchange specialists routinely engage in selling short to accommodate customers and to maintain orderly markets. Short-term traders also engage in selling short in an attempt to take advantage of imbalances in the market place.

Selling SHORT AGAINST THE BOX, a form of **hedging,** involves selling equal shares of a stock owned by a shareholder in order to protect a profit and to carry the profit into a later tax year. In terms of dollar volume, selling short commodities and currencies far exceeds that of stock transactions.

COMMODITY SHORT SALES short sales accomplished in the **futures** market. A speculator wishing to take advantage of an expected decline in a commodity can sell a large quantity of the commodity for future delivery. In such transactions, the required down payment is only 8 percent to 10 percent of the contract value which offers the speculator high **leverage.** A small decline in the commodity results in a large return on the speculator's investment. High risk is involved, since a modest increase in the commodity price can wipe out the speculator's down payment which generates a margin call, that is, a call for additional capital. If the speculator cannot meet the call he or she is sold out, usually at great loss. A long position in commodities involves similar high risk if maximum margin is used.

SENILE DEMENTIA (dĕ-mĕn'-shē-à)—Lat: insanity which occurs as the result of old age and is progressive in character; a progressive, incurable form of fixed insanity resulting in a total collapse of the mental faculties which, in its final state, necessarily deprives one of **testamentary** capacity. With that particular malady, the victim loses the power to think, reason, or act sanely. See **competent; incompetency.**

SENTENCE the punishment ordered by a court to be inflicted upon a person convicted of a crime, usually either a NON-CUSTODIAL SENTENCE such as **probation** and/or a fine, or a CUSTODIAL SENTENCE such as a term of years of imprisonment or a number of months in a county jail. Such an order usually identifies the authority which must carry out the sentence and authorizes and directs such authority to execute the order. See 100 S.E. 2d 681, 683; 128 So. 814, 816. See also **pretrial intervention.**

CONCURRENT SENTENCES sentences that run at the same time as each other, as opposed to a CONSECUTIVE [CUMULATIVE] SENTENCE [see below]. See 255 P. 2d 782, 784; 456 P. 2d 415, 417. Two or more sentences running concurrently need not begin and/ or end at the same time.

CONDITIONAL DISCHARGE SENTENCE see SUSPENDED SENTENCE, below.

CONSECUTIVE [CUMULATIVE] SENTENCE a sentence that runs separately from one or more other sentences to be served by the same individual. The sentence is cumulative to the extent that it begins after an existing sentence has terminated either by expiration of the maximum term of the existing sentence, or by release from the present sentence through parole. If the consecutive sentence is a custodial one, the parole will be to the cell (called CELL PAROLE) so that the consecutive sentence may be served during the period of the parole.

DEFERRED SENTENCE a sentence not imposed unless the defendant violates the conditions of **probation.** 202 N.W. 2d 72, 77.

DETERMINATE SENTENCE a sentence imposed for a definite rather than indefinite term. It may be a MANDATORY SENTENCE (see below) or a sentence imposed within a permissible range by the exercise of judicial discretion. See generally, Campbell, Law of Sentencing §§31-33 (1978).

INDETERMINATE SENTENCE a sentence for the maximum period prescribed by law for the particular offense committed, subject to the provision of the statute that the custodial portion may be sooner terminated by the parole board. 284 P. 323, 325. The sentence may be terminated any time after the expiration of the minimum period required for parole eligibility. See 97 F. 2d 182, 187.

INTERLOCUTORY SENTENCE a temporary or provisional sentence, one pending the imposition of a final sentence; a sentence on an ancillary question derived from the main cause of action.

MANDATORY SENTENCE a custodial sentence that the legislature has required to be imposed upon persons convicted of certain offenses. If the criminal statute requires a certain minimum period of incarceration, no discretion to suspend the sentence exists in the trial court. The legislative command must be unequivocal since courts hesitate to find their judicial discretion curtailed; the legislature normally provides explicitly for the mandatory sentence by stating that a certain minimum sentence shall be imposed and that it may not be suspended nor may the defendant be released on **probation** or **parole** until that minimum term has been served. Only **executive clemency** by way of commutation of the minimum term can relieve the defendant of a mandatory sentence. See generally Campbell, Law of Sentencing §§28-30 (1978).

PRESENTENCE REPORT see **presentence report.**

SPLIT SENTENCE a short custodial sentence served as a condition of probation. See **probation** [SPLIT SENTENCE].

SUSPENDED SENTENCE a sentence whose imposition or execution has been withheld by the court on certain terms and conditions. A defendant sentenced to six months in jail "suspended" is not required to serve that time in jail provided that the defendant does not violate the express or implied conditions of his or her suspension. An implied condition is always that the defendant not commit a further violation of the law during a fixed period. Where no such period is fixed by the court, the practical effect of the suspended sentence is similar to an UNCONDITIONAL DISCHARGE sentence, i.e., the matter is terminated without any real conditions whatsoever. A CONDITIONAL DISCHARGE is a suspended sentence on particular conditions for a period expressly fixed by the court or by statute at generally between one and three years after the sentence is imposed. See, e.g., New York Penal Law §65.05.

UNCONDITIONAL DISCHARGE SENTENCE see SUSPENDED SENTENCE (above).

SEPARABLE CONTROVERSY within **removal** statute, a claim or cause of action that is part of the entire controversy yet by its nature can be severed from the whole, 310 F. Supp. 1340, 1342. For a case to present a separable controversy within the statute providing for removal of causes to the federal court, 28 U.S.C. §1441(c) provides:

"Whenever a separate and independent claim or cause of action, which would be removable if sued upon alone, is joined with one or more otherwise non-removable claims or causes of action, the entire case may be removed and the district court may remand all matters not otherwise within its original jurisdiction." See 200 U.S. 206.

SEPARATE BUT EQUAL a doctrine under which "equality of treatment is accorded when the races are provided substantially equal facilities, even though these facilities are separate." 347 U.S. 483, 488. Although the doctrine has not been **per se** eliminated from American jurisprudence, its application to most aspects of society has been found to violate the **equal protection clause** of the **Fourteenth Amendment.** The violation is not so much directed toward the physical aspects of separate facilities, but rather the intangible harm that results from the segregation which is a by-product of the doctrine. So, for example, the Supreme Court has found that the mere segregation of minority and white students in public education creates a sense of inferiority that tends to "(retard) the educational and mental development" of minority children. Id. at 494.

SEPARATION see **divorce** [SEPARATION [DIVORCE A MENSA ET THORO]].

SEPARATION AGREEMENT a written agreement between spouses who intend to be divorced, which provides for the payment of **alimony,** the division of property, and the **custody** and support of children. A separation agreement is legally enforceable, and is generally not subject to modification due to changed circumstances provided it reasonably supports the children of the marriage and the other spouse does not become a public charge. Clark, Law of Domestic Relations §16.13 (1968).

If the spouses are actually separated, that is, living apart from one another, the separation agreement may control the income tax consequences of payments made pursuant to it. Alimony payments based upon the marital or family relationship are deductible by the spouse making the payments, and must be included in the income of the spouse receiving the payments. I.R.C. §71(a)(2). Child support payments are not tax deductible. Through the characterization of the payments, the parties may agree to shift income in order to achieve tax savings through the use of the lower tax brackets of each spouse. The parties may also agree as to which of them will claim the dependency exemption for each of their children. I.R.C. §152(e). See **divorce** [SEPARATION A MENSA ET THORO]; **post-nuptial agreement; prenuptial agreement.**

SEPARATION OF POWER the doctrine prohibiting one branch of government, either state or local, from infringing or encroaching upon or exercising the powers belonging to another branch. Under this doctrine, for example, the executive branch of government is primarily responsible for determining which violations are to be prosecuted. 722 F. 2d 562. Although the doctrine may not promote efficiency, it is considered a "bulwork against tyranny" and looks to prevent any person or group from imposing its unchecked will. 381 U.S. 437, 443; 103 S. Ct. 2362, 2367.

SEQUESTER to separate from or to hold aside, as in to sequester assets or to sequester witnesses during a trial. See **sequestration.**

SEQUESTRATION in equity, the act of seizing or taking possession of the property belonging to another, and holding it "until the profits have paid the demand for which it was taken." 15 F. 6, 11.

In practice, at **common law,** **juries** (at least in capital cases) were always sequestered, i.e., kept together throughout the trial and deliberations and guarded from improper contact, until they were discharged. This common law right to demand jury sequestration has been replaced in most jurisdictions with a **discretion** in the trial court to grant sequestration "in the interests of justice." The modern view is that locking a jury up during the trial prejudices both the state and the **defendant.** See 117 A. 2d 473, 478. If a case is sensational and major, the jury will likely be sequestered.

The sequestration of **witnesses** involves keeping witnesses apart from one another and outside of the courtroom. It is frequently ordered by the court at the request of one of the parties in order to insure that the in-court testimony of each witness not be colored by what another witness said. The order of sequestration usually forbids the witnesses who have not yet testified from talking with witnesses who have testified.

SERIAL BOND see **bond** [SERIAL BOND].

SERIATIM *(sĕr-ē-ä'-tĭm)*—Lat: in due order, successively; in order, in succession, individually; one by one; separately; severally.

SERIES BOND see **bond** [SERIES BOND].

SERVANT an **agent** who is not an independent contractor. One who works for, and is subject to, the control of the master; a person employed to "perform services in the affairs of another and who with respect to the physical conduct in the performance of the services is subject to the other's control or right to control.

"In determining whether one acting for another is a servant or an independent **contractor,** the following matters of fact, among others, are considered: (1) the extent of control which, by the agreement, the master may exercise over the details of the work; (2) whether or not the one employed is engaged in a distinct occupation or business; (3) the kind of occupation, with reference to whether, in the locality, the work is usually done under the direction of the employer or by a specialist without supervision; (4) the skill required in the particular occupation; (5) whether the employer or the worker supplies the instrumentalities, tools, and the place of work for the person doing the work; (6) the length of time for which the person is employed; (7) the method of payment, whether by the time or by the job; (8) whether or not the work is a part of the regular business of the employer; (9) whether or not the parties believe they are creating the relation of master and servant; and (10) whether the principal is or is not in business." Restatement of Agency (2d) §220, pp. 485-87. A master is in many instances liable, under the theory of **respondeat superior,** for the **torts** of the servant, but not for those of an **independent contractor.** See also **agent; fellow servant rule; master and servant.**

SERVICE delivery of a **pleading, notice,** or other paper in a **suit,** to the opposite party, so as to charge the party with the receipt of it and subject the party to its legal effect. See 178 N.E. 870, 871. The bringing to notice, either actually or constructively. See 74 S.E. 2d 852, 854.

PERSONAL SERVICE actual delivery to the party to be served. Historically, personal service was an outgrowth of **capias,** and, as opposed to all other types of constructive service, is only achieved upon personal delivery. See Green, Basic Civil Procedure 56 (2d ed. 1979).

SERVICE BY MAIL may be permitted either by court rule or, under unusual circumstances, as the court may authorize. For instance, Fed. R. Civ. Proc. 4(c)(ii) allows service by mail on individuals, other than infants or incompetents, and on corporations or partnerships.

SERVICE BY PUBLICATION constructive service accomplished by publishing the notice to be served in a newspaper designated by the court, and in some jurisdictions, by mailing that newspaper to the last known address of the party. See 243 U.S. 90.

SUBSTITUTED SERVICE constructive service accomplished by presenting service to a recognized representative or agent of the party to be served. See Fed. R. Civ. Proc. 4(d)(1); New York C.P.L.R. §308.

SERVICE OF PROCESS the communication of the **process** or the court papers, to the defendant, either by actual delivery, or by other methods whereby defendant is furnished with reasonable notice of the proceedings against him or her to afford the defendant opportunity to appear and be heard. See 296 F. Supp. 1106, 1107. (For the types of service of process, see **service.**)

SERVICES at common law, the acts done by an English **feudal tenant** for the benefit of his lord, which formed the **consideration** for the property granted to him by his lord. Services were of several types, including knight's service, military service, and the more varied kind of certain and determinate service called socage. See also **tenure.**

SERVIENT ESTATE in relation to an **easement,** that **estate** which is **burdened** by the **servitude,** i.e., that estate which is subject to use in some way by the owner of the **dominant estate;** also called SERVIENT TENEMENT.

SERVITUDE, EQUITABLE see **equitable servitude.**

SERVITUDES in constitutional law, a condition of enforced compulsory service of one to another, 203 U.S. 1, 17, which is prohibited by the U.S. Constitution, Amend. XIII, except as punishment for a convicted criminal; charges or incumbrances which follow the land, 147 So. 33, 35, and are distinguishable from **easements** in that easement usually refers to a right enjoyed whereas servitudes refer to a burden imposed. 226 S.E. 2d 559, 563.

SESSION LAWS laws bound in volumes in the order of their enactment by a state legislature, before possible codification. See **code.**

SET ASIDE to annul, or make **void,** as to "set aside" a judgment. When **proceedings** are irregular, they may be set aside on **motion** of the **party** whom they injuriously affect. See **motion** [MOTION TO SET ASIDE JUDGMENT]. See also **reverse.**

SET-OFF a **counterclaim** by **defendant** against **plaintiff** that grows from an independent **cause of action** and diminishes the plaintiff's potential recovery; "a counter-demand arising out of a transaction extrinsic to the plaintiff's cause of action. It, therefore, is not incompatible with the justice of the plaintiff's claim but seeks to balance it in whole or in part by a counter-obligation alleged to be due by the plaintiff to the defendant in another transaction." 67 F. Supp. 212, 215.

"Set-off, both at law and in equity, must be understood as that right which exists between two parties each of whom under an independent contract owes an ascertained amount to the other to set-off his respective debts by way of mutual deduction so that in any action brought for the larger debt, [only] the residue [remaining] after such deduction shall be recovered." 16 A. 2d 804, 806. See also **recoupment.**

For federal tax purposes, a doc-trine that allows the amount of refund that a **taxpayer** could claim (or the amount of deficiency the government could assess) except for the fact that such claim (or assessment) is barred by the Statute of Limitations to be offset against the amount of deficiency which could be properly assessed (or the amount which the taxpayer could properly claim as a refund) for the same **taxable year.** I.R.C. §7422.

SETTLEMENT generally, the conclusive fixing or resolving of a matter; the arrangement of a final disposition of it. See 116 N.J. Super. 390, 397. A compromise achieved by the adverse parties in a **civil suit** before final **judgment,** whereby they agree between themselves upon their respective rights and obligations, thus eliminating the necessity of judicial resolution of the controversy. See **accord and satisfaction; out-of-court settlement; property settlement.** Compare **plea bargaining** in the criminal context.

SETTLOR [DONOR; TRUSTOR] one who creates a **trust** by giving **real** or **personal property** "in trust" to another (the **trustee**) for the benefit of a third person (the **beneficiary**). One who gives such money is said to "settle" it on, or bring **title** to rest with, the trustee, and is also called the **"donor"** or **"trustor."**

SEVENTH AMENDMENT the amendment to the U.S. Constitution that guarantees the right to a **jury trial** in any **civil** case before a federal court if the amount in controversy exceeds $20. Each civil litigant in a federal court is entitled to a jury of twelve persons before a judge capable of instructing them on the law, and a unanimous verdict. 174 U.S. 1. Antieau, Modern Constitutional Law §7:17 (1969). However, trial by jury is not automatic; rather, a party must specifically request it. Fed. R. Civ. Proc. 38. A litigant is not entitled to have a jury decide **equitable** claims.

However, when a case includes both legal and equitable causes of action, each litigant is entitled to have the legal issues decided by the jury prior to the resolution of the equitable issues. 369 U.S. 469. Wright, Law of Federal Courts §92 (4th ed. 1983).

SEVER see **severance.**

SEVERABLE CONTRACT one which, in the event of a **breach** by one of the parties, may be justly considered as several independent agreements expressed in a single **instrument.** Where a **contract** is deemed severable, a breach thereof may constitute a default as to only a part of the contract, saving the defaulting party from the necessity of responding in **damages** for a breach of the entire agreement. See, e.g., U.C.C. §2-612(2) conferring upon a buyer the right to reject one installment of an **installment contract** in the event that installment is substantially impaired. See also U.C.C. §2-612(3) authorizing a party aggrieved by a breach that impairs the value of the whole contract to treat the breach as one affecting only part of the contract by suing for damages with respect to past installments or by demanding future installments.

A severable contract may in fact be a series of DIVISIBLE CONTRACTS so that each part may be supported by a separate **consideration** and involve separate suits for breach of contract. Simpson, Contracts §153 (2d ed. 1965). See also **installment contract.**

SEVERABLE STATUTE a legislative act, the remainder of which is valid when a certain portion has been declared invalid, because the parts of the statute are not wholly interdependent. After the invalid portion of the act has been stricken, if that which remains is self-sustaining and is capable of separate enforcement without regard to that portion of the statute that has been cast aside, then such a statute is said to be severable. Where the legislature intends its enactment to be severable, it often expresses that intention in a SEVERABILITY CLAUSE at the end of the act. 1A Sands, Sutherland Statutory Construction §20.22 (4th ed. 1972); 2 op. cit. §§44.01 et seq. (4th ed. 1973). See also **saving clause.**

SEVERAL [SEVERALLY] separate and apart from; e.g., in a **note,** each who "severally" promises to pay is responsible separately for the entire amount, Simpson, Contracts §§136 et seq. (2d ed. 1965); and in a **judgment** against more than one defendant, arising out of one **action,** each may be severally **liable** for the entire amount of the judgment, thereby permitting the successful plaintiff to recover the entire amount of the judgment from any defendant against whom he or she chooses to institute a suit. See, e.g., Prosser, Law of Torts §47 (4th ed. 1971). See **contribution; joint and several; joint tort-feasor.**

SEVERALTY refers to the holding of property solely, separately, and individually. A tenant in severalty holds the land exclusively and solely for the duration of his or her **estate** without any other person holding joint rights. 2 Bl. Comm.* 179

SEVERANCE the act of separating; the state of being disjoined or separated. In criminal law, severance is the process by which the particular **charge** on which the **defendant** is currently to stand trial is chosen, so that only one charge or only properly joined charges are before the **jury** in one trial. Severance may also refer to the disjoinder, for separate trials, of two or more **defendants** named in the same **indictment** or **information,** who would normally be tried together. It is particularly useful when some prejudice might arise to one or more of the defendants if they were tried together. E.g., Fed. R. Crim. Proc. 14.

Severance of claims or parties is also available in **civil** trials to prevent prejudice or for the convenience of the parties. Not infrequently a court may sever the issue of **liability** from the issue of **damages** and direct that the question of liability be determined first. Once liability is established, the parties may agree upon the question of damages, thereby avoiding a lengthy trial on that issue. Fed. R. Civ. Proc. 21, 42b.

SEVERE of an extreme degree, beyond endurance. For example, in determining whether a plaintiff has succeeded in showing severe emotional distress, both the intensity and duration of the emotional distress suffered must be considered in determining whether the distress is of such substantial quantity or enduring quality that "no reasonable person in a civilized society should be expected to endure it."

SEXUAL ASSAULT see **rape** [SEXUAL ASSAULT].

SEXUAL CONTACT see **rape** [SEXUAL CONTACT].

SEXUAL HARASSMENT see **harassment** [SEXUAL HARASSMENT].

SHALL often used to denote an obligation or direction to do some act, 170 N.W. 2d 433, 440; however, it is sometimes considered to be permissive, and to mean the same as the word "may," 103 N.W. 2d 245, 254.

SHAM PLEADING in civil practice, a pleading that is sufficient on its face but so clearly and indisputably false that it presents no real **issue** of fact to be determined by a **trial**. A **complaint** or **answer** will be stricken as sham only when it is clear and undisputed that the alleged claim or **defense** is wholly unsupported by facts. 174 S.W. 2d 681.

SHAM TRANSACTION see **transaction** [SHAM TRANSACTION].

SHARE a portion of something; an **interest** in a **corporation**, e.g., a stock. See **securities** [STOCK]; **stockholder.**

SHARE AND SHARE ALIKE in equal shares, 312 A. 2d 373, 377. The phrase is normally used to describe the division of property among a class of persons on a **per capita** basis; however, other language in the controlling legal document, such as a **will** or a **trust,** may require the property to be divided **per stirpes.** 207 A. 2d 840, 842.

SHARE, ELECTIVE see **widow's election.**

SHAREHOLDER see **stockholder.** See also **round-lot shareholders.**

SHAREHOLDER'S DERIVATIVE ACTION see **derivative action.**

SHELLEY'S CASE, RULE IN see **Rule in Shelley's Case.**

SHELTER see **tax shelter.**

SHERIFF'S SALE [JUDICIAL SALE] a **sale** of **property** by the sheriff under authority of a court's **judgment** and **writ of execution** in order to satisfy an unpaid judgment, **mortgage, lien,** or other **debt** of the owner **[judgment debtor].** See **sale** [FORCED SALE].

SHERMAN ANTITRUST ACT the federal statute passed in 1890 to prohibit unreasonable restraints upon and monopolization of trade in interstate or foreign commerce. 15 U.S.C. §§1–17. The statute forbids two or more persons from engaging in **monopolistic** practices and **price fixing.** "Some restraints, like price fixing, are illegal **per se,** but the legality of others depends on the 'rule of reason.'" Henn & Alexander, Laws of Corporations §310 (3d ed. 1983).

In 1914, the **Clayton Act** was passed to supplement the Sherman Act by prohibiting tying, exclusive dealing and total requirements agreements, corporate mergers that tend to substantially lessen competition, and interlocking director-ates. 15 U.S.C. §§12-27.

SHIELD LAWS in evidence law, statutes that grant a potential witness a privilege against testifying about certain matters. Shield laws most commonly refer to statutes enacted by most states that allow a journalist or other newsperson to refuse to disclose confidential sources of information and other information, notes, and materials. McCormick, Evidence §77 (2d ed. 1972). Many states also have enacted shield laws to protect rape victims against harassment through questions about past sexual behavior. However, a defendant may ask about the lifestyle of the victim if those questions can be shown to be essential for a fair trial, although permission of court is usually required. See, e.g., N.J.S.A. 2C:14-7. See **journalist's privilege; privileged communication.**

SHIFTING INTEREST see **interest** [SHIFTING INTEREST].

SHIFTING THE BURDEN OF PROOF transferring to the other party in a litigation the burden that one party has in producing evidence to support his or her claim; requires that the person who originally had the burden make out a **prima facie** case or defense by some minimum of evidence. See **burden of proof.**

SHIFTING USE see **use.** See also **interest** [EXECUTORY INTEREST].

SHIPMENT CONTRACT see **tender** [TENDER OF DELIVERY].

SHOP see **closed shop; open shop; union shop.**

SHORT AGAINST THE BOX see **selling short** [SHORT AGAINST THE BOX].

SHORT RATE in insurance law, a term applied to a mutual **rescission** of **insurance** by both parties, who then contract for a new policy which is identical with the original except for a shortened term and lower earned premium. 41 A. 2d 525, 532.

SHORT SELLING see **selling short.**

SHORT SWING PROFITS see **insider** [SHORT SWING PROFITS].

SHORT-TERM CAPITAL GAIN see **capital.**

SHORT YEAR see **taxable year** [SHORT YEAR].

SHOW CAUSE ORDER "an **order** [made upon the **motion** of one party] requiring a party to appear and show cause [argue] why a certain thing should not be done or permitted. It requires the [adverse] party to meet the **prima facie case** made by the applicant's verified **complaint** or **affidavit**." 230 S.W. 2d 444, 447.

An order to show cause is an accelerated method of beginning a litigation by compelling the adverse party to respond in a much shorter period of time than he would normally have under a **complaint.** The order may or may not contain temporary restraints [see **restraining orders**] but will generally be "returnable" in a few days, which means that the opposing party must prepare answering affidavits and persuade the court that an issue of a fact exists requiring a full, plenary trial proceeding. The opposing party may also simply argue on the return date that even if the plaintiff's statements in his or her moving papers are true, they do not state a cause of action or justify the relief prayed for in the order to show cause. Compare **summons.**

SHOW UP a one-to-one confrontation between a suspect and a witness to a crime, 544 P. 2d 289, 290. Although the term is frequently used interchangeably with **line-up,** the two are distinguishable in that line-up refers to a group of persons being shown to a witness.

SICK PAY refers to compensation an employee receives while away from a job due to illness or injury. In general, when an employee receives payments as reimbursement for medical care or for permanent injury, such payments constitute an **exclusion** from **gross income.** If an employee receives wages or payments in lieu of wages under a disability plan provided by the employer, of which payments are made to the employee on account of permanent and total disability, a portion of such payment is not subject to income taxes. I.R.C. §104.

SIDE-BAR the area of the court room that is within the hearing of the judge but out of the hearing of the jury and the witness. When court is in session and the attorneys must discuss with the judge issues that are not appropriate for the jury to hear, the attorneys and the judge will hold a conference at side-bar. Such side-bar conferences are preserved by the stenographer and appear in the transcript for purposes of appeal. 322 A. 2d 495, 499.

SIGHT DRAFT a **bill of exchange** for the immediate payment of money, 405 P. 2d 488, 490. See **demand note; draft** [SIGHT DRAFT].

SIGNATURE a writing or other mark that is placed upon an instrument for the purpose of authenticating it or giving it legal effect. Statutes define "signature" differently in different contexts, such as in corporate documents, wills, books, etc. For instance, under the **Uniform Commercial Code,** a signature "is made by use of any name, including any trade or assumed name, upon an instrument, or by any word or mark used in lieu of a written signature." U.C.C. §3-401(2).

SILENT PARTNER an investor in a business enterprise who either does not take an active role in the management of the business, or whose identity is not revealed to third parties; a principal whose identity is not disclosed by his or her agent. While the identity of a silent partner may or may not be disclosed, the silent partner, nonetheless, participates in the profits or losses of the enterprise. See **principal** [UNDISCLOSED PRINCIPAL].

SILVER PLATTER DOCTRINE the doctrine, now discredited, that allowed evidence seized by state officers in an illegal search and seizure to be used against the defendant in a federal criminal trial. 338 U.S. 74, 79. It was subsequently declared unconstitutional. 364 U.S. 206.

SIMPLE CONTRACT an informal **contract** made without **seal.** See **sealed instrument.**

SIMPLE NEGLIGENCE the failure to exercise ordinary care; to be distinguished from **gross negligence.** 46 S.E. 2d 2, 5. See **negligence.**

SIMPLE TRUST see **trust** [SIMPLE TRUST].

SIMPLICITER simply, directly, summarily.

SIMULTANEOUS DEATH ACT a uniform state law passed in most states providing for the distribution of property when distribution depends upon the time of death of more than one person and it cannot be determined that the persons died other than simultaneously. In cases governed by the Act, the law presumes each person died before the other, with the effect that one half of the property of each passes to the estate of the other. Page, Wills §64.15 (1960). See Uniform Simultaneous Death Act, vol. 8A Uniform Laws Annotated (master ed.).

SINE DIE *(sē'-nā dē'-ā)*—Lat: without day, without time; "a legislative body adjourns 'sine die' when it adjourns without appointing a day on which to appear or assemble again." 300 S.W. 2d 806.

SINE QUA NON *(sē'-nā kwä nōn)*—Lat: without which not; that without which the thing cannot be, i.e., the essence of something; e.g., in **tort** law, the act of the defendant, without which there would not have been a tort. See **cause.**

SINKING FUND an accumulation, by a corporation or governmental body, of money invested for the purpose of repaying a **debt** or replacing equipment. In governmental bodies, a sinking fund is a **fund** arising from taxes, imposts or duties, appropriated toward the payment of interest due on a public loan and for the eventual payment of the **principal.** See 29 A. 387, 389.

S.I.P.C. see **Securities Investor Protection Corporation [S.I.P.C.].**

SITUS the location or place of a thing. 206 P. 2d 218, 220. The situs of **real property** and **tangible personal property** is determined by its physical location. The situs of **intangible** personal property is determined by reference to various factors, and often depends upon the legal context in which it is determined. For instance, the situs of a **debt** may be where the **debtor** or the **creditor** is located. Because of the theoretical nature of the situs of intangibles, the issue of situs frequently becomes one of **jurisdiction,** that is, whether a court has the jurisdiction to issue an order that will affect the rights of persons in the intangible property, and whether the order may be enforced in a practical manner.

SIXTH AMENDMENT the amendment to the U.S. Constitution that entitles the accused in a criminal trial the right to a **speedy trial** by an impartial jury, to be informed of the charges against him or her, to be confronted with witnesses against him or her, to have **compulsory process** for obtaining witnesses in his or her favor, and to have effective assistance of counsel.

Through the process of **selective incorporation,** each of these rights has been applied to the states under the **due process clause** of the **Fourteenth Amendment.** While these rights form the foundation of the accused's right to a fair trial, the accused has been accorded additional rights, such as the right to conduct his or her own defense as necessary to a fair trial under the due process clause. 422 U.S. 806. Schwartz, Constitutional Law §7.12 (1979).

SKY LAWS see **blue sky laws; sunshine laws.**

S.L. session or statute laws.

SLANDER defamation; spoken words that tend to damage the reputation of another. See 260 S.W. 523, 525. Under modern legal and constitutional concepts, slander is limited to false remarks inasmuch as truth is an absolute **defense** to an **action** for slander.

Unlike **libel,** slanderous utterances may not be actionable without proof of actual temporal **damages.** Only where the words impute crime, loathsome disease or unchastity, or when they relate to an individual's business or profession is this requirement of proving "special damages" dispensed with. Prosser, Torts 754 (4th ed. 1971). Slander may take the form of either SLANDER PER SE or SLANDER PER QUOD. If the defamatory meaning is apparent on the face of the statement, then the statement is slanderous per se. If the defamatory meaning arises only from extrinsic facts, not apparent upon the face of the statement, then the statement is slanderous per quod. See id. at 748. See also **defamation; fighting words.** Compare **libel.**

SLIGHT CARE see **care** [SLIGHT CARE].

SLIGHT NEGLIGENCE see **negligence** [SLIGHT NEGLIGENCE].

SMALL CLAIMS COURT a court of **limited jurisdiction,** usually able to adjudicate claims of $500 or less, depending on statute. Proceedings are less formal than in other types of courts and parties usually represent themselves.

SOCAGE in feudal England, a type of tenure founded upon certain and designated services performed by the vassal for his lord, other than military or knight's service. Where the services were considered honorable it was called FREE SOCAGE and where the services were of a baser nature it was called VILLEIN SOCAGE. By the statute 12 Car. 2, c. 24, most all tenures by knight-servants were converted into FREE AND COMMON SOCAGE. See 2 Bl. Comm.*79-80. See also **homage.**

SOCIAL GUEST see **guest** [SOCIAL GUEST].

SODOMY crime **against nature;** made a **felony** in the early sixteenth century by statute and thus considered a **common law** felony in the United States. It was originally only an ecclesiastical offense. Sodomy includes both **bestiality** and buggery [copulation per anus] and in many jurisdictions has been expanded to cover other acts of unnatural sexual intercourse. See Perkins & Boyce, Criminal Law 465 (3d ed. 1982).

Sodomy can be either consensual, by forcible compulsion, or with a physically helpless person, and includes such acts with underaged persons.

Modern statutes may limit the scope of sodomy such as by defining deviate sexual intercourse as "sexual conduct between persons not married to each other consisting of contact between the penis and anus, the mouth and penis, or the mouth and vulva." New York Penal Law §§130.38, 130.00(2).

Some states have removed sodomy from the category of crime except to the extent that criminal sanctions are needed to protect individuals against forcible acts; young persons from sexual advances by older persons; and the public from open and notorious conduct that flouts accepted standards of morality in the community. Ill. Crim. Code of 1961, Art. 11. Perkins & Boyce, Criminal Law 468 (3d ed. 1982).

SOLEMNITY OF CONTRACT the concept that two persons are free and entitled to make whatever **contract** or agreement they wish, and that if the requisite formalities are observed and no defenses exist, their contract should be respected and enforced.

SOLE PROPRIETORSHIP a business or financial venture carried on by a single person and which is not a **trust** or **corporation.** Unlike a corporation or a trust, a sole proprietorship is not a separate taxpayer; instead its income is taxed directly to the proprietor.

SOLICITATION an offense developed by the later common law courts to reach conduct whereby one enticed, incited, or importuned another to commit a **felony** or certain **misdemeanors** injurious to the public welfare. See 102 Eng. Rep. 269 (1801). The common law offense has been codified by only a small minority of American jurisdictions and is sometimes an element in an **attempt** liability. If the actor agrees to join the other in an offense, a **conspiracy** will be established and there will be no need for solicitation liability.

The Model Penal Code defines solicitation as commanding, encouraging, or requesting another person to engage in conduct that constitutes a crime or an attempt to commit a crime (with the intent that the crime be committed). Model Penal Code §5.02(1) (1962). Generally the code provides that solicitation be as punishable as the crime solicited. Id. at §5.05(1).

SOLICITER see **barrister.**

SOLICITOR GENERAL person appointed by the President to assist the Attorney General in performing his or her duties. 28 U.S.C. §505. The Soliciter General may attend to the interests of the United States in any court, 28 U.S.C. §517, and except when otherwise authorized, only the Solicitor General or the Attorney General shall conduct and argue suits and appeals in the Supreme Court and suits, in which the United States is interested, in the court of claims. 28 U.S.C. §518(a).

SOLVENCY the ability to pay all **debts** and just claims as they come due; "generally understood to mean that a person is able to pay his debts as they mature.

[The term further signifies] that one's property is adequate to satisfy his obligations when sold under **execution.** Only clear solvency in the latter sense will uphold a voluntary conveyance against pre-existing debts." 91 S.W. 958, 961. In certain contexts, solvency may consist simply of an excess of assets over liabilities. See 9 S.W. 2d 688, 690. Compare **insolvency.** See **bankruptcy.**

SOUND good physical condition; free from defects. See **sane.**

SOUND AND DISPOSING MIND AND MEMORY language often used in a **will** as a declaration by the **testator** that he had **testamentary capacity** when he executed the will.

SOUND BODY free from disease or infirmity, 115 N.W. 869, 875.

SOUND MIND able to know and understand the nature of one's acts, 181 S.W. 2d 369, 374; synonymous with **testamentary capacity,** 348 S.W. 2d 169, 172.

SOUNDS IN has a connection or association with; is concerned with; thus, though a party to a lawsuit has **pleaded damages** in **tort,** it may be said that the **action** never-

theless "sounds in" **contract** if the elements of the offense charged appear to constitute a contract, rather than a tort, action. Whether the court will consider it a tort or a contract may influence the damage measure since, for example, **punitive damages** are recoverable in tort but not on contract. See Simpson, Contracts 394 (2d ed. 1965).

SOVEREIGN that which is preeminent among all others. 1 Bl. Comm.*241. For instance, in a monarchy, the king as sovereign has absolute power, while in a democracy, the people have the sovereign power. Blackstone, the eighteenth century legal theorist, defined sovereign power to mean "the making of laws." 1 Bl. Comm. *49. In ancient England, the king's word was law; in today's democratic governments, the law-making function has been taken over by representative bodies such as Congress. Other incidents of sovereignty in addition to law-making power are **sovereign immunity,** which prohibits lawsuits against the sovereign without its permission, and **eminent domain,** which allows the sovereign to take private property and put it to public use.

SOVEREIGN IMMUNITY a doctrine precluding the institution of a **suit** against the sovereign [government] without the sovereign's consent. The doctrine was originally based on the maxim "the king can do no wrong." This rationale is inapplicable in the United States since it was rejected in the Declaration of Independence. 440 U.S. 410, 415. Another rationale is that the "sovereign is exempt from suit [on the] practical ground that there can be no legal right against the authority that makes the law on which the right depends." 205 U.S. 349, 353. The state may nevertheless be held liable where the injurious activity was "proprietary" rather than "governmental," i.e., where the injury was caused by the state acting in its capacity as a commercial entity rather than that of sovereign. This doctrine has been partially abrogated by judicial decisions, 115 N.W. 2d 618, and by statutes often called **tort claims acts.**

The doctrine not only controls suits against the sovereign in the courts of the sovereign, but, as expressed in the **Eleventh Amendment,** it also explicitly limits the powers of federal courts to entertain suits against a state brought by citizens of other states or of foreign countries. States are still subject to suit brought by other states or the federal government and to injunctive and declaratory relief in suits in which state officials are the nominal defendants. 440 U.S. 410, 420. Federal courts will not, however, direct state officials to obey state law. 104 S. Ct. 900. Moreover, the doctrine of sovereign immunity does not always protect a state from suit in the courts of a sister state, at least where the sister state is pursuing a legitimate policy and has consented to suit on similar grounds. 440 U.S. 410.

SPACE ARBITRAGE see **arbitrage** [SPACE ARBITRAGE].

SPECIAL APPEARANCE see **appearance.**

SPECIAL ASSUMPSIT see **assumpsit** [SPECIAL ASSUMPSIT].

SPECIAL CONTRACT see **sealed instrument; specialty.**

SPECIAL COURTS-MARTIAL see **court-martial; military law** [COURT-MARTIAL].

SPECIAL DAMAGES see **damages** [CONSEQUENTIAL [SPECIAL] DAMAGES].

SPECIAL DEMURRER see **demurrer** [SPECIAL DEMURRER].

SPECIAL INDORSEMENT see **indorsement.**

SPECIAL JURISDICTION see **jurisdiction** [LIMITED [SPECIAL] JURISDICTION]; **limited jurisdiction.**

SPECIAL LEGISLATION acts of the legislature enacted in the form of private acts, for the benefit of a certain individual, as opposed to general legislation enacted for the general population. Examples include acts to provide recovery otherwise unavailable in the courts, and special laws enacted for a limited group of persons. Special laws may be constitutional if there is a rational basis for limiting the application of the statute to the special group. Several states have constitutional provisions allowing the enactment of special legislation affecting certain classes of persons, such as small municipalities, but usually only if enacted pursuant to a certain procedure. See, e.g., N.J. Const. Art. 4, Sec. 7, paras. 9, 10.

SPECIAL MASTER see **master** [master in chancery; special master].

SPECIAL PROSECUTOR see **prosecutor** [SPECIAL PROSECUTOR].

SPECIAL TRAVERSE see **traverse.**

SPECIALTY common law category of formal **contracts** which were valid without **consideration.** It is synonymous with "SPECIAL CONTRACT." The usual form of the formal contract which was called a "specialty" was an instrument under seal. Other examples include **recognizances, negotiable instruments** and documents, and **letters of credit.** Restat. (Second) Contracts §6; Corbin, Contracts §5 (1952). See **sealed instrument.**

SPECIE money that has an intrinsic value, e.g., gold and silver coins. These are coins made of scarce metals which are usually minted in various denominations differentiated by weight and fineness. Most often these coins are stamped with government seals and insignias signifying their value as currency. See 79 U.S. (12 Wall.) 687, 695. See also **in specie.**

SPECIFIC BEQUEST see **bequest.**

SPECIFIC DENIAL see **denial** [SPECIFIC DENIAL].

SPECIFIC INTENT see **intent.**

SPECIFIC MENS REA see **mens rea.**

SPECIFIC PERFORMANCE an **equitable remedy** available to an aggrieved party when the party's remedy at law is inadequate, consisting of a requirement that the party guilty of a **breach of contract** undertake to perform or to complete performance of his or her obligations under the contract. It is grounded on the equitable maxim that equity regards that as done which ought to have been done. Unlike money **damages** which are enforceable only by a judgment against property, a decree of specific performance requires that the party against whom the decree is directed do a particular act on pain of being imprisoned for contempt. Specific performance is available whenever the subject matter of the contract is unique and "in other proper circumstances." U.C.C. §2-716(1). Thus one can obtain a decree of specific performance for the purchase of a unique chattel such as a rare painting, and in all transactions involving land, which the law presumes to be unique. Restatement, (Second) Contracts §360. Once a purchaser of land has signed a contract, he or she is said to have equitable title because he or she can enforce the contract through a decree of specific performance.

There are cases in which the court of equity will not specifically enforce a contract even though the remedy at law is inadequate. Personal service contracts and construction contracts are common examples, due to the difficulty of the court's overseeing proper performance by the defaulting party. Restatement (Second) Contracts §§366, 367. Several other instances

may also bar this remedy. See generally, id., at §§362 et seq. In these instances a negative injunction can sometimes be obtained, preventing the defaulting party from doing the same act or service for anyone other than the aggrieved party. Also, where the defaulting party is a buyer, an aggrieved seller who has produced specially manufactured goods for the buyer or who is otherwise unable to sell the goods may enjoy a kind of "specific performance" at law by bringing an action for the price. See U.C.C. §2-709.

SPECIFIC RELIEF see **specific performance.**

SPEECH, FREEDOM OF see **freedom** [FREEDOM OF SPEECH].

SPEECH OR DEBATE CLAUSE Art. I, Sec. 6, Cl. 1 of U.S. Constitution that provides that members of Congress, except for treason, felony, and breach of peace, be privileged from prosecution "for any speech or debate in either House." The speech or debate clause was designed to assure the Congress wide freedom of speech, debate, and deliberation without intimidation or threats from the executive branch and to protect members of Congress against prosecutions that directly impinge upon or threaten the legislative process. 408 U.S. 606.

SPEED see **controlled substances.**

SPEED, DELIBERATE see **deliberate speed.**

SPEEDY TRIAL a trial conducted according to prevailing rules, regulations, and proceedings of law free from arbitrary, vexatious, and oppressive delays. 404 P. 2d 683, 685. Under the **Sixth Amendment** of the U.S. Constitution, as implemented by 18 U.S.C. §§3161 et seq., and Fed. R. Crim. Proc. 50, a defendant in a criminal prosecution is entitled to a speedy trial. To decide whether a delay in a trial has violated a defendant's constitutional right four factors must be considered: (1) length of delay; (2) reason for delay; (3) prejudice to defendant; and (4) waiver of right to speedy trial. 407 U.S. 514.

SPENDING POWER the power of Congress to spend money in order to provide for the general welfare of the United States. U.S. Constitution, Art. I, Sec. 8, Cl. 1. At least since 1936, this power has been recognized not only to apply to purposes other than those specifically enumerated in Article I of the Constitution, but to include purposes such as Social Security, desegregation, and environmental control. 297 U.S. 1; 301 U.S. 619; 301 U.S. 548; Antieau, Modern Constitutional Law §§12:56 and 12:57 (1969).

SPENDTHRIFT TRUST a **trust** created to provide a fund for the maintenance of a **beneficiary** which is restricted so as to be secure against the beneficiary's improvidence, see 93 P. 2d 880, 883, and beyond the reach of his or her creditors. See 27 A. 2d 166, 172. The terms of such trusts usually prohibit the beneficiary from transferring his or her interest in the trust for consideration or otherwise. Spendthrift trusts are given varying effect throughout the states. In some, the matter is governed by statute; in others, the courts allow the beneficiary to transfer a partial interest in the trust, such as a right to **principal.** See generally, Scott, Law of Trusts §151 (3d ed. 1967).

SPLIT SENTENCE see **probation** [SPLIT SENTENCE].

SPLITTING A CAUSE OF ACTION practice of bringing an **action** for only part of the **cause of action** in one **suit,** and initiating another suit for another part; consists in dividing a single or individual cause of action into several parts or claims and bringing several actions thereon. See 59 N.W. 2d 74, 78. Under the general policy prohibiting the splitting of causes of action, "the

law mandatorily requires that all **damages** sustained or accruing to one as a result of a single **wrongful act** must be claimed and recovered in one action or not at all." 10 So. 2d 432, 433. However, the practice is allowed under certain circumstances, such as when a demand that was the subject of the second action was not due at the time of the first action. 112 P. 2d 774, 778. See also **multiplicity of suits.** Compare **joinder; misjoinder.**

SPOUSAL DISQUALIFICATION common law rule that disqualified the husband or wife from testifying either for or against the spouse in any civil or criminal case. Today, statutes generally consider a husband or wife fully competent to testify either for or against a spouse, subject to the limitations of the **marital communications privilege.** McCormick, Evidence §§66, 78 et seq. (2d ed. 1972). The witness-spouse alone has a privilege to refuse to testify adversely. The witness may be neither compelled to testify nor foreclosed from testifying. 445 U.S. 40, 53.

SPRINGING INTEREST see **interest.**

SPRINGING USE see **use.** See also **interest** [EXECUTORY INTEREST].

SQUEEZE-OUT in corporate law, any transaction engaged in by the parties in control of a corporation for the purpose of eliminating minority **shareholders.** "The use of corporate control vested in the statutory majority of shareholders or the **board of directors** to eliminate minority shareholders from the enterprise or to reduce to relative insignificance their voting power or claims on corporate assets. . . . Furthermore, it implies a purpose to force upon the minority shareholder a change which is not incident to any other business goal of the corporation. Although the form of such freeze-out transaction may vary and is not confined to merger or consolidation, the policy considerations are generally the same." 370 N.E. 2d 345, 353.

STAKEHOLDER "a third party chosen by two or more persons to keep in deposit **property** or money the right or **possession** of which is contested between them, and to be delivered to the one who shall establish his right to it." 162 S.E. 2d 765, 770. See **interpleader.**

STANDARD DEDUCTIONS see **deductions** [STANDARD DEDUCTIONS].

STANDARD OF CARE the uniform standard of behavior upon which the theory of **negligence** is based. The standard of care requires the actor to do what the "reasonable person of ordinary prudence" would do in the actor's place. 498 S.W. 2d 388, 391. If the actor's conduct falls below the standard that a reasonable person would conform to under like circumstances, the actor may be liable for injuries or damages resulting from his or her conduct.

STANDING the legal right of a person or group to challenge in a judicial forum the conduct of another, especially with respect to governmental conduct. In the federal system, **litigants** must satisfy constitutional standing requirements in order to create a legitimate **case or controversy** within the meaning of Article III of the federal Constitution. A taxpayer will have standing to challenge governmental conduct if the taxpayer can establish (1) "a logical link between that status and the type of legislative enactment attacked," and (2) "a nexus between that status and the precise nature of the constitutional infringement alleged." 392 U.S. 83, 102. "The gist of the question of standing, is whether the party seeking relief has 'alleged such a personal stake in the outcome of the controversy as to insure that concrete adverseness which sharpens the presentation of issues upon which the court so largely depends

for illumination of difficult constitutional questions.' " 418 U.S. 208, 237 citing 369 U.S. 186, 204. See **political question.**

In criminal procedure, under federal constitutional standards only persons aggrieved by a violation of the Fourth Amendment have standing to challenge the police conduct and its fruits. Thus, persons whose "legitimate expectation of privacy" was violated, conversants in a conversation and the owner of premises and property have standing, but third parties not present do not have standing even though the evidence obtained is to be used against them and even if they were the "target" of the investigation. See 439 U.S. 128; 392 U.S. 364; 394 U.S. 165. Some state courts follow a rule of "vicarious standing" whereby any citizen can challenge the legality of the methods employed to obtain evidence against him. See 290 P. 2d 855. Also, some state courts continue to follow a doctrine of AUTOMATIC STANDING first developed by the U.S. Supreme Court, 362 U.S. 257, and later abandoned, 448 U.S. 83, whereby anyone charged with a possessory offense has standing to challenge its validity if the evidence so obtained is to be used against him or her. See, e.g., 88 N.J. 211, 228.

STANDING MUTE in a criminal trial, refusing to **plead;** today held equivalent to a **plea** of **not guilty.** See also **self-incrimination.**

STANDING ORDER see **order** [STANDING ORDER].

STAR CHAMBER an ancient court of England that received its name because the ceiling was covered with stars; it sat with no jury and could administer any penalty but death. The Star Chamber was abolished when its jurisdiction was expanded to such an extent that it became too onerous for the people of England. See Baker, An Introduction to English Legal History 51

(1971). See generally, Holdsworth, A History of English Law 155-214 (1924). The abuses of the star chamber were a principal reason for the incorporation in the federal constitution of the privilege against **self-incrimination.**

STARE DECISIS *(stä'-rä dĕ-sī'-sĭs)*—Lat: to stand by that which was decided; rule by which common law courts "are slow to interfere with principles announced in the former decisions and often uphold them even though they would decide otherwise were the question a new one." 156 P. 2d 340, 345. "Although [stare decisis] is not inviolable, our judicial system demands that it be overturned only on a showing of good cause. Where such a good cause is not shown, it will not be repudiated." The doctrine is of particularly limited application in the field of constitutional law. 298 U.S. 38, 94. See **precedent.**

STATE ACTION generally, term used to describe claims arising under the **due process clause** of the **Fourteenth Amendment** and the **Civil Rights Act** (42 U.S.C. §1983) for which a private party is seeking damages or other proper remedy because the state has violated that party's civil rights. 438 F. Supp. 47. Factors to be considered in determining whether the state is significantly involved in a statutorily authorized private conduct for purposes of constituting "state action" include the source of authority for private action, whether the state is so entwined with the regulation of private conduct as to constitute state activity, whether there is meaningful state participation in the activity, and whether there has been delegation of what has traditionally been state function to private persons. 379 N.E. 2d 1169, 1172. There is no practical distinction between "state action" under the Fourteenth Amendment and the requirements for "under color of state law" under the Civil Rights

Act. 365 U.S. 167; 564 F. 2d 849, 855. See **color of law.**

STATEMENT a declaration of fact; an allegation by a witness. See also **prior inconsistent statement; registration statement.**

CLOSING STATEMENT in litigation, a **summation** made by the attorney, at the end of the case, which sets forth that client's case. In real estate law, a document prepared in the closing of a sale of real estate that summarizes the transaction and sets forth its financial terms.

OPENING STATEMENT in litigation, a statement made by the attorney for each party after the jury has been selected and before any evidence has been presented. A defendant may reserve an opening statement until after the conclusion of the plaintiff's case. An opening statement outlines for the jury the evidence that each party intends to present and informs the jury of the party's theory of the case.

STATE OR MUNICIPAL BONDS state or municipal bonds are debt instruments issued by state or local governments. The interest paid or accrued on such bonds is generally an **exclusion** from **gross income,** and thus not subject to **income tax.** I.R.C. §103.

STATE REMEDIES see **exhaustion of remedies** [EXHAUSTION OF STATE REMEDIES].

STATU QUO see **in statu quo.**

STATUS CRIME an offense where there is no wrongful deed that would render the actor criminally liable if combined with **mens rea.** 261 N.W. 2d 847, 851-52. The imposition of any punishment for such an offense violates the **cruel and unusual punishment** prohibition of the **Eighth Amendment.** For example, although one may be convicted for the use of drugs one may not be convicted for the mere status of addiction to drugs. 370 U.S. 660. See also **vagrancy.**

STATUS QUO (stă'-tŭs kwō)— Lat: the postures or positions which existed; the conditions or situations which existed. The "status quo to be preserved by [a] temporary **injunction** is the last actual, peaceable, noncontested status which preceded the pending controversy." 498 S.W. 2d 42, 48. See **restraining order.** In a **breach of contract** setting, in order for the plaintiff to get **restitution** for the value of his or her performance he or she must return the value of the part performance he or she received from the defendant, since the purpose of the remedy of restitution is to restore the STATUS QUO ANTE, i.e., the situation which existed at the inception of the **contract.** In order to restore the status quo ante, each party must be placed **in statu quo,** i.e., each party must be placed in the position he or she occupied at the inception of the contract. Placing each of the parties in statu quo means restoring each to the status quo; i.e., the position occupied at the making of the contract. See 5 Corbin, Contracts §1114 (1964). 28 P. 764, 767. The status quo ante is in contradiction to the usual "benefit of the bargain" goal of placing the parties in the position they would have been in had the contract been fulfilled. See **damages; rescission.**

STATUTE an act of the legislature, adopted pursuant to its constitutional authority, by prescribed means and in certain form such that it becomes the law governing conduct within its scope. Statutes are enacted to prescribe conduct, define crimes, create inferior governmental bodies, appropriate public monies, and in general to promote the public good and welfare. Lesser governmental bodies adopt **ordinances;** administrative agencies adopt regulations. See **police power.** Compare **common law, judge-made**

law. See also **declaratory statutes; severable statute.**

STATUTE OF FRAUDS statutory requirement that certain contracts be in writing to be enforceable. Most such statutes are patterned after the English statute enacted in 1677. Contracts to answer to a **creditor** for the **debt** of another, contracts made in **consideration** of marriage, contracts for the sale of land or affecting any **interest** in land (except short-term **leases**) and contracts not to be performed within one year from their making, must be evidenced by a written memorandum, and signed by the PARTY TO BE CHARGED, [i.e., by the party sought to be bound by the contract]. Under a separate section of the English statute and as codified in the Uniform Commercial Code, a contract for the sale of goods where the contract price exceeds $500 must likewise be in writing. See U.C.C. §2-201.

Under the MAIN PURPOSE RULE, where one party has agreed to answer for the debt of another and the promisor undertaking the obligation has an independent interest of his or her own in so doing, such contract need not be in writing. Nor is a written contract required "in consideration of marriage" where it is actually only in contemplation of marriage and supported by other consideration. An oral contract that has been fully performed on both sides is "not within the statute," that is, not subject to its requirements. The statute does not apply to contracts implied by law or to **quasi contracts.**

PART PERFORMANCE is another important exception and operates to take an oral contract "out of the statute," i.e., to render it enforceable. In the case of a sale of goods within the statute, acceptance of part or all of the goods by the buyer or payment of all or part of the purchase price by the buyer suffices as part performance as to that portion

of the contract. See U.C.C. §2-201
(3)(c).

STATUTE OF LIMITATIONS
"any law which fixes the time within which **parties** must take judicial action to enforce rights or else be thereafter barred from enforcing them," 116 S.E. 2d 654, 657.

Virtually all actions at law, **civil** or **criminal,** have a statutory time beyond which the action may not be brought. A common exception is murder, which is generally not subject to a statute of limitations. Additionally, equity proceedings are governed by an independent equity doctrine called **laches.** The time limitation is also an essential element of **adverse possession,** prescribing the time at which the adverse possessor's interest in the property becomes unassailable. The policy underlying the enactment of such laws concerns the belief that there is a point beyond which a prospective defendant should no longer need to worry about the possible commencement in the future of an action against him or her, that the law disfavors "stale evidence," and that no one should be able to "sit on his rights" for an unreasonable amount of time without forfeiting his or her claims. See **laches.**

STATUTE OF QUIA EMPTORES see **Quia Emptores, Statute of.**

STATUTE OF USES An English statute (27 Hen. VIII) enacted in 1536, for the purpose of preventing the separation of legal and **equitable estates** in land, a separation that arose whenever a **use** was created at **common law.** The purpose was to unite all legal and equitable estates in the beneficiary [the holder of the equitable estates] and to strip the **trustee** [the holder of the legal **title**] of all interest. See **use** for a discussion of statute's application.

STATUTE OF WILLS an early English statute prescribing the conditions necessary for a valid disposition through a **will.** Today, the term is used broadly to refer to the statutory provisions of a particular jurisdiction relating to the requirements for valid **testamentary** dispositions. Generally, to be valid, a will must be in writing and signed by the testator and by competent witnesses. Page, Wills §19.4 (1960).

STATUTE, TITLE OF A see **title** [TITLE (OF A STATUTE)].

STATUTORY ARSON see **arson.**

STATUTORY CONSTRUCTION the process by which one determines the meaning of statutes by drawing conclusions with respect to subjects that lie beyond the direct expression of the text from elements known from, and given in the text. Construction may be reached by reasoning from extraneous connected circumstances, laws, writings, or legislative history bearing on the same or connected matter by seeking and applying the probable aim and purpose of the statute. 433 N.Y.S. 2d 345, 350. The courts have developed principles of statutory construction such as **ejusdem generis** and **expressio unius est exclusio alterius.** See also **liberal construction; severable statute** [SEVERABILITY CLAUSE]; **strict construction.** See generally Sands, Sutherland Statutory Construction (4th ed. 1972–1973).

STATUTORY EXCEPTIONS see **exceptions** [STATUTORY EXCEPTIONS].

STATUTORY OFFENSE those crimes created by **statutes** and not by **common law;** offenses **malum prohibitum.** See **regulatory offenses.**

STATUTORY RAPE see **rape.**

STAY a judicial **order** whereby some action is forbidden or held in abeyance until some event occurs or the court lifts its order. For instance, a single justice of the U.S. Supreme Court has the power to "stay" an injunction pending an appeal to the entire Supreme Court. See generally Fed. R. Civ. Proc. 62. See **injunction; restraining order.**

STAY OF EXECUTION process whereby a **judgment** is precluded from being executed for a specific period of time. Fed. R. Civ. Proc. 62(a).

STEP TRANSACTION see **transaction** [STEP TRANSACTION].

STEP-UP BASIS see **basis** [STEP-UP BASIS].

STIMULANTS see **controlled substances** [STIMULANTS].

STIPULATION an agreement, admission, or concession made by parties in a judicial proceeding or by their attorneys, relating to business before the court. 235 N.E. 2d 664, 668. At **common law** and under the statutes that now generally govern, in order to bind the parties a stipulation must be in writing unless made on the **record** in a court proceeding. 341 So. 2d 1135, 1136; 223 N.W.2d 557, 562. Unlike a contract, a stipulation does not require **consideration** or **mutuality** to be enforceable. 97 N.E. 1042, 1047, 73 Am. Jur. 2d 536.

A stipulation is generally employed to avoid the delay or expense that might result from the full enforcement of procedural rights requiring the exhaustive presentation of evidence or validation of facts not in dispute. 566 P. 2d 133, 134; 213 S.E. 2d 428. On the other hand, stipulation of a fact by one party does not preclude the other party from introducing evidence to prove that fact. 523 P. 2d 337, 341. Parties may not stipulate to determinations of law or to conclusions of law that might follow from the facts or evidence stipulated. 208 S.E. 2d 422, 425. A stipulation binds only the parties to the agreement, and does not bind third parties.

A stipulation is sometimes termed a JUDICIAL ADMISSION. 98 F. 2d 328, 330; 233 Ill. App. 240, 245.

STIRPES see **per stirpes.**

STOCK see **securities** [STOCK].

STOCKBROKER see **broker** or **registered representative.**

STOCK CERTIFICATE written **instrument** evidencing a share in the ownership of a **corporation.** See **securities.**

STOCK CLEARING a so-called "back office" function in the securities trade that involves physical delivery of securities and money payments between buyers and sellers. Members of the **New York Stock Exchange** and the **American Stock Exchange** have established an efficient, automated stock clearing organization which, through its various subsidiaries, provides depository, delivery, and computerized bookkeeping entries that have greatly reduced the physical movement of stock and money between member firms. Various subsidiaries involved are the Securities Industry Automation Corporation [SIAC], the Depositor Trust Company, [DTC], the Central Certificate Service, and Stock Clearing Corporation.

STOCK CORPORATION see **nonstock corporation.**

STOCK DIVIDEND see **dividend** [STOCK DIVIDEND].

STOCK EXCHANGE a market maintained for the purpose of buying and selling **securities.** Under the **Securities Exchange Act of 1934** ("the 1934 Act") an "exchange" is defined as any organization, association, or group of persons, whether incorporated or unincorporated, that constitutes, maintains, or provides a marketplace or facilities for bringing together buyers and sellers of securities or for otherwise performing with respect to securities the functions commonly performed by a stock exchange as that term is generally understood, and includes the marketplace and the market facilities maintained by such exchange. 15 U.S.C. §78c(a)(1). Several stock exchanges exist throughout the country, the most prominent of which is the **New York Stock Exchange.** Under the 1934 Act, every stock exchange is subject to registration with the **Securities and Exchange Commission,** which may be denied unless the exchange adopts rules providing for the discipline, suspension, or expulsion of a member who engages in conduct inconsistent with just and equitable principles of trade. 15 U.S.C. §78f; Jaffe, Broker Dealers and Securities Markets §§10.01-10.02 (1977). See also **American Stock Exchange; regional stock exchange.**

STOCKHOLDER a holder of one or more **shares** of the stock of a **corporation.** As a stockholder one possesses evidence, usually **stock certificates,** that the holder is the real owner of a certain individual portion of the property in actual or potential existence held by the company in its name as a unit for the common benefit of all the owners of the entire **capital** stock of the company. See 77 Ill. App. 424, 433. See **security.** See also **dummy** [DUMMY STOCKHOLDER].

STOCKHOLDER'S DERIVATIVE ACTION [SUIT] see **derivative action.**

STOCK ISSUE see **issue** [STOCK ISSUE].

STOCK MARKET an organized market where **stocks** and **bonds** are actively traded such as **stock exchanges** or **over-the-counter** markets maintained through the **National Association of Securities Dealers [NASD].** Other types of organized exchanges include the **options** exchanges, **commodities** exchanges including the **futures** market, the **money market,** and the **capital market** [bond market] which is largely handled by the stock market participants. See also **brokers; dealers; securities.**

STOCK OPTION the granting to an individual of the right to purchase a corporate stock at some future date at a price specified at the time the option is given rather than at the time the stock is obtained. The option may be purchased or sold, as in a CALL OPTION, or may be granted to an individual by the company as in an EMPLOYEE STOCK OPTION. The option will always involve a specified number of shares, state a time period within which it may be exercised and state a price to be paid upon exercise. A PUT OPTION is the reverse of a call option in that the holder has a right to compel the seller of the option to purchase his shares at a fixed price during a set time period for a pre-determined price per share.

Such options involve no commitments on the part of the individual to purchase the stock and the option is usually exercised only if the price of the stock has risen above the price specified at the time the option was given.

Stock options are a form of incentive compensation. They are usually given by a corporation in an attempt to motivate an employee or **officer** to continue with the corporation or to improve corporate productivity in a manner which will cause the price of the corporation's stock to rise and thereby increase the value of the option. See **security; see also stock dividend.**

NONQUALIFIED STOCK OPTION for income tax purposes, an option which does not qualify as a qualified stock option. On exercise of a nonqualified stock option, the employee recognizes as ordinary income the difference between the option price and the fair market value of the stock. Subsequent sale or exchange of such stock will constitute the sale or exchange of a **capital asset.** I.R.C. §121 et seq.

QUALIFIED STOCK OPTION for income tax purposes, an option

which qualifies for favorable tax treatment. If an employer gives its employee the right to purchase stock in the employer corporation at the price the stock was selling at the time of the option and meets certain other requirements, such grant of an option constitutes a qualified stock option. If the employee exercises such qualified stock option by buying the stock at some time in the future, the employee will not **recognize income** on the difference between the option price and the value of the stock when such option is exercised. Moreover, if the employee holds the stock for more than a certain period of time, the gain recognized on a **sale or exchange** of the stock will be taxed as a capital gain or loss. I.R.C §§421 et seq.

STOCK RIGHTS see **subscription rights.**

STOLEN PROPERTY see **receiving stolen property.**

STOP AND FRISK in reference to police conduct, a limited search for weapons confined to outer clothing. See 475 P. 2d 702–705. Under the Fourth Amendment as judicially construed, police officers may "stop and frisk" a person only if they have reason to believe that that person is an armed and dangerous individual. If so, they may make a reasonable search for weapons for their own protection regardless of whether they have **probable cause** to **arrest** the individual. The standard for judging if a "stop and frisk" was proper is based on whether a reasonably prudent person in the circumstances would be warranted in the belief that his or her safety or that of others was in danger; but due weight is also given to the reasonable inferences that a police officer is entitled to draw from the facts, in light of his or her professional experience. 392 U.S. 1, 27, 30. See also **search and seizure.**

STRADDLE in the securities trade, refers to an **option** position in which a holder has both a **put** (contract to sell) and a **call** (contract to buy) on the same **stock** or **commodity** at the same or nearly the same exercise price. Profit is gained if the optioned stock has a large price movement in either direction. If the price remains stable, a loss results. Thus, straddles are of interest when the underlying stock or commodity is very volatile, but the direction of the next move is uncertain. See also **hedging.**

STRAIGHT-LINE METHOD see **depreciation** [STRAIGHT-LINE DEPRECIATION].

STRAW MAN [PERSON] a colloquial expression designating those arguments in **briefs** or **opinions** created solely for the purpose of debunking or "discovering" them. Arguments so created are like "straw men" because they are, by nature, insubstantial.

The term is also sometimes referred to in commercial and property contexts when a transfer is made to a third party, the straw man [person], simply for the purpose of retransferring to the transferror in order to accomplish some purpose not otherwise permitted. Thus, if a **covenant running with the land** must be included in the deed in the jurisdiction, such a covenant can be established subsequently by conveying the property to a straw man [person] and obtaining from this person a new grant with the desired covenant now in the deed. See **dummy.**

STREET NAME refers to **securities** held in the name of a **broker** or the broker's nominee instead of the name of the **owner**. This condition is required when securities are purchased on **margin**. Many cash buyers find it convenient to leave their securities with their broker who normally holds them in "street name" although arrangements can be made to hold the securities as custodian in the customer's name.

STRICT CONSTRUCTION as to statutes, or contracts, an interpretation by adherence to the literal meaning of the words used. "Strict **construction** of a statute means simply that it must be confined to such subjects or applications as are obviously within its terms or purposes. . . . It does not require such an unreasonably technical construction that the words used cannot be given their fair and sensible meaning in accord with the obvious intent of the legislature." 68 N.E. 2d 278, 282. See **statutory construction.**

STRICT LIABILITY in tort and criminal law, liability without fault. Often in tort law one who engages in an activity that has an inherent risk of injury such as those classified as **ultrahazardous activities,** is liable for all injuries proximately caused by his or her enterprise, even without a showing of negligence. Thus, one who uses explosives or who harbors wild animals is liable for all resulting injuries even if the utmost care is used. The rationale of the tort law of strict liability is that it tends to discourage dangerous activities while not entirely prohibiting any social benefit they may have. Prosser, Torts 495 (4th ed. 1971). A recently developing area of strict liability concerns consumer **product liability.**

In the criminal law, offenses sometimes do not require any specific or general **mens rea.** The conduct itself, even if innocently engaged in, results in criminal liability. Because of the possible harshness of holding people strictly accountable in this way, the courts require strong evidence of a legislative intent to statutorily create strict liability before the usual requirement of mens rea will be dispensed with; and strict liability crimes are usually limited to minor offenses or **regulatory offenses** such as parking violations and violations of health codes. Penalties for strict liability crimes are usually minimal, except in certain instances such as drug and weapons offenses where the penalties may be quite substantial. In some jurisdictions, strict liability offenses are reduced to "violations" that carry only money fines (and short jail terms) and are not deemed "criminal" offenses. Model Penal Code §2.05.

STRICT SCRUTINY a test to determine the constitutional validity of a statute that creates a classification of persons, including classifications based on nationality or race, 403 U.S. 365. Under this test, if a classification scheme affects fundamental rights, it requires a showing that the classification is necessary to, and the least intrusive means of, achieving the compelling state interest, 405 U.S. 330. Such rights include the right to vote, Id.; to interstate travel, 394 U.S. 618; to education, 411 U.S. 1; and to marriage and procreation, 316 U.S. 535. The governmental body passing the legislation in question bears "a heavy burden of justification" to show that the law is necessary to promote a compelling state interest and is being accomplished by the least drastic and intrusive means. 411 U.S. 1, 16-17. See **equal protection of the laws.**

STRIKE a concerted action or combined effort by a group designed to exert pressure on an individual or entity to accede to certain demands. For instance, the mass refusal to work overtime by a group of employees constitutes a strike. 321 A. 2d 123, 126. The right to strike by employees is generally governed by the **National Labor Relations Act,** 29 U.S.C. §§151 et seq. However, the use of the term "strike" is not limited to the labor context. For instance, the refusal of a group of tenants to pay rent until the landlord makes improvements in the rented property is commonly referred to as a RENT STRIKE. See **no strike clause.**

STRIKE SUIT a suit brought primarily for its nuisance value by a small **shareholder** whose interest in the **corporation** is insignificant. Knowing that the cost of defending such a suit is high, the shareholder sues hoping for a private settlement. Henn & Alexander, Law of Corporations §358 (3d ed. 1983). Strike suits are "shareholder" **derivative actions** begun with the hope of winning large attorney's fees or private settlements, and with no intention of benefitting the **corporation** on behalf of which **suit** is theoretically brought." 210 A. 2d 890, 894. These suits are also called "BLACKMAIL SUITS" and "HOLD-UP SUITS." To prevent such abuses, many states have enacted laws giving defending corporations the option of forcing a plaintiff-shareholder to post security sufficient to cover reasonable expenses of litigation, including attorneys' fees, where the plaintiff-shareholder owns less than 5 percent of the outstanding stock or stock valued at less than $50,000. See, e.g., N.Y. Bus. Corp. Law §627.

SUA SPONTE *(sū'-à spŏn'-tā)*— Lat: of itself or of one's self, without being prompted; i.e., as where the court moves to declare a **mistrial** "sua sponte," that is, through the court's own volition [on its own motion], without such a **motion** being made by either of the **adverse parties.**

SUBCHAPTER S CORPORATION see **corporation** [S CORPORATION].

SUBCONTRACTOR one to whom principal contractor sublets part of, or all of, contract; also refers to portions obtained from other subcontractors. See 183 S.E. 914, 915. One who agrees to perform part of a contract for the principal [general] contractor or another subcontractor.

SUBDIVISION any reduction in size of a parcel or tract of land by division into two or more smaller parcels. 231 A. 2d 553, 557. See **zoning.**

SUBINFEUDATION the process that developed under **feudal** law whereby the **grantee** of an **estate** in land from his lord granted a smaller estate in the same land to another. In 1066, William the Conqueror claimed all the land of England for the crown. Subsequently, he granted land to barons for their use in exchange for **services,** but retained ultimate **ownership,** this grant process being called **infeudation.** Such barons held land **in capite.** Subinfeudation was the process by which barons further divided the land by making grants to knights in return for knight services, and the term also includes all subsequent grants and subdivisions by knights and their grantees. Owners under subinfeudation held land "in service" to their grantor and owed nothing directly to the king. See Cheshire, The Modern Law of Real Property 8-19 (11th ed. 1972).

Subinfeudation was made illegal by the statute, of **Quia Emptores,** 18 Edw. I.C.I., and was replaced by the modern concept of **alienation.** See also **servitudes.**

SUBJACENT SUPPORT "the support of the surface by the underlying strata of the earth," 248 A. 2d 106, 115. Compare **lateral support.**

SUBJECT MATTER the thing in dispute; the nature of the **cause of action;** "the real **issue** of fact or law presented for **trial** as between those **parties,"** 62 P. 2d 1248, 1252; the object of a contract.

SUBJECT MATTER JURISDICTION see **jurisdiction** [SUBJECT MATTER JURISDICTION].

SUBJECT TO MORTGAGE see **mortgage** [SUBJECT TO MORTGAGE].

SUBJECT TO OPEN describes the **future interests** of a class of persons in **real property** or a **trust** when the number of persons who could comprise the class may increase or decrease. For example, A, fee owner, conveys to B for life, remainder to B's children. At the time of the grant, B has a child C. C has a vested remainder subject to open to let in later born children. Thereafter, children D and E are born to B and upon their births the remainder opens and vests in C, D, and E as co-tenants. The term is also known as SUBJECT TO PARTIAL DEFEASANCE. Boyer, Survey of the Law of Property 37, 117 (3d ed. 1981).

SUB JUDICE *(sŭb jū'-dĭ-sā)*—Lat: under a court; before a court or judge for consideration. Thus, the "INSTANT MATTER" or the "CASE AT BAR" will be called the "matter (case) sub judice."

SUBLEASE see **lease** [SUBLEASE [UNDERLEASE]].

SUBLET "to make a **sublease** accompanied by a surrender of the **premises** or at least a part thereof." 413 S.W. 2d 592, 601. See **let.** Compare **assignment.**

SUBMIT to yield to the will of another. 235 N.E. 2d 284, 286; in mediation procedures, committing to discretion of another or presenting for determination. 360 So. 2d 1092, 1095. As used in condition of **probation** pursuant to which a defendant is required to submit to a warrantless search, may be defined as consent to such searches during the probationary period. 587 P. 2d 706.

SUB MODO *(sŭb mō'-dō)*—Lat: under a qualification; subject to a condition or qualification.

SUB NOMINE *(sŭb nō'-mē-nā)*—Lat: under the name; used to indicate that the title of a case has been altered at a later stage in the proceedings, e.g., *Scott v. Duane,* aff'd sub. nom. *Scott v. Robert.*

SUBORDINATION to give one **claim** or **debt** a lower priority in relation to another claim or debt. A SUBORDINATION AGREEMENT is one whereby a **creditor** agrees that claims of other creditors must be fully paid before there is any pay-

ment to himself or herself, the subordinated creditor. In **bankruptcy,** the subordination of a **claim** is generally considered the leveling off of the relative disparity in claim levels to prevent injustice. 144 F. 2d 791, 800. In real estate law, subordination refers to the establishment of priority between different existing interests, claims, **liens,** and **encumbrances** on the same parcel of land. 96 Cal. Rptr. 338.

SUBORNATION OF PERJURY the crime of procuring another to make a false oath. 272 A. 2d 794, 800. Proof of subornation of perjury requires proof of both **perjury** in fact and that the perjured statement was procured by the **accused. Id.** There must also be proof that the suborner knew or should have known that such oaths or **testimony** would be false. See 262 F. 2d 788, 794. See also **false swearing.**

SUBPOENA *(sŭ-pē'-nà)*—Lat: a **writ** issued under authority of a court to compel the **appearance** of a **witness** at a judicial proceeding, the disobedience of which may be punishable as a **contempt** of court. 183 N.Y.S. 2d 125, 129.

SUBPOENA AD TESTIFICANDUM *(äd tĕs'-tĭ-fĭ-kän'-dūm)* subpoena to testify. It "is a technical and descriptive name for the ordinary subpoena." 12 A. 2d 128, 129. Compare **summons.**

SUBPOENA DUCES TECUM *(dū'-chĕs tā'-kūm)* under penalty you shall take it with you. Type of subpoena issued by a court at the request of one of the parties to a suit requiring a **witness** to bring to court or to a **deposition** any relevant **documents** that are under the witness's control. 139 So. 794. See, e.g., Fed. R. Civ. Proc. 45(b).

SUBROGATION "one's payment or assumption of an obligation for which another is primarily liable." McClintock, Equity §123 (2d ed. 1948). "This doctrine is not dependent upon **contract,** nor upon **privity** between the parties; it is the creature of **equity,** and is founded upon principles of natural justice. . . . Subrogation has been generally classified as being either legal or conventional. Legal subrogation arises by **operation of law** where one having a **liability,** or right, or a **fiduciary** relation in the premises, pays a debt due by another under such circumstances that he is in equity entitled to the security or obligation held by the creditor whom he has paid. Conventional subrogation, on the other hand, arises where by express or implied agreement with the **debtor,** a person advancing money to discharge a prior **lien** might be substituted to the security of the prior lienee." 18 S.E. 2d 917, 920.

Subrogation typically arises when an insurance company pays its insured pursuant to a policy; the company is then subrogated to the cause of action of its insured. Similarly, under **worker's compensation acts** the board is subrogated to the injured worker's right (up to the amount of the board's payments) to sue the responsible party.

SUBROGEE one who, by **subrogation,** succeeds to the legal rights or claims of another.

SUBROGOR one whose legal rights or claims are acquired by another through **subrogation.**

SUB ROSA literally "under the rose"; secretly, covertly, privately.

SUBSCRIBER a person who has agreed to take and pay for the original unissued **shares** of a corporation. 219 So. 2d 574, 576.

SUBSCRIPTION RIGHTS the **contractual** right of an existing shareholder to purchase additional **shares** of **stock** of the same kind as that already held when and if new shares are issued by a corporation. See Henn & Alexander, Laws of Corporations §169 (3d ed. 1983).

Also called STOCK RIGHTS. Compare **stock option; warrant** [STOCK WARRANT].

SUBSEQUENT CONDITION see **condition subsequent.**

SUBSIDIARY an inferior portion or capacity; usually used in describing the relationship between **corporations.**

SUBSIDIARY CORPORATION one in which another corporation owns at least a majority of the shares and thus has control, 153 A. 159, 160; it has all of the normal elements of a corporation (charter, by-laws, directors, etc.) but its **stock** is controlled by another corporation known as the PARENT CORPORATION. This relationship of parent and subsidiary often becomes important for tax purposes and for determining whether a court will ignore the corporate existence of the subsidiary and **pierce the corporate veil.**

SUB SILENTIO (*sŭb sĭ-lĕn'-shē-ō*)—Lat: under silence; silently. When a later opinion reaches a result contrary to what would appear to be controlling authority, it is said that the later case has overruled sub silentio the prior holding by necessary implication.

SUBSTANTIAL COMPLIANCE see **substantial performance [compliance].**

SUBSTANTIAL PERFORMANCE [COMPLIANCE] the performance of all the essential terms of a contract so that the purpose of the contract is accomplished; however, unimportant omissions and technical defects may exist in the strict performance of the contract, see 272 S.W. 616, 619; "that performance of a contract which, while not full performance, is so nearly equivalent to what was bargained for that it would be unreasonable to deny the promisee the full contract price subject to the promisor's right to recover whatever damages may have been occasioned him by the promisee's failure to render full performance." 247 So. 2d 72, 75. See **breach of contract.**

SUBSTANTIVE DUE PROCESS see **due process of law.**

SUBSTANTIVE LAW "the **positive law** which creates, defines and regulates the rights and duties of the **parties** and which may give rise to a **cause of action,** as distinguished from **adjective law** which pertains to and prescribes the practice and **procedure** or the legal machinery by which the substantive law is determined or made effective." 192 P. 2d 589, 593-594.

SUBSTITUTED BASIS see **basis** [SUBSTITUTED BASIS].

SUBSTITUTED SERVICE see **service** [SUBSTITUTED SERVICE].

SUBSTITUTION putting in place of another thing, serving in lieu of another. 264 N.Y.S. 336. In respect to **wills,** the putting of one person in the place of another so that he or she may, on failure of the original **devisee** or **legatee** or after such person, have the benefit of the **legacy;** particularly, the act of the **testator** in naming a second legatee who is to take the legacy on failure of the original legatee or after such person. 145 N.E. 2d 566, 567.

SUBTENANT one who **leases** all or part of rented **premises** from the original **lessee** for a term less than that held by the original lessee. 3 P. 2d 1042, 1043. The original lessee becomes the sublessor as to the subtenant. Most leases either prohibit subletting or require the lessor's permission in advance. The original lessee remains responsible for the subtenant's obligations to the lessor. Compare **assignment.**

SUCCESSION refers to the process by which the property or rights of a **decedent** is taken through **descent** or by **will.** It is a word that clearly excludes those who take by **deed, grant, gift,** or any form of purchase or **contract.** 10 S.W. 505, 507. See **hereditary succession; inheritance; intestate succession.**

SUCCESSIVE TERMS a series of terms where one term follows the term immediately preceding it.

SUCCESSOR one who assumes the place of another and fulfills his or her role or continues in his or her position, 53 Cal. Rptr. 551, 557; one who has been duly chosen to accede to some office after its current occupant. A corporate successor is a **corporation** that takes on the burdens and arrogates the rights of a predecessor corporation by merger, acquisition, or other valid legal succession. 224 F. Supp. 347, 351.

SUE OUT "to petition for and take out, or to apply for and obtain" a **writ** or court **order,** as to "sue out" a writ in **chancery.** 21 S.W. 811, 812.

SUFFERANCE see **tenancy** [TENANCY AT SUFFERANCE].

SUFFICIENT CONSIDERATION see **consideration.**

SUICIDE the voluntary and intentional killing of one's self; suicide was a felony at **common law,** but modern statutory law is not unanimous in classifying it as a crime. There is no unanimity on the question of whether **attempted** suicide or **aiding and abetting** suicide is illegal, although the criminalization of aiding and abetting suicide is strongly favored by critical commentators. See Perkins & Boyce, Criminal Law 122 (3d ed. 1982).

Suicide by one in possession of one's mental faculties is often excluded from life insurance coverage. See 9 S.W. 812, 815. However, **non-contestability clauses** mandated by statute preclude the exclusion by the insurer after a period of time (such as two years after purchase).

SUI GENERIS (sū-ē' jěn'-ěr-ĭs)— Lat: of its own kind. Unique; in a class by itself. See also **ejusdem generis.**

SUI JURIS *(sū-ē' jûr' -ĭs)*—Lat: of his own right; a term used to describe one who is no longer dependent, e.g., one who has reached the age of **majority,** or has been removed from the care of a guardian; signifies one capable of caring for himself. See 196 P. 2d 456, 461. See **emancipation; incompetence; non sui juris.**

SUIT "a very comprehensive [word], . . . understood to apply to any **proceeding** in a court of justice by which an individual pursues [a] **remedy** which the law affords. The modes of proceeding may be various; but, if a right is litigated in a court of justice, the proceeding by which the decision of the court is sought is a suit." 91 U.S. 367, 375. Formerly applied only to proceedings in **equity,** and now applicable to proceedings in **courts of law** as well. May also be used in relation to criminal proceedings, but this is a less proper usage than its more frequent appearance in reference to civil cases. See 144 N.W. 491. See also **action; friendly suit; litigation; multiplicity of actions [suits].**

CLASS SUIT see **class action.**

(STOCKHOLDERS')   DERIVATIVE SUIT see **derivative action.**

SUITOR a claimant; a litigant. 15 So. 2d 229, 232. A party to an action in a court of law.

SUM CERTAIN any amount that is fixed, settled, stated or exact. 139 N.W. 421, 425-427. It may refer to the value of a **negotiable instrument,** a price stated in a **contract,** or to a measure of damages in a lawsuit. The sum must be ascertainable at the time the instrument is made and computable solely from examination of it. A claim for damages in an amount to be determined by the **trier of fact,** such as treble damages for an **antitrust** violation, 9 F.R.D. 506, 508, or a claim under a contract containing open price terms, 185 N.E. 77, 78, is not a "sum certain." In commercial law, in order for an instrument to be negotiable, it must contain an unconditional promise to pay a sum certain. U.C.C. §3-104(1)(b); 61 N.W. 854, 855. Whether a claim is for a sum certain is highly important in the area of **default judgments,** since generally a clerk may enter judgment upon the default of a party only if it is for a sum certain and not otherwise. 11 F.R.D. 364, 365.

When damages or a claim is for a sum certain the amount is referred to as LIQUIDATED; when the amount is not for a sum certain or before entry of a **judgment,** the claim is UNLIQUIDATED. See also **liquidated damages.**

SUMMARY COURTS-MARTIAL see **court-martial; military law** [COURT-MARTIAL].

SUMMARY JUDGMENT preverdict **judgment** rendered by the court in response to a **motion** by plaintiff or defendant, who claims that the absence of factual dispute on one or more **issues** eliminates the need to send those issues to the **jury;** a "device designed to effect a prompt disposition of controversies on their **merits** without resort to a lengthy trial, if in essence there is no real dispute as to salient facts or if only a question of law is involved." 172 S.E. 2d 816, 817. See Fed. R. Civ. Proc. 56. Compare **directed verdict, summary proceeding.**

SUMMARY PROCEEDING a form of lawsuit in which ordinary legal procedures are disregarded so that the issue at hand may be resolved in a timely fashion. Usually a summary proceeding is limited to a single issue. For instance, most states have summary proceedings to allow a **creditor** to take possession of property securing an unpaid **debt.** While some aspects of legal process may be abandoned, such as jury trial, other rights, such as **notice** and the opportunity to be heard, must be observed. 419 U.S.

601. Summary proceedings have been commonly used in **arbitration, bankruptcy, landlord-tenant,** and **unlawful entry** and detainer cases. Compare **summary judgment.**

SUMMATION [SUMMING UP] the final step in a **trial,** wherein each party's counsel reviews the **evidence** that has been presented and attempts to show why its position should prevail; also known as CLOSING ARGUMENTS. In a jury trial, this step immediately precedes a judge's **instructions** to a jury. The party with the **burden of proof** always closes or sums up last. Therefore, in a civil case, the defendant closes first and then the plaintiff follows. In criminal cases, though, the prosecution closes first, with the defendant following. In most cases, the prosecution is also afforded an opportunity to rebut the defendant's closing as well.

A prosecutor has a special burden during his or her summation, and must not: comment on a defendant's failure to testify, 380 U.S. 609; refer to evidence not in record, 595 F. 2d 751; interject personal opinions concerning veracity of witnesses, 543 F. 2d 1333; appeal to a jury based on passion or prejudice rather than facts, 664 F. 2d 971; or imply that the prosecutor believes that the defendant is guilty of the crime charged, 558 F. 2d 387. A prosecutor cannot be argumentative in his or her closing and "it is as much [the prosecutor's] duty to refrain from improper methods calculated to produce a wrongful conviction as it is to use every legitimate means to bring about a just one." 295 U.S. 78, 88. Still, the prosecutor is entitled to a certain degree of latitude in summation, 553 F. 2d 1013, and his or her closing must be viewed in the context of the entire trial rather than in the abstract. 666 F. 2d 1227.

SUMMONS "a mandate requiring the **appearance** of said defendant in said **action** under penalty of having

judgment entered [against him] for failure so to do," 294 P. 499, 500. See **default judgment.** The object of the summons is to notify the defendant that he has been sued. See 155 N.E. 254, 255. See **process, service.** Compare **subpoena.**

SUNDAY CLOSING LAWS any state or local laws that restrict activities, such as the sale of goods on Sunday. These laws are rooted in the Christian religious tradition and date back to the Middle Ages. 11 Suffolk L. Rev. 1089. Because of their religious basis, Sunday closing laws have been attacked as violative of the **establishment clause** of the U.S. Constitution, but have been upheld as a valid exercise of the **police power,** mandating a day of rest for workers. 113 U.S. 703, 710. 366 U.S. 617. However, Sunday laws have been successfully attacked for discriminatory effect, 57 A.L.R. 2d 975, for vagueness, 91 A.L.R. 2d 763, and because they may contain numerous and irrational exceptions. 353 N.E. 2d 574, 578.

BLUE LAWS any state or local laws that, for moral or religious purposes, restrict activities on Sunday or that restrict certain activities all the time, such as an ordinance prohibiting the operation of a movie theatre in a municipality. The name "blue laws" was received when the Sunday closing laws of New Haven, Connecticut, were printed on blue paper in 1781. 11 Suffolk L. Rev. 1089.

SUNSHINE LAWS laws that require government agencies and departments to permit the public to attend their meetings. E.g., 5 U.S.C. §552b. Also called OPEN PUBLIC MEETINGS LAWS. See also **Freedom of Information Act.**

SUO NOMINE (sū'-ō-nō'-mē-nā)—Lat: in his own name.

SUPERIOR COURT see **inferior court** [SUPERIOR COURT].

SUPERSEDEAS *(sū-pèr-sē'dē-as)*—Lat: you shall forbear. A **writ** commanding a "stay of proceedings." The purpose of such a writ is to maintain the status quo that existed before the entry of a **judgment** or **decree** of the court below. 183 P. 2d 275, 277.

SUPERSEDING CAUSE see **cause** [SUPERSEDING CAUSE].

SUPERVENING CAUSE see **cause** [INTERVENING [SUPERVENING] CAUSE].

SUPPLEMENTAL something added to cure a deficiency or otherwise complete a document or act. Compare **amendment**.

SUPPLEMENTAL ACT ". . . that which supplies a deficiency, adds to or completes, or extends that which is already in existence without changing or nullifying the original; [an act] designed to improve an existing statute by adding something thereto without changing the original text." 100 N.E. 2d 304, 308.

SUPPLEMENTAL AFFIDAVIT a subsequent affidavit in addition to the original one. Generally used to explain or correct the original affidavit, but may also be used to set up a new and different defense.

SUPPLEMENTAL ANSWER an answer in addition to the original answer which corrects, enhances, or explains the original one.

SUPPLEMENTAL BILL in equity, a bill in addition to the original bill, that brings into controversy some matter that occurred after the original bill was filed, or that corrects a defect in the original bill. 152 So. 459, 461.

SUPPLEMENTAL CLAIM a filed claim seeking additional relief after the filing of the original claim.

SUPPLEMENTAL PLEADING [COMPLAINT] see **pleading** [SUPPLEMENTAL PLEADING].

SUPPLEMENTAL PROCEEDING a proceeding in an action against a **judgment debtor** to discover property of the debtor subject to **execution** and apply such property to the satisfaction of the judgment. 1 P. 2d 924, 925. Such a proceeding is separate from the original action and is generally governed by the rules of the court. See, e.g., Fed. R. Civ. Proc. 69(a).

SUPPORT see **alimony**. See also **lateral support; subjacent support.**

SUPPRESS to effectively prevent; to restrain; to end by force. 94 So. 408, 409. See **suppression of evidence.**

SUPPRESSION OF EVIDENCE the refusal to produce evidence or to allow evidence to be produced for use in litigation. Suppression of evidence refers most commonly to the sanction in a criminal case for an unreasonable **search or seizure** that violates a defendant's constitutional rights. In 1914, the U.S. Supreme Court held that illegally seized evidence must be excluded from use in federal criminal trials. 232 U.S. 383. In 1961, the Court expanded the **exclusionary rule** to include state criminal trials. 367 U.S. 643.

Suppression of evidence also refers either to a party's refusal to produce evidence or to interference by a party with the production of evidence when another party seeks the evidence pursuant to the law. In civil cases, the failure to produce evidence may constitute an admission that the evidence is unfavorable to the party refusing to produce it. McCormick, Evidence §273 (2d ed. 1972).

SUPRA *(sū'pra)*—Lat: above; in a written work, it refers the reader to a part that precedes that which is being read, as compared with the command "infra" which directs the reader forward. See **infra.**

SUPREMACY CLAUSE popular title for Article VI, Section [2] of the United States Constitution, which is the main foundation of the federal government's power over the states, providing in effect that the "acts of the Federal Government are operative as supreme law throughout the Union. They are self-executing, since they prescribe rules enforceable in all courts of the land. The states have no power to impede, burden, or in any manner control the operation of the laws enacted by the Government of the nation. . . . [T]he full import of the Supremacy Clause was made clear after John Marshall became Chief Justice. In the Marshall interpretation, the clause meant essentially two things: (1) the states may not interfere in any manner with the functioning of the Federal Government; and (2) federal action (whether in the form of a statute, a treaty, a court decision, or an administrative act), if itself constitutional, must prevail over state action inconsistent therewith." Schwarz, Constitutional Law 48 (2d ed. 1979).

SUPREME COURT the highest **appellate court** in most **jurisdictions** and in the **federal court** system. It is usually the appellate state court of last resort, and unless a case raises a federal question reviewable in federal court, its decisions cannot be reviewed by other courts and must be followed. 379 U.S. 487; 87 U.S. (20 Wall.) 590. However, in some states, most notably New York, the "Supreme Court" is an inferior court and not the court of last resort. In New York, the court of last resort is called the "Court of Appeals" and in Massachusetts, it is the "Supreme Judicial Court."

In the federal court system, the United States Supreme Court is expressly established by the Constitution, which vests judicial power in "one Supreme Court and such inferior courts as Congress shall establish." U.S. Constitution, Art. III, Sec. 1. It consists of a **Chief** Justice and eight **Associate Justices** appointed by the President with the advice and consent of the United States Senate. Six justices of the Court are necessary to constitute a **quorum.** See 28 U.S.C. §1; U.S. Constitution, Art. II, Sec. 2, Cl. 2. The U.S. Constitution and laws give the Supreme Court both **original jurisdiction,** in all cases affecting ambassadors, other public ministers, and counsels, and all cases in which a state is a party, and **appellate jurisdiction** over all cases decided by the lower federal courts and cases decided by state courts involving issues of federal law. U.S. Constitution, Art. III, Sec. 2, Cl. 2; 28 U.S.C. §§1251 et seq.

SURCHARGE an additional charge that has been omitted from an account stated. Surcharging an account stated means proving the improper omission of certain items therefrom. 219 S.W. 148. The term is also used to signify a penalty exacted for the failure to exercise common prudence, common skill, and common caution in the performance of a **fiduciary**'s duties. 26 A. 2d 320. Similarly, a SURTAX is a tax charged on certain kinds of income in addition to the tax normally imposed. 148 P. 2d 1004.

SURETY "one who undertakes to pay money or perform other acts in the event that his **principal** fails to do so; the surety is directly and immediately liable for the **debt.**" 334 F. Supp. 1009, 1013. See **indorsement.** Compare **guarantor.** See also **Statute of Frauds.**

SURETY BOND see **bond** [SURETY BOND]

SURPLUS the remainder of a fund appropriated for a particular purpose, after the purpose has been accomplished or any monies necessary therefore have been spent; the residue. 67 Cal. Rptr. 104, 107.

In corporations, surplus ordinarily refers to the assets that remain after liabilities and debts, including capital stock, have been deducted from the assets. 431 S.W. 2d 177, 180. If the surplus balance is negative, i.e., its debits exceed its credits, then a deficiency exists. Henn & Alexander, Laws of Corporations 876 (3d ed. 1983).

EARNED SURPLUS that portion of surplus derived from the net earnings, gains, or profits retained by a corporation, rather than paid to shareholders as dividends. See 275 U.S. 215, 219.

PAID-IN SURPLUS that portion of surplus derived from the sale, exchange, or issuance of capital stock at a price above the **par value** of the stock. Par value is the value at which capital stock is carried on the corporate books, and is not necessarily the price received for the stock by the corporation. The difference between the par value and the actual price received is the paid-in surplus. 149 S.E. 2d 642, 644.

In the case of no-par stock, it is the amount received that has been allocated to paid-in surplus. Cox, Corporations 258 (1973). The term is sometimes used interchangeably with "capital surplus," although the latter term is often used generally to denote the entire surplus of a corporation other than its earned surplus. See, e.g., N.Y. Bus. Corp. Law §102(2).

UNEARNED SURPLUS see **unearned surplus.**

SURREBUTTER in **common law pleading,** a **plaintiff**'s answer to the **defendant**'s **rebuttal** [rebutter].

SURREJOINDER in **common law pleading,** a **plaintiff**'s answer to the **defendant**'s **rejoinder.**

SURRENDER the delivery of **possession** or release in response to a demand, 81 N.Y. 242, 244. In landlord-tenant law, the yielding of the **leasehold estate** by the lessee to the **landlord,** so that the estate for years merges in the reversion and no longer exists as a separate estate. 87 A. 112, 108 F. 2d 216. The termination of a lease may be accomplished by the express mutual agreement of the parties called "express surrender," or by **operation of law** when the parties perform some act from which it may be implied that they both agreed to the surrender. 158 A. 88.

In contract law, the surrender of a legal right is a valid consideration to support the contract. Corbin, Contracts § 132 (1952). In criminal law, surrender refers to the act by which an accused is delivered to the authorities. See also **extradition.**

SURROGATE a judicial officer of limited **jurisdiction,** who administers matters regarding decedents' and incompetents' estates and, in some cases, adoptions. See **probate.**

SURROGATE PARENT one who is not a child's parent, but who stands in the place of the parent and is charged with a parent's rights, duties, and responsibilities, either by virtue of voluntary assumption or court appointment. See **guardian; in loco parentis.**

SURROGATE'S COURT see **court** [SURROGATE'S COURT].

SURTAX see **surcharge** [SURTAX].

SURVEILLANCE oversight or supervision. In criminal law, an investigative process by which police gather evidence about crimes or suspected crime through continued observation of persons or places. **Wiretapping,** electronic observation, tailing, or shadowing are examples of this type of law enforcement procedure. See **search and seizure.**

SURVIVAL STATUTE a statute that preserves for a decedent's **estate** a **cause of action** for infliction of **pain and suffering** and related **damages** suffered up to the moment of death. Such a statute is to be contrasted with a **wrongful death**

act, which views causing one's death not as a **tort** as to the decedent himself or herself, but as a wrong with respect to the family, and which gives the decedent's immediate family a cause of action for losses occasioned by his or her death, such as lost wages and lost companionship (**consortium**). One chief difference between a survival statute and a wrongful death statute is that "where death is instantaneous, or substantially so, there can be no cause of action under the survival acts, since the decedent has had no time to suffer any appreciable damages, and so no cause of action ever has vested in him." Prosser, Torts 902 (4th ed. 1971).

SURVIVORSHIP a right whereby a person with an **interest** in property becomes entitled to the whole property by reason of his or her having survived another person who also had an interest in it. 20 N.Y.S. 2d 59, 62. It is one of the elements of a **joint tenancy,** and a tenancy by the entirety. See also **survival statute.**

SUSPECT CLASSIFICATION see **equal protection of the laws.**

SUSPENDED SENTENCE see **sentence** [SUSPENDED SENTENCE].

SUSTAIN to support; to approve; to adequately maintain; e.g., the judge "sustained" the **plea** because he found it to be true. 25 N.E. 2d 230; or the plaintiff "sustained" the **burden** of coming forward with the requisite evidence.

SWEARING, FALSE see **false swearing.**

SWEEPSTAKES see **lottery** [SWEEPSTAKES].

SWITCH see **bait and switch.**

SYLLABUS a **head note** preceding a reported case and summarizing the principles of law as established in that case. See 47 N.E. 2d 627, 629. Under the practice of the United States Supreme Court the headnotes are prepared for the convenience of readers by the Reporter of Decisions; as such the syllabus constitutes no part of the opinion of the Court. 200 U.S. 321, 337.

SYMBOLIC DELIVERY see **delivery.**

SYNDICATE a group of individuals or companies who have formed a joint venture to undertake a project which the individuals would be unable or unwilling to pursue alone. In the **securities** trade, new **offerings** and large **secondary distribution** are routinely marketed by a syndicate of **investment bankers** and **stockbrokers.** Formation of an **underwriting** syndicate is usually required since large offerings involve more capital and more marketing capacity than any single investment banker can supply. Sometimes used to refer to the "mob." See **organized crime.**

T

TACIT implied or indicated, but not actually expressed; arising without express contract or agreement. 158 F. 2d 809, 811. Compare **latent.**

TACKING to add or join together; in property law, the uniting of the periods of **possession** of successive adverse possessors to complete the period necessary to establish title by **adverse possession,** which is possible provided that there is **privity** of estate between the successive adverse possessors. Thus, for tacking to be permitted, the original adverse possessor must transfer the property either by a voluntary conveyance or by inheritance. 305 A. 2d 562.

The term is also sometimes used in a legislative context to denote the practice of attaching onto a general appropriations bill a separate, unrelated bill, that would not likely pass on its own merits, in an effort to compel the legislature to vote for it, 29 A. 297.

The term as applied to **mortgages** refers to the joining of a mortgage in a third priority position with a first mortgage so as to frustrate the second priority position of a second mortgagee.

TAFT-HARTLEY ACT popular name for the LABOR-MANAGEMENT RELATIONS ACT of 1947, 29 U.S.C. §§141 et seq., the principal aim of which was to establish limitations on unions. See Myers, Labor Law and Legislation 413-422 (5th ed. 1975). It amended the **National Labor Relations Act** of 1935, also known as the WAGNER ACT, 29 U.S.C. §§151 et seq., to give more protection to employers involved in labor disputes. The Wagner Act had granted employees the right to join labor unions and bargain collectively with their employers. 29 U.S.C. §157. To protect this right, the Wagner Act prohibited company interference with employee efforts to organize a union, company domination of a labor union, company refusal to hire or tenure anyone because of union membership, company firing or otherwise disfavoring an employee because of the assertion of rights under the Wagner Act, and company refusal to bargain collectively with a labor union. 29 U.S.C. §158. See **collective bargaining; labor organization [union].**

The Taft-Hartley Act's stated purpose is to "prescribe the legitimate rights of both employees and employers," 29 U.S.C. §141. It was adopted to protect employers' rights by broadening their rights to free speech on unionization, 29 U.S.C. §158(c); by permitting them to disregard unions formed by supervisory personnel, 29 U.S.C. §164(a); by outlawing **closed shops;** by permitting employees to refrain from union activity, 29 U.S.C. §157; and by limiting employee elections on whether to unionize to one per year, 29 U.S.C. §§159(c)(1) and 159(c)(1)(3). It also prohibits unions from forcing employees to join, 29 U.S.C. §158(b)(1); from forcing an employer to discriminate against non-union employees, 29 U.S.C. §158(b)(2); from refusing to bargain collectively with the employer, 29 U.S.C. §158(b)(3); from engaging in **wildcat strikes,** 29 U.S.C. §158(b)(4)(i); from charging discriminatory membership fees, 29 U.S.C. §158(b)(5); and from extracting favors or kickbacks from employers, 29 U.S.C. §158(b)(6).

The Taft-Hartley Act also separated the prosecutorial and adjudicative functions of the **National Labor Relations Board** to provide for unbiased decisions by that agency and gave the federal courts of appeals broader powers of review over the board's findings. 29 U.S.C. §160.

TAIL, ESTATE IN see **fee tail.**

TAINTED EVIDENCE see **fruit of the poisonous tree.**

TAKING THE FIFTH the popular term given to a person's assertion of the **Fifth Amendment** right not to give evidence that will incriminate oneself. See **pleading the Fifth; self-incrimination, privilege against.**

TANGIBLE PROPERTY property, either **real** or **personal,** capable of being **possessed;** such as is capable of being apprehended by the senses, which is accessible, identifiable, etc., see 228 S.W. 2d 882; 147 N.Y.S. 465, 469. "Tangible property" is corporeal, as distinguished from intangible property or incorporeal rights in property, such as **franchises, copyrights, easements,** etc. See 57 P. 2d 1022, 1028. For taxation purposes, "tangible property" generally refers to **personalty** [personal property], and is that movable property which has a value of its own, rather than merely the evidence or representative of value, and which has a visible or substantial existence. See 307 U.S. 357.

TARGET CORPORATION see **corporation** [TARGET CORPORATION].

TARIFF tax; used most frequently in reference to taxes on imported and exported goods; a **customs duty**, Tariff Act of 1930, 19 U.S.C. §§1202 et seq. Also, a public document setting forth the services offered of a public utility or carrier, rates and charges with respect to the services, and governing rules, regulations, and practices relating to those services. 433 F. Supp. 352, 357 n. 4.

GATT [GENERAL AGREEMENT ON TARIFFS AND TRADE] an international agreement signed by most of the nations of the free world, including all of the major industrial nations, which establishes rules for the conduct of international trade. The purpose of GATT is to promote the expansion of world trade by the removal of trade barriers such as tariffs and customs duties. Under GATT, each signatory country is granted **most favored nation** status vis-à-vis each other signatory country. Rossides, U.S. Customs, Tariffs, and Trade 12-15 (1977).

TAX a rate or sum of money assessed on a person or property for the support of the government, 86 S.E. 2d 672, 676, and commonly levied upon assets or real property (property tax), or income derived from wages, etc. (income tax), or upon the sale or purchase of goods (sales tax).

AD VALOREM TAX [VALUE ADDED TAX] a tax imposed upon the difference between the cost of an asset to the taxpayer and the present **fair market value** of such asset; a tax based on a percentage of the value of the property subject to taxation, as opposed to a specific tax, which is a fixed sum applied to all of a certain class of articles. See 194 S.E. 151, 154.

AVOIDANCE OF TAX see **avoidance of tax.**

CAPITAL GAINS TAX see **capital** [CAPITAL GAINS].

CLAIM OF RIGHT see **claim of right.**

DEDUCTIONS see **deductions; tax deduction.**

ESTATE TAX tax upon the transfer of property, not upon the property itself; estate taxes imposed upon the net value of a decedent's estate. Estate taxes are based upon the power to transmit or the transmission from the dead to the living. The same tax result is accomplished in some jurisdictions through imposition of INHERITANCE TAXES which are taxes imposed upon the receipt of the deceased's property by the beneficiary. 298 F. 803, 810. See also 244 N.Y.S. 2d 960, 964. Estate taxes and inheritance taxes are both forms of TRANSFER TAXES which are taxes levied upon the passing of title to property. See **inheritance.**

ESTIMATED TAX generally, income taxes paid periodically by a taxpayer on income not subject to withholding taxes, in an amount based upon the taxpayer's projected liability.

EXCISE TAX a federal tax imposed upon the purchase of certain items. See **excise.**

FEDERAL INSURANCE CONTRIBUTION ACT see **F.I.C.A.**

F.I.C.A. see **F.I.C.A.**

FRANCHISE TAX a tax generally imposed by the states upon **corporations.** Often, the franchise tax is divided into two components: (1) a tax upon the net income of the corporation attributable to activities within the state; and (2) the tax on the net worth of the corporation located in the state.

GIFT TAX see **gift tax.**

HIDDEN TAX see **hidden tax.**

INCOME TAX a tax imposed upon income received which is **recognized** for tax purposes by the **taxpayer,** reduced by the allowable **deductions** and **credits.** See **return.**

INHERITANCE TAX see ESTATE TAX above; **inheritance.**

LICENSE TAX see **license tax.**

PERSONAL HOLDING COMPANY TAX see **personal holding company.**

POLL TAX see **poll tax.**

PROGRESSIVE TAX a tax in which rate increases as the amount subject to tax increases. For example, a progressive income tax would be a tax at which on lower income levels the rate of tax was lower than the rate of tax on higher income levels.

PROPERTY TAX generally, tax imposed by municipalities upon owners of property within their jurisdiction based upon the value of such property. The rate of such tax is usually the same regardless of the value of the property.

PROPORTIONAL TAX a tax imposed at a fixed and uniform rate in proportion to the property subject to the tax, 106 N.W. 93, 96.

REFUND see **tax refund.**

REGRESSIVE TAX a tax in which rate decreases as the amount to which the tax is applied increases.

RETURN see **return.**

SALES TAX a tax generally imposed by state or local government on the sale of certain items that are generally not for resale. In general, the sales tax is at a set rate regardless of the purchase price

of the property. Compare USE TAX below.

SURTAX see **surcharge** [SURTAX].

TAX SALE see **sale** [TAX SALE].

TRANSFER TAX see ESTATE TAX above.

UNIFIED ESTATE AND GIFT TAX a federal tax imposed upon the net value of an estate and on gifts of certain amounts. The transferor is liable for the gift taxes but if the transferor fails to pay the gift tax, the transferee may be held liable for its payment. I.R.C. §§2001 et seq. and 2501 et seq.

USE TAX a tax imposed upon property purchased in one jurisdiction but brought into another jurisdiction. The jurisdiction imposing a "use tax" does so to curtail out-of-state purchases made for the purpose of avoiding sales taxes. The rate of a use tax is generally the same as the rate of a sales tax. See SALES TAX above.

VALUE ADDED TAX see AD VALOREM TAX above.

WITHHOLDING TAX the amount of **income tax** withheld from a payment of income. For example, an employer is required to withhold taxes from an employee's salary when the salary is paid to the employee. The amount withheld is a credit against the amount of income taxes that the employee must pay on income earned for the **taxable year.** I.R.C. §§3401-3404.

TAXABLE ESTATE the amount to which the rate of **estate** tax is applied in order to determine the amount of estate tax payable. For federal estate tax purposes, it is the **decedent's** gross estate, i.e., all property in which the decedent had an interest at the time of death as well as specified other property, I.R.C. §§2033 et seq., less the estate tax deductions, such as **marital** and **charitable deductions,**

I.R.C. §§2051 et seq. See **tax** [ESTATE TAX].

TAXABLE GIFT the amount to which the rate of **gift tax** is applied in order to determine the amount of gift tax payable. For federal gift tax purposes, it is the total amount of gifts made, less the gift tax deductions allowed, such as the **marital** and the **charitable deductions,** I.R.C. §2503(a). The aggregate of all lifetime gifts that are taxable is added to the **decedent's estate** to determine the applicable estate tax under the unified estate and gift tax. I.R.C. §2001.

TAXABLE INCOME the amount applied to the rate of income tax in order to determine the income tax payable. For federal income tax purposes, it is defined differently for corporations and individuals. The taxable income of a corporation is its gross income less its income tax deductions. I.R.C. §63(a). The taxable income of an individual is **gross income,** less the deductions allowed in computing the adjusted gross income, I.R.C. §62, less the excess of itemized deductions over the zero bracket amount. I.R.C. §63(b). See **deductions** [ZERO BRACKET AMOUNT].

TAXABLE YEAR the period during which the income tax liability of an individual or entity is calculated, or, in the case of certain non-taxable entities, the period for which tax information is provided. Individuals generally have a calendar year as their taxable year, while other entities are generally free to elect their taxable years. I.R.C. §441(b).

FISCAL YEAR a taxable year other than a calendar year; such taxable years are generally available, to entities other than individuals, such as **corporations, partnerships,** and **trusts.** I.R.C. §441(e).

SHORT YEAR a taxable period which, for a variety of reasons,

consists of less than a full year. I.R.C. §443.

TAX BENEFIT DOCTRINE a theory that provides for the inclusion in **gross income** of amounts deducted in earlier **taxable years** and recovered in later years, but only to the extent that the earlier **deductions** resulted in a reduction in income tax liability for the earlier year. I.R.C. §111.

TAX COURT an independent 16-judge federal administrative agency that functions as a court to hear disputes over proposed tax deficiencies asserted by the Internal Revenue Service. The Tax Court, formerly known as the Board of Tax Appeals, is a court of original jurisdiction. Its jurisdiction is limited to hearing petitions for redetermination of federal income, estate, and gift tax liabilities; it has no investigative, regulatory, or administrative functions. **Trial by jury** is not available and any refund claims must be brought to federal district court or the U.S. **Court of Claims.** Tax court trials are **de novo** and an adverse decision may be appealed as of right to the U.S. Court of Appeals and in rare cases to the U.S. Supreme Court. I.R.C. §§7441 et seq.

TAX CREDIT a dollar for dollar reduction in the amount of tax that a taxpayer owes. Unlike **deductions** or **exemptions,** which reduce the amount of income subject to tax, a credit reduces the actual amount of tax owed.

INVESTMENT TAX CREDIT credits allowed for investments in personal property devoted to business or income-producing activity. I.R.C. §38 and §§46-50.

JOBS CREDIT a credit allowed to businesses for increasing the number of employees they hire. I.R.C. §44B and §51-53.

TAX DEDUCTION an item that may be deducted from a gross amount subject to tax, in order to yield the net amount subject to tax. By reducing the amount subject to tax, a tax deduction will usually reduce the amount of tax imposed. For instance, the Internal Revenue Code allows various deductions from gross income in order to determine the amount of taxable income. I.R.C. §§62-63. See **deduction.**

TAX EVASION the fraudulent and willful underpayment or non-payment of taxes. A term usually applied to activities that constitute criminal tax fraud; generally applied to any of various methods by which a **taxpayer** may pay less than his or her proper tax liability by using illegal methods. Evasion is to be distinguished from tax **avoidance,** which denotes the proper use of interpretation of relevant tax law to legally minimize tax liability.

TAX EXEMPT not subject to tax. Most commonly used to describe tax exempt **interest,** which is interest paid by the states or their subdivisions and is exempt from federal income taxes. I.R.C. §103. Interest paid by the states was initially exempted from federal income taxation in 1913 under the belief that taxing such interest would unconstitutionally interfere with the state's ability to raise funds. The exemption is now retained by Congress as a form of revenue sharing with the states. Bittker, Federal Taxation of Income, Estates and Gifts 15.2.1 (1981).

TAX EXPENDITURE revenue losses suffered by the federal government as a result of provisions of the **Internal Revenue Code** which grant special tax benefits to certain kinds of taxpayers or certain activities engaged in by taxpayers. This approach recognizes that such provisions are the economic equivalent of a collection of the forgiven tax liability and a simultaneous direct budget outlay to the benefited taxpayers.

TAX EXPENDITURE BUDGET a listing or compilation of the various tax expenditures inherent in the tax system for the year in question.

TAXING POWER the power of Congress "to lay and collect taxes, duties, imports and excises . . . [provided that] all duties, imports and excises shall be uniform throughout the United States," U.S. Constitution, Art. I, §8, cl. 1, and "to lay and collect taxes on incomes, from whatever source derived, without apportionment among the several States, and without regard to any census or enumerations," U.S. Const. Amend. XVI. The taxing power is used primarily to raise revenue. However, some taxes, such as the estate, gift and generation-skipping taxes attempt to affect social policy, while other taxes, such as the excise tax on gambling and marijuana are used to regulate or deter certain activities. 340 U.S. 42; 345 U.S. 22. Antieau, Modern Constitutional Law §§12:42-12:44 (1969).

TAXPAYER the person who is determined to bear the tax liability for a given **transaction.** I.R.C. §7701(a) (14). Under a variety of circumstances, the entity that directly engages in a transaction may not be the taxpayer with respect to the transaction. Thus, although a **partnership** may receive **income,** that income is taxed to the partner. See **assignment of income.**

TAX-PREFERENCE ITEMS those items of **income, deduction,** or **tax credit** that are deemed to reflect a preference in the tax law for the **taxpayer** benefited by the item. Since the tax-preference items may result in minimal tax liability for certain taxpayers notwithstanding substantial **gross income,** a minimum tax is imposed on the aggregate of the tax-preference items. This tax provision attempts to insure a minimum tax liability for each taxpayer. I.R.C. §§56-58.

TAX RATE the percentage rate of **tax** imposed on a taxpayer. Tax liability is computed by applying the applicable tax rate to the tax base. In a progressive tax system, tax rates increase (through various "brackets") as the tax base increases. Thus, as more income is received, the last to be received is taxed in a tax rate bracket higher than the earlier income. See **tax** [PROGRESSIVE TAX].

MARGINAL TAX RATE the highest percentage rate at which any part of the taxpayer's income is taxed.

EFFECTIVE TAX RATE the rate at which the taxpayer would be taxed if his or her tax liability were taxed at a constant rate rather than at a progressive rate. This rate is computed by determining what percentage the taxpayer's tax liability is of the taxpayer's total taxable income.

TAX RETURN see **return.**

TAX SALE see **sale** [TAX SALE].

TAX SHELTER a transaction by which a taxpayer reduces his or her tax liability by engaging in activities that provide **deductions** or **tax credits** to apply against his or her tax liability. In such cases, the activities engaged in are said to "shelter" the taxpayer's other income. Abuses in the use of these devices have led to amendments to the **Internal Revenue Code,** which have sharply curtailed the availability and usefulness of these devices, such as the "at-risk" rules (below) and the penalties imposed on abusive tax shelters, I.R.C. §6700.

AT-RISK RULES provisions of the Internal Revenue Code that limit the amount of loss from business and investment activities that a taxpayer may deduct to the total amount that he or she has "at risk" in the activity. A taxpayer is "at risk" in an activity only to the extent of the cash or other property he or she has invested in the activity and to the extent he or she is personally liable for the debts of the activity secured by his or her property. A taxpayer is not at risk for amounts of **nonrecourse debt.** The at-risk rules are generally applicable to most business activities except real estate investment. I.R.C. §465. Chirelstein, Federal Income Taxation §13.01(b) (3d ed. 1982).

TEMPORARY that which is to last for a limited time; ephemeral; transitory; 38 Cal. Rptr 63, 67. Temporary has no fixed meaning in the sense that it designates a fixed period of time, but is used in contradistinction to permanent. 392 S.W. 2d 30, 34. See **injunction; interim financing; interim order; restraining order.**

TEMPORARY INJUNCTION see **injunction** [TEMPORARY INJUNCTION].

TEMPORARY RESTRAINING ORDER see **restraining order.**

TEMPORE *(tĕm'-pō-rā)*—Lat: for the time of; thus, the "President pro tempore" of the United States Senate is the Senate President for the present time (when the Vice President is not presiding over the Senate).

TENANCY a **tenant's** right to possess or occupy an **estate,** whether by **lease** or by **title,** derived from the Latin "tenere," meaning "to hold." See 17 S.W. 546, 547. Tenancy refers generally to any such right to hold property, but in a more limited sense it refers to holding in subordination to another's title, as in the landlord-tenant relationship. The various types of tenancy include the following:

COTENANCY see **cotenancy.**

HOLDOVER TENANCY see TENANCY AT SUFFERANCE (below).

JOINT TENANCY "a single **estate** in **property,** real or personal, owned by two or more persons, under one **instrument** or act of the parties, [with] an equal right in all to share in the enjoyment during their lives; and on the death of a joint tenant, the property descends to the survivor or survivors and at length to the last survivor." 309 P. 2d 1022, 1025. Joint tenancy originally was a technical feudal estate in land, but now applies, through statutes, to **personalty** as well. It is particularly common in the purchase of **stocks** and **bonds** and in bank accounts. At common law, a joint tenancy was found to have been formed when there were the four **unities** of time, title, interest, and possession, and these "four unities" are still referred to as elements of a joint tenancy. The primary characteristic of a "joint tenancy" is the **right of survivorship,** which distinguishes it from a TENANCY IN COMMON (see below). Unlike a TENANCY BY THE ENTIRETY [see below], a joint tenancy may be **partitioned [divided]** by one joint tenant by a **sale** or **incumbrance** (i.e., a joint tenant's interest may be reached by his **creditors**), without the consent of the other(s). When this happens, a "tenancy in common" is created, because (technically) the unities of time and title or interest are broken. See 189 N.E. 576, 578.

PERIODIC TENANCY in landlord-tenant law, a **tenancy** for a particular period (a week, month, year, or number of years), plus the expectancy or possibility that the period will be repeated. In contrast to a "tenancy for years," a periodic tenancy must be terminated by due notice to quit by either the landlord or the tenant, unless one party has failed to perform some part of his obligation. A periodic tenancy is considered a form of TENANCY AT WILL (see below), and is created either by express agreement or by implication from the manner in which rent is paid. For example, if A holds B's land with no express time limitation, and rent is payable with reference to divisions of a year, it will be deemed a tenancy from year to year. See 3 S.E. 2d 484, 485. State statutes govern the time necessary for due notice to be given. A periodic tenancy is also **alienable.**

TENANCY AT SUFFERANCE [HOLDOVER TENANCY] in landlord-tenant law, a tenancy that comes into existence when one at first lawfully possesses land as under a lease, and subsequently "holds over beyond the end of one term of such lease or occupies it without such lawful authority." For example, if A has a tenancy for years for one month, at the end of that month, if A continues in possession, his becomes a tenancy at sufferance [or holdover tenancy]. Thus a tenancy at sufferance cannot arise from an agreement, which distinguishes it from a tenancy at will. A tenant at sufferance differs from a **trespasser** only in that he or she originally entered with the landlord's permission. See 228 P. 2d 705. The landlord has a right to establish a landlord-tenant relationship (i.e., extend the lease) of a tenant at sufferance. Reciprocally, a tenant cannot be sued for trespass as a tenant at sufferance before the landlord enters and demands possession. See 32 A. 2d 247. A tenant at sufferance cannot grant such an estate to a third person.

TENANCY AT WILL in landlord-tenant law, a leased estate which confers upon the tenant the right to possession for an indefinite period such as is agreed upon by both parties. See 284 P. 2d 580, 582. A tenancy at will is characterized primarily by the uncertain term and the right of either party to terminate upon proper notice. However, statutes now govern the time provisions necessary before eviction may be had. A tenancy at will may arise out of an express contract or by implication. Because a tenancy at will is determinable at any time, the tenant cannot **assign** or **grant** his or her estate to another. See 55 Me. 33, 36.

TENANCY BY THE ENTIRETY the ownership of property, real or personal, **tangible** and **intangible**, by a husband and wife together. In addition to the four **unities** of time, title, interest, and possession, **unity of person** must exist. The husband and wife are said to be "seized as one person." See 155 N.E. 787. Neither is allowed to **alienate** any part of the property so held without consent of the other. The survivor of the marriage is entitled to the whole property. See 295 F. 429, 431. A divorce severs the tenancies by the entirety and usually creates a tenancy in common. See 168 S.W. 2d 1087, 1090. Under the MARRIED WOMAN'S ACTS each tenant by the entirety is a "tenant in common" of the **use,** and therefore entitled to one-half of the rents and profits while both are alive. See 125 N.Y.S. 1071, 1072.

TENANCY FOR YEARS an estate in land created by a lease limited to a specified and definite term, whether in weeks, months, or years. It is **determinable** (i.e., it ends) upon the expiration of that term, and does not require **notice** of re-entry by the **landlord** nor notice to quit by the tenant. However, if the tenant stays on, the tenancy may be converted into a TENANCY AT SUFFERANCE (see above), TENANCY AT WILL (see above), or a PERIODIC TENANCY (see above), and determinable as such. See 82 P. 20, 21, 178 A. 113, 115, 94 P. 2d 335, 337. A "tenancy for years" is **alienable,** subject to lease restrictions against **assignment** or **sublease.**

TENANCY FROM YEAR TO YEAR [PERIOD TO PERIOD] see PERIODIC TENANCY (above).

TENANCY IN CAPITE tenancy-in-chief. In feudal law, the holding of land directly from the crown.

TENANCY IN COMMON an interest held by two or more persons, each having a possessory right, usually deriving from a title (though also from a lease) in the same piece of land. "Tenancy in common" also applies to **personalty.** See 107 P. 2d 933, 934. At common law, a tenancy in common was (and still is) characterized by unity of possession. Though co-tenants may have unequal shares in the property, they are each entitled to equal use and possession. Thus, each is said to have an "undivided interest" in the property. See 176 P. 2d 425, 427. An estate held as a tenancy in common may be partitioned, sold or incumbered. See **partition.**

TENANT one who holds land by any kind of **title** or right, whether permanently or temporarily; one who purchases an **estate** and is entitled to **possession,** whether exclusive or to be shared with others; also, one who **leases** premises from the owner **(landlord)** or from a previous tenant, thereby becoming a **subtenant.** See also **tenancy.**

TENANTABLE REPAIR see **good tenantable repair.**

TENANT FOR LIFE see **life tenant.**

TENANT IN FEE (SIMPLE) "a tenant in fee simple who hath lands, tenements, or hereditaments to hold to him and his heirs forever; generally, absolutely and simply without mentioning what heirs, but referring that to his own pleasure, or to the disposition of the law." 78 P. 2d 905, 908. The "word 'fee' alone, without any qualifying words, serves to designate a **fee simple estate,** and is not infrequently used in that sense." Id. at 907.

A tenant in fee simple or fee simple absolute holds the greatest estate known to law. The word "simple" is used to indicate that there are no restrictions with respect to the inheritance characteristics of the estate. The word "absolute" emphasizes that the estate is not defeasible upon the happening of any event. Burby, Real Property 5 (3d ed. 1965).

TENDER an unconditional offer to **perform** coupled with a manifested ability to carry out the offer and production of the subject matter (money, etc.) of the tender, 243 F. Supp. 741, 744; an offer to perform as per an existing contract which, if unjustifiably refused, places the refusing party in default and permits the party making tender to exercise his remedy for **breach (of contract).** 17 P. 2d 952, 953. See also **legal tender; tender offer.**

TENDER OF DELIVERY the seller's placement at the buyer's disposal of goods sold to the buyer. 241 N.W. 2d 521, 522. In the Uniform Commercial Code, the term describes a seller's requirements to satisfy his or her obligation to make a timely **delivery** to the buyer in a sales contract. Under the U.C.C., a seller's failure to tender delivery at the proper place under **contract** may constitute a **breach,** unless the seller has a lawful excuse therefore; similarly, a buyer's refusal to take delivery at the proper place may constitute a breach on the buyer's part. See, generally, White & Summers, Uniform Commercial Code §§3-5 (2d ed. 1980); U.C.C. §§2-301, 2-507. If a contract does not require delivery at any particular destination, it is generally considered a SHIPMENT CONTRACT, with the point of delivery being the point of shipment and the point at which the buyer asumes the **risk of loss.** If a destination is specified, however, it is considered a DESTINA-TION CONTRACT and the risk of loss passes to the buyer only upon the seller's tender at destination. U.C.C. §§2-509(1)(b) and 2-509(4); 442 F. 2d 660. See **C.I.F.** [cost, insurance and freight]; **free alongside [F.A.S.]; free on board [F.O.B.].** See also **bill of lading.**

TENDER OFFER in corporate law, an offer to purchase all shares of **stock** of a **corporation,** up to a specific number, tendered by shareholders within a specified period at a fixed price, usually at a premium above the **market price.** Tender offers are usually made by a party seeking to take control of a corporation, and are often followed by a **merger** proposal. Bloomenthal, Securities Law Handbook §§20.01-20.06 (1981).

Congress passed the WILLIAMS ACT in 1968 to regulate tender offers so that shareholders may make an informed decision whether to tender their shares for purchase. Under its most important provision, any person who becomes the owner of 5 percent or more of the outstanding stock in a corporation must inform both the **Securities and Exchange Commission** and the corporation of such stock holdings. 15 U.S.C. §78m(d) (1).

TENEMENT property of a permanent and fixed nature including both **corporeal** and **incorporeal real property.** In modern usage, "tenement" applies to any house, building or structure attached to land, and also to any kind of human habitation or dwelling inhabited by a **tenant.** Se 203 S.W. 36, 37, 73 N.E. 241, 243. "Tenement" is frequently used to indicate dilapidated or inferior dwellings or those rented to the poor. See 75 N.Y.S. 768, 769. See **dominant estate [tenement]; servient estate.** Compare **premises.**

TENTH AMENDMENT the amendment to the U.S. Constitution, referred to as the RESERVED POWERS AMENDMENT, that reserves to the states or the people any powers not delegated to the United States nor prohibited to the states by the Constitution. It expresses the original framers' intent that the central government be a government of limited powers and was included in the **Bill of Rights** to prevent the federal government from attempting to exercise powers it was not specifically given. Traditionally, the Tenth Amendment has been viewed as a mere truism which restates the relationship between the states and the federal government. However, the Supreme Court has more recently held that the amendment bars Congress from exercising power that impairs a state's integrity or ability to function effectively in the federal system. 426 U.S. 833. Schwartz, Constitutional Law §2.2 (1979).

TENURE right to hold, 39 N.W. 2d 359, 360; in real property, an ancient hierarchical system of holding lands. See 187 N.Y.S. 216, 231.

The term also refers to a statutory right of certain civil servants and teachers in the public schools to retain their positions permanently, subject only to removal for adequate cause, or economic necessity; e.g., the abolition of a department where the enrollment eliminates the demand and the tenured teacher is not qualified to teach another subject taught by a nontenured teacher. In addition, tenure is frequently guaranteed by contract for teachers and professors in private educational institutions. In these situations, the standard clause provides for termination of tenured faculty only for adequate cause or in extraordinary circumstances, in case of demonstrably or bona fide financial exigency. See American Assoc. of Univ. Professors, Statement of Principles on Academic Freedom and Tenure in AAUP Bulletin 44:290-293 (No. 1A, 1958). This is the standard statement of academic tenure for private institutions. See also C. Byse & L. Joughin, Tenure in American Higher Education 172-175 (1959).

Where dismissal is for cause, notice and a hearing according the teacher rudimentary **due process** is required both in the public and the private sector.

TENURIAL   OWNERSHIP see **ownership.**

TERMINABLE INTEREST an **interest** in **property** that will fail or terminate on the lapse of time, on the occurrence of an event or a contingency, or on the failure of an event or a contingency to occur. The term is used to describe a class of property that generally does not qualify for the marital deduction for federal estate and gift **tax** purposes. I.R.C. §§2056(b) and 2523 (b).

TERMINER see **oyer and terminer.**

TERM INSURANCE see **insurance** [TERM INSURANCE].

TERM OF ART see **words of art.**

TERM OF COURT a definite time period prescribed by law for a court to administer its duties. See 190 N.E. 270, 272. "Term" and "session" are often used interchangeably, but technically, "term" is the statutory time prescribed for judicial business and "session" is the time a court actually sits to hear cases. 242 S.W. 993, 994. In general, terms of court no longer have any special significance, fixed periods of days having replaced the stated terms of court.

TERM, SUCCESSIVE see **successive term.**

TERRITORIAL COURT a **court** established by Congress under Art. IV, Sec. 3, Cl. 2 of the Constitution, which gives Congress the power to make "all needful rules and regulations respecting the territory or other property belonging to the United States." 370 U.S. 530; 371 F. 2d 79.

TERRITORIAL JURISDICTION the territory over which a government or a subdivision thereof has **jurisdiction,** 147 P. 2d 858, 861; relates to a tribunal's power with regard to the territory within which it is to be exercised, and connotes power over property and persons within such territory. 94 N.E. 2d 438, 440.

TERRITORIAL WATERS all inland waters, waters between the line of mean high tide and mean low tide, and all waters seaward to a line three geographical miles from the coastline generally constitute the territorial waters of a country. 235 F. Supp. 990, 1002.

TERROREM see **in terrorem.**

TESTACY the state or condition of leaving a valid **will** at one's death, compared to **"intestacy,"** which is the condition of dying without having made a will.

TESTAMENT strictly, a testimonial or statement of a person's wishes concerning the disposition of his or her **personal property** after death, in contrast to a **will,** which is strictly a **devise** of **real estate.** See 21 Wend., N.Y., 430, 436. Commonly, however, "will" and "testament" are considered synonymous. 74 P. 2d 27, 32. The law of "testaments" is statutory. 147 S.W. 2d 644, 647. The word is rarely used today except in the formal heading of one's will, which reads "This is the last will and testament of. . . ."

TESTAMENTARY CAPACITY the mental capacity a person must have at the time of execution of his or her will in order for the will to be valid. Testamentary capacity usually requires that the person comprehend the nature and extent of his or her property, the persons who are the natural objects of his or her bounty and the dispositive effect of the act of executing the will. 271 N.W. 2d 52, 55. It is synonymous with "sound mind." See **sound** [SOUND MIND].

TESTAMENTARY DISPOSITION a gift of property which **vests** [takes effect] at the time of the death of the person making the disposition. It can be effected by **deed,** by an **inter vivos** transaction, or by **will.** See 17 Cal. Rptr. 744, 751. All **instruments** used to make testamentary dispositions must comply with the requirements of the **statute of wills.** See **causa mortis.**

TESTAMENTARY TRUST see **trust** [TESTAMENTARY TRUST].

TESTATOR [TESTATRIX] one who makes and executes a **testament** or **will,** "testator" applying to males, "testatrix" to females. See also **intestate; testacy; testament; testamentary disposition.** Compare **administrator; executor.**

TEST CASE [ACTION] a lawsuit that tests the validity of a law or a legal principle. Usually, the case is one of many similar cases pending, and is chosen for decision prior to the others because its facts are most representative of the issue. Often the case is brought about intentionally by a group interested in determining the validity of the law.
   Such cases are limited by the case or controversy doctrine which prohibits parties from bringing collusive suits before the court. Wright, Federal Courts §12 (4th ed. 1983). See **controversy** [CASE OR CONTROVERSY].

TESTIFY the making of a statement under **oath** or **affirmation** in a judicial proceeding, 107 N.W. 470, 475; to make a solemn declaration under oath or affirmation for the purpose of establishing proof of some fact to the court. 146 N.E. 2d 413, 414. See **examination; false swearing; perjury; testimony; witness.**

TESTIMONIAL IMMUNITY see **self-incrimination, privilege against** [TESTIMONIAL [USE] IMMUNITY].

TESTIMONY a statement made by

a **witness,** under oath, usually related to a legal **proceeding** or legislative hearing. "**Evidence** given by a competent witness under oath or affirmation as distinguished from evidence derived from writing and other sources. . . . Evidence is the broader term and includes all testimony, which is one species of evidence." 470 S.W. 2d 679, 682. See **expert witness.**

THEFT see **larceny.**

THING IN ACTION see **chose** [CHOSE IN ACTION].

THIRD PARTY see **party** [THIRD PARTY].

THIRD PARTY BENEFICIARY "persons who are recognized as having enforceable rights created in them by a **contract** to which they are not **parties** and for which they give no **consideration.** These persons can be loosely grouped into two classes; (1) donee beneficiaries, and (2) creditor (or obligee) beneficiaries. The third person is a DONEE BENEFICIARY if the promisee who buys the promise expresses an intention and purpose to confer a benefit upon him or her as a **gift** in the shape of the promised performance. He or she is a CREDITOR BENEFICIARY if the promisee, or some other person, is under an obligation (a duty or a liability) to him or her and the contract is so made that the promised performance or the making of the executory contract itself will discharge that obligation." Corbin, Contracts §774 (1952). The contract must be primarily for the third person's benefit, so that an incidental beneficiary of a contract would not have sufficient interest under which to enforce the promise. Restatement (Second) Contracts §315.

A third person's interest may be cut off prior to **vesting** by **rescission** between the contracting parties. Once a third person's rights are vested, he or she may sue the promisor in the event of a **breach.** This prevents the promisor from **unjust**

enrichment and avoids multiple litigation in the case of a creditor beneficiary. Any defenses available to the promisor arising from the contract may be asserted against the beneficiary. Corbin, **supra,** §818.

THIRD PARTY PLAINTIFF see **plaintiff** [THIRD PARTY PLAINTIFF].

THIRTEENTH AMENDMENT the amendment to the United States Constitution that prohibits slavery and **involuntary servitude** and empowers Congress to enforce the amendment by appropriate legislation. The Thirteenth Amendment was passed in 1863 during the Civil War. It not only prohibits slavery but also forbids "PEONAGE" which is a condition of involuntary servitude based on indebtedness. 197 U.S. 207. The Thirteenth Amendment is self-enacting as regards slavery, and permits Congress to pass legislation forbidding badges of slavery such as all forms of racial discrimination, private and public, in the sale and rental of property, 392 U.S. 409, 437-44. Further, a state may not enact laws designed to force employees to stay on their jobs by, for example, making it a crime to terminate private employment. However, a state may punish a crime through forced labor, 235 U.S. 133, and may compel labor on behalf of the government, such as highway labor, 240 U.S. 328. See generally Antieau, Modern Constitutional Law §§8:84 et seq. (1969).

THREAT a declaration of an intention or determination to inflict punishment, loss, or pain on another, or to injure another by some wrongful act. 60 F. Supp. 235, 236. A threat may be made by means of innuendo or suggestion as well as by express language. 148 F. Supp. 75, 77. Threats may be the basis of criminal or civil liability. See, e.g., Model Penal Code §211.3; 221.3; Prosser, Law of Torts §12 (4th ed. 1971). Mere words, however violent, have been held not to amount to an **assault**. Id. §10. See **coercion; extortion; fighting words; mental cruelty.**

THRIFT INSTITUTIONS a generic name for savings banks and savings and loan associations. See **bank.**

TIDE LAND land over which the tide ebbs and flows, see 150 F. 840, 842; land covered and uncovered by ordinary tides. See 219 P. 197, 199. The limit of the tide land is usually the mean high tide. See **avulsion; reliction.**

TIME see **reasonable time.**

TIME ARBITRAGE see **arbitrage** [TIME ARBITRAGE].

TIME DRAFT see **draft** [TIME DRAFT].

TIMESHARING a form of ownership of property, under which ownership rights vest in a number of parties, each of which is entitled to use the property for a specific period of time, such as one or more weeks. Also refers to shared use of computer facilities.

TIME OF THE ESSENCE a term used in **contracts** that fixes time of **performance** as a vital term of the contract, the **breach** of which may operate as a discharge of the entire contract, 208 S.W. 2d 392, 407. The phrase emphasizes "that the performance by one party at the time specified in the contract . . . is essential in order to enable him to require performance from the other party." 133 A. 677, 680. A contract for the sale of **land** which sets a specific date of performance but does not contain the clause "time is of the essence" is enforceable within a reasonable period of time even after the date specified. 174 S.W. 2d 642, 645.

TIME, UNITY OF see **unities** [UNITY OF TIME].

TITHE in old English law, a right of the clergy to extract one-tenth of the produce of lands and personal industry of the people for the use of the Church. These tithes have been compared to rent charges or **ground rents**. 3 Steph Com. 731.

TITLE ownership; in property law, "a shorthand term used to denote the facts which, if proved, will enable a **plaintiff** to recover **possession** or a **defendant** to retain possession of a thing." Cribbet, Principles of the Law of Property 15 (2d ed. 1975). Having title to something means having the right to possess the thing. The term is used most often in connection with **real property.** As to the sale of goods, the Uniform Commercial Code limits the effect of title upon the rights, obligations, and remedies covered by the Code. U.C.C. §2-401.

ADVERSE TITLE a title asserted in opposition to another; one claimed to have been acquired by **adverse possession.**

BAD TITLE see **bad title.**

CHAIN OF TITLE see **chain of title.**

CLEAR TITLE see **clear title.**

CLEAR TITLE OF RECORD a **title** that the **record** shows to be an **indefeasible** unencumbered estate. It differs from a **clear title** in that the latter can be demonstrated by evidence independent of the record. See 154 N.E. 920, 921.

CLOUD ON TITLE see **cloud on title.**

COLOR OF TITLE see **color of title.**

DEFECTIVE TITLE see **defective title.**

DOCUMENT OF TITLE see **document of title.**

EQUITABLE TITLE ownership recognized by a court of equity or founded upon equitable principles as opposed to formal legal title. The purchaser of real property can require **specific performance** of a contract for purchase and as a result, prior to the actual conveyance, he or she has an enforceable equitable title that can be terminated only by a **bona fide purchaser.** See **specific performance.**

GOOD TITLE see **good title.**

MARKETABLE TITLE see **marketable title.**

PARAMOUNT TITLE see **paramount title.**

QUIET TITLE see **quiet title.**

TITLE [OF A STATUTE] the heading of a **statute** or legislative bill, which introduces it by giving a brief description or summary of the matters it embraces.

UNITY OF TITLE see **unities** [UNITY OF TITLE].

TITLE JURISDICTION a jurisdiction in which **title** to **mortgaged premises** passes to the **mortgagee,** and only passes back to mortgagor (home owner) when full payment is made. Compare **lien jurisdictions.**

TITLE SEARCH a search made through the records maintained in the public record office to determine the state of a **title,** including all **liens, encumbrances, mortgages, future interests,** etc., affecting the property; the means by which a **chain of title** is ascertained.

TITLE THEORY see **mortgage; title jurisdiction.**

TOLL to bar, defeat, 75 S.W. 1122, 1126. To "toll" the **Statute of Limitations** means to stop its running. 329 S.W. 2d 39, 43.

The term also signifies a charge for the use of another's property, 228 P. 2d 238, 240, or refers to the **consideration** given for the use of roads, bridges, ferries, or similar things of a public nature, 82 P. 2d 120.

TOMBSTONE AD a common expression for a newspaper advertisement announcing the sale or purchase of **securities** in a **corporation.** The term derives from the fact that such advertisements usually consist of all copy and no illustrations, and thus look like a tombstone. A tombstone ad is merely a public announcement concerning such transactions and does not constitute either an offer to sell or to buy the securities. Such offers constitute and may only be made by a **prospectus.** 15 U.S.C. §77b(10)

TONNAGE in commercial usage, the number of tons burden a ship or vessel will carry, as estimated by the official measurement and computation prescribed by public authority. 79 U.S. (12 Wall.) 204.

TONNAGE DUTY a tax imposed on ships that enter the United States; it is called tonnage duty since it is based upon the ship's tonnage. 46 U.S.C. §§121 et seq.

TORT a wrong; a private or **civil** wrong or injury resulting from a breach of a legal duty that exists by virtue of society's expectations regarding interpersonal conduct, rather than by **contract** or other private relationship. 256 N.E. 2d 254, 259. "The word is derived from the Latin 'tortus' or 'twisted'." Prosser, Law of Torts §1 (4th ed. 1971). The essential elements of a tort are the existence of a legal duty owed by a **defendant** to a **plaintiff, breach** of that duty, and a causal relation between defendant's conduct and the resulting damage to plaintiff. See, generally, id. See also **derivative tort.**

TORT CLAIMS ACT statute passed by Congress and most states that waives **sovereign immunity** from liability in tort. The federal act, called the FEDERAL TORT CLAIMS ACT [F.T.C.A.], passed in 1946, confers exclusive **jurisdiction** on United States **District Courts** to hear claims against the United States, "for money **damages,** accruing on and after January 1, 1945, for **injury** or loss of **property,** or personal injury or death, caused by the **negligent** or **wrongful act** or omission of any employee of the government while acting within the scope of his office or employment, under circumstances where the United States, if a private person, would be liable to the claimant in accordance with the law of the place where the act or omission occurred." 28 U.S.C. 1346 (b).

The federal act provides for a number of exceptions to the general waiver of sovereign immunity. Most of the exceptions are specific in nature, such as injuries received by members of the armed forces during war, 340 U.S. 135. Some exceptions, however, are broad. The act excludes liability for **intentional torts** (such as **assault, false imprisonment,** and **slander**); **strict liability,** 406 U.S. 797; and acts done with due care in the execution of a statute or regulation or within the discretionary function of an agency or employee. 346 U.S. 15. See 28 U.S.C. §2680. Prosser, Law of Torts 972 (4th ed. 1971). A 1974 amendment extended the federal act to intentional torts by law enforcement persons. Claims against the United States not sounding in tort are governed by the Tucker Act under the jurisdiction of the United States Claims Court. 28 U.S.C. §§1491-1506. See **Court of Claims** [TUCKER ACT].

TORTFEASOR one who commits a **tort.** See **joint tortfeasors.**

TORTIOUS unlawful; describes conduct that subjects the actor(s) to **tort** liability, 143 N.E. 2d 673, 680.

TOTAL DISABILITY as used in insurance contracts, a person's inability to perform the material duties of some occupation for which he or she is qualified by experience or training; 36 So. 2d 123, 126. Absolute physical disability or helplessness is not necessary for "total disability" to exist. 148 F. 2d 590, 596. See **worker's compensation acts.**

TOTAL INCORPORATION see **selective incorporation** [TOTAL INCORPORATION APPROACH].

TOTALITY OF THE CIRCUMSTANCES TEST a test used to determine whether certain constitutional rights of a defendant have been violated. The test looks to all the circumstances attending the alleged violation, rather than to any particular factors. While some factors may recur more frequently than others, the relative importance of any one factor depends upon the particular facts of a case. The test was originally used to determine whether a confession was coerced from a defendant in violation of his or her privilege against **self-incrimination,** 373 U.S. 503, until the **Miranda** case required that a defendant have his or her rights read to him or her. 384 U.S. 436. The test is currently used to determine whether a defendant consented to a **warrantless** search, 412 U.S. 218, and whether **probable cause** exists for the issuance of a **search warrant,** 103 S. Ct. 2317.

TOTAL LOSS in insurance contracts, the destruction of property such that it is no longer useful for its intended purpose, 24 S.W. 2d 292, or which renders it of little or no value to the owner. 1 Mass. 264, 275.

TOTO see **in toto.**

TOUCH AND CONCERN in real property law, a requirement for a covenant which **"runs with the land"** is that it touch and concern the land involved. A covenant runs with the land when the rights or liabilities of the covenant pass to the succeeding owners with the title to the land. A covenant touches and concerns the land when it enhances the enjoyment of one parcel of real property by burdening the enjoyment of another. Boyer, Survey of the Law of Property 515-520 (3d ed. 1981). For instance, a covenant in a building development that each property owner paint his or her house a specific color would run with the land.

TO WIT namely; that is to say.

TRACT INDEX see **chain of title.**

TRADE FIXTURE property placed on or annexed to rented **real estate** by a **tenant** for the purpose of aiding himself or herself in the conduct of a trade or business. The law makes provisions for the tenant to remove such **fixtures** at the end of his or her tenancy though the tenant is responsible to the landlord for any damage to the premises resulting from such removal, unlike other fixtures considered **improvements** and which the tenant must leave intact. See 175 P. 2d 512, 518; 65 A. 2d 523, 526. See **waste.**

TRADE, FAIR see **fair trade laws.**

TRADEMARK any word, name, symbol, or device used by a manufacturer or merchant to identify his or her goods. 15 U.S.C. §1127. The basis for trademark law lies in the tort of **unfair competition,** under which a seller using a mark similar to one already in use could be liable for the buyer's likely confusion between two products or services due to all of the seller's efforts considered as a whole. The law of trademark addresses the narrower issue of whether the confusion arises from the marks used to identify the goods. At common law, trademark infringement was illegal as a form of unfair competition or commercial **fraud.** In 1946, Congress passed the LANHAM ACT, which provides for the federal registration of trademarks and their protection against infringement by the federal courts. 15 U.S.C. §§1051 et seq. A trademark arises from regular usage of the mark, and only lasts as long as the usage continues. A mark subject to trademark protection may also be protected under **copyright** and **patent** law. 1 McCarthy, Trademarks and Unfair Competition, §§2:2, 5:2, 5:4, 6:1 (1973).

TRADE, RESTRAINT OF see **restraint of trade.**

TRADE SECRETS "[a]ny formula, pattern, machine or process of manufacturing used in one's business which may give the user an opportunity to obtain an advantage over its competitors," 278 N.W. 2d 81, 89-90. "A plan or process, tool, mechanism or compound, known only to its owner and those . . . employees to whom it is necessary to disclose it," 15 A. 212. When trade secrets are obtained and used without the owner's permission, the owner can seek an **injunction** to stop its use as well as money **damages.** To recover, the owner must prove that the idea or item was held in strict secrecy, and that it was obtained by others through fraud or other unfair means. Trade secrets are distinguished from **patents** in that the owner holds no formally established exclusive rights to it as against the public. Once a trade secret is discovered either by analysis of the product or by any other proper method, the discoverer is free to use it for his or her own advantage. 86 A. 2d 283.

TRADE USAGE a practice widely accepted and relied upon in numerous transactions in a particular trade or industry. 386 F. Supp. 1210, 1220. A meaning given to language due to its general acceptance in a trade or industry and the reasonable reliance of the parties on such meaning. 105 N.W. 692, 695. The **Uniform Commercial Code** uses the synonymous term USAGE OF TRADE which is defined as "any practice or method of dealing having such regularity of observance in a place, vocation or trade as to justify an expectation that it will be observed with respect to the transaction in question. The existence and scope of such a usage are to be proved as facts. If it is established that such a usage is embodied in a written trade code or similar writing the interpretation of the writing is for the court." U.C.C. §1-205(2).

A COURSE OF DEALING is to be distinguished from a trade usage in that the course of dealing is based upon "a sequence of previous conduct between the parties to a particular transaction which is fairly to be regarded as establishing a common basis of understanding for interpreting their expressions and other conduct." U.C.C. §1-205(1). The express terms of an agreement and an applicable course of dealing or trade usage should be construed wherever reasonable as consistent with each other; but when such construction is unreasonable, express terms control both course of dealing and trade usage while course of dealing controls trade usage. U.C.C. §1-205(4).

TRADITIONARY EVIDENCE statements of fact based upon tradition, longstanding reputation, and statements made by deceased persons which are admissible to prove pedigree and ancient boundaries when no living witnesses are available to testify about such matters. 25 Colo. 545, 554, Wigmore, Evidence §§1563-1571 (1974).

TRANSACTION the doing or performance of some matter of business between two or more persons, 10 Ohio App. 303, 304. An act or **agreement,** or several acts or agreements that have some connection with each other, in which more than one person is concerned, and by which the legal relations of such persons between themselves are altered. 24 N.E. 2d 228, 234. In tax law, transactions may be characterized in the following ways to describe their tax consequences.

CLOSED TRANSACTION a transaction is closed when all events have occurred so as to allow the transaction to be subject to tax. 283 U.S. 404.

OPEN TRANSACTION a transaction is open if events have not occurred to allow the transaction to be subject to tax. For example, if an **asset** is sold in exchange for an undetermined purchase price, the transaction will not be subject to income tax until the earlier of (a) the purchase price being determined or (b) the payments are received which exceed the taxpayer's **basis** in such asset. 283 U.S. 404.

SHAM TRANSACTION a transaction that will be ignored for tax purposes because it is deemed to have no substance. 267 F. 2d 127.

STEP TRANSACTION a series of interrelated events veiwed as a single transaction; a transaction that consists of a number of interdependent steps but is subject to tax based upon all of the various steps rather than each intermediate step. 302 U.S. 609, 613.

TRANSACTIONAL IMMUNITY see **self-incrimination, privilege against** [TRANSACTIONAL IMMUNITY].

TRANSACTIONS OR OCCURRENCE TEST in civil practice, the requirement that a party must make a **counterclaim** for all **causes of action** arising from the same transaction or occurrence which is the subject matter of the opposing party's claim. Fed. R. Civ. Pro. 13(a). The failure to bring the counterclaim may result in the party being barred from ever litigating his or her claim. See **counterclaim** [COMPULSORY COUNTERCLAIM]. The purpose of the rule is to avoid the expense that would result from a multiplicity of lawsuits. 525 F. 2d 620, 625. "Transaction" is liberally construed to encompass any series of occurrences that are logically connected. 552 F. 2d 1257, 1261.

TRANSCRIPT an official and certified copy of what transpired in **court** or at an out-of court **deposi-**

tion, 194 S.W. 2d 508, 509. The transcript is usually prepared by a court reporter from shorthand notes made during the proceeding. It is most commonly used on **appeal,** when the proceedings of a trial court are reviewed for error.

TRANSFER to convey or remove from one person or place to another; to sell or give; specifically, to take over **possession** or control as in the transfer of **title** to land. 25 N.E. 2d 999, 1001.

In a **securities** context, the transfer of **stock** is a two-stage process. The first step is delivery of stock (or **bonds**) to the buying broker by the selling broker who in turn obtained the securities from the selling customer if they were not held by the broker. The buying broker, in turn, delivers the securities to the **transfer agent** for reissue in the buyer's name.

TRANSFER AGENT individual or firm that keeps a record of the **shareholders** of a **corporation** by name, address, and number of shares owned. When stock is sold, the new owner through an agent presents the shares purchased to the transfer agent who cancels the old certificates and issues new certificates registered in the name of the owner. Every stock transaction does not result in a transfer since a significant portion of most **issues** is held in **street name** to support **margin** or for the convenience of the owner. See also **registrar.**

TRANSFER IN CONTEMPLA- TION OF DEATH see **cause** (CAUSA MORTIS); **gift** (GIFT IN CONTEMPLATION OF DEATH).

TRANSFERRED INTENT a doctrine in **tort** law and **criminal** law that provides that if a defendant intends harm to A but harms B instead, the "intent" is said to be "transferred" to the harm befalling the actual victim as far as defendant's liability to B in tort is concerned. This is only a "fiction," or a legal conclusion, created in order to accomplish the desired result in terms of liability. See Prosser, Law of Torts 32-33 (4th ed. 1971). The doctrine is applicable in criminal law, Model Penal Code §2.03(2)(3), and finds most frequent application in a **homicide** context. 330 A. 2d 176.

TRANSFEREE LIABILITY tax liability imposed upon a person other than the taxpayer actually liable for the tax under specified circumstances wherein the other person is the transferee of property from the taxpayer, and where the taxpayer has been rendered unable to pay his or her tax liability by virtue of the transfer. In general, the transferee can only be liable to the extent of the value of the property transferred, although the liability is personal and can be recovered from any assets of the transferee. "Transferee," for purposes of imposition of this liability, includes **heirs,** donees of **gifts** and **shareholders** of dissolved **corporations** but does not include people who act as mere **agents** for others. I.R.C. §§6901-6905.

TRAVERSE a **common law pleading** that denies the opposing party's **allegations** of fact; "a denial by a party of facts alleged in an adverse **pleading** . . . [or] a denial that he has sufficient knowledge or information to form a belief concerning them." 9 S.W. 281.

GENERAL TRAVERSE a blanket denial, stated in general terms, intended to cover all the allegations.

SPECIAL TRAVERSE a denial that is not absolute, but that seeks to establish or explain a denial through the presentation of supplementary facts (or **new matter**) which, if accurate, would render the allegations untenable. See 13 A. 2d 456. See **absque hoc; confession and avoidance.**

TREASON the crime of "adhering to the enemy and rendering him aid and comfort." 325 U.S. 1. Under the U.S. Constitution, treason may only consist of levying war against the United States or adhering to its enemies and giving them aid and comfort, and a person may only be convicted of treason upon the testimony of two witnesses to the same **overt act** or on a confession in open court. U.S. Constitution, Art. 3, Sec. 3, Cl. 1. While Congress may punish the person convicted of treason, it may not "work **corruption of blood**" or forfeiture except during the life of the person attainted. U.S. Constitution, Art. 3, Sec. 3, Cl. 2.

In England, corruption of blood as a punishment for treason resulted in the disinheritance of the convict's children and the forfeiture of the convicted's property to the crown. The U.S. Constitution prohibits this punishment in order to prevent the injustice of innocent children suffering for the offense of their ancestor. 92 U.S. 202. Congress has adopted the constitutional definition of treason by making it a crime punishable by death, by imprisonment of not less than five years, and by a prohibition against holding public office. 18 U.S.C. §2381.

TREASURE TROVE any item of value found hidden in the earth or in a private place, such as a house, whose owner is unknown. While historically "treasure trove" was only gold or silver, modern cases have treated the paper representations thereof as constituting "treasure trove." 205 P. 2d 562. Treasure trove is distinguished from **lost property** in that it must have been hidden by the owner for safe-keeping and not parted with voluntarily. 33 N.W. 2d 232, 234-235. In the absence of **statute**, the finder of "treasure trove" has a legal claim to it against all the world except the true owner. 178 F. Supp. 854, 856. See also **abandonment.**

TREASURY the subdivision of a government, corporation, or other entity that is responsible for its financial affairs. The United States Department of the Treasury includes the Bureau of Alcohol, Tobacco and Firearms, the Office of the Comptroller of the Currency, the United States Customs Service, the Bureau of Engraving and Printing, the Federal Law Enforcement Training Center, the Bureau of Government Financial Operations, the Internal Revenue Service, the Bureau of the Mint, the Bureau of the Public Debt, the United States Savings Bond Division, and the United States Secret Service. The basic functions of the Department of the Treasury are to develop and propose national and international economic and tax policies; to serve as the government's financial agent, to collect taxes, to disburse funds, and to manage the public debt; to produce currency and coins; and to enforce specific groups of laws.

TREASURY BILL a **promissory note** issued by the U.S. Treasury, having maturity periods up to one year. 240 F. Supp. 867, 897, n. 85. Notes maturing between one and five years are called **Treasury notes** and notes maturing after five years are called **Treasury bonds.** Treasury bills are paid in full at maturity, although they are originally sold at a discount to face value. Denominations are $10,000 or multiples thereof, with smaller denominations offered when money is in short supply. Large dollar amounts of Treasury bills, which are **bearer** instruments, change hands daily as an active component of money market trading.

TREASURY BOND a long-term **debt** instrument issued by the U.S. government. **Issues** of the U.S. government have the highest rating among so-called fixed income or debt **securities** and, therefore, offer the lowest taxable yield of any **bonds.**

The term also refers to bonds that have been bought back by the issuing corporation. See **treasury stock.** Such Treasury bonds are usually retired as part of **sinking fund** requirements or held in the corporate treasury, which reduces interest expense.

TREASURY NOTE an intermediate term (one-to-five years) obligation of the U.S. government that bears interest paid by **coupon.** Like all direct U.S. government obligations, Treasury notes carry the highest domestic credit standing and, thus, have the lowest taxable yield available at equivalent **maturity.**

TREASURY SHARES [STOCK] common or preferred **stock** issued by a company and later reacquired by it. The stock may be used for a variety of corporate purposes such as a stock bonus plan for management and employees or to acquire another company, and it may be held indefinitely, resold, or retired. While held in the company treasury, the stock earns no dividends and has no vote in company affairs. Henn & Alexander, Laws of Corporations §158 (3rd ed. 1983).

TREATY in international law, a compact made between two or more independent nations with a view to the public welfare, 107 F. 2d 819, 827; "an international agreement of the United States must relate to the external concerns of the nation as distinguished from matters of purely internal nature." Restatement 2d, Foreign Relations Law of the United States §40 (1965). Under the Constitution, the President has the sole power to initiate and make treaties, which must be approved by the Senate before they become binding on citizens of the United States as law. Art. II, Sec. 2. An EXECUTIVE AGREEMENT is often substituted for a treaty. In such agreements the President, without the need for Senate approval, may bind the government just as in a treaty. 301 U.S. 324. However, such agreements can reach only narrower topics or be entered into pursuant to formal authority delegated by the Congress in particular legislation. See 69 F. 2d 44, 48. Trade agreements, for example, are often executive agreements rather than treaties. States may not engage in treaties of any kind, and once a treaty becomes law it is binding on the states under the **supremacy clause.** Art. I, Sec. 10, Cl. 1; Art. VI, Cl. 2.

TREBLE DAMAGES see **damages** [DOUBLE [TREBLE] DAMAGES].

TRESPASS at common law, a **form of action** instituted to recover **damages** for any unlawful injury to the plaintiff's person, **property,** or rights, involving immediate force or violence, 235 S.W. 2d 531, 532; also used today to signify the violent act itself that causes such an injury, 266 A. 2d 175, 180. In modern parlance, the term most often connotes a wrongful interference with or disturbance of the **possession** of property, 69 So. 2d 724, 726, and is applied to **personalty** as well as to **realty** 287 S.W. 2d 202, 204.

CONTINUING TRESPASS trespass not intermittent or transient, as where one dumps garbage upon the land of another. In such a case, there is a continuing wrong so long as the offending object remains. Prosser, Law of Torts §13 (4th ed. 1971).

TRESPASS DE BONIS ASPORTATIS a common law action brought to recover damages from a person who has taken away goods or property from its rightful owner. 38 So. 2d 721, 722. To maintain trespass de bonis asportatis, it is not necessary to prove an actual forcible dispossession of the property, but merely the unlawful interference with, or exercise of ownership over, property, to the exclusion of the owner. 10 Mass. 125, 128. In addition, intent is unimportant, as the action may be sustained if the act was committed without justifiable cause or purpose even though it was done accidentally or by mistake. 6 Wis. 317, 321.

TRESPASS ON THE CASE one of the two early English actions at common law dealing with torts (the other being trespass). Trespass on the case, or simply "case," afforded remedy against injury to person or property indirectly resulting from the conduct of the defendant. The action of trespass covered only directly resulting injury. "The classic illustration of the difference between trespass and case is that of a log thrown into the highway. A person struck by the log as it fell could maintain trespass against the thrower, since injury was direct; but one who was hurt by stumbling over it as it lay in the road, could maintain, not trespass, but an action on the case." Prosser, Torts §7 (4th ed. 1971).

TRESPASS QUARE CLAUSUM FREGIT trespass "whereby he broke the close"; where the defendant enters upon the land of the plaintiff, he or she is subject to damages for such entrance under the common law. Sec 57 A. 2d 329, 330. See quare clausum fregit.

TRESPASS VI ET ARMIS trespass with force and arms, or by an unlawful means; a remedy for injuries accompanied with force or violence, or where the act done is in itself an immediate injury to another's person or property. 173 S.W. 2d 606, 613.

TRESPASSER one who enters or remains upon land of another without the owner's permission. Restatement (Second) Torts §329. The owner of the land has no duty to guard against injury of a trespasser and is not liable if a trespasser injures himself or herself unless an unjustified risk of injury to such persons is created, such as by the use of spring guns or human traps. Prosser, Law of Torts §58 (4th ed. 1971). See trespass. Compare invitee; licensee.

TRESPASS ON THE CASE see trespass [TRESPASS ON THE CASE].

TRIAL a judicial examination of issues between parties, whether they are issues of law or of fact, before a court that has jurisdiction over the cause, 158 S.E. 2d 212, 217. Trials are governed by established procedures and court rules, and usually involve offering of testimony or evidence. 168 N.Y.S. 2d 83, 86.

BENCH TRIAL the trial of a matter where the court sits without a jury; trial by a judge. Both parties must waive any constitutional or statutory right to trial by jury. Compare jury trial.

TRIAL BY JURY see jury trial.

TRIAL BY THE RECORD a trial in which a party pleads that a record exists supporting his or her claim, and the adversary denies the record's existence, or pleads NUL TIEL RECORD (no such record). If the record can be produced, it is considered by the court in reaching a verdict. If it is not produced, judgment is given to the adversary.

TRIAL DE NOVO historically described as an appeal from a decision of a court of chancery. It signifies a proceeding in which both issues of law and issues of fact are reconsidered as if the original trial had never taken place. Appeals from probate court or from minor courts, such as local municipal courts, are often by trial de novo. New testimony may be adduced or the matter may be determined de novo on the basis of the evidentiary record already produced. When the trial de novo is "on the record," no new evidence is taken by the reviewing court, but a fresh consideration of the law and facts is nevertheless undertaken without deference to the decision reached in the initial trial.

TRIAL COURT court of original jurisdiction, where matters are to be litigated first and where all evidence relative to a cause is received and considered. A trial court determines both the facts and the law in a particular case whereas an **appellate court** predominantly reviews questions of law and not of facts. 339 P. 2d 398, 400. See **federal courts; question of fact; question of law.**

TRIBUNAL an officer or body having authority to **adjudicate** matters. 75 F. Supp. 486, 487. See also **administrative agency; court; forum; trial court.**

TRIER OF FACT see **fact-finder.**

TRIPARTITE having three parts.

T.R.O. temporary **restraining order.**

TROVER an early common law **tort action** to recover **damages** for a wrongful **conversion** of **personal property** or to recover actual **possession** of such property. See 49 S.E. 2d 500, 504. Originally, the action was limited to cases in which **lost property** had been found and converted by the finder to his own use. See 28 A. 2d 334, 337. Later the action was expanded to include property not actually lost and found, but only wrongly converted. At first, a fiction was created (when the facts revealed otherwise) that such property had been lost and found, but since the distinction was later abandoned, the use of such a fiction became unnecessary. See Prosser, Law of Torts §15 (4th ed. 1971). Compare **detinue; replevin; trespass; unlawful detainer.**

TRUE BILL see **indictment.**

TRUST " 'property, real or personal, held by one party for the benefit of another.' . . . It implies two interests, one legal, and the other **equitable;** the **trustee** holding the legal title or interest; and the **cestui que trust** or **beneficiary** holding the equitable title or interest." 140 P. 2d 335, 338. The one who supplies the property or **consideration [res]** for the trust is the **settlor** [also called trustor or **donor**]. Trust also applies generally to any relationship in which one acts as a **guardian** or **fiduciary** in relation to another's property. Thus a deposit of money in a bank is a "trust," or the receipt of money to be applied to a particular purpose or to be paid to another is a "trust." See 18 A. 1056, 1058.

ACTIVE TRUST a trust in which the trustee has affirmative duties to perform, requiring the exercise of sound personal discretion. 43 A. 201, 202. Compare PASSIVE TRUST (below).

BREACH OF TRUST see **breach (of contract)** [BREACH OF TRUST].

CESTUI QUE TRUST (sĕs'-twē kā)— Old Fr: beneficiary; "one for whose benefit the trust is created. . . . The property given in trust is called the subject matter, or trust **res** [or corpus]." 195 N.E. 557, 564.

CHARITABLE TRUST a trust designated for the benefit of a class or the public generally and created for charitable, educational, religious, or scientific purposes. A court will consider a trust a charitable one whenever its performance will accomplish a substantial amount of social benefit to the public or some reasonably large class thereof. A charitable trust is frequently called a PUBLIC TRUST or a charity. Bogert & Bogert, Law of Trusts §§54-70 (5th ed. 1973).

CLIFFORD TRUST a trust established to pay its income to someone other than its **grantor** for a period of at least 10 years, but which will eventually terminate and return its **corpus** to the grantor. E.g., I.R.C. §673(a). Clifford trusts are created for the purpose of reducing income taxes by shifting the income earned by the trust assets to a person who is taxed at lower rates than the grantor, and who is a natural object of the grantor's bounty. Clifford trusts are named after the well-known case of *Helvering v. Clifford,* 309 U.S. 331 (1940), in which the attempt to shift income for tax purposes failed. The grantor trust rules were enacted in order to clarify the circumstances when a grantor may shift income for tax purposes. See I.R.C. §§671 et seq.

COMPANY see **trust company.**

COMPLEX TRUST a trust which under the instrument of its creation or under state law may either distribute or retain income. I.R.C. §§661-663.

CONSTRUCTIVE [INVOLUNTARY] TRUST one found to exist by operation of law or by "construction" of the court, regardless of any lack of express agreement between or intent by the parties. When one party has been wrongfully deprived either by mistake, fraud, or some other breach of faith or confidence, of some right, benefit, or title to the property, a court may impose upon the present holder of legal title a constructive trust for the benefit of that party. See 219 S.W. 2d 282, 285. Thus in order to prevent the **unjust enrichment** of the legal holder, such person is deemed to hold the property as a trustee for the **beneficial use** of that party which has been wrongfully deprived of its rights. See 25 N.W. 2d 225, 228. Contrast RESULTING TRUST (below).

DECLARATION OF TRUST an instrument by which the owner of property declares that he or she is holding that property in trust, thus making himself or herself a trustee of the property. A declaration of trust creates a valid trust of the property subject to it, even though the settlor receives no consideration for declaring the trust, and even though the property is not formally transferred. The settlor must only satisfy the **Statute of Frauds** to create the trust, unless it is in substance a **testamentary** disposition, in which case the **Statute of Wills** must be satisfied. Scott, Law of Trusts §17.1 (3d ed. 1967).

DEED OF TRUST see **deed of trust; trust deed.**

DIRECT TRUST see EXPRESS [DIRECT] TRUST (below).

DISCRETIONARY TRUST a trust that gives the trustee the discretion to pay to or apply for the benefit of the beneficiary so much or all of the trust income or principal as the trustee deems appropriate. E.g., 19 N.Y.S. 2d 44, 47. Compare **spendthrift trust.**

DISTRIBUTION OF A TRUST see **distribution** [TRUST DISTRIBUTION].

EXPRESS [DIRECT] TRUST a trust created from the free and deliberate act of the parties, including an affirmative intention of the **settlor** [the one granting the property] to set up the trust, usually evidenced by some writing, **deed,** or **will.** See 13 N.W. 2d 749, 751. A **parol** [oral] agreement to create a trust cannot be enforced where the **statute of frauds** requires a written instrument. See 210 S.W. 2d 985, 987, 988. Trusts are generally classified as either "express" or "implied," the latter class including RESULTING TRUSTS (below) and CONSTRUCTIVE [INVOLUNTARY] TRUSTS (above). See 55 S.E. 377, 379.

FIXED INVESTMENT TRUST see **nondiscretionary trust.**

FUND see **trust fund.**

GRANTOR TRUSTS trusts with **bene-ficiaries** other than the **grantor,** but where the income is taxed to the grantor if the grantor is viewed as a substantial owner of the trust. Factors indicating substantial ownership include whether the grantor has retained the power to control the beneficial enjoyment of the trust, I.R.C. §674; if the grantor has a reversionary interest in the trust that will or may be reasonably expected to take effect in possession or enjoyment within ten years of the trust's commencement, I.R.C. §673(a); or if the income of the trust is for the benefit of the grantor, I.R.C. §677. Such a trust is often called a CLIFFORD TRUST (see above). See I.R.C. §§671-79.

IMPLIED TRUST one inferred from the parties' transactions by **operation of law,** in contrast to an express trust which is created by the parties' deliberate acts and/or expression of intent. See 189 P. 396, 398; 149 S.W. 2d 930, 932, 933. Implied trusts can be either "constructive" or "resulting." See 55 S.E. 377, 379.

INDENTURE see **trust indenture.**

INTER VIVOS TRUST a trust created during the grantor's lifetime. 324 N.E. 2d 594, 596.

INVESTMENT TRUST see **investment company [trust].**

INVOLUNTARY TRUST see CONSTRUCTIVE [INVOLUNTARY] TRUST (above).

LAND TRUST see **land trust.**

LIVING TRUST an **inter vivos** trust; a trust established and in operation during the settlor's life. Compare TESTAMENTARY TRUST (below).

NONDISCRETIONARY TRUST see **nondiscretionary trust.**

ORAL TRUST see **oral** [ORAL TRUST].

PASSIVE TRUST a trust imposing no active duties on the trustee, but rather the trustee merely holds legal title to the property. 33 N.W. 2d 510, 515. Under the statute of uses, the legal estate in a passive trust rests in the beneficiary. E.g., 122 N.E. 85, 87.

POUROVER TRUST a trust that either distributes assets to another trust, or that receives assets from another trust or some other source.

PRECATORY TRUSTS trusts created in a **will** by the use of **precatory** words such as "wish" and "desire." For example, "I wish that John takes care of Rudy until he is married." Older cases found the use of these types of words presumptively mandatory and enforced the trusts. Now courts look to whether there is a **testamentary** intent to impose a legal obligation upon the **legatee** named in the will (in the above example, John) to make a particular disposition of property. Restatement (Second) Trusts §25; Scott, Law of Trusts, §25.2 (3d ed. 1967). Courts consider the language in question in the context of the whole will and the facts and circumstances surrounding the will, 95 C.J.S. Wills §602b, but jurisdictions are divided as to whether these words create enforceable trusts. See 487 S.W. 2d 201. Compare 270 N.E. 2d 905. See **precatory.**

PUBLIC TRUST see CHARITABLE TRUST (above).

REAL ESTATE INVESTMENT TRUST see **real estate investment trust [R.E.I.T.].**

RESULTING TRUST a **trust** arising by implication of law when it appears from the nature of the transaction that it was the intention of the parties to create a trust. See 121 N.E. 621, 627. It is therefore to be distinguished from a "constructive trust" in that "a resulting trust is a status that automatically arises by operation of law out of certain circumstances, while a constructive trust is a remedy that **equity** applied in order to prevent injustice or in order to do justice." 89 C.J.S. Trusts §14. Thus, a "resulting trust" involves the element of intent, which, though implied, makes it more like an EXPRESS TRUST (above). A constructive trust, in contrast, is sometimes found contrary to the parties' intent, in order to work equity or frustrate **fraud**. See 53 A. 2d 805.

SAVINGS ACCOUNT [BANK] TRUST see TOTTEN TRUST (below).

SIMPLE TRUST a trust required, by the terms of its creation or under state law, to distribute all of its income currently. I.R.C. §§651-652.

SPENDTHRIFT TRUST see **spendthrift trust.**

TESTAMENTARY TRUST a trust created under a will and which comes into existence after the grantor's death. 324 N.E. 2d 594, 596.

TOTTEN TRUST a bank account established by a depositor who describes himself or herself as trustee for another, other than a trustee under a will, trust agreement, or court order. N.Y.E.P.-T.L. §7-5.1(d). During the depositor's lifetime, a Totten trust is fully revocable; upon the depositor's death, the account is payable to the named beneficiary, subject to the claims of the depositor's creditors. N.Y.E.P.-T.L. §§7-5.1 et seq. The purpose of a Totten trust is to create a testamentary substitute, i.e., a means of passing one's money upon one's death other than by will. Totten trusts are statutorily recognized in some states and are given various effect in others. Bogert & Bogert, Law of Trusts

§20 (5th ed. 1973). Totten trusts are also known as SAVINGS ACCOUNT [BANK] TRUSTS. 179 N.Y. 112.

TRUSTEE see **trustee.**

TRUST INDENTURE ACT OF 1939 see **securities acts** [TRUST INDENTURE ACT OF 1939].

TRUSTOR see **trustor.**

UNIT INVESTMENT TRUST see **unit investment trust.**

VOTING TRUST see **voting trust.**

TRUST COMPANY a financial organization that provides **trust** services such as acting in the capacity of **trustee, fiduciary,** or agent for both individuals and companies; **transfer agents** are typically provided by trust companies. Duties include administering trust funds, acting as custodian for property held in trust, providing investment management for trust funds, executing wills, etc. Trust companies often engage in banking activities as well, and are regulated by state law.

TRUST DEED see **deed of trust.**

TRUSTEE one who holds legal **title** to property "in **trust**" for the benefit of another person, and who is required to carry out specific duties with regard to the property, or who has been given power affecting the disposition of property for another's benefit. "Trustee" is also used loosely as anyone who acts as a **guardian** or **fiduciary** in relationship to another, such as a public officer toward constituents, a state toward citizens, or a partner to co-partner. See **bankruptcy** [BANKRUPTCY TRUSTEE]; **de facto** [DE FACTO TRUSTEE]; **use.** Compare **settlor.**

TRUST FUND real property or **personal property** held "in **trust**" for the benefit of another person; the **corpus [res]** of a trust.

TRUST INDENTURE an instrument that states the terms and conditions of a **trust,** particularly a trust created as **security** for a **bond issue.**

TRUST INDENTURE ACT OF 1939 see **Securities Acts** [TRUST INDENTURE ACT OF 1939].

TRUSTOR one who creates a **trust;** more often called the **settlor.**

TRUTH-IN-LENDING ACT a federal law, requiring that individuals applying for commercial credit be provided with accurate and understandable information relating to the cost of credit, enabling them to decide which credit source offers them the most favorable credit terms. 15 U.S.C. §§1601-1677. Under this law, the commercial lender must inform the borrower of the dollar amount of the interest charges and the interest rate, computed on an annual basis according to the specified formula, and must afford borrowers who pledge **real property** as security for the loan a three-day period in which to **rescind** the transaction. See **Regulation Z.**

TRY TITLE to submit to judicial scrutiny the legitimacy of **title** to property. See also **quiet title.**

TUCKER ACT see **court of claims.**

TURNTABLE DOCTRINE see **attractive nuisance.**

TURPITUDE see **moral turpitude.**

1231 ASSET see **capital** [§1231 ASSET].

TWO FUNDS DOCTRINE see **marshaling [marshalling]** [TWO FUNDS DOCTRINE].

TWO PARTY CONSENT see **wiretap** [TWO PARTY CONSENT].

TYING ARRANGEMENT the sale of one product on the condition that the purchaser also buy another product, or agree to not buy the other product from anyone else. A tying arrangement is a *per se* viola-

tion of the **Sherman Antitrust Act,** 332 U.S. 392, 396, in that it allows the seller to exploit his or her control over the tying product to force the buyer into the purchase of a tied product that the buyer either did not want at all or might have preferred to purchase elsewhere on different terms. 104 S. Ct. 1551, 1558. But, if a seller does not possess sufficient market power to cause an actual adverse effect on competition, a court will not find a tying arrangement and therefore the **per se** rule will not apply. Id. at 1566-68. See **antitrust laws.**

U

UBI (*u'bi*)—Lat: where.

UBI SUPRA (*ū'bē sū'prä*)—Lat: where stated above.

U.C.C. see **Uniform Commercial Code [U.C.C.].**

U.C.C.C. see **Uniform Consumer Credit Code [U.C.C.C.].**

ULTIMATE FACTS facts said to "lie in the area between evidence and a conclusion of law. They are the essential and determining facts on which the final conclusion of law is predicated. They are deduced by **inference** from evidentiary facts, which can be directly established by testimony or evidence," 74 N.E. 2d 563, 567. Compare **mediate data.**

ULTRAHAZARDOUS ACTIVITY an activity which gives rise to **strict liability,** because it "necessarily involves a risk of serious harm to the person, land or **chattels** of others, which cannot be eliminated by the exercise of utmost care" and it "is not a matter of common usage." Restatement, Torts §§519, 520. Blasting is universally recognized as an ultrahazardous activity, and it should be noted that strict liability in this context means the duty owed cannot be **delegated,** e.g., an owner of property who hires an independent **contractor** to perform blasting cannot thereby escape liability for damage resulting from the blasting operation. See Restatement 2d, Torts §§423, 427.

ULTRA VIRES (ūl' trä vi' rēz)— Lat: beyond, outside of, in excess of powers; that which is beyond the power authorized by law for an entity. The term applies especially to an action of a **corporation** which is beyond the powers conferred upon it by its **charter,** or by the statute under which it was created. See 79 S.W. 2d 1012, 1016. Ultra vires activities of a corporation may give rise to an action **quo warranto** by the state **Attorney General** to forfeit the corporation's charter of incorporation.

UNAVOIDABLE ACCIDENT see **accident** [UNAVOIDABLE ACCIDENT].

UNCLEAN HANDS one of the maxims of **equity** embodying the principle that a party seeking redress in a court of equity (equitable relief) must not have done any dishonest or unethical act in the transaction upon which he or she maintains the action in equity, since a court of conscience will not grant relief to one guilty of unconscionable conduct, i.e., to one with "unclean hands." See 171 A. 738. Compare **clean hands.** McClintock, Equity §26 (2d ed. 1948).

UNCONDITIONAL DISCHARGE see **sentence** [SUSPENDED SENTENCE].

UNCONSCIONABLE so unreasonably detrimental to the interest of a contracting party as to render the **contract** unenforceable. The common law rule rendering unconscionable contracts unenforceable was codified in the Uniform Commercial Code in §2-302. "The basic test is whether, in the light of the general commercial background and the commercial needs of the particular trade or case, the clauses involved are so one-sided as to be unconscionable under the circumstances existing at the time of the making of the contract." U.C.C. §2-302 Official Comment.

The term refers to a bargain so one-sided as to amount to an "absence of meaningful choice on the part of one of the parties together with contract terms which are unreasonably favorable to the other party. . . . Ordinarily, one who signs an agreement without full knowledge of its terms might be held to **assume the risk** that he has entered into a one-sided bargain. But when a party of little bargaining power and hence little real choice, signs a commercially unreasonable contract with little or no knowledge of its terms, it is hardly likely that his consent . . . was ever given to all the terms. In such a case the usual rule that the terms of an agreement are not to be questioned should be abandoned and the court should consider whether the terms of the contract are so unfair that enforcement should be withheld." 350 F. 2d 445, 449-50. see also **duress.**

UNCONSTITUTIONAL conflicting with some provision of **constitution,** most commonly the United States Constitution. When a **statute** is found to be unconstitutional, it is considered void or as if it had never been, and consequently all **rights, contracts,** or **duties** that depend on it are void. Similarly, no one can be punished for having refused obedience to the law once it is found to be unconstitutional. Some determinations of unconstitutionality, particularly in the area of law enforcement, are applied prospectively so that previous uses of the unconstitutional practice are not affected. See **retroactive.**

Misconceptions of the term's meaning sometimes arise as a result of the term's dual usage. In the English sense, the term means that legislation is unwise or unsound, while in the American sense, it refers to existing legislation that conflicts with a written constitution. See generally 1 F.2d 1001; 498 P.2d 9, 14; 57 A.L.R.3d 1058. The term also relates to state constitutional provisions and laws that are repugnant to the U.S. Constitution, and to state laws that are repugnant to that state's constitution.

In some instances, part of a statute may be unconstitutional, and if the invalid part can be severed, the constitutional portion continues to stand. 315 U.S. 568, 572. If the unconstitutional portion cannot be severed, however, the whole statute falls.

UNDER COLOR OF LAW see **color of law.**

UNDER COLOR OF TITLE see **color of title.**

UNDERLEASE see **sublease.**

UNDER PROTEST the making of a payment or the doing of an act under an obligation while reserving the right to object to the obligation at a later date. Typically, a party will make the payment or perform the act, but will at the same time inform the other party in writing that the performance is under protest. The statement "under protest" "without prejudice," "with reservation of right," or the like will prevent an **accord and satisfaction** and will prevent prejudice to the rights reserved. U.C.C. §1-207.

UNDER SEAL see **seal; specialty.**

UNDER THE INFLUENCE see **driving while intoxicated [D.W.I.].**

UNDER THE WILL, ELECTION see **election under the will.**

UNDERWRITE to insure the satisfaction of an obligation, such as an **insurance** contract or the sale of **bonds.** To underwrite an insurance contract is to act as the insurer or assume the risk for the loss of life or property of another. See 69 N.W. 141. To underwrite a **stock** or bond issue is to insure the sale of stocks or bonds by agreeing to buy, before a certain date, the entire issue if they are not sold to the public, or any part of the issue remaining after the sale. See 70 F. 2d 815.

Underwriting is one method used by corporations to raise capital. A conventional underwriting is handled by an investment banker who agrees to buy the issue from the seller and who forms a **syndicate** to provide the necessary capital and distribution network. The syndicate then sells the issue to investors and the proceeds of that sale, less an underwriting fee, are paid to the client company. Underwriting services go beyond the very important capital-raising function and include advice as to price and type of security to be offered, and as to when the offering should be made. Both the company and the underwriter cooperate in preparing the **prospectus** required by the **Securities and Exchange Commission.** The prospectus must be approved by the S.E.C. prior to the offering becoming effective, and a copy of it must be given to each investor in the issue.

UNDISCLOSED PRINCIPAL see **principal** [UNDISCLOSED PRINCIPAL].

UNDIVIDED INTEREST [RIGHT] the interest or right in **property** owned by **tenants in common, joint tenants,** or **tenants by the entirety,** whereby each tenant has an equal right to make use of and enjoy the entire property. See 63 F. Supp. 220, 223. An "undivided interest" derives from **unity of possession,** which is essential to the above tenancies. "Undivided interests" in property are to be distinguished from interests that have been **partitioned,** i.e., divided and distributed to the different owners for their use in **severalty.** See 33 Mass. 87, 98. An undivided interest may be of only a fractional share, e.g., "an undivided one-quarter interest,'' in which case the holder is entitled to one-quarter of all profits and sale proceeds but has a right to possession of the whole.

UNDUE INFLUENCE influence of another destroying the requisite free will of a **testator** or **donor,** which creates a ground for nullifying a **will** or invalidating an improvident **gift.** 32 A. 2d 371, 374. It is established by excessive importunity, superiority of will or mind, the relationship of the parties (e.g., priest and penitent or caretaker and senior citizen) or by any other means constraining the donor or testator to do what he is unable to refuse. See 58 A. 2d 31, 33. The elements of undue influence are susceptibility of testator/donor to such influence, the exertion of improper influence, and submission to the domination of the influencing party. See 160 N.W. 2d 49, 50. The strong influence of affection, however, does not constitute undue influence. 159 N.E. 305, 309. A **contract** will not be binding if one party unduly influences the other since the parties have not dealt on equal terms. In such a case, the influencing party is said to have an unfair advantage over the other based, among other things, on real or apparent authority, knowledge of necessity or distress, or a fiduciary or confidential relationship. 4 A. 2d 132. Compare **duress.** See also **unconscionable.**

UNEARNED SURPLUS in finance, surplus not part of earned surplus. It may include **paid-in-surplus,** REVALUATION SURPLUS, which arises upon the revaluation of assets above their cost, or DONATED SURPLUS, which arises from capital contributions other than for shares of **stock.** 570 P. 2d 1156, 1160.

UNETHICAL not ethical; not in accordance with the standards followed in a business or a profession. 42 N.Y.S. 2d 857, 859. See **conflict of interest.** See also **Code of Profes-** sional **Responsibility** and **Model Rules of Professional Conduct** (reproduced in appendix, infra).

UNEXECUTED USE see **use** [UNEXECUTED USE].

UNFAIR COMPETITION representations or conduct that deceive the public into believing that the business name, reputation, or **good will** of one person is that of another, 116 N.E. 796; unfair, untrue, or misleading advertising that is likely to lead the public into believing that certain goods are associated with another manufacturer; imitation of a competitor's product, package, or trademark in circumstances where the consumer might be misled; conduct which is contrary to honest industrial and commercial practice, 479 F. Supp. 792, 798.

Unfair competition is a **tort** and a **fraud** for which the courts may afford a **remedy,** 90 F. Supp. 477, including injunctions against fraudulent or deceptive practices that disparage a competitor's trade or product. In order to make out a case of unfair competition it is not necessary to show that any person has been actually deceived, but merely that such deception will be a natural and probable result of the act. Although it is commonly held that fraudulent intent is a necessary element of unfair competition, such intent may be presumed when it causes actual or probable deception. See Prosser, Law of Torts §130 (4th ed. 1971).

UNFAIR LABOR PRACTICE any activities by either a **labor organization** (union) or an employer which is unlawful under the **National Labor Relations Act.** Unions are specifically forbidden to engage in the following activities: restraint or coercion of employees or employers; coercion of employers to discriminate against employees; refusal to bargain; coercion or inducement of **strikes** or **boycotts** for a specific purpose; excessive or discriminatory initiation fees; **featherbedding;**

picketing for organizational purposes under certain circumstances; in the health care industry, picketing or striking on less than 10 days' notice. 29 U.S.C. §158(b).

Employers are specifically forbidden to engage in the following activities: interference with employees in exercise of their rights; domination of a labor organization; encouragement or discouragement of membership in labor unions through discriminatory terms and conditions of employment; discrimination against employees for filing labor grievances or testifying in regard to them; refusal to bargain collectively with the representative of a majority of the employees; entering into contracts that discriminate against other employers. 29 U.S.C. §158(a) See **collective bargaining.**

UNFIT unsuitable, incompetent, or not adapted for a particular use or service, 522 P. 2d 330, 334. Compare **warranty** [WARRANTY OF FITNESS].

UNIFIED ESTATE AND GIFT TAX see **tax** [UNIFIED ESTATE AND GIFT TAX].

UNIFORM ARBITRATION ACT see **arbitrator** [UNIFORM ARBITRATION ACT].

UNIFORM CODE OF MILITARY JUSTICE see **military law** [[UNIFORM] CODE OF MILITARY JUSTICE].

UNIFORM COMMERCIAL CODE [U.C.C.] a code of laws governing various commercial transactions, including the sale of goods, banking transactions, secured transactions in personal property, and other matters designed to bring uniformity in these areas to the laws of the various states, and that has been adopted, with some modifications, in all states as well as in the District of Columbia and in the Virgin Islands. Due to the influence of **civil law,** Louisiana did not adopt the articles on sales and secured transactions.

UNIFORM CONSUMER CREDIT CODE [U.C.C.C.] one of several **uniform laws** that states may or may not adopt, the U.C.C.C. was passed to simplify and further consumer understanding of all aspects of credit and credit transactions and to encourage the development of sound consumer credit practices. Sometimes called U.3C. U.C.C.C. §1.102(2).

UNIFORM GIFTS TO MINORS ACT [U.G.M.A.] a **uniform law** adopted by every state which creates a statutory method for making a **gift** in **trust** to minors.

The law usually applies only to certain types of personal property, such as securities, annuity, life insurance and endowment policies, partnership interests, or tangibles. The gift is made and the **trust** is created by the donor either by registering the property in the name of the custodian, followed by the language "as custodian for . . ." or by delivering the property to the custodian together with a statement that the property is to be held as custodian under the Uniform Gifts to Minors Act. The statutes set forth the terms of the trust, under which the custodian may apply the trust fund for the benefit of the minor and is obliged to pay over the funds upon the minor attaining age 18, unless the donor indicates at the time of the gift that it is to be held until age 21.

UNIFORM LAWS laws that have been approved by the Commissioners on Uniform State Laws and are proposed to all state legislatures for their consideration and adoption. Some uniform laws are passed by only a few states; others are passed by all the states with minor differences in language. Examples include the Uniform Adoption Act, Uniform Child Custody Jurisdiction Act, Uniform Code of Military Justice (see **military law**), **Uniform Commercial Code, Uniform Consumer Credit Code, Uniform Gifts to Minors Act,** Uniform Limited

Partnership Act, Uniform Probate Code, Uniform Rules of Evidence, Uniform Simultaneous Death Act, and Uniform Testamentary Additions to Trusts Act.

UNILATERAL CONTRACT see **contract** [UNILATERAL CONTRACT].

UNILATERAL MISTAKE see **mistake.**

UNION see **labor organization** [union].

UNION SHOP a work place where all the employees are members of a union. Non-union members may work in such shops provided they agree to join the union. See **closed shop; open shop.**

UNIT see **commercial unit.**

UNITED STATES ATTORNEY see **district attorney.**

UNITED STATES CLAIMS COURT see **Court of Claims.**

UNITED STATES MAGISTRATE see **magistrate** [UNITED STATES [FEDERAL] MAGISTRATE].

UNITED STATES TRUSTEE see **bankruptcy** [UNITED STATES TRUSTEE].

UNITIES the **common law** requirements necessary in order to create a **joint tenancy,** or a **tenancy by the entirety.** A joint tenancy requires the "four unities" of "interest," "possession," "time," and "title," and a tenancy by the entirety, in addition to the four unities, requires "unity of person." Tenants in common, as a result of the kind of estate they hold, have a unity of possession but no unity is required to create such an estate.

UNITY OF INTEREST the requirement that the ownership shares, i.e., **interests** of the co-tenants in a joint tenancy or tenancy by the entirety be equal. An individual joint tenant cannot encumber his or her "share" by **mortgage** without destroying this unity; to preserve the joint tenancy the mort-

gage must be agreed to by all. Tenants in common are not subject to this unity of interest rule and may have unequal shares in the same property.

UNITY OF PERSON the common law requirement for the creation of a tenancy by the entirety that the co-tenants be husband and wife, based on the conception that marriage created a "unity of person." See 103 So. 833, 834.

UNITY OF POSSESSION the equal right of each co-owner of property to the **use** and **possession** of the whole property. See 300 S.W. 2d 379, 383. Unity of possession is necessary for each of the three types of co-tenancies. See **undivided interest.**

UNITY OF TIME the requirement that the interests of the co-tenants in a joint tenancy or tenancy by the entirety must commence (or **vest**) at the same moment in time.

UNITY OF TITLE the requirement that all tenants of a joint tenancy or both tenants of a tenancy by the entirety acquire their interests under the same **title;** thus, such co-tenants cannot hold by different **deeds.** See 126 N.E. 2d 479, 480.

UNIT INVESTMENT TRUST an unmanaged **portfolio** of **bonds** sold to investors in units of $1,000 each. A bank or **trust company** serves as custodian and **trustee** for the portfolio of bonds, and collects and periodically disburses interest payments and principal when bonds mature. Since the portfolio is fixed, the trust is self-liquidating due to both unit holder redemptions and bond maturities. Compare **nondiscretionary trust.**

UNIVERSAL AGENT one authorized to transact all the business of his or her **principal** of every kind. See 10 So. 304, 307. See **agent.**

UNJUST ENRICHMENT principle

in law of contracts by which "a person who has been unjustly enriched at the expense of another is required to make **restitution** to the other." Restatement, Restitution 1. Restitution and unjust enrichment are the modern designations for the older doctrine of **quasi contracts,** which are not true contracts, but are obligations created by the law when money, property, or services have been obtained by one person at the expense of another and under such circumstances that in equity and good conscience he or she ought not retain it. See 209 P. 2d 457, 460. When one receives a benefit, the retention of which would be inequitable, the law will impose a duty to pay compensation in order to prevent unjust enrichment. Retention of a benefit without compensation will not be considered inequitable or unjust if the benefit was conferred without any reasonable basis of compensation and in no event should the compensation ordered exceed the compensation anticipated by the person who rendered the service or delivered the goods. But see **officious intermeddler.** See also **quantum meruit.**

UNLAWFUL ASSEMBLY a **misdemeanor** at common law consisting of "a meeting of three or more persons with a common plan in mind which, if carried out, [would] result in a riot; a meeting with intent to commit a crime by open force or execute a common design lawful or unlawful in an unauthorized manner likely to cause courageous persons to apprehend a **breach of the peace.**" Perkins & Boyce Criminal Law 481 (3d ed. 1982). The right "peaceably to assemble" is constitutionally guaranteed by the First Amendment. See also **association; conspiracy.**

UNLAWFUL DETAINER the act of retaining **possession** without right, as in the case of a tenant whose lease has expired. UNLAWFUL DETAINER STATUTES often create a right to oust by summary process a **holdover tenant** and to determine speedily the right to possession of real property, thus avoiding the judicially disfavored remedy of **self-help.** The **summary proceeding** determines only the question of possession and no ultimate determination of **title** or **estate** can be made in such a proceeding. See 173 P. 2d 343, 348. See **detainer; forcible entry and detainer.**

UNLAWFUL ENTRY the statutory crime of entering onto someone else's property without their consent by fraud or force. Unlawful entry is broader than and should be distinguished from the common law crime of **burglary** which requires the breaking and entry of the dwelling of another at night and with felonious intent. Statutes prohibiting unlawful entry were passed to protect society from acts not prohibited by burglary. See **trespass.** Perkins & Boyce, Criminal Law 269-72 (3d ed. 1982).

UNLAWFUL FORCE see **force** [UNLAWFUL FORCE].

UNLIQUIDATED see **sum certain** [UNLIQUIDATED].

UNLISTED SECURITY a **stock** or **bond** not listed on a **stock exchange** and therefore traded only in the **over-the-counter market.**

UNNATURAL ACT [OFFENSE] see **crime against nature.**

UNNECESSARY HARDSHIP in **zoning** law, a permissible ground for a **variance.** Unnecessary hardship exists when the physical characteristics of the real estate are such that it cannot be used for a permitted purpose, or that it can only be used for a permitted purpose at a prohibitive expense, 401 A. 2d 1240, 1242.

UNREALIZED APPRECIATION see **appreciation** [UNREALIZED APPRECIATION].

UNREASONABLE arbitrary, capricious, absurd, immoderate, or exorbitant, 287 N.W. 122, 131; not conformable to reason, irrational, beyond bounds of reason or moderation, 268 P. 2d 605, 616.

UNREASONABLE PUNISHMENT see **cruel and unusual punishment.**

UNREASONABLE RESTRAINT OF TRADE see **restraint of trade.**

UNREASONABLE SEARCH AND SEIZURE a search and/or seizure of a person, a house, papers or effects that are protected against it by the Fourth and Fourteenth Amendments and state constitutions, where the basis for the search and/or seizure does not meet constitutional requirements. See **search and seizure.**

UNUSUAL PUNISHMENT see **cruel and unusual punishment.**

USAGE OF TRADE see **trade usage.**

USE the right to enjoy the benefits flowing from **real property** or **personal property.** See 446 S.W. 2d 897, 903; 47 A.L.R. 3d 189. It generally means the right to enjoy, hold, occupy, or have the fruits of a thing but not to own the object itself; in other words, **equitable** ownership as distinct from legal title. Consequently, if the object is money, its use is the **interest** earned and if the object is real estate, its use is the rent generated, or the right a person may have to use or enjoy the property of another. 220 N.Y.S. 2d 109, 112; 72 N.W. 2d 324, 326. The term also refers to the right of a **patent holder** or **licensee** to use an invention. A **patent** is infringed upon by unauthorized use or even the threat to use the patented invention during the term of the patent. 35 U.S.C. §271(a). Use also is defined as a continual or repeated practice or accustomed or usual procedure. 240 A. 2d 886, 889. See **patent infringement.**

Historically, the word "use" defined every form of beneficial or equitable ownership and therefore is an "all embracing" term for an **estate** which is less than **legal.** 150 N.Y.S. 2d 911, 912. English usage of the term has developed into what is now known as a **trust** and in this sense "use" refers to a person other than the owner who takes the profits; one who takes the profits, has the use. 62 N.E. 1002, 1003. Uses have been created (1) by express provision in a valid **deed;** (2) by implication to the conveyor when **conveyance** is made without **consideration** [called a RESULTING USE]; (3) by **bargain and sale;** (4) by covenant to stand **seised.** Burby, Real Property 8 (3d ed. 1965). Under the **Statute of Uses,** the party in whom a use was created was deemed seised of a like **estate** as the party had in the use; hence "A to B for the use of C for life" was operative under the statute to convey to C a life estate. It should be noted that not all uses were converted under the statute to legal interests or estates. The statute applied to PASSIVE USES, i.e., instances where the legal titleholder had no obligations with respect to the estate other than to hold title. Thus, A to B for the use of C created a passive use which the statute converted into a legal estate in C. Those not so converted, classified as UNEXE-CUTED USES, were: a use raised on a non-**freehold estate,** i.e., a **tenancy,** "A to B for 10 years for the use of C"; a USE ON A USE, "A to B for the use of C for life then to the use of D"; and ACTIVE USES, which constitute the modern **trusts,** i.e., where a person holds legal title but unlike the passive use the legal titleholder has duties and obligations to perform in connection with his holding. Thus, A to B to invest for the benefit of C creates an active use and legal title does not merge with C's use. See Moynihan, Introduction to the Law of Property 207-212 (1962).

An important effect of the Statute of Uses was the validation of **executory interests** (a species of **future interests**) which had heretofore been recognized only in equity. Two kinds of executory interests so converted into legal estates were the springing and shifting uses. A SHIFTING USE is a use which arises in derogation of another, i.e., "shifts" from one beneficiary to another, depending on some future contingency. A SPRINGING USE is a use that arises upon the occurrence of a future event and that does not take effect in derogation of any interest other than that which results to the grantor, or remains in the grantor in the meantime. Thus, A to B and his heirs to the use of C and his heirs beginning at some future date creates a legal estate in B, a resulting use for the interim period in A, and a springing use in C when his use comes into effect. If A conveys property to B for the use of C unless a contingency occurs in which case D should have the use, C obtains an equitable estate but if the contingency occurs then the equitable estate shifts to D who has a shifting use. "A shifting use is one which cuts short a prior use estate in a person other than the conveyor; a springing use is one which cuts short a use estate in the conveyor." Id. at 178.

BENEFICIAL USE see **beneficial use.**

CESTUI QUE USE see **cestui que** [CESTUI QUE USE].

EXCLUSIVE USE in real property law, one of the elements of a **prescriptive easement.** Exclusive use in this regard means that the rights of the party claiming the easement do not depend upon similar rights in others, and does not mean that no other persons have physically used the property in question. 281 N.W. 2d 892, 898.

In trademark law, exclusive use refers to the exclusive use of both a specific mark or symbol and of any confusingly similar mark or term. 53 F. 2d 1011.

FAIR USE see **fair use.**

PERMISSIVE USE use with the knowledge or consent of the owner; a license terminable at the will of the owner or when the acts contemplated in the permission are completed. 201 S.W. 64, 66.

PUBLIC USE see **public use.**

USE IMMUNITY see **self-incrimination, privilege against** [TESTIMONIAL [USE] IMMUNITY].

USES, STATUTE OF see **Statute of Uses.**

USE TAX see **tax** [USE TAX].

USEFUL LIFE see **depreciation** [USEFUL LIFE].

USE IMMUNITY see **self-incrimination, privilege against** [TESTIMONIAL [USE] IMMUNITY].

USE, PUBLIC see **public use.**

USUFRUCT in the **civil law,** the right to use and enjoy **property** vested in another, "and to draw from the same all the profit, utility, and advantage which it may produce, provided it be without altering the substance of the thing." 75 P. 698, 699. See **beneficial use.**

USURIOUS CONTRACT a contract that imposes **interest** on a debt at a rate in excess of that permitted by law. 76 P. 2d 334, 336. See **loansharking; usury.**

USURY an **unconscionable** or exorbitant rate of **interest;** an excessive and illegal requirement of compensation for **forbearance** on a **debt** [**interest**]; "a bargain under which a greater profit than is permitted by law is paid, or is agreed to be paid to a creditor by or on behalf of the debtor for a loan of money, or for extending the maturity of a pecuniary debt." Restatement, Contracts §526. Although universally deplored, it was not recognized as an offense at **common law.** See Calamari & Perillo, Contracts 560

(1970). The state legislatures today determine the maximum allowable rates of interest that may be demanded in any financial transaction. However, usury laws usually do not apply to corporate borrowers. While in many jurisdictions a usurious contract is a nullity and is hence unenforceable, in some jurisdictions a creditor may recover his or her **principal;** in others, the principal as well as interest at the legally authorized rate may be recovered. 14 Williston, Contracts §1698B (3d ed. 1972).

UTILITY see **public utility.**

UTMOST CARE in tort law, such a degree of care as would be exercised by a very careful, prudent, and competent person under the same or similar circumstances. 118 S.W. 799, 803. See **negligence.**

UTMOST RESISTANCE that degree of resistance that a woman traditionally has been required to offer her attacker in order to charge that she has been raped; the maximum resistance of which a person is capable in resisting attack. 149 N.W. 771, 772. The "utmost resistance" doctrine may not apply if the woman is put in fear of personal violence and so submits to avert serious bodily injury to herself. 143 S.W. 2d 288, 289. See generally Perkins & Boyce, Criminal Law 210-12 (3d ed. 1982). See **rape.**

UTTER to put forth, to execute; especially, to offer, a forged instrument with representations by words or acts, directly or indirectly, that the instrument is valid. See 125. So. 793, 794.

The crime of UTTERING a forged instrument includes the element of fraudulent intent to injure another, see 101 P. 2d 860, 863, and is distinguished from the crime of **forgery,** by the requirement that the utterer pass or attempt to pass the forged instrument. See 419 P. 2d 403, 406. Mere showing of a forged instrument without an attempt to pass it as genuine is not uttering. See 29 N.W. 923, 925. Modern statutes have tended to combine forgery, uttering, and **counterfeiting** under a single statutory offense called forgery. Model Penal Code §224.1.

UXOR see **et ux.**

VACATE to render **void;** to **set aside,** as "to vacate a judgment." See **reverse.**

To move out; to render vacant as in "vacating **premises.**" See **abandonment.**

VAGRANCY a general term for a class of minor offenses such as idleness without employment, having no visible means of support, etc.; roaming, wandering, or loitering; wandering or strolling around from place to place without any lawful purpose or object. Vagrancy statutes developed following the breakup of the English feudal estates. The downfall of the feudal system led to labor shortages. The Statutes of Laborers, 23 Edw. 3, c.1 (1349); 25 Edw. 3, c.1. (1350) were enacted to stabilize the working force by prohibiting increases in wages and prohibiting the movement of workers in search of improved conditions. Later the poor laws included vagrancy provisions to prevent the movement of "wild rogues" and the "notorious brotherhood of beggars." See [1937] 1 K.B. 232, 271.

More recently, the vagrancy statutes have been used by the police as authority for arresting persons who are suspected of some wrongdoing but where **probable cause** for their arrest does not exist. However, these statutes have been open to abuse and have recently found disfavor in the courts. See 282 NYS 2d 739. Courts have declared them unconstitutional as unreasonable, violative of **due process,** and **void for vagueness.** Thus a criminal statute requiring persons who loiter or wander on the streets to provide "credible and reliable" identification was struck down as unconstitutionally vague by failing to clarify the requirement of identification, thereby encouraging arbitrary enforcement. 103 S. Ct. 1855-56. See also 405 U.S. 156.

VAGUENESS see **void for vagueness.**

VALUABLE CONSIDERATION see **consideration.**

VALUE the monetary worth of a thing; marketable price; estimated or assessed worth. 85 A. 2d 109, 110. The method of determining an object's value, and thus the value itself, will vary depending upon the purpose for which it is being determined. For instance, for estate and gift **tax** purposes, "value" is the price a willing buyer would pay a willing seller if neither is compelled to buy or sell and both have reasonable knowledge of the relevant facts. Treas. Reg. §§20.2031-1 (b) and 25.2512-1. However, for insurance purposes, value may refer to REPLACEMENT VALUE, that is, the cost of replacing an object, rather than its fair **market value.** See **book value; capitalized value; cash surrender value; diminution in value; face value; going concern value; net asset value; par value; probative** [PROBATIVE VALUE].

VALUE ADDED TAX see **tax** [AD VALOREM TAX].

VARIANCE in procedure, a discrepancy between what is **charged** or **alleged** and what is proved or offered as proof; not every variance is fatal. 257 A. 2d 814, 817. A FATAL VARIANCE, in both civil and criminal cases, is a material and substantial variance, and, in criminal cases, it must also tend to mislead the defendant in making his or her defense, or tend to expose the defendant to the injury of being put twice in jeopardy for the same offense. 237 P. 2d 162, 165. See **double jeopardy.** The liberalization of pleading rules in civil cases has essentially eliminated variance as a cause for dismissal. See Fed. R. Civ. Proc. 15a.

In zoning law, it is an exemption from the application of a zoning ordinance or regulation permitting a use which varies from that otherwise permitted under the zoning regulation. The exception is granted by the appropriate authority in special circumstances to protect against an undue hardship wrought by strict enforcement of the zoning regulations. See also **non-conforming use.**

VASSAL at common law, a person who was granted **real property** in return for a promise to perform services for his or her **grantor** or lord. For instance, the king of England was the lord of the country and granted land to his nobles; the nobles were then obligated to perform various feudal services for the king, and were vassals to him. Upon a vassal's failure to perform the required services, the property reverted to the lord. 33 A. 1076, 1080. While the nobles were vassals of the king, they also could grant land in return for feudal services, and thus be lords to other vassals. See **subinfeudation.** The abuses of the feudal system led the term to acquire a meaning similar to "slave." 2 Bl. Comm. *53.

VEIL, PIERCING see **piercing the corporate veil.**

VENAL dishonest; readily bribed or corrupted.

VEL NON *(vĕl nŏn)*—Lat: or not; as, "The question of his being guilty, vel non, is for the jury to determine."

VENDEE buyer; purchaser, especially in **contract** for the **sale** of **realty.**

VENDOR seller; especially person

who sells **real property**. The word "seller" is used more often to describe a **personal property** transaction.

VENIRE *(vĕ-nē'rā)*—Lat: to come; refers to the common law process by which jurors are summoned to try a case. 46 A. 2d 921, 923.

VENIRE DE NOVO *(dā nō'-vō)* to come anew; refers to the summoning of a second **jury** for the purpose of proceeding to a second trial. Such a second trial is awarded where a **verdict** [by the jury] or finding [by the court] "is so defective, uncertain, or ambiguous upon its face that no **judgment** can be rendered upon it." 41 N.E. 383, 386. At early common law, the writ of venire de novo (or VENIRE FACIAS DE NOVO, which was the more proper term), issued only in response to a jury's verdict, id., and only where the defect appeared on the face of the record rather than at some place extrinsic to it, 27 N.E. 448; but these technical limitations have been incorporated into the more modern procedure of granting a new trial, which serves the purpose of the old venire de novo. See, e.g., Fed. R. Civ. Proc. 59. The term, when used, generally denotes a new trial. See 171 N.E. 585.

VENUE a neighborhood, a neighboring place; synonymous with "place of trial." It refers to the possible or proper place or places for the trial of a **suit,** as among several places where **jurisdiction** could be established. See 132 N.W. 2d 304, 308; and 257 F. Supp. 219, 224. "Jurisdiction deals with the authority of a court to exercise judicial power. Venue deals with the place where that power should be exercised. Jurisdiction over the **subject matter** cannot be conferred by the parties, and the lack thereof may not be waived. Venue, on the other hand, is bottomed on convenience, and improper venue may be waived," Green, Civil Procedure 64 (2d ed. 1979). Venue "is the right of the party sued to have the action brought and heard in a particular judicial district." 249 A. 2d 916, 918. In a criminal trial where the publicity surrounding the crime would virtually preclude a fair trial, the court will direct a CHANGE OF VENUE, or removal of the proceedings to a different district or county. See **forum non conveniens; removal.**

VERACITY honesty, truthfulness. See **witness** [CHARACTER WITNESS].

VERDICT the opinion of a jury, or of a judge where there is no jury, on a question of fact. See 31 Ill. App. 325, 338. A verdict differs from a judgment in that a verdict is not a judicial determination, but rather a finding of fact which the trial court may accept or reject and utilize in formulating its judgment. See 446 S.W. 2d 243, 244.

COMPROMISE VERDICT a verdict resulting from improper surrender of one juror's opinion to another on a material issue. See 215 P. 887, 889-90. [See QUOTIENT VERDICT below].

DIRECTED VERDICT see **directed verdict.**

FALSE VERDICT a manifestly unjust **verdict;** one not true to the **evidence,** arrived at by any process (such as a coin flip or a **quotient verdict**) that departs from the legitimate methods by which jurors may reach a decision. When such a verdict is rendered, the court can enter a **judgment n.o.v.** ("notwithstanding the verdict").

GENERAL VERDICT ordinary verdict declaring simply which party prevails, without any special findings of fact.

PARTIAL VERDICT in criminal law, a finding that the defendant is guilty of certain charges but innocent of others.

QUOTIENT VERDICT improper and unacceptable kind of compromise verdict resulting from an agreement by the jurors that their verdict will be an award of **damages** in an amount to be determined by the addition of all juror's computations of damages and its division by the number of jurors.

SPECIAL VERDICT one rendered on certain specific factual issues posed by the court. "Instead of a general finding for one party or the other, the special verdict requires the jury to make a specific finding on each ultimate fact put in issue by the **pleadings**. . . . The Court will then apply the law to those found facts." Green, Civil Procedure 208 (2d ed. 1979).

When a trial court in a criminal case directs that the jury answer specific questions and render special verdicts incident to its general verdict of guilty or not guilty as to particular counts of the indictment, it may operate to coerce a particular result by leading the jury to that conclusion. For this reason, special verdicts have been held improperly ordered in criminal cases where rendered against the wishes of the defendant who, it is said, has a right to a general verdict free from the influence of the court's special interrogatories. See 416 F. 2d 165.

VERIFICATION confirmation of correctness, truth, or authenticity of **pleading** or other paper **affidavit**, oath, or **deposition**, 12 F. 2d 81, 83; an affidavit attached to a statement affirming the truth of that statement. See 105 P. 2d 59, 63.

VERTICAL PRICE FIXING see **price fixing.**

VERTICAL PRIVITY see **privity** [VERTICAL PRIVITY].

VESTED fixed, accrued, or abso-lute, see 170 S.W. 885, 888; not contingent; generally used to describe any right or **title** to something that is not dependent upon the occurrence or failure to occur of some specified future event (**condition** precedent). Although sometimes used to refer to an immediate possessory **interest** in property, the more technically proper definition also comprehends interests that will become rights to actual **possession** of the property at some later time [**in futuro**]. See 344 P. 2d 16, 21. Originally applied in reference to estates in **real property,** it has come to be applied to other property interests. See, e.g., 24 N.W. 161, 170-171 (**personal property**); 156 S.W. 2d 146, 151 (**trusts**); 4 N.W. 2d 919, 920 (**alimony** and child support payments). Compare **contingent.**

VESTED ESTATE a property **interest** which is either currently in possession or will necessarily come into **possession** in the future merely upon the **determination** (end) of the **preceding estate.** Thus, for there to be a "vested estate" there must exist a known person who would have an immediate right to possession upon the expiration of the prior estate. See 157 S.W. 2d 429, 436. At common law "vested estate" was one that could be **devised** or **alienated,** whereas a **contingent estate** could not. Unlike a vested estate, a contingent estate depends upon the occurrence of an uncertain event or the future ascertainment of presently unknown takers. See 51 N.Y.S. 1038, 1043. Contingent estates can now be devised and alienated, albeit with the uncertainty that the estate may never pass to the grantee.

VESTED INTEREST "a present right or title to a thing, which carries with it an existing right of alienation, even though the right to possession or enjoyment may be postponed to some uncertain time in the future. . . ." 120 S.W. 2d 778, 781. See **interest.**

VESTED REMAINDER "[a **remainder**] which is limited to an ascertained person in being, whose right to the **estate** is fixed and certain, and [which] does not depend upon the happening of any future event, but whose **enjoyment** [of the estate] is postponed to some future time." 102 S.E. 643, 644. See **contingent remainder.**

VESTED RIGHTS in relation to constitutional guarantces, it is a broad shield of protection consisting of "a vested interest which it is right and equitable that the government should recognize and protect, and of which the individual could not be deprived arbitrarily without injustice." 65 N.W. 2d 785, 791. The term "is frequently used to designate a right which has become so fixed that it is not subject to [being] divested without the consent of the owner." 84 P. 2d 552, 554.

VETO see **pocket veto.**

VEXATIOUS LITIGATION civil **action** shown to have been instituted maliciously and without **probable cause,** and one which may be protected against by **injunction.** See 11 N.Y.S. 2d 768, 772. See **litigious; malicious prosecution.**

VICARIOUS LIABILITY the imputation of **liability** upon one person for the actions of another. In tort law, if an employee, EE, while in the **scope of his employment** for employer, ER, drives a delivery truck, and hits and injures P crossing the street, ER will be vicariously liable, under the doctrine of **respondeat superior,** for injuries sustained by P. In criminal law, in some jurisdiction, if EE, who is employed by ER as a bartender, sells liquor to a minor, ER will be criminally liable for the offense of EE. See 110 N.W. 2d 29, 34. Sometimes this doctrine is called IMPUTED LIABILITY. Compare **strict liability.**

VICINAGE neighborhood; vicinity. Its contemporary meaning denotes a particular area where a crime was committed, a **trial** is being held, or the community from which jurors are called. See **jury** [JURY OF THE VICINAGE].

VICE CRIMES activities such as gambling, prostitution and pornography which are illegal because they offend the moral standards of the community.

VICTUALS prepared food; food ready to eat, 120 N.E. 407.

VICTUALER [VICTUALLER] one who sells food or drink prepared for consumption on the premises. 120 N.E. 407, 409.

VIDELICET see **viz.**

VIDUITATE [VIDUITY] widowhood.

VI ET ARMIS see **trespass** [TRESPASS VI ET ARMIS].

VIEW see **plain view.** See also **line up; show up.**

VILLEIN SOCAGE see **socage.**

VILLENAGE a menial form of feudal **tenure** in which the **tenant** [the **villein**] was required to perform all **services** demanded by the lord of the manor.

VIOLATION OF PROBATION see **probation.**

VIOLENCE [VIOLENT] moving, acting, or characterized by physical force, especially by extreme and sudden or unjust or improper force. 79 S.W. 2d 292, 296. The degree of force implied by the word "violence" depends upon the context in which it is used. For instance, its use in an insurance policy may imply a lesser degree or a different type of force than its use in a criminal statute. Compare 13 A. 2d 651, 656; 68 Cal. Rptr. 657.

VIR (vir)—Lat: man.

VISA a recognition of the validity of a passport, issued by the proper officials of the country which the bearer wishes to enter, 14 F. 2d 679, 682; more broadly, a symbol made on a document certifying that it has been examined and approved.

VISITATION, CONJUGAL see **conjugal rights** [CONJUGAL VISITATION].

VISITATION RIGHTS in family law, the right granted by a court to a parent or other relative who is deprived custody of a child to visit the child on a regular basis. 219 N.E. 2d 300, 302.

VIS MAJOR *(vĭz mä' -yôr)*—Lat: a greater force, superior force; it is used in the civil law to mean **act of God,** see 38 So. 873, 874, and has reference to an "irresistible natural cause which cannot be guarded against by the ordinary exertions of human skill and prudence." 121 S.W. 36, 43. "A loss 'vis major' (superior force) is a loss that results immediately from natural cause, without the intervention of man, and could not have been prevented by the exercise of prudence, diligence and care." 222 F. Supp. 299, 305. "The early authors treated [the phrase] as the equivalent to an **act of God.** Later authority seems to have broadened its meaning to include any insuperable interference." 77 F. 2d 614, 617.

VITALIZED see **quickening.**

VITIATE to void or render a nullity; to impair.

VIZ. *(vĭz)*—Lat: abbreviated form of the Latin word "videlicet," meaning namely, that is to say. It is a term used in relation to **pleadings** "to particularize or explain what goes before it. It may restrain the generality of a preceding word, but cannot enlarge or diminish the preceding subject-matter. In the former case it is merely explanatory of the language which precedes it, while in the latter it is repugnant to it." 48 A. 639, 642. "When any fact alleged in pleading is preceded by 'to wit,' 'that is to say,' or 'namely,' such fact is said to be laid under a 'videlicet,' " the purpose of which is to particularize or specify. 116 N.W. 2d 243, 244.

VOICE EXEMPLAR a recording of a person's voice made for the purpose of identification, usually in a criminal investigation. The Supreme Court has held that requiring a person to make a voice **exemplar** does not violate the privilege against **self-incrimination,** since it is used for identification purposes only, and that it does not constitute an unreasonable **search or seizure.** 410 U.S. 1.

VOID empty, having no legal force, ineffectual, unenforceable, 146 N.E. 2d 477, 479; incapable of being ratified. For example, one who has been adjudicated an **incompetent** and for whom a **guardian** has been appointed has no capacity to contract, and any **contract** entered into is void. Compare **voidable.**

VOIDABLE capable of being later annulled; a valid act which, though it may be rendered void, may accomplish the thing sought to be accomplished until the fatal defect in the transaction has been effectively asserted or judicially ascertained and declared. 152 N.E. 2d 813, 817. For example, an infant has no capacity to contract, hence any contract entered into by the infant is voidable. It is not **void,** however, and until and unless **repudiated** by the minor, it is binding on the **competent** party. The infant may ratify the contract and so be bound thereunder when the disability of infancy is removed, i.e., when the age of **majority** is reached.

In the law of sales, it is possible to get voidable title in **goods** by obtaining them in a fraudulent manner. A person with voidable title in goods has the power to transfer a good title to a good faith purchaser for value. U.C.C. §2-403.

VOIDABLE PREFERENCE see **preference** [VOIDABLE PREFERENCE].

VOID FOR VAGUENESS a criminal statute is constitutionally void for vagueness when it is so vague that persons of common intelligence must necessarily guess at its meaning and differ as to its application. 269 U.S. 385, 391. A statute is void when it is vague either as to what persons fall within the scope of the statute, what conduct is forbidden, or what punishment may be imposed. "**Due process** requires that criminal statutes, administrative crimes, and **common law** crimes be reasonably definite as to persons and conduct within their scope and the punishment which may be imposed for their violation. In determining whether a legislative, judicial or administrative definition is void for vagueness, the following inquiries are appropriate: (1) Does the law give fair notice to those persons potentially subject to it? (2) Does the law adequately guard against arbitrary and discriminatory enforcement? (3) Does the law provide sufficient breathing space for First Amendment Rights?" LaFave and Scott, Criminal Law 83 (1972). Use of this doctrine as a constitutional attack is based upon an assertion that the meaning of the statute in question is so uncertain and unclear as to render it void. The due process clause of the Fifth Amendment requires that criminal statutes give reasonably certain notice that an act has been made criminal before it is committed. Every person should be able to know with certainty when he or she is committing a crime. See 341 U.S. 223, 230; 105 F. Supp. 202; 103 S. Ct. 1855.

FACIAL INVALIDITY doctrine whereby a law will be determined to be VOID ON ITS FACE if it "does not aim specifically at evils within the allowable area of [government] control but . . .

sweeps within its ambit other activities that constitute an exercise [of protected rights]." 310 U.S. 88, 97. In the absence of this doctrine the statute itself will not be considered void but its application to particular conduct may be determined to be invalid on grounds of vagueness in that the actor did not have reasonable notice that the particular conduct was proscribed. In such instances the statute is "invalid or unconstitutional AS APPLIED," rather than on its face. 379 U.S. 559. See also 380 U.S. 479. See **overbreadth; standing.**

VOID, NULL AND see **nullity.**

VOID ON ITS FACE see **void for vagueness** [VOID ON ITS FACE].

VOIR DIRE *(vwŏr dēr)*—Fr: to speak the truth. A VOIR DIRE EXAMINATION usually refers to the examination by the court or by the attorneys of prospective jurors, to determine their qualification for **jury** service, to determine if cause exists for challenge (i.e., to excuse) particular jurors, and to provide information about the jurors so that the parties can exercise their statutory peremptory challenges (objections to particular jurors without the need for any cause to be stated). See Green, Basic Civil Procedure 185-86 (2d ed. 1979).

A voir dire examination during the trial refers to a **hearing** out of the presence and hearing of the jury by the court upon some **issue** of fact or law that requires an initial determination by the court or upon which the court must rule as a matter of law alone. Thus, where a **confession** of the **defendant** is to be introduced by the state in a criminal **trial,** the trial court must conduct a voir dire examination to determine if the statements were voluntarily obtained in compliance with the **Miranda** requirements and thus constitutionally admissible. This determination must be made at least initially by the court before the jury is permitted to hear the confession. 378 U.S. 368; 385 U.S. 538, 543.

VOLENTI NON FIT INJURIA *(vō-lĕn'-tē nŏn fēt ĭn-jū'-rē-à)*— Lat: the volunteer suffers no wrong; no legal wrong is done to the person who consents. 102 P. 2d 213, 218. In tort law, it refers to the fact that one cannot usually claim **damages** when one consented to the activity that caused the damages.

VOLUNTARY APPEARANCE see **appearance.**

VOLUNTARY DISABLEMENT see **anticipatory breach [of contract]** [VOLUNTARY DISABLEMENT].

VOLUNTARY DISSOLUTION see **dissolution** [VOLUNTARY DISSOLUTION].

VOLUNTARY MANSLAUGHTER see **manslaughter** [VOLUNTARY MANSLAUGHTER].

VOLUNTARY NONSUIT see **nonsuit** [VOLUNTARY NONSUIT].

VOLUNTARY WASTE see **waste.**

VOTING see **cumulative voting.**

VOTING RIGHT in corporate law, the right to vote at a shareholder's meeting is inherent in and incidental to the ownership of corporate **stock.** However, a corporation may have more than one class of stock, in which case some of it may be non-voting stock. The laws of most states protect a shareholder's right to vote through statutes requiring annual meetings, notices of such meetings, and **pre-emptive rights.** 5 Fletcher, Cyclopedia Corporations §§2025, 2026, 2049.1, 2064, 2075-2095 (1976). Upon the issuance of new stock, shareholders usually vote to elect the directors of the corporation and vote on fundamental corporate transactions, such as a **merger** or a **dissolution.** If a shareholder does not intend to attend the shareholders' meeting, the shareholder may vote by a **proxy.** Shareholders may enter into agreements to vote their stock a certain way, or to pool their votes in a **voting trust,** so as to establish and maintain control over a corporation.

In constitutional law, the right to vote may not be denied on account of race, color, or previous condition of servitude. U.S. Const. Amend. XV, or on account of sex, U.S. Const. Amend. XIX. Furthermore, the payment of a **poll tax** as a condition to voting in a federal election is forbidden. U.S. Const. Amend. XXIV. Congress enacted the Voting Rights Act of 1965 to further combat attempts to infringe on citizens' rights to vote in public elections. 42 U.S.C. §§1971-1974(e). See also **one man [person] one vote.**

VOTING RIGHTS ACT the federal law passed in 1965 to effectuate the right of each citizen to vote under the **Fifteenth Amendment** to the U.S. Constitution. The law provides that no voting qualification, prerequisite to voting, or standard practice or procedure shall be imposed or applied by any state or political subdivision to deny or abridge the right of any citizen of the United States to vote because of race or color. 42 U.S.C. §1973. The law forbids various restrictions on the right to vote, such as literacy and educational requirements. 395 U.S. 285. Antieau, Federal Civil Rights Acts §§9-18 (1980).

VOTING TRUST the "accumulation in a single hand, or in a few hands, of **shares** of corporate **stock** belonging to many owners in order thereby to control the business of the **company.**" 152 N.E. 609, 611. "A voting trust as commonly understood is a device whereby two or more persons owning stock with voting powers, divorce the voting rights thereof from ownership, retaining to all intents and purposes the latter in themselves and transferring the former to trustees in whom the voting rights of all the depositors in the trust are pooled." 130 A. 2d 338, 344.

W

WAGE EARNER'S PLAN see bankruptcy [WAGE EARNER'S PLAN].

WAGE, MINIMUM see **minimum wage.**

WAGER OF LAW under early English law, the giving of a pledge or **surety** by a **defendant** to appear in court with the required number of COMPURGATORS [character **witnesses**] who would testify that they believed the defendant to be telling the truth. The number of compurgators was usually 11 but could vary. The form of the oath they had to recite was very strict. If one of them used the wrong word, the oath "burst" and the plaintiff won. In England, this procedure had largely died out by the 13th century but was still used occasionally as late as the 18th century in cases of **debt** and **detinue.**

Compurgation orginally became the accepted mode of **trial** adapted to members of the church when the duel and ordeal lost favor. The defendant would then be expected to bring a required number of priests and/or kinsmen as compurgators because they should best know the defendant's character. Later, for practical reasons, neighbors became acceptable compurgators. The compurgators were not witnesses but merely expressed their confidence in the veracity of the defendant. Therefore, a comparative value was attached to their **oaths.** For example, the oath of one competent witness may have outweighed the oaths of six compurgators. H. LEA, Superstition and Force 13-91 (3d ed. 1878). The defense of wager of law was much abused. Since it was only available in actions of debt, the courts permitted the creditor to sue in **assumpsit,** an action in which that defense was not available. Corbin, Contracts 29 (1952).

WAGNER ACT see **labor organization [union]** [NATIONAL LABOR RELATIONS ACT]; **Taft-Hartley Act.**

WAIT see **lying in wait.**

WAITING PERIOD generally, any period of time that must expire before a party may attempt to pursue legal rights. For instance, most states require a waiting period after a blood test or the issuance of a marriage license before a marriage may occur. 52 Am. Jur. Marriage §36 (1970). A waiting period may be unconstitutional if it interferes with a citizen's right to travel freely. For instance, a law requiring that a person be a resident of the state for one year before he or she may be eligible for welfare benefits was held unconstitutional on that ground. 394 U.S. 618. See also **red herring** [WAITING PERIOD].

WAIVER an intentional and voluntary giving up, relinquishment, or surrender of some known right. In general, a waiver may either result from an express agreement or be inferred from circumstances, 200 A. 2d 166, 172, but courts must indulge every reasonable presumption against the waiver of constitutional rights. 304 U.S. 458, 464. To forego a constitutional right, the waiver must be an "intelligent relinquishment or abandonment of a known right." Id. Courts will not imply waiver from a silent **record;** thus, to find a waiver of a constitutional right, the trial court should hold a hearing and make explicit **findings of fact** supporting a valid waiver. In criminal procedure, the defendant should personally participate in a decision to waive a constitutional right whenever his or her consent can be practicably obtained. 405 U.S. 504. Thus, the defendant may be unable to participate in strategic trial waivers but he or she can give intelligent consent to whether or not to appeal his or her conviction. See **informed consent.**

EXECUTORY WAIVER one that affects a still unperformed duty of a contracting party, as in the excuse by A of **performance** by B of something that A has a right to exact. 318 S.W. 2d 456, 459. An executory waiver does not require **consideration** but may be retracted until there has been detrimental reliance upon it. See U.C.C. §2-209(5).

IMPLIED WAIVER the waiver of substantial rights based upon the conduct of the waiving party. For an implied waiver to occur, the party alleging the waiver must have acted in detrimental **reliance** on the conduct constituting the waiver, 627 P. 2d 845, 850, and the conduct relied upon must demonstrate a clear, decisive, and unequivocal purpose to waive the legal rights involved. 420 F. 2d 1119, 1126. Compare **estoppel.**

WANT OF CONSIDERATION see **consideration** [WANT OF CONSIDERATION].

WANT OF PROSECUTION see **prosecution** [WANT OF PROSECUTION].

WANTON grossly **negligent** or careless; extremely **reckless**, etc.; virtually synonymous with reckless. 5 So. 2d 41, 45. **Willful** implies intent or purpose, while wanton expresses a reckless disregard of consequences. 88 A. 895, 896. See **negligence** [WANTON NEGLIGENCE].

WARD a person over whom or over whose property a guardian is appointed, 135 N.W. 2d 832; a person whom the law regards as incapable of managing his or her own affairs, 125 P. 2d 318. A ward retains legal **title** in his or her **property** although he or she may not make any **contracts** respecting the property. See **guardian.**

The term "ward" is also used to refer to one of the sections into which a town is divided for educational or electoral purposes. 117 N.E. 2d 227, 230.

WARDSHIP the office of **guardian.** At common law, a form of guardianship. The guardian was entitled to the wardship of a male **heir** who was under age 21, or a female under age 14. The guardian had custody of both the body and the lands of the heir, and was not required to account to the heir for the profits derived from the land. 2 Bl. Comm *67.

WAREHOUSEMAN'S LIEN see **lien** [WAREHOUSEMAN'S LIEN].

WAREHOUSE RECEIPT a receipt issued by a person (**bailee**) engaged in the business of storing **goods** for hire. U.C.C. §1-201 (45). A warehouse receipt constitutes a **document of title** under the Uniform Commercial Code, which evidences that the person in possession of the document is entitled to receive, hold, and dispose of the document and the goods it covers. U.C.C. §1-201(15). A warehouse receipt may be a **negotiable instrument,** depending upon its terms. White & Summers, Uniform Commercial Code §§20-1 to 20-5 (2d ed. 1980).

WARRANT a written **order** or **writ** from a competent authority directing the doing of a certain act, especially one directing the **arrest** of a person or persons, issued by a court, body, or official, having authority to issue ARREST WARRANTS (see below). See also **bench warrant.** 171 F. Supp. 393, 395.

The word "warrant" is also used in commercial and property law to refer to a particular kind of guarantee or assurance as to the quality and validity of what is being **conveyed** or sold. See **guarantee; merchantability; warranty.**

ARREST WARRANT an order of a court directing the sheriff or other officer to seize a particular person to answer a **complaint** or otherwise appear before the court. If a defendant fails to appear as required in court the judge will issue a **bench warrant** for arrest. For less serious offenses, it is common to issue a **summons** in lieu of an arrest warrant. See, e.g., Fed. R. Crim. Proc. 4(a). An arrest warrant is constitutionally required to enter a person's home to effect an arrest except in **exigent circumstances** such as hot pursuit. 445 U.S. 573. See **arrest; search and seizure.** Compare **warrantless arrest.**

BENCH WARRANT see **bench warrant.**

GENERAL WARRANT see **search warrant** [GENERAL WARRANTS].

SEARCH WARRANT an order that certain premises or property be searched for particularized items which if found are to be seized and used as **evidence** in a criminal **trial** or destroyed as contraband. See **search and seizure; search warrant.**

STOCK WARRANT a certificate that gives the holder the right to purchase shares of the underlying **stock** for a specified price and within a specified time period. Stock warrants usually originate as a bonus with new **issues** of **bonds, notes,** or preferred stock where they serve as an inducement to the buyer. Warrants so offered come attached to the new security and usually cannot be separated for a short period; once separated, the warrants can be traded like any other security. Warrants offer investment **leverage;** that is, for a small initial cost the buyer can participate in the price movement of the underlying and more expensive stock; warrants appeal to speculators and tend to be very volatile.

WARRANT TO SATISFY JUDGMENT

an authorization issued by the **judgment creditor's** attorney to the clerk of the court directing him or her to enter a **satisfaction** of the **judgment** in the official court records.

WARRANTLESS ARREST an **arrest** made without a warrant. At common law, an officer was justified in making an arrest without a warrant if the officer reasonably believed that the defendant had committed a **misdemeanor** in his or her presence or had committed any **felony.** There is a constitutional preference for arrest upon a warrant, however, 379 U.S. 89, and the Supreme Court has held that a warrantless arrest will be judged by a somewhat higher standard of **probable cause** than if the same arrest had occurred under the direction of a neutral and detached magistrate. Id. While warrantless arrests in public places have been upheld, 423 U.S. 411, an arrest in a private residence requires an arrest warrant unless there are exigent circumstances. 445 U.S. 573. See **search and seizure; warrant** [ARREST WARRANT].

WARRANTY an assurance by one **party** to a **contract** of the existence of a fact upon which the other party may rely, intended precisely to relieve the promisee of any duty to ascertain the fact for himself or herself, and which amounts to a promise to **indemnify** the promisee for any loss if the fact warranted proves untrue. 155 F. 2d 780, 784. Such warranties are either made overtly (EXPRESS WARRANTIES) or by implication (IMPLIED WARRANTIES). See U.C.C. §§2-312–2-318.

A **covenant** of warranty in **real property** is a convenant **running with the land,** insuring the continuing validity of **title** and the **breach** of which occurs at the time of conveyance and gives rise to an action by the last vendee against the first or any other warrantor. See 24 N.W. 333, 335.

BREACH OF WARRANTY see **breach** [BREACH OF WARRANTY].

WARRANTY OF FITNESS FOR A PARTICULAR PURPOSE a warranty that the goods are suitable for the special purpose of the buyer, which will not be satisfied by mere fitness for general purposes.

WARRANTY OF HABITABILITY [more properly, an implied or express **covenant** of **habitability**] a promise by landlord that at the inception of the lease there are no **latent defects** in facilities vital to the use of the premises for residential purposes, and that these facilities will remain in usable condition during the duration of the lease. See 56 N.J. 130, 145.

WARRANTY OF MERCHANTABILITY a warranty that the goods are reasonably fit for the general purposes for which they are sold. See U.C.C. §§2-314.

WARRANTY ACT see **Magnuson-Moss Warranty Act.**

WARRANTY DEED a **deed** that warrants that the **grantor** has the **title** he or she claims he or she has. It purports to convey property free and clear of all encumbrances, except those noted in the instrument. As a guarantee of title, the warranty deed creates liability in the grantor if the title transferred is defective. It is distinguished from a **quitclaim deed** which merely conveys whatever title the grantor has or may have, 213 P. 2d 895, 897, and which consequently does not give rise to damages in the event title is defective. The usual warranties contained in the warranty deed are **seisin, quiet enjoyment,** right to convey, freedom from encumbrances, future assurances, and defense of title against all claims. A warranty deed does not necessarily transfer a **fee simple,** but may also pass a **life estate** or a term of years. A general warranty deed warrants that the property being transferred

is not subject to any encumbrances or liens. A specific warranty deed only warrants against the encumbrances or liens specified therein. See **deed.**

WASH SALE the simultaneous buying and selling of significant volumes of a **stock issue** to create the impression of activity in the stock and, thereby, attract the attention of speculators and investors. The **Securities and Exchange Commission** prohibits wash sales along with a number of other manipulative practices. See **manipulation; painting the tape.**

For tax purposes, a sale and repurchase of stock or securities within a relatively short period of time in order to artificially create a tax loss. If a **taxpayer recognizes** a loss from the **sale or exchange** of shares of stock or securities and, within a period beginning 30 days before the date of the sale or disposition and ending 30 days after the date of sale or disposition the taxpayer purchases substantially identical stock or securities, then no loss from such sale or disposition shall be recognized. I.R.C. §1091.

WASTE generally, an act, by one in rightful **possession** of land who has less than a **fee simple** interest in the land, which decreases the value of the land or the owner's **interest** or the interest of one who has an **estate** that may become possessory at some future time (such as a **remainderman, lessor, mortgagee, reversioner**). Waste is "the deterioration or improper deterioration or material alteration of things forming an essential part of the **inheritance,** done or suffered by a person rightfully in possession by virtue of a temporary or partial estate, as, for example, a **tenant** for life or for years. The rightful possession of the wrongdoer is essential, and constitutes a material distinction between waste and **trespass.**" 21 A. 2d 354, 358.

AMELIORATING WASTE a change in the physical structure of the occupied premises by an unauthorized act of the tenant which, though technically "waste" in fact increases the value of the land, e.g., where the tenant tears out all the cabinets in the kitchen and replaces them with new cabinets of better quality. Ameliorating waste is not ordinarily grounds for liability. See 162 N.E. 621, 622.

ECONOMIC WASTE a production practice which, in light of alternatives, reduces net value of mineral resources that may be produced from a reservoir.

EQUITABLE WASTE "such acts as at law would not be [deemed] to be waste under the circumstances of the case, but which in the view of a Court of Equity are so esteemed from their manifest injury to the inheritance, although they are not inconsistent with the legal rights of the party committing them." Story, Eq. Jr. §915 (13th ed. 1886). Thus, conduct will be enjoined where the court finds it to be abusive and where the injunction is required pro bono publico. Id. Courts may be guided by the standard of "that which a prudent man would not do with his own property" in defining the limits of this equity power. See 62 N.E. 210, 214.

PERMISSIVE WASTE injury to the inheritance caused by the tenant's failure to make the reasonable repairs to the premises which are expected of the tenant; e.g., a life tenant or tenant for years, fails to cover a hole in the roof of the dwelling house on the leased premises and as a result the floors and ceilings are damaged by rainfall. A tenant is bound to make ordinary repairs. Id.

PHYSICAL WASTE a production practice which in light of alterna-

tives, reduces the quantity of mineral resources that may be produced from a reservoir.

VOLUNTARY WASTE "injury to the inheritance caused by an affirmative act of the tenant." Id. at 237.

WASTING ASSET an asset that will be consumed through its use, 211 N.Y.S. 128, 133; property exhausted over a period of years through the progressive loss of value or consumption of the property. 71 F. 2d 292, 293. For instance, a coal mine is a wasting asset, since it contains a limited amount of coal that will be exhausted by regular mining activity.

WATERED STOCK in corporate law, shares of stock that have been issued by the corporation for less than full lawful consideration. Traditionally, par value established the consideration for which stock could be issued, and every state enacted a constitutional or statutory provision governing such consideration. However, since the enactment of the federal securities laws during the 1930's requiring the disclosure of financial information of a corporation to a potential investor, the issuance of stock at its par value has become of less importance, and stock is usually issued today with no or only nominal par value. Fletcher, Cyclopedia Corporations §§5199, 5207 and 5207.1 (1971).

WATERS see territorial waters.

WAY, RIGHT OF see right of way.

WEAPON see dangerous weapon [instrumentality]; deadly weapon; force; gun control law.

WEIGHT OF THE EVIDENCE a phrase indicating the relative value of the totality of evidence presented on one side of a judicial dispute, in light of the evidence presented on the other side, see 109 So. 2d 375, 378; refers to the persuasiveness of the testimony of the witnesses. See **against the weight of the evidence; burden of proof.**

WESTLAW see **Lexis.**

WHEN ISSUED short for "when, as, and if issued" which is a conditional trading basis for a new **stock** or **bond issue** that has been authorized for issuance but does not actually exist. WHEN-ISSUED SECURITIES can be bought or sold like ordinary **securities** except that transactions do not settle until the actual security is formally issued and the **stock exchange** involved or the **National Association of Securities Dealers** decides on a specific settlement date. The most common occasion for when-issued trading is in connection with **stock splits.** After the split is announced but before the new shares issue, the split stock may be traded on a when-issued basis. Such trading has speculative appeal since a small down payment of only 25 percent is required and since no **margin** or loan debt is required for the balance until settlement date which might be some weeks in the future.

WHIPLASH INJURY neck injury commonly associated with "rear end"-type automobile collisions; caused by a sudden and unexpected forced-forward movement of the body while the unsupported head of an automobile occupant attempts to remain stationary consistent with the laws of physics, subjecting the neck to a severe strain while in a relaxed position. 320 F. 2d 437, 441. It is a favorite **claim** in **tort** actions arising from such collisions because it is difficult to prove or disprove medically.

WHITE-COLLAR CRIME a phrase connoting a variety of frauds, schemes, corruptions, and commercial offenses committed by business persons, con artists, and public officials. The term was originally intended as a classification of offenders but has expanded to include a broad range of non-violent offenses that have cheating and dishonesty as their central element. Consumer **fraud, bribery,** and stock **manipulation** are examples of white-collar crime.

It has been observed that white-collar criminals are prosecuted sporadically, if at all, and rarely are subjected to jail sentences or any meaningful criminal sanction. A major obstacle to effective sanction is said to be the complexity of the crimes, which require enormous expenditures to prosecute. 11 Amer. Crim. L. Rev. 959, 960. See **organized crime; racketeering.**

WHITE SLAVE TRAFFIC ACT see **Mann Act.**

WHOLE LIFE INSURANCE see **insurance** [WHOLE LIFE INSURANCE].

WHOLESALER middleman; person who buys large quantities of goods and resells to other distributors rather than to ultimate consumers. Compare **jobber.**

WIDOW'S ALLOWANCE see **family allowance.**

WIDOW'S [WIDOWER'S] ELECTION see **right of election.**

WILDCAT STRIKE an unauthorized strike, 70 F. Supp. 996; a strike for which the representing labor union disclaims responsibility. Wildcat strikes are generally strikes in breach of a **collective bargaining** agreement and are usually held to be illegal. The strikers usually retain no vested or contingent interest in their positions, 145 F. 2d 199, and their employer may obtain **damages** either through **arbitration** or by a lawsuit. 370 U.S. 254, 230 F. 2d 576. See **labor organization [union].**

WILD'S CASE, RULE IN see **Rule in Wild's Case.**

WILL a person's [**testator's**] declaration of how he desires his property to be disposed of after his death. Such a declaration is revocable during his lifetime, operative for no purpose until death, and applicable to the situation which exists at his death. A will may also contain other declarations of the testator's desires as to what is to be done after he dies so long as it disposes of some property. Atkinson, Wills 2 (2d ed. 1953).

The difference between a will and a **deed** is that by means of a deed, a present **interest** passes on delivery, while a will takes effect only upon the death of the **testator.** 20 So. 2d 71, 72. "Will" is generally used as synonymous with **testament,** 74 P. 2d 27, 32, but the latter is, technically, confined to the disposition of **personal property.** 54 F. 860, 865. See **codicil; causa mortis; holographic will; noncupative will; revocation of will.** Compare **gift; inter vivos; testamentary disposition.**

JOINT [MUTUAL] WILL a single will executed jointly by two or more persons, the provisions of which are reciprocal and which show on their face that the devises and bequests therein are made one in consideration of the other. 82 N.E. 2d 382, 386.

LAST WILL AND TESTAMENT an expression commonly used to refer to the most recent document directing the disposition of the real and personal property of the party.

RECIPROCAL WILLS one or more wills in which two or more testators make testamentary dispositions in favor of each other. 106 N.W. 2d 637, 639. This can be achieved in separate wills [known as MUTUAL WILLS], 179 N.E. 2d 489, or by one will [known as a JOINT AND RECIPROCAL WILL], 360 N.Y.S. 2d 129. Such wills may be revocable by the surviving testator although some states have created a presumption in favor of irrevocability. 176 N.W. 2d 561. A JOINT WILL may be both "a will contractual in character, and a contract testamentary in nature," 454 P. 2d 438, 440, giving rise to appropriate remedies in contract for any breach thereof.

WILLFUL [WILFUL] in civil proceedings, denotes an act that is intentional, or knowing, or voluntary, as distinguished from accidental. In a criminal statute, it generally means an act done stubbornly, obstinately, perversely, or with a bad purpose; without justifiable excuse. 290 U.S. 389, 394. See Perkins & Boyce Criminal Law 875 (3rd ed. 1982).

WILLFUL NEGLIGENCE see **negligence** [WANTON NEGLIGENCE].

WILLIAMS ACT see **tender offer.**

WILLS, STATUTE OF see **Statute of Wills.**

WINDING UP the process of **liquidating** a **corporation** or **partnership.** It "involves the process of collecting the **assets,** paying the expenses involved, satisfying the creditors' claims and distributing whatever is left—the net assets, usually in cash but possibly in kind, first to any preferred shareholders according to their liquidation preferences and rights, then to any other shareholders with [more] than normal liquidation rights, and finally **pro rata** among the rest of the shareholders." Henn & Alexander, Laws of Corporations 1148 (3rd ed. 1983).

Liquidation procedures are usually prescribed and regulated by states. Partial liquidation is possible, in which case the corporation would not be dissolved. Liquidation is generally to be distinguished from **dissolution,** which refers to the termination of the legal life of the corporation or **partnership.**

WIRETAP "the acquisition of the contents of any wire or oral communication through the use of any electronic, mechanical, or other device." 18 U.S.C. §2510 (4). Federal and state law prohibit the unauthorized use or possession of wiretap devices. Key to the notion of wiretap is the expectation surrounding the communication—that it will not be subject to interception. Thus, wiretap violates federal criminal law only if it occurs by means of an unusual device, such as an electronic "bug" or a transmitter hidden in a room, since the use of telephone equipment furnished to telephone company customers, or used by the telephone company in the normal course of its business, and hearing aids are exempted. 18 U.S.C. §2510 (5). The law also applies only if information revealing the identity of the parties, or the substance, purport, or meaning of their communication is acquired. 18 U.S.C. §2510 (8).

The use of PEN REGISTERS, which record the number dialed on a telephone, have been held to be beyond the law's scope for several reasons, including since it neither hears nor monitors conversations, 565 F. 2d 385 and does not intercept communications, 442 U.S. 735; 434 U.S. 159, 166-67. Some jurisdictions, however, have accorded persons a higher degree of privacy with respect to pen register disclosures. See 450 A. 2d 952.

The use of wiretaps by governmental authorities is subject to the constitutional prohibition against unreasonable **searches and seizures,** and they can only be used after a finding of **probable cause.** 389 U.S. 347. Under federal law, only the United States Attorney General or any specially designated Assistant Attorney General may authorize a wiretap application to a federal judge. 18 U.S.C. §2516.

Use of wiretaps by private citizens against other private citizens constitutes the tort of **invasion of privacy** and gives rise to a claim for **damages.** However, consensual wiretapping by any one participant in an oral communication is not prohibited by the federal statute or the statutes of most states which have incorporated a ONE PARTY CONSENT standard. A minority of states has adopted a TWO PARTY CONSENT standard under which all participants must consent to render lawful a consensual interception.

WITHDRAWAL the removal of money or the like from the place where it is kept, such as a bank. In criminal law, it is the separation of one's self from the criminal activity; to be effective to terminate **liability** for subsequent acts of a continuing **conspiracy,** the withdrawing party's action must evince disapproval of or opposition to the criminal activities, and communicate timely to the other active members. 200 N.E. 2d 11, 14. Compare **renunciation.**

WITHHOLDING that portion of wages earned that an employer deducts, usually for income **tax** purposes, from each salary payment made to an employee. The amount so deducted is then forwarded to the government to be credited against the total tax owed by the employee at the end of the **taxable year.** See **tax** [WITHHOLDING TAX].

WITHHOLDING TAX see **tax** [WITHHOLDING TAX].

WITHOUT FAULT, LIABILITY see **strict liability.**

WITHOUT RECOURSE generally, without further rights in regard to some matter. In finance, without recourse, or "nonrecourse," refers to the fact that the borrower is not personally liable on a loan, and that the lender must look to other **security** for repayment. See **nonrecourse.**

WITH PREJUDICE see **dismissal** [DISMISSAL WITH PREJUDICE]; **prejudice.**

WITHOUT PREJUDICE see **dismissal** [DISMISSAL WITHOUT PREJUDICE]; **prejudice.**

WITH RESERVATION see **under protest.**

WITNESS one who gives evidence in a cause before a court and who **attests** or swears to facts or gives or bears **testimony** under oath, 183 N.Y.S. 2d 125, 129; to observe the execution of, as that of an **instrument** and/or to sign one's name to it to authenticate it [attestation]. 294 N.W. 357, 362.

ADVERSE [HOSTILE] WITNESS one whose relationship to the opposing party is such that his or her testimony may be prejudiced against that party, 313 P. 2d 684, 686. A witness declared to be hostile may be asked **leading questions** and is subject to cross-examination by the party that called him or her. See Fed. R. Evid. 611(c). Such a witness is sometimes described as having an **adverse interest.** See Va. Code Ann. §8.01-401.A.

CHARACTER WITNESS a witness who testifies as to the reputation of another person for truth and veracity in the community where that person lives. Character witnesses are used either to impeach or to support the testimony of a key witness. McCormick, Evidence §44 (2d ed. 1972). Using a character witness is one of three ways to use character evidence at trial. Such evidence is also used to introduce proof that the party in question has been convicted of a crime. McCormick, Evidence §43 (2d ed. 1972). Lastly, the evidence is used to show that the person has engaged in wrongful acts but has not been criminally convicted. This latter type of character evidence is disfavored, and its use is greatly limited by the courts. McCormick, Evidence §42 (2d ed. 1972).

EXPERT WITNESS see **expert witness.**

HOSTILE WITNESS see ADVERSE [HOSTILE] WITNESS (above).

LAY WITNESS see **lay witness.**

MATERIAL WITNESS a witness whose testimony is not only relevant to the matter in issue, but also without which the matter may not be resolved. The government may hold a material witness, whether the victim or an eyewitness, against his or her will in order to insure his or her presence at trial. 18 U.S.C. §3149.

WITNESS AGAINST ONESELF see **self-incrimination, privilege against.**

WORDS OF ART words that have a particular meaning to a particular area of study; e.g., in law, **last clear chance, promissory estoppel, reliance** are all words of art because they have either no or different meanings outside a legal context.

WORDS OF FIGHTING see **fighting words.**

WORDS OF LIMITATION words used in an instrument conveying an interest in property which seems to indicate the party to whom a conveyance is made but which actually indicates the type of estate taken by the grantee; for instance, in a conveyance "to B and his heirs," if "and his heirs" describe the estate taken by B, namely, a fee simple, they are words of limitation. Boyer, Survey of the Law of Property 12 (3d ed. 1981). Compare **words of purchase.**

WORDS OF PURCHASE words in a property transfer that indicate who takes the estate. The term designates the nature of the estate granted, while **words of limitation** define the property rights given to the grantee. For example, if land is transferred to "B and his heirs," a common law court might find that a **fee tail,** and not a **fee simple,** was created, whereby B took a **life estate,** and his **heirs** took succeeding life estates until the line died out. "And his heirs" would then be words of purchase, not limitation, since they describe who took the property and not what property was taken. Boyer, Survey of the Law of Property 12 (3d ed. 1981).

WORKER'S [WORKMEN'S] COMPENSATION ACTS statutes which, in general, establish the liability of an employer for injuries or sicknesses which "arise out of and in the course of employment." Prosser, Torts 532-533 (4th ed. 1971). The liability is created without regard to the fault or **negligence** of the employer. Benefits generally include hospital and other medical payments and compensation for loss of income; if the injury is covered by the statute, compensation thereunder will be the employee's only remedy against his or her employer.

These statutes have had the effect of abolishing the notion that the hazards of a particular job or workplace are voluntarily encountered by the employee by virtue of his or her agreement to work there, and thus could not give rise to liability for negligence on the part of the employer. See 132 A. 2d 505, 511. Also contrary to the common law rule, the employer is generally not exempt from liability under these statutes when the injury is caused by the negligence of a fellow-servant. See Prosser, supra, at 525-537. See **strict liability.** Compare **employers' liability acts.** See also **scope of employment.**

WORKHOUSE see **jail** [WORK-HOUSE].

WORK PRODUCT that work done by an attorney in the process of representing a client which is ordinarily not subject to **discovery;** "work product can generally be defined to encompass writings, statements, or testimony which would substantially reflect or invade an attorney's legal impressions or legal theories as to a pending or reasonably anticipated litigation. An attorney's legal impressions and theories would include . . . tactics, strategy, opin-

ions and thoughts." 34 F.R.D. 212, 213; 329 U.S. 495.

Where special necessity is demonstrated, discovery may nevertheless be had; e.g., where "relevant and non-privileged facts remain hidden in an attorney's file and production of those facts is essential to the preparation of one's case." Id. at 511.

WORTH see **net worth.**

WORTHIER TITLE, DOCTRINE OF early common law rule whereby a **gift** by **devise** [i.e., by **will**] to one's **heir** which amounted to exactly what the heir would have taken under the statutes governing **descent and distribution** had the heir's ancestor died **intestate,** was disregarded and the heir took instead by descent, which was considered as conferring a "worthier," [better] title.

The rule also has an application in **inter vivos** transfers of property; thus, a grantor may not limit a **remainder** to the grantor's own heirs. This has been recognized in many American jurisdictions as a rule of construction effectuating the intent of the grantor. Thus, a **reversion** in the grantor is preferred to a **remainder** in the grantor's heirs. See 122 N.E. 221. Otherwise, the doctrine has been abolished in most jurisdictions. See generally, Moynihan, Introduction to the Law of Real Property 149-162 (1962).

WRAPAROUND MORTGAGE in real estate law, a second **mortgage** which allows the borrower to take advantage of a low interest first mortgage without being subject to the usual cash flow demands of carrying both a first and second mortgage. The face amount of the wraparound mortgage is the amount due on the first mortgage plus the amount due on the second mortgage. Annual payments are computed on this combined amount, and are applied to satisfy the payments due on the first mortgage before being applied to the wraparound mortgage. The wraparound mortgage is frequently used in the purchase and sale of realty when the seller's mortgage is at more advantageous terms than financing available to the buyer. 2 Real Estate Rev. 35 (1972).

WRIT a mandatory precept issued by the authority and in the name of the sovereign or the state for the purpose of compelling a person to do something therein mentioned. It is issued by a court or other competent tribunal, and is directed to the sheriff or other officer authorized to execute it. In every case the writ itself contains directions as to what is required to be done. See **peremptory writ; prerogative writ.**

WRIT OF ASSISTANCE at common law, a general **warrant** under which an officer of the crown, such as a customs official, had blanket authority to search where he or she pleased for goods imported in violation of the British tax laws. Writs of assistance were greatly abused and hated in this country prior to the American Revolution, and ultimately resulted in the adoption of the constitutional ban against unreasonable **searches and seizure** and especially the requirement of particularization. 379 U.S. 476, 481-485.

In modern practice, a writ of assistance is an equitable remedy used to transfer property where the title has been previously adjudicated. 421 N.E. 2d 415, 418. The issuance of a writ of assistance is a **summary proceeding,** not a new lawsuit, which is incidental or auxiliary to a prior judgment or decree and is issued to enforce such judgment or decree. 377 N.E. 2d 1214, 1217.

WRIT OF CAPIAS see **capias.**

WRIT OF CORAM NOBIS *(kôr'-äm nō'-bĭs)*—Lat: before us; in our presence, i.e., in our court. The purpose of the writ "is to bring the attention of the court to, and obtain relief from, errors of fact, such as . . . a valid **defense** existing in the facts of the case, but which, without **negligence** on the part of the defendant, was not made, either through **duress** or **fraud** or excusable mistake; these facts not appearing on the face of the **record** [nor being facts that,] if known in season, would have prevented the rendition and entry of the **judgment** questioned. . . . [Thus,] writ does not lie to correct errors of law." 198 P. 2d 505, 506. It is addressed to the court that rendered the judgment in which injustice was allegedly done, in contrast to **appeals** or review, which are directed to another court. 269 N.Y.S. 2d 983, 986. It is another name for "WRIT OF ERROR CORAM NOBIS." Sometimes it is referred to simply as "CORAM NOBIS." Compare **new trial** motion.

WRIT OF ERROR an early common law **writ** issued out of "the **appellate court** and served on the trial judge ordering him to send up the **record** in the case. The one who sought the review, whether the plaintiff or defendant in the trial court, [is] designated as the 'plaintiff in error.' His opponent [is] the 'defendant in error.' . . . The only function of the appellate court [is] to review alleged errors of law. . . ." Green, Basic Civil Procedure 254 (2d ed. 1979). It is similar to a writ of **certiorari,** but a writ of error, unlike a writ of certiorari, is a writ of right and lies only where jurisdiction is exercised according to the course of the common law. See 29 N.E. 43, 45; and 67 Me. 429, 433.

WRIT OF EXECUTION a routine court order by which the court attempts to enforce the **judgment** that has been granted a **plaintiff** by authorizing a sheriff to levy on the property belonging to the **judgment debtor,** which is located within the county. See Green, Civil Procedure 223 (2d ed. 1979). See also **in rem; sheriff's sale.**

WRIT OF MANDAMUS see **mandamus.**

WRIT, PEREMPTORY see **peremptory writ.**

WRIT, PREROGATIVE see **prerogative writ.**

WRIT OF PROHIBITION a **prerogative writ** issued by a superior court that prevents an inferior court or tribunal from exceeding its **jurisdiction** or usurping **jurisdiction** which it has not been given by law. See 194 N.E. 2d 912, 914; 193 So. 2d 26, 29. "It is an extraordinary writ because it only issues when the party seeking it is without other means of redress for the wrong about to be inflicted by the act of the inferior tribunal." 179 So. 403, 404. Where the action sought to be prohibited is judicial in nature the writ may be exercised against public officers. See 208 S.W. 835, 839. Sometimes it is referred to simply as PROHIBITION.

WRIT OF RIGHT a **writ** generally issued as a matter of course or granted as a matter of right, in contrast to **prerogative writs** that are issued only at the discretion of the issuing authority; also the name of an ancient writ for the recovery of real property.

WRITTEN INSTRUMENT anything reduced to writing; the **agreement** or **contract** the writing contains, 44 So. 2d 184, 188. A document or writing that gives formal expression to some act. 118 N.Y.S. 433, 439. Many acts are required to be set forth in a written instrument in order to have legal effect. See **Statute of Frauds.**

WRONG generally, the violation of the legal rights of another, 175 N.Y.S. 2d 643, 645; the breach of a legal duty, 69 P. 241, 243. See **crime; tort.**

WRONGFUL ACT "[a]ny act which in the ordinary course will infringe upon the rights of another to his **damage,** unless it is done in the exercise of an equal or superior right." 73 N.J.L. 729, 744. Thus, the scope of the term is not limited to acts that are "illegal," but comprehends as well acts that are deemed immoral, anti-social, tortious, etc. See **tort.**

WRONGFUL DEATH STATUTES statutes that create a cause of action for any wrongful act, neglect, or default that causes death. The action may be brought by the **executor** or **administrator** of the **decedent's estate,** or by his surviving family, and is intended to compensate the family for the loss of the economic benefit that it would have received in the form of support, services, or contributions had the decedent lived. Wrongful death statutes are to be distinguished from **survival statutes,** which allow a decedent's estate to sue for pain and suffering, medical expenses, and lost wages resulting from the tortious act leading to death. However, both statutes provide relief from the common law rule that the death of an individual extinguishes a cause of action in a civil suit. Every American state has a wrongful death statute. Prosser, Torts §127 (4th ed. 1971). See also **Lord Campbell Act.**

WRONGFUL LIFE a tort action concerning childbirth, such as the birth of a child after the negligent performance of an operation to sterilize the parent, 356 N.E. 2d 496, 499, or the birth of a child with serious defects due to the doctor's failure to advise the parents properly. 508 F. Supp. 537, 538. Compare **wrongful death statutes.**

X

X a mark that may be used as **signature** by one who is unable to write his or her name. The mark may be placed wherever the signature could be placed and does not have to be attested unless so required by statute. A name may accompany a mark, and the mark will be sufficient even if the name is invalid due to an incorrect spelling or other error. 80 C.J.S. Signatures §4 (1953).

Y

YEAR AND A DAY RULE in criminal law, the common law rule that a death must occur within one year and one day of the act alleged to cause the death, for the death to constitute **murder.** The rule was not incorporated into the Model Penal Code and has been abandoned by most states. See, e.g., N.J.S.A. 2c: 11-2.1; Perkins & Boyce, Criminal Law 47-48 (3d ed. 1982).

YEARLY see **per annum.**

YELLOW DOG CONTRACT an employment contract expressly prohibiting the named employee from joining labor unions under pain of dismissal. See 101 P. 2d 436, 443. Typically, a yellow dog contract will contain the following three provisions: (1) a representation by the employee that he or she is not a member of a labor union; (2) a promise by the employee not to join a labor union; (3) and a promise by the employee to quit his or her job upon joining a labor union, 339 P. 2d 801, 817. Yellow dog contracts are not enforceable in federal courts, 29 U.S.C. §103, and are prohibited under the laws or the constitutions of most states. See, e.g., N.J. Constitution, Art. 1, Sec. 19 (1947). See **labor organization [union].**

YIELD refers to the current return as a percentage of the price of a stock or **bond.** For example, if a stock that sells for $25 pays a dividend of $1.25, the yield is 5 percent. In considering bond yields, the situation is somewhat more complex. The coupon yield is based on the face value of the bond and is used as a key feature along with the maturity date in describing a specific bond issue. For example, a 6 percent bond pays a semi-annual coupon of $30 which gives an annual yield of $60 per $1,000 face value for a 6 percent yield. If the bond sells in the open market for $67, then the current yield is 8.92 percent. A third bond yield is **yield-to-maturity** which takes into account the capital gain potential in a discounted bond over the remaining life of the issue.

YIELD TO MATURITY a calculation of **yield** on a bond that takes into account the **capital gain** on a discount bond or capital loss on a premium bond. In the case of a discount bond, the yield-to-maturity (YTM) is higher than the current yield or the coupon yield. The reverse is true for a premium bond with YTM lower than both current yield and coupon yield. See **yield.**

YOUNG ADULT OFFENDERS ACT see **youthful offender** [YOUNG ADULT OFFENDERS ACT].

YOUTHFUL OFFENDER term generally designating one who is, for purposes of sentencing, older than a juvenile but younger than an adult. The FEDERAL YOUTH CORRECTIONS ACT [FYCA], 18 U.S.C. §§5005-5026, discusses sentencing of persons under the age of twenty-two. The YOUNG ADULT OFFENDERS ACT, 18 U.S.C. §4216, allows for the extension of the FYCA to apply to offenders between 22 and 26 years old, at the discretion of the sentencing judge. The judge must find, however, that the treatment under the FYCA would be of no benefit to a young offender before imposing an adult sentence. 418 U.S. 424. The purpose of the

FYCA is to substitute rehabilitative treatment for retribution as a sentencing goal. 434 U.S. 542, 545. There are three essential features to the program: flexibility in choosing among a variety of treatment settings and programs tailored to individual needs; separation of youth offenders from hardened criminals; and careful and flexible control of the duration of commitment and of supervised release. 434 U.S. 542, 545-46. Further, the offender may obtain, upon successful adjustment, a certificate setting aside the conviction. 18 U.S.C. §5021. "Setting aside" has been held to mean **expungement.** 606 F. 2d 1226; 482 F. Supp. 234. Many states have similar youthful offender programs. See e.g. N.Y. Crim. Proc. L. §720.20; Mich. Comp. Laws Ann. §762.13. Compare **juvenile delinquency.**

ZERO BRACKET AMOUNT see **deductions** [ZERO BRACKET AMOUNT].

ZONE OF EMPLOYMENT that physical area within which injuries to an employee are compensible by **worker's compensation** laws; it denotes the place of employment and surrounding areas, including the means of ingress and egress, which are under control of the employer. 57 N.E. 2d 607, 608. Compare **scope of employment.**

ZONING legislative action, usually on the municipal level, which separates or divides municipalities into districts for the purpose of regulating, controlling, or in some way limiting the use of private property, and the construction and/or structural nature of buildings erected within the zones or districts established. See 198 A. 225. Local zoning authority ordinarily derives from a state constitutional grant of power to the state legislature, which in turn by statutes defers or delegates it to municipalities. See, e.g., N.J. Const. Art. IV, Sec. 6, Cl. 2 (1947) and N.J.S.A. 40:55-32. Zoning is said to be part of the state **police power,** and therefore must be for the purpose of furthering the health, morals, safety, or the general welfare of the populace. See 283 A. 2d 353, 355.

Zoning decisions are subject to judicial review against arbitrariness and compliance with **due process;** zoning ordinances properly adopted are presumed to be valid, 181 A. 2d 129 (upholding exclusion of trailer camps from an industrial district), although equal protection considerations must be satisfied. See, e.g., 75 N.W. 2d 25. Aesthetics as such have been held insufficient to support a zoning ordinance but have been upheld if adopted with "a view of conserving the value of property and encouraging the most appropriate use of land." 29 N.J. 481, 494.

APPENDIX

The Constitution of the United
  States
ABA Model Codes of Professional
  Responsibility (with 1980 amend-
  ments)
ABA Model Rules of Professional
  Conduct (1983)
Federal Judicial Circuits

THE CONSTITUTION OF THE UNITED STATES

PREAMBLE

*We the People of the United
States, in Order to form a more perfect Union, establish Justice, insure domestic Tranquility, provide
for the common defence, promote
the general Welfare, and secure the
Blessings of Liberty to ourselves
and our Posterity, do ordain and
establish this Constitution for the
United States of America.*

ARTICLE I

Section 1. All legislative Powers
herein granted shall be vested in a
Congress of the United States,
which shall consist of a Senate and
House of Representatives.

Section 2. [1] The House of Representatives shall be composed of
Members chosen every second
Year by the People of the several
States, and the Electors in each
State shall have the Qualifications
requisite for Electors of the most
numerous Branch of the State Legislature.

[2] No Person shall be a Representative who shall not have attained to the Age of twenty five
Years, and been seven Years a Citizen of the United States, and who
shall not, when elected, be an
Inhabitant of that State in which he
shall be chosen.

[3] Representatives and direct
Taxes shall be apportioned among
the several States which may be
included within this Union, according to their respective Numbers,
which shall be determined by adding to the whole Number of free
Persons, including those bound to
Service for a Term of Years, and
excluding Indians not taxed, three
fifths of all other Persons. The actual Enumeration shall be made within three Years after the first Meeting of the Congress of the United
States, and within every subsequent Term of ten Years, in such
Manner as they shall by Law
direct. The Number of Representatives shall not exceed one for every
thirty Thousand, but each State
shall have at Least one Representative: and until such enumeration
shall be made, the State of New
Hampshire shall be entitled to
chuse three, Massachusetts eight,
Rhode Island and Providence Plan-
tations one, Connecticut five, New
York six, New Jersey four, Penn-
sylvania eight, Delaware one,
Maryland six, Virginia ten, North
Carolina five, South Carolina five,
and Georgia three.

[4] When vacancies happen in the
Representation from any State, the
Executive Authority thereof shall
issue Writs of Election to fill such
Vacancies.

[5] The House of Representatives shall chuse their Speaker and
other Officers; and shall have the
sole Power of Impeachment.

Section 3. [1] The Senate of the
United States shall be composed of
two Senators from each State, chosen by the Legislature thereof, for

six Years; and each Senator shall have one Vote.

[2] Immediately after they shall be assembled in Consequence of the first Election, they shall be divided as equally as may be into three Classes. The Seats of the Senators of the first Class shall be vacated at the Expiration of the Second Year, of the second Class at the Expiration of the fourth Year, and of the third Class at the Expiration of the sixth Year, so that one third may be chosen every second Year; and if Vacancies happen by Resignation, or otherwise, during the Recess of the Legislature of any State, the Executive thereof may make temporary appointments until the next Meeting of the Legislature, which shall then fill such Vacancies.

[3] No Person shall be a Senator who shall not have attained to the Age of thirty Years, and been nine Years a Citizen of the United States, and who shall not, when elected, be an Inhabitant of that State for which he shall be chosen.

[4] The Vice President of the United States shall be President of the Senate, but shall have no Vote, unless they be equally divided.

[5] The Senate shall chuse their other Officers, and also a President pro tempore, in the Absence of the Vice President, or when he shall exercise the Office of President of the United States.

[6] The Senate shall have the sole Power to try all Impeachments. When sitting for that Purpose, they shall be on Oath or Affirmation. When the President of the United States is tried, the Chief Justice shall preside: And no Person shall be convicted without the Concurrence of two thirds of the Members present.

[7] Judgment in Cases of Impeachment shall not extend further than to removal from Office, and disqualification to hold and enjoy any Office of honor, Trust, or Profit under the United States: but the Party convicted shall nevertheless be liable and subject to Indictment, Trial, Judgment, and Punishment, according to Law.

Section 4. [1] The Times, Places and Manner of holding Elections for Senators and Representatives, shall be prescribed in each State by the Legislature thereof; but the Congress may at any time by Law make or alter such Regulations, except as to the Places of chusing Senators.

[2] The Congress shall assemble at least once in every Year, and such Meeting shall be on the first Monday in December, unless they shall by Law appoint a different Day.

Section 5. [1] Each House shall be the Judge of the Elections, Returns, and Qualifications of its own Members, and a Majority of each shall constitute a Quorum to do Business; but a smaller Number may adjourn from day to day, and may be authorized to compel the Attendance of absent Members, in such Manner, and under such Penalties as each House may provide.

[2] Each House may determine the Rules of its Proceedings, punish its Members for disorderly Behavior, and, with the Concurrence of two thirds, expel a Member.

[3] Each House shall keep a Journal of its Proceedings, and from time to time publish the same, excepting such Parts as may in their Judgment require Secrecy; and the Yeas and Nays of the Members of either House on any question shall, at the Desire of one fifth of those Present, be entered on the Journal.

[4] Neither House, during the Session of Congress, shall, without the Consent of the other, adjourn for more than three days, nor to any other Place than that in which the two Houses shall be sitting.

Section 6. [1] The Senators and Representatives shall receive a Compensation for their Services, to be ascertained by Law, and paid out of the Treasury of the United

States. They shall in all Cases, except Treason, Felony and Breach of the Peace, be privileged from Arrest during their Attendance at the Session of their respective Houses, and in going to and returning from the same; and for any Speech or Debate in either House, they shall not be questioned in any other Place.

[2] No Senator or Representative shall, during the Time for which he was elected, be appointed to any civil Office under the Authority of the United States, which shall have been created, or the Emoluments whereof shall have been increased during such time and no Person holding any office under the United States, shall be a Member of either House during his Continuance in Office.

Section 7. [1] All Bills for raising Revenue shall originate in the House of Representatives; but the Senate may propose or concur with Amendments as on other Bills.

[2] Every Bill which shall have passed the House of Representatives and the Senate, shall, before it becomes a Law, be presented to the President of the United States; If he approve he shall sign it, but if not he shall return it, with his Objections to the House in which it shall have originated, who shall enter the Objections at large on their Journal, and proceed to reconsider it. If after such Reconsideration two thirds of that House shall agree to pass the Bill, it shall be sent together with the Objections, to the other House, by which it shall likewise be reconsidered, and if approved by two thirds of that House, it shall become a Law. But in all such Cases the Votes of both Houses shall be determined by Yeas and Nays, and the Names of the Persons voting for and against the Bill shall be entered on the Journal of each House respectively. If any Bill shall not be returned by the President within ten Days (Sundays excepted) after it shall have been presented to him, the Same shall be a Law, in like Manner as if he had signed it, unless the Congress by their Adjournment prevent its Return in which Case it shall not be a Law.

[3] Every Order, Resolution, or Vote, to Which the Concurrence of the Senate and House of Representatives may be necessary (except on a question of Adjournment) shall be presented to the President of the United States; and before the Same shall take Effect, shall be approved by him, or being disapproved by him, shall be repassed by two thirds of the Senate and House of Representatives, according to the Rules and Limitations prescribed in the Case of a Bill.

Section 8. [1] The Congress shall have Power To lay and collect Taxes, Duties, Imposts and Excises, to pay the Debts and provide for the common Defence and general Welfare of the United States; but all Duties, Imposts and Excises shall be uniform throughout the United States;

[2] To borrow money on the credit of the United States;

[3] To regulate Commerce with foreign Nations, and among the several States, and with the Indian Tribes;

[4] To establish an uniform Rule of Naturalization, and uniform Laws on the subject of Bankruptcies throughout the United States;

[5] To coin Money, regulate the Value thereof, and of foreign Coin, and fix the Standard of Weights and Measures;

[6] To provide for the Punishment of counterfeiting the Securities and current Coin of the United States;

[7] To Establish Post Offices and Post Roads;

[8] To promote the Progress of Science and useful Arts, by securing for limited Times to Authors and Inventors the exclusive Right to their respective Writings and Discoveries;

[9] To constitute Tribunals inferior to the supreme Court;

[10] To define and punish Piracies and Felonies committed on the high Seas, and Offenses against the Law of Nations;

[11] To declare War, grant Letters of Marque and Reprisal, and make Rules concerning Captures on Land and Water;

[12] To raise and support Armies, but no Appropriation of Money to that Use shall be for a longer Term than two Years;

[13] To provide and maintain a Navy;

[14] To make Rules for the Government and Regulation of the land and naval Forces;

[15] To provide for calling forth the Militia to execute the Laws of the Union, suppress Insurrections and repel Invasions;

[16] To provide for organizing, arming, and disciplining, the Militia, and for governing such Part of them as may be employed in the Service of the United States, reserving to the States respectively, the Appointment of the Officers, and the Authority of training the Militia according to the discipline prescribed by Congress;

[17] To exercise exclusive Legislation in all Cases whatsoever, over such District (not exceeding ten Miles square) as may, by Cession of particular States, and the Acceptance of Congress, become the Seat of the Government of the United States, and to exercise like Authority over all Places purchased by the Consent of the Legislature of the State in which the Same shall be, for the Erection of Forts, Magazines, Arsenals, dock-Yards, and other needful Buildings;—And

[18] To make all Laws which shall be necessary and proper for carrying into Execution the foregoing Powers, and all other Powers vested by this Constitution in the Government of the United States, or in any Department or Officer thereof.

Section 9. [1] The Migration or Importation of Such Persons as any of the States now existing shall think proper to admit, shall not be prohibited by the Congress prior to the Year one thousand eight hundred and eight, but a Tax or duty may be imposed on such Importation, not exceeding ten dollars for each Person.

[2] The privilege of the Writ of Habeas Corpus shall not be suspended, unless when in Cases of Rebellion or Invasion the public Safety may require it.

[3] No Bill of Attainder or ex post facto Law shall be passed.

[4] No Capitation, or other direct, Tax shall be laid, unless in Proportion to the Census or Enumeration herein before directed to be taken.

[5] No Tax or Duty shall be laid on Articles exported from any State.

[6] No Preference shall be given by any Regulation of Commerce or Revenue to the Ports of one State over those of another: nor shall Vessels bound to, or from, one State be obliged to enter, clear, or pay Duties in another.

[7] No money shall be drawn from the Treasury, but in Consequence of Appropriations made by Law; and a regular Statement and Account of the Receipts and Expenditures of all public Money shall be published from time to time.

[8] No Title of Nobility shall be granted by the United States: And no Person holding any Office of Profit or Trust under them, shall, without the Consent of the Congress, accept of any present, Emolument, Office, or Title, of any kind whatever, from any King, Prince, or foreign State.

Section 10. [1] No state shall enter into any Treaty, Alliance, or Confederation: grant Letters of Marque and Reprisal; coin Money; emit Bills of Credit; make any Thing but gold and silver Coin a Tender in Payment of Debts; pass any Bill of Attainder, ex post facto Law, or Law impairing the Obligation of Contracts, or grant any Title of Nobility.

[2] No State shall, without the Consent of the Congress, lay any Imposts or Duties on Imports or Exports, except what may be absolutely necessary for executing its inspection Laws: and the net Produce of all Duties and Imposts, laid by any State on Imports or Exports, shall be for the Use of the Treasury of the United States; and all such Laws shall be subject to the Revision and Controul of the Congress.

[3] No State shall, without the Consent of Congress, lay any Duty of Tonnage, keep Troops, or Ships of War in time of Peace, enter into any Agreement or Compact with another State, or with a foreign Power, or engage in War, unless actually invaded, or in such imminent Danger as will not admit of delay.

ARTICLE II

Section 1. [1] The executive Power shall be vested in a President of the United States of America. He shall hold his Office during the Term of four Years, and, together with the Vice President, chosen for the same Term, be elected, as follows:

[2] Each State shall appoint, in such Manner as the Legislature thereof may direct, a Number of Electors, equal to the whole Number of Senators and Representatives to which the State may be entitled in the Congress; but no Senator or Representative, or Person holding an Office of Trust or Profit under the United States, shall be appointed an Elector.

[3] The Electors shall meet in their respective States, and vote by Ballot for two Persons, of whom one at least shall not be an Inhabitant of the same State with themselves. And they shall make a List of all the Persons voted for, and of the Number of Votes for each; which List they shall sign and certify, and transmit sealed to the Seat of the Government of the United States, directed to the President of the Senate. The President of the Senate shall, in the Presence of the Senate and House of Representatives, open all the Certificates, and the Votes shall then be counted. The Person having the greatest Number of Votes shall be the President, if such Number be a Majority of the whole Number of Electors appointed; and if there be more than one who have such Majority, and have an equal Number of Votes, then the House of Representatives shall immediately chuse by Ballot one of them for President; and if no Person have a Majority, then from the five highest on the List the said House shall in like Manner chuse the President. But in chusing the President, the Votes shall be taken by States the Representation from each State having one Vote; A quorum for this Purpose shall consist of a Member or Members from two thirds of the States, and a Majority of all the States shall be necessary to a Choice. In every Case, after the Choice of the President, the Person having the greater Number of Votes of the Electors shall be the Vice President. But if there should remain two or more who have equal votes, the Senate shall chuse from them by Ballot the Vice President.

[4] The Congress may determine the Time of chusing the Electors, and the Day on which they shall give their Votes; which Day shall be the same throughout the United States.

[5] No person except a natural born Citizen, or a Citizen of the United States, at the time of the Adoption of this Constitution, shall be eligible to the Office of President; neither shall any Person eligible to that Office who shall not have attained to the Age of thirty five Years, and been fourteen Years a Resident within the United States.

[6] In case of the removal of the President from Office, or of his Death, Resignation or Inability to discharge the Powers and Duties of

the said Office, the Same shall devolve on the Vice President, and the Congress may by Law provide for the Case of Removal, Death, Resignation or Inability, both of the President and Vice President, declaring what Officer shall then act as President, and such Officer shall act accordingly, until the Disability be removed, or a President shall be elected.

[7] The President shall, at stated Times, receive for his Services, a Compensation, which shall neither be increased nor diminished during the Period for which he shall have been elected, and he shall not receive within that Period any other Emolument from the United States, or any of them.

[8] Before he enter on the Execution of his Office, he shall take the following Oath or Affirmation: "I do solemnly swear (or affirm) that I will faithfully execute the Office of President of the United States, and will to the best of my Ability, preserve, protect and defend the Constitution of the United States."

Section 2. [1] The President shall be Commander in Chief of the Army and Navy of the United States, and of the militia of the several states, when called into the actual Service of the United States; he may require the Opinion, in writing, of the principal Officer in each of the Executive Departments, upon any Subject relating to the Duties of their respective Offices, and he shall have Power to grant Reprieves and Pardons for Offenses against the United States, except in Cases of Impeachment.

[2] He shall have Power, by and with the Advice and Consent of the Senate to make Treaties, provided two thirds of the Senators present concur; and he shall nominate, and by and with the Advice and Consent of the Senate, shall appoint Ambassadors, other public Ministers and Consuls, Judges of the supreme Court, and all other Officers of the United States, whose Appointments are not herein other-

wise provided for, and which shall be established by Law; but the Congress may by Law vest the Appointment of such inferior Officers, as they think proper, in the President alone, in the Courts of Law, or in the Heads of Departments.

[3] The President shall have Power to fill up all Vacancies that may happen during the Recess of the Senate, by granting Commissions which shall expire at the End of their next Session.

Section 3. He shall from time to time give to the Congress Information of the State of the Union, and recommend to their Consideration such Measures as he shall judge necessary and expedient; he may, on extraordinary Occasions, convene both Houses, or either of them, and in Case of Disagreement between them, with Respect to the Time of Adjournment, he may adjourn them to such Time as he shall think proper; he shall receive Ambassadors and other public Ministers; he shall take Care that the Laws be faithfully executed, and shall Commission all the Officers of the United States.

Section 4. The President, Vice President and all civil Officers of the United States, shall be removed from Office on Impeachment for, and Conviction of, Treason, Bribery, or other high Crimes and Misdemeanors.

ARTICLE III

Section 1. The judicial Power of the United States, shall be vested in one supreme Court, and in such inferior Courts as the Congress may from time to time ordain and establish. The Judges, both of the supreme and inferior Courts, shall hold their Offices during good Behavior, and shall, at stated Times, receive for their Services a Compensation, which shall not be diminished during their Continuance in Office.

Section 2. [1] The judicial Power shall extend to all Cases, in Law and Equity, arising under this Constitution, the Laws of the United States, and Treaties made, or which shall be made, under their Authority;—to all Cases affecting Ambassadors, other public Ministers and Consuls;—to all Cases of admiralty and maritime Jurisdiction;—to Controversies to which the United States shall be a Party;—to Controversies between two or more States;—between a State and Citizens of another State;—between Citizens of different States;—between Citizens of the same State claiming Lands under the Grants of different States, and between a State, or the Citizens thereof, and foreign States, Citizens or Subjects.

[2] In all Cases affecting Ambassadors, other public Ministers and Consuls, and those in which a State shall be a Party, the supreme Court shall have original Jurisdiction. In all the other Cases before mentioned, the supreme Court shall have appellate Jurisdiction, both as to Law and Fact, with such Exceptions, and under such Regulations as the Congress shall make.

[3] The trial of all Crimes, except in Cases of Impeachment, shall be by Jury; and such Trial shall be held in the State where the said Crimes shall have been committed; but when not committed within any State, the Trial shall be at such Place or Places as the Congress may by Law have directed.

Section 3. [1] Treason against the United States, shall consist only in levying War against them, or, in adhering to their Enemies, giving them Aid and Comfort. No person shall be convicted of Treason unless on the Testimony of two Witnesses to the same overt Act, or on Confession in open Court.

[2] The Congress shall have Power to declare the Punishment of Treason, but no Attainder of Treason shall work Corruption of Blood, or Forfeiture except during the Life of the Person attainted.

ARTICLE IV

Section 1. Full Faith and Credit shall be given in each State to the public Acts, Records, and judicial Proceedings of every other State. And the Congress may by general Laws prescribe the Manner in which such Acts, Records and Proceedings shall be proved, and the Effect thereof.

Section 2. [1] The Citizens of each State shall be entitled to all Privileges and Immunities of Citizens in the several states.

[2] A Person charged in any State with Treason, Felony, or other Crime, who shall flee from justice, and be found in another State, shall on demand of the executive Authority of the State from which he fled, be delivered up, to be removed to the State having Jurisdiction of the Crime.

[3] No Person held to Service or Labour in one State, under the Laws thereof, escaping into another, shall, in Consequence of any Law or Regulation therein, be discharged from such Service or Labour, but shall be delivered up on Claim of the Party to whom such Service or Labour may be due.

Section 3. [1] New States may be admitted by the Congress into this Union; but no new State shall be formed or erected within the Jurisdiction of any other State; nor any State be formed by the Junction of two or more States, or Parts of States, without the Consent of the Legislatures of the States concerned as well as of the Congress.

[2] The Congress shall have Power to dispose of and make all needful Rules and Regulations respecting the Territory or other Property belonging to the United States; and nothing in this Constitution shall be so construed as to Prejudice any Claims of the United States, or of any particular State.

Section 4. The United States shall guarantee to every State in this Union a Republican Form of Government, and shall protect each of them against Invasion; and on

Application of the Legislature, or of the Executive (when the Legislature cannot be convened) against domestic Violence.

ARTICLE V

The Congress, whenever two thirds of both Houses shall deem it necessary, shall propose Amendments to this Constitution, or, on the Application of the Legislatures of two thirds of the several States, shall call a Convention for proposing Amendments, which, in either Case, shall be valid to all Intents and Purposes, as part of this Constitution, when ratified by the Legislatures of three fourths of the several States, or by Conventions in three fourths thereof, as the one or the other Mode of Ratification may be proposed by the Congress; Provided that no Amendment which may be made prior to the Year One thousand eight hundred and eight shall in any Manner affect the first and fourth Clauses in the Ninth Section of the first Article; and that no State, without its Consent, shall be deprived of its equal Suffrage in the Senate.

ARTICLE VI

[1] All Debts contracted and Engagements entered into, before the Adoption of this Constitution shall be as valid against the United States under this Constitution, as under the Confederation.

[2] This Constitution, and the Laws of the United States which shall be made in Pursuance thereof; and all Treaties made, or which shall be made, under the Authority of the United States, shall be the supreme Law of the Land; and the Judges in every State shall be bound thereby, any Thing in the Constitution or Laws of any State to the Contrary notwithstanding.

[3] The Senators and Representatives before mentioned, and the Members of the several State Legislatures, and all executive and judicial Officers, both of the United States and of the several States, shall be bound by Oath or Affirma-tion, to support this Constitution; but no religious Test shall ever be required as a Qualification to any Office or public Trust under the United States.

ARTICLE VII

The Ratification of the Conventions of nine States shall be sufficient for the Establishment of this Constitution between the States so ratifying the Same.

ARTICLES IN ADDITION TO, AND AMENDMENT OF, THE CONSTITUTION OF THE UNITED STATES OF AMERICA, PROPOSED BY CONGRESS, AND RATIFIED BY THE LEGISLATURES OF THE SEVERAL STATES PURSUANT TO THE FIFTH ARTICLE OF THE ORIGINAL CONSTITUTION.

PREAMBLE
TO
BILL OF RIGHTS
(First Ten Amendments)

The conventions of a number of the States having at the time of their adopting the Constitution, expressed a desire, in order to prevent misconstruction or abuse of its powers, that further declaratory and restrictive clauses should be added: And as extending the ground of public confidence in the Government, will best insure the beneficient ends of its institution.

AMENDMENT I [1791]

Congress shall make no law respecting an establishment of religion, or prohibiting the free exercise thereof; or abridging the freedom of speech, or of the press; or the right of the people peaceably to assemble, and to petition the Government for a redress of grievances.

AMENDMENT II [1791]

A well regulated Militia, being necessary to the security of a free State, the right of the people to keep and bear Arms, shall not be infringed.

AMENDMENT III [1791]

No Soldier shall, in time of peace be quartered in any house, without the consent of the Owner, nor in time of war, but in a manner to be prescribed by law.

AMENDMENT IV [1791]

The right of the people to be secure in their persons, houses, papers, and effects, against unreasonable searches and seizures, shall not be violated, and no Warrants shall issue, but upon probable cause, supported by Oath or affirmation, and particularly describing the place to be searched, and the persons or things to be seized.

AMENDMENT V [1791]

No person shall be held to answer for a capital, or otherwise infamous crime, unless on a presentment or indictment of a Grand Jury, except in cases arising in the land or naval forces, or in the Militia, when in actual service in time of War or public danger; nor shall any person be subject for the same offence to be twice put in jeopardy of life or limb; nor shall be compelled in any criminal case to be a witness against himself, nor be deprived of life, liberty, or property, without due process of law; nor shall private property be taken for public use, without just compensation.

AMENDMENT VI [1791]

In all criminal prosecutions, the accused shall enjoy the right to a speedy and public trial, by an impartial jury of the State and district wherein the crime shall have been committed, which district shall have been previously ascertained by law, and to be informed of the nature and cause of the accusation; to be confronted with the witness against him; to have compulsory process for obtaining witnesses in his favor, and to have the Assistance of Counsel for his defence.

AMENDMENT VII [1791]

In Suits at common law, where the value in controversy shall exceed twenty dollars, the right of trial by jury shall be preserved, and no fact tried by jury, shall be otherwise re-examined in any Court of the United States, than according to the rules of the common law.

AMENDMENT VIII [1791]

Excessive bail shall not be required, nor excessive fines imposed, nor cruel and unusual punishments inflicted.

AMENDMENT IX [1791]

The enumeration in the Constitution, of certain rights, shall not be construed to deny or disparage others retained by the people.

AMENDMENT X [1791]

The powers not delegated to the United States by the Constitution, nor prohibited by it to the States, are reserved to the States respectively, or to the people.

AMENDMENT XI [1798]

The Judicial power of the United States shall not be construed to extend to any suit in law or equity, commenced or prosecuted against one of the United States by Citizens of another State, or by Citizens or Subjects of any Foreign State.

AMENDMENT XII [1804]

The Electors shall meet in their respective states and vote by ballot for President and Vice-President, one of whom, at least, shall not be an inhabitant of the same state with themselves; they shall name in their ballots the person voted for as President, and in distinct ballots the person voted for as Vice-President, and they shall make distinct lists of all persons voted for as President, and of all persons voted for as Vice-President, and of the number of votes for each, which lists they shall sign and certify, and transmit sealed to the seat of the government of the United States, directed to the President of the Senate;—

The President of the Senate shall, in the presence of the Senate and House of Representatives, open all the certificates and the votes shall then be counted;—The person having the greatest number of votes for President, shall be the President, if such number be a majority of the whole number of Electors appointed; and if no person have such majority, then from the persons having the highest numbers not exceeding three on the list of those voted for as President, the House of Representatives shall choose immediately, by ballot, the President. But in choosing the President, the votes shall be taken by states, the representation from each state having one vote; a quorum for this purpose shall consist of a member or members from two-thirds of the states, and a majority of all the states shall be necessary to a choice. And if the House of Representatives shall not choose a President whenever the right of choice shall devolve upon them before the fourth day of March next following, then the Vice-President shall act as President, as in the case of the death or other constitutional disability of the President.—The person having the greatest number of votes as Vice-President, shall be the Vice-President, if such number be a majority of the whole number of Electors appointed, and if no person have a majority, then from the two highest numbers on the list, the Senate shall choose the Vice-President; a quorum for the purpose shall consist of two-thirds of the whole number of Senators, and a majority of the whole number shall be necessary to a choice. But no person constitutionally ineligible to the office of President shall be eligible to that of Vice-President of the United States.

AMENDMENT XIII [1865]

Section 1. Neither slavery nor involuntary servitude, except as a punishment for crime whereof the party shall have been duly convicted, shall exist within the United States, or any place subject to their jurisdiction.

Section 2. Congress shall have power to enforce this article by appropriate legislation.

AMENDMENT XIV [1868]

Section 1. All persons born or naturalized in the United States, and subject to the jurisdiction thereof, are citizens of the United States and of the State wherein they reside. No State shall make or enforce any law which shall abridge the privileges or immunities of citizens of the United States; nor shall any State deprive any person of life, liberty, or property, without due process of law; nor deny to any person within its jurisdiction the equal protection of the laws.

Section 2. Representatives shall be apportioned among the several States according to their respective numbers, counting the whole number of persons in each State excluding Indians not taxed. But when the right to vote at any election for the choice of electors for President and Vice President of the United States, Representatives in Congress, the Executive and Judicial officers of a State, or the members of the Legislature thereof, is denied to any of the male inhabitants of such State, being twenty-one years of age, and citizens of the United States, or in any way abridged, except for participation in rebellion, or other crime, the basis of representation therein shall be reduced in the proportion which the number of such male citizens shall bear to the whole number of male citizens twenty-one years of age in such State.

Section 3. No person shall be a Senator or Representative in Congress, or elector of President and Vice President, or hold any office, civil or military, under the United States, or under any State, who having previously taken an oath, as a member of Congress, or as an officer of the United States, or as a member of any State legislature, or as an executive or judicial officer of any State, to support the Constitution of the United States, shall have engaged in insurrection or rebellion against the same, or given aid or comfort to the enemies thereof. But Congress may by a vote of two-thirds of each House, remove such disability.

Section 4. The validity of the public debt of the United States, authorized by law, including debts incurred for payment of pensions and bounties for services in suppressing insurrection or rebellion, shall not be questioned. But neither the United States nor any State shall assume or pay any debt or obligation incurred in aid of insurrection or rebellion against the United States, or any claim for the loss or emancipation of any slave; but all such debts, obligations and claims shall be held illegal and void.

Section 5. The Congress shall have power to enforce, by appropriate legislation, the provisions of this article.

AMENDMENT XV [1870]

Section 1. The right of citizens of the United States to vote shall not be denied or abridged by the United States or by any State on account of race, color, or previous condition of servitude.

Section 2. The Congress shall have power to enforce this article by appropriate legislation.

AMENDMENT XVI [1913]

The Congress shall have power to lay and collect taxes on incomes, from whatever source derived, without apportionment among the several States, and without regard to any census or enumeration.

AMENDMENT XVII [1913]

[1] The Senate of the United States shall be composed of two Senators from each State, elected by the people thereof, for six years; and each Senator shall have one vote. The electors in each State shall have the qualifications requisite for electors of the most numerous branch of the State legislatures.

[2] When vacancies happen in the representation of any State in the Senate, the executive authority of such State shall issue writs of election to fill such vacancies: *Provided,* That the legislature of any State may empower the executive thereof to make temporary appointments until the people fill the vacancies by election as the legislature may direct.

[3] This amendment shall not be so construed as to affect the election or term of any Senator chosen before it becomes valid as part of the Constitution.

AMENDMENT XVIII [1919]

Section 1. After one year from the ratification of this article the manufacture, sale, or transportation of intoxicating liquors within, the importation thereof into, or the exportation thereof from the United States and all territory subject to the jurisdiction thereof for beverage purposes is hereby prohibited.

Section 2. The Congress and the several States shall have concurrent power to enforce this article by appropriate legislation.

Section 3. This article shall be inoperative unless it shall have been ratified as an amendment to the Constitution by the legislatures of the several States, as provided in the Constitution, within seven years from the date of the submission hereof to the States by Congress.

AMENDMENT XIX [1920]

[1] The right of citizens of the United States to vote shall not be denied or abridged by the United States or by any State on account of sex.

[2] Congress shall have power to enforce this article by appropriate legislation.

AMENDMENT XX [1933]

Section 1. The terms of the President and Vice President shall end at noon on the 20th day of January, and the terms of Senators and Representatives at noon on the 3d day of January, of the years in which such terms would have ended if this article had not been ratified; and the terms of their successors shall then begin.

Section 2. The Congress shall assemble at least once in every year, and such meeting shall begin at noon on the 3d day of January, unless they shall by law appoint a different day.

Section 3. If, at the time fixed for the beginning of the term of the President, the President elect shall have died, the Vice President elect shall become President. If the President shall not have been chosen before the time fixed for the beginning of his term, or if the President elect shall have failed to qualify, then the Vice President elect shall act as President until a President shall have qualified; and the Congress may by law provide for the case wherein neither a President elect nor a Vice President elect shall have qualified, declaring who shall then act as President, or the manner in which one who is to act shall be selected, and such person shall act accordingly until a President or Vice President shall have qualified.

Section 4. The Congress may by law provide for the case of the death of any of the persons from whom the House of Representatives may choose a President whenever the right of choice shall have devolved upon them, and for the case of the death of any of the persons from whom the Senate may choose a Vice President whenever the right of choice shall have devolved upon them.

Section 5. Sections 1 and 2 shall take effect on the 15th day of October following the ratification of this article.

Section 6. This article shall be inoperative unless it shall have been ratified as an amendment to the Constitution by the legislatures of three-fourths of the several States within seven years from the date of its submission.

AMENDMENT XXI [1933]

Section 1. The eighteenth article of amendment to the Constitution of the United States is hereby repealed.

Section 2. The transportation or importation into any State, Territory, or possession of the United States for delivery or use therein of intoxicating liquors, in violation of the laws thereof, is hereby prohibited.

Section 3. This article shall be inoperative unless it shall have been ratified as an amendment to the Constitution by conventions in the several States, as provided in the Constitution, within seven years from the date of the submission hereof to the States by the Congress.

AMENDMENT XXII [1951]

Section 1. No person shall be elected to the office of the President more than twice, and no person who has held the office of President, or acted as President, for more than two years of a term to which some other person was elected President shall be elected to the office of President more than once. But this Article shall not apply to any person holding the office of President when this Article was proposed by the Congress, and shall not prevent any person who may be holding the office of President, or acting as President, during the term within which this Article becomes operative from holding the office of President or acting as President during the remainder of such term.

Section 2. This article shall be inoperative unless it shall have been ratified as an amendment to the Constitution by the legislatures of three-fourths of the several States within seven years from the date of its submission to the States by the Congress.

AMENDMENT XXIII [1961]

Section 1. The District constituting the seat of Government of the United States shall appoint in such manner as the Congress may direct:

A number of electors of President and Vice President equal to the whole number of Senators and Representatives in Congress to which the District would be entitled if it were a State, but in no event more than the least populous state; they shall be in addition to those appointed by the states, but they shall be considered, for the purposes of the election of President and Vice President, to be electors appointed by a state; and they shall meet in the District and perform such duties as provided by the twelfth article of amendment.

Section 2. The Congress shall have power to enforce this article by appropriate legislation.

AMENDMENT XXIV [1964]

Section 1. The right of citizens of the United States to vote in any primary or other election for President or Vice President, for electors for President or Vice President, or for Senator or Representative in Congress, shall not be denied or abridged by the United States, or any State by reason of failure to pay any poll tax or other tax.

Section 2. The Congress shall have the power to enforce this article by appropriate legislation.

AMENDMENT XXV [1967]

Section 1. In case of the removal of the President from office or of his death or resignation, the Vice President shall become President.

Section 2. Whenever there is a vacancy in the office of the Vice President, the President shall nominate a Vice President who shall take office upon confirmation by a majority vote of both Houses of Congress.

Section 3. Whenever the President transmits to the President pro tempore of the Senate and the Speaker of the House of Represen-
tatives his written declaration that he is unable to discharge the powers and duties of his office, and until he transmits to them a written declaration to the contrary, such powers and duties shall be discharged by the Vice President as Acting President.

Section 4. Whenever the Vice President and a majority of either the principal officers of the executive departments or of such other body as Congress may by law provide, transmit to the President pro tempore of the Senate and the Speaker of the House of Representatives their written declaration that the President is unable to discharge the powers and duties of his office, the Vice President shall immediately assume the powers and duties of the office as Acting President.

Thereafter, when the President transmits to the President pro tempore of the Senate and the Speaker of the House of Representatives his written declaration that no inability exists, he shall resume the powers and duties of his office unless the Vice President and a majority of either the principal officers of the executive department or of such other body as Congress may by law provide, transmit within four days to the President pro tempore of the Senate and the Speaker of the House of Representatives their written declaration and the President is unable to discharge the powers and duties of his office. Thereupon Congress shall decide the issue, assembling within forty-eight hours for that purpose if not in session. If the Congress, within twenty-one days after receipt of the latter written declaration, or, if Congress is not in session, within twenty-one days after Congress is required to assemble, determines by two-thirds vote of both Houses that the President is unable to discharge the power and duties of his office, the Vice President shall continue to discharge the same as Acting President; otherwise, the President shall resume the powers and duties of his office.

AMENDMENT XXVI [1971]

Section 1. The right of citizens of the United States, who are eighteen years of age or older, to vote shall not be denied or abridged by the United States or by any State on account of age.

Section 2. The Congress shall have power to enforce this article by appropriate legislation.

PROPOSED CONSTITUTIONAL AMENDMENT*

Section 1. For purposes of representation in Congress, election of the President and Vice President, and Article V of this Constitution,

the District constituting the seat of government of the United States shall be treated as though it were a State.

Section 2. The exercise of the rights and powers conferred under this article shall be by the people of the District constituting the seat of government and shall be as provided by Congress.

Section 3. The twenty-third Amendment to the Constitution is hereby repealed.

Section 4. This article shall be inoperative, unless it shall have been ratified as an amendment to the Constitution by the legislatures of three-fourths of the several States within seven years from the date of its submission.

*Congress submitted this proposed amendment to the states for ratification in August, 1978.

ABA MODEL CODE OF PROFESSIONAL RESPONSIBILITY

Editor's Note: The ABA Model Code of Professional Responsibility was originally adopted in 1969. It was amended several times, with the last amendments adopted in 1980. In August 1983, The ABA replaced the entire Model Code with the Model Rules of Professional Conduct, which appear at page 01:101.The ethics rules of the majority of the states, however, are still patterned after the Model Code. The Model Code is copyrighted by the American Bar Association.

Preamble

The continued existence of a free and democratic society depends upon recognition of the concept that justice is based upon the rule of law grounded in respect for the dignity of the individual and his capac-

ity through reason for enlightened self-government. Law so grounded makes justice possible, for only through such law does the dignity of the individual attain respect and protection. Without it, individual rights become subject to unrestrained power, respect for law is destroyed, and rational self-government is impossible.

Lawyers, as guardians of the law, play a vital role in the preservation of society. The fulfillment of this role requires an understanding by lawyers of their relationship with and function in our legal system. A consequent obligation of lawyers is to maintain the highest standards of ethical conduct.

In fulfilling his professional responsibilities, a lawyer necessarily assumes various roles that require the performance of many difficult tasks. Not every situation which he may encounter can be foreseen, but fundamental ethical principles are always present to guide him. Within the framework of these principles, a lawyer must with courage and foresight be able and ready to shape the body of the law to the ever-changing relationships of society.

The Model Code of Professional Responsibility points the way to the aspiring and provides standards by which to judge the transgressor. Each lawyer must find within his own conscience the touchstone against which to test the extent to which his actions should rise above minimum standards. But in the last analysis it is the desire for the respect and confidence of the members of his profession and of the society which he serves that should provide to a lawyer the incentive for the highest possible degree of ethical conduct. The possible loss of that respect and confidence is the ultimate sanction. So long as its practitioners are guided by these principles, the law will continue to be a noble profession. This is its greatness and its strength, which permit of no compromise.

Preliminary Statement

In furtherance of the principles stated in the Preamble, the American Bar Association has promulgated this Model Code of Professional Responsibility, consisting of three separate but interrelated parts: Canons, Ethical Considerations, and Disciplinary Rules. The Model Code is designed to be adopted by appropriate agencies both as an inspirational guide to the members of the profession and as a basis for disciplinary action when the conduct of a lawyer falls below the required minimum standards stated in the Disciplinary Rules.

Obviously the Canons, Ethical Considerations, and Disciplinary Rules cannot apply to non-lawyers; however, they do define the type of ethical conduct that the public has a right to expect not only of lawyers but also of their non-professional employees and associates in all matters pertaining to professional employment. A lawyer should ultimately be responsible for the conduct of his employees and associates in the course of the professional representation of the client.

The Canons are statements of axiomatic norms, expressing in general terms the standards of professional conduct expected of lawyers in their relationships with the public, with the legal system, and with the legal profession. They embody the general concepts from which the Ethical Consideration and the Disciplinary Rules are derived.

The Ethical Considerations are aspirational in character and represent the objectives toward which every member of the profession should strive. They constitute a body of principles upon which the lawyer can rely for guidance in many specific situations.

The Disciplinary Rules, unlike the Ethical Considerations, are mandatory in character. The Disciplinary Rules state the minimum level of conduct below which no lawyer can fall without being subject to disciplinary action. Within the framework of fair trial, the Disciplinary Rules should be uniformly applied to all lawyers, regardless of the nature of their professional activities. The Model Code makes no attempt to prescribe either disciplinary procedures or penalties for violation of a Disciplinary Rule, nor does it undertake to define standards for civil liability of lawyers for professional conduct. The severity of judgment against one found guilty of violating a Disciplinary Rule should be determined by the character of the offense and the attendant circumstances. An enforcing agency, in applying the Disciplinary Rules, may find interpretive guidance in the basic principles embodied in the Canons and in the objectives reflected in the Ethical Considerations.

CANON 1
A Lawyer Should Assist in Maintaining the Integrity and Competence
of the Legal Profession
DISCIPLINARY RULES

DR 1-101 Maintaining Integrity and Competence of the Legal Profession.

(A) A lawyer is subject to discipline if he has made a materially false statement in, or if he has deliberately failed to disclose a material fact requested in connection with, his application for admission to the bar.

(B) A lawyer shall not further the application for admission to the bar of another person known by him to be unqualified in respect to character, education, or other relevant attribute.

DR 1-102 Misconduct.

(A) A lawyer shall not:

  (1) Violate a Disciplinary Rule.

  (2) Circumvent a Disciplinary Rule through actions of another.

  (3) Engage in illegal conduct involving moral turpitude.

  (4) Engage in conduct involving dishonesty, fraud, deceit, or misrepresentation.

  (5) Engage in conduct that is prejudicial to the administration of justice.

  (6) Engage in any other conduct that adversely reflects on his fitness to practice law.

DR 1-103 Disclosure of Information to Authorities.

(A) A lawyer possessing unprivileged knowledge of a violation of DR 1-102 shall report such knowledge to a tribunal or other authority empowered to investigate or act upon such violation.

(B) A lawyer possessing unprivileged knowledge or evidence concerning another lawyer or a judge shall reveal fully such knowledge or evidence upon proper request of a tribunal or other authority empowered to investigate or act upon the conduct of lawyers or judges.

CANON 2
A Lawyer Should Assist the Legal Profession in Fulfilling Its Duty to
Make Legal Counsel Available
DISCIPLINARY RULES

DR 2-101 Publicity.

(A) A lawyer shall not, on behalf of himself, his partner, associate or any other lawyer affiliated with him or his firm, use or participate in the use of any form of public communication containing a false, fraudulent, misleading, deceptive, self-laudatory or unfair statement or claim.

(B) In order to facilitate the process of informed selection of a lawyer by potential consumers of legal services, a lawyer may publish or broadcast, subject to DR 2-103, the following information in print media distributed or over television or radio broadcast in the geographic area or areas in which the lawyer resides or maintains offices or in which a significant part of the lawyer's clientele resides, provided that the information disclosed by the lawyer in such publication or broadcast complies with DR 2-101(A), and is presented in a dignified manner:

  (1) Name, including name of law firm and names of

professional associates; addresses and telephone numbers;
(2) One or more fields of law in which the lawyer or law firm practices, a statement that practice is limited to one or more fields of law, or a statement that the lawyer or law firm specializes in a particular field of law practice, to the extent authorized under DR 2-105;
(3) Date and place of birth;
(4) Date and place of admission to the bar of state and federal courts;
(5) Schools attended, with dates of graduation, degrees and other scholastic distinctions;
(6) Public or quasi-public offices;
(7) Military service;
(8) Legal authorships;
(9) Legal teaching positions;
(10) Memberships, offices, and committee assignments, in bar associations;
(11) Membership and offices in legal fraternities and legal societies;
(12) Technical and professional licenses;
(13) Memberships in scientific, technical and professional associations and societies;
(14) Foreign language ability;
(15) Names and addresses of bank references;
(16) With their written consent, names of clients regularly represented;
(17) Prepaid or group legal services programs in which the lawyer participates;
(18) Whether credit cards or other credit arrangements are accepted;

(19) Office and telephone answering service hours;
(20) Fee for an initial consultation;
(21) Availability upon request of a written schedule of fees and/or an estimate of the fee to be charged for specific services;
(22) Contingent fee rates subject to DR 2-106(C), provided that the statement discloses whether percentages are computed before or after deduction of costs;
(23) Range of fees for services, provided that the statement discloses that the specific fee within the range which will be charged will vary depending upon the particular matter to be handled for each client and the client is entitled without obligation to an estimate of the fee within the range likely to be charged, in print size equivalent to the largest print used in setting forth the fee information;
(24) Hourly rate, provided that the statement discloses that the total fee charged will depend upon the number of hours which must be devoted to the particular matter to be handled for each client and the client is entitled to without obligation an estimate of the fee likely to be charged, in print size at least equivalent to the largest print used in setting forth the fee information;
(25) Fixed fees for specific legal services,* the description of which would not be misunderstood or be

*The agency having jurisdiction under state law may desire to issue appropriate guidelines defining "specific legal services"

deceptive, provided that the statement discloses that the quoted fee will be available only to clients whose matters fall into the services described and that the client is entitled without obligation to a specific estimate of the fee likely to be charged in print size at least equivalent to the largest print used in setting forth the fee information.

(C) Any person desiring to expand the information authorized for disclosure in DR 2-101(B), or to provide for its dissemination through other forums may apply to [the agency having jurisdiction under state law]. Any such application shall be served upon [the agencies having jurisdiction under state law over the regulation of the legal profession and consumer matters] who shall be heard, together with the applicant, on the issue of whether the proposal is necessary in light of the existing provisions of the Code, accords with standards of accuracy, reliability and truthfulness, and would facilitate the process of informed selection of lawyers by potential consumers of legal services. The relief granted in response to any such application shall be promulgated as an amendment to DR 2-101(B), universally applicable to all lawyers.**

(D) If the advertisement is communicated to the public over television or radio, it shall be prerecorded, approved for broadcast by the lawyer, and a recording of the actual transmission shall be retained by the lawyer.

(E) If a lawyer advertises a fee for a service, the lawyer must render that service for no more than the fee advertised.

(F) Unless otherwise specified in the advertisement if a lawyer publishes any fee information authorized under DR 2-101(B) in a publication that is published more frequently than one time per month, the lawyer shall be bound by any representation made therein for a period of not less than 30 days after such publication. If a lawyer publishes any fee information authorized under DR 2-101(B) in a publication that is published once a month or less frequently, he shall be bound by any representation made therein until the publication of the succeeding issue. If a lawyer publishes any fee information authorized under DR 2-101(B) in a publication which has no fixed date for publication of a succeeding issue, the lawyer shall be bound by any representation made therein for a reasonable period of time after publication but in no event less than one year.

(G) Unless otherwise specified, if a lawyer broadcasts any fee information authorized under DR 2-101(B), the lawyer shall be bound by any representation made therein for a period of not less than 30 days after such broadcast.

(H) This rule does not prohibit limited and dignified identification of a lawyer as a lawyer as well as by name:

(1) In political advertisements when his professional status is germane to the political campaign or to a political issue.

(2) In public notices when the name and profession of a lawyer are required or authorized by law or are reasonably pertinent for a purpose other than the attraction of potential

---

** *The agency having jurisdiction under state law should establish orderly and expeditious procedures for ruling on such applications.*

clients.

(3) In routine reports and announcements of a bona fide business, civic, professional, or political organization in which he serves as a director or officer.

(4) In and on legal documents prepared by him.

(5) In and on legal textbooks, treatises, and other legal publications, and in dignified advertisements thereof.

(I) A lawyer shall not compensate or give any thing of value to representatives of the press, radio, television, or other communication medium in anticipation of or in return for professional publicity in a news item.

DR 2-102 Professional Notices, Letterheads and Offices.

(A) A lawyer or law firm shall not use or participate in the use of professional cards, professional announcement cards, office signs, letterheads, or similar professional notices or devices, except that the following may be used if they are in dignified form:

(1) A professional card of a lawyer identifying him by name and as a lawyer, and giving his addresses, telephone numbers, the name of his law firm, and any information permitted under DR 2-105. A professional card of a law firm may also give the names of members and associates. Such cards may be used for identification.

(2) A brief professional announcement card stating new or changed associations or addresses, change of firm name, or similar matters pertaining to the professional offices of a lawyer or law firm,

which may be mailed to lawyers, clients, former clients, personal friends, and relatives. It shall not state biographical data except to the extent reasonably necessary to identify the lawyer or to explain the change in his association, but it may state the immediate past position of the lawyer. It may give the names and dates of predecessor firms in a continuing line of succession. It shall not state the nature of the practice except as permitted under DR 2-105.

(3) A sign on or near the door of the office and in the building directory identifying the law office. The sign shall not state the nature of the practice, except as permitted under DR 2-105.

(4) A letterhead of a lawyer identifying him by name and as a lawyer, and giving his addresses, telephone numbers, the name of his law firm, associates and any information permitted under DR 2-105. A letterhead of a law firm may also give the names of members and associates, and names and dates relating to deceased and retired members. A lawyer may be designated "Of Counsel" on a letterhead if he has a continuing relationship with a lawyer or law firm, other than as a partner or associate. A lawyer or law firm may be designated as "General Counsel" or by similar professional reference on stationery of a client if he or the firm devotes a substantial amount of professional time in the representation of the client.

The letterhead of a law firm may give the names and dates of predecessor firms in a continuing line of succession.

(B) A lawyer in private practice shall not practice under a trade name, a name that is misleading as to the identity of the lawyer or lawyers practicing under such name, or a firm name containing names other than those of one or more of the lawyers in the firm, except that the name of a professional corporation or professional association may contain "P.C." or "P.A." or similar symbols indicating the nature of the organization, and if otherwise lawful a firm may use as, or continue to include in, its name the name or names of one or more deceased or retired members of the firm or of a predecessor firm in a continuing line of succession. A lawyer who assumes a judicial, legislative, or public executive or administrative post or office shall not permit his name to remain in the name of a law firm or to be used in professional notices of the firm during any significant period in which he is not actively and regularly practicing law as a member of the firm, and during such period other members of the firm shall not use his name in the firm name or in professional notices of the firm.

(C) A lawyer shall not hold himself out as having a partnership with one or more other lawyers or professional corporations unless they are in fact partners.

(D) A partnership shall not be formed or continued between or among lawyers licensed in different jurisdictions unless all enumerations of the members and associates of the firm on its letterhead and in other permissible listings make clear the jurisdictional limitations on those members and associates of the firm not licensed to practice in all listed jurisdictions; however, the same firm name may be used in each jurisdiction.

(E) Nothing contained herein shall prohibit a lawyer from using or permitting the use of, in connection with his name, an earned degree or title derived therefrom indicating his training in the law.

DR 2-103 Recommendation of Professional Employment.

(A) A lawyer shall not, except as authorized in DR 2-101 (B), recommend employment as a private practitioner, of himself, his partner, or associate to a layperson who has not sought his advice regarding employment of a lawyer.

(B) A lawyer shall not compensate or give anything of value to a person or organization to recommend or secure his employment by a client, or as a reward for having made a recommendation resulting in his employment by a client, except that he may pay the usual and reasonable fees or dues charged by any of the organizations listed in DR 2-103(D).

(C) A lawyer shall not request a person or organization to recommend or promote the use of his services or those of his partner or associate, or any other lawyer affiliated with him or his firm, as a private practitioner, except as authorized in DR 2-101, and except that

(1) He may request referrals from a lawyer referral service operated, sponsored, or approved by a bar association and may pay its fees incident thereto.

(2) He may cooperate with the legal service activities of any of the offices or

organizations enumerated in DR 2-103(D)(1) through (4) and may perform legal services for those to whom he was recommended by it to do such work if:

(a) The person to whom the recommendation is made is a member or beneficiary of such office or organization; and

(b) The lawyer remains free to exercise his independent professional judgment on behalf of his client.

(D) A lawyer or his partner or associate or any other lawyer affiliated with him or his firm may be recommended, employed or paid by, or may cooperate with, one of the following offices or organizations that promote the use of his services or those of his partner or associate or any other lawyer affiliated with him or his firm if there is no interference with the exercise of independent professional judgment in behalf of his client:

(1) A legal aid office or public defender office:

(a) Operated or sponsored by a duly accredited law school.

(b) Operated or sponsored by a bona fide nonprofit community organization.

(c) Operated or sponsored by a governmental agency.

(d) Operated, sponsored, or approved by a bar association.

(2) A military legal assistance office.

(3) A lawyer referral service operated, sponsored, or approved by a bar association.

(4) Any bona fide organization that recommends, furnishes or pays for legal services to its members or beneficiaries provided the following conditions are satisfied:

(a) Such organization, including any affiliate, is so organized and operated that no profit is derived by it from the rendition of legal services by lawyers, and that, if the organization is organized for profit, the legal services are not rendered by lawyers employed, directed, supervised or selected by it except in connection with matters where such organization bears ultimate liability of its member or beneficiary.

(b) Neither the lawyer, nor his partner, nor associate, nor any other lawyer affiliated with him or his firm, nor any non-lawyer, shall have initiated or promoted such organization for the primary purpose of providing financial or other benefit to such lawyer, partner, associate or affiliated lawyer.

(c) Such organization is not operated for the purpose of procuring legal work or financial benefit for any lawyer as a private practitioner outside of the legal services program of the organization.

(d) The member or beneficiary to whom the legal services are furnished, and not such organization, is recognized as the client of the lawyer in the matter.

(e) Any member or beneficiary who is entitled to have legal services furnished or paid for by the organization may, if such member or beneficiary so desires, select counsel other than that furnished, selected or approved by the organization for the particular matter involved; and the legal service plan of such organization provides appropriate relief for any member or beneficiary who asserts a claim that representation by counsel furnished, selected or approved would be unethical, improper or inadequate under the circumstances of the matter involved and the plan provides an appropriate procedure for seeking such relief.

(f) The lawyer does not know or have cause to know that such organization is in violation of applicable laws, rules of court and other legal requirements that govern its legal service operations.

(g) Such organization has filed with the appropriate disciplinary authority at least annually a report with respect to its legal service plan, if any, showing its terms, its schedule of benefits, its subscription charges, agreements with counsel, and financial results of its legal service activities or, if it has failed to do so, the lawyer does not know or have cause to know of such failure.

(E) A lawyer shall not accept employment when he knows or it is obvious that the person who seeks his services does so as a result of conduct prohibited under this Disciplinary Rule.

DR 2-104 Suggestion of Need of Legal Services.

(A) A lawyer who has given in-person unsolicited advice to a layperson that he should obtain counsel or take legal action shall not accept employment resulting from that advice, except that:

(1) A lawyer may accept employment by a close friend, relative, former client (if the advice is germane to the former employment), or one whom the lawyer reasonably believes to be a client.

(2) A lawyer may accept employment that results from his participation in activities designed to educate laypersons to recognize legal problems, to make intelligent selection of counsel, or to utilize available legal services if such activities are conducted or sponsored by a qualified legal assistance organization.

(3) A lawyer who is recommended, furnished or paid by a qualified legal assistance organization enumerated in DR 2-103(D)(1) through (4) may represent a member or beneficiary thereof, to the extent and under the conditions prescribed therein.

(4) Without affecting his right to accept employment, a lawyer may speak publicly or write for publication on legal topics so long as

he does not emphasize his own professional experience or reputation and does not undertake to give individual advice.

(5) If success in asserting rights or defenses of his client in litigation in the nature of a class action is dependent upon the joinder of others, a lawyer may accept, but shall not seek, employment from those contacted for the purpose of obtaining their joinder.

DR 2-105 Limitation of Practice.

(A) A lawyer shall not hold himself out publicly as a specialist, as practicing in certain areas of law or as limiting his practice permitted under DR 2-101(B), except as follows:

(1) A lawyer admitted to practice before the United States Patent and Trademark Office may use the designation "Patents," "Patent Attorney," "Patent Lawyer," or "Registered Patent Attorney" or any combination of those terms, on his letterhead and office sign.

(2) A lawyer who publicly discloses fields of law in which the lawyer or the law firm practices or states that his practice is limited to one or more fields of law shall do so by using designations and definitions authorized and approved by [the agency having jurisdiction of the subject under state law].

(3) A lawyer who is certified as a specialist in a particular field of law or law practice by [the authority having jurisdiction under state law over the subject of specialization by lawyers] may hold himself out as such, but only in accordance with the rules prescribed by that authority.

DR 2-106 Fees for Legal Services.

(A) A lawyer shall not enter into an agreement for, charge, or collect an illegal or clearly excessive fee.

(B) A fee is clearly excessive when, after a review of the facts, a lawyer of ordinary prudence would be left with a definite and firm conviction that the fee is in excess of a reasonable fee. Factors to be considered as guides in determining the reasonableness of a fee include the following:

(1) The time and labor required, the novelty and difficulty of the questions involved, and the skill requisite to perform the legal service properly.

(2) The likelihood, if apparent to the client, that the acceptance of the particular employment will preclude other employment by the lawyer.

(3) The fee customarily charged in the locality for similar legal services.

(4) The amount involved and the results obtained.

(5) The time limitations imposed by the client or by the circumstances.

(6) The nature and length of the professional relationship with the client.

(7) The experience, reputation, and ability of the lawyer or lawyers performing the services.

(8) Whether the fee is fixed or contingent.

(C) A lawyer shall not enter into an arrangement for, charge, or collect a contingent fee for representing a defendant in a criminal case.

DR 2-107 Division of Fees Among Lawyers.

(A) A lawyer shall not divide a fee

for legal services with another lawyer who is not a partner in or associate of his law firm or law office, unless:

(1) The client consents to employment of the other lawyer after a full disclosure that a division of fees will be made.

(2) The division is made in proportion to the services performed and responsibility assumed by each.

(3) The total fee of the lawyers does not clearly exceed reasonable compensation for all legal services they rendered the client.

(B) This Disciplinary Rule does not prohibit payment to a former partner or associate pursuant to a separation or retirement agreement.

DR 2-108 Agreements Restricting the Practice of a Lawyer.

(A) A lawyer shall not be a party to or participate in a partnership or employment agreement with another lawyer that restricts the right of a lawyer to practice law after the termination of a relationship created by the agreement, except as a condition to payment of retirement benefits.

(B) In connection with the settlement of a controversy or suit, a lawyer shall not enter into an agreement that restricts his right to practice law.

DR 2-109 Acceptance of Employment.

(A) A lawyer shall not accept employment on behalf of a person if he knows or it is obvious that such person wishes to:

(1) Bring a legal action, conduct a defense, or assert a position in litigation, or otherwise have steps taken for him, merely for the purpose of harassing or maliciously injuring any person.

(2) Present a claim or defense in litigation that is not warranted under existing law, unless it can be supported by good faith argument for an extension, modification, or reversal of existing law.

DR 2-110 Withdrawal from Employment.

(A) In general.

(1) If permission for withdrawal from employment is required by the rules of a tribunal, a lawyer shall not withdraw from employment in a proceeding before that tribunal without its permission.

(2) In any event, a lawyer shall not withdraw from employment until he has taken reasonable steps to avoid foreseeable prejudice to the rights of his client, including giving due notice to his client, allowing time for employment of other counsel, delivering to the client all papers and property to which the client is entitled, and complying with applicable laws and rules.

(3) A lawyer who withdraws from employment shall refund promptly any part of a fee paid in advance that has not been earned.

(B) Mandatory withdrawal.

A lawyer representing a client before a tribunal, with its permission if required by its rules, shall withdraw from employment, and a lawyer representing a client in other matters shall withdraw from employment, if:

(1) He knows or it is obvious that his client is bringing the legal action, conducting the defense, or asserting a position in the litigation, or is otherwise having steps taken for him,

merely for the purpose of harassing or maliciously injuring any person.

(2) He knows or it is obvious that his continued employment will result in violation of a Disciplinary Rule.

(3) His mental or physical condition renders it unreasonably difficult for him to carry out the employment effectively.

(4) He is discharged by his client.

(C) Permissive withdrawal.

If DR 2-110 (B) is not applicable, a lawyer may not request permission to withdraw in matters pending before a tribunal, and may not withdraw in other matters, unless such request or such withdrawal is because:

(1) His client:

   (a) Insists upon presenting a claim or defense that is not warranted under existing law and cannot be supported by good faith argument for an extension, modification, or reversal of existing law.

   (b) Personally seeks to pursue an illegal course of conduct.

   (c) Insists that the lawyer pursue a course of conduct that is illegal or that is prohibited under the Disciplinary Rules.

(d) By other conduct renders it unreasonably difficult for the lawyer to carry out his employment effectively.

(e) Insists, in a matter not pending before a tribunal, that the lawyer engage in conduct that is contrary to the judgment and advice of the lawyer but not prohibited under the Disciplinary Rules.

(f) Deliberately disregards an agreement or obligation to the lawyer as to expenses or fees.

(2) His continued employment is likely to result in a violation of a Disciplinary Rule.

(3) His inability to work with co-counsel indicates that the best interests of the client likely will be served by withdrawal.

(4) His mental or physical condition renders it difficult for him to carry out the employment effectively.

(5) His client knowingly and freely assents to termination of his employment.

(6) He believes in good faith, in a proceeding pending before a tribunal, that the tribunal will find the existence of other good cause for withdrawal.

CANON 3
A Lawyer Should Assist in Preventing the Unauthorized Practice of Law
DISCIPLINARY RULES

DR 3-101 Aiding Unauthorized Practice of Law.

(A) A lawyer shall not aid a nonlawyer in the unauthorized practice of law.

(B) A lawyer shall not practice law in a jurisdiction where to do so

would be in violation of regulations of the profession in that jurisdiction.

DR 3-102 Dividing Legal Fees with a Non-Lawyer.

(A) A lawyer or law firm shall not

share legal fees with a non-lawyer, except that:
   (1) An agreement by a lawyer
       with his firm, partner, or
       associate may provide for
       the payment of money,
       over a reasonable period
       of time after his death, to
       his estate or to one or
       more specified persons.
   (2) A lawyer who undertakes
       to complete unfinished le-
       gal business of a deceased
       lawyer may pay to the
       estate of the deceased
       lawyer that proportion of
       the total compensation
       which fairly represents
       the services rendered by
       the deceased lawyer.

   (3) A lawyer or law firm may
       include non-lawyer em-
       ployees in a compensa-
       tion or retirement plan,
       even though the plan is
       based in whole or in part
       on a profit-sharing ar-
       rangement, providing
       such plan does not cir-
       cumvent another Disci-
       plinary Rule.

**DR 3-103 Forming a Partnership
with a Non-Lawyer.**

(A) A lawyer shall not form a part-
    nership with a non-lawyer if
    any of the activities of the part-
    nership consist of the practice
    of law.

CANON 4
A Lawyer Should Preserve the Confidences and Secrets of a Client
DISCIPLINARY RULES

**DR 4-101 Preservation of Confi-
dences and Secrets of a Client.**

(A) "Confidence" refers to infor-
    mation protected by the attor-
    ney-client privilege under ap-
    plicable law, and "secret" re-
    fers to other information
    gained in the professional rela-
    tionship that the client has
    requested be held inviolate or
    the disclosure of which would
    be embarrassing or would be
    likely to be detrimental to the
    client.
(B) Except when permitted under
    DR 4-101 (C), a lawyer shall
    not knowingly:
    (1) Reveal a confidence or
        secret of his client.
    (2) Use a confidence or se-
        cret of his client to the dis-
        advantage of the client.
    (3) Use a confidence or se-
        cret of his client for the
        advantage of himself or of
        a third person, unless the
        client consents after full
        disclosure.
(C) A lawyer may reveal:
    (1) Confidences or secrets

    with the consent of the cli-
    ent or clients affected, but
    only after a full disclosure
    to them.
    (2) Confidences or secrets
        when permitted under
        Disciplinary Rules or re-
        quired by law or court
        order.
    (3) The intention of his client
        to commit a crime and the
        information necessary to
        prevent the crime.
    (4) Confidences or secrets
        necessary to establish or
        collect his fee or to defend
        himself or his employees
        or associates against an
        accusation of wrongful
        conduct.
(D) A lawyer shall exercise reason-
    able care to prevent his em-
    ployees, associates, and others
    whose services are utilized by
    him from disclosing or using
    confidences or secrets of a cli-
    ent, except that a lawyer may
    reveal the information allowed
    by DR 4-101 (C) through an
    employee.

CANON 5
A Lawyer Should Exercise Independent Professional Judgment on
Behalf of a Client
DISCIPLINARY RULES

DR 5-101 Refusing Employment When the Interests of the Lawyer May Impair His Independent Professional Judgment.

(A) Except with the consent of his client after full disclosure, a lawyer shall not accept employment if the exercise of his professional judgment on behalf of his client will be or reasonably may be affected by his own financial, business, property, or personal interests.

(B) A lawyer shall not accept employment in contemplated or pending litigation if he knows or it is obvious that he or a lawyer in his firm ought to be called as a witness, except that he may undertake the employment and he or a lawyer in his firm may testify:

   (1) If the testimony will relate solely to an uncontested matter.

   (2) If the testimony will relate solely to a matter of formality and there is no reason to believe that substantial evidence will be offered in opposition to the testimony.

   (3) If the testimony will relate solely to the nature and value of legal services rendered in the case by the lawyer or his firm to the client.

   (4) As to any matter, if refusal would work a substantial hardship on the client because of the distinctive value of the lawyer or his firm as counsel in the particular case.

DR 5-102 Withdrawal as Counsel When the Lawyer Becomes a Witness.

(A) If, after undertaking employment in contemplated or pending litigation, a lawyer learns or it is obvious that he or a lawyer in his firm ought to be called as a witness on behalf of his client, he shall withdraw from the conduct of the trial and his firm, if any, shall not continue representation in the trial, except that he may continue the representation and he or a lawyer in his firm may testify in the circumstances enumerated in DR 5-101(B) (1) through (4).

(B) If, after undertaking employment in contemplated or pending litigation, a lawyer learns or it is obvious that he or a lawyer in his firm may be called as a witness other than on behalf of his client, he may continue the representation until it is apparent that his testimony is or may be prejudicial to his client.

DR 5-103 Avoiding Acquisition of Interest in Litigation.

(A) A lawyer shall not acquire a proprietary interest in the cause of action or subject matter of litigation he is conducting for a client, except that he may:

   (1) Acquire a lien granted by law to secure his fee or expenses.

   (2) Contract with a client for a reasonable contingent fee in a civil case.

(B) While representing a client in connection with contemplated or pending litigation, a lawyer shall not advance or guarantee financial assistance to his client, except that a lawyer may advance or guarantee the expenses of litigation, including court costs, expenses of investigation, expenses of medical examination, and costs of obtaining and presenting evidence, provided the client remains ultimately liable for such expenses.

DR 5-104 Limiting Business Relations with a Client.

(A) A lawyer shall not enter into a business transaction with a client if they have differing interests therein and if the client expects the lawyer to exercise his professional judgment therein for the protection of the client, unless the client has consented after full disclosure.

(B) Prior to conclusion of all aspects of the matter giving rise to his employment, a lawyer shall not enter into any arrangement or understanding with a client or a prospective client by which he acquires an interest in publication rights with respect to the subject matter of his employment or proposed employment.

DR 5-105 Refusing to Accept or Continue Employment if the Interests of Another Client May Impair the Independent Professional Judgment of the Lawyer.

(A) A lawyer shall decline proffered employment if the exercise of his independent professional judgment in behalf of a client will be or is likely to be adversely affected by the acceptance of the proffered employment, or if it would be likely to involve him in representing differing interests, except to the extent permitted under DR 5-105(C).

(B) A lawyer shall not continue multiple employment if the exercise of his independent professional judgment in behalf of a client will be or is likely to be adversely affected by his representation of another client, or if it would be likely to involve him in representing differing interests, except to the extent permitted under DR 5-105(C).

(C) In the situations covered by DR 5-105 (A) and (B), a lawyer may represent multiple clients if it is obvious that he can adequately represent the interest of each and if each consents to the representation after full disclosure of the possible effect of such representation on the exercise of his independent professional judgment on behalf of each.

(D) If a lawyer is required to decline employment or to withdraw from employment under a Disciplinary Rule, no partner, or associate, or any other lawyer affiliated with him or his firm, may accept or continue such employment.

DR 5-106 Settling Similar Claims of Clients.

(A) A lawyer who represents two or more clients shall not make or participate in the making of an aggregate settlement of the claims of or against his clients, unless each client has consented to the settlement after being advised of the existence and nature of all the claims involved in the proposed settlement, of the total amount of the settlement, and of the participation of each person in the settlement.

DR 5-107 Avoiding Influence by Others Than the Client.

(A) Except with the consent of his client after full disclosure, a lawyer shall not:
  (1) Accept compensation for his legal services from one other than his client.
  (2) Accept from one other than his client any thing of value related to his representation of or his employment by his client.

(B) A lawyer shall not permit a person who recommends, employs, or pays him to render legal services for another to direct or regulate his professional judgment in rendering such legal services.

(C) A lawyer shall not practice with or in the form of a professional corporation or association authorized to practice law for a profit, if:

   (1) A non-lawyer owns any interest therein, except that a fiduciary representative of the estate of a lawyer may hold the stock or interest of the lawyer for a reasonable time during administration;

   (2) A non-lawyer is a corporate director or officer thereof; or

   (3) A non-lawyer has the right to direct or control the professional judgment of a lawyer.

CANON 6
A Lawyer Should Represent a Client Competently
DISCIPLINARY RULES

DR 6-101 Failing to Act Competently.

(A) A lawyer shall not:

   (1) Handle a legal matter which he knows or should know that he is not competent to handle, without associating with him a lawyer who is competent to handle it.

   (2) Handle a legal matter without preparation adequate in the circumstances.

   (3) Neglect a legal matter entrusted to him.

DR 6-102 Limiting Liability to Client.

(A) A lawyer shall not attempt to exonerate himself from or limit his liability to his client for his personal malpractice.

CANON 7
A Lawyer Should Represent a Client Zealously
Within the Bounds of the Law

DISCIPLINARY RULES

DR 7-101 Representing a Client Zealously.

(A) A lawyer shall not intentionally:

   (1) Fail to seek the lawful objectives of his client through reasonably available means permitted by law and the Disciplinary Rules, except as provided by DR 7-101 (B). A lawyer does not violate this Disciplinary Rule, however, by acceding to reasonable requests of opposing counsel which do not prejudice the rights of his client, by being punctual in fulfilling all professional commitments, by avoiding offensive tactics, or by treating with courtesy and consideration all persons involved in the legal process.

   (2) Fail to carry out a contract of employment entered into with a client for professional services, but he may withdraw as permitted under DR 2-110, DR 5-102, and DR 5-105.

   (3) Prejudice or damage his client during the course of the professional relationship, except as required under DR 7-102 (B).

(B) In his representation of a client, a lawyer may:

   (1) Where permissible, exercise his professional judgment to waive or fail to assert a right or position of his client.

   (2) Refuse to aid or participate in conduct that he

believes to be unlawful, even though there is some support for an argument that the conduct is legal.

DR 7-102 Representing a Client Within the Bounds of the Law.

(A) In his representation of a client, a lawyer shall not:

    (1) File a suit, assert a position, conduct a defense, delay a trial, or take other action on behalf of his client when he knows or when it is obvious that such action would serve merely to harass or maliciously injure another.

    (2) Knowingly advance a claim or defense that is unwarranted under existing law, except that he may advance such claim or defense if it can be supported by good faith argument for an extension, modification, or reversal of existing law.

    (3) Conceal or knowingly fail to disclose that which he is required by law to reveal.

    (4) Knowingly use perjured testimony or false evidence.

    (5) Knowingly make a false statement of law or fact.

    (6) Participate in the creation or preservation of evidence when he knows or it is obvious that the evidence is false.

    (7) Counsel or assist his client in conduct that the lawyer knows to be illegal or fraudulent.

    (8) Knowingly engage in other illegal conduct or conduct contrary to a Disciplinary Rule.

(B) A lawyer who receives information clearly establishing that:

    (1) His client has, in the course of the representation, perpetrated a fraud upon a person or tribunal shall promptly call upon his client to rectify the same, and if his client refuses or is unable to do so, he shall reveal the fraud to the affected person or tribunal, except when the information is protected as a privileged communication.

    (2) A person other than his client has perpetrated a fraud upon a tribunal shall promptly reveal the fraud to the tribunal.

DR 7-103 Performing the Duty of Public Prosecutor or Other Government Lawyer.

(A) A public prosecutor or other government lawyer shall not institute or cause to be instituted criminal charges when he knows or it is obvious that the charges are not supported by probable cause.

(B) A public prosecutor or other government lawyer in criminal litigation shall make timely disclosure to counsel for the defendant, or to the defendant if he has no counsel, of the existence of evidence, known to the prosecutor or other government lawyer, that tends to negate the guilt of the accused, mitigate the degree of the offense, or reduce the punishment.

DR 7-104 Communicating With One of Adverse Interest.

(A) During the course of his representation of a client a lawyer shall not:

    (1) Communicate or cause another to communicate on the subject of the representation with a party he knows to be represented by a lawyer in that matter unless he has the prior consent of the lawyer representing such other party or is authorized by law to do so.

(2) Give advice to a person who is not represented by a lawyer, other than the advice to secure counsel, if the interests of such person are or have a reasonable possibility of being in conflict with the interests of his client.

DR 7-105 Threatening Criminal Prosecution.

(A) A lawyer shall not present, participate in presenting, or threaten to present criminal charges solely to obtain an advantage in a civil matter.

DR 7-106 Trial Conduct.

(A) A lawyer shall not disregard or advise his client to disregard a standing rule of a tribunal or a ruling of a tribunal made in the course of a proceeding, but he may take appropriate steps in good faith to test the validity of such rule or ruling.

(B) In presenting a matter to a tribunal, a lawyer shall disclose:
   (1) Legal authority in the controlling jurisdiction known to him to be directly adverse to the position of his client and which is not disclosed by opposing counsel.
   (2) Unless privileged or irrelevant, the identities of the clients he represents and of the persons who employed him.

(C) In appearing in his professional capacity before a tribunal, a lawyer shall not:
   (1) State or allude to any matter that he has no reasonable basis to believe is relevant to the case or that will not be supported by admissible evidence.
   (2) Ask any question that he has no reasonable basis to believe is relevant to the case and that is intended to degrade a witness or other person.
   (3) Assert his personal knowledge of the facts in issue, except when testifying as a witness.
   (4) Assert his personal opinion as to the justness of a cause, as to the credibility of a witness, as to the culpability of a civil litigant, or as to the guilt or innocence of an accused; but he may argue, on his analysis of the evidence, for any position or conclusion with respect to the matters stated herein.
   (5) Fail to comply with known local customs of courtesy or practice of the bar or a particular tribunal without giving to opposing counsel timely notice of his intent not to comply.
   (6) Engage in undignified or discourteous conduct which is degrading to a tribunal.
   (7) Intentionally or habitually violate any established rule of procedure or of evidence.

DR 7-107 Trial Publicity.

(A) A lawyer participating in or associated with the investigation of a criminal matter shall not make or participate in making an extrajudicial statement that a reasonable person would expect to be disseminated by means of public communication and that does more than state without elaboration:
   (1) Information contained in a public record.
   (2) That the investigation is in progress.
   (3) The general scope of the investigation including a description of the offense and if permitted by law, the identity of the victim.
   (4) A request for assistance in apprehending a suspect or assistance in other mat-

ters and the information necessary thereto.

(5) A warning to the public of any dangers.

(B) A lawyer or law firm associated with the prosecution or defense of a criminal matter shall not, from the time of the filing of a complaint, information, or indictment, the issuance of an arrest warrant, or arrest until the commencement of the trial or disposition without trial, make or participate in making an extrajudicial statement that a reasonable person would expect to be disseminated by means of public communication and that relates to:

(1) The character, reputation, or prior criminal record (including arrests, indictments, or other charges of crime) of the accused.

(2) The possibility of a plea of guilty to the offense charged or to a lesser offense.

(3) The existence or contents of any confession, admission, or statement given by the accused or his refusal or failure to make a statement.

(4) The performance or results of any examinations or tests or the refusal or failure of the accused to submit to examinations or tests.

(5) The identity, testimony, or credibility of a prospective witness.

(6) Any opinion as to the guilt or innocence of the accused, the evidence, or the merits of the case.

(C) DR 7-107 (B) does not preclude a lawyer during such period from announcing:

(1) The name, age, residence, occupation, and family status of the accused.

(2) If the accused has not been apprehended, any information necessary to aid in his apprehension or to warn the public of any dangers he may present.

(3) A request for assistance in obtaining evidence.

(4) The identity of the victim of the crime.

(5) The fact, time, and place of arrest, resistance, pursuit, and use of weapons.

(6) The identity of investigating and arresting officers or agencies and the length of the investigation.

(7) At the time of seizure, a description of the physical evidence seized, other than a confession, admission, or statement.

(8) The nature, substance, or text of the charge.

(9) Quotations from or references to public records of the court in the case.

(10) The scheduling or result of any step in the judicial proceedings.

(11) That the accused denies the charges made against him.

(D) During the selection of a jury or the trial of a criminal matter, a lawyer or law firm associated with the prosecution or defense of a criminal matter shall not make or participate in making an extra-judicial statement that a reasonable person would expect to be disseminated by means of public communication and that relates to the trial, parties, or issues in the trial or other matters that are reasonably likely to interfere with a fair trial, except that he may quote from or refer without comment to public records of the court in the case.

(E) After the completion of a trial or disposition without trial of a criminal matter and prior to the imposition of sentence, a lawyer or law firm associated with the prosecution or defense shall not make or participate in making an extrajudicial statement that a reasonable person would expect to be disseminated by public communication and that is reasonably likely to affect the imposition of sentence.

(F) The foregoing provisions of DR 7-107 also apply to professional disciplinary proceedings and juvenile disciplinary proceedings when pertinent and consistent with other law applicable to such proceedings.

(G) A lawyer or law firm associated with a civil action shall not during its investigation or litigation make or participate in making an extra-judicial statement, other than a quotation from or reference to public records, that a reasonable person would expect to be disseminated by means of public communication and that relates to:

(1) Evidence regarding the occurrence or transaction involved.

(2) The character, credibility, or criminal record of a party, witness, or prospective witness.

(3) The performance or results of any examinations or tests or the refusal or failure of a party to submit to such.

(4) His opinion as to the merits of the claims or defenses of a party, except as required by law or administrative rule.

(5) Any other matter reasonably likely to interfere with a fair trial of the action.

(H) During the pendency of an administrative proceeding, a lawyer or law firm associated therewith shall not make or participate in making a statement, other than a quotation from or reference to public records, that a reasonable person would expect to be disseminated by means of public communication if it is made outside the official course of the proceeding and relates to:

(1) Evidence regarding the occurrence or transaction involved.

(2) The character, credibility, or criminal record of a party, witness, or prospective witness.

(3) Physical evidence or the performance or results of any examinations or tests or the refusal or failure of a party to submit to such.

(4) His opinion as to the merits of the claims, defenses, or positions of an interested person.

(5) Any other matter reasonably likely to interfere with a fair hearing.

(I) The foregoing provisions of DR 7-107 do not preclude a lawyer from replying to charges of misconduct publicly made against him or from participating in the proceedings of legislative, administrative, or other investigative bodies.

(J) A lawyer shall exercise reasonable care to prevent his employees and associates from making an extrajudicial statement that he would be prohibited from making under DR 7-107.

DR 7-108 Communication with or Investigation of Jurors.

(A) Before the trial of a case a lawyer connected therewith shall not communicate with or cause another to communicate with anyone he knows to be a member of the venire from which the jury will be selected for the trial of the case.

(B) During the trial of a case:

(1) A lawyer connected therewith shall not communicate with or cause

another to communicate with any member of the jury.

(2) A lawyer who is not connected therewith shall not communicate with or cause another to communicate with a juror concerning the case.

(C) DR 7-108 (A) and (B) do not prohibit a lawyer from communicating with veniremen or jurors in the course of official proceedings.

(D) After discharge of the jury from further consideration of a case with which the lawyer was connected, the lawyer shall not ask questions of or make comments to a member of that jury that are calculated merely to harass or embarrass the juror or to influence his actions in future jury service.

(E) A lawyer shall not conduct or cause, by financial support or otherwise, another to conduct a vexatious or harassing investigation of either a venireman or a juror.

(F) All restrictions imposed by DR 7-108 upon a lawyer also apply to communications with or investigations of members of a family of a venireman or a juror.

(G) A lawyer shall reveal promptly to the court improper conduct by a venireman or a juror, or by another toward a venireman or a juror or a member of his family, of which the lawyer has knowledge.

DR 7-109 Contact with Witnesses.

(A) A lawyer shall not suppress any evidence that he or his client has a legal obligation to reveal or produce.

(B) A lawyer shall not advise or cause a person to secrete himself or to leave the jurisdiction of a tribunal for the purpose of making him unavailable as a witness therein.

(C) A lawyer shall not pay, offer to pay, or acquiesce in the payment of compensation to a witness contingent upon the content of his testimony or the outcome of the case. But a lawyer may advance, guarantee, or acquiesce in the payment of:

(1) Expenses reasonably incurred by a witness in attending or testifying.

(2) Reasonable compensation to a witness for his loss of time in attending or testifying.

(3) A reasonable fee for the professional services of an expert witness.

DR 7-110 Contact with Officials

(A) A lawyer shall not give or lend any thing of value to a judge, official, or employee of a tribunal except as permitted by Section C(4) of Canon 5 of the Code of Judicial Conduct, but a lawyer may make a contribution to the campaign fund of a candidate for judicial office in conformity with Section B(2) under Canon 7 of the Code of Judicial Conduct.

(B) In an adversary proceeding, a lawyer shall not communicate, or cause another to communicate, as to the merits of the cause with a judge or an official before whom the proceeding is pending, except:

(1) In the course of official proceedings in the cause.

(2) In writing if he promptly delivers a copy of the writing to opposing counsel or to the adverse party if he is not represented by a lawyer.

(3) Orally upon adequate notice to opposing counsel or to the adverse party if he is not represented by a lawyer.

(4) As otherwise authorized by law, or by Section A(4) under Canon 3 of the Code of Judicial Conduct.

CANON 8
A Lawyer Should Assist in Improving the Legal System
DISCIPLINARY RULES

DR 8-101 Action as a Public Official.

(A) A lawyer who holds public office shall not:

    (1) Use his public position to obtain, or attempt to obtain, a special advantage in legislative matters for himself or for a client under circumstances where he knows or it is obvious that such action is not in the public interest.

    (2) Use his public position to influence, or attempt to influence, a tribunal to act in favor of himself or of a client.

    (3) Accept any thing of value from any person when the lawyer knows or it is obvious that the offer is for the purpose of influencing his action as a public official.

DR 8-102 Statements Concerning Judges and Other Adjudicatory Officers.

(A) A lawyer shall not knowingly make false statements of fact concerning the qualifications of a candidate for election or appointment to a judicial office.

(B) A lawyer shall not knowingly make false accusations against a judge or other adjudicatory officer.

DR 8-103 Lawyer Candidate for Judicial Office.

(A) A lawyer who is a candidate for judicial office shall comply with the applicable provisions of Canon 7 of the Code of Judicial Conduct.

CANON 9
A Lawyer Should Avoid Even the Appearance of Professional Impropriety
DISCIPLINARY RULES

DR 9-101 Avoiding Even the Appearance of Impropriety.

(A) A lawyer shall not accept private employment in a matter upon the merits of which he has acted in a judicial capacity.

(B) A lawyer shall not accept private employment in a matter in which he had substantial responsibility while he was a public employee.

(C) A lawyer shall not state or imply that he is able to influence improperly or upon irrelevant grounds any tribunal, legislative body, or public official.

DR 9-102 Preserving Identity of Funds and Property of a Client.

(A) All funds of clients paid to a lawyer or law firm, other than advances for costs and expenses, shall be deposited in one or more identifiable bank accounts maintained in the state in which the law office is situated and no funds belonging to the lawyer or law firm shall be deposited therein except as follows:

    (1) Funds reasonably sufficient to pay bank charges may be deposited therein.

    (2) Funds belonging in part to a client and in part presently or potentially to the lawyer or law firm must be deposited therein, but the portion belonging to the lawyer or law firm may be withdrawn when due unless the right of the

lawyer or law firm to receive it is disputed by the client, in which event the disputed portion shall not be withdrawn until the dispute is finally resolved.

(B) A lawyer shall:
(1) Promptly notify a client of the receipt of his funds, securities, or other properties.
(2) Identify and label securities and properties of a client promptly upon receipt and place them in a safe deposit box or other place of safekeeping as soon as practicable.
(3) Maintain complete records of all funds, securities, and other properties of a client coming into the possession of the lawyer and render appropriate accounts to his client regarding them.
(4) Promptly pay or deliver to the client as requested by a client the funds, securities, or other properties in the possession of the lawyer which the client is entitled to receive.

ABA MODEL RULES OF PROFESSIONAL CONDUCT

The Model Rules of Professional Conduct were adopted by the House of Delegates of the American Bar Association on August 2, 1983.

CONTENTS

Preamble
Scope
Terminology
Rules

CLIENT-LAWYER RELATIONSHIP

Rule
1.1 Competence
1.2 Scope of Representation
1.3 Diligence
1.4 Communication
1.5 Fees
1.6 Confidentiality of Information
1.7 Conflict of Interest: General Rule
1.8 Conflict of Interest: Prohibited Transactions
1.9 Conflict of Interest: Former Client
1.10 Imputed Disqualification: General Rule
1.11 Successive Government and Private Employment
1.12 Former Judge or Arbitrator
1.13 Organization as the Client
1.14 Client Under a Disability
1.15 Safekeeping Property
1.16 Declining or Terminating Representation

COUNSELOR
2.1 Advisor
2.2 Intermediary
2.3 Evaluation for Use by Third Persons

ADVOCATE
3.1 Meritorious Claims and Contentions
3.2 Expediting Litigation
3.3 Candor Toward the Tribunal
3.4 Fairness to Opposing Party and Counsel
3.5 Impartiality and Decorum of the Tribunal
3.6 Trial Publicity
3.7 Lawyer as Witness
3.8 Special Responsibilities of a Prosecutor
3.9 Advocate in Nonadjudicative Proceedings

TRANSACTIONS WITH PERSONS OTHER THAN CLIENTS
4.1 Truthfulness in Statements to Others
4.2 Communication with Person Represented by Counsel
4.3 Dealing with Unrepresented Person
4.4 Respect for Rights of Third Persons

LAW FIRMS AND ASSOCIATIONS

5.1 Responsibilities of a Partner or Supervisory Lawyer
5.2 Responsibilities of a Subordinate Lawyer
5.3 Responsibilities Regarding Nonlawyer Assistants
5.4 Professional Independence of a Lawyer
5.5 Unauthorized Practice of Law
5.6 Restrictions on Right to Practice

PUBLIC SERVICE

6.1 Pro Bono Publico Service
6.2 Accepting Appointments
6.3 Membership in Legal Services Organization
6.4 Law Reform Activities Affecting Client Interests

INFORMATION ABOUT LEGAL SERVICES

7.1 Communications Concerning a Lawyer's Services
7.2 Advertising
7.3 Direct Contact with Prospective Clients
7.4 Communication of Fields of Practice
7.5 Firm Names and Letterheads

MAINTAINING THE INTEGRITY OF THE PROFESSION

8.1 Bar Admission and Disciplinary Matters
8.2 Judicial and Legal Officials
8.3 Reporting Professional Misconduct
8.4 Misconduct
8.5 Jurisdiction

PREAMBLE: A LAWYER'S RESPONSIBILITIES

A lawyer is a representative of clients, an officer of the legal system and a public citizen having special responsibility for the quality of justice.

As a representative of clients, a lawyer performs various functions. As advisor, a lawyer provides a client with an informed understanding of the client's legal rights and obligations and explains their practical implications. As advocate, a lawyer zealously asserts the client's position under the rules of the adversary system. As negotiator, a lawyer seeks a result advantageous to the client but consistent with requirements of honest dealing with others. As intermediary between clients, a lawyer seeks to reconcile their divergent interests as an advisor and, to a limited extent, as a spokesperson for each client. A lawyer acts as evaluator by examining a client's legal affairs and reporting about them to the client or to others.

In all professional functions a lawyer should be competent, prompt and diligent. A lawyer should maintain communication with a client concerning the representation. A lawyer should keep in confidence information relating to representation of a client except so far as disclosure is required or permitted by the Rules of Professional Conduct or other law.

A lawyer's conduct should conform to the requirements of the law, both in professional service to clients and in the lawyer's business and personal affairs. A lawyer should use the law's procedures only for legitimate purposes and not to harass or intimidate others. A lawyer should demonstrate respect for the legal system and for those who serve it, including judges, other lawyers and public officials. While it is a lawyer's duty, when necessary, to challenge the rectitude of official action, it is also a lawyer's duty to uphold legal process.

As a public citizen, a lawyer should seek improvement of the law, the administration of justice and the quality of service rendered by the legal profession. As a member of a learned profession, a lawyer should cultivate knowledge of the law beyond its use for clients, employ that knowledge in reform of the law and work to strengthen legal education. A lawyer should be mindful of deficiencies in the administration of justice and of the fact that the poor, and sometimes persons who are not poor, cannot afford adequate legal assistance, and should therefore devote professional time and civic influence in their behalf. A lawyer should aid the legal profession in pursuing these objectives and should help the bar regulate itself in the public interest.

Many of a lawyer's professional responsibilities are prescribed in the Rules of Professional Conduct, as well as substantive and procedural law. However, a lawyer is also guided by personal conscience and the approbation of professional peers. A lawyer should strive to attain the highest level of skill, to improve the law and the legal profession and to exemplify the legal profession's ideals of public service.

A lawyer's responsibilities as a representative of clients, an officer of the legal system and a public citizen are usually harmonious. Thus, when an opposing party is well represented, a lawyer can be a zealous advocate on behalf of a client and at the same time assume that justice is being done. So also, a lawyer can be sure that preserving client confidences ordinarily serves the public interest because people are more likely to seek legal advice, and thereby heed their legal obligations, when they know their communications will be private.

In the nature of law practice, however, conflicting responsibilities are encountered. Virtually all difficult ethical problems arise from conflict between a lawyer's responsibilities to clients, to the legal system and to the lawyer's own interest in remaining an upright person while earning a satisfactory living. The Rules of Professional Conduct prescribe terms for resolving such conflicts. Within the framework of these Rules many difficult issues of professional discretion can arise. Such issues must be resolved through the exercise of sensitive professional and moral judgment

guided by the basic principles underlying the Rules.

The legal profession is largely self-governing. Although other professions also have been granted powers of self-government, the legal profession is unique in this respect because of the close relationship between the profession and the processes of government and law enforcement. This connection is manifested in the fact that ultimate authority over the legal profession is vested largely in the courts.

To the extent that lawyers meet the obligations of their professional calling, the occasion for government regulation is obviated. Self-regulation also helps maintain the legal profession's independence from government domination. An independent legal profession is an important force in preserving government under law, for abuse of legal authority is more readily challenged by a profession whose members are not dependent on government for the right to practice.

The legal profession's relative autonomy carries with it special responsibilities of self-government. The profession has a responsibility to assure that its regulations are conceived in the public interest and not in furtherance of parochial or self-interested concerns of the bar. Every lawyer is responsible for observance of the Rules of Professional Conduct. A lawyer should also aid in securing their observance by other lawyers. Neglect of these responsibilities compromises the independence of the profession and the public interest which it serves.

Lawyers play a vital role in the preservation of society. The fulfillment of this role requires an understanding by lawyers of their relationship to our legal system. The Rules of Professional Conduct, when properly applied, serve to define that relationship.

SCOPE

The Rules of Professional Conduct are rules of reason. They should be interpreted with reference to the purposes of legal representation and of the law itself. Some of the Rules are imperatives, cast in the terms "shall" or "shall not." These define proper conduct for purposes of professional discipline. Others, generally cast in the term "may" are permissive and define areas under the Rules in which the lawyer has professional discretion. No disciplinary action should be taken when the lawyer chooses not to act or acts within the bounds of such discretion. Other Rules define the nature of relationships between the lawyer and others. The Rules are thus partly obligatory and disciplinary and partly constitutive and descriptive in that they define a lawyer's professional role. Many of the Comments use the term "should." Comments do not add obligations to the Rules but provide guidance for practicing in compliance with the Rules.

The Rules presuppose a larger legal context shaping the lawyer's role. That context includes court rules and statutes relating to matters of licensure, laws defining specific obligations of lawyers and substantive and procedural law in general. Compliance with the Rules, as with all law in an open society, depends primarily upon understanding and voluntary compliance, secondarily upon reinforcement by peer and public opinion and finally, when necessary, upon enforcement through disciplinary proceedings. The Rules do not, however, exhaust the moral and ethical considerations that should inform a lawyer, for no worthwhile human activity can be completely defined by legal rules. The Rules simply provide a framework for the ethical practice of law.

Furthermore, for purposes of determining the lawyer's authority and responsibility, principles of substantive law external to these Rules determine whether a client-lawyer relationship exists. Most of the duties flowing from the client-lawyer relationship attach only after the client has requested the lawyer to render legal services and the lawyer has agreed to do so. But there are some duties, such as that of confidentiality under Rule 1.6, that may attach when the lawyer agrees to consider whether a client-lawyer relationship shall be established. Whether a client-lawyer relationship exists for any specific purpose can depend on the circumstances and may be a question of fact.

Under various legal provisions, including constitutional, statutory and common law, the responsibilities of government lawyers may include authority concerning legal matters that ordinarily reposes in the client in private client-lawyer relationships. For example, a lawyer for a government agency may have authority on behalf of the government to decide upon settlement or whether to appeal from an adverse judgment. Such authority in various respects is generally vested in the attorney general and the state's attorney in state government, and their federal counterparts, and the same may be true of other government law officers. Also, lawyers under the supervision of these officers may be authorized to represent several government agencies in intragovernmental legal controversies in circumstances where a private lawyer could not represent multiple private clients. They also may have authority to represent the "public interest" in circumstances where a private lawyer would not be authorized to do so. These Rules do not abrogate any such authority.

Failure to comply with an obligation or prohibition imposed by a Rule is a basis for invoking the disciplinary process. The Rules presuppose that disciplinary assessment of a lawyer's conduct will be made on the basis of the facts and circumstances as they existed at the time of the conduct in question and in recognition of the fact that a lawyer often has to act upon uncertain or incomplete evidence of the situation. Moreover, the Rules presuppose that whether or not discipline should be imposed for a violation, and the severity of a sanction, depend on all the circumstances, such as the willfulness and seriousness of the violation, extenuating factors and whether there have been previous violations.

Violation of a Rule should not give rise to a cause of action nor should it create any presumption that a legal duty has been breached. The Rules are designed to provide guidance to lawyers and to provide a structure for regulating conduct through disciplinary agencies. They are not designed to be a basis for civil liability. Furthermore, the purpose of the Rules can be subverted when they are invoked by opposing parties as procedural weapons. The fact that a Rule is a just basis for a lawyer's self-assessment, or for sanctioning a lawyer under the administration of a disciplinary authority, does not imply that an antagonist in a collateral proceeding or transaction has standing to seek enforcement of the Rule. Accordingly, nothing in the Rules should be deemed to augment any substantive legal duty of lawyers or the extra-disciplinary consequences of violating such a duty.

Moreover, these Rules are not intended to govern or affect judicial application of either the attorney-client or work product privilege. Those privileges were developed to promote compliance with law and fairness in litigation. In reliance on the attorney-client privilege, clients are entitled to expect that communications within the scope of the privilege will be protected against compelled disclosure. The attorney-client privilege is that of the client and not of the lawyer. The fact that in exceptional situations the lawyer under the Rules has a limited discretion to disclose a client confidence does not vitiate the proposition that, as a general matter, the client has a reasonable expectation that information relating to the client will not be voluntarily disclosed and that disclosure of such information may be judicially compelled only in accordance with recognized exceptions to the attorney-client and work product privileges.

The lawyer's exercise of discretion not to disclose information under Rule 1.6 should not be subject to reexamination. Permitting such reexamination would be incompatible with the general policy of promoting compliance with law through assurances that communications will be protected against disclosure.

The Comment accompanying each Rule explains and illustrates the meaning and purpose of the Rule. The Preamble and this note on Scope provide general orientation. The Comments are intended as guides to interpretation, but the text of each Rule is authoritative. Research notes were prepared to compare counterparts in the ABA Model Code of Professional Responsibility (adopted 1969, as amended) and to provide selected references to other authorities. The notes have not been adopted, do not constitute part of the Model Rules, and are not intended to affect the application or interpretation of the Rules and Comments.

TERMINOLOGY

"Belief" or "Believes" denotes that the person involved actually supposed the fact in question to be true. A person's belief may be inferred from circumstances.

"Consult" or "Consultation" denotes communication of information reasonably sufficient to permit the client to appreciate the significance of the matter in question.

"Firm" or "Law firm" denotes a lawyer or lawyers in a private firm, lawyers employed in the legal department of a corporation or other organization and lawyers employed in a legal services organization. See Comment, Rule 1.10.

"Fraud" or "Fraudulent" denotes conduct having a purpose to deceive and not merely negligent misrepresentation or failure to apprise another of relevant information.

"Knowingly," "Known," or "Knows" denotes actual knowledge of the fact in question. A person's knowledge may be inferred from circumstances.

"Partner" denotes a member of a partnership and a shareholder in a law firm organized as a professional corporation.

"Reasonable" or "Reasonably" when used in relation to conduct by a lawyer denotes the conduct of a reasonably prudent and competent lawyer.

"Reasonable belief" or "Reasonably believes" when used in reference to a lawyer denotes that the lawyer believes the matter in question and that the circumstances are such that the belief is reasonable.

"Reasonably should know" when used in reference to a lawyer denotes that a lawyer of reasonable prudence and competence would ascertain the matter in question.

"Substantial" when used in reference to degree or extent denotes a material matter of clear and weighty importance.

Rules

CLIENT-LAWYER RELATIONSHIP
RULE 1.1 Competence

A lawyer shall provide competent representation to a client. Competent representation requires the legal knowledge, skill, thoroughness and preparation reasonably necessary for the representation.

COMMENT:
Legal Knowledge and Skill
In determining whether a lawyer

employs the requisite knowledge and skill in a particular matter, relevant factors include the relative complexity and specialized nature of the matter, the lawyer's general experience, the lawyer's training and experience in the field in question, the preparation and study the lawyer is able to give the matter and whether it is feasible to refer the matter to, or associate or consult with, a lawyer of established competence in the field in question. In many instances, the required proficiency is that of a general practitioner. Expertise in a particular field of law may be required in some circumstances.

A lawyer need not necessarily have special training or prior experience to handle legal problems of a type with which the lawyer is unfamiliar. A newly admitted lawyer can be as competent as a practitioner with long experience. Some important legal skills, such as the analysis of precedent, the evaluation of evidence and legal drafting, are required in all legal problems. Perhaps the most fundamental legal skill consists of determining what kind of legal problems a situation may involve, a skill that necessarily transcends any particular specialized knowledge. A lawyer can provide adequate representation in a wholly novel field through necessary study. Competent representation can also be provided through the association of a lawyer of established competence in the field in question.

In an emergency a lawyer may give advice or assistance in a matter in which the lawyer does not have the skill ordinarily required where referral to or consultation or association with another lawyer would be impractical. Even in an emergency, however, assistance should be limited to that reasonably necessary in the circumstances, for ill considered action under emergency conditions can jeopardize the client's interest.

A lawyer may accept representation where the requisite level of competence can be achieved by reasonable preparation. This applies as well to a lawyer who is appointed as counsel for an unrepresented person. See also Rule 6.2.

Thoroughness and Preparation

Competent handling of a particular matter includes inquiry into and analysis of the factual and legal elements of the problem, and use of methods and procedures meeting the standards of competent practitioners. It also includes adequate preparation. The required attention and preparation are determined in part by what is at stake; major litigation and complex transactions ordinarily require more elaborate treatment than matters of lesser consequence.

Maintaining Competence

To maintain the requisite knowledge and skill, a lawyer should engage in continuing study and education. If a system of peer review has been established, the lawyer should consider making use of it in appropriate circumstances.

RULE 1.2 Scope of Representation

(a) A lawyer shall abide by a client's decisions concerning the objectives of representation, subject to paragraphs (c), (d) and (e), and shall consult with the client as to the means by which they are to be pursued. A lawyer shall abide by a client's decision whether to accept an offer of settlement of a matter. In a criminal case, the lawyer shall abide by the client's decision, after consultation with the lawyer, as to a plea to be entered, whether to waive jury trial and whether the client will testify.

(b) A lawyer's representation of a client, including representation by appointment, does not constitute an endorsement of the client's political, economic, social or moral views or activities.

(c) A lawyer may limit the objectives of the representation if the cli-

ent consents after consultation.

(d) A lawyer shall not counsel a client to engage, or assist a client, in conduct that the lawyer knows is criminal or fraudulent, but a lawyer may discuss the legal consequences of any proposed course of conduct with a client and may counsel or assist a client to make a good faith effort to determine the validity, scope, meaning or application of the law.

(e) When a lawyer knows that a client expects assistance not permitted by the rules of professional conduct or other law, the lawyer shall consult with the client regarding the relevant limitations on the lawyer's conduct.

COMMENT:
Scope of Representation

Both lawyer and client have authority and responsibility in the objectives and means of representation. The client has ultimate authority to determine the purposes to be served by legal representation, within the limits imposed by law and the lawyer's professional obligations. Within those limits, a client also has a right to consult with the lawyer about the means to be used in pursuing those objectives. At the same time, a lawyer is not required to pursue objectives or employ means simply because a client may wish that the lawyer do so. A clear distinction between objectives and means sometimes cannot be drawn, and in many cases the client-lawyer relationship partakes of a joint undertaking. In questions of means, the lawyer should assume responsibility for technical and legal tactical issues, but should defer to the client regarding such questions as the expense to be incurred and concern for third persons who might be adversely affected. Law defining the lawyer's scope of authority in litigation varies among jurisdictions.

In a case in which the client appears to be suffering mental disability, the lawyer's duty to abide by the client's decisions is to be guided by reference to Rule 1.14.

Independence from Client's Views or Activities

Legal representation should not be denied to people who are unable to afford legal services, or whose cause is controversial or the subject of popular disapproval. By the same token, representing a client does not constitute approval of the client's views or activities.

Services Limited in Objectives or Means

The objectives or scope of services provided by a lawyer may be limited by agreement with the client or by the terms under which the lawyer's services are made available to the client. For example, a retainer may be for a specifically defined purpose. Representation provided through a legal aid agency may be subject to limitations on the types of cases the agency handles. When a lawyer has been retained by an insurer to represent an insured, the representation may be limited to matters related to the insurance coverage. The terms upon which representation is undertaken may exclude specific objectives or means. Such limitations may exclude objectives or means that the lawyer regards as repugnant or imprudent.

An agreement concerning the scope of representation must accord with the Rules of Professional Conduct and other law. Thus, the client may not be asked to agree to representation so limited in scope as to violate Rule 1.1, or to surrender the right to terminate the lawyer's services or the right to settle litigation that the lawyer might wish to continue.

Criminal, Fraudulent and Prohibited Transactions

A lawyer is required to give an honest opinion about the actual consequences that appear likely to result from a client's conduct. The fact that a client uses advice in a course of action that is criminal or fraudulent does not, of itself, make a lawyer a party to the course of action. However, a lawyer may not knowingly assist a client in criminal or fraudulent conduct. There is a critical distinction between presenting an analysis of legal aspects of questionable conduct and recommending the means by which a crime or fraud might be committed with impunity.

When the client's course of action has already begun and is continuing, the lawyer's responsibility is especially delicate. The lawyer is not permitted to reveal the client's wrongdoing, except where permitted by Rule 1.6. However, the lawyer is required to avoid furthering the purpose, for example, by suggesting how it might be concealed. A lawyer may not continue assisting a client in conduct that the lawyer originally supposes is legally proper but then discovers is criminal or fraudulent. Withdrawal from the representation, therefore, may be required.

Where the client is a fiduciary, the lawyer may be charged with special obligations in dealings with a beneficiary.

Paragraph (d) applies whether or not the defrauded party is a party to the transaction. Hence, a lawyer should not participate in a sham transaction; for example, a transaction to effectuate criminal or fraudulent escape of tax liability. Paragraph (d) does not preclude undertaking a criminal defense incident to a general retainer for legal services to a lawful enterprise. The last clause of paragraph (d) recognizes that determining the validity or interpretation of a statute or regulation may require a course of action involving disobedience of the statute or regulation or of the interpretation placed upon it by governmental authorities.

RULE 1.3 Diligence

A lawyer shall act with reasonable

diligence and promptness in representing a client.

COMMENT:

A lawyer should pursue a matter on behalf of a client despite opposition, obstruction or personal inconvenience to the lawyer, and may take whatever lawful and ethical measures are required to vindicate a client's cause or endeavor. A lawyer should act with commitment and dedication to the interests of the client and with zeal in advocacy upon the client's behalf. However, a lawyer is not bound to press for every advantage that might be realized for a client. A lawyer has professional discretion in determining the means by which a matter should be pursued. See Rule 1.2. A lawyer's workload should be controlled so that each matter can be handled adequately.

Perhaps no professional shortcoming is more widely resented than procrastination. A client's interests often can be adversely affected by the passage of time or the change of conditions; in extreme instances, as when a lawyer overlooks a statute of limitations, the client's legal position may be destroyed. Even when the client's interests are not affected in substance, however, unreasonable delay can cause a client needless anxiety and undermine confidence in the lawyer's trustworthiness.

Unless the relationship is terminated as provided in Rule 1.16, a lawyer should carry through to conclusion all matters undertaken for a client. If a lawyer's employment is limited to a specific matter, the relationship terminates when the matter has been resolved. If a lawyer has served a client over a substantial period in a variety of matters, the client sometimes may assume that the lawyer will continue to serve on a continuing basis unless the lawyer gives notice of withdrawal. Doubt about whether a client-lawyer relationship still exists should be clarified by the lawyer, preferably in writing, so that the client will not mistakenly suppose the lawyer is looking after the client's affairs when the lawyer has ceased to do so. For example, if a lawyer has handled a judicial or administrative proceeding that produced a result adverse to the client but has not been specifically instructed concerning pursuit of an appeal, the lawyer should advise the client of the possibility of appeal before relinquishing responsibility for the matter.

RULE 1.4 Communication

(a) A lawyer shall keep a client reasonably informed about the status of a matter and promptly comply with reasonable requests for information.

(b) A lawyer shall explain a matter to the extent reasonably necessary to permit the client to make informed decisions regarding the representation.

COMMENT:

The client should have sufficient information to participate intelligently in decisions concerning the objectives of the representation and the means by which they are to be pursued, to the extent the client is willing and able to do so. For example, a lawyer negotiating on behalf of a client should provide the client with facts relevant to the matter, inform the client of communications from another party and take other reasonable steps that permit the client to make a decision regarding a serious offer from another party. A lawyer who receives from opposing counsel an offer of settlement in a civil controversy or a proffered plea bargain in a criminal case should promptly inform the client of its substance unless prior discussions with the client have left it clear that the proposal will be unacceptable. See Rule 1.2(a). Even when a client delegates authority to the lawyer, the client should be kept advised of the status of the matter.

Adequacy of communication depends in part on the kind of advice or assistance involved. For example, in negotiations where there is time to explain a proposal, the lawyer should review all important provisions with the client before proceeding to an agreement. In litigation a lawyer should explain the general strategy and prospects of success and ordinarily should consult the client on tactics that might injure or coerce others. On the other hand, a lawyer ordinarily cannot be expected to describe trial or negotiation strategy in detail. The guiding principle is that the lawyer should fulfill reasonable client expectations for information consistent with the duty to act in the client's best interests, and the client's overall requirements as to the character of representation.

Ordinarily, the information to be provided is that appropriate for a client who is a comprehending and responsible adult. However, fully informing the client according to this standard may be impracticable, for example, where the client is a child or suffers from mental disability. See Rule 1.14. When the client is an organization or group, it is often impossible or inappropriate to inform every one of its members about its legal affairs; ordinarily, the lawyer should address communications to the appropriate officials of the organization. See Rule 1.13. Where many routine matters are involved, a system of limited or occasional reporting may be arranged with the client. Practical exigency may also require a lawyer to act for a client without prior consultation.

Withholding Information

In some circumstances, a lawyer may be justified in delaying transmission of information when the client would be likely to react imprudently to an immediate communication. Thus, a lawyer might withhold a psychiatric diagnosis of a client when the examining psychiatrist indicates that disclosure would harm the client. A lawyer may not withhold information to serve the lawyer's own interests or convenience. Rules or court orders governing litigation may provide that information supplied to a lawyer may not be disclosed to the client. Rule 3.4(c) directs compliance with such rules or orders.

RULE 1.5 Fees

(a) A lawyer's fee shall be reasonable. The factors to be considered in determining the reasonableness of a fee include the following:

(1) the time and labor required, the novelty and difficulty of the questions involved, and the skill requisite to perform the legal service properly;

(2) the likelihood, if apparent to the client, that the acceptance of the particular employment will preclude other employment by the lawyer;

(3) the fee customarily charged in the locality for similar legal services;

(4) the amount involved and the results obtained;

(5) the time limitations imposed by the client or by the circumstances;

(6) the nature and length of the professional relationship with the client;

(7) the experience, reputation, and ability of the lawyer or lawyers performing the services; and

(8) whether the fee is fixed or contingent.

(b) When the lawyer has not regularly represented the client, the basis or rate of the fee shall be communicated to the client, preferably in writing, before or within a reasonable time after commencing the representation.

(c) A fee may be contingent on the outcome of the matter for which the service is rendered, except in a matter in which a contingent fee is prohibited by paragraph (d) or other law. A contingent fee agreement shall be in writing and shall state the method by which the fee is to be determined, including the percentage or percentages that shall accrue to the lawyer in the event of settlement, trial or appeal, litigation and other expenses to be deducted from the recovery, and whether such expenses are to be deducted before or after the contingent fee is calculated. Upon conclusion of a contingent fee matter, the lawyer shall provide the client with a written statement stating the outcome of the matter and, if there is a recovery, showing the remittance to the client and the method of its determination.

(d) A lawyer shall not enter into an arrangement for, charge, or collect:

(1) any fee in a domestic relations matter, the payment or amount of which is contingent upon the securing of a divorce or upon the amount of alimony or support, or property settlement in lieu thereof; or

(2) a contingent fee for representing a defendant in a criminal case.

(e) A division of fee between lawyers who are not in the same firm may be made only if:

(1) the division is in proportion to the services performed by each lawyer or, by written agreement with the client, each lawyer assumes joint responsibility for the representation;

(2) the client is advised of and does not object to the participation of all the lawyers involved; and

(3) the total fee is reasonable.

COMMENT:
Basis or Rate of Fee
When the lawyer has regularly represented a client, they ordinarily will have evolved an understanding concerning the basis or rate of the fee. In a new client-lawyer relationship, however, an understanding as to the fee should be promptly established. It is not necessary to recite all the factors that underlie the basis of the fee, but only those that are directly involved in its computation. It is sufficient, for example, to state that the basic rate is an hourly charge or a fixed amount or an estimated amount, or to identify the factors that may be taken into account in finally fixing the fee. When developments occur during the representation that render an earlier estimate substantially inaccurate, a revised estimate should be provided to the client. A written statement concerning the fee reduces the possibility of misunderstanding. Furnishing the client with a simple memorandum or a copy of the lawyer's customary fee schedule is sufficient if the basis or rate of the fee is set forth.

Terms of Payment
A lawyer may require advance payment of a fee, but is obliged to return any unearned portion. See Rule 1.16(d). A lawyer may accept property in payment for services, such as an ownership interest in an enterprise, providing this does not involve acquisition of a proprietary interest in the cause of action or subject matter of the litigation contrary to Rule 1.8(j). However, a fee paid in property instead of money may be subject to special scrutiny because it involves questions concerning both the value of the services and the lawyer's special knowledge of the value of the property.

An agreement may not be made whose terms might induce the lawyer improperly to curtail services for the client or perform them in a way contrary to the client's interest. For example, a lawyer should not enter into an agreement whereby services are to be provided only up to a stated amount when it is foreseeable that more extensive services probably will be required, unless the situation is adequately explained to the client. Otherwise, the client might have to bargain for further assistance in the midst of a proceeding or transaction. However, it is proper to define the extent of services in light of the client's ability to pay. A lawyer should not exploit a fee arrangement based primarily on hourly charges by using wasteful procedures. When there is doubt whether a contingent fee is consistent with the client's best interest, the lawyer should offer the client alternative bases for the fee and explain their implications. Applicable law may impose limitations on contingent fees, such as a ceiling on the percentage.

Division of Fee

A division of fee is a single billing to a client covering the fee of two or more lawyers who are not in the same firm. A division of fee facilitates association of more than one lawyer in a matter in which neither alone could serve the client as well, and most often is used when the fee is contingent and the division is between a referring lawyer and a trial specialist. Paragraph (e) permits the lawyers to divide a fee on either the basis of the proportion of services they render or by agreement between the participating lawyers if all assume responsibility for the representation as a whole and the client is advised and does not object. It does not require disclosure to the client of the share that each lawyer is to receive. Joint responsibility for the representation entails the obligations stated in Rule 5.1 for purposes of the matter involved.

Disputes over Fees

If a procedure has been established for resolution of fee disputes, such as an arbitration or mediation procedure established by the bar, the lawyer should conscientiously consider submitting to it. Law may prescribe a procedure for determining a lawyer's fee, for example, in representation of an executor or administrator, a class or a person entitled to a reasonable fee as part of the measure of damages. The lawyer entitled to such a fee and a lawyer representing another party concerned with the fee should comply with the prescribed procedure.

RULE 1.6 Confidentiality of Information

(a) A lawyer shall not reveal information relating to representation of a client unless the client consents after consultation, except for disclosures that are impliedly authorized in order to carry out the representation, and except as stated in paragraph (b).

(b) A lawyer may reveal such information to the extent the lawyer reasonably believes necessary:

(1) to prevent the client from committing a criminal act that the lawyer believes is likely to result in imminent death or substantial bodily harm; or

(2) to establish a claim or defense on behalf of the lawyer in a controversy between the lawyer and the client, to establish a defense to a criminal charge or civil claim against the lawyer based upon conduct in which the client was involved, or to respond to allegations in any proceeding concerning the lawyer's representation of the client.

COMMENT:

The lawyer is part of a judicial system charged with upholding the law. One of the lawyer's functions is to advise clients so that they avoid any violation of the law in the proper exercise of their rights.

The observance of the ethical obligation of a lawyer to hold inviolate confidential information of the client not only facilitates the full development of facts essential to proper representation of the client but also encourages people to seek early legal assistance.

Almost without exception, clients come to lawyers in order to determine what their rights are and what is, in the maze of laws and regulations, deemed to be legal and correct. The common law recognizes that the client's confidences must be protected from disclosure. Based upon experience, lawyers know that almost all clients follow the advice given, and the law is upheld.

A fundamental principle in the client-lawyer relationship is that the lawyer maintain confidentiality of information relating to the representation. The client is thereby encouraged to communicate fully and frankly with the lawyer even as to embarrassing or legally damaging subject matter.

The principle of confidentiality is given effect in two related bodies of law, the attorney-client privilege (which includes the work product doctrine) in the law of evidence and the rule of confidentiality established in professional ethics. The attorney-client privilege applies in judicial and other proceedings in which a lawyer may be called as a witness or otherwise required to produce evidence concerning a client. The rule of client-lawyer confidentiality applies in situations other than those where evidence is sought from the lawyer through compulsion of law. The confidentiality rule applies not merely to matters communicated in confidence by the client but also to all information relating to the representation, whatever its source. A lawyer may not disclose such information except as authorized or required by the Rules of Professional Conduct or other law. See also Scope.

The requirement of maintaining confidentiality of information relating to representation applies to government lawyers who may disagree with the policy goals that their representation is designed to advance.

Authorized Disclosure

A lawyer is impliedly authorized to make disclosures about a client when appropriate in carrying out the representation, except to the extent that the client's instructions or special circumstances limit that authority. In litigation, for exam-ple, a lawyer may disclose information by admitting a fact that cannot properly be disputed, or in negotiation by making a disclosure that facilitates a satisfactory conclusion.

Lawyers in a firm may, in the course of the firm's practice, disclose to each other information relating to a client of the firm, unless the client has instructed that particular information be confined to specified lawyers.

Disclosure Adverse to Client

The confidentiality rule is subject to limited exceptions. In becoming privy to information about a client, a lawyer may foresee that the client intends serious harm to another person. However, to the extent a lawyer is required or permitted to disclose a client's purposes, the client will be inhibited from revealing facts which would enable the lawyer to counsel against a wrongful course of action. The public is better protected if full and open communication by the client is encouraged than if it is inhibited.

Several situations must be distinguished.

First, the lawyer may not counsel or assist a client in conduct that is criminal or fraudulent. See Rule 1.2(d). Similarly, a lawyer has a duty under Rule 3.3(a)(4) not to use false evidence. This duty is essentially a special instance of the duty prescribed in Rule 1.2(d) to avoid assisting a client in criminal or fraudulent conduct.

Second, the lawyer may have been innocently involved in past conduct by the client that was criminal or fraudulent. In such a situation the lawyer has not violated Rule 1.2(d), because to "counsel or assist" criminal or fraudulent conduct requires knowing that the conduct is of that character.

Third, the lawyer may learn that a client intends prospective conduct that is criminal and likely to result in imminent death or substantial bodily harm. As stated in paragraph (b)(1), the lawyer has professional discretion to reveal information in order to prevent such consequences. The lawyer may make a disclosure in order to prevent homicide or serious bodily injury which the lawyer reasonably believes is intended by a client. It is very difficult for a lawyer to "know" when such a heinous purpose will actually be carried out, for the client may have a change of mind.

The lawyer's exercise of discretion requires consideration of such factors as the nature of the lawyer's relationship with the client and with those who might be injured by the client, the lawyer's own involvement in the transaction and factors that may extenuate the conduct in question. Where practical, the lawyer should seek to persuade the client to take suitable action. In any case, a disclosure adverse to the client's interest should be no greater than the lawyer reasonably believes necessary to the purpose. A lawyer's decision not to take preventive action permitted by paragraph (b)(1) does not violate this Rule.

Withdrawal

If the lawyer's services will be used by the client in materially furthering a course of criminal or fraudulent conduct, the lawyer must withdraw, as stated in Rule 1.16(a)(1).

After withdrawal the lawyer is required to refrain from making disclosure of the clients' confidences, except as otherwise provided in Rule 1.6. Neither this Rule nor Rule 1.8(b) nor Rule 1.16(d) prevents the lawyer from giving notice of the fact of withdrawal, and the lawyer may also withdraw or disaffirm any opinion, document, affirmation, or the like.

Where the client is an organization, the lawyer may be in doubt whether contemplated conduct will actually be carried out by the organization. Where necessary to guide conduct in connection with this Rule, the lawyer may make inquiry within the organization as indicated in Rule 1.13(b).

Dispute Concerning Lawyer's Conduct

Where a legal claim or disciplinary charge alleges complicity of the lawyer in a client's conduct or other misconduct of the lawyer involving representation of the client, the lawyer may respond to the extent the lawyer reasonably believes necessary to establish a defense. The same is true with respect to a claim involving the conduct or representation of a former client. The lawyer's right to respond arises when an assertion of such complicity has been made. Paragraph (b)(2) does not require the lawyer to await the commencement of an action or proceeding that charges such complicity, so that the defense may be established by responding directly to a third party who has made such an assertion. The right to defend, of course, applies where a proceeding has been commenced. Where practicable and not prejudicial to the lawyer's ability to establish the defense, the lawyer should advise the client of the third party's assertion and request that the client respond appropriately. In any event, disclosure should be no greater than the lawyer reasonably believes is necessary to vindicate innocence, the disclosure should be made in a manner which limits access to the information to the tribunal or other persons having a need to know it, and appropriate protective orders or other arrangements should be sought by the lawyer to the fullest extent practicable.

If the lawyer is charged with wrongdoing in which the client's conduct is implicated, the rule of confidentiality should not prevent the lawyer from defending against the charge. Such a charge can arise in a civil, criminal or professional disciplinary proceeding, and can be based on a wrong allegedly committed by the lawyer against the client, or on a wrong alleged by a third person; for example, a person claiming to have been defrauded by the lawyer and client acting together. A lawyer entitled to a fee is permitted by paragraph (b)(2) to prove the services rendered in an action to collect it. This aspect of the rule expresses the principle that the beneficiary of a fiduciary relationship may not exploit it to the detriment of the fiduciary. As stated above, the lawyer must make every effort practicable to avoid unnecessary disclosure of information relating to a representation, to limit disclosure to those having the need to know it, and to obtain protective orders or make other arrangements minimizing the risk of disclosure.

Disclosures Otherwise Required or Authorized

The attorney-client privilege is differently defined in various jurisdictions. If a lawyer is called as a witness to give testimony concerning a client, absent waiver by the client, Rule 1.6(a) requires the lawyer to invoke the privilege when it is applicable. The lawyer must comply with the final orders of a court or other tribunal of competent jurisdiction requiring the lawyer to give information about the client.

The Rules of Professional Conduct in various circumstances permit or require a lawyer to disclose information relating to the representation. See Rules 2.2, 2.3, 3.3 and 4.1. In addition to these provisions, a lawyer may be obligated or permitted by other provisions of law to give information about a client. Whether another provision of law supersedes Rule 1.6 is a matter of interpretation beyond the scope of these Rules, but a presumption should exist against such a supersession.

Former Client

The duty of confidentiality continues after the client-lawyer relationship has terminated.

RULE 1.7 Conflict of Interest: General Rule

(a) A lawyer shall not represent a client if the representation of that client will be directly adverse to another client, unless:

(1) the lawyer reasonably believes the representation will not adversely affect the relationship with the other client; and

(2) each client consents after consultation.

(b) A lawyer shall not represent a client if the representation of that client may be materially limited by the lawyer's responsibilities to another client or to a third person, or by the lawyer's own interests, unless:

(1) the lawyer reasonably believes the representation will not be adversely affected; and

(2) the client consents after consultation. When representation of multiple clients in a single matter is undertaken, the consultation shall include explanation of the implications of the common representation and the advantages and risks involved.

COMMENT:
Loyalty to a Client

Loyalty is an essential element in the lawyer's relationship to a client. An impermissible conflict of interest may exist before representation is undertaken, in which event the representation should be declined. If such a conflict arises after representation has been undertaken, the lawyer should withdraw from the representation. See Rule 1.16. Where more than one client is involved and the lawyer withdraws because a conflict arises after representation, whether the lawyer may continue to represent any of the clients is determined by Rule 1.9. See also Rule 2.2(c). As to whether a client-lawyer relationship exists or, having once been established, is continuing, see Comment to Rule 1.3 and Scope.

As a general proposition, loyalty to a client prohibits undertaking representation directly adverse to that client without that client's consent. Paragraph (a) expresses that general rule. Thus, a lawyer ordinarily may not act as advocate against a person the lawyer represents in some other matter, even if it is wholly unrelated. On the other hand, simultaneous representation in unrelated matters of clients whose interests are only generally adverse, such as competing economic enterprises, does not require consent of the respective clients. Paragraph (a) applies only when the representation of one client would be directly adverse to the other.

Loyalty to a client is also impaired when a lawyer cannot consider, recommend or carry out an appropriate course of action for the client because of the lawyer's other responsibilities or interests. The conflict in effect forecloses alternatives that would otherwise be available to the client. Paragraph (b) addresses such situations. A possible conflict does not itself preclude the representation. The critical questions are the likelihood that a conflict will eventuate and, if it does, whether it will materially interfere with the lawyer's independent professional judgment in considering alternatives or foreclose courses of action that reasonably should be pursued on behalf of the client. Consideration should be given to whether the client wishes to accommodate the other interest involved.

Consultation and Consent

A client may consent to representation notwithstanding a conflict. However, as indicated in paragraph (a)(1) with respect to representation directly adverse to a client, and paragraph (b)(1) with respect to material limitations on representation of a client, when a disinterested lawyer would conclude that the client should not agree to the representation under the circumstances, the lawyer involved cannot properly ask for such agreement or provide representation on the basis of the client's consent. When more than one client is involved, the question of conflict must be resolved as to each client. Moreover, there may be circumstances where it is impossible to make the disclosure necessary to obtain consent. For example, when the lawyer represents different clients in related matters and one of the clients refuses to consent to the disclosure necessary to permit the other client to make an informed decision, the lawyer cannot properly ask the latter to consent.

Lawyer's Interests

The lawyer's own interests should not be permitted to have adverse effect on representation of a client. For example, a lawyer's need for income should not lead the lawyer to undertake matters that cannot be handled competently and at a reasonable fee. See Rules 1.1 and 1.5. If the probity of a lawyer's own conduct in a transaction is in serious question, it may be difficult or impossible for the lawyer to give a client detached advice. A lawyer may not allow related business interests to affect representation, for example, by referring clients to an enterprise in which the lawyer has an undisclosed interest.

Conflicts in Litigation

Paragraph (a) prohibits representation of opposing parties in litigation. Simultaneous representation of parties whose interest in litigation may conflict, such as co-plaintiffs or co-defendants, is governed by paragraph (b). An impermissible conflict may exist by reason of substantial discrepancy in the parties' testimony, incompatibility in positions in relation to an opposing party or the fact that there are substantially different possibilities of settlement of the claims or liabilities in question. Such conflicts can arise in criminal cases as well as civil. The potential for conflict of interest in representing multiple defendants in a criminal case is so grave that ordinarily a lawyer should decline to represent more than one codefendant. On the other hand, common representation of persons having similar interests is proper if the risk of adverse effect is minimal and the requirements of paragraph (b) are met. Compare Rule 2.2 involving intermediation between clients.

Ordinarily, a lawyer may not act as advocate against a client the lawyer represents in some other matter, even if the other matter is wholly unrelated. However, there are circumstances in which a lawyer may act as advocate against a client. For example, a lawyer representing an enterprise with diverse operations may accept employment as an advocate against the enterprise in an unrelated matter if doing so will not adversely affect the lawyer's relationship with the enterprise or conduct of the suit and if both clients consent upon consultation. By the same token, government lawyers in some circumstances may represent government employees in proceedings in which a government agency is the opposing party. The propriety of concurrent representation can depend on the nature of the litigation. For example, a suit charging fraud entails conflict to a degree not involved in a suit for a declaratory judgment concerning statutory interpretation.

A lawyer may represent parties having antagonistic positions on a legal question that has arisen in different cases, unless representation of either client would be adversely affected. Thus, it is ordinarily not improper to assert such positions in cases pending in different trial courts, but it may be improper to do so in cases pending at the same time in an appellate court.

Interest of Person Paying for a Lawyer's Service

A lawyer may be paid from a source other than the client, if the client is informed of that fact and consents and the arrangement does not compromise the lawyer's duty of loyalty to the client. See Rule 1.8(f). For example, when an insurer and its insured have conflicting interests in a matter arising from a liability insurance agreement, and the insurer is required to provide special counsel for the insured, the arrangement should assure the special counsel's professional independence. So also, when a corporation and its directors or employees are involved in a controversy in which they have conflicting interests, the corporation may provide funds for separate legal representation of the directors or employees, if the clients consent after consultation and the arrangement ensures the lawyer's professional independence.

Other Conflict Situations

Conflicts of interest in contexts other than litigation sometimes may be difficult to assess. Relevant factors in determining whether there is potential for adverse effect include the duration and intimacy of the lawyer's relationship with the client or clients involved, the functions being performed by the lawyer, the likelihood that actual conflict will arise and the likely prejudice to the client from the conflict if it does arise. The question is often one of proximity and degree.

For example, a lawyer may not represent multiple parties to a negotiation whose interests are fundamentally antagonistic to each other, but common representation is permissible where the clients are generally aligned in interest even though there is some difference of interest among them.

Conflict questions may also arise in estate planning and estate administration. A lawyer may be called upon to prepare wills for several family members, such as husband

and wife, and, depending upon the circumstances, a conflict of interest may arise. In estate administration the identity of the client may be unclear under the law of a particular jurisdiction. Under one view, the client is the fiduciary; under another view the client is the estate or trust, including its beneficiaries. The lawyer should make clear the relationship to the parties involved.

A lawyer for a corporation or other organization who is also a member of its board of directors should determine whether the responsibilities of the two roles may conflict. The lawyer may be called on to advise the corporation in matters involving actions of the directors. Consideration should be given to the frequency with which such situations may arise, the potential intensity of the conflict, the effect of the lawyer's resignation from the board and the possibility of the corporation's obtaining legal advice from another lawyer in such situations. If there is material risk that the dual role will compromise the lawyer's independence of professional judgment, the lawyer should not serve as a director.

Conflict Charged by an Opposing Party

Resolving questions of conflict of interest is primarily the responsibility of the lawyer undertaking the representation. In litigation, a court may raise the question when there is reason to infer that the lawyer has neglected the responsibility. In a criminal case, inquiry by the court is generally required when a lawyer represents multiple defendants. Where the conflict is such as clearly to call in question the fair or efficient administration of justice, opposing counsel may properly raise the question. Such an objection should be viewed with caution, however, for it can be misused as a technique of harassment. See Scope.

RULE 1.8 Conflict of Interest: Prohibited Transactions

(a) A lawyer shall not enter into a business transaction with a client or knowingly acquire an ownership, possessory, security or other pecuniary interest adverse to a client unless:

(1) the transaction and terms on which the lawyer acquires the interest are fair and reasonable to the client and are fully disclosed and transmitted in writing to the client in a manner which can be reasonably understood by the client;

(2) the client is given a reasonable opportunity to seek the advice of independent counsel in the transaction; and

(3) the client consents in writing thereto.

(b) A lawyer shall not use information relating to representation of a client to the disadvantage of the client unless the client consents after consultation.

(c) A lawyer shall not prepare an instrument giving the lawyer or a person related to the lawyer as parent, child, sibling, or spouse any substantial gift from a client, including a testamentary gift, except where the client is related to the donee.

(d) Prior to the conclusion of representation of a client, a lawyer shall not make or negotiate an agreement giving the lawyer literary or media rights to a portrayal or account based in substantial part on information relating to the representation.

(e) A lawyer shall not provide financial assistance to a client in connection with pending or contemplated litigation, except that:

(1) a lawyer may advance court costs and expenses of litigation, the repayment of which may be contingent on the outcome of the matter; and

(2) a lawyer representing an indigent client may pay court costs and expenses of litigation on behalf of the client.

(f) A lawyer shall not accept compensation for representing a client from one other than the client unless:

(1) the client consents after consultation;

(2) there is no interference with the lawyer's independence of professional judgment or with the client-lawyer relationship; and

(3) information relating to representation of a client is protected as required by Rule 1.6

(g) A lawyer who represents two or more clients shall not participate in making an aggregate settlement of the claims of or against the clients, or in a criminal case an aggregated agreement as to guilty or nolo contendere pleas, unless each client consents after consultation, including disclosure of the existence and nature of all the claims or pleas involved and of the participation of each person in the settlement.

(h) A lawyer shall not make an agreement prospectively limiting the lawyer's liability to a client for malpractice unless permitted by law and the client is independently represented in making the agreement, or settle a claim for such liability with an unrepresented client or former client without first advising that person in writing that independent representation is appropriate in connection therewith.

(i) A lawyer related to another lawyer as parent, child, sibling or spouse shall not represent a client in a representation directly adverse to a person who the lawyer knows is represented by the other lawyer except upon consent by the client after consultation regarding the relationship.

(j) A lawyer shall not acquire a proprietary interest in the cause of action or subject matter of litigation the lawyer is conducting for a client, except that the lawyer may:

(1) acquire a lien granted by law to secure the lawyer's fee or expenses; and

(2) contract with a client for a reasonable contingent fee in a civil case.

COMMENT:
Transactions Between Client and Lawyer

As a general principle, all transactions between client and lawyer should be fair and reasonable to the client. In such transactions a review by independent counsel on behalf of the client is often advisable. Furthermore, a lawyer may not exploit information relating to the representation to the client's disadvantage. For example, a lawyer who has learned that the client is investing in specific real estate may not, without the client's consent, seek to acquire nearby property where doing so would adversely affect the client's plan for investment. Paragraph (a) does not, however, apply to standard commercial transactions between the lawyer and the client for products or services that the client generally markets to others, for example banking or brokerage services, medical services, products manufactured or distributed by the client, and utilities services. In such transactions, the lawyer has no advantage in dealing with the client, and the restrictions in paragraph (a) are unnecessary and impracticable.

A lawyer may accept a gift from a client, if the transaction meets general standards of fairness. For example, a simple gift such as a present given at a holiday or as a token of appreciation is permitted. If effectuation of a substantial gift requires preparing a legal instrument such as a will or conveyance, however, the client should have the detached advice that another lawyer can provide. Paragraph (c) recognizes an exception where the client is a relative of the donee or the gift is not substantial.

Literary Rights

An agreement by which a lawyer acquires literary or media rights concerning the conduct of the representation creates a conflict between the interests of the client and the personal interests of the lawyer. Measures suitable in the representation of the client may detract from the publication value of an account of the representation. Paragraph (d) does not prohibit a lawyer representing a client in a transaction concerning literary property from agreeing that the lawyer's fee shall consist of a share in ownership in the property, if the arrangement conforms to Rule 1.5 and paragraph (j).

Person Paying for Lawyer's Services

Rule 1.8(f) requires disclosure of the fact that the lawyer's services are being paid for by a third party. Such an arrangement must also conform to the requirements of Rule 1.6 concerning confidentiality and Rule 1.7 concerning conflict of interest. Where the client is a class, consent may be obtained on behalf of the class by court-supervised procedure.

Family Relationships Between Lawyers

Rule 1.8(i) applies to related lawyers who are in different firms. Related lawyers in the same firm are governed by Rules 1.7, 1.9, and 1.10. The disqualification stated in Rule 1.8(i) is personal and is not imputed to members of firms with whom the lawyers are associated.

Acquisition of Interest in Litigation

Paragraph (j) states the traditional general rule that lawyers are prohibited from acquiring a proprietary interest in litigation. This general rule, which has its basis in common law champerty and maintenance, is subject to specific exceptions developed in decisional law and continued in these Rules, such as the exception for reasonable contingent fees set forth in Rule 1.5 and the exception for certain advances of the costs of litigation set forth in paragraph (e).

This Rule is not intended to apply to customary qualification and limitations in legal opinions and memoranda.

RULE 1.9 Conflict of Interest: Former Client

A lawyer who has formerly represented a client in a matter shall not thereafter:

(a) represent another person in the same or a substantially related matter in which that person's interests are materially adverse to the interests of the former client unless the former client consents after consultation; or

(b) use information relating to the representation to the disadvantage of the former client except as Rule 1.6 would permit with respect to a client or when the information has become generally known.

COMMENT:

After termination of a client-lawyer relationship, a lawyer may not represent another client except in conformity with this Rule. The principles in Rule 1.7 determine whether the interests of the present and former client are adverse. Thus, a lawyer could not properly seek to rescind on behalf of a new client a contract drafted on behalf of the former client. So also a lawyer who had prosecuted an accused person could not properly represent the accused in a subsequent civil action against the government concerning the same transaction.

The scope of a "matter" for purposes of Rule 1.9(a) may depend on the facts of a particular situation or transaction. The lawyer's involvement in a matter can also be a question of degree. When a lawyer has been directly involved in a specific transaction, subsequent representation of other clients with materially adverse interests clearly is prohibited. On the other hand, a lawyer who recurrently handled a type of problem for a former client is not precluded from later representing another client in a wholly distinct problem of that type even though the subsequent representation involves a position adverse to the prior client. Similar considerations can apply to the reassignment of military lawyers between defense and prosecution functions within the same military jurisdiction. The underlying question is whether the lawyer was so involved in the matter that the subsequent representation can be justly regarded as a changing of sides in the matter in question.

Information acquired by the lawyer in the course of representing a client may not subsequently be used by the lawyer to the disadvantage of the client. However, the fact that a lawyer has once served a client does not preclude the lawyer from using generally known information about that client when later representing another client.

Disqualification from subsequent representation is for the protection of clients and can be waived by them. A waiver is effective only if there is disclosure of the circumstances, including the lawyer's intended role in behalf of the new client.

With regard to an opposing party's raising a question of conflict of interest, see Comment to Rule 1.7. With regard to disqualification of a firm with which a lawyer is associated, see Rule 1.10.

RULE 1.10 Imputed Disqualification: General Rule

(a) While lawyers are associated in a firm, none of them shall knowingly represent a client when any one of them practicing alone would be prohibited from doing so by Rules 1.7, 1.8(c), 1.9 or 2.2.

(b) When a lawyer becomes associated with a firm, the firm may not knowingly represent a person in the same or a substantially related matter in which that lawyer, or a firm with which the lawyer was associated, had previously represented a client whose interests are materially adverse to that person and about whom the lawyer had acquired information protected by Rules 1.6 and 1.9(b) that is material to the matter.

(c) When a lawyer has terminated an association with a firm, the firm is not prohibited from thereafter representing a person with interests materially adverse to those of a client represented by the formerly associated lawyer unless:

(1) the matter is the same or substantially related to that in which the formerly associated lawyer represented the client; and

(2) any lawyer remaining in the firm has information protected by Rules 1.6 and 1.9(b) that is material to the matter.

(d) A disqualification prescribed by this Rule may be waived by the affected client under the conditions stated in Rule 1.7.

COMMENT:
Definition of "Firm"

For purposes of the Rules of Professional Conduct, the term "firm" includes lawyers in a private firm, and lawyers employed in the legal department of a corporation or other organization, or in a legal services organization. Whether two or more lawyers constitute a firm within this definition can depend on the specific facts. For example, two practitioners who share office space and occasionally consult or assist each other ordinarily would not be regarded as constituting a firm. However, if they present themselves to the public in a way suggesting that they are a firm or conduct themselves as a firm, they should be regarded as a firm for purposes of the Rules. The terms of any formal agreement between associated lawyers are relevant in determining whether they are a firm, as is the fact that they have mutual access to confidential information concerning the clients they serve. Furthermore, it is relevant in doubtful cases to consider the underlying purpose of the rule that is involved. A group of lawyers could be regarded as a firm for purposes of the rule that the same lawyer should not represent opposing parties in litigation, while it might not be so regarded for purposes of the rule that information acquired by one lawyer is attributed to another.

With respect to the law department of an organization, there is ordinarily no question that the members of the department constitute a firm within the meaning of the Rules of Professional Conduct. However, there can be uncertainty as to the identity of the client. For example, it may not be clear whether the law department of a corporation represents a subsidiary or an affiliated corporation, as well as the corporation by which the members of the department are directly employed. A similar question can arise concerning an unincorporated association and its local affiliates.

Similar questions can also arise with respect to lawyers in legal aid. Lawyers employed in the same unit of a legal service organization constitute a firm, but not necessarily those employed in separate units. As in the case of independent practitioners, whether the lawyers should be treated as associated with each other can depend on the particular rule that is involved, and on the specific facts of the situation.

Where a lawyer has joined a private firm after having represented the government, the situation is governed by Rule 1.11(a) and (b); where a lawyer represents the government after having served private clients, the situation is governed by Rule 1.11(c)(1). The individual lawyer involved is bound by the Rules generally, including Rules 1.6, 1.7, and 1.9.

Different provisions are thus made for movement of a lawyer from one private firm to another and for movement of a lawyer between a private firm and the government. The government is entitled to protection of its client confidences, and therefore to the protections provided in Rules 1.6, 1.9, and 1.11. However, if the more extensive disqualification in Rule 1.10 were applied to former government lawyers, the potential effect on the government would be unduly burdensome. The government deals with all private citizens and organizations, and thus has a much wider circle of adverse legal interests than does any private law firm. In these circumstances, the government's recruitment of lawyers would be seriously impaired if Rule 1.10 were applied to the government. On balance, therefore, the government is better served in the long run by the protections stated in Rule 1.11.

Principles of Imputed Disqualification

The rule of imputed disqualification stated in paragraph (a) gives effect to the principle of loyalty to the client as it applies to lawyers who practice in a law firm. Such situations can be considered from the premise that a firm of lawyers is essentially one lawyer for purposes of the rules governing loyalty to the client, or from the premise that each lawyer is vicariously bound by the obligation of loyalty owed by each lawyer with whom the lawyer is associated. Paragraph (a) operates only among the lawyers currently associated in a firm. When a lawyer moves from one firm to another, the situation is governed by paragraphs (b) and (c).

Lawyers Moving Between Firms

When lawyers have been associated in a firm but then end their association, however, the problem is more complicated. The fiction that the law firm is the same as a single lawyer is no longer wholly realistic. There are several competing considerations. First, the client previously represented must be reasonably assured that the principle of loyalty to the client is not compromised. Second, the rule of disqualification should not be so broadly cast as to preclude other persons from having reasonable choice of legal counsel. Third, the rule of disqualification should not unreasonably hamper lawyers from forming new associations and taking on new clients after having left a previous association. In this connection, it should be recognized that today many lawyers practice in firms, that many to some degree limit their practice to one field or another, and that many move from one association to another several times in their careers. If the concept of imputed disqualification were defined with unqualified rigor, the result would be radical curtailment of the opportunity of lawyers to move from one practice setting to another and of the opportunity of clients to change counsel.

Reconciliation of these competing principles in the past has been attempted under two rubrics. One approach has been to seek per se rules of disqualification. For example, it has been held that a partner in a law firm is conclusively presumed to have access to all confidences concerning all clients of the firm. Under this analysis, if a lawyer has been a partner in one law firm and then becomes a partner in another law firm, there is a presumption that all confidences known by a partner in the first firm are known to all partners in the second firm. This presumption might properly be applied in some circumstances, especially where the client has been extensively represented, but may be unrealistic where the client was represented only for limited purposes. Furthermore, such a rigid rule exaggerates the difference between a partner and an associate in modern law firms.

The other rubric formerly used for dealing with vicarious disqualification is the appearance of impropriety proscribed in Canon 9 of the ABA Model Code of Professional Responsibility. This rubric has a twofold problem. First, the appearance of impropriety can be taken to include any new client-lawyer relationship that might make a former client feel anxious. If that meaning were adopted, disqualification would become little more than a question of subjective judgment by the former client. Second, since "impropriety" is undefined, the term "appearance of impropriety" is question-begging. It therefore has to be recognized that the problem of imputed disqualification cannot be properly resolved either by simple analogy to a lawyer practicing alone or by the very general concept of appearance of impropriety.

A rule based on a functional analysis is more appropriate for determining the question of vicarious disqualification. Two functions are involved: preserving confidentiality and avoiding positions adverse to a client.

Confidentiality

Preserving confidentiality is a question of access to information. Access to information, in turn, is essentially a question of fact in particular circumstances, aided by inferences, deductions or working presumptions that reasonably may be made about the way in which lawyers work together. A lawyer may have general access to files of all clients of a law firm and may regularly participate in discussions of their affairs; it should be inferred that such a lawyer in fact is privy to all information about all the firm's clients. In contrast, another lawyer may have access to the files of only a limited number of clients and participate in discussion of the affairs of no other clients; in the absence of information to the contrary, it should be inferred that such a lawyer in fact is privy to information about the clients actually served but not those of other clients.

Application of paragraphs (b) and (c) depends on a situation's particular facts. In any such inquiry, the burden of proof should rest upon the firm whose disqualification is sought.

Paragraphs (b) and (c) operate to disqualify the firm only when the lawyer involved has actual knowledge of information protected by Rules 1.6 and 1.9(b). Thus, if a lawyer while with one firm acquired no knowledge of information relating to a particular client of the firm, and that lawyer later joined another firm, neither the lawyer individually nor the second firm is disqualified from representing another client in the same or a related matter even though the interests of the two clients conflict.

Independent of the question of disqualification of a firm, a lawyer changing professional association has a continuing duty to preserve confidentiality of information about a client formerly represented. See Rules 1.6 and 1.9.

Adverse Positions

The second aspect of loyalty to client is the lawyer's obligation to decline subsequent representations involving positions adverse to a former client arising in substantially related matters. This obligation requires abstention from adverse representation by the individual lawyer involved, but does not properly entail abstention of other lawyers through imputed disqualification. Hence, this aspect of the problem is governed by Rule 1.9(a). Thus, if a lawyer left one firm for another, the new affiliation would not preclude the firms involved from continuing to represent clients with adverse interests in the same or related matters, so long as the conditions of Rule 1.10(b) and (c) concerning confidentiality have been met.

RULE 1.11 Successive Government and Private Employment

(a) Except as law may otherwise expressly permit, a lawyer shall not represent a private client in connection with a matter in which the law-

yer participated personally and substantially as a public officer or employee, unless the appropriate government agency consents after consultation. No lawyer in a firm with which that lawyer is associated may knowingly undertake or continue representation in such a matter unless:

    (1) the disqualified lawyer is screened from any participation in the matter and is apportioned no part of the fee therefrom; and

    (2) written notice is promptly given to the appropriate government agency to enable it to ascertain compliance with the provisions of this rule.

(b) Except as law may otherwise expressly permit, a lawyer having information that the lawyer knows is confidential government information about a person acquired when the lawyer was a public officer or employee, may not represent a private client whose interests are adverse to that person in a matter in which the information could be used to the material disadvantage of that person. A firm with which that lawyer is associated may undertake or continue representation in the matter only if the disqualified lawyer is screened from any participation in the matter and is apportioned no part of the fee therefrom.

(c) Except as law may otherwise expressly permit, a lawyer serving as a public officer or employee shall not:

    (1) participate in a matter in which the lawyer participated personally and substantially while in private practice or nongovernmental employment, unless under applicable law no one is, or by lawful delegation may be, authorized to act in the lawyer's stead in the matter; or

    (2) negotiate for private employment with any person who is involved as a party or as attorney for a party in a matter in which the lawyer is partici-

pating personally and substantially.

(d) As used in this Rule, the term "matter" includes:

(1) any judicial or other proceeding, application, request for a ruling or other determination, contract, claim, controversy, investigation, charge, accusation, arrest or other particular matter involving a specific party or parties; and

(2) any other matter covered by the conflict of interest rules of the appropriate government agency.

(e) As used in this Rule, the term "confidential government information" means information which has been obtained under governmental authority and which, at the time this Rule is applied, the government is prohibited by law from disclosing to the public or has a legal privilege not to disclose, and which is not otherwise available to the public.

COMMENT:

This Rule prevents a lawyer from exploiting public office for the advantage of a private client. It is a counterpart of Rule 1.10(b), which applies to lawyers moving from one firm to another.

A lawyer representing a government agency, whether employed or specially retained by the government, is subject to the Rules of Professional Conduct, including the prohibition against representing adverse interests stated in Rule 1.7 and the protections afforded former clients in Rule 1.9. In addition, such a lawyer is subject to Rule 1.11 and to statutes and government regulations regarding conflict of interest. Such statutes and regulations may circumscribe the extent to which the government agency may give consent under this Rule.

Where the successive clients are a public agency and a private client, the risk exists that power or discretion vested in public authority might be used for the special benefit of a private client. A lawyer should not be in a position where benefit to a private client might affect performance of the lawyer's professional functions on behalf of public authority. Also, unfair advantage could accrue to the private client by reason of access to confidential government information about the client's adversary obtainable only through the lawyer's government service. However, the rules governing lawyers presently or formerly employed by a government agency should not be so restrictive as to inhibit transfer of employment to and from the government. The government has a legitimate need to attract qualified lawyers as well as to maintain high ethical standards. The provisions for screening and waiver are necessary to prevent the disqualification rule from imposing too severe a deterrent against entering public service.

When the client is an agency of one government, that agency should be treated as a private client for purposes of this Rule if the lawyer thereafter represents an agency of another government, as when a lawyer represents a city and subsequently is employed by a federal agency.

Paragraphs (a)(1) and (b) do not prohibit a lawyer from receiving a salary or partnership share established by prior independent agreement. They prohibit directly relating the attorney's compensation to the fee in the matter in which the lawyer is disqualified.

Paragraph (a)(2) does not require that a lawyer give notice to the government agency at a time when premature disclosure would injure the client; a requirement for premature disclosure might preclude engagement of the lawyer. Such notice is, however, required to be given as soon as practicable in order that the government agency will have a reasonable opportunity to ascertain that the lawyer is complying with Rule 1.11 and to take appropriate action if it believes the lawyer is not complying.

Paragraph (b) operates only when the lawyer in question has knowledge of the information, which means actual knowledge; it does not operate with respect to information that merely could be imputed to the lawyer.

Paragraphs (a) and (c) do not prohibit a lawyer from jointly representing a private party and a government agency when doing so is premitted by Rule 1.7 and is not otherwise prohibited by law.

Paragraph (c) does not disqualify other lawyers in the agency with which the lawyer in question has become associated.

RULE 1.12 Former Judge or Arbitrator

(a) Except as stated in paragraph (d), a lawyer shall not represent anyone in connection with a matter in which the lawyer participated personally and substantially as a judge or other adjudicative officer, arbitrator or law clerk to such a person, unless all parties to the proceeding consent after disclosure.

(b) A lawyer shall not negotiate for employment with any person who is involved as a party or as attorney for a party in a matter in which the lawyer is participating personally and substantially as a judge or other adjudicative officer, or arbitrator. A lawyer serving as a law clerk to a judge, other adjudicative officer or arbitrator may negotiate for employment with a party or attorney involved in a matter in which the clerk is participating personally and substantially, but only after the lawyer has notified the judge, other adjudicative officer or arbitrator.

(c) If a lawyer is disqualified by paragraph (a), no lawyer in a firm with which that lawyer is associated may knowingly undertake or continue representation in the matter unless:

(1) the disqualified lawyer is screened from any participation in the matter and is apportioned no part of the fee therefrom; and

(2) written notice is promptly given to the appropriate tribunal to enable it to ascertain compliance with the provisions of this rule.

(d) An arbitrator selected as a partisan of a party in a multi-member arbitration panel is not prohibited from subsequently representing that party.

COMMENT:

This Rule generally parallels Rule 1.11. The term "personally and substantially" signifies that a judge who was a member of a multimember court, and thereafter left judicial office to practice law, is not prohibited from representing a client in a matter pending in the court, but in which the former judge did not participate. So also the fact that a former judge exercised administrative responsibility in a court does not prevent the former judge from acting as a lawyer in a matter where the judge had previously exercised remote or incidental administrative responsibility that did not affect the merits. Compare the Comment to Rule 1.11. The term "adjudicative officer" includes such officials as judges pro tempore, referees, special masters, hearing officers and other parajudicial officers, and also lawyers who serve as part-time judges. Compliance Canons A(2), B(2) and C of the Model Code of Judicial Conduct provide that a part-time judge, judge pro tempore or retired judge recalled to active service, may not "act as a lawyer in any proceeding in which he served as a judge or in any other proceeding related thereto." Although phrased differently from this Rule, those Rules correspond in meaning.

RULE 1.13 Organization as Client

(a) A lawyer employed or retained by an organization represents the organization acting through its duly authorized constituents.

(b) If a lawyer for an organization knows that an officer, employee or other person associated with the organization is engaged in action, intends to act or refuses to act in a matter related to the representation that is a violation of a legal obligation to the organization, or a violation of law which reasonably might be imputed to the organization, and is likely to result in substantial injury to the organization, the lawyer shall proceed as is reasonably necessary in the best interest of the organization. In determining how to proceed, the lawyer shall give due consideration to the seriousness of the violation and its consequences, the scope and nature of the lawyer's representation, the responsibility in the organization and the apparent motivation of the person involved, the policies of the organization concerning such matters and any other relevant considerations. Any measures taken shall be designed to minimize disruption of the organization and the risk of revealing information relating to the representation to persons outside the organization. Such measures may include among others:

(1) asking reconsideration of the matter;

(2) advising that a separate legal opinion on the matter be sought for presentation to appropriate authority in the organization; and

(3) referring the matter to higher authority in the organization, including, if warranted by the seriousness of the matter, referral to the highest authority that can act in behalf of the organization as determined by applicable law.

(c) If, despite the lawyer's efforts in accordance with paragraph (b), the highest authority that can act on behalf of the organization insists upon action, or a refusal to act, that is clearly a violation of law and is likely to result in substantial injury to the organization, the lawyer may resign in accordance with Rule 1.16.

(d) In dealing with an organization's directors, officers, employees, members, shareholders or other constituents, a lawyer shall explain the identity of the client when it is apparent that the organization's interests are adverse to those of the constituents with whom the lawyer is dealing.

(e) A lawyer representing an organization may also represent any of its directors, officers, employees, members, shareholders or other constituents, subject to the provisions of Rule 1.7. If the organization's consent to the dual representation is required by Rule 1.7, the consent shall be given by an appropriate official of the organization other than the individual who is to be represented, or by the shareholders.

COMMENT:
The Entity as the Client

An organizational client is a legal entity, but it cannot act except through its officers, directors, employees, shareholders and other constituents.

Officers, directors, employees and shareholders are the constituents of the corporate organizational client. The duties defined in this Comment apply equally to unincorporated associations. "Other constituents" as used in this Comment means the positions equivalent to officers, directors, employees and shareholders held by persons acting for organizational clients that are not corporations.

When one of the constituents of an organizational client communicates with the organization's lawyer in that person's organizational capacity, the communication is protected by Rule 1.6. Thus, by way of example, if an organizational client requests its lawyer to investigate allegations of wrongdoing, interviews made in the course of that investigation between the lawyer and the client's employees or other constituents are covered by Rule 1.6. This does not mean, however, that constituents of an organizational client are the clients of the lawyer. The lawyer may not disclose to such constituents information relating to the representation except for disclosures explicitly or impliedly authorized by the organizational client in order to carry out the representation or as otherwise permitted by Rule 1.6.

When constituents of the organization make decisions for it, the decisions ordinarily must be accepted by the lawyer even if their utility or prudence is doubtful. Decisions concerning policy and operations, including ones entailing serious risk, are not as such in the lawyer's province. However, different considerations arise when the lawyer knows that the organization may be substantially injured by action of constituent that is in violation of law. In such a circumstance, it may be reasonably necessary for the lawyer to ask the constituent to reconsider the matter. If that fails, of if the matter is of sufficient seriousness and importance to the organization, it may be reasonably necessary for the lawyer to take steps to have the matter reviewed by a higher authority in the organization. Clear justification should exist for seeking review over the head of the constituent normally responsible for it. The stated policy of the organization may define circumstances and prescribe channels for such review, and a lawyer should encourage the formulation of such a policy. Even in the absence of organization policy, however, the lawyer may have an obligation to refer a matter to higher authority, depending on the seriousness of the matter and whether the constituent in question has apparent motives to act at variance with the organization's interest. Review by the chief executive officer or by the board of directors may be required when the matter is of importance commensurate with their authority. At some point it may be useful or essential to obtain an independent legal opinion.

In an extreme case, it may be reasonably necessary for the lawyer to refer the matter to the organization's highest authority. Ordinarily, that is the board of directors or similar governing body. However, applicable law may prescribe that under certain conditions highest authority reposes elsewhere; for example, in the independent directors of a corporation.

Relation to Other Rules

The authority and responsibility provided in paragraph(b) are concurrent with the authority and responsibility provided in other Rules. In particular, this Rule does not limit or expand the lawyer's responsibility under Rules 1.6, 1.8, and 1.16, 3.3 or 4.1. If the lawyer's services are being used by an organization to further a crime or fraud by the organization, Rule 1.2(d) can be applicable.

Government Agency

The duty defined in this Rule applies to governmental organizations. However, when the client is a governmental organization, a different balance may be appropriate between maintaining confidentiality and assuring that the wrongful official act is prevented or rectified, for public business is involved. In addition, duties of lawyers employed by the government or lawyers in military service may be defined by statutes and regulation. Therefore, defining precisely the identity of the client and prescribing the resulting obligations of such lawyers may be more difficult in the government context. Although in some circumstances the client may be a specific agency, it is generally the government as a whole. For example, if the action or failure to act involves the head of a bureau, either the department of which the bureau is a part or the government as a whole may be the client for purpose of this Rule. Moreover, in a matter involving the conduct of government officials, a government lawyer may have authority to question such conduct more extensively than that of a lawyer for a private organization in similar circumstances. This Rule does not limit that authority. See note on Scope.

Clarifying the Lawyer's Role

There are times when the organization's interest may be or become adverse to those of one or more of its constituents. In such circumstances the lawyer should advise any constituent, whose interest the lawyer finds adverse to that of the organization of the conflict or potential conflict of interest, that the lawyer cannot represent such constituent, and that such person may wish to obtain independent representation. Care must be taken to assure that the individual understands that, when there is such adversity of interest, the lawyer for the organization cannot provide legal representation for that constituent individual, and that discussions between the lawyer for the organization and the individual may not be privileged.

Whether such a warning should be given by the lawyer for the organization to any constituent individual may turn on the facts of each case.

Dual Representation

Paragraph (e) recognizes that a lawyer for an organization may also represent a principal officer or major shareholder.

Derivative Actions

Under generally prevailing law, the shareholders or members of a corporation may bring suit to compel the directors to perform their legal obligations in the supervision of the organization. Members of unincorporated associations have essentially the same right. Such an action may be brought nominally by the organization, but usually is, in fact, a legal controversy over management of the organization.

The question can arise whether counsel for the organization may defend such an action. The proposition that the organization is the lawyer's client does not alone resolve the issue. Most derivative actions are a normal incident of an organization's affairs, to be defended by the organization's lawyer like any other suit. However, if the claim involves serious charges of wrongdoing by those in control of the organization, a conflict may arise between the lawyer's duty to the organization and the lawyer's relationship with the board. In those circumstances, Rule 1.7 governs who should represent the directors and the organization.

RULE 1.14 Client Under a Disability

(a) When a client's ability to make adequately considered decisions in connection with the representation is impaired, whether because of minority, mental disability or for some other reason, the lawyer shall, as far as reasonably possible, maintain a normal client-lawyer relationship with the client.

(b) A lawyer may seek the appointment of a guardian or take other protective action with respect to a client, only when the lawyer reasonably believes that the client cannot adequately act in the client's own interest.

COMMENT:

The normal client-lawyer relationship is based on the assumption that the client, when properly advised and assisted, is capable of making decisions about important matters. When the client is a minor or suffers from a mental disorder or disability, however, maintaining the ordinary client-lawyer relationship may not be possible in all respects. In particular, an incapacitated person may have no power to make legally binding decisions. Nevertheless, a client lacking legal competence often has the ability to understand, deliberate upon, and reach conclusions about matters affecting the client's own well-being. Furthermore, to an increasing extent the law recognizes intermediate degrees of competence. For example, children as young as five or six years of age, and certainly those of ten or twelve, are regarded as having opinions that are entitled to weight in legal proceedings concerning their custody. So also, it is recognized that some persons of advanced age can be quite capable of handling routine financial matters while needing special legal protection concerning major transactions.

The fact that a client suffers a disability does not diminish the lawyer's obligation to treat the client with attention and respect. If the person has no guardian or legal representative, the lawyer often must act as de facto guardian. Even if the person does have a legal representative, the lawyer should as far as possible accord the represented person the status of client, particularly in maintaining communication.

If a legal representative has already been appointed for the client, the lawyer should ordinarily look to the representative for decisions on behalf of the client. If a legal representative has not been appointed, the lawyer should see to such an appointment where it would serve the client's best interests. Thus, if a disabled client has substantial property that should be sold for the client's benefit, effective completion of the transaction ordinarily requires appointment of a legal representative. In many circumstances, however, appointment of a legal representative may be expensive or traumatic for the client. Evaluation of these considerations is a matter of professional judgment on the lawyer's part.

If the lawyer represents the guardian as distinct from the ward, and is aware that the guardian is acting adversely to the ward's interest, the lawyer may have an obligation to prevent or rectify the guardian's misconduct. See Rule 1.2(d).

Disclosure of the Client's Condition

Rules of procedure in litigation generally provide that minors or persons suffering mental disability shall be represented by a guardian or next friend if they do not have a general guardian. However, disclosure of the client's disability can adversely affect the client's interests. For example, raising the question of disability could, in some circumstances, lead to proceedings for involuntary commitment. The lawyer's position in such cases is an unavoidably difficult one. The lawyer may seek guidance from an appropriate diagnostician.

RULE 1.15 Safekeeping Property

(a) A lawyer shall hold property of clients or third persons that is in a lawyer's possession in connection with a representation separate from the lawyer's own property. Funds shall be kept in a separate account maintained in the state where the lawyer's office is situated, or elsewhere with the consent of the client or third person. Other property shall be identified as such and appropriately safeguarded. Complete records of such account funds and other property shall be kept by the lawyer and shall be preserved for a period of [five years] after termination of the representation.

(b) Upon receiving funds or other property in which a client or third person has an interest, a lawyer shall promptly notify the client or third person. Except as stated in this Rule or otherwise permitted by law or by agreement with the client, a lawyer shall promptly deliver to the client or third person any funds or other property that the client or third person is entitled to receive and, upon request by the client or third person, shall promptly render a full accounting regarding such property.

(c) When in the course of representation a lawyer is in possession of property in which both the lawyer and another person claim interests, the property shall be kept separate by the lawyer until there is an accounting and severance of their interests. If a dispute arises concerning their respective interests, the

portion in dispute shall be kept separate by the lawyer until the dispute is resolved.

COMMENT:

A lawyer should hold property of others with the care required of a professional fiduciary. Securities should be kept in a safe deposit box, except when some other form of safekeeping is warranted by special circumstances. All property which is the property of clients or third persons should be kept separate from the lawyer's business and personal property and, if monies, in one or more trust accounts. Separate trust accounts may be warranted when administering estate monies or acting in similar fiduciary capacities.

Lawyers often receive funds from third parties from which the lawyer's fee will be paid. If there is risk that the client may divert the funds without paying the fee, the lawyer is not required to remit the portion from which the fee is to be paid. However, a lawyer may not hold funds to coerce a client into accepting the lawyer's contention. The disputed portion of the funds should be kept in trust and the lawyer should suggest means for prompt resolution of the dispute, such as arbitration. The undisputed portion of the funds shall be promptly distributed.

Third parties such as a client's creditors, may have just claims against funds or other property in a lawyer's custody. A lawyer may have a duty under applicable law to protect such third-party claims against wrongful interference by the client, and accordingly may refuse to surrender the property to the client. However, a lawyer should not unilaterally assume to arbitrate a dispute between the client and the third party.

The obligations of a lawyer under this Rule are independent of those arising from activity other than rendering legal services. For example, a lawyer who serves as an escrow agent is governed by the applicable law relating to fiduciaries even though the lawyer does not render legal services in the transaction.

A "client's security fund" provides a means through the collective efforts of the bar to reimburse persons who have lost money or property as a result of dishonest conduct of a lawyer. Where such a fund has been established, a lawyer should participate.

RULE 1.16 Declining or Terminating Representation

(a) Except as stated in paragraph (c), a lawyer shall not represent a client or, where representation has commenced, shall withdraw from the representation of a client if:

(1) the representation will result in violation of the rules of professional conduct or other law;

(2) the lawyer's physical or mental condition materially impairs the lawyer's ability to represent the client; or

(3) the lawyer is discharged.

(b) Except as stated in paragraph (c), a lawyer may withdraw from representing a client if withdrawal can be accomplished without material adverse effect on the interests of the client, or if:

(1) the client persists in a course of action involving the lawyer's services that the lawyer reasonably believes is criminal or fraudulent;

(2) the client has used the lawyer's services to perpetrate a crime or fraud;

(3) a client insists upon pursuing an objective that the lawyer considers repugnant or imprudent;

(4) the client fails substantially to fulfill an obligation to the lawyer regarding the lawyer's services and has been given reasonable warning that the lawyer will withdraw unless the obligation is fulfilled;

(5) the representation will result in an unreasonable finan-

cial burden on the lawyer or has been rendered unreasonably difficult by the client; or
(6) other good cause for withdrawal exists.
(c) **When ordered to do so by a tribunal, a lawyer shall continue representation notwithstanding good cause for terminating the representation.**
(d) **Upon termination of representation, a lawyer shall take steps to the extent reasonably practicable to protect a client's interests, such as giving reasonable notice to the client, allowing time for employment of other counsel, surrendering papers and property to which the client is entitled and refunding any advance payment of fee that has not been earned. The lawyer may retain papers relating to the client to the extent permitted by other law.**

COMMENT:

A lawyer should not accept representation in a matter unless it can be performed competently, promptly, without improper conflict of interest and to completion.

Mandatory Withdrawal

A lawyer ordinarily must decline or withdraw from representation if the client demands that the lawyer engage in conduct that is illegal or violates the Rules of Professional Conduct or other law. The lawyer is not obliged to decline or withdraw simply because the client suggests such a course of conduct; a client may make such a suggestion in the hope that a lawyer will not be constrained by a professional obligation.

When a lawyer has been appointed to represent a client, withdrawal ordinarily requires approval of the appointing authority. See also Rule 6.2. Difficulty may be encountered if withdrawal is based on the client's demand that the lawyer engage in unprofessional conduct. The court may wish an explanation for the withdrawal, while the lawyer may be bound to keep confidential the facts that would constitute such an explanation. The lawyer's statement that professional considerations require termination of the representation ordinarily should be accepted as sufficient.

Discharge

A client has a right to discharge a lawyer at any time, with or without cause, subject to liability for payment for the lawyer's services. Where future dispute about the withdrawal may be anticipated, it may be advisable to prepare a written statement reciting the circumstances.

Whether a client can discharge appointed counsel may depend on applicable law. A client seeking to do so should be given a full explanation of the consequences. These consequences may include a decision by the appointing authority that appointment of successor counsel is unjustified, thus requiring the client to represent himself.

If the client is mentally incompetent, the client may lack the legal capacity to discharge the lawyer, and in any event the discharge may be seriously adverse to the client's interests. The lawyer should make special effort to help the client consider the consequences and, in an extreme case, may initiate proceedings for a conservatorship or similar protection of the client. See Rule 1.14.

Optional Withdrawal

A lawyer may withdraw from representation in some circumstances. The lawyer has the option to withdraw if it can be accomplished without material adverse effect on the client's interests. Withdrawal is also justified if the client persists in a course of action that the lawyer reasonably believes is criminal or fraudulent, for a lawyer is not required to be associated with such conduct even if the lawyer does not further it. Withdrawal is also permitted if the lawyer's services were misused in the past even if that would materially prejudice the client. The lawyer also may withdraw where the client insists on a repugnant or imprudent objective.

A lawyer may withdraw if the client refuses to abide by the terms of an agreement relating to the representation, such as an agreement concerning fees or court costs or an agreement limiting the objectives of the representation.

Assisting the Client Upon Withdrawal

Even if the lawyer has been unfairly discharged by the client, a lawyer must take all reasonable steps to mitigate the consequences to the client. The lawyer may retain papers as security for a fee only to the extent permitted by law.

Whether or not a lawyer for an organization may under certain unusual circumstances have a legal obligation to the organization after withdrawing or being discharged by the organization's highest authority is beyond the scope of these Rules.

COUNSELOR
RULE 2.1 Advisor

In representing a client, a lawyer shall exercise independent professional judgment and render candid advice. In rendering advice, a lawyer may refer not only to law but to other considerations such as moral, economic, social and political factors, that may be relevant to the client's situation.

COMMENT:
Scope of Advice

A client is entitled to straightforward advice expressing the lawyer's honest assessment. Legal advice often involves unpleasant facts and alternatives that a client may be disinclined to confront. In presenting advice, a lawyer endeavors to sustain the client's morale and may put advice in as acceptable a form as honesty permits. However, a lawyer should not be deterred from giving candid advice by the prospect that the advice will be unpalatable to the client.

Advice couched in narrowly legal terms may be of little value to a client, especially where practical considerations, such as cost or effects on other people, are predominant. Purely technical legal advice, therefore, can sometimes be inadequate. It is proper for a lawyer to refer to relevant moral and ethical considerations in giving advice. Although a lawyer is not a moral advisor as such, moral and ethical considerations impinge upon most legal questions and may decisively influence how the law will be applied.

A client may expressly or impliedly ask the lawyer for purely technical advice. When such a request is made by a client experienced in legal matters, the lawyer may accept it at face value. When such a request is made by a client inexperienced in legal matters, however, the lawyer's responsibility as advisor may include indicating that more may be involved than strictly legal considerations.

Matters that go beyond strictly legal questions may also be in the domain of another profession. Family matters can involve problems within the professional competence of psychiatry, clinical psychology or social work; business matters can involve problems within the competence of the accounting profession or of financial specialists. Where consultation with a professional in another field is itself something a competent lawyer would recommend, the lawyer should make such a recommendation. At the same time, a lawyer's advice at its best often consists of recommending a course of action in the face of conflicting recommendations of experts.

Offering Advice

In general, a lawyer is not expected to give advice until asked by the client. However, when a lawyer knows that a client proposes a course of action that is likely to result in substantial adverse legal consequences to the client, duty to the client under Rule 1.4 may require that the lawyer act if the client's course of action is related to the representation. A lawyer ordinarily has no duty to initiate investigation of a client's affairs or to give advice that the client has indicated is unwanted, but a lawyer may initiate advice to a client when doing so appears to be in the client's interest.

Rule 2.2 Intermediary

(a) A lawyer may act as intermediary between clients if:

    (1) the lawyer consults with each client concerning the implications of the common representation, including the advantages and risks involved, and the effect on the attorney-client privileges, and obtains each client's consent to the common representation;

    (2) the lawyer reasonably believes that the matter can be resolved on terms compatible with the clients' best interests, that each client will be able to make adequately informed decisions in the matter and that there is little risk of material prejudice to the interests of any of the clients if the contemplated resolution is unsuccessful; and

    (3) the lawyer reasonably believes that the common representation can be undertaken impartially and without improper effect on other responsibilities the lawyer has to any of the clients.

(b) While acting as intermediary, the lawyer shall consult with each client concerning the decisions to be made and the considerations relevant in making them, so that each client can make adequately informed decisions.

(c) A lawyer shall withdraw as intermediary if any of the clients so requests, or if any of the conditions stated in paragraph (a) is no longer satisfied. Upon withdrawal, the law-yer shall not continue to represent any of the clients in the matter that was the subject of the intermediation.**

COMMENT:

A lawyer acts as intermediary under this Rule when the lawyer represents two or more parties with potentially conflicting interests. A key factor in defining the relationship is whether the parties share responsibility for the lawyer's fee, but the common representation may be inferred from other circumstances. Because confusion can arise as to the lawyer's role where each party is not separately represented, it is important that the lawyer make clear the relationship.

The Rule does not apply to a lawyer acting as arbitrator or mediator between or among parties who are not clients of the lawyer, even where the lawyer has been appointed with the concurrence of the parties. In performing such a role the lawyer may be subject to applicable codes of ethics, such as the Code of Ethics for Arbitration in Commercial Disputes prepared by a joint Committee of the American Bar Association and the American Arbitration Association.

A lawyer acts as intermediary in seeking to establish or adjust a relationship between clients on an amicable and mutually advantageous basis; for example, in helping to organize a business in which two or more clients are entrepreneurs, working out the financial reorganization of an enterprise in which two or more clients have an interest, arranging a property distribution in settlement of an estate or mediating a dispute between clients. The lawyer seeks to resolve potentially conflicting interests by developing the parties' mutual interests. The alternative can be that each party may have to obtain separate representation, with the possibility in some situations of incurring additional cost, complication or even litigation. Given these and other relevant factors, all the clients may prefer that the lawyer act as intermediary.

In considering whether to act as intermediary between clients, a lawyer should be mindful that if the intermediation fails the result can be additional cost, embarrassment and recrimination. In some situations the risk of failure is so great that intermediation is plainly impossible. For example, a lawyer cannot undertake common representation of clients between whom contentious litigation is imminent or who contemplate contentious negotiations. More generally, if the relationship between the parties has already assumed definite antagonism, the possibility that the clients' interests can be adjusted by intermediation ordinarily is not very good.

The appropriateness of intermediation can depend on its form. Forms of intermediation range from informal arbitration, where each client's case is presented by the respective client and the lawyer decides the outcome, to mediation, to common representation where the clients' interests are substantially though not entirely compatible. One form may be appropriate in circumstances where another would not. Other relevant factors are whether the lawyer subsequently will represent both parties on a continuing basis and whether the situation involves creating a relationship between the parties or terminating one.

Confidentiality and Privilege

A particularly important factor in determining the appropriateness of intermediation is the effect on client-lawyer confidentiality and the attorney-client privilege. In a common representation, the lawyer is still required both to keep each client adequately informed and to maintain confidentiality of information relating to the representation. See Rules 1.4 and 1.6. Complying

with both requirements while acting as intermediary requires a delicate balance. If the balance cannot be maintained, the common representation is improper. With regard to the attorney-client privilege, the prevailing rule is that as between commonly represented clients the privilege does not attach. Hence, it must be assumed that if litigation eventuates between the clients, the privilege will not protect any such communications, and the clients should be so advised.

Since the lawyer is required to be impartial between commonly represented clients, intermediation is improper when that impartiality cannot be maintained. For example, a lawyer who has represented one of the clients for a long period and in a variety of matters might have difficulty being impartial between that client and one to whom the lawyer has only recently been introduced.

Consultation

In acting as intermediary between clients, the lawyer is required to consult with the clients on the implications of doing so, and proceed only upon consent based on such a consultation. The consultation should make clear that the lawyer's role is not that of partisanship normally expected in other circumstances.

Paragraph (b) is an application of the principle expressed in Rule 1.4. Where the lawyer is intermediary, the clients ordinarily must assume greater responsibility for decisions than when each client is independently represented.

Withdrawal

Common representation does not diminish the rights of each client in the client-lawyer relationship. Each has the right to loyal and diligent representation, the right to discharge the lawyer as stated in Rule 1.16, and the protection of Rule 1.9 concerning obligations to a former client.

RULE 2.3 Evaluation for Use by Third Persons

(a) **A lawyer may undertake an evaluation of a matter affecting a client for the use of someone other than the client if:**

> (1) the lawyer reasonably believes that making the evaluation is compatible with other aspects of the lawyer's relationship with the client; and

> (2) the client consents after consultation.

(b) **Except as disclosure is required in connection with a report of an evaluation, information relating to the evaluation is otherwise protected by Rule 1.6.**

COMMENT:
Definition

An evaluation may be performed at the client's direction but for the primary purpose of establishing information for the benefit of third parties; for example, an opinion concerning the title of property rendered at the behest of a vendor for the information of a prospective purchaser, or at the behest of a borrower for the information of a prospective lender. In some situations, the evaluation may be required by a government agency; for example, an opinion concerning the legality of the securities registered for sale under the securities laws. In other instances, the evaluation may be required by a third person, such as a purchaser of a business.

Lawyers for the government may be called upon to give a formal opinion on the legality of contemplated government agency action. In making such an evaluation, the government lawyer acts at the behest of the government as the client but for the purpose of establishing the limits of the agency's authorized activity. Such an opinion is to be distinguished from confidential legal advice given agency officials. The critical question is whether the opinion is to be made public.

A legal evaluation should be distinguished from an investigation of a person with whom the lawyer does not have a client-lawyer relationship. For example, a lawyer retained by a purchaser to analyze a vendor's title to property does not have a client-lawyer relationship with the vendor. So also, an investigation into a person's affairs by a government lawyer, or by special counsel employed by the government, is not an evaluation as that term is used in this Rule. The question is whether the lawyer is retained by the person whose affairs are being examined. When the lawyer is retained by that person, the general rules concerning loyalty to client and preservation of confidences apply, which is not the case if the lawyer is retained by someone else. For this reason, it is essential to identify the person by whom the lawyer is retained. This should be made clear not only to the person under examination, but also to others to whom the results are to be made available.

Duty to Third Person

When the evaluation is intended for the information or use of a third person, a legal duty to that person may or may not arise. That legal question is beyond the scope of this Rule. However, since such an evaluation involves a departure from the normal client-lawyer relationship, careful analysis of the situation is required. The lawyer must be satisfied as a matter of professional judgment that making the evaluation is compatible with other functions undertaken in behalf of the client. For example, if the lawyer is acting as advocate in defending the client against charges of fraud, it would normally be incompatible with that responsibility for the lawyer to perform an evaluation for others concerning the same or a related transaction. Assuming no such impediment is apparent, however, the lawyer should advise the client of the implications of the evaluation, particularly the lawyer's responsibilities to third persons and the duty to disseminate the findings.

Access to and Disclosure of Information

The quality of an evaluation depends on the freedom and extent of the investigation upon which it is based. Ordinarily a lawyer should have whatever latitude of investigation seems necessary as a matter of professional judgment. Under some circumstances, however, the terms of the evaluation may be limited. For example, certain issues or sources may be categorically excluded, or the scope of search may be limited by time constraints or the noncooperation of persons having relevant information. Any such limitations which are material to the evaluation should be described in the report. If after a lawyer has commenced an evaluation, the client refuses to comply with the terms upon which it was understood the evaluation was to have been made, the lawyer's obligations are determined by law, having reference to the terms of the client's agreement and the surrounding circumstances.

Financial Auditors' Requests for Information

When a question concerning the legal situation of a client arises at the instance of the client's financial auditor and the question is referred to the lawyer, the lawyer's response may be made in accordance with procedures recognized in the legal profession. Such a procedure is set forth in the American Bar Association Statement of Policy Regarding Lawyers' Responses to Auditors' Requests for Information, adopted in 1975.

ADVOCATE
RULE 3.1 Meritorious Claims and Contentions

A lawyer shall not bring or defend a proceeding, or assert or controvert an issue therein, unless there is a basis for doing so that is not frivolous, which includes a good faith argument for an extension, modification or reversal of existing law. A lawyer for the defendent in a criminal proceeding, or the respondent in a proceeding that could result in incarceration, may nevertheless so defend the proceeding as to require that every element of the case be established.

COMMENT:

The advocate has a duty to use legal procedure for the fullest benefit of the client's cause, but also a duty not to abuse legal procedure. The law, both procedural and substantive, establishes the limits within which an advocate may proceed. However, the law is not always clear and never is static. Accordingly, in determining the proper scope of advocacy, account must be taken of the law's ambiguities and potential for change.

The filing of an action or defense or similar action taken for a client is not frivolous merely because the facts have not first been fully substantiated or because the lawyer expects to develop vital evidence only by discovery. Such action is not frivolous even though the lawyer believes that the client's position ultimately will not prevail. The action is frivolous, however, if the client desires to have the action taken primarily for the purpose of harassing or maliciously injuring a person or if the lawyer is unable either to make a good faith argument on the merits of the action taken or to support the action taken by a good faith argument for an extension, modification or reversal of existing law.

RULE 3.2 Expediting Litigation

A lawyer shall make reasonable efforts to expedite litigation consistent with the interests of the client.

COMMENT:

Dilatory practices bring the administration of justice into disrepute. Delay should not be indulged merely for the convenience of the advocates, or for the purpose of frustrating an opposing party's attempt to obtain rightful redress or repose. It is not a justification that similar conduct is often tolerated by the bench and bar. The question is whether a competent lawyer acting in good faith would regard the course of action as having some substantial purpose other than delay. Realizing financial or other benefit from otherwise improper delay in litigation is not a legitimate interest of the client.

Rule 3.3 Candor Toward the Tribunal

(a) A lawyer shall not knowingly:

(1) make a false statement of material fact or law to a tribunal;

(2) fail to disclose a material fact to a tribunal when disclosure is necessary to avoid assisting a criminal or fraudulent act by the client;

(3) fail to disclose to the tribunal legal authority in the controlling jurisdiction known to the lawyer to be directly adverse to the position of the client and not disclosed by opposing counsel; or

(4) offer evidence that the lawyer knows to be false. If a lawyer has offered material evidence and comes to know of its falsity, the lawyer shall take reasonable remedial measures.

(b) The duties stated in paragraph (a) continue to the conclusion of the proceeding, and apply even if compliance requires disclosure of information otherwise protected by Rule 1.6.

(c) A lawyer may refuse to offer evidence that the lawyer reasonably believes is false.

(d) In an ex parte proceeding, a lawyer shall inform the tribunal of all material facts known to the lawyer which will enable the tribunal to make an informed decision, whether or not the facts are adverse.

COMMENT:

The advocate's task is to present the client's case with persuasive force. Performance of that duty while maintaining confidences of the client is qualified by the advocate's duty of candor to the tribunal. However, an advocate does not vouch for the evidence submitted in a cause; the tribunal is responsible for assessing its probative value.

Representations by a Lawyer

An advocate is responsible for pleadings and other documents prepared for litigation, but is usually not required to have personal knowledge of matters asserted therein, for litigation documents ordinarily present assertions by the client, or by someone on the client's behalf, and not assertions by the lawyer. Compare Rule 3.1. However, an assertion purporting to be on the lawyer's own knowledge, as in an affidavit by the lawyer or in a statement in open court, may properly be made only when the lawyer knows the assertion is true or believes it to be true on the basis of a reasonably diligent inquiry. There are circumstances where failure to make a disclosure is the equivalent of an affirmative misrepresentation. The obligation prescribed in Rule 1.2(d) not to counsel a client to commit or assist the client in committing a fraud applies in litigation. Regarding compliance with Rule 1.2(d), see the Comment to that Rule. See also the Comment to Rule 8.4(b).

Misleading Legal Argument

Legal argument based on a knowingly false representation of law constitutes dishonesty toward the tribunal. A lawyer is not required to make a disinterested exposition of the law, but must recognize the existence of pertinent legal authorities. Furthermore, as stated in paragraph (a)(3), an advocate has a duty to disclose directly adverse authority in the controlling jurisdiction which has not been disclosed by the opposing party. The underlying concept is that legal argument is a discussion seeking to determine the legal premises properly applicable to the case.

False Evidence

When evidence that a lawyer knows to be false is provided by a person who is not the client, the lawyer must refuse to offer it regardless of the client's wishes.

When false evidence is offered by the client, however, a conflict may arise between the lawyer's duty to keep the client's revelations confidential and the duty of candor to the court. Upon ascertaining that material evidence is false, the lawyer should seek to persuade the client that the evidence should not be offered or, if it has been offered, that its false character should immediately be disclosed. If the persuasion is ineffective, the lawyer must take reasonable remedial measures.

Except in the defense of a criminal accused, the rule generally recognized is that, if necessary to rectify the situation, an advocate must disclose the existence of the client's deception to the court or to the other party. Such a disclosure can result in grave consequences to the client, including not only a sense of betrayal but also loss of the case and perhaps a prosecution for perjury. But the alternative is that the lawyer cooperate in deceiving the court, thereby subverting the truth-finding process which the adversary system is designed to implement. See Rule 1.2(d). Furthermore, unless it is clearly understood that the lawyer will act upon the duty to disclose the existence of false evidence, the client can simply reject the lawyer's advice to reveal the false evidence and insist that the lawyer keep silent. Thus the client could in effect coerce the lawyer into being a party to fraud on the court.

Perjury by a Criminal Defendant

Whether an advocate for a crimi-nally accused has the same duty of disclosure has been intensely debated. While it is agreed that the lawyer should seek to persuade the client to refrain from perjurious testimony, there has been dispute concerning the lawyer's duty when that persuasion fails. If the confrontation with the client occurs before trial, the lawyer ordinarily can withdraw. Withdrawal before trial may not be possible, however, either because trial is imminent, or because the confrontation with the client does not take place until the trial itself, or because no other counsel is available.

The most difficult situation, therefore, arises in a criminal case where the accused insists on testifying when the lawyer knows that the testimony is perjurious. The lawyer's effort to rectify the situation can increase the likelihood of the client's being convicted as well as opening the possibility of a prosecution for perjury. On the other hand, if the lawyer does not exercise control over the proof, the lawyer participates, although in a merely passive way, in deception of the court.

Three resolutions of this dilemma have been proposed. One is to permit the accused to testify by a narrative without guidance through the lawyer's questioning. This compromises both contending principles; it exempts the lawyer from the duty to disclose false evidence but subjects the client to an implicit disclosure of information imparted to counsel. Another suggested resolution, of relatively recent origin, is that the advocate be entirely excused from the duty to reveal perjury if the perjury is that of the client. This is a coherent solution but makes the advocate a knowing instrument of perjury.

The other resolution of the dilemma is that the lawyer must reveal the client's perjury if necessary to rectify the situation. A criminal accused has a right to the assistance of an advocate, a right to testify and a right of confidential communication with counsel. However, an accused should not have a right to assistance of counsel in committing perjury. Furthermore, an advocate has an obligation, not only in professional ethics but under the law as well, to avoid implication in the commission of perjury or other falsification of evidence. See Rule 1.2(d).

Remedial Measures

If perjured testimony or false evidence has been offered, the advocate's proper course ordinarily is to remonstrate with the client confidentially. If that fails, the advocate should seek to withdraw if that will remedy the situation. If withdrawal will not remedy the situation or is impossible, the advocate should make disclosure to the court. It is for the court then to determine what should be done—making a statement about the matter to the trier of fact, ordering a mistrial or perhaps nothing. If the false testimony was that of the client, the client may controvert the lawyer's version of their communication when the lawyer discloses the situation to the court. If there is an issue whether the client has committed perjury, the lawyer cannot represent the client in resolution of the issue, and a mistrial may be unavoidable. An unscrupulous client might in this way attempt to produce a series of mistrials and thus escape prosecution. However, a second such encounter could be construed as a deliberate abuse of the right to counsel and as such a waiver of the right to further representation.

Constitutional Requirements

The general rule—that an advocate must disclose the existence of perjury with respect to a material fact, even that of a client—applies to defense counsel in criminal cases, as well as in other instances. However, the definition of the lawyer's ethical duty in such a situation may be qualified by constitutional provisions for due process and the right to counsel in criminal cases. In some jurisdictions these provisions have been construed to require that counsel present an accused as a witness if the accused wishes to testify, even if counsel knows the testimony will be false. The obligation of the advocate under these Rules is subordinate to such a constitutional requirement.

Duration of Obligation

A practical time limit on the obligation to rectify the presentation of false evidence has to be established. The conclusion of the proceeding is a reasonably definite point for the termination of the obligation.

Refusing to Offer Proof Believed to be False

Generally speaking, a lawyer has authority to refuse to offer testimony or other proof that the lawyer believes is untrustworthy. Offering such proof may reflect adversely on the lawyer's ability to discriminate in the quality of evidence and thus impair the lawyer's effectiveness as an advocate. In criminal cases, however, a lawyer may, in some jurisdictions, be denied this authority by constitutional requirements governing the right to counsel.

Ex Parte Proceedings

Ordinarily, an advocate has the limited responsibility of presenting one side of the matters that a tribunal should consider in reaching a decision; the conflicting position is expected to be presented by the opposing party. However, in an ex parte proceeding, such as an application for a temporary restraining order, there is no balance of presentation by opposing advocates. The object of an ex parte proceeding is nevertheless to yield a substantially just result. The judge has an affirmative responsibility to accord the absent party just consideration. The lawyer for the represented party has the correlative duty to make disclosures of material facts known to the lawyer and that the lawyer reasonably believes are necessary to an informed decision.

RULE 3.4 Fairness to Opposing Party and Counsel

A lawyer shall not:

(a) unlawfully obstruct another party's access to evidence or unlawfully alter, destroy or conceal a document or other material having potential evidentiary value. A lawyer shall not counsel or assist another person to do any such act;

(b) falsify evidence, counsel or assist a witness to testify falsely, or offer an inducement to a witness that is prohibited by law;

(c) knowingly disobey an obligation under the rules of a tribunal except for an open refusal based on an assertion that no valid obligation exists;

(d) in pretrial procedure, make a frivolous discovery request or fail to make reasonably diligent effort to comply with a legally proper discovery request by an opposing party;

(e) in trial, allude to any matter that the lawyer does not reasonably believe is relevant or that will not be supported by admissible evidence, assert personal knowledge of facts in issue except when testifying as a witness, or state a personal opinion as to the justness of a cause, the credibility of a witness, the culpability of a civil litigant or the guilt or innocence of an accused; or

(f) request a person other than a client to refrain from voluntarily giving relevant information to another party unless:

    (1) the person is a relative or an employee or other agent of a client; and

    (2) the lawyer reasonably believes that the person's interests will not be adversely affected by refraining from giving such information.

COMMENT:

The procedure of the adversary system contemplates that the evidence in a case is to be marshalled competitively by the contending parties. Fair competition in the adversary system is secured by prohibitions against destruction or concealment of evidence, improperly influencing witnesses, obstructive tactics in discovery procedure, and the like.

Documents and other items of evidence are often essential to establish a claim or defense. Subject to evidentiary privileges, the right of an opposing party, including the government, to obtain evidence through discovery or subpoena is an important procedural right. The exercise of that right can be frustrated if relevant material is altered, concealed or destroyed. Applicable law in many jurisdictions makes it an offense to destroy material for purpose of impairing its availability in a pending proceeding or one whose commencement can be foreseen. Falsifying evidence is also generally a criminal offense. Paragraph (a) applies to evidentiary material generally, including computerized information.

With regard to paragraph (b), it is not improper to pay a witness's expenses or to compensate an expert witness on terms permitted by law. The common law rule in most jurisdictions is that it is improper to pay an occurrence witness any fee for testifying and that it is improper to pay an expert witness a contingent fee.

Paragraph (f) permits a lawyer to advise employees of a client to refrain from giving information to another party, for the employees may identify their interests with those of the client. See also Rule 4.2.

RULE 3.5 Impartiality and Decorum of the Tribunal

A lawyer shall not:

(a) seek to influence a judge, juror, prospective juror or other official by means prohibited by law;

(b) communicate ex parte with such a person except as permitted by law; or

(c) engage in conduct intended to disrupt a tribunal.

COMMENT:

Many forms of improper influence upon a tribunal are proscribed by criminal law. Others are specified in the ABA Model Code of Judicial Conduct, with which an advocate should be familiar. A lawyer is required to avoid contributing to a violation of such provisions.

The advocate's function is to present evidence and argument so that the cause may be decided according to law. Refraining from abusive or obstreperous conduct is a corollary of the advocate's right to speak on behalf of litigants. A lawyer may stand firm against abuse by a judge but should avoid reciprocation; the judge's default is no justification for similar dereliction by an advocate. An advocate can present the cause, protect the record for subsequent review and preserve professional integrity by patient firmness no less effectively than by belligerence or theatrics.

RULE 3.6 Trial Publicity

(a) A lawyer shall not make an extrajudicial statement that a reasonable person would expect to be disseminated by means of public communication if the lawyer knows or reasonably should know that it will have a substantial likelihood of materially prejudicing an adjudicative proceeding.

(b) A statement referred to in paragraph (a) ordinarily is likely to have such an effect when it refers to a civil matter triable to a jury, a criminal matter, or any other proceeding that could result in incarceration, and the statement relates to:

(1) the character, credibility, reputation or criminal record of a party, suspect in a criminal investigation or witness, or the identity of a witness, or the expected testimony of a party or witness;

(2) in a criminal case or proceeding that could result in incarceration, the possibility of a plea of guilty to the offense or the existence or contents of any confession, admission, or statement given by a defendant or suspect or that person's refusal or failure to make a statement;

(3) the performance or results of any examination or test or the refusal or failure of a person to submit to an examination or test, or the identity or nature of physical evidence expected to be presented;

(4) any opinion as to the guilt or innocence of a defendant or suspect in a criminal case or proceeding that could result in incarceration;

(5) information the lawyer knows or reasonably should know is likely to be inadmissible as evidence in a trial and would if disclosed create a substantial risk of prejudicing an impartial trial; or

(6) the fact that a defendant has been charged with a crime, unless there is included therein a statement explaining that the charge is merely an accusation and that the defendant is presumed innocent until and unless proven guilty.

(c) Notwithstanding paragraph (a) and (b)(1-5), a lawyer involved in the investigation or litigation of a matter may state without elaboration:

(1) the general nature of the claim or defense;

(2) the information contained in a public record;

(3) that an investigation of the matter is in progress, including the general scope of the investigation, the offense or claim or defense involved and, except when prohibited by law, the identity of the persons involved;

(4) the scheduling or result of any step in litigation;

(5) a request for assistance in obtaining evidence and information necessary thereto;

(6) a warning of danger concerning the behavior of a person involved, when there is reason to believe that there exists the likelihood of substantial harm to an individual or to the public interest; and
(7) in a criminal case:
(i) the identity, residence, occupation and family status of the accused;
(ii) if the accused has not been apprehended, information necessary to aid in apprehension of that person;
(iii) the fact, time and place of arrest; and
(iv) the identity of investigating and arresting officers or agencies and the length of the investigation.

COMMENT:

It is difficult to strike a balance between protecting the right to a fair trial and safeguarding the right of free expression. Preserving the right to a fair trial necessarily entails some curtailment of the information that may be disseminated about a party prior to trial, particularly where trial by jury is involved. If there were no such limits, the result would be the practical nullification of the protective effect of the rules of forensic decorum and the exclusionary rules of evidence. On the other hand, there are vital social interests served by the free dissemination of information about events having legal consequences and about legal proceedings themselves. The public has a right to know about threats to its safety and measures aimed at assuring its security. It also has a legitimate interest in the conduct of judicial proceedings, particularly in matters of general public concern. Furthermore, the subject matter of legal proceedings is often of direct significance in debate and deliberation over questions of public policy.

No body of rules can simultaneously satisfy all interests of fair

trial and all those of free expression. The formula in this Rule is based upon the ABA Model Code of Professional Responsibility and the ABA Standards Relating to Fair Trial and Free Press, as amended in 1978.

Special rules of confidentiality may validly govern proceedings in juvenile, domestic relations and mental disability proceedings, and perhaps other types of litigation. Rule 3.4(c) requires compliance with such Rules.

RULE 3.7 Lawyer as Witness
(a) A lawyer shall not act as advocate at a trial in which the lawyer is likely to be a necessary witness except where:
(1) the testimony relates to an uncontested issue;
(2) the testimony relates to the nature and value of legal services rendered in the case; or
(3) disqualification of the lawyer would work substantial hardship on the client.
(b) A lawyer may act as advocate in a trial in which another lawyer in the lawyer's firm is likely to be called as a witness unless precluded from doing so by Rule 1.7 or Rule 1.9.

COMMENT:

Combining the roles of advocate and witness can prejudice the opposing party and can involve a conflict of interest between the lawyer and client.

The opposing party has proper objection where the combination of roles may prejudice that party's rights in the litigation. A witness is required to testify on the basis of personal knowledge, while an advocate is expected to explain and comment on evidence given by others. It may not be clear whether a statement by an advocate-witness should be taken as proof or as an analysis of the proof.

Paragraph (a)(1) recognizes that if the testimony will be uncontested, the ambiguities in the dual role are purely theoretical. Paragraph (a)(2) recognizes that where the testimony concerns the extent and value of legal services rendered in the action in which the testimony is offered, permitting the lawyers to testify avoids the need for a second trial with new counsel to resolve that issue. Moreover, in such a situation the judge has first hand knowledge of the matter in issue; hence, there is less dependence on the adversary process to test the credibility of the testimony.

Apart from these two exceptions, paragraph (a)(3) recognizes that a balancing is required between the interests of the client and those of the opposing party. Whether the opposing party is likely to suffer prejudice depends on the nature of the case, the importance and probable tenor of the lawyer's testimony, and the probability that the lawyer's testimony will conflict with that of other witnesses. Even if there is risk of such prejudice, in determining whether the lawyer should be disqualified due regard must be given to the effect of disqualification on the lawyer's client. It is relevant that one or both parties could reasonably foresee that the lawyer would probably be a witness. The principle of imputed disqualification stated in Rule 1.10 has no application to this aspect of the problem.

Whether the combination of roles involves an improper conflict of interest with respect to the client is determined by Rule 1.7 or 1.9. For example, if there is likely to be substantial conflict between the testimony of the client and that of the lawyer or a member of the lawyer's firm, the representation is improper. The problem can arise whether the lawyer is called as a witness on behalf of the client or is called by the opposing party. Determining whether or not such a conflict exists is primarily the responsibility of the lawyer involved. See Comment to Rule 1.7. If a lawyer who is a member of a firm may not act as both advocate and witness by reason of conflict of interest, Rule 1.10 disqualifies the firm also.

RULE 3.8 Special Responsibilities of a Prosecutor

The prosecutor in a criminal case shall:

(a) refrain from prosecuting a charge that the prosecutor knows is not supported by probable cause;

(b) make reasonable efforts to assure that the accused has been advised of the right to, and the procedure for obtaining, counsel and has been given reasonable opportunity to obtain counsel;

(c) not seek to obtain from an unrepresented accused a waiver of important pretrial rights, such as the right to a preliminary hearing;

(d) make timely disclosure to the defense of all evidence or information known to the prosecutor that tends to negate the guilt of the accused or mitigates the offense, and, in connection with sentencing, disclose to the defense and to the tribunal all unprivileged mitigating information known to the prosecutor, except when the prosecutor is relieved of this responsibility by a protective order of the tribunal; and

(e) exercise reasonable care to prevent investigators, law enforcement personnel, employees or other persons assisting or associated with the prosecutor in a criminal case from making an extrajudicial statement that the prosecutor would be prohibited from making under Rule 3.6.

COMMENT:

A prosecutor has the responsibility of a minister of justice and not simply that of an advocate. This responsibility carries with it specific obligations to see that the defendant is accorded procedural justice and that guilt is decided upon the basis of sufficient evidence. Precisely how far the prosecutor is required to go in this direction is a matter of debate and varies in different jurisdictions. Many jurisdictions have adopted the ABA Standards of Criminal Justice Relating to Prosecution Function, which in turn are the product of prolonged and careful deliberation by lawyers experienced in both criminal prosecution and defense. See also Rule 3.3(d), governing ex parte proceedings, among which grand jury proceedings are included. Applicable law may require other measures by the prosecutor and knowing disregard of those obligations or a systematic abuse of prosecutorial discretion could constitute a violation of Rule 8.4.

Paragraph (c) does not apply to an accused appearing pro se with the approval of the tribunal. Nor does it forbid the lawful questioning of a suspect who has knowingly waived the rights to counsel and silence.

The exception in paragraph (d) recognizes that a prosecutor may seek an appropriate protective order from the tribunal if disclosure of information to the defense could result in substantial harm to an individual or to the public interest.

RULE 3.9 Advocate in Nonadjudicative Proceedings

A lawyer representing a client before a legislative or administrative tribunal in a nonadjudicative proceeding shall disclose that the appearance is in a representative capacity and shall conform to the provisions of Rule 3.3(a) through (c), 3.4(a) through (c), and 3.5.

COMMENT:

In representation before bodies such as legislatures, municipal councils, and executive and administrative agencies acting in a rule-making or policy-making capacity, lawyers present facts, formulate issues and advance argument in the matters under consideration. The decision-making body, like a court, should be able to rely on the integrity of the submissions made to it. A lawyer appearing before such a body should deal with the tribunal honestly and in conformity with applicable rules of procedure.

Lawyers have no exclusive right to appear before nonadjudicative bodies, as they do before a court. The requirements of this Rule therefore may subject lawyers to regulations inapplicable to advocates who are not lawyers. However, legislatures and administrative agencies have a right to expect lawyers to deal with them as they deal with courts.

This Rule does not apply to representation of a client in a negotiation or other bilateral transaction with a governmental agency; representation in such a transaction is governed by Rules 4.1 through 4.4.

TRANSACTIONS WITH PERSONS OTHER THAN CLIENTS

RULE 4.1 Truthfulness in Statements to Others

In the course of representing a client a lawyer shall not knowingly:

(a) make a false statement of material fact or law to a third person; or

(b) fail to disclose a material fact to a third person when disclosure is necessary to avoid assisting a criminal or fraudulent act by a client, unless disclosure is prohibited by Rule 1.6.

COMMENT:
Misrepresentation

A lawyer is required to be truthful when dealing with others on a client's behalf, but generally has no affirmative duty to inform an opposing party of relevant facts. A misrepresentation can occur if the lawyer incorporates or affirms a statement of another person that the lawyer knows is false. Misrepresentations can also occur by failure to act.

Statements of Fact

This Rule refers to statements of fact. Whether a particular statement should be regarded as one of fact can depend on the circumstances. Under generally accepted conventions in negotiation, certain types of statements ordinarily are not taken as statements of material fact. Estimates of price or value placed on the subject of a transaction and a party's intentions as to an acceptable settlement of a claim are in this category, and so is the existence of an undisclosed principal except where nondisclosure of the principal would constitute fraud.

Fraud by Client

Paragraph (b) recognizes that substantive law may require a lawyer to disclose certain information to avoid being deemed to have assisted the client's crime or fraud. The requirement of disclosure created by this paragraph is, however, subject to the obligations created by Rule 1.6.

RULE 4.2 Communication with Person Represented by Counsel

In representing a client, a lawyer shall not communicate about the subject of the representation with a party the lawyer knows to be represented by another lawyer in the matter, unless the lawyer has the consent of the other lawyer or is authorized by law to do so.

COMMENT:

This Rule does not prohibit communication with a party, or an employee or agent of a party, concerning matters outside the representation. For example, the existence of a controversy between a government agency and a private party, or between two organizations, does not prohibit a lawyer for either from communicating with nonlawyer representatives of the other regarding a separate matter. Also, parties to a matter may communicate directly with each other and a lawyer having independent justification for communicating with the other party is permitted to do so. Communications authorized by law include, for example, the right of a party to a controversy with a government agency to speak with government officials about the matter.

In the case of an organization, this Rule prohibits communications by a lawyer for one party concerning the matter in representation with persons having a managerial responsibility on behalf of the organization, and with any other person whose act or omission in connection with that matter may be imputed to the organization for purposes of civil or criminal liability or whose statement may constitute an admission on the part of the organization. If an agent or employee of the organization is represented in the matter by his or her own counsel, the consent by that counsel to a communication will be sufficient for purposes of this Rule. Compare Rule 3.4(f).

This Rule also covers any person, whether or not a party to a formal proceeding, who is represented by counsel concerning the matter in question.

RULE 4.3 Dealing with Unrepresented Person

In dealing on behalf of a client with a person who is not represented by counsel, a lawyer shall not state or imply that the lawyer is disinterested. When the lawyer knows or reasonably should know that the unrepresented person misunderstands the lawyer's role in the matter, the lawyer shall make reasonable efforts to correct the misunderstanding.

COMMENT:

An unrepresented person, particularly one not experienced in dealing with legal matters, might assume that a lawyer is disinterested in loyalties or is a disinterested authority on the law even when the lawyer represents a client. During the course of a lawyer's representation of a client, the lawyer should not give advice to an unrepresented person other than the advice to obtain counsel.

RULE 4.4 Respect for Rights of Third Persons

In representing a client, a lawyer shall not use means that have no substantial purpose other than to embarrass, delay, or burden a third person, or use methods of obtaining evidence that violate the legal rights of such a person.

COMMENT:

Responsibility to a client requires a lawyer to subordinate the interests of others to those of the client, but that responsibility does not imply that a lawyer may disregard the rights of third persons. It is impractical to catalogue all such rights, but they include legal restrictions on methods of obtaining evidence from third persons.

LAW FIRMS AND ASSOCIATIONS

·RULE 5.1 Responsibilities of a Partner or Supervisory Lawyer

(a) A partner in a law firm shall make reasonable efforts to ensure that the firm has in effect measures giving reasonable assurance that all lawyers in the firm conform to the rules of professional conduct.

(b) A lawyer having direct supervisory authority over another lawyer shall make reasonable efforts to ensure that the other lawyer conforms to the rules of professional conduct.

(c) A lawyer shall be responsible for another lawyer's violation of the rules of professional conduct if:

(1) the lawyer orders or, with knowledge of the specific conduct, ratifies the conduct involved; or

(2) the lawyer is a partner in the law firm in which the other lawyer practices, or has direct supervisory authority over the other lawyer, and knows of the conduct at a time when its consequences can be avoided or mitigated but fails to take reasonable remedial action.

COMMENT:

Paragraphs (a) and (b) refer to lawyers who have supervisory authority over the professional work of a firm or legal department of a government agency. This includes members of a partnership and the shareholders in a law firm organized as a professional corporation; lawyers having supervisory authority in the law department of an enterprise or government agency; and lawyers who have intermediate managerial responsibilities in a firm.

The measures required to fulfill the responsibility prescribed in paragraphs (a) and (b) can depend on the firm's structure and the nature of its practice. In a small firm, informal supervision and occasional admonition ordinarily might be sufficient. In a large firm, or in practice situations in which intensely difficult ethical problems frequently arise, more elaborate procedures may be necessary. Some firms, for example, have a procedure whereby junior lawyers can make confidential referral of ethical problems directly to a designated senior partner or special committee. See Rule 5.2. Firms, whether large or small, may also rely on continuing legal education in professional ethics. In any event, the ethical atmosphere of a firm can influence the conduct of all its members and a lawyer having authority over the work of another may not assume that the subordinate lawyer will inevitably conform to the Rules.

Paragraph (c)(1) expresses a general principle of responsibility for acts of another. See also Rule 8.4(a).

Paragraph (c)(2) defines the duty of a lawyer having direct supervisory authority over performance of specific legal work by another lawyer. Whether a lawyer has such supervisory authority in particular circumstances is a question of fact. Partners of a private firm have at least indirect responsibility for all work being done by the firm, while a partner in charge of a particular matter ordinarily has direct authority over other firm lawyers engaged in the matter. Appropriate remedial action by a partner would depend on the immediacy of the partner's involvement and the seriousness of the misconduct. The supervisor is required to intervene to prevent avoidable consequences of misconduct if the supervisor knows that the misconduct occurred. Thus, if a supervising lawyer knows that a subordinate misrepresented a matter to an opposing party in negotiation, the supervisor as well as the subordinate has a duty to correct the resulting misapprehension.

Professional misconduct by a lawyer under supervision could reveal a violation of paragraph (b) on the part of the supervisory lawyer even though it does not entail a violation of paragraph (c) because there was no direction, ratification or knowledge of the violation.

Apart from this Rule and Rule 8.4(a), a lawyer does not have disciplinary liability for the conduct of a partner, associate or subordinate. Whether a lawyer may be liable civilly or criminally for another lawyer's conduct is a question of law beyond the scope of these Rules.

RULE 5.2 Responsibilities of a Subordinate Lawyer

(a) A lawyer is bound by the rules of professional conduct notwithstanding that the lawyer acted at the direction of another person.

(b) A subordinate lawyer does not violate the rules of professional conduct if that lawyer acts in accordance with a supervisory lawyer's reasonable resolution of an arguable question of professional duty.

COMMENT:

Although a lawyer is not relieved of responsibility for a violation by the fact that the lawyer acted at the direction of a supervisor, that fact may be relevant in determining whether a lawyer had the knowledge required to render conduct a violation of the Rules. For exam-

ple, if a subordinate filed a frivolous pleading at the direction of a supervisor, the subordinate would not be guilty of a professional violation unless the subordinate knew of the document's frivolous character.

When lawyers in a supervisor-subordinate relationship encounter a matter involving professional judgment as to ethical duty, the supervisor may assume responsibility for making the judgment. Otherwise a consistent course of action or position could not be taken. If the question can reasonably be answered only one way, the duty of both lawyers is clear and they are equally responsible for fulfilling it. However, if the question is reasonably arguable, someone has to decide upon the course of action. That authority ordinarily reposes in the supervisor, and a subordinate may be guided accordingly. For example, if a question arises whether the interests of two clients conflict under Rule 1.7, the supervisor's reasonable resolution of the question should protect the subordinate professionally if the resolution is subsequently challenged.

RULE 5.3 Responsibilities Regarding Nonlawyer Assistants

With respect to a nonlawyer employed or retained by or associated with a lawyer:

(a) a partner in a law firm shall make reasonable efforts to ensure that the firm has in effect measures giving reasonable assurance that the person's conduct is compatible with the professional obligations of the lawyer;

(b) a lawyer having direct supervisory authority over the nonlawyer shall make reasonable efforts to ensure that the person's conduct is compatible with the professional obligations of the lawyer; and

(c) a lawyer shall be responsible for conduct of such a person that would be a violation of the rules of professional conduct if engaged in by a lawyer if:

(1) the lawyer orders or, with the knowledge of the specific conduct, ratifies the conduct involved; or

(2) the lawyer is a partner in the law firm in which the person is employed, or has direct supervisory authority over the person, and knows of the conduct at a time when its consequences can be avoided or mitigated but fails to take reasonable remedial action.

COMMENT:

Lawyers generally employ assistants in their practice, including secretaries, investigators, law student interns, and paraprofessionals. Such assistants, whether employees or independent contractors, act for the lawyer in rendition of the lawyer's professional services. A lawyer should give such assistants appropriate instruction and supervision concerning the ethical aspects of their employment, particularly regarding the obligation not to disclose information relating to representation of the client, and should be responsible for their work product. The measures employed in supervising nonlawyers should take account of the fact that they do not have legal training and are not subject to professional discipline.

RULE 5.4 Professional Independence of a Lawyer

(a) A lawyer or law firm shall not share legal fees with a nonlawyer, except that:

(1) an agreement by a lawyer with the lawyer's firm, partner, or associate may provide for the payment of money, over a reasonable period of time after the lawyer's death, to the lawyer's estate or to one or more specified persons;

(2) a lawyer who undertakes to complete unfinished legal business of a deceased lawyer may pay to the estate of the deceased lawyer that proportion of the total compensation which fairly represents the services rendered by the deceased lawyer; and

(3) a lawyer or law firm may include nonlawyer employees in a compensation or retirement plan, even though the plan is based in whole or in part on a profit-sharing arrangement.

(b) A lawyer shall not form a partnership with a nonlawyer if any of the activities of the partnership consist of the practice of law.

(c) A lawyer shall not permit a person who recommends, employs, or pays the lawyer to render legal services for another to direct or regulate the lawyer's professional judgment in rendering such legal services.

(d) A lawyer shall not practice with or in the form of a professional corporation or association authorized to practice law for a profit, if:

(1) a nonlawyer owns any interest therein, except that a fiduciary representative of the estate of a lawyer may hold the stock or interest of the lawyer for a reasonable time during administration;

(2) a nonlawyer is a corporate director or officer thereof; or

(3) a nonlawyer has the right to direct or control the professional judgment of a lawyer.

COMMENT:

The provisions of this Rule express traditional limitations on sharing fees. These limitations are to protect the lawyer's professional independence of judgment. Where someone other than the client pays the lawyer's fee or salary, or recommends employment of the lawyer, that arrangement does not modify the lawyer's obligation to the client. As stated in paragraph (c), such arrangements should not interfere with the lawyer's professional judgment.

RULE 5.5 Unauthorized Practice of Law

A lawyer shall not:

(a) practice law in a jurisdiction where doing so violates the regulation of the legal profession in that jurisdiction; or

(b) assist a person who is not a member of the bar in the performance of activity that constitutes the unauthorized practice of law.

COMMENT:

The definition of the practice of law is established by law and varies from one jurisdiction to another. Whatever the definition, limiting the practice of law to members of the bar protects the public against rendition of legal services by unqualified persons. Paragraph (b) does not prohibit a lawyer from employing the services of paraprofessionals and delegating functions to them, so long as the lawyer supervises the delegated work and retains responsibility for their work. See Rule 5.3. Likewise, it does not prohibit lawyers from providing professional advice and instruction to nonlawyers whose employment requires knowledge of law; for example, claims adjusters, employees of financial or commercial institutions, social workers, accountants and persons employed in government agencies. In addition, a lawyer may counsel nonlawyers who wish to proceed pro se.

RULE 5.6 Restrictions on Right to Practice

A lawyer shall not participate in offering or making:

(a) a partnership or employment agreement that restricts the rights of a lawyer to practice after termination of the relationship, except an agreement concerning benefits upon retirement; or

(b) an agreement in which a restriction on the lawyer's right to practice is part of the settlement of a controversy between private parties.

COMMENT:

An agreement restricting the right of partners or associates to practice after leaving a firm not only limits their professional autonomy but also limits the freedom of clients to choose a lawyer. Paragraph (a) prohibits such agreements except for restrictions incident to provisions concerning retirement benefits for service with the firm.

Paragraph (b) prohibits a lawyer from agreeing not to represent other persons in connection with settling a claim on behalf of a client.

PUBLIC SERVICE

RULE 6.1 Pro Bono Publico Service

A lawyer should render public interest legal service. A lawyer may discharge this responsibility by providing professional services at no fee or a reduced fee to persons of limited means or to public service or charitable groups or organizations, by service in activities for improving the law, the legal system or the legal profession, and by financial support for organizations that provide legal services to persons of limited means.

COMMENT:

The ABA House of Delegates has formally acknowledged "the basic responsibility of each lawyer engaged in the practice of law to provide public interest legal services" without fee, or at a substantially reduced fee, in one or more of the following areas: poverty law, civil rights law, public rights law, charitable organization representation and the administration of justice. This Rule expresses that policy but is not intended to be enforced through disciplinary process.

The rights and responsibilities of individuals and organizations in the United States are increasingly defined in legal terms. As a consequence, legal assistance in coping with the web of statutes, rules and regulations is imperative for persons of modest and limited means, as well as for the relatively well-to-do.

The basic responsibility for providing legal services for those unable to pay ultimately rests upon the individual lawyer, and personal involvement in the problems of the disadvantaged can be one of the most rewarding experiences in the life of a lawyer. Every lawyer, regardless of professional prominence or professional workload, should find time to participate in or otherwise support the provision of legal services to the disadvantaged. The provision of free legal services to those unable to pay reasonable fees continues to be an obligation of each lawyer as well as the profession generally, but the efforts of individual lawyers are often not enough to meet the need. Thus, it has been necessary for the profession and government to institute additional programs to provide legal services. Accordingly, legal aid offices, lawyer referral services and other related programs have been developed, and others will be developed by the profession and government. Every lawyer should support all proper efforts to meet this need for legal services.

RULE 6.2 Accepting Appointments

A lawyer shall not seek to avoid appointment by a tribunal to represent a person except for good cause, such as:

(a) representing the client is likely to result in violation of the rules of professional conduct or other law;

(b) representing the client is likely to result in an unreasonable financial burden on the lawyer; or

(c) the client or the cause is so repugnant to the lawyer as to be likely to impair the client-lawyer relationship or the lawyer's ability to represent the client.

COMMENT:

A lawyer ordinarily is not obliged to accept a client whose character or cause the lawyer regards as repugnant. The lawyer's freedom to select clients is, however, qualified. All lawyers have a responsibility to assist in providing pro bono publico service. See Rule 6.1. An individual lawyer fulfills this responsibility by accepting a fair share of unpopular matters or indigent or unpopular clients. A lawyer may also be subject to appointment by a court to serve unpopular clients or persons unable to afford legal services.

Appointed Counsel

For good cause a lawyer may seek to decline an appointment to represent a person who cannot afford to retain counsel or whose cause is unpopular. Good cause exists if the lawyer could not handle the matter competently, see Rule 1.1, or if undertaking the representation would result in an improper conflict of interest, for example, when the client or the cause is so repugnant to the lawyer as to be likely to impair the client-lawyer relationship or the lawyer's ability to represent the client. A lawyer may also seek to decline an appointment if acceptance would be unreasonably burdensome, for example, when it would impose a financial sacrifice so great as to be unjust.

An appointed lawyer has the same obligations to the client as retained counsel, including the obligations of loyalty and confidentiality, and is subject to the same limitations on the client-lawyer relationship, such as the obligation to refrain from assisting the client in violation of the Rules.

RULE 6.3 Membership in Legal Services Organization

A lawyer may serve as a director, officer or member of a legal services organization, apart from the law firm in which the lawyer practices, notwithstanding that the organization serves persons having interests adverse to a client of the lawyer. The lawyer shall not knowingly participate in a decision or action of the organization:

(a) if participating in the decision would be imcompatible with the lawyer's obligations to a client under Rule 1.7; or

(b) where the decision could have a material adverse effect on the representation of a client of the organization whose interests are adverse to a client of the lawyer.

COMMENT:

Lawyers should be encouraged to support and participate in legal service organizations. A lawyer who is an officer or a member of such an organization does not thereby have a client-lawyer relationship with persons served by the organization. However, there is potential conflict between the interests of such persons and the interests of the lawyer's clients. If the possibility of such conflict disqualified a lawyer from serving on the board of a legal services organization, the profession's involvement in such organizations would be severely curtailed.

It may be necessary in appropriate cases to reassure a client of the organization that the representation will not be affected by conflicting loyalties of a member of the board. Established, written policies in this respect can enhance the credibility of such assurances.

RULE 6.4 Law Reform Activities Affecting Client Interests ·

A lawyer may serve as a director, officer or member of an organization involved in reform of the law or its administration notwithstanding that the reform may affect the interests of a client of the lawyer. When the lawyer knows that the interests of a client may be materially benefitted by a decision in which the lawyer participates, the lawyer shall disclose that fact but need not identify the client.

COMMENT:

Lawyers involved in organizations seeking law reform generally do not have a client-lawyer relationship with the organization. Oth-erwise, it might follow that a lawyer could not be involved in a bar association law reform program that might indirectly affect a client. See also Rule 1.2(b). For example, a lawyer specializing in antitrust litigation might be regarded as disqualified from participating in drafting revisions of rules governing that subject. In determining the nature and scope of participation in such activities, a lawyer should be mindful of obligations to clients under other Rules, particularly Rule 1.7. A lawyer is professionally obligated to protect the integrity of the program by making an appropriate disclosure within the organization when the lawyer knows a private client might be materially benefitted.

INFORMATION ABOUT LEGAL SERVICES

RULE 7.1 Communications Concerning a Lawyer's Services

A lawyer shall not make a false or misleading communication about the lawyer or the lawyer's services. A communication is false or misleading if it:

(a) contains a material misrepresentation of fact or law, or omits a fact necessary to make the statement considered as a whole not materially misleading;

(b) is likely to create an unjustified expectation about results the lawyer can achieve, or states or implies that the lawyer can achieve results by means that violate the rules of professional conduct or other law; or

(c) compares the lawyer's services with other lawyers' services, unless the comparison can be factually substantiated.

COMMENT:

This Rule governs all communications about a lawyer's services, including advertising permitted by Rule 7.2. Whatever means are used to make known a lawyer's services, statements about them should be truthful. The prohibition in paragraph (b) of statements that may create "unjustified expectations" would ordinarily preclude advertisements about results obtained on behalf of a client, such as the amount of a damage award or the lawyer's record in obtaining favorable verdicts, and advertisements containing client endorsements. Such information may create the unjustified expectation that similar results can be obtained for others without reference to the specific factual and legal circumstances.

RULE 7.2 Advertising

(a) Subject to the requirements of Rule 7.1, a lawyer may advertise services through public media, such as a telephone directory, legal directory, newspaper or other periodical, outdoor, radio or television, or through written communication not involving solicitation as defined in Rule 7.3.

(b) A copy or recording of an advertisement or written communication shall be kept for two years after its last dissemination along with a record of when and where it was used.

(c) A lawyer shall not give anything of value to a person for recommending the lawyer's services, except that a lawyer may pay the reasonable cost of advertising or written communication permitted by this rule and may pay the usual charges of a not-for-profit lawyer referral service or other legal service organization.

(d) Any communication made pursuant to this rule shall include the name of at least one lawyer responsible for its content.

COMMENT:

To assist the public in obtaining legal services, lawyers should be allowed to make known their services not only through reputation but also through organized information campaigns in the form of advertising. Advertising involves an active quest for clients, contrary to the tradition that a lawyer should not seek clientele. However, the public's need to know about legal services can be fulfilled in part through advertising. This need is particularly acute in the case of persons of moderate means who have not made extensive use of legal services. The interest in expanding public information about legal services ought to prevail over considerations of tradition. Nevertheless, advertising by lawyers entails the risk of practices that are misleading or overreaching.

This Rule permits public dissemination of information concerning a lawyer's name or firm name, address and telephone number; the kinds of services the lawyer will undertake; the basis on which the lawyer's fees are determined, including prices for specific services and payment and credit arrangements; a lawyer's foreign language ability; names of references and, with their consent, names of clients regularly represented; and other information that might invite the attention of those seeking legal assistance.

Questions of effectiveness and taste in advertising are matters of speculation and subjective judgment. Some jurisdictions have had extensive prohibitions against television advertising, against advertising going beyond specified facts about a lawyer, or against "undignified" advertising. Television is now one of the most powerful media for getting information to the public, particularly persons of low and moderate income; prohibiting television advertising, therefore, would impede the flow of information about legal services to many sectors of the public. Limiting the information that may be advertised has a similar effect and assumes that the bar can accurately forecast the kind of information that the public would regard as relevant.

Neither this Rule nor Rule 7.3 prohibits communications authorized by law, such as notice to members of a class in class action litigation.

Record of Advertising

Paragraph (b) requires that a record of the content and use of advertising be kept in order to facilitate enforcement of this Rule. It does not require that advertising be subject to review prior to dissemination. Such a requirement would be burdensome and expensive relative to its possible benefits, and may be of doubtful constitutionality.

Paying Others to Recommend a Lawyer

A lawyer is allowed to pay for advertising permitted by this Rule, but otherwise is not permitted to pay another person for channeling professional work. This restriction does not prevent an organization or person other than the lawyer from advertising or recommending the lawyer's services. Thus, a legal aid agency or prepaid legal services plan may pay to advertise legal services provided under its auspices. Likewise, a lawyer may participate in not-for-profit lawyer referral programs and pay the usual fees charged by such programs. Paragraph (c) does not prohibit paying regular compensation to an assistant, such as a secretary, to prepare communications permitted by this Rule.

RULE 7.3 Direct Contact with Prospective Clients

A lawyer may not solicit professional employment from a prospective client with whom the lawyer has no family or prior professional relationship, by mail, in-person or otherwise, when a significant motive for the lawyer's doing so is the lawyer's pecuniary gain. The term "solicit" includes contact in person, by telephone or telegraph, by letter or other writing, or by other communication directed to a specific recipient, but does not include letters addressed or advertising circulars distributed generally to persons not known to need legal services of the kind provided by the lawyer in a particular matter, but who are so situated that they might in general find such services useful.

COMMENT:

There is a potential for abuse inherent in direct solicitation by a lawyer of prospective clients known to need legal services. It subjects the lay person to the private importuning of a trained advocate, in a direct interpersonal encounter. A prospective client often feels overwhelmed by the situation giving rise to the need for legal services, and may have an impaired capacity for reason, judgment and protective self-interest. Furthermore, the lawyer seeking the retainer is faced with a conflict stemming from the lawyer's own interest, which may color the advice and representation offered the vulnerable prospect.

The situation is therefore fraught with the possibility of undue influence, intimidation, and over-reaching. This potential for abuse inherent in direct solicitation of prospective clients justifies its prohibition, particularly since lawyer advertising permitted under Rule 7.2 offers an alternative means of communicating necessary information to those who may be in need of legal services.

Advertising makes it possible for a prospective client to be informed about the need for legal services, and about the qualifications of available lawyers and law firms, without subjecting the prospective client to direct personal persuasion that may overwhelm the client's judgment.

The use of general advertising to transmit information from lawyer to prospective client, rather than direct private contact, will help to assure that the information flows cleanly as well as freely. Advertising is out in public view, thus subject to scrutiny by those who know the lawyer. This informal review is itself likely to help guard against statements and claims that might constitute false or misleading communications, in violation of Rule 7.1. Direct, private communications from a lawyer to a prospective client are not subject to such third-scrutiny and consequently are much more likely to approach (and occasionally cross) the dividing line between accurate representations and those that are false and misleading.

These dangers attend direct solicitation whether in-person or by mail. Direct mail solicitation cannot be effectively regulated by means less drastic than outright prohibition. One proposed safeguard is to require that the designation "Advertising" be stamped on any envelope containing a solicitation letter. This would do nothing to assure the accuracy and reliability of the contents. Another suggestion is that solicitation letters be filed with a state regulatory agency. This would be ineffective as a practical matter. State lawyer discipline agencies struggle for resources to investigate specific complaints, much less for those necessary to screen lawyers' mail solicitation material. Even if they could examine such materials, agency staff members are unlikely to know anything about the lawyer or about the prospective client's underlying problem. Without such knowledge they cannot determine whether the lawyer's representations are misleading. In any event, such review would be after the fact, potentially too late to avert the undesirable consequences of disseminating false and misleading material.

General mailings not speaking to a specific matter do not pose the same danger of abuse as targeted mailings, and therefore are not prohibited by this Rule. The representations made in such mailings are necessarily general rather than tailored, less importuning than informative. They are addressed to recipients unlikely to be specially vulnerable at the time, hence who are likely to be more skeptical about unsubstantiated claims. General mailings not addressed to recipients involved in a specific legal matter or incident, therefore, more closely resemble permissible advertising rather than prohibited solicitation.

Similarly, this Rule would not prohibit a lawyer from contacting representatives of organizations or groups that may be interested in establishing a group or prepaid legal plan for its members, insureds, beneficiaries or other third parties for the purpose of informing such entities of the availability of and details concerning the plan or arrangement which he or his firm is willing to offer. This form of communication is not directed to a specific prospective client known to need legal services related to a particular matter. Rather, it is usually addressed to an individual acting in a fiduciary capacity seeking a supplier of legal services for others who may, if they choose, become prospective clients of the lawyer. Under these circumstances, the activity which the lawyer undertakes in communicating with such representatives and the type of information transmitted to the individual are functionally similar to and serve the same purpose as advertising permitted under Rule 7.2.

RULE 7.4 Communication of Fields of Practice

A lawyer may communicate the fact that the lawyer does or does not practice in particular fields of law. A lawyer shall not state or imply that the lawyer is a specialist except as follows:

(a) a lawyer admitted to engage in patent practice before the United States Patent and Trademark Office may use the designation "patent attorney" or a substantially similar designation;

(b) a lawyer engaged in admiralty practice may use the designation "admiralty," "proctor in admiralty" or a substantially similar designation; and

(c) (provisions on designation of specialization of the particular state).

COMMENT:

This Rule permits a lawyer to indicate areas of practice in communications about the lawyer's services; for example, in a telephone directory or other advertising. If a lawyer practices only in certain fields, or will not accept matters except in such fields, the lawyer is permitted so to indicate. However, stating that the lawyer is a "specialist" or that the lawyer's practice "is limited to" or "concentrated in" particular fields is not permitted. These terms have acquired a secondary meaning implying formal recognition as a specialist. Hence, use of these terms may be misleading unless the lawyer is certified or recognized in accordance with procedures in the state where the lawyer is licensed to practice.

Recognition of specialization in patent matters is a matter of long-established policy of the Patent and Trademark Office. Designation of admiralty practice has a long historical tradition associated with maritime commerce and the federal courts.

RULE 7.5 Firm Names and Letterheads

(a) A lawyer shall not use a firm name, letterhead or other professional designation that violates Rule 7.1. A trade name may be used by a lawyer in private practice if it does not imply a connection with a government agency or with a public or charitable legal services organization and is not otherwise in violation of Rule 7.1.

(b) A law firm with offices in more than one jurisdiction may use the same name in each jurisdiction, but identification of the lawyers in an office of the firm shall indicate the jurisdictional limitations on those not licensed to practice in the jurisdiction where the office is located.

(c) The name of a lawyer holding a public office shall not be used in the name of a law firm, or in communications on its behalf, during any substantial period in which the lawyer is not actively and regularly practicing with the firm.

(d) Lawyers may state or imply that they practice in a partnership or other organization only when that is the fact.

COMMENT:

A firm may be designated by the names of all or some of its members, by the names of deceased members where there has been a continuing succession in the firm's identity or by a trade name such as the "ABC Legal Clinic." Although the United States Supreme Court has held that legislation may prohibit the use of trade names in professional practice, use of such names in law practice is acceptable so long as it is not misleading. If a private firm uses a trade name that includes a geographical name such as "Springfield Legal Clinic," an express disclaimer that it is a public legal aid agency may be required to avoid a misleading implication. It may be observed that any firm name including the name of a deceased partner is, strictly speaking, a trade name. The use of such names to designate law firms has proven a useful means of identification. However, it is misleading to use the name of a lawyer not associated with the firm or a predecessor of the firm.

With regard to paragraph (d), lawyers sharing office facilities, but who are not in fact partners, may not denominate themselves as, for example, "Smith and Jones," for that title suggests partnership in the practice of law.

MAINTAINING THE INTEGRITY OF THE PROFESSION

RULE 8.1 Bar Admission and Disciplinary Matters

An applicant for admission to the bar, or a lawyer in connection with a bar admission application or in connection with a disciplinary matter, shall not:

(a) knowingly make a false statement of material fact; or

(b) fail to disclose a fact necessary to correct a misapprehension known by the person to have arisen in the matter, or knowingly fail to respond to a lawful demand for information from an admissions or disciplinary authority, except that this rule does not require disclosure of information otherwise protected by Rule 1.6.

COMMENT:

The duty imposed by this Rule extends to persons seeking admission to the bar as well as to lawyers. Hence, if a person makes a material false statement in connection with an application for admission, it may be the basis for subsequent disciplinary action if the person is admitted, and in any event may be relevant in a subsequent admission application. The duty imposed by this Rule applies to a lawyer's own admission or discipline as well as that of others. Thus, it is a separate professional offense for a lawyer to knowingly make a misrepresentation or omission in connection with a disciplinary investigation of the lawyer's own conduct. This Rule also requires affirmative clarification of any misunderstanding on the part of the admissions or disciplinary authority of which the person involved becomes aware.

This Rule is subject to the provisions of the Fifth Amendment of the United States Constitution and corresponding provisions of state constitutions. A person relying on such a provision in response to a question, however, should do so openly and not use the right of nondisclosure as a justification for failure to comply with this Rule.

A lawyer representing an applicant for admission to the bar, or representing a lawyer who is the subject of a disciplinary inquiry or proceeding, is governed by the rules applicable to the client-lawyer relationship.

RULE 8.2 Judicial and Legal Officials

(a) A lawyer shall not make a statement that the lawyer knows to be false or with reckless disregard as to its truth or falsity concerning the qualifications or integrity of a judge, adjudicatory officer or public legal officer, or of a candidate for election or appointment to judicial or legal office.

(b) A lawyer who is a candidate for judicial office shall comply with the applicable provisions of the code of judicial conduct.

COMMENT:

Assessments by lawyers are relied on in evaluating the professional or personal fitness of persons being considered for election or appointment to judicial office and to public legal offices, such as attorney general, prosecuting attorney and public defender. Expressing honest and candid opinions on such matters contributes to improving the administration of justice. Conversely, false statements by a lawyer can unfairly undermine public confidence in the administration of justice.

When a lawyer seeks judicial office, the lawyer should be bound by applicable limitations on political activity.

To maintain the fair and independent administration of justice, lawyers are encouraged to continue traditional efforts to defend judges and courts unjustly criticized.

RULE 8.3 Reporting Professional Misconduct

(a) A lawyer having knowledge that another lawyer has committed a violation of the Rules of Professional Conduct that raises a substantial question as to that lawyer's honesty, trustworthiness or fitness as a lawyer in other respects, shall inform the appropriate professional authority.

(b) A lawyer having knowledge that a judge has committed a violation of applicable rules of judicial conduct that raises a substantial question as to the judge's fitness for office shall inform the appropriate authority.

(c) This rule does not require disclosure of information otherwise protected by Rule 1.6.

COMMENT:

Self-regulation of the legal profession requires that members of the profession initiate disciplinary investigation when they know of a violation of the Rules of Professional Conduct. Lawyers have a similar obligation with respect to judicial misconduct. An apparently isolated violation may indicate a pattern of misconduct that only a disciplinary investigation can uncover. Reporting a violation is especially important where the victim is unlikely to discover the offense.

A report about misconduct is not required where it would involve violation of Rule 1.6. However, a lawyer should encourage a client to consent to disclosure where prosecution would not substantially prejudice the client's interests.

If a lawyer were obliged to report every violation of the Rules, the failure to report any violation would itself be a professional offense. Such a requirement existed in many jurisdictions but proved to be unenforceable. This Rule limits the reporting obligation to those offenses that a self-regulating profession must vigorously endeavor to prevent. A measure of judgment is, therefore, required in complying with the provisions of this Rule. The term "substantial" refers to the seriousness of the possible offense and not the quantum of evidence of which the lawyer is aware. A report should be made to the bar disciplinary agency unless some other agency, such as a peer review agency, is more appropriate in the circumstances. Similar considera-tions apply to the reporting of judicial misconduct.

The duty to report professional misconduct does not apply to a lawyer retained to represent a lawyer whose professional conduct is in question. Such a situation is governed by the rules applicable to the client-lawyer relationship.

RULE 8.4 Misconduct

It is professional misconduct for a lawyer to:

(a) violate or attempt to violate the rules of professional conduct, knowingly assist or induce another to do so, or do so through the acts of another;

(b) commit a criminal act that reflects adversely on the lawyer's honesty, trustworthiness or fitness as a lawyer in other respects;

(c) engage in conduct involving dishonesty, fraud, deceit or misrepresentation;

(d) engage in conduct that is prejudicial to the administration of justice;

(e) state or imply an ability to influence improperly a government agency or official; or

(f) knowingly assist a judge or judicial officer in conduct that is a violation of applicable rules of judicial conduct or other law.

COMMENT:

Many kinds of illegal conduct reflect adversely on fitness to practice law, such as offenses involving fraud and the offense of willful failure to file an income tax return. However, some kinds of offense carry no such implication. Traditionally, the distinction was drawn in terms of offenses involving "moral turpitude." That concept can be construed to include offenses concerning some matters of personal morality, such as adultery and comparable offenses, that have no specific connection to fitness for the practice of law. Although a lawyer is personally answerable to the entire criminal law, a lawyer should be professionally answerable only for offenses that indicate lack of those characteristics relevant to law practice. Offenses involving violence, dishonesty, or breach of trust, or serious interference with the administration of justice are in that category. A pattern of repeated offenses, even ones of minor significance when considered separately, can indicate indifference to legal obligation.

A lawyer may refuse to comply with an obligation imposed by law upon a good faith belief that no valid obligation exists. The provisions of Rule 1.2(d) concerning a good faith challenge to the validity, scope, meaning or application of the law apply to challenges of legal regulation of the practice of law.

Lawyers holding public office assume legal responsibilities going beyond those of other citizens. A lawyer's abuse of public office can suggest an inability to fulfill the professional role of attorney. The same is true of abuse of positions of private trust such as trustee, executor, administrator, guardian, agent and officer, director or manager of a corporation or other organization.

RULE 8.5 Jurisdiction

A lawyer admitted to practice in this jurisdiction is subject to the disciplinary authority of this jurisdiction although engaged in practice elsewhere.

COMMENT:

In modern practice lawyers frequently act outside the territorial limits of the jurisdiction in which they are licensed to practice, either in another state or outside the United States. In doing so, they remain subject to the governing authority of the jurisdiction in which they are licensed to practice. If their activity in another jurisdiction is substantial and continuous, it may constitute practice of law in that jurisdiction. See Rule 5.5.

If the rules of professional conduct in the two jurisdictions differ, principles of conflict of laws may apply. Similar problems can arise when a lawyer is licensed to practice in more than one jurisdiction.

Where the lawyer is licensed to practice law in two jurisdictions which impose conflicting obligations, applicable rules of choice of law may govern the situation. A related problem arises with respect to practice before a federal tribunal, where the general authority of the states to regulate the practice of law must be reconciled with such authority as federal tribunals may have to regulate practice before them.

The Thirteen Federal Judicial Circuits

See 28 U.S.C.A. § 41

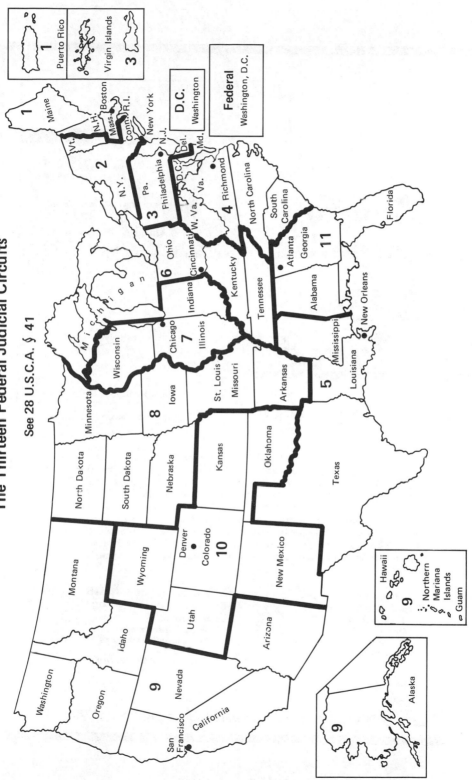

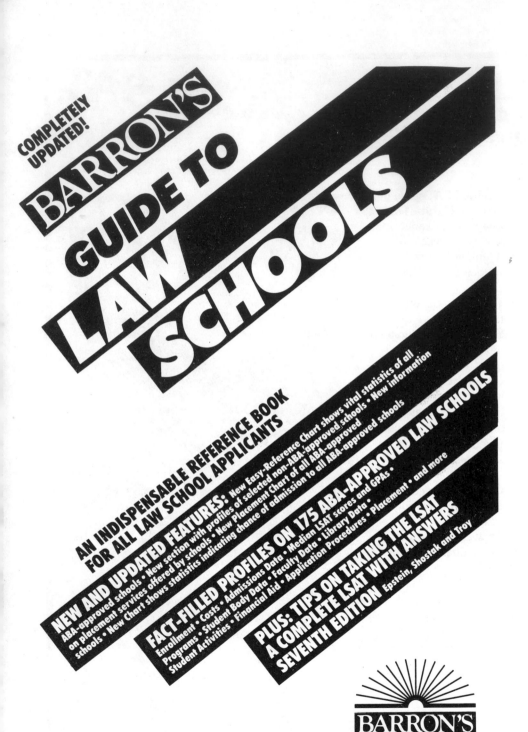

COMPLETELY UPDATED!

BARRON'S GUIDE TO LAW SCHOOLS

AN INDISPENSABLE REFERENCE BOOK FOR ALL LAW SCHOOL APPLICANTS

NEW AND UPDATED FEATURES: New Easy-Reference Chart shows vital statistics of all ABA-approved schools • New section with profiles of selected non-ABA-approved schools • New information on placement services offered by schools • New Placement Chart of all ABA-approved schools • New Chart shows statistics indicating chance of admission to all ABA-approved schools

FACT-FILLED PROFILES ON 175 ABA-APPROVED LAW SCHOOLS Enrollment • Costs • Admissions Data • Median LSAT scores and GPAs • Programs • Student Body Data • Faculty Data • Library Data • Student Activities • Financial Aid • Application Procedures • Placement • and more

PLUS: TIPS ON TAKING THE LSAT A COMPLETE LSAT WITH ANSWERS SEVENTH EDITION Epstein, Shostak and Troy

BARRON'S

Barron's Educational Series, Inc.
250 Wireless Boulevard
Hauppauge, New York 11788

At your bookseller, or order direct adding 10% postage (minimum charge $1.50) plus applicable sales tax.

$10.95 $15.95 Canada